D1223434

# Private Foundations

# Don't Miss Out on Must-Have and Timely New Information!

- Keep up-to-date on relevant changes in IRS forms, requirements, and related tax procedures.
- Learn about new federal, state, and local laws covering tax regulations surrounding private foundations.
- Stay abreast of complicated legal and tax issues.

Subscribe now to make sure you have access to the latest information regarding tax regulations for private foundations.

**Go to**

**www.nonprofitcommunity.com/index.php/ nonprofit-accounting-finance/**

**and sign up today!**

# Private Foundations

## Tax Law and Compliance

## Fourth Edition

**Bruce R. Hopkins**
**Jody Blazek**

PROPERTY OF

AUG 2 6 2014

FOUNDATION CENTER

WILEY

Cover image: ©iStock.com/phleum
Cover design: Wiley

Copyright © 2014 by John Wiley & Sons, Inc. All rights reserved.

Published by John Wiley & Sons, Inc., Hoboken, New Jersey.
Published simultaneously in Canada.

No part of this publication may be reproduced, stored in a retrieval system, or transmitted in any form or by any means, electronic, mechanical, photocopying, recording, scanning, or otherwise, except as permitted under Section 107 or 108 of the 1976 United States Copyright Act, without either the prior written permission of the Publisher, or authorization through payment of the appropriate per-copy fee to the Copyright Clearance Center, Inc., 222 Rosewood Drive, Danvers, MA 01923, (978) 750-8400, fax (978) 646-8600, or on the Web at www.copyright.com. Requests to the Publisher for permission should be addressed to the Permissions Department, John Wiley & Sons, Inc., 111 River Street, Hoboken, NJ 07030, (201) 748-6011, fax (201) 748-6008, or online at http://www.wiley.com/go/permissions.

Limit of Liability/Disclaimer of Warranty: While the publisher and author have used their best efforts in preparing this book, they make no representations or warranties with respect to the accuracy or completeness of the contents of this book and specifically disclaim any implied warranties of merchantability or fitness for a particular purpose. No warranty may be created or extended by sales representatives or written sales materials. The advice and strategies contained herein may not be suitable for your situation. You should consult with a professional where appropriate. Neither the publisher nor author shall be liable for any loss of profit or any other commercial damages, including but not limited to special, incidental, consequential, or other damages.

For general information on our other products and services or for technical support, please contact our Customer Care Department within the United States at (800) 762-2974, outside the United States at (317) 572-3993 or fax (317) 572-4002.

Wiley publishes in a variety of print and electronic formats and by print-on-demand. Some material included with standard print versions of this book may not be included in e-books or in print-on-demand. If this book refers to media such as a CD or DVD that is not included in the version you purchased, you may download this material at http://booksupport.wiley.com. For more information about Wiley products, visit www.wiley.com.

*Library of Congress Cataloging-in-Publication Data:*
Hopkins, Bruce R., author.
  Private foundations : tax law and compliance / Bruce R. Hopkins, Jody Blazek. — Fourth Edition.
    pages cm. — (Wiley nonprofit authority)
  Includes index.
    ISBN 978-1-118-53247-8 (cloth); ISBN 978-1-118-53249-2 (ebk); ISBN 978-1-118-53250-8 (ebk)
  1. Nonprofit organizations—Taxation—Law and legislation—United States.  2. Charitable uses, trusts, and foundations—Taxation—United States.  I. Blazek, Jody, author.  II. Title.
  KF6449.H63 2014
  343.7306'68—dc23
                                                                                          2013046694

Printed in the United States of America

10 9 8 7 6 5 4 3 2 1

*This book is dedicated
to my private foundation clients,
and my friends and colleagues at
Polsinelli Shalton Flanigan Suelthaus PC
who help me serve them.*

BRH

*And also to Blazek & Vetterling clients and colleagues,
seminar and conference participants, and fellow CPAs
and lawyers who serve private foundations, for asking the
questions that provide fuel for new editions of the book.*

JB

# Contents

## CONTENTS

# CONTENTS

# Preface

Private foundations, although constituting a relatively small portion of the charitable community, are burdened with extensive federal tax law requirements that belie their numbers, and that substantially regulate and circumscribe their operations. This body of law has steadily grown since its inception as a considerable portion of the Tax Reform Act of 1969. This book came about in reflection of this expanding and expansive aspect of the law pertaining to these unique forms of tax-exempt organizations. We have attempted to both capture and summarize this law, and to provide guidance as to compliance with it.

As noted, a private foundation is a charitable entity for tax purposes. Technically, this means it is an organization described in section 501(c)(3) of the Internal Revenue Code. This in turn means, of course, that nearly all of the considerable law embodied in and around that section is applicable to private foundations. The law in this area, however, stimulated by a variety of abuses, perceived and otherwise, includes an overlay collection of statutory requirements, in the form of rules applicable only to private foundations. These rules are the principal subject of this book.

Many lawyers and accountants who practice in the exempt organizations field have little or no involvement with private foundations. With their exempt clients being public charities or other types of nonprofit organizations, this is understandable; these practitioners have no reason to master the private foundation rules. As private foundations proliferate, existing ones grow, and the law becomes more encompassing, however, successful understanding of the private foundation rules becomes increasingly important for all tax practitioners. Indeed, as the law in the charitable area evolves, some of these rules are becoming applicable outside the private foundation realm, with emphasis in that regard on supporting organizations and donor-advised funds.

There is more to this dimension of the matter. Until recently, the tax laws specifically applicable to private foundations had no particular practical relationship to the tax laws pertaining to public charities. (Two exceptions of note are the laws concerning functionally related businesses and voter registration projects.) With respect to the self-dealing rules, however, this dichotomy is rapidly and dramatically changing.

With the advent of the intermediate sanctions against excessive compensation, much of the private foundation law pertaining to self-dealing has been grafted onto the public charity rules. This extension of private foundation law into the public charity context amounts to more than the concept of *self-dealing* informing the concept of the *excess benefit transaction*: the law concerning *corrections*, the *amount involved*, and the *highest fiduciary standards* is also now a part of public charity law. For those advising public charities in this area, this book should be helpful.

Earlier, it was said that we have endeavored to "capture" the tax law concerning private foundations. This, in fact, is an impossible task, an elusive goal. The reason for this lies in the inherent nature of the "law" in this field. While the foundation law is framed by detailed statutes and regulations, much of the details are technically not law at all (i.e., hundreds of Internal Revenue Service private determinations: private letter rulings, technical advice memoranda, chief counsel memoranda, and the like). These documents tumble out of the IRS, seemingly by the tons every month. They infuse the law of private foundations with its dynamism, keeping it flowing, changing, expanding. (The field is nearly 45 years of age, yet the IRS is still initiating—and in some instances, reversing—its policy determinations in the area.)

The compliance aspects of these rules provide the key to ongoing qualification of a private foundation's tax-exempt status and avoidance of the excise tax imposed on rule violations. This book thoroughly explores the rules and contains charts and checklists to aid in applying them. It seeks to dispel the myth that private foundations are difficult if not impossible to manage. What can be fascinating about the study of private foundations is the broad latitude of operation actually allowed and the room for creativity in planning and operating them.

The rules are detailed in six Internal Revenue Code sections concerning self-dealing, mandatory distributions, excess business holdings, jeopardizing investments, taxable expenditures, and the excise tax on investment income. The foundation and its managers are subject to a variety of excise taxes if the rules are violated. Some advisors discourage the creation of private foundations because of this potential liability. Until 1984, the sanctions were imposed without exception, making caution a reasonable approach. Except for the penalties for self-dealing, sanctions can now be abated if the failure to meet a requirement is due to reasonable cause. Thus there has been significant easing of the hard and fast rules initially designed by Congress to curtail a private foundation's operations. Caution cannot be thrown to the wind, but potential foundation creators shouldn't be needlessly afraid of incurring excise taxes.

The one unforgivable constraint placed on private foundations prohibits self-dealing, namely, financial transactions between the foundation and its creators, funders, insiders, and certain of their relatives. This rule is applied without regard to the amount of economic benefit received by the foundation. The Code, on the one hand, states that these acts are absolutely prohibited and lists six comprehensive types of transactions that are forbidden. The Code, on the other hand, also lists eight exceptions to the general rule; the tax regulations add more exceptions. So again, while the rules appear draconian, there is room to maneuver. In recent years, the IRS in private letter rulings has considerably broadened and liberally applied the exceptions and permitted transactions that, according to the Code, are self-dealing. When, for example, sharing office space with its creators saves the foundation money as a practical matter, the IRS has approved transactions that on their face constitute self-dealing based upon a literal reading of the tax code. A glance at the subtopics of Chapter 5 provides a clue to the broad range of transactions that entail exceptions and thus are permitted.

Special numerical tests apply to assure that a private foundation does not unduly hoard its money. An amount equal to at least 5 percent of the value of a foundation's investment assets must be paid out annually for charitable purposes. Advisors seeking to assist a private foundation in conserving its endowment must understand the standards for identifying the assets that are counted in making the calculation as distinguished from those assets that need not be included. When and how the assets that comprise the payout base are valued also impacts the results. The authors of this Code provision recognized a foundation would not necessarily always distribute the precisely calculated amount. Thus a carryover of excess distributions to future years is permitted. In its early years, and later under the right circumstances, a foundation can delay or set aside a portion of its annual required payout for up to five years.

A foundation must pay an annual excise tax of 2 percent on its net investment income. With proper timing of its charitable distributions, a foundation can cut this tax in half in some years. A foundation with substantially appreciated property may be able to totally eliminate the tax in regard to capital gains on certain assets. Although the 2 percent tax rate is modest, most foundation representatives are appreciative of the opportunity to apply the kind of tax planning ideas covered in Chapter 10 to reduce the tax.

In addition to observing the fiduciary responsibility standards imposed by laws of the locale in which the foundation is situated, the Code provides that trustees and directors of private foundations must not purchase or hold investments that subject the foundation's capital to jeopardy. What was thought to be a jeopardizing investment in 1970, when the regulation explaining these provisions were written, has significantly evolved over the years. The regulations state, for example, that a foundation may not buy put and call options on marketable securities. Contemporary investment theory nonetheless has it that it is prudent to sell "covered calls" against long-term stock positions in the foundation's investment portfolio; the IRS has privately agreed. Foundations with conservative investment policies based on the regulations may be pleased to understand the evolution of the rules outlined in Chapter 8.

When a private foundation and its creators, funders, and certain of their relatives in combination own more than 20 percent of a business enterprise, the foundation is deemed to have excess business holdings an exception applies, such as foundation ownership of less than 2 percent of the company. Permitted holdings of business enterprises actually vary according to the form of ownership, type of entity, and other variables discussed in Chapter 7. Nicely enough, the foundation has five years to dispose of any excess holdings received as a gift or inheritance. The ownership limitation does not apply to a business, termed functionally related, that accomplishes a charitable purpose, such as a low-income housing project.

So long as it is accomplishing a charitable purpose, a private foundation is essentially permitted to spend its money in a variety of ways. While most foundations make grants to churches, schools, hospitals, museums, and broadly supported charitable organizations, a foundation can conduct its own programs. The rules constraining the fashion in which the foundation spends its money are found in Chapter 9 concerning taxable expenditures. An excise tax is potentially due if the foundation spends money for certain purposes. A foundation, just like all other types of charitable organizations, cannot make an expenditure in support of or in opposition to a candidate for elective office. A public charity can spend a limited amount of money to lobby those that make our laws; a private foundation generally cannot. A foundation, however, may support certain types of voter education efforts, and can study and report on social issues that are customarily the subject of legislative actions, such as the environment or military preparedness. The girth of Chapter 9 illustrates the breadth of issues that might involve a taxable expenditure. Contrary to what some think, these rules allow a foundation to make grants to individuals. To do so, the foundation's plan for choosing the recipients must be approved in advance by the IRS. Similarly, a private foundation can make a grant to another private foundation or to a non–tax exempt organization. In doing so, it must obtain specific documentation of the charitable purposes of the grant and make special reports to the IRS. This enhanced paperwork may reasonably make a foundation reluctant to make such an expenditure, but for some, the process, called exercising expenditure responsibility, is worth the effort. Sample documents and checklists are in Chapter 9 to facilitate the process.

The closest scrutiny the IRS places on exempt organizations occurs when it considers a newly created organization's application for recognition of tax exemption, Form 1023. For a foundation that plans to conduct a grant-making program, approval should be accomplished with ease. The application of a foundation that proposes to conduct active projects must be prepared with the utmost care, with attention to the import of the information submitted. It is advantageous to be aware of the issues of concern to the IRS and to follow the suggestions in Chapter 2.

Because an excise tax can be imposed for violation of the rules, it is important that a private foundation and its advisors have a system for monitoring compliance with the rules. The private foundation sanctions are somewhat interactive; a taxable expenditure can occur in connection with an act of self-dealing. The Form 990-PF, filed annually with the Internal Revenue Service, is designed to measure the private foundation's ongoing satisfaction of the rules. In a sometimes confusing fashion, Form 990-PF is not prepared sequentially. Among one of the most useful bits of information the reader will find in this book is a chart outlining those parts to prepare first, those parts that are dependent on another part, and the order in which the parts should be prepared. In response to the many times we have been asked, a checklist of private foundation organizational issues provides a guide to record keeping and policy issues important to a foundation. Chapter 12 contains a wealth of suggestions for preparing Form 990-PF and accomplishing the foundation's compliance goals.

Some of the additions to the text of the book were occasioned by questions put to the authors during the course of our practices, at seminars and conferences, and by e-mail. These questions are welcome, and we trust they will continue.

Every book summarizing a body of law has to have a cutoff date as to what developments to include. This edition covers events through the close of 2013. Such a limitation is always frustrating, inasmuch as there have been important developments since that period. So, because the law in this field is so dynamic, we have been unable to "capture" it in its entirety; the best we could do is summarize it as of a particular point in time. These subsequent and ongoing developments are certain to provide ample material for our first supplement to this edition.

\*　　\*　　\*

A glance at recent publications such as the IRS's annual report for tax-exempt organizations and the Department of the Treasury/IRS priority guidance plan reveals that private foundations are far from being in the federal government's sights these days. That fact constitutes obviously good news for the leaders and managers of foundations. Yet we can report regulatory rumblings (to keep the lawyers and accountants engaged and happy).

The fluctuation of investment returns yielding increases and declines in the value of foundation assets over the years impacts grantmaking policies. Many foundations now use a "smoothing" design for charitable disbursement planning. The tax-reporting requirements for foundations owning securities through an investment partnership, particularly those based offshore, present serious challenges and enhanced compliance efforts. Valuing these assets for purposes of calculating the mandatory payout is a particular problem discussed in this edition.

Serious issues faced foundations that invested in Ponzi schemes and similar investment frauds. A number of law issues were raised in this context, many of which were nicely identified by lawyers who submitted comments on behalf of the Tax Section of the New York State Bar Association. These issues are summarized in this edition, principally in connection with material concerning the law as to jeopardizing investments, mandatory payouts, and determination of the excise tax on net investment income; brief mention is accorded the self-dealing and taxable expenditures rules from this perspective. The IRS has yet to issue any guidance in this area.

Still other topics discussed in this edition are the regulations issued by the IRS in amplification of the rules concerning Type III supporting organizations that Congress enacted as part of the enactment of the Pension Protection Act of 2006, new private letter rulings concerning asset transfers from one private foundation to another, and an update of a discussion of the use of Form 990 to evaluate grantee financial information.

The IRS in 2011 issued a form styled "Request for Miscellaneous Determinations" to be filed by charitable (IRC § 501(c)(3)) organizations (Form 8940). This form must be used, *inter alia*, when seeking IRS approval of private foundation set-asides under the suitability test, advance approval of foundation voter registration activities, advance approval of foundation scholarship procedures, advance approval that a potential grant (or contribution or bequest) constitutes an unusual grant, change in type (or initial determination of type) of supporting organizations, reclassification of foundation status (including request by a public charity for private foundation status), and termination of private foundation status (including the post-60-months filing).

Organizations that are applying for recognition of tax exemption and are seeking approval of scholarship procedures or Form 990 filing exemption should include the request as part of the application (Form 1023) rather than utilize this new form.

Otherwise, as noted, matters are relatively quiet on the private foundation tax law and compliance front. Some of the more notable other topics discussed in this edition are an interesting legislative proposal to revise the regime imposing an excise tax on foundations' net investment income, a curious IRS ruling allowing a community foundation to sell its grantmaking services within its community without running afoul of the unrelated business income rules, and the holding by the IRS that foundation grants to single-member limited liability companies (disregarded entities) that are wholly owned by U.S. charities are qualifying distributions.

\* \* \*

We have had enormous support from John Wiley & Sons in the preparation of this book. Thanks are extended to Martha Cooley and Robin Sarantos for their assistance in conjunction with the first edition, to Susan McDermott and Louise Jacob for their help with the second edition, to Susan and Natasha A. S. Wolfe in connection with the preparation of the third edition, and to Lia Ottaviano, Claire New, and Mary Daniello for their hard work and invaluable help in connection with this edition. We have had marvelous experiences on other occasions in working with the editors at Wiley, and the support we have received in connection with this book is a continuation of this fine Wiley tradition.

BRUCE R. HOPKINS
JODY BLAZEK

# Book Citations

Throughout this book, 12 books by the authors (in some instances, as co-author), all published by John Wiley & Sons, are referenced in this way:

1. Hopkins, *IRS Audits of Tax-Exempt Organizations: Policies, Practices, and Procedures* (2008): *IRS Audits*.

2. Blazek, *IRS Form 1023 Tax Preparation Guide* (2005): *IRS Form 1023 Tax Preparation Guide*.

3. Hopkins, *The Law of Fundraising, Fifth Edition* (2013): *Fundraising*.

4. Hopkins, *The Law of Intermediate Sanctions: A Guide for Nonprofits* (2003): *Intermediate Sanctions*.

5. Hopkins, *The Law of Tax-Exempt Organizations, Tenth Edition* (2011): *Tax-Exempt Organizations*.

6. Hopkins, *Nonprofit Governance: Law, Practices & Trends* (2009): *Nonprofit Governance*.

7. Blazek, *Nonprofit Financial Planning Made Easy* (2008): *Nonprofit Financial Planning Made Easy*.

8. Hopkins, *Nonprofit Law for Colleges and Universities: Essential Questions and Answers for Officers, Directors, and Advisors* (2011): *Colleges and Universities*.

9. Hopkins, *Planning Guide for the Law of Tax-Exempt Organizations: Strategies and Commentaries* (2004): *Planning Guide*.

10. Hopkins, *The Tax Law of Charitable Giving, Fifth Edition* (2014): *Charitable Giving*.

11. Hopkins, *The Tax Law of Unrelated Business for Nonprofit Organizations* (2005): *Unrelated Business*.

12. Blazek, *Tax Planning and Compliance for Tax-Exempt Organizations, Fourth Edition* (2004): *Tax Planning and Compliance*.

The third, fifth, tenth, and twelfth editions of these books are annually supplemented. Also, updates on all of the foregoing law subjects (plus private foundations law) are available in *Bruce R. Hopkins' Nonprofit Counsel*, a monthly newsletter also published by Wiley.

# Private Foundations

# CHAPTER ONE

# Introduction to Private Foundations

## § 1.1  PRIVATE FOUNDATIONS: UNIQUE ORGANIZATIONS

There are millions of tax-exempt charitable organizations in the United States, yet only about 90,000 of them are classified, for federal tax purposes, as private foundations. This fact alone—this isolation of foundations purely for purposes of government regulation—makes private foundations unique.

The federal tax law segregates private foundations from other charitable entities, these other entities being generically referred to as *public charities*. Congress differentiated private foundations from other charities in 1969, and in so doing triggered a chain of reactions and developments in the tax law that shows no sign of abating. In a move that made life more complicated for nearly all in the charitable community, the federal tax law presumes that all charitable organizations are private foundations. (The burden of proving non–private foundation status rests with each charitable organization; the process of rebutting the presumption is part of the procedure for filing for recognition of tax-exempt status.[1]) As another example of uniqueness, no other type of tax-exempt organization is accorded such a statutory focus.

Certainly the regulatory regime imposed on private foundations is unique. There is no category of tax-exempt organization that is subject to anything like the compliance burdens that comprise the sweep of Chapter 42 of the Internal Revenue Code. Even the origin of this legislation is unique: The mood of Congress during the course of its endeavors in this regard in the years leading up to the 1969 legislation was very anti–private foundation, with the nation's legislature dismayed at the findings presented to it by the Department of the Treasury in a 1965 report and by a series of congressional hearings.[2] The animosity toward, sometimes hostility against, private foundations that motivated members of Congress and the staff at that time is reflected in the legislation that quickly took shape that year.

When Congress targeted privately funded charities and gave them special status, the following sections were added to the Internal Revenue Code. These sections have operational constraints that govern the conduct of private foundations and impose excise taxes for failures to adhere to the rules.

- IRC § 4940, Tax on Investment Income
- IRC § 4941, Taxes on Self-Dealing
- IRC § 4942, Taxes on Failure to Distribute Income
- IRC § 4943, Taxes on Excess Business Holdings
- IRC § 4944, Taxes on Investments That Jeopardize Charitable Purpose
- IRC § 4945, Taxes on Taxable Expenditures
- IRC § 4946, Disqualified Persons
- IRC § 4947, Application of Taxes to Certain Nonexempt Trusts
- IRC § 4948, Foreign Private Foundations

Sanctions for failure to comply with private foundation rules potentially include a tax (called the *Chapter 42 tax*) on both the foundation and its disqualified persons, loss of tax exemption, and repayment of all tax benefits accrued during the life of the foundation for its funders and itself. Under certain circumstances, these taxes can be abated if the violation was due to reasonable

---

1. Internal Revenue Code of 1986, as amended, IRC § 508(b). The procedure for filing for recognition of tax-exempt status is the subject of *Tax-Exempt Organizations*, Chapter 25; *Tax Planning and Compliance*, Chapter 18; and *IRS Form 1023 Tax Preparation Guide.*
2. *See* text accompanied by *infra* notes 18 and 20.

cause, rather than for willful and intentional reasons, and if the violation is properly corrected.[3]

Notwithstanding the turbulence within their legal setting, private foundations are a viable and valuable type of nonprofit organization. They are also unique in that they are often used as a means to accomplish the personal philanthropic goals of individuals. Some professional advisors discourage the formation of private foundations because of the complexity of the regulatory rules underlying and surrounding them. There is no question that the foundation rules are often more complicated than those applicable to public charities and other forms of exempt organizations. The reformation of the donor-advised funds and Type III supporting organization rules by the Pension Protection Act of 2006, however, significantly narrowed the differences between those two types of charitable entities and private foundations. Many constraints on operation and procedural requirements formerly only applicable to private foundations now also apply to donor-advised funds and Type III supporting organizations. Exhibit 1.1 displays a comparison of the applicable rules. Persons who decided against creating a private foundation in the past may change their views after studying this chart. Nevertheless, the creation and operation of a private foundation can be a rewarding experience.

Private foundations are ideal charitable vehicles for many funders. An individual can create a foundation qualified for tax exemption and be its sole trustee or director retaining absolute control. Commonly, a donor and his or her family members comprise the governing board of a private foundation, although financial and other transactions between them and the foundation are tightly constrained by the tax law.

Funders who wish to be flexible in their grant-making programs may prefer a private foundation for a similar reason. While a grant payout requirement must be adhered to, there is considerable latitude in the design of its charitable programs. The foundation can maintain its own programs rather than fund others; this entity is the *private operating foundation*. Here a funder can establish the foundation, hire a staff, and work to further his or her own charitable purposes.

Another potential advantage is the fact that family members or other disqualified persons can be paid reasonable compensation in the form of director or trustee fees for their services on the organization's governing board. Disqualified persons can also be paid salaries for services rendered in their capacity as staff members. Those who learn the rules and plan well to adhere to them need not allow the tax law penalties to serve as a deterrent to creation of a private foundation.

Finally, a private foundation can serve as an ideal income and estate planning device for individuals with charitable interests. The classic example

---

3. IRC § 4962.

**EXHIBIT 1.1**

Comparison of Tax Rules Applicable to Private Foundations,
Donor-Advised Funds, and Type III Supporting Organizations

| | Private Foundation | Donor-Advised Fund | Type III* Supporting Organization |
|---|---|---|---|
| § 4940 Excise Tax on Investment Income | Yes | No | No |
| § 4941 Self-Dealing Prohibitions | Yes | Yes | Yes[†] |
| § 4942 Mandatory Annual Spending | Yes | No | Yes[‡] |
| § 4943 Excess Business Holdings | Yes | Yes | Yes |
| § 4944 Jeopardizing Investments | Yes | No | No |
| § 4945 Taxable Expenditures | Yes | Yes[§] | No |
| **Tax Compliance Issues:** | | | |
| Annual Tax Return | Yes | No | Yes |
| Anonymity for Donor (Sch. B disclosure) | No | Yes | Yes |
| Record-Keeping Responsibility | Yes | No | Yes |
| Tax Deduction 20/30% of AGI | Yes | Higher | Higher |
| Tax Deduction 30/50% of AGI | Lower | Yes | Yes |
| Grants to Individuals | Yes | No | Yes |
| Expenditure Responsibility for Grants to Non-501(c)(3) Organizations | Yes | Yes | No |

* Non–functionally integrated. *See* § 15.7.
[†] IRC §§ 4967 and 4958. *See* § 6.5.
[‡] Proposed Reg. § 1.509(a)-4(i)(1). *See* § 15.7(g-1).
[§] IRC § 4966. *See* § 16.9.

is a philanthropist who has publicly traded stock that is highly appreciated in value. A private foundation can be created, the securities contributed to the foundation and sold by that entity, and the philanthropist claims a charitable contribution deduction based on the full fair market value of the stock and avoids taxation of the capital gain.[4] The foundation can retain the stock and endeavor to expand its base of principal, and essentially spend only the income from its investments for its charitable purposes.

Philanthropists who make charitable bequests by means of their wills can create private foundations to receive a portion of the bequest while they are

4. *See* § 14.4(b) for possible limitations on the deduction.

living. Contributions to the foundations made during the donor's lifetime are deductible, thereby increasing the estate by reducing income tax. The property gifted to the private foundation and the undistributed income accumulating in the private foundation are not subject to estate tax. A private foundation can also be the remainder interest beneficiary of a charitable remainder trust created during the donor's lifetime. This approach usually results in more after-tax money for the foundation and other beneficiaries.

This unique entity known as a private foundation is thus both heavily regulated by a body of extensive and complex law, and a very useful charitable planning vehicle. To achieve the optimum in charitable giving and granting by means of a private foundation, the management and advisors to the foundation must master this body of law. The pages that follow are intended to be a guide to that end.

Philanthropists seeking to avoid the constraints applicable to private foundations should explore the pros and cons of establishing a supporting organization[5] or a donor-advised fund.[6]

## § 1.2  DEFINITION OF *PRIVATE FOUNDATION*

The federal tax law defines the term *private foundation* as a domestic or foreign charitable organization, other than one of the entities collectively known as *public charities*.[7] Thus, one way to view a private foundation is as a charitable organization[8] that cannot or does not qualify as a form of public charity.

Each U.S. and foreign charitable organization is presumed to be a private foundation; this presumption is rebutted by a showing that the entity is a church, school, hospital, medical research organization, publicly supported charity, supporting organization, or organization that tests for public safety.[9] That is, by operation of law, if a charitable organization cannot be classified as a public charity, it is (or becomes) a private foundation.[10]

Despite the absence of a generic definition of the term, a private foundation essentially is a tax-exempt organization that has these characteristics: (1) it is a charitable organization, (2) it is funded from one source (usually an individual, a family, or a business), (3) its ongoing revenue is derived from investments (in the nature of an endowment fund), and (4) it makes grants to other charitable organizations rather than operate its own program (unless it is a private operating foundation). Congress could have crafted an affirmative definition of the term *private foundation*, using these criteria, but the statutory scheme enacted in 1969

---

5. *See* § 15.7.
6. *See* Chapter 16.
7. IRC § 509(a). The details of this definition are the subject of Chapter 15.
8. That is, an organization that is tax-exempt pursuant to IRC § 501(a) as an organization described in IRC § 501(c)(3).
9. IRC § 509(a)(1)–(4).
10. IRC § 508(b).

was, as noted, developed in a strenuously anti–private foundation environment and the "definition" was thus devised in a manner to make it as encompassing as possible. (Indeed, the statutory definition is actually one of what a private foundation *is not*, rather than a definition of what a private foundation *is*.)

If circumstances change, or if its creators wish it, a private foundation can terminate its private foundation status. This happens most frequently where the organization's level or mix of funding is such that it can qualify as a publicly supported charity or where the organization converts to a supporting organization. A private foundation can distribute all of its assets to a public charity and dissolve itself or can merge into one or more other private foundations.[11]

## § 1.3 HISTORY AND BACKGROUND

Private foundations have long been much-maligned entities, not only in the federal tax laws but within society at large. Their history, which is extensive, is rich with many successes and strewn with few abuses.[12] They are vehicles for some of the most humanitarian and progressive acts, yet whenever a list of tax reforms is compiled, private foundations, and/or the tax law rules that apply to them, always seem to attract much attention.

A private foundation is a unique breed of tax-exempt organization, in that while it is recognized as charitable, educational, or the like, it is usually controlled and supported by a single source, for example, one donor, a family, or a company. This one characteristic, which the Internal Revenue Service (IRS) has recognized as an indirect but nonetheless qualifying means of support of charity,[13] has spawned several criticisms, including alleged irresponsive governance and inadequate responses to perceived needs. Private foundations are similarly chastised for being elitist, playthings of the wealthy, and havens for "do-gooders" assuaging their inner needs by dispensing beneficence to others.[14]

More serious criticisms of private foundations are that they further various tax inequities, are created for private rather than philanthropic purposes, and do not actually achieve charitable ends.[15] As will be developed in subsequent chapters, nearly all of the abuses—apocryphal or otherwise—involving private foundations were eradicated as the result of enactment of the Tax Reform Act of 1969.[16]

---

11. *See* Chapter 13.
12. Wormser, *Foundations: Their Power and Influence* (Sevierville, TN: Catholic House Books, 1993); Andrews, *Philanthropic Foundations* (New York: Russell Sage Foundation, 1956).
13. IRS Revenue Ruling (Rev. Rul.) 67-149, 1967-1 C.B. 133.
14. E.g., Branch, "The Case Against Foundations," *Washington Monthly* 3 (July 1971).
15. E.g., Stern, *The Great Treasury Raid* (New York: Random House, 1964), 242–246. *Cf.* Stern, *The Rape of the Taxpayer* (New York: Random House, 1973).
16. As one court stated, Congress enacted these rules "to put an end, as far as it reasonably could, to the abuses and potential abuses associated with private foundations" (*Mannheimer Charitable Trust, Hans S. v. Commissioner*, 93 T.C. 35, 39 [1989]).

The origins of private foundations are traceable to the genesis of philanthropy itself. Foundations as legal entities were recognized in the Anglo-Saxon legal system and were fostered in the United States by the law of charitable trusts. Charitable endowments in America are essentially creatures of common law, although amply sustained in statutory laws concerning taxes, corporations, decedents' estates, trusts, and property.[17] The modern American foundation is of relatively recent vintage, dating back to the mid-nineteenth century. Many of the well-known foundations are reflective of the great fortunes established at the advent of the 1900s. Foundations proliferated after World War II, in large part because of favorable economic conditions and tax incentives. More recently, private foundations founded and funded by those successful in the realm of technology are being added to the list of the nation's largest charities.

Foundations were not defined (albeit indirectly) in the Internal Revenue Code (nor in any other federal statute) until 1969—though not because of lack of interest in them by Congress. They were investigated, for example, by the "Walsh Committee" (the Senate Industrial Relations Committee) from 1913 to 1915 for allegedly large stockholdings, by the "Cox Committee" (House Select Committee to Investigate and Study Educational and Philanthropic Foundations) in 1952, by Representative B. Carroll Reece in 1954 (the House Special Committee to Investigate Tax-Exempt Foundations and Comparable Organizations) for alleged support of subversives, and by Representative Wright Patman throughout the 1960s for allegedly tending more to private interests than public benefit. Congressman Patman's inquiries and others' culminated in the extensive foundation provisions of the Tax Reform Act of 1969,[18] which introduced the first statutory definition of the term *private foundation*. Yet a more expressive definition is: ". . . a nongovernmental, nonprofit organization, with funds and program managed by its own trustees or directors, and established to maintain or aid social, educational, charitable, religious, or other activities serving the common welfare."[19]

Controversy persists over the appropriate role for foundations in America—or whether they should exist at all. Foundations are attacked by some as too uninvolved in current issues and problems and by others as too effective in fomenting social change. The federal government is now spending billions of dollars in the realms of health, education, and welfare, formerly the domain of

---

17. Fremont-Smith, *Foundations and Government, State and Federal Law* (New York: Russell Sage Foundation, 1965), especially Chapter 1.
18. Andrews, *Patman and Foundations: Review and Assessment* (New York: Foundation Center, 1968); Myers, "Foundations and Tax Legislation," *VI Bull. of Found. Lib. Center* (No. 3) 51 (1965). Following a preliminary survey in 1961, Rep. Patman caused publication of "Tax Exempt Foundations and Charitable Trusts: Their Impact on Our Economy," Chairman's Report to (House) Select Committee on Small Business, First Installment, 87th Cong., 1st Sess. (1962). Six additional installments were published over the period 1963 to 1968.
19. The Foundation Center, *The Foundation Directory*, 4th ed. (1971), vii.

private philanthropy. Recent years have also borne witness to intensified drives for tax reform, tax equality, and tax simplification. These and other developments have made the tax treatment for private foundations and their donors even more vulnerable.

Notwithstanding a variety of anti-foundation developments in the regulatory context, Congress and the executive branch of the federal government have, on occasion, affirmed their support for private foundations. For example, the Department of the Treasury had this to say about the value of foundations:

> Private philanthropy plays a special vital role in our society. Beyond providing for areas into which government cannot or should not advance (such as religion), private philanthropic organizations can be uniquely qualified to initiate thought and action, experiment with new and untried ventures, dissent from prevailing attitudes, and act quickly and flexibly.
>
> Private foundations have an important part in this work. Available even to those of relatively restricted means, they enable individuals or small groups to establish new charitable endeavors and to express their own bents, concerns, and experience. In doing so, they enrich the pluralism of our social order. Equally important, because their funds are frequently free of commitment to specific operating programs, they can shift the focus of their interest and their financial support from one charitable area to another. They can, hence, constitute a powerful instrument for evolution, growth, and improvement in the shape and direction of charity.[20]

Private foundations are an integral component of a society that values individual responsibility and private efforts for the public good. One organization championing foundations advances the following rationale:

> Foundations have the particular characteristic of serving as sources of available capital for the private philanthropic service sector of our society in all its range and variety. They thus help make possible many useful public services that would in most cases otherwise have to be provided by tax monies. They offer "the other door on which to knock," without which many volunteer activities would not be initiated and others could not be continued. They are there to respond both to new ideas and [to] shifting social needs with a freedom and flexibility that is not common to or easy for government agencies. Finally, as centers of independent thought and judgment in their own right, they help support freedom of thought, experimentation, and honest criticism directed at pressing needs of the society, including even the scrutiny and evaluation of governmental programs and policies.[21]

The great regulatory surge that swept over private foundations has largely subsided as the regulators have moved on to focus on other types of nonprofit

---

20. Treasury Department Report on Private Foundations, Committee on Finance, United States Senate, 89th Cong., 1st Sess. (1965), 5 (also 11–13).
21. Council on Foundations, Report and Recommendations to the Commission on Private Philanthropy and Public Needs on Private Philanthropic Foundations (1974), 1–8.

organizations. The federal tax laws applicable to foundations remain complex, but, for the most part, the foundation community has learned to coexist with them. Nonetheless, it must be conceded that, as the U.S. Tax Court observed (and subsequent chapters indicate), "classification as a private foundation is burdensome."[22]

## § 1.4 PRIVATE FOUNDATION LAW PRIMER

Private foundations are a type of charitable organization, exempt from federal income tax. As such, they are subject to all of the rules applicable to charitable organizations generally. In addition, private foundations are subject to more detailed and stringent rules.

### (a) Introduction

The federal tax law pertaining to private foundations was enacted as part of the Tax Reform Act of 1969. The ensuing 40-plus years have not brought much substantive change in the statutory framework. These years, however, have brought many pages of tax regulations, hundreds of private letter rulings, and a considerable number of court opinions.

Private foundation statutory law has inspired similar rules for public charities, most notably the intermediate sanctions rules,[23] some of the supporting organizations rules,[24] and the donor-advised fund rules.[25] Recently, Congress has grafted some of the private foundation rules onto the public charity rules, such as application of the excess business holdings[26] rules to donor-advised funds and application of these rules to supporting organizations.

### (b) General Operational Requirements

Private foundations must apply for recognition of tax-exempt status;[27] must file annual information returns with the IRS;[28] must meet a special organizational test;[29] must satisfy certain disclosure requirements;[30] may receive deductible charitable contributions (albeit usually within more stringent limitations than public charities);[31] must adhere to the general rules

---

22. *Friends of the Society of Servants of God v. Commissioner*, 75 T.C. 209, 212 (1980).
23. IRC § 4958. See *Tax-Exempt Organizations*, Chapter 21.
24. *See* § 15.7.
25. *See* § 16.9.
26. *See* Chapter 7.
27. *See* § 2.5.
28. *See* §§ 12.1, 12.2.
29. *See* § 1.7.
30. *See* § 12.3(b).
31. *See* Chapter 14.

imposed on tax-exempt charities, such as the general organizational test, the operational test, the private inurement doctrine, the private benefit doctrine, the limitation on legislative activities, and the prohibition on political campaign activities;[32] must comply with a battery of unique laws, where the sanctions include imposition of one or more excise taxes (most of which are subject to abatement provisions);[33] must pay an excise tax on net investment income[34] and must comply with the unrelated business rules.[35] Sanctions may apply to disqualified persons.

## (c) Disqualified Persons

A variety of persons are considered disqualified persons with respect to a private foundation. These persons are generally equivalent to insiders in connection with the private inurement doctrine.[36]

Disqualified persons with respect to private foundations are (1) substantial contributors, that is, the creator of the foundation if it is a charitable trust or a person that has contributed more than $5,000 to the foundation where the gift amount is in excess of 2 percent of the donee's total support during its existence as measured at the time of the contribution; (2) foundation managers, that is, a foundation trustee, director, officer, or an individual with similar powers or responsibilities; (3) an owner of more than 20 percent of a business where the entity is a substantial contributor; (4) a member of the family of an individual referenced in the foregoing three categories; (5) a corporation, partnership, trust, or estate in which any of the persons referenced in the foregoing four categories have more than a 35 percent ownership or other interest; (6) another private foundation (but only for purposes of the excess business holdings rules); and (7) a government official (but only for purposes of the self-dealing rules).[37]

## (d) Self-Dealing Rules

The self-dealing rules essentially prohibit, by means of excise taxes and a correction requirement, financial transactions between a private foundation and a disqualified person.[38]

Generally, self-dealing transactions are (1) sales, exchanges, or leasing of property between a private foundation and a disqualified person; (2) lending

---

32. *See Tax-Exempt Organizations* §§ 4.3, 4.5, and Chapters 20, 22, and 23, respectively.
33. *See* § 1.10.
34. *See* Chapter 10.
35. *See* Chapter 11.
36. *See Tax-Exempt Organizations* § 20.3.
37. *See* Chapter 4.
38. *See* Chapter 5.

of money or other extension of credit between a private foundation and a disqualified person; (3) furnishing of goods, services, or facilities between a private foundation and a disqualified person; (4) payment of compensation, or payment or reimbursement of expenses, by a private foundation to a disqualified person; and (5) payment by a private foundation to a governmental official (with exceptions).[39]

There are exceptions to these general rules, including (1) payment of compensation by a private foundation to a disqualified person for certain personal services, where the compensation is reasonable and is in furtherance of the foundation's exempt purposes; (2) certain lending and furnishing arrangements without interest or other charge, when done in furtherance of charitable purposes; and (3) certain transactions occurring during the administration of a decedent's estate.[40]

These rules are underlain by a series of excise taxes, beginning with an initial tax on an act of self-dealing equal to 10 percent of the amount involved. Another excise tax is imposed on a foundation manager equal to 5 percent of the amount involved, subject to a $20,000 per act maximum tax. An additional tax may be imposed on a self-dealer equal to 200 percent of the amount involved. There is an additional tax on a foundation manager equal to 50 percent of the amount involved, subject to a $20,000 per act maximum tax. The tax liability on foundation managers is joint and several. Tax abatement is not available in this context. A correction requirement is also involved.[41]

## (e)  Mandatory Payout Rules

The private foundation mandatory payout rules are designed to cause foundations to spend currently rather than indefinitely accumulate income and assets.[42]

A private foundation is generally required to pay out for charitable purposes an amount equal to 5 percent of its noncharitable assets; this involves the concepts of minimum investment return and distributable amount. The amount distributed must be in the form of a qualifying distribution, which can involve a set-aside.[43]

An initial tax is imposed on a private foundation equal to 30 percent of undistributed income. An additional tax may be imposed on a foundation equal to 100 percent of undistributed income. There is a correction requirement. Tax abatement is potentially available.[44]

---

39.  *See* § 5.3.
40.  *See* § 5.3(b), (c).
41.  *See* § 5.15.
42.  *See* Chapter 6.
43.  *See* § 6.5.
44.  *See* § 6.7.

### (f) Excess Business Holdings Rules

The excess business holdings rules are designed to prevent the control of a for-profit business by a private foundation, alone or in conjunction with its disqualified persons.[45]

A private foundation is generally prohibited, by application of excise taxes, from having excess business holdings, which generally means more than a 20 percent interest in a business; where control of the business is elsewhere, the threshold amount is 35 percent. The holdings of disqualified persons are taken into account in calculating these percentages; a 2 percent de minimis rule considers only the foundation's holdings.[46]

An initial tax on a private foundation's excess business holdings is imposed, equal to 10 percent of the value of the holdings. An additional tax may be imposed equal to 200 percent of the value of excess business holdings. There is a correction requirement. Tax abatement is potentially available.[47]

### (g) Jeopardizing Investments Rules

The jeopardizing investments rules imposed on private foundations can be viewed as a federal tax law codification of traditional prudent investment principles. These rules parallel state laws under which the managers of a private foundation have a fiduciary responsibility to safeguard its assets on behalf of its charitable constituents.[48]

A private foundation is subject to sanctions if it invests an amount in a manner that would jeopardize the carrying out of an exempt purpose. There is no per se type of jeopardizing investment. An investment jeopardizes exempt purposes of a private foundation where its foundation managers failed to exercise ordinary business care and prudence, at the time the investment was made, in providing for the short-term and long-term financial needs of the foundation in connection with the conduct of its charitable programs.[49]

These rules are inapplicable to program-related investments, the primary purpose of which is to achieve charitable objectives and no significant purpose of which is the production of income or appreciation in the value of property.[50]

An initial tax is imposed on a private foundation in the amount of 10 percent of the jeopardizing investment. An initial tax is imposed on foundation managers in the amount of 10 percent of the investment, when they knowingly participated in it, subject to a $10,000 per investment maximum tax. An

---

45. *See* Chapter 7.
46. *See* § 7.2.
47. *See* § 7.6.
48. *See* Chapter 8.
49. *See* § 8.1.
50. *See* § 8.3.

additional tax in the amount of 25 percent may be imposed on a private foundation. There is an additional tax on foundation managers, subject to a $20,000 per investment maximum tax. There is a correction requirement. Tax abatement is potentially available.[51]

The Prudent Investor Rules outlined by the American Bar Association in its Restatement of the Law Trust Series contain guidance on this subject.

## (h)   Taxable Expenditures Rules

The taxable expenditures rules place limitations on the types of grants private foundation are permitted to make.[52]

A private foundation makes a taxable expenditure if it pays or incurs an amount to carry on propaganda or otherwise attempts to influence legislation. These rules may be triggered if a foundation makes a grant to a public charity that attempts to influence legislation or if the foundation makes the expenditure directly. A private foundation may, however, engage in nonpartisan analysis, study, or research, as well as make expenditures that are protected by the self-defense exception.[53]

A private foundation makes a taxable expenditure if it pays or incurs an amount to influence the outcome of a public election, although the funding of certain voter registration drives is permitted.[54] A foundation makes a taxable expenditure if it makes certain types of grants to individuals.[55] A foundation makes a taxable expenditure when it makes a grant, loan, or other form of program-related investment, for charitable purposes, to an entity other than a public charity (except a Type III non–functionally integrated supporting organization), unless it exercises expenditure responsibility.[56] A foundation makes a taxable expenditure if it pays or incurs an amount for a noncharitable purpose.[57] Special rules apply in connection with grants to foreign charities.[58]

An initial excise tax of 20 percent is imposed on a private foundation's taxable expenditure. An initial tax of 5 percent is imposed on a foundation manager who agreed to the making of the expenditure, absent reasonable cause, subject to a per-expenditure maximum tax of $10,000. An additional tax may be imposed on a private foundation at the rate of 100 percent. An additional tax may be imposed on a foundation manager at the rate of 50 percent, subject to a

---

51. *See* § 8.4.
52. *See* Chapter 9.
53. *See* § 9.1.
54. *See* § 9.2.
55. *See* § 9.3.
56. *See* § 9.9.
57. *See* § 9.8.
58. *See* § 9.5.

per-expenditure maximum tax of $20,000. There is a correction requirement. Tax abatement is potentially available.[59]

### (i)  Tax on Investment Income

Generally, a private foundation is required to pay an excise tax of 2 percent on its net investment income. Under certain circumstances, this tax is reduced to 1 percent.[60] This tax is not imposed on exempt operating foundations.

### (j)  Termination of Private Foundation Status

Termination rules apply to private foundations, designed to prevent foundations from ceasing to be a charitable organization so that it can use its funds and assets for noncharitable purposes.[61]

A private foundation's status may be voluntarily terminated by transfer of all of its income and assets to one or more public charities or if the foundation becomes a public charity.[62] A foundation's status may be involuntarily terminated if it engages in willful, flagrant, or repeated acts (or failures to act) giving rise to one or more of the private foundation excise taxes; a foundation in this circumstance would be liable for a termination tax.[63]

Special rules apply when a private foundation transfers assets to another private foundation pursuant to a liquidation, merger, redemption, recapitalization, or other adjustment.[64]

### (k)  Record-Keeping and Grant-Making Suggestions

A private foundation should maintain a permanent file for each of its grant recipients that reflects the purpose of the grant. The approval process followed, including verification of grantee's qualification either as a public charity or an entity requiring expenditure responsibility agreement, schedule of required follow-up reports, and other information about the grantee would be kept in the file. Some foundations scan and retain all relevant data in an electronic form.

A private foundation should carefully describe its charitable mission and the specific types of programs it supports. Some foundations develop written grant guidelines to inform interested persons of the purposes for which the foundation will grant funds. A grant application or proposal should be required for each potential grantee.

---

59. *See* § 9.10.
60. *See* Chapter 10.
61. *See* Chapter 13.
62. *See* § 13.1.
63. *See* § 13.2.
64. *See* § 13.5.

From a federal tax law perspective, there is no requirement for a private foundation to keep the paperwork with respect to grants that are not awarded. Some foundations find it useful to retain these materials for a few years for reference in the event an organization replies or there is an inquiry about the grant deliberation process.

### (l)  Charitable Giving Rules

Generally, contributions to private foundations give rise to a federal income tax charitable contribution deduction.[65]

There are percentage limitations on the deductibility, for federal income tax purposes, of gifts by individuals to charitable organizations. These limitations are more stringent than is the case with respect to gifts to public charities: (1) 30 percent of adjusted gross income in instances of gifts of money (as contrasted with 50 percent for such gifts to public charities) and (2) 20 percent of adjusted gross income in instances of gifts of property (as contrasted with 30 percent for such gifts to public charities). For purposes of these percentage limitations, private operating foundations, private foundations where there are certain distributions out of corpus, and common fund private foundations are treated as public charities.[66]

Generally, a contribution of property that has appreciated in value to a charitable organization gives rise to a charitable deduction based on the property's fair market value. This type of gift to a private foundation, however, generally is deductible only to the extent of the donor's basis in the property, although there is an exception for gifts of qualified appreciated securities.[67]

Gifts to private foundations are subject to the general rules for all charitable gifts as to record-keeping, substantiation, appraisal, disclosure, and reporting requirements.[68] These gifts also qualify for the gift and estate tax charitable deductions.

### (m)  Unrelated Business Rules

Private foundations are subject to the unrelated business rules.[69] Because of the excess business holdings rules, however, private foundations are limited in their ability to to directly conduct an unrelated trade or business or to invest in pass-through entities that conduct unrelated businesses. The excess business holdings rules exclude from the definition of business enterprise any activity that derives at least 95 percent of its gross income from passive sources, such as

---

65. *See* Chapter 14.
66. *See* § 14.1(b).
67. *See* § 14.2.
68. *See* § 14.6.
69. *See* Chapter 11.

interest, dividends, royalties, rent, and capital gains. This exclusion ties in with the modifications applicable in the unrelated business context. For these purposes, income does not lose its character as passive income because it is debt-financed. The exceptions to unrelated business income taxation apply with respect to private foundations (although they are infrequently utilized).

## § 1.5 STATISTICAL PROFILE

Private foundations today number, as noted, about 90,000 charitable organizations.[70] These organizations held $588.5 billion in assets for that year.[71] Although more than two thirds of all annual information returns filed by private foundations for 2009 were filed by foundations with less than $1 million in assets, these entities held less than 3 percent of the total assets. The largest foundations, those holding assets valued at $100 million or more, represented less than 1 percent of all returns filed for 2009; these organizations, however, held 58.6 percent of total assets.

Investment assets accounted for almost 92 percent of the total asset value reported by private foundations for 2009. The total amount of investment assets of foundations for that year was $539.8 billion. Revenue of foundations in 2009 totaled $42.4 billion.

Distributions by nonoperating foundations amounted to $43.3 billion. Qualifying distributions, in the form of grants, constituted 88.8 percent of this amount. Another 8.6 percent of qualifying distributions consisted of operating and administrative expenses. Program-related investments, amounts paid to acquire assets, and set-asides accounted for the remaining 2.6 percent of qualifying distributions.

Foundations' qualifying distributions exceeded the required distributable amount of $23.4 billion to varying degrees across each asset-size category. Generally, as asset size increased, the extent to which foundations' qualifying distributions exceeded the required distributable amount decreased. In the aggregate, the small foundations—those with less than $1 million in assets— reported total qualifying distributions that were more than five times larger than their required distributable amount. Foundations with assets between $1 million and $10 million disbursed amounts that were twice their required distributable amount, while those with assets of $10 million or more disbursed slightly less than twice their required distributable amount.

---

70. The most recent data concerning private foundations compiled by the IRS is for tax year 2009. In that year, domestic private foundations filed 92,624 annual information returns (Forms 990-PF). The statistics in this section are derived from Belmonte, "Domestic Private Foundations and Related Excise Taxes, Tax Year 2009," 32 *Statistics of Income Bulletin* 114, no. 3 (Winter 2013).

71. This asset value remains significantly below the prerecession amount of $674 billion (for 2007).

Self-dealing acts, of which there were 294, involved $14.9 million; the average act of self-dealing amount was $51,000. Self-dealing taxes totaled $1.7 million, representing the second-largest excise tax amount. The highest amount was for the tax on undistributed income.

Nonoperating private foundations paid $43.3 billion in total qualifying distributions for 2009, of which 88.8 percent were in the form of grants. Program-related investments, amounts paid to acquire assets, and set-asides accounted for 2.6 percent of qualifying distributions. Foundations' qualifying distributions exceeded the required distributable amount of $23.4 billion to varying degrees across the asset-size category; foundations with assets of $10 million or more disbursed slightly less than twice their required amount. A mere 1,285 private foundations reported a total of $20.8 million of taxable undistributed income.

Five private foundations reported nine excess business holdings (totaling $13.7 million); taxes amounted to $1.4 million. Ninety-eight private foundations reported 153 taxable expenditures, causing total tax of slightly more than $640,000. No jeopardizing investments were reported.

## § 1.6  FOUNDATIONS IN OVERALL EXEMPT ORGANIZATIONS CONTEXT

Within the realm of tax-exempt organizations, there are relatively few private foundations; they account for about 5 percent of exempt organizations.

Nearly all tax-exempt organizations are identified as such by federal statute.[72] Some, mostly governmental entities, are exempt in accordance with a constitutional law doctrine, such as the doctrine of intergovernmental immunity.

Of those tax-exempt organizations that have a statutory authorization, more than 50 percent are *charitable* in nature.[73] The term *charitable* encompasses entities that are charitable in a technical sense as well as those that qualify as educational, religious, scientific, and like entities. Each of these types of entities is defined in the federal tax law.[74]

There are, however, many additional types of tax-exempt organizations other than those that are charitable in nature. Other exempt organizations (often ones that private foundations will encounter) include title-holding corporations,[75]

---

72. Most categories of tax-exempt organizations are the subject of IRC § 501(c). Other types of exempt organizations are referenced in IRC §§ 526–529.
73. That is, they are tax-exempt organizations described in IRC § 501(c)(3).
74. *See* § 1.5.
75. That is, entities described in IRC § 501(c)(2) and (25). *See Tax-Exempt Organizations* § 19.2 and *Tax Planning and Compliance*, Chapter 10.

social welfare organizations,[76] labor organizations,[77] business and professional associations,[78] social clubs,[79] fraternal organizations,[80] veteran's' organizations,[81] and political organizations.[82]

## § 1.7  DEFINITION OF *CHARITY*

A private foundation must be operated for charitable purposes. For the most part, this means that a foundation must confine its grant-making and other programs to charitable ends. One of the many responsibilities, then, of private foundation management is to be certain that each of the foundation's grantees, or its programs, qualify under one or more rationales for being charitable.

The federal tax law definition of the term *charitable* is based on English common law and trust law precepts. Federal income tax regulations recognize this fact by stating that the term is used in its "generally accepted legal sense."[83] At the same time, court decisions continue to expand the concept of *charity* by introducing additional (more contemporary) applications of the term. As one court observed, evolutions in the definition of the word *charitable* are "wrought by changes in moral and ethical precepts generally held, or by changes in relative values assigned to different and sometimes competing and even conflicting interests of society."[84]

The term *charitable* in the federal income tax setting, in the more technical sense, embraces a variety of purposes and activities. These include relief of the poor and distressed or of the underprivileged, the advancement of religion, advancement of education, advancement of science, lessening of the burdens of government, community beautification and maintenance, promotion of health, promotion of social welfare, promotion of environmental conservancy, advancement of patriotism, care of orphans, maintenance of public confidence

---

76. That is, entities described in IRC § 501(c)(4). *See Tax-Exempt Organizations*, Chapter 13, and *Tax Planning and Compliance*, Chapter 6.
77. That is, entities described in IRC § 501(c)(5). *See Tax-Exempt Organizations* § 16.1 and *Tax Planning and Compliance*, Chapter 7.
78. That is, entities described in IRC § 501(c)(6). *See Tax-Exempt Organizations*, Chapter 14, and *Tax Planning and Compliance*, Chapter 8.
79. That is, entities described in IRC § 501(c)(7). *See Tax-Exempt Organizations*, Chapter 15, and *Tax Planning and Compliance*, Chapter 9.
80. That is, entities described in IRC § 501(c)(8) and (10). *See Tax-Exempt Organizations* § 19.4.
81. That is, organizations described in IRC § 501(c)(19). *See Tax-Exempt Organizations* § 19.11.
82. That is, organizations described in IRC § 527. *See Tax-Exempt Organizations*, Chapter 17, and *Tax Planning and Compliance*, Chapter 23.
83. Income Tax Regulations (Reg.) § 1.501(c)(3)-1(d)(2).
84. *Green v. Connelly*, 330 F. Supp. 1150, 1159 (D.D.C. 1971), *aff'd sub nom. Coit v. Green*, 404 U.S. 997 (1971).

in the legal system, facilitating student and cultural exchanges, and promotion and advancement of amateur sports.[85]

*Charitable organizations*, as that term is used in the most encompassing manner, includes *educational* organizations. In addition to institutions such as schools, colleges, universities, museums, and libraries, educational organizations are those that (1) provide instruction or training of individuals in a variety of subjects for the purpose of improving or developing their capabilities or (2) instruct the public on subjects useful to the individual and beneficial to the community.[86]

*Religious* organizations are part of the community of charitable organizations. These entities are churches and other membership and nonmembership religious organizations. For reasons of constitutional law, the terms *religion* and *religious* cannot be accorded a definition applied by governmental agencies.[87]

*Scientific* organizations are, for the most part, those that engage in scientific research. Entities that are scientific in nature may have as their primary purpose the dissemination of scientific information by such means as publications and conferences. These organizations may also be considered educational in nature.[88]

# § 1.8  OPERATING FOR CHARITABLE PURPOSES

A private foundation, as is the case with all tax-exempt charitable organizations, must meet a standard for qualification as a charitable organization, referred to as the *operational test*. This test requires that the private foundation operate *exclusively* to accomplish one or more of the eight purposes referenced in the Internal Revenue Code: religious, charitable, scientific, testing for public safety, literary, or educational purposes, or to foster national or international amateur sports competition, or for the prevention of cruelty to children or animals.[89] The term *exclusively* for purposes of the organizational test does not literally mean exclusively, but rather means *primarily*.[90] Consequently, the conduct of some amount of nonexempt activity is permitted for organizations qualifying for tax exemption as charitable organizations. Due to the application of the private foundation sanctions,[91] however, a private foundation must operate only, or truly exclusively, for one or more of the named charitable

---

85. Reg. § 1.501(c)(3)-1(d)(2). *See Tax-Exempt Organizations*, Chapter 7, and *Tax Planning and Compliance*, Chapter 4.
86. Reg. § 1.501(c)(3)-1(d)(3). *See Tax-Exempt Organizations*, Chapter 8, and *Tax Planning and Compliance*, Chapter 5.
87. *See Tax-Exempt Organizations*, Chapter 10, and *Tax Planning and Compliance*, Chapter 3.
88. Reg. § 1.501(c)(3)-1(d)(5). *See Tax-Exempt Organizations*, Chapter 9.
89. *See* § 1.5.
90. Reg. § 1.501(c)(3)-1(d)(1)(ii).
91. *See* § 1.10.

purposes. The organizational test also requires that the organization's articles of organization provide that no part of the net earnings of the corporation, community chest, fund, or foundation inure to the benefit of any private shareholder or individual.[92] Simply stated, a private foundation may not operate to accomplish the private purposes or serve the private interests of its founders, those who control it, those who fund it, or their families—these persons are termed *disqualified persons*.[93]

A qualifying private foundation promotes the general welfare of society. Evidence for satisfaction of this operational test is found not only in the nature of the nonprofit's activities but also in its sources of financial support, the constituency for whom it operates, and the nature of its expenditures. The presence of a single nonexempt program, if substantial in nature, will destroy the exemption regardless of the number or importance of the truly exempt purposes.[94]

The benefit to an individual participating in a foundation's programs is acceptable when the activity itself is considered a charitable pursuit. Examples of these benefits are the advancement a student receives from attending college and the relief from suffering experienced by a sick person. The standards of permissible individual benefit are different for certain of the eight categories of charitable purpose, and the distinctions are sometimes vague and not necessarily logical. For example, promoting amateur sports competition is treated as an exempt purpose, but maintaining an athletic facility that restricts its availability to less than the entire community is not charitable.[95] A sports club serving only its individual members is not charitable,[96] but a fitness center promoting health and available to the general public may qualify as a charitable organization.[97] Visiting a museum or attending a play is recognized as educational, but attending a semiprofessional baseball game is not.[98]

---

92. *See* § 5.1.
93. *See* Chapter 4. A strange and troublesome opinion from the U.S. Tax Court was based on the operational test. On that occasion, the court held that an organization cannot qualify for tax-exempt status as a charitable or educational entity because its activities and those of its founder, sole director, and officer are essentially identical (*Salvation Navy, Inc. v. Commissioner*, 84 T.C.M. 506 [2002]). The court wrote that the affairs of the organization and this individual are "irretrievably intertwined," so that the "benefits" of tax exemption would "inure" to the individual personally (at 508). Many charities engage in activities that their founders would otherwise personally undertake, and they are under the direct control of these individuals; this is typical of a private foundation.
94. *Better Business Bureau of Washington, D.C. v. United States*, 326 U.S. 279, 284 (1945).
95. Rev. Rul. 67-325, 1967-2 C.B. 113.
96. *I Media Sports League, Inc. v. Commissioner*, 52 T.C.M. 1092 (1986).
97. E.g., IRS Private Letter Ruling (Priv. Ltr. Rul.) 8935061. An important issue in these private rulings is whether fees charged limit the availability of the facility to the general public—a characteristic required to prove that the organization operates for charitable purposes.
98. *Hutchinson Baseball Enterprises, Inc. v. Commissioner*, 73 T.C. 144 (1979), *aff'd*, 696 F.2d 757 (10th Cir. 1982); *Wayne Baseball, Inc. v. Commissioner*, 78 T.C.M. 437 (1999).

To prove that its programs benefit the public, rather than private individuals, a private foundation often must be found to benefit an indefinite class of persons—a charitable class—rather than a particular individual or a limited group of individuals. It may not be "organized or operated for the benefit of private interests such as designated individuals, the creator's family, shareholders of the organization or persons controlled, directly or indirectly, by such private interests."[99] Thus, a trust established to benefit an impoverished retired minister and his wife cannot qualify.[100] Likewise, a fund established to raise money to finance a medical operation, rebuild a house destroyed by fire, or provide food for a particular person does not benefit a charitable class. An organization formed by merchants to relocate homeless persons from a downtown area was found to serve the merchant class and promote their interests, rather than those of the homeless or the citizens.[101] In explaining the meaning of the word *charitable*, the regulations also deem federal, state, and local governments to be charitable entities by stipulating that relieving their burdens is a form of charitable activity qualifying for tax exemption.[102]

A comparatively small group of individuals can be benefited as long as the group is not limited to identifiable individuals. The class need not be indigent, poor, or distressed.[103] A scholarship fund for a college fraternity that provided school tuition for deserving members was ruled to be a tax-exempt foundation,[104] but a trust formed to aid destitute or disabled members of a particular college class was deemed to benefit a limited class. The "general law of charity recognizes that a narrowly defined class of beneficiaries will not cause a charitable trust to fail unless the trust's purposes are personal, private, or selfish as to lack the element of public usefulness."[105] Criteria for selection of eligible beneficiaries should be followed, and evidence used to choose eligible individuals—case histories, grade reports, financial information, recommendations from specialists, and the like—should be maintained.

A genealogical society tracing the migrations to and within the United States of persons with a common name was found to qualify as a tax-exempt social

---

99. Reg. § 1.501(c)(3)-1(d)(1)(iii).
100. *Carrie A. Maxwell Trust, Pasadena Methodist Foundation v. Commissioner*, 2 T.C.M. 905 (1943).
101. *Westward Ho v. Commissioner*, 63 T.C.M. 2617 (1992).
102. Reg. § 1.501(c)(3)-1(d)(2); see § 4.6 of *Tax Planning and Compliance* for discussion of standards for qualifying as "Lessening the Burdens of Government." See also "How the Concept of Charity Has Evolved," presentation for the American Bar Association Exempt Organization Committee, 16 *Exempt Org. Tax Rev.* (No. 3) 403–412 (Mar. 1997).
103. *Consumer Credit Counseling Service of Alabama, Inc. v. United States*, 78-2 U.S.T.C. ¶ 9468 (D.C.1979), but *see El Paso del Aquila Elderly v. Commissioner*, 64 T.C.M. 376 (1992) (making burial insurance available at cost for the elderly is a charitable activity only if distress is relieved, by allowing indigents to participate, and the community as a whole benefits).
104. Rev. Rul. 56-403, 1956-2 C.B. 307.
105. IRS General Counsel Memorandum (Gen. Couns. Mem.) 39876.

club, rather than a charity. Although there was educational merit in the historical information compiled, the private interest of the family group was held to predominate.[106] If membership in the society is open to all and its focus is educational—presenting lectures, sponsoring exhibitions, publishing a geographic area's pioneer history—it may be classified as charitable.[107] In contrast, a society limiting its membership to one family and compiling research data for family members individually cannot qualify for tax exemption.[108]

A simple way to prove that an organization operates to benefit a charitable class is for the organization to regrant its monies only to another public charitable organization. Congress imposed such a system on private foundations in 1969 to constrain their grant-making freedom, as described in the analysis of the expenditure responsibility rules.[109] Private foundations can grant monies to individuals and nonpublic entities for a charitable purpose, but only if they enter into a formal contractual agreement with the grant recipient or obtain IRS approval in advance for individual grant programs. Although there are no such formal rules for public charities, a similar burden to prove that grant funds reach a charitable class exists. The IRS inserts the following language in the determination letters of grant-making public charities:

> This determination is based upon evidence that your funds are dedicated to the purposes listed in section 501(c)(3). To assure your continued exemption, you should maintain records to show that funds are expended only for such purposes. If you distribute funds to other organizations, your records should show whether they are exempt under section 501(c)(3). In cases where the recipient organization is not exempt under section 501(c)(3), there should be evidence that the funds will remain dedicated to the required purposes and that they will be used for those purposes by the recipient.

An organization's tax-exempt status was revoked because it failed to prove that its individual refugee relief payments were made to members of a charitable class. The IRS agreed to reinstate the exemption only if all payments were made directly to charitable organizations, governmental units, or organizations that would otherwise qualify as public charities (presumably foreign relief groups such as the World Health Organization or the United Nations Relief Agency).[110] Similarly, an organization lost its exempt status for lack of evidence that it served a charitable class.[111] The organization operated canteen-style lunch trucks and argued that the food was provided to needy persons on a

---

106. *Callaway Family Association, Inc. v. Commissioner*, 71 T.C. 340 (1978); Rev. Rul. 67-8, 1967-1 C.B. 142.
107. Rev. Rul. 80-301, 1980-2 C.B. 180.
108. Rev. Rul. 80-302, 1980-2 C.B. 182.
109. *See* Chapter 9.
110. Revocation letter dated May 24, 1993, issued to the National Defense Council.
111. *New Faith, Inc. v. Commissioner*, 64 T.C.M. 1050 (1992).

donation or "love offering basis." The evidence found lacking by the court included:

- There was no record of the number of persons, if any, receiving food items for free or below cost nor the number of customers who were impoverished or needy persons.
- No tally of sales below fair market value was maintained.
- Written statements of the organization did not show that food was offered to anybody free or below cost.

The some 9,000 current and former employees, volunteers, and families of an exempt healthcare provider were found by the IRS to be a sufficiently large class of beneficiaries to qualify as a charitable class. Gifts to the assistance fund created by the hospital were ruled deductible as charitable gifts because they were not earmarked for any specific person. The IRS also noted that the contributions were not made with the expectation of individual financial benefit, but instead were voluntary gifts to provide assistance to financially needy persons suffering economic hardship due to accident, loss, or disaster.[112]

The IRS, however, subsequently adopted a contrary position and reversed its ruling that a company foundation's disaster relief program was charitable.[113] Although there was some public benefit from the foundation's provision of assistance in times of disaster or financial crisis, the IRS did not find any assurance that selection of beneficiaries solely among employees of a particular employer serves the best interests of the public. Instead, the foundation was deemed to serve "the private interests of X and its subsidiaries who utilize such benefit programs to recruit and retain a more stable and productive workforce." Because the beneficiaries were a designated or limited group—employees of a specific company—they did not constitute a charitable class, and the foundation could not qualify for a tax exemption. For the same reasons, the disbursements made by the foundation were taxable expenditures[114] of benefit to the company officials and owners. Because the benefit to the company was more than incidental and tenuous, the grants distributed by the foundation also resulted in acts of self-dealing.[115] Additionally, the expenditures did not constitute qualifying distributions[116] because they did not serve a charitable purpose.

---

112. Priv. Ltr. Rul. 9316051, modified and superseded by Priv. Ltr. Rul. 9741047 (with the IRS stressing the facts that the class of eligible beneficiaries is "sufficiently large and open-ended," and that beneficiaries are selected on an "objective and nondiscriminatory basis" designed to provide relief to those who are "needy and distressed").
113. Priv. Ltr. Rul. 199914040, revoking Priv. Ltr. Rul. 9516047.
114. *See* Chapter 9.
115. *See* § 5.8(c).
116. *See* § 6.5.

A similar issue can arise in connection with a company foundation's scholarship plan. To qualify as a charitable program, this type of plan must meet mathematical tests essentially designed to limit the probability of an employee's qualification to assure that such foundations do not overly serve the private interests of an employer.[117]

## § 1.9  ORGANIZATIONAL RULES

One of the fundamental requirements in the law pertaining to tax-exempt organizations, particularly charitable ones, is that these organizations must be *organized* for one or more tax-exempt purposes. This is known as the *organizational test*.[118]

The organizational test for charitable organizations, in general, emphasizes two requirements. One focuses on the organization's statement of purposes, requiring language that articulates a charitable end and forbidding language that may empower the organization to engage, to more than an insubstantial extent, in noncharitable activities or to pursue noncharitable purposes.[119] The other mandates a *dissolution clause*, which directs the passage of the organization's assets and net income, in the event of its dissolution or liquidation, for charitable ends, usually by causing transfer of the assets and income to one or more other charitable organizations.[120]

There is, however, a separate and additional organizational test for private foundations. A private foundation cannot be exempt from federal income tax (nor will contributions to it be deductible as charitable gifts) unless its governing instrument or the provisions of state law applicable to it include provisions, the effects of which are to require distributions at such time and in such manner as to comply with the annual payout rules and prohibit the foundation from engaging in any act of self-dealing, retaining any excess business holdings, making any jeopardizing investments, or making any taxable expenditures.[121] Generally, these provisions must be in the foundation's articles of organization[122] and not merely in its bylaws.[123]

The provisions of the governing instrument of a private foundation or applicable state law must require or prohibit, as the case may be, the foundation to act or refrain from acting so that the foundation, and any foundation

---

117. *See* § 9.3(e).
118. Reg. § 1.501(c)(3)-1(b).
119. Reg. § 1.501(c)(3)-1(b)(1).
120. Reg. § 1.501(c)(3)-1(b)(2).
121. IRC § 508(e)(1); Reg. § 1.508-3(a). *See* Chapters 5–9.
122. *See* § 2.1.
123. Reg. § 1.508-3(c).

managers or other disqualified persons with respect to the foundation, will not be liable for any of the private foundation excise taxes.[124] The governing instrument of a nonexempt split-interest trust[125] must contain comparable provisions in respect to any of the applicable private foundation excise taxes.[126]

Specific reference in the governing instrument to the appropriate sections of the Internal Revenue Code is generally required, unless equivalent language is used that is deemed by the IRS to have the same full force and effect. A governing instrument that contains only language sufficient to satisfy the requirements of the organizational test for charitable organizations in general, however,[127] does not meet the specific requirements applicable with respect to private foundations, regardless of the interpretation placed on the language as a matter of law by a state court.[128] A governing instrument of a private foundation does not meet these organizational requirements if it expressly prohibits the distribution of capital or corpus.[129]

A private foundation's governing instrument is deemed to conform with the requisite organizational requirements if valid provisions of state law have been enacted that require the foundation to act or refrain from acting so as not to subject it to any of the private foundation excise taxes or that treat the required provisions as being contained in the foundation's governing instrument.[130] The IRS ruled as to which state statutes contain sufficient provisions in this regard.[131]

Any provision of state law is presumed to be valid as enacted and, in the absence of state law provisions to the contrary, applies with respect to any private foundation that does not specifically disclaim coverage under state law (either by notification to the appropriate state official or by commencement of judicial proceedings).[132] If a state law provision is declared invalid or inapplicable with respect to a class of foundations by the highest appellate court of the state involved or by the U.S. Supreme Court, the foundations covered by the determination must meet the private foundation organizational

---

124. Reg. § 1.508-3(b)(1). Rev. Rul. 70-270, 1970-1 C.B. 135, contains sample governing instrument provisions.
125. *See* § 13.2.
126. Reg. § 1.508-3(b)(1). Rev. Rul. 74-368, 1974-2 C.B. 390, contains sample governing instrument provisions.
127. *See* text accompanied by *supra* note 116.
128. Reg. § 1.508-3(b)(1).
129. Reg. § 1.508-3(b). In one instance, a charitable testamentary trust was found to have violated the private foundation organizational rules because the trust instrument required the trust to accumulate, rather than distribute, income; a state court ordered modification of the instrument to provide for the requisite distribution of the foundation's income (*Estate of Lee H. Barnes*, 74-1 U.S.T.C. ¶ 9241 [Court of Common Pleas of Lancaster County, Pa. (1973)]).
130. Reg. § 1.508-3(d)(1).
131. Rev. Rul. 75-38, 1975-1 C.B. 161.
132. Reg. § 1.508-3(d)(2)(i).

requirements within one year from the date on which the time for perfecting an application for review by the Supreme Court expires. If this application is filed, these requirements must be met within one year from the date on which the Supreme Court disposes of the case, whether by denial of the application for review or decision on the merits.[133] If a provision of state law is declared invalid or inapplicable with respect to a class of foundations by a court of competent jurisdiction, and the decision is not reviewed by the highest state appellate court or the Supreme Court, and the IRS notifies the general public that the provision has been declared invalid or inapplicable, then all private foundations in the state involved must meet these organizational requirements, without reliance on the statute to the extent declared invalid or inapplicable by the decision, within one year from the date the notice is made public.[134] These rules do not apply to a foundation that is subject to a final judgment entered by a court of competent jurisdiction, holding the law invalid or inapplicable with respect to the foundation.[135]

In one case, a charitable trust created by will in 1967 had its trust instrument amended by court order to enable the trust, a private foundation, to comply with the organizational requirements.[136] In a similar case, the trustees of a private foundation were permitted by a state court to modify a trust document to facilitate compliance by the foundation with these organizational rules.[137]

## § 1.10  PRIVATE FOUNDATION SANCTIONS

The federal tax rules pertaining to private foundations are often stated as if they are laws, in the sense of rules governing human conduct. This is technically not the case, in that these rules—comprising part of the Internal Revenue Code—are cast as tax provisions. Thus, the law states that if a course of conduct is engaged in, the imposition of one or more taxes will be the (or a) result. For example, there is no rule of law that states that a private foundation may not engage in an act of self-dealing; rather, the law is that an act of self-dealing will trigger a tax.

Each of the private foundation rules, then, is underlain with a series of taxes. These are portrayed as excise taxes. The taxes are severe and are intended to deter or stimulate conduct, rather than to raise revenue.

---

133. Reg. § 1.508-3(d)(2)(ii).
134. Reg. § 1.508-3(d)(2)(iii).
135. Reg. § 1.508-3(d)(2)(iv).
136. *Matter of Jeanne E. Barkey*, 71-1 U.S.T.C. ¶ 9350 (Surrogate's Court of New York County, NY [1971]).
137. *William Wikoff Smith Trust Estate, "The W. W. Smith Foundation,"* 72-1 U.S.T.C. ¶ 9271 (C.P. Montgomery County Orphans' Court, Pa. [1971]).

Indeed, these excise taxes are more accurately characterized as penalties. For example, the legislative history of the self-dealing rules is replete with references to the tax sanctions as "penalties." The report of the House Committee on Ways and Means accompanying its version of the 1969 tax legislation stated that the "permissible activities of private foundations . . . are substantially tightened to *prevent* self-dealing between the foundations and their substantial contributors."[138] The Committee added that it "has determined to generally *prohibit* self-dealing transactions and provide a variety and graduation of sanctions."[139] In this report there are numerous references to these sanctions as constituting "prohibitions" or arising out of "prohibited" conduct. Identical or similar language appears in the report of the Senate Committee on Finance in its version of the 1969 legislation.[140] This continues to be the view of Congress on the subject, in that a report of the Ways and Means Committee issued in 1996 refers to the private foundation rules as a "penalty regime."[141]

The courts, as well, view these private foundation tax provisions as penalties. For example, two federal appellate courts rejected the argument that the self-dealing taxes are mere excise levies and held that these taxes are penal in nature.[142] This wide-ranging view that the private foundation rules are sanctioned by penalties inevitably leads to the view that the rules broadly encompass foundations' operations. Certainly the IRS accords the broadest of interpretations to this area of the law and, correspondingly, strict and narrow readings as to the exceptions.

Because of the nature of this statutory tax structure, a person subject to tax does not merely pay it and continue with the transaction and its consequences, as is the case with nearly all other federal tax regimes. This structure weaves a series of spiraling taxes from which the private foundation, and/or disqualified person(s), can emerge only by paying one or more taxes and either correcting (undoing) the transaction involved by repaying the money or returning assets or having the foundation's income and assets confiscated by the IRS.

The private foundation rules collectively stand as devices Congress created for the purpose of curbing what was perceived as a host of abuses being perpetrated through the use of private foundations by those who control or

---

138. H. Rep. No. 91-413, 91st Cong., 1st Sess. (1969), Part I at 4 (emphasis added).
139. *Id.*, Part IV at 21 (emphasis added).
140. S. Rep. No. 91-552, 91st Cong., 1st Sess. (1969).
141. H. Rep. No. 104-506, 104th Cong., 2d Sess. 56 (1996). This observation was made in the context of a discussion of the intermediate sanctions rules applicable with respect to public charities, social welfare organizations, and certain nonprofit insurance issuers (IRC § 4958), which in many ways are structured in the same fashion as the private foundations rules. In general, *see Intermediate Sanctions.*
142. *Mahon v. United States* (In re Unified Control Systems, Inc.), 586 F.2d 1036 (5th Cir. 1978); *United States v. Feinblatt* (In re Kline), 547 F.2d 823 (4th Cir. 1977). Also *Rockefeller v. United States*, 572 F. Supp. 9 (E.D. Ark. 1982), *aff'd per curiam*, 718 F.2d 290 (8th Cir. 1983), *cert. den.*, 460 U.S. 962 (1984); *Estate of Bernard J. Reis v. Commissoner*, 87 T.C. 1016 (1986).

manipulate them (disqualified persons).[143] Congress addressed the problems from several directions, through prohibitions on self-dealing,[144] mandatory payouts for charitable purposes,[145] prohibitions on substantial holdings of business enterprises,[146] prohibitions on engaging in jeopardizing (speculative) investments,[147] and a cluster of other banned activities, the funding of which is considered taxable expenditures.[148] These and other related provisions comprise Chapter 42 of the Internal Revenue Code. Similar constraints were placed on certain supporting organizations and donor-advised funds in 2006.[149]

The taxes imposed for violation of the private foundation rules are structured as a tripartite level of taxation: initial (first-tier) taxes, additional (second-tier) taxes, and the involuntary termination (third-tier or confiscation) taxes. The first and second of these taxes are characterized as excise taxes and are outlined in Exhibit 1.2.[150] The third of these taxes is imposed when the IRS requires termination of the foundation due to flagrant violations of the rules.[151] Form 4720 is filed to report the incidents and calculate any taxes due.[152]

The penalty provisions of these excise taxes do not contain an exception, or excuse, for imposition of the penalty on a private foundation for failure to comply with the specific provisions. The regulations accompanying these provisions, however, contain relief for those foundation managers who do not condone or participate in the decision to conduct a prohibited action. Until 1984, the penalties were strictly applied.[153] Congress in 1984 added statutes[154] to permit abatement of the penalties imposed on both the foundation and its managers if it is established to the satisfaction of the IRS that:

- The taxable event was due to reasonable cause and not to willful neglect, and

- The event was corrected within the correction period for such event.

---

143. *See* Chapter 4.
144. *See* Chapter 5.
145. *See* Chapter 6.
146. *See* Chapter 7.
147. *See* Chapter 8.
148. *See* Chapter 9.
149. *See* Chapters 15 and 16.
150. The specifics of these excise taxes for each of the sets of private foundation rules are the subject of the last sections of Chapters 5–9.
151. *See* Chapter 13.
152. This form is reproduced as Exhibit 12.6 in Chapter 12.
153. *Charles Stewart Mott Foundation v. United States*, 91-2 U.S.T.C. ¶ 50340 (6th Cir. 1991); *Mannheimer Charitable Trust, Hans S. v. Commissioner*, 93 T.C. 35 (1989).
154. IRC §§ 4961– 4963.

**EXHIBIT 1.2**

Private Foundation Excise Taxes

| Sanction | Tax Imposed On | | Initial Tax | | Additional Tax | |
| --- | --- | --- | --- | --- | --- | --- |
| | Private Foundation | Managers | First-Tier Rate | Imposed | Second-Tier Rate | Assessed |
| Section 4940 Investment Income Tax | X | | 2% | Of investment income imposed annually when Form 990-PF filed. | N/A | Not applicable. |
| | X | | 1% | Tax reduced by 1 percent for PFs increasing grants annually. | | |
| Section 4941 Self-Dealing | | On self-dealer X | 10% | Of amount involved for each year transaction outstanding. | 200% | If self-dealing not corrected. |
| | | On manager X | 5% | Of amount involved for each year transaction outstanding. Participating managers jointly and severally liable; can agree to allocate among themselves; maximum for managers $10,000. | 50% | If manager refuses to agree to part or all of correction. Maximum additional tax $10,000. |
| Section 4942 Undistributed Income | X | | 30% | Of undistributed income for each year undistributed. | 100% | For each year income remains undistributed. |
| Section 4943 Excess Business Holdings | X | | 10% | On fair market value of excess holdings each year. | 200% | Of excess holdings at end of "taxable period." |

*(Continued)*

EXHIBIT 1.2 (Continued)

| Sanction | Tax Imposed On | | Initial Tax | | Additional Tax | |
| | Private Foundation | Managers | First-Tier Rate | Imposed | Second-Tier Rate | Assessed |
| --- | --- | --- | --- | --- | --- | --- |
| Section 4944 Jeopardizing Investments | X | | 10% | On amount so invested for each year of taxable period. | 25% | Of amount not removed from jeopardy. |
| | | X | 10% | On amount so invested for each year of investment. Participating managers jointly and severally liable for maximum tax of $5,000 per investment. | 5% | Of amount on managers who refused to agree to part or all of removal from jeopardy; maximum for management $10,000. |
| Section 4945 Taxable Expenditures | X | | 20% | Of each taxable expenditure. | 100% | Of uncorrected expenditure at end of taxable period. |
| | | X | 5% | Of each taxable expenditure for manager who knew of and agreed to the expenditure. Maximum for all managers $5,000. | 50% | Of amount on manager who refuses to correct all or part of taxable amount; maximum amount $10,000. |

To allow abatement, the actions of the responsible foundation officials must be considered. Although one of these provisions[155] is titled "Definitions," neither it nor the regulations define the terms *reasonable cause* or *willful neglect*. There have not been any court decisions and few IRS private determinations[156] concerning abatement of these penalties. In a ruling concerning a taxable expenditure penalty for failure to seek advance approval of a scholarship plan, there was no mention of abatement.[157]

The regulations pertaining to the penalties imposed on self-dealers, on managers approving of self-dealing, jeopardizing investments, and taxable expenditures, however, contain definitions that one must hope can be applied to justify abatement of the penalties. The definitions of *reasonable cause* and *willful* are the same as those listed above. The officials of private foundations must show that they used good business judgment exercised with ordinary business care and prudence. They must show that they made a good faith effort to follow the rules by seeking the advice of qualified professionals. All of the facts and circumstances of the foundation's activities must be fully disclosed to such advisors.

For the foundation's penalty to be abated, its managers must also prove that the failure was due to reasonable cause and not to willful neglect. A bankruptcy judge found that a trustee had not demonstrated conscious, intentional, or reckless indifference in failing to file a return or obtain an extension, so reasonable cause for abating penalties existed.[158]

Under the general rules pertaining to tax penalties,[159] the determination of whether a taxpayer's actions were due to reasonable cause in good faith is made on a case-by-case basis. According these rules, "generally, the most important factor is the extent of the taxpayer's effort to access the taxpayer's proper tax liability. Circumstances that may indicate reasonable cause and good faith include an honest misunderstanding of fact or law that is reasonable in light of all of the facts and circumstances, including the experience, knowledge, and education of the taxpayer." This regulation provides that reliance on the advice of a professional tax advisor does not necessarily demonstrate reasonable cause and good faith. This type of reliance, however, constitutes reasonable cause and good faith if, under all the circumstances, the reliance was reasonable and the taxpayer acted in good faith. Reliance on the opinion or advice of a professional is considered reasonable cause if:

155. IRC § 4962.
156. Tech. Adv. Mem. 9424004. *See* Chapter 7, note 133.
157. Priv. Ltr. Rul. 9825004.
158. *United States Bankruptcy Court of Central District of California re Molnick's, Inc.*, 95-1 U.S.T.C.¶ 95,751 (9th Cir. 1995).
159. Reg. § 1.6664-4(b); *see* also §§ 8.4 and 9.8.

- The taxpayer did not know, or should not have known, that the advisor lacked knowledge in the relevant aspects of federal tax law.

- The advice was based on all pertinent facts and circumstances and the tax law as it relates to the matter involved, including the taxpayer's purpose for entering into the transaction and for structuring a transaction in a particular manner.

- The advice is based on reasonable factual or legal assumptions and does not unreasonably rely on the representations, statements, findings, or agreements of the taxpayer or any other person.

The second-tier taxes may also be abated.[160]

When enacted in 1969, the private foundation rules were unique. The statutory scheme devised by Congress had no precedent in the tax law. (The only other prior occasion when Congress levied a tax on otherwise tax-exempt organizations was on adoption of the tax on unrelated business income, implemented in 1950.)[161] But in the immediate aftermath of enactment of the foundation rules, speculation started as to whether and to what extent this new approach might be extended to other tax-exempt organizations, principally public charities. Since then, the rules engendered to reform the conduct of private foundations have been replicated in varying degrees by Congress four times, principally with respect to the operations of public charities: taxes on lobbying expenditures,[162] taxes on political campaign expenditures,[163] and taxes on the rendering of excess benefits to disqualified persons.[164] Thus, private foundations law set in motion the use of a tax scheme that has been utilized since and undoubtedly will be used again. But the amount of interpretative law built up around these statutory rules is most extensive in respect to private foundations.

---

160. IRC § 4961. A private foundation that failed to make any grants for charitable purposes during its existence, to pay any tax on its net investment income, to pay penalties for late filing of its annual information returns, and to respond to inquiries from the IRS and state officials had its tax exemption revoked (Priv. Ltr. Rul. 201021029).

161. *See* Chapter 11.

162. IRC §§ 4911 and 4912.

163. IRC § 4955.

164. IRC § 4958.

# CHAPTER TWO

# Starting and Funding a
# Private Foundation

Creating a private foundation, while not a simple matter, need not be an overly complicated process and, it is hoped, can be accomplished efficiently using the resources in this book. As a prelude to the specific requirements for forming and funding a foundation, Exhibit 2.1 provides a brief overview of the steps taken in the formation stage of a private foundation's life.

## §2.1 CHOICE OF ORGANIZATIONAL FORM

For the most part, the federal tax law does not mandate a specific organizational form for entities to qualify for tax-exempt status. Certainly there is no

**Exhibit 2.1**  Steps in Creating a Private Foundation

*Step 1:* Establish a nonprofit corporation or trust, the assets of which are permanently dedicated to conducting charitable programs.[1]

To qualify as an organization eligible to receive charitable donations, the foundation must spend its money to accomplish one of eight specific purposes: charitable, educational, religious, scientific, literary, preventing cruelty to children or animals, testing for public safety, or fostering national or international amateur sports competition.

A foundation can conduct its own charitable programs, such as operating a school or a museum or acquiring and restoring historic properties, and be classified as a private operating foundation.[2] Many private foundations instead simply make grants to charities chosen by their funders.[3] The Council on Foundations (www.cof.org) and the Association of Small Foundations (www.smallfoundations.org) both have useful information for creators of private foundations regarding grant programs, funding issues, and legal and compliance issues.

*Step 2:* Prepare a mission statement for the proposed foundation describing the types of activities it will conduct.[4]

To seek IRS approval for tax-exempt status, a complete description of proposed foundation activities must be written in such a fashion to paint a picture of the organization as if it were in existence. For example, if a foundation plans to operate a library, the location, hours, types of books, literary programs, planned relationship to area schools, and other information illustrating the fashion in which the library would operate is described.

*Step 3:* Prepare a three-year financial projection.[5]

Sources of revenues and expected expenditures must be described. Funding solely by the foundation's creator is simply shown. If the foundation plans to seek donations from others, sample fundraising letters and details of any events that would be anticipated are furnished. A detailed budget of planned expenditures—grants, salaries, rents, office expenses, travel, books, and all other types of disbursements—must be projected.[6]

*Step 4:* Consider special rules applicable to private foundations.

Evaluate type of property to be donated for issues of self-dealing[7] distribution requirements,[8] excess business holdings,[9] jeopardizing investments,[10] investment excise tax,[11] and deductibility as charitable donation.[12]

---

1. *See* § 2.1.
2. *See* § 3.1.
3. *See* § 9.4, 9.5
4. *See* Form 1023, Part IV; Exhibits 2.2 and 2.3; and § 6.5.
5. *See* p. 80 for Form 1023, Part IX, example.
6. *See* Chapter 9.
7. *See* Chapter 5.
8. *See* Chapter 6.
9. *See* Chapter 7
10. *See* Chapter 8.
11. *See* Chapter 10.
12. *See* Chapter 14.

**Exhibit 2.1**   (Continued)

---

*Step 5:* File completed Form 1023 with Internal Revenue Service to seek recognition of qualification for tax-exempt status.

*Step 6:* Receive funding from creator and establish financial record-keeping and tax compliance systems sufficient to maintain exempt status.[13]

---

required form for private foundations. The federal law provision describing the exemption criteria for charitable organizations[14] refers to organizations that constitute a "corporation, community chest, fund, or foundation." Except for the word *corporation*, however, these terms do not connote organizational forms. Thus, in determining the organizational form for a private foundation, the statutory law is of no utility, inasmuch as it refers only to *foundation* (or fund).

Generally, the form choices for nonprofit organizations, including private foundations, in relation to tax exemption are nonprofit corporation, trust (lifetime or testamentary), and unincorporated association.[15] Whatever the form, the organization is created by means of a set of *articles of organization.*[16]

An unincorporated association usually is a membership entity, the articles of organization of which are termed a *constitution.* This form is rarely suitable for private foundations. Thus, nearly all private foundations are constituted as trusts or nonprofit corporations.

Traditionally, private foundations have been created as trusts, particularly where their founders are individuals. The type of a trust established during a founder's (grantor's) lifetime is technically known as an *inter vivos trust;* one created by means of an individual's will is a *testamentary trust.* For a testamentary trust, a section of the creator's will constitutes the articles of organization. With a lifetime trust, the articles of organization will be in the form of a *declaration of trust* (where the grantor establishes the trust in a document stating the fact of the trust) or a *trust agreement* (where the grantor contracts with a person, such as a financial institution, to be the trustee of the trust). Some choose to create a trust because their governance provisions often cannot be changed without judicial approval.

While the trust form is still used today, it is common to establish a private foundation as a nonprofit corporation. The principal reason for this is the limitation on personal liability, for directors (trustees) and officers, that the corporate form affords. The nonprofit corporation's *articles of incorporation* commonly can be changed by existing directors. This type of entity almost always has a set of operational rules, usually termed its *bylaws.*

---

13. *See* § 12.3.
14. That is, organizations described in IRC § 501(c)(3) and exempt from federal income taxation by reason of IRC § 501(a).
15. IRS Revenue Procedure (Rev. Proc.) 82-2, 1982-1 C.B. 367.
16. Reg. § 1.501(c)(3)-1(b)(2).

There are other considerations in this regard as well, being matters of state law. Some states have less regulatory oversight over charitable trusts than nonprofit corporations. Thus, for example, the trust organizing document may not have to be filed with the state and/or the state may not have annual reporting requirements. Therefore, a state's regulatory environment may offer greater privacy, perhaps anonymity, to those who operate a private foundation in trust form. State law may permit one trustee of a trust, where three directors of a corporation may be required. All of these factors, of course, should be assessed and weighed when selecting the form of a private foundation in a particular state.[17]

In some instances, such as where the foundation is established as a testamentary trust, the trustee or trustees are given the discretionary authority by the grantor (decedent) to, after the grantor's death, convert the trust to the corporate form.

An alternative to the creation of a private foundation is establishing an account within a charitable organization that is classified as a public charity.[18] These accounts are maintained by community foundations and funds created by financial institutions and are usually referred to as a *donor-advised fund.*[19]

## §2.2 FUNDING A FOUNDATION

Most private foundations are initially funded by contributions from the individuals or for-profit companies that create them. As discussed, private foundations are *private* in nature because they are funded from one source—usually an individual, family, or corporation. Some private foundations receive subsequent and ongoing annual contributions from the original donor and others following the founding gift. A significant, and in many cases sole, source of support for private foundations is income derived from investment of the contributed funds. Less commonly, a public charity ceases to conduct fund-raising activities or fails to qualify as a supporting organization, and consequently becomes a private foundation.

A private foundation created by one or more individuals may be established during the lifetime of one or more of them or by means of their estates. That is, a private foundation can be created entirely by one or more lifetime gifts or it can be created wholly in testamentary form. Some foundations are established as a blend of these approaches: The foundation is initially and annually funded by an individual, and he or she subsequently additionally funds the foundation from his or her estate. Certainly family members and others can fund a foundation established by another, again either during their lifetimes and/or by means of their estates.

---

17. *See Planning Guide,* Chapter 1.
18. *See* Chapter 15.
19. *See* Chapter 16.

There are no limitations in the law as to the amount that can be contributed to a private foundation or the number of persons who may donate to a foundation. There are, however, lower percentages of income limits as to the deductibility of contributions to a private foundation as compared to a public charity.[20] A broad base of economic support is required to qualify as a publicly supported charity.[21]

Private foundations may be funded with money or property; this property can include securities, artwork, real estate, and other assets. There are constraints in this regard as to gifts of property, however. For example, a gift of a business enterprise to a private foundation could cause problems in relation to the rules on excess business holdings, though special rules extend the time that contributed excess holdings may be held by a private foundation.[22] As another illustration, a gift of property with indebtedness could generate unrelated business income or self-dealing.[23]

As another example, assume a married couple wants to leave 1,000 acres of farmland to a private foundation on their death and wishes to stipulate that the property cannot be developed or broken up into small parcels. Several issues must be considered in making such a gift. Again, due to the excess business holdings rules, the foundation is prohibited from operating the farm as a business itself, although it can convert the land to passive investment property by renting the land to someone else to farm or could establish programs to devote the property to agricultural research or other charitable purpose. As investment property, the full fair market value of the farmland would be includible in the foundation's asset base for calculating its annual mandatory payout. If the net rental income, less associated expenses, is below that amount and the foundation has few other income-producing assets, the foundation might find itself unable to meet its mandatory charitable distribution requirement.[24]

One of the chief features of the federal tax rules concerning charitable giving is that the deductible amount for a gift of property is generally equal to the full fair market value of the property at the time of the gift. The amount of appreciation in the property (the amount exceeding the donor's tax basis), which would be taxed if sold, escapes income taxation. Thus, where the property has increased in value (*appreciated property*), the charitable deduction generally is based on that higher value, and the capital gain that would have been recognized had the property been sold is not subject to tax. Yet there are tax rules that are disadvantageous to private foundations, in that gifts of appreciated property to them, except as noted below, are deductible only to the extent of the donor's basis in the property, making the appreciation element in the property not counted in calculating the charitable deduction. At the same time, there is a rule—in the nature of an

---

20. *See* § 14.3.
21. *See* Chapter 15.
22. *See* § 7.2.
23. *See* Chapters 11 and 5.
24. *See* Chapter 6.

exception to the exception—by which most publicly traded securities can be contributed to a private foundation and the deduction based on the full fair market value of the securities as of the date of the gift. The value of shares of readily marketable securities is fully deductible so long as the donation represents no more than 10 percent of the value of the company.[25]

The deduction limitation for appreciated property gifts to a private foundation applies to most types of appreciated property—such as land, collectibles, partnership interests, or closely held company stock. The limitation does not apply if the foundation essentially gives away the property itself or its commensurate value.[26] A foundation with excess distributions carryovers can make an out-of-corpus election to allocate some excess as such a redistribution.[27] A private foundation may be funded by an individual during his or her lifetime by means of a planned gift of a partial interest in property rather than an outright gift. A planned gift may also be made on a testamentary basis.[28]

## § 2.3 ESTATE PLANNING PRINCIPLES

Private foundations are often created out of decedents' estates. One mechanism to accomplish this is the establishment, by will, of a testamentary trust. This trust survives not only the decedent but also the estate of the decedent. (As noted earlier, often the trustee or trustees are given the authority to convert the trust to a nonprofit corporation.) Another approach is to create a nonprofit corporation to receive the money and/or property to be transferred to the foundation as a bequest.

### (a) Decedents' Estates

The assets bequeathed and/or devised by a decedent for a charitable foundation remain in the estate until transferred at the appropriate time from the estate to the foundation. Until this transfer occurs, the assets are those of the estate, not the foundation. This can have certain advantages, such as exclusion of the assets from the asset base used to compute the annual minimum payout amount,[29] protection from certain self-dealing sanctions,[30] and avoidance of the investment income excise tax that applies to the assets of private foundations.[31]

---

25. These charitable giving rules are discussed in detail in Chapter 14.
26. By the fifteenth day of the third month of the year following the gift; IRC § 170(b)(1)(F)(ii).
27. *See* § 6.7.
28. *See* § 2.4.
29. Reg. § 53.4942(a)-2(c)(2)(ii). If the period of administration of an estate is unduly prolonged, however, the estate may be considered terminated for federal income tax purposes (Reg. § 1.641(b)-3(a)), in which instance assets of the estate destined for the private foundation will be deemed then held by the foundation (Reg. § 53.4942(a)-2(c)(2) (ii)). In general, *see* § 6.3.
30. *See* § 5.11.
31. *See* Chapter 10.

An existing estate can be a disqualified person with respect to a private foundation.[32] This means, for example, there is a potential for an act of self-dealing between the two entities.[33] For instance, the purchase of assets of an estate, directly or indirectly, by a private foundation may be self-dealing.[34]

## (b)  Estate and Gift Tax Considerations

Estate planning, by necessity, takes into account the federal estate tax[35] and the federal gift tax.[36] The gift tax may be imposed on transfers of money or property during the donor's lifetime, while the estate tax is levied on transfers at death.[37] These taxes are separate from the federal income tax.

Unlike the federal income tax charitable giving rules,[38] there is no limitation, with respect to estate tax deductibility, as to the amount that can pass to a charitable organization from a decedent's estate. Thus, if desired, the entirety of an estate may be transferred to a private foundation (or other charitable organization), with a full deduction for the value of the assets devoted to charity.[39] Often, however, the decedent's estate entails a range of specific bequests, as well as assets for a foundation.

A tentative plan to phase out the estate tax over a 10-year period ending in 2010 was extended in December 2010.[40]

## § 2.4  FOUNDATIONS AND PLANNED GIVING

A planned gift is generally the most sophisticated type of contribution made to a charitable organization. It is often made with property that has appreciated in value rather than with money. For the most part, private foundations can be the recipients of planned gifts.

There are two basic types of planned gifts. One type is a gift made during the donor's lifetime, using a trust or other agreement. The other type is a gift made by means of a will; the gift comes out of a decedent's estate, as a bequest or devise.

---

32. *See* § 4.7.
33. *See* Chapter 5.
34. Reg. § 53.4941(d)-1(b)(3); *Rockefeller v. United States*, 572 F. Supp. 9 (E.D. Ark. 1982), *aff'd*, 718 F.2d 290 (8th Cir. 1983).
35. IRC § 2001.
36. IRC § 2501.
37. In general, *see Charitable Giving*, Chapter 8.
38. *See* Chapter 14.
39. IRC § 2055(a).
40. Tax Relief, Unemployment Insurance Reauthorization, and Job Creation Act, December 17, 2010; renewed again by the American Taxpayer Relief Act on January 1, 2013.

## (a) Introduction to Planned Giving

Planned giving, usually perceived as the most complex among categories of charitable giving, rests on a very simple precept: Conceptually, an item of property has within it an *income interest* and a *remainder interest.*

The income interest in an item of property is a function of the income generated by the property. The remainder interest within an item of property is the projected value of the property, or the property produced by reinvestments, at a future date.[41] The value of these interests is measured by the value of the property, the age of the donor(s), the amount and frequency of payment of the income interest, and the period of time that the income interest will exist. The actual computation is made by means of actuarial tables, usually those promulgated by the Department of the Treasury.

Most charitable gifts of the planned gift variety are made by use of a *split-interest trust.* This is the mechanism by which the two interests are conceptually separated. These gifts usually involve gifts of remainder interests and frequently utilize the vehicle of the *charitable remainder trust.* This is certainly the case with private foundations, inasmuch as remainder interest given by means of pooled income funds is not available to private foundations.[42] Private foundations may be the recipient of *charitable gift annuities,* however.

## (b) Charitable Remainder Trusts

It is common for a private foundation to be initially funded by means of a charitable remainder trust, which is a form of split-interest trust. Likewise, it is often the case that an existing private foundation is made the beneficiary of a charitable remainder trust. In either instance, the remainder trust is established as a separate legal entity and, by means of the trust, a remainder interest in the property transferred is created for the ultimate benefit of the private foundation.[43]

A charitable remainder trust basically is just that: The entity is a trust that is a vehicle by means of which a charitable remainder interest destined for charity is created.[44] Each charitable remainder trust is arranged specifically for the particular circumstances of the donor(s), with the remainder interest in the gift property designated for one or more charitable organizations.

A qualified charitable remainder trust must provide for a specified distribution of income, at least annually, to or for the use of one or more beneficiaries

---

41. The conceptual underpinnings of planned giving are the subject of § 14.5.
42. The law as to pooled income funds requires, *inter alia*, that a qualified fund be maintained at all times by certain categories of public charities (IRC § 642(c)(5)(A)).
43. The assets in a charitable remainder trust are not part of the asset base of a beneficiary private foundation for mandatory payout purposes (*see* Chapter 6) while they are in the trust (Reg. § 53.4942(a)-2(c)(2)(i)).
44. IRC § 664. A more detailed discussion of charitable remainder trusts is in § 14.5.

(at least one of which is not a charity). The flow of income must be for life or for a term of no more than 20 years, with an irrevocable remainder interest to be held for the benefit of the charitable organization or paid over to it. Again, usually noncharitable (often individual) beneficiaries are the holders of the income interest and the charitable organization has the remainder interest.

How the income interests in a charitable remainder trust are ascertained depends on whether the trust is a *charitable remainder annuity trust* (where income payments are a fixed amount, an annuity) or a *charitable remainder unitrust* (where income payments are an amount equal to a percentage of the annually determined fair market value of the assets in the trust).

All categories of charitable organization—public charities and private foundations—are eligible to be remainder beneficiaries of charitable remainder trusts.

Conventionally, once the income interest expires, the assets in a charitable remainder trust are distributed to the charitable organization that is the remainder beneficiary. If the assets, or a portion of them, are retained in the trust, the trust will be classified as a private foundation, unless it can become qualified as a public charity.

One common pattern in this regard is a charitable remainder trust created during the lifetime of a married couple. A private foundation is established and nominally funded. This foundation is made the remainder interest beneficiary of the remainder trust. The income interest beneficiaries of the trust are the married individuals, who have the interest jointly; the income interest continues for the benefit of the survivor of the two. On the death of the second to die, the assets in the trust are transferred to the private foundation. This approach can also be affected by means of a charitable remainder trust created by will of a married individual. The income interest is established for the benefit of the surviving spouse; at his or her death, the trust assets are transferred to the private foundation.

Another common approach is to utilize a charitable remainder trust in conjunction with a funded, operational private foundation. One or more individuals can establish a remainder trust at any time, for the purpose of creating a remainder interest in the trust for the foundation. Again, the trust may be established during the lifetime of the donor(s) or by means of a will.

For purposes of many of the private foundation rules, a charitable remainder trust is treated as a private foundation.[45]

## (c)  Other Planned Giving Vehicles

Most forms of planned giving have a common element: The donor transfers to a charitable organization the remainder interest in a property, and one or

---

45. IRC § 4947(a)(2). *See* § 3.7.

more noncharitable beneficiaries retain the income interest. A reverse sequence may occur, however—and that is the essence of the *charitable lead trust.* These trusts are frequently utilized in conjunction with private foundations.

The property transferred to a charitable lead trust is apportioned into an income interest and a remainder interest. The income interest in the property is created for the benefit of a private foundation or other charitable organization, either for a term of years or for the life of an individual (or the lives of more than one individual).[46] The remainder interest in the property is reserved to return, at the expiration of the income interest (the end of the *lead period*), to the donor or some other noncharitable beneficiary or beneficiaries; often the property passes from one generation (the donor's) to another.

The charitable lead trust can be used to accelerate into one year a series of charitable contributions that would otherwise be made annually. There may be, then, a single-year deduction for the "bunched" amount of charitable gifts.

In some circumstances, a charitable deduction is available for the transfer of an income interest in property to a charitable organization. There are stringent limitations, however, on the deductibility of charitable contributions of these income interests.

Another form of planned giving is the *charitable gift annuity.* A form of fundraising popular with some public charities, it is infrequently used by private foundations. The annuity is based on an agreement between the donor and donee; there is no use of a split-interest trust. The donor agrees to make a gift and the donee agrees, in return, to provide the donor (and/or someone else) with an annuity.

With one payment, the donor is engaging in two transactions: the purchase of an annuity and the making of a charitable gift. The sum in excess of the amount necessary to fund the annuity is the charitable gift portion; the gift gives rise to a charitable contribution deduction. Because of this duality in the transaction, the charitable gift annuity transfer constitutes a *bargain sale.*

Gifts of life insurance (whole life) may be made to charitable organizations, including private foundations. If the life insurance policy is fully paid up, the donor will receive a charitable contribution deduction for the cash surrender value or the replacement value of the policy. If premiums are still being paid, the donor receives a charitable deduction for the premium payments made during the tax year. For the deduction to be available, however, the donee charitable organization must be both the beneficiary and the owner of the insurance policy.

There is some uncertainty as to whether a gift of a life insurance policy to a charitable organization is valid (and thus enforceable and deductible), because of the necessity of *insurable interest*—the owner and beneficiary of the policy

---

46. The assets in a charitable lead trust are not part of the asset base of a beneficiary private foundation for mandatory payout purposes (*see* Chapter 6) while they are in the trust (Reg. § 53.4942(a)-2(c)(2)(iii)).

must be more economically advantaged with the insured alive rather than dead. In many instances, a charitable organization is advantaged by having a donor of a life insurance policy alive: He or she may be a key volunteer (such as a trustee or officer) or a potential donor of other, larger gifts.

## (d) Interrelationships with Private Foundation Rules

Any contemplated planned gift to a private foundation should, before it is consummated, be evaluated in the context of the federal tax rules uniquely applicable to foundations. For example, the gift should not be made if it would entail an act of self-dealing.[47] Revenue from income-producing property, and untaxed appreciation if sold, will likely be subject to the 2 percent excise tax on investment income.[48]

There are limitations on the extent of business holdings that can be held at any point in time by a private foundation.[49] These rules are pertinent where the planned gift involves a transfer of stock or other manifestation of a business holding to a private foundation. A contribution of a large business holding to a private foundation may cause the foundation to have an excess business holding, potentially subject to tax. There is a special rule by which an excess business holding acquired by a private foundation by gift may be retained by a foundation for a five-year period before the excess holdings rules take effect.[50] In addition, the IRS has the authority to allow an additional five-year period for the disposition of excess business holdings in the case of an unusually large gift or bequest of diverse business holdings, under certain circumstances.[51]

A planned gift may cause a private foundation to have a jeopardizing investment.[52] Although the tax on jeopardizing investments does not apply to investments originally made by a person who later transferred them as gifts to a private foundation,[53] subsequent investment practices involving the assets by the foundation may cause the presence of a jeopardizing investment. For example, the IRS ruled that the contribution of a whole-life insurance policy to a private foundation eventuated in a jeopardizing investment, because the foundation, instead of surrendering the policy for its cash value, continued to pay the policy premiums and interest on a policy loan to the point that the amount it was paying was greater than the insurance proceeds it would derive upon the death of the insured.[54] The tax on jeopardizing investments is

---

47. *See* Chapter 5.
48. *See* Chapter 10.
49. *See* Chapter 7.
50. IRC § 4943(c)(6). *See* § 7.2.
51. IRC § 4943(c)(7). *See* § 7.2.
52. *See* Chapter 8.
53. Reg. § 53.4944–1(a)(2)(ii).
54. Rev. Rul. 80-133, 1980-1 C.B. 258.

inapplicable to investments that are acquired by a private foundation solely as a result of a corporate reorganization.[55]

## § 2.5 ACQUIRING RECOGNITION OF TAX-EXEMPT STATUS

A private foundation is a tax-exempt organization, by reason of being a *charitable* entity. As is the case for nearly all exempt charitable organizations, private foundations are required to seek recognition of exempt status from the IRS. By contrast, as a general rule, an organization desiring exempt status pursuant to any other provision of federal tax law may (but is not required to) secure recognition of that exemption from the IRS.

A charitable organization located anywhere in the world can seek recognition of its tax-exempt status for a variety of reasons. Foreign private foundations with investments in U.S. companies must pay a 4 percent excise tax on the dividends, interest, rents, and royalties earned on such investments.[56] The tax is withheld by the investment company.[57] The rate of withholding on a nonexempt foreign charity is, however, made at the normal rate for taxpaying entities, which is 30 percent.[58] A foreign charity that can satisfy one of the tests for qualification as a public charity[59] may seek recognition of that status if it plans to seek funding from U.S. private foundations. Expenditure responsibility agreements are not required for gifts to a foreign charity with an IRS determination of its public charity status.[60]

The IRS does not *grant* exempt status to an organization. Whether a nonprofit organization is entitled to tax exemption, on an initial or continuing basis, is a matter of law. Thus, it is Congress that, by statute, defines the categories of organizations that are eligible for federal income tax exemption,[61] and it is Congress that determines whether a category of tax exemption should be continued.[62] Congress, then, defines the types of entities eligible for exempt status, while the function of the IRS is to *recognize* exempt status where appropriate. Consequently, when a private foundation or other organization makes application to the IRS for a ruling or determination as to exempt status, it is requesting the IRS to recognize that exemption, which (if the organization is correct) has already been granted by the federal tax laws.

---

55. Reg. § 53.4944–1(a)(2)(ii).
56. *See* § 10.7.
57. IRC § 1443(b).
58. IRS General Counsel Memorandum (Gen. Couns. Mem.) 38840 (unless a tax treaty provides an exemption).
59. *See* Chapter 15.
60. *See* §§ 6.5 and 9.5.
61. E.g., *HCSC-Laundry v. United States*, 450 U.S. 1 (1981).
62. E.g., *Maryland Savings-Share Insurance Corp. v. United States*, 400 U.S. 4 (1970).

The United States–Canadian income tax treaty provides for reciprocal recognition of exemption for religious, scientific, literary, educational, or charitable organizations. The diplomatic notes signed in 1980 when the treaty was approved directed the "Competent Authorities" to review the other country's procedures and requirements for recognition of exemption and to avoid requiring filings that duplicate effort. The agreement provided that the United States would study the Canadian rules for determining qualification to see if they are compatible with U.S. rules. Almost 20 years later, the IRS announced it had entered into a mutual agreement for reciprocal recognition of exempt status.[63] Though the agreement was intended to facilitate cross-border grants, the notice presents a number of issues.

Every Canadian charity registered with Revenue Canada is now automatically treated as a charitable organization with no need to file Form 1023 unless and until the U.S. authorities find some reason to withdraw approval. Unfortunately, all Canadian organizations are presumed to be private foundations "in the absence of receiving certain financial information." The notice says Canadian organizations may provide information to the IRS to establish their public charity status (the Cincinnati processing center). Those that qualify as public charities for reasons of financial support provide Form 8734, which details sources of support and lists private donations and fees.[64] Those organizations treated as inherently public charities[65] (churches, schools, hospitals, and support organizations) would file the appropriate Form 1023 schedules.[66] Revenue Canada's certification of charity status would also be submitted.

## (a)  Preparing Form 1023

An organization seeking recognition of exemption as a charitable organization, including a private foundation, is required to file Form 1023, Application for Recognition of Exemption, under Section 501(c)(3) of the Internal Revenue Code. (See.)[67]

The proper preparation of an application for recognition of tax exemption for a private foundation (or other type of tax-exempt organization) involves far more than merely responding to the questions on a government form. It is a process not unlike the preparation of a prospectus for a business in conformity with securities law requirements. Every statement made in the application

---

63. IRS Notice 99-47, 1999-36 I.R.B. 344.
64. Except for those that report five years of revenue, the form is exactly the same as Part IV-A of Schedule A, Form 990, filed annually by public charities.
65. Discussed in § 15.3.
66. Schedules A–D.
67. *Form 1023 Tax Preparation Guide*, Chapter 18; *see also* Hopkins, "A Practical Guide on How to Apply for Section 501(c)(3) Status," *J. Tax-Exempt Orgs.* (No. 4) 8 (Jan./Feb. 1993); *Tax-Exempt Organizations*, Chapter 23.

should be carefully considered with a view to the issues the IRS considers in reviewing the response to its questions. The application has almost no questions strictly germane to private foundations and does not request any specific information regarding a new foundation's potential violation of the private foundation tax rules. However, certain answers can reflect violations. In one example, Part V, Question 8a, asks, "Do you or will you have any leases, contracts, loans, or other agreements with your officers, directors, trustees, etc.?" The IRS's objectives in asking the question is to obtain information to allow them to determine whether any private inurement will result from such arrangements. For a private foundation, a "yes" response would indicate that self-dealing will result from proposed transactions between the applicant and its creators.[68] Some of the questions may force the applicant organization to focus on matters that good management practices would cause it to consider, even in the absence of the application requirements.

The prime objective must be accuracy; it is essential that all material facts be correctly and fully disclosed. Of course, the determination as to which facts are material and the marshaling of these facts requires judgment. The successful preparer anticipates the reason the IRS is seeking the information requested by each question. Moreover, the manner in which the answers are phrased can be extremely significant; in this regard, the exercise can be more one of art than science. The preparer or reviewer of the application should be able to anticipate the concerns that the contents of the application may cause the IRS and to see that the application is properly prepared, while simultaneously minimizing the likelihood of conflict with the IRS. Organizations that are entitled to exempt status have been denied recognition of exemption by the IRS, or at least have caused the process of gaining the recognition to be more protracted, because of artless phraseology in the application that motivated the IRS to muster a case that the organization does not qualify for exemption. The fact that the application is available for public inspection only underscores the need for its thoughtful preparation.[69]

Successful preparation of Form 1023 involves looking into the future and describing how a new foundation intends to accomplish its mission. The application should paint a well-defined picture of how the foundation will operate in both words and numbers. It is like a business plan—proposed activities are described and sources of revenue and proposed expenditures for the first three years are presented. A charitable organization that expects to receive its support from a particular family, or a limited number of financial supporters, will be classified as a private foundation.[70] Completion of the application for a foundation that plans to make grants to public charities can

---

68. *See* Chapter 5.
69. *See* § 12.3.
70. *See* § 1.2 for an expanded definition.

be a relatively simple matter. Particularly when the creators and trustees plan to donate their time and necessary office space, most of the answers in the lengthy Part V may be *No*.

Applicants must carefully consider the depth of information to provide for *Yes* answers that request an explanation on this form. There are several questions for which the foundation may not yet have information to provide. For example, Part VIII, line 13 asks a series of questions about grant-making activity. Commonly a new foundation has not yet developed its contracts, records, or application forms. This information was not previously requested, and it was sufficient to say that the foundation would develop administrative procedures and policies to adhere to the Minimum Distribution Requirements of IRC § 4942[71] and Taxable Expenditure rules of IRC § 4945.[72] The form requests information to evidence that grants, notes, and other distributions will be paid to further exempt purposes, including a copy of grantee contracts, if any, description of records the foundation keeps with respect to the grants, the selection process for choosing grantees, and grant oversight procedures.[73]

Not all lines explain why the information is requested, though some lines incorporate guidance into the form itself. The new interactive version of the form includes helpful hints and links to help applicants submit a complete application. Nonetheless, the import of some responses is often unclear. Weighing the material facts that must be submitted against their potential for generating controversy with the IRS is an issue. Facts must be accurate, but there is room for judgment in the presentation of a potentially nonexempt activity. If there is a reasonable chance that a potentially unrelated activity might be approved and the foundation is prepared to agree not to undertake the activity if it is not acceptable, inclusion is warranted. Another important aspect to consider is the possibility that the organization will be somewhat constrained to operate in the manner presented in Form 1023.

When the questions involve sensitive issues, such as compensation of disqualified persons, full disclosures with documents are in order. For other matters, it may be suitable simply to say plans are not yet developed despite the tone of some questions that implies a *Yes* answer is expected. The Form 990-PF each year provides a mechanism to explain new programs or structural changes once they are a reality. Finally, many persons will view the application in the future for a number of reasons. The foundation's managers should periodically review the original Form 1023 to be sure everyone understands why the IRS considers the foundation to be exempt, and to see if there has been a "material change" in its operations. The application must also be available for inspection by anyone who asks to see it. Private foundations approved for qualification

---

71. *See* Chapter 6.
72. *See* Exhibits 9.2, 9.3, and 9.4.
73. *See* § 9.4 for examples.

under IRC § 501(c)(3) that file 990-PFs are listed in IRS EO Select Check (successor to Publication 78) available at www.irs.gov and in the IRS Business Master File.[74]

An interactive Form 1023 based on the June 2006 version was released in 2013. The new version contains pop-up boxes for most lines of the form with explanations and links to irs.gov publications. A *Stay Exempt* program explaining the application process and rules for maintaining tax-exemption with links to IRS educational programs is provided. The form will still be physically filed until testing of the new program is complete. See Exhibit 2.2.

## (b)  Suggestions for PF-Sensitive Parts

Many parts of the form are self-explanatory, and the new interactive form has links to guidance on the IRS site. Particular issues a private foundation applicant should note are discussed below.

**Part I—Identification of Applicant.**  This part includes familiar items: name, address, persons to contact, and prior IRS filing history. A question, however, has been added to look for tax-avoidance schemes. Line 8 asks for the name, address, amount paid or promised to be paid, plus a description of the person's role if someone was hired to "help plan, manage, or advise you about the structure or activities or your organization, or about your financial or tax matters." Since it is customary and there is nothing inherently wrong with the new organization engaging advisors, this line is troubling. Some suggest this question is unwarranted.[75] The instructions do not say what "plan and manage" means. Many organizations engage professionals to develop their strategic plan, policy and procedure manual, computer network, website, or school curriculum, for example. The instructions specifically mention a person hired to develop a program to solicit funds and one to "advise you about tax exemption." The accountant, lawyer, or other professional authorized to represent the foundation with Form 2848 need not be listed here.

**Part II—Organizational Structure.**  The opening sentences to this part provide very clear guidance: "You must be a corporation (including a limited liability company), an unincorporated association, or a trust to be tax-exempt. DO NOT file this form unless you can check 'Yes' for lines 1, 2, 3, or 4." Sole proprietorships, partnerships, or loosely affiliated groups of individuals are ineligible. It is welcome news that the IRS officially acknowledges the ability of a limited liability company (LLC) to seek independent tax-exempt status after years of indecision on the matter. A single-member LLC that files its own application is treated as a corporation.

---

74.  www.irs.gov/charities/index.html.
75.  E.g., *Bruce R. Hopkins' Nonprofit Counsel* 22(1) (January 2005).

Active Project Fund                                    33-3333333

# Form 1023 Checklist
## (Revised December 2013)
### Application for Recognition of Exemption under Section 501(c)(3) of the Internal Revenue Code

**Note.** *Retain a copy of the completed Form 1023 in your permanent records. Refer to the* General Instructions *regarding Public Inspection of approved applications.*

**Check each box to finish your application (Form 1023). Send this completed Checklist with your filled-in application. If you have not answered all the items below, your application may be returned to you as incomplete.**

☑ Assemble the application and materials in this order:
- Form 1023 Checklist
- Form 2848, *Power of Attorney and Declaration of Representative* (if filing)
- Form 8821, *Tax Information Authorization* (if filing)
- Expedite request (if requesting)
- Application (Form 1023 and Schedules A through H, as required)
- Articles of organization
- Amendments to articles of organization in chronological order
- Bylaws or other rules of operation and amendments
- Documentation of nondiscriminatory policy for schools, as required by Schedule B
- Form 5768, Election/Revocation of Election by an Eligible Section 501(c)(3) Organization To Make Expenditures To Influence Legislation (if filing)
- All other attachments, including explanations, financial data, and printed materials or publications. Label each page with name and EIN.

☑ User fee payment placed in envelope on top of checklist. DO NOT STAPLE or otherwise attach your check or money order to your application. Instead, just place it in the envelope.

☑ Employer Identification Number (EIN)

☑ Completed Parts I through XI of the application, including any requested information and any required Schedules A through H.
- You must provide specific details about your past, present, and planned activities.
- Generalizations or failure to answer questions in the Form 1023 application will prevent us from recognizing you as tax exempt.
- Describe your purposes and proposed activities in specific easily understood terms.
- Financial information should correspond with proposed activities.

☑ Schedules. Submit only those schedules that apply to you and check either "Yes" or "No" below.

| Schedule A | Yes ___ No ✓ | Schedule E | Yes ___ No ✓ |
| Schedule B | Yes ___ No ✓ | Schedule F | Yes ___ No ✓ |
| Schedule C | Yes ___ No ✓ | Schedule G | Yes ___ No ✓ |
| Schedule D | Yes ___ No ✓ | Schedule H | Yes ___ No ✓ |

**EXHIBIT 2.2**

Form 1023

Active Project Fund                                           33-3333333

☑ An exact copy of your complete articles of organization (creating document). Absence of the proper purpose and dissolution clauses is the number one reason for delays in the issuance of determination letters.

  ● Location of Purpose Clause from Part III, line 1 (Page, Article and Paragraph Number) <u>Pg 1, Art 4, Sec 4.01</u>
  ● Location of Dissolution Clause from Part III, line 2b or 2c (Page, Article and Paragraph Number) or by operation of state law <u>Pg2, Art 4, Sec 4.02c</u>

☑ Signature of an officer, director, trustee, or other official who is authorized to sign the application.
  ● Signature at Part XI of Form 1023.

☑ Your name on the application must be the same as your legal name as it appears in your articles of organization.

Send completed Form 1023, user fee payment, and all other required information, to:

Internal Revenue Service
P.O. Box 192
Covington, KY 41012-0192

If you are using express mail or a delivery service, send Form 1023, user fee payment, and attachments to:

Internal Revenue Service
201 West Rivercenter Blvd.
Attn: Extracting Stop 312
Covington, KY 41011

**EXHIBIT 2.2**

_(Continued)_

| Form **2848**<br>(Rev. March 2012)<br>Department of the Treasury<br>Internal Revenue Service | **Power of Attorney<br>and Declaration of Representative**<br>▶ Type or print.  ▶ See the separate instructions. | OMB No. 1545-0150<br>**For IRS Use Only**<br>Received by:<br>Name _____<br>Telephone _____<br>Function _____<br>Date ___ / ___ / ___ |
|---|---|---|

**Part I**   **Power of Attorney**

**Caution:** *A separate Form 2848 should be completed for each taxpayer. Form 2848 will not be honored for any purpose other than representation before the IRS.*

**1   Taxpayer information.** Taxpayer must sign and date this form on page 2, line 7.

| Taxpayer name and address<br>Active Project Fund<br>1010 Main Street<br>Any Town, TX 77777 | Taxpayer identification number(s)<br>33-3333333 | |
|---|---|---|
| | Daytime telephone number<br>444-444-4444 | Plan number (if applicable) |

hereby appoints the following representative(s) as attorney(s)-in-fact:

**2   Representative(s)** must sign and date this form on page 2, Part II.

| Name and address<br>A Good Accountant<br>1 Main Street<br>Any Town, TX 77777 | CAF No. _ _ _ 5555-55555R _ _ _ .<br>PTIN _ _ _ P01111111 _ _ _ _<br>Telephone No. _ _ 323-222-3333 _ _ _<br>Fax No. _ _ 323-222-3334 _ _ _ . |
|---|---|
| Check if to be sent notices and communications  ☑ | Check if new: Address ☐  Telephone No. ☐  Fax No. ☐ |
| Name and address | CAF No. _ _ _ _ _ _ _ _ _ _ .<br>PTIN _ _ _ _ _ _ _ _ _ _ _<br>Telephone No. _ _ _ _ _ _ _ _<br>Fax No. _ _ _ _ _ _ _ _ _ |
| Check if to be sent notices and communications  ☐ | Check if new: Address ☐  Telephone No. ☐  Fax No. ☐ |
| Name and address | CAF No. _ _ _ _ _ _ _ _ _ _ .<br>PTIN _ _ _ _ _ _ _ _ _ _ _<br>Telephone No. _ _ _ _ _ _ _ _<br>Fax No. _ _ _ _ _ _ _ _ _ |
| | Check if new: Address ☐  Telephone No. ☐  Fax No. ☐ |

to represent the taxpayer before the Internal Revenue Service for the following matters:

**3   Matters**

| Description of Matter (Income, Employment, Payroll, Excise, Estate, Gift, Whistleblower, Practitioner Discipline, PLR, FOIA, Civil Penalty, etc.) (see instructions for line 3) | Tax Form Number<br>(1040, 941, 720, etc.) (if applicable) | Year(s) or Period(s) (if applicable)<br>(see instructions for line 3) |
|---|---|---|
| Income | 1023 | 2014 - 2016 |
| | | |
| | | |

**4   Specific use not recorded on Centralized Authorization File (CAF).** If the power of attorney is for a specific use not recorded on CAF, check this box. See the Instructions for Line 4. **Specific Uses Not Recorded on CAF**  . . . . . . . . . . . . . . . . ▶ ☐

**5   Acts authorized.** Unless otherwise provided below, the representatives generally are authorized to receive and inspect confidential tax information and to perform any and all acts that I can perform with respect to the tax matters described on line 3, for example, the authority to sign any agreements, consents, or other documents. The representative(s), however, is (are) not authorized to receive or negotiate any amounts paid to the client in connection with this representation (including refunds by either electronic means or paper checks). Additionally, unless the appropriate box(es) below are checked, the representative(s) is (are) not authorized to execute a request for disclosure of tax returns or return information to a third party, substitute another representative or add additional representatives, or sign certain tax returns.

☐ Disclosure to third parties;   ☐ Substitute or add representative(s);   ☐ Signing a return;   _____

☐ Other acts authorized: _____
_____ (see instructions for more information)

**Exceptions.** An unenrolled return preparer cannot sign any document for a taxpayer and may only represent taxpayers in limited situations. An enrolled actuary may only represent taxpayers to the extent provided in section 10.3(d) of Treasury Department Circular No. 230 (Circular 230). An enrolled retirement plan agent may only represent taxpayers to the extent provided in section 10.3(e) of Circular 230. A registered tax return preparer may only represent taxpayers to the extent provided in section 10.3(f) of Circular 230. See the line 5 instructions for restrictions on tax matters partners. In most cases, the student practitioner's (level k) authority is limited (for example, they may only practice under the supervision of another practitioner).

List any specific deletions to the acts otherwise authorized in this power of attorney: _ _ _ _ _ _ _ _ _ _ _
_ _ _ _ _ _ _ _ _ _ _ _ _ _ _ _ _ _ _ _
_ _ _ _ _ _ _ _ _ _ _ _ _ _ _ _ _ _ _ _
_ _ _ _ _ _ _ _ _ _ _ _ _ _ _ _ _ _ _ _

For Privacy Act and Paperwork Reduction Act Notice, see the instructions.      Cat. No. 11980J      Form **2848** (Rev. 3-2012)

**EXHIBIT 2.2**

*(Continued)*

**6** **Retention/revocation of prior power(s) of attorney.** The filing of this power of attorney automatically revokes all earlier power(s) of attorney on file with the Internal Revenue Service for the same matters and years or periods covered by this document. If you **do not** want to revoke a prior power of attorney, check here . . . . . . . . . . . . . . . . . . . . . . . . . . . . . . ▶ ☐
YOU MUST ATTACH A COPY OF ANY POWER OF ATTORNEY YOU WANT TO REMAIN IN EFFECT.

**7** **Signature of taxpayer.** If a tax matter concerns a year in which a joint return was filed, the husband and wife must each file a separate power of attorney even if the same representative(s) is (are) being appointed. If signed by a corporate officer, partner, guardian, tax matters partner, executor, receiver, administrator, or trustee on behalf of the taxpayer, I certify that I have the authority to execute this form on behalf of the taxpayer.

▶ IF NOT SIGNED AND DATED, THIS POWER OF ATTORNEY WILL BE RETURNED TO THE TAXPAYER.

| *A. B. Sample* | *5/1/14* | President |
|---|---|---|
| Signature | Date | Title (if applicable) |

| A. B. Sample | ☐☐☐☐☐ | Active Project Fund |
|---|---|---|
| Print Name | PIN Number | Print name of taxpayer from line 1 if other than individual |

---

### Part II    Declaration of Representative

Under penalties of perjury, I declare that:

- I am not currently under suspension or disbarment from practice before the Internal Revenue Service;
- I am aware of regulations contained in Circular 230 (31 CFR, Part 10), as amended, concerning practice before the Internal Revenue Service;
- I am authorized to represent the taxpayer identified in Part I for the matter(s) specified there; and
- I am one of the following:

   **a** Attorney—a member in good standing of the bar of the highest court of the jurisdiction shown below.

   **b** Certified Public Accountant—duly qualified to practice as a certified public accountant in the jurisdiction shown below.

   **c** Enrolled Agent—enrolled as an agent under the requirements of Circular 230.

   **d** Officer—a bona fide officer of the taxpayer's organization.

   **e** Full-Time Employee—a full-time employee of the taxpayer.

   **f** Family Member—a member of the taxpayer's immediate family (for example, spouse, parent, child, grandparent, grandchild, step-parent, step-child, brother, or sister).

   **g** Enrolled Actuary—enrolled as an actuary by the Joint Board for the Enrollment of Actuaries under 29 U.S.C. 1242 (the authority to practice before the Internal Revenue Service is limited by section 10.3(d) of Circular 230).

   **h** Unenrolled Return Preparer—Your authority to practice before the Internal Revenue Service is limited. You must have been eligible to sign the return under examination and have signed the return. **See Notice 2011-6 and Special rules for registered tax return preparers and unenrolled return preparers in the instructions.**

   **i** Registered Tax Return Preparer—registered as a tax return preparer under the requirements of section 10.4 of Circular 230. Your authority to practice before the Internal Revenue Service is limited. You must have been eligible to sign the return under examination and have signed the return. **See Notice 2011-6 and Special rules for registered tax return preparers and unenrolled return preparers in the instructions.**

   **k** Student Attorney or CPA—receives permission to practice before the IRS by virtue of his/her status as a law, business, or accounting student working in LITC or STCP under section 10.7(d) of Circular 230. See instructions for Part II for additional information and requirements.

   **r** Enrolled Retirement Plan Agent—enrolled as a retirement plan agent under the requirements of Circular 230 (the authority to practice before the Internal Revenue Service is limited by section 10.3(e)).

   ▶ IF THIS DECLARATION OF REPRESENTATIVE IS NOT SIGNED AND DATED, THE POWER OF ATTORNEY WILL BE RETURNED. REPRESENTATIVES MUST SIGN IN THE ORDER LISTED IN LINE 2 ABOVE. See the instructions for Part II.

**Note:** For designations d-f, enter your title, position, or relationship to the taxpayer in the "Licensing jurisdiction" column. See the instructions for Part II for more information.

| Designation— Insert above letter **(a–r)** | Licensing jurisdiction (state) or other licensing authority (if applicable) | Bar, license, certification, registration, or enrollment number (if applicable). See instructions for Part II for more information. | Signature | Date |
|---|---|---|---|---|
| b | XX | 99999 | *A. G. Accountant* | *5/1/14* |
| | | | | |
| | | | | |

Form **2848** (Rev. 3-2012)

---

**EXHIBIT 2.2**

*(Continued)*

| Form **1023**<br>(Rev. December 2013)<br>Department of the Treasury<br>Internal Revenue Service | **Application for Recognition of Exemption**<br>**Under Section 501(c)(3) of the Internal Revenue Code**<br>► (Use with the June 2006 revision of the Instructions for Form 1023 and the current Notice 1382) | (00) | OMB No. 1545-0056<br>**Note:** *If exempt status is approved, this application will be open for public inspection.* |

Use the instructions to complete this application and for a definition of all **bold** items. For additional help, call IRS Exempt Organizations Customer Account Services toll-free at 1-877-829-5500. Visit our website at **www.irs.gov** for forms and publications. If the required information and documents are not submitted with payment of the appropriate user fee, the application may be returned to you.

Attach additional sheets to this application if you need more space to answer fully. Put your name and EIN on each sheet and identify each answer by Part and line number. Complete Parts I - XI of Form 1023 and submit only those Schedules (A through H) that apply to you.

**Part I**    **Identification of Applicant**

| 1 Full name of organization (exactly as it appears in your **organizing document**)<br><br>Active Project Fund | 2 c/o Name (if applicable) | |
|---|---|---|
| 3 **Mailing address** (Number and street) (see instructions)<br><br>1010 Main Street | Room/Suite | 4 Employer Identification Number (EIN)<br><br>33-3333333 |
| City or town, state or country, and ZIP + 4<br><br>Any Town, TX 77777 | | 5 Month the annual accounting period ends (01 – 12)<br><br>12 |

6 Primary contact (officer, director, trustee, or **authorized representative**)

| a Name: A Good Accountant | |
|---|---|
| **b** Phone: | (323) 222-3333 |
| **c** Fax: (optional) | (323) 222-3334 |

7 Are you represented by an authorized representative, such as an attorney or accountant? If "Yes," provide the authorized representative's name, and the name and address of the authorized representative's firm. Include a completed Form 2848, *Power of Attorney and Declaration of Representative,* with your application if you would like us to communicate with your representative.
   ☑ Yes    ☐ No    **See attachment**

8 Was a person who is not one of your officers, directors, trustees, employees, or an authorized representative listed in line 7, paid, or promised payment, to help plan, manage, or advise you about the structure or activities of your organization, or about your financial or tax matters? If "Yes," provide the person's name, the name and address of the person's firm, the amounts paid or promised to be paid, and describe that person's role.
   ☑ Yes    ☐ No    **See attachment**

9a Organization's website: www.activeprojectfund.org

   b Organization's email: (optional) info@activeprojectfund.org

10 Certain organizations are not required to file an information return (Form 990 or Form 990-EZ). If you are granted tax-exemption, are you claiming to be excused from filing Form 990 or Form 990-EZ? If "Yes," explain. See the instructions for a description of organizations not required to file Form 990 or Form 990-EZ.
   ☐ Yes    ☑ No

11 Date incorporated if a corporation, or formed, if other than a corporation.  (MM/DD/YYYY)    01 / 15 / 2014

12 Were you formed under the laws of a **foreign country**? If "Yes," state the country.
   ☐ Yes    ☑ No

For Paperwork Reduction Act Notice, see page 24 of the instructions.     Cat. No. 17133K     Form **1023** (Rev. 12-2013)

**EXHIBIT 2.2**

*(Continued)*

Form 1023 (Rev. 12-2013)　　(00)　Name: Active Project Fund　　　　　　　　　EIN: 33 – 3333333　　　Page **2**

## Part II　Organizational Structure

You must be a corporation (including a limited liability company), an unincorporated association, or a trust to be tax exempt. (See instructions.) **DO NOT file this form unless you can check "Yes" on lines 1, 2, 3, or 4.**

1　Are you a **corporation**? If "Yes," attach a copy of your articles of incorporation showing **certification of filing** with the appropriate state agency. Include copies of any amendments to your articles and be sure they also show state filing certification.　☑ Yes　☐ No
See attachment

2　Are you a **limited liability company (LLC)**? If "Yes," attach a copy of your articles of organization showing certification of filing with the appropriate state agency. Also, if you adopted an operating agreement, attach a copy. Include copies of any amendments to your articles and be sure they show state filing certification. Refer to the instructions for circumstances when an LLC should not file its own exemption application.　☐ Yes　☑ No

3　Are you an **unincorporated association**? If "Yes," attach a copy of your articles of association, constitution, or other similar organizing document that is dated and includes at least two signatures. Include signed and dated copies of any amendments.　☐ Yes　☑ No

4a　Are you a **trust**? If "Yes," attach a signed and dated copy of your trust agreement. Include signed and dated copies of any amendments.　☐ Yes　☑ No

b　Have you been funded? If "No," explain how you are formed without anything of value placed in trust.　☐ Yes　☐ No

5　Have you adopted **bylaws**? If "Yes," attach a current copy showing date of adoption. If "No," explain how your officers, directors, or trustees are selected.　☑ Yes　☐ No
See attachment

## Part III　Required Provisions in Your Organizing Document

The following questions are designed to ensure that when you file this application, your organizing document contains the required provisions to meet the organizational test under section 501(c)(3). Unless you can check the boxes in both lines 1 and 2, your organizing document does not meet the organizational test. **DO NOT file this application until you have amended your organizing document.** Submit your original and amended organizing documents (showing state filing certification if you are a corporation or an LLC) with your application.

1　Section 501(c)(3) requires that your organizing document state your exempt purpose(s), such as charitable, religious, educational, and/or scientific purposes. Check the box to confirm that your organizing document meets this requirement. Describe specifically where your organizing document meets this requirement, such as a reference to a particular article or section in your organizing document. Refer to the instructions for exempt purpose language. Location of Purpose Clause (Page, Article, and Paragraph): <u>Pg 1, Art. 4, Sec. 4.01</u>　☑

2a　Section 501(c)(3) requires that upon dissolution of your organization, your remaining assets must be used exclusively for exempt purposes, such as charitable, religious, educational, and/or scientific purposes. Check the box on line 2a to confirm that your organizing document meets this requirement by express provision for the distribution of assets upon dissolution. If you rely on state law for your dissolution provision, do not check the box on line 2a and go to line 2c.　☑

2b　If you checked the box on line 2a, specify the location of your dissolution clause (Page, Article, and Paragraph). Do not complete line 2c if you checked box 2a.　<u>Pg 1, Art. 4, Sec. 4.02c</u>

2c　See the instructions for information about the operation of state law in your particular state. Check this box if you rely on operation of state law for your dissolution provision and indicate the state: _____　☐

## Part IV　Narrative Description of Your Activities　　　　See attachment

Using an attachment, describe your *past, present,* and *planned* activities in a narrative. If you believe that you have already provided some of this information in response to other parts of this application, you may summarize that information here and refer to the specific parts of the application for supporting details. You may also attach representative copies of newsletters, brochures, or similar documents for supporting details to this narrative. Remember that if this application is approved, it will be open for public inspection. Therefore, your narrative description of activities should be thorough and accurate. Refer to the instructions for information that must be included in your description.

## Part V　Compensation and Other Financial Arrangements With Your Officers, Directors, Trustees, Employees, and Independent Contractors

1a　List the names, titles, and mailing addresses of all of your officers, directors, and trustees. For each person listed, state their total annual **compensation**, or proposed compensation, for all services to the organization, whether as an officer, employee, or other position. Use actual figures, if available. Enter "none" if no compensation is or will be paid. If additional space is needed, attach a separate sheet. Refer to the instructions for information on what to include as compensation.

| Name | Title | Mailing address | Compensation amount (annual actual or estimated) |
|---|---|---|---|
| A. B. Sample | President | 1010 Main Street Any Town, TX 77777 | None |
| C. D. Sample | Secretary/Treasurer | 1010 Main Street Any Town, TX 77777 | None |
| E. F. Sample | Vice President | 1010 Main Street Any Town, TX 77777 | None |
| | | | |
| | | | |

Form **1023** (Rev. 12-2013)

**EXHIBIT 2.2**

*(Continued)*

Form 1023 (Rev. 12-2013)   (00) Name: Active Project Fund                    EIN: 33 – 3333333        Page **3**

| **Part V** | Compensation and Other Financial Arrangements With Your Officers, Directors, Trustees, Employees, and Independent Contractors *(Continued)* |

b List the names, titles, and mailing addresses of each of your five highest compensated employees who receive or will receive compensation of more than $50,000 per year. Use the actual figure, if available. Refer to the instructions for information on what to include as compensation. Do not include officers, directors, or trustees listed in line 1a.

| Name | Title | Mailing address | Compensation amount (annual actual or estimated) |
|---|---|---|---|
| Jane Smith | Executive Director | 1010 Main Street Any Town, TX 77777 | 52,000 |
| | | | |
| | | | |
| | | | |
| | | | |

c List the names, names of businesses, and mailing addresses of your five highest compensated **independent contractors** that receive or will receive compensation of more than $50,000 per year. Use the actual figure, if available. Refer to the instructions for information on what to include as compensation.

| Name | Title | Mailing address | Compensation amount (annual actual or estimated) |
|---|---|---|---|
| None | | | |
| | | | |
| | | | |
| | | | |
| | | | |

The following "Yes" or "No" questions relate to *past, present, or planned* relationships, transactions, or agreements with your officers, directors, trustees, highest compensated employees, and highest compensated independent contractors listed in lines 1a, 1b, and 1c.

**2a** Are any of your officers, directors, or trustees **related** to each other through **family** or **business relationships**? If "Yes," identify the individuals and explain the relationship.   ☑ Yes   ☐ No
See attachment

**b** Do you have a business relationship with any of your officers, directors, or trustees other than through their position as an officer, director, or trustee? If "Yes," identify the individuals and describe the business relationship with each of your officers, directors, or trustees.   ☐ Yes   ☑ No

**c** Are any of your officers, directors, or trustees related to your highest compensated employees or highest compensated independent contractors listed on lines 1b or 1c through family or business relationships? If "Yes," identify the individuals and explain the relationship.   ☐ Yes   ☑ No

**3a** For each of your officers, directors, trustees, highest compensated employees, and highest compensated independent contractors listed on lines 1a, 1b, or 1c, attach a list showing their name, qualifications, average hours worked, and duties.   See attachment

**b** Do any of your officers, directors, trustees, highest compensated employees, and highest compensated independent contractors listed on lines 1a, 1b, or 1c receive compensation from any other organizations, whether tax exempt or taxable, that are related to you through **common control**? If "Yes," identify the individuals, explain the relationship between you and the other organization, and describe the compensation arrangement.   ☐ Yes   ☑ No

**4** In establishing the compensation for your officers, directors, trustees, highest compensated employees, and highest compensated independent contractors listed on lines 1a, 1b, and 1c, the following practices are recommended, although they are not required to obtain exemption. Answer "Yes" to all the practices you use.

**a** Do you or will the individuals that approve compensation arrangements follow a conflict of interest policy?   ☑ Yes   ☐ No
**b** Do you or will you approve compensation arrangements in advance of paying compensation?   ☑ Yes   ☐ No
**c** Do you or will you document in writing the date and terms of approved compensation arrangements?   ☑ Yes   ☐ No

Form **1023** (Rev. 12-2013)

**EXHIBIT 2.2**

*(Continued)*

Form 1023 (Rev. 12-2013)　　(00) Name: Active Project Fund　　　　　　　　　EIN: 33 _ 3333333　　　Page **4**

| **Part V** | **Compensation and Other Financial Arrangements With Your Officers, Directors, Trustees, Employees, and Independent Contractors** *(Continued)* | | |
|---|---|---|---|

| | | | |
|---|---|---|---|
| **d** | Do you or will you record in writing the decision made by each individual who decided or voted on compensation arrangements? | ☑ Yes | ☐ No |
| **e** | Do you or will you approve compensation arrangements based on information about compensation paid by **similarly situated** taxable or tax-exempt organizations for similar services, current compensation surveys compiled by independent firms, or actual written offers from similarly situated organizations? Refer to the instructions for Part V, lines 1a, 1b, and 1c, for information on what to include as compensation. | ☑ Yes | ☐ No |
| **f** | Do you or will you record in writing both the information on which you relied to base your decision and its source? | ☑ Yes | ☐ No |
| **g** | If you answered "No" to any item on lines 4a through 4f, describe how you set compensation that is **reasonable** for your officers, directors, trustees, highest compensated employees, and highest compensated independent contractors listed in Part V, lines 1a, 1b, and 1c. | | |
| **5a** | Have you adopted a **conflict of interest policy** consistent with the sample conflict of interest policy in Appendix A to the instructions? If "Yes," provide a copy of the policy and explain how the policy has been adopted, such as by resolution of your governing board. If "No," answer lines 5b and 5c. | ☑ Yes<br>See attachment | ☐ No |
| **b** | What procedures will you follow to assure that persons who have a conflict of interest will not have influence over you for setting their own compensation? | | |
| **c** | What procedures will you follow to assure that persons who have a conflict of interest will not have influence over you regarding business deals with themselves?<br><br>**Note:** A conflict of interest policy is recommended though it is not required to obtain exemption. Hospitals, see Schedule C, Section I, line 14. | | |
| **6a** | Do you or will you compensate any of your officers, directors, trustees, highest compensated employees, and highest compensated independent contractors listed in lines 1a, 1b, or 1c through **non-fixed payments**, such as discretionary bonuses or revenue-based payments? If "Yes," describe all non-fixed compensation arrangements, including how the amounts are determined, who is eligible for such arrangements, whether you place a limitation on total compensation, and how you determine or will determine that you pay no more than reasonable compensation for services. Refer to the instructions for Part V, lines 1a, 1b, and 1c, for information on what to include as compensation. | ☑ Yes<br>See attachment | ☐ No |
| **b** | Do you or will you compensate any of your employees, other than your officers, directors, trustees, or your five highest compensated employees who receive or will receive compensation of more than $50,000 per year, through non-fixed payments, such as discretionary bonuses or revenue-based payments? If "Yes," describe all non-fixed compensation arrangements, including how the amounts are or will be determined, who is or will be eligible for such arrangements, whether you place or will place a limitation on total compensation, and how you determine or will determine that you pay no more than reasonable compensation for services. Refer to the instructions for Part V, lines 1a, 1b, and 1c, for information on what to include as compensation. | ☐ Yes | ☑ No |
| **7a** | Do you or will you purchase any goods, services, or assets from any of your officers, directors, trustees, highest compensated employees, or highest compensated independent contractors listed in lines 1a, 1b, or 1c? If "Yes," describe any such purchase that you made or intend to make, from whom you make or will make such purchases, how the terms are or will be negotiated at **arm's length**, and explain how you determine or will determine that you pay no more than **fair market value**. Attach copies of any written contracts or other agreements relating to such purchases. | ☐ Yes | ☑ No |
| **b** | Do you or will you sell any goods, services, or assets to any of your officers, directors, trustees, highest compensated employees, or highest compensated independent contractors listed in lines 1a, 1b, or 1c? If "Yes," describe any such sales that you made or intend to make, to whom you make or will make such sales, how the terms are or will be negotiated at arm's length, and explain how you determine or will determine you are or will be paid at least fair market value. Attach copies of any written contracts or other agreements relating to such sales. | ☐ Yes | ☑ No |
| **8a** | Do you or will you have any leases, contracts, loans, or other agreements with your officers, directors, trustees, highest compensated employees, or highest compensated independent contractors listed in lines 1a, 1b, or 1c? If "Yes," provide the information requested in lines 8b through 8f. | ☐ Yes | ☑ No |
| **b** | Describe any written or oral arrangements that you made or intend to make. | | |
| **c** | Identify with whom you have or will have such arrangements. | | |
| **d** | Explain how the terms are or will be negotiated at arm's length. | | |
| **e** | Explain how you determine you pay no more than fair market value or you are paid at least fair market value. | | |
| **f** | Attach copies of any signed leases, contracts, loans, or other agreements relating to such arrangements. | | |
| **9a** | Do you or will you have any leases, contracts, loans, or other agreements with any organization in which any of your officers, directors, or trustees are also officers, directors, or trustees, or in which any individual officer, director, or trustee owns more than a 35% interest? If "Yes," provide the information requested in lines 9b through 9f. | ☐ Yes | ☑ No |

Form **1023** (Rev. 12-2013)

**EXHIBIT 2.2**

*(Continued)*

Form 1023 (Rev. 12-2013)  (00) Name: Active Project Fund    EIN: 33 – 3333333    Page 5

**Part V** Compensation and Other Financial Arrangements With Your Officers, Directors, Trustees, Employees, and Independent Contractors *(Continued)*

  **b** Describe any written or oral arrangements you made or intend to make.

  **c** Identify with whom you have or will have such arrangements.

  **d** Explain how the terms are or will be negotiated at arm's length.

  **e** Explain how you determine or will determine you pay no more than fair market value or that you are paid at least fair market value.

  **f** Attach a copy of any signed leases, contracts, loans, or other agreements relating to such arrangements.

**Part VI** Your Members and Other Individuals and Organizations That Receive Benefits From You

The following "Yes" or "No" questions relate to goods, services, and funds you provide to individuals and organizations as part of your activities. Your answers should pertain to *past, present,* and *planned* activities. (See instructions.)

| | | |
|---|---|---|
| **1a** In carrying out your exempt purposes, do you provide goods, services, or funds to individuals? If "Yes," describe each program that provides goods, services, or funds to individuals. | ☐ Yes | ☑ No |
| **b** In carrying out your exempt purposes, do you provide goods, services, or funds to organizations? If "Yes," describe each program that provides goods, services, or funds to organizations. | ☑ Yes<br>See attachment | ☐ No |
| **2** Do any of your programs limit the provision of goods, services, or funds to a specific individual or group of specific individuals? For example, answer "Yes," if goods, services, or funds are provided only for a particular individual, your members, individuals who work for a particular employer, or graduates of a particular school. If "Yes," explain the limitation and how recipients are selected for each program. | ☐ Yes | ☑ No |
| **3** Do any individuals who receive goods, services, or funds through your programs have a family or business relationship with any officer, director, trustee, or with any of your highest compensated employees or highest compensated independent contractors listed in Part V, lines 1a, 1b, and 1c? If "Yes," explain how these related individuals are eligible for goods, services, or funds. | ☐ Yes | ☑ No |

**Part VII** Your History

The following "Yes" or "No" questions relate to your history. (See instructions.)

| | | |
|---|---|---|
| **1** Are you a **successor** to another organization? Answer "Yes," if you have taken or will take over the activities of another organization; you took over 25% or more of the fair market value of the net assets of another organization; or you were established upon the conversion of an organization from for-profit to non-profit status. If "Yes," complete Schedule G. | ☐ Yes | ☑ No |
| **2** Are you submitting this application more than 27 months after the end of the month in which you were legally formed? If "Yes," complete Schedule E. | ☐ Yes | ☑ No |

**Part VIII** Your Specific Activities

The following "Yes" or "No" questions relate to specific activities that you may conduct. Check the appropriate box. Your answers should pertain to *past, present,* and *planned* activities. (See instructions.)

| | | |
|---|---|---|
| **1** Do you support or oppose candidates in **political campaigns** in any way? If "Yes," explain. | ☐ Yes | ☑ No |
| **2a** Do you attempt to influence **legislation**? If "Yes," explain how you attempt to influence legislation and complete line 2b. If "No," go to line 3a. | ☐ Yes | ☑ No |
| **b** Have you made or are you making an **election** to have your legislative activities measured by expenditures by filing Form 5768? If "Yes," attach a copy of the Form 5768 that was already filed or attach a completed Form 5768 that you are filing with this application. If "No," describe whether your attempts to influence legislation are a substantial part of your activities. Include the time and money spent on your attempts to influence legislation as compared to your total activities. | ☐ Yes | ☐ No |
| **3a** Do you or will you operate bingo or **gaming** activities? If "Yes," describe who conducts them, and list all revenue received or expected to be received and expenses paid or expected to be paid in operating these activities. **Revenue and expenses** should be provided for the time periods specified in Part IX, Financial Data. | ☐ Yes | ☑ No |
| **b** Do you or will you enter into contracts or other agreements with individuals or organizations to conduct bingo or gaming for you? If "Yes," describe any written or oral arrangements that you made or intend to make, identify with whom you have or will have such arrangements, explain how the terms are or will be negotiated at arm's length, and explain how you determine or will determine you pay no more than fair market value or you will be paid at least fair market value. Attach copies of any written contracts or other agreements relating to such arrangements. | ☐ Yes | ☑ No |
| **c** List the states and local jurisdictions, including Indian Reservations, in which you conduct or will conduct gaming or bingo. | | |

Form **1023** (Rev. 12-2013)

**EXHIBIT 2.2**

*(Continued)*

Form 1023 (Rev. 12-2013)   (00) Name: Active Project Fund        EIN: 33 – 3333333       Page **6**

**Part VIII   Your Specific Activities** *(Continued)*

**4a** Do you or will you undertake **fundraising**? If "Yes," check all the fundraising programs you do or will conduct. (See instructions.)   ☐ Yes  ☑ No

- ☐ mail solicitations
- ☐ email solicitations
- ☐ personal solicitations
- ☐ vehicle, boat, plane, or similar donations
- ☐ foundation grant solicitations
- ☐ phone solicitations
- ☐ accept donations on your website
- ☐ receive donations from another organization's website
- ☐ government grant solicitations
- ☐ Other

Attach a description of each fundraising program.

**b** Do you or will you have written or oral contracts with any individuals or organizations to raise funds for you? If "Yes," describe these activities. Include all revenue and expenses from these activities and state who conducts them. Revenue and expenses should be provided for the time periods specified in Part IX, Financial Data. Also, attach a copy of any contracts or agreements.   ☐ Yes  ☑ No

**c** Do you or will you engage in fundraising activities for other organizations? If "Yes," describe these arrangements. Include a description of the organizations for which you raise funds and attach copies of all contracts or agreements.   ☐ Yes  ☑ No

**d** List all states and local jurisdictions in which you conduct fundraising. For each state or local jurisdiction listed, specify whether you fundraise for your own organization, you fundraise for another organization, or another organization fundraises for you.

**e** Do you or will you maintain separate accounts for any contributor under which the contributor has the right to advise on the use or distribution of funds? Answer "Yes" if the donor may provide advice on the types of investments, distributions from the types of investments, or the distribution from the donor's contribution account. If "Yes," describe this program, including the type of advice that may be provided and submit copies of any written materials provided to donors.   ☐ Yes  ☑ No

**5** Are you **affiliated** with a governmental unit? If "Yes," explain.   ☐ Yes  ☑ No

**6a** Do you or will you engage in **economic development**? If "Yes," describe your program.   ☐ Yes  ☑ No
**b** Describe in full who benefits from your economic development activities and how the activities promote exempt purposes.

**7a** Do or will persons other than your employees or volunteers **develop** your facilities? If "Yes," describe each facility, the role of the developer, and any business or family relationship(s) between the developer and your officers, directors, or trustees.   ☐ Yes  ☑ No

**b** Do or will persons other than your employees or volunteers **manage** your activities or facilities? If "Yes," describe each activity and facility, the role of the manager, and any business or family relationship(s) between the manager and your officers, directors, or trustees.   ☐ Yes  ☑ No

**c** If there is a business or family relationship between any manager or developer and your officers, directors, or trustees, identify the individuals, explain the relationship, describe how contracts are negotiated at arm's length so that you pay no more than fair market value, and submit a copy of any contracts or other agreements.

**8** Do you or will you enter into **joint ventures**, including partnerships or **limited liability companies** treated as partnerships, in which you share profits and losses with partners other than section 501(c)(3) organizations? If "Yes," describe the activities of these joint ventures in which you participate.   ☐ Yes  ☑ No

**9a** Are you applying for exemption as a childcare organization under section 501(k)? If "Yes," answer lines 9b through 9d. If "No," go to line 10.   ☐ Yes  ☑ No

**b** Do you provide child care so that parents or caretakers of children you care for can be **gainfully employed** (see instructions)? If "No," explain how you qualify as a childcare organization described in section 501(k).   ☐ Yes  ☐ No

**c** Of the children for whom you provide child care, are 85% or more of them cared for by you to enable their parents or caretakers to be gainfully employed (see instructions)? If "No," explain how you qualify as a childcare organization described in section 501(k).   ☐ Yes  ☐ No

**d** Are your services available to the general public? If "No," describe the specific group of people for whom your activities are available. Also, see the instructions and explain how you qualify as a childcare organization described in section 501(k).   ☐ Yes  ☐ No

**10** Do you or will you publish, own, or have rights in music, literature, tapes, artworks, choreography, scientific discoveries, or other **intellectual property**? If "Yes," explain. Describe who owns or will own any copyrights, patents, or trademarks, whether fees are or will be charged, how the fees are determined, and how any items are or will be produced, distributed, and marketed.   ☐ Yes  ☑ No

Form **1023** (Rev. 12-2013)

**EXHIBIT 2.2**

*(Continued)*

Form 1023 (Rev. 12-2013)      (00)  Name: Active Project Fund                      EIN:   33 – 3333333           Page **7**

**Part VIII   Your Specific Activities** *(Continued)*

11   Do you or will you accept contributions of: real property; conservation easements; closely held securities; intellectual property such as patents, trademarks, and copyrights; works of music or art; licenses; royalties; automobiles, boats, planes, or other vehicles; or collectibles of any type? If "Yes," describe each type of contribution, any conditions imposed by the donor on the contribution, and any agreements with the donor regarding the contribution.   ☑ **Yes**   ☐ **No**
See attachment

12a   Do you or will you operate in a **foreign country** or **countries?** If "Yes," answer lines 12b through 12d. If "No," go to line 13a.   ☐ **Yes**   ☑ **No**
   **b**   Name the foreign countries and regions within the countries in which you operate.
   **c**   Describe your operations in each country and region in which you operate.
   **d**   Describe how your operations in each country and region further your exempt purposes.

13a   Do you or will you make grants, loans, or other distributions to organization(s)? If "Yes," answer lines 13b through 13g. If "No," go to line 14a.   ☑ **Yes**   ☐ **No**
See attachment
   **b**   Describe how your grants, loans, or other distributions to organizations further your exempt purposes.
   **c**   Do you have written contracts with each of these organizations? If "Yes," attach a copy of each contract.   ☐ **Yes**   ☑ **No**
   **d**   Identify each recipient organization and any **relationship** between you and the recipient organization.
   **e**   Describe the records you keep with respect to the grants, loans, or other distributions you make.
   **f**   Describe your selection process, including whether you do any of the following:
      **(i)**   Do you require an application form? If "Yes," attach a copy of the form.   ☐ **Yes**   ☑ **No**
      **(ii)**   Do you require a grant proposal? If "Yes," describe whether the grant proposal specifies your responsibilities and those of the grantee, obligates the grantee to use the grant funds only for the purposes for which the grant was made, provides for periodic written reports concerning the use of grant funds, requires a final written report and an accounting of how grant funds were used, and acknowledges your authority to withhold and/or recover grant funds in case such funds are, or appear to be, misused.   ☐ **Yes**   ☑ **No**
   **g**   Describe your procedures for oversight of distributions that assure you the resources are used to further your exempt purposes, including whether you require periodic and final reports on the use of resources.

14a   Do you or will you make grants, loans, or other distributions to foreign organizations? If "Yes," answer lines 14b through 14f. If "No," go to line 15.   ☐ **Yes**   ☑ **No**
   **b**   Provide the name of each foreign organization, the country and regions within a country in which each foreign organization operates, and describe any relationship you have with each foreign organization.
   **c**   Does any foreign organization listed in line 14b accept contributions earmarked for a specific country or specific organization? If "Yes," list all earmarked organizations or countries.   ☐ **Yes**   ☐ **No**
   **d**   Do your contributors know that you have ultimate authority to use contributions made to you at your discretion for purposes consistent with your exempt purposes? If "Yes," describe how you relay this information to contributors.   ☐ **Yes**   ☐ **No**
   **e**   Do you or will you make pre-grant inquiries about the recipient organization? If "Yes," describe these inquiries, including whether you inquire about the recipient's financial status, its tax-exempt status under the Internal Revenue Code, its ability to accomplish the purpose for which the resources are provided, and other relevant information.   ☐ **Yes**   ☐ **No**
   **f**   Do you or will you use any additional procedures to ensure that your distributions to foreign organizations are used in furtherance of your exempt purposes? If "Yes," describe these procedures, including site visits by your employees or compliance checks by impartial experts, to verify that grant funds are being used appropriately.   ☐ **Yes**   ☐ **No**

Form **1023** (Rev. 12-2013)

**EXHIBIT 2.2**

*(Continued)*

Form 1023 (Rev. 12-2013)     (00)  Name: Active Project Fund                                    EIN:  33 – 3333333          Page **8**

| Part VIII | Your Specific Activities *(Continued)* | | |
|---|---|---|---|
| 15 | Do you have a **close connection** with any organizations? If "Yes," explain. | ☐ Yes | ☑ No |
| 16 | Are you applying for exemption as a **cooperative hospital service organization** under section 501(e)? If "Yes," explain. | ☐ Yes | ☑ No |
| 17 | Are you applying for exemption as a **cooperative service organization of operating educational organizations** under section 501(f)? If "Yes," explain. | ☐ Yes | ☑ No |
| 18 | Are you applying for exemption as a **charitable risk pool** under section 501(n)? If "Yes," explain. | ☐ Yes | ☑ No |
| 19 | Do you or will you operate a **school**? If "Yes," complete Schedule B. Answer "Yes," whether you operate a school as your main function or as a secondary activity. | ☐ Yes | ☑ No |
| 20 | Is your main function to provide **hospital** or **medical care**? If "Yes," complete Schedule C. | ☐ Yes | ☑ No |
| 21 | Do you or will you provide **low-income housing** or housing for the **elderly** or **handicapped**? If "Yes," complete Schedule F. | ☐ Yes | ☑ No |
| 22 | Do you or will you provide scholarships, fellowships, educational loans, or other educational grants to individuals, including grants for travel, study, or other similar purposes? If "Yes," complete Schedule H. | ☐ Yes | ☑ No |

**Note: Private foundations** may use Schedule H to request advance approval of individual grant procedures.

Form **1023** (Rev. 12-2013)

**EXHIBIT 2.2**

*(Continued)*

Form 1023 (Rev. 12-2013)   (00)  Name: Active Project Fund          EIN:  33 – 3333333          Page 9

## Part IX  Financial Data

For purposes of this schedule, years in existence refer to completed tax years. If in existence 4 or more years, complete the schedule for the most recent 4 tax years. If in existence more than 1 year but less than 4 years, complete the statements for each year in existence and provide projections of your likely revenues and expenses based on a reasonable and good faith estimate of your future finances for a total of 3 years of financial information. If in existence less than 1 year, provide projections of your likely revenues and expenses for the current year and the 2 following years, based on a reasonable and good faith estimate of your future finances for a total of 3 years of financial information. (See instructions.)

### A. Statement of Revenues and Expenses

| | Type of revenue or expense | Current tax year (a) From 1/15/14 To 12/31/14 | (b) From 1/1/15 To 12/31/15 | (c) From 1/1/16 To 12/31/16 | (d) From __ __ To __ __ | (e) Provide Total for (a) through (d) |
|---|---|---|---|---|---|---|
| Revenues | 1  Gifts, grants, and contributions received (do not include unusual grants) | 300,000 | 400,000 | 500,000 | | 1,200,000 |
| | 2  Membership fees received | | | | | 0 |
| | 3  Gross investment income | 300 | 600 | 3,000 | | 3,900 |
| | 4  Net unrelated business income | | | | | 0 |
| | 5  Taxes levied for your benefit | | | | | 0 |
| | 6  Value of services or facilities furnished by a governmental unit without charge (not including the value of services generally furnished to the public without charge) | | | | | 0 |
| | 7  Any revenue not otherwise listed above or in lines 9–12 below (attach an itemized list) | | | | | 0 |
| | 8  Total of lines 1 through 7 | 300,300 | 400,600 | 503,000 | 0 | 1,203,900 |
| | 9  Gross receipts from admissions, merchandise sold or services performed, or furnishing of facilities in any activity that is related to your exempt purposes (attach itemized list) | 10,000 | 20,000 | 60,000 | | 90,000 |
| | 10  Total of lines 8 and 9 | 310,300 | 420,600 | 563,000 | 0 | 1,293,900 |
| | 11  Net gain or loss on sale of capital assets (attach schedule and see instructions) | | | | | 0 |
| | 12  Unusual grants | | | | | 0 |
| | 13  Total Revenue Add lines 10 through 12 | 310,300 | 420,600 | 563,000 | | 1,293,900 |
| Expenses | 14  Fundraising expenses | | | | | |
| | 15  Contributions, gifts, grants, and similar amounts paid out (attach an itemized list) | | 2,000 | 2,000 | | |
| | 16  Disbursements to or for the benefit of members (attach an itemized list) | | | | | |
| | 17  Compensation of officers, directors, and trustees | | | | | |
| | 18  Other salaries and wages | 65,000 | 147,000 | 183,000 | | |
| | 19  Interest expense | | | | | |
| | 20  Occupancy (rent, utilities, etc.) | 12,000 | 24,000 | 30,000 | | |
| | 21  Depreciation and depletion | 5,000 | 5,000 | 5,000 | | |
| | 22  Professional fees | 16,000 | 4,000 | 4,500 | | |
| | 23  Any expense not otherwise classified, such as program services (attach itemized list) | 77,000 | 64,000 | 50,000 | | |
| | 24  Total Expenses Add lines 14 through 23 | 175,000 | 246,000 | 274,500 | 0 | |

Form **1023** (Rev. 12-2013)

## Exhibit 2.2

*(Continued)*

Form 1023 (Rev. 12-2013)   (00) Name: **Active Project Fund**    EIN: 33 – 3333333    Page **10**

| **Part IX** | **Financial Data** *(Continued)* | | | |
|---|---|---|---|---|

**B. Balance Sheet** (for your most recently completed tax year) — Year End: 12/31/14

**Assets** (Whole dollars)

| | | | |
|---|---|---|---|
| 1 | Cash | 1 | None |
| 2 | Accounts receivable, net | 2 | |
| 3 | Inventories | 3 | |
| 4 | Bonds and notes receivable (attach an itemized list) | 4 | |
| 5 | Corporate stocks (attach an itemized list) | 5 | |
| 6 | Loans receivable (attach an itemized list) | 6 | |
| 7 | Other investments (attach an itemized list) | 7 | |
| 8 | Depreciable and depletable assets (attach an itemized list) | 8 | |
| 9 | Land | 9 | |
| 10 | Other assets (attach an itemized list) | 10 | |
| 11 | Total Assets (add lines 1 through 10) | 11 | 0 |

**Liabilities**

| | | | |
|---|---|---|---|
| 12 | Accounts payable | 12 | |
| 13 | Contributions, gifts, grants, etc. payable | 13 | |
| 14 | Mortgages and notes payable (attach an itemized list) | 14 | |
| 15 | Other liabilities (attach an itemized list) | 15 | |
| 16 | Total Liabilities (add lines 12 through 15) | 16 | 0 |

**Fund Balances or Net Assets**

| | | | |
|---|---|---|---|
| 17 | Total fund balances or net assets | 17 | |
| 18 | Total Liabilities and Fund Balances or Net Assets (add lines 16 and 17) | 18 | None |

19 Have there been any substantial changes in your assets or liabilities since the end of the period shown above? If "Yes," explain.    ☐ Yes  ☑ No

| **Part X** | **Public Charity Status** |
|---|---|

Part X is designed to classify you as an organization that is either a **private foundation** or a **public charity**. Public charity status is a more favorable tax status than private foundation status. If you are a private foundation, Part X is designed to further determine whether you are a **private operating foundation**. (See instructions.)

**1a** Are you a private foundation? If "Yes," go to line 1b. If "No," go to line 5 and proceed as instructed. If you are unsure, see the instructions.    ☑ Yes  ☐ No

**b** As a private foundation, section 508(e) requires special provisions in your organizing document in addition to those that apply to all organizations described in section 501(c)(3). Check the box to confirm that your organizing document meets this requirement, whether by express provision or by reliance on operation of state law. Attach a statement that describes specifically where your organizing document meets this requirement, such as a reference to a particular article or section in your organizing document or by operation of state law. See the instructions, including Appendix B, for information about the special provisions that need to be contained in your organizing document. Go to line 2.    ☑

**2** Are you a private operating foundation? To be a private operating foundation you must engage directly in the active conduct of charitable, religious, educational, and similar activities, as opposed to indirectly carrying out these activities by providing grants to individuals or other organizations. If "Yes," go to line 3. If "No," go to the signature section of Part XI.    ☑ Yes  ☐ No

**3** Have you existed for one or more years? If "Yes," attach financial information showing that you are a private operating foundation; go to the signature section of Part XI. If "No," continue to line 4.    ☐ Yes  ☑ No

**4** Have you attached either (1) an affidavit or opinion of counsel, (including a written affidavit or opinion from a certified public accountant or accounting firm with expertise regarding this tax law matter), that sets forth facts concerning your operations and support to demonstrate that you are likely to satisfy the requirements to be classified as a private operating foundation; or (2) a statement describing your proposed operations as a private operating foundation?    ☑ Yes  ☐ No

**5** If you answered "No" to line 1a, indicate the type of public charity status you are requesting by checking one of the choices below. You may check only one box.

The organization is not a private foundation because it is:

**a** 509(a)(1) and 170(b)(1)(A)(i)—a church or a convention or association of churches. Complete and attach Schedule A.    ☐

**b** 509(a)(1) and 170(b)(1)(A)(ii)—a **school**. Complete and attach Schedule B.    ☐

**c** 509(a)(1) and 170(b)(1)(A)(iii)—a **hospital**, a cooperative hospital service organization, or a medical research organization operated in conjunction with a hospital. Complete and attach Schedule C.    ☐

**d** 509(a)(3)—an organization supporting either one or more organizations described in line 5a through c, f, g, or h or a publicly supported section 501(c)(4), (5), or (6) organization. Complete and attach Schedule D.    ☐

Form **1023** (Rev. 12-2013)

**EXHIBIT 2.2**

*(Continued)*

Form 1023 (Rev. 12-2013)　(00) Name: Active Project Fund　　　　EIN: 33 _ 3333333　　Page **11**

| **Part X** | **Public Charity Status** *(Continued)* |

e  509(a)(4)—an organization organized and operated exclusively for testing for public safety. ☐

f  509(a)(1) and 170(b)(1)(A)(iv)—an organization operated for the benefit of a college or university that is owned or operated by a governmental unit. ☐

g  509(a)(1) and 170(b)(1)(A)(vi)—an organization that receives a substantial part of its financial support in the form of contributions from publicly supported organizations, from a governmental unit, or from the general public. ☐

h  509(a)(2)—an organization that normally receives not more than one-third of its financial support from gross **investment income** and receives more than one-third of its financial support from contributions, membership fees, and gross receipts from activities related to its exempt functions (subject to certain exceptions). ☐

i  A publicly supported organization, but unsure if it is described in 5g or 5h. The organization would like the IRS to decide the correct status. ☐

6  If you checked box g, h, or i in question 5 above, you must request either an **advance** or a **definitive ruling** by selecting one of the boxes below. Refer to the instructions to determine which type of ruling you are eligible to receive.

a  **Request for Advance Ruling:** By checking this box and signing the consent, pursuant to section 6501(c)(4) of the Code you request an advance ruling and agree to extend the statute of limitations on the assessment of excise tax under section 4940 of the Code. The tax will apply only if you do not establish public support status at the end of the 5-year advance ruling period. The assessment period will be extended for the 5 advance ruling years to 8 years, 4 months, and 15 days beyond the end of the first year. You have the right to refuse or limit the extension to a mutually agreed-upon period of time or issue(s). Publication 1035, *Extending the Tax Assessment Period,* provides a more detailed explanation of your rights and the consequences of the choices you make. You may obtain Publication 1035 free of charge from the IRS web site at *www.irs.gov* or by calling toll-free 1-800-829-3676. Signing this consent will not deprive you of any appeal rights to which you would otherwise be entitled. If you decide not to extend the statute of limitations, you are not eligible for an advance ruling.

**Consent Fixing Period of Limitations Upon Assessment of Tax Under Section 4940 of the Internal Revenue Code**

For Organization

------------------------------------------------　------------------------------------------------　------------------------
(Signature of Officer, Director, Trustee, or other　(Type or print name of signer)　　　　　(Date)
authorized official)
　　　　　　　　　　　　　　　　　　　　------------------------------------------------
　　　　　　　　　　　　　　　　　　　　(Type or print title or authority of signer)

For IRS Use Only

------------------------------------------------------------------------------------　------------------------
IRS Director, Exempt Organizations　　　　　　　　　　　　　　　(Date)

b  **Request for Definitive Ruling:** Check this box if you have completed one tax year of at least 8 full months and you are requesting a definitive ruling. To confirm your public support status, answer line 6b(i) if you checked box g in line 5 above. Answer line 6b(ii) if you checked box h in line 5 above. If you checked box i in line 5 above, answer both lines 6b(i) and (ii). ☐

(i) (a) Enter 2% of line 8, column (e) on Part IX-A. Statement of Revenues and Expenses. _____ 0

(b) Attach a list showing the name and amount contributed by each person, company, or organization whose gifts totaled more than the 2% amount. If the answer is "None," check this box. ☐

(ii) (a) For each year amounts are included on lines 1, 2, and 9 of Part IX-A. Statement of Revenues and Expenses, attach a list showing the name of and amount received from each **disqualified person.** If the answer is "None," check this box. ☐

(b) For each year amounts are included on line 9 of Part IX-A. Statement of Revenues and Expenses, attach a list showing the name of and amount received from each payer, other than a disqualified person, whose payments were more than the larger of (1) 1% of line 10, Part IX-A. Statement of Revenues and Expenses, or (2) $5,000. If the answer is "None," check this box. ☐

7  Did you receive any unusual grants during any of the years shown on Part IX-A. Statement of Revenues and Expenses? If "Yes," attach a list including the name of the contributor, the date and amount of the grant, a brief description of the grant, and explain why it is unusual. ☐ Yes  ☐ No

Form **1023** (Rev. 12-2013)

## Exhibit 2.2

*(Continued)*

Form 1023 (Rev. 12-2013)     (00) Name: Active Project Fund                                   EIN:  33 – 3333333          Page **12**

| **Part XI** | **User Fee Information** |
|---|---|

*You must include a user fee payment with this application. It will not be processed without your paid user fee. If your average annual gross receipts have exceeded or will exceed $10,000 annually over a 4-year period, you must submit payment of $850. If your gross receipts have not exceeded or will not exceed $10,000 annually over a 4-year period, the required user fee payment is $400. See instructions for Part XI, for a definition of **gross receipts** over a 4-year period. Your check or money order must be made payable to the United States Treasury. User fees are subject to change. Check our website at www.irs.gov and type "User Fee" in the keyword box, or call Customer Account Services at 1-877-829-5500 for current information.*

1   Have your annual gross receipts averaged or are they expected to average not more than $10,000?       ☐ Yes     ☑ No
    If "Yes," check the box on line 2 and enclose a user fee payment of $400 (Subject to change—see above).
    If "No," check the box on line 3 and enclose a user fee payment of $850 (Subject to change—see above).

2   Check the box if you have enclosed the reduced user fee payment of $400 (Subject to change).         ☐

3   Check the box if you have enclosed the user fee payment of $850 (Subject to change).                 ☑

**I declare under the penalties of perjury that I am authorized to sign this application on behalf of the above organization and that I have examined this application, including the accompanying schedules and attachments, and to the best of my knowledge it is true, correct, and complete.**

Please Sign Here ▶

| *A. B. Sample* | A. B. Sample | 5/5/2014 |
|---|---|---|
| (Signature of Officer, Director, Trustee, or other authorized official) | (Type or print name of signer) | (Date) |
| | President | |
| | (Type or print title or authority of signer) | |

**Reminder:** Send the completed Form 1023 Checklist with your filled-in-application.          Form **1023** (Rev. 12-2013)

## Exhibit 2.2

*(Continued)*

**Active Project Fund**                                                33-3333333
**Attachment to Form 1023**

ARTICLES OF INCORPORATION
Of
**Active Project Fund**
(A Non-Profit Corporation)

I, the undersigned natural person of the age of eighteen (18) years or more, acting as incorporator of a corporation under the Texas Non-Profit Corporation Act, do hereby adopt the following Articles of Incorporation for such Corporation:

ARTICLE ONE
Name

The name of the Corporation is **Active Project Fund.**

ARTICLE TWO
Nonprofit Corporation

The Corporation is a nonprofit corporation.

ARTICLE THREE
Duration

The period of the Corporation's duration is perpetual.

ARTICLE FOUR
Purposes

Section 4.01. The Corporation is organized exclusively for charitable, literary, and educational purposes as defined in Section 501(c)(3) of the Internal Revenue Code. These activities will include, but not be limited to, improving the quality of management and operation of nonprofit organizations.

Section 4.02. Notwithstanding any other provision of these Articles of Incorporation:

a. No part of the net earnings of the Corporation shall inure to the benefit of any director of the Corporation, officer of the Corporation, or any private individual (except that reasonable compensation may be paid for services rendered to or for the Corporation affecting one or more of its purposes); and no director, officer or any private individual shall be entitled to share in the distribution of any of the corporate assets on dissolution of the Corporation. No substantial part of the activities of the Corporation shall be the carrying on of propaganda, or otherwise attempting to influence legislation, and the Corporation shall not participate in, or intervene in (including the publication or distribution of statements) any political campaign on behalf of any candidate for public office.

b. The corporation shall not conduct or carry on any activities not permitted to be conducted or carried on by an organization exempt from taxation under Section 501(c)(3) of the Internal Revenue Code and its Regulations as they now exist or as they may hereafter be amended, or by an organization, contributions to which are deductible under 170(c)(2) of the Internal Revenue Code and Regulations as they now exist or as they may hereafter be amended.

c. Upon dissolution of the Corporation or the winding up of its affairs, the assets of the Corporation shall be distributed exclusively to charitable organizations which would then qualify under the provisions of Section 501(c)(3) of the Internal Revenue Code and its Regulations as they now exist or as they may be hereafter amended.

d. The Corporation is organized pursuant to the Texas Nonprofit Corporation Act and does not contemplate pecuniary gain or profit and is organized for nonprofit purposes which are consistent with the provisions of Section 501(c)(3) of the Internal Revenue Code and its Regulations as they now exist or as they may hereafter be amended.

ARTICLE FIVE

1                                                              Articles of Organization
This model provided by Texas Accountants and Lawyers for the Arts.

**EXHIBIT 2.2**

*(Continued)*

**Active Project Fund**                                          33-3333333
**Attachment to Form 1023**

Membership

The Corporation shall have no voting members.

ARTICLE SIX
Initial Registration Office and Agent

The street address of the initial registered office of the Corporation is 1010 Main Street, Any Town, XX 77777, and the name of the initial registered agent at such address is A.B. Sample.

ARTICLE SEVEN
Directors

The number of Directors constituting the initial Board of Directors of the Corporation is three (3), and the names and addresses of those people who are to serve as the initial Directors are:

| Name | Address |
|---|---|
| A.B. Sample | 1010 Main Street, Any Town, XX, 77777 |
| B.C. Sample | 1010 Main Street, Any Town, XX, 77777 |
| D.E. Sample | 1010 Main Street, Any Town, XX, 77777 |

ARTICLE EIGHT
Indemnification of Directors and Officers

Each Director and each officer or former Director or officer may be indemnified and may be advanced reasonable expenses by the Corporation against liabilities imposed upon him or her and expenses reasonably incurred by him or her in connection with any claim against him or her, or any action, suit or proceeding to which he or she may be a party by reason of his or being, or having been, such Director or officer and against such sum as independent counsel selected by the Directors shall deem reasonable payment made in settlement of any such claim, action, suit or proceeding primarily with the view of avoiding expenses of litigation; provided, however, that no Director or officer shall be indemnified (a) with respect to matters as to which he or she shall be adjudged in such action, suit or proceeding to be liable for negligence or misconduct in performance or duty, (b) with respect to any matters which shall be settled by the payment of sums which independent counsel selected by the Directors shall not deem reasonable payment made primarily with a view to avoiding expense of litigation, or (c) with respect to matters for which such indemnification would be against public policy. Such rights of indemnification shall be in addition to any other rights to which Directors or officers may be entitled under any bylaw, agreement, corporate resolution, vote of Directors or otherwise. The Corporation shall have the power to purchase and maintain at its cost and expense insurance on behalf of such persons to the fullest extent permitted by this Article and applicable state law.

ARTICLE NINE
Limitation On Scope Of Liability

No director shall be liable to the Corporation for monetary damages for an act or omission in the Director's capacity as a Director of the Corporation, except and only for the following:

a.     A breach of the Director's duty of loyalty to the Corporation;

b.     An act or omission not in good faith by the Director or an act or omission that involves the intentional misconduct or knowing violation of the law by the Director;

c.     A transaction from which the Director gained any improper benefit whether or not such benefit resulted from an action taken within the scope of the Director's office; or

d.     An act or omission by the Directors for which liability is expressly provided for by statute.

ARTICLE TEN

2

This model provided by Texas Accountants and Lawyers for the Arts.   Articles of Organization

**EXHIBIT 2.2**

---

*(Continued)*

**Active Project Fund**                                    33-3333333
**Attachment to Form 1023**

<u>Informal Action by Directors</u>

Any action required by law to be taken at a meeting of Directors, or any action which may be taken at a meeting of Directors, may be taken without a meeting if a consent in writing setting forth the action so taken shall be signed by a sufficient number of Directors as would be necessary to take that action at a meeting at which all of the Directors were present and voted. All consents signed in this manner must be delivered to the Secretary or other officer having custody of the minute book within sixty (60) days after the date of the earliest dated consent delivered to the Corporation in this manner. A facsimile transmission or other similar transmission shall be regarded as signed by the Director for purposes of this Article.

ARTICLE ELEVEN
<u>Incorporator</u>

The name and address of the incorporator is:

| <u>Name</u> | <u>Address</u> |
|---|---|
| A.B. Sample | 1010 Main Street, Any Town, XX, 77777 |

IN WITNESS WHEREOF, I have hereunto set my hand, this 15th day of January, 2014.

*Jane Smith*
_____
Jane Smith

This model provided by Texas Accountants and Lawyers for the Arts.
Articles of Organization

**EXHIBIT 2.2**

*(Continued)*

**Active Project Fund**
**Attachment to Form 1023**

33-3333333

BYLAWS OF

**Active Project Fund**

a Texas Non-Profit Corporation
\* \* \* \* \* \* \* \* \* \* \* \* \* \* \* \*
ARTICLE ONE - OFFICES

Section 1.01.    Principal Office. The principal office of the Corporation in the State of Texas shall be located in the City of Any Town, County of Harris. The Corporation may have such other offices, either within or without the State of Texas, as the Board of Directors may determine or as the affairs of the Corporation may require from time to time.

Section 1.02.    Registered Office and Registered Agent. The Corporation shall have and continuously maintain in the State of Texas a registered office, and a registered agent whose office is identical with such registered office may be, but need not be, identical with the principal office of the Corporation in the State of Texas, and the address of the registered office may be changed from time to time by the Board of Directors.

ARTICLE TWO - PURPOSES

Section 2.01.    Organizational Purposes. The Corporation is organized exclusively for charitable, scientific and educational purposes. The corporation is established as a permanent organization in Texas seeking to enrich the local community through activities promoting such provision. The Corporation may engage in any activities that further its purpose.

No part of the net earnings of the Corporation shall inure to the benefit of any Director of the Corporation, officer of the Corporation, or any private individual (except that reasonable compensation may be paid for services rendered to or for the Corporation affecting one or more of its purposes), and no Director or officer of the Corporation, or any private individual shall be entitled to share in the distribution of any of the corporate assets on dissolution of the Corporation. No substantial part of the activities of the Corporation shall be the carrying on of propaganda, or otherwise attempting to influence legislation, and the Corporation shall not participate in, or intervene in (including the publication or distribution of statements) any political campaigning on behalf of any candidate for public office.

Notwithstanding any other provision of these Bylaws, the Corporation shall not conduct or carry on any activities not permitted to be conducted or carried on by an organization exempt from taxation under Section 501(c)(3) of the Internal Revenue Code and its Regulations as they now exist or as they may hereafter be amended, or by an organization, contributions to which are deductible under Section 170(c)(2) of the Internal Revenue Code and Regulations, as they now exist or as they may hereafter be amended.

Upon dissolution of the Corporation or the winding up of its affairs, the assets of the Corporation shall be distributed exclusively to charitable organizations which would then qualify under the provisions of Section 501(c)(3) of the Internal Revenue Code and its Regulations as they now exist or as they may hereafter be amended.

ARTICLE THREE - MEMBERS

Section 3.01.    The corporation shall have no voting members.

ARTICLE FOUR - BOARD OF DIRECTORS

Section 4.01.    General Powers. The affairs of the Corporation shall be managed by its Board of Directors. Directors need not be residents of Texas.

Section 4.02.    Number, Tenure and Qualifications. The number of Directors shall be not less than three (3) nor more than twenty (20). The initial Directors shall serve terms of one, two and three years, as provided by the Board. Afterwards, each director shall serve for three years, thereby providing for staggered terms. The initial terms of additional Directors shall be fixed to ensure than a disproportionate number of Directors (more than one-half) will not be up for election in any given year.

Section 4.03.    Regular Meetings. The Board of Directors shall provide for by resolution the time and place, either within or without the State of Texas, for the holding of the regular annual meeting(s) of the Board, and may provide by resolution the time and place for the holding of additional regular meetings of the Board, without other notice than such resolution. However, there shall never be less than one annual meeting of the Board of Directors.

1

This model provided by the Texas Accountants and Lawyers for the Arts.                    Bylaws

**EXHIBIT 2.2**

*(Continued)*

**Active Project Fund**                                                        33-3333333
**Attachment to Form 1023**

Section 4.04.    Annual Meetings. Beginning in 2014 an annual meeting of the Board of Directors shall be held at the date, time and place determined by the Board of Directors.

Section 4.05.    Special Meetings. Special meetings of the Board of Directors may be called by or at the request of the President, or any two Directors. The person or persons authorized to call special meetings of the Board may fix any place, either within or without the State of Texas, as the place for holding any special meetings of the Board called by them.

Section 4.06.    Meetings Utilizing Electronic Media. Members of the Board of Directors or members of any committee designated by the Board of Directors may participate in and hold a meeting of that Board or committee, respectively, by means of conference telephone or similar communication equipment, provided that all persons participating in such a meeting shall constitute presence in person at such meeting, except where a person participates in the meeting for the express purpose of objecting to the transaction of any business on the ground that the meeting is not lawfully created.

Section 4.07.    Notice. Notice of any special meeting of the Board of Directors shall be given at least (5) business days previously thereto by oral or written notice delivered personally or sent by mail, telegram, facsimile or messenger to each Director at his or her address as shown by the records of the Corporation. If mailed, such notice shall be deemed to be delivered when deposited in the United States mail so addressed with postage thereon prepaid. If notice be given by telegram, such notice shall be deemed to be delivered when the telegram is delivered to the telegram company. Any Director may waive notice of any meeting. The attendance of a Director at any meeting shall constitute a waiver or notice of such meeting, except when a Director attends a meeting for the express purpose of objecting to the transaction of any business because the meeting is not lawfully called or convened. Neither the business to be transacted at, nor the purpose of, any regular or special meeting of the Board need be specified in the notice or waiver of notice of such meeting, unless specifically required by law or by these Bylaws.

Section 4.08.    Quorum. A majority of the Board of Directors, but never less than three (3), shall constitute a quorum for the transaction of business at any meeting of the Board; but if less than a quorum of the Directors is present at said meeting, a majority of the Directors present may adjourn the meeting from time to time without further notice.

Section 4.09.    Manner of Acting. The act of a majority of the Directors present at a meeting at which a quorum is present shall be the act of the Board of Directors, unless the act of a greater number is required by law or by these Bylaws.

Section 4.10.    Vacancies. Any vacancy occurring in the Board of Directors, and any directorship to be filled by reason of an increase in the number of Directors, shall be filled by the Board of Directors. A Director elected to fill a vacancy shall be elected for the unexpired term of his or her predecessor in office. However, vacancies need not be filled unless such a vacancy would result in fewer than three directors remaining on the board.

Section 4.11.    Compensation. Directors as such shall not receive any stated salaries for their services, but by resolution of the Board of Directors a fixed sum and expenses of attendance, if any, may be allowed for attendance at each regular or special meeting of the Board; but nothing herein contained shall be construed to preclude any Director from serving the Corporation in any other capacity and receiving compensation therefore.

Section 4.12.    Informal Action by Directors. Any action required by law to be taken at a meeting of Directors, or any action which may be taken at a meeting of Directors, may be taken without a meeting if a consent in writing setting forth the action so taken shall be signed by a sufficient number of Directors as would be necessary to take that action at a meeting at which all the Directors were present and voted. Each such written consent shall be delivered, by hand or certified or registered mail, return receipt requested, to the Secretary or other officer or agent of the Corporation having custody of the Corporation's minute book. A written consent signed by less than all of the Directors is not effective to take the action that is the subject of the consent unless, within sixty (60) days after the date of the earliest dated consent delivered to the Corporation in the manner required by this Article, a consent or consents signed by the required number of Directors is delivered to the Corporation as provided in this Article. For purposes of this Article, a telegram, telex, cablegram, or similar transmission by a Director or a photographic, photostatic, facsimile or similar reproduction of a writing signed by a Director shall be regarded as signed by the Director.

Section 4.13.    Resignation. Any Director may resign by giving written notice to the President. The resignation shall be effective at the next called meeting of the Board of Directors, of which meeting the resigning Director shall receive notice.

Section 4.14.    Removal. Any Director may be removed with or without cause by a two thirds majority of the remaining Directors.

2
This model provided by the Texas Accountants and Lawyers for the Arts.            Bylaws

## EXHIBIT 2.2

(Continued)

■  69  ■

**Active Project Fund**                                                    33-3333333
**Attachment to Form 1023**

Section 4.15.    Indemnification. The Corporation may indemnify and advance reasonable expenses to directors, officers, employees and agents of the Corporation to the fullest extent required or permitted by Article 2.22A of the Texas Non-Profit Corporation Act, subject to the restrictions, if any, contained in the Corporation's Articles of Incorporation. The Corporation shall have the power to purchase and maintain at its cost and expense insurance on behalf of such persons to the fullest extent permitted by Article 2.22A of the Texas Non-Profit Corporation Act.

### ARTICLE FIVE - OFFICERS

Section 5.01.    Officers. The officers of the Corporation shall be a President, one or more Vice Presidents (the number thereof to be determined by the Board of Directors), a Secretary, a Treasurer, and such other officers as may be elected in accordance with the provisions of this Article. The Board of Directors may elect or appoint such other officers, including one or more Assistant Secretaries and one or more Assistant Treasurers, as it shall deem desirable, such officers to have the authority and perform the duties prescribed, from time to time, by the Board of Directors. Any two or more offices may be held by the same person, except the offices of President and Secretary.

Section 5.02.    Election and Term of Office. The officers of the Corporation shall be elected by the Board of Directors at the alternate Annual meeting of the Board of Directors and shall serve terms of two years duration. If the election of officers shall not be held at such meeting, such election shall be held as soon thereafter as conveniently may be. New offices may be created and filled at any meeting of the Board of Directors. Each officer shall hold office for two years, or until his or her successor shall have been duly elected and shall have qualified.

Section 5.03.    Removal. Any officer elected or appointed by the Board of Directors may be removed with or without cause by a majority vote of the Board of Directors, but such removal shall be without prejudice to the contract rights, if any, of the officer so removed.

Section 5.04.    Vacancies. A vacancy in any office because of death, resignation, disqualification, or otherwise, may be filled by the Board of Directors for the unexpired portion of the term.

Section 5.05.    President. The President shall be the principal executive officer of the Corporation and shall, in general, supervise and control all of the business and affairs of the Corporation. He or she shall preside at all meetings of the Board of Directors. The President may sign, with the Secretary or any other proper officer of the Corporation authorized by the Board of Directors, any deeds, mortgages, bonds, contracts, or other instruments which the Board of Directors has authorized to be executed, except in cases where the signing and execution thereof shall be expressly delegated by the Board of Directors or by these Bylaws or by statute to some other officer or agent of the Corporation; and in general he or she shall perform all duties as may be prescribed by the Board of Directors from time to time, including participating in various committee meetings as a member or chairperson thereof. He or she shall also be responsible for informing the Board of Directors of possible programs, meetings, and functions of the corporation.

Section 5.06.    Vice President. In the absence of the President or in the event of his or her inability or refusal to act, the Vice President (or in the event there be more than one Vice President, the Vice Presidents in order of their election) shall perform the duties of the President, and when so acting shall have all the powers of and be subject to all the restrictions upon the President. Any Vice President shall perform such other duties as from time to time may be assigned to him or her by the President or Board of Directors.

Section 5.07.    Treasurer. If required by the Board of Directors, the Treasurer shall give a bond for the faithful discharge of his or her duties in such sum and with such surety or sureties as the Board of Directors shall determine. He or she shall have charge and custody of and be responsible for all funds and securities of the Corporation; receive and give receipts for moneys due and payable to the Corporation from any source whatsoever, and deposit all such moneys in the name of the Corporation in such banks, trust companies, or other depositories as shall be selected in accordance with the provisions of these Bylaws; he or she shall keep proper books of account and other books showing at all times the amount of funds and other property belonging to the Corporation, all of which books shall be open at all times to the inspection of the Board of Directors; he or she shall also submit a report of the accounts and financial condition of the Corporation at each annual meeting of the Board of Directors; and in general perform all the duties incident to the office of Treasurer and such other duties as from time to time may be assigned to him or her by the President or by the Board of Directors.

Section 5.08.    Secretary. The Secretary shall keep the minutes of the meetings of the Board of Directors in one or more books provided for that purpose; give all notices in accordance with the provisions of these Bylaws or as required by law; be custodian of the corporate records and of the seal of the Corporation, and affix the seal of the Corporation to all documents, the execution of which on behalf of the Corporation under its seal is duly authorized in accordance with the provisions of these Bylaws; and, in general, perform all duties incident to the office of Secretary and such other duties as from time to time may be assigned to him or her by the President or Board of Directors. The Board of Directors and Officers shall give bonds of the faithful discharge of their duties in such sums and with such sureties as the Board of Directors shall determine. The Assistant Treasurer and Assistant Secretaries, in general, shall perform such duties as shall be assigned to them by the Treasurer or the Secretary or by the President or the Board of Directors.

### ARTICLE SIX- COMMITTEES

3

This model provided by the Texas Accountants and Lawyers for the Arts.                                        Bylaws

## EXHIBIT 2.2

*(Continued)*

**Active Project Fund**  33-3333333
**Attachment to Form 1023**

Section 6.01.    Appointment. The Board of Directors shall appoint members of committees established by the Board of Directors. The Board of Directors shall appoint the chairperson of each committee. These committees shall perform such functions and make such reports as the President or Board of Directors shall determine. Both Directors and members of the Advisory Board may serve on all committees except the Executive Committee.

Section 6.02.    Committees of Directors. The Board of Directors, by resolution adopted by a majority of the Directors in office, may designate and appoint one or more committees, each of which shall consist of two or more persons, a majority of who are Directors, which committees, to the extent provided in said resolution shall have and exercise the authority in the management of the Corporation of the Board of Directors. However, no such committee shall have the authority of the Board of Directors in reference to amending, altering, or repealing the Bylaws; electing, appointing, or removing any member of any such committee or any Director or officer of the Corporation; amending the Articles of Incorporation; adopting a plan of merger or adopting a plan of consolidation with another Corporation; authorizing the sale, lease, exchange, or mortgage of all or substantially all of the property and assets of the Corporation; authorizing the voluntary dissolution of the Corporation or revoking proceedings therefor; adopting a plan for the distribution of the assets of the Corporation; or amending, altering, or repealing any resolution of the Board of Directors which by its terms provides that it shall not be amended, altered or repealed by such committee. The designation and appointment of any such committee and the delegation thereof of authority shall not operate to relieve the Board of Directors, or any individual Director, of any responsibility imposed on it or him or her by law.

Section 6.03.    Executive Committee. The Board of Directors may from among its members appoint an Executive Committee consisting of the officers and any additional members as deemed necessary by the Board to serve at the pleasure of the Board. The President, unless absent or otherwise unable to do so, shall preside as Chairperson of the Executive Committee. The Committee shall meet at the call of the President or the Board of Directors, or any two (2) members of the Committee, and shall have and may exercise when the Board of Directors is not in session the power to perform all duties, of every kind and character, not required by law or the charter of the Corporation to be performed solely by the Board of Directors. The Executive Committee shall have authority to make rules for the holding and conduct of its meetings, keep records thereof and regularly report its actions to the Board. A majority but never less than three of the members of the Committee in office shall be sufficient to constitute a quorum at any meeting of the Committee, and all action taken at such a meeting shall be by a majority of those present all acts performed by the Executive Committee in the exercise of its aforesaid authority shall be deemed to be, and may be certified as, acts performed under authority of the Board of Directors. Vacancies in the Executive committee shall be filled by appointment by the Board of Directors. All actions of the Executive Committee shall be recorded in writing in a minute book kept for that purpose and a report of all action shall be made to the Board of Directors at its next meeting. The minutes of the Board of Directors shall reflect that such a report was made along with any action taken by the Board of Directors with respect thereto.

Section 6.04.    Nominating Committee. The President shall, with thirty (30) days advance notice to the Board of Directors, appoint the members of the Nominating Committee created by the Board of Directors. The members shall be members of the Board of Directors and Advisory Board appointed to nominate candidates for officers and directors. Additional nominations may be made by Directors at the annual meeting.

Section 6.05.    Advisory Committee. The function and purpose of the Advisory Committee shall be to advise the Board of Directors on matters relating to the purpose of the organization and to suggest projects, which the Corporation may undertake.

Section 6.06.    Other Committees. Other committees not having and exercising the authority of the Board of Directors in the management of the Corporation may be designated by a resolution adopted by a majority of the Directors present at a meeting at which a quorum is present. Except as otherwise provided in such resolution, the President of the Corporation shall appoint the members of each such committee. Any member thereof may be removed by the person or persons authorized to appoint such member whenever in their judgment the best interests of the Corporation shall be served by such removal. Members of such committee or committees may, but need not be, Directors.

Section 6.07.    Term of Office. Each member of a committee shall continue as such until the next annual meeting of the members of the Board of Directors and until his or her successor is appointed, unless the committee shall be sooner terminated, or unless such member be removed from such committee, or unless such member shall cease to qualify as a member thereof.

Section 6.08.    Chairperson. One member of each committee shall be appointed chairperson by the person or persons authorized to appoint the members thereof.

Section 6.09.    Vacancies. Vacancies in the membership of any committee may be filled by appointments made in the same manner as provided in the case of the original appointments.

## Exhibit 2.2

*(Continued)*

Active Project Fund                                              33-3333333
Attachment to Form 1023

Section 6.10.   Quorum. Unless otherwise provided in the resolution of the Board of Directors designating a committee, a majority of the whole committee shall constitute a quorum and the act of a majority of the members present at a meeting at which a quorum is present shall be the act of the committee.

Section 6.11.   Rules. Each committee may adopt rules for its government not inconsistent with these Bylaws or with rules adopted by the Board of Directors.

Section 6.12.   Committee Dissolution. The Board of Directors may, in its sole discretion, dissolve any committee with or without cause. Except for the Executive Committee, such dissolution shall require approval by a majority of the quorum. The Executive Committee shall only be dissolved by approval of two-thirds or more of all members of the Board of Directors.

## ARTICLE SEVEN - CONTRACTS, CHECKS, DEPOSITS, AND GIFTS

Section 7.01.   Contracts. The Board of Directors may authorize any officer or officers, agent or agents of the Corporation, in addition to the officers so authorized by these Bylaws, to enter into any contract or execute and deliver any instrument in the name of and on behalf of the Corporation. Such authority may be general or confined to specific instances.

Section 7.02.   Checks and Drafts, Etc. All checks, drafts, or orders for the payment of money, notes, or other evidence of indebtedness issued in the name of the Corporation shall be signed by such officer or officers, agent or agents of the Corporation and in such manner as shall from time to time be determined by resolution of the Board of Directors. In the absence of such determination by the Board of Directors, such instruments shall be signed by the Treasurer or an Assistant Treasurer and countersigned by the President or a Vice President of the Corporation.

Section 7.03.   Deposits. All funds of the Corporation shall be deposited from time to time to the credit of the Corporation in such banks, trust companies, or other depositories as the Board of Directors may select.

Section 7.04.   Gifts. The Board of Directors may accept on behalf of the Corporation any contribution, gift, bequest, or devise for the general purposes or for any special purpose of the Corporation.

## ARTICLE EIGHT - BOOKS AND RECORDS

Section 8.01.   Books and Records. The Corporation shall keep correct and complete books and records of account of the activities and transactions of the Corporation including, a minute book which shall contain a copy of the Corporation's application for tax-exempt statue (IRS Form 1023), copies of the organization's IRS information and/or tax returns (For example, Form 990 and all schedules thereto), and a copy of the Articles of Incorporation, Bylaws, and Amendments. The Corporation shall also keep minutes of the proceedings of its Board of Directors and any committees having the authority of the Board of Directors. All books and records of the Corporation may be inspected by any Director or his or her agent or attorney for any proper purpose at any reasonable time. Representatives of the Internal Revenue Service may inspect these books and records as necessary to meet the requirements relating to federal tax form 990. All financial records of the Corporation shall be available to the public for inspection and copying to the fullest extent required by law.

## ARTICLE NINE - FISCAL YEAR

Section 9.01.   Fiscal Year. The fiscal year of the Corporation shall begin on January 1 of each year and conclude on the last day of December of the year.

## ARTICLE TEN - SEAL

Section 10.01. Seal. The Board of Directors may authorize a corporate seal.

## ARTICLE ELEVEN - WAIVER OF NOTICE

Section 11.01. Waiver of Notice. Whenever any notice is required to be given under the provisions of the Texas Non-Profit Corporation Act or under the provisions of the Articles of Incorporation or the Bylaws of the Corporation, a waiver thereof in writing signed by the person or persons entitled to such notice, whether before or after the time therein, shall be deemed equivalent to the giving of such notice.

5

**EXHIBIT 2.2**

*(Continued)*

**Active Project Fund**                                                   33-3333333
**Attachment to Form 1023**

ARTICLE TWELVE - <u>AMENDMENTS TO BYLAWS</u>

Section 12.01.  <u>Amendments to Bylaws</u>.  These Bylaws may be altered, amended, or repealed and new Bylaws may be adopted by a two-thirds majority of the Directors present at any regular meeting or at any special meeting, if at least one day's written notice is given of an intention to alter, amend, or repeal these Bylaws or to adopt new Bylaws at such meeting.

ARTICLE THIRTEEN - <u>AMENDMENTS TO ARTICLES</u>

Section 13.01.  <u>Amendments to Articles</u>.  The Articles of Incorporation of the Corporation may, to the extent allowed by law, be altered, amended, or restated and new Articles of Incorporation may be adopted by a two-thirds majority of the Directors present at any regular meeting or at any special meeting, if at least one day's written notice is given of an intention to alter, amend, or restate the Articles of Incorporation or to adopt new Articles of Incorporation at such meeting.

<u>CERTIFICATE</u>

I HEREBY CERTIFY that the foregoing is a true, complete and correct copy of the By Laws of Active Project Fund, a Texas non-profit corporation, in effect on the date hereof.

IN WITNESS WHEREOF, I hereunto set my hand, this 15th day of January, 2014

*AB Sample*                                     *President*
_____        _____
              Signature                                      Title

This model provided by the Texas Accountants and Lawyers for the Arts.                    Bylaws

**EXHIBIT 2.2**

*(Continued)*

■  **73**  ■

**Active Project Fund**                                                                     33-3333333
**Attachment to Form 1023**

Part I, Line 7

A Good Accountant, Smith & Jones, LLP, 1 Main Street, Any Town, XX 77777.

Part I, Line 8

A Good Accountant, Smith & Jones, LLP, 1 Main Street, Any Town, XX 77777.
The amount to be paid for the preparation of Form 1023 is approximately $3,500-$5,000. The fee for future preparation of required Internal Revenue Service filings such as the Form 990-PF may be $2,000-$3,000 per year. A Good Accountant will help the organization by preparing all required Internal Revenue Service filings.

Part IV

Active Project Fund was created and will operate exclusively for charitable and educational purposes as defined in IRC §501(c)(3). Specifically, Active Project Fund (APF) is dedicated to improving the quality of management and operation of nonprofit organizations classified as tax-exempt charitable organizations under §501(c)(3). APF will accomplish its purpose by conducting seminars, providing technical assistance, and writing and disseminating educational materials.

**Seminars:** APF has hired an executive director with significant experience in nonprofit management. She will develop courses on financial and management issues such as personnel policies, budgeting, fundraising, office efficiency, computer use, and other issues relevant to management of a nonprofit organization. APF will seek to identify qualified professionals in the community who will be willing to volunteer their time as teachers. APF also expects to hire instructors with special expertise. Modest fees will be charged for registration. (20% of total activity)

**Technical Assistance:** APF plans to encourage effective management by facilitating solutions to problems nonprofits face. APF will provide technical assistance in strategic planning, budgeting, organizational policies, bookkeeping, record retention and data storage systems, and other nonprofit management issues. Charges for services will be calculated on a sliding-scale basis dependent upon the organization's ability to pay. APF will develop, and keep open regularly, a library of technical books, publications, and computer programs on nonprofits. APF will seek to foster exchanges of information and encourage networking. For example, roundtable-type meetings will be held, possibly groups with similar concerns will be formed. APF will develop a database of problems faced and solutions found as a reference tool. APF also expects to develop, as a resource tool, lists of companies, professionals, and other information useful to its exempt constituents. Modest charges, that will not recoup cost, will be imposed for publications. (60% of total activity)

**Publications:** APF plans to publish an electronic newsletter that contains technical articles on topics of interest to nonprofits. The newsletter will also serve to announce seminars, roundtable meetings, library news and other information. The newsletter will be distributed free of charge and contain no advertising. APF will seek legal, accounting, and other types of professionals to donate articles and information. The newsletter will only be disseminated through the website to make it available to anyone. (20% of activity)

Part V, Line 2a

The President A.B. Sample is married to the Secretary/Treasurer C.D. Sample. E.F. Sample is their son.

Part V, Line 3a

A.B. Sample is the President. His qualifications include a degree in business. He expects to work 5-10 hours a week for the organization as a volunteer with no compensation. His duties include supervising and conducting APF's activities and operations. He will preside at all meetings and shall keep the Board informed concerning activities of the Fund. He may sign contracts and documents authorized by the Board. He will foster committees and appoint members to serve on committees.

Page 1 of 3                                                                     Attachment to Many Parts

**EXHIBIT 2.2**

*(Continued)*

**Active Project Fund**                                                    33-3333333
**Attachment to Form 1023**

C.D. Sample is the Secretary and Treasurer. Her qualifications include working at an accounting firm that specializes in nonprofit issues. She plans to work 3-5 hours a week for the organization as a volunteer with no compensation. Her duties include acting as Secretary of all meetings and keeping the minutes. In addition, she will have custody of all funds and securities of APF. She will maintain a full and accurate account of receipts and disbursements of the Fund and deposits all money and valuables in the bank or other depositories.

E.F. Sample is the Vice President. His qualifications include an interest in aiding nonprofits. He plans to work 2 hours a week for the organization as a volunteer with no compensation.

Jane Smith is the Executive Director. She is unrelated to the Sample family. Her qualifications include working for ten years at The Big Foundation in a similar capacity. She has lectured throughout the country on the importance of structure within nonprofit organizations. She will work approximately 45 hours per week. Her duties will include managing the daily activities of APF under the guidance of the Board of Directors.

Part V, Line 5a

The Board of Directors of Active Project Fund has adopted a conflict of interest policy consistent with the recommendations of the Internal Revenue Service instructions. Please find a copy of the policy attached.

Part V, Line 6a

The employment agreement with the Executive Director Jane Smith provides that she may be compensated through a non-fixed payment in the form of a discretionary bonus. The Board of Directors has the option of voting to give the executive director a non-fixed bonus if her work has been excellent for the previous year and all goals have been met or exceeded. The optional bonus must be less than 10% of her total compensation for the year. The bonus must be reviewed by the Board of Directors to ensure that the total compensation plus the optional bonus is reasonable compensation for her services.

Part V, Line 7a

APF will purchase management services from highly compensated employee Jane Smith. APF has negotiated these services at arm's length and the fees are at or below the fair market value as determined by bids from similar companies.

Part VI, Line 1b

APF plans to provide an annual grant to a deserving organization that needs assistance in developing its management structure. Before making any grants, APF will verify that the grantee is listed in IRS Business Master File as a public charity other than a Type III non-functionally integrated supporting organization. See Part IV for a description of the services APF plans to provide to charitable organizations classified as §501(c)(3) public charities.

Part VIII, Line 11

APF has not accepted donations other than cash at this time. It is unknown if any of such donations will be given to APF in the future. If APF were offered non-cash donations, it would work with its tax advisors to make sure that it complied with all applicable Internal Revenue Services rules for the organization and the donor.

**EXHIBIT 2.2**

*(Continued)*

**Active Project Fund**                                                          33-3333333
**Attachment to Form 1023**

Part VIII, Line 13b

APF plans to make one grant a year to a deserving organization that needs assistance in developing its management structure. APF's programs focus on improving management situations within nonprofits. The grant would serve to improve the organization's internal structure by providing funds for software, office equipment, necessary training, etc.

Part VIII, Line 13d

No recipients have been determined yet. However, no grants will be provided to organizations that have relationships with disqualified persons. Additionally, once an organization has received a grant, it becomes ineligible to receive further grants.

Part VIII, Line 13e

For each grant, APF plans to keep a file that includes a copy of the organization's IRS determination letter and APF's recommendation of the types of expenditures that would best improve the organization's internal structure.

Part VIII, Line 13f

The selection process will include recommendations from the Executive Director based upon organizations she has dealt with throughout the year during seminars or by providing technical assistance. The Board will then review the nominated organizations' most recent 990 and a letter that explains what the organization would do with the funds if granted them.

Part VIII, Line 13g

Once the organization has been granted the funds, it will be responsible for providing a report at the end of its next fiscal year that describes how the money was put to use.

Page 3 of 3                                          Attachment to Many Parts

**EXHIBIT 2.2**

*(Continued)*

**Active Project Fund**                                                    33-3333333
**Attachment to Form 1023**

### Active Project Fund Conflict of Interest Policy

Article I
Purpose

The purpose of the conflict of interest policy is to protect Active Project Fund's interests when it contemplates entering into a transaction or arrangement that might benefit the private interest of an officer or director of the organization or might result in a possible excess benefit transaction. This policy is intended to supplement but not replace any applicable state and federal laws governing conflict of interest applicable to nonprofit and charitable organizations.

Article II
Definitions

1. **Interested Person**
Any director, principal officer, or member of a committee with governing board delegated powers, who has a direct or indirect financial interest, as defined below, is an interested person.

2. **Financial Interest**
A person has a financial interest if the person has, directly or indirectly, through business, investment, or family:
   **a.** An ownership or investment interest in any entity with which the organization has a transaction or arrangement,
   **b.** A compensation arrangement with the organization or with any entity or individual with which the organization has a transaction or arrangement, or
   **c.** A potential ownership or investment interest in, or compensation arrangement with, any entity or individual with which the organization is negotiating a transaction or arrangement.

Compensation includes direct and indirect remuneration as well as gifts or favors that are not insubstantial.

(A financial interest is not necessarily a conflict of interest. Under Article III, Section 2, a person who has a financial interest may have a conflict of interest only if the appropriate governing board or committee decides that a conflict of interest exists.)

Article III
Procedures

1. **Duty to Disclose**
In connection with any actual or possible conflict of interest, an interested person must disclose the existence of the financial interest and be given the opportunity to disclose all material facts to the directors and members of committees with governing board delegated powers considering the proposed transaction or arrangement.

2. **Determining Whether a Conflict of Interest Exists**
After disclosure of the financial interest and all material facts, and after any discussion with the interested person, he/she shall leave the governing board or committee meeting while the determination of a conflict of interest is discussed and voted upon. The remaining board or committee members shall decide if a conflict of interest exists.

3. **Procedures for Addressing the Conflict of Interest**
   **a.** An interested person may make a presentation at the governing board or committee meeting, but after the presentation, he/she shall leave the meeting during the discussion of, and the vote on, the transaction or arrangement involving the possible conflict of interest.
   **b.** The chairperson of the governing board or committee shall, if appropriate, appoint a disinterested person or committee to investigate alternatives to the proposed transaction or arrangement.
   **c.** After exercising due diligence, the governing board or committee shall determine whether the organization can obtain with reasonable efforts a more advantageous transaction or arrangement from a person or entity that would not give rise to a conflict of interest.

1                                         Attachment to Part V, Line 5a

**Exhibit 2.2**

*(Continued)*

Active Project Fund         33-3333333
Attachment to Form 1023

**d.** If a more advantageous transaction or arrangement is not reasonably possible under circumstances not producing a conflict of interest, the governing board or committee shall determine by a majority vote of the disinterested directors whether the transaction or arrangement is in the organization's best interest, for its own benefit, and whether it is fair and reasonable. In conformity with the above determination it shall make its decision as to whether to enter into the transaction or arrangement.

4. **Violations of the Conflicts of Interest Policy**
   **a.** If the governing board or committee has reasonable cause to believe a member has failed to disclose actual or possible conflicts of interest, it shall inform the member of the basis for such belief and afford the member an opportunity to explain the alleged failure to disclose.
   **b.** If, after hearing the member's response and after making further investigation as warranted by the circumstances, the governing board or committee determines the member has failed to disclose an actual or possible conflict of interest, it shall take appropriate disciplinary and corrective action.

**Article IV**
**Records of Proceedings**

The minutes of the governing board and all committees with board delegated powers shall contain:
   **a.** The names of the persons who disclosed or otherwise were found to have a financial interest in connection with an actual or possible conflict of interest, the nature of the financial interest, any action taken to determine whether a conflict of interest was present, and the governing board's or committee's decision as to whether a conflict of interest in fact existed.
   **b.** The names of the persons who were present for discussions and votes relating to the transaction or arrangement, the content of the discussion, including any alternatives to the proposed transaction or arrangement, and a record of any votes taken in connection with the proceedings.

**Article V**
**Compensation**

   **a.** A voting member of the governing board who receives compensation, directly or indirectly, from the Organization for services is precluded from voting on matters pertaining to that member's compensation.
   **b.** A voting member of any committee whose jurisdiction includes compensation matters and who receives compensation, directly or indirectly, from the Organization for services is precluded from voting on matters pertaining to that member's compensation.
   **c.** No voting member of the governing board or any committee whose jurisdiction includes compensation matters and who receives compensation, directly or indirectly, from the Organization, either individually or collectively, is prohibited from providing information to any committee regarding compensation.

**Article VI**
**Annual Statements**

Each director, principal officer and member of a committee with governing board-delegated powers shall annually sign a statement, which affirms such person:
   **a.** Has received a copy of the conflicts of interest policy,
   **b.** Has read and understands the policy,
   **c.** Has agreed to comply with the policy, and
   **d.** Understands the organization is charitable and in order to maintain its federal tax exemption it must engage primarily in activities that accomplish one or more of its tax-exempt purposes.

**Article VII**
**Periodic Reviews**

To ensure the organization operates in a manner consistent with charitable purposes and does not engage in activities that could jeopardize its tax-exempt status, periodic reviews shall be conducted. The periodic reviews shall, at a minimum, include the following subjects:

2                Attachment to Part V, Line 5a

**EXHIBIT 2.2**

---

*(Continued)*

**Active Project Fund**                                                       33-3333333
**Attachment to Form 1023**

**a.** Whether compensation arrangements and benefits are reasonable, based on competent survey information, and the result of arm's length bargaining.

**b.** Whether partnerships, joint ventures, and arrangements with management organizations conform to the organization's written policies, are properly recorded, reflect reasonable investment or payments for goods and services, further charitable purposes and do not result in inurement, impermissible private benefit or in an excess benefit transaction.

**Article VIII**
**Use of Outside Experts**

When conducting the periodic reviews as provided for in Article VII, the organization may, but need not, use outside advisors. If outside experts are used, their use shall not relieve the governing board of its responsibility for ensuring periodic reviews are conducted.

*Adopted by Board of Directors on May 1, 2014*

3                                                    Attachment to Part V, Line 5a

**EXHIBIT 2.2**

---

*(Continued)*

**Active Project Fund**                                                          33-3333333
**Attachment to Form 1023**

| Part IX - Financial data | 2014 | 2015 | 2016 |
|---|---|---|---|
| **Revenue, Line 1 - Contributions** | $300,000 | $400,000 | $500,000 |

A.B. & C.D. Sample plan to donate shares of Clean Air Industries (listed on NYSE).
The shares will be sold upon receipt and used to support APF programs and provide working capital.

**Revenue, Line 9 - Exempt Function Income**

| | 2014 | 2015 | 2016 |
|---|---|---|---|
| Seminar fees | 5,000 | 10,000 | 30,000 |
| Publication sales | 5,000 | 10,000 | 30,000 |
| | $ 10,000 | $ 20,000 | $ 60,000 |

**Expenses, line 18 - Other salaries & wages**

| | 2014 | 2015 | 2016 |
|---|---|---|---|
| Executive Director (full time) | 18,000 | 52,000 | 55,000 |
| Administrator (full time) | 20,000 | 30,000 | 32,000 |
| Instructors (3-4 part-time) | 10,000 | 20,000 | 24,000 |
| Librarian/publicist (part time) | 6,000 | 12,400 | 16,000 |
| Assistants (2-3 part time) | 5,000 | 20,000 | 40,000 |
| | 59,000 | 134,400 | 167,000 |
| Fringe benefits and payroll tax | 6,000 | 12,600 | 16,000 |
| Total other salaries | $ 65,000 | $ 147,000 | $ 183,000 |

**Expenses, Line 21 - Depreciation**

Active Project Fund plans to spend up to $ 25,000 buying computers,
office furnishings, tables and chairs, projectors, and similar equipment.
The depreciation will be calculated on a five year straight-line basis.

**Expenses, Line 21 -- Professional fees**

| | 2014 | 2015 | 2016 |
|---|---|---|---|
| Legal fees | 4,000 | 1,000 | 1,000 |
| Accounting fees | 2,000 | 3,000 | 3,500 |
| Website designer | 10,000 | | |
| | $ 16,000 | $ 4,000 | $ 4,500 |

**Expenses, Line 22 - Other Expense**

| | 2014 | 2015 | 2016 |
|---|---|---|---|
| Library books and publications | 20,000 | 10,000 | 5,000 |
| Computer programs for teaching purposes | 24,000 | 18,000 | 7,000 |
| Printing & design of seminar materials | 10,000 | 6,000 | 4,000 |
| Website fees and maintenance | 12,000 | 14,000 | 16,000 |
| Seminar refreshments | 4,000 | 6,000 | 7,000 |
| Office supplies & expenses | 5,000 | 8,000 | 9,000 |
| Insurance | 2,000 | 2,000 | 2,000 |
| Total other expenses | $ 77,000 | $ 64,000 | $ 50,000 |

Attachment to Part IX-A

**EXHIBIT 2.2**

*(Continued)*

**Active Project Fund**                                          33-3333333
**Attachment to Form 1023**

Active Project Fund projects the following information
that indicate it will meet the Income and Endowment Tests
and be eligible for classification as an operating foundation.

### Income Test

|  | 2014 | 2015 | 2016 |
|---|---|---|---|
| Line 1a  Adjusted net income | 300 | 600 | 3,000 |
| Line 1b  Minimum investment return | 9,000 | 12,500 | 13,000 |
| Line 2a  Qualifying distributions | 170,000 | 239,000 | 267,500 |
| Line 2b  Acquisition of exempt function assets | 25,000 | | |
| Line 2d  Total qualifying distributions | $ 195,000 | $ 239,000 | $ 267,500 |
| | | | |
| Line 3a  Percentage of qualifying distributions to ANI | > 100% | > 100% | >100% |
| Line 3b  Percentage of qualifying distribution to MDR | > 100% | > 100% | >100% |

### Endowment Test

| | | | |
|---|---|---|---|
| Line 9     Value of assets not used directly in exempt activities. | | | |
| Line 9a  Projected monthly average of investment securities | 0 | 0 | 0 |
| Line 9b  Projected average of cash balances | 180,000 | 250,000 | 260,000 |
| Line 9c  Projected value of other investment property | 0 | 0 | 0 |
| Line 9d   Total | 180,000 | 250,000 | 260,000 |
| Line 10  Acquisition indebtedness | | 0 | 0 |
| Line 11  Balance | 180,000 | 250,000 | 260,000 |
| | | | |
| Line 12  Multiple line 11 by 3-1/3% | $5,994 | $8,325 | $8,658 |

**Note line 2d exceeds the amount on line 12.**

Active Project Fund has made a good faith determination that it will satisfy the income test and
the endowment test set forth above for its first taxable year and and the years thereafter based
upon projections of income and expenditures and the opinion of our counsel. See Part IV for
description of the planned activities.

*A Good Accountant*
_____
A Good Accountant

Attachment to Part X, Line 4

**EXHIBIT 2.2**

*(Continued)*

No application need be filed for an LLC that is treated as a disregarded entity in relation to its single member. An example would be an LLC created by a private foundation to hold title to an investment property on its behalf. In either case, the provisions of the LLC's formation documents must dedicate the assets to charitable purposes.

**Part III—Information about the Required Provisions in Your Organizing Document.**   This part has two lines with check boxes that need a *Yes* answer and a reference to the section of the foundation's documents that contain appropriate language. Some may struggle or misstep here because both questions require reference to the instructions and Appendix B for full understanding. A description of the organizational requirements for a private foundation can be found in the instructions to the form. The tests are described under *Qualification of a Section 501(c))(3) Organization* in the instructions, but only portions are highlighted in the titles for this part. Line 1 asks if the documents "state your exempt purposes, such as charitable, religious, educational, and/or scientific purposes." Four purposes—testing for public safety, literary, fostering national or international amateur sports competition, and prevention of cruelty to children or animals—listed in IRC § 501(c)(3) are not mentioned. It is sufficient that a private foundation say it is organized for charitable purposes, particularly if it plans to make grants to public charities that advance several of the above purposes.

The first box of Line 2 asks if the documents contain a dissolution clause to dedicate the organization's assets permanently to charitable purposes either expressly or by state law. Then it asks the applicant to describe "specifically where your organizational documents meet this requirement." A second box asks if the applicant relies on operation of state law for dissolution provision. It is important to read the specific instructions for this part.

For private foundations, there is another issue. The state laws outlined in Appendix B of the IRS instructions were designed in 1970 to allow private foundations to automatically (as a matter of law) meet the notice requirements.[76] Organizational rules require that the foundation's documents contain provisions that prohibit violation of the private foundation rules.[77] The majority of the states passed legislation that imposed such a requirement on private foundations, existing or newly created, without requiring that such language literally appear in their organizational documents. Line 1b of Part X asks if this requirement was satisfied.

**Part IV—Narrative Description of Your Activities.**   The essence of the applicant's charitable nature should be reflected in the description of activities. The

---

76. *See* § 2.6.
77. *See* § 1.7.

who, what, why, where, when, and how of the ways the foundation will accomplish its exempt purposes should be explained. This part is particularly challenging because it provides an open-ended opportunity to provide information. It does not question; it simply asks for a description. Presenting precise and complete information, in coordination with other parts of the form, is the key. Presenting unnecessary information that instigates questions not asked is not helpful. The IRS suggests a printout of the website page that summarizes the organization's mission could be attached.

Parts VI and VIII and the applicable schedules should be completed prior to this part because they contain questions and instructions germane to the different types of charitable entities that should be considered in completing this part.

**Part V—Information about Compensation and Other Financial Arrangements with Your Officers, Directors, Trustees, Employees, and Independent Contractors.**   The nine detailed questions about financial transactions with the organization's officials early in the application illustrate the key criteria for approval—satisfaction of the test requiring that a charitable organization not operate to benefit private individuals. For a privately funded charity, this requirement is enforced with rules prohibiting most financial transactions between the foundation and its creators, their relations, and others that control the foundation—all referred to as disqualified persons.[78] Chapter 5 discusses this important constraint placed on private foundations by the self-dealing prohibitions. An exception does permit a private foundation to pay a disqualified person compensation for services rendered in managing the foundation assets and its charitable programs. For any compensation proposed to be paid to a disqualified person, detailed information evidencing the amounts paid will be reasonable, and therefore not result in self-dealing, must be attached. Before completing the application, the standards for defining reasonable compensation, information that evidences reasonableness, and a checklist to test the proposed compensation plans using an IRS checklist are critical to review.[79]

Applicants are asked to provide a list of officers, directors, or trustees, their duties and hours worked, and the amount of their expected compensation, if any. The detailed Line 2, 3, and 4 questions must be answered carefully when the foundation reports it will provide such compensation. The creator alone, or with members of his or her immediate family, often constitutes the officer(s), director(s), and trustee(s) of a private foundation. There is no requirement that a private foundation have outside directors or trustees. A private foundation that proposes to compensate its officers, directors, or founders may, however, wish to include unrelated parties in its governing body. Such persons add the

---

78.  *See* Chapter 4.
79.  *See* § 5.6(a).

disinterested element of approval to a related-party transaction under conflict-of-interest standards. Although the form states that it is only a recommendation, a foundation should adopt a conflict-of-interest policy to evidence its good faith intention to avoid excess payments. The model IRS policy provided in the instructions to Form 1023 is displayed in the attachment to Part V, Line 5a of Exhibit 2.2 for Active Project Fund. The provisions are not particularly suited to a private foundation. How can a sole trustee "leave the meeting" as anticipated by Article III of the policy? The self-dealing rules prohibit financial transactions with any entity in which a disqualified person has a financial interest. Nonetheless, when compensation for disqualified persons is proposed, governance policies to avoid self-dealing should be adopted and submitted with the application.

Due to the self-dealing prohibitions, the answers on Lines 6, 7, 8, and 9 will generally be *No.*

**Part VI—Information about Your Members and Other Individuals and Organizations That Receive Benefits from You.**   A private operating foundation that maintains a museum, sponsors research and distributes publications announcing the results thereof, operates low-income housing projects, or conducts any other active program must answer the questions on Lines 1 and 2 in detail. To whom services will be available, how the prices will be established, standards to be applied if the charges are or are not to be made according to a sliding scale, and other relevant information to enable the IRS to evaluate the charitable nature of the programs should be provided. Evidence that the activity is not profit motivated, that a charitable class will be served by the services or goods, and that no unrelated business[80] is involved is essential.

A private foundation that plans to provide scholarships would answer *Yes* to Line 1a and refer to Schedule H where the detailed plans are described. A foundation that plans to make grants to other charities answers *Yes* to Line 1b and refers to Part VIII, Lines 13 (domestic grants) and 14 (foreign grants). The answer to Line 3 for a private foundation can only be *Yes* regarding related-party use of facilities on the same basis they are made available to the general public.[81]

**Part VII—Information about Your History.**   This part asks two very different questions. Line 1 simply asks whether the applicant is a successor to another organization and says answer *Yes* if you:

- Have taken (or will take) over the activities of another organization,
- Have taken 25 percent or more of the fair market value of the net assets of another organization,

---

80. *See* Chapter 11.
81. *See* § 5.9(c).

- Have been converted or merged from another organization, or
- Installed the same officers, directors, or trustees as another organization that no longer exists and that had purpose(s) similar to your purpose(s).

Schedule G must be attached if this answer is *Yes*. Though there are no instructions for this question or Schedule G, the questions asked in Schedule G delve into relationships, assumption of debt, and other impermissible terms of a conversion/combination. The rules applicable when a private foundation merges or splits ups are discussed in Chapter 13.

It is desirable that the answer to Line 2 is *No*—the application was filed in a timely fashion within, rather than after, 27 months of its formation. A charitable § 501(c)(3) organization is not treated as a tax-exempt organization until it notifies the IRS by filing Form 1023. Timely filing is measured from the date the organization is formed, or the date it becomes a legal entity or comes into existence under applicable state law.[82] For a corporation or LLC, this normally will be the date its articles are approved by the appropriate state official. For unincorporated organizations, it is the date the trust instrument, constitution, or articles of association are adopted. When the Form 1023 is timely filed, recognition of exemption retroactively applies to the date of creation.

Applications filed late, as a general rule, are effective only as of the date the application is postmarked. The limited circumstances for automatic extension of the 27-month rule are explained in Schedule E. A late filer that fails to receive retroactive approval may be classified as a (c)(4) organization for the period between formation and filing and thus avoid income tax. The consequence of late filing is primarily a potential obligation to pay federal income and various state taxes on the taxable income received during the prerecognition period. Since voluntary donations are generally gifts under IRC § 103, this exposure may be modest. Of most concern is the fact that many donors, and particularly private foundation grantors, require IRS recognition before they will provide funding to a new organization. Technically, however, the deductibility of charitable contributions under IRC § 170 does not depend on recognition as an IRC § 501(c)(3) organization.

**Part VIII—Information about Your Specific Activities.**  The questions in this part delve into matters that can prevent a new nonprofit's qualification for tax exemption and revisits issues from other parts; cross-references may be in order. For private foundations most of the answers will be *No*, except Lines 13 and 14 where the grant-making programs are described. It is critical that a private foundation answer both Lines 1 and 2 *No*, we will not attempt to influence an election or conduct lobbying.[83]

---

82. Rev. Proc. 2014-9, 2014-2 I.R.B. 281.
83. *See* § 9.1.

The fact that there is no instruction for Line 11 belies the potential for trouble with this question. When the question asks if the foundation will accept contributions of real estate, conservation easements, closely held stock, and the like, several issues arise. A foundation will not commonly be soliciting such gifts from the general public, but may expect to receive them from its creators. The response to this question in Exhibit 2.2 reflects the applicant's awareness of the income tax issues involved.

A foundation that plans to operate in a foreign country must, on Line 12, name the countries and regions, the nature of the program(s), and the fashion in which the activity will advance its exempt purpose. The tax code places no constraints on the geographic location of charitable programs, and the detailed description of programs in Part IV may be sufficient for this line. What is not asked, but is needed, is a description of the procedures the organization will implement to assure its support does not aid persons identified by the government as terrorists in violation of the U.S. Patriot Act.[84] The U.S. Treasury Department has issued voluntary guidelines an organization conducting programs in foreign countries should consider adopting.[85]

Lines 13a to 13g request extensive details if an organization does or will make grants, loans, or other distributions to other organizations. The questions imply the applicant must have sufficient plans—application forms, grant proposals, criteria for selection, evaluation systems including follow-up grantee reports—in place to assure the funds are devoted by the recipients to charitable purposes.[86] Grantee contracts and loan documents are requested, along with a description of the records that will be retained regarding each grant. This line may be troubling for an applicant that has not yet activated its grant program. In the past, it has been sufficient for a private foundation planning to make grants to unrelated public charities, not yet identified, simply to say so. There is no specific provision in the federal tax law that requires the written requests or follow-up reports implied on Line 13g to be necessary. Determining that the grantee is listed in IRS EO Select Check (replaced Publication 78) as a qualified § 501(c)(3) is thought by some to be sufficient proof of the charitable nature of the grantee's activities. Nonetheless, an IRS representative in Cincinnati was of the opinion that lack of proposed grant applications and procedures meant the application was incomplete. Exhibits 9.2, 9.3 and 9.4 serve as minimal examples of the type of documents expected.

---

84. Executive Order 13224 bans humanitarian aid to Specially Designated Nationals and Blocked Persons.
85. "Anti-Terrorist Financing Guidelines: Voluntary Best Practices for U.S. Based Charities" were published on November 7, 2002. Websites with information to assist in developing compliance plans on foreign activities include www.cof.org and www.usig.org; *see* § 9.5.
86. Sample applications for grants-in-aid are illustrated in Appendix 17-1 of Blazek, *Tax Planning and Compliance.*

Plans to make grants to foreign organizations involve the six important issues listed in Lines 14a to 14f. It is imperative that the applicant describe procedures it will adopt to assure that the money will be devoted to charitable purposes and not be used to advance terrorists as described above in Line 12. The answers to Lines 14 c to f must be *Yes*. For Line 14c and d, the applicant must evidence it will not serve to circumvent the income tax rule that disallows a donation deduction for a gift to a foreign organization. Only gifts to domestic organizations, those created or organized in the United States, are deductible as contributions for U.S. tax purposes.[87] This limitation, plus the fact that U.S. tax-exempt organizations are permitted to conduct activities anywhere in the world, prompts creation of domestic *Friends Of* organizations to raise U.S. support for foreign charities. So long as the U.S. charity has control and discretion over the ultimate spending of the money,[88] funds raised for regrant to a foreign organization do qualify as charitable contributions for individuals.

Line 15 asks about the applicant's *Close Connections*. The three types of connections described in the instructions are an applicant controlled by or in control of another organization, an entity created concurrent with another organization, and one that will share facilities. For many, the relationships are explained in responses to other lines. To qualify, a supporting organization(s) must be subject to some control and authority as to budgets and expenditures (Schedule D) by its supported entity. A separate charity formed to conduct fundraising (Part VIII, line 4d) or to hold the investment assets of another charity may possess elements of common control. Economies of scale may be reaped in sharing arrangements and collaborations. Such connections do not necessarily negatively impact, and can facilitate, qualification. An entity formed to conduct services for members of an affiliated group may classify revenue from a business-like service as exempt function. Without the close connection, service revenue might be treated as unrelated business income.

Only one of the last seven lines of Part VIII commonly pertains to a private foundation: Line 22, Scholarships [Schedule H].[89] A private operating foundation could conceivably operate a facility for low-income, elderly, or handicapped persons requiring it to complete Schedule F.[90] Lines 16 to 21 primarily concern programs conducted by public charities.

---

87. IRC § 170(c); in addition, a corporation is only permitted an income tax deduction for gifts to be used within the United States or any of its possessions exclusively for charitable purposes; see Chapter 14.

88. Rev. Rul. 66-79, 1966-1 C.B. 48.

89. The extension discussion in § 9.3 should be studied by any foundation seeking approval for its plans to award scholarships.

90. *See* § 4.2(a) in *Tax Planning and Compliance*. The 2004 IRS CPE Text updated the IRS's policies regarding housing for senior citizens and updates previous articles, and discusses handling of applications and ruling requests for such entities.

**Part IX—Financial Data.** This part of Form 1023 remains mostly unchanged since the prior version and, as the title implies, it presents the prospective foundation's financial information. The data display in this part may differ from financial statements presented in accordance with generally accepted accounting principles (GAAP) and Form 990-PF. The past, present, and future financial projections are a key piece of information that must be coordinated with the literal descriptions presented in the application. The IRS does not say so, but it is acknowledged that the organization's actual financial results may vary from its projected amounts. Form 990-PF each year asks for a description of any new activities and other changes.[91]

- *Section A: Statement of Revenue and Expenses* is required for all organizations, both newly formed ones presenting projected or proposed financial data and those having actual financial history. Details for many revenue and expense categories are not requested, but the author's experience indicates submission of such details will avoid requests by the IRS specialist reviewing the application. In preparing this part, it is important to be conscious that the successful application paints a picture of the organization in the reviewer's mind. Exhibit 2.2 for Active Project Fund reflects a foundation that has had no financial activity to date.

  The IRS requests that a complete fiscal year be presented in each column, with column (a) combining actual and projected revenue for the first year of existence and columns (b), (c), and possibly (d) either actual or projected for full years. Most foundations will be submitting the application prior to a full year of financial activity.

  A summary of the order of years suggested follows:

  ○ New entity created on May 1, 2014, that has not completed a full fiscal year: 2014, 2015, 2016.

  ○ New entity created May 2013 that has completed only one full year: 2013, 2014, 2015, 2016.

  ○ New entity created May 2102 with two or three full years: 2012, 2013, 2014, 2015.

- *Suggestions for Particular Lines*: The attachment in Exhibit 2.2 reflects the type of financial details that the authors suggest be provided to explain proposed financial activity. A brief description of issues presented by those lines of this part that deserve particular attention follows. Most important, the financial data must be coordinated with responses to other parts of the application (shown below in brackets) that ask for literal descriptions of financial matters. It would be a unique and unusual private foundation that has numbers displayed on Lines 2, 5, 6, 7, 12, 14, 16, and 19.

---

91. *See* § 12.2(c).

○ Line 1, Gifts, grants, and contributions received: A display of details for gifts and contributions should be coordinated with the explanation of any fundraising activity [Part VIII, Question 4]. Most private foundations will simply reflect the dollar amount of anticipated donations from their creators.

○ Line 4, Net unrelated business income: Income from unrelated businesses that are regularly carried on in a businesslike manner and reportable as taxable on Form 990-T, such as advertisements in publications or rental of indebted property, is included here. The many exclusions and modifications provided in the tax code make this a complicated subject.[92] Excluded unrelated income is reported on Line 3. The important issue for exemption purposes is that too high an amount on this line in relation to overall revenue indicates the primary purpose of the organization is not necessarily charitable.

○ Line 9, Gross receipts from admissions, merchandise sold, or services performed, or furnishing of facilities in any activity that is related to your charitable, etc. purposes: This line would reflect program fees, sales of books, and other items to be sold. A detailed list of such revenue, as illustrated in the attachment for this line for Active Project Fund (Exhibit 2.2), can be provided. This line should be coordinated with the description of proposed goods and services to be provided, such as circulation and attendance numbers [Line 1b of Part VI].

○ Line 13, Total revenue: A careful applicant uses this line to calculate ratios, such as the percentage of projected expenses to expected revenues. Another comparison would be the total on Line 24 to total assets. A private foundation must spend an amount equal to 5 percent of the average value of its assets annually.[93] Another issue is the percentage of administrative expenses in relation to overall expenses and also to grants. There are currently no specific limitations, but there have been congressional proposals to impose such limits. Certainly compensation of officials on Line 17 is an item that will be scrutinized.

○ Line 15, Contributions, gifts, grants, and similar amounts paid: This line should be the major outlay for a private foundation, other than one with direct operating expenses for its active projects. A foundation that has had actual financial activity is asked to provide a list of grantees. The descriptions of grant-making procedures [Part VIII, Lines 13 and 14, and Schedule H] should be coordinated with this information. An example of the type of supplemental information that might be provided includes:

---

92. *See* Chapter 11 for a presentation of this type of income.
93. *See* Chapter 6.

|                                    | Year 1 | Year 2    | Year 3      |
|------------------------------------|--------|-----------|-------------|
| Grants to public charities         | 0      | $500,000  | $500,000    |
| College scholarships               | 0      | 100,000   | 300,000     |
| Grants-in-aid to needy individuals | 0      | 100,000   | 200,000     |
| Total Grants Projected             | $ 0    | $700,000  | $1,000,000  |

- ○ Line 17, Compensation of officers, directors, and trustees: The instructions for this line, somewhat innocently, only ask for the total amount of compensation paid to officials. Applicants must keep the operational and organizational tests and the self-dealing rules in mind—neither the assets nor income of the organization may be used to provide private benefit to officials. This information should be coordinated with Part V, where the details of each board member's annual compensation, title, address, and duties are described and explanations of why proposed salaries are reasonable should be presented.
- ○ Line 18, Other salaries and wages: Again, private benefit can be an issue. It is advisable to include a detailed listing of positions with a brief job description, compensation to be paid, and expected hours worked per week.
- ○ Line 19, Interest expense: Total interest expense other than that included on Line 20 goes here. When the applicant plans to secure financing for purchase of equipment or buildings, details of the lending terms are requested [Line 14 of the balance sheet]. It would be unusual, but not impermissible, for a new foundation to borrow money to provide working capital. For example, it was funded with closely held stock that must await public registration for the shares or a piece of land that must be sold to raise funds to make grants and pay other expenses. A foundation is prohibited from paying interest to a disqualified person; an explanation of the manner in which the loan serves the organization's exempt purposes is imperative. Evidencing the IRS's concern that such loans not provide private benefits, details of loans are also furnished as an attachment to the balance sheet and explained [Part V, Line 8].
- ○ Line 21, Depreciation and depletion: Assets that have a useful life exceeding one year are capitalized and carried on the balance sheet [Line 7 and/or 8]. A portion of the cost is written off each year; this is called depreciation or depletion. An attachment is not requested for this line; however, the list of assets summarized by type requested for Lines 7 and 8 can contain a column reflecting the useful lives assigned and corresponding depreciation expense.

○ Line 22, Professional fees: Fees charged by accountants, lawyers, building managers, or other nonemployee service providers (independent contractors), other than fundraisers, are presented on this line. In the past, the IRS has routinely requested details if they were not furnished. Now the literal description requested in Part V and Part VIII can be coordinated and reduce the details for this line.

○ Line 23, Any expense not otherwise classified such as program services: In the interest of avoiding questions that may delay the application process, detail is recommended unless the amount is under 5 percent of total expense and is truly miscellaneous. Page 2 of Form II, Statement of Functional Expenses, on Form 990 may be used as a guide to the suitable types of expense categories. Expenses associated with investment properties should be presented on this line to avoid distortion of operational expenses.

○ Line 24, Total expenses: Expense totals are shown for each year without an overall total. Reported expenses in column (a) might include both actual and projected amounts for a foundation that has already had some amount of financial activity. Exhibit 2.2 assumes no activity before the time of filing. No "net income" appears on this page and amounts will not necessarily agree with the net asset total reported on the balance sheet.

• *Section B: The Balance Sheet.* An organization that has completed a full year presents a balance sheet as of its most recent year-end. A new organization presents the most current information available. This balance sheet may be frustrating for accountants because the fund balances do not tie in to the Statement of Income and Expenses in Section A of this part. Unlike Section A, the organization does not make projections for this section. Often a new foundation has no assets and may simply say so.

The instructions for this part do not mention accounting methods. It is suitable, however, for this information to follow the cash or accrual method used to keep the organization's financial records and also used to complete section A. Assets of an unrelated business activity are not mentioned in the instructions. They should not be segregated, but instead are combined with investment assets as is customary for financial reporting purposes. Except for Lines 1, 2, 3, 9, 13, and 17, an itemized list of assets reported on each line is requested.

It is important that Lines 6, 14, and 15 pertaining to loans receivable and payable be coordinated with information provided in other parts. In a straightforward manner, the instructions ask for details about each loan—the borrower's or lender's name, purpose of the loan, repayment terms, interest rate, and the original amount of the loan. What it does not ask is if the lender is a related party—a fact that is to be fully disclosed [Part V, Lines 8 and 9]. It is vital to remember that a no-interest loan to a private foundation from a disqualified person that serves its exempt purposes is permissible. A loan to a disqualified person from the foundation is prohibited.

Organizations owning bonds, notes receivable, stocks, buildings, land, mineral interests, or any other investment assets report them on these lines. Details are requested for all assets, other than government bonds, and in the case of stocks, both the book and fair market value of each holding must be reported. The instructions ask for specifics.

The last line of this part is a question that asks for an explanation if there have been any significant changes since the balance sheet date. For a new organization that has not completed a full year, this answer should be *No* because it is instructed to use the most current information possible. An entity that has completed a full year some months before it makes application may find this situation exists. Say the foundation was created in May 2014, adopts a June 30 fiscal year, devoted the first year to planning, and commenced activity in the fall of 2014. The balance sheet it is instructed to attach would be dated June 30, 2014. If the amount of revenue reported in column (a) significantly exceeds expenses (for a full fiscal ending 2015 that combines actual with projected amounts), it might deserve an explanation.

**Part X—Public Charity Status.** The significance of public charity status for tax-exempt charitable organizations is multifaceted, and is of importance to both private and public exempt organizations. Knowledge of the categories of public charities[94] is the key to understanding this aspect of the law. All charitable organizations other than public charities are private foundations. Public charity status is more favorable as compared to private foundations that must comply with the operational constraints of the private foundation rules. The allowable contribution deductions for gifts to private foundations are less than those afforded for public charities.[95] A private foundation must pay a 1 to 2 percent excise tax annually on its investment income.[96] A private foundation cannot buy or sell property, nor enter into financial transactions (called *self-dealing*) with its directors, officers, contributors, or their family members, under most circumstances.[97] A private foundation's annual spending for grants to other organizations and charitable projects must meet a minimum distribution requirement.[98] A public charity has no specific spending requirement, other than those imposed by its funders. Holding more than 20 percent of a business enterprise, including shares owned by board members and contributors, is generally prohibited for private foundations, as are jeopardizing investments.[99]

---

94. *See* Chapter 5.
95. *See* § 14.1.
96. IRC § 4940; *see* Chapter 10.
97. IRC § 4941; *see* Chapter 5.
98. IRC § 4942; *see* Chapter 6.
99. IRC § 4943–4944; *see* Chapters 7 and 8.

No such tax law limits are placed on public charities, although fiduciary responsibility standards apply. Last, limitations are placed on a private foundation's expenditures.[100] It is therefore very useful for a charitable organization, when possible, to obtain and maintain public status.

The first two lines of this part must be answered by all private foundations. Line 1b asks if the foundation's governing documents meet the organizational requirements that enjoin it to adhere to the federal tax laws that constrain the foundation's activities. This requirement is addressed either with overt language in the foundation's documents or by operation of state law. For private foundations in all states, other than Arizona and New Mexico, this answer is *Yes* because all other states (a list is provided in Appendix B to the instructions) impose statutory provisions that satisfy this requirement.

A private operating foundation declares its intention to conduct active programs that allow it to be so classified by checking Line 2 *Yes*. A private operating foundation is a charity that conducts one or more programs directly, or, in the language of the statute, "actively conducts activities constituting the purpose or function for which it is organized and operated."[101] A private operating foundation sponsors and manages its own charitable projects (and can also make limited grants to other organizations). An example is an endowed institution operating a museum, library, or other charitable pursuit not included in the list of organizations that can qualify as public charities regardless of their sources of support. A private operating foundation must meet two annual distribution requirements: one based on its income levels and another on its assets or sources of its revenues. It must spend the requisite amount in support of its own projects and satisfy an asset or endowment test. Importantly for its funders, donations to a private operating foundation are afforded the higher deductibility limits allowed for gifts to public charities.

A *Yes* on Line 3 indicates the prospective private operating foundation has been in existence for one or more years and is submitting financial information to evidence its qualification. A new private operating foundation answers *Yes* on Line 4 to express its intention to qualify even though it has had no activity. Then it submits either (1) an affidavit or opinion of an attorney, certified public accountant, or accounting firm with expertise in tax matters that contains sufficient facts to likely satisfy the tests or (2) its own statement describing proposed operating (and financial information) that indicates it can qualify as a private operating foundation (POF). For an example, see the attachment to Part X, Line 4 for Active Project Fund (Exhibit 2.2).

Lines 5, 6, and 7 pertain to public charities and are inapplicable for a private foundation.

---

100. IRC § 4945; *see* Chapter 9.
101. IRC § 4942(j)(3); *see* § 3.1.

**Part XI—User-Fee Information.** Form 8718 has been incorporated into the form with this part. An individual authorized by Form 2848 may not sign the application unless that person is also an officer, director, trustee, or other official who is authorized to sign the application.

As shown Exhibit 2.2, Part XI, User Fee Information, Items 1 and 3 reflect an $850 filing fee effective January 2010, still in effect. The IRS-promised Cyber Assistant program for electronic filing of Form 1023 is now in place. The first step taken in the fall of 2013 was an interactive form still filed physically but displayed on their website with instructions, technical information, and helpful hints. Readers should look for required electronic filing in the future.

**The Schedules.** In addition to the 12 pages that all applicants must file, nine special-purpose schedules are provided. Schedules A to D and F pertain to churches, schools, hospitals, supporting organizations, and low-income housing providers and would not be filed by a private foundation. The schedule most commonly filed by a foundation is Schedule H. Exhibit 2.3 illustrates Schedule H, entitled *Organizations Providing Scholarships, Fellowships, Educational Loans, or Other Educational Grants.* An applicant planning to award individual grants should review the law on this point[102] as an aid to completing Schedule H to obtain IRS approval in advance of making awards.

Schedule E, *Organizations Not Filing Form 1023 within 27 Months of Formation*, replaces the page for private operating foundations that has been eliminated.[103] Schedule F, *Homes for the Elderly or Handicapped*, is expanded to include low-income housing. The questions reflected on the lines of this schedule embody the respective revenue procedures applicable to the respective types of charities.[104]

### (c) The Substantially Completed Application

The application for recognition as submitted by a private foundation (or other tax-exempt organization) will not be processed by the IRS until the application is at least *substantially completed.*[105] If an application for recognition of exemption does not contain the requisite information, it usually will be returned to the applicant organization without being considered on its merits, with a letter of explanation. Likewise, for purposes of the declaratory judgment

---

102. *See* § 9.3.
103. A prospective private operating foundation can complete and submit the previous schedule that contains information and calculations necessary to test and furnish an affidavit of its qualification.
104. Rev. Rul. 79-18, 1979-1 C.B. 152 and Rev. Rul. 81-61, 1981-1 C.B. 355 (aged); Rev. Rul. 70-585, 1970-2 C.B. 115. *Housing Pioneers, Inc. v. Commissioner*, 65 T.C.M. 2191 (1993), *aff'd* (9th Cir. 1995); Tech. Adv. Mems. 200218037 and 200151045 (low-income housing).
105. Rev. Proc. 2014-9, 2014-2 I.R.B. 281 § 3.08.

**Schedule H. Organizations Providing Scholarships, Fellowships, Educational Loans, or Other Educational Grants to Individuals and Private Foundations Requesting Advance Approval of Individual Grant Procedures**

| Section I | *Names of individual recipients are not required to be listed in Schedule H.* |
|---|---|

**Public charities and private foundations complete lines 1a through 7 of this section. See the instructions to Part X if you are not sure whether you are a public charity or a private foundation.**

1a  Describe the types of educational grants you provide to individuals, such as scholarships, fellowships, loans, etc.

  b  Describe the purpose and amount of your scholarships, fellowships, and other educational grants and loans that you award.

  c  If you award educational loans, explain the terms of the loans (interest rate, length, forgiveness, etc.).

  d  Specify how your program is publicized.

  e  Provide copies of any solicitation or announcement materials.

  f  Provide a sample copy of the application used.

2  Do you maintain case histories showing recipients of your scholarships, fellowships, educational loans, or other educational grants, including names, addresses, purposes of awards, amount of each grant, manner of selection, and relationship (if any) to officers, trustees, or donors of funds to you? If "No," refer to the instructions.  ☐ Yes   ☐ No

3  Describe the specific criteria you use to determine who is eligible for your program. (For example, eligibility selection criteria could consist of graduating high school students from a particular high school who will attend college, writers of scholarly works about American history, etc.)

4a  Describe the specific criteria you use to select recipients. (For example, specific selection criteria could consist of prior academic performance, financial need, etc.)

  b  Describe how you determine the number of grants that will be made annually.

  c  Describe how you determine the amount of each of your grants.

  d  Describe any requirement or condition that you impose on recipients to obtain, maintain, or qualify for renewal of a grant. (For example, specific requirements or conditions could consist of attendance at a four-year college, maintaining a certain grade point average, teaching in public school after graduation from college, etc.)

5  Describe your procedures for supervising the scholarships, fellowships, educational loans, or other educational grants. Describe whether you obtain reports and grade transcripts from recipients, or you pay grants directly to a school under an arrangement whereby the school will apply the grant funds only for enrolled students who are in good standing. Also, describe your procedures for taking action if the terms of the award are violated.

6  Who is on the selection committee for the awards made under your program, including names of current committee members, criteria for committee membership, and the method of replacing committee members?

7  Are relatives of members of the selection committee, or of your officers, directors, or **substantial contributors** eligible for awards made under your program? If "Yes," what measures are taken to ensure unbiased selections?  ☐ Yes   ☐ No

  **Note.** If you are a private foundation, you are not permitted to provide educational grants to **disqualified persons.** Disqualified persons include your substantial contributors and foundation managers and certain family members of disqualified persons.

| Section II | **Private foundations complete lines 1a through 4f of this section. Public charities do not complete this section.** |
|---|---|

1a  If we determine that you are a private foundation, do you want this application to be considered as a request for advance approval of grant making procedures?  ☐ Yes   ☐ No   ☐ N/A

  b  For which section(s) do you wish to be considered?

    • 4945(g)(1)—Scholarship or fellowship grant to an individual for study at an educational institution  ☐

    • 4945(g)(3)—Other grants, including loans, to an individual for travel, study, or other similar purposes, to enhance a particular skill of the grantee or to produce a specific product  ☐

2  Do you represent that you will (1) arrange to receive and review grantee reports annually and upon completion of the purpose for which the grant was awarded, (2) investigate diversions of funds from their intended purposes, and (3) take all reasonable and appropriate steps to recover diverted funds, ensure other grant funds held by a grantee are used for their intended purposes, and withhold further payments to grantees until you obtain grantees' assurances that future diversions will not occur and that grantees will take extraordinary precautions to prevent future diversions from occurring?  ☐ Yes   ☐ No

3  Do you represent that you will maintain all records relating to individual grants, including information obtained to evaluate grantees, identify whether a grantee is a disqualified person, establish the amount and purpose of each grant, and establish that you undertook the supervision and investigation of grants described in line 2?  ☐ Yes   ☐ No

Form **1023** (Rev. 12-2013)

**EXHIBIT 2.3**

Schedule H

Form 1023 (Rev. 12-2013)    (00)  Name: _____    EIN: _____ – _____    Page **26**

**Schedule H.** Organizations Providing Scholarships, Fellowships, Educational Loans, or Other Educational Grants to Individuals and Private Foundations Requesting Advance Approval of Individual Grant Procedures *(Continued)*

| **Section II** | **Private foundations complete lines 1a through 4f of this section. Public charities do not complete this section.** *(Continued)* |
|---|---|

**4a** Do you or will you award scholarships, fellowships, and educational loans to attend an educational institution based on the status of an individual being an *employee of a particular employer?* If "Yes," complete lines 4b through 4f.  ☐ Yes  ☐ No

**b** Will you comply with the seven conditions and either the percentage tests or facts and circumstances test for scholarships, fellowships, and educational loans to attend an educational institution as set forth in Revenue Procedures 76-47, 1976-2 C.B. 670, and 80-39, 1980-2 C.B. 772, which apply to inducement, selection committee, eligibility requirements, objective basis of selection, employment, course of study, and other objectives? (See lines 4c, 4d, and 4e, regarding the percentage tests.)  ☐ Yes  ☐ No

**c** Do you or will you provide scholarships, fellowships, or educational loans to attend an educational institution to employees of a particular employer?  ☐ Yes  ☐ No  ☐ N/A

If "Yes," will you award grants to 10% or fewer of the eligible applicants who were actually considered by the selection committee in selecting recipients of grants in that year as provided by Revenue Procedures 76-47 and 80-39?  ☐ Yes  ☐ No

**d** Do you provide scholarships, fellowships, or educational loans to attend an educational institution to children of employees of a particular employer?  ☐ Yes  ☐ No  ☐ N/A

If "Yes," will you award grants to 25% or fewer of the eligible applicants who were actually considered by the selection committee in selecting recipients of grants in that year as provided by Revenue Procedures 76-47 and 80-39? If "No," go to line 4e.  ☐ Yes  ☐ No

**e** If you provide scholarships, fellowships, or educational loans to attend an educational institution to children of employees of a particular employer, will you award grants to 10% or fewer of the number of employees' children who can be shown to be eligible for grants (whether or not they submitted an application) in that year, as provided by Revenue Procedures 76-47 and 80-39?  ☐ Yes  ☐ No  ☐ N/A

If "Yes," describe how you will determine who can be shown to be eligible for grants without submitting an application, such as by obtaining written statements or other information about the expectations of employees' children to attend an educational institution. If "No," go to line 4f.

**Note.** Statistical or sampling techniques are not acceptable. See Revenue Procedure 85-51, 1985-2 C.B. 717, for additional information.

**f** If you provide scholarships, fellowships, or educational loans to attend an educational institution to *children of employees of a particular employer* without regard to either the 25% limitation described in line 4d, or the 10% limitation described in line 4e, will you award grants based on facts and circumstances that demonstrate that the grants will not be considered compensation for past, present, or future services or otherwise provide a significant benefit to the particular employer? If "Yes," describe the facts and circumstances that you believe will demonstrate that the grants are neither compensatory nor a significant benefit to the particular employer. In your explanation, describe why you cannot satisfy either the 25% test described in line 4d or the 10% test described in line 4e.  ☐ Yes  ☐ No

Form **1023** (Rev. 12-2013)

**EXHIBIT 2.3**

*(Continued)*

rules, it is the position of the IRS that the 270-day period[106] does not begin until the date a substantially completed application is filed with the appropriate IRS office.[107]

A substantially completed application for recognition of tax exemption for a tax-exempt organization is one that:

- Is signed by an authorized individual,

- Includes an employer identification number,

- Includes information regarding any previously filed federal income and/or exempt organization information returns,

- Includes a statement of receipts and expenditures and a balance sheet for the current year and the three preceding years (or the years the organization was in existence, where that period is less than four years), although if the organization has not yet commenced operations, or has not completed one full accounting period, a proposed budget for two full accounting periods and a current statement of assets and liabilities is acceptable,

- Includes a narrative statement of proposed activities[108] and a narrative description of anticipated receipts and contemplated expenditures.[109]

- Includes a copy of the document by which the organization was established that is signed by a principal officer or is accompanied by a written declaration signed by an authorized individual, certifying that the document is a complete and accurate copy of the original or otherwise meets the requirement that it be a *conformed copy*.[110]

- If the organizing document is a set of articles of incorporation, includes evidence that it was filed with and approved by an appropriate state official (such as a copy of the certificate of incorporation) or includes a copy of the articles of incorporation accompanied by a written declaration signed by an authorized individual that the copy is a complete and accurate copy of the original copy that was filed with and approved by the state, and stating the date of filing with the state,

- If the organization has adopted bylaws,[111] includes a current copy of that document, verified as being current by an authorized individual.

- Is accompanied by the correct user fee.[112]

---

106.  IRC § 7428(b)(2).
107.  Rev. Proc. 2014-9, 2014-2 I.R.B. 281 § 10.02(1).
108.  Also Reg. §§ 1.501(a)-1(b)(1), 1.501(c)(3)–1(b)(1)(v).
109.  Also Reg. § 1.501(a)-1(a)(3).
110.  Rev. Proc. 68-14, 1968-1 C.B. 768.
111.  Reg. § 1.501(a)-1(a)(3).
112.  Rev. Proc. 2014-9, 2014-2 I.R.B. 281 § 3.02.

An English translation of the organizational documents, as well as all other attachments to the application for recognition of exemption, must be furnished by a foreign organization seeking exempt status.

In the case of an organization that appears likely to qualify, the IRS will inform the organization of the time within which the completed application must be resubmitted in order for the application to be considered a timely notice to the IRS.[113]

Where an application for recognition of tax exemption involves an issue for which significant contrary authorities (such as court opinions) exist, the applicant organization is encouraged by the IRS to disclose and discuss them. Failure to do so can result in requests for additional information and may delay action on the application.[114]

If an application for recognition of tax exemption is revised at the request of the IRS, the 270-day period that applies in the declaratory judgment context[115] will not be considered by the IRS as starting until the date the application is refiled with the IRS with the requested information. If the upgraded application is mailed and a postmark is not evident, the period starts on the date the IRS receives the substantially completed application.

Even though an application for recognition of tax exemption is substantially complete, the IRS has reserved the authority to obtain additional information before a determination letter or ruling is issued.[116] The standards for a substantially completed application also apply with respect to the notice requirements for charitable organizations.[117]

The IRS website reports the top 10 reasons why applications are delayed in processing:

1. Incorrect or no user fee included.

2. Missing complete copy of organizing document with any amendments and evidence of filing and approval by the state.

3. Bylaws, with evidence they were adopted, not attached.

4. Signature of a director, trustee, principal officer, or other authorized individual in a similar capacity omitted.

5. Pages or questions incomplete, or schedules for churches, schools, hospitals, scholarships, supporting organizations, or certain other organizations omitted.

---

113. *See* § 2.6.
114. Rev. Proc. 2014-9, 2014-2 I.R.B. 281 § 4.06(1).
115. *See* IRC § 7428.
116. Rev. Proc. 2014-9, 2014-2 I.R.B. 281 § 4.06. Also Reg. §§ 1.501(a)–1(b)(2), 601.201(h)(1)(ii), (iii). *Cf.* text accompanied by notes 78–87.
117. *See* § 2.6.

6. Failure to complete all required schedules, including supporting information requested for financial statements.

7. Description of activities to be conducted to achieve exempt purposes inadequate. Simple restatement from organizational documents insufficient. A "who, what, when, where, and why" approach is necessary to reflect the past, present, and planned activities.

8. Required information on the principal officers and board of directors, including their names, mailing addresses, titles and positions, and annual compensation incomplete.

9. Fiscal year ending date confusion: bylaws say one thing and financials and prior returns filed reflect another.

10. Insufficient financial data.

### (d) Recognition Application Procedure and Issuance of Determination Letters and Rulings

The IRS annually promulgates rules by which a ruling or determination letter may be issued to a private foundation, or other organization, in response to the filing of an application for recognition of tax-exempt status.[118] Most of these documents are *determination letters*, which are letters recognizing exempt status issued by the IRS out of an office other than its National Office.[119] A *ruling* is a letter issued by the National Office of the IRS.

Applications for recognition of tax exemption are filed with the IRS Service Center in Cincinnati, Ohio. A determination letter or ruling recognizing exempt status will be issued by the IRS to an organization, where its Form 1023 and supporting documents establish that it meets the requirements of the category of exemption that it claimed as provided in the Internal Revenue Code and other related law.

Exempt status for a newly created organization will be recognized by the IRS in advance of operations where the entity's proposed activities are described in sufficient detail to permit a conclusion that the organization will clearly meet the pertinent statutory requirements. Ideally, the information submitted with the application allows the reader to imagine or picture the organization as if it were fully operational. A mere restatement of purposes or a statement that proposed activities will be in furtherance of the organization's purposes does not satisfy this requirement. An applicant organization has the burden of proof in this regard; thus, it must fully describe the activities in which it expects to engage, including the standards, criteria, procedures, or other means adopted or planned for carrying out the activities, the anticipated sources

---

118. Rev. Proc. 2014-9, 2014-2 I.R.B. 281.
119. *Id.* § 1.01(6).

of receipts, and the nature of contemplated expenditures.[120] The IRS, generally supported by the courts, usually will refuse to recognize an organization's tax-exempt status unless the entity tenders sufficient information to the government regarding its operations and finances.[121] An organization is considered to have made the required "threshold showing," however, where it describes its activities in "sufficient detail" to permit a conclusion that the entity will meet the pertinent requirements,[122] particularly where it answered all of the questions propounded by the IRS.[123]

One court concluded that an organization failed to meet its burden of proof as to its eligibility for tax exemption because it did not provide a "meaningful explanation" of its activities to the IRS.[124] Another organization suffered the same fate inasmuch as it offered only "vague generalizations" of its ostensibly planned activities.[125] By contrast, the court, in another instance, observed that although the law "requires that the organization establish reasonable standards and criteria for its operation as an exempt organization," the standard does not necessitate "some sort of metaphysical proof of future events."[126]

When the representatives of a would-be tax-exempt organization fail to submit its books and records to the IRS, an inference arises that the facts involved would denigrate the organization's cause.[127] A court concluded that an organization's failure to respond "completely or candidly" to many of the inquiries of the IRS precluded it from receiving a determination as to its tax-exempt status.[128]

Where the organization cannot demonstrate, to the satisfaction of the IRS, its proposed activities will qualify it for tax exemption, a record of actual operations may be required before a determination letter or ruling is issued. In cases where an organization is unable to fully describe its purposes and activities, a refusal by the IRS to issue a determination letter or ruling is considered an initial

---

120. *Id.* § 1.01(6). For example, the foundation might draw up its checklists and procedures for managing its proposed grant-making activity following the examples provided in § 9.4.
121. E.g., *The Basic Unit Ministry of Alma Karl Schurig v. United States*, 511 F. Supp. 166 (D.D.C. 1981).
122. Rev. Proc. 2014-9, 2014-2 I.R.B. 281 § 4.03.
123. E.g., *The Church of the Visible Intelligence That Governs the Universe v. United States*, 83-2 U.S. T.C. ¶ 9726 (Ct. Cl. 1983).
124. *Public Industries, Inc. v. Commissioner*, 61 T.C.M. 1626, 1629 (1991).
125. *Pius XII Academy, Inc. v. Commissioner*, 43 T.C.M. 634, 636 (1982).
126. *American Science Foundation v. Commissioner*, 52 T.C.M. 1049, 1051 (1986).
127. E.g., *New Concordia Bible Church v. Commissioner*, 49 T.C.M. 176 (1984) (*app. dis.*, 9th Cir. [1985]). Also *Chief Steward of the Ecumenical Temples and the Worldwide Peace Movement and His Successors v. Commissioner*, 49 T.C.M. 640 (1985); *Basic Bible Church of America, Auxiliary Chapter11004 v. Commissioner*, 46 T.C.M. 223 (1983).
128. *National Association of American Churches v. Commissioner*, 82 T.C. 18, 32 (1984). Also *United Libertarian Fellowship, Inc. v. Commissioner*, 65 T.C.M. 2178 (1993); *Church of Nature in Man v. Commissioner*, 49 T.C.M. 1393 (1985); *LaVerdad v. Commissioner*, 82 T.C. 215 (1984).

adverse determination from which administrative appeal or protest rights will be afforded.[129]

A determination letter or ruling recognizing tax exemption ordinarily will not be issued if an issue involving the organization's exempt status is pending in litigation or is under consideration within the IRS.[130]

An application for recognition of tax exemption may be withdrawn, on the written request of an authorized representative of the organization, at any time prior to the issuance of an initial adverse determination letter or ruling. Where an application is withdrawn, it and all supporting documents are retained by the IRS.[131]

Pursuant to the general procedures to be updated annually, Exempt Organization (EO) Determinations is authorized to issue determination letters in response to applications for recognition for exempt status. EO Determinations will refer to EO Technical any applications that present issues that are not specifically covered by statute or regulations, or by a ruling, opinion, or court decision published in the Internal Revenue Bulletin. Also, EO Determinations will refer applications that have been specifically reserved by revenue procedure or by other IRS instructions for handling by EO Technical for purposes of establishing uniformity or centralized control of designated categories of cases. EO Technical will notify the applicant organization on receipt of a referred application and will consider each application and issue a ruling directly to the organization.

If at any time during the course of consideration of an application for recognition by EO Determinations, the applicant organization believes that its case involves an issue to which there is no published precedent, or there has been nonuniformity in the IRS's handling of similar cases, the organization may request that EO Determinations either refer the application to EO Technical or seek technical advice from EO Technical. If EO Determinations proposes to recognize the exemption of an organization to which EO Technical had issued a previous contrary ruling or technical advice, EO Determinations must seek technical advice from EO Technical before issuing a determination letter. (This rule does not apply where EO Technical issued an adverse ruling and the organization subsequently made changes to its purposes, activities, or operations to remove the basis for which recognition of exempt status was denied.)[132]

---

129. Rev. Proc. 2014-9, 2014-2 I.R.B. 281 § 7.02.

130. Rev. Proc. 2014-9, 2014-2 I.R.B. 281 § 4.04.

131. *Id*. § 6.01(1).

132. The Director, Exempt Organizations Rulings and Agreements, issued a memorandum, dated March 13, 2008, transmitting guidelines for the processing of applications for recognition of exemption filed by entities seeking classification as supporting organizations; this guidance consisted of a "guide sheet" for Type I and II entities, and a separate guide sheet for Type III entities (*see* §§ 15.7(e)–15.7(g)). The Director, by memorandum dated July 31, 2008, transmitted guidance for the processing of applications for recognition of exemption submitted by supporting organizations that maintain donor-advised funds; this guidance included a donor-advised funds guide sheet (*see* Chapter 16).

## (e)   Application Processing Timeline

After submission of the application, one can go to the IRS website "Where Is My Exemption Application?" at www.irs.gov, to find out which month's received applications are being processed through. As of September 21, 2013, the website showed that cases received through April 2012 were being assigned. This 1½-year gap indicates why the goal in preparing the application is for the first reviewer in Cincinnati to decide the submission can be approved without additional questions, a condition called "merit closing." The IRS reports that 40 percent of all of the applications are "merit closed." That desirable result occurs when the application is approved based on information submitted with no additional information requested so that a determination of exempt status is made without any questions being asked. In that case, the IRS usually issues the determination letter within two to three months. They have created a second screening to address nontechnical issues like those listed in the next subsection. This stage adds a month or two. The remaining 50 percent or so are set aside to be assigned for technical review. In that case, approval (or even correspondence from the IRS with additional questions) can take over a year.

## (f)   Issues Causing Applications to Be Routed to EO Technical

Applications may also be given extra scrutiny or delayed based on the character of activity proposed. Cases that are reserved for EO Technical essentially will not be merit closed. Applications for organizations conducting certain activities are so reserved:[133]

- Provision of commercial-type insurance.
- Potentially discriminatory private school.
- Certain hospitals and health-care providers.
- Requests for advance approval of grant-making procedures that have an agreement for the administration of the scholarship program with certain organizations.
- Churches conducting activities solely through the Internet.
- Organizations whose sole activity is the provision of Internet access.
- Organizations whose fundraising activities occur wholly over the Internet.

The list of applications that will also get special scrutiny includes applicants whose primary activity is gaming, foreign organizations, group exemption requests, farmers' cooperatives, requests under § 501(d), limited liability companies, and disaster relief.

---

133.  Internal Revenue Manual 7.20.5.

The IRS, reputedly because of concerns about terrorists, gives enhanced scrutiny to applications with plans to do foreign grant making or conduct programs overseas. The IRS checks names of individuals mentioned in the application against the U.S. Treasury Office of Foreign Assets Control list.[134] Although not required, such applicants are well advised to state that the voluntary best practices regarding foreign activity will be followed.[135]

In general, an organization can rely on a determination letter or ruling from the IRS recognizing its tax exemption. This is not the case, however, if there is a material change, inconsistent with exemption, in the character, purpose, or method of operation of the organization.[136]

## (g)  Exemption for State Purposes

Many states allow exemption from some or all of their income, franchise, licensing fees, property, sales, or other taxes to religious, charitable, and educational organizations and various other nonprofit organizations. The process for obtaining such exemptions varies with each state and locality. Each newly created private foundation should obtain current information and forms directly from the appropriate state or local authorities in conjunction with seeking recognition of federal tax exemption.

In Texas, by way of example, the state filing schedule starts when a nonprofit certificate of organization is filed with the secretary of state. There is no filing or registration for trusts or unincorporated associations. A status report is next filed with the comptroller of public accounts, indicating which category of federal exemption is being sought. No formal application process is required for exemption. State exemption is automatically granted when the exempt organization furnishes a copy of its federal exemption determination letter to the comptroller's office. The private foundation may furnish a copy of its completed Form 1023 and a letter requesting state exemption, if it desires state recognition prior to receiving the federal approval. The effective date of Texas sales and franchise tax exemption is the date of qualification for federal tax exemption. If the federal exemption process is delayed one year, a franchise tax may be due to be filed. The franchise, but not sales tax, is refundable once the exemption is approved.

By contrast, California has its own application for exemption (Form 3500), which must be filed with the Franchise Tax Board. This form is filed at the same time as the Form 1023. The instructions for Form 3500 indicate that the Franchise Tax Board may require proof of federal exemption before it makes a ruling on state exemption. Approval of Form 3500 grants exemption from sales and franchise tax.

---

134. Comments of Ward Thomas at March 15, 2007, program of the Exempt Organizations section of the District of Columbia Bar Association.

135. *See* § 17.6(d).

136. *Id.* § 11.02.

In New York, Form CT-247 must be filed to request exemption from franchise and sales tax. To be considered tax-exempt, the corporation must be a not-for-profit corporation, it must not have stock, its net earnings must not benefit any disqualified person, and it must be federally exempt. Both California and New York maintain that unrelated business income is not covered under this exemption; separate forms must be filed to report and pay tax on those revenues.

Two significant cases have considered eligibility for exemption from local sales taxes. The Supreme Court decided that a sales tax could be imposed on the sale of religious articles if it is equally imposed on other nonprofit organizations.[137] The argument, focused primarily upon the First Amendment, is protection of the free exercise of religion. The Supreme Court also held that state sales tax exemption for religious publications violates the establishment clause of the First Amendment when religious organizations are the only beneficiaries of the exemption.[138] Most states automatically grant exemption from sales tax when federal exemption has been granted. It is important to remember that exemptions from sales tax usually are related to purchases by the organization; in most cases, the organization is still required to collect and remit sales tax when it makes sales.

Local property tax exemptions may also be available. Some (but not all) charitable organizations qualify under the Texas Property Tax Code for exemption, for example. YWCAs and YMCAs have faced challenges to their local property tax exemptions in California and in Oregon, with conflicting results. The primary issue has been the level of free services furnished to the needy. In Utah and other states, hospital systems' local property tax exemptions have been questioned. Tax authorities in Pennsylvania tried to revoke property tax exemptions for private colleges.

Charitable solicitation registration is required in certain municipalities and states, depending upon the level of activity. Fortunately, the National Association of Attorneys General and the National Association of State Charities Officials (NAAG/NASCO) have aided in the development of a form called the Unified Registration Statement, which can be used to register in all states requiring registration except Colorado and Florida. Some states require other forms in addition to those submitted to the IRS.

## § 2.6 SPECIAL REQUIREMENTS FOR CHARITABLE ORGANIZATIONS

An organization—such as a private foundation—that desires recognition as a tax-exempt charitable organization as of the date of its establishment should notify the IRS that it is applying for recognition of tax exemption on that basis

137. *Swaggart Ministries v. Board of Equalization of California*, 493 U.S. 378 (1990).
138. *Texas Monthly, Inc. v. Bullock*, 489 U.S. 1 (1989).

within 27 months from the end of the month in which it was organized.[139] Thus, where the IRS recognizes the tax exemption of an organization that made a timely filing, the exemption is effective retroactively, as of the date the organization was created. Otherwise, the recognition of tax exemption as a charitable organization by the IRS will be effective only on a prospective basis from the IRS receipt date (assuming a favorable determination).[140] The application can be filed by regular U.S. mail, Express Mail, private delivery service, or, soon, electronically. It is critical that the applicant have proof of the date transmitted by obtaining a certified mail receipt or delivery confirmation from FedEx, DHL Express, or United Parcel Service.[141] Otherwise, the period begins on the date the application is stamped as received by the IRS.[142]

An organization is considered *organized* on the date it becomes a charitable entity.[143] In determining the date on which a corporation is organized for purposes of this exemption recognition process, the IRS looks to the date the entity came into existence under the law of the state in which it was incorporated, which usually is the date its articles of incorporation were filed in the appropriate state office.[144] This date is not the date the organizational meeting was held, bylaws were adopted, or actual operations began.

If an organization makes a nonsubstantive amendment to a governing instrument,[145] that action is not taken into account for purposes of the 27-month rule.[146] For example, an organization may have submitted an application for recognition of tax exemption within the 27-month period and subsequently made a nonsubstantive amendment to its governing instrument; its tax exemption is still effective as of the date of its formation. Likewise, an organization may have submitted an application for recognition of tax exemption after expiration of the 27-month period and thereafter made a nonsubstantive amendment to its governing instrument; its tax exemption is effective as of the date the application was mailed to or received by the IRS, as the case may be. If an organization makes a nonsubstantive amendment to its governing instrument after expiration of the 27-month period and then applies for recognition of exemption within 27 months after the date of the amendment, the organization will be recognized as tax-exempt as of the date the application was mailed to or received by the IRS, not the date the amendment

---

139. IRC § 508(a). This notice is given by the filing of the application for recognition of tax exemption (*see* § 2.5). Reg. § 1.508-1(a)(2)(i) states this rule in terms of a 15-month filing period. The IRS provided an automatic 12-month extension of time for this filing (Rev. Proc. 92-85, 1992-2 C.B. 490 § 4.01), thereby converting it to a 27-month period.
140. E.g., Priv. Ltr. Rul. 8518067.
141. Instructions for Form 1023 should be consulted for current information on transmission instructions, possibly by electronic filing.
142. Rev. Rul. 77-114, 1977-2 C.B. 152.
143. Reg. § 1.508-1(a)(2)(iii). *See* Form 1023, Part I, question 5.
144. Rev. Rul. 75-290, 1975-2 C.B. 215.
145. Rev. Proc. 2007-52, 2007-3 I.R.B. 222 § 11.01 (2).
146. Rev. Proc. 84-47, 1984-1 C.B. 545.

was made. Where a substantive amendment is made to the governing instrument, recognition of exemption is effective as of the date of the change.

The IRS has general discretionary authority, upon a showing of good cause, to grant a reasonable extension of a time fixed by the tax regulations for making an election or application for relief in respect to the federal income tax law.[147] This discretionary authority may be exercised where the time for making the election or application is not expressly prescribed by statute, the request for the extension is filed with the IRS within a period of time the IRS considers reasonable under the circumstances, and it is shown to the satisfaction of the IRS that granting the extension will not jeopardize the interests of the federal government. The IRS acknowledged that it can exercise this discretionary authority to extend the time for satisfaction of the 27-month notice requirement (which, as noted, is not fixed by statute).[148] The IRS outlined the information and representations that must be furnished and some factors that will be taken into consideration in determining whether an extension of this nature will be granted.[149]

An organization's eligibility to receive deductible charitable contributions is also governed by the 27-month rule. Thus, where a private foundation or other charitable organization timely files the application for recognition of tax exemption, and the determination letter or ruling ultimately is favorable, the ability to receive deductible charitable gifts is effective as of the date the organization was formed.

An organization that qualifies for tax exemption as a charitable organization but files for recognition of exemption after the 27-month period can be tax-exempt as a social welfare organization[150] for the period commencing on the date of its inception to the date tax exemption as a charitable organization becomes effective.[151] Contributions to social welfare organizations are, however, generally not deductible as charitable gifts, so this approach is of little utility to private foundations.[152]

---

147. Reg. § 1.9100-1.

148. Rev. Proc. 84-47, 1984-1 C.B. 545 § 4; Rev. Rul. 80-259, 1980-2 C.B. 192.

149. Rev. Proc. 92-85, 1992-2 C.B. 490, mod. by Rev. Proc. 93-28, 1993-2 C.B. 344. A request for this extension is built into the application for recognition of tax exemption (Form 1023, Part III, questions 13(c) and (d)).

150. That is, an organization described in IRC § 501(c)(4). In general, *Tax-Exempt Organizations*, Chapter 13, and *Tax Planning and Compliance*, Chapter 6.

151. Rev. Rul. 80-108, 1980-1 C.B. 119. This is because social welfare organizations are not required to apply for recognition of tax-exempt status. The IRS requests an organization in this circumstance to file Form 1024, page 1, with its application for recognition of exemption (Form 1023, Part III, instructions accompanying line 6).

152. This is because nearly all private foundations are funded at the time of their inception; the charitable contribution deduction is, of course, desired for these initial gifts. If, however, a private foundation is formed and minimally funded during the grantor's lifetime (*see* § 2.3), with the vast bulk of the funding to come later, this preliminary use of the social welfare organization status may be of some utility.

In general, every charitable organization is presumed to be a private foundation unless it is able to rebut the presumption.[153] The rebuttal process entails the filing of the requisite notice with the IRS;[154] this was previously done as part of the application for recognition of tax exemption.[155] Since 2006, the form simply asks that the applicant check a box to declare whether it is or is not a private foundation. Information to allow the IRS to monitor ongoing qualification is submitted on Schedule A of Form 990.

There are statutory exceptions to the 27-month rule, but they are of no general applicability to private foundations.[156]

The IRS promulgated administrative procedures to follow where the filing of an application for recognition of tax exemption by a private foundation (and other exempt organizations) results in an adverse determination.[157] The IRS is empowered to revoke the tax-exempt status of an organization;[158] this can have a variety of tax consequences.[159] A denial of recognition of tax-exempt status or revocation of exempt status can be appealed by the organization, once all administrative remedies are exhausted, to the courts.[160]

## § 2.7   WHEN TO REPORT BACK TO THE IRS

As a foundation grows and changes over the years, it may face the question of when, or if, it must report back to the IRS. Annually, on Form 990-PF, the organization is asked whether substantial changes have occurred. The possibilities are endless and the requirements are vague. Changes that affect an exempt organization's current status need to be reported on Form 990-PF, but a new Form 1023 is not required to be filed. A foundation that has engaged in an activity not previously reported to the IRS is asked to attach a detailed description of the activities in question 2 of Part VII-A. The Form 990-PF instructions are silent on the matter and give no guidance on the consequence of such an attachment to the annual return. The Form 990 instructions for 2012

---

153. IRC § 509(a).
154. IRC § 508(a), (b).
155. Form 1023, Part III, questions 7–14.
156. Churches, their integrated auxiliaries, interchurch organizations, local units of a church, and conventions or associations of churches are not required to file for recognition of tax exemption (IRC § 508(c)(1), (2)). In addition, this notice requirement is inapplicable to organizations the gross receipts of which in each tax year are normally not more than $5,000 (IRC § 508(c)(1)); however, this exception is not available to private foundations. Another exception is for organizations covered by a group exemption (*see Tax-Exempt Organizations* § 25.6); however, private foundations are not permitted to be included in these groups.
157. *See Tax-Exempt Organizations* § 26.1.
158. *Id.* § 26.2.
159. *See* Chapter 13.
160. *See Tax-Exempt Organizations* § 26.2.

state: "An organization must report new, significant program services or significant changes in how it conducts program services on Form 990, rather than in a letter to the IRS letters confirming the tax-exempt status of organizations that report such new services or significant changes." The dilemma is that no written IRS approval will be sent in response to changes described on the Form 990-PF. The IRS has issued Form 8940, Request for Miscellaneous Determination, to seek approval for changes listed on the form. This welcome new tool standardizes changes for which a private foundation is allowed to seek a determination from the Cincinnati office. A change in organizational form from trust to nonprofit corporation or vice versa requires submission of a new Form 1023.

### (a) When Should a Ruling Be Requested?

The procedures described earlier concern reporting changes to the IRS after these changes have already occurred. In terms of IRS procedures, it is important to distinguish between gaining approval in advance of a change, rather than not seeking approval and risking a sanction for a fait accompli.

Once a change has occurred in the form of organization or a major new activity is undertaken, the organization should choose the best method to inform the IRS, based on the preceding discussion. This action is taken when the relevant tax laws are clear and established precedents exist, and there is little or no doubt that the change is acceptable.

There may, however, be proposed changes for which the organization wishes advance approval because there is a lack of published rulings or other authoritative opinions on the subject. The procedure for obtaining sanction for prospective changes is to request a ruling from the assistant commissioner for Employee Plans and Exempt Organizations at the IRS National Office. When significant funds are involved or if disapproval of the change would mean that the organization could lose its exemption, filing of a ruling request may be warranted.

A decision to request a ruling must be made in view of the cost and time involved in the process. The user fee is $10,000.[161] The IRS promulgates guidelines for seeking a ruling or technical advice.[162]

### (b) Changes in Tax Methods

A private foundation may wish (or may be forced) to make a change in its tax filing methods—either changing the fiscal year and its accounting method, or both.

---

161. Rev. Proc. 2014-8, 2014-1 I.R.B. 242.
162. Rev. Proc. 2014-5, 2014-1 I.R.B. 169.

**Fiscal or Accounting Year.** One common change that may occur during the life of a foundation is a change in its tax accounting year. Although commercial, taxpaying businesses must secure advance IRS approval to change their tax year, a streamlined system is available for exempt organizations. The organization simply files a "timely filed short period" Form 990-PF (or 990-EZ, 990, or 990-T).

For example, assume that a calendar-year foundation wishes to change its tax year to a fiscal year spanning July 1 to June 30. A return is filed, reporting financial transactions for the short-period year (the six months ending June 30 of the year of change). The June 30 return would be due to be filed by November 15, the normal due date for a full-year return ending June 30 (due date can be extended).

The minimum distribution requirements are calculated for the short taxable year, applying a percentage prorated for the months in the year. For example, the percentage for a six-month year would be 2.5 percent, or 5 percent times 6/12.[163] A major consideration, however, is the fact that the full amount due for a full year must be paid out before the short year ends. This acceleration of payout may impact the foundation's qualification for the 1 percent investment excise tax.[164]

If the foundation has not changed its year within the past 10 years (backward to include the prior short-period return as a full year), the change is indicated on the return. The words "Change of Accounting Period" are simply written across the top of the front page. If a prior change has occurred within the preceding 10 years, Form 1128 is attached to the return and a copy is separately filed with the Service Center where the return is filed.

Late applications, which are due when an organization wants to change its year after the short-period return filing due date has passed, can also be filed on Form 1128. A user fee of $350 must accompany the Service Center copy, along with a request for Section 9100 relief.[165]

**Accounting Method Change.** Generally accepted accounting principles recommend that the accrual method of accounting be used for financial statement reporting; thus, a certified public accountant cannot issue a clean or unqualified opinion on financial statements prepared on a cash receipts and disbursements basis. Because it is simpler, many foundations in their early years use the cash method, which is perfectly acceptable for filing Form 990-PF and (possibly) for reporting to boards and contributors. Maturing organizations commonly face a decision whether to change to the accrual method, in order to secure an audited statement or to satisfy granting entities' requirements.

To compound the matter, many organizations in the past employed a hybrid method of accounting. For example, they used the cash method for reporting

---

163. Reg. § 53.4942(a)-2(c)(5)(iii).
164. *See* § 10.2.
165. Rev. Proc. 92-75, 1992-2 C.B. 448.

charitable donations, which is required for reporting qualifying distributions on Form 990-PF,[166] and used the accrual method for disbursements. Pledges to pay grants are not legally enforceable in some states, so that many foundations choose not to record pledges because "all events have not occurred" to make recording them as liabilities a prudent reflection of income. For calculating annual payout requirements, the cash basis must be used.

Advance permission from the IRS is requested by income taxpayers on Form 3115. There is no mention of submission of this form in the Form 990-PF instructions, which simply require that the foundation report the financial information on the basis of the accounting method the foundation regularly uses to keep its books and records

### (c) Amended Returns

If a mistake is discovered after Form 990-PF has been filed, the question arises whether an amended return should be filed or whether the change can simply be reflected in the next year's fund balance section as a prior-period adjustment. This decision can be difficult to make. There is usually very little tax involved, so the change is not likely to be considered *material.* Income omitted in the prior year could, for example, be added to the current year's income.

Amendment is appropriate when correction would cause a change in private versus public charity status, when unrelated business income would increase or decrease, and when more than about 10 percent of gross receipts have been omitted. As a rule, for an insignificant correction with no effect on retention of exempt status, complete disclosure on the following year's return is sufficient. The parts of Form 990-PF with historic financial information that impacts the current year should be corrected.

### (d) IRS Guidance and Examinations of Exempt Organizations

The IRS/Treasury Priority Guidance Plan, which is issued each summer, announces the focus issues for the coming year. Details of the plans can be viewed on the IRS website. During the 2013–2014 year, the top priorities for exempt organizations included guidance on the following topics:

- Revenue Procedures updating grantor and contributor reliance criteria under §§ 170 and 509.

- Update of Revenue Procedure 2011–33 for EO Select Check.

- Guidance under § 501(c)(4) relating to measurement of an organization's primary activity and whether it is operated primarily for the promotion

---

166. *See* § 6.5.

of social welfare, including guidance relating to political campaign intervention.

- Final regulations under §§ 501(r) and 6033 on additional requirements for charitable hospitals as added by § 9007 of the ACA.

- Additional guidance on § 509(a)(3) supporting organizations (SOs).

- Guidance under § 4941 regarding a private foundation's investment in a partnership in which disqualified persons are also partners.

- Finalized 2012 proposed regulations on program-related investments.

- Guidance regarding new excise taxes on donor-advised funds and fund management as added by § 1231 of the Pension Protection Act of 2006.

After securing recognition of tax exemption from the IRS and filing Form 990-PF annually with the Internal Revenue Service Center, a call may be received from the field office for the foundation's area. Ongoing qualification as an exempt organization may be questioned by the specialist who wants to look at the organization's financial books and records. The knock on the door comes in the form of a phone call from the IRS agent assigned to the case to the person identified as the contact person on Form 990-PF. The agent will request to arrange an appointment to examine a particular year's return. Many foundations will refer such a call to their professional advisors, usually the accountant who prepared Form 990-PF.

**Examination Procedures.**   The examination procedures are outlined in the IRS's Tax-Exempt Organizations Examination Procedures, a part of the *Internal Revenue Manual*.[167]

IRS agents are directed to perform the following steps:

- *Pre-examination:* Review the returns to identify any large, unusual, or questionable items that should be examined for determining the correct tax liability and exempt status. The balance sheet and revenue sources are to be scrutinized for unidentified unrelated business activity. The return is checked for completeness and to identify any data to be secured in the field.

- *Administrative file:* The exempt organization's administrative file is checked for possible caveats in an exemption letter and to familiarize the agent with the reasons for which the foundation was originally exempt. Prior examinations, technical advice, and correspondence with the foundation, if any, are reviewed. If a prior examination recommended

---

167. *IRM*, Part 4, Chapter 4.75. In general, *IRS Audits*, Chapter 5.

some changes in operations, the agent is to be alert during the current examination to assure that corrective action was taken.

- *Examination guidelines:* Agents are responsible for developing issues raised in the examination. They are to study the relevant portions of the *Exempt Organizations Examination Procedures* concerning the particular type of organization they are examining and are to gather facts to apply the statutes.

- *Preliminary work:* The examination is to be conducted at the foundation's office with an authorized representative. Before the books and records are reviewed, the agent conducts an interview with the principal officer or authorized representative. The agent looks into programs and activities, sources of income, purchases of assets, receipts and payments of loans, noncash transactions, internal controls, and any large or unusual items.

- *On-site tours:* The agent may request a tour of the facilities. During this time, other employees who may be able to provide a more detailed description of operations can be interviewed.

**Location of the Examination.** The first question to ask in connection with the examination is its location. If a professional advisor is involved, the examination may take place in his or her office, depending on the sophistication of the foundation's accounting staff and the volume of records to be examined. If the information cannot be readily moved in a few boxes, the examination should take place in the foundation's offices. In either case, the examiner will want to visit the physical location in which the programs are conducted.

**Types of Examinations.** *Routine examinations:* After the appointment is made, the examiner will send a letter specifically listing the items to be reviewed. The records will be sampled by the auditor. All of the board of directors' meeting minutes are usually read, but not all of the canceled checks are scanned. The breadth of the materials reviewed depends to some extent on the quality of the accounting work papers and ledgers, and on the nature of the foundation's activities. When accounting records and original source documents can easily be traced to the numbers reported on the Form 990-PF being examined, the amount of detailed work will be limited and the examination will flow more smoothly.[168]

*Team Examinations:* For years, one of the mainstays of the IRS tax-exempt organizations examination effort was the *coordinated examination program* (CEP), which focused not only on exempt organizations but also on affiliated entities and arrangements (such as subsidiaries, partnerships, and other joint ventures)

---

168. *See IRS Audits* § 1.6(a), (b).

and collateral areas of the law (such as employment tax compliance and tax-exempt bond financing). The CEP approach, involving relatively sizable teams of revenue agents, was concentrated on large, complex organizations, such as colleges, universities, and health-care institutions. This program has been abandoned, however, and replaced by the *team examination program* (TEP). Both the CEP and TEP approaches nonetheless share the same objective, which is to avoid a fragmenting of the exempt organization examination process by using a multi-agent approach. The essential characteristics of the TEP approach that differentiates it from the CEP approach is that the team examinations are being utilized in connection with a wider array of exempt organizations, the number of revenue agents involved in each examination is smaller, and the revenue agents are less likely to establish audit offices at the exempt organization undergoing an examination.

A TEP case generally is one where the exempt organization's annual information return reflects either total revenue or assets greater than $100 million (or, in the case of a private foundation, $500 million). Nonetheless, the IRS may initiate a team examination where the case would benefit (from the government's perspective) from a TEP approach or where there is no annual information return filing requirement. There is a presumption that a team examination approach carefully scrutinizing charitable activities will be utilized in all cases meeting the TEP criteria.[169]

*Rollover audits:* Sometimes the motivation for the audit is another IRS audit, such as a review of a substantial contributor's or a related organization's return. In such a case, the organization must ask to be informed about all of the facts and circumstances, and should do everything possible to cooperate with the other persons involved.

*Compliance checks:* An overlay to the IRS program of examination of tax-exempt organizations is the agency's *compliance check* program, which focuses on specific compliance issues. Examples of these projects are the IRS's inquiries into the levels and types of compensation provided by exempt organizations, involvement by public charities in political campaign activities, disparities between reported levels of charitable giving and fundraising costs, compliance by exempt organizations in annual information return reporting of any involvement in excess benefit transactions, and adherence by community foundations with the federal tax law rules.[170]

**How to Prepare for the Audit.**   Good judgment is called for in culling an organization's records to prepare for the auditor's appointment. For example, the auditor will ask to see correspondence files. In the case of a sizable foundation with several program offices, this cannot possibly mean every

---

169.  *Id.* § 1.6 (c).
170.  *Id.* § 1.6 (d).

single correspondence file. Perhaps the correspondence of the chief financial officer or the executive director would be furnished, with an offer to furnish more correspondence if desired.

Too often, some of the requested records are not in appropriate condition to be examined. The most troublesome records are often the board minutes. It is important to carefully prepare minutes of the board of directors' meetings. Optimally, these minutes reflect the exempt nature of the organization's overall concerns. If, for example, a commercial-type operation is undertaken as a program-related investment to accomplish exempt purposes, the minutes should reflect that relationship. A thorough discussion of the pregrant inquiry and expenditure responsibility agreements would appropriately appear in the minutes of a foundation approving a grant to another foundation.[171]

Pamphlets, brochures, and other literature also make up an open-ended category. In some cases, the volume of this literature is staggering, so choosing those examples that portray the organization in the best light is acceptable. Obviously, the examiner cannot and will not look at every shred of paper produced by the organization in a three-year period. Someone knowledgeable about the issues involved in ongoing qualification for exempt status should review the materials and choose those most suitable to be furnished to the auditor. Or this type of individual should develop guidelines for persons gathering the information, to assure that the best possible case is presented to the IRS.

The physical space in which the examination is conducted is important. In most cases, a private office should be provided as the examiner's workspace, rather than a nook near the coffee bar or copy machine. Affording some privacy will prevent organization staff from involving themselves in the examination and minimize any distractions that would waste the examiner's time. Particularly when a paid professional is assisting in the examination, it is useful to limit the scope of the work and make the review as efficient as possible, to save professional fees.

### (e) Achieving Positive Results

There are four rules for achieving positive results in an IRS examination:

1.  *Assign a contact person:* One individual should be identified as the lead contact on behalf of the exempt organization, through whom all answers are to be funneled. If an outside professional is involved in the examination, he or she may be this contact.

2.  *The less said the better:* Answer only the specific question asked. Do not provide more information than is requested. The examiner should be

---

171. *See* Chapter 9.

given specific answers to specific questions. He or she should not be allowed to go through the organization's file cabinets.

3.  *Do not answer a question if you are unsure of its import:* Problem issues should be identified ahead of time, and the materials to be furnished to the IRS should be organized for presentation in the most favorable light. New materials, reports, or summaries of information found lacking can be prepared to better reflect the organization's purposes and accomplishments. If you are unsure of the answer to any question, say that you are not sure and that you will find out. Make a list for further consideration, consult a professional, or simply become better prepared to present the best picture of the organization.

4.  *Expect the best from the examiner:* The IRS agents who examine exempt organizations are knowledgeable, experienced, cooperative (usually), and sympathetic with the spirit of the nonprofit community. They perceive their purpose as different from that of income tax examiners. Their examination often can be a positive experience for an organization. It can validate the foundation's qualification and can sometimes help organization staff to understand why in fact the organization is exempt. Another very useful aspect is the reminder it serves of the need to document and preserve a clear record of accomplishments, both from a financial and a philosophical standpoint.

**The Desired Result: A "No Change."**   The desired end product of an IRS examination is a *no-change letter* stating that the organization will continue to qualify for exempt status. If the examiner finds no reason to challenge the status of the organization, he or she will normally convey this conclusion to the organization's representative in the field. The examiner then returns to the office to write up the case. The report is reviewed by the examiner's superiors and, some months later, the organization should receive a letter stating that the foundation's status as a charitable organization continues.

**Changes Suggested.**   In the event that the IRS examiner finds the organization is not operating in an entirely exempt fashion, several consequences may follow.

If the agent finds unreported or underreported unrelated business income (UBI), the consequences depend on the amount of the UBI in relation to the foundation's total revenues. If the UBI is not considered excessive, the organization's exempt status is not challenged. If Form 990-T has not previously been filed, its preparation will be requested and any delinquent income taxes, penalties, and interest will be assessed. Deductions claimed for unrelated business income are also reviewed.[172]

---

172.  *See* Chapter 11.

The calculation of the investment income tax might be adjusted to reallocate expenses claimed as a reduction to income subject to the excise tax.[173] The average fair market value of asset calculations might have been found to be incorrect. Appraisal of real estate might be challenged and found to be low.[174] These issues are resolvable, although they cause an increase in the excise tax and the minimum distribution requirements.

A more serious outcome is that the examiner may suggest that a related party transaction resulted in self-dealing,[175] that the foundation's stock ownership represents excess business holdings,[176] or that a partnership interest the foundation purchased is a jeopardizing investment.[177] In the worst case, a private foundation's ongoing qualification for tax-exempt status could be challenged with a suggestion that the foundation should be involuntarily terminated.[178]

The agent often comments on documentation policies. Are invoices available to evidence all disbursements? What about expense reimbursements reports, particularly for travel and entertainment? Payments for personal services paid to individuals are closely scrutinized to evaluate employee versus independent contractor classifications. If compensation is paid to foundation trustees, directors, or their relatives, the amounts will be carefully examined for reasonableness and in view of the self-dealing rules.

---

173. *See* § 10.4.
174. *See* § 6.3.
175. *See* Chapter 5.
176. *See* Chapter 7.
177. *See* Chapter 8. The ending sections of Chapters 5 through 9 explain and discuss the consequences of and possible abatement of penalties for these private foundation sanctions.
178. *See* Chapter 13.

# CHAPTER THREE

# Types of Private Foundations

The federal tax law definition of the term *private foundation* embraces all charitable entities other than those that are classified as public charities.[1] Although the "standard" private foundation is the most predominant, there are several other varieties of foundations. Moreover, certain nonexempt trusts and foreign entities are subject to some or all of the private foundation rules.

## §3.1 PRIVATE OPERATING FOUNDATIONS

Private operating foundations have long been recognized as nonpublicly supported organizations that devote most of their earnings and much of their assets directly to the conduct of their tax-exempt purposes. This special type of foundation is essentially a blend of a private foundation and a public charitable organization. A private operating foundation is a charitable organization that makes qualifying distributions directly for the active conduct of activities constituting the purpose or function for which it was organized.[2] In the language of the regulations:

---

1. IRC § 509.
2. IRC § 4942(j)(3)(A).

> Qualifying distributions are not made directly for the active conduct of activities constituting its (the private operating foundation's) charitable, educational, or other similar exempt purpose unless such qualifying distributions are used by the foundation itself, rather than by or through one or more grantee organizations which receive such qualifying distributions directly or indirectly from such foundation.[3]

In other words, a private operating foundation (POF) makes its required charitable expenditures by sponsoring and managing its own programs rather than making grants to other organizations. For any year in which it qualifies as a private operating foundation, it is excluded from the excise tax on the failure to make qualifying distributions imposed on standard private foundations.[4] Typically, a private operating foundation is an endowed institution operating a museum, a library, or some other charitable pursuit not included in the specific list of organizations that qualify as public charities without regard to their sources of support (generally churches, schools, hospitals, and certain medical research organizations).[5] Many private operating foundations are privately funded entities created by one or more individuals of means who has strong ideas about the charitable objectives he or she wants to accomplish through self-initiated projects, such as feeding the poor or preserving a wildlife and wetlands area.

A private operating foundation is subject to an annual distribution requirement that it spend, or distribute, a calculated amount annually for its own charitable program. The required distribution amount is measured under a dual system testing its income levels and also the character of its assets or sources of its revenues.[6] Of particular significance for some funders, donations made to a private operating foundation are subject to the more generous contribution deduction limitations allowed for gifts made to public charities.[7]

## (a) Direct Charitable Distributions

The most significant attribute of a private operating foundation is sometimes difficult to achieve. To be considered as *operating*, the foundation must spend a specified annual amount on one or more projects in which it is significantly involved in a continuing and sustainable fashion. Further, the requisite involvement is, as a general rule, evident where the foundation's expenditures are made directly to vendors, employees, and contractors. A POF purchases goods and services that advance its purposes, rather than providing funding for such expenses indirectly through an intermediary organization. A private operating foundation is in this way unlike a standard private foundation

---

3. Reg. § 53.4942(b)-1(b)(1).
4. IRC § 4942(a)(1) though it must meet a distribution test for either three out of four years or an average of four years to retain POF status; *see* Chapter 6.
5. *See* Chapter 15.
6. *See* § 3.1(d), (e).
7. *See* § 3.1(g).

that makes grants to other charitable organizations. It must also make required annual charitable distributions,[8] but it does so in a different fashion. The requisite involvement is present where payments to accomplish the private operating foundation's charitable, educational, or similar tax-exempt purpose are made directly and without the assistance of an intervening organization or agency.

A typical private operating foundation that is significantly involved in its programs maintains a staff of program specialists, researchers, teachers, administrators, or other personnel needed to supervise, direct, and carry out its programs on a continuing basis. The staff can be partly or wholly comprised of volunteers. Depending on the scope and type of the foundation's activities, its funders and (or) its board of trustees can constitute its staff if their work involvement is substantive.

A private operating foundation typically acquires and maintains assets used in its programs, such as buildings, collections of specimens and art objects, or research laboratories. Qualifying direct expenditures also include the purchase of books and publications, supplies, computer programs, and other project supplies, such as food to feed the poor. Such a foundation might pay for travel and equipment used in connection with an archeological study. It might hire an architect to plan and design a historical restoration project, buy and restore buildings, and subsequently maintain the buildings and open them for public viewing. The costs of administering the programs, such as telephone, insurance, professional advisors, occupancy, and other expenses necessary to conduct the programs, are also treated as direct expenses of the foundation's programs.

Expenditures related to administration of the foundation's investment assets are not treated as direct program disbursements. These expenses might include management, custody, or trustee fees, salary and related costs of personnel whose time is partly or wholly devoted to handling investment properties, office space, equipment, supplies, and other facility costs associated with such personnel, real estate operating expenses (rental income properties), professional fees (a geologist and/or a lawyer to evaluate a proposed royalty agreement), market timing service, subscriptions and fees for information services, and any other costs directly connected with maintaining and conserving the foundation's investment assets. Expenses attributable to both program and investment-management activities, such as the executive director's salary and office space, must be allocated on a reasonable and consistently applied basis.[9] Payment of the investment excise tax is treated as a direct program expenditure.[10]

Optimally, a private operating foundation is identified in the public eye with and by its projects. Classic examples of suitable organizational focus include

---

8. *See* discussion of the income test in § 3.1(d).
9. Reg. § 53.4942(b)-1(b)(1).
10. Reg. § 53.4942(b)-1(b)(3).

operating a museum, conducting scientific research, and promoting historical restoration by publishing monographs, sponsoring lectures on the subject, and purchasing, restoring, and maintaining historic buildings. Two contrasting examples found in the regulations illustrate the concept of active programs:[11]

- *Example 1* (does not qualify as operating): M foundation is created to improve conditions in a particular urban ghetto. M spends 10 percent of its income to make a survey of urban ghetto problems (an active disbursement) and grants 90 percent of its income to other nonprofit organizations doing ghetto rehabilitation projects (inactive or passive).

- *Example 2* (qualifies as operating): The same M foundation spends 10 percent of its income on surveying the ghetto problems. Instead of granting funds to other organizations, M spends its other income to maintain a staff of social workers and researchers who analyze its surveys and make recommendations as to methods for improving ghetto conditions. M makes grants to independent social scientists to assist in these analyses and recommendations. M publishes periodic reports indicating the results of its surveys and recommendations. M makes grants to social workers and others who act as advisors to nonprofit organizations, as well as small business enterprises, functioning in the community.

Using a facts and circumstances approach, the regulations provide other examples of actively conducted, or self-initiated, programs:

*Teacher training program:* An entity is formed to train teachers for institutions of higher education. Fellowships are awarded to students for graduate study leading to advanced degrees in college teaching. Pamphlets encouraging prospective college teachers and describing the private operating foundation's activity are widely circulated. Seminars, attended by fellowship recipients, foundation staff and consultants, and other interested parties, are held each summer, and papers from the conference are published. Despite the fact that a majority of the organization's money is spent for fellowship payments, the program is comprehensive and suitable to qualify as an active project.

*Medical research organization:* An organization is created to study heart disease. Physicians and scientists apply to conduct research at the medical research organization's center. Its professional staff evaluates the projects, reviews progress reports, supervises the projects, and publishes the resulting findings.

*Historical reference library:* A library organization is established to hold and care for manuscripts and reference material relating to the history of the

---

11. Reg. § 53.4942(b)-1(d).

region in which it is located. In addition, it makes a limited number of annual grants to enable postdoctoral scholars and doctoral candidates to use its library. Sometimes, but not always, the operating foundation can obtain the rights to publish the scholar's work.

*Set-asides:* Funds set aside for a specific future project involving the active conduct of its tax-exempt activities will qualify as a direct expenditure.[12] An example of qualification involved a private operating foundation, organized to restore and perpetuate wildlife and game animals on the North American continent. It acquired and planned to convert a portion of the new land into an extension of its existing wildlife sanctuary and the remainder into a public park under a four-year construction contract. Payments were made mainly during the last two years.[13] In such a case, the requirements for the amounts set aside must be satisfied to be counted as qualifying distributions.[14] For a newly created entity, a plan to set aside funds for a qualifying activity can be sufficient for classification of the organization as a private operating foundation.[15]

*Limited liability company:* A private operating foundation was ruled able to retain that status notwithstanding expansion of its activities to include control over and management of, by means of a single-member limited liability company,[16] a component of a public charity.[17] Specifically, this foundation assumed responsibility for administering a school of a tax-exempt university. The IRS concluded that qualifying distributions (from the foundation through the company to the university) constituted distributions directly for the active conduct of activities furthering the foundation's exempt purpose, thereby enabling the foundation to satisfy the income test.[18] The agency also ruled that the foundation's use of its assets to operate the program through the limited liability company satisfied the endowment test and that the revenue (including tuition and fees) derived from operation of the university's program may be treated as support from the general public for purposes of the support test.[19]

---

12. IRC § 4942(g)(2); Reg. § 53.4942(b)-1(b)(1).
13. Rev. Rul. 74-450, 1974-2 C.B. 388.
14. *See* § 6.5(c).
15. Gen. Couns. Mem. 39442.
16. A single-member limited liability company is an entity that is generally disregarded for federal tax purposes (*see Tax-Exempt Organizations* § 4.1(b)).
17. Priv. Ltr. Rul. 200431018.
18. *See* § 3.1(d).
19. *See* § 3.1(e).

## (b) Grants to Other Organizations

While one or more other charities may be involved in some manner, the private operating foundation must expend a prescribed amount of its funds on its own direct charitable programs rather than by or through one or more grantee organizations. The regulations provide that:

> Qualifying distributions are not made by a foundation directly for the active conduct unless such distributions are used by the foundation itself, rather than by or through one or more grantee organizations.[20]

A grant to another organization is presumed to be indirect conduct of exempt activity, even if the activity of the grantee organization helps the operating foundation accomplish its goals and its own exempt purposes.

This prohibition against mere distributions to grantees and the requirement of significant involvement by the private operating foundation in its programs nearly deprived one organization of private operating foundation status but for a liberal construction by the IRS of the rules. A private foundation (a trust) that operated a cultural center formed a corporation, controlled by it, to act in a fiduciary capacity on its behalf in conducting the operations of the center. An amount equal to substantially all of the foundation's net income was turned over each year to the corporation and disbursed in the operation of the center. The corporation held income and property from the foundation as a fiduciary and not as an absolute owner. The IRS ruled that the corporation was not a grantee organization that received qualifying distributions from the trust but was a trustee of the trust, thereby enabling the private foundation to qualify as a private operating foundation.[21]

A private foundation that was originally created to operate residential living quarters for seniors changed its focus. It converted a former living space into a senior citizens' center to serve as a central intake and assessment point for identifying and addressing the needs of seniors in the area.[22] Part of the space was rented on a reduced rate to program partners, namely, other tax-exempt organizations that provided services to senior citizens. The remaining space was used for foundation programs benefiting the elderly: support group meeting rooms, training and placement center, resources and information room, and classrooms. The foundation reimbursed the partners for expenses incurred in assisting the foundation with its own or jointly operated programs. The foundation sought approval of its ongoing classification as a private operating foundation. The IRS found rental of space on a low-cost basis and partnering

---

20. Reg. § 53.4942(b)-1(b).
21. Rev. Rul. 78-315, 1978-2 C.B. 271; Priv. Ltr. Rul. 9203004.
22. Priv. Ltr. Rul. 9723047.

programs with other exempt organizations to be an actively conducted program.

As another example of program-related investments, the IRS ruled that a private foundation made such an investment when it invested in a for-profit company, the purpose of which was to encourage the creation of jobs and economic development in a region targeted for this purpose by a state government,[23] and when a private foundation made loans and other investments for the purpose of promoting economic development in a foreign country.[24]

It is important to note, however, that a private operating foundation is not prohibited from making grants to other organizations. Grants of this nature simply are not counted in calculating satisfaction of the income test.[25] So long as it distributes the requisite annual amount for the programs it actively conducts, a private operating foundation may, in addition, make grants to other organizations. Administrative expenses attributable to both active programs and grants to other organizations should be allocated on a reasonable basis between the two types of program in presenting financial information on Part XIV of Form 990-PF to evidence qualification as a POF.

### (c)  Individual Grant Programs

Payments to individuals in connection with a scholarship program, a student loan fund, a minority business enterprise capital fund, or similar charitable effort may be classified as a distribution for the active conduct of a private operating foundation's tax-exempt purposes.[26] To qualify as a direct program activity, the facts and circumstances surrounding the making or awarding of the grants must indicate that they are an integral part of, and essentially necessary to, accomplishing an active program in which the foundation is *significantly involved.* Merely selecting, screening, and investigating applicants for grants and scholarships is insufficient to support operating foundation status. When the grant recipients perform their work or studies solely for their own purposes, such as in the pursuit of a doctoral degree, or exclusively under the direction of some other organization, the grants are not considered as a direct qualifying expenditure.

A significantly involved foundation has a focused exempt mission or purpose. The regulations state that the test of whether individual grants are direct program expenditures is qualitative, rather than strictly quantitative. To explain the meaning of this suggestion, the regulations provide that, although a

---

23. Priv. Ltr. Rul. 199943044.
24. Priv. Ltr. Rul. 199943058.
25. *See* § 3.1(c).
26. Reg. § 53.4942(b)–1(b)(2)(i).

foundation's grant to one or more grantee organizations or individuals might be in support of its own active programs, these grants are considered as indirect, rather than direct (active), distributions. In one instance, a foundation was found to maintain a significant involvement in its ongoing attempt to ameliorate poverty in a rural area. The fund assisted needy young people in a county by providing scholarships, finding them summer jobs, getting students involved with local civic affairs, and other activities designed to educate and improve the circumstances of young people and make it possible for them to remain in the area.[27] The fact that a foundation screened, investigated, and tested the applicants to make sure they complied with academic and financial requirements set for scholarship recipients was insufficient activity to constitute an educational program.[28] Evaluating their needs and providing counseling and financial aid prior to referral of needy individuals to another agency was, on the other hand, deemed an active program.[29]

Even though the amount of the grants or scholarships are not counted in calculating qualification for the income test,[30] the administrative expenses of screening and investigating grants (as opposed to the grants or scholarships themselves) may be counted as active program expenditures.[31]

*Significant involvement* of the operating foundation and its staff exists when the individual grants are a part of a comprehensive program. The regulations provide two examples of these programs.[32] In one, the foundation's purpose is to relieve poverty and human distress, and its exempt activities are designed to ameliorate conditions among the poor, particularly during national disasters. The foundation provides food and clothing to these indigents, without the assistance of an intervening organization or agency, under the direction of a salaried or voluntary staff of administrators, researchers, and other personnel who supervise and direct the activity.

In the second example, an operating foundation develops a specialized skill or expertise in scientific or medical research, social work, education, or the social sciences. A salaried staff of administrators, researchers, and other personnel supervises and conducts the work in its particular area of interest. As part of the program, the foundation awards grants, scholarships, or other payments to individuals to encourage independent study and scientific research projects and to otherwise further their involvement in its field of interest. The foundation sponsors seminars, conducts classes, and provides direction and supervision for the grant recipients. Based on these facts, the individual grants are treated as active and thus qualify under the income test.

27. *The Miss Elizabeth D. Leckie Scholarship Fund v. Commissioner,* 87 T.C. 250 (1986).
28. Reg. § 53.4942(b)-1(d), Example (10).
29. Priv. Ltr. Rul. 9203004.
30. *See* § 3.1(d).
31. Reg. § 53.4942(b)-1(b)(2)(i).
32. Reg. § 53.4942(b)-1(b)(2)(ii).

## (d)  Income Test

To qualify as a private operating foundation, a foundation must satisfy numerical tests intended to ensure that it conducts its exempt activities directly, rather than by supporting other organizations. The two categories of tests are:

1.  *Income Test:* This test requires that a specific amount be spent on directly conducted charitable programs determined by either its actual income or hypothetical minimum investment return.

2.  *Asset, Endowment, or Support Test:* One of three tests regarding its assets and sources of revenues apply as described in the next subsection.

The *income test* gauges whether a private operating foundation has spent sufficient funds for its own programs, or direct charitable distributions. As a general concept, the foundation need not actually (or in an accounting sense) trace the source of funds it uses to satisfy this test. Qualifying distributions that count toward meeting the income test may be made from current or accumulated income, including capital gains, or from current or accumulated contributions;[33] they can be made in cash or property.[34] In determining satisfaction of the income test, the foundation computes its adjusted net income[35] and its minimum investment return,[36] and tallies its qualifying distributions.[37]

*Adjusted net income* is calculated using this formula:

$$A - B - C - D + E = \text{Adjusted net income}$$

- A = Gross income for the year, including investment income such as dividends, interest, short-term capital gains, royalties; fees, tuition, product sales, and other revenues from charitable activities including short-term gain from sale of charitable- and unrelated-use assets; income from a functionally related business and program-related investments; other unrelated trade or business income; and tax-exempt interest.

- B = Long-term capital gains from sale of assets held for investment, for charitable use, and for conduct of an unrelated business. The tax basis for property received by the foundation as a gift is equal to the tax basis of the donor. For property held by the foundation on December 31, 1969, basis is equal to the value on that date.

---

33.  Reg. § 53.4942(b)-1(c).
34.  Reg. § 53.4942(a)-(3).
35.  IRC § 4942(f); Reg. § 53.4942(a)-2(d); Form 990-PF, page 1, column C, illustrated and explained in Chapter 12.
36.  IRC § 4942(e); *see* § 6.3 and Part XI of Form 990-PF.
37.  *See* § 6.4 and Part XII of Form 990-PF.

- C = Gifts, grants, and contributions received, including income distributed from an estate (unless the estate is treated as terminated for federal tax purposes because its administration has been prolonged for tax avoidance reasons).

- D = Ordinary and necessary expenses paid or incurred for the production or collection of amounts treated as gross income for this purpose, including the management, conservation, or maintenance of property held for the production of this income. Depreciation is allowed and computed on a straight-line basis; cost depletion (no percentage) is permitted. Salaries, rents, taxes, repairs, and other expenses of operating income-producing properties are included, as are expenses associated with tax-exempt interest. Where a foundation expense is related both to income production and program activities, only that portion directly attributable to includible income is deducted, following some reasonable and consistent allocation method. Direct program disbursements reduce adjusted net income to the extent of income produced by the program.

- E = Modifications, or additions to the current year spending requirement, are made for any recovery or refund of amounts treated as a qualifying distribution in a previous year, including proceeds of the sale of assets, to the extent the purchase cost of which was treated as a qualifying distribution in a prior year. The addition is limited to the lower of the actual sales price or the amount previously reported as a qualifying distribution. A previously set-aside obligation is added back or increases the distributable amount if plans change or the funds are no longer needed for the purposes for which the set-aside was allowed and treated as a distribution in a past year.[38]

Over the years, a few IRS rulings have been published to clarify the amounts includible in adjusted net income. A brief summary follows.

- Bond premium amortization is permitted.[39]

- Annuity, IRA, and other employee benefit plan payments are includible to the extent that the amount exceeds the value of the right to receive the payment on the decedent's date of death.[40]

- Capital gain dividends paid or credited for reinvestment by a mutual fund are not included, because they are considered long-term.[41]

---

38. Reg. § 53.4942(a)–2(d)(4); see § 3.1(b).
39. Rev. Rul. 76-248, 1976-1 C.B. 363; IRC § 171.
40. Rev. Rul. 75-442, 1975-2 C.B. 448.
41. Rev. Rul. 73-320, 1973-2 C.B. 385; IRC § 852(b)(3)(B).

*Minimum investment return* for this purpose is the same as for a standard private foundation; it equals 5 percent of the average fair market value of the foundation's noncharitable, or investment assets, not including its charitable-use assets.

*Qualifying distributions* of a private operating foundation are defined by the federal tax law in the same fashion as for a traditional foundation. Confusion can arise in completing Form 990-PF because direct and indirect charitable disbursements are presented together on page one and in Part XII. To complete Part XIV, where the private operating foundation tests are presented, a distinction must be made between expenditures eligible to be classified as directly expended for the active conduct of a foundation's charitable programs and those distributions that are made indirectly either by grant to another organization or to an individual.[42]

Traditional foundations are required to distribute a minimum investment return amount.[43] Under the definition for private operating foundations, the amount that must be annually expended for the active conduct of charitable activities equals substantially all, meaning 85 percent, of the lesser of its:

- Adjusted net income (ANI), or

- Minimum investment return (MIR) (essentially results in a 4.25 percent payout if this factor applies).

A special rule applies to a private operating foundation that makes grants to other organizations in addition to its active-program expenditures.[44] The rule applies if two conditions exist: (1) the foundation's adjusted net income is higher than its minimum investment return, and (2) its total qualifying distributions exceed minimum investment return but are less than adjusted net income. To meet the income test and qualify as a private operating foundation, a foundation in that circumstance must meet a test that requires it spend at least 85 percent of its adjusted net income for its own projects. Effectively, indirect grants to other organizations are not counted at all in meeting the distribution requirements and can be paid only in addition to substantially all of the foundation's adjusted

---

42. *See* § 3.1(a).
43. *See* Chapter 6.
44. Reg. § 53.4942(b)-1(a)(1)(ii). A special caveat was added to IRC § 4942(j)(3) when the test was revised to permit a foundation distributing a lower income amount to qualify as an operating foundation. A cryptic sentence was added to the end of the subsection, reading: "Notwithstanding the provisions of subparagraph (A) [the revised income test], if the qualifying distributions of an organization for the taxable year exceed the minimum investment return for the taxable year, clause (ii) of this subparagraph [permitting the minimum investment return be the test if it is lower] shall not apply unless substantially all of such qualifying distributions are made directly for the active conduct. . . ."

gross income. This rule is intended to prevent a private operating foundation from reducing its expenditures on its active programs to a lower minimum investment return level while expending the balance of its distributions in the form of grants to other organizations. Importantly, this rule does not prohibit grants to other organizations; it simply raises the required payout when ANI is high than MIR.

In summary, to satisfy the income test, a private foundation must annually expend an amount equal to substantially all (85 percent) of the lesser of its adjusted net income or its minimum investment return in the form of qualifying distributions directly for the active conduct of its tax-exempt activities.

A private operating foundation must, in addition to satisfying the income test, meet one of the three other tests regarding its assets and sources of revenue, as next described. The tests must be fulfilled within specific time frames. One of the tests, the *endowment test*, requires a private operating foundation to normally make qualifying distributions directly for the active conduct of its charitable activities equal to at least $66\frac{2}{3}$ percent of its minimum investment return, which equals $3\frac{1}{3}$ percent of MIR (possibly less than required by the alternative income test described earlier).

### (e) Asset, Endowment, or Support Test

A private operating foundation must also meet one of three alternative tests, an asset, endowment, or support test, for each year or three out of four average years.[45] Just like the income test that imposes a requirement that the private operating foundation spend the majority of its income for active programs, these tests determine whether the foundation's assets and income therefrom are so devoted.

**Asset Test.** The first of the three tests, the asset test, requires that substantially all (meaning at least 65 percent) of the private operating foundation's assets be active-use assets of any of these types:[46]

- Program assets devoted directly to the active conduct of its tax-exempt activities, to functionally related businesses, or to a combination of both.

- Stock of a corporation that is controlled by the private operating foundation, the assets of which are 65 percent or more so devoted.

- Partly assets, described in the first category, and partly stock, described in the second category.

---

45. *See* § 3.1(f).
46. IRC § 4942(j)(3)(B); Reg. § 53.4942(b)-2(a)(1)(i).

An asset, to qualify under this test, must actually be used by the organization directly for the active conduct of its tax-exempt purpose(s).[47] The determination of a particular asset's character in this regard is, however, a question of fact. The concepts applied in identifying these exempt function and dual-use assets are the same as those used to identify assets excluded in calculating a foundation's minimum investment return.[48] To the extent assets are used directly for the active conduct of the foundation's exempt activities, they are counted for this test.[49] Thus, an asset may be apportioned between its exempt and nonexempt use. For example, if the foundation's building is used 50 percent for active programs and their administration, with the other 50 percent rented to tenants not involved in the programs, one half of the value would be treated as qualifying for the asset test. The basis of the allocation is the fair rental value of the two portions rather than the respective square footage.[50] An asset that is used 95 percent or more of the time for exempt functions can be fully counted as a qualifying asset.[51] Assets held for the production of income, investment, or other similar purpose, such as stocks and bonds, interest-bearing notes, endowment funds, or leased real estate, are generally not considered as devoted to the active conduct of the foundation's programs and are not counted. Conversely, these assets are counted for purposes of the endowment test and form the basis on which the minimum investment return is calculated.

Classic examples of active-use assets include the art collections of a museum, performance halls and studios of a music conservatory, and the laboratories and library of a research organization. Intangible assets, such as patents, copyrights, and trademarks, are also counted if used in connection with active programs.

A *functionally related business* is a department or separate entity that sells goods or renders services that accomplish the foundation's tax-exempt purposes. Technically, it should be treated for tax purposes as a related trade or business.[52] Although a functionally related business may coincidentally produce profits the foundation uses to pay for other exempt activities, its primary purpose must be to advance the foundation's charitable, educational, or other exempt purposes. A museum gift shop and a library's bookstore that sell educational materials are examples of functionally related businesses operated alongside the exempt activities. For example, a wholly owned, separately incorporated taxable entity that holds lodging facilities and other accommodations for rental to visitors to the foundation's historical area can qualify as

---

47. *See* § 6.2(c).
48. *See* § 6.2(d); Internal Revenue Manual 7.26.6.3.3.1.
49. Reg. § 53.4942(b)-2(a)(2)(i).
50. Rev. Rul. 82-137, 1982-2 C.B. 303.
51. *Id.*
52. *See* Chapter 11.

a functionally related business. Its value would be taken into account in calculating the asset test. The income from the property is included in adjusted net income required to be distributed.

The foundation may treat property it acquires for future active-program use as a qualifying asset even though it is rented, in whole or part, during the reasonable period of time it takes to make arrangements to use or otherwise ready the property for active use. One year is generally considered a reasonable time frame.

Rental property provided to tenants that serves to accomplish an exempt purpose (e.g., housing for low-income families, studio spaces for community art groups, or a hotel adjacent to the foundation's historical village) may be treated as an active-use asset in a specific circumstance—the rent is essentially below the prevailing market rate. The property is treated as an active-use asset if the rental income derived from the property is less than the amount that would be required to be charged in order to recover the cost of purchasing the property and annual upkeep and maintenance expenses, such as insurance and painting. Although the regulations provide no specific time frame permitted for the cost recovery, the number of years in which a prudent investor buying similar property in the same area would expect to recoup the investment should be acceptable. The equipment necessary to maintain a computerized database of information on endangered species, accessible on the Internet for a fee to those studying this subject, could also qualify under this test, dependent on the fee levels.

Conversely, loans receivable from members of a charitable class (students or minority business owners) or funds placed on deposit with a lending institution to guarantee these loans are not treated as actively used assets.[53] Even though the making of the loan itself is considered an active program expense, the loan itself, as an interest-bearing receivable, is not to be treated as devoted to active use. Similarly, program-related investments that produce investment income would not be treated as active-conduct assets. If the rate of interest is below market, a foundation might argue that the rule pertaining to below-market rental property be applied.

Funds set aside, or earmarked for specific active program expenditures in the future, are essentially treated as investment assets, so set-aside reserves are specifically not treated as active-use assets. Assets either acquired or disposed of during the year, and therefore held for less than a full year, are only partly includable in the asset test calculations. The included amount is the fractional part calculated by multiplying the asset's value times the ratio of the number of days in the year the assets were held, divided by 365 or 366.[54]

---

53. Reg. § 53.4942(b)-2(a)(2)(ii).
54. Reg. § 53.4942(b)-2(a)(3).

The asset test is calculated based on, as a general rule, the fair market value of the assets[55] and following the rules for determining the annual minimum investment return.[56] Certain active-use assets, according to the regulations, may not necessarily be capable of valuation using standard methods. Examples of these assets include art objects, historical buildings, and botanical gardens. Where the foundation can demonstrate that these special-purpose assets are not readily marketable, the asset's historical cost, unadjusted for depreciation, is the amount included to calculate satisfaction of the asset test.

**Endowment Test.** A private operating foundation satisfies the endowment test when it normally expends its funds, in the form of qualifying distributions, directly for the active conduct of its tax-exempt activities, in an amount equal to at least two thirds of its minimum investment return.[57] Thus, this payout requirement obligates the private operating foundation to distribute annually an amount equal to:

$3\frac{1}{3}\%$ ($\frac{2}{3}$ of 5%) of the value of investment or nonactive-use assets

The endowment test specifies a lower percentage than the income test, which requires at least 4.25 percent (85 percent × 5 percent) of the value of investment assets be distributed. Assume a private operating foundation has $10 million of investment assets at year-end. To satisfy the endowment test, however, it must spend $333,333 on active program expenditures. To satisfy the income test, this foundation must spend the lower of $425,000 (85 percent of 5 percent of $1 million), or 85 percent of its adjusted net income. Assume its adjusted net income is lower and equals $250,000. Based on these facts, it would be required by the income test to spend only $212,500 (85 percent of $250,000) on programs. Because its adjusted net income is lower than the minimum investment return, its distributions for endowment test purposes will exceed the amount required for income test purposes. Conversely, if its adjusted net income was greater than the minimum investment return, say $600,000, the direct expenditures required by the income test would automatically allow it to satisfy the endowment test.

The endowment test applies to determine qualification for foundations holding investment assets that amount to more than 35 percent of their total assets or, conversely, to a foundation with program or active-use assets equaling less than 65 percent of its total assets, as required to meet the asset test. Correspondingly, such a foundation's programs would typically be service

---

55. Reg. § 53.4942(b)-2(a)(4).
56. The valuation rules discussed in § 6.2 and applied for calculation of the minimum investment return are also used for this purpose.
57. Reg. § 53.4942(b)-2(b)(1).

intensive or product oriented, such as those of a self-help provider, educational publisher, or performing arts foundation that would normally have modest amounts of program assets in relation to its investment assets. The concept of expenditures directly for the active conduct of tax-exempt activities under the endowment test is the same as that under the income test.[58] The foundation is not required to trace the source of these expenditures to determine whether they were derived from investment income or from contributions.

An organization that, on May 26, 1969, and at all times after that date and before the close of the tax year involved, operated and maintained, as its principal functional purpose, facilities for the long-term care, comfort, maintenance, or education of permanently and totally disabled persons, elderly persons, needy widows, or children qualifies as an operating foundation if the organization meets the requirements of the endowment test.[59] This rule applies only for purposes of the foundation distributions to this type of organization and means they are determined as if the organization is not a private operating foundation (unless it meets a definition of a public or publicly supported charity or otherwise qualifies as a private operating foundation).

**Support Test.** The third alternative test imposes three concurrent tests, all of which must be met. The private operating foundation applying this test must satisfy each of these requirements:[60]

- Substantially all (85 percent) of its support (other than gross investment income) is normally received from the general public and from at least five tax-exempt organizations that are not disqualified persons[61] in respect to each other or the recipient private operating foundation.

- Not more than 25 percent of its support (other than gross investment income) is normally received from any one of these organizations.

- Not more than 50 percent of its support is normally received from gross investment income.

The support received by an organization from any one tax-exempt organization may be counted toward satisfaction of the support test only if the organization receives support from at least four other exempt organizations. The regulations permit an organization to receive support from five exempt organizations and no support from the general public, although the statute

---

58. Reg. § 53.4942(b)-1(b)(1); § 3.1(b).
59. IRC § 4942(j)(5).
60. IRC § 4942(j)(3)(B)(iii). Support for this purpose is defined by IRC § 509, discussed in Chapter 15.
61. IRC § 4946(a)(1)(H), discussed in Chapter 4.

appears to require both.[62] Support received from an individual, trust, or corporation (other than a tax-exempt organization) is taken into account as support from the general public only to the extent that the total amount received from any sources (including attributed sources) during the compliance period does not exceed 1 percent of the organization's total support (other than gross investment income) for the period. Support from a governmental unit, however, while treated as being from the general public, is not subject to this 1 percent limitation.[63]

Organizations meeting the support test have often developed an expertise in a particular area and thus are able to attract charitable contributions and grants from other foundations to enable them to sustain programs in their areas of specialization. Support received from related parties[64] is added to apply the 1 percent limitation so that their combined support is treated as if it were provided by one person.

## (f) Compliance Period

The income test and either the asset, endowment, or support test are applied each year for a four-year period that includes the current and past three years, although the methods may be alternated as respects a subsequent tax year.[65] The private operating foundation has a choice of two methods to calculate its compliance with the tests for each year:

1. All four years can be aggregated, that is, the distributions for four years are added together. The private operating foundation must use only one of the asset, endowment, or support tests for this aggregate test.

2. For three of the four years, the private operating foundation meets the income test and any one of the asset, endowment, or support tests.

Although a private operating foundation has a choice of method 1 (aggregation) or method 2 (three years out of four standing alone), the same method must be applied for purposes of calculating its income test and its asset, endowment, or support test for each year. There is no requirement in the regulations or the tax code that the foundation choosing to apply method 2 must make up any deficiency of active distributions in the one year they fail to meet the tests.[66] A private foundation that applies method 1 for measuring its qualification is essentially allowed to carry forward excess distributions from

---

62. Reg. § 53.4942(b)-2(c)(2)(iii).
63. Reg. § 53.4942(b)-2(c)(2)(iv).
64. As defined in IRC § 4946(a)(1)(C)-(G).
65. Reg. § 53.4942(b)-3(a).
66. *See* Priv. Ltr. Rul. 9509042.

one year. It is important to note, however, that use of the three-out-of-four-year method, or method 2, eliminates the benefit, or carryover, of any excess distributions from a prior year.

If the private operating foundation fails to qualify for a particular year, it is treated as an ordinary private foundation for that year. It can return to private operating foundation classification as soon as it again qualifies under both the income test and the asset, endowment, or support test. Importantly, distributions during that year would have to satisfy both the test for an ordinary PF status and its restored POF status. The tax on the failure to make qualifying distributions[67] does not apply to private operating foundations, and the deficiency of distributions need not be corrected.

New organizations generally are expected to meet the tests in their first year. Once a new organization satisfies the test in the first year, it continues to qualify for its second and third taxable years of existence only if it satisfies the dual tests described above by the aggregation method for all the years it has been in existence.[68]

A special rule allows the new foundation to be treated as qualifying if such organization has made a good faith determination that it is likely to satisfy both tests. If application for recognition of exemption is made prior to the completion of the proposed private operating foundation's first fiscal year, the IRS will accept the organization's assertion, based on a good faith and determination that it plans to qualify.[69] Form 1023 and its instructions contain a work paper for submitting the appropriate information, as shown in Exhibit 2.2, attachment for Part X, question 4. Failure in the first year can be remedied if the foundation does in fact qualify in its second, third, and fourth years.

Generally, the status of grants or contributions made to a private operating foundation is not affected until notice of change of status of the organization is communicated to the general public. This is not the case, however, if the grant or contribution was made after (1) the act or failure to act that resulted in the organization's inability to satisfy the requirements of one or more of the previously mentioned tests, and the grantor or contributor was responsible for or was aware of the act or failure to act, or (2) the grantor or contributor acquired knowledge that the IRS had given notice to the organization that it would be deleted from classification as a private operating foundation.[70] A grantor or contributor will not be deemed to have the requisite responsibility or awareness under the first of the aforementioned categories, however, if the grantor or contributor made his or her grant or contribution in reliance on a written statement by the grantee organization containing sufficient facts to the

---

67. IRC § 4942(2).
68. Reg. § 53.4942(b)-3(b).
69. Reg. § 53.4942(b)-3(b)(2).
70. Reg. § 53.4942(b)-3(d)(1).

effect that the grant or contribution would not result in the inability of the grantee organization to qualify as a private operating foundation.[71]

## (g)   Advantages and Disadvantages of Private Operating Foundations

Private operating foundations have certain advantages.

*Contribution Deduction Limits Are Preferential.* The percentage limits for charitable deductions are higher for private operating foundations than for private foundations and are the same as the deductions permitted for public charities. A full 50 percent of an individual's adjusted net income can be sheltered by cash contributions to an operating foundation, as compared with the 30 percent of one's adjusted net income that can be deducted for cash gifts to a standard private foundation.

A deduction is permitted, as a general rule, for the appreciation component of all types of property donated to a private operating foundation. The deduction for a gift of real estate, artwork, or other similar property to a normal private foundation is generally limited to the donor's tax basis in the property.[72] A special exception permits a deduction for the full fair market value of readily marketable securities.[73] With or without the exception, a gift of property to a private operating foundation is fully deductible, subject to the 30 percent limitation on capital gain property.

*Distribution Amount May Be Lower.* The minimum distribution requirement for an operating foundation may be lower than for standard private foundations. In some cases, given a sufficient return on investment, a private operating foundation can accumulate a higher endowment over the years.

Because a private operating foundation is required to meet the income tests described above for the active conduct of charitable purposes, it is not subject to the same minimum payout requirements imposed on standard private foundations. Moreover, a private operating foundation can be the recipient of grants from a standard private foundation without having to spend the funds within the following year, with the funds nevertheless qualifying as expenditures of income by the donating foundation for purposes of its mandatory distribution requirements.[74]

The income test requires an operating foundation to distribute only the 85 percent of the lower of its adjusted net income or its minimum investment return. Where the adjusted net income is less than the minimum investment return, the endowment test would require it pay out only $66\frac{2}{3}$ percent of its minimum investment return.[75]

---

71. Reg. § 53.4942(b)-3(d)(2).
72. IRC § 170(e)(1)(B)(ii). *See* § 14.4.
73. IRC § 170(e)(5).
74. *See* Chapter 6.
75. *See* § 3.1(d) and (e).

The primary disadvantage of a private operating foundation is loss of the one-year time delay afforded to normal private foundations in meeting the minimum distribution requirement. For each year, a private foundation calculates a minimum distribution requirement based on 5 percent of the average value of its investment assets for that year and has until the end of the next succeeding year to make qualifying distributions in that amount. The private operating foundation, instead, must meet the income test and the asset, endowment, or support test each year as of the last day of the particular year or cumulatively for three out of the four years then ended. The need to sustain self-initiated programs and manage the staff or volunteers that conduct the active projects is for some a disadvantage, or certainly a requirement that can be an obligation some funders wish to avoid.

A private foundation is required to serve as a conduit to enable a donor to receive a contribution deduction for gifts of certain appreciated property. Charitable contributions to conduit private foundations qualify as deductible items eligible for the 50 percent and 30 percent limitations.[76]

## (h) Conversion to or from Private Operating Foundation Status

An IRS advance ruling is not technically required for a private foundation to convert itself into an operating foundation or, conversely, for an operating foundation to become a standard private foundation, since the qualification is based on numerical tests. Any foundation is qualified if it meets the tests by changing its method of operation or mix of assets. Many directors and trustees, however, seek the comfort of an IRS determination to sanction the conversion. The impact of the conversion on the cumulative qualifying distribution tests must be reviewed.

An operating foundation must meet its minimum distribution requirements within the year; a private foundation, one year later, as discussed earlier. An operating foundation converting to a normal private foundation gains a one-year grace period; converting to an operating foundation accelerates required distributions. Funders of an operating foundation can be adversely affected by conversion to a private foundation. As explained above, an operating foundation is treated like a public charity for charitable donation percentage limitations, making donations to operating foundations more favorable. In view of the favorable deduction rule, conversion to an operating foundation can be an important consideration.

A private foundation can seek IRS approval for its conversion to a private operating foundation by submitting Form 8940 to the IRS Service Center in Cincinnati, Ohio, requesting a "reclassification of its foundation status." A $400 filing fee is required. A revised determination letter will be issued. A regular

---

76. IRC §§ 170(b)(1)(A)(vii), 170(b)(1)(E)(ii).

private foundation converting to a private operating foundation submits a completed Form 990-PF, Part XIV, Private Operating Foundation, reflecting its good faith determination that is will satisfy the requisite tests.[77] The Active Projects Fund application shown in Exhibit 2.2, attachment for Part X, question 4, can be referred to as a guide. A listing and description of distributions for the active conduct of its own programs or activities is requested.[78] The effective date for conversion to operating foundation classification is not clearly set out in the tax code or in the regulations. The calculations are made for the foundation's tax year essentially resulting in year-end conversions. The code simply provides that a private operating foundation must meet a *qualifying distribution test* by spending the requisite amount in support of its own projects and that it normally satisfy the asset test or the endowment test. A new organization submits an affidavit of its intention to so qualify as a private operating foundation prospectively before it conducts any activity. Special rules for organizations in existence in 1969 allowed a first-year effective date for qualification as a private operating foundation.[79] The requirements for a foundation converting to a private operating foundation are not mentioned.

The endowment test must be "normally" met.[80] The term *normally*, however, is essentially defined as the four-year compliance period.[81] An existing foundation does not get the fresh start permitted for new foundations. The IRS concluded that "a private foundation that has been in existence for at least four years and has not heretofore qualified for operating foundation status may satisfy the operating foundation requirements by showing that it has met the income test and one of the three alternative tests over a four-year period." Further, such a foundation will be "considered an operating foundation effective the final year of the four-year period."[82] Because a converting private foundation is not a new organization, this conclusion is logical. A foundation was able to qualify in the year of its conversion by receiving approval for a single, but substantial, set-aside to operate a facility to assist persons with limited employability due to temporary or permanent disabilities.[83] Despite the fact that it could not meet the tests during its first through third years, it met the test on an aggregate basis of all four years.

---

77. *See* § 3.1(d) and 3.1(e).
78. The instructions to the form also request a statement describing any adverse impact if you do not receive the requested status.
79. Reg. § 53.4942(b)-3(c).
80. IRC § 4942(j)(3).
81. *See* § 3.1(f).
82. IRS Exempt Organizations CPE Technical Program textbook for Fiscal Year 1984, at 249, citing Reg. § 53.4942-3(a).
83. Priv. Ltr. Rul. 9108001. A set-aside for summer enrichment program scholarships was approved by the IRS (Priv. Ltr. Rul. 9018033).

The four-year time frame for a change in classification established by the regulations can be frustrating to a foundation funder whose charitable deduction limitations would be improved by the conversion. Assume a calendar-year foundation makes a decision to start a conversion in June and by year-end has made the level of direct program expenditures required to qualify as an operating foundation. Even though it had not yet made direct expenditures during the period January through May, the entire year will be counted. Nonetheless, a donation of noncash assets, such as land or art, prior to the end of the fourth year is not eligible for the more generous deduction limitations afforded to a private operating foundation.[84] This timing can be important to a foundation that plans the conversion to make use of appreciated assets its funders wish to donate.

New operating foundations generally must meet the special test in their first year. If application for exemption is made prior to the completion of the proposed operating foundation's first fiscal year, the IRS will accept the organization's assertion, based on a good faith determination, that it plans to qualify.[85] Form 1023 and its instructions contain a work paper for submitting the appropriate information. Failure in the first year may be remedied if the operating foundation does in fact qualify in its second, third, and fourth years, or based on an average of the years. A new operating foundation delayed in the commencement of its active programs might qualify to use the *cash distribution test*.[86] If the operating foundation fails to qualify in one particular year, it is treated as an ordinary private foundation for that year. It can return to operating foundation classification as soon as it again qualifies under both the income test and the asset, endowment, or support test.

## (i) Exempt Operating Foundations

Certain private foundations are able to qualify as *exempt operating foundations*.[87] These entities are exempt from the tax on private foundations' net investment income and from the requirement that grants to them must be the subject of expenditure responsibility,[88] which constitutes the meaning of the term *exempt* in this context.

An exempt operating foundation is one that qualifies as a private operating foundation, has been publicly supported for at least 10 years, has a board of directors that is representative of the public and most of whom are not disqualified individuals, and does not have an officer who is a disqualified individual.

---

84. *See* §§ 3.1(g), § 14.4.
85. Reg. § 53.4942(b)-3; *see* Exhibit 2.3.
86. *See* Chapter 6.
87. IRC § 4940(d).
88. The expenditure responsibility requirements are the subject of § 9.6.

## § 3.2   CONDUIT FOUNDATIONS

A standard private foundation (i.e., not a private operating foundation) becomes a *conduit foundation* for any year in which it makes qualifying distributions,[89] which are treated[90] as distributions out of corpus,[91] in an amount equal in value to 100 percent of contributions received in the year involved, whether as cash or property.[92] To enable the donor to claim a charitable deduction, the distributions must be made not later than the fifteenth day of the third month after the close of the private foundation's tax year in which the contributions were received, and the private foundation must not have any remaining undistributed income for the year. The point is any current-year qualifying distributions are first offset against the amount required to be paid out based on the prior year calculations. In a sense, the conduit-type private foundation is not a separate category of private foundation but is instead a term used to refer to a treatment given a particular type of contribution to a private foundation.

A foundation may be a conduit foundation for only that year when it receives a donation for which the donor desires a higher deduction limitation. A conduit foundation is sometimes referred to as a "pass-through foundation" because it usually receives, but does not keep, and instead redistributes donations. As discussed below, a foundation with an excess distributions carryover may use the excess to satisfy the redistribution requirement. Status as a conduit foundation applies on a year-by-year basis. The election to treat the gifts as being made out of corpus does not impact the succeeding year distributions.

The qualifying distribution may be of the contributed property itself, the proceeds of the sale of contributed property, or cash or other assets of the foundation of equal value. In making the calculation in satisfaction of the 100 percent requirement, the amount of this fair market value may be reduced by any reasonable selling expenses incurred by the foundation in the sale of the contributed property. An excise tax, however, will be due on any gain from the sale.

This tax is not imposed if the property is redistributed rather than sold.[93] Moreover, at the choice of the private foundation, if the contributed property is sold or distributed within 30 days of its receipt by the private foundation, the amount of the fair market value is either the gross amount received on the

---

89. IRC § 4942(g), other than IRC § 4942(g)(3). In general, *see* Chapter 6.
90. This treatment is after the application of IRC § 4942(g)(3). This means that every contribution described in IRC § 4942(g)(3) (*see* § 6.2) received by the conduit foundation in a particular tax year must be distributed by it by the fifteenth day of the third month after the close of that year in order for any other distribution by the foundation to be counted toward the 100 percent requirement.
91. IRC § 4942(h); *see* § 12.2(k).
92. IRC § 170(b)(1)(E)(ii); Reg. § 1.170A-9(g)(1).
93. *See* § 10.4(b).

sale of the property (less reasonable selling expenses) or an amount equal to the fair market value of the property on the date of its distribution to a public charity.[94]

Excess distribution carryovers[95] can also be counted as a qualifying distribution by a conduit foundation.[96] The regulations allow a foundation to elect to treat as a current distribution out of corpus any amount distributed within one of the five prior taxable years, which was treated as a distribution out of corpus, and not availed of for any other purpose.

A conduit foundation must attach a statement to Form 990-PF for the year in which it treats distributions as being made out of corpus for purposes of permitting a donor to claim a full fair market deduction.

These distributions are treated as made first out of contributions of property and then out of contributions of cash received by the private foundation in the year involved. The distributions cannot be made to an organization controlled directly or indirectly by the private foundation or by one or more disqualified persons[97] with respect to the private foundation or to a private foundation that is not a private operating foundation.

These rules may be illustrated by the following example:

> X is a private foundation reporting on a calendar-year basis. As of January 1, 2014, X had no undistributed income for 2013. X's distributable amount for 2014 was $600,000. In July 2014, A, an individual, contributed $500,000 of appreciated property (which, if sold, would give rise to long-term capital gain) to X. X did not receive any other contributions in either 2013 or 2014. During 2014, X made qualifying distributions of $700,000, which were treated as made out of the undistributed income for 2014 (of $600,000) and the balance ($100,000) out of corpus. The gift will qualify as made to a conduit foundation for 2014 if the private foundation made additional qualifying distributions of $400,000 out of corpus by March 15, 2015.
>
> If the facts were as stated in the preceding description, except that as of January 1, 2014, X had $100,000 of undistributed income for 2013, the $700,000 distributed by X in 2014 would be treated as made out of the undistributed income for 2013 and 2014 ($700,000). X would, therefore, have had to make additional qualifying distributions of $500,000 out of corpus between January 1, 2015, and March 15, 2015, if X was to qualify as a conduit foundation for 2015.[98]
>
> If the facts were as stated in the foregoing paragraph, but the calendar years involved were 2016 and 2017 (or subsequent years) (assuming the law does not change), the qualifying distributions that would otherwise have to total $500,000 may be less than that amount if the contributed property is sold or distributed within 30 days of its receipt by the private foundation.

---

94. Reg. § 1.170A-9(g)(2)(iv).
95. *See* § 6.6.
96. Reg. § 53.4942(a)-3(c)(2)(iv).
97. *See* Chapter 4.
98. Reg. § 1.170A-9(g)(4).

The contributor must obtain adequate records or other sufficient evidence from the private foundation showing that the private foundation made the qualifying distributions.[99] The value of the contributed property will be included in the calculation of the foundation's distributable income for the period of time it holds the property between receipt of the gift and redistribution of either the property itself, cash equal to the fair market value of the property, or proceeds of sale of the property.[100] To offset what might appear to be an unfair result, the foundation may retain any income earned on the property during the time it holds the gift. The donor receives a charitable deduction for a gift of this nature, as if the gift were to a public charity, assuming the special rule is elected; the IRS can exercise its discretionary authority to grant relief to extend the time needed to make the election.

## § 3.3  COMMON FUND FOUNDATIONS

A special type of standard private foundation (i.e., one not a private operating foundation) is one that pools contributions received in a common fund but allows the donor or his or her spouse (including substantial contributors)[101] to retain the right to designate annually the organizations to which the income attributable to the contributions is given (as long as the organizations qualify as certain types of entities that are not private foundations)[102] and to designate (by deed or will) the organizations to which the corpus of the contributions is eventually to be given. Moreover, this type of private foundation must pay out its adjusted net income to public charities by the fifteenth day of the third month after the close of the tax year in which the income is realized by the fund, and the corpus must be distributed to these charities within one year after the death of the donor or his or her spouse.[103]

In the sole instance of the IRS to publicly rule on the status of a private foundation as a common fund private foundation, the IRS considered a tax-exempt trust that was operated, supervised, and controlled by the distribution committee of a community trust.[104] Its function was to receive and pool contributions and to distribute its income to public and publicly supported charities. Every donor had the right to designate the charitable recipients of the trust's income and of the corpus of the fund attributable to his or her contribution. All of the other requirements of the common fund foundation rules were satisfied in this instance, and, therefore, the IRS concluded that the trust

---

99. Reg. § 1.170A- 9(g) (1), Examples (1) and (2); *see* also Priv. Ltr. Rul. 200311033.
100. *See* § 6.2.
101. *See* § 4.1.
102. IRC § 509(a)(1). *See* §§ 1.1 and 1.2.
103. IRC § 170(b)(1)(E)(iii).
104. *See* § 15.4(d).

qualified as a common fund private foundation.[105] (Were it not for the fact that the donors had the right to designate the recipients, the trust would have qualified as a supporting organization[106] and not as a private foundation.)

Contributions to this type of private foundation qualify for the 50 percent and 30 percent limitations on the charitable deduction.[107]

## §3.4  RESEARCH AND EXPERIMENTATION FUNDS

One of the purposes of Congress in enacting the Economic Recovery Tax Act of 1981 was to provide incentives for an increase in the conduct of research and experimentation. Consequently, a tax credit was created for certain research and experimental expenditures paid in carrying on a trade or business.[108] The tax credit is allowable to the extent that current-year expenditures exceed the average amount of research expenditures in a base period (generally, the preceding three tax years). Subject to certain exclusions, the term *qualified research* used for purposes of the tax credit is the same as that used for purposes of the deduction rules for research expenses.[109]

Research expenditures qualifying for this tax credit consist of two basic types: in-house research expenses and contract research expenses. In-house research expenditures are those for research wages and supplies, along with certain lease or other charges for research use of computers, laboratory equipment, and the like. Contract research expenditures are 65 percent of amounts paid to another person (for example, a research firm or university) for research.

A tax credit is also available for 65 percent of an amount paid by a corporation to a qualified organization for basic research to be performed by the recipient organization, where the relationship is evidenced by a written research agreement. (This research is a form of contract research.) The term *basic research* means "any original investigation for the advancement of scientific knowledge not having a specific commercial objective, except that such term shall not include (A) basic research conducted outside the United States, and (B) basic research in the social sciences or humanities."[110]

For purposes of the rules concerning basic contract research, a *qualified organization* is either (1) an institution of higher education[111] that is a tax-exempt

---

105. Rev. Rul. 80-305, 1980-2 C.B. 71.
106. *See* § 15.7.
107. IRC §§ 170(b)(1)(A)(vii), 170(b)(1)(E)(iii).
108. IRC § 41.
109. A taxpayer may elect to deduct currently the amount of research or experimental expenditures incurred in connection with the taxpayer's trade or business or may elect to amortize certain research costs over a period of at least 60 months (IRC § 174). These rules apply to the costs of research conducted on behalf of the taxpayer by a research firm, university, or the like.
110. IRC § 41.
111. IRC § 3304(f).

educational organization[112] or (2) any other type of charitable, educational, scientific, or similar tax-exempt organization[113] that is organized and operated primarily to conduct scientific research and is not a private foundation.[114]

A special provision allows certain funds organized and operated exclusively to make basic research grants to institutions of higher education to be considered as qualifying organizations, even though the funds do not themselves perform the research. To qualify, a fund must be a charitable, educational, scientific, or similar tax-exempt organization, not be a private foundation, be established and maintained by an organization that is a public or publicly supported charity and was created prior to July 10, 1981, and make its grants under written research agreements. Moreover, a fund must elect to become this type of a qualified fund; by making the election, the fund becomes treated as a private foundation, except that the investment income excise tax[115] is not applicable.[116]

Thus Congress has created a category of organizations that, because of the nature of their programs (rather than the nature of their support or degree of public involvement), are regarded as private foundations. Apparently, this status as a private foundation continues only as long as the fund makes the qualified basic research grants, and the fund can revert to a form of public charity when and if it ceases making the grants.

## §3.5 OTHER TYPES OF FOUNDATIONS

The *community foundation* is in essence a fund created by contributions to support charitable activities primarily in a single geographical area. This type of organization is not a private foundation but, rather, a publicly supported charity.[117] These foundations customarily create donor-advised funds that accept gifts subject to the donor's right to recommend recipients of distributions from their fund. Importantly the community foundation retains dominion and

---

112. IRC § 170(b)(A)(ii). *See* § 1.5.

113. IRC § 501(c)(3).

114. One of the questions thus posed by this provision is whether private operating foundations (*see supra* § 1) are eligible to participate in this contract research program. Certainly these types of foundations that conduct their own research should be qualified organizations for this purpose, notwithstanding the general prohibition against the involvement of private foundations (IRC § 41(e)(6)(B)(iii)). By contrast, for purposes of the provision allowing an estate and gift tax charitable contribution deduction for the transfer of a work of art to a qualified charitable organization, irrespective of whether the copyright therein is simultaneously transferred to the charitable organization, a private operating foundation is expressly included as a qualified organization (IRC § 2055(e)(4)(D)) even though "private foundations" are excluded.

115. IRC § 4940. *See* Chapter 10.

116. Once this election is made, it can be revoked only with the consent of the IRS.

117. *See* § 15.4(d)

control over decisions regarding the distributions.[118] Some financial institutions, including Schwab, Fidelity, and Vanguard, have obtained IRS recognition for their donor-advised funds.

Many for-profit corporations have related foundations that perform charitable activities (e.g., research, community development) that are related to the business of or undertaken with use of the name of the corporation. These are almost always private foundations.

Most public colleges and universities have related foundations, usually public charities, used to attract charitable contributions for activities of the respective institutions.[119] Comparable organizations are often created for private educational institutions, hospitals, and other institutions, but these entities usually find their nonprivate foundation designation under the general rules for publicly supported or supporting organizations.[120] These organizations are almost never private foundations.

Trusts that are not exempt from federal tax are generally subjected to the same requirements and restrictions that are applicable to private foundations if they have any unexpired interests that are devoted to charitable purposes.[121] The reason for this rule is to prevent these trusts from being used to avoid certain requirements and restrictions imposed on private foundations.[122] Many of the private foundation rules are applicable to nonexempt trusts, in which all or part of the unexpired interests are devoted to one or more charitable purposes—certain *charitable trusts* and *split-interest trusts*. The basic purpose of this requirement is to prevent these trusts from being used to avoid the requirements and restrictions applicable to private foundations.[123]

## §3.6  NONEXEMPT CHARITABLE TRUSTS

For certain purposes,[124] a nonexempt charitable trust is treated as an organization that is a charitable entity. This type of trust[125] is a trust that is not tax-exempt, all of the unexpired interests in which are devoted to one or more charitable purposes, and for which a deduction is allowed.[126]

---

118. *See* Chapter 16.
119. IRC § 170(b)(1)(A)(iv). *See* § 15.3(d).
120. This type of organization would find its public or publicly supported charity status under IRC § 170(b)(1)(A)(vi), 509(a)(2), or 509(a)(3); *see* § 15.4.
121. IRC § 4947. *See* §§ 3.6, 3.7.
122. IRC § 4947.
123. Reg. § 53.4947-1(a). E.g., the discussion in *Peters v. United States*, 624 F.2d 1020 (Ct. Cl. 1980).
124. IRC §§ 507–509 (except IRC § 508(a)–(c)), 4940–4948.
125. IRC § 4947(a)(1).
126. The deduction is that allowed by IRC §§ 170, 545(b)(2), 556(b)(2), 642(c), 2055, 2106(a)(2), or 2522. Reg. § 53.4947-1(b)(1).

This rule for charitable trusts usually applies to trusts in which all unexpired interests consist only of charitable income and remainder interests (regardless of whether the trustee is required to distribute corpus to, or hold corpus in trust for the benefit of, any remainder beneficiary) or to trusts in which all unexpired interests consist of charitable remainder interests where the trustee is required to hold corpus in trust for the benefit of any charitable remainder beneficiary. An estate from which the executor or administrator is required to distribute all of the net assets (free of trust) to charitable beneficiaries is generally not considered to be a charitable trust during the period of estate administration or settlement. However, in the case of an estate from which the executor or administrator is required to distribute all of the net assets (free of trust) to charitable beneficiaries, if the estate is considered terminated for federal income tax purposes,[127] then the estate will be treated as a charitable trust between the date on which the estate is considered terminated and the date on which final distribution of all of the net assets is made to the charitable beneficiaries. Similarly, in the case of a trust in which all of the unexpired interests are charitable remainder interests that have become entitled to distributions of corpus (free of trust) upon the termination of all intervening noncharitable interests, if after the termination of the intervening interests the trust is considered terminated for federal income tax purposes,[128] the trust will be treated as a charitable trust, rather than a split-interest trust,[129] between the date on which the trust is considered terminated and the date on which final distribution (free of trust) of all of the net assets is made to the charitable remainder beneficiaries.[130]

As noted, a nonexempt charitable trust is treated as a charitable organization. As discussed, an organization that is a charitable entity is a private foundation unless it meets the requirements of one or more rules by which private foundation classification is avoided.[131] Therefore, a nonexempt charitable trust is considered to be a private foundation unless it meets one of these requirements. A nonexempt charitable trust that was originally a private foundation and subsequently became qualified as a public or publicly supported charity must first terminate its private foundation status[132] before it can

---

127. Reg. § 1.641(b)-3(a).
128. Reg. § 1.641(b)-3(b).
129. *See* § 3.7.
130. Reg. § 53.4947-1(b)(2). By enactment of legislation in 1980 (P. L. 96-603, 96th Cong., 2d Sess. (1980)), Congress subjected nonexempt charitable trusts to the same reporting and disclosure requirements as are imposed on tax-exempt charitable organizations. Also Reg. § 1.6012-3(a)(7).
131. *See* Chapter 15.
132. *See* Chapter 13.

be excluded from private foundation status as a public or publicly supported entity.[133]

The regulations accompanying these statutory rules[134] state that, for these purposes, the term *charitable* includes not only the conventional tax law meaning of the term[135] but the meaning for governmental purposes[136] as well. A court held that the government cannot validly enforce this broadened definition and that a trust that was established in part to further "public" purposes is not an "exclusively charitable" entity and thus not subject to the private foundation requirements.[137]

Not every trust with charitable beneficiaries constitutes a nonexempt charitable trust. The IRS occasionally rules that a trust will not be treated as a private foundation by virtue of these rules.[138]

A nonexempt charitable trust must pay normal income tax.[139] This type of trust, all of the unexpired interests of which are devoted to charity, is treated as a charitable organization if tax deductions were allowed for gifts to it.[140] Therefore, it is not qualified as tax-exempt until it seeks recognition of its tax-exempt status by filing Form 1023.[141] Until it files for exemption, it is a taxable entity. Unless it was created prior to 1970 or meets the organizational provision described below, the charitable contribution deduction of a nonexempt charitable trust is limited to 50 percent of its income in calculating its taxable income.[142] Thus, even if, pursuant to its governing instrument, it pays out all of its income to another charitable organization, half of its income is taxed when it files Form 1041.

A nonexempt charitable trust is subject to all of the rules applicable to private foundations.[143] It must file Form 990-PF[144] and pay an excise tax on its investment income. Additionally, it must file Form 1041 and pay normal income tax if it has any taxable income. An unlimited deduction, rather than the 50 percent of income limit, applies to nonexempt trusts that meet the

---

133. Rev. Rul. 76-92, 1971-1 C.B. 92.
134. Reg. § 53.4947-1(a).
135. IRC § 170(c)(2).
136. IRC § 170(c)(1).
137. *Hammond v. United States*, 84-1 U.S.T.C. ¶ 9387 (D. Conn. 1984), *aff'd*, 764 F.2d 88 (2d Cir.1985). In general, Appert, "Nonexempt Charitable Trusts under the Tax Reform Act of 1969," 25 *Tax Lawyer* 99 (1971).
138. E.g., Priv. Ltr. Rul. 9742006.
139. IRC § 4940(b).
140. IRC § 4947(a)(1).
141. IRC 508(a); effective retroactively to date of creation of the trust if the application is filed within 27 months of its creation.
142. IRC § 642(c)(6) refers to IRC § 170 limitations.
143. *See* Chapters 4–10.
144. IRC § 6033(d).

organizational rules for qualifying as a private foundation.[145] Form 1041 need not be filed if the trust has no taxable income under Subtitle A of the Code.[146] When the IRS receives Form 990-PF from a nonexempt trust, it customarily requests that the trust file Form 1023 to establish its tax-exempt status.[147]

The IRS, from time to time, issues rulings classifying a trust as a nonexempt charitable trust.[148]

## § 3.7 SPLIT-INTEREST TRUSTS

Certain of the private foundation rules likewise apply to nonexempt split-interest trusts.[149] A *split-interest trust* is a trust that is not tax-exempt, not all of the unexpired interests in which are devoted to one or more charitable purposes, and that has amounts in trust for which a deduction was allowed.[150] This type of trust is subject to the termination rules, the organizational requirements to the extent applicable, the self-dealing rules, the excess business holdings rules, the jeopardizing investments rules, and the taxable expenditures rules, as if it were a private foundation.[151]

The foregoing rule is inapplicable to any amounts payable under the terms of a split-interest trust to income beneficiaries, unless a charitable deduction was allowed[152] with respect to the income interest of any beneficiary.[153] The rule is inapplicable to any assets held in trust (together with the income and capital gains derived from the assets), other than assets held in trust with respect to

---

145. Under IRC § 642(c), an income tax deduction is allowed for amounts paid or permanently set aside (including income) for charitable purposes, without limitation, pursuant to the terms of the governing instrument. *See* § 1.7; an unlimited charitable deduction should be available to those nonexempt trusts located in states that automatically impose the organizational requirements.

146. Rev. Proc. 83-32 and instructions to Form 990-PF for 2013.

147. In INFO 2000-0260 (released December 29, 2000), the IRS discussed a social welfare organization claiming, on the Form 990 that it filed, to qualify as an IRC § 501(c)(4) organization. The IRS stated that it will not accept returns filed by organizations that have not filed Form 1024. IRC § 508, which requires Form 1023 be filed by charities seeking recognition as 501(c)(3) organizations, has no counterpart for other categories of exempt organizations. Thus, the IRS was attempting to force organizations to file Form 1024, even though they are not, by law, required to do so, as a condition for accepting their Form 990s. It is understood that this policy (which was wholly contrary to law) has been abandoned.

148. E.g., Priv. Ltr. Rul. 200043051.

149. IRC § 4947(a)(2).

150. *See supra* note 118. The IRS ruled that an ordinary complex trust (IRC § 661 et seq.) was not a split-interest trust simply because the trust proposed to make income distributions to charitable organizations (Priv. Ltr. Rul. 200714025).

151. Reg. § 53.4947-1(c)(1). For these rules, *see* Chapters 13, 1, 5, 7, 8, and 9, respectively.

152. IRC §§ 170(f)(2)(B), 2055(e)(2)(B), or 2522(c)(2)(B).

153. IRC § 4947(a)(2)(A), Reg. § 53.4947-1(c)(2).

which a deduction was allowed,[154] if the other amounts are segregated from the assets for which no deduction was allowable.[155] For these purposes, a trust with respect to which amounts are segregated must separately account for the various income, deductions, and other items properly attributable to each segregated asset in the books of account and separately to each of the beneficiaries of the trusts.[156] If any amounts held in trust are segregated, the value of the net assets for purposes of the termination rules[157] is limited to the segregated amounts.[158] The foregoing is inapplicable to any amounts transferred in trust before May 27, 1969.[159]

In the case of a trust created before May 27, 1969, the trust can avoid the private foundation rules if it can establish that it is a split-interest trust rather than a charitable trust. The issue in this instance is likely to be whether there is a noncharitable beneficiary of the trust. One opinion concerned a pre-1969 trust that was established to run a business following the owner's death, with income made available to both the company and a private foundation; the court gave an expansive reading to the term *beneficial interest*, writing that it means any right given by a trust instrument to receive a benefit from the trust in some contingency.[160] In that case, the company was held to be a noncharitable beneficiary of the trust, causing the trust to thus be a split-interest trust and not subject to the private foundation requirements.

Notwithstanding the foregoing, the excess business holdings rules[161] and the jeopardizing investment rules[162] do not apply to a split-interest trust if:

- All the income interest[163] (and none of the remainder interest) of the trust is devoted solely to one or more charitable purposes, and all amounts in the trust for which a deduction was allowed[164] have an aggregate value (at the time the deduction was allowed) of not more than 60 percent of the aggregate fair market value of all amounts in the trust (after the payment of estate taxes and all other liabilities), or

---

154. *See supra* note 118.
155. IRC § 4947(a)(2)(B), Reg. § 53.4947-1(c)(3).
156. IRC § 4947(a)(3), Reg. § 53.4947-1(c)(3).
157. IRC § 507(c)(2), (g). *See* Chapter 13.
158. Reg. § 53.4947-2(a).
159. IRC § 4947(a)(2)(C), Reg. § 53.4947-1(c)(5).
160. *Hammond v. United States*, 84-1 U.S.T.C. ¶ 9387 (D. Conn. 1984), *aff'd*, 764 F. 2d 88 (2d Cir. 1985).
161. *See* Chapter 7.
162. *See* Chapter 8.
163. Reg. § 53.4947-2(b)(2)(i).
164. *See supra* note 118.

- A deduction was allowed under one of these provisions for amounts payable under the terms of the trust to every remainder beneficiary but not to any income beneficiary.[165]

An estate from which the executor or administrator is required to distribute all of the net assets in trust or free of trust to both charitable and noncharitable beneficiaries is generally not considered to be a split-interest trust during the period of estate administration or settlement.[166] When the estate is terminated, it is treated as a split-interest trust (or, if applicable, a charitable trust)[167] between the date on which the estate is considered terminated and the date on which final distribution of the net assets to the last remaining charitable beneficiary is made.[168]

Once all of the noncharitable interests in a split-interest trust expire, the trust becomes a (nonexempt) charitable trust.[169]

Not every trust with charitable beneficiaries constitutes a split-interest trust. The IRS occasionally rules that a trust will not be treated as a private foundation by virtue of these rules.[170]

## § 3.8  FOREIGN PRIVATE FOUNDATIONS

In lieu of the tax on the net investment income of private foundations,[171] there is, for each tax year, on the gross investment income[172] derived from sources within the United States,[173] by every foreign organization that is a private foundation for the year, a tax equal to 4 percent of income.[174] A *foreign organization*, for these purposes, means any organization that was not created or organized in the United States or any U.S. possession, or under the law of the United States, any state, the District of Columbia, or any possession of the United States.[175]

Whenever a tax treaty exists between the United States and a foreign country, and a foreign private foundation subject to these rules is a resident of that country or is otherwise entitled to the benefits of the treaty, if the

---

165. IRC § 4947(b)(3); Reg. § 53.4947- 2(b)(1). The term *income beneficiary* is defined in Reg. § 53.4947-2(b)(2)(ii).
166. Reg. § 53.4947-1(c)(6)(i).
167. *See* § 13.1.
168. Reg. § 4947-1(c)(6)(ii).
169. E.g., Priv. Ltr. Rul. 8220101.
170. E.g., Priv. Ltr. Rul. 9742006.
171. *See* Chapter 10.
172. IRC § 4940(c)(2). Also Rev. Rul. 72-244, 1972-1 C.B. 282.
173. IRC § 861.
174. IRC § 4948(a).
175. Reg. § 53.4948-1(a)(1). Also IRC § 170(c)(2)(A).

treaty provides that any item or items of gross investment income are exempt from income tax, the item or items need not be taken into account by the private foundation in computing the foreign foundation tax.[176] Thus, Canadian private foundations, exempt from the Canadian income tax and qualifying under the rules for charitable organizations generally, are exempt from the foreign private foundation tax by virtue of the U.S.-Canada Income Tax Convention.[177] The U.S.–Canadian tax treaty presumes that Canadian charities that can qualify as public charities are to be treated as private foundations unless they seek recognition of public status.[178] Nonetheless, a foreign charitable organization (private or public) is required to file Form 990 or 990-PF only when its U.S. source gross income exceeds $25,000 and it has significant U.S. activity.[179] By contrast, a Belgian foundation, which derived only interest income from the United States, was ruled to not be exempt from the foreign private foundation tax because neither the U.S.-Belgium Income Tax Convention nor the Treaty of Friendship, Establishment, and Navigation with the Kingdom of Belgium provides the requisite exemption.[180]

The termination tax[181] and notice requirements[182] of the special organizational rules[183] and the sanctions imposed on domestic private foundations[184] are inapplicable to any foreign organization that, from the date of its creation, has received substantially all (i.e., at least 85 percent) of its support (other than gains from sale of capital assets) from sources outside the United States.[185] For this purpose, gifts, grants, contributions, or membership fees directly or indirectly from a United States person[186] are from sources within the United States.[187]

A foreign organization that can qualify for classification as a public charity, however, can be excused from the rules pertaining to private foundations. A foreign public charity can seek a determination of its qualification as a public charity by filing an application for recognition of exemption.[188]

---

176. Reg. § 53.4948-1(a)(3).
177. Rev. Rul. 74-183, 1974-1 C.B. 328.
178. The implication of this notice is discussed in § 2.5.
179. Rev. Proc. 94-17, 1994-1 C.B. 579.
180. Rev. Rul. 76-330, 1976-2 C.B. 488; Rev. Rul. 77-289, 1977-2 C.B. 490.
181. *See* § 13.5.
182. *See* § 2.6.
183. *See* § 1.6.
184. *See* Chapters 5–9.
185. IRC § 4948(b).
186. IRC § 7701(a)(30).
187. Reg. § 53.4948-1(b).
188. Rev. Rul. 66-177, 1966-1 C.B. 132; Form 1023 is discussed and illustrated in § 2.5.

Though it does not become eligible to receive donations deductible for U.S. income tax purposes,[189] it will receive proof of its eligibility to receive deductible donations for gift and estate tax purposes. If it wishes to seek funding from U.S. private foundations, it will also have proof that it qualifies as a public charity so that foundation grantees need not exercise expenditure responsibility nor require an affidavit of public charity equivalency in regard to grants it receives.[190] Finally, the foreign organization can claim exemption from the withholding tax on any U.S. source investment income that will be paid at the normal rate of 4 percent absent proof of exemption.[191]

Nonetheless, a foreign private foundation is not regarded as a tax-exempt organization if it has engaged in a *prohibited transaction* after December 31, 1969.[192] A *prohibited transaction*[193] is any act or failure to act (other than in respect to the minimum investment return requirements)[194] that would subject the private foundation or a disqualified person[195] in respect to it, to a penalty in respect to any private foundation excise tax liability[196] or a termination tax[197] if the private foundation were a domestic private foundation.[198]

A foreign private foundation will be denied exemption from taxation for all tax years beginning with the tax year during which it is notified by the IRS that it has engaged in a prohibited transaction.[199] In the case of an act or failure to act, before giving notice the IRS will warn the foreign private foundation that the act or failure to act may be treated as a prohibited transaction. The act or failure to act will not, however, be treated as a prohibited transaction if it is corrected within 90 days after the issuing of the warning. The organization may, in respect to the second tax year following the tax year in which it was given a prohibited transaction notice, apply for tax exemption. If the IRS is satisfied that the organization will not knowingly again engage in a prohibited transaction, the organization will be so notified in writing. In that case, the organization will not, in respect to tax years beginning with the tax year in respect to which a claim for tax exemption is filed, be denied exemption from taxation by reason of any prohibited transaction that was engaged in before the date on which notice was given.[200]

---

189. IRC § 170(c).
190. *See* §§ 6.5, 9.5.
191. Gen. Couns. Mem. 38840.
192. IRC § 4948(c)(1).
193. IRC § 4948(c)(2).
194. *See* Chapter 6.
195. *See* Chapter 4.
196. IRC § 6684.
197. *See* Chapter 13.
198. *See* Reg. § 53.4948-1(c)(2).
199. IRC § 4948(c)(3).
200. Reg. § 53.4948-1(c)(3).

No gift, bequest, legacy, devise, or transfer will give rise to a charitable contribution deduction if made to a foreign private foundation in two circumstances. One is where the transaction occurred after the date on which the IRS published notice that it notified the organization that it engaged in a prohibited transaction. The other is where the transaction took place in a tax year of the organization for which it is not exempt from taxation by reason of having engaged in a prohibited transaction.[201]

---

201. IRC § 4948(c)(4), Reg. § 53.4948-1(d).

# CHAPTER FOUR

# Disqualified Persons

A basic concept of the tax laws relating to private foundations is that of the *disqualified person.* An understanding of the meaning of this term is essential to appreciation of the scope of the rules defining permitted sources, controlled organizations, prohibited self-dealing, and the other private foundation rules. Essentially, a disqualified person is a person[1] (including an individual, corporation, partnership, trust, estate, or other private foundation) standing in one or more particular relationships with respect to a private foundation, its trustees, and its founders.

## § 4.1  SUBSTANTIAL CONTRIBUTORS

One category of disqualified person[2] is a *substantial contributor* to a private foundation.[3] The term means any person who contributed[4] or bequeathed an aggregate amount of more than the higher of 2 percent of the total contributions and bequests received by the private foundation before the close of its tax year in which the contribution or bequest is received by the private foundation from that person or $5,000 to the private foundation. In computing the $5,000/2 percent threshold, all contributions and bequests to the private foundation since its creation are taken into account. The following example illustrates this rule:[5]

> Individual A, on January 1, 2014, contributes $3,000 to private foundation M (the tax year of which is the calendar year). This is A's first gift to M. As of that date, M has

---

1. IRC § 7701(a)(1).
2. IRC § 4946(a)(1)(A).
3. IRC § 507(d)(2)(A).
4. Reg. § 1.507- 6(c).
5. *See* Exhibit 4.1.

# DISQUALIFIED PERSONS

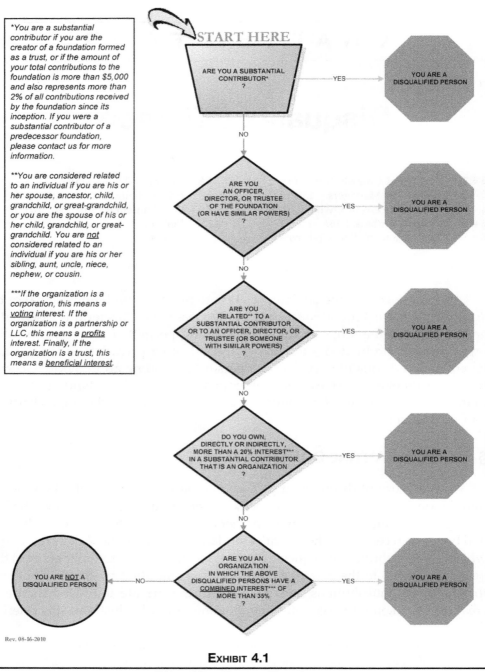

*You are a substantial contributor if you are the creator of a foundation formed as a trust, or if the amount of your total contributions to the foundation is more than $5,000 and also represents more than 2% of all contributions received by the foundation since its inception. If you were a substantial contributor of a predecessor foundation, please contact us for more information.

**You are considered related to an individual if you are his or her spouse, ancestor, child, grandchild, or great-grandchild, or you are the spouse of his or her child, grandchild, or great-grandchild. You are not considered related to an individual if you are his or her sibling, aunt, uncle, niece, nephew, or cousin.

***If the organization is a corporation, this means a voting interest. If the organization is a partnership or LLC, this means a profits interest. Finally, if the organization is a trust, this means a beneficial interest.

START HERE

ARE YOU A SUBSTANTIAL CONTRIBUTOR* ? — YES → YOU ARE A DISQUALIFIED PERSON

NO

ARE YOU AN OFFICER, DIRECTOR, OR TRUSTEE OF THE FOUNDATION (OR HAVE SIMILAR POWERS) ? — YES → YOU ARE A DISQUALIFIED PERSON

NO

ARE YOU RELATED** TO A SUBSTANTIAL CONTRIBUTOR OR TO AN OFFICER, DIRECTOR, OR TRUSTEE (OR SOMEONE WITH SIMILAR POWERS) ? — YES → YOU ARE A DISQUALIFIED PERSON

NO

DO YOU OWN, DIRECTLY OR INDIRECTLY, MORE THAN A 20% INTEREST*** IN A SUBSTANTIAL CONTRIBUTOR THAT IS AN ORGANIZATION ? — YES → YOU ARE A DISQUALIFIED PERSON

NO

YOU ARE NOT A DISQUALIFIED PERSON ← NO — ARE YOU AN ORGANIZATION IN WHICH THE ABOVE DISQUALIFIED PERSONS HAVE A COMBINED INTEREST*** OF MORE THAN 35% ? — YES → YOU ARE A DISQUALIFIED PERSON

Rev. 08-16-2010

## EXHIBIT 4.1

Disqualified Persons Flowchart

throughout its existence received gifts and bequests totaling $200,000. Since A's gift is less than $5,000 and also is below the 2 percent threshold (2 percent of $200,000 being $4,000), A has not become a substantial contributor to M because of this gift. A makes a second gift to M, on July 1, 2014, in the amount of $3,000. M does not receive any more gifts and grants in 2014. As of the close of 2014, the cumulative total of gifts and bequests to M is $230,000 (2 percent of which is $4,600). A became a substantial contributor to M, as of that date, as the result of the second gift, which caused her cumulative gifts to M to total $6,000, thereby exceeding the threshold of $5,000.

In determining whether a contributor is a substantial contributor, the total of the amounts received from the contributor and the aggregate total contributions and bequests received by the private foundation must be accumulated as of the last day of each tax year. Generally, all contributions and bequests made before October 9, 1969, are deemed to have been made on that date. Each contribution or bequest made after that is valued at its fair market value on the date received and an individual is treated as making all contributions and bequests made by his or her spouse.[6] Thus, each private foundation must maintain a running tally of contributions and bequests from persons, taking into account the attribution rules.[7] There is no provision for exclusion of unusual grants to calculate aggregate contributions for purposes of identifying substantial contributors.[8] See Exhibit 4.2 for a workpaper that can be used to maintain cumulative donation information from year to year to identify new substantial contributors.

A donor becomes a substantial contributor as of the first date when the private foundation received from him, her, or it an amount sufficient to make him, her, or it a substantial contributor,[9] so the private foundation should tabulate accumulating totals as the contributions and bequests are received, lest it inadvertently commit an act of self-dealing or otherwise violate one or more of the other rules regulating the activities of private foundations. The determination as to substantial contributor status is not made, however, until the last day of the tax year, so that contributions and bequests made subsequent to the gifts of the contributor in question but within the same tax year may operate to keep him, her, or it out of substantial contributor status even though that status was temporarily obtained at an earlier point during the year. These rules may be illustrated as follows:

On July 21, 2012, X corporation contributed $2,000 to private foundation Y (the tax year of which is the calendar year). As of the close of 2013, Y had received $150,000 in contributions and bequests. On September 17, 2014, X gave Y $3,100. As of that date, Y had received a total of $245,000 in contributions and bequests. Between September 17, 2014, and December 31, 2014, Y received $50,000 in contributions from others.

---

6. IRC § 507(d)(2)(B)(i)-(iii).
7. *See* § 4.4.
8. IRC § 507(d)(2); Reg. § 1.507-6.
9. Reg. § 1.507-6(b)(1).

**EXHIBIT 4.2** Cumulative List of Substantial Contributors

## SAMPLE FOUNDATION
### Cumulative List of Substantial Contributors

This report is updated annually to maintain historic data needed to identify PF donors who have become substantial contributors

|  | Cumulative Donations |  | 2% floor |
| --- | --- | --- | --- |
| All years to date | 12,000,000 |  | 240,000 |
| Current year | 1,000,000 |  |  |
| New cumulative amount | 13,000,000 |  | 260,000 |

|  | Cumulative Donations to Date | Donations This Year | Updated Cumulative Donations |
| --- | --- | --- | --- |
| Donor ABC | 5,000,000 | 1,000,000 | 6,000,000 |
| Donor DEF | 100,000 | 200,000 | 300,000* |
| Donor GHI | 1,000,000 |  | 1,000,000 |
| Donor JKL | 50,000 |  | 50,000 |

*Under IRC § 507(d)(2), this donor became a substantial contributor.

> X "temporarily" was a substantial contributor to Y on September 17, 2014, because X's gifts totaling $5,100 were at that time in excess of $5,000 and the 2 percent threshold amount (2 percent of $245,000 being $4,900). X is not a substantial contributor to Y, however, as of the close of 2014 because its total gifts to Y of $5,100 were less than the 2 percent threshold amount, which is $5,900 (2 percent × $295,000).

In the case of a trust, the term *substantial contributor* also means the creator of the trust without regard to amounts donated.[10] The term *person* generally includes tax-exempt organizations[11] but does not include governmental units[12] and also includes a decedent, even at the point in time preceding the transfer of

---

10. Reg. § 1.507-6(a)(1).
11. That is, organizations encompassed by IRC § 501(a).
12. That is, entities described in IRC § 170(c)(1).

any property from the estate to the private foundation.[13] With one exception, once a person becomes a substantial contributor to a private foundation, he, she, or it can never escape that status,[14] even though he, she, or it might not be so classified if the determination were first made at a later date.[15]

The one exception enables a person's status as a substantial contributor to terminate if, after 10 years, he or she has no connection with the private foundation.[16] To become disconnected, three factors must be present during the 10-year period:

1. The person (and any related persons) did not make any contributions to the private foundation.

2. Neither the person, nor any related person, was a foundation manager of the private foundation.

3. The aggregate contributions made by the person (and any related persons) are determined by the IRS "to be insignificant when compared to the aggregate amount of contributions to such foundation by one other person,"[17] taking into account appreciation on contributions while held by the private foundation. For these purposes, the term *related person* means related disqualified persons, and in the case of a corporate donor includes the officers and directors of the corporation.[18]

For certain purposes,[19] the term *substantial contributor* does not include most organizations that are not private foundations[20] or an organization wholly owned by a public or publicly supported charity. Moreover, for purposes of the self-dealing rules, the term does not include any charitable organization,[21] since to require inclusion of charitable organizations for this purpose would preclude private foundations from making large grants to or otherwise interacting with other private foundations.[22] In computing the support fraction for purposes of

---

13. *Rockefeller v. United States*, 572 F. Supp. 9 (E.D. Ark. 1982), *aff'd*, 718 F.2d 290 (8th Cir. 1983), *cert. den.*, 466 U.S. 962 (1984).
14. IRC § 507(d)(2)(B)(iv).
15. Reg. § 1.507-6(b)(1).
16. IRC § 507(d)(2)(C).
17. IRC § 507(d)(2)(C)(i)(III).
18. IRC § 507(d)(2)(C)(ii).
19. IRC §§ 170(b)(1)(D)(iii), 507(d)(1), 508(d), 509(a)(1) and (3), and IRC Chapter 42.
20. Reg. § 53.4946–1(a)(7). That is, organizations described in IRC § 509(a)(1), (2), or (3). *See* Chapter 15.
21. Reg. § 53.4946-1(a)(8). For these purposes, a charitable organization is an organization described in IRC § 501(c)(3), other than an organization that tests for public safety (IRC § 509(a)(4)). *See* § 15.12.
22. Reg. § 1.507-6(a)(2). This exception also applies to IRC § 4947(a)(1) trusts (*see* § 3.6) (Rev. Rul. 73-455, 1973-2 C.B. 187).

one category of publicly supported organization,[23] however, the term *substantial contributor* includes public charities where the $5,000/2 percent test is exceeded, although the support may qualify as a material change in support or an unusual grant.

In the only court decision on the point, the U.S. Tax Court concluded that the self-dealing rules[24] did not apply to certain transactions involving a private foundation because the ostensible disqualified person was not such a person in that he was not (albeit barely) a substantial contributor to the foundation.[25] This outcome, which turned in part on the court's valuation of the property involved, enabled this individual to escape $2.7 million in taxes and penalties.

## § 4.2 FOUNDATION MANAGERS

Another category of disqualified persons[26] is a *foundation manager*, defined to mean an officer, director, or trustee of a private foundation, or an individual having powers or responsibilities similar thereto.[27] An individual is considered an *officer* of a private foundation if he or she is specifically so designated under the constitutive documents of the private foundation or he or she regularly exercises general authority to make administrative or policy decisions on behalf of the private foundation. A person who has authority merely to make recommendations pertaining to administrative or policy decisions, but lacks authority to implement them without approval of a superior, is not considered a manager. Independent contractors, such as lawyers, accountants, and investment managers and advisors, acting in that capacity, are also not managers or officers.[28] In one case, however, the IRS determined that employees of a bank that was the trustee of a private foundation were foundation managers, because "they [were] free, on a day-to-day basis, to administer the trust and distribute the funds according to their best judgment."[29] It is important to reiterate the point that a manager must have authority or responsibility to be considered a disqualified person.[30]

Even if an individual lacks the authority to be classified as a manager on an overall basis, he or she can be treated as a foundation manager in respect to a particular act (or failure to act) over which he or she does have authority. A public charity's managers are called *key employees* for Form 990 reporting purposes. The definition of a key employee is precisely the same as the

---

23. IRC § 509(a)(2)(A). *See* Chapter 15.
24. *See* Chapter 5.
25. *Graham v. Commissioner*, 83 T.C.M. 1137 (2002).
26. IRC § 4946(a)(1)(B).
27. IRC § 4946(b)(1); Reg. § 53.4946-1(f)(1).
28. Reg. § 53.4946-1(f)(2).
29. Rev. Rul. 74-287, 1974-1 C.B. 327.
30. IRC § 4946(b)(2); Reg. § 53.4946-1(f)(4).

definition for a foundation manager quoted earlier. Although the IRS does not suggest its application, a private foundation that has difficulty in identifying its managers might refer to the following additional explanatory information provided in the Form 990 instructions for Part VII-A (2008 version):

> A "key employee" is any person having responsibilities, power, or influence over the organization as a whole similar to those of officers, directors, or trustees. The term includes the chief management and administrative officials of an organization (such as an executive director, chief financial officer, or chancellor) and managers of a discrete segment or activity or authority to control capital expenditures, operating budgets, or compensation for employees.

## § 4.3  CERTAIN 20 PERCENT OWNERS

An owner of more than 20 percent of the total combined voting power of a corporation, the profits interest of a partnership, or the beneficial interest of a trust or unincorporated enterprise, any of which is (during the ownership) a substantial contributor to a private foundation, is a disqualified person.[31]

The term *combined voting power*[32] includes voting power represented by holdings of voting stock, actual or constructive,[33] but does not include voting rights held only as a director or trustee.[34] Thus, for example, an employee stock ownership trust[35] that held 30 percent of the stock of a corporation that was a substantial contributor to a private foundation on behalf of the corporation's participating employees (who direct the manner in which the trust votes the shares) was held to have merely the voting power of a trustee and not the ownership of the stock, and thus to not be a disqualified person in respect to the private foundation.[36]

The term *voting power* includes outstanding voting power but does not include voting power obtainable but not obtained, such as voting power obtainable by converting securities or nonvoting stock into voting stock, by exercising warrants or options to obtain voting stock, or voting power that will vest in preferred stockholders only if and when the corporation has failed to pay preferred dividends for a specified period of time or has otherwise failed to meet specified requirements.[37]

For the purpose of determining the combined voting power, profits interest, or beneficial interest of an individual, there are certain attribution rules.

---

31. IRC § 4946(a)(1)(C).
32. IRC § 4946(a)(1)(C)(i).
33. *See* IRC § 4946(a)(3).
34. Reg. § 53.4946-1(a)(5).
35. IRC § 4975(e).
36. Rev. Rul. 81-76, 1981-1 C.B. 516.
37. Reg. § 53.4946-1(a)(6).

In respect to combined voting power,[38] stock (or profits or beneficial interests) owned directly or indirectly by or for a corporation, partnership, estate, or trust is considered as being owned proportionately by or for its shareholders, partners, or beneficiaries.[39] Moreover, an individual is considered as owning the stock owned by members of his or her family, as discussed.[40] Any stockholders that have been counted once (whether by reason of actual or constructive ownership) in applying these rules[41] are not counted a second time.[42] Essentially, the attribution rules are the same as the federal tax rules generally,[43] and there is a special rule for constructive ownership of stock.[44] In respect to profits or beneficial interests, ownership thereof is similarly taken into account in determining whether an individual is a disqualified person.[45]

For purposes of the excess business holdings rules[46] only, the term *disqualified person* does not include an employee stock ownership plan,[47] in respect to grandfathered business holdings acquired pursuant to a pre-1969 will, as respects tax years beginning after July 18, 1984.[48]

Constructive ownership of rights and interests must be determined in accordance with the applicable attribution rules.

In one instance, involving three national trade associations that elect the directors of a private foundation, the 30 local association members of one of the three national associations (which thus is a federation of associations), and another national association controlled by the three associations, the IRS held that the private foundation could make grants to the local associations without committing an act of self-dealing, even though the controlled national association was a substantial contributor and the federation of associations held more than 20 percent of the combined voting power of the controlled association, inasmuch as the federation of associations had no ownership interest in its local association members and they were not otherwise disqualified persons in respect to the private foundation.[49]

---

38. IRC § 4946(a)(1)(c)(i), (a)(1)(E).
39. IRC § 267(c)(1); Reg. § 53.4946-1(d)(1).
40. IRC § 267(c)(4), as modified by IRC § 4946(a)(4); Reg. § 53.4946-1(d)(1)(i); *see* § 4.4.
41. IRC § 4946(a)(1)(E).
42. Reg. § 53.4946-1(d)(1)(ii).
43. IRC § 267(c) is applied without regard to IRC § 267(c)(3).
44. Stock constructively owned by an individual by reason of the application of IRC § 267(c)(2) is not treated as owned by him or her if he or she is described in IRC § 4946(a)(1)(A), (B), or (C). Also Reg. § 53.4946-1(d)(1).
45. Reg. § 53.4946-1(e).
46. *See* Chapter 7.
47. IRC § 4975(e)(7).
48. IRC § 4943(d)(4).
49. Priv. Ltr. Rul. 8525075.

The profits interest[50] of a partner is that equal to his or her distributive share of income of the partnership as determined under special federal tax rules.[51] The term *profits interest* includes any interest that is outstanding but not any interest that is obtainable but has not been obtained.[52]

The beneficial interest in an unincorporated enterprise (other than a trust or estate) includes any right to receive a portion of distributions from profits of the enterprise or, in the absence of a profit-sharing agreement, any right to receive a portion of the assets (if any) upon liquidation of the enterprise, except as a creditor or employee.[53] A right to receive distribution of profits includes a right to receive any amount from the profits other than as a creditor or employee, whether as a sum certain or as a portion of profits realized by the enterprise. Where there is no agreement fixing the rights of the participants in an enterprise, the fraction of the respective interests of each participant therein is determined by dividing the amount of all investments or contributions to the capital of the enterprise made or obligated to be made by the participant by the amount of all investments or contributions to capital made or obligated to be made by all of them.[54]

A person's beneficial interest in a trust is determined in proportion to the actuarial interest of the person in the trust.[55] The term *beneficial interest* includes any interest that is outstanding but not any interest that is obtainable but has not been obtained.[56]

## § 4.4   FAMILY MEMBERS

Another category of disqualified person is a member of the family of an individual who is a substantial contributor, a foundation manager, or one of the previously discussed 20 percent owners.[57] The term *member of the family* is defined to include an individual's spouse, ancestors, children, grandchildren, great-grandchildren, and the spouses of children, grandchildren, and great-grandchildren.[58] Thus, these family members are themselves disqualified persons.

---

50.  IRC § 4946(a)(1)(c)(ii).
51.  IRC §§ 707(b)(3), 4946(a)(4); Reg. § 53.4946-1(a)(2).
52.  Reg. § 53.4946-1(a)(6).
53.  IRC § 4946(a)(1)(C)(iii).
54.  Reg. § 53.4946-1(a)(3).
55.  Reg. § 53.4946-1(a)(4).
56.  Reg. § 53.4946-1(a)(6).
57.  IRC § 4946(a)(1)(D).
58.  IRC § 4946(d).

A legally adopted child of an individual is treated for these purposes as a child of the individual by blood.[59] A brother, sister, aunt, or uncle of an individual is not, for these purposes, a member of the family.[60]

## §4.5 CORPORATIONS OR PARTNERSHIPS

A corporation is a disqualified person if more than 35 percent of the total combined voting power in the corporation (including constructive holdings)[61] is owned by substantial contributors, foundation managers, 20 percent owners, or members of the family of any of these individuals.[62] The phrase *combined voting power* includes the voting power represented by holdings of voting stock, actual or constructive, but does not include voting rights held only as a director or trustee.[63] Employing that rule, the IRS concluded that stock held in a voting trust, which was related to a bank and held stock of a company for a private foundation and other entities, was excludable in computing the 35 percent threshold because it was being held by the trust only in a fiduciary capacity (thereby enabling the IRS to rule that the company was not a disqualified person with respect to the foundation and that proposed stock redemptions would not be acts of self-dealing).[64]

A partnership is a disqualified person if more than 35 percent of the profits interest in the partnership (including constructive holdings)[65] is owned by substantial contributors, foundation managers, 20 percent owners, or members of the family of any of these individuals.[66]

## §4.6 TRUSTS OR ESTATES

A trust or estate is a disqualified person if more than 35 percent of the beneficial interest in the trust or estate (including constructive holdings)[67] is owned by substantial contributors, foundation managers, 20 percent owners, or members of the family of any of these individuals.[68]

It is the position of the chief counsel of the IRS that an estate is not a disqualified person with respect to a trust funded by the estate solely because the estate is a continuation of the decedent who was a disqualified person. Where the disqualified person-decedent's children and grandchildren (thus,

---

59. Reg. § 53.4946-1(h).
60. *Id.*
61. IRC § 4946(a)(3).
62. IRC § 4946(a)(1)(E).
63. Reg. § 53.4946-1(a)(5).
64. Priv. Ltr. Rul. 200750020.
65. IRC § 4946(a)(4).
66. IRC § 4946(a)(1)(F).
67. IRC § 4946(a)(4).
68. IRC § 4946(a)(1)(G).

also disqualified persons)[69] are beneficiaries of trusts funded by the estate and these beneficial interests are more than 35 percent of the beneficial interest in the estate, however, the estate is a disqualified person.[70]

## §4.7 PRIVATE FOUNDATIONS

A private foundation may be a disqualified person with respect to another private foundation but only for purposes of the excess business holdings rules.[71] The disqualified person private foundation must be effectively controlled,[72] directly or indirectly, by the same person or persons (other than a bank, trust company, or similar organization acting only as a foundation manager) who control the private foundation in question, or must be the recipient of contributions substantially all of which were made, directly or indirectly, by substantial contributors, foundation managers, 20 percent owners, and members of their families who made, directly or indirectly, substantially all of the contributions to the private foundation in question.[73] One or more persons are considered to have made *substantially all* of the contributions to a private foundation for these purposes if the persons have contributed or bequeathed at least 85 percent of the total contributions and bequests that have been received by the private foundation during its entire existence, where each person has contributed or bequeathed at least 2 percent of the total.[74] For example:

> Foundation A has received contributions of $100,000 throughout its existence, as follows: $35,000 from X, $51,000 from Y (X's father), and $14,000 from Z (an unrelated person). During its existence, foundation B has received $100,000 in contributions, as follows: $50,000 from X and $50,000 from Q (X's wife). For excess business holdings purposes, A is a disqualified person as to B and B is a disqualified person as to A.

## §4.8 GOVERNMENTAL OFFICIALS

A governmental official may be a disqualified person with respect to a private foundation but only for purposes of the self-dealing rules.[75] The term *governmental official* means (1) an elected public official in the U.S. Congress or executive branch, (2) presidential appointees to the U.S. executive or judicial branches, (3) certain higher-compensated or ranking employees in one of these three branches, (4) House of Representatives or Senate employees earning at

---

69. *See* text accompanied by *supra* note 58.
70. Gen. Coun. Mem. 39445.
71. IRC § 4946(a)(1)(H). *See* Chapter 7.
72. Reg. § 1.482-1(a)(3).
73. Reg. § 53.4946-1(b)(1).
74. Reg. § 53.4946-1(b)(2).
75. IRC § 4946(a)(1)(I). *See* Chapter 5.

least $15,000 annually, (5) elected or appointed public officials in the U.S. or District of Columbia governments (including governments of U.S. possessions or political subdivisions or areas of the United States) earning at least $15,000 annually, (5) elected or appointed public officials in the executive, legislative, or judicial branch of a state, the District of Columbia, a U.S. possession, or political subdivision or other areas of the foregoing, receiving gross compensation at an annual rate of at least $20,000, (6) the personal or executive assistant or secretary to any of the foregoing, or (7) a member of the IRS Oversight Board.[76]

In defining the term *public office* for purposes of the fifth category of governmental officials, this term must be distinguished from mere public employment. Although holding a public office is one form of public employment, not every position in the employ of a state or other governmental subdivision[77] constitutes a public office. Although a determination as to whether a public employee holds a public office depends on the facts and circumstances of the case, the essential element is whether a significant part of the activities of a public employee is the independent performance of policy-making functions. Several factors may be considered as indications that a position in the executive, legislative, or judicial branch of the government of a state, possession of the United States, or political subdivision or other area of any of the foregoing, or of the District of Columbia, constitutes a public office. Among the factors to be considered, in addition to that already set forth, are that the office is created by Congress, a state constitution, or a state legislature, or by a municipality or other governmental body pursuant to authority conferred by Congress, state constitution, or state legislature, and the powers conferred on the office and the duties to be discharged by the official are defined either directly or indirectly by Congress, a state constitution, or a state legislature, or through legislative authority.[78]

For example, a lawyer appointed by a state's attorney general to perform collection services on a part-time basis for the attorney general's office was held not to be a governmental official.[79] Likewise, the IRS ruled that the holder of the office of county attorney is not a governmental official for these purposes.[80] Similarly, an individual appointed by the president of the United States to serve as director of an entity was ruled not to be a government official, because of her status as a special government employee (based on the number of days of employment).[81] By contrast, a chief administrative officer serving a city's mayor was ruled to be a government official.[82]

---

76. IRC § 4946(c).
77. IRC § 4946(c)(5).
78. Reg. § 53.4946-1(g)(2).
79. E.g., Priv. Ltr. Rul. 8508097.
80. Priv. Ltr. Rul. 8533099.
81. Priv. Ltr. Rul. 9804040.
82. Priv. Ltr. Rul. 200605014.

In a rather astounding private letter ruling, the IRS concluded that a state district court judge was not a government official for purposes of these rules.[83] The agency was moved to reach this conclusion because of a state statute providing that district court judges must apply existing law to the facts of each case; by statute, these judges cannot write new law or policy and must apply the law as created by the state's legislature or appellate courts. The IRS held that the judge in this instance "does not exercise significant independent policy-making powers, even though he may independently perform his duties as a government employee."[84] Quite appropriately, soon after this ruling was issued, it was revoked.[85]

Further, in applying the rules concerning the fifth category of governmental officials, the $15,000 amount is the individual's *gross compensation*.[86] This term refers to all receipts attributable to public office that are includible in gross income for federal income tax purposes. For example, an elected member of a state legislature may receive a salary of less than $15,000 each year, but also receive an expense allowance that, when added to the salary, results in a total amount of more than $15,000 per year; where the expense allowance is a fixed amount given to each legislator regardless of actual expenses and there is no restriction on its use and no requirement that an accounting for its use be made to the state, the expense allowance is part of the legislator's gross compensation and the legislator becomes a disqualified person.[87]

A private foundation maintained a director-initiated grant program (enabling directors to direct grants that are not processed through the usual staff review system) and a matching gifts program (with respect to gifts by directors and staff). These director-initiated grants cannot be made to fulfill a director's charitable pledge or if the director receives a benefit. One of the foundation's directors is a government official. The IRS ruled that this individual's participation in these programs do not entail any payments to the director and that none of these payments constitutes compensation to this individual.[88]

---

83. Priv. Ltr. Rul. 200542037.
84. It is almost impossible for a judge to write an opinion without creating "new law," despite what a state statute may stipulate; the likelihood that a given case will have a precisely applicable precedent is remote. Being human, a judge is not a legal opinion-crunching automaton. This ruling suggested that, in the absence of such a statute, a state district court judge would be a governmental official for this purpose; it also indicated that state appellate court judges are government officials.
85. Priv. Ltr. Rul. 200604034.
86. IRC § 4946(c)(5).
87. Rev. Rul. 77-473, 1977-2 C.B. 421.
88. Priv. Ltr. Rul. 200605014. Thus, this director's participation in these programs was ruled to not amount to self-dealing (*see* § 5.10).

## §4.9 TERMINATING DISQUALIFIED PERSON STATUS

It is certainly possible for a person that is a disqualified person with respect to a private foundation to terminate his, her, or its status as a disqualified person. There is, however, little law on the point. In one instance, a corporation made an exchange offer to a private foundation concerning certain shares of the corporation's nonvoting stock. This corporation was once a disqualified person with respect to the foundation solely because an individual who was a manager of the foundation[89] owned more than 35 percent of the total combined voting power of the corporation.[90] Five years before the exchange occurred, the foundation manager resigned that position. The IRS ruled that the resignation of the foundation manager terminated the status of the corporation as a disqualified person with respect to the private foundation, noting that all aspects of the exchange occurred after the separation of the foundation manager and that he was not connected with the proposed exchange while serving in that capacity.[91] This ruling gave the impression that some reasonable period of time had to pass to cause the termination of status to be respected.

That impression was erased, years later, when the IRS concluded that an individual was not a foundation manager (or any other type of disqualified person) with respect to a private foundation, in connection with a prospective sale of businesses by the foundation, even though the individual resigned from the foundation's board of directors the day before he bid on the assets.[92] He had been an employee of one of the principal businesses for 25 years and was the chief operating officer of it for many of those years. Even after he retired, he was persuaded to become reinvolved in corporate management, as a consultant to a newly formed holding company, because of his knowledge and expertise. He was overseeing the process of selling the businesses until he decided to be a bidder. Nonetheless, several factors led the IRS to its conclusion that this individual would not exercise undue influence over the sale of the assets, including an open bidding process, evaluation of bids by a bank and an investment firm, supervision of the sale by a court, and approval of the transaction by the attorney general of the state involved. The ruling enabled this individual, should his bid prevail, to acquire the businesses from the foundation without engaging in one or more acts of self-dealing.[93]

The IRS ruled that two trustees of a private foundation, who resigned their positions over three years beforehand, were no longer disqualified persons with

89. *See* § 4.2.
90. *See* § 4.5.
91. Rev. Rul. 76-448, 1976-2 C.B. 368. Thus, this exchange was able to take place without causing an act of self-dealing under IRC § 4941(d)(1)(A). *See* § 5.4.
92. Priv. Ltr. Rul. 199943047.
93. This ruling may be contrasted with Rev. Rul. 80-207, 1980-2 C.B. 193, discussed in § 15.7(h), text accompanied by note 308.

respect to the foundation, so that an exchange of property that was about to occur would not constitute self-dealing.[94] The transaction was an exchange of houses, one of which was owned by one of the former trustees. The IRS emphasized that these individuals were not disqualified persons in any other capacity, the house would be used for exempt purposes, and there were no discussions about the proposed exchange while they served as trustees. As a result of the exchange of houses, this former trustee may become a substantial contributor to the foundation, thus again becoming a disqualified person with respect to it.[95] Nonetheless, the transaction would not be self-dealing because the disqualified person status arose only as a result of the transaction.[96]

---

94. Priv. Ltr. Rul. 201130008.
95. *See* § 4.1.
96. Reg. § 53.4941(d)-1(a).

# CHAPTER FIVE

# Self-Dealing

Tax-exempt charitable organizations, including private foundations, are subject to the federal tax law rules prohibiting private inurement and non-incidental private benefit.[1] Particularly in the case of private inurement, the law imposes standards of reasonableness with respect to transactions involving members of the board and other insiders with respect to the charitable organization, entailing payment of compensation, provision of services, purchases and sales, loans, rental arrangements, and other transfers of income or assets. The sanctions for violation of either of these doctrines are the revocation or denial of exempt status and loss of the ability to attract tax-deductible contributions.

Congress, in 1969, decided that, with respect to private foundations, these two doctrines were inadequate. Among the practices Congress found troublesome were loans and stock bailouts between certain privately funded organizations and their creators and creator's families. Former law[2] permitted these transactions as long as they were reasonable, such as charging a reasonable rate of interest or payment of fair market value. Nevertheless, Congress believed that private foundations were being used as pocketbooks for funds not necessarily available from other sources, so it set out to eliminate self-interested financial activity between a private charity and its insiders. As the following quotation from the 1969 legislative history indicates, the arm's-length approach embodied in the prior law was deemed no longer sufficient, resulting in the enactment of self-dealing rules:

> Arm's-length standards have proved to require disproportionately great enforcement efforts, resulting in sporadic and uncertain effectiveness of the provisions. On occasion the sanctions are ineffective and tend to discourage the expenditure of enforcement effort. On the other hand, in many cases the sanctions are so great in comparison to the offense involved, that they cause reluctance in enforcement, especially in view of the element of subjectivity in applying arm's-length standards. Where the Internal Revenue Service does seek to apply sanctions in such circumstances, the same factors encourage extensive litigation and a noticeable reluctance by the courts to uphold severe sanctions.
>
> Consequently, as a practical matter, prior law did not preserve the integrity of private foundations. Also, the Congress concluded that compliance with arm's-length standards often does not in itself prevent the use of a private foundation to improperly benefit those who control the foundations. This is true, for example, where a foundation (1) purchases property from a substantial donor at a fair price, but does so in order to provide funds to the donor who needs cash and cannot find a ready buyer; (2) lends money to the donor with adequate security and at a reasonable rate of interest, but at a time when the money market is too tight for the donor to readily find alternate sources of funds; or (3) makes commitments to lease property

---

1. *See* §§ 5.1, 5.2.
2. IRC § 503 (repealed).

from the donor at a fair rental when the donor needs such advance leases in order to secure financing for construction or acquisition of the property.

To minimize the need to apply subjective arm's-length standards, to avoid the temptation to misuse private foundations for noncharitable purposes, to provide a more rational relationship between sanctions and improper acts, and to make it more practical to properly enforce the law, the [Tax Reform] Act [of 1969] generally prohibits self-dealing transactions and provides a variety and graduation of sanctions. . . . This is based on the belief by the Congress that the highest fiduciary standards require complete elimination of all self-dealing rather than arm's-length standards.[3]

Any determination that the sanctions with respect to self-dealing are to be imposed requires the existence of three elements: a private foundation,[4] a disqualified person (DP),[5] and an act of self-dealing between the two.[6] It is usually immaterial whether a self-dealing transaction results in a benefit or a detriment to the private foundation.[7] A self-dealing transaction does not include a transaction between a private foundation and a disqualified person, however, where the disqualified person status arises only as a result of the transaction.[8]

Notwithstanding enactment of the self-dealing rules, the private inurement and private benefit doctrines remain applicable with respect to private foundations. Thus, for example, if self-dealing is pervasive and ongoing, the tax-exempt status of a private foundation can be revoked.[9] Likewise, even if an exception to the self-dealing rules is applicable, the private benefit doctrine may nonetheless apply.[10]

## § 5.1   PRIVATE INUREMENT DOCTRINE

The federal tax law states that no part of the net earnings of tax-exempt charitable organizations, including private foundations, may inure to the benefit of persons in their private capacity.[11] This rule is known as the *private inurement doctrine*. Thus, this doctrine is a statutory criterion for federal income tax exemption for charitable organizations. Indeed, it is the

---

3. Joint Committee on Internal Revenue Taxation, *General Explanation of Tax Reform Act of 1969*, 91st Cong., 2d Sess. 30–31 (1970).
4. *See* § 1.2.
5. *See* Chapter 4.
6. Thus, for example, transactions between a private foundation and a fund are not acts of self-dealing, where the fund is not a separate legal entity (Priv. Ltr. Rul. 8623080).
7. *Leon A. Beeghly Fund v. Commissioner*, 35 T.C. 490 (1960), *aff'd*, 310 F.2d 756 (6th Cir. 1962).
8. Reg. § 53.4941(d)-1(a).
9. E.g., Tech. Adv. Mem. 9335001.
10. *See* § 5.2.
11. IRC § 501(c)(3); Reg. § 1.501(c)(3)-1(c)(2).

fundamental defining principle distinguishing *nonprofit organizations* from *for-profit organizations*.[12]

The peculiarly phrased (and thoroughly antiquated) language of the private inurement doctrine requires that the tax-exempt organization be organized and operated so that "no part of . . . [its] net earnings . . . inures to the benefit of any private shareholder or individual." This provision reads as if it were proscribing the payment of dividends. In fact, it is rare for an exempt organization to have shareholders, let alone make any payments to them. The contemporary, and broad and wide-ranging, meaning of the statutory language[13] is barely reflected in its literal form and transcends the nearly century-old formulation: None of the income or assets of a charitable organization may be permitted to directly or indirectly unduly benefit an individual or other person who is in a position to exercise a significant degree of control over it.

Essentially, the doctrine forbids ways of causing the income or assets of charitable (and certain other) tax-exempt organizations to flow away from the organization (*inure*) and to one or more persons who are related to the organization (*insiders*) for nonexempt purposes. The Office of Chief Counsel of the IRS bluntly summarized the doctrine: "The inurement prohibition serves to prevent anyone in a position to do so from siphoning off any of a charity's income or assets for personal use."[14]

The essence of the private inurement rule is to ensure that the tax-exempt organization involved is serving a public interest and not a private interest. That is, to be tax-exempt, it is necessary for an organization to establish that it is not organized and operated for the benefit of private interests such as designated individuals, the creator of the organization or his or her family, shareholders of

---

12. An oddity in this area is the fact that, in a sense, the private inurement proscription in the Internal Revenue Code is redundant and thus unnecessary, in that this proscription is inherent in the concept of a nonprofit organization. Thus, the U.S. Supreme Court wrote that a "non-profit entity is ordinarily understood to differ from a for-profit corporation principally because it is barred from distributing its net earnings, if any, to individuals who exercise control over it, such as members, officers, directors, or trustees" (*Camps Newfound/Owatonna, Inc. v. Town of Harrison, Maine et al.* 520 U.S. 564, 585 (1997) (internal quotation marks omitted)). It may be noted that this proscription extends to persons other than just individuals and that, since an insider is required to have a private inurement transaction, this type of a transaction rarely occurs simply because it is with an organization's member.

13. A court wrote that the "boundaries of the term 'inures' have thus far defied precise definition" (*Variety Club Tent No. 6 Charities, Inc. v. Commissioner*, 74 T.C.M. 1485, 1494 (1997)).

14. Gen. Couns. Mem. 39862. A gentler explication of the doctrine by the agency's lawyers was that "[i]nurement is likely to arise where the financial benefit represents a transfer of the organization's financial resources to an individual solely by virtue of the individual's relationship with the organization, and without regard to accomplishing exempt purposes" (Gen. Couns. Mem. 38459).

the organization, persons controlled (directly or indirectly) by these private interests, or any other persons having a personal and private interest in the activities of the organization.[15]

In determining the presence of any proscribed private inurement, the law looks to the ultimate purpose of the organization. If the basic purpose of the organization is to benefit individuals in their private capacity, then it cannot be tax-exempt even though exempt activities are also performed. Conversely, incidental benefits to private individuals, such as those that are generated by reason of the organization's program activities, will usually not defeat the exemption if the organization otherwise qualifies under the appropriate exemption provision.[16]

The IRS and the courts have recognized a variety of forms of private inurement. These include:

- Excessive or unreasonable compensation (the most common form of private inurement);
- Unreasonable or unfair rental arrangements;
- Unreasonable or unfair lending arrangements;
- Provision of services to persons in their private capacity;
- Certain assumptions of liability;
- Certain sales of assets to insiders;
- Certain participations in partnerships and other joint ventures;
- Certain percentage payment arrangements; and
- Varieties of tax avoidance schemes.

The doctrine of private inurement does not prohibit transactions between charitable organizations and those who have a close relationship with it. As the IRS wrote, "There is no absolute prohibition against an exempt section 501(c)(3) organization dealing with its founders, members, or officers in conducting its economic affairs."[17] Rather, the private inurement doctrine requires that these transactions be tested against a standard of *reasonableness*.[18] The standard calls for a roughly equal exchange of benefits between the parties; the law is designed to discourage what the IRS termed a "disproportionate share of the benefits of the exchange" flowing to an insider.[19]

---

15. Reg. §§ 1.501(a)-1(c), 1.501(c)(3)-1(c)(1)(ii), 1.501(c)(3)-1(c)(2), 1.501(c)(3)-1(d)(1)(ii).
16. Reg. § 1.501(c)(3)-(c)(1).
17. Priv. Ltr. Rul. 9130002. To this group may be added directors and trustees.
18. In contrast, the private foundation self-dealing rules generally and essentially forbid these types of transactions.
19. Priv. Ltr. Rul. 9130002.

Generally, an *insider*[20] is a person who has a unique relationship with the charitable organization, by which that person can cause application of the organization's funds or assets for the private purposes of the person by reason of the person's exercise of control or influence over, or being in a position to exercise that control or influence over, the organization.[21] The scope of the concept of the *insider* continues to be the subject of litigation.[22]

The sanction for violation of the private inurement doctrine is denial or revocation of the charitable organization's tax-exempt status.

## §5.2 PRIVATE BENEFIT DOCTRINE

The federal tax law concerning tax-exempt charitable organizations, including private foundations, imposes an *operational test*, which looks to see whether the organization is conducting programs in furtherance of its tax-exempt purposes rather than for private individuals.[23] This standard has spawned the *private benefit doctrine*. As one court stated the matter, the private benefit proscription "inheres in the requirement that [a charitable] organization operate exclusively for exempt purposes."[24]

This doctrine is potentially applicable with respect to all persons, including those who are not insiders; that is, the doctrine embraces benefits provided to "disinterested persons"[25] or "unrelated" persons.[26] Or, as the IRS stated the matter, the private benefit doctrine applies with respect to "all kinds of persons and groups."[27] Indeed, the IRS has written that "[t]here is general agreement that [private] inurement is a subset of private benefit."[28] Thus, it is broader than the private inurement doctrine and, in many respects, subsumes that doctrine. The private benefit doctrine essentially is intended to prevent a charitable organization from benefiting private interests in any way, other than to an

---

20. The federal tax law has appropriated the term from the federal securities laws that prohibit, for example, insider trading.
21. *American Campaign Academy v. Commissioner*, 92 T.C. 1053 (1989). It was subsequently stated that the "case law [as to private inurement] appears to have drawn a line between those who have significant control over the organization's activities and those who are unrelated third parties" (*Variety Club Tent No. 6 Charities, Inc. v. Commissioner*, 74 T.C.M. 1485, 1492 (1997)).
22. E.g., *United Cancer Council, Inc. v. Commissioner*, 165 F.3d 1173 (7th Cir. 1999), *rev'g* 109 T.C. 326 (1997). In general, *see Tax-Exempt Organizations* § 20.3; *Intermediate Sanctions* § 2.3.
23. Reg. § 1.501(c)(3)-1(b). *See Tax-Exempt Organizations* § 4.3.
24. *Redlands Surgical Services v. Commissioner*, 113 T.C. 47, 74 (1999), *aff'd*, 242 F.3d 904 (9th Cir. 2001).
25. *American Campaign Academy v. Commissioner*, 92 T.C. 1053, 1069 (1989).
26. *Redlands Surgical Services v. Commissioner*, 113 T.C. 47, 74 (1999), *aff'd*, 242 F.3d 904 (9th Cir. 2001).
27. Priv. Ltr. Rul. 200635018.
28. Priv. Ltr. Rul. 201044025.

insubstantial extent. The IRS does not recognize the notion of incidental private inurement.

One of the few cases fully explicating the private benefit doctrine concerned an otherwise tax-exempt school that trained individuals for careers as political campaign professionals.[29] Nearly all of the school's graduates became employed by or consultants to organizations or candidates of a national political party. A court concluded that the school did not primarily engage in activities that accomplished educational purposes, in that it benefited private interests to more than an insubstantial extent. That is, the school was found to be substantially benefiting the private interests of the political party's entities and candidates.

The heart of this opinion is the analysis of the concept—not previously or subsequently articulated—of *primary* private benefit and *secondary* private benefit. In that setting, the beneficiaries of primary private benefit were the school's students; the beneficiaries of secondary private benefit were the employers of the graduates. The existence of this secondary private benefit was what caused this school to fail to acquire tax-exempt status.

The court accepted the IRS's argument that "where the training of individuals is focused on furthering a particular targeted private interest, the conferred secondary benefit ceases to be incidental to the providing organization's exempt purposes."[30] The beneficiaries, at the secondary level, were found to be a "select group."[31]

The school unsuccessfully presented as precedent several IRS rulings holding tax-exempt, as educational organizations, entities that provide training to individuals in a particular industry or profession.[32] The court accepted the IRS's characterization of these rulings, which was that the "secondary benefit provided in each such ruling was broadly spread among members of an industry . . . as opposed to being earmarked for a particular organization or person."[33] The court said that the secondary benefit in each of these rulings was, because of the spread, "incidental to the providing organization's exempt purpose."[34]

This court subsequently held that a nonprofit organization that audited structural steel fabricators in conjunction with a quality certification program conducted by a related trade association did not constitute a charitable organization, in part because it yielded inappropriate private benefit to the association

---

29. *American Campaign Academy v. Commissioner*, 92 T.C. 1053 (1989).
30. *Id.* at 1074.
31. *Id.* at 1076.
32. E.g., Rev. Rul. 75-196, 1975-1 C.B. 155; Rev. Rul. 72-101, 1972-1 C.B. 144; Rev. Rul. 68-504, 1968-2 C.B. 211; Rev. Rul. 67-72, 1967-1 C.B. 125.
33. *American Campaign Academy v. Commissioner*, 92 T.C. 1053, 1074 (1989).
34. *Id.*

and to the fabricators that were inspected.[35] The court wrote that the "development and administration of a quality certification program, at the request of and for the structural steel industry, would appear to be consistent with [the association's] mission as a business league."[36] It added that the "focus thus seems to be on aiding industry participants, with any benefit to the general public being merely secondary."[37] The court thus saw more than insubstantial private benefit in two contexts: the extent to which the purported charitable organization served the association's interests in carrying out its role of industry betterment and the benefit accruing to the steel fabricators that requested audits and whose facilities were inspected by the organization.

The most significant of the private benefit court cases[38] concerned the matter of whole entity joint ventures, in this case a nonprofit subsidiary of a health-care facility, where the entity places its entire operations in a venture with a for-profit entity, perhaps ceding authority over all of its resources to the co-venturer.[39] A fundamental concept in this context is control, with the IRS and the courts examining relationships between public charities and for-profit organizations to ascertain if the charity has lost control of its facilities and programs to the for-profit. Examples include relationships reflected in management agreements, leases, fundraising contracts, and, of course, partnership, limited liability company, or other joint venture agreements. In this context, it can be irrelevant if the public charity is in fact engaging substantially in exempt activities and if fees (if any) paid by the exempt organization to a for-profit entity are reasonable.

The sweeping rule of law in this regard was articulated, in one of the two most radical of these cases, by a federal court of appeals, which wrote that the "critical inquiry is not whether particular contractual payments to a related for-profit organization are reasonable or excessive, but instead whether the entire enterprise is carried on in such a manner that the for-profit organization benefits substantially from the operation of" the tax-exempt organization.[40] This opinion articulates the outer reaches of the ambit of the private benefit doctrine: the thought that there can be unwarranted private benefit, conferred on a person who is not an insider, even if the terms and conditions of the arrangement are reasonable and substantial exempt functions are occurring.

---

35. *Quality Auditing Co. v. Commissioner*, 114 T.C. 498 (2000).
36. *Id*. at 510.
37. *Id*.
38. *Redlands Surgical Services v. Commissioner*, 113 T.C. 47 (1999), *aff'd*, 242 F.3d 904 (9th Cir. 2001).
39. *See Tax-Exempt Organizations* § 32.5.
40. *Church by Mail, Inc. v. Commissioner*, 765 F.2d 1387, 1392 (9th Cir. 1985), *aff'g* 48 T.C.M. 471 (1984).

In the other of these cases, two for-profit organizations that did not have any formal structural control over the nonprofit entity, the tax exemption of which was at issue, nevertheless were found to have exerted "considerable control" over its activities.[41] The for-profit entities set fees that the nonprofit organization charged for training sessions, required the nonprofit organization to carry on certain types of educational activities, and provided management personnel paid for and responsible to one of the for-profit organizations. Pursuant to a licensing agreement with the for-profit organizations, the nonprofit entity was allowed to use certain intellectual property for 10 years; at the end of the license period, all copyrighted material, including new material developed by the nonprofit organization, was required to be turned over to the for-profit organizations. The nonprofit organization was mandated to use its excess funds for the development of its program activities or related research. The for-profit organizations also required that trainers and local organizations sign an agreement to not compete with these activities for two years after terminating their relationship with the organizations involved.

The trial court, in this case, concluded that the nonprofit organization was "part of a franchise system which is operated for private benefit and . . . its affiliation with this system taints it with a substantial commercial purpose."[42] The "ultimate beneficiaries" of the nonprofit organization's activities were found to be the for-profit corporations; the nonprofit organization was "simply the instrument to subsidize the for-profit corporations and not vice versa."[43] The nonprofit organization was held to not be operating exclusively for charitable purposes.

These two court opinions have framed this analysis. Even without formal control over the ostensible tax-exempt organization by one or more for-profit entities, the ostensible tax-exempt organization can be viewed as merely the instrument by which a for-profit organization is subsidized (benefited). The nonprofit organization's "affiliation" with a for-profit entity or a "system" involving one or more for-profit entities can taint the nonprofit organization, actually or seemingly imbuing it with a substantial commercial purpose. The result is likely to be a finding of private benefit (or, if an insider is involved, private inurement),[44] causing the nonprofit organization to lose or be denied tax-exempt status.

Matters worsen in this context where there is actual control. This is the principal message of the decision concerning whole entity joint ventures. In that case, a public charity (a subsidiary of an exempt hospital) became a

---

41. *est of Hawaii v. Commissioner*, 71 T.C. 1067, 1080 (1979), *aff'd*, 647 F.2d 170 (9th Cir. 1981).
42. *Id.*, 71 T.C. at 1080.
43. *Id.*
44. The private inurement doctrine was invoked in a case concerning a charitable organization in a partnership in *Housing Pioneers, Inc. v. Commissioner*, 65 T.C.M. 2191 (1993).

co–general partner with a for-profit organization in a partnership that owned and operated a surgery center. A for-profit management company affiliated with the for-profit co–general partner managed the arrangement. The public charity's sole activity was participation in the partnership. The court termed this relationship "passive participation [by the charitable organization] in a for-profit health-service enterprise."[45] The court concluded that it was "patently clear" that the partnership was not being operated in an exclusively charitable manner. The income-producing activity of the partnership was characterized as "indivisible" as between the non-profit and for-profit organizations. No "discrete part" of these activities was "severable from those activities that produce income to be applied to the other partner's profit."[46]

The heart of this whole entity joint venture decision is this: To the extent that a public charity "cedes control over its sole activity to for-profit parties [by, in this case, entering into the joint venture] having an independent economic interest in the same activity and having no obligation to put charitable purposes ahead of profit-making objectives," the charity cannot be assured that the partnership will in fact be operated in furtherance of charitable purposes.[47] The consequence is the conferring on the for-profit party in the venture "significant private benefits."[48]

The IRS is making much of the private benefit doctrine, as two examples illustrate. The agency is of the view that private benefit is present when the founders of an otherwise tax-exempt school also are directors of a for-profit company that manages the school; the nature of the benefit is largely financial, and the IRS asserted that the educational activities of the school could be undertaken without conferring the benefit (i.e., by use of employees or volunteers).[49] The agency also believes that certain scholarship-granting foundations are ineligible for tax exemption, by reason of the private benefit doctrine, because the recipients are individuals who are participants in beauty pageants operated by tax-exempt social welfare organizations; private benefit is thought to be bestowed on the social welfare organizations because the

---

45. *Redlands Surgical Services v. Commissioner*, 113 T.C. 47, 77 (1999), *aff'd*, 242 F.3d 904 (9th Cir. 2001).

46. *Id.*

47. *Id.* at 78.

48. *Id.* This decision was a major victory for the IRS, which earlier staked out, in Rev. Rul. 98-15, 1998-1 C.B. 718, the position adopted by the court. The agency, however, did not prevail in a whole hospital joint venture case (*St. David's Health Care System, Inc. v. United States*, 2002-2 U.S.T.C. ¶ 50,452 (W.D. Tex. 2002), *vacated and remanded (for trial)*, 349 F.3d 232 (5th Cir. 2003) No. 101CV-046 (W.D. Tex. Mar. 4, 2004)).

49. "Private Benefit Under IRC [§] 501(c)(3)," Topic H in the IRS Exempt Organizations Continuing Professional Education Technical Instruction Program textbook for fiscal year 2001.

grant programs serve to attract contestants to enter the pageants and on the for-profit entities that are corporate sponsors of the pageants.[50]

Although tax-exempt charitable organizations may provide benefits to persons in their private capacity, benefits of this nature must—to avoid jeopardizing exempt status—be incidental both quantitatively and qualitatively in relation to the furthering of exempt purposes. To be quantitatively incidental, the private benefit must be insubstantial, measured in the context of the overall tax-exempt benefit conferred by the activity.[51] To be qualitatively incidental, private benefit must be a necessary concomitant of the exempt activity, in that the exempt objectives cannot be achieved without necessarily benefiting certain individuals privately.[52]

The private benefit doctrine applies to private foundations, inasmuch as they are tax-exempt, charitable organizations. Nonetheless, there is only one known instance of application of the doctrine in the private foundation context.

In that instance, an individual who was not a disqualified person with respect to the foundation[53] desired access to an archive of valuable documents held by the foundation, for the purpose of writing a commercial trade book about the individual who was the subject of the archive. The foundation was holding the archive for the purpose of organizing, preserving, and cataloging it, and ultimately transferring the archive to a public charity. The IRS ruled that although providing this individual access to the collection would not amount to self-dealing (because she was not a disqualified person), the foundation would confer impermissible private benefit to the individual: The private interests of the individual would be served by the commercial profit gained because the book would be enhanced by the information contained in the foundation-owned archive.[54]

---

50. "Beauty Pageants: Private Benefit Worth Watching," Topic B in the IRS Exempt Organizations Continuing Professional Education Technical Instruction Program textbook for fiscal year 2002. As still another illustration of this point, the IRS is ruling that a small board of directors, particularly one consisting of related individuals, is inherently an instance of unwarranted private benefit, so that an organization with a governing board of this nature cannot qualify as a tax-exempt charitable organization (*see Tax-Exempt Organizations* § 5.7(b)). Were this law (and it is not), there would be few exempt private foundations and no exempt family foundations.

51. E.g., *Ginsburg v. Commissioner*, 46 T.C. 47 (1966); Rev. Rul. 75-286, 1975-2 C.B. 210; Rev. Rul. 68-14, 1968-1 C.B. 243.

52. E.g., Rev. Rul. 70-186, 1970-1 C.B. 128.

53. *See* Chapter 4.

54. Priv. Ltr. Rul. 200114040. The IRS ruled that, when a private foundation commenced a scholarship program and collaborated in this regard with community foundations, it did not transgress the private inurement and private benefit doctrines simply because relatives of some of the directors of the community foundations received assistance (the scholarships were held to be qualifying distributions and the recipients members of a charitable class) (Priv. Ltr. Rul. 200332018).

Traditionally, the private benefit doctrine has been largely applied in cases concerning relationships between public charities and individuals. The application of this doctrine, however, is being expanded to encompass arrangements between charitable organizations and for-profit entities and charitable organizations and other categories of tax-exempt organizations.[55]

The sanction for violation of the private benefit doctrine is denial or revocation of the charitable organization's tax-exempt status.

The private benefit doctrine can apply in a factual situation even where the private inurement rules or the self-dealing rules do not apply, such as where the transaction does not involve an insider or a disqualified person.[56]

## § 5.3 DEFINITION OF SELF-DEALING

Basically, all direct and indirect financial transactions between a private foundation and its disqualified persons—persons who control and fund the foundation[57]—are prohibited. Although there are exceptions, most of these rules are draconian. It is usually immaterial whether the transaction results in a benefit or a detriment to the private foundation.[58] There is no de minimis threshold (at least, not yet adopted by a court); for example, even if only $1 was paid by a private foundation for a disqualified person's $1 million building, this bargain sale is prohibited, notwithstanding the economic advantage to the

---

55. The appellate court that reversed the Tax Court in *United Cancer Council, Inc. v. Commissioner*, 165 F.3d 1173 (7th Cir. 1999), *rev'g*, 109 T.C. 326 (1997), also remanded the case for consideration in light of the private benefit doctrine, inasmuch as the Tax Court previously held that an act of private inurement is also an act of private benefit (*American Campaign Academy v. Commissioner*, 92 T.C. 1053 (1989)), the *United Cancer Council* case was shaping up to be a significant private benefit case. The case, however, was settled before the Tax Court could rule on the private benefit aspects.

56. In *Graham v. Commissioner*, 83 T.C.M. 1137 (2002), the self-dealing rules were held inapplicable because the party to the transaction with a private foundation was not a disqualified person; the transaction was otherwise a self-dealing one, however, yet the IRS did not pursue revocation of the foundation's tax-exempt status because of the private benefit. Likewise, the IRS ruled that the sale of a parcel of real estate to a private foundation by the nephews of the founder of the foundation was not self-dealing, in that they were not disqualified persons with respect to the foundation (Priv. Ltr. Rul. 200333030).

57. *See* Chapter 4.

58. Reg. § 53.4941(d)-1(a). Occasionally, the concept of *reasonableness* is factored into the analysis (other than in connection with the personal services exception; *see* § 5.6(a)). For example, an early termination of a charitable remainder trust (which is subject to the self-dealing rules; *see* § 3.7) was held to not be self-dealing because the method of allocating assets of the trust on its termination to the beneficiaries was reasonable, the income beneficiaries had life expectancies reflecting average longevity, state law allowed the early termination, and all of the beneficiaries favored the early termination (Priv. Ltr. Rul. 200252092). *See* Rev. Rul. 2008-41, 2008-30 I.R.B. 170.

foundation. In certain circumstances, however, an incidental or tenuous benefit is disregarded.[59]

A sale can occur between a private foundation and a person who at the time of the sale is not a disqualified person, even though the transaction causes the person to become a substantial contributor and, consequently, a disqualified person. *Indirect acts* of self-dealing are also covered by these rules; such acts are those between disqualified persons and organizations controlled by the private foundation, or vice versa.[60] The complex subject of self-dealing may be addressed from different perspectives by presenting:

- Six specific prohibitions stated in the Internal Revenue Code.
- Exceptions to the six specific prohibitions rules found in the statute and in the regulations.
- Examples of acceptable and unacceptable self-dealing transactions.
- Suggestions for documenting relationships that could produce self-dealing.
- Procedures and rules to follow if self-dealing occurs.

### (a)  Six Specific Acts

Six acts of prohibited self-dealing between a private foundation and a disqualified person are referenced in the statute.[61] As a general rule, the specified transactions cannot occur directly between a private foundation and one or more of its insiders, nor indirectly through an entity controlled by such disqualified persons or by the foundation. These transactions are:

1. Sale, exchange, or leasing of property.
2. Lending of money or other extension of credit.
3. Furnishing of goods, services, or facilities.
4. Payment of compensation (or payment or reimbursement of expenses).
5. Transfer to, or use by or for the benefit of, a disqualified person of any income or assets of the foundation.
6. Agreement to pay a government official.

### (b)  Statutory Exceptions

Statutory *Special Rules* provide both clarification and certain exceptions, remove some of the absoluteness in the six prohibitions, and bring some reasonableness to the rules. The basic concept underlying these exceptions is to permit

---

59. *See* § 5.8(d).
60. *See* § 5.11.
61. IRC § 4941(d)(1).

certain transactions that provide benefit to a foundation without producing gain to any disqualified persons. The following transactions are permitted:[62]

- Transfer of indebted real or personal property is considered a permitted sale to a private foundation if the foundation does not assume a mortgage or similar debt, or if it takes the property subject to a debt placed on the property by the disqualified person before the 10-year period ending on the date of gift.[63]

- A disqualified person can make a loan that is without interest or other charge to the foundation if the funds are used exclusively for the private foundation's tax-exempt purposes.[64]

- Offering a no-rent lease or furnishing free use of a disqualified person's goods, services, or facilities to the private foundation is permissible, as long as they are used exclusively for tax-exempt purposes.

- Furnishing a disqualified person with exempt-function goods, facilities, or services that the private foundation regularly provides to the general public is not self-dealing, if conditions and charges for the transaction are the same as those for the public.[65]

- Reasonable compensation, payment of expenses, and reimbursement of expenses for a disqualified person can be paid by the private foundation to a disqualified person, if the amounts are reasonable and necessary to carry out the private foundation's exempt purposes.[66] The definition of *reasonable compensation* relied on by the IRS says that reasonable compensation is "such amount as would be ordinarily be paid for like services by like enterprises under like circumstances."[67]

- Proceeds of a corporate liquidation, merger, redemption, recapitalization, or other corporate adjustment, organization, or reorganization can be received by a foundation if "all securities of the same class as that held by the foundation are subject to the same terms and such terms provide for receipt by the foundation of no less than fair market value."

- Certain scholarship, travel, and pension payments to elected or appointed federal and state government officials are not considered self-dealing.[68]

---

62. IRC § 4941(d)(2).
63. *See* § 5.5(a).
64. *See* § 5.5.
65. *See* § 5.9.
66. *See* § 5.6.
67. Reg. § 1.165-7(b)(3).
68. *See* § 5.10.

- Leasing by a disqualified person to a foundation of space in a building with other unrelated tenants is acceptable if
  - The lease was binding on October 9, 1969, or including renewals.
  - The lease was not a prohibited transaction under former law.[69]
  - The lease terms and its renewals reflect an arm's-length transaction.

## (c)  Exceptions Provided in Regulations

In general, a transaction between a private foundation and a disqualified person is not an act of self-dealing if (1) the transaction is a purchase or sale of securities by a private foundation through a stockbroker, where normal trading procedures on a stock exchange or recognized over-the-counter market are followed, (2) neither the buyer nor the seller of the securities nor the agent of either knows the identity of the other party involved, and (3) the sale is made in the ordinary course of business and does not involve a block of securities larger than the average daily trading volume of that stock over the previous four weeks.[70]

Additional exceptions to the (at first glance) six specific, and seemingly absolute, rules are found in the regulations, which provide that the following types of *indirect* transactions do not constitute acts of self-dealing:[71]

- Certain business transactions between an organization controlled by the private foundation and its disqualified persons. *Control*, for purposes of these exceptions, means that the foundation or its managers, acting in their capacity as such, can cause the transaction to take place.

- A grant to an uncontrolled intermediary organization that plans to use the funds to make payments to governmental officials is not self-dealing, as long as the intermediary is in fact in control of the selection process and makes its decision independently.

- Transactions during administration of an estate or revocable trust in which the private foundation has an interest or expectancy, if certain specific requirements are satisfied.[72]

- Transactions totaling up to $5,000 a year and arising in the *normal course* of a retail business are permitted between a disqualified person and a business controlled by the foundation, as long as the prices are the same as for other customers.

---

69.  IRC § 503 (repealed).
70.  Reg. § 53.4941(a)-1(a)(1).
71.  Reg. § 53.4941(d)-1(b).
72.  *See* § 5.11.

- Stocks owned on May 26, 1969, and required to be distributed to avoid the tax on excess business holdings[73] were allowed to be sold, exchanged, or otherwise disposed of to a disqualified person.[74]

- A private foundation converting to classification as a public charity is not treated as a private foundation for self-dealing purposes during its 60-month termination period; therefore, transactions prohibited for private foundations otherwise may be allowed.[75]

## §5.4 SALE, EXCHANGE, LEASE, OR FURNISHING OF PROPERTY

The sale, exchange, lease, or furnishing of property between a private foundation and a disqualified person with respect to the foundation generally constitutes self-dealing.[76] Thus, for example, the sale of incidental supplies by a disqualified person to a foundation or the sale of stock by a disqualified person to a foundation for a bargain price is an act of self-dealing, regardless of the amount paid.[77] A private foundation's purchase of a mortgage held by its bank trustee that was a disqualified person was found to be self-dealing, even though the rate was much more favorable than would otherwise have been available; the self-dealing occurred because the bank (disqualified as a trustee) was selling its own property, not simply handling the purchase of an investment instrument from an independent source.[78] Conversely, even though the same banking institution served as trustee for both parties, a sale to a foundation by a testamentary trust (which was not disqualified in relation to the foundation) was not self-dealing.[79] A sale to the bank itself by either party would be self-dealing, however, because the bank is disqualified as to both parties, even though neither trust is related to the other trust. The sale by a private foundation to an unrelated party of an option to buy shares in a corporation that is a disqualified person in regard to the foundation is not self-dealing, even though the exercise of the option by the foundation would be.[80]

---

73. *See* Chapter 7.
74. Reg. § 53.4941(d)-4(b).
75. Reg. § 1.507-2(f)(2); Priv. Ltr. Rul. 199911054. In general, *see* Chapter 13. Also, the self-dealing rules do not apply with respect to amounts payable by a split-interest trust to its income beneficiaries for which a charitable deduction was allowed (Reg. § 53.4947-1(c)(2)(i)). Indeed, the self-dealing rules are not implicated where a charitable remainder trust is declared void and the assets returned to the donor (e.g., Priv. Ltr. Rul. 9816030).
76. IRC § 4941(d)(1)(A).
77. Reg. § 53.4941(d)-2(a)(1).
78. Rev. Rul. 77-259, 1977-2 C.B. 387.
79. Rev. Rul. 78-77, 1978-1 C.B. 378.
80. Priv. Ltr. Rul. 8502040.

An installment sale may be an act of self-dealing either as a sale of property[81] or an extension of credit.[82]

The transfer of real or personal property by a disqualified person to a private foundation is treated as a sale or exchange for these purposes if the private foundation assumes a mortgage or similar lien that was placed on the property prior to the transfer, or takes the property subject to a mortgage or similar lien that a disqualified person placed on the property within the 10-year period ending on the date of transfer.[83] A *similar lien* includes, but is not limited to, deeds of trust and vendors' liens, but does not include any other lien if it is insignificant in relation to the fair market value of the property transferred.[84]

If a transaction is not a sale or exchange between a private foundation and a disqualified person, it will not be an act of self-dealing (unless some other definition of the term applies). In one instance, the IRS ruled that, where the previously undivided interests of a foundation and disqualified person trusts in parcels of real estate are divided on a pro rata basis in accordance with the fair market value of the common interests surrendered and the separate interests received, the division of the properties will not constitute a sale or exchange of the properties, so that the partition will not amount to an act of self-dealing.[85] In another case, a contribution by disqualified persons of units in a limited liability company to a private foundation was ruled to not be self-dealing, because liabilities placed on the company did not constitute a similar lien (in that they were insignificant),[86] so that the transfer did not constitute a sale or exchange;[87] this characterization of the transaction facilitated a side-stepping of the rule that the sale of securities by a disqualified person to a foundation in a bargain sale is self-dealing.[88]

A contribution to a private foundation by a person who is a disqualified person with respect to the private foundation is not an act of self-dealing.[89]

---

81. IRC § 4941(d)(1)(A).
82. IRC § 4941(d)(1)(B).
83. IRC § 4941(d)(2)(A). Also Reg. § 53.4941(d)-2(a)(2); *Harold and Julia Gershman Family Foundation v. Commissioner*, 83 T.C. 217 (1984); Rev. Rul. 78-395, 1978-2 C.B. 270.
84. By reason of the Tax Reform Act of 1984 § 312, the self-dealing rules do not apply with respect to certain sales by the Wasie Foundation, as described in *Wasie v. Commissioner*, 86 T.C. 962 (1986).
85. Priv. Ltr. Rul. 200350022. In this ruling, the IRS relied on Rev. Rul. 56-437, 1956-2 C.B. 507 (holding that the severance of a joint tenancy in stock of a corporation, under a state's partition statute, and the issuance of separate stock certificates in the names of each of the joint tenants was a nontaxable exchange).
86. *See* text accompanied by *supra* note 82.
87. Priv. Ltr. Rul. 201012050.
88. *See* text accompanied by *supra* note 75.
89. E.g., Priv. Ltr. Rul. 8234149.

## (a) Transactions by Agents

The fact that an intermediary person or agent handles the transaction does not circumvent the rules, and self-dealing occurs when a disqualified person buys private foundation property from an agent through whom the foundation is selling property. In a case involving an art object consigned to a commercial art auction house, the purchase of the object by a disqualified person constituted self-dealing.[90] Similarly, the leasing of property to a disqualified person by a management company resulted in self-dealing when the foundation controlled the manager's actions through a retained veto power.[91]

## (b) Exchanges

An exchange of property, such as the transfer of shares of stock in payment of an interest-free loan, is tantamount to a sale or exchange.[92] Similarly, a transfer of real estate equal to the amount of the disqualified person's loan (in an effort to correct self-dealing) was ruled to be a second act of self-dealing.[93] On the other hand, a transfer of real estate in satisfaction of a pledge to pay cash or readily marketable securities was held not to be a sale or exchange, because the pledge was not legally enforceable and because a pledge is not considered a debt.[94] Essentially, self-dealing does not result from this type of a transfer because it is a gift.[95]

The IRS ruled that a split-dollar life insurance arrangement, involving a private foundation and its chief executive officer, included as part of a comprehensive compensation package, would not entail self-dealing.[96] The premiums to be paid by the executive and the private foundation will be sent directly to the insurance company; the IRS ruled that this would not be an exchange of property between the parties. The arrangement would permit the executive to assign his rights under the agreement to another party, such as an irrevocable life insurance trust. The IRS ruled that an assignment by this executive of his rights under the insurance arrangement, and the assignee's exercise of the rights and assumptions of obligations under the agreement, would not involve a sale, exchange, or other transfer of property between the executive and the private foundation.[97]

---

90. Rev. Rul. 76-18, 1976-1 C.B. 355.
91. Priv. Ltr. Rul. 9047001.
92. Rev. Rul. 77-379, 1977-2 C.B. 387.
93. Rev. Rul. 81-40, 1981-1 C.B. 508.
94. *See* § 5.8.
95. Priv. Ltr. Rul. 8723001.
96. Priv. Ltr. Rul. 200020060.
97. The IRS also ruled that this split-dollar insurance arrangement is not the type of insurance arrangement that is subject to IRC § 170(f)(10) or IRS Notice 99-36, 1999-26 I.R.B. 3 (concerning certain forbidden charitable split-dollar life insurance plans).

An exchange of a private foundation's securities in a reorganization or merger of a corporation that is a disqualified person is not necessarily an act of self-dealing. If all of the securities of the same class as those held by the foundation (prior to the transaction) are subject to the same, or uniform, terms and the foundation receives full fair market value for its securities, prohibited self-dealing does not occur.[98]

The partition of property held as tenants-in-common with a disqualified person did not produce reportable gain nor constitute self-dealing for a private foundation.[99] Without having explicitly said so, the IRS does not deem a partition as a prohibited sale or exchange. The foundation had received the undivided interest in the unproductive property as a gift from the disqualified person. Local law prohibited a nonprofit corporation from holding unproductive property, and the foundation wanted to make the property marketable by creating a divided interest.

## (c)  Leasing of Property

The leasing of property between a private foundation and a disqualified person generally constitutes self-dealing.[100] The leasing of property by a disqualified person to a private foundation without charge, however, is not an act of self-dealing. A lease is considered to be without charge even though the private foundation pays its portion of janitorial services, utilities, or other maintenance costs, as long as the payment is not made directly or indirectly to a disqualified person.[101]

As an example of permitted rent-free use, assume a private foundation borrows at no cost an art object from its creator to display in the foundation's museum. The foundation pays the maintenance and insurance on the object directly to the vendors. Thus, the foundation is essentially allowed to pay the disqualified person's costs of owning the art object during the time the works are on public display. The reason for permitting this arrangement is that the public benefits: Art that is otherwise not available can now be seen. On the other hand, placement of a foundation's art in its creator's home, away from public view, would be self-dealing.[102] Displaying art on the creator's property that is open to the public has been permitted, but only because the foundation's

---

98. Reg. § 53.4941(d)-3(d)(1). *See* discussion in § 5.13.
99. E.g., Priv. Ltr. Rul. 8038049; *see* § 5.4(e).
100. IRC § 4941(d)(1)(A); Reg. § 53.4941(d)-2(b)(1).
101. Reg. § 53.4941(d)–2(b)(2). *See* § 5.11.
102. Rev. Rul. 74-600, 1974-2 C.B. 385.

collection was displayed throughout the city, primarily on public lands, as part of a comprehensive outdoor museum program.[103]

A private foundation desired to dispose of ranch land it had owned for over 30 years to acquire other income-producing property to carry out its grant programs. An engineer advised that the foundation would maximize the ranch's value by developing the property—a process expected to take considerable time and requiring someone to live on the ranch during its development. The IRS approved a plan for the foundation to lease to its executive vice president, for a nominal sum, 1 percent of the ranch acreage, on which he would, at his expense, construct a residence. The lease provided for the foundation to pay the officer the then fair market value of any improvements upon the termination of the lease. The primary purpose of the transaction was to "ensure the foundation's interests in the ranch were safeguarded." The IRS decided that although the officer and his wife were disqualified persons, the duties were reasonable and necessary to accomplishing the foundation's purposes, and therefore the lease and subsequent payment to the officer would not result in self-dealing.[104]

A foundation's rental of a charter aircraft from a charter aircraft company, which is itself a disqualified person, was found to be an act of self-dealing.[105] Donating use of the airplane to the foundation, however, would be allowed. As long as the airplane is used for bona fide foundation business, the foundation can directly pay for fuel or hangar rental in the city visited, as long as the goods and services are purchased from an independent party.[106] Thus, the IRS ruled that disqualified persons may, without engaging in an act of self-dealing, lend works of art to a private foundation, inasmuch as the loan was without charge.[107]

---

103. Tech. Adv. Mem. 9221002. But see Priv. Ltr. Rul. 8824001 for the opposite result when, due to the fact that sculptures were placed on a disqualified person's private residential grounds not physically open to the public but available only for viewing from the street, self-dealing was ruled to have occurred. In evaluating display of foundation artwork in the lobby of a building owned by a disqualified person, the answer may depend on a number of facts. Is it sufficient that the building is open to the general public? Should the number and type of visitors be considered? Do unrelated parties occupy part or all of the building? Does the fact that the artwork is not visible from the street change the result? Would it change the answer if the foundation publicized the availability of the sculpture for public viewing, and/or should it include educational information about the work to building visitors?

104. Priv. Ltr. Rul 9327082.

105. Rev. Rul. 73-363, 1973-2 C.B. 383. Reg. § 53.4941(d)–2(d)(1).

106. See § 5.9.

107. Priv. Ltr. Rul. 200014040. Likewise, where a lease by a private foundation of property for charitable purposes was guaranteed by a disqualified person, the guarantee was characterized by the IRS as the provision of services without charge (Priv. Ltr. Rul. 199950039).

## (d)  Furnishing of Goods, Services, or Facilities

As a general rule, self-dealing includes any direct or indirect furnishing of goods, services, or facilities between a private foundation and disqualified persons.[108] The law, however, also contains special rules, one of which allows the furnishing without charge of a disqualified person's goods, services, or facilities to the private foundation as long as they are used exclusively for tax-exempt purposes.[109] Thus, the use of office space, an automobile, an auditorium, laboratory and office supplies, telephone equipment, and the like can be donated.[110] The foundation must require and actually use the donated property in conducting its charitable programs. The permitted furnishing is considered as *without charge*, even though the foundation pays for transportation, insurance, maintenance, and other costs it incurs in obtaining or using the property, so long as the payment is not made directly or indirectly to the disqualified person.[111]

Another special exception permits a foundation to furnish a disqualified person with exempt function goods, facilities, or services that the private foundation regularly provides to the public, such as a park, a museum, or a library. Such furnishing is not self-dealing if the conditions and charges made to the public are at least on as favorable a basis as the goods or services are made available for the disqualified person's use.[112] This exception is intended to apply to functionally related facilities,[113] such as a public park that a substantial number of persons, other than disqualified persons, use. A director of a private foundation that operates a museum, for example, could pay the normal price for his or her admission into an exhibition and to purchase a book in the museum bookstore.

For example, the IRS ruled that the use of a private foundation's meeting room by a disqualified person was not an act of self-dealing inasmuch as the room was made available to the disqualified person on the same basis that it was made available to the general public and was functionally related to the performance of a tax-exempt purpose of the private foundation.[114] Similarly, the IRS held that it was not an act of self-dealing for a museum, which was a private foundation, to allow a corporation, which was a disqualified person with respect to the private foundation, to use its private road for access to the corporation's headquarters. The road was made available to the general public

---

108. IRC § 4941(d)(1)(C).
109. IRC § 4941(d)(2)(C).
110. E.g., Priv. Ltr. Rul. 9805021 (use of foundation's facility for overnight stays by disqualified person when done to carry out the foundation's business).
111. Reg. § 53.4941(d)-2(d)(3). The IRS, in private letter rulings, has relaxed this rule somewhat, as discussed in § 5.9.
112. IRC § 4941(d)(2)(D); Reg. § 53.4941(d)-3(b).
113. IRC § 4941(j)(5). *See* §§ 3.1(e), 6.2(c).
114. Rev. Rul. 76-10, 1976-1 C.B. 355.

on a comparable basis, a substantial number of (nondisqualified) persons actually used the road, and the use of the road as an entrance to the museum was functionally related to the private foundation's tax-exempt purpose. The corporation had agreed to maintain the road, although that did not entitle it to any special privileges with respect to the use of the road.[115] In another instance, however, because the rental of office space to disqualified persons did not contribute importantly to a private foundation's tax-exempt purpose of conducting agricultural research and experimentation, the rental was held to be self-dealing, even though the disqualified persons conducted business activities in the same subject area of the private foundation's research.[116] Likewise, the IRS concluded that self-dealing occurred when a disqualified person lived rent-free in a manor house as a resident curator of a historic plantation, which was a national historic landmark, because the private foundation that owned and operated the property insufficiently made the grounds open to the public.[117]

Although the special exceptions in the statutory law do not address the point, the regulations expand this exception to allow a foundation to furnish goods, services, or facilities to its managers in recognition of their services as employees.[118] The value of the services or goods must be reasonable and necessary to the performance of their tasks in carrying out the exempt purposes of the foundation. Whether or not reportable as taxable income, the value of facilities and goods provided must not, when added to other amounts provided to a manager, cause him or her to receive excessive compensation. Accordingly, the IRS found that the furnishing of living quarters in a historical district to a substantial contributor (who worked 25 to 35 hours a week overseeing the complex and managing the foundation's financial affairs) was not self-dealing, again, because the value of the personal living quarters when combined with other compensation was reasonable.[119]

Providing a residence to a private foundation's president and his wife, who also served as the foundation's treasurer, on foundation property while they supervised the development of a retreat, conference, and ministry center was found to serve the foundation's exempt purposes.[120] The couple was said to be uniquely qualified to manage the project because they had shaped the ministry's vision and the president was a civil engineer familiar with the zoning and other local property law. Once the project was complete, a retreat-center director would be hired and the disqualified persons would move out. Because their

---

115. Rev. Rul. 76-459, 1976-2 C.B. 369.

116. Rev. Rul. 79-374, 1979-2 C.B. 387.

117. Tech. Adv. Mem. 9646002, revoking Priv. Ltr. Rul. 8651087. Indeed, the transgression was found to amount to unwarranted private benefit (*see* § 5.2).

118. Reg. § 53.4941(d)-2(d)(2).

119. Priv. Ltr. Rul. 8948034.

120. Priv. Ltr. Rul. 199913040.

overall compensation, including the value of the rent-free housing, was reasonable and their services were integral to the accomplishment of the exempt mission, the IRS concluded that impermissible self-dealing would not result from this furnishing of housing.

A trust created to promote open space, recreation, and education on a reserve did not commit acts of self-dealing when its work impacted land partly owned by its disqualified persons. The reserve is owned 54 percent by a company that was a substantial contributor to the foundation, 31 percent by a political subdivision, and 15 percent by other public and private owners.[121] The trust had extensive plans to produce a comprehensive plan for the reserve, to study its habitat and wildlife, to promote stewardship, to conduct public education activities, and to facilitate educational and recreational public access to the reserve. Due to the public nature of the project, the IRS decided any direct or indirect transfer to, or use of, foundation assets by the disqualified person (developer) was incidental and tenuous.[122]

### (e)  Co-Owned Property

Mere co-ownership of a property by a private foundation and its disqualified person(s) does not, in and of itself, represent self-dealing.[123] Therefore, a private foundation can receive and hold a gift or bequest of an undivided interest in property from its disqualified person(s). The difficulty is that only the foundation can *use the property*, because the statute specifically prohibits the use of any foundation income or assets by its disqualified persons.[124] A transitional exception to the rule provided by Congress applies only to property jointly owned before October 9, 1969.

---

121.  Priv. Ltr. Rul. 200527020. Though not provided in the facts of the ruling, the reserve seems to be a very large tract of land that includes subdivisions developed by the disqualified person.

122.  Citing Example 1 in Reg. § 53.4941(d)-2(f)(9) that deems a foundation's work to improve a ghetto in which the disqualified persons own property yielded only incidental benefit.

An IRS private letter ruling illustrates the blending of some of these rules. Although self-dealing generally includes the furnishing of goods between a private foundation and a disqualified person, this type of furnishing is allowed if it is without charge. Pursuant to this exception, a foundation was permitted to borrow an art collection from a disqualified person trust and display it to the public (Priv. Ltr. Rul. 201346011). The exception also extended to the provision of exhibit space to the foundation (*see* § 5.4(c)). Compensation paid to those providing "special technological services" for the conservation of exhibits, being "similar to the services an anthropologist or archeologist would provide with respect to artifacts," were held eligible for the personal services exception (*see* § 5.6(a)). Participation by other disqualified persons in certain event activities was held to not be self-dealing because of the incidental benefit exception (*see* § 5.8(d)).

123.  Priv. Ltr. Rul. 7751033.

124.  IRC § 4941(d)(1)(E).

Essentially, a foundation may hold and use co-owned property, but the disqualified person co-owner can only hold, but cannot use or otherwise reap any benefit from, the property. A number of private rulings have illustrated why limited-use or shared ownership can still be of some advantage to persons holding this type of an interest. In one case, an individual and his spouse owned an extensive art collection that they planned to bequeath to a museum they were creating. On the husband's death, the private foundation museum and the spouse became joint tenants holding an undivided interest in each object in the art collection. The IRS would not permit the spouse to display a small portion of the co-owned objects in her home and strictly applied the statute to prohibit her use of the art.[125] The IRS nonetheless permitted the spouse to display a portion of art works in her home, holding that the spouse's "private use of the small percentage of her separate property art works not loaned to you [the museum] at any one time will not constitute an act of self-dealing." The ruling, by stipulating that only her separate property could be displayed in her home, indirectly concluded that her tenant-in-common interest in the extensive art collection could not be displayed in her home.[126]

In this case, the spouse and the foundation asked the IRS to approve an agreement that the foundation has the "duty, and will make all expenditures necessary, to insure and adequately care for, maintain, conserve, and provide security for [the spouse's] separate property art works and the art works held by you and [the spouse] as tenants-in-common as long as they are on your premises or are otherwise in Foundation's possession." Similarly, the spouse bore the cost of insuring and maintaining art works that were in her possession. The ruling adopted a policy regarding sharing of property and stated that "insuring the art works in your [museum] custody affords you protection against the risk of financial loss in the event the works are damaged or destroyed. As in the supplemental submissions to your ruling request, it is more economical for you to obtain a single policy covering all art works in your possession rather than a multiplicity of separate short term policies covering different sets of art works which may be displayed from time to time in your museum. While [the spouse] may receive a benefit from your being the policy holder, the benefit will not be consequential in a financial sense since [the spouse] will pay the portion of the insurance premium attributable to her private use and enjoyment of her separate property art works. Therefore, such benefits as may accrue to [the spouse] from your obtaining the insurance policy are merely incidental or tenuous benefits. Finally, the loan of art work from [the spouse] furthers your educational and charitable purposes of having available these items for public display, and any benefit to [the spouse] from your payment of transportation,

---

125. Priv. Ltr. Rul. 8842045.
126. Gen. Couns. Mem. 39770 was more specific in holding that no portion of the co-owned art could be displayed in this individual's home.

maintenance, or insurance is merely incidental to the achievement of this charitable and educational goal."[127]

A gift of an undivided interest in property the donor planned to subsequently sell was sanctioned.[128] The donor relinquished all rights to use the improved real estate and retained only the right to inspect the property. Expenses were to be shared proportionately between the donor and the foundation. On subsequent sale of the co-owned property, the proceeds were divided proportionately. Self-dealing did not result from the gift, from holding the property jointly, or from the eventual sale by the foundation to an independent party.

Participation in a condominium association, as compared to owning an undivided interest in property, was found by the IRS to not constitute an act of self-dealing, and importantly, the disqualified persons could use their separately owned spaces.[129] The private foundation, which focuses on acquisition, display, and distribution of works of fine art, wished to acquire an art gallery space. Its creators purchased a warehouse building that was converted to a condominium consisting of five units. The largest unit was donated (free of encumbrances) to the foundation plus an undivided interest in the common areas and parking lot. Another unit was donated to the foundation to be used as an investment rental property. The remaining three units, comprising only 15 percent of the total square footage, were retained to be used as offices for the disqualified persons. The offices would also be available, plus a secretary/receptionist, free of charge to the foundation.

In this instance, common costs, such as maintenance, repairs, and operational (presumably utilities and janitorial) costs, were to be shared on an "objective basis according to the respective square footage of each owner's unit." Though not said to be a requirement in the decision, the foundation owned a majority of the building's square footage and, thereby, voting control of the association. If instead this foundation had been given an undivided interest in 85 percent of the property, the disqualified persons would not have been able to use the property.

The restrictions on use have also been found to include the making of improvements to a property. In one instance, a foundation jointly held property bequeathed to it by the co-owner's spouse prior to 1969, so she was permitted to receive income on her undivided share under the transitional rule. The co-owners wanted to make substantial improvements in the property to enhance its income-producing potential. Despite the fact the foundation and the spouse were to carefully divide the income and costs on a strict proportional basis, the

---

127. *See* §§ 5.8(d), 5.9.
128. Priv. Ltr. Rul. 7751033.
129. Priv. Ltr. Rul. 200014040.

IRS ruled that the improvement of the co-owned property would result in self-dealing and that the transitional rule could no longer apply.[130]

In another instance, sharing the cost of improvements to a residence in which the foundation had a remainder interest with the life tenant (spouse of donor), who was over 90 years old, was found not to result in self-dealing. The IRS noted that the repairs were capital in nature and necessary to maintain the condition of the property, which was a valuable foundation asset. Payment of the entire cost of improvement by the foundation could have been considered an impermissible use of foundation assets by its disqualified person; payment of its actuarially determined share of the cost was not. The ruling did not mention the fact that the relationship was not technically one of co-ownership; the tenant was not occupying foundation property. Finally, any benefit was found to be tenuous and incidental due to the life tenant's age.[131]

An alternative to holding property as co-owners—becoming partners—has been sanctioned by the IRS.[132] A limited partnership interest given to a foundation is different from the "jointly owned property" contemplated by the regulations. In the IRS's opinion, the "holding and use of separate interests in a limited partnership is not the use of jointly owned property." Instead of donating an undivided interest in a shopping center, the donors transferred the property to and became general partners in a limited partnership. Then they gave a freely transferable limited partnership interest to an independent corporate trustee to hold in a charitable remainder trust.[133] Caution must be used in planning these arrangements, however, to assure that the terms of the partnership agreement permit each partner to have exclusive control, or use, of their respective interests and do not create any common or shared interests.

Although the IRS, as reflected in some private letter rulings, has forbidden disqualified persons from using property co-owned with a private foundation, in other rulings the IRS has permitted types of passive investment holdings that might be considered self-dealing based on a literal reading of the rules. For example, the IRS labeled permitted co-ownership of real property an *investment relationship*.[134] The foundation and its disqualified persons each received their ownership by gift, held property as tenants in common, and had separate interests in a 40-year lease on the property. Because there was no sale, lease, or transfer of the property between the private foundation and its disqualified persons, self-dealing did not occur as to the holding of the property. As for the lease, the private foundation received its portion of the rental payment directly,

---

130. Priv. Ltr. Rul. 8038049.
131. Priv. Ltr. Rul. 200149040.
132. E.g., Priv. Ltr. Rul. 7810038.
133. This type of a trust is treated as a private foundation under IRC § 4947; *see* § 3.7.
134. Priv. Ltr. Rul. 9651037.

thereby "precluding its interest in the lease from being used by a disqualified person."

A private foundation's purchase of limited partnerships and interests in limited liability companies, in which an investment fund managed by the foundation trustees and investment advisor also invested, was not considered by the IRS to be self-dealing because there was no direct or indirect transfer of assets to or for the use of disqualified persons.[135] The factors on which the IRS based its approval were that (1) the foundation and the funds will not pool their investments to meet any minimum investment requirement, (2) the funds' investment return will not vary based on the foundation's investments, (3) the foundation's investment will not affect the cost of the funds' investment, (4) the funds will not advertise the foundation's participation in or connection to the investment or use it to attract other investors, (5) unrelated parties control and operate the partnerships and limited liability companies, and (6) the foundation trustee will not receive additional fees from the foundation attributable to these investments.

The primary focus in evaluating a coinvestment situation is whether the disqualified persons receive more than incidental or tenuous benefit by having the foundation invest in the same investment vehicle. In one instance, the following benefits were said to accrue to both the foundation and its disqualified persons:

- Reduction of administrative costs.

- Obtaining access to investments and investment funds that might otherwise be unavailable to the individual partners.

- Facilitating diversification of the assets for all partners.

- Obtaining economies of scale and cost savings as well as greater negotiating power through a coinvestment model. In the case of any fees or expenses of third-party investment managers based on a percentage of assets managed, the foundation would pay the lowest possible percentage and the disqualified persons would pay the remaining higher fees.

The IRS ruled that any benefits the DPs received from the PF's participation in the investment would be incidental and tenuous. Also, the PF's coinvestment was held not be a transfer to, or use by or for the benefit of, the PF's income or assets by any DP.[136]

No self-dealing was found when a limited liability company (the Land LLC) formed by three unrelated private foundations leased its land to a limited

---

135. Priv. Ltr. Rul. 9844031.
136. Priv. Ltr. Rul. 200551025.

liability company (the Building LLC) owned by disqualified persons with respect to the foundations.[137] The key to this conclusion was the fact that each of the disqualified persons owned less than 35 percent of the Building LLC. The leasing did not result in self-dealing because the Building LLC was therefore not a disqualified person. The carefully constructed arrangement was intended to give the foundations access to the management skills of their disqualified persons that would enable the foundations to invest in real estate at relatively low risk. Conversely, self-dealing was found to occur if a foundation and its disqualified persons were to jointly develop two tracts of land that they already co-owned 50/50. The foundation had received its one-half interest through an inheritance. The planned development was to be extensive and require substantial additional investment by the co-owners for such items as utilities, streets, drainage, and construction of buildings to be rented after completion. Costs would be paid one half by each owner, and future profits were to be shared equally.

The use of foundation income and assets for the proposed development was deemed self-dealing. The IRS further stated that "it is immaterial whether or not a transaction itself results in a benefit or a detriment to the private foundation."[138]

The consequences of transactions during the life of the partnership or joint venture deserve careful attention when the partnership or venture itself is a disqualified person[139] and other disqualified persons are also partners. Although the IRS has sanctioned such arrangements, there has been very little consideration of the transactions throughout the life and on dissolution of the entity.[140] It seems clear that proportional distributions of income to all partners should not represent a sale or exchange that creates self-dealing,[141] but special allocations could. Redemption of the foundation's interest could also result in self-dealing. If the terms for redemption apply equally to all partners, the IRS has concluded that the corporate redemption exception could apply.[142]

## § 5.5  LOANS AND OTHER EXTENSIONS OF CREDIT

The lending of money or other extension of credit between a private foundation and a disqualified person generally constitutes an act of self-dealing.[143] The lending cannot be direct or indirect, and the fact that the rate

---

137. Priv. Ltr. Rul. 200517031.
138. Priv. Ltr. Rul. 8038049.
139. IRC § 4946(a)(1)(E).
140. *See* Kirk, "Self-Dealing and the Lobster Pot of Joint Ventures," *Exempt Org. Tax Rev.* 221–232. (Aug. 2005).
141. Priv. Ltr. Rul. 200420029.
142. IRC § 4941(d)(2)(F); Priv. Ltr. Rul. 9237032; Field Service Adv. 200015007.
143. IRC § 4941(d)(1)(B).

of interest is better than the foundation could otherwise receive does not eliminate the self-dealing.[144] Even if a circuitous route is taken so that the first borrower is not an insider, indebtedness payable to or from the foundation by an insider is prohibited. For example, if a foundation sells property to an unrelated third party, who thereafter resells the property to a party related to the foundation, and if this disqualified person assumes liability for the first mortgage or takes the property subject to the mortgage payable to the foundation, self-dealing occurs with the second sale. Similarly, the transfer of a disqualified person's obligation by an unrelated party to a foundation results in self-dealing if the foundation becomes a creditor under the note.[145] A private foundation's payment of an obligation or debt of its disqualified person, such as a pledge to make church tithes, constitutes self-dealing.

In the instance of a self-dealing transaction that is a loan, an additional self-dealing transaction is deemed to occur on the first day of each tax year in the taxable period[146] after the tax year in which the loan occurred. An IRS ruling illustrates how the private foundation self-dealing taxes are calculated in an instance of a foundation loan to a disqualified person that spans more than one year and thus constitutes multiple acts of self-dealing.[147]

A loan by a private foundation to an individual, before he or she becomes a foundation manager (and thus a disqualified person),[148] may not be an act of self-dealing, because the self-dealing rules do not apply, in that the disqualified person status arose only following completion of the negotiation of the compensation package.[149] Where the loan principal remains outstanding once the individual becomes a disqualified person, however, an act of self-dealing occurs;[150] indeed, an act of self-dealing takes place in each year in which there is an uncorrected extension of credit.[151]

## (a) Gifts of Indebted Property

A transfer of indebted real or personal property to a private foundation is considered an impermissible sale or exchange if the foundation assumes a mortgage or similar lien that was placed on the property prior to the transfer, or takes the property subject to a mortgage or similar lien that the disqualified

---

144. Priv. Ltr. Rul. 9222052.
145. Reg. § 53.4941(d)–2(c)(1).
146. *See* § 5.15(d)(i), text accompanied by notes 460-461.
147. Rev. Rul. 2002-43, 2002-2 C.B. 85.
148. *See* Chapter 4.
149. Priv. Ltr. Rul. 9530032. *See* text accompanied by *supra* note 8.
150. Priv. Ltr. Rul. 9530032. Previously, the IRS ruled that there was no self-dealing in these circumstances, because the loan was created before the individual became a disqualified person (Priv. Ltr. Rul. 9343033). This ruling was reconsidered (Priv. Ltr. Rul. 9417018), however, and thereafter revoked (Priv. Ltr. Rul. 9530032).
151. *See* § 5.14.

person placed the loan on the property within a 10-year period ending on the date of the transfer.[152] The date on which the loan is made, not when the loan or line of credit was approved, is the date from which the 10-year exception is measured. It is normally the date a lien is actually placed on the property, even though the loan is part of a multiphase financing plan started more than 10 years before the transaction.[153]

In one instance, a disqualified person transferred to a private foundation a parcel of real property that was subject to a lien placed on the property by the disqualified person within the 10-year period ending on the transfer date. When the property was originally acquired, the lien created by the deed of trust executed in conjunction with the purchase of the property was placed on the property prior to the 10-year period. Within the 10-year period, however, the disqualified person obtained another loan, and the lien created by the deed of trust executed in conjunction with this new loan was placed on the land within the 10-year period. The IRS said that, for purposes of the self-dealing rules, "it [did] not matter that the taxpayer placed the second lien on the property as part of a multi-phased financing program begun more than 10 years before the date of transfer."[154]

The IRS accords these rules broad application, as evidenced by its determination that the contribution to a private foundation by a disqualified person of a life insurance policy subject to a policy loan was an act of self-dealing. This conclusion rested on the analysis that a life insurance policy loan is sometimes characterized as an advance of the proceeds of the policy, with the loan and the interest on it considered charges against the property, rather than amounts that must be paid the insurer.[155] The IRS concluded that the effect of the transfer was essentially the same as the transfer of property subject to a lien, in that the transfer of the policy relieved the donor of the obligation to repay the loan, pay interest on the loan as it accrues, or suffer continued diminution in the value of the policy. Application of the self-dealing rules to this type of transaction was completed by a finding that the amount of the loan was significant in relation to the value of the policy.[156]

A future obligation to pay expenses to maintain gifted property is not indebtedness for this purpose. A loan by a foundation to a trustee's client is self-dealing because the transaction confers benefit on the trustee by providing service to the trustee's client.[157]

A gift of stock in a rental property holding company that was indebted to the substantial contributor was ruled not to result in self-dealing. The loan was

---

152. IRC § 4941(d)(2)(A).
153. Rev. Rul. 78-395, 1978-2 C.B. 270.
154. *Id.* at 270.
155. E.g., *Dean v. Commissioner*, 35 T.C. 1083 (1961).
156. Rev. Rul. 80-132, 1980-1 C.B. 255.
157. Tech. Adv. Mem. 8719004.

made for business reasons prior to the transfer of the shares and the foundation is not personally obligated.[158]

## (b) Interest-Free Loans

The lending of money or other extension of credit without interest or other charge (determined without regard to the imputed interest rules) by a disqualified person to a private foundation is permitted if the proceeds of the loan are used exclusively in carrying out the foundation's exempt activities.[159] Thus, the making of a promise, pledge, or similar arrangement to a private foundation by a disqualified person, whether evidenced by an oral or written agreement, a promissory note, or other instrument of indebtedness, to the extent motivated by charitable intent and unsupported by consideration, is not an *extension of credit* before the date of maturity.[160]

The payment of expenses on behalf of a foundation by a disqualified person can be considered as an interest-free loan to the foundation. If expense advances are treated as loans without charge and are paid in connection with its exempt activities, a foundation can repay the loan and essentially make a reimbursement. Limited advances and reimbursements of expenses are permitted for foundation managers.[161] The regulations explaining the facility-sharing exception, however, prohibit a foundation's payment of costs it incurs in using the property directly or indirectly, to the disqualified person.[162] Despite this possible conflict, the IRS has taken a practical approach and permitted reimbursement in circumstances where the transaction clearly allows the foundation to better accomplish its exempt purposes.[163]

This exception is effectively voided where a private foundation repays or cancels the debt by transferring property other than cash (e.g., securities) to repay the loan. The IRS takes the position that the transfer, when viewed together with the making of the loan, is tantamount to a sale or exchange of property between the foundation and the disqualified person, and thus constitutes an act of self-dealing.[164]

---

158. Priv. Ltr. Rul. 8409039.
159. IRC § 4941(d)(2)(B); Reg. § 53.4941(d)-2(c)(2).
160. Reg. § 53.4941(d)-2(c)(3). E.g., Priv. Ltr. Rul. 200232036 (concerning the role of a private foundation as a conduit in paying premiums on a term life insurance policy on the life of a disqualified person) and Priv. Ltr. Rul. 200112064 (concerning the pledge by a disqualified person corporation to a private foundation of an option to purchase shares of the corporation's stock).
161. *See* § 5.6(d).
162. Reg. § 53.4941(d)-2(d).
163. The IRS permitted reimbursements in connection with a foundation's sharing of facilities and personnel as discussed in § 5.9.
164. *Supra* notes 87 and 88.

An individual who was a disqualified person with respect to a private foundation made an interest-free loan to a tax-exempt school to enable it to complete construction, purchase furniture and other materials, and hire staff; this individual also was the president of the school. The private foundation planned to make a grant to the school with the understanding that the school would use the funds to repay the loan. The IRS ruled that the making of this grant would not constitute self-dealing because the prospective grant was "unrestricted," in that the school "may" repay the loan, the proceeds of which were used for exempt purposes.[165] The disqualified person was said to have "no control" over the school to compel it to repay his loan; the school was characterized by the IRS as being "under no [legal] requirement to use the loan to repay" the disqualified person lender.[166]

## § 5.6 PAYMENT OF COMPENSATION

The payment of compensation by a tax-exempt charitable organization triggers potential application of various bodies of the federal tax law. Most of these areas of the law require that this type of compensation be reasonable. For example, the doctrine of private inurement,[167] applicable to private foundations, incorporates this requirement when compensation is paid to insiders, as does the doctrine of private benefit,[168] also applicable to private foundations, when compensation is paid to anyone. The sanction for violation of either doctrine can be loss of tax-exempt status. The intermediate sanctions rules,[169] while not formally applicable to foundations, entail much law on the subject that can also inform this matter of payment of compensation by charitable entities, including whether the compensation is reasonable. The sanctions in this context are imposition of excise taxes on disqualified persons.

The payment of compensation, including payment or reimbursement of expenses, by a private foundation to a disqualified person generally constitutes an act of self-dealing.[170] An extremely important and frequently used exception

---

165. Priv. Ltr. Rul. 200443045.

166. This position of the IRS may be contrasted with its diametrically opposite position in the charitable gift substantiation area (*see* § 16.2, footnote 9). In that context, the IRS successfully asserted that an *expectation* or an *understanding* on the part of a donor amounts to a *service* for purposes of these substantiation requirements (e.g., *Addis* v. *Commissioner*, 118 T.C. 528 (2002), *aff'd*, 374 F.3d 881 (9th Cir. 2004), *cert. den.*, 543 U.S. 1151 (2005)). These decisions not only erroneously cast an expectation or understanding as the equivalent of *consideration* for purposes of the substantiation rules (IRC § 170(f)(8)), they inappropriately graft language from the charitable split-dollar insurance plan rules (IRC § 170(f)(10)) onto the substantiation rules. For more on this point, *see Fundraising* § 8.15.

167. *See* § 5.1.

168. *See* § 5.2.

169. IRC § 4958. *See Tax-Exempt Organizations*, Chapter 21; *Intermediate Sanctions.*

170. IRC § 4941(d)(1)(D); Reg. § 53.4941(d)-2(e).

to the general rule allows payment of compensation to a disqualified person for services actually rendered in carrying out foundation affairs, except in the case of a government official. The performance of personal services must be reasonable and necessary to carrying out the tax-exempt purposes of the foundation, and the total amount of the compensation paid, including reimbursements, must not be excessive.[171] Thus, for this capacious exception to be available, the compensation must be for personal services, the compensation must be reasonable, and the compensation must be necessary for advancement of the private foundation's exempt purposes.

## (a)  Definition of Personal Services

The term *personal services* is not defined by statute or regulations; the boundaries of this exception are not precisely drawn. The IRS observed that the personal services exception is a "special rule that should be strictly construed," for, if not, the "fabric woven by Congress to generally prohibit insider transactions [involving private foundations] would unravel."[172] Examples in the regulations make it clear that the services of lawyers and investment managers, as such, are personal services. This exception is available irrespective of whether the person who receives the compensation (or payment or reimbursement) is an individual; thus, personal services can be provided by a corporation, partnership, or other type of service provider.[173]

In one of these illustrations, two partners in a 10-partner law firm served as trustees of a private foundation. These lawyers and the firm are disqualified persons. The firm provides legal services for the foundation. Assuming the services are reasonable and necessary for carrying out the foundation's exempt purposes, and assuming that the amount paid for these services is not excessive, these services are personal services and do not constitute impermissible self-dealing.[174] Similarly, the IRS ruled that unwarranted self-dealing did not occur when a foundation paid reasonable legal fees awarded by a court to a lawyer representing one of the foundation's managers; the lawsuit was filed against the other managers to require them to carry out the foundation's charitable program and was necessary to accomplish the foundation's exempt purposes.[175]

In another illustration provided in the regulations, a manager of a private foundation owns an investment counseling business. This individual manages the foundation's investment portfolio, for which he receives reasonable compensation. The payment of this compensation to this disqualified person is

---

171.  IRC § 4941(d)(2)(E); Reg. § 53.4941(d)-3(c).
172.  Priv. Ltr. Rul. 9325061.
173.  Reg. § 53.4941(d)-3(c)(1).
174.  Reg. § 53.4941(d)-3(c)(2), Example (1).
175.  Rev. Rul. 73-601, 1973-2 C.B. 385.

not an impermissible act of self-dealing.[176] A third illustration concerns a commercial bank that serves as a trustee for a private foundation. This bank also maintains the foundation's checking and savings accounts, and rents a safety deposit box to the foundation. The use of the funds by the bank and the payment of compensation by the foundation to the bank for the performance of these services, which are reasonable and necessary to the carrying out of the foundation's exempt purposes, are not impermissible acts of self-dealing if the compensation is not excessive.[177]

In the last of these illustrations, a substantial contributor to a private foundation owns a factory that manufactures microscopes. This person contracts with the foundation to manufacture 100 microscopes for the foundation. Even if the foundation uses the microscopes in furtherance of its exempt purposes and even if the compensation paid by the foundation is reasonable, any payment under this contract by the foundation constitutes an act of self-dealing, inasmuch as such payments are not compensation paid for the performance of personal services.[178]

The term *personal services* includes the services of a broker serving as agent for a private foundation but not the services of a dealer who buys from the private foundation as a principal and sells to third parties.[179]

There is one court decision on the point, based on the foregoing illustrations, holding that the services sheltered by this exception are confined to those that are "essentially professional and managerial in nature."[180] That case involved the provision of janitorial services, which were ruled to not be professional and managerial in nature.

A wide range of services provided by disqualified person banks and other financial institutions is covered by this exception. The IRS ruled that the management and investment of the funds of two private foundations by the trust department of a financial institution were personal services.[181] Likewise, the personal services exception was held to encompass investment counseling, financial planning, custodial, legal, and accounting services provided by a bank.[182] Further, a bank assisting a private foundation in connection with its securities-lending program was held to not be engaged in prohibited self-dealing by reason of the personal services exception.[183]

---

176. Reg. § 53.4941(d)-3(c)(2), Example (2).
177. *Id.*, Example (3).
178. *Id.*, Example (4).
179. Reg. § 53.4941(d)-3(c)(1). This exception was ruled to apply with respect to services provided by disqualified persons in connection with the sale of a private foundation's art work (Priv. Ltr. Rul. 9011050).
180. *Madden, Jr. v. Commissioner*, 74 T.C.M. 440, 449 (1997).
181. Priv. Ltr. Rul. 9503023.
182. Priv. Ltr. Rul. 9114036.
183. Priv. Ltr. Rul. 200501021.

This exception, however, is by no means confined to financial institutions. IRS rulings refer to disqualified person corporations, partnerships, and limited liability companies that provide personal services to private foundations. These services include management of real estate,[184] cash and debt management,[185] other forms of investment management,[186] other types of financial services,[187] coordination of tax matters,[188] accounting services,[189] types of administrative services,[190] and other types of management services.[191] The IRS permitted a management company to provide services to a private foundation under these rules, notwithstanding the fact that the company was owned by a disqualified person.[192] Services provided by employees of private foundations, such as selection of grant projects, can be encompassed by the exception.[193]

By contrast, the IRS ruled that maintenance, repair, janitorial, cleaning, landscaping, and similar "operational" services do not qualify for this exception.[194] Similarly, services by a general contractor, brokerage for the sale and leasing of real property, insurance brokerage, and certain marketing and advertising services were held to not constitute personal services.[195]

A topic that is rarely discussed in the law is the matter of compensation paid to the members of the board of trustees of a private foundation for their services as such. This is a common practice; the assumption seems to be that services of this nature constitute *personal services*. An IRS ruling concerned compensation paid to trustees who performed services normally provided by officers and outside professionals, as well as services in fields such as investments, personnel, and grant-making. Noting that these trustees' fees were less than those charged by financial institutions for similar

---

184. E.g., Priv. Ltr. Rul. 200326039.
185. E.g., Priv. Ltr. Rul. 200315031.
186. E.g., Priv. Ltr. Rul. 9237035.
187. E.g., Priv. Ltr. Ruls. 200116047, 200217056.
188. E.g., Priv. Ltr. Rul. 9703031.
189. E.g., Priv. Ltr. Rul. 9702036.
190. E.g., Priv. Ltr. Rul. 200228026.
191. E.g., Priv. Ltr. Rul. 9238027. The distinctions in this area turn more on what is *managerial* than what is *professional*. For example, while janitorial services are not protected by this exception (*see* text accompanied by *supra* note 180), services that constitute the management of janitorial services are within the exception (e.g., Priv. Ltr. Rul. 200326039).
192. Priv. Ltr. Rul. 200238053.
193. E.g., Priv. Ltr. Rul. 199927046.
194. Priv. Ltr. Rul. 200315031. In one instance, the IRS concluded that secretarial services were embraced by the personal services exception (Priv. Ltr. Rul. 9238027), yet on another occasion, the agency required a private foundation to provide an amended services agreement that specifically precluded such services (Priv. Ltr. Rul. 200217056). The provision of secretarial services by a disqualified person to a private foundation is generally regarded as self-dealing (*see* § 5.9(a)).
195. Priv. Ltr. Rul. 9325061.

services, the agency ruled that the fees were reasonable and thus the payment of them were not self-dealing.[196] This ruling assumed—but does not hold—that the services to be provided by these trustees were personal services. The matter of compensation of private foundation trustees who serve solely in that capacity has not been addressed by a court decision or IRS ruling.[197]

### (b) Definition of Compensation

The term *compensation* in this setting generally means a salary or wage, any bonuses, fringe benefits, retirement benefits, and the like. Occasionally, however, other economic benefits are treated as compensation for purposes of application of the self-dealing rules. For example, under certain circumstances, the value of an indemnification by a private foundation of a foundation manager, or the payment by a foundation of the premiums for an insurance policy for a foundation manager, must be treated as compensation so as to avoid self-dealing. Likewise, the IRS ruled that a split-dollar life insurance arrangement established by a private foundation for the benefit of a key employee was a form of compensation to the employee.[198] By contrast, when the self-dealing rules are explicit in prohibiting a particular type of transaction between a private foundation and a disqualified person, the rules cannot be sidestepped by treating the value of the economic benefit provided as part of the disqualified person's total (reasonable) compensation.[199]

This topic is accorded more expansive treatment in the intermediate sanctions setting. In that context, the term *compensation* generally includes all

---

196. Priv. Ltr. Rul. 200135047.
197. Nonetheless, the IRS ruled that the trustees of a private foundation may cause the foundation's trust agreement to be amended to eliminate a trust termination date and extend the duration of the trust indefinitely, thereby concomitantly elongating the period of time they serve and receive compensation, without engaging in self-dealing (Priv. Ltr. Rul. 200343026); that a private foundation may compensate its board members for their participation in a conference sponsored by the foundation (Priv. Ltr. Rul. 200324056); and that a private foundation may compensate its foundation managers for attendance at board meetings (Priv. Ltr. Rul. 200007039).
198. Priv. Ltr. Rul. 200020060.
199. *See* § 5.7(b). For example, a loan by a private foundation to a disqualified person is an act of self-dealing (*see* § 5.5). The self-dealing rules cannot be avoided by regarding the value of this type of loan as compensation (Priv. Ltr. Rul. 9530032). By contrast, this characterization of a loan as compensation is permissible in the case of a public charity dealing with an insider (*id.*). Under the intermediate sanctions rules, however, this practice is impermissible when done in hindsight, in that an economic benefit cannot be treated as consideration for the performance of services unless the organization clearly indicated its intent to so treat the benefit (IRC § 4958(c)(1)(A)). This approach thus imposes a more rigorous standard in this regard on public charities than is the case with private foundations.

economic benefits provided by a charitable organization, to or for the use of a person, in exchange for the performance of services.[200] These benefits include (but are not limited to) (1) all forms of cash and noncash compensation, including salary, fees, bonuses, severance payments, and certain deferred compensation; (2) the payment of liability insurance premiums for, or the payment or reimbursement by the organization of, (a) any penalty, tax, or expense of correction owed in connection with the intermediate sanctions rules, (b) any expense not reasonably incurred by the person in connection with a civil judicial or civil administrative proceeding arising out of the person's performance of services on behalf of the organization, or (c) any expense resulting from an act, or failure to act, with respect to which the person has acted willfully and without reasonable cause; and (3) all other compensatory benefits, whether or not included in gross income for income tax purposes, including payments to welfare benefit plans, such as plans providing medical, dental, life insurance, severance pay, and disability benefits, and both taxable and nontaxable fringe benefits (other than certain fringe benefits),[201] including expense allowances or reimbursements (other than expense reimbursements pursuant to an accountable plan),[202] and the economic benefit of a below-market loan.[203]

The compliance questionnaire sent by the IRS in 2008 to about 400 tax exempt colleges and universities[204] also provides a comprehensive list of types of remuneration that may be paid to executives of tax-exempt organizations, including private foundations: salary; bonus; contributions to employee benefit plans (e.g., health benefit plans); incentives (short-term and long-term); contributions to life, disability, and/or long-term care insurance: split-dollar life insurance (where the organization pays the premiums); loans or other extensions of credit (in the case of forgone interest or debt forgiveness); stock or stock options (equity-based compensation); severance or change-of-control payments; personal use of the organization's credit card (where there is no reimbursement); personal use of the organization's owned or leased vehicles; personal travel for the individual and/or spouse/other family member (where there is no reimbursement); expense reimbursements pursuant to a nonaccountable plan; value of organization-provided housing and utilities; value of organization-provided vacation home; personal services provided at individual's residence (e.g., housekeeper, lawn service, maintenance or repair services);

---

200. Reg. § 53.4958-4(b)(1)(ii)(B).
201. That is, those described in IRC § 132.
202. Reg. § 1.62-2(c).
203. IRC § 7872(e)(1). This inventory of the elements of compensation is in Reg. § 53.4958-4(b)(1)(ii)(B).
204. Form 14018. See *Tax-Exempt Organizations* §§ 5.7(c), 8.3(a)(i); *Colleges and Universities,* Chapters 2, 5, 6, 7, 10, and 15.

other personal services provided (e.g., legal, financial, retirement services); payment of health and/or social club dues; personal use of organization's aircraft or boat; first-class travel;[205] scholarship and/or fellowship grants (if taxable); executive fringe benefits;[206] contributions to deferred compensation plans; and any other form of compensation.

The determination as to whether any of these items is included in the gross income of a disqualified person for federal income tax purposes is made on the basis of standard federal tax principles, irrespective of whether the item is taken into account for purposes of determining the reasonableness of compensation.[207]

## (c)  Definition of Reasonable

The self-dealing regulations lack a definition of the phrase *reasonable compensation*, but instead direct a foundation to consult the body of law pertaining to the deductibility of compensation as a business expense to determine whether pay is excessive. In application of that law, a private foundation has the burden of showing that a compensation package is equal to "such amount as would ordinarily be paid for like services by like enterprises under like circumstances."[208] A private foundation that compensates disqualified persons is well advised, however, to follow developments regarding the excess benefit transactions rules, which are applicable with respect to public charities. These rules impose penalties on persons receiving, and in some instances approving of, excessive compensation.[209]

An excess benefit, in the public charity context, occurs when the economic benefit paid by the charitable organization to a disqualified person exceeds the value of the consideration received—such as for services performed or property transferred. Similarly, self-dealing occurs when a private foundation pays unreasonable compensation to a disqualified person.

Although the excess benefit transactions rules are somewhat different from the self-dealing rules, many of the terms are the same. The excess benefit transactions rules contain criteria for assessing the reasonableness of compensation that can be applied in the private foundation setting. These elements are

---

205. Payment of first-class travel, however, is not a form of compensation.
206. Other than IRC § 132 fringe benefits.
207. Reg. § 53.4958-4(b)(1)(ii)(C).
208. Reg. § 1.162-7(b)(3).
209. The intermediate sanctions rules follow the same formula as is used in the business expense deduction rules (*see supra* note 208) (Reg. § 53.4958 4(b)(1)(ii)(A)). This alchemy used in determining the reasonableness of compensation is termed an "accumulation and assessment of data as to comparability" (Reg. § 53.4958-6(c)(2)). The IRS wrote that "exemption from federal income tax of an organization is not jeopardized where agreements on compensation are entered into through negotiations conducted at arm's-length and are not considered to be excessive based on a person having similar responsibilities and comparable duties" (Priv. Ltr. Rul. 200944055).

contained as part of a unique feature of the excess benefit transactions rules: a rebuttable presumption that compensation (and other transactions) is reasonable.[210] Pursuant to that presumption, relevant information as to reasonableness of compensation includes (1) compensation levels paid by similarly situated organizations, both taxable and tax-exempt for functionally comparable positions, (2) the availability of similar services in the geographic area of the tax-exempt organization, (3) current compensation surveys compiled by independent firms, and (4) actual written offers from similar institutions competing for the services of the disqualified person.[211]

The IRS, in the college and university questionnaire,[212] identified the following factors to use in setting an individual's compensation: the compensation levels paid by similar organizations, the level of the individual's education and experience, the specific responsibilities of the position involved, the individual's previous salary or compensation package, similar services in the same geographic or metropolitan area, the number of the organization's employees, and the organization's annual budget and/or gross revenue and assets.

The IRS, in this questionnaire, also identified the following sources to be used in obtaining comparability data as to an individual's compensation: published surveys of compensation paid by similar organizations, Internet research on compensation paid by similar organizations, telephone survey(s) of compensation paid by similar organizations, use of an outside expert hired to provide a report on comparable compensation data, a report prepared by an expert compensation analyst employed by the organization involved, written offers of employment from similar organizations, and annual information returns filed by similar organizations.

Courts develop criteria as to the reasonableness of compensation; often the cases involve for-profit employers. This is because a payment of compensation, to be deductible as a business expense,[213] must be an outlay that is ordinary and necessary. The concepts of reasonable and ordinary and necessary are essentially identical.[214] There is inherent tension in this context, however, in that the "judges of the Tax Court are not equipped by training or experience to determine the [reasonableness of] salaries of corporate officers; no judges are."[215]

---

210. Reg. § 53.4958-6.

211. Reg. § 53.4958-6(c)(2)(i).

212. *See* text accompanied by *supra* note 204.

213. IRC § 162.

214. *Rapco, Inc. v. Commissioner*, 85 F.3d 950 (2nd Cir. 1996).

215. *Exacto Spring Corp. v. Commissioner*, 196 F.3d 833, 835 (7th Cir. 1999). In one case, the Tax Court found that the reasonable compensation for an executive for a year was $98,000; revisiting the case following a partial reversal, the court concluded that the reasonable compensation amount for the same executive and year was $500,000 (*E. J. Harrison and Sons, Inc. v. Commissioner*, 86 T.C.M. 240 (2003), *rev'd and rem'd*, 2005-2 U.S.T.C. ¶ 50, 493 (9th Cir. 2005), *on rem.*, 91 T.C.M. 1301 (2006), *aff'd*, 2008-1 U.S.T.C. ¶ 50, 244 (9th Cir. 2008)).

A private foundation may decide to utilize the services of an independent consulting firm in determining the reasonableness of compensation for one or more of its employees. If it does, the foundation should be certain that the company is reputable, should consider the cost (fees and expenses), should obtain the report as a draft and have it reviewed and if necessary edited by competent legal counsel, and should verify (or have the lawyer do so) that all relevant criteria are identified and discussed in the report. The foundation should be careful to avoid the phenomenon "created [by some consultants] by their willingness to use their resumes and their skills to advocate the position of the party who employs them without regard to objective and relevant facts, contrary to their professional obligations."[216]

To prove that compensation is reasonable applying these concepts, a foundation must show that the pay is equal to "such amount as would ordinarily be paid for like services by like enterprises under like circumstances."[217] For example, an annual salary 75 percent higher than the average for private foundations of comparable size listed in one of the Council on Foundations' *Foundation Management Reports*, which also represented 35 percent of the foundation's grant expense, was found to be excessive and an act of self-dealing.[218] The factors used in evaluating whether private inurement has occurred[219] are also relevant in determining whether compensation paid by a private foundation is reasonable for purposes of the self-dealing rules.

A foundation striving to prove that compensation payments are not excessive for the work performed can consider these points:

- Is the amount of any payment for personal services excessive or unreasonable?[220]

- Are the payments ordinary and necessary to carry out the exempt purposes of the foundation?[221]

- What are the individual's responsibilities and duties? Is there a written job description, a contract for services, or personnel procedures?

- Is the person qualified for the position through experience, education, or other special expertise?[222]

---

216. *Boltar, LLC v. Commissioner*, 136 T.C. 326 (2011). This observation by the court pertained to appraisers but applies equally in this setting.
217. Reg. § 1.162-7(b)(3).
218. Priv. Ltr. Rul. 9008001.
219. In general, *see Tax-Exempt Organizations* § 19.4(a); *Tax Planning and Compliance*, Chapter 5.
220. *The Labrenz Foundation v. Commissioner*, 33 T.C.M. 1374 (1974).
221. *Enterprise Railway Equipment Company v. United States*, 161 F. Supp. 590 (Ct. Cl. 1958). This case concerned a commercial business but is cited by the IRS as an example of application of the IRC § 162 standards for the reasonableness of salaries paid by exempt organizations.
222. *B.H.W. Anesthesia Foundation, Inc. v. Commissioner*, 72 T.C. 681 (1979).

- How much time is devoted to the position?

- Are time sheets or other evidence of time devoted to the foundation's work maintained?

- To evaluate compensation accurately, count not only salary but all benefits, including:[223]

  - Salary or fees (current and deferred),

  - Fringe benefits,

  - Contribution to pension or profit-sharing plans,[224]

  - Housing or automobile allowances,

  - Directors' and officers' liability insurance,[225]

  - Expense reimbursements,

  - Clubs, resort meetings, or other lavish items, and

  - Compensation to family members.

- How does the compensation structure for an individual compare with those of organizations of similar size and similar activities? Employees and consultants serving a charitable organization can be provided compensation commensurate with that paid by for-profit businesses.[226]

- To evaluate the reasonableness of compensation accurately, a private foundation should take into account all economic benefits provided.[227]

- How does the individual's compensation package compare with those of other members of the staff and the organization's overall budget?

- Are there sharp increases (spikes) in compensation levels?[228]

- Be cautious with large bonuses.[229]

- Salary increases may successfully be cast as payments, in whole or in part, for prior years' services, where the individual was undercompensated in those years.[230] Documentation is critical to the success of this position.

---

223. *John Marshall Law School v. United States*, 81-2 U.S.T.C. ¶ 8514 (Ct. Cl. 1981).
224. Rev. Rul. 74-591, 1974-2 C.B. 385.
225. *See* § 5.7 regarding indemnification of disqualified persons and payments of liability insurance premiums.
226. The House Committee on Ways and Means report accompanying the intermediate sanctions legislation states that "an individual need not necessarily accept reduced compensation merely because he or she renders services to a tax-exempt, as opposed to a taxable, organization" (H. Rep. 104-506, 104th Cong., 2nd Sess. 56, note 5 (1996)).
227. *John Marshall Law School v. United States*, 81-2 U.S.T.C. ¶ 8514 (Ct. Cl. 1981).
228. *Miller and Son Drywall, Inc. v. Commissioner*, 196 F.3d 833 (7th Cir. 1999).
229. *Haffner's Service Stations, Inc. v. Commissioner*, 326 F.3d 1 (1st Cir. 2003).
230. Reg. § 53.4958-4(a)(1); *Devine Brothers, Inc. v. Commissioner*, 85 T.C.M. 768 (2003).

- Is compensation percentage-based or otherwise in commission form? This is not likely to occur in the foundation context, but contingent compensation arrangements have been upheld in the courts where the compensation is reasonable and the conditional nature of the compensation is beneficial to the organization (e.g., percentage-based fundraising compensation).[231] It usually is prudent to place a cap on this form of compensation.[232]

- The law in the nonprofit context does not openly take into account, in assessing the reasonableness of compensation, the leadership skills of an individual in advancing the cause of an organization. In a for-profit business case, the court portrayed an executive as the "locomotive" of the company, observing that the business would not have succeeded without this executive's "devotion, dedication, intelligence, foresight, and skill."[233] In another instance, a court wrote that an executive was the "driving force" behind the company's success, recognizing the executive's "dedication and hard work."[234]

- The emergence of nonprofit governance principles and practices is informing this subject. A private foundation may consider adoption of a compensation policy.[235] Ideally, an interested party should abstain from voting on his or her compensation.

A court opinion provides another version of the IRS's standards for determining reasonable compensation. A private foundation with about $200,000 in assets paid its sole trustee annual compensation of $45,000 and furnished him with two automobiles and a fully equipped office. An expert witness for the IRS testified that the compensation for this individual should range from $1,450 to $2,000 during the years at issue, based on a formula to determine annual trustee compensation of $4 to $5 per $1,000 of foundation assets, plus 5 percent of foundation income. The court found the compensation to be self-dealing, and also revoked the tax-exempt status of the foundation on the ground of private inurement.[236]

A *Compensation of Disqualified Person Checklist* can be found in Exhibit 5.1 to serve as a foundation's guide to properly documenting reasonableness of compensation paid to disqualified persons. A checklist published by the IRS in the context of the intermediate sanctions rules offers further guidance as to the process for establishing the reasonableness of compensation paid to private foundation personnel.

---

231. *National Foundation, Inc. v. United States*, 87-2 U.S.T.C. ¶ 9602 (Ct. Cl. 1987).
232. *People of God Community v. Commissioner*, 75 T.C. 1053 (1989).
233. *Beiner, Inc. v. Commissioner*, 88 T.C.M. 297, 324, 325 (2004).
234. *Multi-Pak Corp. v. Commissioner*, 99 T.C.M. 1567, 1579 (2010).
235. *See Nonprofit Governance* §§ 4.2(c), 6.3(e).
236. *Kermit Fischer Foundation v. Commissioner*, 59 T.C.M. 898 (1990).

**Exhibit 5.1**  Compensation of Disqualified Person Checklist

This checklist can serve as a guide to documenting the reasonableness of compensation a private foundation (PF) pays to the persons that create, control, and manage it. The general rule prohibits such payments [§ 5.3]. A statutory exception permits the payment of reasonable compensation to such persons for personal services rendered in carrying out the tax-exempt purposes of the foundation.

Name of Foundation_____

**Self-dealing occurs,** and penalties can be imposed, when a disqualified person receives unreasonable compensation for services rendered.

**Unreasonable compensation** results when the total economic benefit provided directly or indirectly to a disqualified person (DP) exceeds value of personal services provided by the DP.

**Disqualified Person** is one with substantial influence over the PF's affairs, including a substantial contributor [§ 4.1], officer, director, trustee, or one with similar responsibilities [§ 4.2], owners of certain businesses that contribute to the PF [§ 4.3], and their family members [§ 4.4].

**Question 1. Is the Compensation Paid to a Disqualified Person Reasonable?**

- Is there a job description, employment contract, engagement letter, or other agreement that fully describes the duties, hours, responsibilities of the disqualified person? [§ 5.6(a)]
- Are all types of compensation, including benefits, fringes, and allowances, taken into account to determine total annual compensation?
- If commission or other type of revenue sharing (incentive pay) is paid, has evidence been obtained showing that the rate is in line with industry standards? [§ 5.6(c)]

**Question 2. Is the Reasonableness of Compensation Properly Documented?**

- Is comparable data—surveys, offers DP received from others, availability of others for job, opinion of consultants, and other evidence of value gathered? [§ 5.6(b)]
- Is the compensation reported to the IRS on Forms W-2 or 1099?
- Is compensation approved (when possible) by nondisqualified persons?
- Are written records of meeting (minutes) when engagement was approved kept with notations of votes, abstentions (conflict), and any other discussions?
- Is all compensation reported on Part VIII of Form 990-PF, including taxable and non-taxable fringe benefits? [See § 12.2(e).]

Prepared by_____

with (PF representative)_____

Date_____

**Intermediate Sanctions IRS Rebuttable Presumption Checklist**

Name of disqualified person: _____
Position under consideration: _____
Duration of contract (1 year, 3 years, etc.): _____
Proposed compensation:_____
    Salary: _____
    Bonus: _____
    Deferred Compensation: _____

*(Continued)*

Eʜɪʙɪᴛ **5.1** (Continued)

---

Fringe benefits (list, excluding § 132 fringes):

_____  _____  _____

_____  _____  _____

Liability insurance premiums: _____

Forgone interest on loans: _____

Other: _____

Description of types of comparability data relied upon (e.g., association survey, phone inquiries, etc.):

    a. _____

    b. _____

    c. _____

    d. _____

Sources and amounts of comparability data:

    Salaries: _____

    Bonuses: _____

    Deferred compensation: _____

    Fringe benefits (list, excluding § 132 fringes):

    Liability insurance premiums: _____

    Forgone interest on loans: _____

    Other: _____

Office of file where comparability data kept:

Total proposed compensation:

Maximum total compensation per comparability data:

Compensation package approved by authorized body:

    Salary: _____

    Bonus: _____

    Fringe benefits (list, excluding § 132 fringes):

    Deferred compensation: _____

    Liability insurance premiums: _____

    Forgone interest on loans: _____

    Other: _____

Date compensation approved by authorized body:

Members of the authorized body present (indicate with X if voted in favor):

Comparability data relied upon by approving body and how data was obtained:

Names of and actions (if any) by members of authorized body having conflict of interest:

Date of preparation of this documentation (must be prepared by the latter of next meeting of authorized body, or 60 days after authorized body approved compensation):

Date of approval of this documentation by Board (must be within reasonable time after preparation of documentation above):

*Source:* Information letter from Steve T. Miller, Director, IRS Exempt Organization Division, May 1, 2001.

---

## (d) Finding Salary Statistics

Comparative information is extremely useful, and sometimes critical, in evaluating the reasonableness of the compensation of a disqualified person. The most appropriate comparison is made with similar foundations in the same field of endeavor (e.g., a grant-making foundation with a similar amount of endowment, another private operating foundation that operates a library, or a medical foundation conducting competitive research projects).

Perhaps the easiest way to secure reliable compensation information is to inspect the annual information returns filed by comparable foundations. Form 990-PF is required to be made available on request at each foundation's office and can be viewed on the Internet.[237] All forms of compensation paid to each officer, director, trustee, and foundation manager must be presented for each of these persons, along with his or her title and average amount of time devoted to the position each week. In addition, similar information is reported for the five highest-paid foundation employees and the five highest-paid independent contractors. For this purpose, a person paid more than $50,000 is highly paid. In some cases, the comparable organization might be a public charity, in which case the Form 990 would be reviewed; it contains similar information.

The Council on Foundations publishes a biennial *Foundation Management Report* for its members, which contains private foundation compensation levels by size of foundation, position, and area of the country. An Urban Institute report updated periodically is available at www.urbaninstitute.org entitled "Foundation Expenses and Compensation." The Association for Small Foundations annually publishes *Foundation Operations and Management Survey*, a comprehensive survey of salaries and benefits by size of organization, region of the country, and by positions (executive director, controller, clerical assistant, program manager, and the like). The *Nonprofit Times* and *The Chronicles of Philanthropy* publish annual salary surveys. Abbott, Langer & Associates publishes and sells an annual survey entitled "Compensation in Nonprofit Organizations," which includes a variety of statistical information. A foundation may also find a survey containing information pertinent to its own area or state published by associations of regional or affinity grant-makers.

### (e)  Commissions or Management Fees

Compensation based on a percentage of sales of a private foundation's goods or property or the value of the property managed is permitted as long as the amount of the commission or fee is not so excessive as to be considered unreasonable. The regulations cite, as an example of disqualified persons who can be paid in this manner, an investment counselor.[238] This regulation does not

---

237. *See* § 12.3(a), www.guidestar.org. The Guidestar Nonprofit Compensation Report provides detailed information indexed by job category, gender, geography, type of nonprofit, budget size, state, and more. National, state, and regional reports are also available.
238. Reg. § 53.4941(d)-3(c)(2), Example (2).

specify the fashion in which the counselor's fee is to be calculated. Instead, the concepts discussed earlier are applied to measure what is reasonable. Particularly when paying this type of compensation, a foundation should become familiar with the market in which similar property is normally sold. The range of commission for the sale of art versus securities exemplifies the need to document comparative pricing. Although the commission charged by a fine arts dealer can range between 10 percent and 50 percent of the selling price, a commission of less than 1 percent is charged for the sale of marketable securities through an established brokerage company.

The IRS outlined what it called *comparability factors* that it recommends a foundation use to evaluate whether commissions are reasonable.[239] The commissions paid to an art dealer that was also a disqualified person were ruled not to be self-dealing when the terms of the commissions were based: on a customary scale prevailing in the work's normal market (i.e., the amount was reasonable). The ruling was sought by the private foundation created by an artist. After the artist's death, the artwork was to be sold by the same dealer who had represented the artist while living, to fund the foundation's programs. The ruling suggested consideration of these factors:

- Commissions charged by nondisqualified persons for selling the (same) artist's work.

- Commissions paid by the artist during his or her lifetime to persons who are now disqualified persons and to others.

- Commissions that agents charge to sell art of the same school as the artist's.

- Commissions that are received by agents who sell art generally from the foundation's geographic area.

In another private ruling, concerning the brokerage commissions paid to a related-party investment manager, the IRS deemed the amount to be customary and normal for the industry. Total compensation, including the normal transaction fees, plus 50 percent of the account's annual equity value increases in excess of 15 percent, was found to be reasonable, because it was comparable with practices in the industry.[240]

---

239. Priv. Ltr. Rul. 9011050.
240. Priv. Ltr. Rul. 9237035. In a situation involving services provided to maintain a historic site, the personal services were found by the IRS to be compensated at a reasonable rate, which was a "rate consistent with and no greater than the rates charged to its other clients" (Priv. Ltr. Rul. 9307026).

## (f) Expense Advances and Reimbursements

Advances that are "reasonable in relation to the duties and expense requirements of a foundation manager" are permitted.[241] Cash advances should not ordinarily exceed $500, according to the regulations. When a foundation chooses to exceed this $500 threshold, appropriate documentation should be gathered. Such a report could reflect the number of days and details of expected expenses. To mitigate the amount needed as an advance, the foundation can also purchase airline tickets and lodging hotels directly. For extended travel time or trips to places where it is not secure to carry cash, the foundation might obtain and allow disqualified persons to use a credit card. Personal use of the card, of course, should be prohibited. If the advance is to cover anticipated out-of-pocket current expenses for a reasonable period, such as a month, self-dealing will not occur:

- When the foundation makes an advance,
- When the foundation replenishes the funds upon receipt of supporting vouchers from the manager, or
- If the foundation temporarily adds to the advance to cover extraordinary expenses anticipated to be incurred in fulfillment of a special assignment, such as long-distance travel.

Thus, the IRS ruled that the payment by a private foundation of legal fees, which were not excessive, awarded by a court to the lawyer for one of the private foundation's managers (and thus a disqualified person), who had initiated litigation against the other managers to require them to carry on the private foundation's charitable program, did not constitute an act of self-dealing, inasmuch as the service performed by the manager in filing the suit was reasonable and necessary to carry out the private foundation's tax-exempt purpose.[242]

A subset of this question arises when a disqualified person expends funds on behalf of the foundation and wishes to be reimbursed. For example, a disqualified person buys office supplies or writes a grant check on behalf of the foundation. Reasonable and necessary expenses incurred by a disqualified person to perform a professional service for a foundation, such as a translation fee for a legal document in connection with a foundation grant to a foreign organization, can also be reimbursed. An architect's charges might include blueprints. Expenses paid by the disqualified person in these circumstances can be classified as loans, bearing no interest, from the disqualified person to the foundation. Complete

---

241. Reg. § 53.4941(d)-3(c)(1).
242. Rev. Rul. 73-613, 1973-2 C.B. 385. A pension paid by a private foundation to one of its directors (a disqualified person), whose total compensation including the pension was not excessive, was not an act of self-dealing (Rev. Rul. 74-591, 1974-2 C.B. 385).

documentation, of course, should evidence the nature of the expenditure and the fact that it advanced the exempt purposes of the foundation.

Expenses of travel and meals incurred in connection with conducting foundation affairs can also be paid or reimbursed. A foundation with directors and personnel in different locations, for example, can pay for the cost of travel to attend a meeting in one of the locations. The expense of site visits to potential grantees can be paid. When a foundation pays such expenses on behalf of its disqualified persons, a written policy should describe the terms for reimbursement and documentation required should be developed. For example, it is prudent for a foundation to adopt a policy against payment of lavish traveling expenses. Limiting the reimbursement to prevailing per diem rates published by the IRS might be considered. Full and complete reports of the expenditures, along with descriptions of the nature of the work performed, meetings held, or other foundation business that necessitated the travel, should be compiled to document the expenditure.

Reimbursement for vehicle mileage should be made based on the prevailing standard mileage rates. Beginning January 1, 2014, the rate was 56 cents per mile for business miles driven and 14 cents for service to a charitable organization. The level of reimbursement by a private foundation would depend, therefore, on the person's position in the foundation. A compensated employee, director, or trustee would be reimbursed at the higher rate. A volunteer director or person working on foundation programs on a pro bono basis would receive the lower rate.

The documentation process and required reports are referred to as an *accountable plan*. Amounts paid under an accountable plan are not reported as compensation to the person being reimbursed.[243] Importantly, these expenses are also not reported as compensation for purposes of completing Form 990-PF, Part VII.

### (g) Bank Fees

Banks and trust companies frequently serve as trustees for private foundations and, in this role, often face the possibility of self-dealing. Certain banking functions that a bank performs for all of its customers can be performed for the private foundations for which it serves as trustee without amounting to self-dealing.[244] Taking into account a fair interest rate for the use of the funds by the bank, reasonable compensation can be paid. The *general banking services* permitted are:

- Checking accounts, as long as the bank does not charge interest on any overdrafts. Payment of overdraft charges not exceeding the bank's cost of processing an overdraft have been ruled to be acceptable,[245]

---

243. Reg. § 1.162-2(c)(4).
244. Reg. § 53.4941(d)-2(c)(4).
245. Rev. Rul. 73-546, 1973-2 C.B. 384.

- Savings accounts, as long as the foundation may withdraw its funds on no more than 30 days' notice without subjecting itself to a loss of interest on its money for the time during which the money was on deposit, and

- Safekeeping activities.

Transactions outside the scope of these three relationships may be troublesome. For example, if a private foundation left excess funds, which were not earning interest, in a bank that is a disqualified person, self-dealing generally would occur.[246] Nonetheless, the IRS ruled that a non–interest bearing clearing account arrangement between a private foundation and a disqualified person bank, being a "common business practice for trust departments," was protected by this exception.[247] A bank trustee's purchase of securities owned by independent parties for a foundation's account is not self-dealing, but purchase of the bank's own mortgage loans would be.[248] The purchase of certificates of deposit by a foundation is unacceptable should the certificates provide for a reduced rate of interest if they are not held to the full maturity date.[249]

By contrast, the IRS ruled that a bank assisting a private foundation in connection with its securities-lending program will not be engaged in prohibited self-dealing by reason of this banking services exception. The foundation had an investment trustee (a bank with trust administration services) that was charged with generally managing and investing the foundation's assets. The IRS observed that the investment trustee, in arranging securities loans for this foundation, is acting merely as the foundation's agent; the bank and its affiliates are not borrowers as part of this program.[250]

## (h) IRS Executive Compensation Study

The IRS, on March 1, 2007, published a report on its findings as a consequence of its Executive Compensation Compliance Initiative that it launched in 2004.[251]

**Background.** The Exempt Organizations Office of the IRS's TE/GE Division implemented this initiative, managed by an Executive Compensation Compliance Initiative Team. This project used the Exempt Organizations Compliance

---

246. Rev. Rul. 73-595, 1973-2 C.B. 384.
247. Priv. Ltr. Rul. 200727018.
248. Rev. Rul. 77-259, 1977-2 C.B. 387.
249. Rev. Rul. 77-288, 1977-2 C.B. 388. By reason of Tax Reform Act of 1984 § 312, the self-dealing rules do not apply to certain financing involving the Wasie Foundation, as described in *Wasie v. Commissioner*, 86 T.C. 962 (1986).
250. Priv. Ltr. Rul. 200501021.
251. IR 2004-106.

Unit (EOCU) and the Data Analysis unit, which were created in 2004. This project encompassed review of Forms 990 and 990-PF, and related returns, for tax years beginning in 2002. The IRS contacted 1,826 charitable organizations to seek information about their executive compensation procedures and practices; 1,428 were public charities and 398 were private foundations. The EOCU sent compliance check letters to 1,223 charitable organizations whose annual information returns were missing information; this entailed 1,023 public charities and 200 private foundations. An examination phase of this project involved 603 organizations, including 179 entities that provided unsatisfactory responses to compliance checks.

**Findings.** This project led the IRS to the following findings:

- Over 30 percent of compliance check recipients were required to amend their annual information returns.
- 15 percent of compliance check recipients were selected for examination.
- "Examinations to date do not evidence widespread concerns other than reporting."
- 25 examinations resulted in proposed excise tax assessments under IRC Chapter 42, aggregating in excess of $21 million, against 40 disqualified persons or organization managers (over $4 million in connection with public charities and over $16 million in connection with private foundations).
- "Although high compensation amounts were found in many cases, generally they were substantiated based on appropriate comparability data."
- Additional education and guidance, and training for agents, are needed in the areas of reporting requirements and use of the rebuttable presumption procedure (the latter for public charities).
- Changes in annual information returns are needed to reduce errors in reporting and provide sufficient information to enable IRS to identify compensation issues.
- This effort utilized "new compliance contact techniques," which have been refined in subsequent projects (e.g., those concerning credit counseling and down payment assistance organizations).

**Methodology.** Organizations (1,223) that received these compliance check letters constituted six categories:

1. 50 public charities with assets of at least $1 million and revenues of at least $5 million that reported "significant total compensation" but failed to provide "complete detailed information" about that compensation.

2. 100 public charities of all sizes reporting receivables/loans from trustees, directors, officers, and key employees exceeding $100,000.

3. 378 public charities that either answered "yes" or failed to respond to the question on the annual return as to whether they participated in an excess benefit transaction.

4. 497 public charities that either answered "yes" or failed to respond to the question about transactions with disqualified persons.

5. 188 private foundations that did not report any officers' compensation on their returns.

6. 12 private foundations were contacted regarding loans to officers.

**Examination Phase.** The general purpose of the examination phase of this project was a determination of whether the compensation of disqualified persons was reasonable. During this process, revenue agents also considered the private foundation rules concerning loans to disqualified persons, and the purchase and sale of foundation assets by and to disqualified persons.

This phase involved the following 782 organizations:

- 100 small public charities (assets of less than $1 million and revenues of less than $5 million) that reported significant amounts of compensation for one or more officers.

- 208 larger public charities (at least $1 million in assets and $5 million in revenues) that reported significant amounts of compensation for one or more officers.

- 97 public charities with completed returns chosen pursuant to a sampling procedure.

- 198 private foundations reporting significant officers' compensation.

- The 179 organizations that provided unsatisfactory responses to the compliance checks.

**Conclusions.** The compliance checks uncovered significant reporting errors and omissions in specific areas, particularly excess benefit transactions and foundation transactions with disqualified persons, yet the examinations indicated that those organizations selected for review generally were compliant with the intermediate sanctions and self-dealing rules. Fifty public charities initially failed to file schedules detailing compensation paid; 10 percent of the private foundations reviewed were referred for examination for this reason. Of the 100 public charities involved in loan-making, 37 were referred for examination; 7 private foundations provided loans or pledged collateral to or for the benefit of disqualified persons, resulting in self-dealing.

Seventy-seven examinations remain open; 705 have been completed (of the latter, 115 were closed with a written advisory suggesting modifications of future behavior and review by the Review of Operations office). The excise taxes assessed were for (1) excessive salary and incentive compensation; (2) payments for vacation homes, personal legal fees, or personal automobiles that were not treated (reported) as compensation; (3) payments for personal meals and gifts to others on behalf of disqualified persons that were not treated as compensation; and (4) payments to an officer's for-profit corporation in excess of the value of the services provided by the corporation. Eleven percent of the disqualified persons involved in private foundation self-dealing transactions reported the transactions; none did so in the public charity excess benefit transactions cases. Thirteen percent of the self-dealing transactions and 11 percent of the excess benefit transactions were corrected before examination.

Of the 27 private foundations that were formally examined, 5 percent paid excessive compensation to officers and directors; 86 percent required recusals of officers and directors from discussion and approval of their compensation; 59 percent had written conflict-of-interest policies; 49 percent commissioned a survey to establish compensation; and 92 percent set compensation within the survey range.

**Lessons Learned and Recommendations.** This report includes the following lessons learned and recommendations:

- The size of this project and the "diverse universe" created logistical difficulties. Future initiatives of this nature should consider breaking the project into components, such as separating public charities and private foundations.

- Using correspondence as the exclusive method of conducting single-issue examinations for "factually sensitive and complicated issues," such as self-dealing and excess benefit transactions, should be reconsidered. Although it is appropriate to use broad contacts to identify cases to be examined, an up-front field visit or other contact with the examined organization might substantially reduce the volume of records needed to be reviewed and the time spent on the examination.

- Compliance check questions must be "clear and focused" so as to produce responses that can be readily analyzed and enable the IRS to select appropriate cases for examination.

- Annual information return compensation reporting needs to be revised to "facilitate accurate and complete" reporting. The Form 990 redesign project should focus on reducing the number of places where the same information is required to be reported on the return, providing clearer instructions regarding what needs to be reported, and requesting specific information to identify potential noncompliance areas, such as loans to officers and directors.

- The Exempt Organizations Office (EO) needs to revisit the issue of when penalties should be assessed for filing incomplete annual information returns.

- EO should communicate to the public the most common return preparation errors identified during the compliance checks and examinations.

- EO should further educate the public charity sector about the intermediate sanctions rebuttable presumption as to reasonableness and how to satisfy its requirements.

- Future initiatives should focus on the correlation between satisfaction of the rebuttable presumption by an organization and the reasonableness of compensation paid to its disqualified persons.

- EO should change its process for monitoring excise taxes collected for the payment of excess compensation to better distinguish between the different types of excise taxes collected from public charities and private foundations.

- The relatively small percentage of corrections made by disqualified persons before contact by EO illustrates the need for a continued enforcement presence in this area. EO should continue to review compensation issues in more focused projects and should "pursue baselining general compliance with the compensation rules."[252]

## § 5.7  INDEMNIFICATION AND INSURANCE

It is common for a private foundation to provide officers' and directors' liability insurance to, or to indemnify, foundation managers in connection with civil proceedings arising from the managers' performance of services for the foundation. The general rule is that indemnification by a private foundation, or the provision of insurance for the purpose of covering the liabilities of an

---

252. This is an impressive undertaking by the IRS, and the agency should be commended by the charitable sector for its efforts. All of this work and reporting is marred, however, by a gaping absence of the obvious: the criteria used by the IRS for determining reasonableness of compensation. Despite the need for understanding and clarification in this area (whether it be the rules as to private inurement, private benefit, self-dealing, or excess benefit transactions), the law (other than court opinions) is basically silent as to these criteria. The recommendation about educating the sector about the rebuttable presumption as to reasonableness (used in the public charity context) is a good idea; an even better one is educating the sector about reasonableness of compensation in the first instance.

individual in his or her capacity as a manager of the foundation, is not self-dealing. Moreover, the amounts expended by a private foundation for insurance or indemnification generally are not included in the compensation of the disqualified person for purposes of determining whether the disqualified person's compensation is reasonable.

Indemnification payments and insurance coverage are divided into non-compensatory and compensatory categories. This body of law is a component of the general statutory scheme by which transfers to, or use by or for the benefit of, a disqualified person of the income or assets of a private foundation generally constitute self-dealing.[253]

## (a) Noncompensatory Indemnification and Insurance

Self-dealing does not occur, as a general rule, when a private foundation indemnifies a foundation manager with respect to the manager's defense in any civil judicial or civil administrative proceeding arising out of the manager's performance of services (or failure to perform services) on behalf of the foundation. This indemnification may be against all expenses (other than taxes, including any of the private foundation taxes, penalties, or expenses of correction) and can include payment of lawyers' fees, judgments, and settlement expenditures. The following conditions must exist, however, for the indemnification to not be considered self-dealing:

- The expenses must be reasonably incurred by the manager in connection with the proceeding, and

---

253. *See* § 5.8. The tax regulation was amended in this regard in 1995 (T.D. 8639). Previously, the provision of insurance for the payment of private foundation taxes by a private foundation for a foundation manager was self-dealing unless the premium amounts were included in the compensation of the manager (prior Reg. § 53.4941(d)-2(f)(1)). Also previously, the regulations provided that the indemnification of certain expenses by a private foundation for a foundation manager's defense in a judicial or administrative proceeding involving private foundation taxes was not, under certain circumstances, self-dealing (prior Reg. § 53.4941(d)-2(f)(3)). The IRS interpretations of these prior rules are contained in Rev. Rul. 82-223, 1982-2 C.B. 301 (concerning indemnification or insurance for coverage of foundation managers for liabilities arising under state law concerning mismanagement of funds; self-dealing found where foundation indemnified a foundation manager for an amount paid in settlement); Rev. Rul. 74-405, 1974-2 C.B. 384 (concerning insurance provided for foundation managers against liability for claims under the federal securities laws in connection with their role in preparing the registration statement and prospectus for a public offering of securities); Priv. Ltr. Rul. 8503098 (holding that indemnification and insurance against foundation tax liability and state mismanagement law liability was not self-dealing); Priv. Ltr. Rul. 8202082 (stating that the rules in the regulations, as to indemnification and insurance, apply with respect to all civil proceedings). There was confusion in this area of the law, occasioned in part by inconsistent rulings from the IRS.

- The manager must not have acted willfully or without reasonable cause with respect to the act or failure to act that led to the proceeding or liability for a private foundation tax.[254]

Likewise, the self-dealing rules do not apply to the payment of premiums for insurance to cover or to reimburse a foundation for this type of indemnification payment.[255] These payments are viewed as expenses for the foundation's administration and operation, rather than compensation for the manager's services. An indemnification or payment of insurance of this nature is not regarded as part of the compensation paid to the manager in the context of determining whether the compensation is reasonable for purposes of the private foundation rules.[256] The IRS ruled that this exception to the self-dealing rules was available in connection with service by some of the managers of a private foundation as trustees of charitable remainder trusts as to which the foundation was the remainder interest beneficiary.[257]

## (b)  Compensatory Indemnification and Insurance

The indemnification of a foundation manager against payment of a penalty tax, and the associated defense, is considered to be part of the manager's compensation. This type of payment by a private foundation is an act of self-dealing, unless, when the payment is added to other compensation paid to the manager, the total compensation is reasonable. A *compensatory expense* of this nature includes payment of any of the following:

- Any penalty, tax (including a private foundation tax), or expense of correction that is owed by the foundation manager,

- Any expense not reasonably incurred by the manager in connection with a civil judicial or civil administrative proceeding arising out of the manager's performance of services on behalf of the foundation, or

- Any expense resulting from an act or failure to act with respect to which the manager has acted willfully and without reasonable cause.[258]

Likewise, the payment by a private foundation of the premiums for an insurance policy providing liability insurance to a foundation manager for any of these three categories of expenses is an act of self-dealing, unless when the

---

254. Reg. § 53.4941(d)-2(f)(3)(i).
255. Reg. § 53.4941(d)-2(f)(3)(ii).
256. *Id.*
257. Priv. Ltr. Rul. 200649030.
258. Reg. § 53.4941(d)-2(f)(4)(i).

premiums are added to other compensation paid to the manager the total compensation is reasonable for purposes of the private foundation rules.[259] If the total compensation is not reasonable, the foundation will have engaged in an act of self-dealing. These payments are viewed as being exclusively for the benefit of the managers, not the private foundation.

A private foundation is not engaged in an act of self-dealing if the foundation purchases a single insurance policy to provide its managers both non-compensatory coverage and compensatory coverage, as long as the total insurance premium is allocated and each manager's portion of the premium attributable to the compensatory coverage is included in that manager's compensation for purposes of determining reasonable compensation.[260]

The term *indemnification* includes not only reimbursement by the foundation for expenses that a foundation manager has already incurred or anticipates incurring, but also direct payment by the foundation of these expenses as the expenses arise.[261]

## (c)  Fringe Benefit Rules and Volunteers

The determination as to whether any amount of indemnification or insurance premium is included in a manager's gross income for individual income tax purposes is made on the basis of general federal tax law principles and without regard to the treatment of the amount for purposes of determining whether the manager's compensation is reasonable for self-dealing purposes.[262] Any property or service that is excluded from income under the de minimis fringe benefit rules[263] may be disregarded for purposes of determining whether the recipient's compensation is reasonable under the private foundation rules.[264]

---

259. Reg. § 53.4941(d)-2(f)(4)(ii).

260. Reg. § 53.4941(d)-2(f)(5). Comments on these regulations in proposed form included the thought that allocation of insurance premiums should not be required, because doing so places an undue burden on private foundations. In deciding to retain the allocation provision in the final regulations, the IRS—in the preamble to the regulations—once again articulated its view of this body of law: "The self-dealing rules were meant to discourage foundations from relieving managers of penalties, taxes and expenses of correction, as well as expenses ultimately resulting from the manager's willful violation of the law. A rule that did not require an allocation to determine whether the disqualified person's compensation is reasonable for purposes of [IRC] chapter 42 could have the opposite effect" (60 Fed. Reg. 65566 (Dec. 20, 1995)).

261. Reg. § 53.4941(d)-2(f)(6).

262. Reg. § 53.4941(d)-2(f)(7).

263. IRC § 132(a)(4).

264. The IRS, on September 14, 2011, announced that employees' use of cell phones for business purposes is a working condition fringe benefit and that use of these phones for personal purposes is a de minimis fringe benefit (Notice 2011-72, 2011-38 I.R.B. 407).

The IRS adopted amended regulations concerning certain fringe benefits[265] relating to the exclusion from gross income of benefits known as *working condition fringe benefits*,[266] which clarified the treatment, in this regard, of bona fide volunteers who perform services for private foundations and other tax-exempt organizations. These regulations, which do not directly address the self-dealing aspects of this matter, apply with respect to volunteers (including directors and trustees) who provide services to exempt organizations and who receive directors' and officers' liability insurance and/or indemnification protection from these organizations.

The federal tax law excludes certain fringe benefits from an individual's gross income.[267] Generally, these fringe benefits are excludable by those who are employees, whether these individuals are compensated or working as volunteers (where the tax-exempt organization has the right to direct or control the volunteers' services). For certain purposes, the term *employee*[268] includes independent contractors. For other purposes,[269] however, independent contractors are not treated as employees. Thus, bona fide volunteers, like their paid counterparts, could not (prior to the adoption of these regulations) exclude no-additional-cost services from their gross income (unless there was an employer-employee relationship, which was unlikely).[270] That is, although volunteers who were employees could exclude from gross income these fringe benefits, and all volunteers (including independent contractors) could exclude de minimis fringe benefits, the language of the regulations relating to working condition fringes did not encompass bona fide volunteers.

The difficulty in this connection regarded the business expense deduction rules. An individual engaged in carrying on a trade or business has the requisite profit motive for business expense deduction purposes. An individual who performs services as a bona fide volunteer, however, does not have a profit motive and thus cannot claim an expense deduction for amounts incurred in connection with the volunteer work. For example, the value of directors' and officers' insurance provided to a volunteer was not excludable as a working condition fringe benefit, even though the same insurance coverage is excludable

---

265. IRC § 132.
266. A working condition fringe benefit is any property or service provided to an employee of an employer to the extent that, if the employee were paid for the property or service, the amount paid would be allowable as a business expense deduction (IRC § 162) or a depreciation deduction (IRC § 167) (IRC § 132(d); Reg. § 1.132-5(a)(1)).
267. IRC § 132(a), encompassing (in addition to working condition fringe benefits [*see supra* note 240]) "no-additional-cost services," "qualified employee discounts," and "de minimis fringe" benefits.
268. Reg. § 1.132-1(b).
269. IRC § 132(a)(1) concerning no-additional-cost services (IRC § 132(b)) and (2) concerning qualified employee discounts (IRC § 132(c)).
270. IRC § 132(a).

from the income of a paid employee or director who has a profit motive. The amended regulations are designed to eliminate this distinction, that is, to ensure that, like their paid counterparts, bona fide volunteers may exclude working condition fringe benefits—including directors' and officers' liability insurance—from their gross income.

The regulations provide that, solely for these purposes, a bona fide volunteer (including a director or officer) who performs services for a tax-exempt organization[271] (or for a governmental unit) is deemed to have a profit motive for purposes of the business expense deduction.[272] An individual is a *bona fide volunteer* only if the total value of the benefits provided with respect to the volunteer services is substantially less than the total value of the volunteer services the individual provides to the organization.[273] The value of liability insurance coverage (or indemnification for liability) is deemed to be substantially less than the value of an individual's volunteer services to the organization, provided that the insurance coverage is limited to acts performed in the discharge of official duties or the performance of services on behalf of the tax-exempt organization (or government) employer.[274]

As noted, these regulations do not directly address the self-dealing aspects of this issue. The preamble accompanying these regulations, however, states that "like other tax-exempt organizations, private foundations need not allocate portions of D & O insurance premiums to individual directors or officers or include any such allocable amounts" as reportable compensation, "provided such amounts are excludable from gross income under the[se] final regulations," and that "whether or not such allocable amounts need to be treated as compensation for the limited purpose" of the self-dealing rules, "no employer should issue [compensation tax form] 1099 or W-2 for any such amount that is excludable from gross income as a working condition fringe benefit." Consequently, while a foundation manager still must (to avoid the self-dealing rules) be certain that this form of compensation is reasonable, the amount involved is excludable from the manager's gross income.

The IRS ruled that a private foundation may amend its articles of incorporation, in conformity with a change in state law, to limit the liability of volunteers who are not directors without engaging in an act of self-dealing.[275] In this ruling, it was concluded that the limitation of nondirector volunteers (principally officers and committee chairs) "is essential in acquiring and retaining capable volunteers who are necessary" to the carrying out of the

---

271. That is, an organization that is tax-exempt pursuant to IRC § 501(a).
272. Reg. § 1.132-5(r)(1), (2).
273. Reg. § 1.132-5(r)(3)(i).
274. Reg. § 1.132-5(r)(3)(ii).
275. Priv. Ltr. Rul. 9440033.

foundations' exempt function; this situation was held to fall within the "reasonable and necessary" exception.[276]

## § 5.8   USES OF INCOME OR ASSETS BY DISQUALIFIED PERSONS

The transfer to, or use by or for the benefit of, a disqualified person of the income or assets of a private foundation generally constitutes self-dealing.[277]

For example, disqualified persons with respect to a private foundation had assets in an investment company that had a collateralization obligation used to satisfy margin requirements. The foundation also had investment assets placed with the same company, which were taken into account in determining the disqualified persons' compliance with the collateralization requirement. This was found by the IRS to constitute self-dealing, as being use of the foundation's assets for the benefit of disqualified persons.[278]

As this and subsequent examples illustrate, the IRS has an expansive view of the scope of this provision. In one instance, the IRS observed that this prohibition is intended to be "extremely broad."[279]

### (a)   Securities Transactions

The purchase or sale of stock or other securities by a private foundation is an act of self-dealing under these rules, if the purchase or sale is made in an attempt to manipulate the price of the stock or other securities to the advantage of a disqualified person.[280]

---

276.  This body of law is not confined to instances involving insurance and indemnification; the principles may be applicable in analogous circumstances. For example, a private foundation acquired partnership interests from a decedent's estate and thereafter engaged in various transactions to avoid receiving unrelated debt-financed income (*see* § 11.4). This foundation sought rulings from the IRS, including one that its payment of the legal and accounting costs for preparing and obtaining the rulings would not be self-dealing. The IRS so ruled, inasmuch as the rulings benefited the foundation to a "large extent" (Priv. Ltr. Rul. 9719041). The IRS analogized these payments to reimbursements to a private foundation for indemnification of a foundation manager with respect to the manager's defense in a civil administrative proceeding arising out of the manager's performance of services for reasonable compensation (Reg. § 53.4941(d)-2(f)(3)).

277.  IRC § 4941(d)(1)(E).

278.  Tech. Adv. Mem. 9627001.

279.  Tech. Adv. Mem. 9825001. Yet, on that occasion, the IRS held that the purchase by a charitable remainder trust of deferred annuity contracts from a commercial life insurance company, where the named annuitants were disqualified persons, did not constitute self-dealing under these rules because, under the facts (including an assignment of the disqualified person's interest in the policy to the trust), the disqualified persons did not receive any present value under the policies.

280.  Reg. § 53.4941(d)-2(f)(1).

An issue on which the IRS has not directly ruled concerns the sale of stock or other securities by a private foundation in a redemption (where the purchasing corporation is not a disqualified person)[281] or in a secondary public offering (where the offering would not take place but for the involvement of the private foundation), where one or more disqualified persons desire to also participate in the securities transaction. To allow the disqualified person(s) to participate in the transaction would be an act of self-dealing under these rules, either as an attempt to manipulate the price of the stock to the advantage of the disqualified persons or to otherwise use the assets of the foundation for the benefit of the disqualified persons. In one instance, a public offering of stock made to enable a private foundation to sell its shares, where disqualified persons were excluded from the transaction, was ruled not to be an act of self-dealing.[282]

## (b)  Payment of Charitable Pledges

Self-dealing in the form of use of a private foundation's assets for the benefit of a disqualified person occurs if the foundation makes a grant that satisfies the disqualified person's legally enforceable pledge to pay the amount. Where this type of pledge qualifies as a debt under local law, payment of the pledge by the foundation relieves the person or company of its obligation and constitutes self-dealing.[283] Payment of church membership dues for a disqualified person was found, for example, to be self-dealing when the membership provided a personal benefit to the individual.[284] Similarly, the IRS ruled that the payment of pledges by a private foundation, which were legally binding before the foundation was created, was self-dealing.[285] The foundation was established by several corporations to serve as a conduit for their contributions. Part of the foundation's initial funding was received on the condition that the foundation use the funds to pay certain charitable pledges that the corporations had previously made.

This would seem to be a harsh rule, where the foundation was established and funded solely for the purpose of satisfying the charitable pledges of the sponsoring corporations—the funds involved, after all, came from the corporations,

---

281.  As discussed in § 5.14, an exception from the self-dealing rules is available for certain redemptions and other corporate transactions where the purchasing corporation is a disqualified person.

282.  Priv. Ltr. Rul. 9016003; Priv. Ltr. Rul. 9114025 (where the sale of limited partnership interests by charitable remainder trusts was held not to constitute an act of self-dealing as long as the trustee of the trusts acted independently of the disqualified persons holding similar interests); Priv. Ltr. Rul. 8944007 (where the managers of a private foundation were precluded from dealing in a corporation's stock during the planning and implementation of a stock redemption; the stock transaction was ruled not to be an act of self-dealing).

283.  Reg. § 53-4941(d)-2(f)(1).

284.  Rev. Rul. 77-160, 1977-1 C.B. 351.

285.  Priv. Ltr. Rul. 8128072.

which could have paid the pledges directly. A more lenient view was adopted by the IRS in 1995, holding that the use of assets of a private foundation, contributed to it specifically for the purpose of satisfying the charitable pledges of sponsoring corporations (which are disqualified persons), was not self-dealing in that the resulting benefit to the corporations was incidental and tenuous.[286] On reconsideration, however, the IRS realized that the assets, once transferred to the foundation under any circumstances, became charitable property in the foundation's hands that cannot be used for the benefit of disqualified persons—and revoked the 1995 ruling,[287] concluding that the pledge payments were self-dealing.[288]

The making of a promise, pledge, or similar arrangement to a private foundation by a disqualified person, whether evidenced by an oral or written agreement, a promissory note, or other instrument of indebtedness, to the extent motivated by charitable intent and unsupported by consideration, is not an extension of credit before the date of maturity.[289]

Modification of a disqualified person's charitable pledge to a foundation prior to its maturity is also acceptable. The IRS looked at the case of a foundation that operated both with current contributions from its substantial contributor and with loans made by a bank against pledges made periodically by that person. When the disqualified person reduced his current promised payments before their maturity, but pledged a larger amount later, self-dealing was held to not occur.[290]

### (c)   For the Benefit of Transactions

An act of self-dealing can occur where a benefit is not provided *to* a disqualified person. This type of an act can take place where a private foundation engages in a transaction with a person (or persons) who is not a disqualified person, where the income or assets of a private foundation are utilized *for the benefit of* a disqualified person (or persons).[291]

For example, where a lawyer who was the sole trustee of a private foundation caused the foundation to make a loan to an individual (who was not a disqualified person) who had substantial dealings with the lawyer and his law firm, the lending transaction amounted to an act of self-dealing because the loan enhanced the lawyer's reputation in the view of his client and thus provided an economic benefit to him.[292]

---

286. Priv. Ltr. Rul. 9540042.
287. Priv. Ltr. Rul. 9610032.
288. Priv. Ltr. Rul. 9703020.
289. Reg. § 53.4941(d)-2(c)(3).
290. Tech. Adv. Mem. 8723001.
291. IRC § 4941(d)(1)(E).
292. Tech. Adv. Mem. 8719004.

Likewise, a bank, which extended credit to large corporations and tax-exempt organizations, where notes were to be purchased by private foundations for which the bank acted as trustee (and thus was a disqualified person), was held to be engaging in a substantial activity that enhanced the reputation of the bank and significantly increased its goodwill, so that the transactions were (or would be) acts of self-dealing.[293] Similarly, marketing benefits provided to a disqualified person by means of a transaction of this nature could entail self-dealing.[294]

Consequently, it is not enough to analyze a transaction to determine if one or more disqualified persons were directly provided a benefit by a private foundation; the analysis needs to continue to see if some advantage was provided for the benefit of a disqualified person. This concept is in the intermediate sanctions rules' definition of an *excess benefit transaction*, so developments in that setting will inform this aspect of the self-dealing rules. Yet, in one instance, the IRS concluded that a benefit was not provided to disqualified persons and thus the transaction was not an excess benefit transaction, without also analyzing whether one or more benefits were provided for the use of disqualified persons (even though the agency concluded that the "main benefit" flowing to them was "intangible public benefit," which presumably akin to enhanced reputation and increased goodwill).[295] A similar ruling was issued in the self-dealing rules setting.[296]

Likewise, the IRS analyzed a situation where a private foundation proposed to lease excess parking space in a garage it owns to tenants in an adjoining building owned by a disqualified person. The IRS concluded that self-dealing would not take place because the disqualified person will not be involved in a leasing transaction.[297] The agency, however, did not discuss the issue as to whether this leasing arrangement nonetheless would confer a benefit on the disqualified person; if it did, self-dealing would take place (unless the benefit was incidental).

### (d) Incidental or Tenuous Benefits

The fact that a disqualified person receives an incidental or tenuous benefit from the use by a private foundation of its income or assets will not, by itself, make the use an act of self-dealing.[298] The IRS ruled that an incidental or tenuous benefit occurs when the general reputation or prestige of a disqualified

---

293. Gen. Couns. Mem. 39107.
294. Priv. Ltr. Rul. 9726006.
295. Priv. Ltr. Rul. 200335037.
296. Priv. Ltr. Rul. 200123072.
297. Priv. Ltr. Rul. 201301015.
298. Reg. § 53.4941(d)-2(f)(2).

person is enhanced by public acknowledgment of some specific donation by such person, when a disqualified person receives some other relatively minor benefit of an indirect nature, or when such a person merely participates to a wholly incidental degree in the fruits of some charitable program that is of broad public interest to the community.[299]

Thus, the public recognition a person may receive, arising from the charitable activities of a private foundation to which the person is a substantial contributor, is not in itself the product of an act of self-dealing.[300] For the same reason, a private foundation grant to a tax-exempt hospital for modernization, replacement, and expansion was deemed not to be an act of self-dealing even though two of the trustees of the private foundation served on the board of trustees of the hospital.[301] Similarly, a contribution by a private foundation to a public charity does not constitute an act of self-dealing notwithstanding the fact that the contribution is conditioned on the agreement of the public charity to change its name to that of a substantial contributor to the private foundation.[302] The right of a corporate foundation official (or any corporate employee) to recommend grants to be made by the corporation's foundation in his or her name provides an intangible benefit that does not result in self-dealing unless the foundation is satisfying an obligation of the employee. Likewise, a program that matches employee gifts with a gift from the corporate foundation is an intangible and incidental benefit to an employee. Similarly, a foundation grant made in honor of a disqualified person's child, relative, or any other person does not result in self-dealing.

A grant by a private foundation to a university to establish an educational program providing instruction in manufacturing engineering is not an act of self-dealing, although a disqualified person corporation intends to hire graduates of the program and encourage its employees to enroll in the program, as long as the corporation does not receive preferential treatment in recruiting graduates or enrolling its employees.[303] In still another of these situations, the

---

299. Rev. Rul. 77-331, 1977-2 C.B. 388.
300. Reg. § 53.4941(d)-2(f)(2). A closely held corporation's donation of its debentures, representing 14 percent of the value of its net assets, to a private foundation, managed by the corporation's employees and shareholders for the promotion of charitable activities in the locality of the corporation and for which it receives public recognition, was not a constructive dividend to the shareholders (Rev. Rul. 75-335, 1975-2 C.B. 107). Cf. Rev. Rul. 68-658, 1968-2 C.B. 119.
301. Rev. Rul. 75-42, 1975-1 C.B. 359. The IRS also ruled that a grant by one private foundation to another private foundation is not an act of self-dealing even though a bank served as the sole trustee of both private foundations (Rev. Rul. 82-136, 1982-2 C.B. 136). This type of a grant may not be counted, however, as a qualifying distribution unless the funds are expended for charitable purposes in the next succeeding year of the recipient foundation; see Chapter 6.
302. Rev. Rul. 73-407, 1973-2 C.B. 383.
303. Rev. Rul. 80-310, 1980-2 C.B. 319.

IRS ruled that the loan program of a private foundation that provided financing to publicly supported organizations for construction projects in disadvantaged areas did not result in acts of self-dealing merely because some contractors and subcontractors involved in the construction projects, their suppliers, and employees of those involved may have had ordinary banking and business relationships with a bank that was a disqualified person with respect to the private foundation.[304] Moreover, a private foundation was able to assume and operate a charitable program previously conducted by a for-profit company, which was a disqualified person with respect to the foundation, as a public service, without engaging in prohibited self-dealing, because the benefit to the company was incidental.[305] In an illustration of what may be the outer reaches of this exception, the IRS ruled that impermissible self-dealing will not occur when a private foundation establishes, funds, and operates an educational institute that has a name similar to that of a company owned by disqualified persons with respect to the foundation, which will plan the programs of the institute.[306]

A park open to the public created adjacent to a corporation's plant reception area was found to further an exempt purpose. The company retained the right to "continued use of its identifying symbol in its advertising and public relations programs in connection with the establishment of the park." The IRS decided the benefit to be derived from the corporation's gifts, which include maintenance and operation costs, flow principally to the general public through access to and use of the park. Though the words "incidental and tenuous" were not used, the ruling concluded no private benefit (by analogy no self-dealing) inured to the company.[307] A similar result was reached for a replica of an early American village named after its corporate supporter.[308] Addressing the same issue from another vantage point, the IRS decided grants paid by a private foundation to match a gift made personally by a director were not self-dealing. The fact that the director was a government official did not change the conclusion.[309]

Other instances of incidental benefits in the private foundation setting include the transfer to and use by a disqualified person (a limited liability company) of an asset of a private foundation, the asset being the foundation's contractual rights pertaining to certain charitable activities.[310] As another example, the programs of a private foundation concerning public health-care

---

304. Rev. Rul. 85-162, 1985-2 C.B. 275.
305. Priv. Ltr. Rul. 9614002.
306. Priv. Ltr. Rul. 199939049.
307. Rev. Rul. 66-358, 1966-2 C.B. 218.
308. Rev. Rul. 77-367, 1977-2 C.B. 193.
309. Priv. Ltr. Rul. 200605014.
310. Priv. Ltr. Rul. 199950039.

education and publication and distribution of a booklet of statistics and a physicians' reference book were ruled to not involve prohibited self-dealing, in that the benefits provided to a disqualified person company were incidental and tenuous.[311] Likewise, a bank, a trustee of a private foundation, sold its investment management division to another bank; because the amount of foundation assets formerly managed by the first bank's division was insubstantial in relation to the total assets sold and because the assets of the foundation invested in the funds involved are insubstantial in relation to the total assets of the foundation, the IRS ruled that the fee payment by one bank to the other, reflecting the foundation's investment, will involve an incidental and tenuous benefit and thus not impermissible self-dealing.[312] Similarly, the IRS ruled that a private foundation established to promote public awareness and appreciation of a type of art could display certain works of this art in a shopping center owned by disqualified persons with respect to the foundation, without engaging in impermissible self-dealing because the display was in furtherance of exempt purposes, only a small amount of art will be displayed, the displayed art otherwise would be held in storage, and none of the art is identified with any disqualified persons.[313]

The IRS ruled, however, that the guarantee of loans made to disqualified persons under a student loan guarantee program established by a private foundation for the children of its employees constituted an act of self-dealing.[314] The program was operated by a public charity, which received a $10,000 grant from the private foundation and agreed to guarantee $100,000 in loans to the children, including the children of a few of the private foundation's employees who were disqualified persons with respect to it. In so ruling, the IRS based its position on the general rule that the indemnification (of a lender) or guarantee (of repayment) by a private foundation with respect to a loan to a disqualified person is treated as a use, for the benefit of the disqualified person, of the income or assets of the private foundation, as is a private foundation grant or other payment that satisfies the legal obligation of a disqualified person.[315] Moreover, the IRS held that this use of the private foundation's income and assets involved more than an incidental or tenuous benefit for the disqualified persons involved, because an act of self-dealing occurred each time a loan involving a disqualified person was made.[316]

A private foundation grant to a private tax-exempt school with the expectation, but with no binding obligation, that the school will use the funds to repay

---

311. Priv. Ltr. Rul. 200309027, as amended by Priv. Ltr. Rul. 200316042.
312. Priv. Ltr. Rul. 200620029.
313. Priv. Ltr. Rul. 201029039.
314. Rev. Rul. 77-331, 1977-2 C.B. 388.
315. Reg. § 53.4941(d)-2(f)(1).
316. An act of self-dealing did not take place when a public charity paid fees to a bank for services as trustee of its pooled income fund (Priv. Ltr. Rul. 8226159).

a loan made to a disqualified person in relation to the foundation was found not to result in self-dealing.[317]

A company foundation's disaster and financial relief program provided, according to the IRS, more than an incidental benefit to its sponsoring corporation and thus resulted in acts of self-dealing.[318] Although there was some public benefit resulting from the foundation's provision of assistance in times of disaster or financial crisis, the IRS was not assured that selection of beneficiaries solely among employees of a particular employer served the best interests of the public. Instead, according to the agency, the foundation served the "private interests of [the corporation] and its subsidiaries who utilize such benefit programs to recruit and retain a more stable and productive workforce." Because the beneficiaries were a designated or limited group—employees of the company—they did not constitute a charitable class and the foundation could not qualify for tax exemption as a charitable entity. For the same reasons, the disbursements made by the foundation were said to be taxable expenditures[319] of benefit to the company officials and owners. Because the benefit to the company was more than incidental and tenuous, the grants distributed by the foundation also resulted in acts of self-dealing. Additionally, the expenditures did not constitute qualifying distributions,[320] because they did not serve a charitable purpose. While the implications in the private foundation setting are not clear, the IRS ruled that a corporation with a large number of employees may maintain a payroll deduction plan for the purpose of collecting contributions for a public charity, which is not controlled by the corporation, and which makes grants and loans to the corporation's employees with a demonstrated need.[321]

The designation of one fifth of the office space in a building for use as a personal office for a private foundation's 90-year-old donor was found to be incidental and tenuous use by the donor. An office building was to be constructed on land she planned to contribute to the foundation. Although this transaction technically constituted self-dealing, the IRS generously concluded that, inasmuch as the donor's health was such that it was unlikely she would live long enough to use the space, the potential use of the space did not have a value.[322]

The goodwill enjoyed by a corporation from recognition of its sponsorship of public television programs is considered an incidental benefit.[323] Likewise, a grant by a private foundation for charitable purposes, where a consequence of

---

317. Priv. Ltr. Rul. 200443045.
318. Priv. Ltr. Rul. 199914040, revoking Priv. Ltr. Rul. 9516047.
319. *See* Chapter 9.
320. *See* § 6.5.
321. Priv. Ltr. Rul. 200307084.
322. Priv. Ltr. Rul. 9604006.
323. Priv. Ltr. Rul. 8644003.

the grant was a likely increase in the value of adjacent land owned by a disqualified person, was found to not be impermissible self-dealing because it conferred only an incidental and tenuous benefit.[324] Similarly, a grant by a private foundation as part of a project to renovate a public library site, where two disqualified persons owning adjacent property might economically benefit, where a bank trustee might benefit as a lending institution, and where another disqualified person might benefit by being a member of the management committee of a limited liability company that was the major funder of the project, was held to not be impermissible self-dealing, because any resulting benefits would be merely incidental and tenuous.[325]

A foundation was created to continue to produce public service television programs of interest to senior citizens for broadcast on a cable television network owned by its creator and her family.[326] The network had previously funded the programs. The plan was to hire an independent producer with no relationship to the family, at fair market, under a requirement that the content be educational and charitable, to assist the creator in developing the programs. The creator would provide her services for free. The foundation would not receive any advertising or other commercial revenue from the broadcasts and the network was prohibited, with exceptions for bonus advertisers, from marketing advertising spots for the program. The ruling request asserted that broadcast over the cable network was absolutely essential to most effectively communicate the information provided in the programs to its target audience.

The IRS found that self-dealing did not occur for two reasons: The foundation creator was donating her services, and the production company was not a disqualified person. Presumably (though not stated) the new foundation did not assume any binding obligations of the creator and her family. Further, the television programs were made available to the public and would be made available to other cable networks. Due to the educational nature of the programs, the costs were deemed direct charitable expenses and, therefore, qualifying distributions[327] that were not taxable expenditures.[328] Although it may be suggested that self-dealing occurred when the network and family members were relieved of paying for the program out of their own pockets, the IRS did not address the question. The agency also did not consider whether any more than incidental benefits were provided to the family and its network.[329]

---

324. Priv. Ltr. Rul. 9819045. A significant element in this ruling, however, was the fact that the foundation's grant was not a substantial part of the overall funding of the project.
325. Priv. Ltr. Rul. 200129041.
326. Priv. Ltr. Rul. 200425051.
327. See § 6.4.
328. See § 9.8.
329. See § 5.8(d).

The IRS has not issued any private or published rulings on the personal use of mileage accumulated on a foundation credit card. In 2002, the IRS admitted there were numerous technical and administrative issues relating to the timing and valuation of such usage. Due to the unresolved issues, the IRS has not "pursued a tax enforcement program with respect to promotional benefits such as frequent flyer miles."[330] The announcement said the IRS would not assert that any taxpayer has understated his or her federal tax liability by reason of the receipt or personal use of frequent flyer miles or other in-kind promotional benefit attributable to the taxpayer's business or official travel. Last, any future guidance on the taxability of these benefits will be applied prospectively.

From time to time, the IRS issues private letter rulings concerning benefits that are or are not forms of incidental or tenuous benefit.[331] Occasionally the facts are such that an involvement of a private foundation in a transaction does not confer any benefit on a disqualified person with respect to the foundation.[332]

### (e) Memberships

A private foundation engages in an act of self-dealing when it pays membership dues or fees on behalf of a disqualified person and thereby relieves him or her of that obligation. The benefit to the person is then direct and economic in nature, not tenuous or incidental. In one instance, a foundation paid its trustee's church dues, thereby enabling him to maintain his membership in and otherwise participate in the religious activities of the congregation. The dues payment was ruled to constitute self-dealing, with the IRS concluding the foundation's payment of the dues "result[ed] in a direct economic benefit to the disqualified person because that person would have been expected to pay the membership dues had they not been paid by the foundation."[333]

It is common for grant recipient organizations to identify their contributors as members eligible for special privileges. When a private foundation makes this type of grant, the individual trustees or other foundation representatives are sometimes involuntarily provided these member benefits. The question is whether the individual can accept these benefits as a representative of the foundation. The IRS, in the church ruling cited above, observed that the benefits provided by reason of the church membership might be described as incidental or tenuous. Nonetheless, self-dealing occurs where a personal obligation is satisfied on behalf of the disqualified person. Some foundations have adopted a policy of disclaiming membership privileges; others specifically require that their disqualified persons pay their own memberships to avoid the issue.

---

330. Ann. 2002-18.
331. E.g., Priv. Ltr. Rul. 9619027.
332. E.g., Priv. Ltr. Rul. 200148071.
333. Rev. Rul. 77-160, 1977-1 C.B. 351, 352, Cf. Rev. Rul. 70-47, 1970-1 C.B. 49; Rev. Rul. 68-432, 1968-2 C.B. 104.

## (f)  Benefit Tickets

Self-dealing was found when a joint purchase of benefit tickets was made by sharing the ticket cost. The private foundation paid the deductible, or charitable contribution, portion of the ticket; the disqualified person paid that part of the ticket price allocable to the fair market value of the dinner, entertainment, and other benefits provided to contributors in connection with the fundraising event.[334]

The IRS held that self-dealing occurred because the benefits were more than tenuous or incidental. To be able to attend the benefit, foundation representatives would have been required to individually pay the full ticket price. Thus, they reaped direct economic benefit to the extent that the foundation paid that portion of the ticket, and self-dealing occurred. Some foundations, however, argue that it is appropriate for their managers to attend fundraising events as representatives of the foundation to evidence their support and that private benefit does not result.

There is no easy answer to this question of foundation purchases of tickets, where foundation representatives attend the event. As a practical matter, if the representatives truly want to attend the event (such as because of the nature of the entertainment or the popularity of a speaker or to invite their friends), the payment and attendance is probably self-dealing. Conversely, if the representatives do not want to attend the event and are doing so only out of obligation, payment by the foundation for the tickets is probably not self-dealing.

Discussions about the potential for self-dealing when disqualified persons attend benefit functions continue. Many speculate that no self-dealing should occur if the disqualified persons purchase their own tickets directly from the charity with the charity correspondingly sitting them at the table paid for by their private foundation. Some talk about the "fun factor," also known as the "rubber chicken" rule. If the disqualified persons do not have any fun, there is no self-dealing. The bottom-line questions that the foundation officials should consider in deciding to accept tickets in connection with foundation sponsorship of an event include:

- Is it appropriate for officials to attend to represent the foundation?
- What charitable purpose is served by attendance of the friends of officials at the function? Are officials introducing them to the charity with the hope that they too will support the charity?
- Does the foundation purchase of the tickets relieve the insiders of an obligation they would otherwise incur?

---

334. Priv. Ltr. Rul. 9021066.

## (g) Other Acts

The indemnification of a lender or guarantee of repayment by a private foundation with respect to a loan to a disqualified person is treated as a use for the benefit of a disqualified person of the income or assets of the foundation.[335]

The IRS ruled that a private foundation committed an act of self-dealing when it placed paintings owned by it in the residence of a substantial contributor.[336] Likewise, self-dealing was found when a private foundation permitted the placement of its sculpture on the private property of a disqualified person.[337] A court held, however, that the making of a charitable contribution to a private foundation by one of its trustees, on the condition that any non-deductible portion of the gift would be returned to him, was not an act of self-dealing, nor was its return.[338]

It is relatively common for the IRS to allow reformation of a charitable remainder trust to enable the trust to be converted to a type envisioned by the donor or donors at the outset but that was incorrectly prepared (due to what the IRS generously describes as a scrivener's error).[339] Occasionally, the IRS rules that this type of trust revision does not entail self-dealing.[340]

The IRS also issues rulings concerning divisions of charitable remainder trusts.[341] Occasionally, the IRS rules that this type of trust division does not entail self-dealing.[342]

## § 5.9 SHARING SPACE, PEOPLE, AND EXPENSES

As a practical matter, many private foundations are operated alongside their creators, whether these are corporations or family groups. At least until a foundation achieves a certain volume of assets with consequential grant activity (and perhaps thereafter), rental of a separate office and engagement of staff is beyond the foundation's reasonable economic capability, particularly when these expenditures take funds away from grant-making activity.

---

335. Reg. § 53.4941(d)-2(f)(1).
336. Rev. Rul. 74-600, 1974-2 C.B. 385.
337. Gen. Coun. Mem. 39741. Indeed, this private benefit was found to be sufficiently egregious to warrant revocation of the foundation's tax-exempt status.
338. *Underwood v. United States*, 461 F. Supp. 1382 (N.D. Tex. 1978). Presumably, the returned portion of the original gift becomes gross income to the donor recipient in the year of the restoration, pursuant to the "tax benefit rule." E.g., *Rosen v. Commissioner*, 71 T.C. 226 (1978) *aff'd*, 80-1 U.S.T.C. ¶ 9138 (1st Cir. 1980).
339. *See Charitable Giving* § 12.4(i).
340. E.g., Priv. Ltr. Rul. 200850046. *See* § 3.7.
341. *See Charitable Giving* § 12.6.
342. E.g., Priv. Ltr. Rul. 200831029.

## (a)  Determining What the Private Foundation Can Pay

The law is not particularly clear as to when a private foundation can pay for its portion of the expenses in a sharing situation involving disqualified persons. The law prohibits the "furnishing of goods, services, or facilities" between (to or from) a foundation and a disqualified person.[343] The types of property intended to be covered by this rule include office space, automobiles, auditoriums, secretarial help, meals, libraries, publications, laboratories, and parking lots.[344]

When Congress imposed these strict rules in 1969, it provided a transitional period until 1980, during which existing contractual sharing arrangements could be phased out.[345] As time passed and the costs of the absolute rule became unreasonable in certain circumstances, the IRS in private letter rulings relaxed what looked like an impenetrable barrier to any arrangements in which a foundation and its creators and funders share the expenses of space, staff, and the like.

## (b)  Office Space and Personnel

A number of private foundations sought and received approval for shared office space and personnel. In one IRS ruling, it was held that self-dealing did not occur when a private foundation rented contiguous space with a common reception area (which constituted sharing), but with separate offices, from its disqualified person. Separate leases were entered into, and the disqualified persons did not receive any benefit in the form of reduced rent because of the foundation's rental of the related space.[346] In another ruling, a foundation and a disqualified person together bought a duplicating machine and hired a shared employee. Time records were kept to determine each entity's share of the cost of the machine and the allocable time of the employee. Because "nothing was paid directly or indirectly to" the disqualified person and there was "independent use" by the foundation that was measurable and specifically paid for to outside parties, self-dealing was held to have not resulted from what certainly appears to have been a "sharing arrangement," supposedly phased out and consequentially prohibited by the self-dealing rules.[347]

Similarly, a "time-sharing arrangement" of a disqualified person management company's employees was condoned by the IRS. The basis for the favorable ruling was the fact that the law permits a foundation to pay reasonable compensation to a disqualified person for the performance of personal services necessary to carry out its exempt purposes. Interestingly, and perhaps

---

343.  IRC § 4941(d)(1)(C).
344.  Reg. § 53.4941(d)-2(d)(1).
345.  Reg. § 53.4941(d)-4(d).
346.  Priv. Ltr. Rul. 8331082.
347.  Tech. Adv. Mem. 7734022; Priv. Ltr. Rul. 8824010.

more important, the IRS found that the benefit to the management company in being relieved from paying a percentage of the salaries of its employees was incidental and tenuous.[348]

The IRS sanctioned cost and property sharing arrangements between members of a group including (1) a public charity that will, for no rent, lease its half-interest in a historical site and associated personal property to a foundation, (2) a foundation whose creators also own the other half-interest, (3) a private operating foundation created by the same disqualified persons to preserve and operate this site, and (4) a business corporation owned more than 35 percent by disqualified persons (making it a disqualified person in relation to both foundations) that would furnish security services and maintenance and repair the site and its utilities. Again, the IRS recommended that foundations be billed and pay their share of costs directly to unrelated parties if possible. The agency wrote that "each owner will pay an allocable share of utility costs, using reasonable methods of allocation."[349] A foundation can pay a disqualified person corporation for personal security services it renders if they are reasonable and necessary to its operation of the site. Easements for use of a disqualified person's property granted to a foundation also did not result in self-dealing, because the foundation's exempt purpose of operating the site was served and rent was not charged.

Another office space arrangement between a foundation and its creators was approved, with slightly different language to permit the sharing.[350] "As long as any payments for the use are made directly to the vendor on a proportional basis," the IRS ruled, self-dealing does not take place. Separate employment contracts were to be entered into with shared employees. Checks in payment of the respective share of employee group insurance were deposited into a joint bank account, from which premiums were paid to the insurer. The telephone system was jointly purchased. Separate maintenance agreements were entered into and separately paid for the foundation's and the disqualified person's respective shares of the equipment. Usage records would be maintained to evidence the portions. Payment of a private foundation's share of costs directly to an independent vendor was not required in a situation where the expenses were paid directly by a condominium association.[351]

A private foundation's payment of the direct flight costs associated with its use of a disqualified person's airplane was found to not be self-dealing.[352] The foundation did not pay any portion of the disqualified person's maintenance or acquisition costs or relieve the disqualified person of a financial obligation. The

---

348. Priv. Ltr. Rul. 9226067.
349. Priv. Ltr. Rul. 9307026.
350. Priv. Ltr. Rul. 9312022.
351. *See* Exhibit 5.1.
352. Priv. Ltr. Rul. 9732031.

airplane use was considered to "further the [private foundation's] exempt purposes by facilitating meetings among various individuals active in its charitable, scientific, and educational programs."[353]

Different and safer terminology was used to secure IRS approval for payment to a disqualified person's family management corporation for rendering accounting, tax, and asset management services.[354] The corporation operated on a cost-recovery basis to serve the business needs of "family assets held in trusts, foundations, and partnerships." While the arrangement is essentially a sharing one, the IRS ruled payment of a fee based on costs was reasonable compensation for services rendered and not an act of self-dealing.[355]

Addition of a supporting organization to the mix of private foundation and disqualified person expense sharing arrangements was approved by the IRS.[356] The ruling stated that "based on the representation that expenses will be allocated and paid at fair market value to S1 (a supporting organization), the participation of T/C (private foundation), D1 and D2 (disqualified persons) with S1 and S2 in the above arrangement will not result in excess benefit transactions." The ruling also declared no self-dealing would occur as it regarded the private foundation.

The IRS allowed disqualified persons and a private foundation to each own office units in a condominium office building and to share common costs on an allocable basis, but only because the disqualified persons used their offices solely for charitable purposes.[357]

A private foundation conducted an Internet-based education and training program providing educational services to teachers and students nationwide. A for-profit company, which is a disqualified person with respect to this foundation, had a charitable program, using innovative technologies, strategies, and employee time and talent, to improve the education of youth. The foundation is among the educational entities served by the company's employees. Guidelines established by the company ban discussion of the company's business activities when engaging in the programs; both entities strive to keep the identities of their respective programs separate and distinct. The IRS ruled that the conduct of the two programs will not constitute self-dealing.[358]

Exhibit 5.2 illustrates an expenditure documentation agreement between a disqualified person and a private foundation. The example assumes that the foundation occupies office space donated by the disqualified person. The foundation maintains records to document its payment for its independent use of the equipment, staff, and other systems in the office.

---

353. Thus, these outlays also did not constitute taxable expenditures (*see* Chapter 9).
354. Priv. Ltr. Rul. 9019064.
355. Due to the exception in IRC § 4941(d)(2)(E).
356. Priv. Ltr. Rul. 200421010.
357. Priv. Ltr. Rul. 200014040.
358. Priv. Ltr. Rul. 200536027.

**Exhibit 5.2** Expenditure Documentation Policy

---

**SAMPLE FOUNDATION**

**Introduction** As a private foundation (PF), Sample Foundation (Sample) is responsible for proving that all of its expenditures are made for charitable purposes and that it makes no expenditures on behalf of, nor has any financial transactions with, its disqualified persons (DPs), meaning major contributors and managers. Sample will establish its headquarters and laboratory in the office building owned by its president and contributor, XYZ, who is a DP in relation to Sample. Therefore, Sample wishes to adopt procedures to meet its responsibility. Specifically, the "self-dealing" provisions of the tax code prohibit the following:

- Sale, exchange, or lease of property between a PF and a DP, except at no charge.
- Lending of money or extension of credit between a PF and a DP.
- Furnishing of goods, services, or facilities between a PF and a DP, unless the DP furnishes them to the PF without charge.
- Payment of compensation or reimbursement of expenses from a PF to a DP, unless such payments are reasonable and necessary to carrying out the exempt purposes of the PF.

**Policy** To ensure adherence to these requirements, Sample adopts the following rules:

**Office space** Sample is entering into a lease agreement with XYZ stipulating that the space is furnished to Sample at no charge. Maintenance, repair, and utilities attributable to the space occupied by Sample will be paid by Sample directly. For example, the space leased to Sample represents percent of the total square footage of the building. Therefore, percent of the utility bill will be paid by Sample. Any expenses not directly attributable to Sample space will be paid by XYZ.

**Personnel** Sample will hire a project manager, and possibly other personnel, to work exclusively on foundation projects. Because Sample is new with modest activity, it does not need a full-time secretary or accountant. Therefore, it will hire the current employees of XYZ on a part-time basis. It is estimated that the receptionist and business manager will devote approximately half of their time to Sample's business. Therefore, half of their salaries, employee benefits, and taxes will be paid by Sample. Each person will maintain a record of his or her actual time, and the ratio will be evaluated periodically.

**Office furnishings and equipment** XYZ owns a telephone system, copy machine, computers, and other equipment that Sample is allowed to use rent-free. To the extent that Sample incurs direct costs in connection with this equipment, it will pay the bills directly. For example, long-distance telephone calls, photocopy paper, and other expendable supplies directly related to foundation activities will be paid by Sample.

**Automobile** XYZ is furnishing Sample with a vehicle for its use in connection with foundation projects. Sample will pay the expenses attributable to its actual use of the vehicle. A mileage log will be maintained to evidence the usage.

**Asset purchases, sales, and debt payments** Sample hereby adopts a policy that it will not engage in any financial transactions with XYZ or with any other DP that would cause it to "self-deal," as that term is defined in Chapter 42 of the Internal Revenue Code.

---

## (c)  Group Insurance

Group insurance policies present similar sharing situations. Corporate and other conglomerate groups funding private foundations have been allowed to include their private foundation employees in a common health insurance policy. The foundation pays directly for the premiums allocable to its employees, or reimburses the company. As discussed above, direct payment is strongly preferred, but if it is impossible, the IRS may allow reimbursement. The rationale is found in the *Special Rules*, which provide that the lending of money by a disqualified person to a private foundation will not be an act of self-dealing if the loan is without interest or other charge and if the proceeds of the loan are used exclusively for the foundation's tax-exempt purposes.[359]

## (d)  Public Facilities

A private foundation that operates a museum, maintains a wildlife preserve, produces an educational journal, or engages in comparable programs is faced with the decree that it not furnish goods, services, or facilities to its insiders. Taken literally, the rule prevents disqualified persons from visiting the sites, purchasing the journal, and similar interrelationships. A foundation's furnishing of goods, services, or facilities normally open to the general public, to a disqualified person, however, falls within another of the useful exceptions to the general rules. This type of activity is not self-dealing under the following circumstances:

- The property involved is functionally related to the exercise or performance by the foundation of its charitable, educational, or other purpose or function forming the basis for its exemption.

- The number of persons (other than the disqualified persons) who use the facility is substantial enough to indicate that the general public is genuinely the primary user.

- The terms for disqualified person usage are not more favorable than the terms under which the general public acquires or uses the property.[360]

## §5.10  PAYMENTS TO GOVERNMENT OFFICIALS

The statutory law prohibits a payment by a private foundation to a government official.[361] There are, nonetheless, a number of exceptions.

---

359.  IRC § 4941(d)(2)(B).
360.  Reg. § 53.4941(d)-3(b)(2). Also *see* § 5.4(d) for examples of particular circumstances in which a private foundation is permitted to use facilities of a disqualified person and vice versa.
361.  IRC § 4941(d)(1)(F).

An agreement by a private foundation to make any payment of money or other property to a government official generally constitutes self-dealing, unless the agreement is to employ a government official for a period after termination of his or her government service and he or she is terminating his or her service within a 90-day period.[362] An individual who otherwise meets the definition of government official is treated as a government official while on leave of absence from the government without pay.[363]

Certain de minimis payments to government officials are permitted, as follows:[364]

- A prize or award that is not includible in gross income,[365] if the government official receiving the prize is selected from the general public. (The prize must be paid over to a charitable institution.)

- A scholarship or fellowship grant that is excludable from gross income[366] and that is to be utilized for study at a qualified educational institution[367] (but only for tuition, fees, and books).[368]

- Certain types of pension plans and annuity payments.[369]

- Any contribution or gift (other than a contribution or gift of money) to, or services or facilities made available to, a government official, if the aggregate value of such gifts, contributions, services, and facilities provided total no more than $25 in any calendar year.

- Government employee training program payments.

- Reimbursement of the actual cost of travel, including meals and lodging, solely within the United States for attendance at a charitable function, not to exceed 125 percent of the prevailing per diem rate.

In regard to the last item, the exception operates only with respect to expenses for travel from one point in the United States to another point in the United States.[370] Consequently, reimbursement by a private foundation for travel expenses incurred by a member of Congress it selects to participate in a

---

362. *Id.*
363. Reg. § 53.4941(d)-2(g).
364. IRC § 4941(d)(2)(G); Reg. § 53.4941(d)-3(e).
365. The rules in this regard are the subject of IRC § 74(b).
366. The rules in this regard are the subject of IRC § 117(a).
367. That is, an entity described in IRC § 151(c)(4).
368. IRC § 4941(d)(2)(G); Reg. § 53.4941(d)-3(e). For this purpose, the definition of scholarships and fellowships is that in the federal tax law prior to the amendment of the income tax exclusion of IRC § 117 in 1986, by reason of § 1001(d)(1)(A) of the Technical and Miscellaneous Revenue Act of 1988.
369. E.g., Priv. Ltr. Rul. 9510073.
370. Reg. § 53.4941(d)-3(e)(7).

conference it cosponsors in a foreign country constitutes an act of self-dealing.[371] Taking the position that the term *United States* is used only in a geographical sense in this context, the IRS ruled that the Commonwealth of Puerto Rico is not a "point in the United States."[372]

The payment or reimbursement, by a private foundation to a government official, of traveling expenses for travel solely from one point to another in the United States is not self-dealing as long as the payment or reimbursement does not exceed the actual cost of the transportation involved plus an amount for all other traveling expenses not in excess of 125 percent of the maximum amount payable for like travel by employees of the United States government.[373] The amendment of this law superseded the per diem rates previously used by the IRS.[374]

## § 5.11   INDIRECT SELF-DEALING

An act of self-dealing may be direct or indirect. An *indirect* act of self-dealing generally occurs as a transaction between a disqualified person and an organization controlled by a private foundation.[375] There are two basic tests for determining whether an organization is controlled by a private foundation for these purposes.[376] The following is an illustration of an indirect self-dealing transaction:

> Private foundation P owns the controlling interest of the voting stock of corporation X, and as a result of this interest, elects a majority of the board of directors of X. Two of the foundation managers, A and B, who are also directors of X, form corporation Y for the purpose of building and managing a country club. A and B receive a total of 40 percent of Y's stock, making Y a disqualified person with respect to P. In order to

---

371. Rev. Rul. 74-601, 1974-2 C.B. 385.
372. Rev. Rul. 76-159, 1976-1 C.B. 356.
373. IRC § 4941(d)(2)(G)(vii). This maximum amount is the subject of 5 U.S.C. § 5702(a).
374. Rev. Rul. 77-251, 1977-2 C.B. 389. At the time of this ruling, the per diem rate for like travel was $35. The IRS ruled in a situation involving a private foundation that wanted to provide a $50 per diem allowance (plus reimbursement of actual transportation costs) for a government official traveling from Washington, D.C., to New York City, to participate in a three-day seminar. The law (5 U.S.C. § 5702(c)) provides for an allowance of up to $50 for travel to "high-rate geographical areas," which includes New York City. Reasoning that because Congress referred only to the general reimbursement rules and not to this particular provision when it enacted the self-dealing rules, the IRS held that the private foundation could pay a per diem allowance of only $43.75 (125 percent of $35) and not the desired $50. Thus, without engaging in self-dealing, a private foundation may reimburse a government official for his or her actual costs of travel plus 125 percent of the "Federal Travel Rate Prescribed Maximum per Diem Rates for CONUS" ("coterminous United States"). This change in this aspect of the self-dealing rules is discussed in Priv. Ltr. Rul. 8911063.
375. Reg. § 53.4941(d)-1(b).
376. Reg. § 53.4941(d)-1(b)(5); Rev. Rul. 76-158, 1976-1 C.B. 354.

finance the construction and operation of the country club, Y requests and receives a loan in the amount of $4,000,000 from X. The making of the loan by X to Y constitutes an indirect act of self-dealing.[377]

A transaction between a private foundation and an organization that is not controlled by the foundation, where those who are disqualified persons[378] with respect to the foundation own less than 35 percent of the voting power of or beneficial interest in the organization, is not an act of *indirect self-dealing* between the foundation and a person considered to be a disqualified person solely because of the ownership interests of those persons in the organization.[379] For purposes of the indirect self-dealing rules, an organization is *controlled* by a private foundation if the foundation or one or more of its foundation managers may, by aggregating their votes or positions of authority, require the organization to engage in a transaction which, if engaged in with the private foundation, would constitute self-dealing.[380] Additionally, an organization is controlled by a private foundation in the case of what would be a self-dealing transaction between the organization and a disqualified person if the person, together with one or more persons who are disqualified persons by reason of the person's relationship with the disqualified person, may, by aggregating their votes or positions of authority with that of the foundation, require the organization to engage in such a transaction.[381] An organization is considered to be controlled by a private foundation, or by a foundation and disqualified persons, if such persons are in fact able to control the organization (even if their aggregate voting power is less than 50 percent of the total voting power of the organization's governing body) or if one or more of such persons has the right to exercise veto power over the actions of the organization that are relevant to any potential acts of self-dealing.[382] In the case of a private foundation that owned 35 percent of the voting stock of a corporation and whose foundation manager owned the remaining 65 percent of the stock but did not hold a position of authority in the corporation by virtue of being a foundation manager, the IRS ruled that the foundation did not control the corporation for self-dealing purposes because it did not have the right to exercise veto control over the actions of the corporation and had no authority over the corporation's actions (other than that represented by its stock ownership).[383] The phrase *combined voting power* includes the voting

---

377. Reg. § 53.4941(d)-1(b)(8), Example (1).
378. That is, are disqualified persons by reason of IRC § 4946(a)(1)(A)–(D). *See* §§ 4.1–4.4.
379. Reg. § 53.4941(d)-1(b)(4).
380. Reg. § 53.4941(d)-1(b)(5).
381. *Id.*
382. *Id.*
383. Rev. Rul. 76-158, 1976-1 C.B. 354.

power represented by holdings of voting stock, actual or constructive, but does not include voting rights held only as a director or trustee.[384]

The controlled organization need not be a private foundation. It may be any type of tax-exempt organization, such as a school, hospital, social welfare organization, business league, or (as noted in the above example) a social club. It may also be a for-profit organization.

The IRS ruled that employees of a bank, which is itself the trustee of a private foundation, who have fiduciary responsibility for administering the foundation and, although they are ultimately responsible to the bank's board and its executive officers for actions taken with respect to the foundation, are free on a day-to-day basis to administer the foundation and distribute its funds according to their best judgment, have powers or responsibilities similar to those of trustees of the private foundation.[385] Nonetheless, the IRS carefully considered the facts surrounding two proposed stock redemptions, where a private foundation would be the seller, and concluded that the foundation and/or its founder did not control the company by virtue of stock ownership or any influence over some of the company's directors, and thus that the redemptions would not be indirect self-dealing transactions.[386]

Private foundations' investments in Ponzi and other fraudulent investment schemes[387] are raising several issues in the federal tax law contexts.[388] A report by the New York State Bar Association, submitted to the federal government,[389] explores these issues. This report concluded that there are no self-dealing issues "that are unique to Ponzi schemes." The report posited a situation where a foundation and a disqualified person with respect to the foundation invested in a Ponzi scheme; the disqualified person withdrew from the scheme. This question was asked: Did an act of indirect self-dealing occur? The report concluded that, if the disqualified person was a qualified investor,[390] "no act of self-dealing should arise in this situation."[391]

The first self-dealing case under the private foundation rules to be decided by a court involved acts of indirect self-dealing.[392] The individual involved wholly owned a corporation (Corporation A) that transferred two encumbered

---

384. Reg. § 53.4946-1(a)(5). The IRS observed that the Internal Revenue Code and the tax regulations "do not systematically define all manner of 'indirect' self-dealing; instead, the facts and circumstances must be considered in each case" (Priv. Ltr. Rul. 200727019).

385. Rev. Rul. 74-287, 1974-1 C.B. 327.

386. Priv. Ltr. Rul. 200750020.

387. *See* § 8.4.

388. *See* §§ 6.3(g); 8.4; 9.8, text accompanied by notes 388, 390; 10.3(j).

389. *See* § 8.4(b).

390. Rev. Proc. 2009-1 C.B. 749. *See* § 8.4, text accompanied by note 86.

391. The report cited, as authority for this conclusion, Reg. § 53.4941(d)-1(b)(4). *See* text accompanied by *supra* note 379.

392. *Adams v. Commissioner*, 70 T.C. 373 (1978), *aff'd* (in an unpublished opinion), 2nd Cir. 1982. Also *Adams v. Commissioner*, 70 T.C. 446 (1978).

properties to another corporation (Corporation B), which was a wholly owned subsidiary of a private foundation (C), of which the individual was a trustee. This individual was a foundation manager by virtue of being a trustee of private foundation C and, thus, a disqualified person with respect to the private foundation, as was A because the individual owned more than 35 percent of the total combined voting power in the corporation.[393] Therefore, the court ruled that the sale of one of the properties by A to B constituted an act of self-dealing.[394] (The transfer of the other property was deemed not to be an act of self-dealing because, as to that property, A was acting merely as a nominee for B.) Another act of self-dealing was found[395] by reason of the fact that even though the properties conveyed were encumbered, B paid the full purchase price for them, with the understanding that either the individual involved or A would satisfy the outstanding mortgage liabilities on the properties; the court agreed with the government's contention that the failure by A to immediately satisfy the liabilities upon receipt of the funds from B gave rise to an implied loan to A from private foundation C in the amount of the outstanding mortgage liabilities.

In the facts of a court case, an individual, a trustee of a private foundation and a director of a for-profit corporation, incurred a large bill at a hotel owned by the corporation, which was 50 percent owned by the foundation (permissible at the time) and 50 percent by a family trust. The foundation was billed for these expenses; the foundation refused to reimburse for the expenses because the individual failed to substantiate a business purpose for them. Following the filing of bankruptcy by this individual, the hotel unsuccessfully sought, as part of the bankruptcy proceedings, to collect its bill from the foundation. The court concluded that the foundation or its managers acting in that capacity did not control the corporation, reasoning (1) that 50 percent ownership is ordinarily insufficient to constitute control; (2) that this individual, together with others who were disqualified persons by virtue of their relationship to him (there were none), could not require the corporation to engage in self-dealing only by aggregating their influence with that of the foundation; (3) that this individual lacked actual control, or a veto power, over the activities of the corporation; and (4) that, to the contrary, the corporation exercised considerable independence from the individual and the foundation in seeking payment from them.[396]

The IRS ruled that loans to an entity, owned 50 percent by a private foundation and 50 percent by a split-interest trust, from a publicly traded company, which was a disqualified person with respect to the foundation,

---

393. *See* § 4.5.
394. IRC § 4941(d)(1)(A).
395. IRC § 4941(d)(1)(B).
396. *Moody v. Commissioner*, 69 T.C.M. 2517 (1995).

were not acts of indirect self-dealing because there were no persons who were disqualified persons by reason of an ownership relationship to the company and the trust controlled the entity without the assistance of the foundation.[397]

The term *indirect self-dealing* does not include a transaction between a disqualified person and an organization controlled by a private foundation, even if it is one of the following enumerated types of self-dealing transactions:

- The transaction results from a business relationship that was established before the transaction constituted an act of self-dealing under the federal tax rules,

- The transaction was at least as favorable to the private foundation-controlled organization as an arm's-length transaction with an unrelated person, and

- Either (a) the private foundation-controlled organization could have engaged in the transaction with someone other than a disqualified person only at a severe economic hardship to the organization, or (b) because of the unique nature of the product or services provided by the private foundation-controlled organization, the disqualified person could not have engaged in the transaction with anyone else or could have done so only by incurring severe economic hardship.[398]

Moreover, the term *indirect self-dealing* does not include a transaction engaged in by an intermediary organization with a governmental official where the organization is a recipient of a grant from a private foundation if:

- The private foundation does not control the organization,

- The private foundation does not earmark the use of the grant for any named governmental official, and

- There does not exist an agreement, oral or written, by which the private foundation may cause the selection of the governmental official by the intermediary organization. A grant by a private foundation will not constitute an indirect act of self-dealing even though the private foundation had reason to believe that certain governmental officials would derive benefits from the grant as long as the intermediary organization exercises control, in fact, over the selection process and actually makes the selection completely independently of the private foundation.[399]

---

397. Priv. Ltr. Rul. 200727019.
398. Reg. § 53.4941(d)-1(b)(1).
399. Reg. § 53.4941(d)-1(b)(2).

Further, *indirect self-dealing* does not include a transaction involving one or more disqualified persons to which a private foundation is not a party, in any case in which the private foundation, by reason of certain rules,[400] could itself engage in the transaction. Thus, for example, even if a private foundation has control of a corporation, the corporation may pay to a disqualified person, except a governmental official, reasonable compensation for personal services.[401]

*Indirect self-dealing* also does not include any transaction between a disqualified person and an organization controlled by a private foundation or between two disqualified persons, where the private foundation's assets may be affected by the transaction, if:

- The transaction arises in the normal and customary course of a retail business engaged in with the general public,

- In the case of a transaction between a disqualified person and an organization controlled by a private foundation, the transaction is at least as favorable to the organization controlled by the private foundation as an arm's-length transaction with an unrelated person, and

- The total of the amounts involved in the transactions with respect to any one disqualified person in any tax year does not exceed $5,000.[402]

An individual who was a disqualified person with respect to a private foundation made an interest-free loan to a tax-exempt school to enable it to complete construction, purchase furniture and other materials, and hire staff; this individual also was the president of the school. The private foundation planned to make a grant to the school with the understanding that the school would use the funds to repay the loan. The IRS ruled that indirect self-dealing would not be involved, because the school was not controlled by the private foundation or the disqualified person. The agency also ruled that even if the school was controlled by the foundation, there would not be indirect self-dealing in that the grant funds were not "earmarked" for the use of a disqualified person, inasmuch as the school will have "ultimate control" of the grant funds and will "not be bound to use any of the contributed funds for repayment of the loan."[403]

The IRS, from time to time, issues private letter rulings as to whether a transaction or arrangement constitutes an indirect act of self-dealing.[404]

---

400. IRC § 4941(d)(2).
401. Reg. § 53.4941(d)-1(b)(7).
402. Reg. § 53.4941(d)-(b)(6). Also Reg. § 53.4941(d)-1(b)(4).
403. Priv. Ltr. Rul. 200443045.
404. E.g., Priv. Ltr. Rul. 200620030.

# § 5.12  PROPERTY HELD BY FIDUCIARIES

A trustee or estate executor may find that property given or bequeathed to a private foundation, such as an undivided interest in property, is not suitable to be held by the foundation.[405] At times, the best solution in this situation results in a self-dealing transaction, either direct or indirect. Because the property has not yet become the property of the foundation, the regulations grant a fair degree of leeway to the estate or revocable trust officials in allocating or selling assets among beneficiaries.

## (a)  General Rules

Transactions during administration regarding the foundation's interest or expectancy in property (whether or not encumbered) held by the estate (regardless of when title vests under local law) are not self-dealing, if all of these conditions are met:[406]

- The executor, administrator, or trustee has authority to either sell the property or reallocate it to another beneficiary, or is required to sell the property by the terms of the trust or will,

- A probate court having jurisdiction over the estate approves the transaction,[407]

- The transaction occurs before the estate or trust is terminated,

- The estate or trust receives an amount equal to or in excess of the fair market value of its interest or expectancy in the property at the time of the transaction, taking into account the terms of any option subject to which the property is acquired by the estate or trust, and

- The foundation receives (a) an interest at least as liquid as the one given up, (b) an exempt function asset, or (c) an amount of money equal to that required under an option binding upon the estate or trust.

This exception to the self-dealing rules is known as the *estate administration exception*. This exception was ruled to be available in (and is nicely illustrated by) a situation in which a private foundation was being liquidated into two new private foundations as part of a plan to settle litigation between two feuding siblings.[408] The settlement plan included reorganization of corporations, some

---

405. *See* § 5.4(e).
406. Reg. § 53.4941(d)-1(b)(3).
407. The regulations do not state that this approval must be granted specifically for the transaction, so the court's acceptance of the final estate accounting and its release of the parties should be sufficient.
408. *See* § 13.7.

of the stock of which was in an estate and destined for (i.e., was an expectancy of) the private foundation. Because the executors of the estate (the siblings) possessed the requisite power of sale, the probate court involved approved the transactions, the foundation was to receive liquid assets in excess of the value of the property it would be giving up, and the transactions were to occur before the estate was considered terminated for tax purposes, the IRS ruled that the estate administration exception was available.[409] Thus, despite considerable benefits to the disqualified persons/siblings—which somewhat troubled the IRS—the transactions were not considered indirect self-dealing. In a similar situation, the IRS ruled that the estate administration exception was available in connection with a series of transactions, pursuant to settlement of litigation, involving a reallocation of assets destined for a private foundation and disqualified persons with respect to it.[410]

Generally, then, where these circumstances are not involved, a prohibited transaction involving an estate or trust, holding property destined for a private foundation, almost always constitutes indirect self-dealing. In one instance, a disqualified person with respect to a charitable trust purchased property from the estate of the decedent who created the trust. The property was destined to be a substantial part of the trust corpus. The disqualified person contended that reliance on the exception was appropriate. The IRS concluded, however, that the purchase was an act of self-dealing because the disqualified person had not paid the estate an amount equal to the fair market value of the property. The matter was litigated, with the trial court and the court of appeals concluding that the IRS was correct and that the regulation in this area was constitutional.[411]

Subsequently, another court had occasion to discuss this carve-out rule. It wrote that "in the absence of those exceptions, such transactions would have been covered by section 4941" (i.e., would have been self-dealing).[412] The court added that it is "clear that transactions affecting the assets of an estate generally are treated as also affecting the assets of any private foundation which, as a beneficiary of the estate, has an expectancy interest in the assets of the estate."[413]

This exception is available only with respect to transactions during administration of an estate, with a disqualified person, regarding a private foundation's "interest or expectancy in property" held by an estate or trust. It seems to be

---

409. Priv. Ltr. Rul. 200117042.
410. Priv. Ltr. Rul. 200132037.
411. *Rockefeller v. United States*, 572 F. Supp. 9 (E.D. Ark. 1982), *aff'd*, 718 F.2d 291 (9th Cir. 1983), *cert. den.*, 466 U.S. 962 (1984).
412. *Estate of Bernard J. Reis v. Commissioner*, 87 T.C. 1016, 1022 (1986).
413. *Id.* The principal issue in the case, not resolved by the court, was whether executors of the state of an artist engaged in acts of self-dealing when they purchased art from the estate.

confined to the sale or other disposition of property by the estate or trust. It does not apply in connection with transactions involving payment of compensation.

These rules have been interpreted by IRS private letter rulings. One ruling involved the division of properties owned by an artist's estate in order to fund a statutory one-third life estate in favor of his wife. The IRS found that self-dealing did not occur, despite the exchanges of property inherent in the settlement, where the agreement satisfied the five basic requirements in the regulations. A substitution of art they preferred, instead of objects specifically bequeathed to the artist's daughters, however, resulted in self-dealing.[414]

Where a foundation is bequeathed the residuary of an estate, a provision that estate taxes are to be paid from the portion given to the foundation was ruled not to result in self-dealing. The IRS ruled that the taxes were being paid from property not owned by the foundation, because it had only a vested interest in the estate after the payment of taxes.[415]

In another ruling, a business corporation operated to promote and produce a musician's work during his life was bequeathed to private foundations formed to perpetuate the musician's name and compositions. The gift was accompanied by a promissory note because the estate was partly insolvent. This non–pro-rata distribution was sanctioned by the IRS since it was approved by the probate court.[416] The IRS also ruled that the operation of the business would be *functionally related* to the purposes of the foundations and would not result in excess business holdings.[417] Likewise, the IRS ruled that a private foundation's holding of a promissory note issued by a disqualified person, and its receipt of note payments from the person after the period of estate administration terminates, will not be deemed acts of self-dealing, by reason of the estate administration exception.[418]

Payments out of an estate's residuary funds made pursuant to the settlement of a will contest were also ruled not to constitute an act of self-dealing. The decedent had left his residuary estate entirely to a private foundation. The will left nothing to his son but gave the son an option to purchase certain assets from the residuary estate. After controversy surrounding the purchase, a settlement was entered into giving the son part of the assets and placing other assets in a 20-year charitable remainder unitrust for the son's benefit, with the remainder given to the foundation. Because the regulation requirements outlined earlier

---

414. Priv. Ltr. Rul. 9242042.
415. Priv. Ltr. Rul. 9307025.
416. Priv. Ltr. Rul. 9308045.
417. *See* § 7.3.
418. Priv. Ltr. Rul. 201129049. The IRS now has a no-rule position as to self-dealing issues involving the issuance of a promissory note by a disqualified person during the administration of an estate or trust (Rev. Proc. 2014-4, 2014-1 I.R.B. 125 § 6.18); this private letter ruling request was submitted prior to announcement of this position.

were met, the IRS ruled that self-dealing did not occur.[419] Subsequent rulings indicate that the IRS is often of the view that will settlements are analogous to estate administration exception circumstances and thus do not entail self-dealing.[420]

It is sometimes difficult, if not impossible, to wrap up matters during administration of an estate. Two examples of difficult situations follow.

1. An estate holds a note receivable from the foundation creator's son. The foundation receives all of the estate assets, including the note. The regulations provide that an act of self-dealing occurs "where a note, the obligor of which is a disqualified person, is transferred by a third party to a private foundation which becomes the creditor under the note."[421] The sentence literally says retention and collection of the note by the foundation is self-dealing. Prudence would recommend that the estate, if possible, be held open until the son can satisfy the obligation.

2. Alternatively, assume a decedent's will provides payments to a former employee. The obligation arose in connection with an on-the-job accident; payments are to continue until the employee recovers from the malady. Because the person is not a disqualified person, assumption of the debt by the foundation should not result in self-dealing. More troubling is the question as to whether payment of the debt is a qualifying distribution[422] or a taxable expenditure because it is not a charitable expenditure.[423] During the estate planning process, such entanglements should be anticipated.

From time to time, the IRS issues private letter rulings as to circumstances where the estate administration exception applies[424] and when it is inapplicable.[425] The IRS has begun issuing rulings in connection with settlement agreements involving property in estates and sales to disqualified persons, finding an absence of self-dealing because of the reasonableness of the settlement and its benefits to the private foundation involved, such as the cessation of litigation and more immediate access to property passing from the estate, without expressly invoking the estate administration exception.[426]

---

419. Priv. Ltr. Rul. 8929087.
420. E.g., Priv. Ltr. Rul. 200218036.
421. Reg. § 53.4941(d)-2(c)(1).
422. *See* Chapter 15.
423. *See* Chapter 17.
424. E.g., Priv. Ltr. Rul. 200117042.
425. E.g., Priv. Ltr. Rul. 9252042.
426. Priv. Ltr. Ruls. 201316021, 201321027.

## (b)  Control Situations

The term *indirect self-dealing* does not include a transaction between a disqualified person and an organization controlled by a private foundation if (1) the transaction results from a business relationship that was established before the transaction constituted an act of self-dealing, (2) the transaction was at least as favorable to the organization controlled by the private foundation as an arm's-length transaction with an unrelated person, and (3) either (a) the organization controlled by the private foundation could have engaged in the transaction with someone other than a disqualified person only at a severe economic hardship to the organization or (b) because of the unique nature of the product or services provided by the organization controlled by the foundation, the disqualified person could not have engaged in the transaction with anyone else, or could have done so only by incurring severe economic hardship.[427]

An organization is *controlled* by a private foundation if the foundation or one or more of its foundation managers may, by aggregating their votes or positions of authority, require the organization to engage in a transaction that, if engaged in with the private foundation, would constitute self-dealing.[428]

Also, an organization is controlled by a private foundation in the case of such a transaction between the organization and a disqualified person, if the disqualified person, together with one or more persons who are disqualified persons by reason of such person's relationship (such as a member of the family)[429] to the disqualified person, may, by aggregating their votes or positions of authority with that of the foundation, require the organization to engage in such a transaction.[430]

As to this second rule, an organization is considered to be controlled by a private foundation, or by a foundation and disqualified persons with respect to it, if such persons are able, in fact, to control the organization (even if their aggregate voting power is less than 50 percent of the total voting power of the organization's governing body) or if one or more of such persons has the right to exercise veto power over the actions of the organization relevant to any potential acts of self-dealing.[431]

Generally, then, where the above three circumstances are not involved, the transaction almost always constitutes indirect self-dealing.[432] Caution should be exercised when relying on the estate administration exception in that it does not

---

427.  Reg. § 53.4941(d)-1(b)(1).
428.  Reg. § 53.4941(d)-1(b)(5).
429.  *See* § 4.4.
430.  *Id.*
431.  *Id.*
432.  Two other exceptions may be available: (1) the benefit to a disqualified person is incidental or tenuous (*see* § 5.8(c)) or (2) the benefit is compensation for personal services where the compensation is reasonable and in furtherance of charitable purposes (*see* § 5.6).

shelter payments of excess compensation, loans, or indirect self-dealing between a company owned by an estate and the foundation.[433]

## §5.13 EARLY TERMINATIONS OF CHARITABLE REMAINDER TRUSTS

A charitable remainder trust[434] may be terminated sooner than is provided in the trust instrument. There are several reasons for the premature termination of this type of trust, such as a desire to transfer the trust assets earlier to the remainder interest beneficiary[435] or an income beneficiary's dissatisfaction with the level of income payments.[436]

The IRS tends to scrutinize proposed early terminations of charitable remainder trusts. The principal concern is that the early termination will result in greater allocation of the trust assets to the income beneficiary, to the detriment of the charitable remainder interest beneficiary, than would be the case if the termination instead occurred at the initially prescribed time.[437] The self-dealing rules potentially apply to the transaction.[438]

Nonetheless, in appropriate circumstances, the IRS will permit an early termination of a charitable remainder trust. The elements the agency reviews are whether (1) the trustee will be distributing to the income and remainder interest beneficiaries lump sums equal to the present value of the irrespective interests as of the termination date, (2) the income and remainder interests are vested, (3) all income beneficiaries are of full legal capacity, (4) all of the beneficiaries favor early termination, (5) any of the income beneficiaries has a medical condition that is expected to result in a shorter period of longevity for the beneficiary,[439] (6) the trust instrument prohibits early termination, and (7) state law (and/or state regulatory authorities) permits early termination.

---

433. When an estate transfers money or property to a private foundation in satisfaction of a bequest, the estate becomes a disqualified person with respect to the foundation when the amount or property value transferred reaches the requisite amount to cause it to have granted more than 2 percent of the total contributions the foundation has received (*see* § 4.1).

434. *See* § 2.4(b).

435. E.g., Priv. Ltr. Rul. 200304025.

436. E.g., Priv. Ltr. Rul. 200208039.

437. An early termination of a charitable remainder trust would, if the terms of the transfers were not reasonable, deprive the charitable remainder beneficiary's of the benefit to which it is entitled, inconsistent with the charitable contribution deduction allowed to the donor or donors.

438. *See* § 3.7.

439. It is the practice of the IRS to require an affidavit from a physician stating that the income beneficiary's does not have a medical condition that would unduly shorten the beneficiary's life.

The self-dealing rules apply except with respect to amounts payable under the terms of such trust to income beneficiaries.[440] The trust instrument may be silent on the point, but state law allowing early terminations of trusts may be considered implied terms of the instrument. Also, the early termination may not be discretionary with the trustee.[441] The foregoing factors are taken into account in the self-dealing context, with early termination of a charitable remainder trust, where a private foundation is the remainder interest beneficiary, found not to be impermissible self-dealing when the method of allocating assets of the trust on its termination was reasonable, the income beneficiaries had life expectancies reflecting average longevity, state law allowed the early termination, and all the beneficiaries favored the early termination.[442] The IRS, from time to time, issues private letter rulings as to early terminations of charitable remainder trusts.[443]

Notwithstanding the foregoing, the IRS appears to be reevaluating its position as to whether an early termination of a charitable remainder trust, where the remainder interest beneficiary is a private foundation, constitutes self-dealing.[444]

## § 5.14  ADDITIONAL EXCEPTIONS

Any transaction between a private foundation and a corporation that is a disqualified person with respect to the private foundation is not an act of self-dealing if the transaction is engaged in pursuant to a liquidation, merger, redemption, recapitalization, or other corporate adjustment, organization, or reorganization.[445] For this exception to apply, however, all the securities of the same class as that held (prior to the transaction) by the private foundation must be subject to the same terms, and the terms must provide for receipt by the private foundation of no less than fair market value.[446] For example, the IRS ruled that this transaction exception is available with respect to a reorganization,[447] where there is only one class of voting stock involved and the shares received will reflect a market value as determined by independent investment bankers.[448]

---

440. IRC § 4947(a)(2)(A).
441. Reg. § 53.4947-1(e).
442. This, then, is one of the few instances in which the concept of reasonableness is factored into a self-dealing law analysis.
443. E.g., Priv. Ltr. Rul. 200124010. In one instance, the income interest was also sold to the remainder interest beneficiary's (Priv. Ltr. Rul. 200310024).
444. E.g., Priv. Ltr. Rul. 200614032, revoking Priv. Ltr. Rul. 200525014. *See* Rev. Rul. 2008-41 2008-30 I.R.B. 170.
445. IRC § 4941(d)(2)(F).
446. Reg. § 53.4941(d)-3(d).
447. IRC § 368(a)(1)(C).
448. Priv. Ltr. Rul. 7847049.

A court held that acts of self-dealing took place when a company, which was a disqualified person with respect to a private foundation, redeemed shares from a private foundation under a treasury share acquisition program; because officers and directors of the company were excluded from participation in the redemption, the requirement of the exception that *all* securities involved in a redemption must be subject to the same terms was found not to have been met.[449] This decision was reversed on appeal, however, with the appellate court holding that this *same terms* rule does not require a corporation that is a disqualified person to include in a redemption program the shares held by its officers and directors, reasoning that this result was in harmony with the federal securities law impact on shareholding insiders.[450]

Generally, a transaction between a disqualified person and a private foundation will not constitute an act of self-dealing if (1) the transaction is a purchase or sale of securities by a private foundation through a stockbroker, where normal trading procedures on a stock exchange or recognized over-the-counter market are followed, (2) neither the buyer nor the seller of the securities, nor the agent of either, knows the identity of the other party involved, and (3) the sale is made in the ordinary course of business and does not involve a block of securities larger than the average trading volume of the stock over the previous four weeks.[451]

Further, the Tax Reform Act of 1969 contains five "savings provisions"[452] or transitional rules rendering the self-dealing rules inapplicable to various pre-1969 and other transactions.[453]

One of these provisions embodied in the 1969 Act excluded from the proscriptions of the self-dealing rules the disposition of a private foundation's excess and nonexcess business holdings,[454] owned by the private foundation on May 26, 1969, to a disqualified person, where the private foundation was required to dispose of the property in order to avoid the taxes on excess holdings,[455] the private foundation received an amount that at least equaled the fair market value of the property, and (in the case of nonexcess holdings) the transaction occurred before January 1975.[456] This exception was allowed in recognition of the fact that in the case of many closely held companies, the only ready market for a foundation's holdings is one or more disqualified persons.

---

449. *Deluxe Check Printers, Inc. v. United States*, 88-1 U.S.T.C. ¶ 9311 (Cl. Ct. 1988).
450. *Deluxe Corporation v. United States*, 885 F.2d 848 (Fed. Cir. 1989). The IRS elected to not further appeal this decision (AOD 1990–08).
451. Reg. § 53.4941(a)-1(a)(1).
452. Tax Reform Act of 1969 § 101(1)(2).
453. Reg. § 53.4941(d)-4.
454. *See* § 7.2(d).
455. IRC § 4943.
456. Tax Reform Act of 1969 § 101(1)(2)(B); Rev. Rul. 75-25, 1975-1 C.B. 359.

This transitional rule concerning the disposition of holdings owned by a private foundation on May 26, 1969, does not have an effective date, as illustrated by a situation where the holdings were not excess holdings as of 1969, so that the exception was not then available, but subsequently became excess holdings. For example, where at least 95 percent of the income of a corporation, wholly owned by a private foundation and its disqualified persons on May 26, 1969, consisted of rents from real property, thus constituting passive income,[457] the corporation was not considered a business enterprise[458] so that the holdings could not be excess holdings. Years later, less than 95 percent of the corporation's gross income was being derived from real property rentals, with the balance coming from the leasing of equipment to unrelated third parties, causing the corporation to become a business enterprise and thus allowing the excess holdings to be sold to disqualified persons pursuant to the exception, inasmuch as all of the other requirements of the transitional rule were met.[459]

Another transitional rule adopted in 1969[460] enabled a private foundation to lease (through 1979) property under certain circumstances to a disqualified person without violating the self-dealing rules.

Congress, in 1980, created a permanent exemption from the self-dealing rules for office space leasing arrangements between a private foundation tenant and a disqualified person where (1) the lease was pursuant to a binding contract in effect on October 9, 1969, even though it had been renewed, (2) at the time of execution the lease was not a prohibited transaction,[461] (3) the space was leased to the private foundation on a basis no less favorable than that on which the space would be made available in an arm's-length transaction, and (4) the leased space was in a building in which there were tenants who were not disqualified persons with respect to the private foundation. These rules are effective for tax years beginning after December 31, 1979.[462]

To enable private foundations to sell property presently being leased to a disqualified person at its maximum value, Congress in 1976 devised another transitional rule allowing a private foundation to dispose of nonexcess property to a disqualified person if at that time it is leasing substantially all of the property under the lease transitional rule and it receives an amount that at least equals the property's fair market value.[463] This rule applied to dispositions occurring before January 1, 1978, and after October 4, 1976.

---

457. IRC § 512(b)(3).
458. IRC § 4943(d)(3)(B).
459. Rev. Rul. 86-53, 1986-1 C.B. 326.
460. Tax Reform Act of 1969 § 101(1)(2)(C).
461. *See* § 5.3.
462. IRC § 4941(d)(2)(H); Reg. § 53.4941(d)-2(b)(3). The specific beneficiary of these rules is the Moody Foundation in Galveston, Texas.
463. Tax Reform Act of 1969 § 101(1)(2)(F).

# §5.15  ISSUES ONCE SELF-DEALING OCCURS

The prohibitions against self-dealing—like the other private foundation rules—are enforced by excise taxes that are, in reality, penalties for what Congress has characterized as wrongful conduct. One court described these sanctions as follows: "The language of the [Tax Reform] Act [of 1969], its legislative history, the graduated levels of the sanctions imposed, and the almost confiscatory level of the exactions assessed, convince us that the exactions in question were intended to curb the described conduct through pecuniary punishment."[464]

Once it has been determined that self-dealing has occurred, the self-dealing must be corrected, an excise tax return must be filed (Form 4720), and tax due must be paid. The steps involved in repairing the damage include *undoing* the transaction, assigning an *amount* attributable to the self-dealing, deciding who has to *pay an excise tax*, and advancing any claim of reasonable cause to reduce or avoid any additional tax. This is a self-enforcement system; the parties should not merely await the possibility of an IRS examination.

## (a)  Undoing the Transaction

To undo a self-dealing transaction, the transaction must be corrected and rescinded (i.e., the property returned) if possible. The term *correction* means undoing the transaction to the extent possible, but, in any case, placing the private foundation in a financial position not worse than that in which it would be if the disqualified person were dealing under the highest fiduciary standards.[465] Specific rules govern sales by or to the foundation, uses of property, and compensation deals.[466]

---

464. *In re Unified Control Systems, Inc.*, 586 F.2d 1036, 1039 (5th Cir. 1978). One court has twice held that the IRC § 4941 "taxes" are penalties for the purpose of assessment of interest (under IRC § 6601(e)(3)) (*Farrell v. United States*, 484 F. Supp. 1097 (E.D. Ark. 1980), followed in *Rockefeller v. United States*, 572 F. Supp. 9 (E.D. Ark. 1982), *aff'd*, 718 F.2d 291 (9th Cir. 1983), *cert. den.*, 466 U.S. 962 (1984)).

465. IRC § 4941(e)(3); Reg. § 53.4941(e)-1(c)(1).

466. If a foundation manager or government official is excused from paying an initial tax, on the ground that the person participated in the act of self-dealing unknowingly (*see* §§ 5.15(d), 5.15(e), the act nonetheless occurred, yet there would not be a basis for imposition of an initial tax. Thus, there would not be any need to correct the act because the correction requirement comes into being, in connection with an additional tax, only where the initial tax is imposed. (There is, however, nothing in the statute or tax regulations on this point, and there is no known such holding in a public or private IRS ruling.) If, moreover, aside from that point, the transaction was a transfer or use of the income or assets of the private foundation (*see* § 5.8), and the benefit was incidental or tenuous (*see* § 5.8(c)), correction would not be entailed because the receipt of an incidental or tenuous benefit is not an act of self-dealing in the first instance. This would also be the outcome in any other instance where a transaction is defined to not be an act of self-dealing (as opposed to merely an exception to a self-dealing tax).

**Sales by the Foundation.** In the case of a sale of property by a private foundation to a disqualified person, undoing the transaction includes rescission of the sale. If the purchaser still holds the property, the foundation must take back the property.[467] The foundation then repays the purchaser the sales price or the current fair market value of the property at the time of the correction, whichever is less. Any income earned by the disqualified person/buyer from the property in excess of the private foundation's earnings on the money (from investment of the sales proceeds) during the self-dealing period should be restored to the foundation, essentially reducing the repayment of the purchase price by the foundation. If the property has been resold, the foundation is to receive the greater of the original proceeds that it received or what the disqualified person received upon the resale.

**Sales to the Foundation.** In the case of a sale of property to a private foundation by a disqualified person, rescission of the sale is required. Fair market value and resale considerations similar to those mentioned previously are taken into account, to assure that the foundation is restored to the financial position in which it would have been had it not purchased the property.[468] For example, assume a foundation sold 100 shares of stock to a disqualified person for $4,000 in 2013, at a time when the value of the shares was $3,500. Further assume that person sells the shares in 2014 for $6,000 and that the shares were selling at $6,700 at one point during the year. The foundation must be paid $6,700 to cure the transaction. The first-tier tax will be charged based on the $4,000. If the self-dealing is not corrected and the second-tier tax applies, the tax is calculated based on $6,700, as described in the next section.

A transaction between a private foundation and a disqualified person is not an act of self-dealing if (1) the transaction is a purchase or sale of securities by a foundation through a stockbroker where normal trading procedures on a stock exchange or recognized over-the-counter market are followed, (2) neither the buyer nor the seller of the securities nor the agent of either knows the identity of the other party involved, and (3) the sale is made in the ordinary course of business and does not involve a block of securities larger than the average daily trading volume of that stock over the previous four weeks. Nonetheless, this exception is inapplicable to a transaction involving a dealer who is a disqualified person acting as a principal or to a transaction involving an extension of credit between a foundation and a disqualified person.

Caution should be exercised in an attempt to effect correction of an act of self-dealing, so that the attempt is not itself regarded as an act of self-dealing. This nearly occurred when a disqualified person, in attempting to correct a self-

---

467. Reg. § 53.4941(e)-1(c)(2).
468. Reg. § 53.4941(e)-1(c)(3).

dealing act in the form of a loan to him from a private foundation,[469] proposed to transfer to the private foundation a parcel of real estate with a fair market value equal to the amount of the loan. The IRS held that (1) the transfer would constitute self-dealing because, since the self-dealer's indebtedness to the private foundation would be canceled, the transaction would be a sale of property by the disqualified person to the private foundation, which would be an act of self-dealing,[470] and (2) the minimum standards for an authentic correction[471] would not be met because "it [would] be generally less advantageous to the foundation to receive the property than to have the loan repaid since it may be both difficult and costly for the foundation to convert the property to cash and thus restore its position."[472] The IRS noted that a transfer of property could be an acceptable correction of a self-dealing loan transaction where the property had substantially appreciated in value and could be readily converted into an amount of money in excess of the debt.

In another example, a private foundation decided to cease operating a home for troubled children. The real estate involved, which had been improved by the foundation as part of its exempt use of the property, was being leased to the foundation by disqualified persons. Closing the home involved cancellation of the lease, which provided that improvements to the property would revert to the landlords. Generally, the transfer of the improvements to disqualified persons would be an act of self-dealing. The IRS, however, permitted the disqualified persons to pay to the foundation the greater of the fair market value of the transferred property at the date the correction occurred or the original cost of the property, thereby placing the foundation in the position of not having expended any of its charitable funds in connection with the property and preventing the disqualified persons from benefiting from the transaction.[473]

**Loans.** Where a loan has been made, the amount involved, and therefore subject to penalty, is the greater of the amount paid for the use of the funds (interest actually paid) or the fair market value of the use (prevailing market rate) for the period of time the money was lent.[474] To correct the self-dealing, the principal of the loan, plus the interest deferential, must be repaid. For an interest-free demand loan, the fair value for use of the money would reasonably be equal to the prevailing federal short-term rate for funds. The authors have seen instances in which the foundation inadvertently paid expenses on behalf of a disqualified person, essentially making a loan that results in self-dealing. In

---

469. IRC § 4941(d)(1)(B); *see* § 5.5.

470. IRC § 4941(d)(1)(A); *see* § 5.4.

471. Reg. § 53.4941(e)-1(c)(4).

472. Rev. Rul. 81-40, 1981-1 C.B. 508, 509.

473. Priv. Ltr. Rul. 9601048.

474. Reg. § 53.4941(e)-1(b)(2)(ii).

this type of a situation, the penalty is imposed on the interest factor, or the prevailing short-term interest rate times the amount of the expenses paid or loan advanced to the disqualified person.

**Uses of Property.** Whether the property is being used by a foundation or a disqualified person, the impermissible use must be stopped. If the rent paid exceeds the fair market value, an imputed rent factor based on fair market differentials, if any, must be repaid to the foundation. Different corrections are specified in the regulations, depending on whether the foundation or the disqualified person rented the property.[475]

**Unreasonable Compensation.** When excessive or unreasonable salaries have been paid to a disqualified person, the excess must be repaid to the foundation. Termination of the employment or independent contractor arrangement, however, is not required.[476]

Corrections of acts of self-dealing that meet these minimum standards of correction are not themselves acts of self-dealing.[477] While the IRS generally has the discretionary authority to abate the private foundation initial taxes in the case of certain taxable events, this authority does not extend to the self-dealing tax.[478]

### (b) Amount Involved

The penalties for entering into a self-dealing transaction are based on the *amount involved*, which is defined as the "greater of the amount of money and the fair market value of the other property given or the amount of money and the fair market value of the other property received."[479]

Where a transaction entails the use of money or other property, the amount involved is the greater of the amount paid for the use or the fair market value of the use for the period for which the money or other property is used.[480] If, for example, a private foundation leases office space from a disqualified person for $30,000, but the fair market value of the space is $25,000, the amount involved is $30,000. If a foundation lends money to a disqualified person at a below-market interest rate, the amount involved equals the difference between the interest actually paid and the amount that would have been charged at the prevailing market rate at the time the loan was made.[481] The highest fair market value

---

475. Reg. § 53.4941(e)-1(c)(4).
476. Reg. § 53.4941(e)-1(c)(6).
477. Reg. § 53.4941(e)-1(c)(1).
478. *See* § 5.15(f).
479. IRC § 4941(e)(2); Reg. § 53.4941(e)-1(b)(1).
480. Reg. § 53.4941(e)-1(b)(2)(ii).
481. Reg. § 53.4941(e)-1(b)(4), Example 2.

during the correction period is the amount involved in the case of the second- and third-tier taxes.[482]

**Compensation.** In the case of compensation paid for personal services to persons other than government officials, the amount involved is the portion of the total compensation in excess of the amount that would have been reasonable.[483]

The term *compensation* in this setting generally means a salary or wage, any bonuses, fringe benefits, retirement benefits, and the like. Occasionally, however, other economic benefits are treated as compensation for purposes of application of the self-dealing rules. For example, under certain circumstances, the value of an indemnification by a private foundation of a foundation manager, or the payment by a foundation of the premiums for an insurance policy for a foundation manager, must be treated as compensation to avoid self-dealing.[484] By contrast, when the self-dealing rules are explicit as to a particular type of prohibited transaction between a private foundation and a disqualified person, the rules cannot be sidestepped simply by treating the value of the economic benefit provided as part of the disqualified person's total (reasonable) compensation.[485]

**Stock Redemptions and Other Permitted Dealings.** A transaction that is permitted by a statutory exception may nonetheless go amiss,[486] resulting in imposition of a penalty tax. This occurs particularly often under exceptions for which the value is determinative. In these cases, the amount involved, or the taxable self-dealing, is only the amount by which the redemption price is deficient (i.e., the amount by which the property was undervalued). For example, a corporation that is a disqualified person in regard to a foundation redeems the foundation's stock for $200,000. Assume that the correct valuation is later determined to be $250,000. Self-dealing has occurred in the amount of $50,000.

---

482. IRC § 4941(e)(2)(B); Reg. § 53.4941(e)-1(b)(3). *See* § 5.15(c).
483. Reg. § 53.4941(e)-1(b)(2)(iii).
484. *See* § 5.7(b).
485. For example, a loan by a private foundation to a disqualified person is an act of self-dealing (*see* § 5.5). The self-dealing rules cannot be avoided by regarding the value of this type of loan as compensation (Priv. Ltr. Rul. 9530032). By contrast, this characterization of a loan as compensation is permissible in the case of a public charity dealing with an insider (*id.*). Under the intermediate sanctions rules, however, this practice is impermissible when done in hindsight, in that an economic benefit cannot be treated as consideration for the performance of services unless the organization clearly indicated its intent to so treat the benefit (IRC § 4958(c)(1)(A)). This approach thus imposes a more rigorous standard in this regard on public charities than is the case with private foundations.
486. IRC § 4941(d)(2); *see* § 5.3(b).

Two conditions must be present to show that the parties made a good faith effort to determine the fair market value:

1.  The appraiser who arrived at the value must be competent to make the valuation, must not be a disqualified person, and must not be in a position, whether by stock ownership or otherwise, to derive an economic benefit from the value utilized; and

2.  The method used in making the valuation must be a generally accepted method for valuing comparable property, stock, or securities for purposes of arm's-length business transactions in which valuation is a significant factor.[487]

## (c)  Date of Valuation

To calculate the *first-tier* tax initially imposed on a sale, exchange, or lease of property, the amount involved is determined as of the date on which the self-dealing occurred.[488] An act of self-dealing *occurs* on the date on which all the terms and conditions of the transaction and the liabilities of the parties have been fixed.[489] If the self-dealing goes uncorrected and the additional or *second-tier* tax is calculated, the valuation is equal to the highest value during the period of time the self-dealing continued uncorrected.

In one case, the need to correct an act of self-dealing gave rise to a peculiar series of transactions. Upon being advised by the IRS that a sale of real estate in 1971 by a disqualified person to a private foundation was an act of self-dealing that required correction, the private foundation in 1973 sold the land back to the disqualified person for the original sale price. Immediately after this transaction, the disqualified person transferred the property to a "straw person" for the same price, who in turn sold it back to the private foundation for the same price. In 1975, the land was transferred by the private foundation to the straw person for the same price. The court involved rejected the disqualified person's assertion that the transfers in 1973 were shams and thus should be ignored for tax purposes, and that any taxes applicable with respect to the 1971 transaction were barred by the statute of limitations. Instead, the court held that the 1973 transfer of the land back to the disqualified person was intended to correct the initial act of self-dealing in 1971, and thus was separate from the other 1973 transaction. The court did not, at the time, rule on the question as to whether the retransfer of the land to the private foundation in 1973 via the straw person constituted an act of self-dealing.[490]

---

487.  Reg. § 53.4941(e)-1(b)(2)(i).
488.  IRC § 4941(e)(2)(A); Reg. § 53.4941(e)-1(b)(3).
489.  Reg. § 53.4941(e)-1(a)(2).
490.  *Dupont v. Commissioner*, 74 T.C. 498 (1980).

## (d) Payment of Tax

There are three taxes that are potentially applicable in the self-dealing context: the first-tier tax, the second-tier tax, and the third-tier tax.

**First-Tier Tax.** Two types of initial taxes are imposed on each act of self-dealing between a private foundation and a disqualified person, and are sometimes identified by the Internal Revenue Code subsection in which they appear, as shown in the following chart. The foundation involved does not pay any self-dealing taxes. Several persons may be taxed at the following rates:

| Tax Is Called | Who Pays | Rate |
| --- | --- | --- |
| 4941(a)(1) tax | Self-dealer | 10% |
| 4941(a)(2) tax | Participating managers | 5% |

The self-dealer, or the disqualified person (other than a foundation manager acting only in that capacity) who participates, pays a 10 percent tax on the amount involved with respect to the act of self-dealing for each year (or part of a year) in the taxable period. The self-dealer is taxed even if he, she, or it was unaware that a rule was being violated. A self-dealer also acting as a foundation manager can be subject to both taxes.[491]

Foundation managers that participate in an act of self-dealing are subject to the lesser rate of 5 percent of the taxable amount. This tax may be imposed, however, only where:

- The initial tax on the self-dealer is imposed,
- The foundation manager knows[492] that the act is an act of self-dealing, and
- The participation by the foundation manager is willful and not due to reasonable cause.[493]

For purposes of this tax, a manager is treated as *participating* in an act of self-dealing in any case in which the person engages or takes part in the transaction by himself, herself, or itself, or directs any person to do so.[494] In this context, the term *participation* includes silence or inaction on the part of a foundation manager where he or she is under a duty to speak or act, as well as any affirmative action by the manager. A foundation manager is not considered to

---

491. IRC § 4941(a)(1); Reg. § 53.4941(a)-1(a)(1); Rev. Rul. 78-76, 1978-1 C.B. 377.
492. *See* text accompanied by *infra* notes 498–499.
493. IRC § 4941(a)(2); Reg. § 53.4941(a)-1(b)(1).
494. Reg. § 53.4941(a)-1(a)(3).

have participated in an act of self-dealing, however, where he or she has opposed the act in a manner consistent with the fulfillment of his or her responsibilities to the private foundation.[495]

Participation by a foundation manager is deemed *willful* if it is voluntary, conscious, and intentional. No motive to avoid the restrictions of the law or the incurrence of any tax is necessary to make the participation willful. Participation by a foundation manager is not willful, however, if he or she does not know that the transaction in which he or she is participating is an act of self-dealing.[496]

A foundation manager's participation is due to *reasonable cause* if he or she has exercised his or her responsibility on behalf of the foundation with ordinary business care and prudence.[497] A manager having a reasonable cause (that under the third factor listed above might excuse above imposition of the tax) would be one found to be attentive to the affairs of the foundation, to be aware of the private foundation sanctions, and to remain sufficiently informed of the foundation's activities to prevent any violations of the sanctions.

The term *knowing* does not mean "having reason to know." Evidence tending to show that an individual has reason to know of a particular fact or particular rule, however, is relevant in determining whether he or she had actual knowledge of that fact or rule. For example, evidence tending to show that an individual has reason to know of sufficient facts so that, based solely on those facts, a transaction would be an act of self-dealing is relevant in determining whether he or she has actual knowledge of those facts.[498]

An individual is considered to have participated in a transaction *knowing* that it is an act of self-dealing only if:

- He or she has actual knowledge of sufficient facts so that, based solely on those facts, the transaction would be an act of self-dealing,

- He or she is aware that the act under these circumstances may violate the self-dealing rules, and

- He or she negligently fails to make reasonable attempts to ascertain whether the transaction is an act of self-dealing, or he or she is in fact aware that it is this type of act.[499]

In the case of a government official,[500] a tax can be imposed only if the official, as a disqualified person, participated in the act of self-dealing knowing

---

495. Reg. § 53.4941(a)-1(b)(2).
496. Reg. § 53.4941(a)-1(b)(4).
497. Reg. § 53.4941(a)-1(b)(5).
498. *Id.*
499. Reg. § 53.4941(a)-1(b)(3).
500. *See* § 4.8.

that it was this type of an act.[501] Otherwise, the tax is imposed on a disqualified person even though the person did not have knowledge at the time of the act that it constituted self-dealing.[502]

The *taxable period* is, with respect to an act of self-dealing, the period beginning with the date on which the act of self-dealing occurred and ending on the earliest of the following dates:

- The date of mailing of a notice of deficiency with respect to the initial tax,[503]
- The date on which the tax is assessed, or
- The date on which correction of the act of self-dealing is completed.[504]

If a transaction between a private foundation and a disqualified person concerns the leasing of property, the lending of money or other extension of credit, other use of money or property, or payment of compensation, the transaction will generally be treated as giving rise to an act of self-dealing on the day the transaction occurs, plus an act of self-dealing on the first day of each applicable tax year after that date.[505]

If more than one person is liable for one of these initial taxes, all of them are jointly and severally liable for the tax with respect to the act of self-dealing involved, up to a maximum of $10,000 for all.[506]

If joint participation in a transaction by two or more disqualified persons constitutes self-dealing (such as a joint sale of property to a private foundation), the transaction is generally treated as a separate act of self-dealing with respect to each disqualified person.[507]

---

501. IRC § 4941(a)(1); Reg. § 53.4941(a)-1(a)(2). There is a (perfectly reasonable) assumption that the rule, as to reliance on advice of counsel in connection with the concept of knowing (*see* § 5.15(e)), is identical in the foundation manager and government official settings. Yet the regulations are improvidently written in this regard, in that reference is made to the fact that a "person's participation in such act will ordinarily not be considered 'knowing' or 'willful' and will ordinarily be considered 'due to reasonable cause' within the meaning of section 4941(a)(2)" (Reg. § 53.4941(a)-1(b)(6)). The reference to knowing, however, in connection with government officials is in IRC § 4941(a)(1). In general, the concept of knowing is the same in both contexts (Reg. § 53.4941(a)-1(a)(2)).

502. Reg. § 53.4941(a)-1(a)(1).

503. The basic rules as to notices of deficiency are the subject of IRC § 6212.

504. IRC § 4941(e)(1); Reg. § 53.4941(e)-1(a). A private foundation lent money to a disqualified person with a tax year different from that of the foundation; the disqualified person must compute the tax payable under IRC § 4941 on account of self-dealing based on his or her own tax year (Rev. Rul. 75-391, 1975-2 C.B. 446).

505. Reg. § 53.4941(e)-1(e)(1).

506. IRC § 4941(c)(1); Reg. § 53.4941(c)-1.

507. Reg. § 53.4941(e)-1(e).

This self-dealing tax is imposed annually (at the 5 percent rate), rather than merely with respect to the year in which the self-dealing took place.[508] For example, if a private foundation made a multiyear loan to a disqualified person, there would be an act of self-dealing with respect to each year there was an outstanding principal balance on the loan.[509]

**Second-Tier Tax.** Where the initial tax is imposed and the self-dealing is not corrected in a timely fashion, an additional tax of 200 percent of the amount involved is imposed on the self-dealer. A foundation manager who refuses to agree to the correction faces a penalty of 50 percent of the amount involved. Again, if more than one manager is liable for one of these taxes, all of them are jointly and severally liable for the tax with respect to the act of self-dealing involved.[510]

**Third-Tier Tax.** The ultimate tax, called third-tier tax, is the termination tax that can be charged if the transactions are never cured.[511] This tax provides that a foundation that conducts repeated and willful violations of the sanctions is liable to be terminated, with all tax benefits it and its contributors have ever received being repaid to the government—very likely, all of the assets held in the foundation.[512]

## (e) Advice of Counsel

If a foundation manager, after full disclosure of the factual situation to legal counsel (including house counsel), relies on the advice of that counsel expressed in a reasoned written legal opinion that an act is not an act of self-dealing—even if that act is subsequently held to be self-dealing—the individual's participation in the act will ordinarily not be considered knowing or willful and will ordinarily be considered due to reasonable cause. This document provided by legal counsel is not required to be a formal *opinion letter* (as the legal profession defines that term); rather, it can be a letter or memorandum containing the views of counsel on the point or points involved.[513] A written legal opinion is considered *reasoned*, even if it reaches a conclusion that is subsequently determined to be incorrect, as long as the opinion addresses itself to the facts and applicable law. A written legal opinion is not considered

---

508. Reg. § 53.4941(a)-1(a)(1); Gen. Couns. Mem. 39066.
509. Priv. Ltr. Rul. 9530032.
510. IRC § 4941(c)(1); Reg. § 53.4941(c)-1.
511. In general, Chapter 13.
512. IRC § 507.
513. In one instance, the IRS wrote that disqualified persons avoided self-dealing taxes because they "relied on the advice of counsel," who "reviewed and approved their activities" (Tech. Adv. Mem. 9408006).

*reasoned*, however, if it does nothing more than recite the facts and express a conclusion. The absence of advice of counsel with respect to an act does not, by itself, give rise to any inference that a person participated in the act knowingly, willfully, or without reasonable cause.[514]

## (f)  Abatement

The IRS generally has the authority to abate the private foundation first-tier taxes where reasonable cause can be shown, as well as in the absence of willful neglect.[515] This authority does not, however, extend to the self-dealing taxes.[516]

Nonetheless, in one instance, the IRS found acts of self-dealing on audit of a private foundation, yet worked with foundation management to revise the organization's operations so as to correct the activities that gave rise to the transgression. The IRS used its general authority to grant relief[517] to do so retroactively for the benefit of the foundation (because tax-exempt status was also at issue) and its management on the self-dealing issues.[518]

## (g)  Court Jurisdiction as to the Tax

The effectiveness of these additional taxes was temporarily in jeopardy as the result of U.S. Tax Court decisions holding that the court lacked the jurisdiction to ascertain whether these taxes should be imposed. The matter first arose in 1978, in connection with the tax court's first self-dealing case,[519] where the court ordered the submission of briefs by the parties as to its authority to determine the 200 percent additional tax.[520] Subsequently, the court found that it did not have jurisdiction to determine whether this second-level tax should be imposed.[521]

The tax court reasoned that its jurisdiction[522] is generally confined to authority to redetermine the correct amount of a deficiency,[523] which is the amount by which the tax imposed (in this instance, by the various private foundation excise taxes)[524] exceeds the tax shown on the return.[525] In these

---

514. Reg. § 53.4941(a)-1(b)(6).
515. IRC § 4962(a).
516. IRC § 4962(b).
517. IRC § 7805(b).
518. Tech. Adv. Mem. 9646002.
519. *Adams v. Commissioner*, 70 T.C. 373 (1978), *aff'd* (in an unpublished opinion), 2nd Cir. 1982.
520. *Adams v. Commissioner*, 70 T.C. 466 (1978).
521. *Adams v. Commissioner*, 72 T.C. 81 (1979).
522. IRC § 7442.
523. IRC § 6214(a).
524. IRC Chapter 42.
525. IRC § 6211(a).

cases, however, said the court, there is yet no deficiency for the court to redetermine, since the second-level tax cannot be imposed until the first-level tax is imposed and the act of self-dealing is corrected, and since the correction period does not expire until the court's decision is final.[526] By the time the second-level tax deficiency arises, the court held, the IRS has already mailed a deficiency notice as respects the act of self-dealing. But since the IRS is precluded from issuing a second deficiency notice for the same self-dealing act,[527] it is, the court held, barred from issuing a deficiency notice for a second-level tax.[528]

Legislation to resolve this unintended void in tax court jurisdiction was adopted by Congress in 1980.[529] Under this approach, the second-tier excise taxes will be imposed at the end of the *taxable period*, which begins with the event giving rise to the self-dealing tax and ends on the earliest of (1) the date a notice of deficiency with respect to the first-tier tax is mailed, (2) the date the first-tier tax is assessed if no deficiency notice is mailed, or (3) the date the taxable act is corrected.[530] Where the act or failure to act that gave rise to the second-tier tax is corrected within the *correction period*,[531] the tax will not be assessed, or if assessed will be abated, or if collected will be credited or refunded.[532] The collection period is suspended during any litigation.[533]

Subsequently, the tax court decided that the 1980 revisions in the statutory law modifying the second-tier tax rules are applicable to a docketed and untried case where the second-tier taxes have not been assessed.[534] The new rules apply with respect to taxes assessed after the date of enactment of the 1980 law, which was December 24, 1980; a statutory notice of deficiency was mailed to the person, alleged to be a self-dealer with a private foundation, on May 14, 1980. The court said that the litigant in the case "confused two distinct events by equating the mailing of the notice of deficiency with the assessment of the tax."[535] Noting that "no assessment can be made where a petition has been timely and validly filed in this Court until the decision of this Court becomes final,"[536] the court decided that the 1980 amendments "are applicable in this

---

526. IRC § 4941(a)(4).
527. IRC § 6212(c).
528. Presumably, this line of reasoning also precluded tax court jurisdiction over cases involving similar taxes in IRC §§ 4942, 4943, 4944, 4945, 4947, 4951, and 4952. As respects IRC § 4945, the Tax Court so held (*Larchmont Foundation, Inc. v. Commissioner*, 72 T.C. 131 (1979)).
529. P.L. 96-596, 94 Stat. 3469.
530. IRC § 4941(e)(1); Reg. § 53.4941(e)-1.
531. IRC § 4962(e); Reg. § 53.4962-1(d), (e).
532. IRC § 4961(a); Reg. § 53.4961-1.
533. IRC § 4961(c); Reg. § 53.4961-2.
534. *Howell v. Commissioner*, 77 T.C. 916 (1981).
535. *Id*. at 920.
536. IRC § 6213(a).

case to the second-tier taxes imposed by Section 4941 because such taxes have not been 'assessed' and the doctrine of res judicata clearly does not apply where the case has not yet been tried and decided on its merits."[537]

Similar rules apply, in the private foundation context, to foundation managers. There are self-harbor rules for managers who disclose the factual situation to a lawyer and rely on a reasoned written legal opinion that the particular transaction is not a prohibited transaction.[538] The IRS is thinking about expanding the private foundation regulations, for purposes of the self-dealing rules (and the expenditure responsibility rules),[539] to parallel the *advice of counsel* safe harbors contained in the intermediate sanctions rules.

Although not expressly mentioned by the IRS, other features of the intermediate sanctions rules that should be considered as additions to the private foundation rules are the rebuttable presumption of reasonableness,[540] the initial contract exception,[541] and the details as to the correction process.[542]

---

537. *Howell v. Commissioner*, 77 T.C. 916, 920 (1981). This opinion also rejected the contention that this interpretation of the 1980 law gave it a retroactive effect and that it is being applied in a manner in violation of due process requirements because its retroactivity was not clearly expressed by the setting of a fixed date. Cf. Judge Fay's dissent. Also *The Barth Foundation v. Commissioner*, 77 T.C. 1008 (1981); *Applestein Foundation Trust v. Commissioner*, 42 T.C.M. 1635 (1981); *The Barth Foundation v. Commissioner*, 42 T.C.M. 1580 (1981). In general, intent or motive is not required for self-dealing to be found. As the tax regulations state, the initial tax for self-dealing "shall be imposed on a disqualified person even though he [or she] had no knowledge at the time of the act that such act constituted self-dealing" (Reg. § 53.4941(a)-1(a)(1)). Also, compliance with state fiduciary law principles is not a defense for self-dealing (cf. § 8.1, text accompanied by note 25). In denying a motion to compel the IRS to produce documents in an action to recover taxes imposed for acts of self-dealing, a court held that the language of IRC § 4941 and the regulations thereunder are "unambiguous" (*Deluxe Check Printers, Inc. v. United States*, 84-2 U.S.T.C. ¶ 9647 (Ct. Cl. 1984)). Another court held that the IRC § 4941 taxes are constitutional, in that they are not an impermissible extension of congressional taxing power (under U.S. Const. Art. 1 § 8, clause 1) nor a transgression of states' rights (U.S. Const., Tenth Am.), and that the underlying regulations are consistent with the statute, are reasonable, are not arbitrary, and are not unconstitutionally vague (*Rockefeller v. United States*, 572 F. Supp. 9 (E.D. Ark. 1982), *aff'd*, 718 F.2d 291 (9th Cir. 1983), *cert. den.*, 466 U.S. 962 (1984)). Also *Estate of Bernard J. Reis v. Commissioner*, 87 T.C. 1016 (1986).
538. *See* § 5.15(e).
539. *See* Chapter 9.
540. *See Intermediate Sanctions*, Chapter 5.
541. *Id.*, § 4.4.
542. *Id.*, § 6.4.

# CHAPTER SIX

# Mandatory Distributions

## §6.1 DISTRIBUTION REQUIREMENTS—IN GENERAL

Prior to enactment of the Tax Reform Act of 1969, the tax law provided that a charitable organization, including a private foundation, would lose its tax-exempt status if its aggregate accumulated income was "unreasonable in amount or duration in order to carry out the charitable, educational, or other purpose or function constituting the basis for [its] exemption. . . ."

This statutory sanction was deemed ineffective by Congress with respect to private foundations, as the following indicates:

> Under prior law, if a private foundation invested in assets that produced no current income, then it needed to make no distributions for charitable purposes. As a result,

while the donor may have received substantial tax benefits from his contribution currently, charity may have received absolutely no current benefit. In other cases, even though income was produced by the assets contributed to charitable organizations, no current distribution was required until the accumulations became "unreasonable." Although a number of court cases had begun to set guidelines as to the circumstances under which an accumulation became unreasonable, in many cases the determination was essentially subjective. Moreover, as was the case with self-dealing, it frequently happened that the only available sanction (loss of exempt status) either was largely ineffective or else was unduly harsh.[1]

Consequently, Congress, in enacting the Tax Reform Act of 1969, repealed this law and substituted rules requiring certain distributions, for charitable purposes, by private foundations.

Private foundations are required to distribute, with respect to each year, grants to other charitable organizations and otherwise spend a certain amount of money and/or property for charitable purposes.[2] There are four of these mandatory distribution rules; the applicable one is dependent on the type of private foundation involved. The general mandatory distribution requirement is the subject of this chapter. The distribution rules for private operating foundations, conduit private foundations, common fund private foundations and certain supporting organizations are discussed elsewhere.[3]

The general purpose of this mandatory payout requirement is to force private foundations to transfer some money and/or property into charitable programs.[4] Another reason for the requirement is to induce avoidance of imprudent or private-interest investment practices, or eliminate the private foundations that engage in those practices. The mandatory payout requirement does not forbid the making of investments with low- or no-current yield (such as raw land). When a private foundation invests in this manner, however, it periodically may have to sell some assets to meet the distribution requirements or distribute property for charitable objectives in satisfaction of the payout rules. Unless the value of its investments is increasing, the private foundation would be chipping away at its asset base, hastening the day when its investment approach causes its decline and perhaps ultimate extinction. This is one of the reasons the "death knell" provision in the Senate version of the 1969 tax legislation, by which foundations would have to terminate their existence after

1. Joint Committee on Internal Revenue Taxation, *General Explanation of Tax Reform Act of 1969*, 91st Cong. 2d Sess. 36 (1970); also Rev. Rul. 67-5, 1967-1 C.B. 123. Prior law was IRC § 504(a)(1).
2. With one exception, the federal tax law does not impose a mandatory distribution requirement on any other type of tax-exempt organization. The exception is the distribution requirement applicable to Type III non–functionally related supporting organizations that have an annual spending requirement as described in § 15.7(g).
3. *See* Chapter 3.
4. *See* text accompanied by *supra* note 1.

a stated period of years, was abandoned in favor of the mandatory distribution requirement.[5]

A private foundation's mandatory distribution requirement principally is a function of the value of its noncharitable-use assets.[6] The mandatory amount that must be annually distributed is ascertained by computing the private foundation's distributable amount,[7] which is equal to the sum of its minimum investment return, plus certain additional amounts, reduced by the sum of the foundation's unrelated business income taxes[8] and the excise tax on investment income[9] for that year.[10] The foundation's *minimum investment return* basically is an amount equal to 5 percent of the value of its noncharitable assets, reduced by any outstanding debt.[11] That amount must be distributed in the form of one or more qualifying distributions.[12] The concept is that an amount equivalent to a reasonable economic return on a private foundation's investments must be spent, transferred, or used for charitable purposes.

## §6.2 ASSETS USED TO CALCULATE MINIMUM INVESTMENT RETURN

Stated most simply, a private foundation annually is required to spend (or pay out) for charitable and administrative purposes an amount equal to at least 5 percent of the average fair market value for the preceding year of its investment assets, reduced by the amount of any debt incurred to acquire the property.

$$(\text{Private foundations investment assets} - \text{debt} - \text{cash reserve}) \times 5\%$$
$$= \text{Minimum investment return}$$

---

5. E.g., Fritchey, "Should Foundations Be Granted Immortality?" *The Washington Star*, Aug. 4, 1969, A-7; also *see* § 8.2 for investment yield concepts.
6. *See* § 6.2.
7. *See* § 6.3.
8. *See* Chapter 11.
9. *See* Chapter 10.
10. IRC § 4942(d); Reg. § 53.4942(a)-2(b)(1)(ii).
11. This rule is often misstated, both in the popular literature and in court opinions. As an example of the latter, the United States Court of Appeals for the Ninth Circuit wrote that a private foundation "must give away at least 5% of its assets annually in order to retain its tax-exempt status" (*Ann Jackson Family Foundation v. Commissioner*, 15 F.3d 917, 921, n. 10 (9th Cir. 1994), *aff'g* 97 T.C. 534 (1991)). The law, however, is that (1) the distributable amount (*see* § 6.4) generally is an amount equal to 5 percent of the average value of the assets (i.e., the assets themselves need not be distributed) and (2) the sanction is the tax(es) for failure to meet the payout requirement (*see* § 6.7(c)), not revocation of tax-exempt status.
12. *See* § 6.5.

The 5 percent applicable percentage is reduced for a foundation with a short taxable year.[13] If the foundation's tax year is less than 12 months, the percentage is calculated by multiplying the number of days in the year by 5 percent and dividing the result by 365. The result is a lower percentage. For example, assume a foundation is created on September 1 and chooses to close its tax year on December 31. Its minimum distribution amount for the first short year is calculated as:

$$\frac{\text{Days in its year of 122 days}}{\text{Days in whole year or 365 days}} \times 5\% = 1.67\%$$

Assume instead that a foundation is created on September of one year, receives its first assets on March 1 of the following year, and adopts a calendar tax year. Since it has no assets for the first four months of its existence, it will have no payout requirement for its first partial year, but it would file a return.[14] For the next, or second, year, it would have been in existence for a full year, even though it received assets in March. Thus its payout percentage would be a full 5 percent. Correspondingly the average value of its assets would be calculated by considering it had zero assets for two months, thereby effectively reducing the asset base to which the percentage is applied.[15]

The partial year allocation of the payout percentage also applies to an existing foundation that changes its year-end. Assume a foundation changes its financial reporting year-end from August 31 to December 31. The change of year requires no permission from the IRS and is accomplished by filing a short period annual information return for the four months ending in December.[16] The percentage applied to calculate its minimum distribution requirement for the next succeeding full calendar year would be 1.67 percent, as shown in the calculation above. Although the reduced percentage could be thought of as an advantage, the normal 5 percent minimum distribution amount attributable to the foundation's last full year ending in August would have to be distributed within the four months of the foundation's short tax year.

## (a) What Are Investment Assets?

An accurate calculation of minimum investment return depends on distinguishing investment assets from exempt function assets. This concept of exempt function versus investment is an important key to understanding minimum investment return. If the foundation holds an asset as an investment, an amount equal to 5 percent of its value is payable annually for

---

13. Reg. § 53.4942(a)-2(c)(5)(iii).
14. *See* Chapter 12.
15. *See* example in § 6.3(c).
16. *See* § 12.3(c).

charitable purposes, even if it is not producing any current income. This regime is different from that of the rules concerning the tax on net investment income, under which income from certain types of investment assets is excluded and not taxed.[17]

The minimum investment return is calculated based on the "excess of the fair market value of all assets of the foundation, other than those that represent future interests or expectations and exempt function assets."[18] Although referred to as an "investment return," neither the tax code nor the regulations define the word *investment* for this purpose. Instead, all assets are included in the calculation unless they are specifically excluded. The included assets are reduced by acquisition indebtedness with respect to those assets and a cash reserve for operations presumed to equal 1½ percent of the total includible assets.[19]

The typical private foundation investment portfolio of stocks, bonds, certificates of deposit, and rental properties forms the basis for calculating the distributable amount. All types of funds—unrestricted, temporarily restricted, permanently restricted, deferred revenues, capital, endowment, and similar types of reserves—are includible in the formula, whether or not current income is produced by the property. Where property is used for both tax-exempt purposes and investment purposes, it is called dual-use property. The value of this dual-use property must be allocated as described below.[20]

## (b)  Future Interests or Expectancies

Certain assets provide beneficial support to a foundation in an indirect fashion. Assets over which the foundation has no control and in which it essentially holds no present interest are not included in the minimum investment return formula. These assets most often are not in the possession or under the control of the foundation, nor are they customarily included in the financial records or statements of the foundation. These future interests are:[21]

- Interests in charitable remainder trusts and other future interests in property (whether legal or equitable) created by someone other than the foundation. These interests are not included in the minimum investment return formula until the intervening interests expire or are otherwise set apart for the foundation. If the foundation is able to take possession of the property at its will or to acquire it readily on giving notice, the property is included. The rules of constructive receipt for determining when a cash-basis taxpayer receives an item of income are relevant.

---

17. IRC § 4940; *see* Chapter 10.
18. Reg. § 53.4942(a)-2(c), further discussed in § 6.2(b), (c).
19. Discussed in § 6.2(c), (f).
20. Reg. § 53.4942(a)-2(c)(3); *see* § 6.2(d).
21. Reg. § 53.4942(a)-2(c)(2).

- The value of present interests in a trust, usually called a charitable lead trust, is also excluded. Income attributable to principal placed in these trusts after May 26, 1969, is includible in the adjusted net income and impacts a private operating foundation's required distributions.[22]

- Pledges of money or other property to the foundation, whether or not the pledges are legally enforceable.[23]

- Property bequeathed to the foundation is excluded while it is held by the decedent's estate. If and when the IRS treats the estate as terminated because the period of administration is prolonged, the assets are treated as foundation assets from the time of the IRS determination.[24]

- Options to sell property that are not readily marketable, such as a nontransferable right to buy real estate, are excluded. Listed options to buy or sell marketable securities or other future obligations that are traded on a stock exchange that have ascertainable value are treated as includible investment assets.

## (c) Exempt Function Assets

Income need not be imputed to property held and actually used by the foundation in conducting its charitable programs. These assets are called *exempt function assets* and are not usually held for the production of income (although they may be).[25] These assets are those used (or held for use) directly in conducting the foundation's programs. An asset must actually be used by the foundation in carrying out its charitable, educational, or other similar purpose that gives rise to its tax-exempt status. The most common type of assets excluded from the minimum investment return formula follow.[26]

*Administrative offices, furnishings, equipment, and supplies* used by employees and consultants in working on the foundation's charitable projects are not included in the asset base for determining the mandatory payout amount. However, the same property, if used by persons who manage the investment properties or endowments, is treated as investment property. Where property is used for both purposes, an allocation is required to be made.[27]

---

22. *See* § 6.4(a), for possible impact on a traditional private foundation.
23. A stock option pledged to a foundation was not counted as an investment asset (Priv. Ltr. Rul. 8315060).
24. Reg. § 1.641(b)-3, for circumstances under which the length of time for administering an estate is considered excessive.
25. *See* § 10.3, income may be reported as investment income.
26. Reg. § 53.4942(a)-2(c)(3)(ii); also *see* § 3.1, where the attributes of exempt function assets and direct program activities are discussed in regard to private operating foundations.
27. *See* § 6.2(d). *See* Exhibit 10.2, *Allocation of Costs by Private Foundations*, that contains accounting policies and procedures to apply in identifying costs by the various functions.

*Buildings, equipment, and facilities* used directly in projects are clearly not counted as investment property. Examples include:

- Real estate, including the portion of a building used by the foundation directly in its charitable, educational, or other similar exempt activities.[28]

- Historic buildings, libraries, and the furnishings in these buildings.

- Collections of objects on educational display, such as works of art or scientific specimens, including artworks loaned to museums, universities, or other charitable institutions.[29]

- Research facilities and laboratories, including a limited-access island held vacant to preserve its natural ecosystem, history, and archaeology.[30]

- Computer programs, books, and other resources used to conduct projects.

- Print shops and educational classrooms.

- Property used for a nominal or reduced rent by another charity. For this purpose, the regulations do not contain a definition of the term *nominal*.[31]

- Buildings of historical significance and land of environmental importance being held for ultimate use as a center for environmental and cultural conservation.[32]

*Reasonable cash balances* are considered to be necessary to carry out a foundation's exempt functions. One and one-half percent of the included investment assets is presumed to be a reasonable cash balance, even if a smaller cash balance is actually maintained.[33] If the facts and circumstances indicate that the foundation needs to maintain a higher amount of money on hand to cover its expenses and disbursements, the foundation can apply to the IRS to permit a higher amount.

*Future use property.* An asset acquired by the foundation for future use may be treated as exempt function property where the foundation has definite plans to commence exempt function use within a limited period of time (one year is considered reasonable), even if the property produces some interim income. An example is a rental building with existing tenants with unexpired leases that a foundation acquires to convert to a community service space for local relief

---

28. Reg. § 53.4942((a)-2(c)(3)(ii)(b).
29. Rev. Rul. 74-498, 1974-2 C.B. 387.
30. Rev. Rul. 75-207, 1975-1 C.B. 361.
31. Reg. § 53.4942(a)-2(c)(3)(ii)(f). The asset test for private operating foundations, however, does define a rental property leased to carry out an exempt purpose. That definition says the property is considered to be exempt property if the rent is less than the amount that would be required to be charged in order to recover the cost of property purchase and maintenance.
32. Priv. Ltr. Rul. 200136029.
33. Reg. § 53.4942(a)-2(c)(3)(iv).

agencies. If the future use is delayed, a set-aside attributable to the acquisition costs could be sought.[34]

*Program-related investments and functionally related businesses* that further the foundation's exempt purposes are also not counted in the asset base for minimum investment return calculation purposes. The primary motivation for acquiring these investments is not the production of income. Examples include a low-income housing project,[35] a student loan fund, and a bookstore operated within a larger aggregate of charitable endeavors. A restaurant and hotel complex operated within a historic village and an educational journal for which advertising is sold are given as examples in the regulations.[36] The properties used in conducting these businesses are not included in investment assets because they are related businesses.[37]

By definition, a functionally related business is one that is charitably motivated, or related.[38] A business in which the performance of service is a material income-producing factor, such as a retail shop, is excluded from the definition of an unrelated business if substantially all of the work (about 85 percent) is performed without compensation.[39] Thus, the value of a business run by volunteers is not counted as an investment asset for purposes of calculating the minimum investment return.[40] A capital-intensive business, such as long-term leasing of heavy equipment or a parking lot, may be treated as an unrelated business even if the management is donated (unless the use advances an exempt purpose).[41] An unrelated business fragmented from within a larger aggregate of exempt activities does not necessarily cause inclusion of the associated related activity assets. Notwithstanding the fact that advertising sold for a journal creates taxable unrelated business income, the publication program overall can be considered a functionally related business.[42] The larger complex of a medical research foundation's publication program determines its character as a related business.

In one instance, a private foundation received, by bequest, intellectual property used in connection with television programming and related educational services directed to the promotion of emotional and intellectual development of children. The foundation desired to license the property, on a no-royalty basis, to a public charity in furtherance of its charitable and educational purposes. The public charity agreed to pay any expenses necessary to protect

---

34. *See* § 6.5(d).
35. Priv. Ltr. Rul. 7823072.
36. Reg. § 53.4942(a)-2(c)(3)(i). Also *see* Chapters 7, 8.
37. *See* Chapter 11.
38. Reg. § 53.4942(a)-2(c)(3)(iii)(a)(1).
39. IRC § 513(a)(1), discussed in Chapter 11.
40. Rev. Rul. 76-85, 1976-1 C.B. 357.
41. Rev. Rul. 78-144, 1978-1 C.B. 168.
42. Reg. § 53.4942(a)-2(c)(3)(iii)(b), Example 2.

and defend the property. The IRS ruled that the value of this intellectual property may be excluded from the foundation's asset base for purposes of computing its minimum investment return.[43]

In another instance, a private foundation, owning a sheep ranch, conducted educational, research, and development programs intended to enhance the quality and increase the production of range sheep in the western United States by developing and introducing into the market sheep with genetically desirable traits, and furthered educational and scientific inquiry concerning the production of sheep. It sold culled sheep to slaughterhouses, along with wool; this undertaking was operated at a significant loss. The foundation represented to the IRS that no portion of the ranch was held for the production of income or for investment. The IRS ruled that the ranch was exempt function property, so that the value of the property was not taken into account in determining the foundation's mandatory payout amount.[44]

Likewise, an artist created a for-profit corporation to house his artistic enterprise. This corporation acquired and stored the materials used by the artist in the creation of his artwork; handled the creation, fabrication, shipment, storage, and insurance of this work; and managed its sale, reproduction, and licensing. The artist died; all of the stock of this corporation is to be transferred to a private operating foundation established by the artist. The function of the corporation will change to curatorial activities and management of the artist's legacy. The foundation will use these resources to increase public exposure and understanding of the broad scope of this artist's work, advance scholarship of his work, and encourage artists' involvement in civic issues by showing that they can change the world. The IRS ruled that the operations of this corporation are a functionally related business and that the value of the foundation's interest in the corporation will be excluded in calculating its minimum investment return.[45]

## (d)  Dual-Use Property

In many cases, a foundation owns and uses property for managing and conducting both its investments and its charitable projects. Whether or not an asset is used (or held for use) in carrying out the foundation's exempt purposes is a question of fact. The correct classification of dual-use assets impacts the calculation of minimum investment return[46] and the resulting mandatory payout requirements. In dual-use situations, an allocation between these two uses must be made. For assets used 95 percent or more for one purpose, the remaining 5 percent is ignored. An office building housing the foundation

---

43. Priv. Ltr. Rul. 200414050.
44. Priv. Ltr. Rul. 201315031.
45. Priv. Ltr. Rul. 201323029.
46. *See* § 15.4(c), which explains that exempt-function assets are not treated as investment assets for purposes of this calculation.

would be allocated based on the functions performed by the persons occupying the spaces. Consider this example:

*Space Allocation Formula*

| Investment department | 1,125 square feet | 25% |
|---|---|---|
| Program offices | 3,375 square feet | 75 |
| | 4,500 square feet | 100% |

In this case, 25 percent of the building's value would be treated as an investment asset. For a large foundation, the formula may be more complicated. A third category, administration, may have to be included in the formula when the staff is sophisticated, and separate personnel, accounting, and central supply departments serve the investment and program groups. For property that is partly used by the foundation and partly rented to others, the IRS has ruled that an allocation based on the fair rental value of the respective spaces, rather than the square footage, is appropriate.[47] Changes in the use of a property to or from an exempt-function use results in an addition to or subtraction from the distributable amount.

## (e)  Assets Held for Future Charitable Use

Sometimes it takes a number of years to piece together a project using hard assets like land, buildings, and equipment. When a foundation has future plans for the use of property and obtains an IRS determination that its immediate use of the property is impractical, an asset held for future use is not included in the payout calculation. Definite plans must exist to commence use within a reasonable period of time, and all of the facts and circumstances must prove the intention to devote the property to this type of use. The concepts for earmarking property of this nature are similar to those pertaining to set-asides.[48]

Property acquired to be devoted to exempt purposes may be treated as exempt function property from the time it is acquired, even if it is temporarily rented.[49] Its acquisition is also treated as a qualifying distribution.[50] The rental, or other nonexempt-use status must be for a reasonable and limited period of time, and only while the property is being made ready for its intended use, such as during remodeling or acquisition of adjacent pieces of property. IRS approval is not necessary if the property conversion takes only one year. If the property is rented for more than a year, however, it is treated as investment property

47.  Rev. Rul. 82-137, 1982-2 C.B. 303.
48.  Reg. § 53.4942(a)-2(c)(3)(i); *see* § 6.5(d).
49.  *Id.*
50.  *See* § 6.5(b).

during the second year and thereafter, until it is devoted to exempt purposes. This change from an investment asset to an exempt function asset is reflected for qualifying distribution purposes. Property reclassified as investment property, conversely, is treated as a negative distribution by adding back the amount previously claimed as a qualifying distribution to the amount required for the annual distributable amount.[51]

## (f) Acquisition Indebtedness

The formula for calculation of the minimum investment return allows a reduction in includible assets by the amount of any acquisition indebtedness "with respect to such assets[52] without regard to the taxable year in which the indebtedness was incurred."[53] To qualify as a timely distribution, it should be emphasized that it is only the aggregate sum of these amounts that must be distributed before the end of the start-up period (end of the fourth year). There is no requirement that any part be distributed in any particular tax year of the start-up period.[54] Also, while the aggregate sum satisfies the cash distribution test, the amount is *not* in lieu of the normal 5 percent minimum distributable amount, but simply a deferral. Nowhere under the requirements for the cash distribution test does it indicate that if those tests are met, the normal 5 percent distributable amounts are superseded. The cash distribution test distributable amounts must be met in order for the foundation to claim a qualifying distribution for its initial set-aside, nothing more.

The regulations repeat this phrase but provide no additional guidance for determining eligible debt for this purpose.[55] Thus, a foundation looks to IRC § 514(c)(l) to identify acquisition indebtedness. That provision states that this type of debt equals the unpaid amount of indebtedness incurred by a foundation in acquiring or improving a property.[56] The most common type of acquisition debt incurred by a foundation is a mortgage on investment real estate. A margin account created to purchase securities would constitute such debt, but private foundations seldom borrow on margin because income from indebted investments is subject to the unrelated business income tax and possibly violates the jeopardizing investment prohibitions.[57]

Some foundations with significant portfolios of marketable securities enter into security lending transactions to enhance the return on those investment assets. The foundation lends its securities to a financial institution, which in

---

51. *See* § 6.4; IRC § 4942(e)(B).
52. Determined under IRC § 514(c)
53. Reg. § 53.4942(a)-2(c)(1)(i).
54. Reg. § 53.4942(a)-3(b)(4)(iii).
55. *See* § 11.4.
56. IRC § 514(c)(8)(C).
57. *See* § 8.1.

return customarily provides the foundation with cash collateral equal to the value (or more) of the securities. The foundation retains its right to receive dividends or interest from the securities and also is entitled to invest the cash it holds as collateral. "For purposes of *this section* [emphasis added] an obligation to return collateral security shall not be treated as acquisition indebtedness.[58] Income earned in connection with such security loans is thereby excluded from the unrelated business income tax."[59]

Under generally accepted accounting standards, the securities and the cash collateral are both reported as a foundation asset. The obligation to repay the cash is reflected as a liability for financial statement purposes, essentially allowing the deposit and the loan to be netted. As a result, the foundation's net assets reflect only the value of the securities it has lent and do not include the collateral cash or corresponding loan. It seems appropriate to allow a similar presentation for purposes of calculating the foundation's minimum investment return—to reduce the cash held as collateral by the collateral loan. However, IRC § 4942(e)(1)(B) refers to IRC § 514(c) to define *acquisition indebtedness*, and that provision provides that the collateral security debt is not acquisition indebtedness. The reason for this exclusion stems from the fact that the unrelated business income rules exclude payments with respect to securities loans, including income from investment of the collateral security, from income tax.

A private foundation, pursuant to a securities lending and guaranty agreement with a bank, loaned certain securities in its investment portfolio to approved borrowers. The bank served as the custodian in these transactions, receiving collateral, which it invested in commingled cash management funds. The foundation could not acquire access to, sell, or pledge this collateral, which was to be returned to the borrower except in the case of a default. On termination of a lending arrangement, the foundation was entitled to receive back from the borrower either the original securities or securities identical to those loaned. The foundation, as compensation, received a percentage of the earnings on the collateral.

The private foundation auditors determined that, for financial statement purposes, the private foundation's transfers of securities to the bank in conjunction with the securities lending transactions must be disclosed on the foundation's financial statements by means of offsetting asset and liability entries on the balance sheet. Thus, the foundation reflects, on its financial statements, the collateral received and the corresponding obligation to return it pursuant to these transactions as assets and liabilities.

The IRS ruled that this foundation, in computing its minimum investment return for purposes of calculating its annual payout obligation, did not have to include as an asset the collateral received in connection with its securities

---

58. *See* also IRC § 512(b)(1).
59. IRC § 4942(e)(1)(A).

lending program, inasmuch as the collateral amount was offset by the requirement to return the collateral on termination of the lending transaction.[60]

## §6.3 MEASURING FAIR MARKET VALUE

In computing its annual distributable amount, a private foundation must determine its minimum investment return, which requires, in part, computation of the aggregate fair market value of all assets of the foundation other than those devoted to its exempt purposes.[61] The minimum investment return is based on 5 percent of the average fair market value of the includible investment assets.[62]

Different methods, revaluation times, and frequencies are provided for various types of investment assets that a private foundation may need to value. Mistakes in valuation can cause the foundation to incorrectly calculate its required distributable amount. When the mistakes are unintentional, penalties may not necessarily be assessed.[63]

### (a) Valuation Methods

Any commonly acceptable method of valuation may be used, as long as it is reasonable and consistently used. Valuations made in accordance with the methods prescribed for estate tax valuation are acceptable. Presumably, the rules governing valuation of charitable gifts would also be appropriate.

Certified, independent appraisals are required only for real property the foundation chooses to revalue on a five-year basis. For all other assets,[64] the foundation itself can establish a consistent method for making a good faith determination of the value of most of its assets.

### (b) Date of Valuation

Different valuation dates are prescribed for different kinds of assets:

*Asset Valuation Dates*

| | |
|---|---|
| Cash | Monthly |
| Marketable securities | Monthly |
| Real estate | Every five years |
| All other assets | Annually |

---

60. Priv. Ltr. Rul. 200329049.
61. Since 1976, the rate has been 5 percent. *See* § 6.8 for the history of the payout rules.
62. *See* § 6.8 for the history of this calculation.
63. Reg. §§ 1.2031 and 53.4942(a)-2(c)(4)(i)(b) and (iv)(c); *see* § 6.7(d).
64. Including real estate.

Assets valued annually can be valued on any date, as long as the same date is consistently used each year. Likewise, real estate and mineral valuation should be done on approximately the same date every fifth year.[65] Cash is valued on a monthly basis by averaging the amount of cash on hand as of the first day of each month and the last day of each month.[66]

The valuation date for real estate received as a gift or a transfer from an estate or trust, or purchased by the foundation, may technically be valued on any date of the year after acquisition of the property. As a practical matter, however, the acquisition date often becomes the date used for investment return valuation purposes, because an appraisal is prepared on that date for the donor or transferor.

## (c) Partial Year

The average value of an asset held by the foundation for part of a year is calculated by using the number of days in the year that the asset was held as the numerator and 365 as the denominator (or the number of days in the tax year if less than 365). The includible value is thereby reduced to equate to the partial-year holding period. For example, for a $100,000 piece of real estate acquired on July 1, by a foundation with a full tax year, the includible amount would be:

*Partial-Year Asset Calculations*

$$\$100,000 \times 184/365, \text{ or } \$50,410$$

A new foundation begins its first year on the date it is created, not the day it first receives assets. Assume the example above applied to a new foundation created on March 1 that received the gift of real estate on July 1. The formula for calculating the includible amount of the real estate value would instead be:

$$\$100,000 \times 184/306, \text{ or } \$60,130$$

## (d) Readily Marketable Securities

Securities for which market quotations are readily available must be valued monthly, using any reasonable and consistent method. Securities include (but

---

65. Reg. § 53.4942(a)-2(c)(4)(ii). If the foundation chooses to value real estate annually, the date chosen should be consistent,
66. *Supra* note 25; Reg. §§ 53.4942(a)-2(c)(4)(i)(a), 53.4942(a)-2(c)(4)(v).

are not limited to) common and preferred stocks, bonds, and mutual fund shares.[67] The monthly security valuation method applies to:

- Stocks listed on the New York Stock Exchange, the American Stock Exchange, or any city or regional exchange in which quotations appear on a daily basis, including foreign securities listed on a recognized foreign national or regional exchange.

- Stocks regularly traded in a national or regional over-the-counter market, for which published quotations are available.

- Locally traded stocks for which quotations can readily be obtained from established brokerage firms.

Stock traded on the Over-the-Counter Bulletin Board (OTCBB) is qualified appreciated stock for purposes of allowing a contribution deduction for the value of the shares rather than the deduction being limited to basis.[68] The IRS noted that the regulations on readily available market quotations were written before the Internet disclosed values. Correspondingly, securities traded on OTCBB constitute readily marketable securities for monthly valuation purposes.

The *quotation system* can be one of a variety of methods, again, as long as a consistent pattern is followed. The following examples are given in the regulations:

- The classic method, averaging the high and low quoted price on a particular day each month, which could be the first, fifth, last, or any other day.

- A formula averaging the first, middle, and last day closing prices for each month.

- The average of the bid and asked price for over-the-counter stocks or funds on a consistent day, using the nearest day if no quote is available on the regular day.

*Portfolio reports* generated by a computer pricing system and prepared monthly for securities held in custody or trust by a bank or other financial institution may be acceptable. The bank's or investment advisor's system must use a valid method for valuing securities for federal estate tax purposes. The foundation has a responsibility to inquire of the bank as to its method of valuation, and to obtain evidence that its system is approved. Banks commonly have certification from bank examiners, and investment advisory firms have

---

67. Reg. § 53.4942(a)-2(c)(4)(i)(c).
68. Priv. Ltr. Rul. 200702031. Also *see* § 14.4(b).

their license renewals from the Securities and Exchange Commission. If these systems conform to the quotation system previously outlined, in the authors' experience, the IRS does not require proof that the bank's system has specific IRS approval, even though the regulations require it.

*Blockage discounts* of up to 10 percent are permitted to reduce the valuation of securities when a foundation can show that the quoted market prices do not reflect fair market value[69] for one or more of the following reasons:

- The block of securities is so large in relation to the volume of actual sales on the existing market that it could not be liquidated in a reasonable time without depressing the market.

- Sales of the securities are few or sporadic in nature, and the shares are in a closely held corporation.

- The sale of the securities would result in a forced or distress sale because the securities cannot be offered to the public without first being registered with the Securities and Exchange Commission.

Essentially, a foundation is permitted to use the price at which the securities could be sold by an underwriter outside the normal market. The IRS admits that if the securities to be valued represent a controlling interest, either actual or effective, in a going business, the price at which other lots change hands may have little relation to the true value of the securities.[70] The IRS also privately ruled that a foundation that did not, over the years, utilize a blockage discount in valuing its securities, but currently wishes to do so, and do so retroactively, can recompute its minimum investment return and distributable amounts for the years that are still open under the statute of limitations. Unlisted securities in which no one "makes a market," so that price quotations are not available, are valued annually like other assets described below.

### (e) Unique Assets

*Nonmarketable investments*: Valuation of so-called alternative investments, such as hedge funds, offshore partnerships, and stock investments, for purposes of calculating the foundation's minimum investment return, is often a challenge. Hedge funds and partnerships often hold several types of investments, including marketable securities and options that would be valued monthly if held outside of the partnership and nonlisted venture capital stocks and loans subject to annual valuation. Unless the fund is itself readily marketable, such as a publicly traded partnership, such investments should be valued annually. What if, however, the foundation gets valuations

---

69. Reg. § 53.4942(a)-2(c)(4)(i)(c)(3).
70. Priv. Ltr. Rul. 9233031.

more than once a year? Can the quarterly, for example, valuations be averaged throughout the year? There does not appear to be any guidance on this question. Since the purpose of the market value calculations is to arrive at the foundation's payout requirement, it seems logical that a nonmarketable fund could be valued more often than once a year when a portion of partnership assets has daily valuations available. Nonetheless, the regulations provide for annual valuation.

The IRS said that "a taxpayer's profits interest in a partnership is analogous to the voting stock of an issuer of unlisted securities."[71] The regulations, adopted in 1972, call for monthly valuations of an asset other than marketable securities in two specific situations:[72]

1. Common trust funds that are "administered under a plan providing for the periodic valuation of participating interests during the fund's taxable year and the reporting of such valuations to participants."

2. Private foundation owns voting stock of an issuer of unlisted securities and has, alone or together with disqualified persons or another private foundation, "effective control of the issuer . . . , then to the extent that the issuer's assets consist of shares of listed securities issues, such assets shall be valued monthly on the basis of market quotations."

Foundations owning securities through an investment partnership found that the minimum investment return calculation produced an unrealistically high payout amount for 2008, depending on the date historically used to value the partnership. The payout requirement for 2009, based on a date early in the year, was often much higher than if the year-end value could be used. The significant decline in security values revived the argument that these partnerships should be valued using periodic valuations, either monthly or quarterly, based on the value of readily marketable securities the partnership holds. The initially proposed regulation stated that, even in cases where the private foundation held only a small minority interest in the unlisted holding company, any listed and readily marketable securities were to be valued using monthly market quotations. In response to objections to this broad approach, the final regulations[73] limited the required monthly valuation of underlying securities to situations where the private foundation had effective control of the unlisted company.

An interest in an investment partnership is an "other asset" valued in accordance with estate tax valuation principles.[74] When the terms of the

---

71. Priv. Ltr. Rul. 200548026.
72. Reg. § 53.4942(a)-2(c)(iii) and (iv).
73. *Id.*
74. IRC § 2031.

partnership restrict withdrawals from the partnership or sale of the interest, the value may be less than the fair market value of the underlying assets. In considering valuation of a partnership controlled by a private foundation and its disqualified persons, the IRS observed that a "taxpayer's profits interest in a partnership is analogous to the voting stock of an issuer of unlisted securities."[75] A discount due to lack of marketability may be appropriate. The 10 percent limitation on value reduction does not apply.[76]

A parallel issue is whether the value of a private foundation's interest in a limited partnership that holds only marketable securities should be reported on the 990-PF in Part X, Minimum Investment Return, on (1) line 1a—Average monthly fair market value of securities, or (2) line 1c—Fair market value of all other assets. Some 990-PF filers report alternative investments that hold marketable securities with available monthly valuations on line 1a, based on the phraseology in the line.[77]

*Difficult to sell assets*: A private foundation may have an *asset* for which neither a ready market nor a standard valuation method exists, in which case different valuation rules may apply. For example, if a private foundation can establish that the value of certain of its securities, determined on the basis of the selling or the bid and asked prices, does not reflect fair market value, then some reasonable modification of that basis or other relevant facts and elements of value should be allowable in determining fair market value. Thus, where a private foundation's unique asset is securities, it may be appropriate for the private foundation to take into account the fact that the block of securities is unusually large. In this instance, the private foundation would have to demonstrate that the block to be valued is so large in relation to actual sales in the existing securities markets that it could not be liquidated within a reasonable time without depressing the market (*blockage*).[78] If so, the price at which the block could be sold outside the market may be a more accurate indication of value than market quotations.[79]

In writing the final version of the Tax Reform Act of 1976, the House-Senate conferees refined the general securities valuation rule by adding a provision restricting the use of a blockage or discount factor in determining the fair market value of private foundations' securities for payout purposes. The provision prohibits a reduction in value, unless and only to the extent that the securities could not be liquidated within a reasonable period of time, except at a price less

---

75. Priv. Ltr. Rul. 200548026.
76. *Id*. *See* § 6.3(e).
77. Only line 1a uses the word "securities."
78. Regs. §§ 53.4942(a)-2(c)(4)(i)(b), 20.2031-2(e). The IRS promulgated guidelines for the valuation of securities that cannot be immediately resold because they are restricted from resale pursuant to the federal securities laws (Rev. Rul. 77-287, 1977-2 C.B. 319). Also Rev. Rul. 78-367, 1978-2 C.B. 249.
79. IRC § 4942(e)(2).

than fair market value, due to (1) the size of the block of the securities, (2) the fact that the securities are those of a closely held corporation, or (3) the fact that the sale of the securities would result in a forced or distress sale. Even where one or more of the foregoing criteria are met, however, the reduction in value of a private foundation's securities may not exceed 10 percent of their otherwise determined fair market value.[80]

This restriction on the use of a discount factor is applicable only to securities for which market quotations are readily available. It does not apply to securities that are restricted from trade on an exchange because of the federal securities laws and are thus *other assets*. These restricted securities may be valued annually, with use of a blockage discount where appropriate, and the valuation may be made by employees of the private foundation or others.

### (f) Cash and Other Types of Assets

Cash is valued by taking the average of the cash on hand at the beginning and end of each month. Thus, a private foundation cannot easily manipulate its cash balance. The calculation of average cash balances adds together the 24 beginning and ending month-end balances for all accounts and divides the result by 24. By comparison, the average value of securities instead adds together 12 valuations on the date chosen by the foundation (usually last trading day of month) and divides the result by 12. Note that even though that portion of the foundation's cash balances determined to be necessary to conduct the foundation's affairs is excluded from the formula used to calculate minimum investment return, the actual cash balances are included to arrive at total investment assets. Most other assets are valued annually, using a reasonable and consistent method, on the bases described in the following paragraphs. The valuation may be made on any day so long as the foundation values that asset on the same day each year.[81]

*Common trust funds:* Foundation funds invested in a common trust fund[82] can use the fund's valuation reports. Fund participants typically receive periodic valuations of their interests from the fund manager throughout the year, and can calculate the average of these valuation reports. If the fund issues

---

80. Priv. Ltr. Rul. 7933084. Pursuant to the rules of the Securities and Exchange Commission (SEC) (Rule 144), a holder of restricted securities may periodically sell a small portion of the securities without regard to the general restriction. Specifically, the holder may sell, in a six-month period on an exchange, a number of shares equal to the lesser of 1 percent of the outstanding stock or an amount equal to the average of trading volume for the four weeks immediately preceding notification to the SEC of a proposed sale. The amount of securities that can be freely sold under Rule 144 is restricted to securities for which market quotations are readily available, thus subjecting them to the 10 percent limitation on discount; the balance of the securities may be valued without regard to that limitation.
81. Reg. § 53.4942(a)-2(c)(3)(iv).
82. Defined by IRC § 584.

valuations quarterly, the simple average of the four reported valuations is the fair market value reportable as an investment asset. If valuations are issued monthly, the sum of 12 months of value would be divided by 12.

Investment real property held by a foundation may be valued on an annual basis or it may be valued by means of a written, certified, and independent appraisal prepared every five years. The five-year valuation method based on an appraisal of real estate provided in the regulations[83] reflects the fact that real estate is often difficult to value and appraisals are costly. The regulations, however, use the word *may* and do not require a five-year appraisal. The IRS will not disturb a properly prepared valuation during the five-year period, even if the value of the property has increased materially, unless it is shown that the valuation was outside the range of reasonable values for the property.

If the five-year valuation method is used, the appraiser must be qualified and may not be a disqualified person with respect to, or an employee of, the foundation. An appraisal is considered certified only if it includes a statement that, in the opinion of the appraiser, the values placed on the land appraised were determined in accordance with valuation principles regularly employed in making appraisals of such property using all reasonable valuation methods.

More frequent valuations can be made when circumstances dictate, as, for example, when real estate has declined substantially in value. A five-year appraisal may be replaced during the five-year period by a new five-year appraisal or with an annual valuation. Annual valuations based on reasonable evidence, such as the local appraisal district value for purposes of imposing property tax or listing prices of contiguous property, can be used. A valuation must, however, use commonly accepted methods of valuation in making an appraisal. Valuations can be made following the principles used for estate tax purposes.[84]

Valuations of mineral interests typically are based on reserve studies conducted by independent petroleum evaluation engineers. These studies are customarily updated every five years, as is the case with the real estate surface and buildings. It also is a common industry practice to value a mineral interest at anywhere from two to three times annual income, particularly where the annual income is relatively small and formal appraisals would be unduly expensive. In one situation, however, a court rejected the annual income approach in favor of a more sophisticated appraisal.[85]

The IRS found in two instances that real estate held in a wholly owned title holding company[86] and a limited liability partnership[87] could be valued using a

---

83. Reg. § 53.4942(a)-2(c)(4)(iv)(b).
84. Reg. § 53.4942(a)-2(c)(4)(iv)(c).
85. *Estate of Juanita C. Smith v. Commissioner*, 65 T.C.M. 2808 (1993).
86. Priv. Ltr. Rul. 9347041.
87. Priv. Ltr. Rul. 200548026.

qualified appraisal made every five years, according to the general rule for real estate valuation, even though the form of ownership was essentially an "other asset" required to be valued annually.

*Valuation of computers, office equipment, and other tangible assets* used in managing investment activity can be determined from the local newspaper's classified advertisements for used equipment, or by obtaining a quotation from a used office furniture dealer.

The value of a *whole-life insurance* policy is its cash surrender value.

*Notes and accounts receivable* are included at their net realizable value, or at their face value discounted for any uncollectible portion. Though it seems logical that a note receivable for which the foundation receives monthly principal payments that reduce the principal amount of the loan be valued on a monthly basis, the regulations provide for annual valuation.[88]

*Collectibles* such as gold, paintings, and gems are valued under estate tax valuation rules.

## (g)  Investment Frauds

Some private foundations faced valuation concerns in calculating their distribution requirement, given what turned out to have been a gross over-valuation of assets due to investment fraud during 2008 and before. The New York State Bar Association Tax Section[89] report stated that a "critical initial question" relevant to the payout rules "is whether a foundation should go back in time and measure its income and asset values for prior years based on current knowledge and information or whether the foundation should view prior year income and asset values as correct and deal with Ponzi scheme losses only in the year of discovery."

This report posed questions: How are Ponzi scheme losses to be taken into account in calculating a foundation's distributable amount? How are prior year investments to be valued? May foundations amend prior year returns, in order to recalculate asset values for prior years, taking into account the fraud (theft) that was discovered in 2008 (or later)? The report observed that this amendment approach "could provide significant relief [for] a number of private foundations." If this recomputation of asset values and amendment of prior year returns is permitted, it would likely generate a significant carryforward for these foundations.[90]

---

88.  Reg. § 53.4942(a)-2(c)(4)(iv).
89.  *See* § 8.4 for additional aspects of this issue.
90.  *See* § 6.7(b).

EXHIBIT **6.1** Formula for Distributable Income

| | |
|---|---|
| Average value of noncharitable assets for the year | $1,000,000 |
| – Acquisition indebtedness* | –50,000 |
| | 950,000 |
| – Cash deemed held for charitable activities (1.5% $950,000) | –14,250 |
| Net value of noncharitable assets | 935,750 |
| Minimum investment return (5% of net value) | 46,787 |
| + Recovery of amounts previously treated as qualifying distributions | +3,000 |
| – Excise and income tax | –2,200 |
| Distributable Amount | $47,587 |

*See § 6.2(f).

## §6.4 DISTRIBUTABLE AMOUNT

A nonoperating private foundation is subject to an excise tax if it fails to spend, or annually pay out, a minimum specified amount for charitable purposes. It may, without penalty, spend more, but not less, than the minimum distributable amount calculated in Exhibit 6.1.[91] Excess distributions in one year can be carried over to a subsequent year as shown in Exhibit 6.2. To arrive at what the Internal Revenue Code calls the *distributable amount*, or minimum amount of qualifying distributions required to be paid out annually, a private foundation applies a formula that combines portions of two different code provisions:

$$A + B - C = \text{Distributable amount}$$

A = Minimum investment return.[92]
B = Any amounts previously included as qualifying distributions,[93] but now not qualifying, such as:

- Grants, student loans, or program-related investments, repaid or returned to the foundation for some reason.

- An asset that ceases to be an exempt function asset, whose purchase or conversion to exempt use was previously included as a qualifying distribution. The sales proceeds or the fair market value at the time of conversion of the asset is the amount added back.

---

91. IRC § 4942(d).
92. IRC § 4942(e); *see* § 6.2.
93. IRC § 4942(g); *see* § 6.5.

- Unused set-aside funds that are no longer earmarked for a charitable project or that are ineligible because the time period allowed has lapsed.[94]

C = The excise tax on investment income and income tax on unrelated business income for the year.

To illustrate how the formula for calculation of the distributable amount works, assume a private foundation has the following facts, reflected in Exhibit 6.1.

This formula applies to a normal, nonoperating, private foundation. The minimum investment return that equals the majority of the required payout has absolutely no relationship to the foundation's actual investment income.[95] The minimum investment return is simply 5 percent of the foundation's average investment assets and is not influenced by the foundation's actual income.[96] Confusion sometimes arises because the regulations still contain the rules applicable before 1982, when a normal private foundation was required to distribute its actual adjusted net income or the minimum investment return, whichever was higher. A foundation that is required to accumulate its income, or is prohibited from distributing its capital or corpus by its governing instruments in effect and unchanged since May 26, 1969, is not subject to the normal payout rules.[97]

Between 1982 and 2003, the IRS Form 990-PF, instructions to the form, and the regulation required that income paid or payable to a foundation by certain trusts be added to the distributable amount, despite the fact that the federal statutory law does not.[98] The Ann Jackson Family Foundation challenged this IRS position and convinced the Tax Court that the regulation was an "unwarranted extension of a statutory position."[99]

## (a)  Application of Distributions

Exhibit 6.2 provides an illustration of the way in which excess distributions are applied. The IRS Chief Counsel, however, has issued a memorandum entitled *Adjustments of Excess Distribution Carryovers from Closed Years*, taking

---

94. *See* § 3.1(d) for discussion of tests based on "adjusted net income" applicable to private operating foundations.
95. Reg. § 53.4942(a)-2(e).
96. *See* § 6.2.
97. Reg. § 53.4942(a)-2(b)(2). IRS Publication 578, *Tax Information for Private Foundations and Foundation Managers* (last revised in January 1989) also contains this requirement.
98. Reg. § 53.4942(a)-2(b)(2). IRS Publication 578, *Tax Information for Private Foundations and Foundation Managers* (last revised in January 1989) also contains this requirement that only applied to amounts placed in trust prior to May 26, 1969.
99. *Ann Jackson Family Foundation v. Commissioner*, 97 T.C. 534, 537 (1991), *aff'd*, 15 F.3d 917 (9th Cir. 1994).

**Exhibit 6.2** Application of Qualifying Distributions and Carryovers

| | 2014 | 2015 | 2016 | 2017 | 2018 | 2019 | Cumulative Excess Distributions |
|---|---|---|---|---|---|---|---|
| Qualifying distributions for year | 0 | 250 | 70 | 40 | 160 | 100 | |
| Distributable amount for year | 100 | 100 | 100 | 100 | 100 | 100 | |
| Net distributions for year | −100 | +150 | −30 | −60 | +60 | 0 | |
| Application: | | | | | | | |
| Apply 2015 to 2014 | +100 | −100 | | | | | +50 (2015 year-end) |
| Apply 2015 to 2016 | | −30 | +30 | | | | +20 (2015 year-end) |
| Apply 2015 to 2017 | | −20 | | +20 | | | 0 |
| Apply 2018 to 2017 | | | | +40 | −40 | | +20 (2018 year-end) |
| 2018 excess can be carried as far as 2023 | 0 | 0 | 0 | 0 | +20 | 0 | +20 (2018 year-end) |

the position that adjustments to years closed by the statute of limitations is permissible.[100] The memorandum recognized the fact that when a nonoperating foundation has excessive or deficient distributions in any one year, the carry-over of excess distributions is essentially an accumulation of all post-1969 years. It is an unusual foundation that pays out the exact minimum distribution amount each year.

### (b) Distribution Deadline

The distributable amount must be paid out by a private foundation—to avoid a penalty—by the close of the year immediately following the year for which the amount was determined. For example, a calendar-year foundation must, by December 31, 2015, distribute the amount calculated as due to be paid out for the year ending December 31, 2014. This deadline essentially gives a newly created foundation almost a two-year period of time in which to establish its grant systems and to earn the income to be distributed. Under a cash distribution test, the new foundation's distributable amount may be further reduced.[101] It would be rare for a foundation to spend the precise distributable

100. Gen. Coun. Mem. 39808.
101. *See* § 6.5(d).

amount. Commonly, a foundation has excess qualifying distributions from one year to the next and is entitled to carry over the excess.[102]

A private foundation that, subsequent to its first year, has a short tax year of less than 12 months must pay out its distributable amount prior to the end of the short period.[103] Thus, a foundation that wishes to change its fiscal year ending must do so in view of the acceleration of the distribution deadline that results. Though the shorter deadline may cause a temporary financial burden, the short year's distribution amount will be based on a reduced percentage prorated according to the number of days in the short year in relation to 365 days.[104] Thus, the amount required to be distributed by the end of the full year following the short year will be a reduced partial-year amount.

### (c)   Inability to Distribute

The federal tax law is silent as to what happens when a private foundation lacks the funds (including principal) to comply with a payout obligation for one or more tax years (other than imposition of the penalty excise taxes). This matter can arise because of an inability to sell nonliquid assets or to poor investment outcome subsequent to computation of the payout amount, including one or more investments induced by fraud.[105] A foundation may also have difficult-to-sell assets or assets it does not wish to sell. This is not a problem that can be cured through an abatement process, unless there is an issue as to asset valuation.[106] A cure might be found in the fact that a foundation is entitled to satisfy its payout requirement with a qualifying distribution of properties other than cash.

This tax regime does not include a tax on foundation managers; thus, there is no potential for tax liability in that context.[107] Perhaps all that can be done is to pay the first-tier tax for an insufficient distribution, distribute the foundation's remaining assets and accumulated income in the form of qualifying distributions,[108] and dissolve the foundation.

## §6.5   QUALIFYING DISTRIBUTIONS

Amounts expended and property transferred by a private foundation to meet the mandatory payout requirement must be in the form of qualifying distributions. The excise tax that is levied on failure to make the requisite

---

102. Rev. Rul. 74-315, 1974-2 C.B. 386.
103. Reg. § 53.4942(a)-2(c)(5)(iii).
104. Reg. § 53.4942(a)-3(a).
105. *See* §§ 6.3(g) and § 8.4.
106. *See* § 6.7(d).
107. There is, however, the potential for tax in the jeopardizing investment area (*see* Chapter 8).
108. *See* § 6.5.

distribution is imposed on the *undistributed income*, defined as the *distributable amount* for the year less qualifying distributions. Qualifying distributions are to be determined solely by a cash receipts and disbursements method of accounting.[109] The amount of a qualifying distribution made in the form of property other than cash is the fair market value of the property on the date the distribution is made. Unless the set-aside rule applies, the distribution requirement can be satisfied only by an actual payout or property distribution; a mere commitment or pledge of funds is inadequate. For this reason, the annual return filed by private foundations, Form 990-PF, instructs that qualifying distributions be determined following the cash method of accounting.

Not all contributions or disbursements qualify, or count, when a foundation tallies up its expenses to see whether it meets the minimum distribution requirements. Two tests must be met. Of primary importance, the expenditure must be in pursuit of a charitable purpose.[110] Second, the foundation must actually relinquish the funds; that is, it cannot retain control over the use of the funds nor restrict them for its own purposes. The rules are designed to assure that the distributable amount is used to serve broad charitable purposes each year. The term *qualifying distributions* is specifically defined to include:[111]

- Any amount, including reasonable and necessary administrative expenses, paid to accomplish one or more tax-exempt purposes, other than a contribution to an organization controlled by the distributing private foundation or by one or more disqualified persons with respect to the private foundation or to a private foundation that is not a private operating foundation (except as noted below in section (a)),

- Any amount paid to acquire an asset used or held for use directly in carrying out one or more tax-exempt purposes,[112] and

- Qualified set-asides[113] and program-related investments.[114]

From time to time, the IRS issues private letter rulings concerning the eligibility of a distribution by a private foundation as a qualifying distribution.[115]

---

109. *See* Chapter 12.
110. IRC § 4942(g)(1). A noncharitable expenditure is treated as a taxable expenditure; *see* IRC § 4945(d) and Chapter 9.
111. Reg. § 1.53.4942(a)-3(a)(2).
112. IRC § 4942(g)(1)(B).
113. *See* § 6.5(c).
114. *See* § 8.3.
115. E.g., Priv. Ltr. Ruls. 200041037 and 201029040.

## (a) Direct Grants

Grants made directly to public charities,[116] for general support or for a wide range of specific charitable purposes, comprise by far the majority of qualifying distributions made by private foundations.[117] A qualifying grant can be paid to an instrumentality of the government on a national, state, or local level. Support for charitable programs of any type of exempt or nonexempt organization anywhere in the world can conceivably qualify if the proper procedures are followed.[118] Payments to three particular types of organizations do not offset, or count toward, meeting the distributable amount. A private foundation is not prevented from making these grants (though it must exercise expenditure responsibility to avoid making a taxable expenditure), but the disbursements do not count toward meeting the distribution requirement. Specifically, these grants are not counted:

1. A grant to another private foundation, unless it is an operating foundation[119] or the recipient foundation redistributes the funds. A grant by a private foundation to an unrelated private operating foundation constitutes a qualifying distribution.[120]

2. A grant to a controlled organization, either private or public, again, unless the funds are properly redistributed.

3. A grant to a nonfunctionally integrated Type III supporting organization.[121]

**Community Foundation Grants.** The extraordinary increase in the value of private foundation investment portfolios in the late 1990s created ever-increasing minimum distribution obligations for many private foundations.[122]

---

116. *See* Chapter 15.
117. The IRS stated, in an information letter made public on July 9, 2010, that private foundations may make grants for charitable purposes to limited liability companies (that are disregarded entities for federal tax purposes) the sole member of which is a tax-exempt public charity that is not related to the grantor, without the need for exercise of expenditure responsibility (INFO 2010-0052). This position of the IRS was augmented by more formal guidance when the agency held that contributions to a single-member limited liability company, that is a disregarded entity, where the limited liability company is wholly owned and controlled by a U.S. charity, are deductible, with the gift treated as being made to a branch or division of the charity (Notice 2012-52, 2012-35 I.R.B. 317). *See Tax-Exempt Organizations* §§ 4.1(b)(ii) and 9.6.
118. *See* Chapter 3.
119. Reg. § 53.4942(a)-3(a)(3).
120. IRC § 4942(g)(1)(A)(ii). Nonetheless, unless the grantee is an exempt operating foundation (*see* § 3.1(i)), the grantor private foundation must exercise expenditure responsibility over the grant (*see* § 9.6).
121. *See* §§ 6.6, 15.7(g).
122. Priv. Ltr. Rul. 9807030. *See* § 10.2(a) for consideration of the impact of nonqualifying grants on the calculation of the 1 percent excise tax on investment income.

A foundation needing to make grant payments to satisfy its payout levels is allowed to make a grant to a community foundation so long as it does not retain control over the funds. This type of grant is not a qualifying distribution if the grantor retains control over the grantee. The following question was added to Form 990-PF for 2012: "Did the foundation make a distribution to a donor-advised fund over which the foundation or a disqualified person had advisory privileges?" If the answer was "Yes," the filer was asked to attach a statement to explain how the distribution will be used to accomplish a charitable purpose and whether the payment was treated as a qualifying distribution. Results of the IRS analysis of the answers should be studied.[123]

The IRS considered whether a donor-advised fund created by a private foundation within a community trust qualified as a component part of the grantee community foundation. The IRS found that it did and that the grant constituted a qualifying distribution.[124] The ruling applied transition rules written for community trusts in existence before November 1976, that were unable to meet all of the requirements of the then-issued community trust regulations.[125] The standards imposed on the asset transfer intend to divest the private foundation of any control or discretion over the fund it creates. In brief, these facts must exist:

- The trust is a publicly supported organization.

- The community trust's governing body is comprised of members who may serve a period of not more than 10 years.

- No person may serve within a period consisting of the lesser of five years or the number of consecutive years the member has immediately completed serving.

- The transferor private foundation may not impose any material restriction or condition that prevents the transferee public charity from freely and effectively employing the transferred assets, or the income derived therefrom, in furtherance of its exempt purposes. Whether a restriction or condition is material depends on the facts and circumstances. Some of the more significant facts are:

  ○ Whether the transferee public charity or participating trustee is the owner in fee of the assets received.

  ○ Whether such assets are to be held and administered by the public charity in a manner consistent with one or more of its exempt purposes.

---

123. As of December 2013 no report has been issued.
124. Reg. § 1.170A-9(e)(12), (13).
125. IRC § 4942(g)(3); Reg. § 53.4942(a)-3(c). This regulation contains five examples that should be reviewed by a foundation claiming a qualifying distribution based on a donee's redistribution of its grant.

○ Whether the governing body of the public charity has ultimate control over the assets and income.

○ Whether and to what extent the public charity's governing body is organized and operated so as to be independent of the transferor.

A cautious private foundation making a grant to a community trust might follow the listed criteria to ensure that such a grant will be treated as a qualifying distribution to an uncontrolled entity.

The IRS's private letter determination that a private foundation's grant to a community foundation is a qualifying distribution leaves unanswered questions. Can a private foundation make a grant to a donor-advised fund (DAF) created by a disqualified person in relation to the foundation? Does the transaction result in self-dealing? Is the grant a qualifying distribution? Is expenditure responsibly required?

The policies and procedures of a DAF must prohibit any dominion or control over the funds by the disqualified person.[126] He or she should have the right only to make recommendations. Self-dealing would occur if the grant funds are used to give rights and privileges of value to the disqualified person— a prohibited transaction.[127] The private foundation grants to the DAF should count as qualifying distributions since neither the disqualified person nor the private foundation has any control over the DAF.

To reinforce the lack of control and show evidence of the absence of self-dealing, the foundation documents transmitting the grant to the DAF should contain stipulations that there are no restrictions on the use of the money. The terms should provide that the money may not be used to provide benefits to the donor advisor, his or her family members, or a 35 percent controlled entity of a disqualified person, such as payment of a personal pledge or purchase of tickets to an event. Further, the foundation should require its customary follow-up reports regarding use of the funds, although formal expenditure responsibility procedures are not required inasmuch as a DAF is a public charity.[128]

**Redistributions.** If the controlled organization or unrelated private foundation redistributes, or essentially does not keep the grant money it receives, the grantor foundation can claim its payment as a qualifying distribution. Three factors must be present:[129]

1. The controlled grantee must be a charitable organization, and the grantee must distribute an amount equal in value to the full amount of the

---

126. *See* Chapter 16.
127. IRC § 4967 prohibits a DAF expenditure that provides more than incidental and tenuous benefit to a disqualified person.
128. *See* § 9.6.
129. IRC § 4942(h). E.g., Rev. Rul. 78-45, 1978-1 C.B. 378.

contribution not later than the close of the first taxable year after the controlled grantee's taxable year in which the contribution is received.

2. The grantee may not count the distribution toward satisfying its own distribution requirements, but instead must treat its regranting of the money as a payment out of its corpus.

3. The donor private foundation must obtain adequate records or other evidence from the grantee proving that the redistribution was accomplished. The donee's report should describe the name and addresses of the recipients of the redistributions and the amount of each. Most important, the donor must receive a statement verifying that the distribution was not treated as a qualifying distribution by the grantee, but instead as a distribution out of corpus.[130]

If all or part of the funds are not suitably redistributed by the grantee by the next year-end, the grantor's distribution amount for the subsequent year must be increased as shown in Exhibit 6.1. Essentially, a grant treated as qualifying in the year it is paid because of expected redistribution by the grantee is added back in the subsequent year in which the failure occurred. If more than one payment was granted, a proration is made.[131]

**Earmarked Grants.** Earmarked grants can be troublesome. As discussed earlier, it is acceptable for a private foundation to direct the purpose for which the funds are used by a grant recipient. The creation of a separate fund or special budgetary controls can be required. There must, however, be no material restriction on their use. The recipient must be free to use the grant for its own exempt purposes. Funds cannot be earmarked for lobbying, a specific individual grant, or any other expenditure the private foundation itself would not be permitted to make.[132]

A foundation's gift of the use of, or lending of, a property, such as artwork or office space, is a transaction of economic value. Because the income tax rules do not allow a contribution deduction for such a gift, such gifts are not generally treated as qualifying distributions. However, there is no specific guidance that says the value of such gift cannot be counted as a qualifying distribution.

**Pledges.** Pledges to make a grant in the future, likewise, do not qualify as an actual distribution. The word *paid* means that a distribution is counted in the year in which it is actually paid out in cash or property, not the year in which a

---

130. Reg. § 53.4942(a)-3(c)(2)(i).
131. *See* Chapter 9.
132. Priv. Ltr. Rul. 8839003; *see* also Priv. Ltr. Rul. 8750006, concerning reporting deferred grant awards.

grant is approved or promised.[133] Thus, a foundation that pledged a grant to a public charity in support of a museum building program could not count the grant until the funds were actually paid. Holding the funds to earn interest for a three-year period before construction begins to enable the foundation to earn interest precludes treating the funds as distributed in the year the pledge is made.[134] Sometimes such a pledge itself can qualify as a set-aside distribution.[135]

**Noncash Grants.** Qualifying distributions can be paid in cash or other property. The fair market value of noncash assets or the distributable amount of dispersal is treated as a qualifying distribution. Because property the foundation receives by gift retains the same tax basis as that of the donor, some private foundations have assets with a value significantly higher than the basis. These appreciated noncash assets held for investment purposes, particularly marketable securities or real estate, provide a tax-planning opportunity. The excise tax on investment income does not include the capital gain inherent in property that is distributed. Thus, it is sometimes desirable for the foundation to grant property, rather than selling the property to raise cash to make the distribution in cash.[136]

When an asset previously used by the foundation in its own exempt activities is subsequently granted to another charity, the grant is still a qualifying distribution. If the foundation had previously considered the purchase of the building as a qualifying distribution, only the current value of the building in excess of the purchase cost is counted.[137]

**Borrowed Funds.** If a private foundation uses borrowed money to make expenditures for a tax-exempt purpose, a qualifying distribution is made when the grant or expense is paid, not when the debt is created nor when the debt is repaid.[138] A foundation cannot, however, borrow from itself, as demonstrated by the unsuccessful attempt by a private foundation to offset one year's large grant, treated as made out of its corpus, with its income as received in subsequent years being applied as qualifying distributions to restore its corpus.[139] Interest on indebtedness incurred to enable the foundation to make charitable distributions is not itself treated as a qualifying distribution. This interest can be taken into account as a deduction in calculating adjusted net

---

133. Rev. Rul. 79-319, 1979-2 C.B. 388; but also *see* Rev. Rul. 77-7, 1977-1 C.B. 354.
134. *See* § 10.4.
135. *See* § 6.5(e).
136. Rev. Rul. 79-375, 1979-2 C.B. 389.
137. *H. Fort Flowers Foundation, Inc. v. Commissioner*, 72 T.C. 399 (1979).
138. Reg. § 53.4942(a)-3(a)(4)(i).
139. Reg. § 53.4942(a)-3(c)(2)(iii), (a)-2(d)(I)(ii).

income,[140] but is not taken into account as a reduction in investment income for purposes of calculating the investment income excise tax.

**Noncharitable Organization.** A grant or other expenditure made to a non-charitable organization can be qualifying so long as the payment is made for a charitable purpose.[141] Private foundation grants to tax-exempt social fraternities specifically earmarked for educational purposes have been condoned in a number of IRS letter rulings. One such grant was paid to build a study room in the chapter house that would contain exclusively educational equipment and furniture, along with computers linked to the university's mainframe. The private foundation was entitled to the return of any funds not so expended and retained the right to inspect the room annually.[142]

## (b) Concept of Control

As stated, as a general rule, a grant by a private foundation to an entity it controls, directly or indirectly, is not a qualifying distribution. In the tax-exempt organizations context, the concept of control of one organization by another is sometimes difficult to determine. In the context of for-profit organizations, control can be measured by stock ownership (or comparable beneficial interest). In the nonprofit setting, mechanisms of control are usually memberships (unlikely in the case of a private foundation) or overlapping directorates (by elections or appointments).

Pursuant to the mandatory payout rules, an organization is considered to be controlled by a private foundation or by one or more of its disqualified persons if any of these persons may, by aggregating their votes or positions of authority, require the grantee organization to make an expenditure or prevent it from making an expenditure.[143] This is the case regardless of the method by which the control is exercised or exercisable. Control does not actually need to be exercised; it is sufficient if control *can* be exercised. It is not necessary that disqualified persons constitute a majority of the grantee organization's board for the organization to be controlled. The issue is a factual question of control; the existence of interlocking directors between the foundation and the grantee organization is not sufficient to deem an organization to be controlled.[144] The grantor foundation will be deemed to control the recipient organization if all of

---

140. As described in § 10.4(b); such interest is not treated as attributable to the production of investment income and is, accordingly, not a reduction in investment income for investment income excise tax purposes.

141. These grants must be made utilizing the expenditure responsibility procedures explained in § 9.4.

142. These purposes are those described in IRC §§ 170(c)(1), 170(c)(2)(B).

143. Reg. § 53.4942(a)-3(a)(3).

144. E.g., Priv. Ltr. Ruls. 8232051, 7828012.

the facts and circumstances demonstrate that a material restriction or condition prevents the recipient from freely and effectively employing the distribution, or the income to be derived therefrom, in furtherance of the recipient's exempt purposes. In general, it is the grantee, not the distribution, that must be controlled by the grantor private foundation.

As to *direct* control, this definition thus has two components. One is that an entity is a controlling entity if it can direct at least 51 percent of the votes or authority to cause the controlled entity to make an expenditure. As an obvious example of this form of control, four of the six directors of two private foundations served as trustees of a charitable trust; the IRS correctly concluded that the foundations controlled the trust.[145] Likewise, the IRS ruled that, where one of the twelve directors of a grantee foundation was a member of the board of directors of the grantor foundation, the grantor foundation did not control the grantee foundation.[146] In another case, the sole donor to a foundation had the right to appoint two of the foundation's five directors; therefore, the foundation's donor did not control the foundation.[147]

The other component of the definition of direct control is that an entity is a controlling entity if it can combine its votes or positions of authority to prevent the controlled entity from making an expenditure. Generally, this approach requires that the controlling entity have the ability to muster at least 50 percent of the votes or positions. In one instance, a private foundation provided financial support to a tax-exempt medical research organization. The medical research organization was governed by an 18-person board of directors, three of whom were appointed by the private foundation. The private foundation–appointed directors did not have veto power over decisions made by the medical research organization's board. The IRS ruled that, therefore, the medical research organization did not control the private foundation; distributions from the private foundation to the medical research organization were treated as qualifying distributions.[148]

An example of indirect control arises where a control person has control or similar influence over another person who is not, viewed alone, a control person.[149] The vote or position of authority of this type of non-control person is taken into account in determining the presence of indirect control. It would seem that an appointment power, alone, is insufficient to create an element of indirect control, although there is no authority on the point.

Informal authority suggests that these control issues can be favorably resolved by means of provisions in governing documents or corporate resolutions

---

145. Priv. Ltr. Rul. 8713056.
146. Priv. Ltr. Rul. 9551037.
147. Priv. Ltr. Rul. 8812046.
148. Priv. Ltr. Rul. 8606040.
149. Rev. Rul. 80-207, 1980-2 C.B.193.

that suitably curb the extent of what would otherwise be a private foundation's control powers.[150]

This definition thus has two components. One is that an entity is a controlling entity if it can muster at least 51 percent of the votes or authority to cause the controlled entity to make an expenditure. The other is that an entity is a controlling entity if it can combine its votes or authority to prevent the controlled entity from making an expenditure. These are forms of direct control.

An example of indirect control arises where a control person has control or similar influence over another person who is not, viewed alone, a control person. The vote or position of authority of this type of noncontrol person is taken into account in determining the presence of indirect control.

## (c) Direct Charitable Expenditures

Any amount, including that portion of reasonable and necessary administrative expenses, paid to accomplish one or more charitable purposes[151] is eligible to be treated as a qualifying distribution.[152] The following expenditures are examples of qualifying distributions.

**Exempt Function Assets.** The purchase of assets used, or held for use, in carrying out the foundation's tax-exempt purposes is treated as a charitable disbursement.[153] Assets of this nature are not held for investment, but instead for use in conducting the foundation's programs. The full purchase price of an exempt function asset is included as a qualifying distribution at the time of purchase even if part or all of the purchase price is borrowed. Amounts expended to make improvements on property can also be qualifying distributions, where charitable ends are being pursued.[154] Depreciation is not counted for this purpose because it would be redundant.[155]

Assume a foundation acquires a building for its own use to house its program and administrative functions. The building has space for expansion that will be rented for the foreseeable future. In the year of acquisition, the foundation is entitled to report a qualifying distribution equal to a portion of the acquisition price, plus any improvements it makes to the property, in the year acquired. The qualifying charitable distribution will be the percentage of the building devoted to administrative and charitable programs. That portion held for investment purposes, either rented to others or housing the investment

---

150. Priv. Ltr. Rul. 200937038.
151. IRC § 4942(g)(1)(A).
152. IRC § 4942(g)(1)(B). *See* § 6.2(c).
153. Priv. Ltr. Rul. 9702040.
154. Rev. Rul. 74-560, 1974-2 C.B. 389.
155. Priv. Ltr. Rul. 9834033.

management department, can be depreciated for excise tax purposes.[156] Assume further the foundation holds the property for three years and then donates the property to another charitable organization. The foundation can report an additional qualifying distribution equal to the increase, if any, in the fair market value of the property over that amount originally treated as a qualifying distribution.[157]

A private foundation's $1 million program-related investment to acquire a 50 percent interest in a partnership was treated as a qualifying distribution. A venture was formed by a foundation and a public charity to provide long-term care for foster home children. Thus, the expenditures were charitable, and the IRS ruled that the $500,000 charitable distributions made by the partnership were qualifying distributions. Some commentators say this result is too good to be true. The ruling does not stipulate the source of the $500,000. If it was from the $1 million investment, it looks like a double dip and seems an impossible result. If the funds came from charges for exempt services provided, the disbursement would be reported net of the revenue on a Form 1065, Schedule K-1. Form 990-PF instructs that current-year charitable disbursements be reduced by any income generated in that activity.[158]

*Conversion* of an asset previously held for investment, an active business property, or a future exempt purpose, to use as an exempt function asset is counted as a qualifying distribution.[159] For example, a building rented to commercial tenants may become an exempt function asset. In this form of conversion, a foundation may enter into a *charitable lease*, at a nominal rate, to allow a public charity to use the property for its charitable purposes.[160] The foundation would properly treat as a qualifying distribution that portion of its building let for a charitable lease based on the amount of rent forsworn in relation to fair rental value of the entire property. The distribution amount for a converted asset is equal to the fair market value on the date of change in the asset's use. The date on which the foundation approves the plan for conversion, rather than the date the actual physical change or occupancy is completed, is the effective date of change.[161] The amount previously claimed as a qualifying distribution when an asset was converted to exempt use must be added back to the distributable amount if the asset is sold. If, instead, the asset is donated to another charitable organization, the difference between the amount previously

---

156. *See* § 10.4(e).
157. IRS Publication 578 (revised January of 1989), page 23 (out of print).
158. E.g., Priv. Ltr. Rul. 8906062. Likewise, the adoption of a plan of conversion of real property to an exempt use by a private operating foundation was considered to be a qualifying distribution, as was a transfer of land to the operating foundation by another private foundation (Priv. Ltr. Rul. 9247036).
159. Reg. § 53.4942(a)-2(c)(3).
160. Rev. Rul. 78-102, 1978-1 C.B. 379.
161. *See* filled-in Form 990-PF in Exhibit 12.1.

claimed and the value at the time of the grant can be treated as a qualifying distribution.

The actual date a foundation converts an asset is sometimes unclear when improvements must be made to the property. Assume a foundation buys a building that it intends to donate to a school as an academic facility. It is expected the remodeling may take at least two years. For financial reasons, the foundation borrows the money to make the acquisition. Title to the property is not transferred to the school until the renovations are complete two years after the date the property is acquired. Although it was not until the title transferred that the school actually began to use the property, the date the asset is considered as devoted to exempt use is the date the foundation adopted the plan.[162] Since the property was effectively committed to exempt use on the date of purchase, that date is the date of conversion of the property.[163]

The date of dedication to exempt purposes may be difficult to pinpoint when a foundation receives property through a donation. The foundation may need some time to evaluate its capability to devote assets to exempt purposes by preparing financial projections and other strategic plans addressing the viability of the choice. One ruling described a bequest from a person who died in 1998.[164] The property, including residences, artwork, and furnishings, was distributed over a period of time. As a fact, the ruling stated artwork was distributed on January 12, 2000, and that the foundation took possession of all of the assets by May 2000. The ruling said, "At that time it decided that instead of selling them, it would use them for charitable programs operated either by the foundation or by other charitable organizations." One presumes this statement refers to May 2000. In classifying the assets for mandatory payout purposes, the ruling does not mention the character of the artwork between January and May 2000. A foundation anticipating receipt of assets that potentially may be classified as exempt function will wish to do as much advance planning as possible to avoid any period of uncertainty.

**Administrative Expenses.**  A portion of the organization's personnel, occupancy, office expense, and overhead, expended to accomplish the foundation's exempt purposes are includible as qualifying distributions. The portion of the foundation's administrative expenses allocable to management of properties held for the production of income, such as investment advisory and rental property management fees, are not considered allocable to the foundation's exempt activities. Legal, accounting, and other professional fees may need to be allocated between those attributable to investments and charitable programs. Legal, accounting, state registration, and other fees and expenses paid in

---

162. Reg. § 53.4942(a)-3(a)(5). Rev. Rul. 78-102, 1978-1 C.B. 379.
163. Reg. § 53.4942(a)-3(a)(5).
164. Priv. Ltr. Rul. 200136029.

connection with creation and qualification of a new private foundation as a tax-exempt organization can also be treated as disbursements for charitable purposes. The design of Form 990-PF prompts the foundation to make this distinction in its expenditures as it fills in the columns in Part I.[165]

Administrative expenses must be reasonable and necessary to accomplishing the foundation's tax-exempt purposes.[166] Expenses directly connected with managing a foundation's grant-making programs may include a computerized grant request tracking system, a program officer's travel to grantee sites, and an allocable portion of the salary of personnel directly involved in the grant-making process. Organizational administrative costs not directly related to grants, such as fundraising expenses, preparation of Form 990-PF and annual reports, and technical assistance to grantees or governments also qualify.[167] Furthermore, legal fees paid in a suit involving an exempt charitable trust seeking to clarify its beneficiaries were treated as a qualifying distribution.[168]

---

165. In the conference committee report accompanying the Tax Reform Act of 1984, it is stated that "the mere fact that a State attorney general, or other State government official, has approved the amount of director fees or other expenditures by a foundation does not establish that such amounts or expenditures are reasonable or not excessive for purposes of any of the private foundation tax provisions" (H. Rep. 98-861, 98th Cong., 2d Sess. 1087 (1984)).

166. IRC § 4942(g)(1)(A).

167. Rev. Rul. 75-495, 1975-2 C.B. 449.

168. IRC § 4942(g)(4), added by Tax Reform Act of 1984 § 304, was allowed to expire and is no longer applicable. This provision recognized four general types of private foundation outlays: (1) grants and contributions, (2) administrative expenses incurred in making grants and contributions, (3) expenditures for the conduct of charitable functions directly by the private foundation, and (4) administrative expenses incurred directly for the conduct of the charitable functions; the limitation was essentially applicable to the second of these types of qualifying distributions.

After nearly 15 years' experience with these rules, Congress concluded that the administrative expenses of private foundations were absorbing an excessive portion of qualifying distributions and placed a limitation on the extent to which grant administrative expenses may be taken into account in determining compliance with the payout requirement. Thus, for years beginning after December 31, 1984, but not for years beginning after December 31, 1990, a private foundation was required to timely pay out, as qualifying distributions, an amount equal to 4.35 percent of its noncharitable assets as grants or contributions, expenditures directly for the active conduct by it of its tax-exempt activities, or qualified administrative expenses incurred directly in making the direct operating expenditures. Congress directed the IRS to modify the private foundation annual information return to facilitate the collection of more information about operating and nonoperating private foundations' administrative expenses (H. Rep. No. 98-861, *supra* note 129, at 1086).

Congress directed that, "to the extent practicable," the study is "to examine (1) the amount of qualifying distributions which actually reach charitable beneficiaries; (2) the administrative costs of such payouts; (3) the effect of the revised general definition . . . [IRC § 4942 (g)(1)(A)] on those administrative expenses which are eligible to be qualifying

Legal fees and associated expenses paid by a foundation in connection with a mediation agreement to distribute the foundation's assets to two new foundations created to resolve a dispute between two remaining directors after the death of a director were treated as a qualifying distribution.[169]

For years beginning after 1984 and before 1991, a limitation was placed on the amount of administrative expense allowed to be treated as qualifying distributions. During that time, no more than 0.65 percent of the foundation's average net investment assets over a three-year period could be claimed.

*Self-sponsored program*, also called *direct charitable activity*, expenses paid directly (of the sort a private operating foundation incurs) by the traditional private foundation also count as qualifying distributions. There are many examples of this type of expenditure, including the costs of operating a museum or a library, running a summer camp for children, conducting research and publishing books, buying food for the hungry, and preserving historic houses. Charitable projects can be carried out in any location. There is no constraint against a private foundation conducting activities outside the United States.[170]

*Individual grants* count as qualifying distributions if they are paid under a program meeting the requirements pertaining to these programs in the taxable expenditures context.[171] Academic grants are considered to be fully counted when the recipients can expend a portion of the funds granted on child care, as long as that spending enables the grantees to continue research and is not made in accordance with individuals' personal or family needs.[172]

---

distributions, subject to the new limitation; and (4) the additional information provided by the revised form concerning categories and types of administrative expenses, and the basis for allocating such expenses among categories of foundation expenditures," and that the study "is intended to provide more detailed information concerning foundation administrative expenditures than is now available" (*id*. at 1087). On the basis of this information, the Department of the Treasury, in January 1990, submitted an analysis of the subject to the House Committee on Ways and Means and the Senate Committee.

The report ("Private Foundation Grant-Making Administrative Expenses Study") concluded that this limitation on grant administrative expenses should be allowed to terminate with respect to the years beginning after December 31, 1990. The IRS concluded that the limit "was not an effective method of discouraging foundations from incurring excessive amounts of these administrative expenses" and that "computations regarding the grant-making administrative expenses limit were complex and burdensome to private foundations." Congress did not act to extend this limitation on grant administrative expenses.

169. Priv. Ltr. Rul. 200725043.
170. *See* § 6.5(e).
171. *See* § 9.3.
172. Priv. Ltr. Rul. 9116032.

*Program-related investments* that meet the requirements of law pertaining to jeopardizing investments[173] and taxable expenditures,[174] including interest-free or low-interest loans to other exempt organizations or individuals, also are counted as qualifying distributions.

## (d)  Use of Single-Member Limited Liability Companies

Use of single-member limited liability companies, where they are disregarded entities for federal tax purposes, by various types of tax-exempt organizations has become common.[175] Private foundations are not excepted from this phenomenon.

In the private foundation setting, matters in this regard were set in motion when the IRS issued guidance stating that a foundation may make a qualifying distribution to a single-member limited liability company that is wholly owned by an unrelated public charity.[176] As the IRS wrote on that occasion, this "disregarded entity generally receives the benefit of its owner's tax-exempt status." This development led to further guidance from the IRS, that contributions to a single-member limited liability company, that is a disregarded entity for federal tax purposes, where the company is wholly owned and controlled by a U.S. charity, are deductible, with the gift treated as being to a branch or division of the charitable donee.[177]

This use of single-member limited liability companies in the private foundations context is not confined to grantees. Foundations can utilize them in lieu of direct grants. In a fine example of this approach, a private foundation, rather than making grants directly to a tax-exempt university to financially salvage an educational program, acquired control over the program by means of a company, appointing a majority of the overseers of the program, purchasing program assets, and becoming responsible for funding the activity. Because the program became conducted under the authority and direction of the foundation, expenditures of the limited liability company were treated as active program expenses, enabling the foundation to qualify as a private operating foundation.[178] In a similar situation, a private foundation utilized a single-member limited liability company to acquire real estate and fund the construction of a tax-exempt school, to be operated by an unrelated party.[179]

---

173. *See* Chapter 8.
174. *See* Chapter 9.
175. *See Tax-Exempt Organizations* § 31.6.
176. INFO 2010-0052.
177. Notice 2012-52, 2012-35 I.R.B. 317.
178. Priv. Ltr. Rul. 200431018. *See* § 3.1.
179. Priv. Ltr. Rul. 201134023.

## (e) Set-Asides

Money set aside or saved for specific future charitable projects, rather than being paid out currently, can be considered to be a qualifying distribution by a private foundation for mandatory payout purposes.[180] An amount set aside in one year for a specific project that is for a tax-exempt purpose or purposes may be treated as a qualifying distribution, if payment for the project is to be subsequently made over a period not to exceed 60 months. The funds set aside are credited, for purposes of the qualifying distribution requirements, as if paid in the tax year the set-aside is made, thus reducing the actual amount of the mandatory payout in that year.

The amount set aside need not be increased by accumulation of income on the amount. The set-aside would be reflected as a liability on the foundation's financial records indicating the amount must be paid out of corpus by the end of the set-aside period.[181] The amount set aside, plus income, is included in the asset base for purposes of calculating minimum investment return.

A specific project includes, but is not limited to, situations where relatively long-term grants or expenditures must be made in order to ensure the continuity of particular projects or program-related investments, or where grants are made as part of a matching-grant program.[182] The concept of this type of project may encompass, for example:

- A plan to erect a building to house a tax-exempt activity of a private foundation (e.g., a museum building in which paintings are to be hung, even though the location of the building and architectural plans have not been finalized).

- A plan to purchase an additional group of paintings offered for sale only as a unit that requires an expenditure of more than one year's income.

- A plan to fund a specific research program that is of such magnitude as to require an accumulation prior to commencement of the research.[183]

- A plan to fund the development and improvement of a family camping facility operated by a charitable organization, where the construction of some of the facilities was unavoidably delayed.[184]

- A plan to postpone a private foundation's grant-making activities until litigation, which prohibits distributions from the foundation, is resolved.[185]

---

180. IRC § 4942(g)(2); Reg. § 53.4942(a)-3(b)(1).
181. Rev. Rul. 78-148, 1978-1 C.B. 380.
182. Reg. § 53.4942(a)-3(b)(2).
183. *Supra* note 109.
184. Priv. Ltr. Rul. 200327062.
185. Priv. Ltr. Rul. 200328049.

- A plan to fund a supporting organization's history exhibits, with the set-aside necessary to enable the foundation to oversee the construction process and integrate the use of proceeds from a planned issuance of bonds.[186]

For example, conversion by a private foundation of newly acquired land, partially to its existing wildlife sanctuary and partially to a park for public use under a four-year construction contract, under which no payment was required until years three and four, was ruled to be a specific project, and the amounts set aside were treated as a qualifying distribution as long as a timely justifying application was filed.[187] By contrast, a private foundation, which made renewable scholarships and fixed-sum research grants that usually ran for three years, proposed to set aside the full amount to be given to each grantee and make annual payments to them from a set-aside account, rather than take the payments out of its current income. The IRS ruled that the amounts were not qualifying distributions within the meaning of the set-aside rules.[188]

Nonetheless, the IRS subsequently allowed a set-aside for a scholarship grant program where the private foundation was newly created, students who would benefit from its grants could not be identified during the grant period, the request was for a one-time set-aside, the foundation's program does not promise future grants, and the foundation advises its grantees to not expect further funding.[189]

**Type 1.** The first of the two types of set-asides originated in 1969 and is based on the suitability test.[190] This test is satisfied where the general set-aside rules are met and where the private foundation is successful in convincing the IRS that the project can be better accomplished by a set-aside rather than by the immediate payment of funds. A ruling from the IRS is necessary for this type of set-aside, and the private foundation must apply for the ruling before the end of the year in which the amount is set aside.[191] The request for the ruling must include the amount of the intended set-aside, the reasons that the project can be better accomplished by a set-aside, and a detailed description of the project.

According to the IRS, a private foundation's desire to retain control over the funds so as to receive income from them is not a persuasive reason for utilizing a

---

186. Priv. Ltr. Rul. 200347018.
187. Rev. Rul. 74-450, 1974-2 C.B. 388.
188. Rev. Rul. 75-511, 1975-2 C.B. 450.
189. Priv. Ltr. Rul. 200434026.
190. IRC § 4942(g)(2)(A), (B)(i); Reg. § 53.4942(a)-3(b)(2).
191. Reg. § 53.4942(a)-3(b)(7)(i).

qualified set-aside, where the private foundation can make the grants out of current or future income.[192]

For good cause shown, the period for paying an amount set aside under the suitability test may be extended by the IRS.[193] For example, a private foundation permitted a set-aside to construct a youth camp was granted a two-year extension to pay out the funds, because of the institution of a building moratorium that caused a delay in acquiring the necessary property.[194] More-over, a private foundation will not incur any taxes under these rules where it disregards a set-aside ruling it received and instead adheres to the general distribution requirements.[195]

Funds set aside by a foundation for two challenge matching-grant programs were treated as qualifying distributions.[196] The foundation pledged to match a grant to a private school and another to a charity providing social and rehabilitation services. This ruling is contrary to other private rulings discussed under "Pledges" and departs from the accepted meaning of the word *paid*.[197] Maybe this ruling signals a move by the IRS toward accounting rules that require promises to grant to be reported as grants in the pledge year.

Construction of new foundation headquarters that would be mostly rented at below cost to other tax-exempt organizations;[198] redevelopment of a city block as a part of a downtown rejuvenation;[199] construction of facilities in Central America for abandoned and underprivileged children;[200] and the making of guarantees of below-market bank loans to public charities to advance charitable child-care programs, and loan deposits and interest-rate subsidy arrangements for the same purpose,[201] were ruled to constitute suitable pro-grams for which a private foundation can set aside funds that will be treated as qualifying distributions.

A private foundation may, the IRS ruled, use borrowed funds to satisfy all or portions of previously approved set-asides for a project, enabling the set-asides to continue to constitute qualifying distributions.[202] The IRS observed that the law does not "specify or limit the source of the funds expected to be used for completion of a project, other than that it must be disclosed at the time the private foundation submits its written request for a set-aside." The tax

---

192. *Supra* note 109.
193. Reg. § 53.4942(a)-3(b)(1).
194. Priv. Ltr. Rul. 7821141.
195. Priv. Ltr. Rul. 8830070.
196. Priv. Ltr. Rul. 9524033.
197. *See* § 6.5(a).
198. Priv. Ltr. Rul. 199907028.
199. Priv. Ltr. Rul. 199906053.
200. Priv. Ltr. Rul. 199905039.
201. Priv. Ltr. Rul. 200043050.
202. Priv. Ltr. Rul. 201152021.

regulations provide that, if a private foundation borrows money to make expenditures for a charitable purpose, a qualifying distribution out of the borrowed funds will generally be deemed to have been made only at the time that the borrowed funds are actually distributed for the exempt purpose.[203] The IRS noted that this regulation "implicitly recognizes that expenditures for qualifying distributions may be made out of borrowed funds."

Advance approval from the IRS of this type of set-aside should be sought by means of filing an IRS form.[204]

From time to time, the IRS issues private letter rulings with respect to these set-aside rules.[205]

**Type 2.** This type of set-aside is based on the *cash distribution test*[206] and may be utilized by a private foundation only in its early years. It originated in 1976, because of the general reluctance of the IRS to approve set-aside requests—a dilemma that was particularly acute for new or newly funded private foundations that were attempting to institute long-term supervised projects in the face of IRS inaction. This test is satisfied where the general set-aside rules are met and where the private foundation actually distributes the *start-up period minimum amount* and subsequently actually distributes the *full-payment period minimum amount*. Approval from the IRS is not required where the cash distribution approach is correctly utilized.

A private foundation's *start-up period* is generally the four years following the year in which the private foundation was created.[207] The start-up period minimum amount that must be timely distributed, in cash or its equivalent, is at least the sum of:

1.  20 percent of the private foundation's distributable amount for the first year of the start-up period.

2.  40 percent of its distributable amount for the second tax year of the start-up period.

3.  60 percent of its distributable amount for the third year of the start-up period.

4.  80 percent of its distributable amount for the fourth year of its start-up period.[208]

---

203. *See* § 6.5(a), text accompanied by *supra* note 111.
204. Form 8940.
205. E.g., Priv. Ltr. Rul. 8627055.
206. IRC § 4942(g)(2)(A), (B)(ii)(I)–(III); Reg. § 53.4942(a)-3(b)(3).
207. Reg. § 53.4942(a)-3(b)(4)(i).
208. IRC § 4942(g)(2)(B)(ii)(II), (III); Reg. § 53.4942(a)-3(b)(4)(ii), (iii).

To qualify as a timely distribution, it should be emphasized that it is only the aggregate sum of these amounts that must be distributed before the end of the start-up period (end of the fourth year). There is no requirement that any part be distributed in any particular tax year of the start-up period.[209] Also, while the aggregate sum satisfies the cash distribution test, the amount is *not* in lieu of the normal 5 percent minimum distributable amount, but simply a deferral. Nowhere under the requirements for the cash distribution test does it indicate that if those tests are met, the normal 5 percent distributable amounts are superseded. The cash distribution test distributable amounts must be met in order for the foundation to claim a qualifying distribution for its initial set-aside, nothing more.

Under certain circumstances, distributions made during the year preceding the private foundation's start-up period and/or made within 5½ months following the start-up period are deemed part of the start-up period minimum amount.[210]

The years of a private foundation's existence after expiration of the start-up period are termed the *full-payment period*.[211] The full-payment period minimum amount that must be timely distributed, in cash or its equivalent, is at least its distributable amount determined under the general rules.[212] Moreover, a private foundation has a five-year carryover of certain distributions that are in excess of the full-payment period minimum amount.[213]

The design of the start-up period amounts that reflect a 20 percent, 40 percent, 60 percent, and 80 percent distributable amount for years 1, 2, 3, and 4 imply that this test applies only to newly created private foundations. The congressional record also describes the test as designed for start-up foundations and existing foundations that have recently received a dramatic influx of new assets.[214] In the two private letter rulings described below, the IRS sanctioned the use of the cash distribution set-aside provisions for foundations that had been in existence well beyond their initial start-up period and had not received an influx of funding. In one instance, cash distribution set-asides were allowed in 1986 and 1988 for a private foundation that was created in 1952.[215] Since the foundation's start-up period had long since passed, it was under the full-payment period minimum distribution requirements. Based on the facts of the ruling, it was apparent that the foundation had met its distribution requirements for purposes of the 5 percent minimum distribution test. It sought, however, and was allowed to qualify for the 1 percent versus 2 percent excise

---

209. Reg. § 53.4942(a)-3(b)(4)(iii).
210. Reg. § 53.4942(a)-3(b)(4)(iv).
211. Reg. § 53.4942(a)-3(b)(5)(i).
212. Reg. § 53.4942(a)-3(b)(5)(ii); *see* § 6.4.
213. IRC § 4942(g)(2)(D), (E); Reg. § 53.4942(a)-3(b)(5)(iii).
214. S. Rep. No. 94-938 (Part 1), 94th Cong., 2d Sess. 593 (1976).
215. Priv. Ltr. Rul. 9301022.

tax on investment income. By making use of the cash distribution test for some grants that were not paid by the end of the foundation's taxable year, the foundation was able to claim additional set-aside amounts as qualifying distributions for purposes of meeting the 1 percent excise tax requirements.

In the second ruling, the foundation wanted the ability to use the cash distribution test for multi-installment grants that covered more than one taxable year.[216] By claiming set-aside amounts as qualifying distributions prior to actual disbursement of the cash, the foundation was allowed to monitor the multi-year grants and get progress reports before the foundation made further distributions to the recipient. Again, the IRS approved use of the cash distribution test for current and *future* taxable years for a foundation that included years well after the foundation's start-up period had expired. Although the two private rulings sanctioned use by an existing foundation, caution should be exercised in considering this approach.

For the years involved in a cash distribution set-aside, a private foundation must include, as part of its annual information return, statements describing the specific project involved and showing the start-up period and the full-payment period minimum amounts.[217] For good cause shown, the period for paying an amount set aside under the cash distribution test may be extended by the IRS.[218]

The IRS provides an IRC 4942(g)(2) Set-Asides Reference Guide Sheet for Processing Set-Aside Requests, "Law at a Glance," and sample private letter rulings for its personnel. The guide and samples are designed to assist in the processing of requests for advance approval of set-asides. Private foundations and their advisors should carefully study them before seeking approval for a set-aside.

From time to time, the IRS issues private letter rulings concerning compliance with these set-aside rules.[219]

### (f) Distributions to Foreign Recipients

A private foundation may make a qualifying distribution to a charitable organization located in a country other than the United States.[220] The IRS ruled that an organization can serve beneficiaries in foreign countries without adversely affecting its tax-exempt status.[221] The general definition of the

---

216. Priv. Ltr. Rul. 9129006.
217. Reg. § 53.4942(a)-3(b)(7)(ii).
218. Reg. § 53.4942(a)-3(b)(1).
219. E.g., Priv. Ltr. Rul. 8627055.
220. That is, an organization described in IRC § 501(c)(3) other than an IRC § 509(a)(4) organization.
221. Rev. Ruls. 68-165, 1968-1 C.B. 253; 68-117, 1968-1 C.B. 251; 71-460, 1971-2 C.B. 231.

term *qualifying distribution*, as discussed earlier, applies to foreign charity grants as well.[222] Grants may be made to foreign governments as well as to foreign charitable organizations.[223]

Additional requirements must be met when a private foundation is making grants to foreign charities, however, to avoid the sanctions for failure to adhere to these distribution requirements. A private foundation that supports charitable activities outside the United States faces a documentation dilemma. It must obtain information that evidences two important facts:

1. The foundation must be able to prove that its money is spent to accomplish a charitable purpose, whether it spends the money directly to conduct a program or makes a grant.

2. If funds are granted to a foreign organization, the foundation must be able to prove the recipient is an uncontrolled entity that would qualify as a public charity or exercise expenditure responsibility.

These two factors stem from the minimum distribution requirements discussed in this chapter and also the taxable expenditure rules.[224]

If the foreign charitable organization has a ruling or a determination letter from the IRS that it is a public charity or a private operating foundation, the grantor private foundation can make a distribution (i.e., a qualifying one) to the foreign organization by following the rules applicable with respect to qualifying distributions to domestic organizations. If the foreign organization does not have a ruling or determination letter (which is more likely to be the case), however, a distribution for charitable purposes is treated as if made to the equivalent of a U.S. public charity or private operating foundation only if the distributing foundation has made a *good faith determination* that the grantee organization is a public charity or private operating foundation.[225] A good faith determination ordinarily is considered as made where the determination is based on an affidavit of the grantee organization or an opinion of legal counsel (of the distributing foundation or the grantee organization) that the grantee organization qualifies as a public charity or private operating foundation. This affidavit or opinion must set forth sufficient facts concerning the operations and support of the grantee organization for the IRS to determine that the grantee

---

222. The general definition of a charitable donee for charitable giving purposes includes a requirement that the organization be created under U.S., state, or similar domestic law (IRC § 170(c)(2)(A)). Thus, the reference to a foreign charity is to an organization that does not satisfy that requirement (Reg. § 53.4942(a)-3(a)(6)(ii)).

223. E.g., Priv. Ltr. Rul. 200031053.

224. *See* Chapter 9.

225. Reg. § 53.4942(a)-3(a)(6)(i). *See* § 9.5 for an explanation of these rules.

organization would be likely to qualify as a public charity or private operating foundation.[226] Based on the details, the management of a private foundation in this circumstance must make a reasonable judgment that the potential grantee is a charitable organization[227] and then make a good faith determination that the entity is either a public charity or private operating foundation.

The IRS developed a simplified procedure enabling U.S. private foundations to make distributions to foreign charitable organizations, relying solely on an appropriate affidavit.[228] This procedure is not available where the grant is a transfer of assets pursuant to any liquidation, merger, redemption, recapitalization or other similar adjustment, organization, or reorganization.[229] Both this reasonable judgment and good faith determination may be made on the basis of a *currently qualified* affidavit prepared by the grantee for the prospective grantor or for another grantor or prospective grantor.[230] This procedure requires that the affidavit be written in English and state the substantive information that is required. An affidavit is considered currently qualified as long as the facts in it are up-to-date, either because they reflect the grantee's latest complete accounting year or (in the case of public charities or private operating foundations whose public charity or operating foundation status is not dependent on public support) if the affidavit is updated at the request of the prospective grantor to reflect the grantee's current data.

An illustration of this procedure was provided by the case of a private foundation that operated a museum. The foundation became unable to pay for the display or maintenance of certain items and decided to grant them to a museum in a foreign country. The U.S. foundation obtained the requisite affidavit from the grantee; that documentation revealed that the grantee was an instrumentality of the foreign nation's government. Consequently, the grant was a qualifying distribution (and not a taxable expenditure).[231]

## § 6.6 DISTRIBUTIONS TO CERTAIN SUPPORTING ORGANIZATIONS

A nonoperating private foundation may not treat as a qualifying distribution an amount paid to a Type III supporting organization that is not a functionally integrated Type III supporting organization or to any other type of supporting organization[232] if a disqualified person with respect to the foundation directly or indirectly controls the supporting organization or a

---

226. *Id.*
227. *See* Chapter 15.
228. Rev. Proc. 92-94, 1992-2 C.B. 507.
229. *Id.* § 4.01. These reorganizations and the like are the subject of IRC § 507(b)(2) (*see* § 13.1).
230. Rev. Proc. 92-94, 1992-2 C.B. 507.
231. Priv. Ltr. Rul. 9839036; *see* § 9.5.
232. Supporting organizations are the subject of § 15.7.

supported organization of the supporting organization.[233] An amount that does not count as a qualifying distribution under this rule can also result in a taxable expenditure.[234] Expenditure responsibility steps are required for a grant to a nonfunctionally integrated supporting organization that does not count as a qualifying distribution.

Pursuant to interim guidance issued by the IRS,[235] a grantor, acting in good faith, may, in determining whether a grantee is a public charity, rely on information from the IRS Business Master File or the grantee's current IRS determination letter recognizing the grantee's tax exemption and indicating the grantee's public charity status. In addition, a grantor, acting in good faith, may rely on a written representation from a grantee and certain specified documents (see bullet points below) in determining the grantee's supporting organization type. In any event, the grantor must verify that the grantee is listed in the IRS's Publication 78 or obtain a copy of the grantee's determination letter.

To establish that a grantee is a Type I or II supporting organization, a grantor, acting in good faith, may rely on a written representation signed by a trustee, director, or officer of the grantee that the grantee is a Type I or II supporting organization, provided that:

- The representation describes how the grantee's trustees, directors, and/ or officers are selected, and references any provision in the governing documents that establish a Type I or II relationship between the grantee and its supported organization(s).

- The grantor collects and reviews copies of the governing documents of the grantee and, if relevant, of the supported organization(s).

To establish that a grantee is a functionally integrated Type III supporting organization, a grantor, acting in good faith, may rely on a written representation signed by a trustee, director, or officer of the grantee that the grantee is a functionally integrated Type III supporting organization, provided that:

- The grantee's representation identifies the one or more supported organizations with which the grantee is functionally integrated.

- The grantor collects and reviews copies of governing documents of the grantee (and, if relevant, of the supported organization(s)) and any other documents that set forth the relationship of the grantee to its supported

---

233. IRC § 4942(g)(4)B. As to the second element of this rule, a payment also is not a qualifying distribution if the IRS determines by regulation that the distribution "otherwise is inappropriate" (IRC § 4942(g)(4)(ii)(II)).
234. IRC § 4945(d)(4). *See* § 9.6.
235. Notice 2006-109, 2006-51 I.R.B. 1121 § 3.01.

organization(s), if the relationship is not reflected in the governing documents.

- The grantor reviews a written representation signed by a trustee, director, or officer of each of the supported organizations with which the grantee represents that it is functionally integrated, describing the activities of the grantee and confirming that, but for the involvement of the grantee engaging in activities to perform the functions of, or to carry out the purposes of, the supported organization, the supported organization would normally be engaged in those activities itself (see below).

As an alternative to the foregoing, a grantor may rely on a reasoned written opinion of counsel of either the grantor or the grantee concluding that the grantee is a Type I, Type II, or Type III functionally integrated supporting organization.

A private foundation considering a grant to a Type I, Type II, or Type III functionally integrated supporting organization may need to obtain a list of the grantee's supported organizations to determine whether any of the supported organizations is controlled (see below) by disqualified persons with respect to the foundation. Likewise, a sponsoring organization considering a grant from a donor-advised fund to one of these types of supporting organizations may need to obtain such a list to determine whether any of the supported organizations is controlled by the fund's donor or donor advisor (and any related parties).[236]

Pursuant to interim guidance issued by the IRS, in determining whether a disqualified person with respect to a private foundation controls a supporting organization or one of its supported organizations, the standards as to control established in the mandatory payout regulations apply.[237] Under these standards, an organization is controlled by one or more disqualified persons with respect to a foundation if any of these persons may, by aggregating their votes or positions of authority, require the supporting or supported organization to make an expenditure or prevent the supporting or supported organization from making an expenditure, regardless of the method by which the control is exercised or exercisable.[238]

---

236. The authors are fearful that private foundation grants to supporting organizations will be considerably reduced as the consequence of these new statutory and regulatory rules, because of the difficulties and risks associated with compliance with them. Private foundations may simply adopt a policy of not making grants to supporting organizations. (This would be unfortunate in that many supporting organizations have fundraising as a principal function.) In this regard, an analogy may be made with respect to expenditure responsibility grants (*see* § 9.6): Private foundations may make them but, because of the intricacies of the rules and the potential for penalties, few do.
237. Reg. § 53.4942(a)-3(a)(3). *See* § 6.5(b).
238. Notice 2006-109, 2006-51 I.R.B. 1121 § 3.02.

## §6.7 SATISFYING THE DISTRIBUTION TEST

Each year, a private foundation is required to spend a calculated minimum amount for charitable purposes based on the value of its assets during the previous year.[239] A new $1 million foundation created on January 1, 2014, and adopting a calendar year, for example, would be required to pay out $50,000 by December 31, 2015.[240] Such a foundation would be subject to an excise tax if it failed to pay out its distributable amount in a timely fashion and, therefore, had undistributed income. An initial tax of 30 percent is imposed for each year that the deficit goes uncorrected.[241]

Not only is a penalty assessed, but a private foundation with undistributed income must correct the deficit with the payment of additional qualifying distributions. An inadvertent deficiency may, in circumstances explained in the following sections, be made up without the imposition of the excise tax. Failure to correct a deficiency, and certainly repeated deficiencies, can result in imposition of excise tax and possibly loss of exemption. The formula for calculation of undistributed income for a particular year follows:

*Calculation of Undistributed Income*

> Current-year distributable amount[242]
>
> Less
>
> Current-year qualifying distributions[243] that are
> not applied either to offset prior deficits or to corpus

### (a) Timing of Distributions

To identify a deficiency in the distributions and to correct it, one must understand how payments are applied. A private foundation's charitable expenditures that are considered qualifying distributions are totaled for each year in which they are paid, but they are not necessarily applied in that year. The terminology can be confusing, because the current-year distributable amount is

---

239. *See* § 6.4.
240. Unless a set-aside distribution applies as explained in § 6.5(c).
241. IRC § 4942(a)(1).
242. *See* § 6.4.
243. *See* § 6.5.

based on the prior year's minimum investment return. Nevertheless, qualifying distributions are applied as follows:[244]

- First, the remaining qualifying distributions are applied to the current year's distributable amount (which is essentially the prior year's adjusted minimum investment return).

- Next, the foundation can make an election to apply qualifying distributions to make up any prior year's deficiency of distributable amount (for a year in which the foundation has undistributed income subject to the excise tax).

- Next, an election can be made to treat distributions as out of corpus for the purpose of the redistribution of (1) a grant received by one foundation from another foundation or (2) a gift from a contributor who wishes to receive a higher percentage contribution deduction limitation must be paid from corpus.[245]

- Next, any remaining distributions are applied to the current year's minimum investment return (which is essentially the next year's payout requirement).

- Finally, any remaining distributions are treated as excess distributions carryover to the next year.

Distributions in excess of the distributable amount that are applied to corpus are carried forward for five years, a period of time called the *adjustment period*. Exhibit 6.2 provides an illustration of the way in which excess distributions are applied. The IRS Chief Counsel issued a memorandum entitled *Adjustments of Excess Distribution Carryovers from Closed Years*, taking the position that adjustments to years closed by the statute of limitations are permissible.[246] The memorandum recognized the fact that if a nonoperating foundation has excessive or deficient distributions in any one year, the carryover of excess distributions is essentially an accumulation of all post-1969 years. It is an unusual foundation that pays out the exact minimum distribution amount each year.

A single error in calculating the qualifying distributions or the amount required to be distributed in any one year causes all years impacted by the mistake to be wrong. Thus, the IRS takes the position, as yet unchallenged in court, that the years from 1970 forward are open years for purposes of distribution carryovers.[247] As shown in the exhibit, the excess applied to corpus

---

244. IRC § 4942(h); Reg. § 53.4942(a)-3(d).
245. IRC § 170(b)(1)(E); *see* § 14.4.
246. Gen. Couns. Mem. 39808; also *see* § 6.4(a).
247. Priv. Ltr. Rul. 9116032.

is available to be carried forward for five years. The excesses shown in the first version are applied in the order in which they occur so that by 2018, no 2011 excess remains, because it offset the 2014, 2015, and 2017 deficits. The 2019 excess of $20 can be carried to 2019.

An operating foundation is expected to make active program distributions beginning in its first year of qualification; it is not allowed the one-year delay[248] for making qualifying distributions permitted for standard private foundations. An operating foundation may calculate its required distributions using either a four-year average method, or a three-out-of-four test.[249] For an operating foundation choosing the three-out-of-four test, the required distributions must be made each year without an allowance for any carryover resulting from excessive expenditures (though it can fail the test in one year out of the four). Application of the four-year average method instead essentially allows the operating foundation to carry over excess qualifying distributions from year to year, similar to the rules for standard private foundations.

Excess distributions cause no particular federal tax consequence but can result in a *substantial contraction* of the private foundation. Certain information must be submitted with Form 990-PF by a private foundation that has a partial or complete liquidation, dissolution, termination, or substantial contraction.[250] If a private foundation distributes all of its net assets, the transfer may constitute a voluntary termination of its private foundation status and require special reporting.[251] A transfer of less than 25 percent of the fair market value of the foundation's net assets, as a general rule, is not treated as a substantial contraction, nor are transfers for full and adequate consideration or distributions out of current income. Where more than 25 percent of the net assets are paid out in a series of related distributions, the facts and circumstances of the transactions must be studied to determine whether a substantial contraction occurred. Special rules apply where the transferee is another private foundation.[252]

## (b) Planning for Excess Distributions

For a number of reasons, many private foundations accumulate excess qualifying distributions. Foundations used as a vehicle for disbursing a philanthropist's annual giving often make grants totaling much more than the mandatory 5 percent payout amount. Some foundations plan to disburse their principal funds over a period of time rather than retain their assets into perpetuity. Other foundations conduct programs that require excess

---

248. Illustrated in Exhibit 6.2.
249. *See* § 3.1(f).
250. Reg. § 1.6043-3(a)(1); General instructions to Form 990-PF for 2012, page 10.
251. *See* Chapter 13.
252. IRC § 507(b)(2); Reg. § 1.507-3(c)(1), (2); *see* Chapter 13.

distributions for a period of a few years. The charitable expenditures of such foundations paid out in excess of the required annual amount are carried over to reduce the distributable amount for the five succeeding years.

A foundation with excess distributions from past years has planning opportunities. One choice is for the foundation to reduce its current spending until the excess is absorbed. Another choice is use of the excess to enhance deductibility of gifts of noncash assets to such foundations. As a general rule, only gifts of cash and readily marketable securities to a private foundation are fully deductible.[253] The deduction for a gift of land, art, closely held company shares, and similar property is limited to the donor's tax basis. For the donor to receive the maximum deduction, the foundation essentially cannot keep the amount of the donated property and must become for the year what is called a conduit foundation.[254] A foundation that has made excess distributions in past years can allocate those past expenditures to a current year's required donation redistribution.

Excess distributions can be treated as qualifying distributions for purposes of increasing the charitable deduction of a donor's gift of noncash assets to full fair market value.[255] Such a foundation exercises its right to elect to treat as a current distribution out of corpus any amount distributed in a prior taxable year that has not otherwise been availed for any other purpose (such as a carryover offset to current distribution requirement).

The foundation timing its annual distributions to take advantage of the reduced excise tax on its investment income will also be able to take advantage of excess distribution carryovers.[256] For example, a foundation may accelerate its grant payments to reach the hypothetical payout percentage level necessary to pay a 1 percent, rather than 2 percent, excise tax. The excess qualifying distributions, unreduced by the tax savings, are available in the following year to satisfy the foundation's distribution requirements.

## (c)  Calculating the Tax

A foundation that fails to make the required charitable expenditures in a timely manner is subject to an excise tax of 30 percent on the undistributed amount. The tax is charged for each year or partial year that the deficiency remains *uncorrected*. Essentially, the tax calculation starts on the first late date and continues until a notice of the deficiency is issued by the IRS (but in whole-year increments). This *taxable period* also closes on the date of voluntary payment of the tax.[257]

---

253.  *See* §§ 3.2, 14.3.
254.  *See* § 3.2.
255.  Reg. 53.4942(a)-3(c)(2)(iv).
256.  *See* § 10.2.
257.  Reg. § 53.4942(a)-2(e)(1)(i).

Assume that a calendar-year foundation fails to distribute $100,000 of its distributable amount by December 31, 2014. If the amount is distributed within the first year after the deadline (by December 31, 2015), a 30 percent tax is due. If the correction takes two years, or is not accomplished until the second year after it was due (on or after January 1, 2016), another 30 percent is due, or a total of 60 percent. If the foundation is able to partially correct the deficiency, the tax is assessed only on the amount remaining undistributed at the end of the year. An additional 100 percent tax is triggered if the foundation fails to make up the deficient distributions within 90 days of receiving IRS notification of the problem. The *allowable correction period* is 90 days after the date of mailing of the deficiency notice.[258]

The notice date is critical to calculating the tax. If the deficiency is self-admitted on the face of Form 990-PF, Part XIII or XIV, an accompanying Form 4720 is due to be filed to calculate the tax due. If the deficiency is not self-admitted, the IRS computers may recognize the problem and generate a notice within a few months beyond the return filing date. In the more common situation, the underdistribution is found by the IRS upon examination and the notice is mailed when the examination is completed. The foundation has 90 days from the date of the notice to correct the problem by making grants. If it does not, a second-tier, 100 percent additional penalty tax is imposed. Payment of these taxes is in addition to, not in lieu of, making the required distributions.[259] The termination tax serves as a third-tier tax.[260]

## (d) Abatement of the Tax

**Valuation Mistakes.** Where a private foundation fails to make the required annual charitable distributions due solely to an incorrect valuation of assets, the statutory sanction may be excused. In the interest of being fair, the tax does not apply, and the underdistribution can essentially be corrected if four conditions for abatement listed in the code are satisfied:[261]

1. Failure to value the assets properly was not willful and was due to reasonable cause.

---

258. Prior IRC § 504 provided, in general, that an organization described in IRC § 501(c)(3) would be denied exemption under IRC § 501 for the tax year involved if amounts accumulated out of income during the tax year or any prior tax year and not actually paid out by the end of the tax year are unreasonable in amount or duration in order to carry out the charitable purpose or function constituting the basis for the organization's tax exemption. For instances of unreasonable accumulation, see Rev. Rul. 67-108, 1967-1 C.B. 127; Rev. Rul. 67-106, 1976-1 C.B. 126.

259. Reg. § 53.4942(a)-2(e)(1)(ii).

260. Reg. § 53.4942(a)-2(e)(3). E.g., *Trust Under the Will of Bella Mabury v. Commissioner*, 80 T.C. 718, 733-741 (1983).

261. IRC § 4942(a)(2).

2. The deficiency is distributed as a qualifying distribution by the foundation within 90 days after receipt of IRS notice of deficiency.

3. The foundation notifies the IRS of the mistake by submitting information on its Form 990-PF and recalculating its qualifying distributions.

4. The extra distribution made to correct the deficiency is treated as being distributed in the deficiency year.

To prove that the undervaluation was *not willful* and *due to reasonable cause*, the foundation must show it made all reasonable efforts in good faith to value the assets correctly.[262] A consistently followed system for collecting the necessary information would satisfy this requirement. A foundation with a portfolio of marketable securities might, for example, retain the month-end copy of stock quotations published in the newspaper to use at year-end. In seeking relief of the penalty for undervaluation of assets that have no readily available value, such as real estate or mineral interests, the foundation must explain the reasons that the fair market value was wrong. Reliance on an invalid appraisal prepared by a qualified appraiser with no relationship to the foundation or its disqualified persons, based on full disclosure of information by the foundation, should be considered reasonable.[263]

**Underdistribution Mistakes.**  The IRS has the discretion to abate the first-tier tax, or 30 percent penalty, for distribution mistakes. Thus, a private foundation failing to meet the minimum distribution requirement may be excused from penalty where it can show it intended to comply with the rules. Abatement may be permitted if the foundation is able to prove that:

- The taxable event (the underdistribution) was due to reasonable cause and not to willful neglect.

- The event was corrected within the correction period for such an event.

In any case in which an initial tax is imposed on the undistributed income of a private foundation for any tax year, an additional tax, equal to 100 percent, is imposed on any portion of the income remaining undistributed at the close of the correction period.[264] Where the underdistribution, called the taxable event,

---

262. Reg. § 53.4942(a)-1(c)(1)(ii).
263. IRC § 4942(j)(2).
264. Reg. § 53.4942(a)-1(a)(3). One court held that the IRC § 4942 taxes are constitutional, in that they are not an impermissible extension of congressional taxing power (under U.S. Const. Art. I § 8, clause 1) nor a violation of Const. Art. I § 9, the Fifth Amendment, or the Sixteenth Amendment (*Stanley O. Miller Charitable Fund v. Commissioner*, 89 T.C. 1112 (1987)).

**Exhibit 6.3** Request for Abatement Regarding Underdistribution

---

SAMPLE FOUNDATION                                          # 44-4444444

ATTACHMENT TO FORM 4720

STATEMENT REGARDING UNDERDISTRIBUTION OF INCOME

During the fiscal year ending June 30, 2014, the SAMPLE FOUNDATION (SAMPLE) inadvertently distributed $70,000 less than the required amount. This mistake was discovered when SAMPLE's annual form 990-PF was being prepared by its accountants on October 28, 2014. During the period July 1, 2014, through October 31, 2014, SAMPLE has in fact already distributed more than the deficient amount of $70,000 for charitable purposes.

Each year during June, SAMPLE's accountants are provided an 11-month report of financial activity. The accountants then calculate the distributable amount, compare that amount with the actual payments to date, look at pledges for grants due to be paid, and advise what additional amount, if any, must be paid out. Due to calculation mistakes and a misunderstanding about a particular grant payment, the amount deemed to be distributable was wrong. SAMPLE's officers intended to pay out, and thought they were paying out, the correct amount.

Pursuant to Internal Revenue Code § 4962, SAMPLE respectfully requests that the first-tier § 4942 penalty for underdistribution of income, or initial tax of $21,000, be abated because the underdistribution was due to reasonable cause and without willful neglect. By the time the mistake was discovered four months after SAMPLE's year-end, SAMPLE had made the required distributions and was no longer deficient. Therefore, SAMPLE submits it is entitled to an abatement of the tax because it meets the requirements of § 4962.

I swear that this information is true and correct and that the foundation's underdistribution of income was inadvertent, accidental, and without intention or knowledge on my part or on the part of any of SAMPLE's other officers.

_____

A. B. Sample, President

---

is corrected within the correction period, any additional tax imposed with respect to the event becomes abated.[265]

A private foundation seeks abatement of this penalty by filing Form 4720 along with an explanation of the reasons that the penalty should be forgiven. A suggested explanation for attachment to the form is shown in Exhibit 6.3.

---

265. *See* Chapter 13.

In the authors' experience, the IRS has responded favorably to such requests.[266]

## (e)  Exception for Certain Accumulations

The mandatory payout rules do not apply to a private foundation to the extent that its income is required to be accumulated pursuant to the mandatory terms (as in effect on May 26, 1969, and at all subsequent times) of an instrument executed before May 27, 1969, with respect to the transfer of income-producing property to the private foundation.[267] The exception to this exception, however, is that the rules are applicable where the organization would have been denied tax exemption by reason of former law if that law had not been repealed by the Tax Reform Act of 1969.[268]

The payout rules also do not apply to a private foundation that is prohibited by its governing instrument or other instrument from distributing capital or corpus to the extent the requirements of the section are inconsistent with the prohibition.[269] However, this exception applies only during the pendency of any judicial proceeding by the private foundation that is necessary to reform or to excuse it from compliance with its instrument in order to comply with the mandatory payout rules.[270] The limited applicability of these two exceptions was illustrated by the IRS in 1977.[271]

## § 6.8  HISTORY OF THE MANDATORY DISTRIBUTION REQUIREMENT

Of all the private foundation rules, none has been more extensively revised since its original enactment than these mandatory distribution requirements. The evolution of these revisions is of assistance in understanding the purpose and mechanics of the rules in their contemporary form.

The definition of the minimum amount that must, under the general rules, be distributed by a private foundation was, as noted,[272] originally enacted in 1969 and revised in 1976 and 1981.

---

266. E.g., Tech. Adv. Mem. 200347023 (where a private foundation relied, in good faith, on incorrect legal advice.) More recently, however, the IRS refused to abate first-tier excise taxes assessed due to a private foundation's insufficient payout over a four-year period (since corrected) on the ground that the foundation failed to demonstrate that it acted with reasonable cause (where the foundation relied, in good faith, on incorrect advice from an accountant). Tech. Adv. Mem. 201129050.
267. Reg. § 53.4942(a)-1(b)(2).
268. *See* § 6.3(a).
269. IRC §§ 4942(b), 4942(j)(2); Reg. § 53.4942(a)-1(c)(3).
270. IRC § 4961.
271. Rev. Rul. 77-74, 1977-1 C.B. 352.
272. *See* the introduction to the chapter.

The percentage used to determine a private foundation's minimum investment return was, at the initiation of this requirement, set at 6 percent of noncharitable assets, for tax years beginning in 1970 or 1971, in the case of a private foundation created after May 26, 1969.[273] The Department of the Treasury was authorized to adjust this rate prospectively from time to time, based on changes in money rates and investment yields, using as the standard the 6 percent rate, given rates and yields for 1969. The subsequent applicable percentages were 5.5 percent for tax years beginning in 1972,[274] 5.25 percent for 1973,[275] and 6 percent for 1974[276] and 1975.[277] The rate for 1976 and thereafter was set at 5 percent.[278]

To afford private foundations organized before May 27, 1969, an opportunity to revise their investment and payout practices, a phase-in period with respect to the 6 percent rate was instituted.[279] The minimum payout was 4.125 percent for tax years beginning in 1972,[280] 4.375 percent for tax years beginning in 1973,[281] 5.5 percent for 1974,[282] and 6 percent for 1975. The Department of the Treasury set the applicable percentage for 1976 at 6.75 percent.[283] This was, however, a dual (or alternative) distribution test, in that the amount to be distributed was the greater of a private foundation's minimum investment return (computed using the applicable year's percentage rate) or its adjusted net income.

Congress, as part of enactment of the Tax Reform Act of 1976, lowered the private foundation mandatory distribution rate. It was lowered, for years beginning after December 31, 1975, to the greater of a foundation's adjusted net income or a minimum investment return of 5 percent;[284] this amount was reduced by any taxes on unrelated business income[285] and the excise tax on net investment income.[286] The authority in the Department of the Treasury to annually adjust the rate was eliminated; this change nullified the prospective increase in the applicable percentage for 1976 to 6.75 percent.

---

273. Reg. § 53.4942(a)-2(c)(5)(i)(a).
274. Reg. § 53.4942(a)-2(c)(5)(i)(b); Rev. Rul. 72-625, 1972-2 C.B. 604.
275. Reg. § 53.4942(a)-2(c)(5)(i)(c); Rev. Rul. 73-235, 1973-1 C.B. 519.
276. Reg. § 53.4942(a)-2(c)(5)(i)(d); Rev. Rul. 74-238, 1974-1 C.B. 326.
277. Reg. § 53.4942(a)-2(c)(5)(i)(d); Rev. Rul. 75-270, 1975-2 C.B. 449.
278. Reg. § 53.4942(a)-2(c)(5)(i)(e).
279. Reg. § 53.4942(a)-2(c)(5)(ii).
280. Reg. § 53.4942(a)-2(c)(5)(ii)(b); Rev. Rul. 72-625, 1972-2 C.B. 604.
281. Reg. § 53.4942(a)-2(c)(5)(ii)(c); Rev. Rul. 73-235, 1973-1 C.B. 519.
282. Reg. § 53.4942(a)-2(c)(5)(ii)(d); Rev. Rul. 74-238, 1074-1 C.B. 326.
283. Rev. Rul. 76-193, 1976-1 C.B. 357.
284. Reg. § 53.4942(a)-2(c)(5)(i)(e).
285. *See* Chapter 11.
286. Reg. § 53.4942(a)-2(b)(1)(ii). This excise tax is the subject of Chapter 10.

Thus, under the post-1969, pre-1982 regime, a private foundation had to determine its adjusted net income in computing its annual distributable amount.[287] The contemporary distribution requirement does not utilize the element of a private foundation's adjusted net income.[288] This concept of adjusted net income concept remains in the law, however, because it is used in determining whether a private foundation constitutes a private operating foundation.[289] The term *adjusted net income* means the excess (if any) of the gross

---

287. In this connection, the IRS ruled that repayments of principal received by a private foundation in tax years beginning after 1969, on loans made in prior years to individuals for charitable purposes, were not includible in its gross income to determine its adjusted net income for these purposes; however, payments of interest on the loans were held to be items of adjusted net income (Rev. Rul. 75-443, 1974-2 C.B. 449). Repayments of a loan made by a private foundation need not be treated as gross income where the loan amounts were not used in meeting the private foundation's distribution obligations, and the repayments may be returned to the corpus (Rev. Rul. 77-252, 1977-2 C.B. 390).

The IRS issued two other rulings in this context. In one case, a private foundation receiving annual payments as a beneficiary of a decedent's deferred incentive compensation income plan was advised to include each payment as gross income to the extent that it exceeded the amount attributable to the value of the right to receive the payment on the decedent's date of death (Rev. Rul. 75-442, 1975-2 C.B. 448). In the other instance, the IRS ruled that capital gain dividends received by a private foundation from a regulated investment company (IRC § 851) are excluded from the private foundation's adjusted net income, because the dividends are statutorily treated as long-term capital gains (IRC § 852 (b)(3)(B); Rev. Rul. 73-320, 1973-2 C.B. 385).

Only net short-term capital gains are included in private foundations' gross income for this purpose (IRC § 4942(f)(2)(B)). Thus, the amount of undistributed income is not reduced for long-term capital losses or for short-term capital losses in excess of capital gains (*Stanley O. Miller Charitable Fund v. Commissioner*, 89 T.C. 1112 (1987)). Interest on government obligations that is normally excludible from gross income (under IRC § 103) is included as private foundation gross income. Generally, deductions are limited to ordinary and necessary expenses paid or incurred for the production or collection of gross income, or for the management, conservation, or maintenance of property held for the production of income. Amortizable bond premiums are deductible (to the extent permitted by IRC § 171) (Rev. Rev. 76-248, 1976-1 C.B. 353).

Imputed interest (IRC § 483) is included within this concept of adjusted gross income. However, some private foundations sold property, prior to the enactment of the private foundation rules in 1969, on an installment sales basis that did not call for a stated rate of interest. The Senate Finance Committee, when developing its version of the Tax Reform Act of 1976, regarded as "onerous" the fact that a private foundation had to distribute income imputed to it as the result of pre-1969 sales, thereby causing it to drastically expand its ongoing active program or forcing it to make one-time grants (which, in the case of a private operating foundation, could cause it to fail to meet the income test, in that grant-making does not constitute the "active conduct" of tax-exempt activities (*see* § 3.1) (S. Rep. No. 94-938 (Part 2), 94th Cong., 2d Sess. 89 (1976)). Accordingly, Congress in 1976 changed the definition of adjusted net income for these purposes to exclude imputed interest in the case of sales made before 1969 (IRC § 4942 (f)(2)(D)). However, imputed income from pre-1969 transactions is included in the net investment income of private foundations for purposes of the investment income tax (*see* Chapter 10).

288. *See* § 6.1.

289. *See* § 3.1.

income for the tax year determined with certain income modifications over the sum of the deductions determined with certain deduction modifications.[290] Gross income does not include gifts, grants, or contributions received by a private foundation; it does include income from a functionally related business.[291]

When Congress adopted the Economic Recovery Tax Act of 1981, it revised the private foundation mandatory distribution rules again, causing the requirement to utilize solely the minimum investment return rate of 5 percent. The law on the point was revised in 1981 because of the dramatically high interest rates paid on bonds and other debt instruments during the late 1970s.[292] The previous requirement, that private foundations distribute the entirety of their adjusted net income for charitable purposes, contributed to a rapid erosion of the resources of private foundations[293] and imposed an artificial, distortive pressure on the investment practices of private foundations.[294] (By contrast, other forms of charitable and other tax-exempt organizations were able to take advantage of these high-income yields to buttress their income and asset base and combat inflation.) During these economic conditions, the income payout requirement forced private foundations to either accept damaging erosion of their assets or engage in investment considerations dictated by federal tax rules rather than prudent investing strategies. The first course of action forced a private foundation to distribute its entire income yield; the second course of action forced the foundation to skew its investment decisions to select its holdings largely from those with low current yields, frequently including relatively risky holdings such as growth stocks and commodities.

The revision of the payout rules in 1981—the use of a single percentage standard—was designed to simultaneously enable private foundations to

---

290. IRC § 4942(f)(2); Reg. § 53.4942(a)-2(d)(1)–(4).

291. Reg. § 53.4942(a)-2(d)(1). The concept of the *functionally related business* is the subject of § 7.3.

292. When the mandatory distribution rules were enacted in 1969, income yields were below 5 percent, inflation had averaged between 2 percent and 3 percent during the 1960s, and stocks were appreciating in value more rapidly than inflation. By 1981, interest rates on debt investments (such as Treasury bills and certificates of deposit) ranged from 13 percent to 17 percent, inflation persisted at the 10 percent to 12 percent level, and stock values had declined sharply.

293. Data from The Foundation Center show that the value of the assets of private foundations (taking inflation into account) declined by nearly 30 percent during the period 1972 to 1977. A survey by the Council on Foundations found an additional decline of 11 percent during the period 1977 to 1979. At the close of that decade, one private foundation published a report entitled *Foundations: Scheduled for Extinction?* (Flint, MI: Charles Stewart Mott Foundation, 1981).

294. E.g., Reilly and Skadden, *Private Foundations: The Payout Requirement and Its Effect on Investment and Spending Policies* (1981); Williamson, "Inflation and the Foundation Payout Rate," 22 *Foundation News* 18 (Mar./Apr. 1981); Williamson, "Investment Expectations and the Foundation Payout Rate," 17 *Foundation News* 13 (Jan./Feb. 1976).

adequately support charitable activities currently and allow them to maintain their ability to do so in the future. This law revision meant that private foundations could return to more traditional, prudent investment practices. This process usually entails the definition of specific investment objectives, a forecast of desired economic returns, and the allocation of assets over a range of investment opportunities that are most likely to achieve the desired rate of return consistent with the investor's risk tolerance and income needs. Unlike the conventional investor, however, a private foundation, in its investment program, must take into account not only the mandatory distribution requirement (both the 5 percent payout requirement and the distinction between charitable and noncharitable assets), but also the jeopardizing investment rules[295] and the investment excise tax (which is imposed on net investment income, including capital gain).[296]

Between 1982 and 2003, the IRS Form 990-PF, instructions to the form, and the regulation required that income paid or payable to a foundation by certain trusts be added to the distributable amount, despite the fact that the federal statutory law does not.[297] The Ann Jackson Family Foundation challenged this IRS position and convinced the tax court that the regulation was an "unwarranted extension of a statutory position."[298] A private foundation that is a beneficiary of such a trust has faced a reporting dilemma in view of this controversy. The problem was created when, in an effort to preserve the principal of private foundations, Congress lowered the annual distribution requirement.[299] Prior to 1982, a private foundation with actual income higher than its hypothetical investment return was required to distribute the higher amount rather than the minimum investment return shown in the above formula.[300] Income for this purpose includes income distributions with respect to amounts placed into a split-interest trust after May 26, 1969. After the change, this section became primarily applicable to private operating foundations.[301]

The IRS, in April 2004, announced a Treasury Department intention to amend the regulations to conform with the tax court decision.[302] The notice states that "until further guidance is promulgated, private foundations should compute the distributable amount under section 4942(d) without regard to Treas. Reg. § 53.4942(a)-2(b)(2)." In other words, line 4b of Part XI of

---

295. *See* Chapter 8.
296. *See* Chapter 10.
297. Reg. § 53.4942(a)-2(b)(2). IRS Publication 578, *Tax Information for Private Foundations and Foundation Managers* (last revised in January 1989) also contains this requirement that only applied to amounts placed in trust prior to May 26, 1969.
298. *Ann Jackson Family Foundation v. Commissioner*, 97 T.C. 537 (1991), *aff'd*, 15 F.3d 917 (9th Cir. 1994).
299. IRC § 4942(c).
300. IRC § 4942(f).
301. *See* § 3.1.
302. Notice 2004–36, 2004–19 I.R.B. 889.

Form 990-PF for years 2003 and prior should be ignored. For purposes of calculating the distributable amount, the addition of income distributions from split-interest trusts is not required by the statute. The Treasury Department and the IRS admit that the regulations, unchanged since 1971, are incorrect due to statutory revisions in 1982. The 2004 Form 990-PF omits the line in Part XI on which such trust distributions were previously added to mandatory distributions.

Importantly, the notice anticipated that private foundations that had added such income to their distributable amounts in the past might wish to recompute the current amount to reduce it by trust income previously included. An amended return was not to be filed to reflect the change; instead, the notice suggests "a schedule to show how the information provided on such return varies from prior year returns as filed."

For 2003 tax returns, the notice instructed private foundations omitting the add-back to mark the front page of their return "Filed pursuant to Notice 2004-36." If any penalties had been paid in the past for reasons of a failure to treat such income as currently distributable, Forms 4720 could be amended. Foundations that followed the tax court reasoning and not added such trust amounts to required annual distributions could rest easy that the IRS and Treasury have conceded the correctness of their filing position under the tax code.

A foundation that instead chose to comply with the controversial regulation in past years had an opportunity to reduce its distributable amount. What the notice did not mention was the fact that the recalculation could involve years since 1983. Distributions in excess of the distributable amount are applied to corpus each year and carried forward for five years, a period of time called the *adjustment period*.

# CHAPTER SEVEN

# Excess Business Holdings

## §7.1  GENERAL RULES

A private foundation's ability to own a business—one that is not conducted as an exempt function—is limited by rules concerning *excess business holdings*. The basic rule is that the combined ownership, by a private foundation and those who are disqualified persons with respect to it,[1] of a business enterprise in any form—corporation, partnership, joint venture, sole proprietorship, or other type of unincorporated company—may not exceed 20 percent. There are rules enabling foundations to, without penalty, receive and dispose of excess holdings when the excess is acquired by the foundation by means of a contribution or inheritance subject to limitations on purchasers imposed by the self-dealing rules.[2]

The rationale underlying these rules was summarized as follows:

> Those who wished to use a foundation's stock holdings to acquire or retain business control in some cases were relatively unconcerned about producing income to be used by the foundation for charitable purposes. In fact, they might have become so interested in making a success of the business, or in meeting competition, that most of their attention and interest was devoted to this with the result that what was supposed to be their function, that of carrying on charitable, educational, etc., activities was neglected. Even when such a foundation attains a degree of

---

1.  *See* Chapter 4.
2.  *See* Chapter 5.

independence from its major donor, there is a temptation for its managers to divert their interest to the maintenance and improvement of the business and away from their charitable duties. Where the charitable ownership predominates, the business may be run in a way which unfairly competes with other businesses whose owners must pay taxes on the income that they derive from the businesses. To deal with these problems, Congress concluded it is desirable to limit the extent to which a business may be controlled by a private foundation.[3]

## (a) Definition of Business Enterprise

The term *business enterprise* is broadly defined to include the active conduct of a trade or business, including any activity that is regularly carried on for the production of income from the sale of goods or the performance of services, and that constitutes an unrelated trade or business.[4] Where an activity carried on for profit is an unrelated business, no part of it may be excluded from classification as a business enterprise merely because it does not result in a profit.[5]

A private foundation proposed to build, maintain, and lease a public ice arena to promote the health and welfare of its community and to lessen the burdens of local government.[6] This facility, which will conform to National Hockey League and college rink specifications, will include a pro shop, coffee shop, concession area, day care center, and lounge. It may also include a conference center, gymnastics facility, and an athletic medicine center. This arena will be leased to third parties at a fair rental value rate. The IRS ruled that the development, ownership, and leasing of the arena will further the foundation's charitable purposes; these activities were held to not constitute a business enterprise for excess business holdings rule purposes.[7]

A bond or other evidence of indebtedness is not a holding in a business enterprise unless it is otherwise determined to be an equitable interest in the enterprise.[8] Thus, an ostensible indebtedness will be treated as a business holding if it is essentially an equity holding in disguise. A leasehold interest in real property is not an interest in a business enterprise, even if the rent is based on profits, unless the leasehold interest is an interest in the income or profits of an unrelated trade or business.[9]

---

3. Joint Committee on Internal Revenue Taxation, *General Explanation of the Tax Reform Act of 1969*, 91st Cong., 2d Sess. 41 (1970).
4. Reg. § 53.4943-10(a)(1). The unrelated business income rules are the subject of Chapter 11.
5. *Id.*
6. *See* § 1.5, text accompanied by note 46.
7. Priv. Ltr. Rul. 200532058.
8. Reg. § 53.4943-10(a)(2).
9. *Id.*

## (b)    Passive Income Businesses

The term *business enterprise* does not include a functionally related busi-ness,[10] a program-related investment,[11] or a trade or business of which at least 95 percent of the gross income is derived from passive sources.[12] An alternative to this passive-source gross income rule is a multiyear averaging mechanism.[13] Thus, stock in a passive holding company is not considered a holding in a business enterprise even if the company is controlled by the foundation; the foundation is treated as owning its proportionate share of any interests in a business enterprise held by the company.[14]

The concept of *passive source income* is derived from the unrelated business rules. Thus, passive income includes items considered passive in nature for purposes of those rules,[15] including:

- Dividends, interest, and annuities.

- Royalties, including overriding royalties, whether measured by produc-tion or by gross or taxable income from the property (working interests in mineral properties are active businesses).[16]

- Rental income from real property and from personal property leased with real property, if the rent attributable to the personal property is incidental (less than 50 percent of the total rent).

- Gains or losses from sales, exchanges, or other dispositions of property other than stock in trade held for regular sale to customers.

- Income from the sale of goods, if the seller does not manufacture, produce, physically receive or deliver, negotiate sales of, or keep inven-tories in the goods.[17]

Tax-exempt title-holding companies[18] can be utilized to house passive business operations.[19]

The fact that the unrelated debt-financed income rules[20] may apply to an item of passive income does not alter the character of the income as passive.[21]

---

10. *See* § 7.3.
11. Reg. § 53.4943-10(b). *See* § 8.3.
12. IRC § 4943(d)(3)(B); Reg. § 53.4943-10(c)(1).
13. Reg. § 53.4943-10(c)(1).
14. *Id.*
15. IRC § 512(b)(1), (2), (3), and (5).
16. Priv. Ltr. Rul. 8407095.
17. Reg. § 53.4943-10(c)(2).
18. Organizations that are tax-exempt by reason of IRC § 501(c)(2) or (25).
19. E.g., Priv. Ltr. Rul. 8840055.
20. IRC §§ 512(b)(4), 514.
21. Reg. § 53.4943-10(c)(2).

## (c)   Certain Investment Partnerships

According to the IRS, the term *business enterprise* "may not encompass certain partnerships that engage solely in investment activities,"[22] even though less than 95 percent of the partnership's income may be derived from passive sources.[23] The matter involved the formation and operation of an investment partnership by 15 private foundations, each of which is a disqualified person with respect to the others.[24] The partnership agreement prohibits the admission of partners that are not private foundations; one of the foundations will serve as the managing general partner. An investment management company that provides services to the manager foundation is to provide investment management and administrative services to this investment partnership without charge. Each foundation's investment in and capital commitment to the investment partnership will not exceed 20 percent of the value of its investment portfolio.[25]

The purpose of this investment partnership is to enable each of these private foundations to invest in equity interests in private businesses and private equity funds not otherwise available to them and to achieve greater diversification in investments. The investments generally will be made in other (lower-tier) limited partnerships, to which this investment partnership will subscribe as a limited partner. The investment partnership's gross income from nonpassive sources (such as income from partnerships engaged in an active business) may not exceed 5 percent a year.[26]

The partnership agreement prohibits this investment partnership from making any investments that would cause any of the foundations to be involved in jeopardy investments.[27] The partnership may not directly engage in an operating business. The agreement forbids the partnership from making any investment that would cause the combined interests of any partner and all disqualified persons with respect to that partner in any business enterprise to exceed the permitted business holdings of the partner.[28] The investment partnership will not purchase property from, sell property to, exchange property with, or lease property to or from a disqualified person with respect to any of the foundation partners.[29] The partnership will not receive credit from or extend

---

22. Priv. Ltr. Rul. 199939046.
23. *See* § 7.1(b).
24. *See* § 4.7.
25. *See* § 7.1(d).
26. A foundation in this instance treats its proportionate share of income of this nature as unrelated business income and may have to pay the resulting tax if the underlying property is debt-financed (IRC § 512 (c)(1)). *See* § 11.4.
27. *See* Chapter 8.
28. *See* § 7.2(b).
29. *See* § 5.3.

credit to a disqualified person with respect to any of the foundation partners.[30] The partnership will not purchase or sell investments in an attempt to manipulate the price of the investments to the advantage of a disqualified person.[31]

If this investment partnership were a business enterprise, then the investment of each of the participating foundations would be an excess business holding, because the combined profits interests of each foundation and its disqualified persons would be in excess of 20 percent,[32] and the 2 percent de minimis rule[33] would be inapplicable. The IRS observed that a "strict reading" of the tax regulations would limit the concept of the passive business to organizations receiving at least 95 percent of their gross income from passive sources. Nonetheless, because the partnership's activities will consist of investing in private business, mostly as a limited partner in other limited partnerships, and because limited partnership interests "may represent passive investments," the IRS ruled that the investment partnership will not be treated as a business enterprise for purposes of the excess business holdings rules.

In a buttressing of its position, the IRS reviewed the legislative history of the excess business holdings rules.[34] The agency said that Congress "only sought to prevent private foundations from engaging in active businesses." The IRS observed that a contrary conclusion would prevent a participating private foundation indirectly investing in limited partnership interests through the partnership, even though it could invest in such interests directly. There was, as noted, a representation that the investment partnership would not acquire more than a 20 percent interest in any limited partnership. The IRS said that the "mere interposition" of this investment partnership "should not produce a different result."

The IRS wrote that "this is a situation that calls for the application of the constructive ownership rule." Under this rule,[35] the investment partnership will not hold an impermissible interest in any business enterprise that would result in indirect excess business holding for any of its foundation partners. The IRS concluded that, given that the foundation partners could directly hold these interests in business enterprises, and given that the investment partnership is formed for "valid business reasons," the foundations should be allowed to form and hold interests in the partnership to achieve the same result indirectly.[36]

---

30. *See* § 5.4.
31. *See* § 5.8(a).
32. *See* § 7.1(d), text accompanied by note 44.
33. *Id.*, text accompanied by notes 51–53.
34. E.g., S. Rep. No. 91-552, 91st Cong., 1st Sess. 2066–2072 (1969).
35. *See* § 7.2(c).
36. This type of investment partnership has been the subject of proposed legislation, by which its tax exemption, and terms and conditions of operation, would be prescribed by statute, somewhat along the lines of IRC § 501(f), which is an exempt investment pool for schools, colleges, and universities (*see Tax-Exempt Organizations* § 10.5). The most recent manifestation of this legislative proposal was in the Revenue Reconciliation Act of 1995, which was vetoed.

A foundation's limited partnership interest in the lower tier of a fund-of-funds partnership was found by the IRS to qualify for the "business enterprise" exception and thereby not to be a business holding. The IRS reasoned that limited partner distributions should also be viewed as passive source income, similar to stock dividends.[37] The ruling does not consider the question of whether the income would be treated as unrelated business income.

## (d) Percentage Limitations

The excess business holdings rules generally limit to 20 percent the permitted ownership of a corporation's voting stock or other interest in a business enterprise that may be held by a private foundation and all disqualified persons combined.[38] Thus, as a general rule, a private foundation and its substantial contributors, managers, their family members, and the like cannot collectively own more than 20 percent of a corporation.

Usually ownership of a corporation is accomplished by means of voting stock. For these purposes, the percentage of voting stock held by a person in a corporation is normally determined by reference to the power of stockholders to vote for the election of directors, with treasury stock and stock that is authorized but unissued disregarded.[39]

Where all disqualified persons with respect to a private foundation together do not own more than 20 percent of the voting stock of an incorporated business enterprise, the foundation can own any amount of nonvoting stock.[40] Equity interests that do not have voting power attributable to them are classified as nonvoting stock.[41] Stock carrying contingent voting rights is treated as nonvoting stock until the event triggering the right to vote occurs.[42] (An illustration is preferred stock that can be voted only if dividends are not paid; these shares are considered nonvoting until the voting power is exercisable.)[43]

In the case of a partnership, including a limited partnership, or a joint venture, the terms *profits interest* and *capital interest* are substituted for *voting stock* and *nonvoting stock* respectively.[44] On at least two occasions the IRS

---

37. Priv. Ltr. Rul. 200611034, citing Reg. § 53.4943-10(c)(2).
38. IRC § 4943(c)(2)(A); Reg. §§ 53.4943-1, 53.4943-3(b)(1)(i).
39. Reg. § 53.4943-3(b)(1)(ii).
40. IRC § 4943(c)(2). An illustration of this rule is provided in Priv. Ltr. Rul. 201013072. This percentage can be as high as 35 percent if effective control lies outside the foundation and its disqualified persons (*see* text accompanied by *infra* note 50).
41. Reg. § 53.4943-3(b)(2)(i).
42. Reg. § 53.4943-3(b)(2)(ii).
43. Thus, the intrinsic character of stock, and not any side agreements, determines whether a stock is voting stock. For example, entering into a binding agreement (scripted on the shares and transferable to any purchaser of the shares) not to vote a private foundation's stock does not reduce excess business holdings (e.g., Priv. Ltr. Rul. 9124061).
44. Reg. § 53.4943-3(c)(2).

has indicated that a private foundation's holdings as a limited partner are not equivalent to nonvoting stock.[45] In the case of a sole proprietorship, a private foundation may not have any permitted holdings.[46] For any other unincorporated business or for a trust, the term *beneficial interest* is substituted for *voting stock*, but no amount of an equivalent to nonvoting stock is allowed.[47]

If effective control of a business enterprise can be shown to the satisfaction of the IRS to be elsewhere (i.e., other than by the private foundation and its disqualified persons), a 35 percent limit may be substituted for the 20 percent limit.[48] The term *effective control* means possession of the power, whether direct or indirect, and whether or not actually exercised, to direct or cause the direction of the management and policies of a business enterprise.[49] Effective control can be achieved through ownership of voting stock, the use of voting trusts, contractual arrangements, or otherwise. It is the reality of control that is decisive rather than its form or the means by which it is exercisable. For this 35 percent rule to apply, a private foundation must demonstrate by affirmative proof that some unrelated third party, or group of third parties, does in fact exercise control over the business enterprise involved.[50]

A private foundation must, however, hold, directly or indirectly, more than 2 percent of the voting stock or other value of a business enterprise before either of these limitations becomes applicable.[51] The holdings of related private foundations[52] are aggregated for the purpose of computing this 2 percent amount,[53] so as to preclude the use of multiple private foundations as a means of converting this de minimis rule into a method of evading the excess business holdings rules.

## §7.2 PERMITTED AND EXCESS HOLDINGS

The *permitted business holdings* of a private foundation are those that are within the previously described 20 percent or 35 percent limitations.[54] Thus, *excess business holdings* constitute the amount of stock or other interest in a

---

45. Priv. Ltr. Rul. 8407095; Gen. Coun. Mem. 39195.

46. Reg. § 53.4943-3(c)(3).

47. Reg. § 53.4943-3(c)(4).

48. IRC § 4943(c)(2)(B); Reg. § 53.4943-3(b)(3)(i).

49. Reg. § 53.4943-3(b)(3)(ii).

50. Rev. Rul. 81-111, 1981-1 C.B. 509.

51. IRC § 4943(c)(2)(C); Reg. § 53.4943-3(b)(4). In 1991, the IRS ruled that a private foundation could split the 2 percent *de minimis* holding allotment between itself and a new private foundation formed to receive one-half of the original foundation's assets (Priv. Ltr. Rul. 9117070); following a review of the issue, however, the IRS revoked its ruling in 1993 (Priv. Ltr. Rul. 9333051).

52. *See* § 4.7.

53. Reg. § 53.4943-3(b)(4).

54. *See* § 7.1(d).

business enterprise that a private foundation would have to dispose of by transferring it to a person (other than a disqualified person) in order for the remaining holdings of the foundation in the enterprise to constitute permitted holdings.[55]

## (a) General Rules

When a purchase, by a disqualified person, of stock or other interest in a business enterprise creates an excess business holding, the private foundation involved has 90 days—from the date it knows, or has reason to know, of the event that caused it to have the excess holdings—to dispose of the excess holdings.[56] The penalty taxes[57] are not applied if the holdings are properly reduced within this 90-day period. The period can be extended to include any period during which a foundation is prevented by federal or state securities law from disposing of the excess holdings.[58]

An interest purchased by a private foundation that causes the ownership of a business holding (combined with that of disqualified persons) to exceed the permissible limits must be disposed of immediately, and the foundation is subject to tax. If the foundation had no knowledge, nor any reason to know, that its holdings had become excessive, the 90-day-period rule applies, and the tax is not assessed.[59]

Whether a private foundation is treated as knowing or having reason to know of the acquisition of holdings by a disqualified person depends on the facts and circumstances of each case. Factors to be considered are the fact that the foundation did not discover acquisitions made by disqualified persons through the use of procedures reasonably calculated to discover the holdings, the diversity of foundation holdings, and the existence of large numbers of disqualified persons who have little or no contact with the foundation or its managers.[60]

If a private foundation disposes of an interest in a business enterprise with any material restrictions or conditions that prevent free use of or prevent disposition of the transferred shares, the foundation is treated as owning the interest until the restrictions or conditions are eliminated.[61]

These rules have a complex past. They were initiated in 1969; interests held as of that year were termed *present holdings*.[62] The excess business holdings rules

---

55. IRC § 4943(c)(1); Reg. § 53.4943-3(a)(1).
56. Reg. § 53.4943-2(a)(1)(ii).
57. *See* § 7.4.
58. Reg. § 53.4943-2(a)(1)(iii).
59. Reg. § 53.4943-2(a)(1)(ii).
60. Reg. § 53.4943-2(a)(1)(v).
61. Reg. § 53.4943-2(a)(1)(iv).
62. Reg. § 53.4943-4(d)(1).

did not apply to present interests; a 50 percent limitation applied or, if lower, the actual percentage of holdings.[63] If a private foundation with present holdings reduced its percentage holdings in a business enterprise, it could not thereafter increase the holdings (the *downward rachet rule*); however, if the reduction caused the holdings to fall below the 20 percent (or 35 percent) level, they could be increased to those levels.[64] Any excess ownership held at that time had to be divested by the foundation, with the period of disposition (or phase) being 10, 15, or 20 years, depending on the percentage of combined ownership.[65] These rules, which played out in 1989, caused major dispositions of securities holdings by private foundations during the 1970s and 1980s. An interest received from a trust that was irrevocable as of May 26, 1969, or from a will in effect and not revised since that date remains subject to these divestiture requirements.[66]

## (b)  Partnerships, Trusts, and Proprietorships

The excess business holdings rules often focus on holdings in the form of stock in incorporated businesses. These rules, however, also apply with respect to holdings in unincorporated business entities, such as partnerships, joint ventures, and trusts.[67] In these contexts, the terms identifying the nature of the ownership are different. In a general or limited partnership or a joint venture, the terms *profit interest* and *capital interest* are substituted for *voting stock* and *nonvoting stock*.[68] For trusts, the term *beneficial interest* is used to define ownership.[69]

The interest of a private foundation and its disqualified persons in a partnership is determined using the federal tax law's distributive share concepts.[70] Absent a formal partnership agreement, the private foundation's ownership is measured by the portion of assets that the foundation is entitled to receive on withdrawal or dissolution, whichever is greater.[71]

For example, a private foundation owning 45 percent of a partnership is considered to own 45 percent of the property owned by the partnership; thus, if the partnership owned 50 percent of the outstanding stock of a corporation, the foundation would be treated as owning 22.5 percent of the corporation (50 percent of 45 percent). Therefore, in this example, the foundation would have

---

63. IRC § 4943(c)(4)(A)(i). Also Rev. Rul. 75-25, 1975-1 C.B. 359.
64. IRC § 4943(c)(4)(A)(ii); Reg. § 53.4943-4(d)(4).
65. The tax law is detailed as to these procedures (IRC § 4943(c)(4)(B)–(D); Reg. § 53.4943-4).
66. IRC § 4943(c)(5); Reg. § 53.4943-5.
67. IRC § 4943(c)(3); Reg. § 53.4943-3(c)(1), (2), (4).
68. IRC § 4943(c)(3)(A); Reg. § 53.4943-3(c)(2).
69. IRC § 4943(c)(3)(C); Reg. § 53.4943-3(c)(4).
70. IRC § 704(b).
71. Reg. § 53.4943-3(c)(2).

excess holdings of 2.5 percent, unless the 35 percent limitation was applicable.[72] This may be the case where a foundation holds a limited partnership interest, which normally does not accord the foundation the requisite power to direct or cause the direction of the management and policies of a business enterprise.[73] A right on the part of the limited partner private foundation to veto the general partner's actions may, however, constitute sufficient control to cause the 20 percent limitation to be applicable.[74]

A private foundation may not operate a business enterprise (other than a functionally related or otherwise exempted one) as a sole proprietorship,[75] because that arrangement by definition entails a 100 percent ownership.[76]

### (c)  Constructive Ownership

In computing the holdings of a private foundation or a disqualified person with respect to a private foundation in a business enterprise, any stock or other interest owned, directly or indirectly, by or for a corporation, partnership, estate, or trust is considered as being owned proportionately by or for its shareholders, partners, or beneficiaries.[77] Exempted from this constructive ownership rule (subject to certain exceptions) are holdings of corporations that are engaged in an active trade or business (the *myopia rule*).[78] A passive parent of an affiliated group of active businesses is treated as an active business for these purposes.[79]

Any interest in a business enterprise over which a private foundation or a disqualified person has a power of appointment, exercisable in favor of the foundation or disqualified person, is treated as owned by the foundation or disqualified person holding the power of appointment.

Stock in a split-interest trust[80] is not considered constructively owned by a private foundation where the foundation's sole relationship with the trust is that it has an income or remainder interest in it.[81]

---

72. *See* § 7.1(c), text accompanied by note 48.
73. Reg. § 53.4943-3(b)(3)(ii).
74. Priv. Ltr. Rul. 9250039.
75. IRC § 4943(c)(3)(B); Reg. § 53.4943-3(c)(3).
76. If a private foundation owns a sole proprietorship and subsequently divests itself of a portion of the interest in it (so that the foundation has less than a 100 percent interest in the equity of the business enterprise), the resulting business enterprise is treated as a partnership (Reg. § 53.4943-10(e)).
77. IRC § 4943(d)(1); Reg. § 53.4943-8(a), (b), (d).
78. Reg. § 53.4943-8(c)(1)–(3).
79. Reg. §§ 53.4943-8(c)(4), 53.4943-10(c)(3).
80. *See* § 3.7.
81. IRC § 4943(d)(1); Reg. § 53.4943-8(b)(2).

## (d) Disposition Periods

If a private foundation obtains holdings in a business enterprise *other than by purchase* by the foundation or by disqualified persons with respect to it, and the additional holdings would result in the foundation's having excess business holdings, the foundation has five years to reduce these holdings to permissible levels.[82] This is because the excess holdings (or an increase in excess holdings) resulting from the transaction are treated as being held by a disqualified person—rather than by the foundation—during the five-year period beginning on the date the foundation obtained the holdings.

Acquisitions by gift, devise, bequest, legacy, or intestate succession are the subjects of this five-year rule,[83] as are certain increases in holdings in a business enterprise that are the result of a readjustment of the enterprise.[84] In the case of an acquisition of holdings in a business enterprise by a private foundation pursuant to the terms of a will or trust, the five-year period does not commence until the date on which the distribution of the holdings from the estate or trust occurs.[85]

A newly created private foundation was allowed five years to dispose of its for-profit subsidiaries purchased during the time it operated as the parent organization (classified as a supporting organization) in a healthcare conglomerate.[86] It was not treated as having acquired the subsidiary shares on the date it converted to a private foundation, but instead at the time of purchase, while it was a supporting organization. The shares were treated as a gratuitously transferred holding.

This five-year rule does not apply to any transfer of holdings in a business enterprise by one private foundation to another private foundation that is related to the first foundation.[87] The rule does not apply to an increase in the holdings of a private foundation in a business enterprise that is part of a plan by which disqualified persons will purchase additional holdings in the same enterprise during the five-year period beginning on the date of the change (e.g., for the purpose of maintaining control of the enterprise).[88] The purchase of holdings by an entity whose holdings are treated as constructively owned by a private foundation, its disqualified persons, or both[89] is treated as a purchase by

---

82. IRC § 4943(c)(6); Reg. § 53.4943-6(a)(1).
83. Reg. § 53.4943-6(a)(2).
84. Reg. § 53.4943-6(d). A *readjustment* may be a merger or consolidation, a recapitalization, an acquisition of stock or assets, a transfer of assets, a change in identity, form, or place of organization, a redemption, or a liquidating distribution (Reg. § 53.4943-7(d)(1)).
85. Reg. § 53.4943-6(b)(1).
86. Priv. Ltr. Rul. 9852023. Also *see* § 10.4(c).
87. Reg. § 53.4943-6(c)(1). *See* § 4.8.
88. Reg. § 53.4943-6(c)(2).
89. *See* text accompanied by *supra* notes 56–58.

a disqualified person if the foundation, its disqualified persons, or both have effective control of the entity or otherwise can control the purchase.[90]

If a private foundation, its disqualified persons, or both hold an interest in specific property under the terms of a will or trust, and if the foundation and/or its disqualified persons agree to the substitution of holdings in a business enterprise for the property, the holdings are regarded as a purchase by a disqualified person.[91]

When a private foundation has a program-related investment (and thus does not have an interest in a business enterprise)[92] and subsequently the investment fails to qualify as a program-related one (so that the holding becomes an interest in a business enterprise), for purposes of this five-year rule, the interest becomes one acquired other than by purchase as of the date of nonqualification.[93] A similar rule applies with respect to passive holdings[94] and to other circumstances in which an interest not originally a business enterprise becomes a business enterprise.[95]

The IRS has the authority to allow an additional five-year period for the disposition of excess business holdings in the case of an "unusually large gift or bequest of diverse business holdings or holdings with complex corporate structures" if:

- The private foundation establishes that diligent efforts to dispose of the holdings were made within the initial five-year period and disposition within the initial five-year period was not possible (except at a price substantially below fair market value) by reason of the size and complexity or diversity of the holdings.

- Before the close of the initial five-year period, the private foundation submits to the IRS a plan for disposition of all of the excess business holdings involved in the extension, submits the plan to the appropriate state attorney general or similar official, and submits to the IRS any response received by the foundation from the state official to the plan during the initial five-year period.

- The IRS determines that the plan can reasonably be expected to be carried out before the close of the extension period.[96]

Private letter rulings illustrate situations in which the IRS has granted extensions of this nature for private foundations that have made the requisite

---

90. Reg. § 53.4943-6(c)(3).
91. Reg. § 53.4943-6(c)(4).
92. *See* text accompanied by *supra* note 8.
93. Reg. § 53.4943-10(d)(1).
94. Reg. § 53.4943-10(d)(2)(i). *See* text accompanied by *supra* note 10.
95. Reg. § 53.4943-10(d)(2)(ii).
96. IRC § 4943(c)(7).

diligent effort.[97] A plan developed by an independent financial consultant to assist a private foundation in selling its holdings, in conjunction with the substantial contributor's family members who owned the same holdings, was approved by the IRS.[98] Likewise, the IRS granted the extension of time, where a foundation made "diligent and continuous" efforts to sell real estate but was impeded by the need for substantial capital improvements and conversions in order to secure a purchaser.[99] Further, a foundation garnered this extension of time where disposition of the foundation's interest in a business during the initial five-year period was not feasible and an investment banker advised the foundation that the interests in the enterprise should be able to be sold for their true value over the coming three to four years.[100] The IRS, by contrast, concluded that a private foundation was not adequately diligent and thus denied a request for an extension.[101]

## § 7.3  FUNCTIONALLY RELATED BUSINESSES

The taxes on excess business holdings do not apply with respect to holdings in a *functionally related business*.[102] This type of business is not considered a *business enterprise*.[103] A functionally related business is a business or activity:

- The conduct of which is substantially related (aside from the mere provision of funds for the tax-exempt purpose) to the exercise or performance by the private foundation of its charitable, educational, or other tax-exempt purpose,

- In which substantially all the work is performed for the foundation without compensation,[104]

- Carried on by the foundation primarily for the convenience of its employees, members, patients, visitors, or students (such as a cafeteria or shop operated for a hospital or museum),

- That consists of the selling of merchandise, substantially all of which has been received by the foundation as contributions, or

- Carried on within a larger aggregate of similar activities or within a larger complex of other endeavors that is related to the tax-exempt purposes of the foundation (other than the need to simply provide funds for these purposes).[105]

---

97. E.g., Priv. Ltr. Rul. 8508114.
98. Priv. Ltr. Rul. 9115061.
99. Priv. Ltr. Rul. 200332020.
100. Priv. Ltr. Rul. 200438042.
101. Priv. Ltr. Rul. 9029067.
102. IRC § 4942(j)(4); Reg. § 53.4943-10(b).
103. IRC § 4943(d)(3)(A).
104. Rev. Rul. 76-85, 1976-1 C.B. 357.
105. Reg. § 53.4942(a)-2(c)(3)(iii).

As an example of the first of these types of businesses, the IRS concluded that a music publishing company that concentrated on classical music was related to the purposes of a private foundation promoting music education and the choice of music as a career, and thus was a functionally related business.[106] Likewise, a racetrack and a campground were ruled by the IRS to constitute functionally related businesses, inasmuch as they were conducted in conjunction with a museum operated by a private foundation.[107] Similarly, a farm in a foreign country, previously conducted as a for-profit operation by the founder of a private foundation, became operated by the foundation after his death as an exempt demonstration project and thus a functionally related business.[108] Also, a grant by a private foundation to a for-profit corporation for the purpose of funding a medical malpractice reinsurance program, to enable physicians in an area to continue to practice, constituted a qualifying distribution because the reinsurance company was a functionally related business.[109]

Likewise, a supporting organization[110] functioning as a qualified scholarship funding corporation made an election[111] to transfer all of its student loan notes to a taxable corporation in exchange for all of the corporation's senior stock and operated thereafter as a private foundation; the IRS ruled that the holding of this stock is a functionally related business.[112] Moreover, the IRS ruled that a taxable subsidiary of a private foundation, formed to provide consulting services to other foundations and exempt organizations about program-related and other investments, to assist in locating investors for community development venture capital funds or rural business investment companies, to provide certain asset management services, and to manage a public mutual fund to facilitate investments in public companies the business practices of which support the foundation's mission, is a functionally related business.[113] This latter ruling, however, was revoked by the IRS without explanation.[114]

In another instance, an artist created a for-profit corporation to house his "artistic enterprise." This corporation acquired and stored the materials used by the artist in the creation of his artwork; handled the creation, fabrication, shipment, storage, and insurance of this work; and managed its sale, reproduction, and licensing. The artist died; all of the stock of this corporation is to be

---

106. Priv. Ltr. Rul. 8927031. *See* § 11.1(c).
107. Priv. Ltr. Rul. 200202077.
108. Priv. Ltr. Rul. 200343027.
109. Priv. Ltr. Rul. 200347017.
110. *See* § 15.7.
111. IRC § 150(d)(3).
112. Priv. Ltr. Rul. 200434028.
113. Priv. Ltr. Rul. 200709065.
114. Priv. Ltr. Rul. 201006032.

transferred to a private operating foundation established by the artist. The function of the corporation will change to curatorial activities and management of the artist's legacy. The foundation will use these resources to increase public exposure and understanding of the broad scope of this artist's work, advance scholarship of his work, and encourage artists' involvement in civic issues by showing that art can change the world. The IRS ruled that the operations of this corporation are a functionally related business, so that the foundation's holding of the stock will not be excess business holdings.[115]

In what apparently is the sole IRS ruling on the point, the IRS ruled that a private foundation can have a functionally related business in the form of a partial ownership of a for-profit business.[116] The foundation in this instance promoted the cause of music education and encouraged the choice of music as a profession. It held 80 percent of the stock of a music publishing company that concentrated its activities in the field of classical and other serious music, publishing and distributing concert music and instructional materials. This publisher published the works of little-known composers. Losses were incurred from these activities, which were subsidized by the functions of acting as a major U.S. distributor of domestic and foreign catalogs representing serious and educational music publishers.[117]

These rules may be utilized as part of a plan to eliminate excess business holdings. For example, a private foundation developed a restructuring plan to enable it to reduce its interests in the voting stock of various companies, held by a single-member limited liability company (a disregarded entity,[118] to permissible levels. The core of this plan was placement of 80 percent of this stock with public charities. The companies were recapitalized, so that the foundation owns, by means of this limited liability company (considered a holding company), 100 percent of a class of stock entitled to elect 20 percent, and zero percent of a class of stock entitled to elect 80 percent, of the companies' directors. The voting stock was designed so that if it or any of its disqualified persons (or anyone who becomes a disqualified person) acquires a share, it automatically converts into nonvoting stock. Additionally, owners of the voting stock are entitled to vote for only one of five directors, so that any increase in the foundation's equity in the

---

115. Priv. Ltr. Rul. 201323029.

116. Priv. Ltr. Rul. 8930047.

117. Given the development of the commerciality doctrine (*see Tax-Exempt Organizations* § 4.10) over recent years, the ongoing validity of this ruling may be in some doubt. The catalog distribution function is likely to be commercial by today's standards, if only because, presumably, the publishers were for-profit businesses. Or, the IRS would assert impermissible private benefit (*see* § 5.2). Even so, a business more commercial in nature than this one may not qualify the partial ownership of it by a private foundation as a functionally related business. This may be the basis for the ruling referenced in *infra* note 119.

118. *See Tax-Exempt Organizations* § 4.1(b)(i).

companies will not result in an increase in any voting rights. The IRS ruled that this foundation timely shed sufficient holdings in the companies' stock to avoid excess business holdings penalties and that the holding company, owning facilities that are used for charitable purposes, is a functionally related business.[119]

## §7.4 RULES APPLICABLE TO CERTAIN SUPPORTING ORGANIZATIONS

The excess business holdings rules are applicable to Type III supporting organizations, other than functionally integrated Type III supporting organizations.[120] In applying these rules, the term *disqualified person* is defined under the intermediate sanctions rules and includes substantial contributors, related persons, and any organization that is effectively controlled by the same person or persons who control the supporting organization or any organization substantially all of the contributions to which were made by the same person or persons who made substantially all of the contributions to the supporting organization.[121]

These rules also apply to a Type II supporting organization[122] if the organization accepts a contribution from a person (other than a public charity, that is not a supporting organization) who controls, either alone or with family members and/or certain controlled entities, the governing body of a supported organization of the supporting organization.[123] Nonetheless, the IRS has the authority to not impose the excess business holdings rules on a supporting organization if the organization establishes that the holdings are consistent with the organization's tax-exempt status.[124]

## §7.5 RULES APPLICABLE TO DONOR-ADVISED FUNDS

The excess business holdings rules are applicable to donor-advised funds.[125] For this purpose, the term *disqualified person* means, with respect to a donor-advised fund, a donor, a donor advisor, member of the family of either, or a 35 percent controlled entity of any of these persons.[126]

---

119. Priv. Ltr. Rul. 200825050.
120. IRC § 4943(f)(1), 3(A). *See* §§ 15.7, 15.7(g).
121. IRC § 4943(f)(4).
122. *See* § 15.7(f).
123. IRC § 4943(f)(1), (3)(B). Temporary standards for determining *control* in this context were provided by the IRS (Notice 2006-109, 2006-51 I.R.B. 1121 § 3.02).
124. IRC § 4943(f)(2).
125. IRC § 4943(e)(1). *See* Chapter 16, particularly § 16.9.
126. IRC § 4943(e)(2). An illustration of application of the excess business holdings rules in this context is in Priv. Ltr. Rul. 201311035.

# §7.6 EXCISE TAXES ON EXCESS HOLDINGS

An initial excise tax is imposed on a private foundation in an instance of excess business holdings in a business enterprise for each tax year that ends during the taxable period.[127] The amount of this tax is 10 percent of the total value of all of the foundation's excess business holdings in each of its business enterprises.[128] This tax is determined using the greatest value of the foundation's excess holdings in the enterprise during the year.[129] Form 4720 is used to calculate and report the tax due. The valuation is determined under the estate tax rules.[130]

The *taxable period* is the period beginning with the first day on which there are excess holdings and ending on the earliest of the following dates:

- The date on which the IRS mails a notice of deficiency with respect to the initial tax[131] in respect of the excess holdings.

- The date on which the excess holding is eliminated.

- The date on which the initial tax in respect of the excess holdings is assessed.[132]

If the deficiency is self-admitted by filing Form 4720, the period ends when the return is filed.

The IRS has the discretionary authority to abate this initial tax where the private foundation establishes that the violation was due to reasonable cause and not to willful neglect, and timely corrects the violation.[133]

If the initial tax is imposed and the excess business holdings are not disposed of by the close of the taxable period, an additional tax is imposed on the private foundation.[134] The amount of this tax is 200 percent of the value of the excess business holdings.[135]

---

127. IRC § 4943(a)(1). This tax is also known as a *first-tier tax* (IRC § 4963(a); Reg. § 53.4963-1(a)).
128. *Id.*; Reg. § 53.4943-2(a)(1)(i).
129. IRC § 4943(a)(2); Reg. § 53.4943-2(a)(2).
130. Reg. § 53.4943-2(a)(1)(i).
131. IRC § 6212.
132. IRC § 4943(d)(2); Reg. § 53.4943-9(a)(1).
133. IRC § 4962. In one instance, the IRS declined to abate initial taxes imposed on a private foundation, in an amount in excess of $200,000, for excess business holdings because of a lack of showing reasonable cause (Tech. Adv. Mem. 9424004). In another instance, however, the IRS abated the tax, where a private foundation relied, in good faith, on incorrect legal advice (Tech. Adv. Mem. 200347023). *See* Exhibit 6.3 for an example of a letter requesting abatement.
134. IRC § 4943 (b). This tax is also known as a *second-tier tax* (IRC § 4963(b); Reg. § 53.4963-1(b)).
135. *Id.*; Reg. § 53.4943-2(b).

The additional taxes are imposed at the end of the taxable period. Where the act or failure to act that gave rise to the additional tax is corrected within the correction period, the tax will not be assessed, or if assessed will be abated, or if collected will be credited or refunded.[136] The *correction period* is the period beginning on the date on which the *taxable event* occurs and ending 90 days after the date of mailing of a notice of deficiency with respect to the additional tax imposed on the event, extended by any period in which a deficiency cannot be assessed[137] and any other period that the IRS determines is reasonable and necessary to bring about correction of the taxable event.[138] In this setting, a taxable event is an act or failure to act giving rise to liability for tax under the excess business holdings rules.[139] This event occurs on the first day on which there are excess business holdings.[140] *Correction* means complete elimination of the excess holdings.[141]

The collection period is suspended during any litigation.[142]

The termination taxes[143] serve as third-tier taxes.

136. IRC § 4961(a); Reg. § 53.4961-1.
137. IRC § 6213(a).
138. IRC § 4963(e)(1); Reg. § 53.4963-1(e)(1).
139. IRC § 4963(c); Reg. § 53.4963-1(c).
140. IRC § 4963(e)(2)(B); Reg. § 53.4963-1(e)(7)(ii).
141. IRC § 4963(d)(2)(B); Reg. § 53.4963-1(d)(2)(ii).
142. IRC § 4961(c); Reg. § 53.4961-2.
143. *See* § 13.3.

# CHAPTER EIGHT

# Jeopardizing Investments

A private foundation has limitations—albeit not particularly stringent ones—on its investment options. Basically, investments that jeopardize a foundation's corpus are not permitted. Investments of this nature are termed *jeopardizing investments.* The rationale underlying these rules was summarized as follows:

> The grant of current tax benefits to donors and exempt organizations usually is justified on the basis that charity will benefit from the gifts. However, if the organization's assets are used in a way which jeopardizes their use for the organization's exempt purpose, this result is not obtained. Prior law recognized this concept in the case of income, but not in the case of an organization's principal.[1]

Under prior law, a private foundation manager might invest the assets in warrants, commodity futures, and options, or might purchase on margin or otherwise expose the corpus of the foundation to risk of loss without being subject to sanction. (In one case, however, a court held that the consistent practice of making these investments constituted operation of the foundation for a substantial nonexempt purpose and would result in loss of tax exemption.)

---

1. Joint Committee on Internal Revenue Taxation, *General Explanation of Tax Reform Act of 1969*, 91st Cong., 2d Sess. 46 (1970).

The purpose, then, of these jeopardizing investment rules is to shield foundation assets from a high degree of risk, so as to maximize both capital and income available for charitable purposes. This body of federal law generally parallels that of state law, where the directors and trustees of private foundations have a fiduciary responsibility to safeguard a charitable entity's assets on behalf of its charitable constituency by following prudent investor standards.

## §8.1 GENERAL RULES

A private foundation cannot invest any amount (income or principal) in a manner that would jeopardize the carrying out of any of its tax-exempt purposes.[2] The statute is silent as to what constitutes this type of investment, other than to exclude from the concept investments that are program-related ones.[3] The regulations state, however, that an investment is considered to jeopardize the carrying out of the tax-exempt purposes of a private foundation if it is determined that the foundation managers, in making the investment, failed to exercise ordinary business care and prudence, under the facts and circumstances prevailing at the time the investment was made, in providing for the long- and short-term financial needs of the private foundation to carry out its exempt purposes.[4] Congress contemplated that the determination as to whether investments jeopardize the carrying out of a private foundation's charitable purposes is to be made as of the time of the investment, in accordance with the prudent trustee approach,[5] and not subsequently on the basis of hindsight.

A determination as to whether the making of a particular investment jeopardizes the tax-exempt purposes of a private foundation is to be made on an investment-by-investment basis, in each case taking into account the private foundation's portfolio as a whole. It is considered prudent for the foundation managers to take into account the expected returns (income and appreciation of capital), the risks of rising and falling price levels, and the need for diversification within the investment portfolio. As to this third criterion, a private foundation manager should consider the type of security involved, the type of industry, the maturity of the company, the degree of risk, and the potential for return. To avoid the imposition of the applicable penalty tax, however, a careful analysis of potential investments must be made and good business judgment must be exercised.[6]

---

2. IRC § 4944(a)(1).
3. *See* § 8.3.
4. Reg. § 53.4944-1(a)(2)(i). Thus, where a private foundation and its managers took reasonable measures, and exercised ordinary business care and prudence prior to entering into the investment, the jeopardizing investment excise taxes (*see* § 8.4) can be avoided (e.g., Tech. Adv. Mem. 200218038).
5. S. Rep. No. 91-552, 91st Cong., 1st Sess. 46 (1969).
6. Reg. § 53.4944-1(a)(2)(i).

Once it has been ascertained that an investment does not jeopardize the carrying out of a private foundation's tax-exempt purposes, the investment is never considered to jeopardize the carrying out of exempt purposes, even though, as a result of the investment, the private foundation subsequently realizes a loss.[7]

## (a) Defining *Jeopardy*

No category of investments is treated as a per se violation of these rules. However, the types or methods of investment that are closely scrutinized to determine whether foundation managers have met the requisite standard of care and prudence include trading in securities on margin, trading in commodity futures, investments in oil and gas syndications, the purchase of puts, calls, and straddles, the purchase of warrants, and selling short. More latitude is permissible in today's sophisticated financial markets, which were not anticipated when the regulations were written in 1970. In 1992, the American Law Institute revised its *Restatement of the Law, Trusts—Prudent Investor Rule*,[8] containing the basic rules governing the investment of trust assets. This update is a useful guide that reflects modern investment concepts and practices. The *prudent investor rule* recognizes that return on investment is related to risk, that risk includes the risk of deterioration of real return owing to inflation, and that the risk/return relationship must be taken into account in managing trust assets.

The IRS has made only one public determination as to whether an investment constitutes a jeopardizing investment. This occurred where the IRS considered a situation involving the contribution to a private foundation of a whole-life insurance policy, which was subject to a policy loan, by a donor (the insured) who at the time of the gift had a life expectancy of 10 years. The private foundation did not surrender the policy for its cash value but continued to pay the annual premiums and interest due on the policy and the loan. Finding that the combined premium and interest payments were such that, by the end of eight years, the private foundation would have invested a greater amount in premiums and interest than it could receive as a return on the investment (as insurance proceeds upon the death of the insured), the IRS concluded that "the foundation managers, by investing at the projected rate of return prevailing at the time of the investment, failed to exercise ordinary business care and prudence in providing for the long-term and short-term financial needs of the foundation in carrying out its exempt purposes." Therefore, under the circumstances, the IRS held that each payment made by the private foundation

---

7. *Id.*
8. American Law Institute Publishers, St. Paul, Minn.; *see* § 8.2.

for a premium on the policy and interest on the policy loan was a jeopardizing investment.[9]

In a hospital reorganization,[10] the IRS considered whether the for-profit subsidiaries of a support organization converting to private foundation status were in jeopardy. There seemed to be no question but that the closely held insurance company, health maintenance organization, and practice management company were risky ventures. The IRS answer to whether the now-private foundation's continued ownership would be considered to have made the investments was no. The for-profit subsidiaries were created by the supporting organization before it became a private foundation, so there was no penalty. Under excess business holdings provisions, the shares would, however, be required to be distributed.[11]

The purchase of gold stocks to protect a portfolio as a hedge against inflation was not treated as jeopardizing, despite a net loss of $7,000 on a $14,500 investment. The private foundation involved bought the shares over three years; it made money on one block and lost on two others. The ruling noted that the foundation had realized $31,000 in gains and $23,000 in dividends during the same period on its whole portfolio. The portfolio performance as a whole was found to enable the foundation to carry out its purposes, and the investments were found not to be jeopardizing.[12] Selling options against the foundation's portfolio in a "covered option trading" program is considered to be a prudent way to enhance yield without risk. Conceivably, failure to conduct this type of program could be considered to create a jeopardizing investment.

A "managed commodity trading program" was found to give diversity to a private foundation's marketable security portfolio and not to be a jeopardizing investment. Since commodity futures have little or no correlation to the stock market, the added diversity may provide less risk for the foundation's overall investment. The foundation proposed to invest 10 percent of its portfolio.[13]

In one case, the manager of a private foundation invested the entire corpus of the foundation in a Bahamian bank without inquiring into the integrity of the bank. Unknown to the manager was the fact that the bank's license to do business had been revoked, as had its charter. Interest payments to the foundation were irregular. The IRS concluded, and a court agreed, that the investment was a jeopardizing one.[14] In another case, investment of nearly all of a foundation's assets in a single partnership was ruled not to be a jeopardizing investment because the partnership's assets were diversified.[15]

---

9. Rev. Rul. 80-133, 1980-1 C.B. 258.
10. Priv. Ltr. Rul. 9852023.
11. *See* § 7.1.
12. Priv. Ltr. Rul. 8718006.
13. Priv. Ltr. Rul. 9237035.
14. *Thorne v. Commissioner*, 99 T.C. 67 (1992).
15. Priv. Ltr. Rul. 200318069.

A limited partnership trading in the futures and forward markets was found not to be a jeopardizing investment in the first private ruling on the subject since 1992 (the only published ruling was in 1980).[16] Even though the foundation invested a "significant amount" of its total assets (numbers not disclosed), the investment was found not to be jeopardizing. The examining agent had argued the foundation could have received a better return with less risk in another investment vehicle. Nonetheless, the IRS found that the foundation managers took reasonable measures and exercised ordinary business care and prudence prior to entering into the partnership based on these facts:

- Foundation managers were actively involved in establishing the partnership and choosing the four different advisors to make allocations to counterbalance the investments.

- Special conditions were negotiated that allowed the foundation to withdraw its funds at any time on written notice prior to the end of the normal term of the partnership.

- Two separate legal opinions concluding the establishment of the partnership was not a jeopardizing investment had been secured by the foundation prior to making the investment.

- There was no relationship among the foundation, its managers, or the chosen investment advisors that would have been furthered by the investment.

This ruling is frustrating. The facts seem to indicate that the foundation placed a substantial portion of its assets in high-risk investment. The IRS found that:

> Neither of these elements [big portion of assets and high risk] are necessarily dispositive of the issue of whether a jeopardizing investment was present. Consideration must be given at the time the investment is made and merely because the end result is not as beneficial to the financial interests of a private foundation as another investment might have been is not grounds in itself for finding that a jeopardizing investment was made. Nor should the percent of assets invested in one investment area be a sole consideration. Diversification is as being one factor to be considered. The determination as to whether something is a jeopardizing investment should be made on an investment-by-investment inquiry based on the prevailing facts and circumstances taking into account the foundation's portfolio as a whole. The key element is whether the foundation managers exercised ordinary business care and prudence.[17]

---

16. Tech. Adv. Mem. 200218038.
17. Reg. § 53.4941-1(a)(2)(i)

In finding the partnership investment not to be jeopardizing, the IRS concluded the key element above was present. The fact that the managers relied on the opinion of outside counsel evidenced their exercise of ordinary business care and prudence. The IRS considered a situation where a private foundation wanted to accept a contribution of a working interest in an oil and gas exploration and development venture. There was no public market for sale of this interest; any liquidation of it would entail sale to the other investors in the project at a substantial discount. Additionally, the project had been highly profitable and the foundation's interest would represent only 1 percent of the venture. The interest was not itself a jeopardizing investment because the foundation received it without consideration, or in other words, did not make an investment.[18] The foundation was, however, subject to calls for capital and payment of expenses in connection with its interest. The IRS did not consider the question of whether such amounts paid by the foundation subsequent to the gift might result in a jeopardizing investment.

The IRS ruled that "approval of an investment procedure governing investments to be made in the future is not possible."[19] This position reflects the fact that advance approval of investment procedures would constitute a determination prior to the investment, would not be on an investment-by-investment basis, and would necessarily preclude application of the "prudent trustee" approach. The IRS, however, will rule as to a *currently proposed investment.*[20]

In general, if a private foundation changes the form or terms of an investment, it is considered to have entered into a new investment on the date of the change. Thus, a determination as to whether the change in the investment causes the investment to be a jeopardizing one is made as of that time.[21]

The IRS occasionally issues private letter rulings as to whether an investment constitutes a jeopardizing investment.[22]

## (b) Donated Assets

The jeopardizing investment rules do not apply to investments made by a person who later transferred them as gifts to a private foundation.[23] Further,

---

18. Priv. Ltr. Rul. 200621032.
19. Rev. Rul. 74-316, 1974-2 C.B. 389.
20. In one instance, the IRS ruled that *nontraditional investments* by a private foundation in four partnerships would not be jeopardizing investments, because the amount of the investment in each partnership would be only 1 percent of the foundation's investment portfolio, there was a diversity of investments among the partnerships, and the investments were based on professional advice; the IRS also approved of an investment by the foundation in a market neutral fund (Priv. Ltr. Rul. 9451067).
21. Reg. § 53.4944-1(a)(2)(iii).
22. E.g., Priv. Ltr. Rul. 200637041.
23. Reg. § 53.4944-1(a)(2)(ii)(a).

these rules do not apply to an investment that is acquired by a private foundation solely as a result of a corporate reorganization.[24] If a foundation furnishes any consideration to a person in connection with this type of transfer, the foundation is treated as having made an investment in the amount of the consideration. Moreover, these rules are inapplicable to investments made before January 1, 1970, unless the form or terms of the investments are later changed or they are exchanged for other investments.[25] Essentially, the foundation is not treated as having made the investment. Though the excess business holding rules might require disposition of such investment, the jeopardizing investment penalty is not imposed.

In one instance, an estate (the decedent being the founder of a foundation) proposed to gratuitously transfer assets to the foundation. The IRS ruled that since the foundation, in acquiring these assets, was not incurring any obligation to use its resources in the future in connection with maintenance of these assets and (at least with respect to one of the assets) it would be "in a position in which it only [stood] to gain and [had] nothing to lose," the jeopardy investment rules would not be implicated.[26]

The private foundation rules are not exclusive. For example, if a private foundation purchases a sole proprietorship in a business enterprise, it may be liable for tax under the excess business holdings rules[27] as well as the rules pertaining to jeopardizing investments.[28]

# §8.2  PRUDENT INVESTMENTS

The jeopardizing investment rules do not exempt or relieve any person from compliance with any federal or state law imposing any obligation, duty, responsibility, or other standard of conduct with respect to the operation or administration of an organization or trust to which this body of law applies. Nor does any state law exempt or relieve any person from any obligation, duty, responsibility, or other standard of conduct provided in these rules.[29] In choosing prudent investments, foundation managers must take into account their need to meet the mandatory charitable distribution rules.[30]

The managers of a private foundation's investments can be guided by the *prudent investor* rules in evaluating proposed investments for jeopardy. An

---

24. Reg. § 53.4944-6.
25. Reg. § 53.4944-1(a)(2)(ii)(b). The corporate reorganization must be one described in IRC § 368(a).
26. Priv. Ltr. Rul. 9614002.
27. *See* Chapter 7.
28. Reg. § 53.4944-1(a)(2)(iv).
29. Reg. § 53.4944-1(a)(2)(i).
30. *See* § 6.7. As investment returns vary throughout the years since 1969, the annual payout percentage has varied. In response to the increase in returns during the late 1990s, there were suggestions to raise the rate; in 2002, there were requests that it be reduced.

investment policy following these rules should theoretically prevent the making of a jeopardizing investment. These standards are compiled by the American Bar Association and were formerly referred to as the *prudent man rules*.[31]

These standards state that "a trustee is under a duty to the beneficiaries to invest and manage the funds of the trust as a prudent investor would, in light of the purposes, terms, distribution requirements, and other circumstances of the trust."[32] The *business judgment rule* requires essentially the same standard for nonprofit corporations and trustees in regard to the management of endowment funds and restricted gifts or bequests.[33]

The prudent investor rules have been codified and adopted by many states. The Uniform Prudent Investor Act was finalized in 1995 and is applicable to trusts. The Uniform Management of Institutional Funds Act (UMIFA) was finalized in 1972 to apply incorporated and unincorporated charitable organizations and certain government organizations. Most all of the states have adopted this standard.[34]

In July 2006, a Uniform Prudent Management of Institutional Funds Act (UPMIFA) was approved by the National Conference of Commissioners on Uniform State Laws to replace UMIFA. A major goal of UPMIFA is to apply the same standards for the management and investment of charitable funds to those organized as a trust, a nonprofit corporation, or any other type of entity. As of April 2012, Mississippi became the 51st state or territory to approve.[35]

UPMIFA requires that the organization consider both the charitable purposes of the institution and the purposes of the fund, subject to the intent expressed by the donor, adhering to the following standards:

- The person responsible for managing and investing an institutional fund must manage and invest the fund in good faith and with the care an ordinarily prudent person in a like position would exercise under similar circumstances.

- Managers are subject to the duty of loyalty imposed by other laws.

- The institution may incur only reasonable costs in relation to the fund assets, purposes of the institution, and the skills available to the institution.

---

31. *Prudent Investor Rules*, Restatement of the Law of Trusts adopted by The American Law Institute at Washington, D.C., May 18, 1990, St. Paul, Minn.: American Law Institute Publishers.
32. *Id.*, p. 8.
33. Overton, ed., *Guidebook for Directors of Nonprofit Corporations*, Nonprofit Corporations Committee, Section of Business Law, American Bar Association, p. 41.
34. The version of UMIFA passed by Texas specifically exempts private foundations from its provisions.
35. Uniform Law Commission April 23, 2012 report; National Association of College and University Business Officers report of status also available at www.nacubo.org.

- An institution must diversify the investments unless special circumstances exist in which the purposes of the fund are better serviced without diversification.

UPMIFA eliminates the concept of historic dollar value. Instead the institution can set an appropriate level of expenditures and accumulation as it deems prudent for the uses, benefits, purposes, and duration for which the endowment fund is established.

The tax rules suggest an investment-by-investment approach.[36] According to the IRS, the "prudent trustee" approach of the regulations could be viewed as neither entirely consistent with nor entirely inconsistent with the Prudent Investor Rule and the UMIFA.[37] The published, and particularly private, rulings issued by the IRS[38] acknowledge the prudent nature of diversification[39] and the need to consider each investment's relationship to the whole to reach this goal. Foundation officials must acknowledge the inconsistency between the tax and local law and take both into account in meeting their obligation to prudently invest the foundation's funds.

The predecessor prudent man rule was first set forth in 1830 and directed trustees to "observe how men of prudence, discretion, and intelligence manage their own affairs, not in regard to speculation, but in regard to the permanent disposition of their funds, considering the probable income, as well as the probable safety of the capital to be invested."[40] In explaining the rules, the guide cautions that the facts and circumstances of each investor (the foundation) must be taken into account in choosing appropriate investments.[41] The foundation's financial managers must familiarize themselves with basic investment strategies and terms reflected in modern investment concepts and practices. Unless the trustees or directors individually possess expertise and time to manage an investment with care, skill, and caution (avoiding jeopardy), they have a duty to delegate management of these funds. The fees charged by professional investment managers are often modest when viewed in relation to the possibility of enhanced yield over a period of time and protection from excise taxes that can be imposed if investment decisions are found to jeopardize the foundation's capital.

---

36. *See* discussion accompanying *supra* notes 2–6.
37. *Public Charity Classification and Private Foundation Issues: Recent Emerging Significant Developments*, p. 241, Exempt Organizations Continuing Professional Education Technical Instruction Program for FY 2000.
38. *See* text accompanying *supra* notes 9–15.
39. The IRS, on one occasion in this context, observed: "Generally, diversification is a prudent strategy for management of investment assets" (Priv. Ltr. Rul. 200433028).
40. *Harvard College v. Amory*, 9 Pick (26 Mass) 446, 461 (1830). In 1959, the rule was changed to direct trustees "to make such investment and only such investments as a prudent man would make of his own property having in view the preservation of the estate and the amount and regularity of the income to be derived."
41. *See supra* note 32.

## (a) Evaluating Investment Alternatives

In striving to avoid jeopardy situations, a foundation's financial managers must evaluate the portion of the foundation's funds that can be invested suitably in a permanent fashion.[42] Depending on the answers to the following questions, the managers might prudently keep only a portion of the foundation's assets in cash-type interest-bearing accounts. Alternatively the foundation might be fully invested in bonds, equities, real estate, and alternative investments. The questions that can form the basis for investment decisions include:

1. *What rate of return should the foundation reasonably expect on its investments?* The mandatory distribution rules require that a private foundation pay out (in cash or other assets) basically 5 percent of the fair market value of its investment assets (a private operating foundation's minimum may be as low as $3\frac{1}{3}$ percent). Thus, without regard to other factors, such as a goal to expand programs or to allow the principal to keep pace with inflation, a private foundation tries to achieve at least a 5 percent current, or nominal, return on its investment. Before 1982, foundations were required to distribute the higher of the computed minimum return or actual current income (not including long-term capital gains). Because of this rule, some foundations focused on capital appreciation rather than current return (and, as a consequence, many saw the value of their principal increase). Foundations that invested in fixed-dollar obligations during that time instead saw their principal value remain static or decline, even though their grant-making levels might have been higher.

2. *Should the foundation use a total return investment policy?*[43] How a foundation answers this question is related to its answer to question 1. A foundation investing for *total return* defines its income to include dividends, rent, interest, and other current payments plus increase in the value of its asset or minus a decline in value. Such a foundation would expect to make grant payments with its dividends and its capital gains. Since the total return method typically embodies capital gains, this policy can have a modest excise tax advantage if the foundation distributes the appreciated property rather than sell it to make cash distributions.[44]

3. *For what length of time can the funds be invested?* The foundation's liquidity needs must be projected into the future for a number of years. To choose prudent investments, the foundation must know when, or if, funds might

---

42. Chapter 5 in Blazek, *Financial Planning for Nonprofit Organizations Made Easy* (Hoboken, NJ: John Wiley & Sons, 2008).
43. *See* § 8.2(d).
44. *See* § 10.2(b).

be needed to meet its annual distribution requirements, to buy a needed asset, or to meet some other financial obligation or program goal. Many investment partnerships, hedge funds, and funds of funds are not readily marketable. Some have a "lock-up period" of one or more years during which the foundation may not withdraw funds. For a foundation with these illiquid investment assets or real estate, this question is particularly relevant. The value of the investment or real estate is included in the minimum investment base of which a foundation must distribute 5 percent even if the property yields no currently disposable income. In this situation, it is highly desirable that the foundation's other investment assets bear a return that is above the minimum investment percentage.

4.  *Can the foundation afford a loss in its principal?* The answer to this question measures the level of risk the foundation perceives prudent. The rate of return from interest, dividends, and/or increase in underlying value of the asset is related to the possibility that the original investment, also called the *principal sum*, can be lost. The higher the risk of loss, the higher the expected return.[45] The possibility that an investment might decline (instead of increase as anticipated) is not necessarily evidence that the investment is a jeopardizing one. The issue here is primarily to evaluate the foundation's ability to meet its financial obligations.

5.  *How secure are the foundation's funding sources?* Though many private foundations are endowed, some foundations are dependent (partly or fully) on new funding to conduct their programs. Each foundation must evaluate the stability of its funding sources to project the level of contingency, or emergency, reserves it may require. Suppose a foundation that sponsors ongoing programs receives annual funding from family members of its creators that is dependent on their income level and consequentially allowed contribution deductions. Assume further that the foundation commonly makes annual disbursements well in excess of the required amount[46] and, in some years, in excess of its current annual funding plus the income from its investment. Such a foundation might prudently maintain its funds in investments with a low risk of loss in principal value (since the funds might be needed at a time when the value is low).

6.  *Is the foundation's staff capable of overseeing the investments?* Absent a Midas touch, special talents and training are required to successfully manage a fully diversified investment portfolio. This question has two different aspects. As evidenced by stock market fluctuations over the years, no one knows when or whether stock values will go up or down. A foundation's financial managers must evaluate their own knowledge and experience

---

45.  *See* § 8.2(c).
46.  *See* § 6.4.

and consider the need to engage outside professional investment managers. In questioning an investment that resulted in a loss, the fact that the foundation engaged a qualified independent manager might serve to excuse the tax sanction.

7. *How will economic conditions impact the investment?* Fixed money investments, such as certificates of deposit and U.S. Treasury obligations, fluctuate in value in relation to the prevailing interest rate and overall economic factors, but have a determinable value if held to maturity (the original principal invested should be returned). Conversely, the value of common stocks, real estate, and tangibles rise or fall in relation to a multitude of factors, including a specific company's earnings, investor mood, and inflationary or deflationary conditions. The foundation must project expected economic conditions to properly diversify its investments.

Many private foundations are choosing to place some of their investment assets in "alternative investments," such as hedge funds and offshore partnerships. These investments embody a number of tax and legal considerations not present in a portfolio of marketable securities. Exhibit 8.1 prompts foundation representatives to ask those questions in evaluating these alternative investment vehicles.[47]

**Exhibit 8.1**  Tax-Exempt Organizations, Including Private Foundations: Checklist for Alternative Investments

---

This checklist is designed to make tax-exempt organizations aware of the tax issues posed by investments in ventures not taxed as normal corporations. Investors must report the income and corresponding deductions from such entities on Form 990-PF and possibly Form 990-T, according to information reported on Form K-1.

**FORM OF INVESTMENT ENTITY**

- Is the investment entity a partnership or LLC taxed as a partnership (income passes through with same character, i.e., ordinary, dividend, interest, capital gain)?
- Is the investment entity a Subchapter S corporation (all income taxed as unrelated business income (UBI))?
- Is the investment entity a corporation taxed itself on the income generated (no UBI)?
- Is the entity an offshore company that reports no U.S. taxable income?

**CHARACTER OF INCOME**

- Is the organization's share of distributable income comprised of passive interest, dividends, rents, and royalties? [IRC § 512(b) and § 4940]
- If ordinary taxable income distributed, are there any deductible (allocable) expenses, such as the investment management, legal, and accounting fees?

---

47. *See* § 12.3(f).

**EXHIBIT 8.1** (Continued)

- Is current income or gains from options, futures, derivatives, currency transactions, and types of alternative investment income taxable?
- Does the venture have indebtedness or operate an active business (creates UBI)?
- Does the partnership agreement provide UBI protection for exempt partners?
- Does the venture operate outside the United States (special rules apply)?

**FIDUCIARY RESPONSIBILITY/JEOPARDIZING INVESTMENT**

- Does the organization engage independent investment advisors?
- Were the investments purchased under a plan to diversify the organization's investments following the prudent investor rules? [IRC § 4943]
- What portion of the organization's overall investment assets do the alternative investments comprise?
- If purchased by a private foundation, was an opinion of independent counsel that the investments would not be jeopardizing sought? [IRC § 4944]
- Is the investment readily marketable? A *no* answer means more risk. Does lock-in (cannot withdraw money from venture) mean valuation should be discounted?

**TAX BASIS/GAIN ON DISPOSITION**

- Does the capital account reported on Form K-1 reflect the organization's actual tax basis? Is a system in place to record annual changes in tax basis?
- Does the venture record increases and decreases in value into the capital accounts?
- Do special allocations of deductions apply?
- Does the investment entity have assets purchased with indebtedness? [IRC § 514]
- Will gain on sale be taxable due to acquisition indebtedness?

**VALUATION ISSUES**

- Does the manager provide periodic valuation information for calculation of average values for minimum investment return [IRC § 4942] and financial reporting purposes?
- Is the investment marketable? Do the terms of the investment limit sale of withdrawal so that a discount in value is indicated?
- For PF purposes, must the investment be valued monthly or annually?

**EXCESS BUSINESS HOLDINGS**

- Does the organization own more than 2 percent of the venture? What percentage do the organization's insiders own? [IRC § 4943]
- Is more than 95 percent of the income produced by the investment passive?

**TAX FILING REQUIREMENTS**

- Must the income be reported and taxed on Form 990-T?
- Was Form K-1 received for partnership investment that reports unrelated business character of distributions?
- If more than $100,000 was transferred to a foreign corporation or partnership, complete Part II to determine if Form 5471 and other forms must be filed.
- Must the organization make deposits of estimated income tax?

Completed by _____

Discussed with client_____(name)_____date_____

*(Continued)*

EXHIBIT **8.1** (Continued)

---

CHECKLIST FOR ALTERNATIVE INVESTMENTS, PART 2: FILING REQUIREMENTS

1. **Answer the following questions if the investment entity is a foreign corporation:**
   - ○ Was more than $100,000 transferred to the corporation within a 12-month period? (Form 926 may be required if *Yes*.) _____
   - ○ Does the investment represent at least 10 percent ownership in corporation? (Forms 926 and 5471 may be required if *Yes*.) _____
   - ○ During the tax year, was the investment interest reduced from more than 10 percent to less than 10 percent? (Form 5471 may be required if *Yes*.) _____
   - ○ Did the exempt organization own 50 percent or more of the corporation for at least 30 consecutive days during the tax year? (Form 5471 may be required if *Yes*.) _____
   - ○ Is the entity a passive foreign investment company (PFIC)? (Form 8621 may be required if *Yes*.) _____

2. **Answer the following questions if the investment entity is a foreign partnership:**
   - ○ Was more than $100,000 transferred to the partnership within a 12-month period? (Form 8865 may be required if *Yes*.) _____
   - ○ Is investment in partnership ownership at least 10 percent? (Form 8865 may be required if *Yes*.) _____
   - ○ During the tax year, did partnership interest increase or decrease by at least 10 percent—e.g., from 11 percent to 21 percent or vice versa? (Form 8865 may be required if *Yes*.) _____
   - ○ During the tax year, did the partnership interest decrease from 10 percent or more to less than 10 percent—e.g., from 12 percent to 8 percent? (Form 8865 may be required if *Yes*.) _____

3. **Is the investment entity a foreign *disregarded entity*? (Form 8858 may be required if *Yes*. )** _____
   - ○ Does EO have a financial interest in or signatory authority over foreign financial accounts, the aggregate value of which exceeds $10,000? (Form 90–22.1 may be required if *Yes*.) _____
   - ○ Does EO own more than 50 percent of stock of a corporation that has foreign financial accounts, the aggregate value of which exceeds $10,000? (Form 90–22.1 may be required if *Yes*.) _____
   - ○ Does EO hold a more than 50 percent partnership interest that has legal title to foreign financial accounts the aggregate value of which exceeds $10,000? (Form 90–22.1 may be required if *Yes*) _____

---

CAVEAT: These questions represent a brief summary of potential reporting obligations for foreign investments. The lengthy set of rules governing the reporting of foreign investments is highly technical. Each foreign investment should be reviewed to determine whether there is a reporting obligation.

## (b) Facing the Unknown

In seeking to answer the questions in Exhibit 8.1, a healthy dose of skepticism and an appreciation of the uncertainty that abounds is important for a foundation attempting to avoid jeopardizing investments. As one writer noted in describing the Federal Reserve Board's deliberations about the interest rate, "no word seems to appear more frequently in the transcripts than *uncertainty*."[48] The financial markets in which a foundation must choose to place its funds are influenced daily by international forces beyond its control. Who knows whether the stock market will go up, whether a global stock fund will sustain its yield, or whether the U.S. dollar will go up against the Japanese yen? The significant declines in the equity markets accompanied by a drastic decline in interest rates during 2001–2002 evidence the need for great caution in making decisions about future market performance.

Diversification is an important technique designed to face the unknown. It essentially entails this fundamental principle: "Don't put all the eggs in one basket." A prudently balanced investment portfolio contains a variety of financial instruments—stocks, bonds, real estate, and so on. The mix of investments assumes that some go up, some go down, and in the long run the averages will provide a desirable stream of income. It is not necessarily conservative or prudent to maintain all the funds invested in fixed-money or interest-bearing securities or all in equities. To conserve the principal in its original dollar amount, inviolate and permanent into perpetuity, may not necessarily be safeguarding the fund for the donor's intentions. It should be remembered that fixed-return investments do have some inherent risk; in 1994 some bond values fell more than 10 percent as the interest rates changed quickly. Conversely, during 2001 and 2002, the market value of some fixed-money obligations rose 10 percent in response to interest rate declines.

The investment alternatives available to a foundation are the same as those available to a for-profit investor. Because the foundation pays a modest excise tax on its income, certain choices, such as municipal bonds or deferred annuities, may not be suitable. The types of investments from which the foundation chooses include those outlined in Exhibit 8.2.

A classically diversified investment portfolio would contain some investments in each of the categories. What portion of the total investments is held in each category depends on the foundation's risk tolerance and life phase, as discussed in the following sections. Suppose a foundation has $1 million to invest permanently. If the board adopts the historically conservative approach, it would invest $100,000 in short-term cash and bonds, $400,000 in long-term bonds, $500,000 in common stocks, and nothing in real estate, gold, or commodities, such as oil.

---

48. Uchitelle, "At the Fed It Looks Like Deja Vu, Again," *New York Times*, July 2, 1995.

**EXHIBIT 8.2**  Investment Alternatives

---

**FIXED MONEY VALUE (PRINCIPAL DOLLAR AMOUNT FIXED)**

Interest-bearing checking account
Money market account
Certificate of deposit
Treasury bills
Series EE bonds
Fixed annuities

**VARIABLE MONEY VALUE (PRINCIPAL VALUE FLUCTUATES WITH PREVAILING INTEREST RATES, BUT INTEREST RATE ON INVESTMENT USUALLY FIXED)**

Treasury notes and bonds
Mortgage-backed bonds
Corporate bonds
Municipal bonds
Annuities or universal life insurance policies
Derivatives of the above variable securities

**EQUITY INVESTMENTS (PRINCIPAL VALUE AND DIVIDEND RATE VARIES)**

Common stock
Preferred stock
Convertible bonds
Stock options

**REAL ESTATE**

Commercial real estate (office, store, hotel, or factory building)
Residential real estate (single-family or multiperson apartment building)
Raw land
Agricultural land

**TANGIBLES (THE FIRST THREE ARE ALSO CALLED COLLECTIBLES)**

Gold and silver
Antiques
Art
Minerals
Commodities

**ALTERNATIVE INVESTMENTS**

Venture capital funds
Hedge funds
Offshore entities
Distressed securities
Emerging market securities
Derivatives

---

The investments within each category might be further diversified. A fixed-money portfolio, for example, would have debt instruments with staggered maturity dates and credit ratings, since fixed-return investments can also fluctuate in value and have inherent risk of loss. The $400,000 in the preceding example might include $133,000 of 5-year bonds, $133,000 of 7-year bonds, and $133,000 of 30-year bonds. Similarly, a common stock portfolio would include stock of companies in different types of businesses—auto manufacturer, drug company, computer software, home building, banking, and so on. Professional investment managers today add commodities, minerals, venture capital, and hedge funds.

## (c) Risk versus Return

A foundation must carefully identify those funds that are suitable for each category of investment type. The possibility for a higher yield or overall return provided by common stock is not always worth the inherent risk of the investment. Funds received as a donation to build a museum over the next two years should earn some interest, but would not prudently be invested in technology stocks.

The relationship of risk to investment return must be understood. The reason a six-month certificate of deposit pays the lowest available interest rate is that no risk is taken. Without question, the face amount of the certificate plus a stated amount of interest will be paid (absent a bank collapse or other banking system crisis). As uncertainty about the final outcome, or risk of loss, increases, the yield (in theory) increases. Correspondingly, a lower yield comes with less uncertainty. The conflict between risks the foundation is willing (or reasonably able) to take and the return on investment needed to pay its annual charitable disbursements is the same as for individuals and for-profit companies. The pyramid in Exhibit 8.3 illustrates the concept. Note that the jeopardy to principal is thought to increase from bottom to top. Some advisors, however, recommend a mixture of the lowest- to highest-risk investments to achieve diversification that ultimately achieves a higher yield.

## (d) Total Return Investing

The financial markets expect low dividend yields equal to a small portion of a company's annual income. This *current return* is accepted to allow the corporation to reinvest most of its earnings in expansion and conglomeration. The desired result is a consequential appreciation in underlying value of the securities. Investors today anticipate annual income will be earned from a combination of dividends and interest, plus gains resulting from appreciation in the value of the underlying security. The objective is to achieve what is called *total return* on the capital invested. What formerly was treated as an addition to

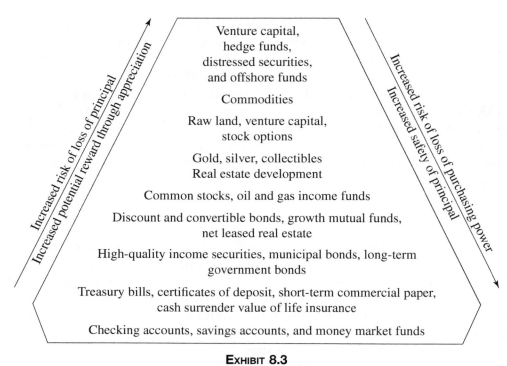

Venture capital,
hedge funds,
distressed securities,
and offshore funds

Commodities

Raw land, venture capital,
stock options

Gold, silver, collectibles
Real estate development

Common stocks, oil and gas income funds

Discount and convertible bonds, growth mutual funds,
net leased real estate

High-quality income securities, municipal bonds, long-term
government bonds

Treasury bills, certificates of deposit, short-term commercial paper,
cash surrender value of life insurance

Checking accounts, savings accounts, and money market funds

**EXHIBIT 8.3**

Investment Risk Pyramid

the principal—the appreciation in value of the asset(s)—is now treated as income under this theory of investing.

The trend toward following a total return concept for endowment funds was encouraged by the Ford Foundation as early as 1969.[49] In a study, Ford concluded, "We find no authoritative support in the law for the widely held view that the realized gains on endowment funds can never be spent. Prudence would call for the retention of sufficient gains to maintain purchasing power in the face of inflation and to guard against potential losses, but subject to the standards which prudence dictates, the expenditure of gains should lie within the discretion of the institution's directors." The study investigated whether "the directors of an educational institution are circumscribed by the law or are free to adopt the investment policy they regard as soundest for their institution,

---

49. Cary and Bright, *The Law and the Lore of Endowment Funds: A Report to the Ford Foundation* (New York: Ford Foundation, 1969). The study was commissioned to examine the law governing the endowment funds of colleges and universities with the goal of conveying new knowledge and informed commentary about charitable investments to strengthen the efforts of the institutions to improve their endowment income. The Uniform Management of Institutional Funds Act permits trustees to treat capital gains as income.

unhampered by legal impediments, prohibitions or restrictions." An illustration of the *total return method* follows:

| Total return | = | Dividends Interest Rent, etc. | + or − | Realized gains or losses | + or − | Unrealized appreciation or depreciation in value of investments |
|---|---|---|---|---|---|---|

### (e)  How Income Is Reported

According to financial analysis theories, long-term investment income may be reported for financial purposes in at least four different ways. The term *realized* is used to denote capital gain or loss from transactions that actually occurred. Realized capital gain is the excess of actual sales proceeds over the amount paid for a security. *Unrealized* capital gain is the hypothetical gain calculated assuming securities still held as investments were sold on the report date. Measures of investment income include:

1. *Current return method.* Using this method, actual interest, dividends, rents, and royalties paid are treated as income (called *unrestricted* for accounting purposes). Any realized or unrealized gains or losses are added back to or subtracted from the principal fund (unrestricted or restricted).

2. *Overall return method.* This method classifies the current return (identified in the preceding item) plus realized capital gains and losses (those resulting from actual sales of the investment asset) as operating (unrestricted) income.

3. *Total return method.* This method reports overall return actually received, plus or minus unrealized gains and losses, as unrestricted income.

4. *Constant return.* Based on a historical average amount, a fixed annual percentage of the value of the investment pool is treated as unrestricted income.

### (f)  Measuring Investment Return

For some investments, the return, or income earned, is easy to calculate. A certificate of deposit pays 5 percent yields, or returns 5 percent to its purchaser. Others are more complicated. The basic formula for an asset, the value of which may fluctuate, arrives at income by dividing the current income received in a year—the interest paid or accrued, dividends, capital gain distributions or other profit share (for partnership), plus the increase in value of the underlying investment less any decrease in value. The return, or yield, is then determined by dividing the income by the value of the investment at the beginning of the period.

Fixed-money investments whose principal values fluctuate with the prevailing interest rates require an additional step. They are often purchased at what is called a *premium* (paying $102 for a $100 bond) or *discount* (paying $95 for a $100 bond). When a premium is paid, the stated yield on the bond is usually higher than the prevailing rate. Conversely, a bond selling at a discount is likely paying a lower percentage than the current rate. Each year the bond is held, a ratable portion of the premium or discount is added to or deducted from income to reflect the true yield, as shown in Example 4 below. Similarly, a bond originally purchased with a coupon interest rate of 8 percent does not yield 8 percent in a year when its principal value declines 2 percent; instead, it yields 6 percent, as reflected in Example 5:

*Example 1.* For a one-year certificate of deposit issued at 5 percent the yield is:

$$\frac{\text{Interest}}{\text{Principal of CD}} \frac{\$5,000}{100,000} = 5\%$$

*Example 2.* Common stock worth $100,000 on first day of year, paying out $2,000 of dividends and selling for $110,000 at year-end.

$$\frac{\text{Dividend} + \text{Increase in value}}{\text{Value of year's beginning}} \frac{\$12,000(2,000 + 10,000)}{100,000} = 12\%$$

*Example 3.* Same as example 2, except stock declined to $98,000 in value.

$$\frac{\text{Dividend} - \text{Decrease in value}}{\text{Value of year's beginning}} \frac{\$0(2,000 - 2,000)}{100,000} = 0\% \text{ (none)}$$

*Example 4.* A five-year bond with principal sum of $100,000 bearing a 5 percent coupon is purchased for $95,000 and at year-end is still worth $95,000. The brokerage or investment manager's report listing this bond would likely reflect that the yield is 5 percent, the face coupon amount.

$$\frac{\text{Interest paid} + \text{Discount*}}{\text{Original cost of bond}} \frac{\$6,000(5,000 - 1,000*)}{\$95,000} = 6.3\%$$

*The purchase discount of $5,000 is divided by five years.

*Example 5.* A five-year bond with principal sum of $100,000 bearing an 8 percent coupon is purchased for $100,000 on the day the bond is originally issued. By year-end the value of the bond has decreased to $98,000 (because the current rate rose).

$$\frac{\text{Interest paid} - \text{Decline in value}}{\text{Original cost of bond}} \quad \frac{\$6,000(8,000 - 2,000)}{\$100,000} = 6\%$$

*Example 6.* For the bond in Example 5, assume in the second year the value increased to $99,000. Note that for the two-year period, the overall total yield might be averaged to determine that the cumulative yield was 7.6 percent (6% + 9.18% divided by 2).

$$\frac{\text{Interest paid} - \text{Increase in value}}{\text{Beginning of year value}} \quad \frac{\$9,000(8,000 + 1,000)}{\$98,000} = 9.2\%$$

Professional investment managers and mutual funds governed by the Securities and Exchange Commission must conform to similar unified standards for reporting investment yield.

## §8.3  PROGRAM-RELATED INVESTMENTS

A *program-related investment* is not considered a jeopardizing investment.[50] A program-related investment is an investment, the primary purpose of which is to accomplish one or more charitable purposes, and no significant purpose of which is the production of income or the appreciation of property.[51] The regulations add a third characteristic, in that no purpose of the investment may be the furthering of substantial legislative or any political activities.[52] Conspicuously absent from the elements of the program-related investment is the proscription on private inurement,[53] simply because private individuals necessarily benefit from the investment, albeit in the course of achieving a larger (charitable) purpose.

An investment is considered as made primarily to accomplish one or more charitable purposes if it significantly furthers the accomplishment of a private foundation's tax-exempt activities and if the investment would not have been made but for the relationship between the investment and the activities.[54] An investment in a functionally related business[55] is considered as made

---

50. Reg. § 53.4944-3(a)(1).
51. IRC § 4944(c); Reg. § 53.4944-3(a)(1).
52. Reg. § 53.4944-3(a)(1)(iii). Also IRC § 170(c)(2)(D); *see* §§ 9.1, 9.2. The regulations provide that an investment shall not be considered as a substantial involvement in an attempt to influence legislation if the recipient of the investment appears before or communicates to any legislative body with respect to legislation or proposed legislation of direct interest to the recipient, as long as the expenses associated with those activities are deductible as a business expense (Reg. § 53.4944-3(a)(2)(iv)). The rules as to deductibility of these types of expenses have been, however, significantly narrowed (IRC § 162 (e)).
53. IRC § 170(c)(2)(C). *See* § 5.1.
54. Reg. § 53.4944-3(a)(2)(i).
55. *See* § 7.3.

primarily to accomplish one or more charitable purposes.[56] In determining whether a significant purpose of an investment is the production of income or the appreciation of property, it is relevant to determine whether investors for profit would be likely to make the investment on the same terms as the private foundation. The fact, however, that an investment produces significant income or capital appreciation is not, in the absence of other factors, conclusive evidence of this type of significant purpose.[57] A program-related investment can be made by investment in a limited liability company.[58]

Illustrations of program-related investments include:

- Low-interest or interest-free loans to needy students.
- High-risk investments in nonprofit low-income housing projects.
- Low-interest loans to small businesses owned by members of economically disadvantaged groups, where commercial funds at reasonable interest rates are not readily available.
- Investments in businesses in deteriorated urban areas under a plan to improve the economy of the area by providing employment or training for unemployed residents.
- Investments in nonprofit organizations combating community deterioration.

Likewise, the IRS ruled that low-interest-rate loans by a private foundation, established to aid the blind in securing employment, which are made to blind persons who desire to establish themselves in business but who are unable to obtain funds through commercial sources, constitute program-related investments.[59] The following IRS examples from regulations and rulings illustrate the concept:[60]

- A small business enterprise, X, is located in a deteriorated urban area and is owned by members of an economically disadvantaged minority group. Conventional sources of funds are unwilling or unable to provide funds to the enterprise. A private foundation makes a below-market-interest-rate loan to the enterprise to encourage economic development.
- The private foundation described in the previous instance allows an extension of X's loan in order to permit X to achieve greater financial stability before it is required to repay the loan. Since the change is not

---

56. Reg. § 53.4944-3(a)(2)(ii); *see* § 1.5.
57. Reg. § 53.4944-3(a)(2)(iii).
58. E.g., Priv. Ltr. Rul. 199910066.
59. Rev. Rul. 78-90, 1978-1 C.B. 380.
60. Reg. § 53.4944-3(b) first five bullets.

motivated by attempts to enhance yield, but by an effort to encourage success of an exempt project, the altered loan is also considered to be program-related.

- Assume instead that a commercial bank will loan X money if it increases the amount of its equity capital. A private foundation's purchase of X's common stock, to accomplish the same purposes as the loan described earlier, is a program-related investment.

- Assume instead that substantial citizens own X, but continued operation of X is important for the economic well-being of the low-income persons in the area. To save X, a private foundation lends X money at below-market rates to pay for specific projects benefiting the community. The loan is program-related.

- A private foundation wants to encourage the building of a plant to provide jobs in a low-income neighborhood. The foundation lends the building funds at below-market rates to SS, a successful commercial company that is unwilling to build the plant without this inducement. Again, the loan is program-related.

- A loan program established to make low-interest-rate loans to blind persons unable to obtain funds through commercial sources constitutes a program-related investment.[61]

- Land purchased for land conservation, wildlife preservation, and the protection of open and scenic spaces is program-related.[62]

- Investment in a for-profit company, the purpose of which is to encourage the creation of jobs in a region targeted for this purpose by a state government.[63]

- Loans and investments to promote economic development in a foreign country, which has a low standard of living, energy and food shortages, and natural disasters.[64]

- A series of low-interest or interest-free loans to organizations in the media field (most of which, if not all, were for-profit businesses), located principally in Central and Eastern Europe and the former Soviet Union, Latin America, Southeast Asia, and Africa, for the purpose of speeding the institution-building process toward open societies and democratic systems.[65]

---

61. Rev. Rul. 78-90, 1978-1 C.B. 380.
62. Priv. Ltr. Rul. 8832074.
63. Priv. Ltr. Rul. 199943044.
64. Priv. Ltr. Rul. 199943058.
65. Priv. Ltr. Rul. 200034037.

- A foundation's investment in a for-profit venture capital fund limited to achieving environmental and economic development goals, subject to environmental guidelines and oversight, accomplishes an exempt purpose. The foundation supports biodiversity and sustainability and believes there is a link between economic development and reduction of poverty and conservation of the biological resources on which nearly all economics are based. Therefore, the foundation's fund investment qualified as a program-related one. The investment was not thereby jeopardizing and the expenditure not a taxable one.[66]

- Loans by a private foundation to promote development and construction of housing in a downtown area were ruled to be program-related investments.[67]

- Operation of a farm in a foreign country, previously conducted as a for-profit operation by the founder of a private foundation, that became operated by the foundation after his death as an exempt demonstration project and thus a program-related investment.[68]

- A grant by a private foundation to a for-profit medical malpractice reinsurance company was held to be a program-related investment because it promoted health by enabling physicians to continue to practice in or locate to a community.[69]

- To stimulate participation of private industry to discover interventions for the developing world, a private foundation will grant funding to commercial companies. Proposals must evidence research that will achieve a charitable objective, a strategy for making the results readily available at affordable prices to those without access, an evaluation of ownership and resulting intellectual property rights, and an outline of a global access plan. Grant recipients must have a reasonable strategy and principles for managing innovation for the purpose of facilitating the future availability and affordability in the developing world. The results of early stage research found impractical or unreasonable to be published and made available to the general public. The ruling finds the expense will constitute a qualifying distribution.[70] It also notes expenditure responsibility will occur.[71] There is no mention of terms for returning the "investment"; the ruling refers to the payments as "transactions," and also refers to "making of grants, contracts, or program-related investments."

---

66. Priv. Ltr. Rul. 200136026.
67. Priv. Ltr. Rul. 200331005.
68. Priv. Ltr. Rul. 200343027.
69. Priv. Ltr. Rul. 200347014.
70. Priv. Ltr. Rul. 200603031.
71. *See* § 9.6.

- Investments by a private foundation in an angel investment fund for businesses owned by members of disadvantaged groups in low-income communities were held to be program-related investments.[72]

- Royalty interest held by a private foundation, arising out of a research agreement with a tax-exempt hospital, pursuant to which the foundation makes grants to the hospital, was held to qualify as a program-related investment; the royalty interest will arise if the hospital or its licensing affiliate receives payments in return for the use of any invention resulting from the funded research.[73]

The IRS, on April 18, 2012, issued proposed regulations that provide additional guidance to private foundations as to program-related investments.[74] This proposal does not add to the substantive rules for qualifying program-related investments but provides nine new examples of these types of investments, illustrating a wider range of them.

The new examples demonstrate that a program-related investment may accomplish a variety of charitable purposes, such as advancing science, combating environmental deterioration, and promotion of the arts. Several examples demonstrate that an investment that funds activities in one or more foreign countries, including investments that alleviate the impact of a natural disaster or that fund educational programs for poor individuals, may further the accomplishment of charitable purposes and qualify as a program-related investment.

An example illustrates that the existence of a potential high rate of return on an investment does not, by itself, prevent it from qualifying as a program-related investment. Another example illustrates that a private foundation's acceptance of an equity position in conjunction with making a loan does not necessarily prevent the investment from qualifying as a program-related investment. Two examples illustrate that a private foundation's provision of credit enhancement can qualify as a program-related investment.

The last of these examples demonstrates that a guarantee arrangement may qualify as a program-related investment. Although the proposed regulations do not address the matter of qualifying distributions,[75] the preamble to the proposal states that the Treasury and the IRS have concluded that there would not be a qualifying distribution at the time the foundation enters into the guarantee arrangement. Under certain circumstances, however, the preamble continues, a private foundation may treat payments made pursuant to a guarantee arrangement as qualifying distributions.

---

72. Priv. Ltr. Rul. 200610020.
73. Priv. Ltr. Rul. 201145027.
74. REG-144267-11.
75. *See* § 6.5.

The proposed regulations include examples illustrating that loans and capital may be provided to individuals or entities that are not themselves members of a charitable class, if the recipients are the instruments by which the private foundation accomplishes its exempt activities.

Once it has been determined that an investment is a program-related one, it does not cease to qualify as this type of investment, provided that any changes in the form or terms of the investment are made primarily for tax-exempt purposes and not for any significant purpose involving the production of income or the appreciation of property. A change made in the form or terms of a program-related investment for the prudent protection of a private foundation's investment ordinarily will not cause the investment to cease to qualify as program-related.[76] Under certain circumstances, a program-related investment may cease to be this type of investment because of a critical change in circumstances, such as where it is serving an illegal purpose or the private purpose of the foundation or its managers. An investment that ceases to be a program-related one because of a critical change in circumstances will not subject the foundation to the tax on jeopardizing investments before the thirtieth day after the date on which the foundation (or any of its managers) has actual knowledge of the critical change in circumstances.

An investment that jeopardizes the carrying out of a private foundation's tax-exempt purposes is considered to be removed from jeopardy when the foundation sells or otherwise disposes of the investment and the proceeds therefrom are not themselves investments that jeopardize the carrying out of exempt purposes.[77]

A program-related investment constitutes a qualifying distribution for a private foundation. Expenditure responsibility must be exercised for most program-related investments and reports made to the IRS on Form 990-PF throughout the life of the investment.[78]

A program-related investment made with a low-profit limited liability company (L3C) also requires an expenditure responsibility agreement because an L3C is not a public charity. An L3C is a hybrid nonprofit/for-profit organization designed to facilitate investments by private foundations in social programs that advance a charitable mission. Unlike a tax-exempt charitable organization, an L3C may distribute its after-tax profits to its investors or owners. Vermont was the first state to recognize this form of organization, in April 2008, followed by Michigan in January 2009 and Wyoming in February 2009.

Loan programs referred to as *recoverable grants* are treated by some advisors as program-related investments and by others as grants. These grants are most commonly made in support of affordable housing, neighborhood centers in low-income areas, and community development initiatives. The Council on

---

76. Reg. § 53.4944-3(a)(3).
77. IRC § 4944(e)(2); Reg. § 53.4944-5(b).
78. *See* § 6.5.

Foundations suggests: "Recoverable grants are grants that function as interest-free loans. They are made by foundations from their grantmaking budget, and are entered on the books as 'recoverable grants.' If repayment is not received, they are converted to grant status."[79]

Treating such a grant as a current-year expense seems to require a decision that the funds will not be recovered. There are no IRS rulings on the subject. It is important to remember such grants paid to an entity that is not a public charity require an expenditure responsibility agreement. Application forms and information about recoverable grants can be found on the websites of The Ford Foundation, JPMorgan Chase, Boston LISC (Local Initiatives Support Corp.), Minnesota Housing Partnership, and other agencies and foundations that provide such funding. The website of the Grantsmanship Center has some information on recoverable grants in its "Answers to Some Frequently Asked Questions About PRIs" and "What Do PRIs Fund?" Because program-related investments perform a similar function, you may want to look at our Frequently Asked Questions (FAQ), "What is a program-related investment (PRI)?"

Expenditure responsibility agreements are not, however, required for investments placed with public charities. For example, a loan to a public school at a low or no-interest rate would qualify as a program-related investment, but expenditure responsibility would not be required because of the borrower's public charity status.[80]

# §8.4  INVESTMENT FRAUDS

The federal tax law essentially is silent on the consequences in law of private foundations' investments in fraudulent schemes, such as Ponzi schemes.

## (a)  Background

There are several issues in this regard, most of them brought to light as a result of several foundations' investments by means of the Bernard L. Madoff Investment Securities firm. Mr. Madoff admitted to running a Ponzi scheme, through his investment firm, involving losses, concerning foundations and other entities, in excess of $50 billion. According to a report referenced in a major newspaper article, at least 147 foundations invested with the Madoff firm.[81] One foundation invested $958 million with the Madoff firm—virtually all of its assets; three other foundations lost $244 million, $199 million, and $178 million. One of the federal tax law issues of the day is whether some of these investments

---

79. Freeman and the Council on Foundations, *Handbook on Private Foundations*, published by the Foundation Center in 1993.
80. *See* § 9.6(c).
81. Browning, "For Investing with Madoff, Private Foundations Could Face Tax Fines," *New York Times*, Feb. 12, 2009, at B4.

constitute jeopardizing investments. As this article put the matter, some foundations "bet the farm—which some tax lawyers say could signal the lack of due diligence and fiduciary responsibility."[82]

A tax law assistant to Sen. Charles Grassley (R-IA), the ranking member of the Senate Finance Committee, said, a few weeks before this article was published, that members of the boards of private foundations may be liable for jeopardizing investment taxes in situations where their foundations invested with the Madoff firm.[83] She noted that some charitable organizations decided not to invest with Madoff after engaging in due diligence, raising the question as to whether those who invested with his company violated the jeopardy investment standard. Brushing aside the argument that these foundations and other investors were defrauded, she said that, "[w]ith respect to charities that apparently have had to close their doors or stop issuing grants because of the losses on their Madoff investments, it would seem hard to argue that these investments did not jeopardize the carrying on of their exempt purpose."

The IRS published general guidance to taxpayers who invested in Ponzi schemes. One element of this guidance is that an individual investor in a Ponzi scheme is entitled to a theft loss deduction in the year the fraud is discovered.[84] The other component of the guidance is a safe-harbor approach for taxpayers to claim a theft loss for Ponzi scheme investments.[85] To avail themselves of this safe harbor, taxpayers must agree not to file amended returns.

The Tax Section of the New York State Bar Association (NYSBA) submitted a report to the Department of the Treasury and the IRS in response to the government's request for assistance in identifying and addressing issues confronting private foundation investors in Ponzi schemes and other frauds.[86]

The NYSBA report identified the relevant issues that private foundations and the IRS need to address in this context. One of the questions posed was whether IRS guidance should impose a single approach that foundations must follow in resolving issues arising from Ponzi scheme investments or whether IRS guidance should give foundations a choice of actions. The report's initial conclusion was that "there are too many differences between foundations (multibillion dollar foundations vs. small family foundations; foundations with minor losses from a Ponzi scheme vs. foundations with all or most of their assets lost in a Ponzi scheme, etc.) to come out with a one-size-fits-all

82. *Id.*
83. Bureau of Nat'l Affairs interview with Theresa Pattera, Daily Tax Report (no. 16) G-2 (Jan. 28, 2009).
84. Rev. Rul. 2009-9, 2009-14 I.R.B. 735.
85. Rev. Proc. 2009-20, 2009-1 C.B. 749.
86. Letter and accompanying report submitted to the Treasury Department and the IRS, dated May 7, 2009, reproduced in *Daily Tax Report*, May 11, 2009, TaxCore. This letter observed that this IRS guidance (*see supra* notes 85, 86) "is not aimed at exempt organizations and does not squarely address the issues facing private foundations."

approach." Also: "Different institutions inevitably will have different needs and administrative capabilities for dealing with Ponzi scheme losses."

As this report observed, private foundations with losses from Ponzi scheme investments "face many difficult reporting and compliance issues for which there is little or no precedent or guidance." The report treats these issues as falling into two categories. One set of these issues concerns the measurement of income and asset values.

This matter arises in two settings: calculation of the required payout amount[87] and determination of net investment income for purposes of the excise tax on that income.[88] The second category of issues "address or relate to the foundation's process for making the Ponzi scheme investment in the first place." Here, the critical question "is whether making the investment involved some prohibited conduct that should be punished by the imposition of a penalty excise tax." The principal issue in this area is whether one or more of the jeopardizing investments rules were transgressed. Of secondary importance are the self-dealing rules[89] and the taxable expenditures rules.[90]

## (b)  NYSBA Report

The NYSBA report stated that application of the jeopardizing investment rules in the Ponzi scheme context is a "key issue" for foundations that made investments of this nature.

The first issue posed by the NYSBA report was: What are the standards to be applied to Ponzi scheme investments that appeared legitimate at the time the investment was made? The report states that, inasmuch as jeopardy investment determinations are not to be based on hindsight, "it would appear that if a foundation or a foundation manager conducted proper due diligence, there should be no penalty." Then: "The key question is what constitutes adequate due diligence" under the circumstances of Ponzi scheme investments. After sketching some of the pertinent factors, the report observed that "frauds are structured and documented in ways to avoid detection and so by definition a Ponzi scheme may not be discovered by a foundation that conducts reasonable diligence."[91]

The second of these issues is: Is placement of a substantial portion or all of a foundation's assets with one fund manager (who represents that its investments are prudent and diversified) an indication of a jeopardizing investment? The report concluded that the examples in the existing jeopardizing investments regulations are "outdated" and thus "do not provide helpful guidance for private foundations

---

87.  See § 6.4.
88.  See § 10.3.
89.  See § 5.11, text accompanied by notes 387–391.
90.  See § 9.8.
91.  This view is buttressed by the IRS's position that these schemes involve thefts (see text accompanied by *supra* notes 85, 86).

in today's market." Stating that the "better view" may be that investing with one manager "is not per se a jeopardizing investment if the foundation uses due diligence in selecting and monitoring the manager and its actual investments," the report concluded that "[h]aving clear guidance on what constitutes a jeopardizing investment would be helpful to foundation managers."

The third issue (actually a cluster of issues) assumes that a Ponzi scheme investment is a jeopardizing investment. Question: How many years may the IRS go back to impose the excise tax(es)? Question: If the Ponzi scheme investment is exchanged for cash, where the cash continues to be the subject of a clawback obligation, does the jeopardizing investments rules taxable period continue?[92] The report stated that it is "unclear" as to how these issues should be resolved.

What about discovery of the Ponzi scheme? Does that mean that the investment was actually removed from jeopardy?[93] The tax regulations appear to treat the investment as removed from jeopardy when the foundation actively does something to change, exchange, or dispose of the investment. Therefore, the report observes, in a Ponzi scheme situation, which is "discovered and collapses on its own, it is unclear whether the foundation has disposed of a jeopardizing investment."

## § 8.5  EXCISE TAXES FOR JEOPARDIZING INVESTMENTS

If a private foundation invests any amount in a manner as to jeopardize the carrying out of any of its tax-exempt purposes, an initial tax is imposed on the private foundation on the making of the investment, at the rate of 10 percent of the amount so invested for each tax year or part thereof in the taxable period.[94] The IRS has the discretionary authority to abate this initial tax where the private foundation establishes that the violation was due to reasonable cause and not to willful neglect, and timely corrects the violation.[95] In any case in which this initial tax is imposed, a tax is also imposed on the participation of any foundation manager in the making of the investment, knowing that it is jeopardizing the carrying out of any of the private foundation's tax-exempt purposes, equal to 5 percent of the amount so invested for each tax year of the private foundation (or part of the tax year) in the taxable period.[96] With respect to any one jeopardizing investment, the maximum amount of this tax is $10,000.[97] Managers found guilty

---

92. See text accompanied by *infra* note 97.
93. See § 8.5(c).
94. IRC § 4944 (a)(1), Reg. § 53.4944-1(a)(1). This tax is also known as a *first-tier tax* (IRC § 4963 (a); Reg. § 53.4963-1(a)).
95. IRC § 4962. E.g., Tech. Adv. Mem. 200347023 (where a private foundation relied, in good faith, on incorrect legal advice). *See* Exhibit 6.3 for an example of a letter requesting abatement.
96. IRC § 4944(e)(1); Reg. § 53.4944-1(b)(1).
97. IRC § 4944(d)(2); Reg. § 53.4944-4(b).

under these rules are jointly and severally liable for the tax.[98] This tax, which must be paid by any participating foundation manager, is not imposed where the participation is not willful and is due to reasonable cause.[99]

## (a) When a Manager *Knows*

A foundation manager is considered to have participated in the making of an investment *knowing* that it is a jeopardizing one only if the manager:

- Has actual knowledge of sufficient facts so that, based solely on those facts, the investment would be a jeopardizing one,

- Is aware that the investment under these circumstances may violate the federal tax law rules governing jeopardizing investments, and

- Negligently fails to make reasonable attempts to ascertain whether the investment is a jeopardizing one, or is in fact aware that it is a jeopardizing investment.[100]

The word *knowing* does not mean "having reason to know." Evidence tending to show that a foundation manager has reason to know of a particular fact or particular rule is relevant, however, in determining whether he or she had actual knowledge of the fact or rule. Evidence tending to show that a foundation manager has reason to know of sufficient facts so that, based solely on the facts, an investment would be a jeopardizing one is relevant in determining whether the manager has actual knowledge of the facts.[101] Thus, the pertinent facts and circumstances are examined to find out why the manager did not know of the relevant facts or law. To be excused of tax liability, the foundation manager essentially must be ignorant of the pertinent facts or law.

For example, the board of trustees of a private foundation may consist of 10 members, three of whom comprise a finance committee. The written investment policy of the foundation provides that the board approves investment decisions proposed by the finance committee, based on the advice of independent counselors. Those members of the board who are not on the finance committee should not be expected to be aware of details discussed in finance committee meetings.

A foundation manager's participation in the making of a jeopardizing investment is *willful* if it is voluntary, conscious, and intentional. A motive to avoid the restrictions of the law or the incurrence of a tax is not necessary to make this type of participation willful. A foundation manager's participation in

---

98. IRC § 4944(d)(1); Reg. § 53.4944-4(a).
99. IRC § 4944(a)(2); Reg. § 53.4944-1(b)(1).
100. Reg. § 53.4944-1(b)(2)(i).
101. *Id.*

a jeopardizing investment, however, is not willful if the manager does not know that it is a jeopardizing investment.[102]

A foundation manager's actions are due to reasonable cause if the manager has exercised his or her responsibility on behalf of the foundation with ordinary business care and prudence.[103] The *participation* of any foundation manager in the making of an investment consists of any manifestation of approval of the investment.[104] Clearly, a vote as a board member to approve an investment is participation. Board members who do not attend meetings but sanction investment decisions may be derelict as to their fiduciary responsibility, but their inability to participate in the investment decision and resulting lack of knowledge may shield them from the tax. If members of the board of directors receive a board information packet revealing the investment under scrutiny, they have the requisite knowledge; however, the tax applies only if they participate in the approval.

## (b) Reliance on Outside Advisors

If a foundation manager, after full disclosure of the factual situation to legal counsel (including house counsel), relies on the advice of that counsel, expressed in a reasoned written legal opinion, that a particular investment would not jeopardize the carrying out of any of the foundation's exempt purposes, the foundation manager's participation in the investment will ordinarily not be considered knowing or willful, and will ordinarily be considered due to reasonable cause. This is the case even where the investment is subsequently held to be a jeopardizing one. A lawyer is not qualified to pass on the appropriateness of an investment as such. Thus, a legal opinion from a lawyer must address a situation where, as a matter of law, the investment is excepted from classification as a jeopardizing investment, such as because it is a program-related investment.[105]

A written legal opinion is considered *reasoned*, even if it reaches a conclusion that is subsequently determined to be incorrect, as long as the opinion addresses itself to the facts and applicable law. A written legal opinion will not be considered reasoned if it does nothing more than recite the facts and express a conclusion. The absence of advice of legal counsel or qualified investment counsel with respect to an investment, however, does not, by itself, give rise to any inference that a foundation manager participated in the investment knowingly, willfully, or without reasonable cause.

Likewise, if a foundation manager, after full disclosure of the factual situation to qualified investment counsel, relies on the advice of that counsel, the foundation manager's participation in failing to provide for the long- and

---

102. Reg. § 53.4944-1(b)(2)(ii).
103. Reg. § 53.4944-1(b)(2)(iii).
104. Reg. § 53.4944-1(b)(2)(iv).
105. Reg. § 53.4944-1(b)(2)(v). *See* § 5.15(e).

short-term financial needs of the foundation will ordinarily not be considered knowing or willful, and will be considered due to reasonable cause. For this rule to apply, the advice must have been derived in a manner consistent with generally accepted practices of individuals who are qualified investment counsel and expressed in writing that a particular investment will provide for these financial needs of the foundation. Again, this is the case even where the investment is subsequently held to be a jeopardizing one.[106]

## (c)  Removal from Jeopardy

An additional tax is imposed in any case in which the initial tax is imposed and the investment is not removed from jeopardy during the taxable period.[107] An investment that jeopardizes the carrying out of exempt purposes is considered to be removed from jeopardy when the investment is sold or otherwise disposed of, and the proceeds from the sale or other disposition are not investments that jeopardize the carrying out of exempt purposes.[108] Correction of a jeopardizing investment may be difficult—if not impossible—where the asset is not marketable. An effort to maximize available funds from the investment may help to avoid the additional tax.

A change by a private foundation in the form or terms of a jeopardizing investment results in the removal of the investment from jeopardy if, after the change, the investment no longer jeopardizes the carrying out of the foundation's exempt purposes. The making of one jeopardizing investment by a foundation and a subsequent change by the foundation of the investment for another jeopardizing investment generally is treated as only one jeopardizing investment. A jeopardizing investment cannot be removed from jeopardy by a transfer from a private foundation to another foundation that is related to the transferor foundation[109] unless the investment is a program-related investment in the hands of the transferee foundation.[110]

The *taxable period* is the period beginning with the date on which the amount is invested in a jeopardizing manner and ending on the earliest of the following dates:

- The date on which the IRS mails a notice of deficiency with respect to the initial tax[111] imposed on the foundation.
- The date on which the initial tax is assessed.
- The date on which the amount invested is removed from jeopardy.[112]

---

106. *Id.*
107. IRC § 4944(b)(1); Reg. § 53.4944-5(d).
108. IRC § 4944(e)(2); Reg. § 53.4944-5(b).
109. *See* § 4.8.
110. Reg. § 53.4944-5(b).
111. IRC § 6212.
112. IRC § 4944(e)(1); Reg. § 53.4944-5(a).

This additional tax, which is to be paid by the foundation, is at the rate of 25 percent of the amount of the investment.[113] Where this tax is imposed and a foundation manager refuses to agree to part or all of the removal of the investment from jeopardy, a tax is imposed on the manager at the rate of 5 percent of the amount of the investment.[114] With respect to any one investment, the maximum amount of this tax is $20,000.[115] Where more than one foundation manager is liable for an additional tax with respect to any one jeopardizing investment, all of the managers are jointly and severally liable for the tax.[116]

Where the act or failure to act that gave rise to the additional tax is corrected within the correction period, the tax will not be assessed, or if assessed will be abated, or if collected will be credited or refunded.[117] The *correction period* is the period beginning on the date on which the *taxable event* occurs and ending 90 days after the date of mailing of a notice of deficiency with respect to the additional tax imposed on the event, extended by any period in which a deficiency cannot be assessed[118] and any other period that the IRS determines is reasonable and necessary to bring about correction of the taxable event.[119] In this setting, a taxable event is an act or failure to act giving rise to liability for tax under the jeopardizing investment rules.[120] This event occurs on the date a jeopardizing investment takes place.[121] *Correction* means removing the investment from jeopardy.[122]

The collection period is suspended during any litigation.[123]

The termination taxes[124] serve as third-tier taxes.

---

113. IRC § 4944(b)(1); Reg. § 53.4944-2(a). This tax is also known as a *second-tier tax* (IRC § 4963 (b); Reg. § 53.4963-1(b)).

114. IRC § 4944(b)(2); Reg. § 53.4944-2(b). This tax cannot be imposed until the individual involved has received adequate notice and had an opportunity to remove a jeopardizing investment (*Thorne v. Commissioner*, 99 T.C. 67 (1992)).

115. IRC § 4944(d)(2); Reg. § 53.4944-4(b).

116. IRC § 4944 (d)(1); Reg. § 53.4944-4(b).

117. IRC § 4961(a); Reg. § 53.4961-1.

118. IRC § 6213(a).

119. IRC § 4963(e)(1); Reg. § 53.4963-1(e)(1).

120. IRC § 4963(c); Reg. § 53.4963-1(c).

121. IRC § 4963(e)(2)(D); Reg. § 53.4963-1(e)(7)(iv).

122. IRC § 4963(d)(2)(C); Reg. § 53.4963-1(d)(2)(iii).

123. IRC § 4961(c); Reg. § 53.4961-2.

124. *See* Chapter 13.

# CHAPTER NINE

# Taxable Expenditures

The federal tax law regards private foundations as trusts that must serve public ends and their trustees as stewards of charitable assets that must be solely devoted to advancement of these purposes. Consequently, the activities for which private foundations may expend their funds are restricted by limitations that are far more stringent than those applicable to charitable organizations generally. These rules, in effect, impose a standard that forbids a private foundation to incur any expenditure for a variety of purposes or functions. Other types of tax-exempt organizations can engage in some amount of nonexempt activity without loss of exempt status or other penalty, but private foundations are not accorded any such leeway. Impermissible expenditures are termed *taxable expenditures.* The private foundation and some, if not all, of its disqualified persons are subject to an excise tax, and can possibly cause loss of the foundation's exemption, if any amount is paid or incurred for one of the following categories of *taxable expenditures:*[1]

1.  To carry on propaganda or otherwise attempt to influence legislation.

2.  To influence the outcome of any specific election, or to carry on any voter registration drive (except efforts of at least five states in scope, as described below).

3.  As a grant to an individual for travel, study, or other similar purpose, unless it meets the conditions listed below.

4.  As a grant to an organization unless:

    o  It is a public charity described in IRC § 509(a)(1) or (2), or

    o  It is a public charity described in IRC § 509(a)(3), other than a non–functionally integrated supporting organization[2] or a supporting organization controlled by a disqualified person,[3] or

    o  It is an exempt operating foundation,[4] or

    o  The private foundation making the grant exercises expenditure responsibility.[5]

These prohibitions apply where a private foundation either directly makes the expenditure itself for the impermissible activity or makes a grant to an organization (usually a public charity) with the funds targeted for an impermissible expenditure by the grantee. The taxable expenditures rules,

---

1.  IRC § 4945(d).
2.  IRC § 4942(g)(4)(a)(i); *functionally integrated* is defined in IRC § 4943(f)(5)(B) and discussed in § 15.7. This type of supporting organization subject to expenditure responsibility rules was created by the Pension Protection Act of 2006, effective for tax years beginning after August 18, 2006 (the day of its passage), with no explanation in legislative history. Many foundations were caught by surprise to find they incurred a taxable expenditure because they failed to exercise expenditure responsibility for this type of a grant.
3.  IRC § 4942(g)(4)(A)(ii).
4.  IRC § 4940(d)(2).
5.  *See* § 9.6.

like so many of the other private foundation rules, were enacted as part of the Tax Reform Act of 1969. Prior to that legislation, the only sanctions available in response to legislative, political, or other activity deemed inappropriate for private foundations were revocation of tax exemption and denial of charitable donee status—sanctions the IRS is usually reluctant to deploy. Moreover, it was thought that the standards under prior law as to the permissible level of activities were so vague as to encourage subjective application of the sanctions.

One summary of the rationale for these rules stated:

> In recent years (before 1969), private foundations had become increasingly active in political and legislative activities. In several instances called to the Congress's attention, funds were spent in ways clearly designed to favor certain candidates. In some cases, this was done by financing registration campaigns in limited geographical areas. In other cases contributions were made to organizations that then used the money to publicize the views, personalities, and activities of certain candidates. It also appeared that officials of some foundations exercised little or no control over the organizations receiving the funds from the foundations.[6]

It was also called to the Congress's attention that prior law did not effectively limit the extent to which foundations could use their money for "educational" grants to enable people to take vacations abroad, to have paid interludes between jobs, and to subsidize the preparation of materials furthering specific political viewpoints.

Congress concluded that more effective limitations must be placed on the extent to which tax-deductible and tax-exempt funds can be dispensed by private persons and that these limitations must involve more effective sanctions. Accordingly, Congress determined that a tax should be imposed on expenditures by private foundations for activities that should not be carried on by exempt organizations (such as lobbying, electioneering, and grassroots campaigning). Congress also believed that granting foundations should take substantial responsibility for the proper use of the funds they give away.[7]

## §9.1 LEGISLATIVE ACTIVITIES

A private foundation, as a charitable organization, is limited by the federal tax law in the extent to which it can engage, without endangering its tax exemption, in attempts to influence legislation. These undertakings are often referred to as *lobbying activities*. Private foundations are subject to an overlay of additional, more stringent, law in this regard. It is often critical for a private foundation to understand the lobbying activities permitted by a public charity

---

6. Joint Committee on Internal Revenue Taxation, *General Explanation of Tax Reform Act of 1969*, 91st Cong., 2d Sess. 47–48 (1970).

7. *Id.*

or charities to which it makes grants. Despite the severity of these rules, however, private foundations can support programs involving public policy and social advocacy issues so long as the activities do not involve attempts to influence legislation. Educational and scientific efforts involving these subjects are not necessarily legislative efforts, even if the problems are of a type with which government would be ultimately expected to deal.[8]

## (a) Law Applicable to Charities Generally

No substantial part of the activities of a charitable organization may consist of carrying on propaganda or otherwise attempting to influence legislation.[9] The term *legislation* means action by Congress, a state legislature, a local council or similar governing body, or the public in a referendum, initiative, constitutional amendment, or similar procedure.[10] It also includes a proposed treaty, required to be submitted by the president to the Senate for its advice and consent from the time the president's representative begins to negotiate its position with the prospective parties to the treaty.[11]

One definition of the term *influence legislation* is any attempt (1) to influence any legislation through an attempt to affect the opinion of the general public or any segment of it or (2) to influence any legislation through communication with any member or employee of a legislative body, or with any government official or employee who may participate in the formulation of the legislation.[12] Another is (1) to contact, or urge the public to contact, members of a legislative body for the purpose of proposing, supporting, or opposing legislation, or (2) to advocate the adoption or rejection of legislation.[13] The word *substantial* in this setting is essentially undefined, although it is measured by the expenditures of money, time spent, and other facts and circumstances of the particular organization's activities.[14] A charitable organization that engages in legislative activities to a substantial extent is an *action organization* and thus cannot qualify as or remain federally tax-exempt.[15]

This rule as to lobbying is termed the *substantial part test*. Public charities that engage in extensive lobbying, and their management, can become subject to a

---

8. *See* exceptions at § 9.1(d).

9. IRC § 501(c)(3). In general, *see Tax-Exempt Organizations*, Chapter 22; *Tax Planning and Compliance*, Chapter 23.

10. IRS § 4911(e)(2); Reg. §§ 1.501(c)(3)-1(c)(3)(ii), 56.4911-2(d)(1)(i).

11. Reg. § 56.4911-2(d)(1)(i).

12. IRC § 4911(d)(1).

13. Reg. § 1.501(c)(3)-1(c)(3)(ii).

14. E.g., *The Nationalist Movement v. Commissioner*, 102 T.C. 558 (1994), *aff'd*, 37 F.3d 216 (5th Cir. 1994).

15. Reg. § 1.501(c)(3)-1(c)(3).

penalty tax under the substantial part test.[16] Most public charities can elect[17] an alternative set of rules that have the advantage of specifically measuring allowable lobbying; this package of rules[18] is known as the *expenditure test.* This test allows a charitable organization to spend stated percentages for lobbying, but taxes any excess lobbying outlays. Many of the rules pertaining to private foundations in this area are the same as those formulated as part of the expenditure test for public charities.

Charitable organizations that engage in lobbying may also have to comply with the Lobbying Disclosure Act of 1995,[19] which in part utilizes some of these federal tax rules.

## (b) Law Specifically Applicable to Private Foundations

A private foundation may not pay or incur any amount to carry on propaganda or otherwise attempt to influence legislation.[20] To do so would be to make a taxable expenditure. Thus, though private foundations are subject to the general test of *substantiality* applicable to charitable organizations as a condition of tax exemption, they are also subject to more specific prohibitions. There are two types of lobbying embraced by the prohibition:

1.  An attempt to influence legislation through communication with any member or employee of a legislative body or with any other governmental official or employee who may participate in the formulation of legislation.[21] This is *direct lobbying.*

2.  An attempt to influence any legislation through an attempt to affect the opinion of the general public or any segment of it.[22] This is *grassroots lobbying.*

An expenditure is an attempt to influence legislation if it is for a direct lobbying communication or a grassroots lobbying communication.[23] A *direct lobbying communication* means an attempt to influence legislation through communication with (1) a member or employee of a legislative body, or (2) a government official or employee (other than a member or employee of a legislative body) who may participate in the formulation of the legislation, but only if the

---

16. IRC § 4912.
17. IRC § 501(h).
18. IRC § 4911.
19. 2 U.S.C. §§ 1601–1602.
20. IRC § 4945(d)(1); Reg. § 53.4945-2(a)(1); this regulation was amended in 1990 to cross-reference the definitions to the Reg. § 1.501(h) rules found in Reg. § 53.4911-2.
21. IRC § 4945(e)(2).
22. IRC § 4945(e)(1).
23. Reg. § 53.4945-2(a)(1).

principal purpose of the communication is to influence legislation.[24] Moreover, to be a direct lobbying communication, it must refer to specific legislation and reflect a view on that legislation.[25]

The phrase *specific legislation* means:

- Legislation that has been introduced in a legislative body or a specific legislative proposal that the organization supports or opposes, and

- In the case of a referendum, ballot initiative, constitutional amendment, or other measure that is placed on the ballot by petitions signed by a required number or percentage of voters, an item becomes specific legislation when the petition is first circulated among voters for signature.[26]

A *grassroots lobbying communication* is an attempt to influence any legislation through an attempt to affect the opinions of the general public or any segment of it.[27] To be a grassroots lobbying communication, the communication must refer to specific legislation, it must reflect a view on the legislation, and it must encourage its recipient to take action with respect to the legislation.[28] The phrase *encouraging recipient to take action* with respect to legislation means that the communication specifically:

- States that the recipient should contact a legislator, staff member, or other government official,

- Gives the address, telephone number, or similar information about the individual(s) to be contacted,

- Provides some material to facilitate the contact (such as a petition or postcard), or

- Identifies one or more legislators who will vote on the legislation as opposing the communication's view of the legislation, being undecided with respect to it, being the recipient's representative in the legislature, or being a member of the committee or subcommittee that will consider the legislation.[29]

## (c) Grants to Charities That Lobby

A general support grant by a private foundation to a public charity that conducts lobbying activities is not a taxable expenditure to the extent that the

---

24. Reg. § 56.4911-2(b)(1)(i).
25. Reg. § 56.4911-2(b)(1)(ii).
26. Reg. § 56.4911-2(d)(1)(ii).
27. Reg. § 56.4911-2(b)(2)(i).
28. Reg. § 56.4911-2(b)(2)(ii).
29. Reg. § 56.4911-2(b)(2)(iii).

grant is not *earmarked* to be used to influence legislation.[30] The word *earmarked* means an agreement, oral or written, that the grant will be used for specific purposes.[31] Whether the public charity has elected to measure its permissible lobbying under the expenditure test is irrelevant.

A grant by a private foundation to fund a specific project of a public charity is not a taxable expenditure to the extent that the grant is not earmarked for a legislative purpose and the amount of the grant (aggregated with other grants by the foundation for the same project in the same year) does not exceed the amount budgeted, for the year of the grant, by the grantee for activities of the project that are not attempts to influence legislation.[32] There are rules for multiyear grants.

Due to the reluctance on the part of some private foundations to support public charities that conduct lobbying activity, the organization Charity Lobbying in the Public Interest[33] engaged the law firm of Caplin & Drysdale to prepare a letter addressing a series of questions about such grants. Some of the questions answered in the memo include the following:

Q: What constitutes "earmarking" of a grant for lobbying?

A: "Earmarking" a grant for lobbying is making a grant with an oral or written agreement that the grant will be used for lobbying.

Q: Absent a specific agreement to the contrary, will the recitation in a grant agreement that "there is no agreement, oral or written, that directs that the grant funds be used for lobbying activities" be sufficient to establish to the satisfaction of the IRS that there has been no earmarking for lobbying?

A: Yes, absent evidence of an agreement to the contrary.

Q: Is a foundation required to include a specific provision in its grant agreements that no part of the grant funds may be used for lobbying?

---

30. Reg. § 53.4945-2(a)(6)(i). These rules were written in the aftermath of adoption of the final regulations (in 1990) underlying the expenditure test enacted in 1976. It was thought that, as a consequence of this body of law, the scope and extent of lobbying by public charities would increase. These prospects gave the private foundation community pause; there was fear that the legislative activities of a grantee public charity electing under the expenditure test would be attributed to the grantor private foundation, causing a taxable expenditure. (The likelihood of this result was present before enactment of the expenditure test, but it was heightened following the introduction of that test and the foundation community's perception of it.) In fact, so few public charities have elected the expenditure test that the risk of lobbying by a grantor public charity being attributed to a grantee private foundation is scarcely greater today than it was before 1976.
31. Reg. § 53.4945-2(a)(5)(i).
32. Reg. § 53.4945-2(a)(6)(ii).
33. Reports describing all 16 questions with IRS responses can be found at the Center for Lobbying in the Public Interest (www.clpi.org).

A: A specific provision is required only if the grantee organization is not a public charity, or if the private foundation earmarks the grant for use by an organization that is not a public charity.

Q: Under what circumstances can a foundation make a grant to public charity for a specific project that includes lobbying?

A: Such a grant can be made if (1) no part of the grant is earmarked for lobbying, (2) the foundation obtains a proposed budget signed by an officer of the public charity showing that the amount of the grant, together with other grants by the same foundation for the same project and year, does not exceed the amount budgeted, for the year of the grant, by the public charity for activities of the project that are not lobbying, and (3) the foundation has no reason to doubt the accuracy of the budget.

Q: Similarly, does it matter that the public charity's proposal indicates that it will be seeking funds for the specific project from other private foundations without referring to other additional sources of funds?

A: No, the specific project grant rules in § 53.4945–2(a)(6)(ii) of the regulations do not require the foundation to concern itself about the other sources of funding for the project in such situations.

Q: What if, in the conduct of the project, the public charity actually makes lobbying expenses in excess of its estimate in the grant proposal?

A: If there was no earmarking and no reason to doubt the original accuracy of the budgets, no taxable expenditure occurs. However, knowledge of the excess may provide a reason to doubt the accuracy of subsequent budgets submitted by the public charity.[34]

In this connection, the private foundation may rely on budget documents or other sufficient evidence supplied by the prospective grantee—unless the foundation doubts or reasonably should doubt the accuracy or reliability of the documents.[35] Again, whether the public charity has elected to be under the expenditure test is irrelevant.

The prohibition against electioneering and lobbying, though absolute for the foundation itself, does not apply to foundation officials acting on their own behalf. Although officials are closely identified with the foundation they have created or direct, the rules do not constrain acts of individuals acting as such. Certainly it is prudent for the officials to overtly state that they are not acting on behalf of the foundation, and foundation monies or facilities should never be used to advance a candidate or promote legislative initiatives. IRS Publication

---

34. This situation is addressed in Reg. § 53.4945-2(a)(7)(ii), Example 13.
35. Reg. § 53.4945-2(a)(6)(iii).

1828, *Tax Guide for Churches and Religious Organizations,* contains guidelines for determining when a minister represents him- or herself rather than the church. The concepts should be studied by a foundation official who actively participates in public affairs.[36]

If the public charity grantee loses its tax exemption because of excessive lobbying, the private foundation grantor will not be considered as having made a taxable expenditure if it was unaware of the revocation and does not control the grantee.[37] A private foundation may want to protect itself from any question about whether it pays for lobbying by specifically requiring that its public charity grantees agree not to do so. For grantees significantly involved in public affairs, the prudent foundation should retain financial information reflecting the portion of the public charities' budget spent on lobbying and also document its efforts with the grants checklist found in Exhibit 9.2. As additional evidence that its funds will not be spent for lobbying, the foundation can request signature of the grant payment transmittal letter provided in Exhibit 9.5. It is important to note that these precautions are not required by law.

A private foundation does not make a taxable expenditure merely because it makes a grant on the condition that the grantee obtain a matching support appropriation from a governmental body.[38]

A private foundation does not make a taxable expenditure when it pays or incurs expenditures in connection with carrying on discussions with officials of government bodies as long as:

- The subject of the discussions is a program that is jointly funded by the foundation and the government or is a new program that may be so jointly funded.

- The discussions are undertaken for the purpose of exchanging data and information on the subject matter of the program.

- The discussions are not undertaken by foundation managers in order to make any direct attempt to persuade governmental officials or employees to take particular positions on specific legislative issues other than the program.[39]

An amount paid or incurred by a recipient of a program-related investment[40] in connection with an appearance before or communication with a

---

36. Also *see* Rev. Rul. 2007-41, 2007-1 C.B. 1421, in which the IRS provided 21 examples of voter education versus electioneering and instances where an individual may speak personally rather than as a representative of an organization.
37. Reg. § 53.4945-2(a)(7)(i).
38. Reg. § 53.49452(a)(3).
39. *Id.*
40. *See* § 8.3.

legislative body, with respect to legislation or proposed legislation of direct interest to the grantee, is not attributed to the investing foundation as long as the foundation did not earmark the funds for legislative activities and the recipient was allowed a business expense deduction for the expenditure.[41] There is no business expense deduction for lobbying unless it is done at the local level.[42]

A private foundation is highly unlikely to have a membership base; if it does, communications to members must be tested against the rules concerning direct lobbying communications.[43] A private foundation may make a grant to an electing public charity earmarked for a communication from the public charity to its members; where special rules[44] apply, the grant is not a taxable expenditure.[45] A grant to a nonelecting public charity for a communication to its members must be tested against the rules concerning direct lobbying communications.

### (d) Nonpartisan Study of Social Issues

Sponsoring discussions or conferences, conducting research, and publishing educational materials about matters of broad social and economic subjects, such as human rights or war, are appropriate and permissible activities for a private foundation. These topics are often the subject matter of legislation, involve public controversy, and raise the possibility of the private foundation's being treated as conducting prohibited legislative activity. A private foundation is safe in sponsoring discussions on such topics and examining these issues, however, as long as the activity constitutes engaging in nonpartisan analysis, study, or research and making available the results of the work to the general public, a segment of the public, or to governmental bodies, officials, or employees.[46] Examinations and discussions of societal problems are not necessarily direct nor grassroots lobbying communications, even where the problems are of the type with which government would be expected to deal ultimately.[47] Thus, expenditures in connection with public discussion or communications with

---

41. Reg. § 53.4945-2(a)(4).

42. IRC § 162(e)(2).

43. Reg. § 53.4945-2(a)(2).

44. Reg. § 56.4911-5. Under these rules, in certain instances, expenditures for a membership communication are not regarded as lobbying expenditures (even where the expenditures would be lobbying expenditures if the communication was with nonmembers). In other instances, expenditures for a membership communication are treated as direct lobbying expenditures even though they would be grassroots lobbying expenditures if the communication was with nonmembers. There is a set of more lenient rules that apply for communications that are directed only to members, and one for communications that are directed primarily to members.

45. Reg. § 53.4945-2(a)(2).

46. IRC § 4945(e); Reg. § 53.4945-2(d)(1)(i).

47. Reg. § 53.4945-2(d)(4).

members of legislative bodies or governmental employees, concerning an issue currently being considered by a legislative body, are not taxable expenditures as long as the discussion does not address itself to the merits of a specific legislative proposal, nor directly encourage recipients to take action with respect to legislation.

The phrase *nonpartisan analysis, study, or research* means an independent and objective exposition or study of a particular subject matter.[48] This definition embraces an activity that is considered educational;[49] this means the exposition can advocate a particular position or viewpoint as long as there is a sufficiently full and fair exposition of the pertinent facts to enable an individual or the public to form an independent opinion or conclusion. A foundation could, for example, issue a communiqué distributing the results of a study reaching the conclusion that oil tankers should have double hulls to lessen the possibility of oil spills, so long as the information forming the basis for the viewpoint is unbiased.

Normally, a publication or a broadcast is evaluated on a presentation-by-presentation basis. If a publication or a broadcast is one of a series prepared or supported by a private foundation and the series as a whole meets the standards of this exception, however, any individual publication or broadcast within the series will not result in a taxable expenditure even though the individual broadcast or publication does not, by itself, meet the standards. Whether a broadcast or a publication is part of a series will ordinarily depend on all the facts and circumstances of each particular situation.[50]

As to the *making available test*, a private foundation can do this by distributing reprints of articles and reports, conferences, meetings, and discussions, and by dissemination to the news media and other public forums. These communications, however, may not be confined to or be directed solely toward those who are interested in one side of a particular issue.[51]

Subsequent use of nonpartisan analysis, study, or research in grassroots lobbying (usually by a public charity grantee) may cause publication of the results to become a grassroots lobbying communication and thus not shielded from this exception.[52] There are rules detailing how this can occur, where the materials are *advocacy communications or research materials*.[53] In this connection, there is a primary purpose test, with a "safe harbor" rule to facilitate it.[54] A

---

48. Reg. § 53.4945-2(d)(1)(ii).
49. Reg. § 1.501(c)(3)-1(d)(3). *See Tax-Exempt Organizations*, Chapter 7.
50. Reg. § 53.4945-2(d)(1)(iii).
51. Reg. § 53.4945-2(d)(1)(iv).
52. Reg. § 53.4945-2(d)(1)(v)(A).
53. Reg. § 56.4911-2(b)(2)(v). These are materials that refer to and reflect a view on specific legislation but do not, in their initial format, contain a direct encouragement for recipients to take action with respect to legislation.
54. Reg. § 56.4911-2(b)(2)(v)(C), (E).

foundation grant is converted to a taxable expenditure under the *subsequent use rule*, however, only where the foundation's primary purpose in making the grant is for lobbying or where the foundation knows (or should know) that the public charity's primary purpose in preparing the communication to be funded by the grant is for use in lobbying.[55]

A communication that reflects a view on specific legislation is not within this exception if the communication directly encourages the recipient to take action with respect to the legislation.[56] A communication can encourage the recipient to take action with respect to legislation, but not do so *directly*,[57] thereby preserving this exception.[58]

Amounts paid or incurred in connection with providing technical advice or assistance to a governmental body, a governmental committee, or a subdivision of either, in response to a written request from that entity (but not just from an individual member of it), do not constitute taxable expenditures.[59] The response to the request must be available to every member of the requesting entity. The offering of opinions or recommendations ordinarily is shielded by this exception if the opinions or recommendations are specifically requested by the entity or are directly related to the requested materials.[60]

## (e)   Self-Defense Exception

The taxable expenditures rules do not apply to any amount paid or incurred in connection with an appearance before or communication with any legislative body with respect to a possible decision of that body that might affect the existence of the foundation, its powers and duties, its tax-exempt status, or the deductibility of contributions to it.[61] Under this exception, known as the *self-defense exception*, a foundation may communicate with anyone (legislature, committees, individual legislators, staff members, or executive branch representatives)—as long as the communication is confined to the prescribed subjects. A foundation may make expenditures in order to initiate legislation, without there being taxable expenditures, if the legislation concerns *only* matters that are the prescribed ones listed above. It is not enough, however, that the legislation merely bear on the scope of the foundation's program activities in the future. Examples of the type of legislative proposal that might threaten the foundation's existence or its powers include:

---

55. Reg. § 53.4945-2(d)(1)(v)(B).
56. Reg. § 53.4945-2(d)(1)(vi). *See supra* text accompanied by notes 26–27.
57. Reg. § 56.4911-2(b)(2)(iv).
58. Reg. § 53.4945-2(d)(1)(vi).
59. IRC § 4945(e)(2); Reg. § 53.4945-2(d)(2)(i).
60. Reg. § 53.4945-2(d)(2)(ii).
61. IRC § 4945(e)(2); Reg. § 53.4945-2(d)(3)(i).

- A rule that would require the inclusion of outside directors on a foundation's governing body.

- A provision that would restrict the power of a foundation to engage in transactions with certain related persons.

- A change in permitted holdings for excess business holding purposes that would cause the foundation to have a self-dealing transaction.

- A law to limit the life of a foundation to some term certain.

Examples of the type of legislative proposal that is not considered to threaten the life or powers of the foundation include:

- An appropriation bill to decrease government funding for programs that the foundation normally funds that would place a financial burden on the foundation by increasing demand for its support by grantees conducting such programs.

- A proposal for a state to assume certain responsibilities for nursing care of the aged that are currently performed by a foundation that believes that it and other private organizations can better accomplish the job.

## § 9.2 POLITICAL CAMPAIGN ACTIVITIES

A private foundation, as a charitable organization, is basically forbidden by the federal tax law to engage, without jeopardizing its tax-exempt status, in political campaign activities. There are more specific rules in this regard for private foundations. It can be important for a private foundation to know the applicability of the federal tax laws relating to political campaign activities as they apply to the public charity or charities to which it makes grants.

### (a) Law Applicable to Charities Generally

A charitable organization, whether public charity or private foundation, may not participate in or intervene in (including the publishing or distributing of statements) any political campaign on behalf of or in opposition to any candidate for public office.[62] Activities that constitute *participation or intervention* in a political campaign, for or against a candidate, include the publication or distribution of written or printed statements or the making of oral statements on behalf of or in opposition to a candidate.[63] For example, a charitable organization making political campaign statements in its fundraising literature

---

62. IRC § 501(c)(3). In general, *see Tax-Exempt Organizations,* Chapter 23; *Tax Planning and Compliance,* Chapter 23.
63. Reg. § 1.501(c)(3)-1(c)(3)(iii).

transgresses these rules.[64] These activities also embrace campaign contributions and the provision of facilities and other resources to political candidates (although that type of support is likely to also be a violation of federal or state campaign finance laws).

The term *candidate for public office* means an individual who offers himself or herself, or is proposed by others, as a contestant for an elective public office, whether the office be national, state, or local.[65] As to the word *campaign*, a federal court observed that "a campaign for a public office in a public election merely and simply means running for office, or candidacy for office, as the word is used in common parlance and as it is understood by the man in the street."[66] While these rules lack a definition of the term *public office*, that term is defined in the context of defining disqualified persons;[67] this is a facts-and-circumstances determination that focuses on whether a significant part of the activities of a public employee is the independent performance of policy-making functions.[68]

A charitable organization that engages in political campaign activities is an *action organization* and thus cannot qualify as or remain federally tax-exempt.[69] Public charities that engage in political campaign activities, and their management, can become subject to penalty taxes.[70] Moreover, a public charity in this circumstance can have its tax year involved immediately terminated and taxes assessed on an accelerated basis,[71] and willful and repeated violations may result in a court-imposed injunction, pursued by the IRS.[72]

Charitable organizations that engage in *political* activities (which may not be political campaign activities) may become ensnared in the political organizations rules, whereby the expenditures involved are taxed.[73]

## (b)  Law Specifically Applicable to Private Foundations

In general, a private foundation may not pay or incur any amount to influence the outcome of any specific public election or carry on, directly or indirectly, any voter registration drive.[74] To do so would be to make a taxable expenditure.

---

64. E.g., Tech. Adv. Mem. 9609007.
65. Reg. § 1.501(c)(3)-1(c)(3)(iii).
66. *Norris v. United States*, 86 F.2d 379, 382 (8th Cir. 1936), *rev'd on other grounds*, 300 U.S. 564 (1937).
67. *See* § 4.9.
68. Reg. § 53.4946-1(g)(2)(i).
69. Reg. § 1.501(c)(3)-1(c)(3).
70. IRC § 4955.
71. IRC § 6852.
72. IRC § 7409.
73. IRC § 527(f)(1).
74. IRC § 4945(d)(2); Reg. § 53.4945-3(a)(1).

A grant by a private foundation to a public charity is not a taxable expenditure, however, if the grant is not earmarked[75] to be used for political campaign activities.[76] Thus, if a public charity were to use foundation funds for a political campaign activity under these circumstances, no portion of the grant would be a taxable expenditure, assuming no agreement, oral or written, by which the foundation may cause the grantee organization to engage in the prohibited activity.[77]

A private foundation is considered to be influencing the outcome of a specific public election if it participates or intervenes, directly or indirectly, in any political campaign on behalf of or in opposition to any candidate for public office.[78] The phrase *participation or intervention* in a political campaign includes:

- Publishing or distributing written or printed statements or making oral statements on behalf of or in opposition to a candidate for public office.

- Paying salaries or expenses of campaign workers.

- Conducting or paying the expenses of conducting a voter registration drive limited to the geographic area covered by the campaign.[79]

- Making a campaign contribution for the benefit of a candidate for public office (which may also be a campaign financing law violation).

## (c)  Voter Registration Drives

The taxable expenditure rule as to political campaign activities is inapplicable to any amount paid or incurred by a tax-exempt charitable organization, including a private foundation, where:

- Its activities are nonpartisan, not confined to one specific election period, and are carried on in at least five states.

- Substantially all (at least 85 percent) of its income is expended directly for the active conduct of its exempt function activities.

- Substantially all of its support (other than gross investment income)[80] is received from tax-exempt organizations, the general public, governmental units, or any combination of these sources, as long as no more than 25 percent of this support is received from any one exempt organization and as long as no more than one-half of its support is received from gross

---

75. *See* text accompanied by *supra* note 30.
76. Reg. §§ 53.4945-3(a)(1), 53.4945-2(a)(5)(i).
77. Reg. § 53.4945-2(a)(5)(i).
78. Reg. § 53.4945-3(a)(2).
79. *Id.*
80. IRC § 509(e).

investment income, with these computations made on the basis of the most recent five tax years of the organization.[81]

- Contributions to the organization for voter registration drives are not subject to conditions that they may be used only in specified states, possessions of the United States, or political subdivisions or other areas of any of these jurisdictions, or the District of Columbia, or that they may be used in only one specific election period.[82]

An advance ruling may be obtained as to the status of an organization under these rules.[83] Where these requirements are satisfied, an amount paid or incurred by a private foundation for the activity is not a taxable expenditure.[84]

Advance approval from the IRS of these types of voter registration activities should be sought by means of filing an IRS form.[85]

## §9.3 GRANTS TO INDIVIDUALS

A private foundation may make grants to individuals for travel, study, or other similar purposes, but to do so it must first obtain approval from the IRS for its written procedures for making the grants. A taxable expenditure results if grants of this nature to individuals are paid without an approved plan.[86] Grants to individuals for shelter and food following a disaster, no-strings-attached awards for achievement, and certain other types of grants to individuals may not require a preapproved plan.[87]

A grant to an individual for travel, study, or other similar purposes is not a *taxable expenditure*, however, if the grant is awarded on an objective and nondiscriminatory basis pursuant to a procedure approved in advance by the IRS and it is demonstrated to the satisfaction of the IRS that:

- The grant constitutes a scholarship or fellowship grant that is excluded from gross income[88] and is to be used for study at an educational institution that normally maintains a regular faculty and curriculum and normally has a regularly organized body of students in attendance at the place where the educational activities are carried on,

---

81. IRC § 4945(f), penultimate sentence.
82. IRC § 4945(f); Reg. § 53.4945-3(b)(1), (3).
83. IRC § 4945(f); Reg. § 53.4945-3(b)(4).
84. IRC § 4945(f), last sentence; Reg. § 53.4945-3(b)(1), (2).
85. Form 8940, plus a $1,000 filing fee (Rev. Proc. 2014-8, 2014-1 I.R.B. 242).
86. Reg. § 53.4945-4(a)(1).
87. *See* discussion in § 9.3(b).
88. As provided by IRC § 117(a) before amendment in 1986; *see infra* note 89.

- The grant constitutes a prize or award that is excluded from gross income,[89] if the recipient of the prize or award is selected from the general public, or

- The purpose of the grant is to achieve a specific objective, produce a report or other similar product, or improve or enhance a literary, artistic, musical, scientific, teaching, or other similar capacity, skill, or talent of the grantee.[90]

For the first of these purposes, the broader definition of an excludable scholarship grant is that used in the federal income tax law before its amendment in 1986.[91] From time to time, the IRS issues private letter rulings concerning grants of this nature.[92]

## (a)  Grants for Travel, Study, or Other Purposes

Only grants paid to individuals for the three aforementioned specified purposes are subject to the prior plan approval rules. The IRS provided an illustration of the concepts in a ruling containing three scenarios.[93] In the first, the grant is not subject to IRS approval, but in the second and third, approval is required.

---

89. IRC § 74(b), without regard to IRC § 74(b)(3).

90. IRC § 4945(g); Reg. § 53.4945-4(a)(3)(ii). The IRS ruled that grants by a private foundation to college students who plan to adhere to a "moral commitment" to teach in a particular state after graduation are not scholarships under IRC § 117(a), and thus are not IRC § 4945 (b)(1) grants but are instead IRC § 4945(g)(3) grants (Rev. Rul. 77-44, 1977-1 C.B. 355). This position stems from the insistence of the IRS that a tax-excludable scholarship cannot exist where there is a requirement of a substantial quid pro quo from the recipient (e.g., *Bingler v. Johnson*, 394 U.S. 741 (1969); Rev. Rul. 73-256, 1973-1 C.B. 56, as modified by Rev. Rul. 74-540, 1974-2 C.B. 38; *Miss Georgia Scholarship Fund, Inc. v. Commissioner*, 72 T.C. 267 (1979)).

91. That is, for purpose of these individual grant rules, the term *scholarship* embraces payments for tuition, fees, living expenses, and allowances for travel, research, clerical help, or equipment. The Tax Reform Act of 1986 revised the IRC § 117 exclusion, so that it is available only for qualified scholarships, which are grants for tuition and fees required for enrollment or attendance, and fees, books, supplies, and equipment required for courses of instruction, thereby leaving outside the reach of the exclusion payments for room and board. However, Congress, in narrowing the scope of the IRC § 117 exclusion, did not intend to correspondingly narrow the scope of the private foundation individual grant rules. That is, in this context, it is the pre-1986 scholarship and fellowship rules that are applicable. The IRS, from the outset of this matter, recognized that the pre-1986 rules remain applicable in the private foundation individual grant setting (Notice 87-31, 1987-1 C.B. 475), as did the staff of the Joint Committee on Taxation in the "General Explanation of the Tax Reform Act of 1986" (p. 42, n. 21). This clarity was subsequently incorporated into the Internal Revenue Code (IRC § 4945(g)(1)).

92. E.g., Priv. Ltr. Rul. 9632024.

93. Rev. Rul. 77-380, 1977-2 C.B. 419.

**Scenario 1.** A private foundation organized to promote the art of journalism makes awards to persons whose work represents the best example of investigative reporting on matters concerning the government. Potential recipients are nominated; they do not apply for the award.[94] The awards are granted in recognition of past achievement and are not intended to finance any specific activities of the recipients or to impose any conditions on the manner in which they are expended by the recipient. Therefore, since the payments are not to finance study, travel, or a similar purpose, the awards project is not subject to prior approval.

**Scenario 2.** Assume instead that the annual award recipients are required to take a three-month summer tour to study government at educational institutions. These awards are subject to prior approval, because the payment is required to be used for study and travel.

**Scenario 3.** The facts are the same as in Scenario 1, except that the award must be used to pursue study at an educational institution and qualifies as a scholarship. Again, prior approval is required.

A similar conclusion was reached in a ruling concerning grants to science fair winners that required them to use the prizes for their education. The program was a scholarship plan requiring approval.[95]

**Other Purposes.** The meaning of grants for *other similar purposes* is elusive. The regulations provide that student loans and program-related investments constitute grants of this nature.[96] If the payment is given with the expectation or requirement that the recipient perform specific activities not directly of benefit to the foundation, a grant occurs. Research grants and payments to allow recipients to compose music or to choreograph a ballet are examples of awards for *similar purposes* when the recipient must perform to earn the award.

**Type of Financial Support.** The IRS approved the amendment of a foundation's research grant program to include payments for infant and child care.[97] The existing program granted funds for equipment, supplies, graduate student support, technical and secretarial services, travel, summer salary, and salary offset for released time from teaching. The foundation wished to encourage young women to embark upon academic careers. Provision of child care funds was intended to enhance the ability of young women fellows to continue to do

---

94. Thus, the IRC § 74(b) exclusion can potentially apply if the recipient transfers that award to a qualifying organization.
95. Rev. Rul. 76-461, 1976-2 C.B. 371.
96. Reg. § 53.4945-4(a)(2). *See* § 8.3.
97. Priv. Ltr. Rul. 9116032.

research work at universities and encourage more women scientists and engineers.

## (b) Other Individual Grants

A private foundation need not receive advance approval from the IRS to make grants to individuals for charitable purposes other than grants for travel, study, or similar purpose when the grant recipient is not required to perform specific actions, services, or meet some requirements. Thus, a plan to make payments to indigent individuals for the purchase of food or clothing does not require prior IRS approval. Similarly, a program to award grants to individuals in recognition of past achievement, such as a competition among students, not intended to finance any future activities of the individual grantee, and under circumstances where no conditions are imposed on the manner in which the awards may be expended by the recipients, does not require prior approval.[98]

**Food, Shelter, and Aid for the Poor or Distressed.** Programs to make grants-in-aid to individuals who lack the resources to satisfy their basic human needs are not required to be preapproved by the IRS. Nonetheless, the foundation has a burden of proving the recipients are chosen in a nondiscriminatory fashion. The criteria for awarding such grants for food, shelter, and medical care should be designed to award funds only to those who are indeed qualified for charitable assistance or persons also referred to as members of a charitable class. To document the charitable nature of the program, it is advisable that a written policy, perhaps including an application form, be used by the foundation to describe the basis for the decision to grant aid. Facts such as income levels, cause of the hardship, recommendations of a government agency, or referrals from a church are among the factors that might be used to make the choice.

For many years, the IRS approved, as exempt functions, of private foundations' (and other charities') disaster relief and hardship programs, including those where the beneficiaries were employees (or perhaps also former employees), and their families, of related companies or other organizations. In these situations, any private benefit, to the beneficiaries or any related entities, was deemed by the IRS to be incidental and thus not to adversely affect the grantor's tax-exempt status.[99] Then, in the late 1990s, the IRS reversed this policy, concluding that company foundation disaster and emergency relief programs were not exempt charitable functions because of private inurement accruing to the sponsoring company in the form of promotion of a loyal and stable employee base.[100] Specifically in the private foundation context, these payments

---

98. *See supra* note 84; Reg. § 53.4945-4(a)(3)(i); Rev. Rul. 76-460, 1976-2 C.B. 371.
99. *See* § 5.8(d).
100. E.g., Priv. Ltr. Rul. 199914040, revoking Priv. Ltr. Rul. 9516047.

pursuant to these programs were not, according to the IRS, qualifying distributions in that they were not made in advancement of charitable purposes,[101] were forms of self-dealing,[102] and were taxable expenditures.

This was the status of the IRS's policy as to disaster relief programs at the time of the terrorist attacks on September 11, 2001. There was considerable confusion, including misunderstanding of applicable law, as to who was eligible for monetary relief and/or services being provided by charities in the immediate aftermath of the attacks. This turmoil was compounded by the IRS's proclamations that, to be eligible for this aid, an individual must demonstrate a financial need. This, however, is not the law; this type of assistance can be provided to those who are distressed, irrespective of financial condition.[103]

Legislation enacted in 2001 introduced rules for provision of assistance by charitable organizations to individuals who are victims of terrorism.[104] Pursuant to this enactment, charitable organizations that make payments to individuals by reason of the death, injury, wounding, or illness of an individual incurred as a result of the September 11, 2001, attacks, or as the result of an attack involving anthrax occurring on or after September 11, 2001, and before January 1, 2002, are not required to make a specific assessment of need for the payments to be considered made for charitable purposes. The grantor organization must make the payments in good faith using a reasonable and objective formula that is consistently applied.

A summary of this legislation, prepared by the staff of the Joint Committee on Taxation,[105] provided examples of these rules.[106] This analysis addressed the matter of the provision of disaster relief assistance by a private foundation controlled by an employer where those who are assisted are employees of the employer. It articulated this standard: "If payments in connection with a qualified disaster are made by a private foundation to employees (and their family members) of an employer that controls the foundation, the presumption that the charity acts consistently with the requirements of section 501(c)(3) applies if the class of beneficiaries is large or indefinite and if recipients are selected based on an objective determination of need by an independent committee of the private foundation, a majority of the members of which are persons other than persons who are in a position to exercise substantial influence over the affairs of the controlling employer (determined under principles similar to those in effect under section 4958)."[107] A qualified disaster

---

101. *See* § 6.1

102. *See* § 5.8(d).

103. *See Tax-Exempt Organizations*, § 7.2, text accompanied by notes 46–51.

104. *Victims of Terrorism Tax Relief Act*, Pub. L. No. 107-124, 107th Cong., 1st Sess. (2001).

105. JCX-91-01.

106. *See Tax-Exempt Organizations*, § 7.2, pp. 200–202.

107. The reference to "section 4958" is to the intermediate sanctions rules. *See Tax-Exempt Organizations*, Chapter 21, *Intermediate Sanctions*; and *Tax Compliance*, Chapter 20.

means a disaster that results from a terroristic or military action, a presidentially declared disaster, an accident involving a common carrier, and any other event that the IRS determines is catastrophic.[108] This legislative history stated that the IRS is expected to reconsider its ruling position, in connection with private foundations and disaster relief programs, in light of this paradigm.

The IRS returned to this matter of disaster relief programs provided by charitable organizations by means of a publication issued in 2005.[109] Disaster programs of company-sponsored charities may be treated as charitable activities where (1) the awards are paid to "needy and distressed persons" pursuant to appropriate standards; (2) the charitable organization's program does not relieve the company of any legal obligation, such as an obligation under a collective bargaining agreement or written plan to provide insurance benefits; and (3) the company does not use the program to recruit employees, induce employees to continue their employment, or otherwise follow a course of action sought by the company. The destruction of an employee's home by fire or medical emergency attributable to a health condition does not constitute an eligible disaster.

A financial assistance program was found not to be a charitable undertaking, because a substantial portion of the charitable class to be aided consisted of employees of a related for-profit corporation, thus causing unwarranted private benefit and self-dealing involving a private foundation that would have conducted the program.[110] The substantial private benefit was described as enabling employees of the corporation to "realize a real and significant benefit because they have recourse to funds in times of financial hardship as a result of their employment when other revenues have been exhausted." (The foundation estimated it would award 5 to 10 grants each year; the potential beneficiaries totaled 20,000.)

The IRS wrote that this program is "essentially an assistance benefit that provides protection and security whether or not used," and that the corporation can "utilize this benefit program to recruit and retain a more stable and productive workforce." The IRS thus concluded that this program would provide far more than incidental private benefit to the employer corporation and that the foundation, if it conducted the program, would be engaging in self-dealing that is much more than incidental or tenuous.[111] The above-referenced IRS publication, revised in 2009 to recognize employer-sponsored public charities, employer-sponsored donor-advised funds, and employer-sponsored private foundations, states that "[l]ike public charities, private foundations can make need-based distributions to victims of disasters or to the poor or

---

108. IRC § 139(c).
109. *Disaster Relief: Providing Assistance Through Charitable Organizations* (Pub. 3833).
110. Priv. Ltr. Rul. 200926033.
111. *See* § 5.8(d).

distressed." It observes that the IRS previously ruled that "because the availability of the disaster relief programs aided employers in recruiting and retaining a stable workforce, such programs conferred a significant private benefit on the sponsoring companies." The publication, taking into account congressional intent following the terrorist attacks in 2001, states: "Accordingly employer-sponsored private foundations may provide assistance to employees or family members affected by a qualified disaster . . . , as long as certain safeguards are in place to ensure that such assistance is serving charitable purposes, rather than the business purpose of the employer. Employer-sponsored private foundations can only make payments to employees or their family members affected by qualified disasters, not in nonqualified disasters or in emergency hardship situations."

A financial assistance program conducted by a tax-exempt charitable organization was approved where the potential beneficiaries were members of a related association because this membership constituted a "large and indefinite number" of individuals.[112]

The need to establish criteria to evidence the charitable nature of such programs was also indicated in the IRS refusal to approve a program to grant funds to ministers to pay outstanding educational loan balances related to studying for their ministry.[113] It is important to note that the proposed grant was not one requiring prior IRS approval, if the ministers were not required to perform any specific acts. The factors the IRS found lacking included:

- The foundation did not request that the ministers establish that the funds would be used for charitable purposes. (With the right words in their grant documents, it could have been asserted that the program served religious purposes.)

- Grantee ministers were not required to provide any follow-up reports or accounting of the fashion in which they used the grant. (In connection with awards made in honor of achievement, no follow-up reporting is required.)

- Grantees were not required to evidence financial need to qualify for the grant. (Since the grants were not awarded on the basis of achievement, this factor should have been present.)

**Awards for Achievement.** Grants to individuals made in recognition of their accomplishments are also not necessarily treated as "grants for travel, study or similar purpose" that require prior IRS approval. Again, the criteria for choosing recipients must be designed to be fair, to achieve a charitable purpose, and

---

112. Priv. Ltr. Rul. 201221024.
113. Priv. Ltr. Rul. 9927047.

not to give favoritism to persons related to the foundation creators and managers. The Nobel Peace or MacArthur Lifetime Achievement Awards are good examples of prizes that serve to acknowledge persons who work to advance science, education, culture, health, and other charitable pursuits that benefit all. The awards honor past achievements and do not require that the monetary award be expended for a particular purpose or that the recipient perform a specific action. Examples of award plans that do not require preapproval versus one that does follow:

- Award by a private foundation to the person who had written the best work of literary criticism during the preceding year, not imposing any future condition on the recipient, was held not to be a taxable expenditure.[114]

- Grants made in recognition of past achievements in the field of journalism were ruled to not constitute taxable expenditures.[115]

- Grants to basketball coaches and their schools, based on overall win/loss records, grade point averages of the teams, and total community service hours of the players.[116]

- Periodic award by a private foundation to individuals for practical accomplishments in the field of commercial space activities, in recognition of past outstanding achievements.[117]

- By contrast, a cash prize to a high school senior whose exhibit received top honors in a local science fair constituted a taxable expenditure because it was intended to finance future educational activities of the grantee and conditions were imposed on the manner in which the award might be expended by the recipient.[118]

A renewal of a grant that satisfied the foregoing requirements is not treated as a grant to an individual that is subject to the requirements of these rules if (1) the grantor has no information indicating that the original grant is being used for any purpose other than that for which it was made, (2) any reports due at the time of the renewal decision pursuant to the terms of the original grant have been furnished, and (3) any additional criteria and procedures for renewal are objective and nondiscriminatory. An extension of the period over which a grant is to be paid is not itself regarded as a grant or a renewal of a grant.[119]

---

114. Rev. Rul. 75-393, 1975-2 C.B. 451.
115. Rev. Rul. 77-434, 1977-2 C.B. 420; Rev. Rul. 77-380, 1977-2 C.B. 419.
116. Priv. Ltr. Rul. 200327060.
117. Priv. Ltr. Rul. 200349007.
118. Rev. Rul. 76-461, 1976-2 C.B. 371.
119. Reg. § 53.4945-4(a)(3)(iii).

## (c) Compensatory Payments

The term *grants* does not include payments for personal services, such as salaries, consultant fees, and reimbursement of travel and other expenses incurred on behalf of the foundation, if paid to persons (regardless of whether the persons are individuals) working on a private foundation project.[120] A private foundation can, without engaging in grant-making, hire persons to assist it in planning, evaluating, or developing projects and program activity by consulting, advising, or participating in conferences organized by the foundation.[121] Persons hired to develop model curricula and educational materials are not considered grant recipients.[122] Likewise, a private foundation can retain the services of an individual to manage the implementation of its grant programs, with the payments treated as compensation for personal services rather than grants.[123]

In 1986, Congress narrowed the tax-free treatment of scholarships, fellowships, and prizes. As a result, all payments to grant recipients, other than those paid for tuition, books, and fees, are taxable. In addition, certain scholarships and, particularly, fellowships are taxable for the reason that the recipient is expected to render services in return for receiving the grant. Where there is a quid pro quo, the grant is made primarily for the benefit of the grantor private foundation, and the approval rules do not apply. A private foundation formed to aid worthy college students intending to teach in a particular state's public schools plans to make scholarship grants. As a condition of the grant, recipients must indicate that they are willing to teach for two years in state public schools after receiving their degrees. Even though the obligation carries no financial guarantee and is only a moral obligation of the student, the IRS found that these scholarships were not described in the federal tax definition of the term *scholarship* and, therefore, that prior approval was not required.[124]

## (d) Selection Process

Once a private foundation chooses to make grants subject to the approval process, it must adopt a suitable plan. In order for a foundation to establish that its grants to individuals for study, travel, or other purposes are made on an objective and nondiscriminatory basis, the grants must be awarded in accordance with a program that, if it were a substantial part of the private foundation's

---

120. Reg. § 53.4945-4(a)(3)(i). Cf. *Westward Ho v. Commissioner*, 63 T.C.M. 2617 (1992). Similarly, the purchase and distribution of gifts to underprivileged children during a holiday season constitute expenditures for charitable activities (namely, relief of the poor and distressed) and thus are not subject to these rules (Priv. Ltr. Rul. 9252031).
121. Reg. § 53.4945-4(a)(2).
122. Rev. Rul. 74-125, 1974-1 C.B. 327.
123. E.g., Priv. Ltr. Rul. 200408033.
124. Rev. Rul. 77-44, 1977-1 C.B. 118.

activities, would be consistent with (1) the existence of the private foundation's tax-exempt status, (2) the allowance of deductions to individuals for contributions to it, and (3) the following three additional requirements, relating to candidates for grants, selection of potential grantees, and the persons making selections.[125]

The primary criterion for approval of a plan for making individual grants is that the grants must be awarded on an "objective and nondiscriminatory basis." The plan must contain the following provisions:

- An *objective and nondiscriminatory* method of choice, consistent with the private foundation's exempt status and the purpose of the grant, is used.

- The group from which grantees are selected is sufficiently broad so as to constitute a charitable class.[126] The size of the group may be small if the purpose of the grant so warrants, such as research fellows in a specialized field.

- Criteria used in selecting the recipients include (but are not limited to) academic performance, performance on tests designed to measure ability and aptitude motivation, recommendations from instructors, financial need, and conclusions the selection committee might draw from a personal interview as to an individual's potential ability and personal character.

- Selection committee members are not in a position to derive a private benefit, directly or indirectly, if one person or another is chosen.

- Grants are awarded for study at an academic institution, fellowships, prizes or awards, or study or research involving a literary, artistic, musical, scientific, or teaching purpose.

- A system to obtain reports is provided for scholarships, fellowships, and research or study grants.[127]

The second item in the preceding list requires the group from which the grantees are chosen to be sufficiently broad. A group including all students in a city or all valedictorians in a state clearly qualifies. The regulations sanction a plan to grant 20 annual scholarships to members of a certain ethnic minority living within a state.[128] A group of girls and boys, however, with at least one-quarter Finnish blood, living in two particular towns, was found to be a discriminatory group and not sufficiently broad.[129] Likewise, a plan that

---

125. Reg. § 53.4945-4(b)(1). Also Rev. Rul. 76-340, 1976-2 C.B. 370.
126. *See Tax Planning and Compliance*, § 2.2(a).
127. IRC § 4945(g); Reg. § 53.4945-4(b) and (c).
128. Reg. § 53.4945-4(b)(5), Example 2.
129. Priv. Ltr. Rul. 7851096.

gave priority to family members and relatives of the trust's creator, if their qualifications were substantially the same as an unrelated party, was found to be discriminatory.[130] A scholarship program established for students attending two named universities failed to qualify for the estate tax charitable contribution deduction because an additional criterion was that the grantees have the same surname as the decedent; inasmuch as there are only about 600 families in the United States with that surname, the IRS concluded that a charitable class was not present (i.e., that the group of potential grantees was too small) and denied the charitable deduction.[131]

In one instance, a private foundation proposed to administer a scholarship program on behalf of a tax-exempt boarding school. All scholarships are to be funded according to the financial needs of the students; the grants are to be made without regard to race, creed, or national origin. The IRS approved the foundation's scholarship granting procedures as being in compliance with these taxable expenditures rules, notwithstanding the fact that this school is an all-boys institution.[132]

There are plenty of private letter rulings seeking approval for scholarship plans that contain selection criteria based on scholastic performance and leadership potential. Fewer in number are rulings that seek approval for fellowships and "other similar purposes." The following criteria were approved for a foundation granting prizes and awards to achieve a specific result, produce a report, or improve or enhance literary, artistic, musical, scientific, or other skill or capacity:[133]

- Potential benefit to the proposed activities to the community and specific population to be served.

- Capacity of the organization or individual to achieve the result.

- Adequacy of proposed financial and time budgets for achieving the desired result.

- Evidence of cooperation and coordination with other organizations and individuals working in the same field.

- Likelihood of ongoing support from other sources for the program.

- Other factors indicating that the program will accomplish the foundation's charitable purposes.

---

130. Rev. Rul. 85-175, 1985-2 C.B. 276.
131. Priv. Ltr. Rul. 9631004. Another private foundation administered a scholarship program, one of the criteria of which was that recipients had to be related to trustees of the foundation! For that and other reasons, its tax-exempt status was retroactively revoked (Priv. Ltr. Rul. 201022030).
132. Priv. Ltr. Rul. 200603029.
133. Priv. Ltr. Rul. 200009053.

Importantly, the ruling also confirmed the distinctions between grants for future performance and past accomplishments.[134] Prizes and awards the foundation proposed to award for past achievements were not subject to preapproval.

## (e)  Employer-Related Programs

A matter of some controversy is the extent to which grants made by a private foundation under an employer-related grant program[135] to an employee or to an employee's child constitute qualifying scholarships, fellowship, or aid grants.

**Scholarships.**  A company foundation was acutely reminded of the importance of requesting approval for a company's scholarship program and also of the need to comply with the participation requirements. Scholarship payments made prior to the date on which it sought IRS approval were taxable expenditures, not only because of the lack of approval but also because the company had insufficient data to prove that the plan was objective and nondiscriminatory.[136]

The IRS has promulgated guidelines[137] for use in determining whether the grants so qualify (and thus are not taxable expenditures).[138] These guidelines also consider whether educational loans made by a private foundation to employees of a particular company or to their children are made for a purpose inconsistent with the private foundation's tax-exempt purposes, because the loans serve the private interests of the employer rather than charitable purposes. The issue with these plans is whether they discriminate in favor of the corporate executives or shareholders and thus represent a means of paying additional compensation. Where certain conditions are satisfied, the IRS will assume that employer-related educational loans are made on the requisite objective and nondiscriminatory basis, and otherwise are not taxable expenditures. These eight conditions include:

1.  The scholarship plan must not be used by the employer, the foundation, or the organizer of it, to recruit employees or to induce continued employment.

2.  The selection committee must be wholly made up of totally independent persons, not including former employees, and preferably including persons knowledgeable about education.

---

134.  *See* § 9.3(b).
135.  Rev. Rul. 79-131, 1979-1 C.B. 368; Rev. Rul. 79-365, 1979-2 C.B. 389.
136.  Priv. Ltr. Rul. 9825004.
137.  Sanders, "New Guidelines Tell When IRS Will Approve Company Foundation Scholarship Grants," 46 *J. Tax* 212 (1977); Sacher, "Rev. Proc. 76-47: Guidelines for Advance Approval of Company Foundation Grants," 116 *Trusts & Estates* 541 (1977).
138.  Rev. Proc. 76-47, 1976-2 C.B. 670, as clarified by Rev. Proc. 85-51, 1985-2 C.B. 717.

3. Identifiable minimum requirements for grant eligibility must be established. Employees, or children of employees, must meet the minimum standards for admission to an educational institution[139] for which the grants are available and are reasonably expected to attend such an institution. Eligibility should not depend on employment-related performance, although up to three years of service for the parent can be required.

4. Selection criteria must be based on substantial objective standards such as prior academic performance, tests, recommendations, financial need, and personal interviews, and unrelated to job performance.

5. A grant may not be terminated because the recipient or parent terminates employment. If the grant award is subject to annual review to continue support for a subsequent year, the recipient cannot be ineligible for renewal because the individual or his or her parent is no longer employed.

6. The courses of study for which grants are available must not be limited to those of particular benefit to the employer.

7. The terms of the grant and course of study must serve to allow recipients to obtain an education in their individual capacities solely for their personal benefit and must not include any commitments, understandings, or obligations of future employment.

8. The number of employees, or children of employees, that may annually receive grants and loans under the program must be stated. Alternately, if the program can satisfy a facts-and-circumstances test in lieu of the applicable percentage test, the loans may not be regarded as taxable expenditures.[140] In its original ruling on this subject, the IRS imposed a percentage test limiting the number of award recipients to 10 percent of the eligible employee applicants and 25 percent of the eligible employee children considered by the selection committee.[141]

Notwithstanding these guidelines, the IRS subsequently indicated its understanding "that for an employer-related educational grant or loan program to fulfill its intended purpose, it is necessary to inform the eligible employees of its availability."[142] Thus, the IRS ruled that a private foundation's employer-related

---

139. As defined in IRC § 151(e)(4).
140. Rev. Proc. 80-39, 1980-2 C.B. 772, as modified by Rev. Proc. 83-36, 1983-1 C.B. 763, and clarified by Rev. Proc. 85-51, 1985-2 C.B. 717. E.g., Rev. Rul. 86-90, 1986-2 C.B. 184. The IRS announced a *rounding convention* to be used in connection with these percentage tests, permitting a rounding up of the number of allowable grants as long as the number otherwise is at least four (Rev. Proc. 94-78, 1994-2 C.B. 833).
141. Rev. Rul. 76-340, 1976-2 C.B. 370. *See supra* note 125.
142. Rev. Proc. 81-65, 1981-2 C.B. 690, 691.

grant or loan program may be publicized in the employer's newsletter without causing a violation of the rules promulgated in either 1976 or 1980,[143] if the private foundation is "clearly identified" as the grantor of the awards.[144] The IRS also ruled that "making public announcements of the grants or loans in the employer's newsletter" is not a violation of either set of rules[145] if the private foundation or the independent selection committee is "clearly identified" as the grantor of the awards.[146]

An individual grant program administered by a company-related private foundation thus may be able to qualify for exemption from treatment as taxable expenditures where the grants are scholarships or fellowships used for study at a qualified educational institution and the grants satisfy these guidelines.[147] Even if the grants cannot meet those requirements, they may avoid classification as taxable expenditures by constituting grants made to achieve a specific objective, produce a product, or improve or enhance some capacity, skill, or talent of the grantees.[148]

**Disaster Relief and Hardship Grants.** The IRS has not developed formal guidelines for private foundations, similar to those promulgated in connection with related company scholarship programs, for employee disaster relief and hardship programs. Nonetheless, there have been significant law developments in this area enabling private foundations to discern some IRS guidance as to employee disaster relief efforts.[149]

- Awards are paid to "needy and distressed persons" pursuant to standards set out in IRS Publication 3833.

- The foundation's program does not relieve the company of any legal obligation, such as an obligation under a collective bargaining agreement or written plan to provide insurance benefits.

- The company does not use the program to recruit employees, to induce employees to continue their employment, or to otherwise follow a course of action sought by the company.[150]

---

143. Rev. Proc. 76-47, 1976-2 C.B. 670, § 4.01; Rev. Proc. 80-39, 1980-2 C.B. 772, § 4.03.
144. Rev. Proc. 81-65, 1981-2 C.B. 690, 691.
145. Rev. Proc. 76-47, 1976-2 C.B. 670 § 4.02; Rev. Proc. 80-39, 1980-2 C.B. 772, § 4.04.
146. Rev. Proc. 81-65, 1981-2 C.B. 690, 691.
147. IRC § 4945(g)(1).
148. IRC § 4945(g)(3); *Beneficial Foundation, Inc. v. United States*, 85-2 U.S.T.C. ¶ 9601 (Cl. Ct. 1985); *see* § 9.3(b). The IRS ruled that educational grants made by a private foundation pursuant to an employer-related grant program, to employees and children of employees who are victims of a qualified disaster, are not taxable expenditures (Rev. Rul. 2003-32, 2003-1 C.B. 689).
149. *See* § 9.3(b), text accompanied by note 109. Also *see* § 17.5(d).
150. *See* § 9.3(c) for more details.

Application of the rules concerning private foundation grants for individuals where the grants are made to a public charity,[151] as they interrelate with the rules concerning employer-related grants,[152] is illustrated by the case of a private foundation program whereby the private foundation made grants to a public charity in partial funding of a scholarship program, with the stipulation that the grants be expended on behalf of children of employees of a particular company who were finalists as determined by the public charity. As a variation of this program, a similar approach required that any excess funds be made available as grants to the next most highly rated children of employees of the company, even though they were not finalists. The IRS concluded that the grants were amounts paid to individuals for study and were taxable expenditures unless made pursuant to a procedure approved in advance by the IRS.[153] An exception for foundation grants to public charities[154] was deemed inapplicable, in that the public charity did not select the scholarship recipients completely independently of the private foundation and merely functioned as an evaluator of the grant program of the private foundation.[155]

Many private letter rulings issued by the IRS contain illustrations of scholarship programs that have been reviewed under these guidelines.[156] Application for approval is the same as for other scholarship plans, although satisfaction of the eight tests listed earlier must be outlined.

## (f)  Reports and Monitoring

The private foundation must maintain, and keep available for IRS examination, documentation that the grant recipients are chosen in a nondiscriminatory manner and that proper follow-up is accomplished. The following records must be kept:[157]

- Information used to evaluate the qualification of potential grantees.

- Reports of any grantee/director relationships.

- Specification of amount and purpose of each grant.

- Grade reports and diversion investigation reports.

---

151. For these purposes, an organization described in IRC § 509(a)(1), (2), or (3). *See* Chapter 15.
152. *See supra* notes 137–140.
153. Rev. Rul. 81-217, 1981-2 C.B. 217.
154. *See* text accompanying *infra* notes 186 and 187.
155. For charitable organizations, other than private foundations, that make grants to individuals, the criteria set out in Rev. Rul. 56-304, 1956-2. C.B. 306, must be followed.
156. E.g., Priv. Ltr. Rul. 8807002.
157. Reg. § 53.4945-4(c)(6).

**Scholarships and Fellowships.**  Generally, with respect to any scholarship or fellowship grant, a private foundation must make arrangements to receive a report of the grantee's work in each academic period. A report of the grantee's courses taken and grades earned in each academic period must be received at least once annually and verified by the educational institution. For grantees whose work does not involve classes but only the preparation of research papers or projects, such as a doctoral thesis, the foundation should receive an annual report approved by the faculty members supervising the grantee, or other school official. Upon completion of a grantee's study, a final report must also be obtained.

**Research or Study Grants.**  With respect to a grant made for travel, study, or other similar purposes, a private foundation must require reports on the use of the funds and the progress made by the grantee toward achieving the purposes for which the grant was made. These reports must be made at least once annually and upon completion of the funded undertaking. This final report must describe the grantee's accomplishments and contain an accounting of the funds received.[158]

**Monitoring.**  Where the requisite reports or other information (including the failure to submit the reports) indicates that all or any part of a grant is not being used in furtherance of the purposes of the grant, the grantor private foundation has a duty to investigate. While conducting its investigation, the private foundation must withhold further payments to the extent possible until any delinquent reports have been submitted.[159] In cases in which the grantor private foundation determines that any part of a grant has been used for improper purposes and the grantee has not previously diverted grant funds to any use not in furtherance of a purpose specified in the grant, the private foundation will not be treated as having made a taxable expenditure solely because of the diversion as long as the private foundation:

- Is taking all reasonable and appropriate steps either to recover the grant funds or to ensure restoration of the diverted funds and the dedication of other grant funds held by the grantee to the purposes being financed by the grant, and

- Withholds any further payments to the grantee after the grantor becomes aware that a diversion may have taken place, until it has received the grantee's assurances that future diversions will not occur and requires the grantee to take extraordinary precautions to prevent future diversions from occurring.[160]

---

158.  Reg. § 53.4945-4(c)(3).
159.  Reg. § 53.4945-4(c)(4)(i).
160.  Reg. § 53.4945-4(c)(4)(ii).

All reasonable and appropriate steps may include appropriate legal action, but need not include a lawsuit if its likely funds would not be recouped in satisfaction of a judgment.[161]

If a private foundation is treated as having made a taxable expenditure in these circumstances, then—unless the foundation takes the steps described in the first of the preceding items—the amount of the taxable expenditure is the amount of the diversion plus any further payments to the grantee. If the foundation complies with the first requirement but not the second, however, the amount of the taxable expenditure is the amount of the further payments.[162]

In cases where a grantee has previously diverted funds received from a grantor private foundation and the grantor foundation determines that any part of a grant has again been used for improper purposes, the private foundation is not treated as having made a taxable expenditure solely by reason of the diversion so long as the private foundation again meets the two requirements listed earlier.[163]

The same rule as to the appropriateness and necessity of legal action applies in this context. If a private foundation is treated as having made a taxable expenditure in a case to which these rules apply, then—unless the private foundation meets the first requirement—the amount of the taxable expenditure is the amount of the diversion plus the amount of any further payments to the grantee. If the private foundation complies with the first requirement, but fails to withhold further payments until the second requirement is met, however, the amount of the taxable expenditure is the amount of the further payments.[164]

The previously discussed rules relating to supervision of scholarship and fellowship grants and investigations of jeopardized grants are considered satisfied with respect to scholarship or fellowship grants under the following circumstances: (1) the scholarship or fellowship grants are made pursuant to an approved plan;[165] (2) the grantor private foundation pays the scholarship or fellowship grants to an operating educational institution;[166] and (3) the educational institution agrees to use the grant funds to defray the recipient's expenses or to pay the funds (or a portion of them) to the recipient only if the recipient is enrolled at the educational institution and his or her standing at the educational institution is consistent with the purposes and conditions of the grant.[167]

---

161. Reg. § 53.4945-4(c)(4)(iv).
162. Reg. § 53.4945-4(c)(4)(ii).
163. Reg. § 53.4945-4(c)(4)(iii).
164. Id.
165. IRC § 4945(g)(1).
166. See supra note 89.
167. Reg. § 53.4945-4(c)(5).

## (g) Seeking Approval

Grants to individuals for travel, study, or similar purposes must be made pursuant to a procedure approved in advance.[168] To secure this approval, a private foundation must demonstrate to the satisfaction of the IRS that:

- Its grant procedure includes an objective and nondiscriminatory selection process.

- The procedure is reasonably calculated to result in performance by grantees of the activities that the grants are intended to finance.

- The private foundation plans to obtain reports to determine whether the grantees have performed the activities that the grants are intended to finance. No single procedure or set of procedures is required. Procedures may vary depending on factors such as the size of the private foundation, the amount and purpose of the grants, and whether one or more recipients are involved.[169]

A request for advance approval of a foundation's grant procedures must fully describe the foundation's procedures for awarding grants and for ascertaining that the grants are used for the proper purposes. The approval procedure does not contemplate specific approval of particular grant programs but, instead, one-time approval of a system of standards, procedures, and follow-up designed to result in grants that meet these rules. Thus, the approval applies to a subsequent grant program as long as the procedures under which it is conducted are not materially different from those described in the request.[170] Examples of such changes would be an extension of a four-year scholarship program to five years when circumstances indicate a necessity for the student or providing apartment rental subsidy in addition to the original dormitory portion of the award when campus housing is limited.

---

168. IRC § 4945(g); Reg. § 53.4945-4(c)(1). One court held that this requirement is a mandatory, substantive provision of federal law, rather than a mere ministerial filing requirement (*John Q. Shunk Association v. United States*, 85-2 U.S.T.C ¶ 9830 (S.D. Ohio 1986)).

169. Reg. §§ 53.4945-4(c)(1), 53.4945-4(d). One court held that a private foundation that awarded scholarships without first obtaining approval of its grant-making procedures and that subsequently received retroactive approval of the procedures is nonetheless liable for the initial excise tax imposed by IRC § 4945(a)(1) (*infra* note 338), in that the corrective measures taken relieved the private foundation only from liability for the additional tax imposed by IRC § 4945(b) (*German Society of Maryland, Inc. v. Commissioner*, 80 T.C. 741 (1983)). Another court apparently was of the view that approval of a private foundation's grant program procedures is automatically retroactive where the features of the program have not changed (*The Addison H. Gibson Foundation v. United States*, 91-1 U.S. T.C. ¶ 50,178 (W.D. Pa. 1991), *aff'd in unpub. opinion* (3rd Cir. 1992)).

170. Reg. § 53.4945-4(d)(1).

This ruling request must contain the following:

- A statement describing the selection process, which must be sufficiently detailed for the IRS to determine whether the grants are made on an objective and nondiscriminatory basis.

- A description of the terms and conditions under which the foundation ordinarily makes these grants, which is sufficient to enable the IRS to determine whether the grants awarded under the procedures would meet one of the basic three requirements.[171]

- A detailed description of the private foundation's procedure for exercising supervision over grants.[172]

- A description of the foundation's procedures for review of grantee reports, for investigation where diversion of grant funds from their proper purposes is indicated, and for recovery of diverted grant funds.[173]

Advance approval from the IRS of these scholarship procedures should be sought by means of filing an IRS form, including a $1,000 filing fee.[174] The foundation submits its proposed procedures for awarding grants, including the methods of meeting the selection process requirements, as illustrated in Exhibit 9.1. Newly created foundations can seek approval for their plans in connection with the filing of their application for recognition of tax exemption.

**Silence Signifies Approval.** Written approval is not sent by the IRS to successful applicants; instead, silence signifies approval. If, by the 45th day after a request for approval of grant procedures has been properly submitted, the private foundation has not been notified that the procedures are unacceptable, it may be considered approved from the date of submission until any receipt of actual notice from the IRS that it does not meet the requirements. The request for approval can be submitted in conjunction with an application for recognition of tax exemption. Schedule H of Form 1023 prompts disclosure of an organization's grant-making procedures and is considered equivalent to a request for advance approval.[175] Recognition of an organization as a tax-exempt charitable organization does not in itself constitute approval of the organization's grant procedures,[176] but if a private foundation does not receive, by the 45th day after submission of its application for recognition of tax exemption, notification that its procedures were not

---

171. *See supra* text accompanied by notes 86–90.
172. *See supra* text accompanied by notes 149 and 150.
173. Reg. § 53.4945-4(d)(1).
174. Form 8940; currently, Rev. Proc. 2014-8, 2014-1 I.R.B. 242.
175. *See* § 2.5(a) and Exhibit 2.2.
176. Rev. Rul. 86-77, 1986-1 C.B. 334.

**Exhibit 9.1**   Request for IRS Approval of Individual Grant Program

---

Internal Revenue Service TE/GE
Exempt Organization Determinations
P.O. Box 2508, Cincinnati, OH 45201

> RE: Sample Foundation
> EIN 44–4444444
> Request for Approval
> of Scholarships

Dear IRS Representative,

From 1988 to 2008, the Sample Foundation operated a medical research facility and was classified as a public charity pursuant to Internal Revenue Code (IRC) § 509(a)(1). During that time a scholarship fund was established in the memory of Dr. XYZ, one of the founders of Sample. For the past 20 years, scholarship grants have been paid annually. During 2008, Sample discontinued the research facility and was reclassified as a private foundation. Your approval for the scholarship program is hereby sought.

The XYZ Scholarship will further Sample's educational purposes by enabling deserving men and women to complete a medical-related education in the graduate schools of their choice, so that they will be able to serve honorably and effectively in their chosen medical field.

The scholarship will be a "grant" within the meaning of IRC § 4945 (d) (3) and will satisfy the requirements of IRC § 4945 (g) in all respects.

The grant will be awarded on an objective and nondiscriminatory basis. The grant will be excluded from gross income under IRC § 117 (a), to the extent that it is used for tuition, books, and equipment required for educational courses. The purpose of the grant is to promote medical-related education for graduate degree candidates, and the recipient of the grant will be selected from the population of medical school graduate students.

As required in Schedule H of Form 1023, the grant-making procedures will be as follows:

*Grantee class.* Any graduate college student seeking a degree in medical-related education may be considered for the scholarship.

*Selection criteria.* The selection criteria for the scholarship will include, but not be limited to, the student's demonstrated academic ability and desire, character, good citizenship, and economic necessity. A recipient cannot be related to a member of the committee or to any "disqualified persons" in relation to Sample.

*Selection committee.* The selection committee will be composed of members of the board of directors of Sample. Members of the selection committee will not be in a position to receive private benefit, directly or indirectly, if certain potential grantees are selected over others.

*Progress reports.* The scholarships will be about $2,500 per semester and can be renewed annually for a maximum of three years, provided that the student is not on academic or disciplinary probation and is making satisfactory progress toward completion of a medical-related degree. A student need not have an "A" average, but should be of a caliber to indicate an ability to profit from and be intellectually equal to work on a graduate level. Progress reports will be obtained and verified with the educational institution each semester. Upon completion of the grantee's study, a final report will be collected from the grantee.

---

*(Continued)*

Exhibit 9.1  (Continued)

---

*Report follow-up.* If no report is filed by the student, or if reports indicate that the funds are not being used in furtherance of the scholarship purpose, a member of the board of directors will investigate the grant. While conducting this investigation, Sample will withhold further payments from the grantee and will take reasonable steps to recover grant funds until it has determined that the funds are being used for their intended exempt purpose.

*Record-keeping.* The foundation will retain all records submitted by the grantees and their educational institutions. Sample will obtain and maintain in its file evidence that no recipient is related to the foundation or to any members of the selection committee.

Sample trusts that the above criteria and purpose for its educational scholarship satisfy the requirements of IRC § 4945 and respectfully requests your approval of its procedures.

Under penalties of perjury, I declare that I have examined this request, including accompanying documents, and to the best of my knowledge and belief, the facts presented in support of the request are true, correct, and complete.

Date _____   Sample Officer _____

---

approved, the private foundation's procedures are considered to have been approved from the date of its application.

A private foundation may find itself in the position of initiating its grant-making procedures approved because of passage of the 45-day period, make grants accordingly, and then subsequently receive notification from the IRS that the procedures do not conform to the statutory requirements. In this situation, a grant made prior to the adverse notice is not a taxable expenditure. Even where the grant is structured as installment payments of a fixed amount, payments of the installments remaining after the notification will not result in taxable expenditures—the payments are considered merely the satisfaction of the private foundation's obligation under the grants that were deemed approved. A renewal of a grant made during the prenotification period would, however, be a taxable expenditure—this type of payment would be within the discretion of the private foundation, and, thus, a new grant.[177]

The IRS issues rulings approving procedures, established to comply with these rules.[178]

## (h)  Individual Grant Intermediaries

For foundations wishing to avoid the administrative burden and cost of applying for approval and disbursing scholarships directly, an alternative is to fund a grant program at an independent public charity. A grant by a private foundation to another organization, which the grantee organization uses to

---

177. Rev. Rul. 81-46, 1981-1 C.B. 514.
178. E.g., Priv. Ltr. Rul. 7830122.

make payments to an individual for purposes described in these rules, is not regarded as a grant by the foundation to the individual grantee if (1) the foundation does not earmark the use of the grant for any named individual and (2) there does not exist an agreement, oral or written, by which the grantor foundation may cause the selection of the individual grantee by the grantee organization. A grant is not regarded as a grant by the private foundation to an individual grantee, even though the foundation has reason to believe that certain individuals will derive benefits from the grant, so long as the grantee organization exercises control, in fact, over the selection process and actually makes the selection completely independently of the foundation.[179]

A grant by a private foundation to a public charity to support individual grants is not regarded as a grant by the foundation to the individual grantee (regardless of the application of the rules in the preceding paragraph) if the grant is made for a project that is supervised by the public charity that also controls the selection of the individual grantee. This rule applies regardless of whether the name of the individual grantee is first proposed by the private foundation, but only if there is an objective manifestation of control by the public charity over the selection process. Essentially, the selection need not be made completely independently of the foundation.[180] If, however, a private foundation makes grants for scholarships to a public charity that is controlled by the foundation, the grants are treated as if made directly to the individual recipients of the scholarships.[181] An illustration of these rules was provided in the case of a private foundation that made grants to vocational high schools (all operating educational organizations), in a certain geographical area, to be used to purchase the basic tools of a trade for students to enable them to better learn their trades and to enter into those trades upon graduation. Because the individual grant recipients were selected by representatives of the private foundation, rather than the schools, the grants were deemed to be made directly to the individual students.[182] Since the purpose of the grants was to aid needy and talented students in the completion of their vocational education, the grants were to individuals for study or similar purposes within the meaning of these rules and constituted taxable expenditures unless the private foundation's grant-making procedures satisfied the requirements of the exception to the general rules.[183]

If a private foundation makes a grant to a governmental agency and the grant is earmarked for use by an individual for travel, study, or other similar purposes, the grant is not subject to the taxable expenditures rules if the agency satisfies the IRS in advance that its grant-making program is in furtherance of a charitable purpose, requires that the individual grantee submit suitable reports

---

179. Reg. § 53.4945-4(a)(4)(i).
180. Reg. § 53.4945-4(a)(4)(ii).
181. E.g., Priv. Ltr. Rul. 200209061.
182. Rev. Rul. 77-212, 1977-1 C.B. 356.
183. *See supra* note 112.

to it, and requires that the organization investigate jeopardized grants in a manner substantially similar to a stipulated procedure.[184]

From time to time, the IRS issues private letter rulings concerning these rules.[185]

A grant by a private foundation to an individual, which meets the requirements of these general rules yet qualifies for an exception, is a taxable expenditure only if (1) the grant is earmarked to be used for any legislative, electioneering, or noncharitable activity,[186] or is earmarked to be used in a manner that would violate the rules concerning grants to individuals or the expenditure responsibility requirement;[187] (2) there is an agreement, oral or written, whereby the grantor private foundation may cause the grantee to engage in any prohibited activity and the grant is in fact used in a manner that violates these rules; or (3) the grant is made for a noncharitable purpose.[188]

## §9.4 GRANTS TO PUBLIC CHARITIES

The federal tax law pertaining to private foundations favors grant-making to public charities, rather than to other types of organizations or to individuals. The most dramatic evidence of this bias is the exemption of grants to public charities from the expenditure responsibility requirements.[189] Furthermore, grants to public charities may be exempt from the individual scholarship and lobbying expense rules that would otherwise be applicable, particularly where the grant funds are not earmarked for those specific purposes that if paid by the foundation itself, would trigger applicability of the restraints.

In the interest of efficiency and to streamline its operations, a private foundation asked the IRS if it was acceptable that its grant-making activity records be maintained only in electronic form.[190] Grant requests and correspondence and reports to and from grantees would be conveyed electronically. Grant agreements would be signed both by foundation and grantee officials. The state in which the foundation operates permits the use of electronic records and signatures in most contracts and other writings of legal significance, plus the origination and maintenance of all books and records for tracking investments, charitable activities, and all other matters. The IRS determined that the

---

184. Reg. § 53.4945-4(a)(4)(iii). The report requirement is the subject of the text accompanied by *supra* notes 132–133; the investigation requirement is the subject of the text accompanied by *supra* notes 134–136.
185. E.g., Priv. Ltr. Rul. 8826029.
186. IRC § 4945(d)(1), (2), and (5). *See* §§ 9.1, 9.2.
187. IRC § 4945(d)(3) and (4). As to the latter, *see* § 9.6.
188. Reg. § 53.4945-4(a)(5).
189. *See* § 9.6.
190. Priv. Ltr. Rul. 200324057, citing Rev. Rul. 71-20, 1971-1 C.B. 392, and Rev. Proc. 98-25, 1998-1 C.B. 689, as well as the Electronic Signatures Act of 2000.

record-keeping requirements[191] would not, of themselves, provide a reason to find that the foundation had not complied with the expenditure responsibility requirements.[192]

## (a) Rationale for Public Charities Grants

Because of the favoritism in the tax rules, most private foundations make grants that are "safe," that is, grants to public charities. That these grants are safe is true, in part, because of the vast amount of charitable work that is performed by public charities. A staple feature of the charitable sector is the funding by private foundations of the programs of public charitable institutions. This element of safety, however, is also attributable to the legal requirements and restrictions involved, most notably the expenditure responsibility rules.

It is important, however, to note that a private foundation is permitted to make a grant to accomplish a charitable purpose to any type of organization, exempt or nonexempt, if it properly documents its purposes in making the grant and ensures the transaction with expenditure responsibility agreements. Grants to public charities may be preferred simply because they require less documentation. Public charities often serve a broad constituency that monitors their responsiveness to public needs and assures that their funds are used for charitable purposes. The purpose of the taxable expenditure rules is to see that private foundation funds are used for these purposes, rather than for private interests.

## (b) Documenting Public Charity Grants

The concept of *public charity* embraces charitable organizations that are in one of five categories:

1. § 509(a)(1) *institutions,* such as churches, universities, colleges, schools, hospitals, medical research organizations, and governmental units and agencies,[193] which are considered to be public because of the activities they conduct.

2. § 509(a)(1) or (2) publicly supported entities, either *donative charities* or *service provider charities,*[194] because they receive revenues from many sources.

3. § 509(a)(3) *supporting organizations*[195] *classified as Type I or II* that exist to benefit one or more other public charities.

---

191. IRC § 6001.
192. *See* § 9.6.
193. *See* § 15.3(e). For more information on tribal governments, visit Native American Philanthropy's website at www.nativephilanthropy.org.
194. *See* §§ 15.4, 15.5.
195. *See* § 15.7.

4. § 509(a)(3) *supporting organizations*[196] *classified as Type III functionally integrated* because they conduct active programs on behalf of one or more other public charity.

5. § 509(a)(3) *supporting organizations*[197] *classified as Type III nonfunctionally integrated* that exist to benefit one or more other public charity (now treated for some purposes as private foundations).[198]

Grants to the first four categories of public charities listed above and to *exempt operating foundations*[199] do not require the granting foundation to exercise expenditure responsibility. A grant to an instrumentality of a foreign government is considered to be a grant to a public charity, as long as it is made for charitable purposes.[200] Likewise, an instrumentality of a U.S. political subdivision is treated as a public charity.[201]

It is troubling to some foundations that wish to support a project of a governmental entity that it has no determination letter and is not classified as a tax-exempt charitable organization. It is sometimes also difficult to determine whether a program qualifies as an instrumentality of the government.[202] Private foundations fund public charities for another reason: simplicity of administration. Exercising expenditure responsibility takes considerable effort and increases the possibility of a taxable expenditure. Nonetheless, even though private foundation grants to public charities have this mantle of preferred status, the private foundation still has the burden of proving that its grantees are in fact public in nature and that the grants will be used for charitable purposes. A discussion of the consequences of a private foundation grant to a public charity that conducts lobbying activities appears elsewhere,[203] as does a discussion of control issues involved in payment of scholarship grants to intermediary organizations.[204]

Successful completion of the checklist in Exhibit 9.2 should assist the private foundation in avoiding a situation where its public charity grants are treated as taxable expenditures. A Certification of Type, which a supporting organization should provide in seeking a grant from a public charity, is shown in Exhibit 9.3. This certification provides information that the private foundation needs to verify whether the supporting organization is a Type I, II, or III. Use of one of the

---

196. *Id.*
197. *Id.*
198. *See* § 6.5(a). Private foundation grants in this context do not constitute qualifying distributions.
199. *See* §§ 3.1(i), 10.6, IRC § 4942(g)(1)(A).
200. Reg. § 53.4945-5(a)(4).
201. Rev. Rul. 81-125, 1981-1 C.B. 515.
202. *See* § 9.4(c); *Tax Planning and Compliance*, Chapter 10.
203. *See* § 9.1(c).
204. *See* § 9.3(c).

**EXHIBIT 9.2** Grant Approval Checklist

---

This checklist should be completed by a private foundation to obtain documentation before it issues a check for a grant.

**OBTAIN DOCUMENTATION OF CHARITABLE PURPOSES OF GRANT**

- Obtain a grant request indicating the exempt purpose of the program(s) to be funded. If the PF is unilaterally giving a grant to an established public charity, a transmittal letter accompanying the grant check that states that it is for general support may suffice. A grant agreement and completion of this checklist are recommended in either case.
- Ascertain, either from a grant request or from interviews with grantee representatives, that funding will not be spent for electioneering, lobbying, an individual grant, or a regrant to another private foundation.

**OBTAIN PROOF THAT GRANTEE IS AN ELIGIBLE PUBLIC CHARITY**

A private foundation must determine a proposed grant recipient organization's IRS tax classification to ascertain the level of documentation and procedures to follow. Though the grantee's IRS determination letter will reflect its § 509 status, the letter is not necessarily sufficient proof of current exempt status. To complicate matters, the IRS Exempt Organizations Business Master File (BMF)* is updated every few weeks (an improvement over the former quarterly updating), contains insufficient data and is challenging to use. Fortunately, two Internet sources of tax status are available:

GrantSafe at www.foundationsource.com
CharityCheck at www.guidestar.org (A fee is charged to access this information.)

Certain status information is available at http://apps.irs.gov/app/eos/. The IRS Select Check (Publication 78 data) indicates that gifts to the organization are eligible for income tax deductibility, and identifies private foundations, but does not disclose whether the public charity is a supporting organization. Another difficulty involves those organizations that lose exemption for failure to file Form 990 and apply for reinstatement. Select Check provides a search feature to identify revoked entities, which is also updated every couple of weeks. Therefore, there can be a delay between issuance of a new determination letter for a reinstated entity and its listing in Select Check as an eligible organization. A new determination letter dated on or after the revocation date can be accepted as proof of tax status even though Select Check has not yet been updated.

Last, churches and governmental entities, if they meet specific criteria, are treated as eligible public charities for this purpose even though they are not required to seek IRS recognition of exempt status and may, therefore, not have an IRS determination letter. Contact us if you have any questions about criteria that define a church or governmental entity.

**EXTRA STEPS FOR APPROVAL OF GRANT TO SUPPORTING ORGANIZATION**

A private foundation cannot make a grant to a § 509(a)(3) supporting organization (SO) without additional information. SOs are categorized as being a Type I, Type II, or Type III SO, but, sadly enough, until very recently that identity was not entered on the SO's IRS determination letter, Form 990, IRS BMF, or Publication 78 (it is still not entered on BMF or Pub. 78). If you are interested in making a grant to a § 509(a)(3) organization, please ask us for our memo regarding Certification of Type [Exhibit 9.3] and reports needed to perform expenditure responsibility. Many foundations have suspended grants to SOs for the additional reason that such grants may not count as qualifying distributions.

---

**Exhibit 9.3** Supporting Organization Certification of Type

NAME OF SUPPORTING ORGANIZATION
ADDRESS
CITY, STATE ZIP

Dear Director, Executive Officer, or Financial Officer,

The Pension Protection Act of 2006 (PPA), signed into law on August 17, 2006, contains several provisions that impact charitable organizations. One of the provisions concerns grants made by private foundations to supporting organizations (SOs). We have identified your organization as one that is classified as a supporting organization under Internal Revenue Code § 509(a)(3).

### WHAT IS A SUPPORTING ORGANIZATION?

All § 501(c)(3) charities are classified as either public charities or private foundations. Some types of charities, such as churches, schools, and hospitals, are classified as public charities because of the nature of their activities. Others qualify as public charities because they meet a "public support test" that indicates they receive support from a broad base of contributors. A supporting organization qualifies as a public charity because it has a close relationship with another § 501(c)(3) public charity. A supporting organization provides meaningful support—financial, programmatic, or both—and gives some degree of structural and operational control to the public charity it supports.

### TYPES OF SUPPORTING ORGANIZATIONS

In general, supporting organizations fall into one of three categories depending on the nature of the relationship between the SO and the charity being supported.

Type I—Operated, supervised, or controlled by: This type is often described as a parent-subsidiary relationship and generally involves the supported charity's officers, directors, trustees, or members having the right to appoint a majority of the officers, directors, or trustees of the supporting organization.

Type II—Supervised or controlled in connection with: This type usually has an overlapping board relationship where at least a majority of the members of the SO's governing board are also members of the supported charity's governing board.

Type III—Operated in connection with: This type may have no, or minimal, board overlap. Accordingly, it operates with a greater degree of independence from the organization it supports, but it is required to have procedures designed to ensure that the supporting organization is responsive to the supported organization.

### LIMITATIONS ON GRANTS TO TYPE III SUPPORTING ORGANIZATIONS

Before August 17, 2007, private foundations could treat a grant to any type of supporting organization as a qualifying distribution just as they would any other public charity grant. Under the PPA, Type III SOs are essentially treated as private foundations. Grants to Type III SOs do not count toward a foundation's mandatory payout requirements.[205] A deficiency in the percent payout results in a penalty of 30 percent (of the deficiency) a year until grants are paid to eliminate the underdistribution. In addition, expenditure responsibility (ER) procedures, including a written agreement, must be entered into before the grant is paid. Failure to follow ER procedures results in a taxable expenditure for which the penalty is 20 percent of the

---

205. *See* § 15.7.

**EXHIBIT 9.3** (Continued)

grant each year until the ER is in place. The impediment on foundation grants to Type III supporting organizations does not apply if the SO qualifies as a "functionally integrated" Type III supporting organization.

## YOUR ORGANIZATION

As noted above, the IRS determination letter evidencing your tax exemption identifies your organization as a supporting organization. Unfortunately, the IRS database does not indicate whether your organization qualifies as a Type I, II, or III supporting organization. Determining which type of SO your organization is will require a review of its governing documents in view of the specific requirements we have outlined.

It may be clear that your organization is a Type I supporting organization. As an example of a Type I supporting organization, the Houston Parks Board is a supporting organization to the City of Houston (the public charity in this example). The mayor appoints, with City Council approval, all of the members of the board of directors of the Houston Parks Board.

If your governance structure does not provide that a majority of the members of the board of your supporting organization are appointed or elected by the supported organization, you may want to confer with legal counsel or a tax advisor to determine which type of supporting organization your organization is. If the legal counsel or tax advisor who originally helped obtain your exempt status with the IRS is available, that would be a good place to start. If not, you may want to engage legal counsel or a tax advisor with expertise in the law of tax-exempt organizations to advise you.

If your organization is a Type III supporting organization, additional documentation will be required to determine whether it is a "functionally integrated" Type III supporting organization.

The enclosed form will allow us to comply with IRS Rev. Proc. 2009–32, Guidance Regarding Supporting Organizations and Donor-Advised Funds. Before we can continue processing your grant application [or make payment on your previously approved grant], we must receive the enclosed form and the additional documents indicated. The form must be signed by the president or chief executive officer of your organization.

Sincerely,

Foundation Representative

## REPRESENTATION OF SUPPORTING ORGANIZATION STATUS

[NAME OF SUPPORTING ORGANIZATION] hereby represents that it qualifies as a public charity because it is a supporting organization as defined by § 509(a)(3).

1. The organization supports _____.
2. The organization represents that its SO type is:
   Type I "Operated, supervised, or controlled by" one or more publicly supported organizations—a majority of the governing board is elected or appointed by the supported organization(s).
   Type II "Supervised or controlled in connection with" one or more publicly supported organizations—a majority of the governing board consists of individuals who also serve on the governing board of the supported organization(s).
   Type III "Operated in connection with" one or more publicly supported organizations—not a Type I or Type II SO.

*(Continued)*

**Eхнівіт 9.3** (Continued)

3. Describe the process by which your governing board is appointed and elected.

   Attach Articles of Incorporation, bylaws, or other documents that detail the process. Please highlight the article(s) or section(s) of the material that prescribe (s) the process.

   *If the organization is a Type I or Type II supporting organization, skip section 4 and go to the signature section that follows. If the organization is a Type III supporting organization, complete section 4.*

4. Type III supporting organizations are either functionally integrated or not functionally integrated with the organization(s) they support.

   a. As a Type III supporting organization, the organization represents that it is

   _____ Functionally integrated with one or more supported organizations.

   _____ Not functionally integrated with one or more supported organizations.

   *If not functionally integrated, skip the remainder of section 4. If functionally integrated, complete the rest of section 4.*

   b. If the organization represents that it is functionally integrated, identify the one or more supported organizations with which it is functionally integrated:

   _____

   _____

   _____

   c. If the organization represents that it is functionally integrated, it must provide one of the following documents. Please indicate which one of the following is attached.

   A written representation signed by an officer, director, or trustee of each of the supported organizations with which the grantee represents that it is functionally integrated describing the activities of the grantee and confirming that but for the involvement of the grantee engaging in activities to perform the functions of, or to carry out the purposes of, the supported organization, the supported organization would normally be engaged in those activities itself. Such written representation must meet the requirements outlined in Section 3 of Rev. Proc. 2009–32.

   A reasoned written opinion of counsel representing the organization concluding that the grantee is a functionally integrated Type III supporting organization.

NAME OF SUPPORTING ORGANIZATION

By:

_____ Signature

_____ Printed Name

_____ Title

_____ Date

**Exhibit 9.4** Grant Agreement

---

This letter requests tax status information before a grant is paid.

GRANTEE ORGANIZATION
ADDRESS

DEAR GRANT RECIPIENT:

As a private foundation, Sample Foundation must ascertain that your organization is exempt from income tax under Internal Revenue Code § 501(c)(3) and whether it is classified as a public charity under IRC § 509(a)(1), (2), or (3).

According to information furnished to us with the proposal, your organization is so qualified. Please inform us only if there has been a change in your tax status since then.

In addition, we must be assured that our grant will be expended for an educational, scientific, literary, or other charitable purpose. We ask that you use our funds exclusively to carry out the project described in the application. Also, we ask you not to use any of our funds to influence legislation, to influence the outcome of any election, or to carry on any voter registration drive.

Finally, we ask that any funds not expended for the purposes for which the grant is being made be returned to us.

Please signify your agreement with these conditions by returning a signed copy of this letter to us.

Thank you.

For Sample Foundation _____

Acknowledged by: _____

Date: _____

---

letters shown in Exhibits 9.4 and 9.5 should also help the foundation avoid having its grants treated as expenditure responsibility grants.

## (c) The Reliance Problem

The regulations provide that a private foundation can rely on a grantee organization's proof, or its determination letter stating that it is a public charity, until a notice of its revocation is published in the weekly *Internal Revenue Bulletin* or is otherwise made public.[206] Therefore, a foundation cannot necessarily accept the determination letter, sometimes dated many years in the past, as proof of a grantee's public status. Unfortunately, the IRS databases, determination letters, and Publication 78 do not reflect whether a charitable entity is a Type I, II, or III supporting organization. Under law changes that took effect as of August 18, 2006, a private foundation must establish this fact to determine

---

206. Reg. §§ 1.170A–9(e)(4)(v)(b), 1.509(a)-3(c)(1)(iii)(a).

**Exhibit 9.5** Grant Payment Transmittal

---

This letter conveys the grant payment check for repeating grant recipients.

GRANTEE ORGANIZATION
ADDRESS

DEAR GRANT RECIPIENT:

We are happy to enclose our check for $_____ in payment of a grant for [name] project as described in your request dated [date].

As a private foundation, we must document that our grant is expended for a charitable or educational purpose. We must ask that you use our funds exclusively to carry out the project described in your request. You must not use any of our funds to influence legislation, to influence the outcome of any election, or to carry on any voter registration drive.

Please verify that your organization continues to be exempt under Internal Revenue Code § 501(c)(3) and is still classified as a public charity pursuant to IRC § 509(a)(1), (2), or (3). Kindly send us a copy of your most recent Internal Revenue Service tax determination letter, your financial statements, Form 990, and any annual report for the year in which our grant funds are expended.

Finally, we must ask that any funds not expended for the purposes for which the grant is being made be returned to us. Please indicate your agreement with these conditions by returning a signed copy of this letter.

Thank you.

For Sample Foundation _____

Acknowledged by: _____

Date: _____

---

whether a grant to the organization will be a qualifying distribution[207] or expenditure responsibility is required.[208] Prudent foundations for years have used the Internet to verify the most current status.

Publication 78 has been incorporated into Exempt Organizations Select Check (EO Select Check), which is now the online search tool for finding information on organizations eligible to receive tax-deductible contributions. The list provides essentially the same data on eligible organizations that was previously searched for using the electronic Publication 78 web page. Users can rely on EO Select Check to determine whether a charitable contribution to an exempt organization is tax-deductible if the organization is not listed on the "Were automatically revoked" portion of that site BUT an organization's public charity status is not reflected.

---

207. *See* § 6.6.
208. *See* § 9.6.

The several issues to consider in establishing the foundation's procedures for identifying supporting organizations that are qualified public charity grantees can be found in § 15.11(a).

If the grantee organization is not controlled by the private foundation (i.e., the PF cannot cause it to act or prevent its acts), the private foundation need not investigate the effect of its grant on the recipient.[209]

**Controlled Grantee.** When the private foundation has a relationship with the grantee organization, and certainly if the foundation controls it, the foundation also has a responsibility to determine whether its grant will cause the recipient organization to lose its public status. When a public entity undergoes a *substantial and material change*, the private foundation has three choices if it chooses to make a grant:

1. The private foundation can satisfy itself that it was not responsible for the change by reviewing financial information from the grantee's officers. The grantor is not responsible if its grant in a year is less than 25 percent of the recipient's total grants and gifts for the immediately preceding four years.

2. The private foundation can ascertain that the grant is an unusual one that will not cause the grantee to lose public status.[210]

3. The private foundation can exercise expenditure responsibility.[211]

**No IRS Exempt Status or Letter.** Churches and their integrated auxiliaries and governmental units do not commonly receive recognition of exemption as public charities, although some seek such a letter to aid in fundraising. When a private foundation wishes to support such entities, it must take the steps listed in Exhibit 9.2 to document the grantee's qualification. Many church groups have certification issued by a national or area association of the member parishes and congregations. For example, Catholic churches, schools, and affiliated auxiliaries are listed in a maroon leather-bound national directory of affiliates. For a church lacking this type of proof, the foundation can gather information directly from the church to determine if the church satisfies a majority of the factors in the 14-point test for qualification as a church.

Verification that a program is a division of the government would involve similar steps. A certificate from the local municipality, school district, county, or other authority would be obtained. A governmental unit is a body that possesses at least three capabilities: the power to assess and collect taxes, police powers to enforce the law, and sovereign powers of eminent domain.[212]

---

209. Rev. Proc. 89-23, 1989-1 C.B. 844.
210. *See* § 15.5(c).
211. Rev. Proc. 81-6, 1981-1 C.B. 620.
212. *See Tax Planning and Compliance,* Chapter 10.

Last, members of an affiliated group of organizations centralized under the common supervision and control of a parent organization do not individually obtain a determination letter and are not listed in Publication 78. Therefore, to verify their public charity status, the foundation should request documentation that the entity is indeed a member of a group (most issue a certificate), look up the parent organization on www.guidestar.org or Publication 78, and observe whether the front page of the grantee's Form 990 indicates it is a member of such group.

### (d)  Intermediary Grantees

A private foundation grant to an intermediary organization may be treated as a grant by the foundation to the ultimate grantee.[213] The rules are identical to the individual grantee rules.[214] Thus a *look-through rule* applies when the private foundation earmarks its grant in an oral or written manner. If the regrant from the intermediary is to another public charity, there is no problem. If the regrant is to another private foundation or for some other purpose referenced in these rules, a taxable expenditure may occur.

## §9.5  GRANTS TO FOREIGN ORGANIZATIONS

With respect to a grant to a foreign organization (other than one described in the public charity rules),[215] the rules prohibiting the use of funds for taxable expenditures are deemed satisfied if the requisite grant agreement imposes restrictions on the use of the grant that are substantially equivalent to the limitations imposed on a domestic private foundation by the taxable expenditures rules. These restrictions may be phrased in appropriate terms under foreign law or custom and ordinarily will be considered sufficient if an affidavit or opinion of qualified counsel is obtained stating that under foreign law or custom, the agreement imposes restrictions on the use of the grant substantially equivalent to the restrictions imposed on a domestic private foundation.[216]

A foreign government and any agency or instrumentality thereof is treated as a public organization for this purpose. Certain international organizations also qualify as public charities, such as the World Health Organization, the United Nations, the International Bank for Reconstruction and Development, the International Monetary Fund, and others designated by the president.[217]

---

213.  Reg. § 53.4945-5(a)(5).
214.  *See* § 9.3.
215.  *See* § 9.4(b).
216.  Reg. § 53.4945-5(a)(5).
217.  Reg. § 53.4945-5(a)(4)(iii). The international organizations are designated by executive order under 22 U.S.C. § 288.

A foreign charitable organization that does not have an IRS determination letter, but that is equivalent to and would in fact qualify as a public charity if it sought approval, may also be treated as a public entity. A private foundation is allowed to make a good-faith determination of the foreign organization's status. An affidavit from the foreign entity or an opinion of counsel should be obtained, and sufficient facts concerning the operations and support of the grantee should be revealed in a manner that would allow the IRS to determine whether the organization would qualify as a public charity.[218] Proposed Regulations were issued on September 24, 2012, to revise certain of the requirements for establishing equivalency of a foreign grantee.[219] The requirement that a determination be made based on the opinion of counsel of the grantor or the grantee was expanded to include written advice from a qualified tax practitioner. A qualified tax practitioner is defined to include an attorney, CPA, or an enrolled agent. It is important to note not only that the type of person who can write the opinion is expanded to include non-attorneys, but also that the requirement that the writer of the opinion be engaged by the grantor or the grantee has been removed. This potentially means that equivalency opinions written for one grantor could be shared with other grantors so that each would not have to hire counsel to form an opinion. Ultimately, many hope that a database of foreign grantees with opinions of equivalency could be created making it easier for foundations to make grants to foreign entities. A private foundation may rely on the proposed regulations with respect to grants made on or after September 24, 2012.[220]

Illustrations of this procedure were provided in the case of a private foundation that provided financial assistance to a tax-exempt charitable orphanage located in a foreign country[221] and in the case of a private foundation that made grants to an exempt church in a foreign country.[222]

The Department of the Treasury, on September 23, 2012, issued proposed regulations in connection with these good-faith determination standards.[223] These proposed regulations would modify the rules to identify a broader class of tax practitioners on whose written advice a private foundation may base a good-faith determination. That is, under this proposal, a private foundation's good-faith determination ordinarily could be based on written advice from a *qualified tax practitioner*, defined as a lawyer, certified public accountant, or enrolled agent.

The preamble to the proposed regulations states that "these practitioners generally provide advice to clients with respect to taking positions on tax returns, and these practitioners are generally authorized to represent their

---

218. *See* § 9.4(b).
219. Prop. Reg. § 53.4945-5(a)(5).
220. Prop. Reg. § 53.4945-5(a)(5)(iii).
221. Priv. Ltr. Rul. 200121078.
222. Priv. Ltr. Rul. 200209055.
223. REG-134974-12.

clients before the IRS without limitations applicable to other types of practitioners (such as enrolled actuaries)." The Treasury Department and the IRS are of the view that "expanding the class of practitioners on whose written advice a private foundation may base a good-faith determination will decrease the cost of seeking professional advice regarding these determinations, enabling foundations to engage in international philanthropy in a more cost-effective manner." Also, the preamble states, "expressly allowing reliance on a broader spectrum of professional tax advisors may encourage more private foundations to obtain written tax advice, thus promoting the quality of the determinations being made."

The equivalency method of proving public status does not necessarily apply to a foreign organization that receives more than 15 percent of its support from U.S. sources. Notice to the IRS is required from these organizations to prove their public status.

**Documentation Choices.** The IRS issued procedures in 1992 intended to simplify the process of securing adequate documentation for foreign grantees.[224] Detailed financial information, organizational documents, program activity descriptions, and other information that evidences the foreign charity's ability to qualify as a public charity under the U.S. tax code must be obtained. The information must be translated into English and accompanied by a sworn statement of validity from the grantee. Additionally, the foundation must obtain follow-up reports that its grant was, in fact, spent for the purposes for which it was awarded.

As a practical matter, these documentation requirements are often difficult to satisfy. Differences in accounting systems, language, cultural patterns, and reporting system in their own countries can lead to confusion. Although the foreign grantee may readily agree to fulfill the requirements described in the grant agreement, misunderstanding of the English terms often leads to an unintended result. In an effort to gain clarity, the Council on Foundations, in December 1999, asked for the following guidance from the IRS:

**Issue 1**

*Classifying Governmentally Supported Foreign Charities*: Establish that a foreign charity receiving substantial support from its government, as many do, could readily qualify as a public charity without further inquiry into its sources of support as Rev. Proc. 92–94 currently requires.

**Issue 2**

*Choosing Expenditure Responsibility Rather than the Out-of-Corpus Rules*: Clarify that a private foundation may elect to treat grants to foreign organizations as grants to noncharities, rather than following the special out-of-pocket rules for grants to other private foundations, even if the private foundation has determined that the foreign organization could qualify as a § 501(c)(3) equivalent but cannot determine whether it

---

224. Rev. Proc. 92-94, 1992-2 C.B. 507; outlined in § 6.5(f).

is a public charity equivalent. Although Rev. Proc. 92–94 clearly states that the equivalency procedure is optional, it does not offer clear guidance on what to do if a private foundation begins the procedure and gets as far as establishing 501(c)(3) equivalence but cannot get any further. Private foundations would like written assurance that they can disregard whatever information they have gathered on § 501 (c)(3) equivalence and make an expenditure responsibility grant to a noncharity rather than a grant meeting the out-of-corpus requirements.

**Issue 3**

*Duration of Expenditure Responsibility for Capital Equipment and Endowment Grants*: Clarify the number of years expenditure responsibility will be required for grants to foreign grantees for capital equipment or endowment.

The IRS did not respond to Issues 1 and 3. The answer to Issue 2 was "yes." The IRS responded by saying: "Neither the Internal Revenue Code nor the Regulations require the foundation to determine whether a foreign grantee is described in § 501 (c)(3) of the Internal Revenue Code. Therefore a U.S. private foundation may elect to treat a foreign grantee as not being described in § 501(c)(3)."[225] The information letter quoted all of the relevant statutes and regulations, and concluded there is no provision in the statute or regulations that compels the foundation to determine the foreign organization's status. The letter stipulated that "a grant from a private foundation to a foreign grantee will be treated as a qualifying distribution for purposes of section 4942 of the Code and not a taxable expenditure for purposes of section 4945 under each of the following three circumstances":

**Option 1**

After making a good faith determination that the foreign grantee is described in §§ 501 (c)(3) and 509(a) of the Code, the foreign grantee is the equivalent of a public charity, the private foundation makes the grant without exercising expenditure responsibility.

**Option 2**

After making a good faith determination that the foreign grantee is described in § 501 (c)(3) of the Code and would be classified as a private foundation because it is not described in § 509(a), the private foundation exercises expenditure responsibility with respect to the grant as prescribed by § 4945(h) and the regulations thereunder, and obtains records verifying that the grantee distributes the full amount of the grant out of corpus by the end of the year following.

**Option 3**

The private foundation treats the grantee as not being described in § 501(c)(3) of the Code and exercises expenditure responsibility with respect to the grant as prescribed in § 4945(h) and the regulations thereunder, including the requirement that the grantee maintain the grant funds in a separate fund dedicated for § 170(c)(2)(B) purposes, in accordance with § 53.4945–6(c) of the Regulations.

Thus the IRS essentially weighed in on the side of exercising the expenditure responsibility procedures described in the following subchapter § 9.6. Exhibit 9.6

---

225. IRS Information Letter to Council on Foundations, April 18, 2001.

**EXHIBIT 9.6** International Grants/Activity Checklist

---

This checklist first lists procedures that all tax-exempt organizations should follow in conducting programs and making grants outside the United States. The purpose is twofold: ensure the expenditures serve an exempt purpose and document intent to avoid support of groups the U.S. Treasury Department identifies as a threat to domestic security. Also, additional steps a private foundation must take are listed.

**Name of Organization** _____

**Name of Grantee/Cooperating Organization** _____

Step 1.  Obtain proposal that includes the following detailed information at a minimum:
  - Two years of financial reports, preferably audited by chartered or certified accountants.
  - Budget of activity to be supported that shows compensation of officials and details of major costs.
  - Organizational documents and proof of charitable or nonprofit status, if any.
  - List of names and positions of officials and key employees.
  - Description of operating procedures recipient uses to protect funding, including internal controls and conflicts of interest policies.
  - Timeline for accomplishment of programs to be supported.

Step 2.  Consider support for specific projects rather than grants for general support of the organization to narrow scope of due diligence and oversight required.

Step 3.  Consider a grant to a U.S. "Friends of" or other cross-border giving organizations.

Step 4.  Go to www.treas.gov/offices/enforcement/ofac/sdn/ and search for names of officials associated with the organization. Print page where names would have appeared alphabetically to evidence absence. Study latest version of the *Anti-Terrorist Financial Guidelines: Voluntary Best Practices for U.S.-Based Charities* on the site.

Step 5.  Prepare agreement with grantee that describes the project and tax-exempt purposes that will be served, terms for transfers of money, for programs to be conducted in stages, what is required for release of additional funds, and reports and evaluations that are required upon completion of program. Agreement should require funds be returned if they are not spent for the intended purpose.

Step 6.  Prepare resolution for approval of project to evidence U.S. organization's "dominion and control" over the decision to provide the financial support.

***Private Foundation Step.*** Obtain public charity equivalency or formal expenditure responsibility agreement, submit enhanced information required on Form 990-PF, and monitor receipt of reports from grant recipient as described in § 9.6.

Prepared by _____ Approved by _____ Date _____

---

can be used to verify that appropriate approval steps are taken before the grant is disbursed.

**Future Development.** There may be changes in procedures required to document grants to foreign organizations and foreign programs. The U.S. Treasury Department on November 7, 2002, issued a voluntary set of best practice guidelines for U.S.-based charities to follow to reduce the likelihood that charitable funds will be diverted to finance terrorist activities. The guidelines address four areas: (1) Governance, (2) Disclosure/Transparency in Governance and Finances, (3) Financial Practice/Accountability, and (4) Anti-Terrorists Financing Procedures.[226] The suggested due diligence steps are detailed and would require much-enhanced documentation, including on-site audits, verification of all of the jurisdictions and sites in which the foreign organization conducts programs, and vetting of public information by Internet-type searches and proof it does not appear on lists of persons linked to terrorism or money laundering.

**Canadian Organizations.** The treaty between Canada and the United States provides that Canadian charities are given reciprocal classification under U.S. rules. However, unless the Canadian organization provides proof of its public charity status, it is presumed to be a private charity. Expenditure responsibility can be exercised to avoid classification of such a grant as a taxable expenditure. The grant to a Canadian organization that has not sought classification as a public charity, however, may not be treated as a qualifying distribution unless the money is passed through.[227]

**Mexican Organizations.** The treatment of grants made by a U.S.-based private foundation to a charitable organization in Mexico is governed by the U.S.-Mexico Income Tax Convention[228] and an accompanying protocol.[229] These two countries recognize each other's public charities on a reciprocal basis, for purposes of tax exemption and public charity status. Thus, a U.S. private foundation can, if the Mexican authorities have granted the requisite authorization to a Mexican charity, treat that charity as a public charity for expenditure responsibility and other purposes. A U.S. private foundation, however, must request proof of that status from the Mexican charity.[230]

**Charitable Deduction Connection.** Among the reasons that a private foundation would involve itself in foreign projects is the rule that precludes income

---

226. U.S. Department of the Treasury, *Anti-Terrorist Financing Guidelines: Voluntary Best Practices for U.S.-Based Charities* (Nov. 7, 2002), reprinted at 39 *Exempt Orgs. Tax Rev.* (No. 1) 120 (Jan. 2003). As of January 2008, no new procedures have been adopted. See Harris, "New Treasury Guidelines on Terrorist Funding Draw Criticism," *id.* at 23. Also, Rambler, "New Developments for International Charitable Giving: The War Against Terrorist Financing," *id.* at 33.
227. The classification of foreign organizations as private or public charities is determined by applying the same rules that apply to domestic organizations, discussed in Chapter 15; Rev. Rul. 75-435, 1975-2 C.B. 215; also IRS Notice 99-47, 1999-2 C.B. 391.
228. Article 22 of this treaty.
229. Paragraph 17 of the protocol.
230. INFO 2003-0158.

deductions for gifts to foreign charities.[231] When a U.S. charity's board (private or public) has control and discretion as to the use of the funds raised, the fact that the funds are raised for projects outside the United States does not render contributions to the U.S. foundation in support of a foreign project nondeductible.

In a ruling concerning deductibility of gifts to a charity with foreign projects, the IRS allowed deductions and, by reference, sanctioned the exempt status for a pair of organizations established to build a basketball stadium in a foreign country and to sponsor and operate the games in the foreign country. Only one organization was designed to qualify for U.S. charitable deductions. Organization 1 raised funds to regrant to organization 2 and to build and own the stadium in which organization 2 would operate. The ruling continues the tax policy regarding charity that recognizes that the exempt nature of an activity is determined by its character, regardless of the location in which it is conducted.[232]

## § 9.6   EXPENDITURE RESPONSIBILITY

### (a)   General Rules

The term *taxable expenditure can* also include any amount paid or incurred by a private foundation as a grant, loan, or program-related investment[233] to an organization that is not a qualified[234] public charity,[235] unless the private foundation exercises expenditure responsibility with respect to the grant.[236] The term *expenditure responsibility* means that the private foundation is responsible to exert all reasonable efforts and to establish adequate procedures to (1) see that the grant is spent solely for the purpose for which it was made, (2) obtain full and complete reports from the grantee on how the funds were spent, and (3) make full and detailed reports with respect to the expenditures to the IRS.[237]

---

231. IRC § 170(a); Rev. Rul. 63-252, 1953-2 C.B. 101; Rev. Rul. 66-79, 1995-1 C.B. 48; Rev. Rul. 75–65, 1975-1 C.B. 79.
232. Priv. Ltr. Rul. 9129040.
233. *See* § 8.3.
234. *See* § 9.6(b).
235. Specifically, an organization is not an expenditure responsibility grantee if it is a public charity, that is, described in IRC § 509(a)(1), (2), or (3) (*see* Chapter 15) or an exempt operating foundation described in IRC § 4940(d)(2); *see* § 3.1(i). Thus, a private foundation grant to a private operating foundation is an expenditure responsibility grant unless the grantee qualifies as an exempt operating foundation (*see* § 6.5(a)).
236. IRC § 4945(d)(4); Reg. § 53.4945-5(a)(1). Thus, for these rules to apply, the payment involved must be a *grant*, rather than, for example, the payment of administrative expenses (e.g., Priv. Ltr. Rul. 200019044).
237. IRC § 4945(h); Reg. § 53.4945-5(b)(1).

Thus, to ensure accountability for grants and program-related investments by private foundations, record-keeping requirements are more stringent when a grant is made to another private foundation (including a private operating foundation), a nonfunctionally integrated Type III supporting organization, an organization that is tax-exempt for reasons other than being charitable, or a for-profit business. In any event, the grant must constitute a direct charitable act or a program-related investment.[238] This type of grant-making was illustrated when the IRS ruled that a private foundation may make a grant for scientific purposes to another private foundation, which in turn will make grants to a third private foundation, without endangering its tax-exempt status and without making any taxable expenditures, where the first and third of these foundations adhered to the expenditure responsibility requirements.[239]

These grants are not prohibited. A private foundation is not an ensurer of the activities of the grantee.[240] A private foundation can make a grant to one of these entities as long as it exerts all reasonable efforts and establishes adequate procedures to see that the grant is spent solely for the charitable purpose for which it was made and submits full and complete reports with respect to the expenditures to the IRS.

**Non-(c)(3) Organization.** As an example of a private foundation grant to a noncharitable tax-exempt organization, a private foundation may make a grant to a social club[241] where the grant is suitably dedicated to charitable purposes. For example, a private foundation made a grant to a social fraternity's title-holding organization[242] to build a study room in the chapter house. The facility was to contain exclusively educational equipment and furniture, along with computers linked to the university's mainframe. The university sanctioned the grant by certifying in writing that the room would benefit the school by supplementing its resources, alleviating overcrowding in its library and study areas, and providing additional computer terminals. The fraternity agreed to return any grant funds not used for construction of the study space. There was no time period stipulated for this guarantee, but the foundation required that it be able to inspect the room annually.[243]

---

238. Reg. § 53.4945-6(c).
239. Priv. Ltr. Rul. 201143022.
240. Reg. § 53.4945-5(b)(1).
241. An organization described in IRC § 501(c)(7).
242. An organization described in IRC § 501(c)(2).
243. Priv. Ltr. Rul. 9050030. Another example of this type of grant was a grant by a private foundation to a local house corporation for a chapter of a national fraternity, which is a tax-exempt social organization, for the purpose of renovating the educational areas of a chapter house (Priv. Ltr. Rul. 9306034).

**Governmental Unit.** For purposes of the expenditure responsibility rules exception, an organization is treated as a publicly supported donative charity[244] if it is an organization described in the charitable giving rules concerning contributions to governmental units[245] or if it is a foreign government or any agency or instrumentality of a foreign government, even if (in either case) it is not considered a charitable organization under the rules pertaining to United States tax-exempt organizations,[246] as long as the grant by the private foundation is made exclusively for charitable purposes.[247] In the case of a grant by a private foundation, made exclusively for charitable purposes, to a wholly owned instrumentality of a political subdivision in a state, the IRS reasoned that if a grant to an instrumentality of a foreign government is treated as a grant to a public charity, a grant to an instrumentality of a domestic political subdivision should likewise be treated as a grant to a public charity.[248] Therefore, the private foundation was held to not be required to exercise expenditure responsibility with respect to the grant.

**Secondary Grantee.** A grant by a private foundation to a grantee organization that the grantee organization uses to make payments to another organization (the *secondary grantee*) is not regarded as a grant by the private foundation to the secondary grantee if the private foundation does not earmark the use of the grant for any named secondary grantee and there does not exist an agreement, oral or written, by which the grantor private foundation may cause the selection of the secondary grantee by the organization to which it has given the grant. A grant is not regarded as a grant by the private foundation to the secondary grantee, even though the private foundation has reason to believe that certain organizations would derive benefits from the grant, as long as the original grantee organization exercises control, in fact, over the selection process and actually makes the selection completely independently of the private foundation.[249]

The grantor private foundation does not have to exercise expenditure responsibility with respect to amounts granted to organizations pursuant to the previously discussed voter registration drive rules.[250] The IRS developed a procedure for private foundations to follow in making grants to foreign charitable organizations, referred to as an affidavit of public status. Due to the

---

244. *See* § 15.3.
245. IRC § 170(c)(1).
246. IRC § 501(c)(3).
247. Reg. § 53.4945-5(a)(4); by contrast, there is no authority allowing a foreign government to be treated as a public charity for purposes of the supporting organization rules (*see* § 15.7).
248. Rev. Rul. 81-125, 1981-1 C.B. 515.
249. Reg. § 53.4945-5(a)(6)(i).
250. Reg. § 53.4945-5(a)(1); *see* § 9.2(c).

difficulties and more recent evolving issues involving terrorist activities, many foundations now choose to exercise expenditure responsibility over grants to foreign organizations.[251]

When one private foundation that has expenditure responsibility grants outstanding merges into another private foundation, the surviving foundation must exercise expenditure responsibility with respect to these grants.[252]

If a private foundation makes a grant to a governmental unit and the grant is earmarked for use by another organization, the grantor foundation need not exercise expenditure responsibility with respect to the grant if the governmental entity satisfies the IRS in advance that its grant-making program is in further-ance of a charitable purpose and the governmental entity exercises expenditure responsibility. Nonetheless, a foundation in this situation would have to make the requisite report to the IRS,[253] unless the grant is earmarked for a public charity or exempt operating foundation.[254]

## (b)  Pre-Grant Inquiry

When a private foundation makes a grant for which it must exercise expenditure responsibility, specific steps must be taken to fulfill its responsi-bilities. Each and every step is required and must be performed sequentially, as outlined in the checklist in Exhibit 9.7. The steps, listed in the order to be taken, include:

1.  Conduct a pre-grant inquiry.

2.  Establish proper terms for the grant or program-related investment.

3.  Enter into a written agreement requiring the terms to be followed and establishing a reporting system for the grantee.

4.  Prepare grant timetable.

5.  Issue payment that refers to written expenditure responsibility agreement.

6.  Follow up by receiving and reviewing grantee reports.

7.  Investigate any diversions of funds.

8.  Annually disclose proper information on the annual information return, Form 990-PF, evidencing compliance with the steps.

9.  Keep documentation of these steps for IRS inspection.

---

251.  Rev. Proc. 92-94, 1992-2 C.B. 507. A summary of this issue is in §§ 6.5(e), 9.5.
252.  Priv. Ltr. Rul. 9331046; *see* § 13.5(b).
253.  *See* text accompanied by *infra* notes 262–268.
254.  Reg. § 53.4945-5(a)(6)(ii).

**Exhibit 9.7** Expenditure Responsibility Control Checklist

| | | |
|---|---|---|
| **Sample Foundation** | | |

**Do Not Proceed to Next Step Until Answers Are Yes!**

| | Date | Initial |
|---|---|---|
| Step 1. Pre-grant inquiry completed. | _____ | _____ |
| Step 2. Establish proper terms for grant or program-related investment. | _____ | _____ |
| Step 3. Expenditure responsibility contract signed. | _____ | _____ |
| Step 4. Grant timetable prepared. | _____ | _____ |
| Step 5. Issue payment that refers to written expenditure responsibility agreement. | _____ | _____ |
| Step 6. Form 990-PF attachment prepared and submitted (Reg. § 53.4945–5(d)). | _____ | _____ |
| Step 7. Delinquent reports or diversions investigated. | _____ | _____ |
| Step 8. Withhold payments if diversions occur. | _____ | _____ |
| Step 9. Segregate documents in a manner to assure that they are saved for four years. | _____ | _____ |
| Approved By: _____ | Date: _____ | |

The first step to take is to investigate the potential grantee organization and its proposed project. A *pre-grant inquiry* is a limited inquiry directed at obtaining enough information to give a reasonable person assurance that the grantee will use the grant for the proper purposes.[255] The inquiry should concern itself with matters such as:

- The identity, prior history, and experience (if any) of the grantee organization and its managers. Is the grantee capable of accomplishing the grant purposes?
- Information about the management, activities, and practices of the grantee organization, obtained either through the private foundation's prior experience and association with the grantee or from other readily available sources.

---

255. Reg. § 53.4945-5(b)(2).

The scope of the inquiry is expected to be tailored to the particular grantee's situation, the period over which the grant is to be paid, the nature of the project, and the private foundation's prior experience with the grantee. If the proposed grantee has previously received an expenditure responsibility grant and successfully satisfied all of the reporting requirements,[256] the pre-grant inquiry might be simplified. Here are two profiles of successful inquiries:

- A private foundation is considering a grant to a newly created drug rehabilitation center located in a neighborhood clinic and classified as a tax-exempt social welfare organization. One of its directors, the foundation is informed, is an ex-convict. The foundation determines that he is fully rehabilitated and that the board as a whole is well qualified to conduct the program, since they are members of the community and more likely to be trusted by drug offenders.

- A grant recipient provides medical research fellowships. It has conducted the program for years and receives a large number of other grants. Another foundation that supports this recipient informs the private foundation that it is satisfied that its grants have been used for the purposes for which they were made.[257]

If the grantee has received prior expenditure responsibility grants from the private foundation and has satisfied all of the reporting requirements, a pre-grant inquiry is not necessary. In the case of a grant to a split-interest trust, which is required by its instrument to make payments to a specified public charity, a less extensive inquiry would be necessary.[258] Exhibit 9.8 can be used to monitor the information gathered and form the basis for the grant decision as a result of the pre-grant inquiry.

## (c)  Grant Terms

An officer, director, or trustee of the grant recipient must sign a written commitment that, in addition to stating the charitable purposes to be accomplished, obligates the grantee to (see Exhibits 9.9 and 9.10):

1.  Repay any portion of the amount granted that is not used for the purposes of the grant,

2.  Submit full and complete annual reports on the manner in which the funds are spent and the progress made in accomplishing the purposes of the grant,

---

256.  Reg. § 53.4941(d)-2(f)(2).
257.  Reg. § 53.4945-5(b)(2)(ii).
258.  *Id.*

**EXHIBIT 9.8**  Pre-Grant Inquiry Checklist

---

Sample Foundation

Name of Proposed Grantee: _____

Tax status?　　　　501(c)(3) ___　501(c)(4) ___　Other ___　(describe)

Category of public　509(a)(1) ___　509(a)(2) ___　509(a)(3) ___　Type I or II[*]
charity

[*] See § 9.4(b) and Exhibit 9.2; for Type III SO see Exhibit 9.3.

Copy of IRS determination letter obtained:　　　　　yes _____　　　no _____

Verified in IRS Charity Check _____ or GrantSafe _____

Written request with full details:　　　　　　　　　yes _____　　get one _____

Complete financial information submitted:　　　　　 yes _____　　　no _____

Form 990 received or reviewed on Guidestar.org:　　 yes _____　　　no _____

Other sources of support: _____

_____

Contacts:　　　　　　　Name　　　　　　　　　Date of meeting/call

　　　　　　　_____　　_____

　　　　　　　_____　　_____

　　　　　　　_____　　_____

References: _____

_____

Prior grants: _____ Date _____

Prior grants: _____ Date _____

Reports on time:　 yes _____　　no; if not, why? _____

Reasons grantee is qualified: _____

Charitable nature of project/program _____

Is project achievable? _____

Supplemental information (not required, but helpful):

Organizational history　　Publications/reports of projects

List of board members　　Projects of grantee

Letters of reference　　　Annual report

Organization budgets　　Needs analysis

---

**EXHIBIT 9.9** Expenditure Responsibility Agreement—Version 1

---

Sample Foundation
_____

Name of Grantee Organization _____

Address _____

Dear _____

_____ (Name of Grantor) is pleased to inform you that its Board of Directors has approved a grant of $_____ to the _____ (Name of Grantee) pursuant to the grant application dated _____. Since your organization and ours are private foundations, we must enter into an expenditure responsibility agreement.

Use of Funds

Our grant must be expended for charitable, scientific, literary, or educational purposes as defined under Internal Revenue Code § 501(c)(3), and more specifically for _____ (Description of purpose of grant, title if any, or general support of the grantee). ANY FUNDS NOT SO EXPENDED MUST BE RETURNED TO _____ (Grantor). Funds may not be used to influence legislation or the outcome of any election, to carry on a voter registration drive, or to make grants to individuals for travel or study.

Annual Report

_____ (Grantee) will provide a narrative and financial report to us by _____ (Date). The narrative portion should include a copy of publications, catalogs, and other materials describing the accomplishments of the program or project. The financial report must be attested to by an outside accountant and must contain details of expenditures, such as salaries, travel, supplies, and the like.

Although grant funds need not be physically separated, records of receipts and expenditures under the grant, as well as copies of the report furnished to us, should be kept available for our inspection until _____ (four years from grant).

Payment Terms

Payments under the grant will be made on the following dates, after receipt of a signed copy of this agreement:

(Date) _____                    (Amount) _____

Sign and Return

If this agreement meets with your approval, kindly sign it and return one copy to us. On behalf of _____ (Grantor), I extend every good wish for the success of this endeavor.

Acknowledged by:


For Sample Foundation                          For Grantee Organization

Date                                           Date

---

**Exhibit 9.10** Expenditure Responsibility Agreement—Version 2

---

Sample Foundation—Grant Agreement

---

Grantee: _____

Amount of Grant Grant Payment Dates

$ _____ _____ _____

$ _____ _____ _____

$ _____ _____ _____

$ _____ _____ _____

Total Grant Awarded     $ _____ _____

Grant Term in Years: _____

Purpose of Grant:

_____ and as further described in your grant request dated _____

Terms of Grant:

A. Funds granted will be expended only for the purposes for which the grant is being made. You will notify us if there are any changes in your plans. ANY FUNDS NOT SO USED MUST BE RETURNED TO SAMPLE FOUNDATION.

B. A financial report attested to by an independent accountant must be furnished annually by (date), along with a narrative report of accomplishments and any reports, publications, or other materials prepared in connection with the project.

C. Financial records pertaining to the grant must be maintained in accordance with generally accepted accounting principles. Receipts and other documentation in connection with the grant will be maintained for at least four years and be open to our inspection at any time during that period.

D. No funds may be used to:

  1. Carry on propaganda, or otherwise attempt to influence legislation (as defined by IRC § 4945);

  2. Influence the outcome of any specific public election, or carry on, directly or indirectly, any voter registration drive (as defined in IRC § 4945);

  3. Make an individual grant or regrant funds to another organization unless the requirements of IRC § 4945 are met; or

  4. Advance any purpose other than one specified in IRC § 170(c)(2)(B).

E. If Sample Foundation becomes aware that the funds are not being used for the purposes described above, we reserve the right to ask to be reimbursed for the amounts so diverted, and will withhold any future grant payments.

Acknowledged by:

For Sample Foundation     For Grantee Organization

Date                      Date

3. Maintain records of the receipts and expenditures, and make its records available to the grantor at reasonable times, and

   ○ Not use any of the funds to carry on propaganda or otherwise to attempt to influence legislation,

   ○ To influence the outcome of any specific public election, or to carry on, directly or indirectly, any voter registration drive,

   ○ To make any grant to an individual or organization, or

   ○ To undertake any activity for any noncharitable purpose, to the extent that use of the funds would be a taxable expenditure if made directly by the private foundation.[259]

The agreement must also clearly specify the purposes of the grant. These purposes may include contributing for capital endowment, for the purchase of capital equipment, or for general support, provided that neither the grants nor the income from them may be used for noncharitable purposes.[260]

*Program-related investments.*[261] In addition to the preceding requirements, the recipient of program-related investment funds must also agree to:

- Repay the funds not invested in accordance with the agreement, but only to the extent permitted by applicable law concerning distributions to holders of equity interests.

- At least once a year during the existence of the PRI, submit financial reports of a type ordinarily required by commercial investors under similar circumstances, and a statement that it has complied with the terms of the investment.

- Maintain books and records of a type normally required by commercial investors.[262]

Program-related investments often provide financing for projects of a business nature, such as real estate development or scientific research. Presumably, funds expended by these projects might not necessarily be considered charitable expenditures if the foundation paid the expenses itself. Therefore, the expenditure responsibility agreement for such investments does not have to contain a requirement that the grantee not use the funds to engage in any activity for any purpose other than charitable ones. Such an investment with a public charity does not require expenditure responsibility process.

---

259. Reg. § 53.4945-5(b)(3)(i), (ii), (iii), and (iv).
260. E.g., Priv. Ltr. Rul. 199952092.
261. *See* § 8.3.
262. Reg. § 53.4945-5(b)(4).

*Foreign grants.* The agreement should phrase the restrictions in appropriate terms under foreign law or custom. While not specifically required, an affidavit or opinion of counsel stating that the agreement is valid under the foreign laws is "sufficient."[263]

### (d)  Monitoring System

Since a private foundation is not an ensurer of the activity of the organization to which it makes a grant, satisfaction of the expenditure responsibility requirements ordinarily means the grantor foundation has not violated the rules pertaining to lobbying or political campaign activity.[264] A private foundation is considered to be exercising expenditure responsibility as long as it exerts the requisite reasonable efforts and establishes the requisite adequate procedures.[265] These rules have been given strict construction by the U.S. Tax Court, which, in concluding that a private foundation's grants failed each of them, wrote that they reflect a "Congressional determination to leave no loophole by imposing strict and detailed conditions to make sure that a private foundation's grants would not be used for proscribed purposes."[266] Before making a grant to an organization where expenditure responsibility must be exercised, a private foundation should establish a system for monitoring the requirements. Again, refer to Exhibit 9.7 for a checklist that can be used as a guide to gather information and assure that suitable steps are taken.

### (e)  Reports from Grantees

In the case of expenditure responsibility grants, except in respect to certain capital endowment grants, the grantor private foundation must require reports on the use of the funds, compliance with the terms of the grant, and progress made by the grantee toward achieving the purposes for which the grant was made. The grantee must make the reports as of the end of its annual accounting period within which the grant or any portion of it is received and all subsequent periods until the grant funds are expended in full or the grant is otherwise terminated. The reports must be furnished to the grantor within a reasonable period of time after the close of the annual accounting period of the grantee for which the reports are made. Within a reasonable period of time after the close of

---

263. Reg. § 53.4945-5(b)(5). *See* §§ 6.5(e), 9.5.
264. *See* §§ 9.1, 9.2.
265. *See* text accompanied by *supra* note 237.
266. *Mannheimer Charitable Trust, Hans S. v. Commissioner*, 93 T.C. 35, 51 (1989). The foundation argued unsuccessfully that all of its internal documents, meeting transcriptions, and actual observations of the activities amounted to the exercise of expenditure responsibility. Despite the facts and the foundation's argument that its failure to report was due to an oversight, the penalty assessment was upheld.

its annual accounting period during which the use of the grant funds is completed, the grantee must make a final report with respect to all expenditures made from the funds (including salaries, travel, and supplies) and indicating the progress made toward the goals of the grant. The grantor need not conduct any independent verification of the reports unless it has reason to doubt their accuracy or reliability.[267] Exhibit 9.11 provides sample grantee reports for annual support and for an endowment grant.

**Endowment Grants.** If a private foundation makes a grant to another private foundation or non-(c)(3) organization for endowment, for the purchase of capital equipment, or for other capital purposes, the grantor foundation must require reports from the grantee on the use of the principal and any income from the grant funds. The grantee must make these reports annually for its fiscal year in which the grant was received and the immediately succeeding two years, generally three years. Only if it is reasonably apparent to the grantor that, before the end of the second succeeding taxable year, neither the principal, the income from the grant funds, nor the equipment purchased with the grant funds has been used for any purpose that would result in liability for a taxable expenditure, the grantor foundation may then allow discontinuance of the reports.[268] Reports of program-related investments must be received and reported throughout the life of the investment.

A private foundation that distributes part of its assets to another private foundation in a termination distribution also has a duty to exercise expenditures responsibility indefinitely. This responsibility ceases when the foundation disposes of all of its assets.[269]

## (f) Grantee's Procedures

A grantee of a private foundation (including the recipient of a program-related investment) need not segregate grant funds nor separately account for them on its books unless either practice is required by the grantor. If neither practice is followed, grants received within a year are deemed to be expended before grants received in a succeeding year. In that event, expenditures of grants received within any year must be prorated among all the grants.

In accounting for grant expenditures, private foundations may make the necessary computations on a cumulative annual basis (or, where appropriate, as of the date on which the computations are made). These rules are to be applied in a manner consistent with the available records of the grantee and with the grantee's treatment of qualifying distributions. The records of expenditures, as

---

267. Reg. § 53.4945-5(c)(1).
268. Reg. § 53.4945-5(c)(2).
269. Regs. §§ 53.4945-5(b)(7) and 1.507-3(a)(7), (8); *see* Chapter 13.

**EXHIBIT 9.11**   Grantee Reports

---

The Anna Jane Smith Memorial Library
1444 Smith Terrace
Anytown, USA 44444

Ms. Jane Sample,
Treasurer SAMPLE
FOUNDATION101 First
Main Plaza Anytown, USA
44444

RE: Annual Report #1 of
grant funds expended
under Expenditure
Responsibility Agreement

Dear Ms. Sample,

On behalf of the Anna Jane Smith Memorial Library, I want to again say how grateful our library is for the significant support we receive from your foundation. The minds of Anytown's children are challenged and expanded by the enrichment your funds allow. The specific purpose of this letter is to report in accordance with our expenditure responsibility agreement dated December 23, 20XX.

Your annual support gift of $200,000 was expended during our fiscal year ending June 30, 20XX, for the library's educational programs. As reflected in our audited financial statements furnished to you with our endowment grant report, total expenditures this year were $429,000. We spent $204,000 on lending library activities, $56,000 for purchasing new books and publications, $72,000 for a school outreach program, and $97,000 on administration and fundraising. Your annual gift and others from our community defrayed all but $92,000 of the total expenditures, meaning that we were able to set aside $24,000 as a reserve for the future.

Additionally, as required by our agreement, all of the income earned on your endowment gift was either currently expended for the library's educational programs or reserved to be spent for such purpose in the future. No portion of the gift was expended for a non-charitable purpose; particularly, no amounts were expended to carry on propaganda or otherwise to attempt to influence legislation, to attempt to influence an election, or to make a grant to an individual. We maintain detailed documentation evidencing the nature of our expenditures and would welcome your inspection of the records if you so desire.

Thank you again for your financial support. If any additional information is required, please let us know.

November 21, 20XX

_____
Mary Kay Anderson
Chief Financial Officer

*(Continued)*

**Exhibit 9.11** (Continued)

The Anna Jane Smith Memorial Library
1444 Smith Terrace
Anytown, USA 44444

Ms. Jane Sample,
Treasurer SAMPLE
FOUNDATION101
First Main Plaza Anytown,
USA 44444

RE: Annual Report # 2
under Endowment
Expenditure Responsibility
Agreement

Dear Ms. Sample,

On behalf of the Anna Jane Smith Memorial Library, I want to first say how grateful our library is for the significant support we receive from your foundation. The minds of Anytown's children are challenged and expanded by the enrichment your funds allow. The purpose of this letter is to again report in accordance with our expenditure responsibility agreement dated December 28, 20XX.

Your generous endowment gift of $100,000 was added to the Anna Jane Smith Memorial Library Endowment Fund to be conserved and prudently invested so as to produce income to support our educational programs. The balance of the endowment as of June 30, 20XX, was $920,000. During our fiscal year then ended, current income of $119,000 was realized on the endowment. Out of this income, $92,000 was expended for library operations and $24,000 was set aside in the temporarily restricted funds to assure support of operations in any future years in which current yield might be lower. A copy of our audited financial statements is enclosed for a full report of our financial activity.

As required by our agreement, all of the income earned on your endowment gift was either currently expended for the library's educational programs or reserved to be spent for such charitable purposes in the future. None of the endowment fund or its income was expended for a noncharitable purpose; particularly, no amounts were expended to carry on propaganda or otherwise to attempt to influence legislation, to attempt to influence an election, or to make a grant to an individual. We maintain documentation evidencing the nature of our expenditures and welcome your inspection of the records, if you so desire.

Thank you again for your financial support. If any additional information is required, please let us know.

November 21, 20XX

Mary Kay Anderson
Chief Financial Officer

well as copies of the reports submitted to the grantor, must be kept for at least four years after completion of the use of the grant funds.[270]

## (g) Reliance on Grantee Information

A private foundation exercising expenditure responsibility with respect to its grants may rely on adequate records or other sufficient evidence supplied by the grantee showing, to the extent applicable, the information that the foundation must report to the IRS.[271] Other sufficient evidence includes a statement by an appropriate trustee, director, or officer of the grantee.[272]

## (h) Reports to IRS

A private foundation making expenditure responsibility grants must provide specific information, as part of its annual information return Form 990-PF, for each tax year in which these grant(s) are made. A report of monitoring steps must also be provided on subsequent return(s) with respect to each expenditure responsibility grant for which any amount or any report is outstanding at any time during the tax year. With respect to any grant made for endowment or other capital purposes, the grantor must provide the required information in the tax years for which the grantor must require a report from the grantee under the rules conceding capital grants to private foundations, typically the grant year plus two subsequent years. Program-related investments must be reported for the life of the loan or for as many years as the investment is outstanding.[273] If a grantee's report contains the required information, the reporting requirement with respect to that grant may be satisfied by submission with the foundation's return of the actual report received from the grantee.[274]

These reports must include the following data with respect to each grant:

- Name and address of the grantee.
- Date and amount of the grant.
- Purpose of the grant.
- Amounts expended by the grantee (based on the most recent report received from the grantee).
- Whether, to the knowledge of the grantor private foundation, the grantee has diverted any funds from the purpose of the grant.

---

270. Reg. § 53.4945-5(c)(3).
271. *See* § 9.6(h).
272. Reg. § 53.4945-5(c)(4).
273. *See* § 8.3, text accompanied by note 75.
274. Reg. § 53.4945-5(d)(1).

EXHIBIT **9.12**   Report to IRS on Form 990-PF

---

SAMPLE
FOUNDATION                                         #ein 444444444

---

Attachment to Form 990-PF Part VII-A, Question 5c on page 5

**Expenditure Responsibility Statement for the year 20XX**

Pursuant to IRC Regulation § 53.4945–5(d)(2), the SAMPLE FOUNDATION provides the
following information:

| | |
|---|---|
| (i) Grantee: | The Anna Jane Smith Memorial Library, 1444 Smith Terrace, Anytown, USA 44444 |
| (ii) Amount of Grants: | December 28, 20XX $100,000 (endowment); December 23, 20XX $10,000 (general support) |
| (iii) Purpose of Grants: | Endowment or general support for the Anna Jane Smith Memorial Library, an education foundation operating a library free and open to the general public in Anytown, in amounts listed above. |
| (iv) and (vi) Reports: | The Anna Jane Smith Memorial Library submitted full and complete reports of its expenditure of December 20XX operating support grant on November 21, 20XX. The Anna Jane Smith Memorial Library also submitted a report on the 20XX endowment grant on November 21, 20XX. The endowment report reflected that the grant was properly added to the Library's endowment, the income from which is devoted exclusively to its educational programs. |
| (v) Diversions: | To the knowledge of the grantor, no funds have been diverted to any activity other than the activity for which the grant was originally made. |
| (vii) Verification: | The grantor has no reason to doubt the accuracy or reliability of the report from the grantee; therefore, no independent verification of the report was made. |

- Dates of any reports received from the grantee.
- Date and results of any verification of the grantee's reports undertaken by or at the direction of the grantor private foundation.[275]

Exhibit 9.12 illustrates a sample 990-PF report.

The IRS once took a strict position on this point, relating to timely reporting of expenditure responsibility grants to the IRS. In one instance, a private foundation made a grant but failed to include it among the list of grants made during that year, required to be supplied as part of its annual information return. Later, the private foundation discovered the omission of the grant from

---

275. Reg. § 53.4945-5(d)(2).

the return and filed a corrected amended return. The failure to comply with the reporting requirement caused the grant to be a taxable expenditure (although the private foundation was able to correct the expenditure). Under the pre-1984 rules, a penalty tax was levied, because "while the subsequent filing of the amended return may have accomplished correction, . . . the untimeliness of such filing precluded it from nullifying the foundation's failure to exercise expenditure responsibility in connection with the grant."[276] Effective beginning in 1984, this type of a mistake may be corrected without penalty.[277]

### (i)  Retention of Documents

In addition to the information included on the annual information return, a grantor private foundation must make available to the IRS, at the foundation's principal office, a copy of the agreement as to each expenditure responsibility grant made during the year, a copy of each report received during the year from each grantee on any expenditure responsibility grant, and a copy of each report made by the grantor's personnel or independent auditors of any audits or other investigations made during the year with respect to any expenditure responsibility grant.[278]

Data contained in these reports, where the reports are received by a private foundation after the close of its accounting year but before the due date of its annual information return for that year, need not be reported on that return, but may be reported on the grantor's information return for the year in which the reports are received from the grantee.[279]

### (j)  Grantee Diversions

Any diversion of grant funds (including the income from the funds in the case of an endowment grant) by the grantee to any use not in furtherance of a purpose specified in the grant may result in the diverted portion of the grant being treated as a taxable expenditure of the grantor. However, the fact that a grantee does not use any portion of the grant funds as indicated in the original budget projection is not treated as a diversion if the use to which the funds are committed is consistent with the purpose of the grant as stated in the grant

---

276. Rev. Rul. 77-213, 1977-1 C.B. 357. Likewise, the penalty was levied where a private foundation reported for three years following the capital grant time frame, but failed to submit reports to the IRS for the full duration of a program-related investment as required by Reg. § 53.4945-5(b)(4)(ii) (*Charles Stewart Mott Foundation v. United States*, 938 F.2d 58 (6th Cir. 1991)).

277. *See* § 9.10(b).

278. Reg. § 53.4945-5(d)(3).

279. Reg. § 53.4945-5(d)(4).

agreement and does not result in a violation of the required terms of the agreement.[280]

In any event, a grantor will not be treated as having made a taxable expenditure solely by reason of a diversion by the grantee, if the grantor has complied with one of the two next-discussed requirements.[281] In cases in which the grantor private foundation determines that any part of a grant has been used for improper purposes and the grantee has not previously diverted grant funds, the private foundation will not be treated as having made a taxable expenditure solely by reason of the diversion as long as the private foundation can show that it:

1. Is taking all reasonable and appropriate steps either to recover the grant funds or to ensure the restoration of the diverted funds and the dedication of the other grant funds held by the grantee to the purposes being financed by the grant, and

2. Withholds any further payments to the grantee after it becomes aware that a diversion may have taken place, until it has received the grantee's assurances that future diversions will not occur and requires the grantee to take extraordinary precautions to prevent future diversions.

If a private foundation is treated as having made a taxable expenditure in this type of situation, then, unless the private foundation meets the requirements of the first of these conditions, the amount of the taxable expenditure is the amount of the grant plus the amount of any further payments to the same grantee. If the private foundation complies with the requirements of this first condition, however, but not the requirements of the second, the amount of the taxable expenditure is the amount of the further payments.[282]

In cases where a grantee has previously diverted funds received from a grantor private foundation, and the grantor foundation determines that any part of a grant has again been used for improper purposes, the private foundation will not be treated as having made a taxable expenditure solely by reason of the diversion as long as the private foundation can show that it has complied with the two previously listed conditions.

If a private foundation is treated as having made a taxable expenditure in this circumstance, then, unless the private foundation meets the requirements of the first of these conditions, the amount of the taxable expenditure is the amount of the diversion plus the amount of any further payments to the same grantee. If the private foundation complies with the first requirement,

---

280. Reg. § 53.4945-5(e)(1)(i).
281. Reg. § 53.4945-5(e)(1)(ii).
282. Reg. § 53.4945-5(e)(1)(iii).

however, but fails to withhold further payments until the second requirement is met, the amount of the taxable expenditure is the amount of the further payments.

As to either of these scenarios, the phrase *all reasonable and appropriate steps* includes legal action where appropriate, but need not include a lawsuit if the action would in all probability not result in the satisfaction of execution on a judgment.[283]

A failure by the grantee to make the required reports (or the making of inadequate reports) will result in treatment of the grant as a taxable expenditure by the grantor unless the grantor has made the grant in accordance with the several expenditure responsibility requirements, has complied with the applicable reporting requirements, makes a reasonable effort to obtain the required report, and withholds all future payments on this grant and on any other grant to the same grantee until the report is furnished.[284] In addition, a grant that is subject to the expenditure responsibility requirements is considered a taxable expenditure of the grantor private foundation if the grantor fails to make the requisite pre-grant inquiry, fails to make the grant in accordance with a procedure consistent with the previously cited requirements, or fails to report to the IRS.[285]

While "reaffirm[ing] the central purpose of the expenditure responsibility rules—to ensure that private foundation grants will be properly used by the recipient organization solely for tax-exempt purposes," the House-Senate conferees, in finalizing the Tax Reform Act of 1984, expressed concern about any "unduly burdensome or unnecessary requirements in some respects (which may operate to deter grants by some foundations to newly formed, community-based foundations)."[286] Accordingly, the conference report directed the Department of the Treasury "to review its expenditure responsibility regulations for purposes of modifying any requirements which are found to be unduly burdensome or unnecessary" and, specifically, to modify the required grantor private foundation reports to the IRS.[287] However, the expenditure responsibility regulations have not been revised.

From time to time, the IRS issues rulings as to whether a private foundation has complied with the expenditure responsibility requirements.[288]

283. Reg. § 53.4945-5(e)(1)(iv), (v).
284. Reg. § 53.4945-5(e)(2).
285. Reg. § 53.4945-5(e)(3). *See* § 9.6(h).
286. H. Rep. No. 98-851, 98th Cong., 2d Sess. 1091 (1984).
287. *Id*. The conferees also directed the Treasury Department to report to the House Committee on Ways and Means and the Senate Committee on Finance on its review and modifications. In general, Grumbach and Paul, "Expenditure Responsibility Is Alive and Well Says Tax Court," 129 *Trusts & Estates* (No. 8) 38 (1990).
288. E.g., Priv. Ltr. Rul. 8717024.

# §9.7   INTERNET AND PRIVATE FOUNDATIONS

Private foundations are using the Internet as a means of conveying and accomplishing their mission. Opportunities to provide links between a foundation's website and other sites on the World Wide Web abound, making it increasingly important that private foundations and their advisors familiarize themselves with the impact of the use of electronic communication systems on their tax-exempt status. Application of existing tax rules and standards to activities conducted on the World Wide Web, including e-mail and other forms of electronic transmission, is an evolving issue.

The IRS, in October 2000, solicited public comment concerning application of the federal tax law governing exempt organizations to activities they conduct on the Internet.[289] They received scores of suggestions, but have been issuing guidance as to application of the federal tax laws to use of the Internet by private foundations and other tax-exempt organizations in only a piecemeal fashion.

## (a)   Exempt Status Issues

To obtain recognition and to maintain tax-exempt status, a private foundation must be dedicated to and devote its primary energies to conducting activities that accomplish a charitable purpose.[290] The standards for defining charitable activities are documented in Treasury regulations, Internal Revenue Manuals for Private Foundations, in countless published and private IRS rulings, and in court decisions. The IRS agrees that existing standards that are used to evaluate print and broadcast communications also apply in determining the character of electronic communication activities.[291] Logically, the tax code and regulations should be applied consistently without regard to the medium in which activities are conducted.

Electronic communication is nonetheless still a relatively unexplored area of activity for tax-exempt organizations beyond a ruling that provides examples of impermissible political intervention.[292] In 1974, the IRS approved exemption for

---

289. IRS Ann. 2000-84, 2000-42 I.R.B. 385.

290. *See* § 1.5.

291. Chasin, Ruth, and Harper, *IRS Exempt Organization Continuing Professional Education Text for Fiscal Year 2000*, Chapter 1.

292. To date, only a few private rulings even mention the word *Internet*. In all instances, the Internet access mentioned in the ruling was to be used as a communication device for the organization's program activity, with no associated revenue generation. Priv. Ltr. Rul. 199913042 considered a private foundation's computer training program for teachers and students. The program was to provide computers and access to the Internet; no revenues were to be generated by the activity, and a charitable class was served by the program. The question was whether the expenditures were taxable under IRC § 4945. The ruling concluded that the educational program, with its Internet-access component, served a charitable or educational purpose. A host of other issues have not been considered to date. In Priv. Ltr. Rul. 9723046, Internet activity was condoned as related, and advertising on the site was noted, but no ruling was requested regarding its unrelatedness or taxability.

a regional computer network for a consortium of colleges and universities based on theory that it advanced education.[293] In 1981, a computer network to exchange bibliographic information between libraries was also ruled to be a charitable organization even though some of its members were not tax-exempt.[294] The IRS training materials say, "Internet Service Providers (ISP) have usually been denied exemption because they are viewed as carrying on a trade or business for profit, or conferring an unmixed private benefit, or both."[295] "Providing communication services of an ordinary commercial nature in a community, even though the undertaking is conducted on a nonprofit basis, is not regarded as conferring a charitable benefit on the community unless the service directly accomplishes one of the established categories of charitable purposes."[296] IRS technicians were told to peruse the ISP's home page to evaluate its exempt character as a source of public information and to see if placards, banners, and links to commercial sites constitute advertising that create unrelated business income.

### (b) Providing Information

The publication of information pertaining to the foundation's mission and program activities for free on its own website is certainly an exempt activity. A site containing basic information about the foundation—grant applications, deadlines, admission standards, locations, examples of grants awarded, and any other information describing the programs it supports—simply replaces brochures and reports now available on paper. Thus, dissemination of information through the Internet to advance the accomplishment of a foundation's exempt purposes is permitted. A site might also contain a bulletin board for constituent communication, such as a parent forum concerning child care issues. The cost of establishing, designing, and maintaining a site that advances the foundation's mission should be considered a qualifying disbursement and not a taxable expenditure.[297]

Linking the organization's website to sites of other tax-exempt organizations that contain reference materials, services, or resources pertaining to a foundation's mission, direct exempt functions, and organizations the foundation financially supports should also be considered an exempt activity. For example, a foundation that focuses on child care issues should be able to link its site to a mental health agency, to the school district, to an association of child

293. Rev. Rul. 74-614, 1974-2 C.B. 164.
294. Rev. Rul. 81-29, 1981-1 C.B. 328.
295. Moore and Harper, *IRS Exempt Organization Continuing Professional Education Text for Fiscal Year 1999*, Chapter C, "Internet Service Providers Exemption Issues."
296. Chasin and Harper, *IRS Exempt Organization Continuing Professional Education Text for Fiscal Year 1997*, Chapter A, "Computer-Related Organizations," pp. 9–12.
297. Expenditures treated as taxable are listed in introduction to this chapter.

psychiatrists, and to the child protective service agency. Links that might cause concern regarding exempt status or produce unrelated business income are discussed later. Publishing information pertaining to legislation and elections on a foundation's website would have to be carefully developed with a view to the special constraints placed on private foundations, discussed in §§ 9.1 and 9.2.

### (c)  Providing Services

Rendering services and information that advance its mission to a private foundation's exempt constituents should similarly be considered an exempt activity. Again, the standards for identifying services that promote the mission are well documented. A private operating foundation that provides counseling, resource information, and transportation assistance to the handicapped and elderly should be able to do so through its website.[298] A foundation focused on legal aid to indigents could provide advice and documents electronically.[299] Providing bibliographic information to libraries has been found to be an exempt function that by reference can be an exempt service if provided on the Internet.[300]

### (d)  Links

The one issue unique to the Internet may be the capability of linking an organization's website instantly and without any charge to another website. It is important to ask whether the organization's interests are served by the link. If revenues are generated as a result of the link, the unrelated business income tax issues must be considered. IRS guidance regarding political intervention says the organization can be held responsible for the content of the linked organization's site and provides the linking organization is responsible to evidence the exempt purposes served by links and to trace the links.[301] The sponsorship regulations look to the content of the page reached by a link from the organization's site to a sponsor site to evaluate whether the link represents an advertisement.[302] If the linked page contains an endorsement of the sponsor's product by the exempt organization or other words indicating that the charity promotes sales of the sponsor's product, the value of the link creates unrelated business income. By analogy, a link from a company foundation's site

---

298. Rev. Rul. 77-246, 1977-2 C.B. 190.
299. Rev. Ruls. 78-428, 1978-2 C.B. 177, and 76-22, 1976-1 C.B. 148.
300. *Council for Bibliographic & Information Technologies v. Commissioner*, 63 T.C.M. 3186 (1992); Rev. Rul. 70-79, 1970-1 C.B. 127.
301. Rev. Rul. 2007-41, 2007–1 C.B. 1421; also see Political Activities Compliance Initiative (2008) at www.irs.gov.
302. Reg. § 1.513-4(f), Example 11.

to the company's home page should be a permissible thank-you and acknow-ledgment as described below. Links can be considered from the vantage point of several different tax consequences, as follows:

**Links That Serve an Exempt Purpose.** An organization's motivation for placing a link on its site should be determinative in evaluating whether a link serves its exempt purposes. If the link is to a site—for-profit or nonprofit—that provides information that enables a viewer to learn, get aid, pray, sign up for classes, or a myriad of other exempt purposes, the link should be considered to serve an exempt purpose. The child care–supporting foundation mentioned earlier would be making related links when it connects its site to a mental health agency, to the school district, to an association of child psychiatrists, or to the child protective service agency.

**Links That Might Create Self-Dealing.** Links to the website of a founda-tion's creators or major donors could possibly be considered an act of self-dealing. The IRS has yet to opine on this question. If the link is deemed to provide public recognition to a donor, the link would be treated as an incidental or tenuous benefit.[303] The issue is whether a monetarily measurable benefit is provided to the donor, rather than a simple public announcement. A link to a donor's home page should represent an acceptable announcement. So long as the linked page is not promoting the donor's products, the corporate sponsor-ship rules say that no substantial benefit occurs.[304] Advisors, particularly those of company foundations, should look for continuing developments in this regard.

**Links That Might Create Unrelated Business Income.** When the organi-zation receives revenue in connection with providing a link, the motivation again must be questioned. Links to the sites of a foundation's business donors as a thank-you to acknowledge their financial support does not necessarily create unrelated advertising revenue as described in the previous paragraph. When information, goods, or consulting services are sold on a foundation's website, the revenues may or may not be considered exempt function income. For all categories of tax-exempt organizations, the character of revenues generated through a website and delivery of services in connec-tion with electronic communication will depend on the relationship between the activity generating the revenue and accomplishment of the organiza-tion's exempt purposes.[305] The charges made by the foundations described above would represent exempt function revenues related to mission. In

---

303. Discussed in § 5.7(c).
304. IRC § 513(i) and Reg. § 1.513-4; *see Tax Planning and Compliance*, § 21.8(e).
305. IRC § 513(a), Reg. § 1.513-1.

considering other situations, the standards for defining relatedness under IRC § 513 and the labyrinth of exceptions and modifications applied in calculating taxable income under IRC § 512 can provide answers. The irregular activity exception will not apply to items continually available for sale on a publicly accessible site. Also without question, to the extent an organization exploits its own website in a commercial fashion or provides Internet services to the general public, the activity would be unrelated,[306] and expenditures of the site might possibly be treated as taxable expenditures and impermissible business activity.

**Links That Cause Penalties.** A link that unilaterally promotes the private interests of the organization's disqualified persons will constitute a nonexempt activity and result in both self-dealing and a taxable expenditure. An example of a situation in which self-dealing could occur is a cancer treatment research group that only links to the private clinic site of its creator, an oncologist. Linking an exempt organization's site to a privately owned business(es) for reasons other than to promote exempt purposes or recognize a contributor would not only result in a penalty but could also endanger the exempt status. The cost associated with links that constitute political expenditures would be reportable as taxable income on Form 1120-POL and also subject to the tax penalty for political expenditures[307] and reported on Form 4720.[308]

**Other Internet Issues.** There are a number of issues beyond the scope of this book that should be mentioned for the sake of completeness. Exhibit 9.13 surveys exemption issues private foundations conducting activities from a web page may have. Additionally a foundation might need to seek assistance in answering the following questions:

- Must any state sales tax be collected for sales of goods or products on the site?

- Do the materials published on the organization's site, or sites to which it is linked, involve legal issues concerning intellectual property rights, invasion of privacy or defamation of character issues, and so on?

- If contributions or memberships are solicited on the website, must the organization report its fundraising activity in any states? Must special disclosures about the organization's financials be shown on the site?

---

306. Discussed in Chapter 11.
307. IRC § 4955.
308. *See* § 12.3(d).

**EXHIBIT 9.13** Checklist for Website Exemption Issues

---

Foundation Name: _____

Website Address: _____

Prepared By: _____ Date: _____

1. Print Home Page and other representative pages from PF's site to _____
   review scope of information presented on site.

2. Does the site reflect the PF's mission and programs as described in _____
   Form 990-PF?

3. Are goods and services offered for sale on the site? _____

   a. Are products or services sold related to exempt purposes? _____

   b. Does site link to a commercial site for sale of its goods or services? _____

   c. Is revenue produced from "hits" on the linked site or some other site? _____

4. Does the organization solicit contributions and/or memberships on _____
   its site?

   a. If so, is state registration required? _____

   b. Are disclosures for quid pro quo transactions provided? _____

   c. Is qualitative and quantitative sponsor information displayed on _____
      the site, creating advertising (UBI) rather than acknowledgment
      (donation)?

5. Can the accounting system capture costs related to the site? _____

6. Can revenues be fragmented by related and unrelated sources? _____

7. Does the site contain discussion of public or civic affairs? _____

   a. If so, is there a "call to action" urging viewers to contact legislators _____
      that constitutes grassroots lobbying?

   b. Does the information presented regarding issues of public policy _____
      (gun control, abortion, etc.) present a biased viewpoint?

8. Is the site linked to other sites? (Be cautious if § 501(c)(4) or PAC sites.) _____

   a. Do links provide information/resources pertaining to mission? _____

   b. Are there links to the organization's sponsors or contributors? _____

   c. If so, does the link represent advertising for the sponsor? _____

   d. Is there a link to a political party? (Prohibited for § (c)(3)'s but OK for _____
      others)

9. Review organization's information reported on Guidestar and IRS _____
   Exempt Organization Select Check.

---

## §9.8 SPENDING FOR NONCHARITABLE PURPOSES

The term *taxable expenditure* includes any amount paid or incurred by a private foundation for any *noncharitable purpose.*[309] The purposes that are considered charitable are those that are religious, charitable, scientific, literary, or educational, the fostering of national or international sports competition, and the prevention of cruelty to children or animals (but not testing for public safety).[310] Thus, ordinarily, only an expenditure for an activity that, if it were a substantial part of the organization's total activities, would cause loss of tax exemption is a taxable expenditure.[311] A private foundation can make a grant to a public charity and earmark the funds for a specific project and not make a taxable expenditure as long as the project itself constitutes a charitable undertaking.[312]

Expenditures not treated as taxable expenditures under these rules are purchases of investments to obtain income to be used in furtherance of charitable purposes, reasonable expenses with respect to investments, payment of taxes, any expenses that qualify as deductions in the computation of unrelated business income tax,[313] any payment that constitutes a qualifying distribution[314] or an allowable deduction pursuant to the investment income tax rules,[315] reasonable expenditures to evaluate, acquire, modify, and dispose of program-related investments,[316] and business expenditures by the recipient of a program-related investment. Conversely, expenditures for unreasonable administrative expenses—including compensation, consultants' fees, and other fees for services rendered—are ordinarily taxable expenditures, unless the private foundation can demonstrate that the expenses were paid or incurred in the good-faith belief that they were reasonable and that the payment or incurrence of the expenses in the amounts involved was consistent with

---

309. IRC § 4945(d)(5); Reg. § 53. 4945-6(a). For these purposes, the term *charitable purposes* means purposes encompassed by IRC § 170(c)(2)(B).
310. *See* § 1.5.
311. Reg. § 53.4945-6(a). E.g., Rev. Rul. 80-97, 1980-1 C.B. 257, where the IRS held that an unrestricted grant from a private foundation to a cemetery company exempt by reason of IRC § 501(c)(13) was a taxable expenditure because the grantee is not described in IRC § 170(c)(2)(B), even though contributions to it are deductible under IRC § 170(c)(5). Also *Gladney v. Commissioner*, 745 F.2d 955 (5th Cir. 1984), where the court held that the transfer of assets to noncharitable recipients upon dissolution of an organization, where the IRC § 507 termination rules were not satisfied, constituted a taxable expenditure.
312. E.g., Tech. Adv. Mem. 9240001.
313. *See* § 11.5.
314. *See* § 6.4.
315. *See* § 10.3.
316. *See* § 8.3.

ordinary business care and prudence.[317] The determination as to whether an expenditure is unreasonable is dependent on the facts and circumstances of the particular case.

An investment may subsequently be discovered to be a Ponzi scheme or other fraud.[318] A report submitted to the government by the New York State Bar Association[319] concluded that an outcome such as this "may be indicative of a failure of [due] diligence or business judgment, but does not indicate the foundation's purpose was not to earn a profit." As to whether this type of an amount paid constitutes a taxable expenditure, this report observed that "it is not at all clear that there is any benefit in stretching the statute to punish a foundation for an investment in a Ponzi scheme where there has been no self-dealing and where the investment was not a jeopardizing investment, based on facts known at the time the investment was made." The report posed three questions in the taxable expenditures context, pertaining to fictitious income reported and reinvested in the arrangement. One, are these amounts considered paid or incurred for taxable expenditures law purposes? Two, are amounts paid, as investment advisory or management fees, in connection with investments in a fraudulent investment scheme, considered taxable expenditures when paid to the operator of the fraudulent arrangement or to a person unaware of the fraud who invested the private foundation's funds in the scheme? Three, what criteria are to be applied in evaluating the reasonableness of the expenses?

A private foundation may utilize these rules even where an expenditure constitutes an act of self-dealing.[320] In one instance, a private foundation made a loan to a disqualified person to generate income to be used solely for the private foundation's charitable purposes—an act of self-dealing.[321] Because the loan was, however, made to the disqualified person at a reasonable rate of interest, was adequately secured, and otherwise met prudent investment standards, and

---

317. *See* § 53.4945-6(b). E.g., *Kermit Fischer Foundation v. Commissioner*, 59 T.C.M. 898 (1990) (payment of unreasonable compensation). Also *Underwood v. United States*, 461 F. Supp. 1382 (N.D.Tex. 1978) (return of contingent contributions held to not be a noncharitable expenditure). In Rev. Rul. 82-223, 1982-2 C.B. 301, the IRS held that a private foundation may, without making a taxable expenditure, indemnify and/or purchase insurance to cover its managers for liabilities arising under state law concerning mismanagement of funds, as long as the payments are treated as part of the foundation manager's compensation and the compensation is reasonable, but that the private foundation would make a taxable expenditure if it indemnified a foundation manager for an amount paid in settlement of a state proceeding. The IRS ruled that a private foundation may amend its articles of incorporation, in conformity with a change in state law, to limit the personal liability of volunteers who are not directors, without making a taxable expenditure (Priv. Ltr. Rul. 9440033).
318. See § 8.4.
319. See § 8.4(b).
320. *See* Chapter 5.
321. IRC § 4941(d)(1)(B).

was designed solely to provide income for the private foundation's charitable purposes, the IRS concluded that it was not a taxable expenditure.[322]

Since a private foundation is not permitted to make an expenditure for a noncharitable purpose, a private foundation may not make a grant to an organization other than a charitable organization unless the making of the grant itself constitutes a direct charitable act or the making of a program-related investment, or the grantor is reasonably assured that the grant will be used exclusively for charitable purposes.[323] In a reversal of its approval of a company foundation employee relief program, the IRS provided a comprehensive review of the private foundation sanctions that can result when a foundation is found to have made a noncharitable expenditure. A discussion of the interaction between the self-dealing, mandatory payout, and tax expenditures rules is a feature of the ruling.[324]

If a private foundation makes a grant (which is not a transfer of assets pursuant to a liquidation, merger, redemption, recapitalization, or other adjustment, organization, or reorganization)[325] to an organization other than a charitable one,[326] the grantor can be reasonably assured that the grant will be used exclusively for charitable purposes only if the grantee organization agrees to maintain and, during the period in which any portion of the grant funds remains unexpended, continuously maintains the grant funds (or other assets transferred) in a separate fund dedicated to one or more charitable purposes.[327]

A foreign organization that does not have a ruling or determination letter that it is a charitable organization is treated as a charitable organization if, in the reasonable judgment of a foundation manager of the grantor private foundation, the grantee organization is a charitable organization. The term *reasonable judgment* is given its generally accepted legal sense within the outlines developed by judicial decisions in the law of trusts.[328]

If a private foundation makes a transfer of assets (other than as part of a direct charitable act or as a private foundation) pursuant to one of these adjustments or reorganizations, to any person, the transferred assets are not considered used exclusively for charitable purposes unless the assets are transferred to a charitable fund or organization.[329]

---

322. Rev. Rul. 77-161, 1977-1 C.B. 358. In this ruling, the IRS observed that "a given set of facts can give rise to taxes under more than one provision of Chapter 42 of the Code," citing Reg. § 53.4944-1(a)(2)(iv).
323. Reg. § 53.4945-6(c)(1).
324. Priv. Ltr. Rul. 199914040.
325. *See* IRC § 507(b)(2), which is the subject of § 13.4.
326. For this purpose, a charitable organization is one described in IRC § 501(c)(3) other than IRC § 509(a)(4); *see* Chapter 15.
327. Reg. § 53.4945-6(c)(2)(i).
328. Reg. § 53.4945-6(c)(2)(ii); *see* § 9.5.
329. Reg. § 53.4945-6(c)(3).

More than any other aspect of the private foundation rules, the taxable expenditures rules reflect the nearly unbridled anti–private foundation emotionalism that gripped Congress as it legislated in this area in 1969. Several of these provisions are directly traceable to specific events that fomented the legislators' unhappiness, many of which came to widespread public attention in the wake of the testimony early in 1969 by Ford Foundation president McGeorge Bundy before the House Committee on Ways and Means.[330] The restrictions on individual grants trace their heritage to the "travel and study awards" that the Ford Foundation made to staff assistants to Senator Robert F. Kennedy following his assassination.[331] The rules concerning private foundations' involvement in public elections and voter registration drives are a reflection of the Ford Foundation financing of voter registration projects, including a grant to Cleveland CORE, travel grants to members of Congress, and the school decentralization experiments in New York (the subject of city-wide teachers' strikes),[332] and of the spending interests of the Frederick W. Richmond Foundation at the time Mr. Richmond was seeking election to Congress.[333] These and similar incidents triggered many critical commentaries on private foundations in the general media,[334] which added to the reaction against private foundations in Congress.

## § 9.9 DISTRIBUTIONS TO CERTAIN SUPPORTING ORGANIZATIONS

A private foundation must exercise expenditure responsibility[335] when it makes a grant to a nonfunctionally integrated Type III supporting organization[336] and will incur a *taxable expenditure* if it fails to do so. Additionally, such a grant does not count as a qualifying distribution.[337]

## § 9.10 EXCISE TAX FOR TAXABLE EXPENDITURES

An initial excise tax is imposed on each taxable expenditure of a private foundation, which is to be paid by the foundation at the rate of 20 percent of the

---

330. "Many in Congress Ready to Tax All Foundations, Curb Their Operations," *Wall Street Journal*, Feb. 28, 1969, at 1.
331. E.g., "5 RFK Aides Defend Grants," *Washington Post*, Feb. 27, 1969, at G1.
332. E.g., "Ford Fund Hints No Retreat on Financing of Disputed Projects, No Fear on Taxes," *Wall Street Journal*, March 3, 1969, at 12.
333. "Rooney Cites Tax-Free Aid Used by Foe," *Washington Star*, Feb. 19, 1969, at A-1.
334. E.g., White, "Congress Girding to Reduce Vast Power of Foundations," *Washington Post*, Feb. 22, 1969, at A-15; McGrory, "Stylist Bundy Sprinkles Snow," *Washington Star*, Feb. 2, 1969, at A-3.
335. *See* § 9.6(a)
336. *See* § 15.7(g).
337. IRC § 4945(d)(4). *See* § 6.5(a).

amount of each taxable expenditure.[338] This excise tax is also imposed on any foundation manager that agreed to the making of a taxable expenditure by a private foundation,[339] equal to 5 percent of the amount involved up to a maximum of $10,000. This initial tax on a manager is imposed only where the foundation initial tax is imposed, the manager knows that the expenditure to which he or she agrees is a taxable expenditure, and the agreement is willful and not due to reasonable cause.[340]

## (a)  Tax on Managers

The 5 percent tax with respect to any particular expenditure applies only to those foundation managers who are authorized to approve, to exercise discretion in recommending approval of, or who agreed to the making of the expenditure by the foundation, and to those foundation managers who are members of a group (such as the foundation's board of directors or trustees) that is so authorized.[341]

The *agreement* of a foundation manager to the making of a taxable expenditure consists of any manifestation of approval of the expenditure that is sufficient to constitute an exercise of the foundation manager's authority to approve, or to exercise discretion in recommending approval of, the making of the expenditure by the foundation, whether or not the manifestation of approval is the final or decisive approval on behalf of the foundation.[342]

A foundation manager is considered to have agreed to an expenditure, *knowing* that it is a taxable one, only if he or she (1) has actual knowledge of sufficient facts so that, based solely on those facts, the expenditure would be a taxable one; (2) is aware that the expenditure under these circumstances may violate the federal tax law governing taxable expenditures; and (3) negligently fails to make reasonable attempts to ascertain whether the expenditure is a taxable one, or he or she is in fact aware that it is such an expenditure. While the term *knowing* does not mean "having reason to know," evidence tending to show that a foundation manager has reason to know of a particular fact or particular rule is relevant in determining whether he or she had actual knowledge of that fact or rule.[343]

A foundation manager's agreement to a taxable expenditure is *willful* if it is voluntary, conscious, and intentional. No motive to avoid the restrictions of the law or the incurrence of any tax is necessary to make an agreement willful. A

---

338. IRC § 4945(a)(1); Reg. § 53.4945-1(a)(1). This tax is also known as a *first-tier tax* (IRC § 4963 (a); Reg. § 53.4963-1(a)).
339. IRC § 4945(a)(2); Reg. § 53.4945-1(a)(2)(vii).
340. Reg. § 53.4945-1(a)(2)(i).
341. *Id.*
342. Reg. § 53.4945-1(a)(2)(ii).
343. Reg. § 53.4945-1(a)(2)(iii).

foundation manager's agreement to a taxable expenditure is not willful, however, if he or she does not know that it is a taxable expenditure.[344] A foundation manager's actions are due to reasonable cause if he or she has exercised his or her responsibility on behalf of the private foundation with ordinary business care and prudence.[345]

> If a foundation manager, after full disclosure of the factual situation to legal counsel (including house counsel), relies on the advice of counsel expressed in a *reasoned* legal opinion that an expenditure is not a taxable one (or that expenditures conforming to certain guidelines are not taxable ones), although the expenditure is subsequently held to be a taxable one, the foundation manager's agreement to the expenditure will ordinarily not be considered *knowing* or *willful* and will ordinarily be considered *due to reasonable cause*. This rule also applies with respect to an opinion that proposed reporting procedures concerning an expenditure will satisfy the taxable expenditure rules, even though the procedures are subsequently held to not satisfy the rules, and to grants made with provisions for such reporting procedures that are taxable solely because of such inadequate reporting procedures. A written legal opinion is considered *reasoned* even if it reaches a conclusion that is subsequently determined to be incorrect as long as the opinion was addressed to the facts and applicable law. By contrast, a written legal opinion is not a reasoned one if it merely recites the facts and expresses a conclusion. The absence of advice of counsel with respect to an expenditure, however, does not alone give rise to an inference that a foundation manager agreed to the making of the expenditure knowingly, willfully, or without reasonable cause.[346]

## (b)  Paying or Abating the Tax

The IRS has the discretionary authority to abate this initial tax where the private foundation establishes that the violation was due to reasonable cause and not to willful neglect, and timely corrects the violation.[347] For example, a private foundation failed to make the requisite expenditure responsibility reports,[348] a fact that was discovered by a subsequent tax advisor who filed a corrective return; the IRS abated the taxable expenditures initial tax.[349] The ruling contains very few other facts, including whether or not expenditure responsibility agreements were properly executed. Likewise, this tax was abated where a private foundation relied, in good faith, on incorrect legal advice.[350] What is interesting is the fact that these are the only IRS missives on the subject of abatement.

---

344.  Reg. § 53.4945-1(a)(2)(iv).
345.  Reg. § 53.4945-1(a)(2)(v).
346.  Reg. § 53.4945-1(a)(2)(vi).
347.  IRC § 4962.
348.  *See* § 9.6(h).
349.  Tech. Adv. Mem. 200452037.
350.  Tech. Adv. Mem. 200347023.

The tax is calculated and reported on Form 4720, Return of Certain Excise Taxes on Charities and Other Persons Under Chapters 41 and 42 of the Internal Revenue Code.[351] Until 1985, the tax was imposed without exception and was strictly enforced. The failure to present required details of an expenditure responsibility grant in the amount of $2 million, for example, cost a foundation $200,000 and could not be corrected in an amended return.[352] As explained above, a 5 percent tax is also imposed on involved managers.

### (c)  Additional Tax

An additional excise tax is imposed in any case in which an initial tax is imposed on a private foundation because of a taxable expenditure and the expenditure is not timely corrected.[353] This additional tax is to be paid by the private foundation and is at the rate of 100 percent of the amount of each taxable expenditure.[354] In any case in which an additional tax has been levied on a private foundation, an excise tax is imposed on a foundation manager because of a taxable expenditure where the foundation manager has refused to agree to part or all of the correction of the expenditure.[355] This additional tax, which is at the rate of 50 percent of the amount of the taxable expenditure, is to be paid by the foundation manager.[356] Where a taxable event is corrected within the correction period, any additional tax imposed with respect to the event becomes abated.[357]

A request for such abatement is submitted on Form 4720. The second question asked on this form is whether or not "any corrective action has been taken on any transaction that resulted in Chapter 42 taxes being reported on this form." If so, complete details about the type of action taken and the value of recovered property are to be described. If the problem has not been cured or remains uncorrected, an explanation is attached. This information must be prepared carefully, because it forms the basis upon which the IRS can permit abatement of the tax. Exhibit 9.14 illustrates the type of statement that would be attached to Form 4720 to explain why the violation was due to reasonable causes and should be abated.

### (d)  Correcting the Expenditure

A taxable expenditure must be corrected. The *correction period* is the period beginning on the date on which the *taxable event* occurs and ending 90 days

---

351. Reproduced in Exhibit 12.6.
352. *See* discussion at *supra* notes 274 and 277.
353. IRC § 4945(b)(1). This tax is also known as a *second-tier tax* (IRC § 4963(b); Reg. § 53.4963-1(b)).
354. Reg. § 53.4945-1(b)(1).
355. IRC § 4945(b)(2).
356. Reg. § 53.4945-1(b)(2).
357. IRC § 4961.

**EXHIBIT 9.14** Request for Abatement of Penalty

---

Sample Foundation # 44–4444444

ATTACHMENT TO FORM 4720 for Fiscal Year Ending June 30, 20XX

STATEMENT regarding CORRECTION OF TAXABLE EXPENDITURE

In submitting its Form 990-PF for the fiscal year ending June 30, 20XX, the SAMPLE FOUNDATION (Sample) inadvertently failed to submit information regarding an expenditure responsibility grant. This failure is corrected in this return by making a complete report of the seven required items properly included as an attachment to Part VII-B, Statement Regarding Activities for Which Form 4720 May Be Required, of this year's Form 990-PF.

Sample, during its fiscal year ending June 30, 20XX, made an endowment grant to ABC FOUNDATION (ABC), a private foundation. The required expenditure responsibility agreement was executed in a timely fashion and the grant information reported in Sample's 20XX Form 990-PF. In addition, ABC reported that the endowment and its income were dedicated to charitable purposes as its agreement with Sample required. Sample duly submitted the seven points of information on its 2006 Form 990-PF for the fiscal year ending June 30, 20XX. ABC further made a second year's report for the 2007 fiscal year.

A taxable expenditure occurred, however, when Sample failed to include a statement of the required information on its 20XX Form 990-PF. Sample had made expenditure responsibility grants in past years, but had not previously made an endowment grant that required multiple-year reporting. Sample's controller who prepared the return failed to include the report because he was following the pattern established for nonendowment grants. Sample's grant department had engaged outside counselors to prepare the agreement regarding the grant. They were advised Sample needed to receive and submit to the IRS two years of monitoring reports and also to report the grant in the year in which it was made. The controller was not furnished a copy of the counselors' letter describing this requirement.

Pursuant to Internal Revenue Code § 4962, Sample respectfully requests that the first-tier § 4945 penalty for failure to report, or initial tax of $15,000, be abated because the failure was due to reasonable causes and without willful neglect. The mistake was discovered by Sample's executive director when she was reviewing the 20XX Form 990-PF prior to submitting it to me for signature. The inclusion of the proper report in this 20XX return effectively corrects the failure to report. Therefore, Sample submits it is entitled to an abatement of the tax because it meets the requirements of § 4962 and the instructions to Form 4720.

I swear that this information is true and correct and that the foundation's failure to make the third year's report of ABC's endowment grant was inadvertent, accidental, and without intention or knowledge on my part or on the part of any of Sample's other officers.

A.B. Sample, President

---

after the date of mailing of a notice of deficiency with respect to the additional tax imposed on the event.[358] This period is extended by any period in which a deficiency cannot be assessed[359] and any other period that the IRS determines

---

358. IRC § 4963(e)(1); Reg. § 53.4963-1(e)(1).
359. IRC § 4963(e)(1)(A); Reg. § 53.4963-1(e)(2). The rules as to nonassessment of a deficiency are those of IRC § 6213(a).

is reasonable and necessary to bring about correction of the taxable event.[360] In this setting, a taxable event is an act or failure to act giving rise to liability for tax under the taxable expenditures rules.[361] This event occurs on the date on which the event occurred.[362]

In general, *correction* of a taxable expenditure is accomplished by recovering part or all of the expenditure to the extent recovery is possible. Where full recovery cannot be accomplished, correction entails any additional corrective action that the IRS may prescribe. This additional corrective action is to be determined by the circumstances of each case and may include requiring that any unpaid funds due the grantee be withheld, that no further grants be made to the grantee, periodic (such as quarterly) reports from the foundation (in addition to other reports that may be required) with respect to all of its expenditures,[363] improved methods of exercising expenditure responsibility, and improved methods of selecting recipients of individual grants. The IRS may prescribe other measures in a particular case. The private foundation making the expenditure is not under any obligation to attempt to recover the expenditure by legal action if the action would in all probability not result in the satisfaction of execution on a judgment.[364]

If the expenditure is taxable only because of a failure to obtain a full and complete report[365] or because of a failure to make a full and detailed report,[366] correction may be accomplished by obtaining or making the report in question. Exhibit 9.14 provides an example of a statement seeking abatement of penalty for failure to properly exercise expenditure responsibility due to a mistake of an independent grants administrator. See also Exhibit 9.15. In addition, if the expenditure is taxable only because of a failure to obtain a full and complete report and an investigation indicates that grant funds were not diverted to a use not in furtherance of a purpose specified in the grant, correction may be accomplished by exerting all reasonable efforts to obtain the report in question and reporting the failure to the IRS, even though the report is not finally obtained.[367]

Where an expenditure is taxable under the rules concerning grants to individuals[368] only because of a failure to obtain advance approval of procedures with respect to grants, correction may be accomplished by obtaining

---

360.  IRC § 4963(e)(1)(B); Reg. § 53.4963-1(e)(3).
361.  IRC § 4963(c); Reg. § 53.4963-1(c).
362.  IRC § 4963(e)(2)(B); Reg. § 53.4963-1(e)(7)(iv).
363.  These reports must be equivalent in detail to those the private foundation is required to file with the IRS (*see* text accompanied by *supra* notes 269, 270).
364.  Reg. § 53.4945-1(d)(1).
365.  *See* text accompanied by *supra* notes 267–269.
366.  *See* text accompanied by *supra* notes 273–276.
367.  Reg. § 53.4945-1(d)(2).
368.  *See* § 9.3.

**Exhibit 9.15**  Penalty Abatement Request—Error by Grant Administrator

---

The ABC Foundation ("Foundation") uses a third-party administrator to verify the public charity status of potential grantees before making grants. During 20XX, the administrator did not accurately verify the public charity status of a particular grantee and allowed the Foundation to make a grant to a nonqualifying grantee.

The Foundation made a single grant in the amount of $XXX to XYZ, a private foundation. Because the Foundation relied upon its administrator to verify the public charity status of grantees, it was unaware that XYZ was not a public charity. Therefore, expenditure responsibility was not exercised, and a taxable expenditure occurred. Upon realizing this error, the Foundation's administrator immediately took steps to begin the expenditure responsibility process and to remedy the flaw in the verification process that caused the grant to occur. The required information regarding the grant has been reported on the Foundation's 20XX Form 990-PF.

Pursuant to Internal Revenue Code § 4962, the Foundation respectfully requests that the first-tier § 4945 penalty for making a taxable expenditure, or initial tax of $XXX, be abated because the failure was due to reasonable causes and without willful neglect. Exercising expenditure responsibility after the fact effectively corrects the taxable expenditure. Therefore, the Foundation submits it is entitled to an abatement of the tax because it meets the requirements of § 4962 and the instructions to Form 4720.

Additionally, at the time the extension for Form 4720 was due, May 15, 20XX, the Foundation's tax advisors lacked any information indicating the need to file that form. Subsequently, while preparing the 20XX 990-PF, they discovered that the Foundation would need to file Form 4720 for that taxable year. Thus, no extensions had been filed by the Foundation prior to the filing of Form 4720. According to the standards set forth in Rev. Proc. 92–85, the Foundation believes its actions were reasonable and in good faith. Moreover, the Foundation prepared and filed Form 4720 as soon as it become aware of the need to do so and, therefore, is entitled to abatement of late filing and payment penalties. The Foundation requests the abatement of the late filing and payment penalties because, as demonstrated above, the late filing and payment was due to reasonable cause.

I swear that this information is true and correct and that the Foundation's failure to enter into expenditure responsibility was inadvertent, accidental, and without intention or knowledge on my part or on the part of any of the Foundation's other officers.

_____

Authorized Official

---

approval of the grant-making procedures and establishing to the satisfaction of the IRS that grant funds have not been diverted to any use not in furtherance of a purpose specified in the grant, the grant-making procedures instituted would have been approved if advance approval of the procedures had been properly requested, and where advance approval of grant-making procedures is subsequently required, the approval will be properly requested.[369]

---

369. Reg. § 53.4945-1(d)(3).

Where more than one foundation manager is liable for an excise tax with respect to the making of a taxable expenditure, all the foundation managers are jointly and severally liable for the tax.[370] The maximum aggregate amount collectible as an initial tax from all foundation managers with respect to any one taxable expenditure is $10,000, and the maximum aggregate amount so collectible as an additional tax is $20,000.[371]

The additional excise taxes are imposed at the end of the *taxable period*, which begins with the date on which the taxable expenditure occurs and ends on the earliest of:

- The date a notice of deficiency with respect to the initial tax is mailed.
- The date the initial tax is assessed if no deficiency notice is mailed.[372]

Where the act or failure to act that gave rise to the additional tax is corrected within the correction period,[373] the tax will not be assessed, or if assessed will be abated, or if collected will be credited or refunded.[374] The collection period is suspended during any litigation.[375]

The termination taxes[376] serve as third-tier taxes.[377]

---

370. IRC § 4945(c)(1); Reg. § 53.4945-1(c)(1).
371. IRC § 4945(c)(2); Reg. § 53.4945-1(c)(2).
372. IRC § 4945(i)(2); Reg. § 53.4945-1(e)(1).
373. *See* text accompanied by *supra* notes 358, 359.
374. IRC § 4961(a); Reg. § 53.4961-1.
375. IRC § 4961(c); Reg. § 53.4961-2.
376. *See* Chapter 13.
377. In general, Sacher, "How IRS's Internal Rules Work for Advance Approval of Company Foundation Grants," 40 *J. Tax.* 363 (1974); Sanders, "Final Regs on Section 4945: Working with the New Rules Restricting Foundations' Activities," 38 *J. Tax.* 130 (1973); Sanders, "Private Foundations: Final Regs on 4945 Clarify and Bring Order to Operating Rules," 38 *J. Tax.* 246 (1973); Sanders, "How Grants to Organizations by Private Foundations Are Affected by the Final Regs," 38 *J. Tax.* 299 (1973); Gregory and Moorehead, "Suggestions for Preventing Taxable Expenditures by Foundations," 19 *Prac. Lawyer* (No. 6) 45 (1973); Moorehead, "Qualifying Distributions: Do Your Grants and Activities Comply?" 11 *N.Y. U. Conf. on Char. Fdns.* 203 (1973); Treitler, "Prop. Regs on 'Taxable Expenditures': Useful Guidelines for Foundation Managers," 34 *J. Tax.* 338 (1971); Wright, "Grantee Selection and Supervision: Legal Requirements and Practical Problems," 10 *N.Y.U. Conf. on Char. Fdns.* 127 (1971); Schilling and Thomson, "Tax Problems of Private Foundations in Receiving and Making Grants," 10 *N.Y.U. Conf. on Char. Fdns.* 277 (1971).

# CHAPTER TEN

# Tax on Investment Income

The private foundation is one of the few types of tax-exempt organizations that are required to pay a tax on investment income.[1] The revenue derived from this tax is intended to offset the cost of enforcing the sanctions imposed on private foundations and other exempt organizations. As one analysis stated, private foundations are to "share some of the burden of paying the cost of government, especially for more extensive and vigorous enforcement of the tax laws relating to exempt organizations."[2] To preserve the concept

---

1. Three other types of tax-exempt organizations are required to pay an investment income tax: social clubs (described in IRC § 501(c)(7)), political organizations (described in IRC § 527), and homeowners associations (described in IRC § 528); this tax is paid as an unrelated business income tax. Furthermore, under certain circumstances, all tax-exempt organizations, including private foundations, are subject to the unrelated business income tax on investment income to the extent that the income is derived from debt-financed property (IRC § 514). However, only private foundations must pay a tax on investment income that is the subject of a statute solely on this point. E.g., *Auen v. United States*, 99-1 U.S.T.C. ¶ 50,247 (9th Cir. 1999).
2. Joint Committee on Internal Revenue Taxation, *General Explanation of Tax Reform Act of 1969*, 91st Cong., 2d Sess. 29 (1970).

that private foundations are exempt entities, this tax is cast as an excise tax rather than an income tax.[3]

Indeed, the tax was intended to be in the nature of an audit fee.[4] These taxes are not actually earmarked for auditing and supervising foundations but are mingled with the general federal revenues.

## § 10.1 RATE OF TAX

An excise tax of 1 or 2 percent is imposed on the net investment income of all domestic tax-exempt private foundations for each tax year.[5] This tax is also imposed on private operating foundations[6] and nonexempt wholly charitable trusts.[7] When adopted in 1969, this tax was set at 4 percent; because the receipts from this tax exceeded the actual costs of the enforcement efforts of the IRS, the tax was reduced to 2 percent in 1978, and the 1 or 2 percent rate illustrated in Exhibit 10.1 was effective for post-1984 years.[8,9] Proposals to reduce the tax to 1 percent and to 1.32 percent,[10] and to eliminate it have been introduced in Congress in recent years. The tax is calculated each year on Form 990-PF,

---

3. It has been held that the application of this tax does not violate equal protection rights (*Williams Home, Inc. v. United States*, 540 F. Supp. 310 (W.D. Va. 1982)).
4. H. Rep. No. 91-413, 91st Cong., 1st Sess 18 (1969); S. Rep. No. 91-552, 91st Cong., 1st Sess. 27 (1969). Because the tax imposed by IRC § 4940(a) is an excise tax, rather than an income tax, the tax is not treated as a covered tax under United States income tax treaties unless a treaty expressly provides otherwise (Rev. Rul. 84-169, 1984-2 C.B. 216).
5. *See* § 10.2; IRC § 4940(a); Reg. § 53.4940-1(a). In one case, however, a private law enacted by Congress in 1875 was found to exempt a private foundation from the IRC § 4940 excise tax (*Trustees of the Louise Home v. Commissioner*, 46 T.C.M. 1494 (1983)).
6. *See* § 3.1.
7. *See* § 3.6.
8. Deficit Reduction Act of 1984.
9. *See* § 10.2. Subsequent to enactment of the Tax Reform Act of 1969, which set the administration tax on private foundations at 4 percent for each tax year beginning after December 31, 1969 (through 1977), representatives of the private foundation community urged reduction of the private foundation tax to the actual level of the cost of auditing and supervision, and an earmarking of the receipts for these purposes. The late Representative Wright Patman, a longtime foe of private foundations, proposed the establishment of an account in the Treasury for excise tax revenues, with at least 50 percent of the receipts to be used by the IRS for supervision of private foundations and the remainder for the states for independent oversight of private foundations' activities (H.R. 5728, 93rd Cong., 2d Sess. (1973)). This approach, however, was never seriously entertained. The Senate version of the Tax Reform Act of 1976 would have lowered the private foundation net investment income tax to 2 percent, but that approach was not taken at that time, because Congress lowered the mandatory payout percentage to a flat 5 percent (*see* Chapter 6) and did not want to have too much legislation favorable to private foundations in one tax act. The reduction in the private foundation investment income tax was delayed until adoption of the Revenue Act of 1978.
10. *See* § 10.7.

Part VI. The tax is paid annually following the estimated tax system applicable to income tax returns.[11]

The tax is also imposed on a nonexempt private foundation if the 2 percent tax on investment income plus any unrelated business income tax[12] exceeds the normal corporate or trust income tax it would pay.[13] The purpose of this latter tax is to ensure that a private foundation will not attempt to reduce its tax liability by intentionally losing its tax-exempt status.

Notwithstanding the reduction of the excise tax rate, the tax-law-writing committees of Congress remain concerned that the IRS devote adequate resources to the administration of the law of tax-exempt organizations.[14] This is relevant in this context, because this tax was instituted to ensure the availability of these resources. In 1974, Congress made a permanent authorization of appropriations to further ensure the availability of sufficient resources to administer this law.[15] However, the change in the private foundation tax rate does not affect the amount of that permanent authorization.

In discussing this law change, the tax committees expressed their expectation that the IRS will annually report to Congress on (1) the extent to which audits are conducted as to the tax liabilities of tax-exempt organizations, (2) the extent to which examinations are made as to the continued qualification of exempt organizations for their exempt status, (3) the extent to which IRS personnel are given initial and refresher instruction in the relevant portions of the law and administrative procedures, (4) the extent to which the IRS cooperates with and receives cooperation from state officials with regard to supervision of tax-exempt organizations, (5) the costs of maintaining the programs at levels that would produce proper compliance with the laws, (6) the amounts requested by the executive branch for the maintenance of the programs, and (7) the reasons for any difference between the needed funds and the requested amounts. In addition, these committees required the IRS to notify Congress "of any administrative problems that [are] experienced in the course of this enforcement of the internal revenue laws with respect to exempt organizations."[16]

---

11. *See* § 12.2(b).
12. *See* Chapter 11.
13. IRC § 4940(b); Reg. § 53.4940-(b).
14. H. Rep. No. 95-842, 95th Cong., 2d Sess. (1978), to accompany H.R. 112, which is the original legislation containing the private foundation excise tax reduction that was made part of the Revenue Act of 1978.
15. Employee Retirement Income Security Act of 1974, 88 Stat. 829 § 1052.
16. H. Rep. No. 95-842, 95th Cong., 2d Sess. (1978); S. Rep. No. 94-938, 94th Cong., 2d Sess. 598–599 (1976).

## § 10.2 REDUCING THE EXCISE TAX

As the rate was reduced over the past 25 years, the private foundation excise tax has become a generally accepted cost of retaining private control over donated funds. Its relatively immaterial annual amount mitigates the need to hire skilled professional advisors to perform year-end tax planning. Nevertheless, substantial savings can result from taking advantage of relatively simple tax planning methods systematically over a period of years.

### (a) Qualification for 1 Percent Rate

The excise tax rate on a private foundation's net investment income is reduced to 1 percent for each year during which the foundation's qualifying distributions[17] equal a hypothetical distribution amount, based upon the past five-year average qualifying distributions, plus 1 percent of net investment income.[18] Thus, in effect, a foundation can essentially choose to distribute 1 percent of its investment income to charitable recipients rather than to the U.S. Treasury. Basically, a reduction is permitted for a foundation whose current-year distributions exceed its payout percentage for the past five years times the average fair market value of its current-year investment assets, plus half of the normal 2 percent tax it is excused from paying. A foundation cannot qualify for the 1 percent tax in its first year. For the second through fourth years, the average is calculated for the period of time the private foundation has been in existence.[19] In the case of a private foundation that is a successor to another private foundation, these rules are applied with respect to the successor by taking into account the experience of the other private foundation.[20]

The instructions for Form 990-PF and regulations do not address inclusion of grants not treated as qualifying distributions in Part XIII, referred to as out of corpus grants, for this purpose.[21] The intention of the 1 percent rate was to allow private foundations that maintained a specified level of distributions to benefit from a reduced tax. The issue is whether the out of corpus grant payments made to allow the donor a higher deduction level (and consequently not counted as qualifying distributions for mandatory payout purposes) can be counted in calculating qualification for the 1 percent tax rate. Part XII of Form 990-PF does not separate, and instead includes, the redistribution amounts. Part V (where

---

17. Essentially, grants and other disbursements for charitable purposes, adjusted for amounts set aside or recovered from past years, as discussed in Chapter 6, and calculated in Part XII of the Form 990-PF, illustrated in Exhibit 12.1.
18. IRC § 4940(e); Reg. § 53.4940-1(d)(1).
19. IRC § 4940(e)(2)-(4).
20. IRC § 4940(e)(6)(A); Priv. Ltr. Rul. 200644050.
21. *See* § 6.5(a) for discussion of rule treating grants out of corpus as disqualifying distributions.

qualification for a reduced tax rate is calculated) refers to Part XII. The authors find no guidance on this position, but the form design allows it.

A private foundation can qualify for this rate reduction only if it has met its mandatory payout requirements and has not been subject to a sanction for underdistribution[22] during the base period.[23] This does not, however, mean the historic payout rate must be above 5 percent. In studying Part V of Form 990-PF, one sees that the payout formula compares the qualifying distributions (based on preceding-year values) to the current-year average value of the assets.[24] It is common, during a period of rising asset value, for the historic payout rate to be less than 5 percent. The original committee reports for this section contained this sentence: "The rate is not reduced for a year if the foundation's average percentage payout for the base period is less than five percent (3 percent in the case of a private operating foundation)."[25] The tax code, the form design, and the IRS instructions to the form do not contain this provision, possibly because someone recognized the good possibility that the result could be less than 5 percent.

The qualifying formula, as illustrated in the following example, basically recalculates the minimum distribution requirement by applying the past five-year average percentage of distributions to the current endowment value and adding half of the normal tax. If the private foundation is sustaining a distribution percentage equal to and $1 more than the past percentage (times the current average value of its investment assets), it can qualify for a reduced tax of 1 percent, rather than 2 percent. The calculation briefly compares:

| | |
|---|---|
| This year's average monthly FMV × 5-year average payout: ($2,000,000 × 5 percent) | $100,000 |
| + 1 percent of private foundation's net investment income | $1,000 |
| Baseline to compare to current distributions | $101,000 |
| Qualifying distributions for the year | $102,000 |

Because the qualifying distributions in this example equal or exceed $101,000, the foundation's tax rate is reduced to 1 percent. Because the calculation is based on the average monthly value of the foundation's investment assets, including the last day of its year, planning for the savings is not easy. Since this tax reduction opportunity came into effect in 1985, foundations that realize the reduction often do so by accident, rather than by specific planning.

Except and unless the value of the foundation's assets fluctuates widely, it is possible to deliberately time grant payments to reduce the tax to 1 percent in alternate years. For a foundation normally paying about $20,000 in tax, a $10,000 biannual savings may be worth the trouble. Exhibit 10.1 illustrates a

---

22. *See* § 6.6.
23. IRC § 4940(e)(2)(B).
24. *See* § 12.2(a) for a filled-in version of this part.
25. House Committee Report for P. L. 98-369, Deficit Reduction Act of 1984.

## Exhibit 10.1

### Distribution Timing Plan to Reduce Excise Tax

**XYZ FOUNDATION—2014**

|  | Qualifying Distribution | FMV Inv. Assets | Distribution Ratio |
|---|---|---|---|
| 2013 | 1,000,000 | 20,000,000 | 5.00% |
| 2012 | 950,000 | 19,000,000 | 5.00% |
| 2011 | 1,100,000 | 22,000,000 | 5.00% |
| 2010 | 1,000,000 | 20,000,000 | 5.00% |
| 2009 | 900,000 | 18,000,000 | 5.00% |
| Average—five years |  |  | 5.00% |
| Average FMV investment assets 2014 |  |  | 21,000,000 |
| Year-end FMV times average |  |  | 1,050,000 |
| Add 1% taxable income |  |  | 20,000 |
| Baseline for qualification |  |  | 1,070,000 |
| 2014 distributions |  |  | 1,300,000 |

**XYZ FOUNDATION—2015**

|  | Qualifying Distribution | FMV Inv. Assets | Distribution Ratio |
|---|---|---|---|
| 2014 | 1,300,000 | 21,000,000 | 6.19% |
| 2013 | 1,000,000 | 20,000,000 | 5.00% |
| 2012 | 950,000 | 19,000,000 | 5.00% |
| 2011 | 1,100,000 | 22,000,000 | 5.00% |
| 2010 | 1,000,000 | 20,000,000 | 5.00% |
| Average—five years |  |  | 5.24% |
| Average FMV investment assets 2009 |  |  | 22,000,000 |
| Year-end FMV times average |  |  | 1,152,381 |
| Add 1% taxable income |  |  | 20,000 |
| Baseline for qualification |  |  | 1,172,381 |
| 2015 distributions |  |  | 850,000 |

**Exhibit 10.1** (Continued)

## XYZ FOUNDATION—2016

|  | Qualifying Distribution | FMV Inv. Assets | Distribution Ratio |
|---|---|---|---|
| 2015 | 850,000 | 22,000,000 | 3.86% |
| 2014 | 1,300,000 | 21,000,000 | 6.19% |
| 2013 | 1,000,000 | 20,000,000 | 5.00% |
| 20012 | 950,000 | 19,000,000 | 5.00% |
| 2011 | 1,100,000 | 22,000,000 | 5.00% |
| Average—five years | | | 5.01% |
| Average FMV investment assets 2010 | | | 23,000,000 |
| Year-end FMV times average | | | 1,152,489 |
| Add 1% taxable income | | | 30,000 |
| Baseline for qualification | | | 1,182,489 |
| 2016 distributions | | | 1,200,000 |

## XYZ FOUNDATION—2017

|  | Qualifying Distribution | FMV Inv. Assets | Distribution Ratio |
|---|---|---|---|
| 2016 | 1,200,000 | 23,000,000 | 5.22% |
| 2015 | 850,000 | 22,000,000 | 3.86% |
| 2014 | 1,300,000 | 21,000,000 | 6.19% |
| 2013 | 1,000,000 | 20,000,000 | 5.00% |
| 2012 | 950,000 | 19,000,000 | 5.00% |
| Average—five years | | | 5.05% |
| Average FMV investment assets 2011 | | | 23,500,000 |
| Year-end FMV times average | | | 1,187,761 |
| Add 1% taxable income | | | 30,000 |
| Baseline for qualification | | | 1,217,761 |
| 2017 distributions | | | 950,000 |

*(Continued)*

**Exhibit 10.1**   (Continued)

## XYZ FOUNDATION—2018

|  | Qualifying Distribution | FMV Inv. Assets | Distribution Ratio |
|---|---|---|---|
| 2017 | 950,000 | 23,500,000 | 4.04% |
| 2016 | 1,200,000 | 23,000,000 | 5.22% |
| 2015 | 1,182,489 | 22,000,000 | 5.37% |
| 2014 | 1,300,000 | 21,000,000 | 6.19% |
| 2013 | 1,000,000 | 20,000,000 | 5.00% |
| Average—five years |  |  | 5.17% |
| Average FMV investment assets 2012 |  |  | 22,000,000 |
| Year-end FMV times average |  |  | 1,136,316 |
| Add 1% taxable income |  |  | 30,000 |
| Baseline for qualification |  |  | 1,166,316 |
| 2018 distributions |  |  | 1,250,000 |

## XYZ FOUNDATION—2019

|  | Qualifying Distribution | FMV Inv. Assets | Distribution Ratio |
|---|---|---|---|
| 2018 | 1,250,000 | 22,000,000 | 5.68% |
| 2017 | 950,000 | 23,500,000 | 4.04% |
| 2016 | 1,200,000 | 23,000,000 | 5.22% |
| 2015 | 850,000 | 22,000,000 | 3.86% |
| 2014 | 1,300,000 | 21,000,000 | 6.19% |
| Average—five years |  |  | 5.00% |
| Average FMV investment assets 2013 |  |  | 22,000,000 |
| Year-end FMV times average |  |  | 1,099,819 |
| Add 1% taxable income |  |  | 30,000 |
| Baseline for qualification |  |  | 1,129,819 |
| 2019 distributions |  |  | 950,000 |

six-year projection for XYZ Foundation that potentially redirects $48,000 in tax. Note in 2014, 2016, and 2018, the baseline for qualification is below the amount of actual distributions for the year. For those years, the excise tax is 1 percent.

## (b)  Distributing, Rather than Selling, Property

Reducing the tax rate from 1 to 2 percent is just one of the ways a private foundation can reduce the excise tax on investment income. There are opportunities embodied in the interaction between the excise tax on investment income, the minimum distribution requirements,[26] and the deduction for appreciated property donations.[27]

For two very different—but interacting—reasons, a foundation might sell assets that result in recognized capital gains subject to tax. A typical foundation, according to the Council on Foundations,[28] invests its assets for *total return*.[29] Under this investment philosophy, a security portfolio, on average, often is comprised of securities with low current income payments and an expectation for underlying appreciation in the value of the securities, typified by common stocks. The aim is a combined income from current dividends, interest, and enhancement in the capital values. It is expected that capital gains will be regularly earned as portfolio holdings are sold in response to market changes. When the desired result—capital gain—occurs, excise tax is due.

A foundation with a 2 percent current dividend and interest yield on its total return portfolio needs to use additional assets to meet its annual payout requirements. A private foundation must annually pay out funds for charitable purposes equal to approximately 5 percent of the average fair market value of its assets for the previous year, or meet a *minimum distribution requirement*.[30] A foundation with such a portfolio essentially distributes a portion of its capital gains to meet the payout requirement. Thus, tax may occur for the second reason—securities are sold to raise the cash to make qualifying distributions. Herein also lies the possibility for tax savings. If instead the securities (rather than cash from their sale) are distributed to grantees, the capital gain earned on the securities is not taxed. The regulations provide that this type of a distribution is not treated as a sale or other distribution.[31]

For example, suppose that one-half, or $500,000, of a foundation's $1 million of income is capital gains on highly appreciated securities. Assume also that the

---

26. *See* Chapter 6.
27. *See* Chapter 14.
28. Council on Foundations, *Foundation Management Report*, 8th ed. (Washington, DC: 1996).
29. *See* § 8.2.
30. *See* § 6.4.
31. Reg. § 53.4940-1(f)(1). The tax regulations provide that, "[f]or purposes of this paragraph, a distribution of property for purposes described in section 170(c) (1) or (2) (B) which is a qualifying distribution under section 4942 shall not be treated as a sale or other disposition of property."

foundation makes grants of $100,000 each to five charitable grantees. As much as $10,000 in tax is saved if the grants are paid with the securities themselves ($500,000 × 2 percent tax). The higher the untaxed gain in a foundation's portfolio, the greater the possibility for savings. The tax basis for calculating the gain for donated securities is equal to the donor's basis—meaning that some foundations have a good chance to realize the savings. Readily marketable securities are most suitable for delivery to grantees because of the ease with which they can be converted to cash. Any appreciated property is, however, subject to this special tax exception. Before 2007, gains from the foundation's sale of exempt function and investment assets that did not produce dividends, interest, rents, and royalties were not subject to the excise tax. Now that almost all of a foundation's gains are taxed,[32] this saving opportunity can also apply to grants of art objects, historic houses, and other types of assets that might be suitable for granting, rather than selling.

Implementing the savings requires some advanced planning and cooperative grantees. Grants are normally pledged and paid in round numbers (e.g., $50,000 or $500,000). Securities do not usually sell for round numbers, and the price changes constantly. The grantee, rather than the granting foundation, will have to pay the sales commission. The foundation may want to round up the number of shares to be delivered or send a check to fill out a pledged amount (if needed) to assure that the grantee receives the intended funding. The potential savings can be compared with the costs before such noncash grants are made. The size of the grant and the likelihood that the grantee may retain the securities in its own portfolio can enhance the attractiveness of this medium for grant funding.

Consider an example. A foundation is funded with zero-basis shares donated by a now publicly traded company's founding family. The foundation keeps a supply of stock certificates in a variety of share numbers. When a grant is due to be paid, one or more certificates for the number of shares approximating the amount pledged are delivered to the grantee. If the shares are selling for $60 and a $100,000 grant is due, approximately 1,670 shares would be delivered (the few extra shares cover the commission). The full fair market value of the shares on the delivery date is treated as a qualifying distribution, and the difference between the value and the foundation's basis ($100,000 of capital gain in this example) is not taxed, saving the foundation $2,000.

## (c)  Another Tax Reduction Possibility

A donation to a nonoperating private foundation is not necessarily fully deductible under a number of statutory constraints. The fair market value of

---

32. *See* § 10.3(b).

noncash gifts, other than readily marketable securities, to nonoperating private foundations[33] is not fully deductible. For a contributor to receive an income tax deduction for a gift of long-term capital gain property, such as land or a collectible (the fair market value of property is in excess of the donor's tax basis), the foundation essentially must give away the full value of the gift (or the gift itself) by the fifteenth day of the third month after the end of its year in which the donation is received.[34] If the noncash donation is retained by the foundation and essentially added to its endowment, the donor's deduction is limited to the tax basis for calculating gain or loss for federal income tax purposes.[35]

During the years 1984 to 1994 and since July 1, 1996, the redistribution issue was not relevant for gifts of certain securities. A special exception to encourage inter vivos gifts to build endowments for private foundations is in effect. A full fair market value deduction is permitted for the donation of *qualified appreciated stock*, or shares of a corporation for which "market quotations are readily available on an established securities market."[36]

A nonoperating private foundation that receives a donation of any type of appreciated property subject to a redistribution requirement has an important tax reduction opportunity. The foundation must choose whether to redistribute the property itself or cash from the sale of another asset(s) or from the sale of the property itself. Choosing the first option—redistribution of the property—presents the third circumstance under which a private foundation may avoid paying the tax by distributing the property itself rather than the cash from its sale.

For the redistribution to "not be treated as a sale or other distribution of property" so as to qualify the gain for exclusion from excise tax, the foundation must grant the property in a manner that is considered a *qualifying distribution*.[37] The grant must be made for charitable purposes[38] and basically be made payable to an unrelated and uncontrolled public charity. In addition, the charitable deduction rules require that the gift be treated as a distribution out of corpus. A foundation can also use any excess distribution carryovers to satisfy this requirement.[39] The fact that the distribution is charged to corpus (to meet the deduction requirement), rather than applied as a current distribution,

---

33. *See* Chapter 14.
34. IRC § 170(b)(1)(E)(ii).
35. IRC § 170(e)(1)(A)(ii).
36. IRC § 170(e)(5). *See* § 14.4(b).
37. IRC § 4942(g).
38. IRC § 170(c)(1) or (2). The IRS concluded that a private foundation that terminated its foundation status before the end of its first tax year by distributing its assets to public charities (*see* § 13.3) was not liable for the tax on net investment income for that year because distributions do not constitute investments for this purpose (Rev. Rul. 2003-13, 2003-1 C.B. 305) (Tech. Adv. Mem. 200613038).
39. *See* § 6.7(b).

should not cause the redistribution to fail as a *qualifying distribution*. Thus, a literal reading of the two applicable tax code sections and the referenced regulation allows the gain inherent in the redistributed property to be excluded from the excise tax.

Another unanswered question in the authors' experience is whether assets redistributed to allow the donor an enhanced charitable deduction that are reported on Part XII of Form 990-PF as an out of corpus distribution can be counted as a qualifying distribution for purposes of calculating qualification for the 1 percent tax rate. See § 6.5(a), Direct Grants, for further consideration of treating redistributions of donated assets as qualifying distributions.

## § 10.3 FORMULA FOR TAXABLE INCOME

The excise tax is imposed on net investment income for each tax year. A private foundation's *net investment income* is the amount by which the sum of its gross investment income and net capital gain exceeds the allowable deductions.[40] That is:

> Gross investment income + Net capital gain − Deductions = Net investment income

### (a) Gross Investment Income

The term *gross investment income* means the gross amount of income from interest, dividends, rents, payments with respect to securities loans (as defined in § 512(a)(5)), and royalties, but not including any such income to the extent included in computing the tax imposed by § 511. Such terms also include income from sources *similar* to those in the preceding sentence.[41] The last sentence is new for fiscal years beginning after August 18, 2006. The somewhat vague word *similar* is intended to expand the definition to include income from peripheral security transactions that do not produce dividends or interest, such as options to sell (a put) or buy (a call) securities, commodity transactions, derivatives, and other investment not anticipated when § 4940 was written. These similar items also include income from notional principal contracts, annuities, and other substantially similar income from ordinary and routine investments, and, with respect to capital gain net income, capital gains from

---

40. IRC § 4940(c)(1); Reg. § 53.4940-1(c)(1), (2).
41. IRC § 4940(c)(2), as revised by the Pension Protection Act of 2006 and by Sec. 3(f) of the Tax Technical Corrections Act of 2007, Pub. L. No. 110-172, 110th Cong., 1st Sess. (2007). Reg. § 53.4940-1(d).

appreciation, including capital gains and losses from the sale or other disposition of assets used to further an exempt purpose.[42]

The income is reportable using the method of accounting normally used by the foundation for financial statement purposes, with certain exceptions as discussed in the following paragraphs.[43] Income of the specified types that is produced by both investment assets and exempt function assets is taxed.[44] Therefore, interest income from student loans or dividends from a program-related corporate stock are included.

Income reported to a private foundation on Form K-1 for partnership investments in which it holds an interest often presents reporting issues. The distributions reported as interest, dividends, rents, and royalties are combined and reported with the foundation's other investment income of that character and unquestionably subject to the excise tax. The other lines, entitled, for example, "Ordinary Income," may be difficult to classify to reach the proper tax result.[45]

## (b)  Capital Gains and Losses

The tax code, effective for fiscal years beginning after August 17, 2006, defines net capital gains subject to the excise tax broadly and essentially says most capital gains are taxed, including those resulting from the sale of exempt function assets. In a negative fashion, the code provides that "[t]here shall not be taken into account any gain or loss from the sale or other disposition of property to the extent that such gain or loss is taken into account for purposes of computing the tax imposed by section 511."[46] A second exception provides for a nontaxable exchange by saying:

> Except to the extent provided by regulation, under rules similar to the rules of section 1031 (including the exception under subsection (a)(2) thereof), no gain or loss shall be taken into account with respect to any portion of property used for a period of not less than 1 year for a purpose or function constituting the basis of the private foundation's exemption if the entire property is exchanged immediately following such period solely for property of like kind which is to be used primarily for a purpose or function constituting the basis for such foundation's exemption.

Net losses from sales or other dispositions of property are only allowed to the extent of gains from such sales or other dispositions and no capital loss

---

42. Joint Committee on Taxation, "Technical Explanation of H.R. 4, the 'Pension Protection Act of 2006,' as Passed by the House on July 28, 2006, and as Considered by the Senate on August 3, 2006," (JCX-38-06) ("Joint Committee Explanation"), at 324.
43. Reg. § 53.4940-1(c).
44. Reg. § 53.4940-1(d)(1).
45. These reporting and compliance issues are discussed in § 10.3(h), § 11.3, Exhibits 11.2 and 12.4.
46. IRC § 4940(c)(4), as revised by the Pension Protection Act of 2006 and § 3(f) of the Tax Technical Corrections Act of 2007, Pub. L. No. 110-172, 110th Cong., 1st Sess. (2007).

carryovers or carrybacks are allowed.[47] This loss limitation requires the prudent foundation to review its current year investment results prior to its year end so as to take steps, if possible, to avoid loss of the tax benefit from any capital losses. Gain from property used in an unrelated trade or business, if it is subject to the unrelated business income tax, is not taxed again under these rules.[48] Mutual fund capital gain dividends, both short and long term, are classified as capital gain, not dividends.[49] Certain types of gains will continue to be excluded from the excise tax:

- Gain inherent in appreciated property distributed as a grant to another charity.[50] The reason is that distribution of property for charitable purposes is not considered a sale or other disposition for purposes of this tax.

- Gain from disposition of excess business holdings held on December 31, 1969 (or received as a bequest under a trust irrevocable on May 26, 1969) and sold to or redeemed by a disqualified person to reduce the holdings pursuant to the excess business holdings rules.[51]

- Gain realized in a merger or corporate reorganization ruled to be tax free.[52]

- Distributions of capital gains from a charitable lead trust.[53]

The basis for calculating gain or loss on a purchased asset is equal to the amount paid by a private foundation for the assets to acquire or construct it, less any allowable depreciation or depletion. Assets acquired by gift, on the other hand, retain the donor's, or a carryover, basis and asset holding period. To follow accounting principles, a private foundation may record the donation at its value on the date the property is given. For tax purposes, however, it may not "step up" the tax basis to this value. Essentially, the foundation pays the tax unpaid by the donor. The basis of inherited property is equal to its value as reported on the federal estate tax return,[54] which ordinarily is its value on the date of the decedent's death. The normal income tax rules[55] are used to measure the carryover basis.[56]

---

47. IRC § 4940(c)(4)(C); before revision, the regulations, but not the tax code disallowed carrybacks.
48. A similar rule operates for nonexempt charitable trusts described in IRC § 4947 (§ 3.6); Rev. Rul. 74-497, 1974-2 C.B. 383.
49. Rev. Rul. 73-320, 1973-2 C.B. 385.
50. Reg. § 53.4940-1(f)(1); see § 10.2(b).
51. Reg. § 53.4940-1(d)(3); Priv. Ltr. Rul. 8214023.
52. IRC § 368 or other provision of IRC Subchapter C. E.g., Priv. Ltr. Rul. 8730061.
53. Tech. Adv. Mem. 9724005.
54. Form 706.
55. IRC § 1015.
56. Reg. § 53.4940-1(f)(2).

For property held by a private foundation on December 31, 1969—the date when the tax became effective—special rules apply. The tax basis for any property held on that date is equal to its December 31, 1969, valuation, unless a loss is realized on the sale using such a value.[57] Property held in a trust or in an estate created before 1969 may also use the 1969 basis.[58] A trust created in 1935, subject to a life estate expiring in 1970, was ruled to be constructively received in 1935 and therefore to be owned by the private foundation in 1969. The basis of the shares received upon the life tenant's death was stepped up to the 1969 value, rather than retaining the 1935 basis.[59]

**Wash Sales.**  A private foundation is subject to limitations on certain capital loss transactions called wash sales.[60] A wash sale is a security sale that results in a loss occurring within 30 days before or after a purchase of the same security. Since net capital losses are not deductible against other investment income, it is important for the timing of losses and gains to be coordinated in view of both of these rules. Gains from security sales are not subject to the wash sale limitation, providing an opportunity to realize a gain to offset losses (that cannot be deducted) and immediately repurchase the security. A comparison of tax savings with cost of the sale should be made.

**Technical Corrections.**  With the PPA revisions, Congress attempted unsuccessfully to expand the private foundation investment income tax base. The concept of *gross investment income* was revised to encompass income items "similar to" those previously enumerated.[61] The Congressional Joint Committee of Taxation's (JCT) technical explanation of the private foundation investment income tax law revisions under the Pension Protection Act of 2006 said:

> The provision amends the definition of gross investment income (including for purposes of capital gain net income) to include items of income that are *similar* to the items presently enumerated in the Code. Such similar items include income from notional principal contracts, annuities, and other substantially similar income from ordinary and routine investments, and, with respect to capital gain net income, capital gains from appreciation, including capital gains and losses from the sale or other disposition of assets used to further an exempt purpose.

As originally revised, § 4940 presented the same dilemma foundations faced regarding capital gains before the *Zemurray* case.[62] Before revision through technical corrections, the code still contained a definition of capital gains tied to

---

57.  IRC § 4940(c)(4)(B); Rev. Rul. 74-403, 1974-2 C.B. 381.
58.  Rev. Rul. 76-424, 1976-2 C.B. 367.
59.  Priv. Ltr. Ruls. 8539001 and 8150002.
60.  IRC § 1091.
61.  IRC § 4940(c)(2), second sentence.
62.  *See* discussion in § 10.3(b).

those properties that produce dividends, interest, rents, royalties, and other similar income. Undoubtedly, the JCT intended to add all capital gains to the § 4940 taxable income. Apparently, they thought capital gains through appreciation to be "similar" to capital gains on property held for the production of dividends, given that both types are property held for investment purposes.

An important question occurred for foundations with capital gains resulting from the expanded definition between August 18 and December 31, 2006. Since the technical correction was not approved until December 29, 2007, some would have omitted gains that then needed to be reported in an amended return.

**Ponzi Scheme Losses.** The disallowance of any current deduction or carryover for capital losses presents a difficult situation for private foundations with losses due to theft or fraud, caused by investments in Ponzi schemes.[63] The IRS, in March 2009, addressed the tax rules that determine the character of such a loss.[64] Issues considered and their determination included:

- Is a loss from criminal fraud or embezzlement in a transaction entered into for profit a theft loss or capital loss? [Answer: Theft loss]

- Is such a loss subject to either the personal loss limits[65] or the limits on itemized deductions?[66] [No]

- In what year is such a loss deductible? [The year in which it is discovered]

- How is the amount of such a loss determined? [The amount invested plus amounts "reinvested" and reported as income less reasonably expected recovery]

- Can such a loss create or increase a net operating loss?[67] [Yes]

- Does such a loss qualify for the computation of tax for the restoration of an amount held under a claim of right?[68] [Yes]

- Does such a loss qualify for adjustment of tax liability in years that are otherwise barred by the period of limitations[69] on filing a claim for refund?[70] [No]

In reaching a conclusion that Ponzi scheme losses are ordinary, rather than capital, losses, the IRS stated: "The character of an investor's loss related to

---

63. See § 8.4(a).
64. Rev. Rul. 2011-9, 2011-2 I.R.B. 283.
65. IRC § 165(h).
66. IRC §§ 67, 68.
67. IRC § 172.
68. IRC § 1341.
69. IRC §§ 1311-1314.
70. IRC § 6511.

fraudulent activity depends, in part, on the nature of the investment." A loss sustained from the worthlessness or other disposition of stock acquired on the open market for investment results in a capital loss, even if the decline is attributable to fraudulent activities of the corporation's officers. The distinction between a capital and ordinary loss in the circumstance rests on the intention of the company officials, namely, whether they had the specific intent to deprive the shareholder of money or property.[71] When the officials intended to, and did, deprive the investors of money by criminal acts, the loss results from a theft treated as a casualty, and thereby ordinary loss. How a private foundation reports theft loss is considered elsewhere;[72] it is not treated as a capital loss. The mandatory payout calculation for years prior to discovery of the loss could be recalculated.[73]

**Losses on Exempt Function Assets.** The federal tax statutory law does not address an issue presented by the new capital gain rules: Does a loss from the sale of an exempt function asset offset gains from the sale of investment securities? The Joint Committee on Taxation's explanation seems to provide an answer:

The provision amends the definition of gross investment income (including for purposes of capital gain net income) to include items of income that are similar to the items presently enumerated in the Code. Such similar items include income from notional principal contracts, annuities, and other substantially similar income from ordinary and routine investments, and, with respect to capital gain net income, capital gains from appreciation, including capital gains and losses from the sale or other disposition of assets used to further an exempt purpose.

There is no expressed limit on offsetting losses from assets used to further an exempt purpose or vice versa. Similarly, there is no distinction between reclassifications of exempt-use asset gains as ordinary rather than capital gain income. This result is reasonable since a private foundation pays the same rate of tax on all of its taxable income. There is also no distinction between long- and short-term goals and losses, except for private operating foundations.[74]

**Basis.** The regulations that address basis issues for private foundations do not provide an answer for an important question: Must a foundation use the

---

71. Rev. Rul. 77-17, 1977-1 C.B. 44.
72. See § 10.4.
73. See § 6.7(a).
74. For private operating foundation purposes, net short-term gains defined by IRC § 1222(5), but not long-term or IRC § 1231 gains, are treated as adjusted gross income, but losses do not reduce income. Reg. § 53.4942(a)-2(d)(2)(ii).

trade or the settlement date in accounting for gains and losses on sales of its marketable security investments? A foundation is to follow the tax rules in subchapter O of the Internal Revenue Code for purposes of determining gain or loss on sale or other disposition of property.[75] This directive means the carry-over basis rules apply to donated property received by a private foundation. The answer to the question posed about the trade date is not addressed, but rulings have held that the trade date is used to determine the holding period and also the sale date.[76] Further, the trade date is required for recognition of a loss on a stock transaction.[77] Lastly, the trade, rather than settlement, date is used by a private foundation following either the cash or accrual method of accounting.[78] Financial institutions that issue gain or loss statements for accounts they hold should use the trade date.

A private foundation that has used the settlement date may need to consider whether a change to use of the trade date is a change in its accounting method to be reported.[79] It may be sufficient for the foundation to simply disclose the change in an attachment to its annual information return.

## (c) Interest

Interest income is taxed if it is earned on the following types of obligations and investments:

- Bank savings or money market accounts, certificates of deposit, commercial paper, and other temporary cash investment accounts.

- Commercial paper, U.S. Treasury bills, notes, bonds, and other interest-bearing government obligations, and corporate bonds.

- Interest on student loans receivable,[80] on mortgage loans to purchasers in low-income housing projects, and loans to minority business owners as a program-related investment.

- Payments on collateral security loans.[81]

- Interest income need not be imputed on a no- or low-interest-bearing loan made and held for exempt purposes, essentially those loans classified as program-related investments.[82]

---

75. Reg. § 53.4940-1(f)-2(i).
76. Rev. Rul. 66-97, 1966-1 C.B. 190; Rev. Rul. 93-84, 1993-2 C.B. 225.
77. Rev. Rul. 70-344, 1970-2 C.B. 50.
78. *Charles Schwab v. United States*, 99-1 U.S.T.C. ¶ 50,109 (9th Cir. 1999).
79. IRS Form 3115.
80. Reg. § 53.4940-1(d)(1).
81. IRC § 512(a)(5).6
82. Reg. § 1.7872-5T(b)(ii); program-related investments are the subject of § 8.3.

A distribution of income from an estate does not retain its character as income and is not taxed when it is received by a private foundation.[83] Where, however, a private foundation receives Series E United States savings bonds from an estate, and no part of the periodic increase in the value of the bonds was reported as income by the estate,[84] the private foundation must report the interest. The right to receive income upon redemption of the bonds is called *income in respect of a decedent.*[85] Therefore, the interest income derived by the private foundation upon redemption of the bonds received from the estate is gross investment income, as is all the interest income accrued on the bonds from the date of purchase by the decedent until the date of redemption by the private foundation.[86]

Municipal bond interest paid by state and local governments is excluded and is not taxed, even though it is included in adjusted income for private operating foundations. Expenses relating to such income are not deductible.[87]

The proceeds of a pension plan are deferred compensation and not one of the specified types of taxable investment income. The IRS specified the plan proceeds paid to a charitable remainder trust were nontaxable income in respect of a decedent.[88] The character of the plan proceeds was the same as they would have been in the hands of the decedent. It found that the proceeds of a Keogh plan in excess of the contributions made to the account were taxable investment income to the decedent. Because the proceeds were income in respect of a decedent, the private foundation was not subject to normal income tax because of its tax exemption.

The IRS also ruled that the proceeds of a donated retirement account were not taxable to a private foundation as investment income because the excise tax is limited in its application to the specifically listed types of income: dividends, interest, rents, and royalties.[89]

Another unanswered question is whether income earned on an annuity contract is subject to the investment income tax. The increase in the annual value of an annuity contract is thought of as interest and calculated at an expressed rate. The annual increase, however, is not taxed as interest under normal income tax rules. The increase is taxable to holders other than natural persons, such as a private foundation, as ordinary income from the annuity contract.[90] When a

---

83. *See* 10.3(g).
84. IRC § 454.
85. Rev. Rul. 64-104, 1964-1 (Part 1) C.B. 223, cited in Rev. Rul. 68-145, 1968-1 CB 203.
86. Rev. Rul. 80-118, 1980-1 C.B. 254; also Rev. Rul. 79-340, 1979-2 CB 320.
87. IRC § 4940(c)(5).
88. Priv. Ltr. Rul. 9237020.
89. Priv. Ltr. Rul. 9838028. The IRS also ruled that proceeds of this nature constitute income in respect of a decedent (IRC § 691) to the recipient private foundation (Priv. Ltr. Rul. 9818009).
90. IRC § 72(u)(1); if the contract is gifted to a private foundation, the excess fair market value of contract over donor's tax basis is taxable as ordinary income to the donor under IRC § 72(e)(4)(C)(III).

private foundation holds an annuity, several questions arise. The increase in value of the annuity should not be reportable for § 4940 purposes because it is not interest, nor is it a dividend or rental or royalty income. Second, the unrelated business income tax rules specifically modify or exclude annuity income from the tax.[91] Last, the proceeds of redemption of the annuity contract would similarly be the disposition of an asset that does not produce the type of income subject to the investment income tax resulting in a nontaxable gain for that purpose. Similarly the gain, or difference between the tax basis of the contract and the proceeds, would not be subject to the unrelated business income tax.[92]

## (d)  Dividends

Dividends that are taxable include the following:

- Dividends paid on all types of securities, whether listed and marketable or privately held and unmarketable.

- Mutual fund dividends (not including the portion reported as capital gain).

- For-profit subsidiary dividends.

- Corporate liquidating distributions classified as dividends,[93] but not including payments on complete redemption of shares that are classified as capital gains.[94]

The redemption of stock from a private foundation to the extent necessary for it to avoid the excess business holdings tax[95] is a sale or exchange not equivalent to a dividend, and the proceeds will not be taxed as investment income.[96] Similarly, a conversion of shares of a corporation owned by a private foundation for shares of another corporation, where the conversion occurs pursuant to a tax-free corporate reorganization,[97] does not constitute net investment income.[98] Dividends on paid-up insurance policies that were donated to a private foundation, however, constitute net investment income.[99] Dividends and other distributions of income from a subchapter S corporation are subject to the unrelated business income, rather than the excise, tax.

---

91. IRC § 512(b)(1).
92. *See* Chapter 11.
93. IRC § 302(b)(1).
94. E.g., Priv. Ltr. Rul. 8001046.
95. *See* Chapter 7.
96. Rev. Rul. 75-336, 1975-2 C.B. 110.
97. IRC § 368.
98. Priv. Ltr. Rul. 7847049.
99. Priv. Ltr. Rul. 8449069.

## (e) Rentals

Amounts paid in return for the use of real or personal property, commonly called rent, are taxable—whether the rental is related or unrelated to the private foundation's exempt activities.[100] The portion of rental income from debt-financed rental property includible in unrelated business income is excluded from the excise tax on investment income.[101]

## (f) Royalties

Payments received in return for assignments of mineral interests owned by a foundation, including overriding royalties, are taxed. Only cost, not percentage, depletion is permitted as an expense. Royalty payments received in return for use of a private foundation's intangible property, such as the foundation's name or a publication containing a literary work commissioned by the foundation, are also taxable.

## (g) Estate or Trust Distributions

Payments to a foundation from an estate or trust do not generally "retain their character in the hands" of the foundation. In other words, these payments do not pass through to the foundation as taxable income.[102] Income earned during administration of an estate and set aside for a foundation is not taxable to either the estate or the foundation (unless administration is unreasonably continued).[103] This is true even if the income earned by the estate is recognized for financial purposes because the foundation follows the accrual method of accounting. The estate assets, including accumulated income, are also not treated as foundation assets for the purpose of calculating grant payout requirements. Part of the reason for this rule lies in the fact that a wholly charitable, also referred to as a nonexempt, trust pays its own 2 percent investment income tax,[104] and its distributions are not taxed again to the foundation upon their receipt. Income earned during administration of a trust estate that is set aside, or earmarked for payment to a foundation, is deductible as a charitable contribution. Such income is not taxable to

---

100. Instructions to Form 990-PF, Part I, column (b), at p. 6.
101. IRC §§ 514(a)(1), 4940(1)(2).
102. Reg. § 53.4940-1(d)(2). The portion of this regulation that requires distributions from a split-interest trust to be subject to the investment excise tax was found invalid in the *Ann Jackson Family Foundation* case (*see* § 6.4(a)); this regulation remains unchanged. Until 2004, Form 990-PF contained a line to report this type of income.
103. Priv. Ltr. Rul. 8909066.
104. IRC § 4947(a)(1); *see* § 3.6.

either the estate or the foundation (unless administration is unreasonably continued).[105]

## (h)  Partnerships

When a private foundation buys, or is given, an interest in a partnership, its proportionate share of interest, dividends, rents, royalties, and capital gains earned by the partnership is reportable for excise tax purposes. The partnership income retains the same character in the foundation's hands. Form K-1 must be provided each year to reflect each partner's income earned by the partnership. Detailed information to allow a tax-exempt partner, including a private foundation, to report its share of unrelated business income and calculate its tax liability must also be provided. Rentals from indebted real estate are the most common type of unrelated income distributed from partnerships.[106] As mentioned in § 10.3 (d), dividends, income distributed to a foundation from a subchapter S corporation and reported on Form K-1 is all subject to the unrelated business income tax, rather than the excise tax, even if the character of the income in the hands of the corporation is interest, dividends, rent, or royalty. Exempt function expenses reported by a program-related investment partnership are reportable in column (c), not (b).

Income reported to a private foundation on Form K-1 for partnership investments in which it holds an interest are often reported incorrectly. It is important that capital gains distributed by the partnership be reported on line 6 to offset any losses the foundation might have realized otherwise. The total of other types of partnership income and expense, including unrelated business income, are reported on lines 11 and 23 of Part I of Form 990-PF in column (a), respectively.[107] Unrelated business income is omitted from column (b). Exhibit 11.3, a checklist

---

105.  Priv. Ltr. Rul. 9724005. The rationale for this position is that net investment income of a private foundation is determined under the principles of IRC subtitle A (income taxes), except to the extent inconsistent with the provisions of IRC § 4940 (IRC § 4940(c)(1); Reg. § 53.4940-1(c)(1)). A charitable lead trust is a *complex trust* because its terms require distributions to charity; thus, the amount includible in gross income and the character of distributions to a private foundation are determined by IRC § 662. Distributions to charity pursuant to the governing instrument are excluded from the income of the beneficiaries (IRC §§ 642(c), 663(a)(2)). Therefore, capital gain distributions from a charitable lead trust to a private foundation are not includible in a private foundation's net investment income under general trust taxation principles. For purposes of the investment income tax, the term *gross investment income* is defined in Reg. § 53.4940-1(d). *Capital gains and losses* are defined in Reg. § 53.4940-1(f). The first of these regulations provides that the income of a split-interest trust retains its character in the hands of a distributee private foundation, but that distributions from these trusts do not otherwise retain their character (Reg. § 53.53.4940-1(d)(2)). (That is, the distributions are treated as contributions rather than income to the private foundation.) There is no counterpart provision in the second of these regulations. Thus, the IRS is of the view that the retention-of-character concept does not apply to capital gains.

106.  *See* § 11.4.

107.  *See* Exhibit 12.1 for filled-in form.

entitled Form K-1 Analysis for Unrelated Business Income Reporting Purposes, can be used to analyze each line of the form.[108]

## (i)   Questionable Taxable Gains before 2007

Gain from sale of property that is capable of producing the specific types of income listed earlier (interest, dividends, rent, security loans, and royalties) is taxed even if the property is disposed of immediately after the foundation receives it. Since the statute before amendment by the Pension Protection Act applied to "property used for the production" of the specified income, astute private foundations in the early days escaped tax on highly appreciated property gifts by selling them as soon as the property was given.[109] These foundations argued that they never held the property to produce the specified types of income, so therefore the tax should not apply.

The Department of the Treasury provided by regulation that the tax applies even if the property was immediately disposed of on its receipt, *if* "the property was of a type which generally produces interest, dividends, rents, royalties, or capital gain through appreciation, such as rental real estate, stocks, bonds, mineral interests, mortgages, and securities."[110] The courts agreed with this interpretation of the tax law by the IRS.[111]

The Treasury Department also attempted to expand the tax code concerning the taxation of capital gain net income by including "capital gains from appreciation" resulting from the disposition of all investment-type assets not used by a private foundation for charitable purposes. Litigation concerning the scope of this regulation occurred, regarding the sale by a private foundation of its interest in timberland from which it never received any income. A federal court of appeals ruled that *capital gains* is not an *independent basis* for taxation and that the regulation is invalid to the extent it would cause that result.[112] The appellate court concluded, however, that "property that is ordinarily of a type that produces interest, dividends, rents, or royalties, and thus falls within one of the first four categories, but which is being held in the particular instance for capital gains through appreciation, is nevertheless taxable" as net investment income. The standard, then, as established by the lower court, is whether it is "economically prudent or reasonable" to use property in a way that produces

---

108. The reporting and compliance issues resulting from offshore investments are discussed in § 12.3(f). Also *see* Exhibit 8.1, Tax-Exempt Organizations, Including Private Foundations: Checklist for Alternative Investments.

109. Rev. Rul. 74-404, 1974-2 C.B. 382.

110. Reg. § 53.4940-1(f)(1).

111. *Ruth E. and Ralph Friedman Foundation, Inc. v. Commissioner*, 71 T.C. 40 (1978); *Greenacre Foundation v. United States*, 762 F.2d 965 (Fed. Cir. 1985), *aff'g* 84-2 U.S.T.C. ¶ 9789 (Ct. Cl. 1984); *Balso Foundation v. United States*, 573 F. Supp. 191 (D. Conn. 1983). Also *Balso Foundation v. United States*, 80-2 U.S.T.C. ¶ 9581 (D. Conn. 1980).

112. *Zemurray Foundation v. United States*, 755 F.2d 404 (5th Cir. 1985).

taxable income, not whether the property is "theoretically susceptible" of this use.[113] Consequently, the tax on the net income of private foundations did not fall on the dispositions of all noncharitable assets but only on those assets that can be reasonably expected to generate one or more of the four types of income. The Congressional Joint Committee of Taxation, effective for tax years beginning after August 17, 2006, codified taxation of capital gains from appreciation, including capital gains and losses from the sale or other disposition of assets used to further an exempt purpose as discussed in § 10.3(b).[114]

---

113. *Zemurray Foundation v. United States*, 84-1 U.S.T.C. ¶ 9246 (E.D. La. 1983). The regulation to accompany this provision states that net capital gains are capital gains and losses from the sale or other disposition of property held by a private foundation for investment purposes or for the production of income (Reg. § 53.4940-1(f)(1)). One court held that this regulation is "overly broad" in three respects: (1) while the statute employs the term *used*, the regulation utilizes the term *held*, so that the regulation wrongfully "allows taxation of gains from the sale of property regardless of whether that property was used for the production of interest, dividends, rents, or royalties"; (2) the regulation would subject to taxation the disposition of property momentarily in a private foundation's possession even though it was never used for investment purposes; and (3) the regulation improperly includes property that produces "gains through appreciation" with the types of property the sale of which results in taxable capital gains. Consequently, the court concluded that the property at issue in the case (an undivided one-half interest in a tract of land, subject to a usufruct, that generated income from timber sales paid solely to the usufructuary) was not used by the private foundation to produce any interest, dividends, rents, or royalties and, thus, that the sale of the property did not produce investment income subject to the IRC § 4940 tax (*Zemurray Foundation v. United States*, 509 F. Supp. 976 (E.D. La. 1981)). This decision, however, was overruled by the U.S. Court of Appeals for the Fifth Circuit, which concluded that the regulation "is not perceived as unreasonable or plainly inconsistent with the statute" (*Zemurray Foundation v. United States*, 687 F.2d 97 (5th Cir. 1982)). Yet the Fifth Circuit concurrently remanded the case to the district court for a determination as to whether the private foundation's timberland was the type of property that generally produces interest, dividends, rents, or royalties. On remand, the district court held that the private foundation was not liable for the net investment income tax, since the property was not the type that generally produces this income and that, while the Fifth Circuit held that the timberland was property that generally produces capital gains through appreciation (a category of property the disposition of which triggers the tax, under the regulations), the property must also be property that produces at least one of the four types of income (*Zemurray Foundation v. United States*, 84-1 U.S.T.C. ¶ 9246 (E.D. La. 1984)). The Chief Counsel of the IRS recommended against seeking Supreme Court review of the Fifth Circuit's decision (AOD 1987-018), and the government generally conceded this issue (Gen. Couns. Mem. 39538). Thus, the IRS now follows this approach (e.g., Priv. Ltr. Rul. 200148066 (holding that proceeds from the sale of a stock option by a private foundation were not subject to the tax)). In general, *Balso Foundation v. United States, supra* note 111; Webster, "Ca-5's Latest Decision Restricts Imposition of Section 4940 Tax on Private Foundations," 64 *J. Tax* (No. 3) 138 (1986). This body of law was amended, however, in an effort to expand the base of this tax, effective for years beginning after August 17, 2006 (*see* § 10.3(b)).

114. IRC § 4940(c)(4) revisions included in the Pension Protection Act did not contain this change that was added by the Technical Correction Act approved on December 27, 2007.

Appreciation of assets held by a newly classified private foundation attributable to the time it was a supporting organization may not necessarily be subject to the excise tax on capital gains.[115] A healthcare conglomerate asked the IRS to consider the issue concerning its reorganization. The parent supporting organization planned to sell its assets—charitable health centers, a publicly traded health maintenance organization, a for-profit physician practice management group, and insurance subsidiary—over a period of years, in a plan to convert itself into a grant-making private foundation. Though the federal tax law does not contain any rule regarding the basis of assets of a converted public charity, the IRS privately adopted a generous position. It allowed a step-up of basis to fair market value on the date a public charity was converted to a private foundation. Essentially, it treated the built-in gains as if they had been realized during the period the organization was a public charity (and therefore free of the excise tax). The ruling cited the transition rule allowing a step-up to value as of December 31, 1969, when the excise tax was first imposed, as the rationale for not requiring recognition of gain realized while the now-private foundation was classified as a supporting organization.[116]

## § 10.4  REDUCTIONS TO GROSS INVESTMENT INCOME

For purposes of computing net investment income, there is allowed, as a deduction from gross investment income, all the ordinary and necessary expenses paid or incurred for the production or collection of gross investment income and for the management, conservation, or maintenance of property held for the production of income.[117] These expenses include that portion of a private foundation's operating expenses that is paid or incurred for the production or collection of gross investment income. Not every expenditure associated with the receipt of income by a private foundation is deductible in determining net investment income, such as the trustee's termination fee where the private foundation is the sole remainder beneficiary of a trust.[118] That is, there must be a *nexus* or an *integral relationship* between the expenses and the earning of gross investment income, as was found with interest expense incurred by a private foundation on a debt underlying a bond issue

---

115. Priv. Ltr. Rul. 9852023; the ruling also cited Rev. Rul. 76-424, 1976-2 C.B. 367, which allowed the basis of property received by a foundation from an estate created before 1970 to be stepped up to December 31, 1969.
116. *See* §§ 7.2(d), concerning associated issues involving excess business holdings, and 8.1 regarding acquisition of jeopardizing investments.
117. IRC § 4940(c)(3)(A).
118. *Lettie Pate Whitehead Foundation, Inc. v. United States*, 606 F.2d 534 (5th Cir. 1979), *aff'g* (on the issue), 77-1 U.S.T.C. ¶ 9157 (N.D. Ga. 1977).

while the bond proceeds, destined for use in furthering charitable purposes, were temporarily invested.[119]

A private foundation's operating expenses include compensation of officers, other salaries and wages of employees, outside legal, accounting, and other professional fees, interest, and rent and taxes on property used in the private foundation's operations. Where a private foundation's officers or employees engage in activities on behalf of the private foundation for both investment purposes and for tax-exempt purposes, compensation and salaries paid to them must be allocated between the investment activities and the tax-exempt activities, referred to as functions.[120] All other operating expenses of a private foundation are subject to allocation where paid or incurred for investment, program services, and foundation administration.[121] Exhibit 10.2 contains accounting policies and procedures to apply in identifying costs by the various functions.

**EXHIBIT 10.2** Allocation of Costs by Private Foundations

A private foundation's excise tax liability (§ 4940) and satisfaction of the mandatory payout of 5 percent of the value of its assets (§ 4942) depend on a proper allocation of its expenses. We have observed over the years that the tendency of Form 990-PF preparers is a preference for allocating expenses to investment income (presumably because it is "deductible"). This practice indeed does save the foundation 1 to 2 percent of its net investment income. Importantly, however, identification of and allocation of expenses to program service, grant-making, and foundation administration costs saves the foundation essentially 100 percent of the expenditure in the foundation's fund balances. Thus we recommend a foundation establish policies for allocating expenses with a view to this fact in accordance with the following standards.

**GUIDELINES**

IRS Form 990-PF and the Statement of Financial Accounting Standards No. 117 require private foundations to report expenses by what is known as their functional classification. The three primary functional classifications are expenses pertaining to investments, program services and grants, and supporting activities. A foundation's supporting activities are comprised of management and general activities with little, if any, fundraising expenses. Statement No.117, Paragraphs 27 and 28 defines these classifications as follows:

**Program services** are activities that pertain to the foundation's grant-making activities and its direct conduct of programs, such as managing a historic village, designing new educational systems, or training community volunteers. These expenses are incurred directly to fulfill the purposes or mission for which the foundation exists. The existing Form 990-PF presents all of these expenses, plus supporting activity costs, in column (d) of Form 990-PF.

---

119. *Indiana University Retirement Community, Inc. v. Commissioner*, 92 T.C. 891 (1989). The court distinguished the situation from that of Rev. Rul. 74–579, 1974-2 C.B. 383, in which "the proceeds of the loan were not a source of investment income."
120. Reg. § 53.4940-1(e)(1).
121. *Julia R. & Estelle L. Foundation, Inc. v. Commissioner*, 70 T.C. 1 (1978), *aff'd*, 598 F.2d 755 (2d Cir.1979). *See* § 12.1(c).

**EXHIBIT 10.2** (Continued)

Costs of directly conducted programs are separately reported in total—without details—in Part IX-A.

**Supporting activities** are a foundation's activities other than program services and include **management and general activities** such as governance and oversight, business management, record-keeping, budgeting, financial reporting and tax compliance, personnel functions, and related administrative activities except for direct conduct of program services, including fundraising activities, if any.

## DIFFERENT SOURCES RECOMMEND DIFFERING PRACTICES AND POLICIES

The IRS Form 990-PF instructions for expenses attributable to investment income subject to the excise tax (column (b) on page 1 of the form) say:

Investment expenses include, in column (b), all ordinary and necessary expenses paid or incurred to produce or collect investment income

*OR*

for the management, conservation, or maintenance of property held for the production of income taxable under § 4940.

If any of the expenses listed in column (a) are paid or incurred for both investment and charitable purposes, they must be allocated on a reasonable basis between the investment activities and the charitable activities so that only expenses from investment activities appear in column (b).

The tax code says unrelated business income tax is imposed on gross income less expenses directly connected with the carrying on of such trade or business.[a]

The Treasury regulations say for unrelated business income reporting purposes that:[b]

Expenses, depreciation, and similar items attributable solely to the conduct of unrelated business activities are proximately and primarily related to that business activity, and therefore qualify for deduction to the extent that they meet the requirements of § 162 (ordinary and necessary business expense), § 167 (depreciation), and other relevant provisions of the Code.

**Generally Accepted Accounting Principles (GAAP) requirements** stipulate there are three types of costs—program, management and general, and fundraising—and provide for guidelines concerning the allocation of those costs among the functional categories of financial statements. GAAP does not specify any method of allocation, nor does it require detailed records to support the allocation (although it is wise to keep records for audit purposes). It does specify that the allocation method must be reasonable and consistently applied, and it may be based on estimates.

Documentation and cost accounting records must be designed to capture revenues and costs by function: directly conducted programs, grants to other organizations, investment management, and administration. Costs that can be directly identified as associated with a specific function are direct costs. When expenses are attributable to more than one function, the foundation must develop techniques to allocate expenses. At a minimum, a foundation might maintain the following:

- A salary/fee allocation system to record the time compensated directors or trustees, employees, and consultants spend on different functions. The possibilities are endless.

*(Continued)*

Each staff member should maintain an individual computer database or fill out a time sheet. The reports should be completed often enough to ensure accuracy, preferably weekly. In some cases, as when personnel perform repetitive tasks, preparing one week's report for each month or one month each year might be sufficient. Percentages of time spent on various functions can then be tabulated and used for accounting allocations. The regulations refer to this condition as dual use.[c]

- Office/program space utilization charts to assign occupancy costs can be prepared. All physical building space rented or owned should be allocated according to its usage. Floor plans must be tabulated to arrive at square footage of the space allocable to each activity center. In some cases, the allocation is made by using staff/time ratios, or the converse. For dual-use space, records must reflect the number of hours or days the space is used for each purpose. If space costs are being allocated to unrelated business income, the *Rensselaer Polytechnic* case[d] should be studied.

- Direct program or activity costs should be captured. The advantages include reduction of unrelated business income and proof of qualifying distributions for direct program activity. A minimal amount of additional time should be required by administrative staff to accumulate costs by programs. A departmental accounting system is imperative. Merchants may assist by establishing separate accounts for different departments.

- Supporting, administrative, or other management costs should be allocated to departments to which the work is directly related. The organization's size and the scope of administrative staff involvement in actual programs determine the feasibility of such cost attributions. Staff salaries are most often allocable. Say, for example, the executive director is also the editor of the foundation's research journal. Based on a record of time spent, his or her salary and associated costs could be attributed partly to the publication. When allocating expenses to unrelated business income, an exploitation of exempt functions rule may apply to limit such an allocation.[e]

- A computer-based fund accounting system is preferable, in which department codes are automatically recorded as moneys are expended. The cost of the software is easily recouped in staff time saved, improved planning, and possibly tax savings due to a reduction in income and excise taxes.

The lack of standard allocation practices makes functional accounting a somewhat unreliable measure of nonprofit efficiency and effectiveness. Given the lack of clear guidelines, a foundation is free to define which expenses are legitimately programmatic and which are supportive. As long as the internal guidelines are reasonable and consistently followed, they are likely to be accepted by auditors and donors.

[a] IRC § 512(a).

[b] Reg. § 1.512(a)-1(b).

[c] Reg. § 1.512(a)-1(c).

[d] IRS and the college argued about allocation of stadium costs over the number of days the facility was actually used versus the number of days in the year; U.S.T.C. ¶ 967, CA-2 1984, 53 AFTR 2d 84–1167.

[e] Reg. § 1.512(a)-1(d).

## (a) Deductions Allowed

The following deductions are permitted:

- Depreciation using a straight-line method calculated over the estimated useful life of the property; accelerated systems are not allowed.[122] The basis for calculating depreciation for purchased or constructed assets is equal to their cost. Donated property retains the donor's, or carryover, basis. The normal income tax rules[123] are used to measure this basis. Special rules apply to assets held by a foundation before 1969 when it began to claim depreciation for the first time in 1970.

- Cost, but not percentage, depletion.[124]

- Investment management or counseling fees, except the portion allocable to tax-exempt interest.[125]

- Legal, accounting, and other professional fees allocable to investment income activity. A private foundation can ask its advisors to render billings specifically identifying this type of an allocation based on time actually spent or another reasonable basis.[126]

- Taxes, insurance, maintenance, and other direct and specifically identifiable costs paid for property producing rental or royalty income, and an allocable part of these costs for administrative offices. Space rental is similarly treated.

- A proportionate part of operating expenses, including director, trustee officer, and staff fees, salaries and associated costs, occupancy costs, office and clerical costs, meetings, dues, administrative fees, and bank trustee fees.

---

122. IRC §§ 167, 4940(c)(3)(B)(i).
123. IRC § 1015.
124. IRC § 4940(c)(3)(B) (ii). In the case of a private foundation that held royalty interests in oil and gas properties, which (prior to 1970) did not claim a depletion deduction, and which recorded depletion on its books using the percentage method (of IRC § 613), the IRS advised the private foundation to determine the basis of its depletable property as of January 1, 1970, and reduce its basis in the property by an amount equal to the potential cost depletion (as provided by IRC § 611; e.g., *Beal Foundation v. United States*, 76-1 U.S.T.C. ¶ 9149 (W.D. Tex. 1975), *aff'd*, 559 F.2d 359 (5th Cir. 1977)). Since the private foundation did not claim any depletion deduction on this royalty interest, however, the IRS held that the private foundation did not have to further reduce the basis by the amount of the percentage of depletion recorded on its books (Reg. § 53.4940-1(e)(2) (iii); Rev. Rul. 79-200, 1979-2 C.B. 364).
125. IRC § 265.
126. Rev. Rul. 75-410, 1975-2 C.B. 446.

- An allocable portion of expenses paid or incurred incident to a charitable program that produces investment income is deductible to the extent of the income earned.[127]
- Bond premium amortization that is deductible.[128]
- Allocable portion of cost of setting up the foundation.

## (b)  Deductions Not Allowed

As a general rule, a deduction is not permitted for costs associated with a foundation's grant-making and other charitable or exempt-function projects. When a project or asset produces or is operated to produce income, the deductions associated with the activity are allocated between the exempt and investment uses.[129] With these joint-purpose activities, however, the primary motivation for undertaking the project (investment or program) must be determined. When the expenses are incurred in connection with an exempt-function project, the regulations provide that allocable expenses are deductible only to the extent of the gross investment income from the project.[130] An investment project conceivably could result in a deductible loss. Clearly, few historical building restorations are undertaken to produce net income. Since admission charges for visiting these buildings are normally incidental to the overall cost of the project, it may be difficult to prove that the building loss is deductible.

The IRS ruled that interest expense to borrow funds to lend interest free to another exempt organization was not an investment expense for purposes of calculating the § 4940 excise tax.[131] The loan was not intended to, and did not, produce gross income, so the conclusion was that the interest paid was an administrative rather than an investment expense. Similarly, the link between the investment income and interest expense was missing because the borrowed funds were used to make a grant with no intention of receiving income in return.[132] The general rule to report deductions against investment income does not reference tax code sections,[133] although certain portions of the regulations refer to income tax sections.[134] Inasmuch as an expense allocation method is not

---

127. Reg. § 53.4940–1(e)(2)(iv); Priv. Ltr. Rul. 8047007.
128. Rev. Rul. 76-248, 1976-1 C.B. 353. This deduction is pursuant to IRC § 171.
129. Reg. § 53.4940-1(e)(1)(ii).
130. Reg. § 53.4940-1(e)(1).
131. Rev. Rul. 74-579, 1974-2 C.B. 383; Gen. Coun. Mem. 35554.
132. *Infra* note 135.
133. E.g., IRC §§ 62, 162, 165, or 212.
134. Reg. § 53.4940-1(c)(2) states that the provisions of IRC §§ 103 and 265 are applicable for interest on certain government obligations and related expenses; Reg. § 53.4940-1(d)(3) refers to IRC § 301 for reporting distributions in redemption of stock; Reg. § 53.4940-1(f)(2) states that the basis for purposes of calculating capital gains and losses is determined under part II of Subchapter O.

prescribed, a foundation is free to use any reasonable method consistently (from year to year). When personnel costs have to be allocated, the preferred method is for the employees involved to maintain actual records of their time devoted to investment and exempt activities. The concepts and rules applicable to deductible expenses for unrelated business income tax purposes can be used as a guideline.[135] Documentation should be maintained as evidence of the manner in which the allocations are made. The following items are examples of non-deductible expenses for investment income purposes:

- Charitable distributions and administrative expenses associated with grant-making program costs are not deductible as investment expense.[136] A charitable deduction[137] is not permitted. Similarly, expenses of programs directly conducted by the foundation are not deductible.

- Purchase of exempt-function assets, depreciation of their cost, and cost of their maintenance, repair, or conservation are not deductible except to the extent of taxable receipts from the assets.[138]

- Capital losses in excess of capital gains are not deductible, nor is a carryover permitted to the succeeding year.[139] This is a potentially costly rule for a private foundation that does not properly time its asset dispositions.

- Operating losses incurred in a preceding year do not carry forward from year to year.[140]

- The allocable portion of expenses of an exempt-function income-producing property, or activity, in excess of the income produced therefrom and reportable as investment income is not deductible.[141]

- Expenses allocable to taxable unrelated business income are not deductible. (The income is also not includible.)[142]

- Interest paid on borrowing to acquire exempt-function assets is not deductible. For example, interest paid on a bond issue floated to finance building a retirement community is not paid on behalf of an investment.[143] If the financed building is rental property, however, the interest

---

135. *See* § 11.5 and Exhibit 10.2.
136. *Julia R. and Estelle L. Foundation, Inc. v. Commissioner*, 70 T.C. 1 (1978), *aff'd*, 598 F.2d 755 (2d Cir. 1979).
137. IRC §§ 170, 642(c).
138. *Historic House Museum Corp. v. Commissioner*, 70 T.C. 12 (1978). The purchase of these types of assets may be treated as a qualifying distribution; *see* § 6.5(b).
139. Reg. § 53.4940-1(f)(3).
140. Reg. § 53.4940-1(e)(1)(iii).
141. *See* § 10.4(a); the excess expense is, however, treated as a qualifying distribution.
142. Reg. § 53.4940-1(e)(1)(i).
143. Rev. Rul. 74-579, 1974-2 C.B. 383; Priv. Ltr. Rul. 8802008.

and other property maintenance and operational expenses should be to the extent of the income deductible.[144]

- A trust termination fee paid by a sole beneficiary private foundation was not paid for the production of income, nor were the unused deductions from the final trust return (customarily deductible to a noncharitable beneficiary)[145] deductible to the private foundation.[146]

- The special corporation deductions, including the dividends received deduction, are not allowed.[147]

## (c) Changing Accounting Method or Tax Year

Many private foundations follow the cash method of accounting since qualifying distributions must be reported on a cash basis. The instructions accompanying the annual information return under Accounting Methods state that, except for Part I, Column D, the financial information should be reported "on the basis of the accounting method the foundation regularly uses to keep its books and records." There is no instruction regarding a change in accounting method. Absent an instruction, the question is whether a private foundation should file the prescribed form with the IRS[148] when the foundation changes its accounting method for financial reporting purposes. The rules for taxpayers in general provide for an automatic accounting method change from accrual to cash for an entity with average annual gross receipts of $10 million or less.[149] The instructions accompanying the unrelated business income tax return[150] contain a provision entitled "Change in accounting method" and state that Form 3115 must be filed to change the method of accounting used to report taxable income. Thus, a private foundation would file this form in connection with reporting of its taxable unrelated business income. An unanswered question is whether such a filing impacts the accounting method used for annual information return purposes. It is arguable that the net investment income is not taxable income within the meaning of the filing instructions. Due to the modest 1–2 percent tax rate imposed on investment income, in many cases the net increase or decrease in reportable income resulting from a change can reasonably be reported in the year of change on the annual information return. When the 1 percent

---

144. *See* text accompanied by *supra* note 102.
145. IRC § 642(h)(2).
146. *Lettie Pate Whitehead Foundation, Inc. v. United States*, 606 F.2d 534 (5th Cir. 1979).
147. IRC § 4940(c)(3); Reg. § 53.4940-1(e)(1)(iii).
148. IRS Form 3115.
149. Rev. Proc. 2002-9, 2002-1 C.B. 327, §§ 5.01 and 5.02.
150. See § 11.5.

difference in the tax rate results is significant, recalculation of the past year might be desirable.

A change in the tax reporting year, when the private foundation has not previously changed its year with the past 10 years, is accomplished simply by filing a short-period return. For example, a June 30 fiscal-year reporting foundation wishes to change to a calendar-year reporting cycle. A six-month return reporting activity from July 1 through December 31 would be filed to achieve a new December 31 year-end. Three consequences must be considered in deciding to make the change:

1. Acceleration of qualifying distribution deadline: The entire annual payout requirement calculated for the full year that would have ended the following June must be satisfied within six months.[151]

2. Potential impact on 1–2 percent: The higher level of expenditures to meet the qualifying distributions requirement during the six-month period in comparison to the average value of the assets could cause a higher than usual payout percentage for the short period that would impact the calculation for several years.[152]

3. Forms 1099 and K-1 provided to the private foundation by financial institutions and partnerships and used in preparing Form 990-PF are issued on a calendar-year basis so that reporting on calendar year may ease the compliance effort.

## § 10.5  FOREIGN FOUNDATIONS

As a general rule, foreign private foundations are taxed at a rate of 4 percent on their U.S. source[153] investment income, calculated under the rules discussed earlier.[154] Tax treaties with some foreign countries, including Canada, provide an exemption from the tax.[155]

The excise tax must be specifically mentioned in a tax treaty for an exemption to apply.[156] Though the excise tax is applied to all investment income earned by a foreign private foundation, those that receive substantially all (at least 85 percent) of their support (other than capital gains) from sources

---

151. Unless the foundation has excess distribution carryovers that can be used to meet the payout requirement.
152. *See* Exhibit 10.1.
153. IRC § 861.
154. IRC §§ 4940(c)(2), 4948(a).
155. Rev. Rul. 74-183, 1974-1 C.B. 328.
156. Rev. Rul. 84-169, 1984-2 C.B. 216.

outside the United States are not subject to the sanctions imposed on domestic private foundations.[157] The termination tax[158] and notice requirements are also inapplicable.[159]

The U.S. source investment income of foreign organizations, both privately and publicly supported, is subject to a 4 percent tax withholding requirement.[160] Because they are ineligible to receive deductible contributions and have no U.S. source taxable income, foreign charities do not normally seek recognition of exempt status for U.S. purposes. To avoid the withholding tax, however, and to more easily receive grants from private foundations,[161] a foreign organization that can qualify as a public charity due either to its activities or to its sources of support might wish to apply for recognition of its public character.[162] A nonexempt charitable organization is subject to normal income tax withholding on its foreign-source U.S. income.

This body of law is the substitute, for foreign organizations, for the conventional investment income tax applicable to private foundations.[163] This law does not, however, affect the category of U.S. tax exemption under which a foreign organization can be classified. For example, a foreign private foundation receiving 84 percent of its support from sources outside the United States could be recognized as an exempt social welfare organization,[164] assuming it was not in existence on October 9, 1969.[165] This type of foreign private foundation however, could not be recognized as an exempt social welfare organization if it were in existence on that date.[166]

## § 10.6 EXEMPTION FROM TAX ON INVESTMENT INCOME

A private foundation that qualifies as an *exempt operating foundation* is exempt from the tax on investment income.[167] To be an exempt operating foundation for any year, a private foundation must have the following characteristics:

---

157. *See* Chapters 5–9.
158. *See* § 13.6.
159. *See* § 3.8.
160. IRC § 1443(b).
161. Foreign organizations must furnish proof of their public status to relieve the grantor foundation of the need to perform expenditure responsibility, as discussed in § 9.5.
162. The process of seeking recognition of exemption is discussed in § 2.5.
163. *See* § 10.1.
164. *See* § 1.4.
165. *See* § 15.2, text accompanied by notes 25–27.
166. E.g., Priv. Ltr. Rul. 200846041.
167. IRC § 4940(d)(1).

1. It qualifies as a private operating foundation.[168]

2. It has been publicly supported for at least 10 years.[169]

3. At all times during the year involved, the governing body of the private foundation consisted of individuals of whom at least 75 percent were not *disqualified individuals*,[170] and was broadly representative of the general public.

4. At no time during the tax year did the private foundation have an officer who was a disqualified individual.[171] The purpose of this exemption[172] is to eliminate this tax liability for organizations that are inherently not private foundations, such as museums and libraries.[173]

Also (although, in a sense, this is not really an "exemption"), a private foundation that is on the accrual method of accounting is not required to recognize income, for purposes of the tax on investment income, received by a trust containing assets destined for the foundation, where the foundation lacks control over the assets.[174]

## § 10.7 LEGISLATIVE PROPOSAL

Legislation has been introduced to simplify the excise tax regime applicable to the net investment income of private foundations.[175] The proposal would substitute a 1.32 percent excise tax rate (a preliminary number, believed to be a revenue-neutral rate) for the current general tax rate of 2 percent.[176] The legislation would also repeal the alternative 1 percent excise tax, available for a year in which a foundation substantially increases its level

---

168. *See* § 3.1(i).
169. IRC § 4940(d)(3)(A). *See* Chapter 15. A private foundation that was a private operating foundation as of January 1, 1983, is deemed to meet the public support requirement, by reason of the Tax Reform Act of 1984 § 302(c)(3). A private foundation that constituted an operating foundation for its last tax year ending before January 1, 1983, is treated as constituting an operating foundation as of January 1, 1983, by reason of the Technical and Miscellaneous Revenue Act of 1988, § 6204.
170. Namely, substantial contributors (*see* § 4.1) and certain related persons. IRC § 4940(d)(3) (B)–(E).
171. IRC § 4940(d)(2). Every organization that desires classification as an exempt operating foundation must request a ruling to that effect from the IRS and, if favorable, attach a copy of it to its annual return (Ann. 85-88, 1985-25 I.R.B. 21).
172. Added by Tax Reform Act of 1984, § 302(a).
173. H. Rep. No. 98-861, 98th Cong., 2d Sess. 1084 (1984).
174. Priv. Ltr. Rul. 200224035.
175. S. 676, 111th Cong., 1st Sess. (2009); S. 593, 112th Cong., 1st Sess. (2011).
176. *See* § 10.1.

of grant-making.[177] An essential point of this legislation, in addition to the simplification feature, is to eliminate the current-law incentive to dramatically increase grant-making in a year (to qualify for the 1 percent tax), which in turn is disadvantageous for foundations because it raises the five-year rolling average, used to calculate eligibility for the smaller tax, causing foundations to pay the higher rate on higher amounts in subsequent years. Also, the hope is that this law change would increase overall foundation grant-making.

---

177. *See* § 10.2.

# CHAPTER ELEVEN

# Unrelated Business Income

The unrelated business income rules constitute a significant component of the general federal tax law for tax-exempt organizations.[1] These rules, however, are of limited concern to private foundations because of the prohibition on excess business holdings,[2] which essentially bars foundations from actively engaging in an unrelated business. Nonetheless, certain aspects of the unrelated business income rules are applicable to private foundations.

A private foundation may receive unrelated business income, for example, from a permitted minority interest in a partnership. During the period of time a private foundation is allowed to dispose of an excess business interest, it might receive business income. Those private operating foundations that charge fees or sell the products of their programs must understand whether this income-producing activity qualifies as a permitted functionally related business activity. A private foundation may have a mortgaged rental property. Finally, the exceptions to these rules are important to all private foundations because, according to the literal definition, investment income is unrelated business income.

---

1. E.g., *Tax-Exempt Organizations*, Chapter 24; *Unrelated Business; Tax Planning and Compliance*, Chapter 21.
2. *See* Chapter 7.

## § 11.1 GENERAL RULES

### (a) Overview

Taxation of a tax-exempt organization's unrelated business income is based on the concept that the approach is a more effective and workable sanction for enforcement of this aspect of the tax law. Rather than deny or revoke the exempt status, the law requires an otherwise tax-exempt organization to pay tax on certain types of income. This body of law is fundamentally simple: The unrelated business income tax applies only to business income that arises from an activity—technically known as a *trade or business*—that is *unrelated* to the organization's tax-exempt purposes. The purpose of the unrelated business income tax is to place a tax-exempt organization's business activities on the same tax basis as the nonexempt business endeavors with which they compete.[3]

The term *unrelated trade or business* means any trade or business, the conduct of which is not substantially related to the exercise or performance, by the tax-exempt organization carrying on the trade or business, of its exempt purpose or function. The conduct of a trade or business is not substantially related to an organization's tax-exempt purpose solely because the organization needs the income or because the profits derived from the business are used for its exempt purposes.

Absent one or more exceptions,[4] gross income of a tax-exempt organization subject to the tax on unrelated income—and most exempt organizations are—is includible in the computation of unrelated business taxable income if three factors are present:

1. The income is from a *trade or business*.
2. The trade or business is *regularly carried on*.
3. The conduct of the business is not *substantially related* to the organization's performance of its tax-exempt purposes.[5]

### (b) Trade or Business Income

To have unrelated business income, a private foundation must first be found to be engaging in a *trade or business*, defined to include any activity carried on for the production of income from the sale of goods or performance of services.[6] The U.S. Tax Court held that a *business* is conducted with "continuity and regularity" and in a "competitive manner similar to commercial enterprises."[7]

---

3. Reg. § 1.513-1(b).
4. *See* § 11.2.
5. Reg. § 1.513-1(a).
6. IRC § 513; Reg. § 1.513-1(b).
7. *National Water Well Association, Inc. v. Commissioner*, 92 T.C. 75, 84 (1989).

Voluntary contributions and grants paid to the foundation with donative intention are, by contrast, not business income. A foundation does, however, receive business income when it invests its assets in return for interest, dividends, rents, or royalties. Although embodied in the definition of a business, income received from passive investments is exempt from the unrelated business income tax.[8]

A few foundations use their assets to conduct an active business in which services and goods are provided to accomplish their exempt purposes. Private foundations operate museums, publish educational materials, manage low-income housing projects, and conduct other programs that, according to the literal definition, constitute a trade or business.[9] These foundations ask visitors to pay admission fees, to pay tuition to attend educational seminars, and to pay rent and other forms of business income. This chapter considers situations when this income becomes unrelated business income subject to income tax.

Some courts have embellished the definition of a business with another criterion, which is that an activity, to be considered a business for tax purposes, must be conducted with a *profit motive*.[10] Under this test, an activity conducted simply to produce some revenue, but without an expectation of producing a profit (similar to that considered under the hobby loss rules), is not a business.[11] Thus, excess expenses (losses) generated in a fundamentally exempt activity, such as an educational publication undertaken without the intention of making a profit, cannot be deducted against the profits from a profit-motivated project, such as a mortgaged rental property. Courts have also applied a *commerciality test*, which looks at the characteristics of a business as illustrated in Exhibit 11.1. If an activity is carried on in a manner similar to that of a commercial business, it may constitute a trade or business.[12]

Historically, the IRS almost always prevailed on the issue as to whether an activity rose to the level of a *trade or business*. One of the rare exceptions to this phenomenon is a federal court of appeals decision in 1996. On that occasion, where the appellate court held that a tax-exempt organization must carry out extensive activities over a substantial period of time for the activities to be considered a business, the court ruled that an income-producing activity was

---

8. *See* § 11.2. The IRS ruled that a tax-exempt university was not engaged in unrelated business when it enabled charitable remainder trusts, as to which it was trustee and remainder interest beneficiary, to participate in the investment return generated by the university's endowment fund, inasmuch as the university was not receiving any economic return by reason of the arrangements (e.g., Priv. Ltr. Rul. 200703037).

9. *See* § 3.1.

10. IRC § 513(c); Reg. § 1.513-1(b).

11. *West Virginia State Medical Association v. Commissioner*, 882 F.2d 123 (4th Cir. 1989), *aff'g* 91 T.C. 651 (1988).

12. IRC § 513(c); Reg. § 1.513-1(b); *Better Business Bureau v. United States*, 326 U.S. 279, 283 (1945); *Scripture Press Foundation v. United States*, 285 F.2d 800 (Ct. Cl. 1961); *Greater United Navajo Development Enterprises, Inc. v. Commissioner*, 74 T.C. 69 (1980).

**Exhibit 11.1**

Commerciality Test Checklist

"YES" answers to these questions are warnings that signal the EO's exposure to a challenge that the organization operates in a commercial manner and may not be exempt.

|  | Yes | No |
|---|---|---|
| COMPETITIVENESS: Does the exempt organization's activity compete with for-profit businesses conducting the same activity? Is there a counterpart for the activity in the business sector, particularly a *small* business? | ☐ | ☐ |
| PERSONNEL MOTIVATION: Do managers receive generous compensation? Is the activity run by well-paid staff members? | ☐ | ☐ |
| SELLING TECHNIQUES: Are advertising and promotional materials utilized? Are retailing methods, such as mail-order catalog or display systems, similar to those of for-profit enterprises? | ☐ | ☐ |
| PRICING: Is the highest price the market will bear charged for goods and services? There are no scaled or reduced rates available for members of a charitable class. | ☐ | ☐ |
| CUSTOMER PROFILE: Are the organization's services and goods for sale to anyone? Are they available to the general public on a regular basis, rather than only for persons participating in the organization's other exempt activities? | ☐ | ☐ |
| ORGANIZATION'S FOCUS/GOOD WORKS RATIO: Does the organization conduct significant other charitable program activity? Is the income-producing activity its primary focus rather than exempt ones? | ☐ | ☐ |
| CHARACTER OF ORGANIZATION'S SUPPORT: Is very little or none of the organization's support from voluntary contributions, grants, or other unearned sources? | ☐ | ☐ |

not a business for unrelated business purposes.[13] In other instances, courts have regarded an economic activity of a tax-exempt organization as something less than a *business,* relying on an absence of competition and lack of profits.[14]

An organization regularly operating an investment service business, even though its customers were other tax-exempt organizations, was also not found to qualify for tax exemption because providing investment services on a regular basis for a fee is a trade or business ordinarily carried on for profit.[15] Similarly, because a conference center was operated in a commercial manner on a break-even basis, it

---

13. *American Academy of Family Physicians v. United States,* 91 F.3d 1155 (8th Cir. 1996).
14. *Laborer's International Union of North America v. Commissioner,* 82 T.C.M. 158 (2001); *Vigilant Hose Company of Emmitsburg v. United States,* 2001-2 U.S.T.C. ¶ 50,458 (D. Md. 2001).
15. Rev. Rul. 69-528, 1969-2 C.B. 127; *see Tax Planning & Compliance* discussion of "Services" in § 21.8(b) and Gen. Coun. Mem. 34369.

was also denied exemption.[16] It organized and sponsored more than 600 educational conferences a year in areas as diverse as civil and human rights, international relations, public policy, the environment, medical education, mental health, and disability. Twenty percent of the events were held for government clients, 50 percent for nonprofit and/or educational clients, and 30 to 40 percent for other users, including a large number of weddings and other private events. Only a few of the events were financially subsidized with lower prices. The court said, "as it is clear from the facts that plaintiff engages in conduct of both a commercial and exempt nature, the question whether it is entitled to tax-exempt status turns largely on whether its activities are conducted primarily for a commercial or for an exempt purpose" and decided the former was true.[17] The fact that Airlie was seeking to recover tax-exempt status previously lost due to private inurement issues may have influenced the case.

The IRS is empowered to fragment a tax-exempt organization's operations, run as an integrated whole, into its component parts in search of one or more unrelated businesses. That is, an activity does not lose identity as a trade or business merely because it is carried on within a larger aggregate of similar activities or within a larger complex of other endeavors that may, or may not, be related to the exempt purposes of the organization.[18] This fragmentation rule enables the IRS to ferret out unrelated business activity that is conducted with, or as a part of, related business activity. The rule is intended to prevent exempt organizations from hiding unrelated business activities within a cluster of related ones.

The operation of a typical museum shop is a classic example of a related business that can be fragmented and found to embody an unrelated segment. The shop itself is undoubtedly a trade or business, often established with a profit motive and operated in a commercial manner. While the books and art reproductions sold serve an educational purpose, the souvenirs and handicrafts that also are often sold are not necessarily treated as educational. Exhibit 11.2 lists factors that may be used to identify related sales of merchandise. The fragmentation rule requires that all items sold be analyzed to identify the educational, or related, items from which the profit is not taxable, and the unrelated souvenir items that may not only be taxable but also impermissible under the excess business holdings rules.[19] Likewise, the IRS applied the fragmentation rule to determine when the making and sales of caskets by an exempt monastery were and were not unrelated business.[20]

---

16. *Airlie Foundation v. IRS*, 283 F. Supp. 2d 58, (D.D.C. 2003).
17. *Id.* at 64.
18. IRC § 513(c); Reg. § 1.513-1(b).
19. *See* Chapter 7.
20. Priv. Ltr. Rul. 200033049.

EXHIBIT **11.2** Identifying Related Sales of Merchandise

---

A foundation that actively conducts a charitable program, such as a museum or a village of historic buildings, may sell physical items that are used in connection with conducting programs. Sales that are clearly related to exempt purposes might include reproductions of art works sold by a museum, a library's charges for copies of bibliographic data, and a historic preservation foundation's sale of tapes of endangered ethnic music to culture seekers. In deciding why and when the sale of such merchandise is treated as an activity has a causal relationship, or is related, to an organization's mission, several factors can be considered. The following questions can be asked to evaluate the relatedness of merchandise sold.

**NATURE OF ITEMS SOLD**

Are the objects actually used by the purchaser to participate in the organization's exempt activities? Asked another way, what is the intended use of the merchandise by the purchaser?

**METHODOLOGY OF SALES ACTIVITY**

Does the manner in which the sales activity is conducted evidence commerciality?

Are a large number of souvenirs or other unrelated items sold?

Are items sold in a shop open to the general public or accessible only to visitors or participants in foundation programs?

Are sales made on the foundation's website or through links from its site to a commercial site?

**MOTIVATION FOR SALES ACTIVITY**

Was a gift shop established to generate profits or to distribute educational items?

Does the shop sell both related and unrelated items?

Standards have been provided by the IRS for use in museum shops to fragment, or identify, those objects that qualify as related to exempt purposes and those that do not.[a]

**NONCOMMERCIAL CHARACTER**

Does one of the exceptions apply evidencing the noncommercial nature of the sales activity?

Are the shop personnel volunteers?

Is merchandise donated?

Is the sales activity irregularly conducted?[b]

[a] Rev. Rul. 73–104, 1973–1 C.B. 263; Rev. Rul. 73–105, 1973–1 C.B. 265; Priv. Ltr. Ruls.8303013, 8326003, 82360, 8328009; and Tech. Adv. Mem. 9550003.

[b] See § 11.1(d).

---

The IRS also uses the fragmentation rule in the context of the provision of services by tax-exempt organizations. For example, the IRS determined that the use of the golf course of a university by its students and employees was not unrelated business, while use of the course by alumni of the university, members of its President's Club, other major donors, and guests of these individuals was unrelated business.[21] As another example, the IRS used the

---

21. Tech. Adv. Mem. 9645004; *see* § 11.3(d).

fragmentation rule to differentiate between related and unrelated educational and religious tours conducted by a tax-exempt organization.[22]

Where an activity carried on for profit constitutes an unrelated trade or business, no part of the business may be excluded from that classification merely because it does not result in profit.[23]

## (c) Substantially Related Activity

Generally, gross income derives from unrelated trade or business if the regular conduct of the trade or business that produces the income is not *substantially related* to the purposes for which tax exemption is granted.[24] This requirement necessitates an examination of the relationship between the business activities that generate the particular income in question—the activities, that is, of producing or distributing the goods or performing the services involved—and the accomplishment of the organization's tax-exempt purposes.[25] The fact that an organization uses revenue for one or more exempt purposes does not itself make the underlying business activity a related one.[26]

A trade or business is related to an organization's tax-exempt purposes only where the conduct of the business activity has a causal relationship to the achievement of its tax-exempt purpose(s) and the relationship is a substantial one.[27] Thus, for the conduct of a trade or business from which a particular amount of gross income is derived to be substantially related to the purposes for which tax exemption is granted, the conduct must contribute importantly to the accomplishment of the particular organization's exempt purposes. If the activity does not accomplish an exempt purpose, the income from the sale of the goods or the performance of the services is not derived from the conduct of related trade or business. The finding of such a causal relationship depends, in each case, on the facts and circumstances involved.[28] The following are examples of related income-producing activities that a private foundation might conduct:

- Sale of educational materials and publications.
- Sale of tickets for a cultural performance or lecture.
- Conference or seminar fees.
- Scientific research consultations or publication.
- Student academic counseling fees.

---

22. Tech. Adv. Mem. 9702004.
23. IRC § 513(c); Reg. § 1.513-1(b).
24. IRC § 513(a); Reg. § 1.513-1(d)(1).
25. Reg. § 1.513-1(d)(1).
26. IRC § 513(a).
27. Reg. § 1.513-1(d)(2).
28. *Id.*

- Sale of museum admission tickets.
- Art exhibition loan charges.

The size and extent of the activities involved are considered in relation to the nature and extent of the tax-exempt function that they purport to serve.[29] If an organization conducts related activities on a larger scale than is reasonably necessary for performance of the functions, the gross income attributable to that portion of the activities in excess of the needs of tax-exempt functions constitutes unrelated business income. For example, a college was found to emphasize "revenue maximization" in the promotion of rock concerts in its multipurpose college auditorium to the exclusion of other considerations, indicating that the trade or business was not operated as an integral part of educational programs and that the activity, therefore, failed the substantially related test.[30] This type of income is not derived from the production or distribution of goods or the performance of services that contribute importantly to the accomplishment of any tax-exempt purpose of the organization.[31] The sale of literature, evaluation equipment, and instructional tapes on use of devices designed to measure the extent of a child's developmental deficiencies was ruled to produce related income to an organization devoted to helping children.[32]

Gross income derived from charges for the performance of exempt functions constitutes gross income from the conduct of a *related trade or business*.[33] For revenues to be treated as *related*, the service or product resulting from exempt functions must ordinarily be sold in substantially the same state they were in on completion of the exempt functions.[34] If, however, a product is utilized or exploited in further business endeavors, beyond those reasonably appropriate or necessary for disposition in the state it is in on completion of tax-exempt functions, the gross income derived from these endeavors is considered to be derived from the conduct of unrelated business.[35]

An asset or facility necessary to the conduct of tax-exempt functions and so used may also be utilized in a commercial endeavor. This is called a *dual use* arrangement. An illustration of this type of use is museum gallery space rented out for private parties in the evening. The mere fact that the gallery is used during the day for educational exhibits does not, by itself, make the income from

---

29. Reg. § 1.513-1(d)(3).
30. Priv. Ltr. Rul. 9147008.
31. *Id.*
32. Priv. Ltr. Rul. 9851052. Likewise, the operation of a guest house, used only by attendees at conferences conducted by a private operating foundation (*see* § 3.1), was ruled to be a related business (Priv. Ltr. Rul. 200030027).
33. Reg. § 1.513-1(d)(4)(i).
34. Reg. § 1.513-1(d)(4)(ii).
35. *Id.*

the commercial rental related income. The test, instead, is whether the rental to private individuals contributes importantly to the accomplishment of the museum's tax-exempt purposes or qualifies for the rental exception.[36]

Activities carried on by an organization in the performance of exempt functions may generate goodwill or other intangibles that are capable of being exploited in commercial endeavors. Where an organization exploits an intangible such as its mailing list or logo, in a commercial fashion, the mere fact that the resultant income depends in part on an exempt function of the organization does not make it related income. In these cases, unless the commercial activities themselves contribute importantly to the accomplishment of an exempt purpose, the income that they produce is gross income from the conduct of unrelated business.[37] Another example of exploitation is advertising in a foundation's periodical that contains reports from a drug abuse study it conducted.[38]

## (d)  Regularly Carried On

To be taxable, an unrelated business must be *regularly carried on.*[39] In determining whether a particular business is regularly carried on by a tax-exempt organization, consideration must be given to the frequency and continuity with which the activities that are productive of the income are conducted and the manner in which they are pursued.[40] This requirement is applied in light of the purpose of the unrelated business income tax, which, as noted, is to place tax-exempt organization business activities on the same tax basis as the nonexempt business endeavors with which they compete. Thus, specific business activities of a tax-exempt organization will ordinarily be deemed to be *regularly carried on* if they manifest a similar frequency and continuity, and are pursued in a manner similar to comparable commercial activities of nonexempt organizations.[41]

Where income-producing activities are of a kind normally conducted by nonexempt commercial organizations on a year-round basis, their conduct by a tax-exempt organization over a period of only a few weeks does not constitute the regular carrying on of a trade or business.[42] Where income-producing activities are of a kind normally undertaken by nonexempt commercial organizations only on a seasonal basis, however, the conduct of the activities by a

---

36.  Reg. § 1.513-1(d)(4)(iii); if unrelated *see* § 11.2(b) for a rental income exception which depends on the level of service the organization provides to the renter.
37.  Reg. § 1.513-1(d)(4)(iv); *see* § 11.2(b) for a royalty income exception.
38.  Reg. § 1.512(a)-1(d)(1), (f).
39.  IRC § 512(a)(1).
40.  Reg. § 1.513-1(c)(1).
41.  *Id.*
42.  Reg. § 1.513-1(c)(2)(i).

tax-exempt organization during a significant part of the season ordinarily constitutes the regular conduct of trade or business.[43] Compare the following activities, for example:

| Irregular | Regular |
| --- | --- |
| Sandwich stand at annual county fair | Café open daily |
| Annual golf tournament | Racetrack operated during racing season |
| Nine-day antique show | Antique store |
| Gala ball held annually | Monthly dance |
| Program ads for annual fundraising event | Advertisements in quarterly magazine |

In determining whether intermittently conducted activities are regularly carried on, the manner in which the activities are conducted must be compared with the manner in which commercial activities are normally pursued by nonexempt organizations. In general, exempt organization business activities that are engaged in only discontinuously or periodically are not considered regularly carried on if they are conducted without the competitive and promotional efforts typical of commercial endeavors.[44] Sales that are systematically and consistently promoted and carried on are deemed to be regularly carried on.[45]

Certain intermittent income-producing activities, such as a benefit golf tournament, occur so infrequently that neither their recurrence nor the manner of their conduct will cause them to be regarded as a business activity that is regularly carried on.[46] Likewise, activities are not regarded as regularly carried on merely because they are conducted on an annually recurrent basis.[47]

When a museum rented an airplane to a company to use for testing purposes, the IRS contended that the personal property rents paid by the company were taxable unrelated business income. A court disagreed with the IRS's position, held that the lease was not a business *regularly carried on*, and agreed with the museum that the transaction was a "one-time, completely fortuitous lease of unique equipment."[48]

## (e) Real Estate Activities

A tax-exempt organization may acquire real property under a variety of circumstances and for a variety of reasons. The acquisition may be by purchase or by contribution and be undertaken to advance exempt purposes or to make

---

43. *Id.*
44. Reg. § 1.513-1(c)(2)(ii).
45. *Id.*
46. E.g., Priv. Ltr. Rul. 200128059.
47. Reg. § 1.513-1(c)(2)(iii).
48. *Museum of Flight Foundation v. United States*, 99-1 U.S.T.C. ¶ 50,311 (D. Wash. 1999).

an investment. The activity may be, or may be seen as being, part of dealings in the ordinary course of a business. Where exempt functions are not involved, the dichotomy becomes whether the exempt organization is a passive investor or is a dealer in property. Often the issue arises when the property, or portions of it, is being sold; is the exempt organization liquidating an investment or selling property to customers in the ordinary course of business?

The elements to take into account in this evaluation are many. One is the purpose for which the property was acquired. Others are the length of time the property was held, the purpose for which the property was held, the proximity of the sale to the purchase of the property, the activities of the exempt organization in improving and disposing of the property, and the frequency, continuity, and size of the sales of the property.

In the absence of use of the property for exempt functions, the factor of frequency of sales tends to be the most important of the criteria.[49] Even in this context, the activity may not be characterized as a business if the sales activity results from unanticipated, externally introduced factors that make impossible the continued preexisting use of the property. The IRS places emphasis on the presence of and the reasons for improvements on the land.

The exception from unrelated income taxation for capital gain,[50] which interrelates with these rules, is not available when the property is sold in circumstances in which the exempt organization is a dealer in the property. Where dealer status exists or is imposed, the property is considered to be property sold in the ordinary course of business, giving rise to ordinary income.

The standard followed in making these determinations, as to whether property is held primarily for sale in the ordinary course of business or is held for investment, is a primary purpose test. In this setting, the word *primary* has been interpreted to mean "of first importance" or "principally."[51] By this standard, the IRS ruled, ordinary income would not result unless a "sales purpose" is "dominant."[52]

In a typical instance, the IRS reviewed a proposed sale of certain real estate interests held by a public charity. In this case, substantially all of the property was received by bequest and had been held for a significant period of time. The decision was made to sell the property (liquidate the investment) due to the enactment of legislation adverse to the investment, so as to receive fair market value. Availability of the property for sale was not advertised to the public. Applying the primary purpose test, the IRS concluded that the proposed sales did not involve property held primarily for sale to customers in the ordinary course of business.[53]

---

49. In part, this is due to the regularly carried on test (*see* § 11.1(d)).
50. *See* § 11.2.
51. *Malat v. Riddell*, 383 U.S. 569 (1966).
52. Priv. Ltr. Rul. 9316032.
53. *Id.*

By contrast, a charitable organization purchased real estate, divided it into lots, and improved the lots. The project evolved into the equivalent of a municipality. Lots were sold to the general public pursuant to a marketing plan involving real estate companies. The IRS concluded that the subdivision, development, and sale of the lots was a business that was regularly carried on, "in a manner that is similar to a for-profit residential land development company." The organization advanced the argument that the land development and sales were done in furtherance of exempt purposes, by attracting members who participate in its educational programs.[54] But the IRS concluded that the relationship between the sales of lots for single-family homes and the organization's goal of increasing program attendance was "somewhat tenuous." Therefore, the IRS held that the resulting sales income was unrelated business income.[55] The IRS, however, approved exclusion of gain on the sale of farmland owned by an orphanage. The sales were expected to involve as many as nine separate parcels over a period of several years. The organization characterized its proposed marketing as "patient and passive" without improvements being made to enhance sale to developers. The fact that the property would not be advertised through real estate brokers was also noted as a fact evidencing nonbusiness nature of the sales activity.[56] In a comparable instance, a "liquidity challenged" charitable trust that wanted to sell leased fee interests in three condominium properties was held by the IRS to be able to utilize the capital gain exclusion; the underlying land was acquired by the trust by gift nearly 100 years before the proposed transaction, and most of the land had been maintained to produce rental income in support of the trust's exempt activities.[57]

Even if the primary purpose underlying the acquisition and holding of real property is advancement of exempt purposes, the IRS may apply the fragmentation rule[58] in search of unrelated business. As the IRS stated the matter in one instance, a charitable organization "engaged in substantial regularly carried on unrelated trade [or] business as a component of its substantially related land purchase activity."[59] The IRS looked to substantial and frequent sales of surplus land that were not intended for exempt use, and found that those sales were unrelated businesses. The same factors were used to reach that conclusion as are used in the general context, such as the sale of land shortly after its purchase and the extent of improvements.

---

54. An argument of this nature was accepted in *Junaluska Assembly Housing, Inc. v. Commissioner*, 86 T.C. 1114 (1986).
55. Tech. Adv. Mem. 200047049.
56. Priv. Ltr. Rul. 200210029.
57. Priv. Ltr. Rul. 200728044.
58. *See* § 11.1(b).
59. Priv. Ltr. Rul. 200119061.

## § 11.2  EXCEPTIONS

A variety of types of income or activities is exempt from taxation under the unrelated business income rules, though some of these exceptions are of little or no utility to private foundations.

The fact that forms of *passive income* are exempt from unrelated business income taxation, however, is significant to private foundations.[60] This type of income is exempt from unrelated income taxation by virtue of a host of *modifications.*[61] For private foundations, the following types of income that are protected by passive income modifications are the most pertinent:

- Dividends, interest, payments with respect to securities loans, amounts received or accrued as consideration for entering into agreements to make loans, income from notional principal contracts, annuities, and other substantially similar income from ordinary and routine investments.[62]

- Royalties, including overriding royalties, whether measured by production or by gross or taxable income from a property.[63]

- Rents from real property and rents from personal property leased with real property (where the rent from personal property is incidental to the total rent).[64]

- Capital gains and gains recognized from the lapse or termination of options to buy or sell securities.[65]

In one instance, amounts realized from the disposition of timber on timberland owned by a private foundation were held to be excludible capital gain,[66] because of a special rule treating this type of economic gain or loss as capital in nature.[67] Some sales of property that may appear to yield capital gain may, in fact, not, if it is determined that the sales amount to an activity of selling property to customers in the ordinary course of business.[68] The IRS developed factors to consider in making this determination: the purpose for which the

---

60. *See* § 3.3.
61. IRC § 512(b). These items of income and capital gain are likely, however, to be subject to a excise tax on net investment income (*see* Chapter 10).
62. IRC § 512(b)(1); Reg. § 1.512(b)-1(a)(1).
63. IRC § 512(b)(2); Reg. § 1.512(b)-1(b).
64. IRC § 512(b)(3)(A); Reg. § 1.512(b)-1(c)(2)(i), (ii).
65. IRC § 512(b)(5); Reg. § 1.512(b)-1(d).
66. Priv. Ltr. Rul. 9252028.
67. IRC § 631(b).
68. E.g., Priv. Ltr. Rul. 9619068 (where a community foundation was able to sell its interests in developed real estate without participating in a commercial business of sales to customers).

property was acquired; the cost of the property to be sold; the frequency, continuity, and size of the sales; the activities of the owner in the improvement and disposition of the property; the extent of improvements made to the property; the proximity of the time of sale in relation to the date of purchase; the purpose for which the property was held; and the prevailing market conditions.[69]

## (a) Royalties

The exception for royalties has proven to be the most contentious of these exclusions for forms of passive income. The IRS and the U.S. Tax Court have different views concerning the scope of this exception. The tax court defined a royalty as a payment for the use of valuable intangible property rights; it rejected the thought that a royalty must be passive in nature to be excludible from unrelated income taxation.[70] Thus, for example, it is the view of that court that certain payments for the use of mailing lists constitute royalties.[71] It also extended its rationale in this regard to revenue derived from the use of affinity credit cards.[72] The IRS, by contrast, was of the view that when an exempt organization performs services to or for the benefit of the payor, or otherwise is actively involved in the activity that generates the income—such as a partnership or in maintaining a membership list—the entity is participating in a joint venture, so that the exclusion is unavailable. For some time, the IRS continued to insist that the only royalties that are statutorily excluded from unrelated business income are those that are forms of investment income or otherwise are passive in nature.[73]

One court of appeals is of the view that the tax court's definition of the term is too broad, in that a royalty "cannot include compensation for services rendered by the owner of the property."[74] This position, then, is a compromise between the approach of the tax court and that of the IRS on the point. Thus, the appellate court wrote that, to the extent the IRS "claims that a tax-exempt organization can do nothing to acquire such fees," the agency is "incorrect."[75] Yet the court continued, "to the extent that . . . the exempt organization involved appears to argue that a 'royalty' is any payment for the use of a

---

69. E.g., Priv. Ltr. Rul. 9619069.
70. This view was first articulated in *Disabled American Veterans v. Commissioner*, 94 T.C. 60 (1990), *rev'd on other grounds*, 942 F.2d 309 (6th Cir. 1991).
71. *Sierra Club, Inc. v. Commissioner*, 65 T.C.M. 2582 (1993); *Disabled American Veterans v. Commissioner*, 94 T.C. 60 (1990), *rev'd on other grounds*, 942 F.2d 309 (6th Cir. 1991). These cases involve situations where the statutory exclusion for mailing list revenue is unavailable (*see* text accompanied by *infra* note 104).
72. *Sierra Club, Inc. v. Commissioner*, 103 T.C. 307 (1994).
73. E.g., Tech. Adv. Mem. 9509002.
74. *Sierra Club, Inc. v. Commissioner*, 86 F.3d 1526, 1532 (9th Cir. 1996).
75. *Id.* at 1535.

property right—such as a copyright—regardless of any additional services that are performed in addition to the owner simply permitting another to use the right at issue, we disagree."[76] Following this and subsequent defeats, the IRS, by the end of 1999, instructed its agents to cease attempts to apply its definition of the term *royalty* in cases of this nature.

Mineral royalties are excluded from taxation, whether measured by production or by gross or taxable income from the mineral property. Where, however, a tax-exempt organization owns a working interest in a mineral property, even if it is relieved of its share of the development costs by the terms of any agreement with an operator, income received from the interest is not excluded from taxation. Payments in discharge of mineral production payments are treated in the same manner as royalty payments for the purpose of computing unrelated business taxable income. To the extent that the carve-out is treated as a loan, the portion of each production payment that is the equivalent to interest is excluded as interest for purposes of unrelated business income taxation.[77]

## (b) Rents

The exclusion for rent is not available where more than 50 percent of the total rent received or accrued under the lease is attributable to personal property.[78] Moreover, rental income is not excluded where the determination of the amount of the rent depends, in whole or in part, on the income or profits derived by any person from the property leased (other than an amount based on a fixed percentage or percentages of gross receipts or sales).[79] Further, in the

---

76. *Id.* The U.S. Court of Appeals for the Ninth Circuit affirmed the opinion in *Sierra Club, Inc. v. Commissioner*, 65 T.C.M. 2582 (1993), because of the organization's minimal involvement in the royalty generation process. By contrast, the court reversed and remanded *Sierra Club, Inc. v. Commissioner*, 103 T.C. 307 (1994) (*see supra* note 72) for a trial of the case in light of the court's revised definition of the term *royalty*. Even with that revised definition, however, the tax court held that the affinity card payments were royalties (*Sierra Club, Inc. v. Commissioner*, 77 T.C.M. 1569 (1999)); the government elected not to appeal this decision. *See* also *Oregon State University Alumni Association, Inc. v. Commissioner; Alumni Association of the University of Oregon, Inc. v. Commissioner*, 99-2 U.S.T.C. ¶ 50,879 (9th Cir. 1999).

77. Reg. § 1.512(b)-1(b).

78. IRC § 512(b)(3)(B)(i); Reg. § 1.512(b)-1(c)(2)(iii)(a).

79. IRC § 512(b)(3)(B)(ii); Reg. § 1.512(b)-1(c)(2)(iii)(b). A classic illustration of the lines to be drawn in this area is the litigation over the issue of sharecrop lease arrangements; the courts have held that the income from these arrangements received by tax-exempt organizations is rent within the scope of the exclusion, rather than income generated out of a joint venture that is not in furtherance of exempt purposes (e.g., *Harlan E. Moore Charitable Trust v. United States*, 812 F. Supp. 130 (C.D. Ill. 1993), *aff'd*, 9 F.3d 623 (7th Cir. 1993); *Trust U/W Emily Oblinger v. Commissioner*, 100 T.C. 114 (1993); *Independent Order of Odd Fellows Grand Lodge of Iowa v. United States*, 93-2 U.S.T.C. ¶ 50,448 (S.D. Iowa 1993); *White's Iowa Manual Labor Institute v. Commissioner*, 66 T.C.M. 389 (1993)).

view of the IRS, the exclusion for rent is unavailable in the case of payments for the use or occupancy of rooms and other space where services are rendered to the occupants that are primarily for their convenience and are other than those usually or customarily rendered in connection with the rental of rooms or other space for occupancy only.[80] Thus, apartment rentals are normally excluded, while hotel room rentals are included.

Examples of rentals that have been deemed to involve the provision of services and thereby treated as unrelated business income not excludible as passive rents include:

- The storage of trailers, campers, motor homes, boats, and cars in the exhibition halls not being used during winter months by an exempt agricultural organization was found to involve the provision of services on a level that caused the rentals to be treated as taxable unrelated income.[81]

- Substantial services were found to be provided to corporate and business patrons who rented a museum's facilities for receptions in the evenings. The services provided included maintenance and security personnel and liquor service (because the museum held the license). The IRS was not convinced that the rentals served an exempt purpose in finding the programs were primarily social- or business-oriented and included such items as cocktails, dinner-dances, awards presentations, and holiday celebrations. While there was some educational benefit to the attendees of viewing exhibits, they were ancillary to the events' principal purpose.[82] The IRS noted that the holding would be different if request was for the organization to create an educational event in its space, with the food and services provided only incidentally.

- Sharecrop arrangements for farmland owned by a foundation may or may not be treated as excludible from unrelated business income under the rent exception. The method for calculating the rent and risk inherent in the agreement is determinative. The issue is whether the foundation is a joint venturer participating in the farming operations. The following factors were considered in court cases on the subject:[83]

  ○ The organization is not involved in the day-to-day operation of the farm; it simply provides the land and buildings.

  ○ The organization bears no risk of loss from accidents.

---

80. Reg. § 1.512(b)-1(c)(5).
81. Tech. Adv. Mem. 9822006.
82. Priv. Ltr. Rul. 9702003.
83. See the court opinions referenced in *supra* note 79.

- ○ The organization is not required to contribute to any losses from the operation, but pays only an agreed portion of the operating expenses (in one case 50 percent).
- ○ The rent is equal to a fixed percentage of the gross sale of the crop or a fixed amount, not a percentage of net profits.[84]

Parking lot rental presents a similar situation. Rental of the bare real estate to another party that operates the lot (where the foundation has no relationship or responsibility to the parkers) clearly produces passive rental income.[85] If the foundation provides some services to the operator, the passive income exclusion may not apply.

Operation of a parking lot for the benefit of employees and persons participating in an exempt organization's functions, rather than disinterested persons, may be a related activity.[86] A parking rate structure "not consistent with commercially operated for-profit facilities in the same metropolitan area" was found to reflect an organization's desire to provide a necessary service to the public.

Income that is passive in nature may nonetheless be subject, in whole or in part, to unrelated income taxation in one of two circumstances:

1. Where the income is debt-financed income.[87]
2. Where the income is derived from a controlled corporation.[88]

As to the latter, the rule applies where there is the appropriate degree of control of the subsidiary by the parent. This type of control requires the ownership of stock possessing more than 50 percent of the total combined voting power of all classes of stock entitled to vote and more than 50 percent of the total number of shares of all other classes of stock of the corporation.[89]

## (c) Research

Any income derived from research performed for any person is excluded from the unrelated business tax, where the organization is operated primarily for the purpose of carrying on fundamental research the results of which are freely available to the public.[90] Likewise, income derived from research for the

---

84. IRC § 512(b)(3)(A)(ii).
85. Priv. Ltr. Rul. 9301024.
86. IRC § 513(a)(2); Priv. Ltr. Rul. 9401031.
87. IRC § 512(b)(4); Reg. § 1.512(b)-1(a)(2). *See* § 11.4.
88. IRC § 512(b)(13); Reg. § 1.512(b)-1(l)(1). These rules are inapplicable to the payment of dividends.
89. IRC § 368(c). The tax regulations extend this definition of control to "non-stock" organizations (Reg. § 1.512(b)-1(l)(4)(i)(b)).
90. IRC § 512(b)(9); Reg. § 1.512(b)-1(f)(3).

federal government (including any of its agencies or instrumentalities) or a state government (or a political subdivision of it), is also excluded.[91]

Critical to the scope of this exclusion is the meaning of the term *research*. As noted, the exclusion emphasizes *fundamental* (or basic) research; it usually is not available for applied research.[92] For example, scientific research does not include activities ordinarily carried on incidental to commercial operations, such as the testing or inspection of materials or products or the designing or construction of equipment or buildings.[93] Also illustrative is the case of an organization that tested drugs for commercial pharmaceutical companies, which was held to not qualify for tax exemption as a scientific organization because the testing was regarded as principally serving the private interests of the manufacturers.[94] Likewise, an organization that inspected, tested, and certified safety shipping containers used in the transport of cargo, and engaged in related research activities, was found to not be engaged in scientific research because the activities were incidental to commercial or industrial operations.[95]

### (d)  Nonbusiness Activities

Income may be excluded from unrelated business income taxation because the nature of the activity that produced the income is not similar to that of activities conducted by businesses. Exclusions of this nature that can be of relevance to a private foundation are:

- Income derived from a business in which substantially all of the work in carrying it on is performed for the organization by volunteers.[96]
- Income from a business that sells merchandise, substantially all of which has been received by the organization as contributions.[97]
- Income from a business conducted primarily for the convenience of the organization's students, patients, members, officers, or employees.[98]

---

91.  IRC § 512(b)(7); Reg. § 1.512(b)-1(f)(1).
92.  Reg. § 1.501(c)(3)-1(d)(5)(i).
93.  Reg. § 1.501(c)(3)-1(d)(5)(ii). In one case, this type of activity was described as "generally repetitive work done by scientifically unsophisticated employees for the purpose of determining whether the item tested met certain specifications, as distinguished from testing done to validate a scientific hypothesis" (*Midwest Research Institute v. United States*, 554 F. Supp. 1379, 1386 (W.D. Mo. 1983), *aff'd*, 744 F.2d 635 (8th Cir. 1984)).
94.  Rev. Rul. 68-373, 1968-2 C.B. 206.
95.  Rev. Rul. 78-426, 1978-2 C.B. 175.
96.  IRC § 513(a)(1); Reg. § 1.513-1(e)(1).
97.  IRC § 513(a)(3); Reg. § 1.513-1(e)(3).
98.  IRC § 513(a)(2); Reg. § 1.513-1(e)(2). The IRS ruled that an educational institution's provision of living quarters for its students is an activity protected from taxation by the convenience doctrine (Priv. Ltr. Rul. 200625035); this ruling is incorrect, however, inasmuch as the provision of housing by an educational institution to its students is a related business (*see Tax-Exempt Organizations*, § 24.5(a)), thus there is no need to rely on an exception from the unrelated business rules.

- Income from the conduct of entertainment at certain fairs and expositions.[99]

- Income from the conduct of certain convention activities and trade shows.[100]

- Income from the conduct of qualified bingo games.[101]

- Income from the distribution of certain low-cost articles incidental to the solicitation of charitable contributions.[102]

- Income from the exchange or rental of mailing lists with or to other charitable organizations.[103]

- Payments from a business sponsor that are acknowledged in a fashion that does not contain quantitative or qualitative language are treated as contributions rather than unrelated advertising business income.[104] Even if the "thank you" is limited to the permissible language, an acknowledgment printed in the monthly newsletter is treated as producing unrelated income.

## (e)  Revenue Produced on the Internet

The character of revenues paid to a private foundation from the sales of its own goods and services on the Internet and payments from Internet merchants is an evolving issue. Many aspects of Internet activities are yet to be considered by the IRS. While there is no question that the law, regulations, court decisions, and rulings that apply to identify and tax unrelated business off the Internet can be applied to online activities, certain unique aspects of the Internet prompt unique and unanswered questions. Some practitioners joke about a one-click rule to suggest the first click to a linked site may not produce unrelated income, but two clicks might. The following is a list of questions that a foundation producing revenue from its site should ask.[105] Exhibit 9.13, Checklist for Website Exemption Issues, can be used to survey the many questions.

- *Do the goods and services sold through the site advance the foundation's exempt purposes?* They certainly can. This determination is made in reference to the mission and the purposes for which the foundation was originally found to be exempt. Registration for the Latin class and purchase of

---

99. IRC § 513(d)(1).
100. *Id.*; Reg. § 1.513-3.
101. IRC § 513(f); Reg. § 1.513-5.
102. IRC § 513(h).
103. *Id.*
104. Reg. § 1.513(i)(2)(a); Reg. § 1.513-4(c).
105. *Tax Planning & Compliance*, Chapter 21.

study tapes on the Internet should be treated no differently from physical registration and purchases from the book store.[106]

- *Does the foundation recognize its sponsors or contributors on its website? If so, do the rules delineating donor acknowledgments versus advertisements apply to links to sponsors?[107] When does the link represent advertising for the sponsor?* A simple banner placed on the foundation's site containing information allowed under the sponsorship regulations represents a permitted acknowledgment that is not advertising. Advertising and possibly self-dealing result when the foundation's links to the sponsor's site that contains promotional material indicating the exempt organization endorses the sponsor's products. Simply linking to a sponsor's home, or other page on which promotional material does not appear, does not create an advertisement[108] and should be treated as incidental and tenuous benefit that is not self-dealing.[109]

- *What is the character of income received as "referral fees" from online vendors, such as Amazon.com, to their nonprofit associates? Does it matter whether the payments are referred to as donations, commissions, revenue share, referral fees, or even advertising? Can such payments be characterized as royalties? Does the result change if the link is established to allow the site visitor to purchase books published by the foundation itself?* There should be little doubt that the payments received from licensing the use of a foundation's mailing list and name and logo are royalties.[110] Further, passive royalty income received in an arrangement that does not require the foundation to perform services is not taxable (whether or not it is unrelated). A foundation will therefore compose agreements with commercial distributors that designate such transactions as licensing transactions under which the foundation is not required to provide any services. Certainly very little effort on the foundation's part is involved, so that arguably the passive royalty modification should apply.

## § 11.3  RULES SPECIFICALLY APPLICABLE TO PRIVATE FOUNDATIONS

The principal reason, from a law standpoint, that private foundations have minimal entanglement with the unrelated business income rules is the limitation on

---

106. *See* § 11.1(c).

107. IRC § 513(i)(2)(A).

108. Links to service provider website were approved for an agricultural association in Priv. Ltr. Rul. 200303062.

109. *See* § 5.8(c).

110. See § 11.2(a).

excess business holdings.[111] For tax-exempt organizations generally, it is common for an unrelated business to be conducted by the organization itself, as one of its many activities. When an exempt organization does that, it is operating the business function as a sole proprietorship; the exempt organization is the sole "owner" of the business enterprise.[112] A private foundation cannot, however, "own" 100 percent of a business operated as a sole proprietorship.[113] Therefore, because of this rule, a private foundation generally cannot engage in an unrelated business activity.[114]

## (a) Business Enterprises

The concept of the *business enterprise* is integral to the excess business holdings rules. In general, that term means the active conduct of an unrelated trade or business, including any activity that is regularly carried on for the production of income from the sale of goods or the performance of services.[115] Where an activity carried on for profit constitutes an unrelated business, no part of the business may be excluded from the classification of a business enterprise merely because it does not result in a profit.[116]

There are several ways in which a private foundation can, without adverse tax consequences, engage in a business (or businesslike) activity. These ways are founded on the concept that the activity does not constitute a *business enterprise.*

The principal way to engage in allowable and nontaxable business activity is to engage in a business activity in which at least 95 percent of the gross income of the business is derived from *passive sources.*[117] Gross income from passive

---

111. *See* Chapter 7.
112. A sole proprietorship is any business enterprise (*see* § 11.1(a)) that is actually and directly owned by a private foundation, in which the foundation has a 100 percent equity interest, and that is not held by a corporation, trust, or other business entity for the foundation (Reg. § 53.4943-10(e)).
113. IRC § 4943(c)(3)(B); Reg. 53.4943-3(c)(3).
114. Some exempt organizations participate in unrelated business activity by means of partnerships. The principles of the excess business holdings rules apply, however, to holdings by a private foundation by means of a partnership, joint venture, or other business enterprise that is not incorporated (IRC § 4943(c)(3)). *See* § 7.2(b). As noted (*see* text accompanied by *supra* note 112), for a proprietorship owned by a private foundation to be a sole proprietorship, the foundation must have a 100 percent interest in the equity of the business enterprise. Thus, if a private foundation sells an interest in a sole proprietorship, the business enterprise becomes treated as a partnership (Reg. § 53.4943-10(e)).
115. Reg. § 53.4943-10(a)(1).
116. *Id*. This language, and that of the previous sentence, is identical to that defining a trade or business in the unrelated business income setting (*see supra* notes 7–24).
117. IRC § 4943(d)(3)(B); Reg. § 53.4943-10(c)(1). These types of undertakings are discussed in § 7.1(b). Also *see* Priv. Ltr. Rul. 199952086 in which a charitable remainder unitrust's wholly owned foreign subsidiary's distributive share of U.S. partnership's income was found not to be unrelated business income. Conversely, gain from the sale of an interest in a partnership that held indebted real estate was treated as gain subject to the unrelated business income tax.

sources includes the items excluded under the modification rules for dividends, interest, payments with respect to securities loans, amounts received as consideration for entering into agreements to make loans, annuities, royalties, rents, capital gains, and gains from the lapse or termination of options to buy or sell securities.[118] For example, a private foundation held, as an investment, a fee ownership interest in several thousand acres of timberland and received capital gain pursuant to timber cutting contracts; the IRS ruled that the foundation's ownership of the timberland was not a business enterprise, inasmuch as at least 95 percent of the gross income from the property was capital gain.[119]

There are two refinements as to these rules:

1.  A bond or other evidence of indebtedness does not constitute a holding in a business enterprise, unless the bond or evidence of indebtedness is otherwise determined to be an equitable interest in the enterprise.[120]

2.  A leasehold interest in real property does not constitute an interest in a business enterprise, even though rent payable under the lease is dependent, in whole or in part, on the income or profits derived by another person from the property, unless the leasehold interest constitutes an interest in the income or profits of an unrelated business.[121]

Thus, as long as the income is generated as one or more forms of these or other types of passive activity, the income will not—a general rule—be taxed as unrelated business income. This exception, then, usually shields from unrelated income taxation most forms of investment income.

Consequently, as a general proposition, a private foundation may freely invest in (or receive as a contribution and retain) securities without becoming subject to the unrelated business income rules. The same is generally true with respect to rental property, although the income may be taxed if the rental property is used in an active business operation, if the rent is based on the lessee's net income or profits, or if the property is indebted. As to royalties, as long as the income is passive in nature, it is not taxable; otherwise, understanding of the scope of the exclusion must await the outcome of litigation.[122]

Gross income from passive sources also includes income from the sale of goods (including charges or costs passed on at cost to purchasers of the goods or income received in settlement of a dispute concerning or in lieu of the exercise of the right to sell the goods) if the seller does not manufacture, produce, physically receive or deliver, negotiate sales of, or maintain inventories in

---

118.  IRC § 4943(d)(3), last sentence; Reg. § 53.4943-10(c)(2). *See* § 11.2, text accompanied by notes 60–67.
119.  Priv. Ltr. Rul. 9252028.
120.  Reg. § 53.4943-10(a)(2).
121.  *Id.*
122.  *See* text accompanied by *supra* note 77.

the goods.[123] For example, where a corporation purchases a product under a contract with the manufacturer, resells it under contract at a uniform markup in price, and does not physically handle the product, the income derived from that markup meets the definition of passive income.[124] By contrast, income from individually negotiated sales, such as those made by a broker, would not meet the definition, even if the broker did not physically handle the goods.[125]

If, in a year, less than 95 percent of the income of a trade or business is from passive sources, a private foundation may, in applying this 95 percent test, substitute for the passive source gross income in the year, the average gross income from passive sources for the 10 years immediately preceding the year in question.[126] Thus, stock in a passive holding company is not to be considered a holding in a business enterprise even if the company is controlled by the foundation; instead, the foundation is treated as owning its proportionate share of any interests in a business enterprise held by the company.[127]

A private foundation should be cautious when attempting to maximize the value of real property that it holds, whether it is property originally invested in by the foundation or acquired by gift. A private foundation can own or have an expectancy interest in this type of property for years, then be tempted to improve it, sell it, or otherwise generate maximum value for the holding. A plan of maximizing value may have been initiated while the property was held by a prior owner, such as a donor or property in an estate that was protected by the estate administration exception.[128] The private foundation may want to continue that plan or initiate one of its own; its trustees may believe that, as a matter of prudent management of assets, that is the proper course of conduct. Nonetheless, unless the property is being (or will be) used for exempt purposes, the foundation should be wary about being classified, for tax purposes, as a dealer in the property. This classification not only raises difficult unrelated business issues—it also entails excess business holdings issues.[129]

## (b) Permitted Businesses

There are two other ways in which a private foundation can, without adverse tax consequences, actively engage in a business activity:

1. Operate a *functionally related business* that accomplishes its exempt purposes, such as a research institute or publication program.[130]

---

123. IRC § 4943(d)(3), last sentence.
124. *See* § 5.11.
125. *Id.*
126. Reg. § 53.4943-10(c)(2).
127. *Id.*
128. *See* § 5.11.
129. *See* Chapter 7.
130. IRC § 4943(d)(3)(A); Reg. § 53.4943-10(b). *See* § 7.3.

**2.** Own business holdings that include *program-related investments*,[131] which are related undertakings.[132]

Passive income from controlled subsidiaries is generally taxable as unrelated business income.[133] Generally, a private foundation cannot own a subsidiary because of the excess business holdings rules.[134] A private foundation may, however, be able to own a controlled organization that generates passive income. For some time, a private foundation could avoid unrelated income taxation in this context either by owning less than 80 percent of the interest in the subsidiary (often an impracticality) or by sharing ownership of the subsidiary with another foundation. For example, two private foundations could each own 50 percent of the subsidiary. Or one foundation could own all of the stock entitled to vote (common stock), and the other foundation could own all of the stock of another class (such as nonvoting preferred stock). Tax avoidance on either of these bases was, however, eliminated by a change in the law in 1997, which reduced the control standard to a more-than-50 percent test and introduced an indirect control rule.[135]

These exceptions may be obviated where a private foundation incurred debt to acquire or improve a property.[136] That is, the resulting income may be taxed, in whole or in part, as unrelated business income, notwithstanding the fact that it is passive income. (This type of income nonetheless retains its character as passive income for purposes of the excess business holdings rules.)[137]

### (c)  Partnerships and S Corporations

A private foundation's share of unrelated business income from a partnership, whether or not distributed or paid to the foundation, flows through to and retains its character as unrelated business income received by the foundation.[138] If the partnership conducts a trade or business that is unrelated to the foundation's exempt purpose, the foundation's share of the business income, less associated deductions, must be reported as unrelated business taxable income on Form 990-T and income tax be paid on the income. The exceptions and modifications pertaining to passive income apply to exclude the foundation's

---

131.  Reg. § 53.4943-10(b).
132.  *See* § 8.3.
133.  *See* text accompanied by *supra* notes 89–90.
134.  *See* Chapter 7.
135.  *See supra* note 90. The indirect control rule utilizes the constructive ownership rules in IRC § 318.
136.  *See* § 11.4.
137.  Reg. § 53.4943-10(c)(2).
138.  IRC § 512(c)(1).

share of interest or other passive income distributed by the partnership. This rule applies to foundations that are general and limited partners.[139] The instructions to Form 1065 filed by partnerships require that the entity provide sufficient information to tax-exempt partners to allow them to correctly report unrelated income items. In the authors' experience, however, such information is sometimes found lacking or confusing. See Exhibit 11.3 for a checklist to use in reviewing K-1 reporting issues.

Financial advisors to institutional investors have created sophisticated forms of investment vehicles in recent years. Some trade securities, some buy rental buildings, some buy security hedges, and some invest in venture capital. The income tax rules pertaining to the character of income earned are sometimes complex. Those that invest in real estate (both partnerships and real estate investment trusts) commonly distribute income attributable to indebted property that may be taxable as unrelated income.[140] A partnership that elects to use the mark-to-market rules[141] for security trading reports the income on line 1 of Form K-1, "ordinary income from trade or business," to its partners although it actually has realized short-term capital gain. This type of income is not, however, treated as unrelated business income to a foundation (and other tax-exempt organizations).[142] Dividends, interest, payments with respect to securities loaned, annuities, income from notional principal contracts, or other substantially similar income from ordinary and routine investment[143] are modified or excluded from unrelated business income. Income from the sale of property "other than stock in trade or other property of a kind which would properly be included in the inventory of the organization if on hand at the close of the tax year" is also excluded.[144] Thus, the gain or loss is specifically excluded from the computation of unrelated business income unless the partnership is a dealer in securities. Additionally, gain from the lapse or termination (sale) of options to buy or sell securities written in connection with the organization's investment activity is excluded from unrelated business income.[145]

Until January 1, 1994, distributions from publicly traded partnerships were fully taxable to the tax-exempt partner, including retirement plans. After 1994, the partnership's income is fragmented to allow each type of income to flow through to the tax-exempt partner according to the general rule. Thus, partnership income or loss retains its character as either taxable business income or

---

139. *Service Bolt Nut Co. Profit Sharing Trust v. Commissioner*, 724 F.2d 519 (6th Cir. 1983), *aff'g* 78 T.C. 812 (1982).
140. *See* § 11.4.
141. IRC § 475.
142. Reg. § 1.512(b)-1(d)(1), (2).
143. Reg. § 1.512(b)-1(a)(1).
144. Reg. § 1.512(b)-1(d)(1).
145. Reg. § 1.512(b)-1(d)(2).

**Exhibit 11.3**

---

Form K-1 Analysis for Unrelated Business Income Reporting Purposes

---

**Name of Partnership** _____

**Prepared by:** _____     **Reviewed by:** _____

| | Check if Yes | |
|---|---|---|
| Part III, line 20 lists Code V | ☐ | Yes here indicates UBI, amounts should be shown and explained. |
| Part II, Line K type not exempt organization | ☐ | If corporation, trust, or individual listed, K-1 preparer should be asked to furnish Code V information, if any. |
| Part II, Line M reflects indebtedness | ☐ | Acquisition debt turns otherwise non-UBI passive income (lines 5–9) into UBI. Partnership should be asked to provide Code V information. |
| Part II, Line N checks box "Tax basis" or "704(b) basis" | ☐ | Capital account cannot be used for MIR calculations. Foundation should request partnership to provide annual valuations of net assets and/or overall partnership values. |
| Part II, Line N checks box "GAAP basis" | ☐ | Capital account *can* be used for MIR calculations. |
| Part III, line 1 reflects "Ordinary income" | ☐ | Certain security transactions realized by a security trader may pass through as UBI, but the PF should rely on Code V info. |
| Part III, line 2, Net rental income (loss) | ☐ | Indebted real property or unindebted hotel or service-providing facilities produce UBI. Again, PF should be able to rely on Code V information. |
| Part III, line 3, Other net rental income (loss) | ☐ | Rental of personal property produces UBI whether or not there is debt. PF can rely on the Code V info unless it has knowledge personal property is rented. |
| Part III, line 4, Guaranteed payments | ☐ | If PF renders no services, such as family limited partnership, no UBI results. |
| Part III, lines 5–9 reports investment income | ☐ | Interest, dividends, rents, royalties, and capital gains normally not UBI (see Part II, line M). |
| Part III, line 10, § 1231 gain | ☐ | This gain results from sale of business-use assets and could be UBI, but again PF should be able to rely on Code V absent other information. |
| Part III, line 11, Other income | ☐ | Codes C (Contracts/straddles) and F (Other income) probably deserve investigation if amount is more than 10% of PF's income, or $10,000, whichever is lower. |
| Part III, line 20, Other information | ☐ | Code V identifies UBI income, but some K-1s present UBI with Code W. |

**Exhibit 11.3**   (Continued)

| Instructions | • Complete this form for each K-1 PF receives. |
|---|---|
| | • Combined unrelated income/loss of $1,000 necessitates filing Form 990-T. |
| | • Total of all income/deductions on K-1 should be reported on Line 11 of Form 990-PF, except for capital gains (report on lines 6–7). |
| | • If no Code V or UBI information is provided and indebtedness is shown, K-1 preparer should be asked to provide UBI information. |

passive investment income in the hands of the tax-exempt partner.[146] A *publicly traded partnership* is one for which interests in it are traded on an established securities market or are readily tradable on a secondary market.[147]

Tax-exempt charitable organizations are eligible, effective for tax years beginning after December 31, 1997, to become shareholders of an S corporation.[148] Stock in an S corporation, however, represents an interest in an unrelated trade or business.[149] Unlike a partnership, all of the income distributed to an exempt organization by an S corporation flows through to it as unrelated business income, including passive income otherwise modified from tax. Gain or loss on the sale of S corporate shares is also treated as unrelated business income. Thus, whenever possible, a foundation's investment in an entity that will produce significant amounts of passive income should preferably be held in partnership form.

### (d)   Community Foundations' Grant-Making Services

The IRS held that the sale of grant-making services by a community foundation[150] to charitable organizations in its community is a related business, while the sales of administrative and clerical services to them are unrelated businesses.[151]

A community foundation engages, in furtherance of its grant-making, in various internal grant management and administrative functions, including undertaking research of potential grantees, designing and operating strategic

---

146.  IRC § 512(c)(2).
147.  IRC § 469(k)(2).
148.  The Small Business Job Protection Act of 1996, § 1316.
149.  IRC § 512(e).
150.  *See* § 15.4(d).
151.  Priv. Ltr. Rul. 200832027. The law as to the sale of services by tax-exempt organizations, in the unrelated business setting, is summarized in *Tax-Exempt Organizations*, § 24.5(j). In essence, the general sale of services (such as consulting services) to the public is an unrelated business, while the sale of services to related parties is disregarded for purposes of tax law analysis.

grant-making programs, exercising proper oversight over the grants made, and numerous routine administrative, accounting, and clerical tasks necessary for the daily operation of the organization. The sources of funding of the foundation's grants are component funds and certain affiliated noncomponent funds, the latter being supporting organizations, pooled income funds, and other split-interest trusts.

This community foundation proposed to sell its internal grant management and administrative services to other grant-making charities, primarily private foundations, that operate independently in the community and lack the staff, expertise, or resources to conduct their own internal grant-making functions. The foundation's goal in providing these services was to educate and assist these entities to enable them to provide more efficient support to the citizens of the community and ultimately for them to establish cooperative relationships with the community foundation that would maximize the pool of charitable resources available for the strategic funding of community-based programs. The foundation advised the IRS that education will be a core component of all the services it intends to sell and that every participating entity will receive, on a continuing basis, instruction and educational materials from it on tactics for strategic and effective grant-making in the community.

The foundation intended to charge a reasonable fee based on its staff's hourly rate in providing the services. Each participating charitable organization will be required to execute a sales contract with the community foundation, pursuant to which it becomes an "enrollee organization." This contract will include a menu of core organizational functions that the foundation agrees to perform for the enrollee organization. Although the community foundation will generally contract only with organizations located and operating in this community, it conceded that exceptions may be made where an organization is located elsewhere but retains it to administer funds to be distributed within the community.

The following nine services were proposed to be sold to enrollees:

1. Assistance with establishment of a grant-making program (such as development of guidelines and procedures for reviewing requests).

2. Review and evaluation of grant requests and preparation of written reports on findings; this may include the conduct of site visits and pre-grant inquiries to obtain information necessary to evaluate proposals (such as interviews).

3. Preparation of research in specific grant-making areas of interest and/or identification of nonprofit organizations conducting programs in interest areas.

4. Design and/or maintenance of a system of monitoring funded programs.

5. Identification of opportunities for collaboration with other funders.

6. Handling day-to-day inquiries from potential grant recipients.

7. Printing checks for approved grants and expenses, and balancing an enrollee's checking account.

8. Organization and staffing of board and grant committee meetings.

9. Tracking of all grant applications and grants awarded, and generating related reports.

The IRS ruled that these proposed services will constitute the conduct of a variety of businesses that will be regularly carried on.[152] The focus thus was on the question of whether these businesses will be substantially related to the community foundation's exempt purpose.[153] The IRS's analysis began with a review of the primary objective of the unrelated business rules, which is to eliminate unfair competition by placing the unrelated business activities of tax-exempt organizations on the same tax basis as the nonexempt business endeavors with which they compete.[154]

Review by the IRS of the "foundation management industry" as a whole revealed that there are "dozens of for-profit companies that provide services similar to those [the community foundation] intends to sell." These companies provide a "diverse array of services," which the IRS enumerated in great detail, ranging from grant-making services to check-writing and reconciliation services. The agency concluded that these services are "nearly identical to those you propose to sell and that you are in direct competition with the for-profit foundation management industry."

Nonetheless, wrote the IRS, the "fact that commercial entities may also provide similar services, in and of itself, is not determinative as to whether a particular service is or is not substantially related to exempt functions." The agency said that, if the provision of a service "contributes importantly to benefiting the charitable class served by an organization's activities, the commercial nature of the service should not be controlling." If, however, "commercial alternatives are available, the argument that a service is substantially related to an organization's exempt function because the organization is uniquely qualified to provide a particular service to help charitable organizations address unmet charitable needs in the community served by the organization would be difficult to sustain."

The IRS classified the proposed services as *grant-making, administrative,* and *clerical.* The grant-making services, said the IRS, are those referenced in items 1 through 5. These services were ruled to be those that contribute importantly to

---

152. *See* § 11.1(d).
153. *See* § 11.1(c).
154. *See Tax-Exempt Organizations,* § 24.1.

the accomplishment of the community foundation's exempt purpose. By providing this package of services, the foundation was said to be able to "uniquely coordinate" the enrollees' grant-making activities for the benefit of the community, provide advice about unmet charitable needs in the community, and provide advice about how to effectively advance those needs. Noting that "similar services are available from the for-profit foundation management industry," the IRS wrote that the community foundation's grant-making services are "uniquely tailored" to enable it to achieve its exempt purpose "effectively and efficiently." These services, then, ruled the IRS, are related businesses.

The administrative services, held the IRS, are those in item 4 (this class of service is classified twice and differently). The "skill set required to conduct these activities is not," said the IRS, "unique" to the charitable sector. These activities are "conducted throughout the business community on a daily basis by individuals such as office administrators, personnel managers, and executive assistants." The clerical services are said to be those in items 6 through 9. These activities are said to require office staff "trained in general office procedures, including word processing, data entry, and bookkeeping entries." These are the functions of "secretaries, receptionists, and bookkeepers." The IRS held that the administrative and clerical services do not contribute importantly to accomplishment of the community foundation's exempt purposes. Some of these services, which are "generic and routine commercial services," amount, it is said, to "back office administration."

Another element of the law that the IRS considered is the inquiry as to whether an activity is conducted on a scale larger than is reasonably necessary to achieve an organization's tax-exempt purpose.[155] The IRS wrote that an organization's income will be subject to the unrelated business income tax where the activities generating the income are not "narrowly tailored" to accomplishment of exempt purposes. The community foundation's grant-making services were found to be so narrowly tailored; the administrative and clerical services were not. As to the latter, the proposed sales of these services are activities that "encompass a wide range of services and are too broadly conducted." This is a separate rationale for concluding that these activities are unrelated businesses.

The IRS noted that, if the community foundation provided these administrative and clerical services at substantially below its cost to charitable organizations, such as by charging 15 percent of its costs and subsidizing 85 percent of its costs to deliver these services,[156] the resulting income would not be taxable. None of the foundation's services are to be provided at substantially below cost, however.

---

155. *Id.,* § 24.4(b).
156. E.g., Rev. Rul. 72-369, 1972-2 C.B. 245. *See,* e.g., *Tax-Exempt Organizations,* § 7.13.

The IRS reminded the community foundation that it must make a reasonable allocation of the fees it receives from the enrollee organizations, and of the expenses involved, as between the related and unrelated business activities.[157]

## § 11.4 UNRELATED DEBT-FINANCED INCOME

The modifications exempting passive investment income, such as dividends and rent, from the unrelated business income tax do not apply to the extent that the investment is made with borrowed funds, that is, the purchase is *debt-financed.* A classic example of a permitted foundation investment impacted by this rule is a rental building financed with a mortgage.

### (a) Acquisition Indebtedness

The term *debt-financed property* means, with certain exceptions, property that is held to produce income (usually dividends, interest, or rent) and with respect to which there is an *acquisition indebtedness* at any time during the tax year (or during the preceding 12 months if the property is disposed of during the year).[158] Acquisition indebtedness, with respect to debt-financed property, means the unpaid amount of the indebtedness incurred:

- By the foundation in acquiring or improving the property,

- Before any acquisition or improvement of the property if the indebtedness would not have been incurred but for the acquisition or improvement of the property, and

- After the acquisition or improvement of the property if the indebtedness would not have been incurred but for the acquisition or improvement, and the incurring of the indebtedness was reasonably foreseeable at the time of the acquisition or improvement.[159]

If property is acquired by a private foundation subject to a mortgage or other similar lien, the indebtedness thereby secured is considered an acquisition indebtedness incurred by the organization when the property is acquired, even

---

157. *See Tax-Exempt Organizations*, § 24.14. This ruling is inconsistent, in many ways, with the general precepts of the commerciality doctrine, which places great emphasis on exempt organizations' program activities that are in direct competition with counterpart for-profit entities (*see Tax-Exempt Organizations*, § 4.11). No court has made the IRS's distinction among program, administrative, and clerical functions. Also, the notion that the charitable entities purchasing the services are members of a charitable class is inconsistent with the IRS's position in similar circumstances (*id.*, § 7.13). Further, the IRS often seizes on fee-charging as a basis for asserting nonexempt activity (*id.*, § 24.2(e)).

158. IRC § 514(b)(1).

159. IRC § 514(c)(1).

though the organization did not assume or agree to pay the indebtedness.[160] In the case of mortgaged property acquired as a result of a bequest or devise, however, the indebtedness secured by this type of mortgage is not treated as an acquisition indebtedness during the 10-year period following the date of acquisition.[161] A like rule applies with respect to mortgaged property received by gift, where the mortgage was placed on the property more than five years before the gift and the property was held by the donor more than five years before the gift.[162] In order to qualify for the above exclusions, the foundation must not agree to pay the indebtedness on the gifted or bequeathed property.[163] Indebted property not producing any recurrent annual income but held to produce appreciation in underlying value is subject to this rule; thus, the capital gains are taxable.[164]

Income from a short sale of publicly traded stock through a broker is not considered unrelated debt-financed income for an exempt organization.[165] Essentially, the transaction does not involve borrowing to acquire an asset, but instead to sell. The code applies to indebtedness incurred to acquire or improve property. Though it does not seem entirely logical, the ruling describes an exempt organization that "borrows 100 shares of a stock and sells the shares." The broker retains the sales proceeds, plus $250x cash and any income earned on the proceeds, as collateral for the organization's obligation to return the borrowed shares. Although the short sale creates an obligation, it does not create acquisition indebtedness.[166]

The same type of reasoning may be applied to a line of credit secured by the foundation's investment portfolio. Assume, for example, that expected proceeds from an asset sale are delayed and the foundation prefers not to sell its securities to meet its payroll or pledged grants. The proceeds of a margin loan are not used to acquire an income-producing asset, but rather to provide working capital to pay for operating expenses. It could be argued that the loan is equivalent to acquisition because it allows the organization not to sell its investments temporarily. Technically, however, no purchase occurs. The IRS labels such indebtedness as "transitory" and part of a "routine investment program" falling short of acquisition indebtedness.[167]

Some foundations with depressed portfolios beginning in 2008 chose to obtain "transitory" indebtedness. A decision to borrow funds to be able to meet the foundation's mandatory payout requirements is not treated as acquisition of

---

160. IRC § 514(c)(2)(A).
161. IRC § 514(c)(2)(B).
162. *Id*.
163. *See* Priv. Ltr. Rul. 9241064.
164. Reg. § 1.514(b)-1(a).
165. Rev. Rul. 95-8, 1995-1 C.B. 107.
166. *Deputy v. du Pont*, 300 U.S. 488, 497–98 (1940).
167. Priv. Ltr. Ruls. 8721107 and 9644063.

the asset the foundation is choosing not to sell. It is important that the foundation records, such as in minutes of the finance committee or trustees, document the purpose for the borrowing.[168]

Similarly a foundation may hold assets that it does not wish to, or cannot, sell for a number of reasons. When a foundation fully invests its assets in equity securities, the cash flow from dividends may not provide sufficient cash to meet its minimum distribution requirements.[169] If a foundation in these circumstances borrows money to meet its obligations, rather than selling its shares, it could be considered to have borrowed the money to keep the shares. In general, securities purchased on margin by a tax-exempt organization constitute debt-financed property,[170] and borrowing against securities on margin is generally deemed a jeopardizing investment.[171] If instead the foundation holds an unmarketable asset, such as real estate, that it is unable to sell, the debt should not be associated with the property. Temporary borrowing by a trust fund, which collectively invests assets of tax-exempt organizations, was found not to give rise to unrelated debt-financed income.[172]

## (b) Related-Use Exceptions

Acquisition indebtedness does not include indebtedness with respect to property where substantially all (at least 85 percent) of its use is related to the exercise or performance by the organization involved of its exempt purpose or, if less than substantially all of its use is related, to the extent that its use is related to exempt purposes.[173] For example, proceeds received by a private foundation from loans do not constitute taxable income from debt-financed property where the funds will be distributed, in the forms of grants, by the foundation for charitable purposes.[174] Further, acquisition indebtedness does not include an obligation to pay a qualified charitable gift annuity.[175] Also excepted from treatment as debt-financed property are the following types of properties:

- Property to the extent that the income is derived from research activities and therefore excluded from taxation.[176]

---

168. Priv. Ltr. Ruls. 8721107, 9644063, and 200235042.
169. *See* Chapter 6.
170. E.g., *Henry E. & Nancy Horton Bartels Trust for the Benefit of the University of New Haven v. United States*, 209 F.3d 147 (2nd Cir. 2000).
171. *See* § 8.1(a).
172. Priv. Ltr. Rul. 200010061.
173. IRC § 514(c)(4).
174. Priv. Ltr. Rul. 200432026.
175. IRC § 514(c)(5).
176. *See* text accompanied by *supra* notes 90–95.

- Property to the extent that its use is in a business exempted from tax because substantially all the work is performed without compensation.[177]

- Property to the extent that its use is in a business carried on primarily for the convenience of the organization's members, students, patients, officers, or employees.[178]

- Property to the extent that its use is in a business that is the selling of merchandise, substantially all of which was donated to the organization.[179]

- Property to the extent that its income is already subject to tax as income from the conduct of an unrelated trade or business.[180]

The *neighborhood land rule* provides another exemption from the debt-financed property rules for interim income from neighborhood real property acquired for a tax-exempt purpose. This rule states that where an exempt organization acquires real property for the principal purpose of using the land in the performance of its exempt functions commencing within 10 years of the time of acquisition, the property will not be treated as debt-financed property for tax purposes as long as the property is in the neighborhood of other property owned by the exempt organization, which is used for exempt ends, and the organization does not abandon its intent to use the land in an exempt manner within the 10-year period.[181] This rule applies after the first 5 years of the 10-year period only if the exempt organization satisfies the IRS that future use of the acquired land in furtherance of its exempt purposes before the expiration of the period is reasonably certain. This process is to be initiated by a timely filing of a ruling request,[182] although the IRS may provide administrative relief[183] in a situation where a ruling request was not timely submitted.[184]

## (c)  Includible Income

In computing unrelated business taxable income of a private foundation (or any other tax-exempt organization), there must be included with respect to each debt-financed property that is unrelated to the organization's exempt

---

177. *See* text accompanied by *supra* note 96.
178. *See* text accompanied by *supra* note 98.
179. *See* text accompanied by *supra* note 97.
180. IRC § 514(b)(1).
181. IRC § 514(b)(3)(A).
182. Reg. § 1.514(b)–1(d)(1)(iii).
183. Reg. § 301.9100–1(a).
184. E.g., Priv. Ltr. Rul. 9603019.

function—as an item of gross income derived from an unrelated trade or business—an amount of income from the property, subject to tax in the proportion in which the property is financed by the debt. Basically, deductions are allowed with respect to each debt-financed property in the same proportion.[185]

The formula for calculation of income subject to tax is:

$$\text{Net income for property} \times \frac{\text{Average acquisition indebtedness}}{\text{Average adjusted basis}}$$

The average acquisition indebtedness equals the arithmetic average of each month or partial month of the tax year. The average-adjusted basis is similarly calculated, and only straight-line depreciation is allowed.

## § 11.5 CALCULATING AND REPORTING THE TAX

*Unrelated business taxable income* means the gross income derived by an organization from an unrelated trade or business (UBI), regularly carried on by the organization, less business deductions that are directly connected with the carrying on of the business.[186] The foundation becomes a normal taxpayer subject to provisions in the income tax code for purposes of reporting UBI. As discussed, for purposes of this determination, gross income and business deductions are computed with certain modifications.[187] Generally, to be directly connected with the conduct of an unrelated business, an item of deduction must have a *proximate and primary relationship* to the carrying on of that business.[188] Expenses, depreciation, and similar items attributable solely to the conduct of an unrelated business are proximately and primarily related to that business and therefore qualify for deduction to the extent that they meet the requirements of relevant provisions of the federal income tax law.[189]

Where facilities and/or personnel are used both to carry on tax-exempt activities and to conduct unrelated trade or business, the expenses, depreciation, and similar items attributable to the facilities and/or personnel (such as overhead and items of salary) must be allocated between the two uses on a reasonable basis.[190] Despite the statutory rule that an expense must be directly

---

185. IRC § 514(a)(1). These rules are summarized in greater detail in *Tax-Exempt Organizations*, Chapter 29.
186. IRC § 512(a)(1).
187. *See* § 11.2.
188. IRC § 162.
189. Reg. § 512(a)-1(b). The business expense deduction rules are the subject of IRC § 162; the depreciation rules are in IRC § 167. *See* § 10.4 and Exhibit 10.2.
190. Reg. § 1.512(a)-1(c).

connected with an unrelated business, the regulations merely state that the portion of the expense allocated to the unrelated business activity is, where the allocation is on a "reasonable basis," proximately and primarily related to the business activity. Once an item is proximately and primarily related to a business undertaking, it is allowable as a deduction in computing unrelated business income in the manner and to the extent permitted by the federal income tax law generally.[191]

Gross income may be derived from an unrelated trade or business that exploits a tax-exempt function. Generally, in these situations, expenses, depreciation, and similar items attributable to the conduct of the exempt function are not deductible in computing unrelated business taxable income. Since the items are incident to a function of the type that is the chief purpose of the organization to conduct, they do not possess a proximate and primary relationship to the trade or business. Therefore, they do not qualify as being directly connected with that business.[192]

In the case of an exempt organization that derives gross income from the regular conduct of two or more unrelated business activities, unrelated business taxable income is the aggregate of gross income from all unrelated business activities, less the aggregate of the deductions allowed with respect to all unrelated business activities.[193]

The unrelated business income tax rates payable by most tax-exempt organizations, including private foundations that are not trusts, are the corporate rates.[194] Private foundations that are trusts are subject to the trust income tax rates.[195] A charitable donation deduction equal to 10 percent of a nonprofit corporation's net income and 50 percent of a trust's income is allowed for grants paid to other charitable organizations.[196]

The tax law features a four-bracket structure for corporations: taxable income of $50,000 or less is taxed at a 15 percent rate, income in the range of $50,001 to $75,000 is taxed at a 25 percent rate, income in the range of $75,001 to $10 million is taxed at a 34 percent rate, and income in excess of $10 million is taxed at a 35 percent rate. An additional 5 percent surtax is imposed on taxable income between $100,000 and $335,000, causing a marginal tax rate of 39 percent on taxable income in that range. A similar 3 percent surtax is imposed on taxable income over $15 million, resulting in a marginal tax rate of 40 percent on taxable income in that range.[197]

---

191.  *Id.*
192.  Reg. § 1.512(a)-1(d).
193.  Reg. § 1.512(a)-1(a).
194.  IRC § 11.
195.  IRC § 1(e).
196.  IRC § 170.
197.  IRC § 11(b), as of January 1, 2008.

The tax rate for a trust is 15 percent on the first $2,400, 25 percent on $2,400–$5,600, 28 percent on $5,600–8,500, 22 percent on $8,500–$11,650, and 35 percent on taxable income over $11,650.

Private foundations and other tax-exempt organizations must make quarterly estimated payments of the tax on unrelated business income.[198] The installments are calculated using Form 990-W.

Unrelated business taxable income is reported to the IRS on Form 990-T. See Exhibit 12.4 for a filled-in example. In computing taxable unrelated income, an organization can utilize all related deductions and is entitled to a specific deduction of $1,000.[199]

The instructions accompanying the unrelated business income tax return state that the return must be filed when the foundation has gross income from an unrelated trade or business of $1,000 or more for the taxable year. Note the article *an*. Gross income means the proceeds of sale of an asset, not the resulting gain once the cost basis is deducted to arrive at taxable income. A question arises when a foundation invests in several different unrelated businesses. For example, a foundation receives three Form K-1s from partnerships reflecting a net loss of ($40,000). If one of the K-1s reflects income in excess of $1,000, it is not clear whether the filing of the tax return is required. The regulations refer to "combined" gross income, which seems to indicate that the amounts of the K-1s should be combined.[200] It is customarily prudent to file in such a situation for two reasons: (1) to record the loss to be carried back or forward to offset income and (2) to start the running of the statute of limitations with regard to the tax return. When there is an overall loss, the exposure to a penalty for failure to file is minimal because it is based on tax due.

*Unrelated Losses from Unrelated Business:* A private foundation may have a net operating or capital loss from unrelated activities for the reporting year. Such losses are commonly distributed by hedge funds and partnerships that purchase real estate, securities, and other assets with debt and reported to the foundation on Form 1065 K-1. Gains and losses from different types of unrelated business activities and ownership interests held by the foundation, plus activities conducted directly by the foundation itself, are netted to arrive at the reportable gain or loss. A net operating loss realized in a tax year from an unrelated business activity may be carried back to prior returns when operating gains were reported and taxed. Conversely, net operating losses are not reduced by related income.

As a general rule the operating loss can be carried back 2 years and forward 20 years.[201] Tax years in which no unrelated business activity was realized are

---

198. IRC § 6154(h); Reg. § 1.6302-1(a).
199. IRC § 512(b)(12). See IRS Form 990, Preparation Guide for Nonprofits, for filled-in Form 990-T and detailed suggestions regarding preparation of the form and allocating deductions. In general, *Unrelated Business.*
200. Reg. § 1.6012-2(e).
201. IRC § 172(b)(1).

counted in calculating the number of years for permissible carrybacks and carryovers. Congress extended this period as a part of economic recovery legislation in 2009.[202] A foundation was entitled to carry back a net operating loss from any one year beginning or ending in 2008 or 2009 for three, four, or five years. In the fifth year, the net operating loss carryback can only offset a maximum of 50 percent of the income. The election to file beyond the normal two-year carryback allowed was irrevocable and had to be made by the extended filing date of the taxpayer's last tax year beginning in 2009.

*Capital Losses:* A foundation organized as a charitable trust that has net capital losses from disposition of unrelated business assets and losses distributed from a partnership(s) for the tax year is entitled to offset up to $3,000 of the loss against its other unrelated business income. Such a charitable trust is also allowed to carry forward net capital losses indefinitely to succeeding years to use as an offset against future net capital gains, plus an annual $3,000 deduction against other types of income.[203] A foundation with such losses that is organized as a nonprofit corporation is not entitled to offset the losses against any of its other unrelated business income, but is allowed both a three-year carryback and five-year carryforward to offset past and future capital gains.[204] The loss is treated as a short-term capital loss in each such taxable year. The entire amount of the net capital loss for any taxable year is carried to the earliest of the taxable years to which such loss may be carried, and the portion of such loss that is carried to each of the other taxable years to which such loss may be carried is the excess, if any, of such loss over the total of the capital gain net income for each of the prior taxable years to which such loss may be carried.

*Passive Activity Loss Limitation:* When the exempt organization has reportable losses from indebted real estate properties, such losses may not necessarily be deductible against other types of unrelated taxable income. The instructions to Form 990-T provide: "[F]or limitations on losses for certain activities, see Form 6198 and, for trusts, Form 8582, or, for corporations, Form 8810, Corporate Passive Activity Loss and Credit Limitations, and sections 465 and 469." However, these instructions raise a question about the applicability of the limitation to a nonprofit corporation. The statute states that it applies to trusts, closely held C corporations, and any personal services corporations. A nonprofit corporation with no shareholders and no personal service activity would not seem to meet the definition in the statute.[205] See Exhibit 11.4.

---

202. Worker, Homeownership, and Business Assistance Act of 2009, Pub. L. No. 111-92, 111th Cong., 1st Sess.
203. IRC § 1211(b).
204. IRC § 1212(a).
205. IRC § 469(a)(2)(A).

**EXHIBIT 11.4**

Comparison of Form 990-T Reporting for Corporation versus Trust

| | Corporation | Trust |
|---|---|---|
| Form 8868 | One automatic 6-month extension. *See IRC Reg. 1.6081–9(a).* | One automatic 3-month extension and one additional 3-month extension. *See IRC Reg. 1.6081–9(a).* |
| Contribution deduction[a] | 10% of taxable income. *See IRC 170(b)(2)(A) and 512(b)(10).* | 50% of taxable income. *See IRC 512(b)(11) and IRC 170(b)(1)(A) and (B).* |
| Unused contribution carryover[b] | Allowed to be carried forward for 5 years. *See IRC 170(d)(2)(A).* | Allowed to be carried forward for 5 years. *See IRC 512(b)(11) and IRC 170(b)(1)(B).* |
| Capital loss deduction | Deduction for capital losses limited to capital gains. The loss can be carried back 3 years and forward 5 years. *See IRC 1212(a)(1).* | Allowed a deduction for capital losses up to $3,000. Any remaining losses are carried forward indefinitely until used up. *See IRC 1211(b) and 1212(b)(1).* |
| Net operating loss deduction | The loss can be carried back 2 years and forward for 20 years. *See IRC 172(b)(1)(A).* | The loss can be carried back 2 years and forward for 20 years. *See IRC 172(b)(1)(A).* |
| 2012 tax rates on ordinary income | *See IRC 511(a)(1) and IRC 11(b).* | |
| | 50,000–75,000 (25%) | 2,300–5,350 (25%) |
| | 75,000–100,000 (34%) | 5,350–8,200 (28%) |
| | 100,000–335,000 (39%) | 8,200–11,200 (33%) |
| | 335,000–10,000,000 (34%) | 11,200 + (35%) |
| | 10,000,000–15,000,000 (35%) | |
| | 15,000,000–18,333,333 (38%) | |
| | 18,333,333 + (35%) | |
| | *See IRC 511(a)(1) and IRC 11(b).* | *See IRC 511(b)(1) and IRC 1(e)(2).* |

*(Continued)*

[a] Limited to actual grants paid to charitable organizations not counting directly conducted charitable programs.
[b] To the extent actual grants exceed the deduction allowed, the excess is carried to future years.

**Eхнibit 11.4** (Continued)

|  | Corporation | Trust |
|---|---|---|
| 2012 tax rates on long-term capital gains | Same as above. | If the trust's overall taxable income puts it in the 15% tax bracket, capital gains are taxed at 5%. Otherwise, capital gains are taxed at 15%. *See IRC 1(h)(1)(B) & (C).* |
| Required to provide preparer's identification number on Form 990-T | Yes. *See IRC 6109(a)(4) and 6696(e)(1).* | Yes. *See IRC 6109(a)(4) and 6696(e)(1).* |

# CHAPTER TWELVE

# Tax Compliance and Administrative Issues

The significance the IRS places on the annual information return for private foundations—Form 990-PF—is indicated by the fact that all foundations, even those without assets or revenues, are required to file the form. Equally important, a private foundation is required to make Form 990-PF available for inspection by anyone who asks to see it.[1] Although private foundations no longer need to announce the availability of Form 990-PF in a newspaper, the return is now available for public inspection throughout the entire year rather than the 180 days after the return is filed. Additionally, the return is available for all to see, and print out if they choose, on the Internet at www.guidestar.org and is also displayed on Foundation Center's website at foundationcenter.org.

The foundation must also furnish Form 990-PF to any and all states in which the foundation is registered or qualified to operate and must tell the IRS that it has done so by answering *Yes* to question 8 in Part VII-A. Therefore, most of this chapter is devoted to explaining part by part and, sometimes line by line, the why and the how of completing this important government form. A filled-in Form 990-PF is provided at the end of the chapter. Footnotes are provided in this chapter to refer to other chapters containing detailed explanation of the rules involved.

Clear, correct, and concise preparation of Form 990-PF is vital for a private foundation. It is critical that the form be prepared not only as a financial document, but also as a tool for communicating the foundation's mission and accomplishments to the public. Form 990-PF is designed to accomplish many purposes that go far beyond mere reporting to the IRS. The form provides a wealth of financial and programmatic information to enable government regulators, funders, journalists, and the interested public to measure a foundation's performance as a charitable entity dedicated to benefiting the general public. Therefore, it is crucial that these annual returns be prepared not only as financial documents, but also as tools for communicating an organization's mission and accomplishments to the public.[2] Among others, there are three very important reasons why 990-PF filers need to be diligent in preparing the forms:

**1. IRS Audit Capability:** The IRS is an important player throughout the life of a private foundation. Eligibility to receive tax-deductible donations, the privilege of receiving (mostly) tax-free income, and other special advantages granted by federal, state, and local governments give significant economic value to a private foundation. Tax-exempt status typically begins with recognition of qualification by the IRS in response to the filing of Form 1023. This often arduous process is often the highest scrutiny a foundation will receive from the

---

1. *See* § 12.3.
2. The forms provided some of the information used by the *Boston Globe* and other publications to report salaries and benefits paid to disqualified persons during 2003.

IRS. Form 1023 effective June 2006 is used for this step.[3] Because of staff attrition due to budget cuts and the significant number of exempt status revocations for failure to file returns explained below, the approval time can be lengthy. It is important that the form be completed with great care to achieve a merit close on the first look by IRS representatives.

IRS oversight of a private foundation continues with the annual filing and potential scrutiny of the Form 990-PF, making it important to understand how that division of the IRS functions. Though a selection of the largest foundations were subject to examination in 2012–2013,[4] there have been very few examinations of modest foundations.

A Tax-Exempt and Government Entities (TE/GE) Division serves exempt organizations, employee plans, and government taxpayers.[5] This division was expected to enhance accountability, technical excellence, and interactive customer service. The intention was to simplify the IRS hierarchy and eliminate regions and districts and their directors and assistant commissioner positions.[6] Since that time, exempt organization matters are handled by the following centralized offices:

- Cincinnati, Ohio, office responsible for determination of exempt status by handling Forms 1023 and 1024 and subsequent issues involving changes in exempt status.

- Ogden, Utah, office responsible for processing Forms 990 filed annually.

- Dallas, Texas, office responsible for examinations.

- Washington, DC, office responsible for technical guidance, training, and overall supervision of exempt organization matters.

As a part of the reorganization, an Advisory Committee on Tax-Exempt and Government Entities (ACT) was established to make recommendations on ways to improve tax administration, policies, and procedures for the TE/GE Division. ACT membership includes a broad cross section of exempt organization representatives plus lawyers, state and tribal government representatives, and university and church officials. ACT, under the leadership of Victoria Bjorklund,[7] designed two charts for the IRS website, entitled *Life Cycle of a Public Charity* and *Life Cycle of a Private Foundation*, which are linked to information and

---

3. The form is discussed and a filled-in example provided in § 2.5; also *see IRS Form 1023 Preparation Guide*. The IRS has issued an electronic prototype of the application.

4. Update of IRS website article May 17, 2013, entitled Exempt Organizations Examinations— Audits of Private Foundations.

5. The Internal Revenue Service Restructuring and Reform Act of 1998.

6. Report of consultants, Booz-Allen & Hamilton, reported in 21 *Exempt Org. Tax Rev.* 179–184 (August 1998).

7. Tax lawyer with Simpson, Thacher & Bartlett, New York.

documents needed to comply with the tax law. The charts resemble a subway map and have lines linking the initial application process with annual filing issues with IRS communications.

**2. Public Disclosure of 990 forms:** A private foundation's reporting responsibilities have entered another dimension and deserve careful attention. The Form 990-PF, 990-T, plus Form 1023 and all IRS correspondence, for all tax-exempt charitable organizations are accessible for one and all to view on the Internet at www.guidestar.org and foundationcenter.org.

Additionally, anyone who contacts a private foundation in person must be allowed to view the return and obtain a copy if they can afford to pay the price.[8] Thus a second reason why accurate and complete preparation of the forms should be given top priority.

A private foundation that files at least 250 returns in a calendar year, including income (a 990-T), excise (990-PF), and employment tax and information returns must e-file their Form 990-PF without regard to assets size.[9] Unfortunately, the instructions to the form do not contain this provision.

**3. Form 990-PF Is Complicated:** Prior to its availability for public inspection and viewing on the Internet, too many Forms 990-PF were poorly and incorrectly prepared. When the authors are asked to review returns prepared by others, we still see significant mistakes and omissions of requested information. The following exhibits are provided at the end of this chapter as tools to enhance understanding of the complex issues and calculations presented on the forms. Use of these guides can aid foundation managers who seek to maintain the foundation's tax-exempt status whole and intact. At the least, the use of these checklists can evidence that the foundation's managers have good faith and intention to comply with the rules.

Exhibit 12.1 Mock-up of Form 990-PF, Return of Private Foundation (beginning with a chart that ties each respective part of the form to the book text on the matter)

Exhibit 12.2 Annual Tax Compliance Checklist for Private Foundation (long version)

Exhibit 12.3 Annual Tax Compliance Checklist for Private Foundation (short version)

Exhibit 12.4 Mock-up of Form 990-T, Exemption Organization Business Income Tax Return

Exhibit 12.5 Description of Major Private Foundation Organizational Issues (grants program, documentation and record-keeping, and compliance with private foundation sanctions)

---

8. The specific rules are summarized in § 12.3(a).
9. IRS website article entitled *e-file for Charities and Non-Profits*, updated August 12, 2013.

The extensive and well-written instructions to Form 990-PF are also a helpful reference. In addition to using this book, one can call 1-877-829-5500 to get an IRS opinion on filing matters for which a ready answer cannot be found or a question on which one simply wants to know their viewpoint. Return preparers might also find that the new "plain language" publications available on the IRS website help explain the rules applicable to tax-exempt nonprofits.

All tax-exempt organizations that are classified as private foundations must file Form 990-PF, and all others are required to file a Form 990, 990-EZ, or 990-N, depending on the amount of their gross income. The Form 990-N, an e-postcard entitled "Annual Electronic Filing Requirement for Small Exempt Organizations," is required for those organizations that normally receive $25,000 or less in annual gross revenue and can only be filed electronically. Failure to file these returns for three consecutive years results in revocation of exemption as of the filing date of the third year.

The IRS, on June 8, 2011, announced that approximately 275,000 organizations have lost their tax-exempt status pursuant to this law.[10] The IRS also announced transitional relief for small organizations;[11] issued guidance as to how organizations can apply for reinstatement, including retroactively, of their exempt status;[12] and rules as to payment of a reduced user fee;[13] and published rules as to allowance of grants and contributions to these entities.[14]

Automatic revocation of a private foundation's tax-exempt status for failure to file annual Form 990-PF is effective on the filing due date of the third year's return unless retroactive recognition is allowed for reasonable causes for failure to file returns. Restoration of exemption is accomplished only by filing a new application for exemption, Form 1023. During the period exemption is lost, the private foundation remains a private foundation required to file Form 990-PF and remains subject to excise taxes outlined in Chapters 5 to 9. Additionally, it must file either Form 1120, U.S Corporate Income Tax Return, or Form 1041, U.S. Income Tax

---

10. Announcement 2011-63, 2011-41 I.R.B. 503.

11. Notice 2011-43, 2011-25 I.R.B. 882.

12. Notice 2011-44, 2011-25 I.R.B. 883. These rules were updated in 2014 (Rev. Proc. 2014-11, 2014-3 I.R.B. 411.

13. Rev. Proc. 2011-36, 2011-25 I.R.B. 915.

14. Rev. Proc. 2011-33, 2011-25 I.R.B. 887.

Return for Estates and Trusts, and pay applicable income tax. The IRS FAQs did not give a citation for this seeming double taxation requirement.

## § 12.1 SUCCESSFUL PREPARATION OF FORM 990-PF

Form 990-PF is designed to accomplish a number of purposes. First, the basic financial information—the revenues, disbursements, assets, and liabilities—are classified into meaningful categories to allow the IRS to statistically evaluate the scope and type of foundation activity, to measure the foundation's taxable investment income, and to tally those disbursements counted in meeting the foundation's 5 percent payout requirement. Second, the form has special parts with information and questions that fish for failures to comply with the federal requirements for maintenance of tax-exempt status for private foundations. The issues addressed by the information presented include, among others, questions such as:

- Are the officers' salaries reported in Part VIII reasonable in relation to the foundation's resources and scope of activity, and if not, has prohibited self-dealing occurred?
- Does Part XIII or Part XIV show that the foundation has made the required amount of qualifying distributions by the end of the year?
- Is the foundation required to pay its investment income tax in quarterly installments because the liability shown in Part VI exceeds $500?
- Does the difference between the book value and the fair market value of the assets reported in Part II indicate that the foundation made jeopardizing investments?
- Do the programs described in Part IX-A constitute direct charitable activity? For a private operating foundation, do the descriptions indicate that the programs are directly carried out by the foundation? Or, similarly, do the program-related investments described in Part IX-B serve a charitable purpose?

In addition to reporting financial activity for the year, the 13-page Form 990-PF enables the IRS to evaluate a private foundation's compliance with the sanctions found in the federal private foundation tax rules and special limitations on activities embodied therein. The technical aspects of those sanctions are presented in Chapters 5 through 9 of this book, which should be studied along with the following suggestions for completion of the form. Sections of those chapters in which the relevant issues are discussed are referenced with footnotes throughout this chapter and on the tax compliance checklist. Form 990-PF, reproduced in Exhibit 12.1, illustrates the depth and girth of information provided with the form. Form 990-PF instructions are 32 pages in length and exemplify the complexity of reporting and compliance requirements for a private foundation. Exhibit 12.1

begins with a cross-reference table connecting the 17 parts of the return with chapters that discuss the issues presented therein. The booklet sent to private foundations by the IRS contains more than 100 pages in total and includes:

- Form 990-PF, *Return of Private Foundation*
- Schedule B, *Schedule of Contributors*
- Form 990-T, *Exempt Organization Business Income Tax Return*
- Form 4720, *Return of Certain Excise Taxes on Charities and Other Persons under Chapters 41 and 42 of the Internal Revenue Code*
- Form 990-W, *Estimated Tax on Unrelated Business Taxable Income for Tax-Exempt Organizations and on Investment Income for Private Foundations*
- Form 8868, *Application for Extension of Time to File an Exempt Organization Return*

If for some reason the forms package is not received, one can request that physical copies of the forms and instructions be mailed by calling 1-800-829-3676. Forms that can be downloaded, filled in, printed, and saved (in Adobe Acrobat format) are also available at www.irs.gov/forms.

Form 990-PF has evolved, over more than 40 years as the law of private foundations has developed, retaining original concepts and adding new ones. Certain interdependent calculations do not follow in logical order, and the return cannot be prepared from front to back sequentially. The most efficient order in which to prepare the form is:

| Step | Part | Step | Part |
|------|------|------|------|
| 1 | IV | 8 | XII, lines 1–4 |
| 2 | I and II | 9 | V and VI |
| 3 | Heading | 10 | XII, lines 5–6 |
| 4 | III | 11 | XI |
| 5 | VII-A | 12 | XIII |
| 6 | VIII | 13 | VII-B |
| 7 | IX-A–X | 14 | XIV–XVII |

Information specific to the foundation is entered in the boxes at the top of page 1 of Form 990-PF. The boxes are self-explanatory, with one exception. There are no instructions for Box C, entitled "If exemption application is pending, check here." A dilemma arises when a new foundation reaches its first filing deadline before the application for exemption[15] has been filed. The word *pending* is not defined. Fortunately, the regulations provide:

---

15. This form is displayed and described in Exhibit 2.2.

> An organization claiming an exempt status under § 501(a), prior to the establishment of such exempt status under § 501 and § 1.501(a)-1, shall file a return required by this section [Form 990-PF if a private foundation] in accordance with the instructions applicable thereto. In such case, the organization must indicate on such return that it is being filed in the belief that the organization is exempt under § 501(a), but that the Internal Revenue Service has not yet recognized such exemption.[16]

A recommendation has been made that the IRS change the instructions and that the description of Box C be changed to replace the words "application pending" with "exemption not yet established."

## (a)  Part I, Analysis of Revenue and Expenses

Part I of Form 990-PF may be the most challenging and difficult part, because some discretion is involved in presenting the information, particularly the expenses. The instructions for this part, in a very helpful fashion, begin by informing the preparer that the three right-hand columns may not necessarily equal the total amount of expenses shown in the leftmost column. Each of the columns in Part I serves a different purpose in the IRS regulatory scheme for private foundations. Deciding what goes where and why is not a logical process. Different accounting methods are used for reporting information in the columns, and some items are included in more than one column, while others are not.

**Column (a). Revenue and Expenses per Books.**  This column agrees with financial reports prepared for the board and for public dissemination by the organization. Either the cash method or the accrual method of accounting is permitted, in keeping with the system regularly used to prepare financial statements for other purposes. Occasionally a foundation changes its accounting method for financial, and correspondingly for tax, purposes. Form 3115 must be filed to seek IRS approval for changing the tax reporting method from cash to accrual basis while the change is essentially automatic. For a foundation adopting the accounting literature set out in Statements of Financial Accounting Standards (SFAS) No. 116 (concerning the time for reporting contributions received and paid out) and SFAS No. 124 (covering the reporting of investments), this change was allowed automatically.

Even though the foundation is instructed as a general rule to follow the same method of reporting income and expense it utilizes for financial reporting purposes, the tax rules require different reporting in certain respects. In-kind contributions of services and the use of property or facilities are not included for tax purposes. The basis of property the foundation received as a donation may be different for tax purposes from what it is for financial purposes, as reflected in

---

16. Reg. § 1.6033-2(c).

the following discussion of Lines 6 and 7. Thus, the capital gains shown in column (a) calculated using book basis may be different from that shown in columns (b) and (c) using the tax basis. Moreover, columns (b) and (c) reflect no losses, and there is no provision for carryover of a net loss for the year.

**Column (b). Net Investment Income.**  Every private foundation and wholly charitable trust is required to pay an excise tax on certain investment income.[17] Column (b) reports the four specific types of income and capital gains subject to excise tax, less associated deductions used to arrive at income subject to the excise tax. The title to this column belies the fact that capital gain from the sale of exempt function assets, not held for investment, is taxable.[18] Column (b) does not include any of the following:

- Unrelated business income separately reported on Form 990-T.[19]
- Program service revenue.[20]
- Profits from fundraising events.
- Net losses from sale of assets.
- Unrealized investment gains or losses recognized under SFAS No. 124.

Expenses directly attributable to the income are deducted in this column.[21] Expenses related to tax-exempt interest income that is excluded from lines 3 and 4 should not be included on Lines 13–23 of column (b). Neither income nor the associated expenses pertaining to unrelated business income are reported in this column. Exhibit 12.1 is a sample completed 2013 private foundation annual information return, and Exhibit 12.4 is a companion unrelated business income tax return that illustrates this situation. These expenses are also not reportable as charitable expenditures in column (d).

**Column (c). Adjusted Net Income.**  This column became obsolete for most foundations in 1976 when only private operating foundation (POF) payout requirements were based partly on the adjust net income. The column is still important for two types.

POFs[22] must spend 85 percent of their adjusted net income on charitable projects they conduct directly. This column calculates what is called *adjusted gross income* by adding up investment income plus net short-term capital gains

---

17. *See* § 10.3.
18. *See* § 10.3(b).
19. *See* § 11.5.
20. *See* § 11.1(c).
21. *See* § 12.1(b).
22. *See* § 3.1.

in excess of losses (a net loss is not entered) and unrelated business income, less expenses attributable to producing the includible income.

Private foundations receiving program service revenues[23] use column (c) to report the income from the performance of its exempt functions. For these organizations, this column is basically used to reduce the expenditures from this income by the income produced so that only the excess expenses in excess of the revenues from program services are reported in column (d).

**Column (d). Disbursements for Charitable Purposes.** The cash method must be used for this column. Under SFAS No. 116, foundations following generally accepted accounting principles (GAAP) report grants approved or pledged for future payment when the promise is made, rather than when the grant is actually disbursed. Such foundations must maintain a parallel accounting system that can prepare a report of grants paid on both the cash (for column (d)) and the accrual basis (for column (a)). For foundations with expenses for the conduct of active programs, the same type of dual reporting is required.

As the title of this column indicates, amounts reported in this column are significant because they count toward calculation of the mandatory charitable payout rules.[24] As a basic concept, any expenses claimed as allocable to investment income are not also reportable in this column. Direct charitable expenditures such as medical care, food, clothing, or cash to indigents or other members of a charitable class, books for a literacy program, printing expenses for producing the books, or other expenses associated with direct program activities are included here. Grants paid to other charitable organizations, fundraising costs, and administrative expenses not allocable to investment income or to adjusted gross income are reported in this column.

### (b)  Line-by-Line Instructions

**Line 1. Contributions, Gifts, and Grants Received.** The total amount of voluntary donations the foundation receives during the year is reported on this line. Schedule B, Schedule of Contributors, is completed if there are contributions of money, stocks, or other property valued at $5,000 or more for the year from an individual or organization. When one donor makes several gifts during the tax year, only smaller gifts of $1,000 or more are added together to determine whether total gifts reach the $5,000 level. The name and address of the donor plus the amount and date of the gift and, in the case of property other than cash, a description of the property, must be entered. An accrual reporting foundation would reflect the present value of pledges for future support reported in accordance with SFAS No. 116 on this line. Distributions from split-interest

---

23.  *See* §§ 6.2(c), 15.5.
24.  *See* § 6.4.

trusts are included here for column (a) purposes. In-kind donations of time, services, or the use of property are not reported as support on page 1. They are not reported even if the services are recorded for financial reporting purposes in accordance with GAAP rules.

The instructions to this line remind the foundation that it must adhere to certain disclosure rules if it solicits contributions of more than $75 for which it gives the donor in return something of value (caution: such a transaction might constitute self-dealing).[25] Similarly, to enable its donors to claim a charitable contribution deduction for gifts to it, the foundation must provide a receipt acknowledging all gifts of $250 or more and indicating whether or not it provided goods and services to the contributor.[26] Penalties are imposed on an organization that does not give a proper disclosure for each quid pro quo contribution. Unless reasonable cause is present, the penalty for each failure to disclose is $10, not to exceed $5,000 for any particular fundraiser.

**Line 3. Interest on Savings and Temporary Cash Investments.**  This line is mostly self-explanatory. The interest earned in a bank money market, checking, or savings account, or other investment accounts of the type reported on Line 2 in the balance sheet on page 2, is reported on this line; interest on a money market mutual fund is instead reported on Line 4. Interest earned on a program-related investment, on a note receivable from the sale of a foundation asset, or on an employee loan would be reported as other income on Line 11.

**Line 4. Dividends and Interest from Securities.**  Income payments from investments in stocks, bonds, security loans, and other financial instruments regulated by state or federal securities law (of the type reported on Line 10 of the balance sheet) are reported here, plus dividends and interest reported on Form K-1 for a partnership in which the foundation holds an interest. Dividends paid by a subsidiary operated as a program-related investment would be reported on Line 11. Capital gain dividends paid by a mutual fund are reported on Line 6. Amounts received from tax-exempt government obligations are included only in columns (a) and (c), not in (b).

**Line 5. Gross and Net Rental Income.**  Gross rents received from investment real or personal property of the type reported on line 11 of the balance sheet are reported on this line. Rents produced through exempt function programs, such as low-income housing, are included on Line 11 of the front page. Rental of office space to other unaffiliated exempt organizations is usually reportable as rents on this line. These rents are reported on Line 11 only if the rental rate is well below the fair rental value of the property and the rental activity is conducted

---

25. *See* Chapter 5.
26. Illustrated in Exhibit 12.6.

for a charitable purpose. Expenses directly connected with the rental income are deducted on Lines 13 through 23.

**Line 6. Net Gain (or Loss) from Sale of Assets.** The gains or losses reported by the foundation for financial purposes from sales or other dispositions of all types of capital assets, including those held for investment, those held for exempt purposes, and those that produce unrelated business income, are reported on Line 6 in column (a) only. By comparison, Line 7 reports, in column (b) only, the gain subject to investment income tax. For sales of assets not subject to tax and therefore not shown in Part IV, a detailed schedule is attached, reflecting the date acquired and sold, gross sales price and selling expenses, cost basis, and any depreciation. Unrealized gains reported for financial statement purposes under SFAS No. 124 are not included here but, instead, are shown as a reconciling item in Part III.

**Line 7. Capital Gain Net Income.** Short- and long-term gains from the sale of foundation property are taxed unless the gain is subject to the unrelated business income tax. Effective for tax years beginning after August 17, 2006, all foundation capital gains may be taxed.[27] A summary of sales reported on Line 7 is entered in Part IV. Importantly, beginning in 2007, for 2006 returns, a detailed list of the sales of publicly traded securities is no longer required. Instead total proceeds and costs for each category of securities may be entered. For planning purposes, it is important to note that property received by the foundation as a donation retains the donor's basis.[28] Since the wealth of a foundation's creator often comes from business interests that are highly appreciated, the foundation receiving such wealth through gifts ends up paying tax on its contributor's gains, albeit at a much lower rate. When market conditions allow, making sales of highly appreciated property in concert with achieving the 1 percent tax rate is desirable.[29] If appreciated property is distributed to the foundation's grant recipients, rather than cash from sale of the property, the gain is not taxed.[30] Gain on investment property sold immediately after its receipt and before the foundation receives current income is taxed.[31]

A foundation with marketable securities may benefit from year-end tax planning because of the rule that does not permit deduction of net capital losses against other investment income. Capital losses are deductible only to the extent of gains, and a net loss expires at year end with no carryover, but wash sales of assets with appreciation may produce allowable gains to offset the losses.

---

27. *See* § 10.3(b).
28. *Id*.
29. *See* § 10.2(a).
30. *See* § 10.2(b).
31. *See* § 10.3(i).

**Line 8. Net Short-Term Capital Gains.** Private operating foundations that complete column (c) separately report net short-term capital gains. The gain increases the adjusted net income of a private operating foundation. If the bottom Line 27c of column (c) is more than Line 6 of Part X, adjusted net income determines the required distributions for a private operating foundation.

**Line 9. Income Modifications.** This line also pertains exclusively to column (c) and mostly impacts the required distributions for private operating foundations. Repayments of amounts previously treated as qualifying distributions,[32] proceeds of sales of assets the purchase of which were treated as qualifying distributions, and the unused portion of funds previously set aside and claimed as a qualifying distribution must be added to income.

Any amounts that were not redistributed by a grantee organization, but were treated as a qualifying distribution in prior years, are also added back on this line in column (c).

**Line 10. Gross Sales.** This line is used by a foundation conducting a self-initiated project(s) that generates sales of inventory, such as an educational bookstore or disabled worker handicrafts. Inventory items are those items the foundation either makes or buys for sale in connection with its charitable programs. Inventory-type items sold in connection with a fundraising event (contribution portion is reported on line 1) are also reported on this line. A detailed attachment grouping the revenue and associated cost by the respective types of items sold is requested. Sales of assets, such as land, buildings, collectibles, or other assets are reported on Lines 6 and 7.

Because the excess business holdings rules[33] generally prohibit a foundation's operation of a business, it is important that these revenues be reported as program-related business income. The gross profit reported in column (c) is reported in Part XVI-A in column (e). This revenue also increases a private operating foundation's annual distribution requirement. This income is not entered into column (b), because it is not subject to the excise tax.

**Line 11. Other Income.** All other types of income, taxable and nontaxable, are reported on this line. The four types of investment income subject to excise tax and not reported on Lines 2 through 7 are entered on this line in columns (a), (b), and (c) (if applicable). Examples of such investment income include mineral royalties,[34] interest on student or economic development loans not reported on Line 3 or 4, rentals from low-cost housing or historical property, and interest,

---

32. *See* § 6.5.
33. *See* § 7.1.
34. *See* § 10.3(f).

dividends, rents, or royalties distributed from a partnership or Subchapter S corporation.

Other kinds of income that are not subject to the investment income tax are also entered on Line 11, but entered only in columns (a) and (c). Fees for services generated in an exempt activity, such as student tuition, testing fees, and ticket sales for cultural events, are good examples of this type of income. Income of this type is entered in column (e) of Part XVI-A, and its relationship to the foundation's exempt activities must be explained. Unrealized gains or losses on investments carried at market value are reported in Part III, not here.

**Lines 13–14. Compensation.** Compensation of officers, directors, trustees, and the like is reported on Line 13. Column (a) of this line should agree with the detailed information in Part VIII reporting compensation paid to each and every officer, trustee, director, and foundation manager. The foundation has a burden to prove that amounts on this line are reasonable and do not result in self-dealing.[35] The amounts paid for compensation on Lines 13 to 15 must be apportioned between that paid in connection with managing and collecting investment income (column (b)) and managing the foundation's charitable programs (columns (c) and (d)).[36] A reasonable and consistently used method for allocating costs to the columns should be followed for this and all the other expense lines.[37]

**Line 15. Employee Benefits.** The cost of providing benefits to employees, such as medical and dental insurance, pension contributions, and the like, are reported on this line. The rules that allow an income tax–paying employer to deduct 401(k) or IRA/SEP plan contributions if paid before the tax return is filed do not apply to allow deduction for such accruals in column (d). The employer portion of federal, state, and local payroll taxes are reported here as well, rather than on Line 18 called "Taxes." The instructions remind the foundation it may also need to file Form 5500 for qualified retirement plans.

**Line 16. Legal, Accounting, and Other Professional Fees.** Fees paid to outside consultants, who are not employees, for services are reported here. A schedule showing the type of service performed for the foundation and amount of expense for each of the three types of services is requested for amounts reported on this line. For example, legal fees paid to create new bylaws, or to prepare property purchase documents, grant agreements, or employment contracts could be so described. Accounting fees for tax compliance services or financial recordkeeping similarly could be so described. Fees to an editor

---

35. *See* § 5.6.
36. *See* § 10.4.
37. *See* Exhibit 10.2 and § 12.1(c).

and designer of an educational brochure would be described and reported on line 16c.

**Line 18. Taxes.**   All types of taxes, except payroll taxes, are reported in column (a), including excise taxes on investment income, property taxes on real estate, and any unrelated business income tax. Only taxes paid on investment property are reported in column (b). Private operating foundations include both excise taxes and taxes paid on investment property in column (c). Only taxes paid on exempt function property are reported in column (d). For nonoperating foundations, the excise tax reduces the foundation's distributable amount in Part XI, Line 2a. Payroll taxes are reported on Line 15.

**Line 19. Depreciation.**   Depreciation is reported in column (a) using the method the foundation follows for financial reporting purposes. Columns (b) and (c) depreciation must be calculated using the straight-line method, and for mineral properties cost depletion, but not percentage depletion, is allowed. The basis of property for this purpose is the same as that for calculating gain. Depreciation is entered in columns (b) and (c) only for the depreciation attributable to investment properties the income of which is reported in those columns.

Depreciation cannot be entered in column (d). The total acquisition cost of an asset used in conducting the foundation's charitable programs[38] is treated as a qualifying distribution during the year in which the asset is acquired. The purchase price of exempt function assets is reported in Part XII, Line 2, and adds to amounts treated as qualifying distributions for the year. The schedule of depreciation expense detail provided for Line 19 can also serve as the schedule for Part II, Line 11, showing investments and accumulated depreciation on the balance sheet. Importantly the depreciation detail can be presented with broad categories of assets, such as office equipment and building rather than a list of each individual computer, desk, or other item.

**Line 20. Occupancy.**   This line should include the rent paid for lease of space or other facilities or, if the property is owned, the mortgage interest, real estate taxes, maintenance, and similar expenses. Utilities and expenses, such as heat, electric, telephone, and trash removal associated with occupied space, are also reported here. Occupancy costs attributable to different types of properties may be reportable on this line. A foundation may pay for space that it occupies itself to administer its investments and charitable programs. An allocation of the occupancy cost must be made between that portion of the space used by persons who manage the foundation's investments (reported in column (b)) and those that manage the grants programs (reported in column (c) and/or (d)). Such an allocation must be made on some reasonable basis (customarily on space used).

38. *See* § 6.5(c).

A foundation might also pay occupancy costs for conduct of its charitable programs, such as a museum building or historic house. Last, a foundation might pay occupancy costs for rental property (reported in column (b)).

**Line 21. Travel, Conferences, and Meetings.** Transportation fares, hotels, meals, and other costs of officers, employees, or volunteers participating in meetings and conferences, conducting active programs, and making grantee site visits are reported here. Only 50 percent of the cost of meals paid in connection with investment income management activities is deductible in columns (b) and (c), a limitation that parallels the individual income tax rules for deductible meals. Honoraria or other fees paid to persons for services rendered in connection with conferences or meetings should be reported on Line 13, 14, or 16.

A foundation reporting travel expense should use a system of documentation designed to prove the travel's exempt purpose. Expense vouchers should reflect the programmatic nature of the expenditures and evidence the absence of any personal expenses. Staff members using a foundation's vehicles or being reimbursed for use of a personal auto should maintain a mileage log to prove that auto usage is devoted to the foundation's affairs. Auto allowances for officers, directors, managers, and key and highly paid employees are included in column (e) of Part VIII. To ensure that traveling costs are reasonable, some foundations adopt a policy of only reimbursing costs at the prevailing per diem allowance provided for IRS expense reporting purposes.[39]

**Line 22. Printing and Publications.** The cost of producing and disseminating information, such as stationery, newsletters, brochures, and websites, about the foundation is reported on this line. A foundation might also report here the cost of publishing and distributing educational materials and books, except to the extent such items are tracked as inventory with the cost reported on Line 10(b). Moreover, subscriptions to outside newsletters such as investment information can be included.

**Line 23. Other Expenses.** Any expenses that cannot be properly reported on the expense lines above should be reported as other expenses, and a schedule must be attached to provide detailed information. Office supplies, membership dues, postage, equipment rental, and amortization of software costs are examples of the type of expenses that commonly are reported on this line.

**Line 25. Contributions, Gifts, Grants Paid.** The total contributions or grants paid (or accrued) to other charitable organizations are reported on this line. Column (d) generally must be reported on a cash basis and include only those contributions and grants actually paid by the organization during the year.

---

39. IRC § 274.

Grants or other payments that are not counted in calculating the foundation's qualifying distributions are not included in column (d). The following types of grant omissions and adjustments are made:

- Returned grant funds are not entered as a reduction, but added back in calculating net qualifying distributions for the year in Part XII, line 4.

- Set-asides are also not entered on line 25, but instead in line 3 of Part XII.[40]

- An accounting adjustment to write off a program-related investment (PRI) is also not treated as an expenditure because such investments are reported in Part XII in the year the investment is made.

- Money received for selling or redeeming a PRI or an exempt function asset is added back in Part XI, line 4, to the extent of the amount claimed as a qualifying distributions when acquired.

- Grant to a controlled organization or another private foundation to the extent not expended by the grantee is added back to the distributable amount since the redistribution requirements are not met.[41]

- Grant to § 509(a)(3), Type III, nonfunctionally integrated organization.

A detailed list, prepared in a way that summarizes each class of activity (e.g., healthcare, education, and disaster relief) and containing the following information, is reported on Part XV, Line 3(a). The total for line 3(a) should agree with column (d) of line 25.

- Name and address of each grantee.

- For individual grant recipients, the relationship by blood, marriage, adoption, or employment to any disqualified person (should be None).[42]

- Tax status of each grantee organization as a public charity. Due to the recent legislation impacting grants to supporting organizations, disclosure of the precise public charity status (i.e., § 509(a)(1) or (2)) is preferable to simply stating "public." If the grantee is another private foundation or a nonexempt organization, this schedule reveals that status and triggers a requirement that additional Expenditure Responsibility information be attached, as explained below in discussion of question 5, Part VII-B.

- Purpose of grant.

---

40. *See* § 6.5(e).
41. *See* § 6.5(a).
42. *See* Chapters 4 and 5.

For column (a) of this line, the foundation reports contributions and grants following the accounting method used for financial purposes. Column (d), however, must be prepared on a cash basis. As a result of the SFAS No. 116 accounting standards, many foundations are now required to book unconditional pledges of support to other organizations in the year a pledge is made; consequently, these foundations now have a significant difference between columns (a) and (d).

**Line 26. Total Expenses and Disbursements.** The total disbursements for charitable purposes shown in column (d) are transferred to Part XII, Line 1a, to measure compliance with the minimum distribution requirement test.

**Line 27a. Excess of Revenues over Expenses and Disbursements.** The difference between revenues and expenses shown here is carried to Part III, the analysis of changes in net assets or fund balances.

**Line 27b. Net Investment Income.** This amount shown in column (b) is the foundation's taxable income that is carried to Part VI to calculate the excise tax on investment income.

**Line 27c. Adjusted Net Income.** Only private operating foundations reflect an amount in this box. This number, if it is more than the amount shown in Line 6 of Part X, is carried to Part XIV, Line 2a, to determine satisfaction of the income test.[43]

## (c) Expense Allocations

Proper identification of expenses directly attributable to management of the foundation's affairs in general, its investments, and its grant-making and active charitable programs is a significant aspect of preparing Form 990-PF. The ordinary and necessary expenses of managing, accounting for, and reporting on investments producing the investment income subject to excise tax are deductible to arrive at net investment income subject to the excise tax. Basically, the rules are the same as the tax rules pertaining to deductible business and investment expenses.[44] A foundation often incurs expenses that are attributable to investments, charitable activities, and services that support both of those functions, such as the salary of its executive director and its office space. The question becomes, then, what portion of the compensation and fees paid to those persons is allocable to each function they perform? In the best situation, foundation personnel keep track of the time they spend performing different

---

43. *See* § 3.1(d).
44. IRC §§ 162, 212.

functions, as described in the following list. At a minimum, a foundation can claim a reasonable portion, such as one fourth to one-half of the total expense of its personnel and advisors, as attributable to its investment income and deducted in columns (b) and (c) (if applicable). The other three quarters or half is reflected in column (d) and adds to the amount of the foundation's qualifying distributions for the year. Upon examination, the IRS will request substantiation of these allocations.

Good accounting is the key to successful completion of the columns on page 1 of Form 990-PF. The accounting rules for allocation of expenses are discussed in Exhibit 10.2. For those foundations with unrelated business income,[45] the allocations can be extremely important, as the foundation must pay tax on that income at normal taxpayer rates. Proper identification of allocable expenses is the goal. Documentation and cost accounting records can be developed to capture revenues and costs in categories and to report them by function. When expenses are attributable to more than one function, a foundation must develop techniques that provide verifiable bases on which expenses may be related to its grant-making and active charitable programs, its investment management activity, and its support service functions. To evidence this functional classification of expenses, a foundation must maintain the following:[46]

- A staff salary allocation system for recording the time employees spend on tasks each day. The possibilities are endless. Each staff member might maintain an individual computer database or fill out a time sheet. The reports should be completed often enough to assure accuracy, preferably weekly. In some cases, as when personnel perform repetitive tasks, preparing one week's report for each month, or one month each year, may be sufficient. Percentages of time spent on various functions can then be tabulated and used for accounting allocations.

- Space utilization charts to assign occupancy costs can be prepared. All physical building space rented or owned can be allocated according to its usage. Floor plans can be tabulated to arrive at square footage of the space allocable to each activity center. In some cases, the allocation is made by using staff/time ratios. For dual-use space, records must reflect the number of hours or days the space is used for each purpose.

- Direct investment management and grant program costs should be captured whenever possible. A computer-based fund accounting system is preferable, in which department codes are automatically recorded as

---

45. *See* § 11.1.
46. For more information, see *Nonprofit Financial Planning Made Easy*, Chapters 6 and 7.

monies are expended. A number of good programs are available, and the cost of the software is easily recouped in staff time saved, improved planning, and, possibly, tax savings. Even the simplest computerized accounting systems permit reporting of revenues and expenses by departments or codes. A minimal amount of additional time should be required by administrative staff to accumulate costs in the desired categories. Some long-distance telephone companies aid the process by providing billing code systems that identify calls by department or function. A large foundation might establish separate accounts with its vendors for each department.

- For costs that cannot be specifically identified, cost allocations must be made on a reasonable and fair basis, recognizing the cause-and-effect relationship between the cost incurred and where it is allocated. Four possible methods of allocating include:

  1. Activity-based allocations (identifying departmental costs).

  2. Equal sharing of costs (e.g., if three projects, divide by three).

  3. Cost allocated relative to stand-alone cost (e.g., what it would cost if a certain department had to hire and buy independently).

  4. Cost allocated in proportion to cost savings.

From 1985 through 1990, Congress placed a limit on a foundation's administrative expenses. General and administrative expense over a limitation equal to .65 percent of the foundation's assets essentially fell through the cracks—it did not reduce income subject to excise tax or count toward the distribution requirements. Based on a study of returns filed during that time, the IRS found the limits ineffective. They were designed to curb abusive situations often found in larger organizations, such as excessive compensation, but the formula missed that mark. The IRS found that it was the smaller foundations that had high administrative expenses, but also had correspondingly high qualifying distributions. Finally, the IRS admitted that the calculations were complicated and burdensome to foundations, and did not recommend their continuance.

## (d)  Part II, Balance Sheets

Both the book value of the foundation's assets and liabilities, and the ending fair market value are presented in Part II. The total in column (c), Line 16, must agree with item I on page 1, top left side. Column (c) need not be completed for a private foundation with assets of less than $5,000. A considerable amount of detail is requested. Certain lines in this part alert the IRS to problem issues, and in those cases detailed schedules are requested. The instructions should be read carefully for the following lines on the balance sheet.

Line 6 Insider Receivables
Line 10 Investments—Securities
Line 11 Investments—Land, Buildings, and Equipment
Line 13 Investments—Other
Line 14 Land, Buildings, and Equipment (devoted to exempt purposes)
Line 15 Other Assets
Line 19 Support and Revenue Designated for Future Periods
Line 20 Loans from Officers, Directors, Trustees, or Other Disqualified Persons
Line 21 Mortgages and Other Notes Payable

For most loans receivable or payable by the foundation, 10 detailed items of information are required: borrower's name and title, original amount, balance due, date of note, maturity date, repayment terms, interest rate, security provided by borrower, purpose of the loan, and description and fair market value of consideration furnished by the lender. This information is submitted to enable the IRS to ascertain the presence of self-dealing.[47]

The schedule for depreciable assets should be prepared to coordinate with the information required to be attached for Part I, Line 19, and Part II, Lines 11 and 14. Likewise, receivable and payable information should bear a reasonable relationship to the amount reported on Line 11 for interest revenue and Line 17 of Part I for interest expense.

The same method used by the foundation for maintaining its normal accounting books and records is followed in completing this part. The fair market value for each category of asset is reported in column (c) for all foundations with assets of $5,000 or more.[48] Only a total is entered on Line 16 for a foundation with less than $5,000. If detailed schedules are requested, they must be furnished only for the year-end numbers. The instructions for this part are quite good and need not be repeated here. Note that foundations following SFAS No. 124 may have essentially identical numbers in columns (b) and (c).

## (e)  Part III, Analysis of Changes in Net Worth or Fund Balances

The information reported on page 1 for Form 990-PF purposes is reconciled to the Part II balance sheet in this part. The information in Part II is reported according to the accounting method under which the foundation keeps its financial records, which may not match the tax reporting rules applicable to Part I. The revenues (Line 3) and expenses (Line 5) that may be reported differently for tax and book purposes include:

- Donated services associated with a capitalized asset, such as fees donated by the architects in connection with a foundation building.

---

47. *See* § 5.4.
48. *See* § 6.2.

- Unrealized gain or loss in the carrying value of marketable securities and other investment assets under SFAS No. 124.

- Change in the accounting treatment of charitable pledges receivable or payable, as required under SFAS No. 116.

- A prior-period accounting adjustment not corrected on an amended return because it was immaterial.[49]

Sometimes a foundation will discover that a mistake was made in a prior-year return that requires correction. Depending on the significance of the mistake, an amended return must be considered. An under- or overreporting of investment income calculated in Part VI signals a need for amendment. As a practical matter, a modest mistake can be adjusted in the currently filed return. A prior-year mistake that impacts a foundation's excess distribution carryover can also be corrected by attaching an explanation of the adjustment to the return and accurately reflecting the carryover in Part XIII. A change affecting unrelated business income tax would necessitate the filing of an amended return.

## (f) Part IV, Capital Gains and Losses for Tax on Investment Income

Effective for tax years beginning after August 17, 2006, capital gains and losses for excise tax purposes are imposed on the sale or exchange of all of the foundation's property unless the transaction qualifies as a nontaxable exchange.[50] As discussed more fully elsewhere,[51] property that is distributed to charitable recipients, rather than sold, is not reported, and any gain is not taxed. For a foundation with substantially appreciated property, this rule provides an important tax planning opportunity.

The gain or loss is calculated by subtracting the amount the foundation paid to purchase the property, adjusted for depreciation reserves, amortization, and selling expenses from the amount of sales proceeds the foundation received.[52] Basis, however, for property the foundation received as a gift is reported in column (g) and is equal to the amount the donor paid for the gifted property, or what is called the donor's tax basis. Property received through a bequest is valued as of the date of death or the alternate valuation date for the decedent.[53]

Notice that only the total capital gain net income is carried from this schedule to column (b) and added to taxable investment income. The short-term portion of the gain is reported in column (c) and increases the amount of adjusted gross income that impacts the amount of direct charitable activity

---

49. *See* § 2.7(c).
50. *See* § 10.3.
51. *See* § 10.2(b).
52. IRC §§ 1011, 1012, 1014, 1015, and 1016 apply in completing this part (IRC § 4940(c)(3)(B)).
53. Reg. § 53.4940-1(f)(2)(i)(B), which refers to IRC § 1015.

expenditures a private operating foundation is required to pay out for the year.[54] A net capital loss for the year is not carried to Part I and is not deductible against other investment income, and no capital loss carryover to a subsequent year is allowed.[55]

As of 2007, for 2006 returns, details of the sales of publicly traded securities are no longer required in this part. Instead one line item for such sales may be entered.

## § 12.2 REPORTS UNIQUE TO PRIVATE FOUNDATIONS

To measure compliance with and enforce the special rules unique to private foundations, Form 990-PF contains 17 parts. The first four discussed to this point[56] essentially report the financial transactions for the year in a financial statement format. The other 13 parts explore particular issues, ask questions that indicate satisfaction of requirements, and prompt attachments of additional information. Failure to furnish a complete expenditure responsibility report for example, results in a taxable expenditure.[57] Each foundation should seek to clearly reflect its mission in completing these parts. Its charitable programs are described and detailed to furnish the reader with a clear picture of the type of grants and activities it supports. Not only is Form 990-PF open to public inspection[58] to anyone who personally asks to see it, but the information is widely available in directories—paper and electronic—published throughout the country as an aid to grant-seekers. The volume and quality of grant requests a foundation receives is influenced by the information submitted on its Form 990-PF.

### (a)  Part V, Qualification for Reduced Tax on Net Investment Income

A private foundation can cut its tax in half (from 2 percent to 1 percent of net investment income) by essentially giving the tax amount to charity.[59] If the foundation's current-year qualifying distributions (Part XII) exceed a hypothetical number (past five-year average payout percentage times average fair market value of assets for the year of calculation plus 1 percent tax for the current year), the tax is reduced to 1 percent. Achieving this reduction is complicated, because the two most important factors are not known until the last day of the taxable year—Line 4 (the average month-end value of investment assets) and probably Line 8 (qualifying distributions). Except for

---

54.  *See* § 3.1.
55.  Reg. § 53.4940-1(f)(3).
56.  *See* § 12.1.
57.  *See* § 9.6.
58.  *See* § 12.3(a).
59.  *See* § 10.2(a) for illustration of the calculations. Proposals to reduce this tax to a single 1.32 percent rate or and eliminate it have been introduced in Congress.

the most generous foundations whose distributions continually increase year to year, reducing the excise tax requires very careful planning. A private foundation cannot qualify for the reduced tax rate in its first year.

## (b) Part VI, Excise Tax on Investment Income

Except for exempt private operating foundations and certain terminating foundations, private foundations pay a tax of 1 to 2 percent, on their net investment income reported in Part I, column (b), Line 27b. Foreign foundations that receive more than 15 percent of their investment income from U.S. sources pay a 4 percent tax on this income. A foundation converting itself to a public charity under the 60-month termination rules[60] is excused from paying the excise tax. Such a foundation signs an agreement to extend the statute of limitations for collecting the excise tax in the event it fails to receive sufficient amounts of public support. A copy of the signed consent agreement is attached to the return each year during the termination period, and Part VI, Line 1, should refer to the attachment and state that the tax is not applicable.

If the annual tax is less than $500, it can be paid with a check accompanying the return as it is filed. If the tax is more than $500, it is paid in advance through the estimated tax system, using depository receipts.

Estimated excise tax on investment income reported on Form 990-PF and unrelated business income reported on Form 990-T must be paid quarterly. Large foundations whose annual income was $1 million or more in any one of its three preceding years can base only the first quarterly payment on the prior year tax. For the second, third, and fourth installments, the tax must be based on annualized actual income and deductions earned through the end of each quarter. Form 990-W contains worksheet and instructions that do not answer the following questions:

- Can the private foundation use the 1 percent tax rate when its projections indicate that the lower rate will apply?

As mentioned in § 10.1, achieving a 1 percent tax rate can be difficult because the calculation is based on financial information for the entire year. Definite numbers are not known until year-end results are finalized, which is much later than the estimated tax payments are due.

- Must the private foundation annualize unusual capital gains that are not expected to reoccur?

Assume capital gain is realized in January and no more gains are expected during the tax year. Most foundations in that circumstance choose to override, or not annualize the capital gain earned in the early part of the year. This

---

60. *See* § 13.4.

solution acknowledges the fact that the penalty is based on the actual tax ultimately paid.

- Should the foundation use the "Standard Option or Option 1 for annualizing income"?

Income distributable by a partnership raises another dilemma since the income is often not received regularly throughout the foundation's tax year, if at all. In some instances, no cash distribution is paid from a partnership, and the foundation only becomes aware of reportable income after year-end when it receives Form 1065 K-1. To accurately calculate expected tax, such income items are not included in items of "extraordinary" income and "need not be annualized."[61] Essentially a foundation must request periodic data from a partnership in which it holds an interest.[62] Often such information is difficult to obtain. In those instances, the foundation may need to make the projection of estimated tax based on prior-year information, a practice not addressed in the regulations.

Penalties are due for failure to pay a sufficient amount by the quarterly due dates.[63] The form used to calculate the penalty for underpayment of estimated excise tax[64] bases any penalty on the applicable tax rate that is determined by information presented in Part V of the annual information return as of the last day of the year. Penalties are also imposed for failure to deposit taxes electronically. The foundation enrolls and makes payments at www.eftps.gov.

## (c) Part VII-A, Statements Regarding Activities

The information desired by the IRS to evaluate a private foundation's qualification for ongoing tax exemption is solicited by 15 questions in this part and 7 in Part B. Certain answers can cause serious problems for the foundation. The questions essentially "fish" for failures to comply with the tax code and regulations and IRS policy rules pertaining to private foundations. The IRS is reportedly guided by the answers to certain questions in choosing suitable candidates for examination. Certain questions, such as in Lines 1 and 4, indicate that other filings are required. Therefore, attention to the impact of the answer to each question is desirable. The IRS instructions to the form provide no guidance regarding the answers to questions in Lines 2, 4, 5, 7, and 14.

**Line 1. Did the Foundation Intervene in an Election or Conduct Any Lobbying?** Answering any of the five parts of this question *Yes* is tantamount to admitting that the exempt status should be questioned and that certainly a

---

61. Instructions for Form 990-W.
62. Reg. § 6654-2(d)(2).
63. IRC § 6655.
64. Form 2210 or 2220.

taxable expenditure has occurred.[65] The answers to all of the parts of this question, including (c), should be *No*, because a private foundation, as outlined in Chapter 9, is absolutely prohibited from engaging in these activities.

Items 1(d) and 1(e) ask the foundation to report the amount of any excise tax imposed by § 4955 on its political expenditures or reimbursements it paid to its managers for such tax. Again the answer must be *Zero* or *None*.

### Line 2. Did the Foundation Have Activities Not Previously Reported to the IRS?
A *Yes* answer to this question alerts the IRS to review organizational changes that the form instructs the foundation to explain in a detailed attachment. The question is sometimes hard to answer when the foundation's activity has evolved or expanded, but it has not necessarily dramatically or totally changed in its focus or overall purpose. As an example, assume a grant-making foundation previously supported soup kitchen programs to feed the poor and has begun to redirect its grants to community gardens that teach the poor to raise their own food. This type of change in grantees is not a new activity. Such a change in the category of public charities a foundation supports has no impact on its tax-exempt status or classification, and the grant details are also displayed in Part XV, so the answer can be *No*.

A *Yes* response does not constitute a request for IRS approval for the new activity, but simply a mechanism to keep the IRS informed with a detailed description of the changes that are attached. In fact, a *Yes* answer does not customarily result in an IRS response. If the foundation board or trustees desire written IRS approval for conduct of the new projects or change in purpose, a formal ruling request must be filed with the EO Determination's Group in Cincinnati, Ohio. This submission, however, is not required, nor encouraged, by the IRS.[66]

The 2012 instructions to Form 990-PF are silent on the matter of reporting changes in activities and organizational documents to the IRS. The private foundation determination letters direct the organization to see Publication 4221-PF, Compliance Guide for 501(c)(3) Private Foundations, for "some helpful information about your responsibilities as an exempt organization." That publication, on page 23, simply states: "A private foundation must report name, address, structural and operational changes on its annual information return, Form 990-PF." It continues to state that a private foundation may also report these changes to the EO Determinations Office with a caution that reporting such changes to the EO Determinations Office does not relieve the organization from reporting the changes on its annual return.

---

65. *See* § 9.1.
66. *See* § 2.7(c).

Activity changes that should be communicated on Form 8940 submitted with a fee to the IRS Exempt Organizations Determinations Office include the following:

- Change in classification of private foundation status.

- Advance approval of a private foundation's grant-making procedures.[67]

- Classification as exempt operating foundation or private operating foundation.[68]

- Advance approval of voter registration activities.[69]

- Approval for set-asides for qualifying distribution purposes.[70]

**Line 3. Have the Organizational Documents Been Changed?** When a foundation revises its charter, trust instrument, or bylaws, the answer to this question is *Yes* and a "conformed" copy of the new organizational document must be attached. "Conformed" means a copy that agrees with the original document and all of the amendments. The copies should be signed, or if not, a written declaration certifying that the copies are complete and accurate or the original documents must be signed by an officer authorized to sign for the foundation. The same issues regarding a desire for IRS positive approval for such changes, as discussed for Line 2, are raised by a *Yes* answer to this question.

**Line 4. Did the Foundation Have More Than $1,000 of Unrelated Business Gross Income?** If question 4(a) is answered *Yes*, question 4(b) must also be answered *Yes*. The answer to this question should be coordinated with Part XVI-A. If an amount in excess of $1,000 appears in column (b), the answer to this question should be *Yes*. This question can be confusing, since the investment income that private foundations earn is technically defined as unrelated trade or business income.[71] Most investment income, however, is modified, or excluded, from unrelated business taxable income,[72] is not required to be reported on Form 990-T, and should appear in column (d) of Part XVI-A.

**Line 5. Did the Foundation Liquidate, Terminate, Dissolve, or Substantially Contract?** The rules governing when, and if, a private foundation should give notification to the IRS prior to distributing all of its assets is a complex subject. Chapter 13 should be studied if the answer to this question is *Yes*. Prior

---

67. *See* § 9.3(g).
68. *See* § 3.1.
69. *See* § 9.2(c).
70. *See* § 6.5(e).
71. IRC § 513. Chapter 11 defines unrelated income and the many exceptions to taxation for certain types of unrelated income, including unindebted investment properties.
72. IRC § 512.

notification of a foundation's intention to dissolve is not necessarily required. If the IRS is not notified, a statement reporting all of the facts and circumstances of its termination must be attached.[73] For a full liquidation or termination, a certified copy of the plan with a schedule listing the names and addresses of all recipients of assets, along with a description of the nature and value of such assets, is required.

According to the IRS general instructions, Part T, disposition of 25 percent or more of the fair market value of the foundation's assets is a substantial contraction. Prior permission to make a substantial contraction, short of totally terminating the foundation, is not literally required by the law or the IRS instructions, although the foundation managers may deem it prudent to seek approval.

### Line 6. Does the Foundation's Governing Instrument Satisfy § 508(e) Requirements?
This question must be answered *Yes*. A private foundation cannot qualify and be recognized as an exempt organization by the IRS unless its governing instruments prohibit its engaging in transactions that would cause it to incur excise taxes for entering into a self-dealing transaction, making taxable expenditures, maintaining excess business holdings, or buying a jeopardizing investment.[74]

The requirement can be met in two ways. Many foundations' governing instruments actually contain required language. Some foundations rely instead on local law. Most states passed legislation in the early 1970s to automatically incorporate the required language for private foundations based in the particular states.

### Line 7. Did the Foundation Have at Least $5,000 in Assets During the Year?
If the answer to this question is *Yes*, the foundation must report the fair market value of its assets in Part II by completing column (c). Such a modestly sized foundation is also excused from completing Part XV. The data submitted in Part XV are compiled and published in directories containing information for grant-seekers.

### Line 8. Submit Information Regarding State Filings.
This request has two parts:

1.  The foundation must enter the name(s) of state(s) to which the foundation reports and in which the foundation is registered as a charitable organization. Even if a private foundation is not registered to do business in a particular state, state filings may be required if the foundation has solicited and received donations from certain states.

---

73. IRC § 507(a).
74. *See* § 2.1.

2.  A foundation with assets of $5,000 or more (answers question 7 *Yes*) is required to furnish a copy of Form 990-PF and of Form 4720, if one is being filed, to the attorney general of:

    ○  Each state listed in the answer to question 8(a),

    ○  The state in which its principal office is located, and

    ○  The state in which the foundation was incorporated or created.

The state copy must be submitted at the same time the federal form is filed. The foundation must also furnish a copy of its Form 990-PF to the attorney general of any state that requests it, whether or not it is registered in that state.[75]

**Line 9. Is This Organization a Private Operating Foundation?**[76]   A *Yes* answer to this question alerts the IRS that the foundation will complete Part XIV, instead of Part XIII, to determine satisfaction of charitable payout tests, and that the foundation must complete column (c) of Part I.

**Line 10. Did Any Person(s) Become Substantial Contributors During the Year?**   If the answer to this question is *Yes*, the foundation is prompted to attach a schedule listing the names and addresses of these contributors.[77] Note that for those contributing $5,000 or more during the year, the same information plus details regarding the gift are provided in Schedule B. Foundation managers that are substantial contributors are also listed in Part XV.

**Line 11. Did the Foundation Own a Controlled Entity Within the Meaning of Section 512(b)(13) and If So, Was a Binding Contract in Effect on August 17, 2006?**   This question pertains to the taxability of payments the foundation receives from a controlled for-profit subsidiary in the form of interest, rents, royalties, or annuities that may be subject to the unrelated business income tax. The instructions to the form should be studied if the answer is *Yes*.

**Line 12. Did the Foundation Acquire an Interest in Any Applicable Insurance Contracts?**   Again, if *Yes*, the instructions should be studied. Certain transactions of this type result in self-dealing.

**Line 13. Public Inspection Copy.**   This question asks whether the foundation complied with the requirement that it allow anyone who asks to see, and receive a copy if they are willing to pay copy charges, the foundation's Forms 990-PF and 1023. The answer to this question should always be *Yes*. Following this

---

75.  Form 990-PF instructions for 2012, General Instruction G.
76.  See § 3.1.
77.  *See* § 4.1.

question is a blank line on which the foundation is now asked to enter its website address.

**Line 14. Who to Contact.**   This line asks for the name and phone number of the person "the books are in care of" and also their location. It is suitable to submit contact information for that person who can be responsive to questions from persons seeking information about the foundation. In the authors' experience, it is this person whom the IRS calls when it wants to schedule an examination.

### (d)   Part VII-B, Statements Regarding Activities for Which Form 4720 May Be Required

It is vital that this part be prepared with great care because the penalties were doubled by the Pension Protection Act of 2006. The series of questions ask whether the foundation has violated any rules that may cause it and its managers to be penalized.[78] A *Yes* answer to a question in this part signals the IRS that the foundation has violated a tax rule.[79] An entry in the *Yes* column requires that the foundation file Form 4720 (Exhibit 12.6) and possibly pay an excise tax for a forbidden act. A *Yes* answer to question 5(c) requires attachment of an Expenditure Responsibility Report of information provided by grantee.[80]

The labyrinth of don'ts (but dos may be okay) should be studied carefully if any of the answers are *Yes*. To avoid an excise tax for self-dealing, the foundation must be able to answer *No* to question 1(b) if 1(a) contains any *Yes* answers. Similarly, any *Yes* answers to the (a) portions of questions 2, 3, and 5 need to be answered with a *No* in 2(b), 3(b), and 5(b) to signal that, though a potential violation of the rules occurred, an exception applied. The answer to both questions 4(a) and 4(b) should be *No*.[81]

The IRS added questions 6(a) and (b) regarding payment of premiums on personal benefit contracts beginning with the 2000 tax return. A personal benefit contract is a life insurance, annuity, and endowment contract that benefits the transferor or his family. If the organization paid premiums on a personal benefit contract, then Line 6(b) is answered *Yes*, and Form 8870 must be filed.

The penalty provisions for violation of the private foundation rules contain few exceptions, or excuses, for imposition of the penalty on the private foundation itself for failure to comply with the specific provisions of these

---

78. In answering the items in question 1, consult Chapter 5; for question 2, Chapter 6; for question 3, Chapter 7; for question 4, Chapter 8; and for question 5, Chapter 9.
79. IRC §§ 4941–4945.
80. Illustrated in Exhibit 9.11.
81. Consult Chapter 6 for aid in answering question 2, Chapter 7 for question 3, Chapter 8 for question 4, and Chapter 9 for question 5.

rules.[82] Some relief from the penalties is allowed for foundation managers who do not condone, or participate in the decision to conduct, a prohibited action. The standards for forgiving the penalty are somewhat different for each type of violation. Before a penalty can be forgiven, the violation must also be corrected by undoing the impermissible transaction or making up the deficiency.

Until 1984, the penalties were strictly applied.[83] Congress in 1984 added code sections[84] to permit abatement of the penalties, not including the self-dealing sanctions, imposed on both the foundation and its managers if it is established to the satisfaction of the IRS that:

- The taxable event was due to reasonable cause and not to willful neglect, and

- The event was corrected within the correction period for such event.

To allow abatement, the actions of the responsible foundation officials must be considered. Although the statute[85] is entitled "Definitions," neither it nor the regulations define the terms *reasonable cause* and *willful neglect*.[86]

### (e) Part VIII, Information about Officers, Directors, Trustees, Foundation Managers, Highly Paid Employees, and Contractors

To assist the IRS in detecting self-dealing and private inurement, details of compensation are reported. Line 1 of this part must be completed to list all of the foundation's officials, regardless of the number, and whether or not they received any compensation or expense reimbursements. Foundation managers are defined by the instructions to include those persons who have responsibilities or powers similar to those of officers, directors, and trustees. A foundation's executive director and chief financial officer are managers, for example.[87] The address at which officials would prefer the IRS contact them (it can be the foundation's address) is requested.

It is extremely important that the foundation use good documentation procedures to evidence the reasonableness of compensation paid to its managers. The checklist found in Exhibit 5.1 should be completed for all compensated officials.

---

82. *See* §§ 6.6, 7.4, 8.4, 9.8.
83. *Charles Stewart Mott Foundation v. United States,* 91-2 U.S.T.C. ¶ 50,340 (6th Cir. 1991); *Mannheimer Charitable Trust, Hans S. v. Commissioner,* 93 T.C. 5 (1989).
84. IRC §§ 4961, 4962, 4963.
85. IRC § 4962.
86. If there is a *Yes* answer to any of the questions, the following sections should be carefully studied to compose the explanations that must be attached to the required Form 4720: question 1—§ 5.13; question 2—§ 6.6; question 3—§ 7.4; question 4—§ 8.4; question 5—§ 9.8.
87. *See* § 4.2.

On Line 1, column (b), of this part, a foundation is expected to report the actual time both its volunteer and compensated officials "devote per week to the position." It is not sufficient to say persons devote "part time" or "as needed" for the number of hours worked. When possible, board members should keep time records particularly for those that receive paid compensation. Absent that, an estimate of hours persons devote to board and committee meetings, site visits, and other foundation affairs should be prepared. For an official who is compensated, the entry in column (b) has other import and should always be entered with some precision. The relationship between the amount of time spent and the compensation paid could indicate that the foundation has made a taxable expenditure[88] and had a self-dealing transaction.[89]

Moreover, on Lines 2 and 3, the foundation must report the compensation of the five highest-paid employees (over $50,000 in compensation) and the five highest-paid independent contractors (paid over $50,000) of professional services, respectively. This reporting should be presented with the same attention to detail discussed above for columns (b), (c), (d), and (e) to officer and director information.

Total compensation paid to persons serving on the governing board, for all services rendered, is to be reported, whether they are employees or independent contractors. For persons serving in more than one position, for instance, both as a director and as an officer or staff member, the compensation for each respective position should be separately presented. Three distinct types of pay are reported in one of three columns.

**Column (c). Compensation.** Salary, fees, vacation pay, sick leave, severance pay, deferred compensation (whether or not reported in column (d) in a prior year), and any other amounts paid for personal services rendered are reported here. The totals for this column may not equal the totals on Part I, Line 13 because certain benefits are reported differently for 990 reporting purposes. The Form 990 for 2008 requires that W-2 compensation be reported by both calendar and fiscal year reporting organizations.

**Column (d). Contributions to Employee Benefit Plans and Deferred Compensation.** All forms of deferred compensation, whether funded or unfunded, whether pursuant to a qualified or an unqualified plan, are reported in this column. Qualified pension plans include defined contribution, defined benefit, and money purchase plans,[90] employee annuity plans,[91]

---

88. *See* § 9.7.
89. *See* § 5.2.
90. IRC § 401(a).
91. IRC § 403(b).

IRA/SEP plans,[92] and a cash or deferred arrangement.[93] Accrued benefits under an unqualified and unfunded deferred compensation arrangement, such as a rabbi trust, are also reported.

Payments under welfare benefit plans on behalf of each official, comprising medical, life, dental, and other types of insurance, scholarships, training, child care, severance pay, and disability payments, are included. In a duplicative manner, the current-year amount set aside is reported in this column as it accrues, while the actual payment made in a later year is reported in column (c).

**Column (e). Expense Account, Other Allowances.** This column is particularly troublesome, because the title does not adequately describe those amounts the instructions direct the foundation to report. The IRS instructions first say taxable and nontaxable fringe benefits and allowances are to be reported, but in a parenthesis to that sentence provide that de minimis fringe benefits excluded from gross income[94] can be excluded in this column. Essentially, the instructions omit most amounts that are not taxable to the individual. As examples of allowances that are included, the instructions stipulate amounts for which the official does not account to the foundation and those that were more than the payee spent on serving the organization. Finally, they say to include payments made in connection with indemnification arrangements, the value of the personal use of housing, autos, or other assets owned, leased, or provided for the organization's use without charge.

An entry should be made in each of the three column (c)s in this part, even if the answer is *None*. If an attachment is required for Line 1, the totals of each column should be entered on page 6. The total gross wages or fees reported as paid to an individual should be corroborated with Forms 941, W-2, and 1099 separately filed with the IRS to report the individual's compensation and tax withholding.

## (f)  Part IX-A, Summary of Charitable Activities

In this part the foundation has an opportunity to describe its exempt purposes and the achievements of the direct charitable programs it actively conducts itself. Grants to other organizations are reported in Part XV. To describe the foundation's accomplishments, the services provided are summarized along with numerical data. How many children were counseled, classes taught, meals served, patients healed, sites restored, books published, conferences convened, research papers produced, and similar data are reported for the foundation's four major projects.[95]

---

92.  IRC § 408.
93.  IRC § 401(k).
94.  IRC § 132(e).
95.  *See* §§ 6.5(b), 3.1(a).

If numerical results are not pertinent or are unavailable, the project objectives and the long-range plans can be described. Reasonable estimates can be furnished if the exact number of recipients is not known. A foundation conducting research on heart disease and testing a controlled group of 100 women over a five-year period would say so. Similarly, a foundation that commissions a study of an area's history and expects the project to take 10 years, could report that four scholars have been hired to deliver annually a minimum of 100 pages each, with citations and appropriate photographic documentation or other archival materials. How the documents will eventually be published is not known, so the number of copies and eventual public benefit cannot be measured. The research modality, however, can be described to evidence the work's educational nature.

The total expenses (including asset acquisitions) for the largest four active programs the foundation conducts is reported alongside the program descriptions. Such expenses are reported in column (d) of page 1 on the generic line describing its nature, such as printing, salaries, and the like. Both direct and indirect (an allocable portion of someone's salary or a portion of the rent, for example) are included. The numbers reflected in Part IX-A do not normally agree with the numbers appearing on the first page. Except for significantly involved grant programs,[96] grant payments to other organizations or individuals are not included in this part.

### (g)  Part IX-B, Summary of Program-Related Investments

Program-related investments[97] made during the year are reported in Part IX-B. Investments made in a prior year should not be reported, even if the foundation still retains an interest in the program that is reflected on the current year balance sheet. Lines 1 and 2 should detail the largest program-related investments of the current tax year regardless of whether held at year-end. Line 3 combines all the remaining investments with an attached detailed schedule, if necessary. The total reported in this section must equal the amount on Line 1(b) of Part XII, but will not necessarily agree with the amount shown on the balance sheet and expenditure responsibility reports.

### (h)  Part X, Minimum Investment Return

Line 6 represents the foundation's required amount of annual charitable granting.[98] The number on Line 6 is entered in Part XI, Line 1. The amount in Part X, Line 5, is entered in Part V, Line 4.

---

96. *See* § 3.1(a).
97. *See* § 8.3.
98. Refer to Chapter 6 for definitions and parameters before completing this part.

## (i)  Part XI, Distributable Amount

This part begins with the calculated minimum investment return from Part X. The excise and income tax imposed on income is next allowed to reduce the required charitable payout. Recoveries of grants claimed as a distribution in a past year are added back. Private operating foundations do not complete this part.

## (j)  Part XII, Qualifying Distributions

In this part, the foundation tallies up the amount of its current-year disbursements that are counted toward its mandatory distribution requirement, which is calculated in Parts XIII and XIV (for private operating foundations).[99] The number on Line 4 carries to Part V, Line 8; Part XIII, Line 4; and Part XIV, Line 2(c).

## (k)  Part XIII, Undistributed Income

This part surveys five years of grant-making history to determine whether the foundation has expended sufficient funds on charitable giving to meet the payout requirements. If this schedule reflects a balance remaining on Line 6(d) or 6(e) indicating a deficiency of qualifying distributions, Form 4720 should be filed to calculate the penalty on underdistributions. The order in which distributions are applied is important.[100]

Qualifying distributions entered on Line 4 should be the same as on Line 4 of Part XII, and the trick is knowing how to apply the total among the four columns and when a distribution is charged to corpus. As the form's design indicates, current-year distributions are first applied to column (c), the remaining undistributed income from the immediately preceding year. The current-year required payout amount (shown in column (c) and based on prior-year calculations) must first be satisfied before any prior-year deficiencies or corrections can be offset, or made up. The form also tracks excess charitable distributions that can be carried over for a five-year period to offset future payout requirements.

A foundation might choose to apply current-year grants as a distribution out of corpus on Line 7, column (a), under certain circumstances. For example, this is appropriate for a foundation that is redistributing a donation for which the contributor desires the maximum deduction, or a grant from a private foundation that has stipulated the grant must be redistributed in order to take a qualifying distribution. The point is that the foundation cannot count a gift attributable to a pass-through contribution as part of its qualifying distributions.

---

99. *See* Chapter 6 for definition and discussion of the terms used on each line.
100. The order in which qualifying distributions are applied is illustrated in § 6.6.

Normally, a foundation must reduce undistributed income in column (d) even though this amount is not technically due until the end of the following year, before applying an amount to Line 7. For a foundation wishing to skip applying current-year distributions (or a portion of them) to the next year's payout requirement, an out of corpus election on Line 4(c) is made. To make the corpus election, a foundation manager signs a statement declaring that the foundation is making an election and designating a specific amount from the current year's distributions as out of corpus. Similarly, an election to skip the next year's payout is made on Line 4(b) in order to apply current distributions toward a deficiency from prior years.

A private foundation must meet its distribution requirements[101] in the year in which it terminates its existence. The distributable amount includes both the remaining amount unpaid from the year preceding the termination year plus the amount calculated to be paid out before the end of the year following termination. The total amount of the assets distributed is "counted towards satisfaction of such *requirements to the extent the amount transferred meets the requirements of section 4942(g)*" (emphasis added).[102] When the foundation is terminating by distributing its assets to another private foundation, the assets transferred can count as a qualifying distribution only if the recipient foundation is not controlled by the terminating foundation and regrants, or pays out, the terminating foundation's grant within its next succeeding taxable year.[103]

Different rules apply for transfers to foundations controlled by the terminating foundation. The IRS, in private letter rulings, directs a transferee organization that is controlled by the terminating foundation to add any undistributed amounts to its distributable amount.[104] Additionally, the surviving foundation must maintain documentation that it has met this requirement. If the transferor foundation has excess qualifying distributions, the amount is instead allowed to be deducted from the transferee foundation's required distribution amount.

## (l)  Part XIV, Private Operating Foundations

Private operating foundations submit information to calculate their ongoing qualification based on four years of their qualifying distributions, income, and assets.[105]

This part determines whether the operating foundation's active project expenditures meet an income test and additionally whether it meets one of three very different tests based upon its assets and support. The tests must be

---

101. Defined in § 6.4.
102. Reg. § 1.507-3(a)(5).
103. *See* § 13.5.
104. E.g., Priv. Ltr. Ruls. 200115038 and 200028014.
105. *See* § 3.1.

met by taking either all four years into account on an overall basis or each of three years out of the four.

## (m)  Part XV, Supplementary Information

*Line 1* is completed by foundations with assets of $5,000 or more, except those foreign foundations whose U.S.-source income is entirely investment income. The name of any foundation manager[106] who is also a substantial contributor[107] and has donated more than $5,000 to the foundation is listed. Those foundation managers who own 10 percent or more of the stock of a corporation in which the foundation also has a 10 percent or greater interest are also listed.[108]

For Line 2, the foundation reveals information regarding its grant programs and therefore, it should be prepared with great care. The address to which requests are to be sent, including for many foundations their website, must be provided along with the form (if any) in which applications should be submitted, what should be attached, the deadlines, and any restrictions and limitations on awards, such as a geographic area, subject, kinds of institutions, and so on. Grant-seekers use the information submitted in this part to select the private foundations to which they will make applications for funding. The Foundation Center and other organizations publish books and electronic media that contain this information. Public libraries in many cities cooperate in making Forms 990-PF available for public inspection. Most often, inspectors look at this and the following parts to find out what kind of grants a private foundation makes.

Foundations that make grants only to preselected charities and do not accept unsolicited requests for funds can check the box on line 2. Because the paper load for some foundations is immense, there is a temptation in some cases to check the box even though it does not necessarily apply. There are ongoing philosophical discussions about the pros and cons of using the box: Should a foundation with unrestricted funds close the door to grant applicants by checking the box?

Line 3 contains five columns listing information about grants paid during the year and approved for future payment. The total under 3(a) should agree with the amount reported on Line 25 of Part I. The Line 3(b) total of future grant commitments is provided for public inspection purposes only, and does not necessarily carry to any other part of the form. A foundation using generally accepted accounting principles would reflect a liability on the balance sheet in Part II, Line 18, for grants payable, with which the number may agree. Note that this amount for SFAS No. 116 financial purposes will be equal to the discounted

---

106. *See* § 4.2.
107. *See* § 4.1.
108. *See* § 7.1.

present value of the pledges, not necessarily the gross face amount of the pledges.

The presentation of this information is extremely important for several reasons. Grant information contained here is widely circulated in the local, state, and national directories published for grant-seekers in books and electronic media. Form 990-PF is also posted on www.guidestar.org, a site that grant-seekers, public regulators, and others now visit to get information about the foundation and the type of programs it supports. The foundation has an opportunity to paint a picture of its mission and reflect the scope and depth of its grant-making. Organizing the grant payments to arrive at subtotals for categories, such as feeding the poor, crime prevention, education, culture, and so on, can result in improved grant applications. At the same time, it satisfies the IRS request that the purpose of the grant be described in the second-from-the-right column.

From a tax standpoint, the middle column in this part is very important and informs the IRS of "Foundation status of the recipient." What this means is the grantee's classification as a public or private charity.[109] If the grantee is a public charity (other than a § 509(a)(3) Type III, nonfunctionally integrated organization),[110] no other information is reported in Form 990-PF concerning the grant. If, instead, the grantee is another private foundation, question 5(a)(4) in Part VII-B will be answered *Yes*. In addition, the foundation must exercise expenditure responsibility and answer question 5(c) *Yes*. Finally, a statement of the sort illustrated in Exhibit 9.11 must be submitted with the return.

The relationship, if any, between individual grant recipients and any foundation manager or substantial contributor is also revealed. Any answer other than *None* in this column raises several issues. The first question is whether self-dealing may have occurred because a payment was made to a disqualified person.[111] In addition, payment to related individuals may indicate that the foundation's scholarship payments are not made on the required "objective and nondiscriminatory basis."[112]

### (n) Part XVI-A, Analysis of Income-Producing Activity and Part XVI-B, Relationship of Activities

At the behest of Congress, Part XVI-A was added to Form 990-PF in 1989 as an audit trail to find unrelated business income. Unrelated income is reported alongside related income in Part I, and this part is designed to fragment the two different types and alert the IRS when to expect that Form 990-T should be filed.

---

109. *See* §§ 15.3, 15.4, 15.5.
110. *See* § 15.7.
111. *See* § 5.2.
112. *See* § 9.3.

The IRS instructions contain a helpful chart comparing the lines of Part I with the lines for entry in this part.

Selection of the appropriate code to identify income is sometimes difficult and can have adverse consequences for the unwary. Some choices are not absolute, and discretion can be important. For example, code 41 highlights activities conducted for nonexempt purposes and operated at a loss, potentially representing use of a foundation's funds for private purposes and the possibility that the IRS should revoke its exemption. It may be useful to review the unrelated business income provisions before completing this part.[113] An understanding of the terms *regularly carried on, related* and *unrelated,* and *fragmented* is absolutely necessary for correct completion of column (b). The form forces the foundation to report items of income appearing on Part I, Lines 3 through 11 (excluding contributions), in one of three categories by column.

**Columns (a) and (b). Unrelated Business Income.** Income from unrelated business activities is reported in column (b). Any amounts included in this column signal the IRS that they must be reported on Form 990-T and are subject to income tax if a profit is generated from the activity. Because a foundation is prohibited ownership in most types of business enterprises,[114] rental income from indebted property is the most common type of unrelated income a foundation would enter in this column. In contrast to Part I, net rental income is entered here.

Column (a) codes are the same as those used in Form 990-T to identify the type of business conducted—finance, real estate, services, and so on. The codes are very similar to those used in Forms 1120 and 1065 for corporate and partnership income tax returns. There is little harm in choosing the wrong code here, because the foundation is already admitting that the income is unrelated business income.

**Columns (c) and (d). Revenues Excluded or Modified from Tax.** Income from investments, fundraising events, and business activities statutorily excluded from tax are included in these columns. The reason for exclusion of the income from tax is claimed by inserting one of 43 code numbers in column (c). The codes explain that, while the foundation is admitting it has unrelated business income, it claims that the unrelated income is not taxable for one of 43 different reasons. If more than one exclusion code applies, the lowest applicable code number is used.

**Column (e). Related or Exempt Function Income.** Income generated by the foundation through charges for services rendered on items sold in connection

---

113. *See* Chapter 11.
114. *See* § 7.1.

with its underlying exempt (program) activities are entered in column (e). Admission fees, publication sales, seminar registrations, and all other revenues received in return for providing exempt functions are included. This column is a safe harbor, because it contains income not potentially subject to the unrelated business income tax. An explanation of the related aspect of each type of income in this column must be entered in Part XVI-B.

Some exempt function income is also described by specific exclusion codes. Rentals from low-income housing fits into code 16 and can also properly be entered in columns (c) and (d). It may be preferable to place such an item in column (e), because the taint of unrelated character is removed. Interest income earned under a student loan program or by a credit union and royalties from scientific research patents are other examples of potential dual classifications.

**Completing the Lines.** For certain lines, gross income before any deductions is reported, and for Lines 5, 6, and 9, net income is reported. The typical private foundation completes Lines 3, 4, and (perhaps) 5 and 7 of this part—the lines for investment income earned on its endowment funds. As explained earlier, some foundations, particularly operating foundations, will have entries on Part XVI-A, Line 1, column (e), for charges made for charitable programs they conduct. This program service revenue is reported on Lines 5 or 11 in Part I, but on Line 1 in this part.

Rental income, reported gross on Part I, is reported net of expenses on this page and is separated into three categories. Real estate rentals can be classified under one of 10 codes, and careful study of the unrelated business income rules[115] may be necessary to assure correct property classification under particular facts and circumstances. For real property rentals received on unindebted property held for investment, the income is reported in column (d) and identified with code 16. Lease rentals dependent on the tenants' profits are classified as unrelated income and must be reported in column (b). Rents on program-related real estate properties are placed in column (e) on Line 5. Codes 30–38 apply specifically to debt-financed income reportable in column (d) but excludable from the unrelated classification because of a statutory exception. The portion of income attributable to acquisition indebtedness that is not excluded is reported in column (b), Line 5.

Royalty income from mineral or intellectual property interests is entered on Line 7. In most cases, this income is entered in column (d) and identified with modification code 15. Royalties from educational publications or research patents may be classed as program service revenue on Line I and entered in column (e) instead. Unrealized gain or loss on an investment portfolio is not considered as current income on page 1 or page 5, but is entered as a surplus adjustment on Lines 3 or 5 of Part III.

---

115. *See* Chapter 11.

Capital gains and losses reported on Line 6 of page 1, from the disposition of assets other than inventory, are reported on this line in column (d) and identified with code 18. Gains and losses from the sale of investment portfolio assets, real estate, office equipment, program-related assets, partnership interests, and all sorts of property are included. Gains from the sale of debt-financed property must be shown in column (b). Gain or loss on the purchase, sale, or lapse of security options can be reported on this line and identified with code 19. Some suggest that revenue attributable to lapsed options, as distinguished from options sold or covered before maturity, should be reportable on Line 11. The IRS instructions, however, are silent, and, for convenience, any option activity can be combined with the security transactions with which they are associated.

Net income from special fundraising events, excluding any portion allocated to donations (not reported in this part), is technically unrelated activity reportable in column (d). Profits from the typical charitable event are not treated as taxable, because they are irregular activities (identified in column (c) with code 01) or run by volunteers (code 02), and the net profit is reported in column (d). When the primary purpose of an event is educational or otherwise exempt, such as a cultural festival, it is conceivable that the profits could be reported as related income in column (e).

A foundation that conducts educational activities, such as a museum or seminar sponsor, may sell inventory—books, art reproductions, and the like. The gross profit from the sales is entered on Line 10 in column (e). A foundation that inherited an active business might conceivably have these inventory sales reportable in column (b) during the period of time it was allowed to maintain the excess business holding.[116] A foundation selling donated goods or materials reports the gross profit in column (d), identified with code 05.

As one may discern from reading the codes, this part is designed for reporting types of income a private foundation commonly lacks—that from county fairs, bingo games, advertising revenues, and mailing list rentals, for example. Among other reasons, including the character of their funding sources, a private foundation is actually constrained from conducting income-producing activities that are essentially equivalent to conducting a proprietary business.[117] Nevertheless, versions of these activities may occur. A foundation could enter into a licensing agreement to exploit the use of its name, logo, or mailing list and receive royalty income that is not treated as business income. This income is reported in column (d) and identified with code 15.[118] The income from the rental or exchange of one foundation's mailing list with another foundation or

---

116.  *See* § 7.1.
117.  *See* § 7.2(b).
118.  *Sierra Club, Inc. v. Commissioner*, 103 T.C. 307 (1994), *aff'd in part, rev'd in part, and remanded*, 86 F.3d 1526, 1532 (9th Cir. 1996); *see* § 11.2(a).

with a public charity is excepted from the unrelated business provisions, entered in column (d) and identified with code 13.

Part XVI-B describes the foundation's charitable activities that produce revenue reported in column (e) of Part XVI-A. The information should explain how the programs accomplish the foundation's mission. For example, if the foundation charges admission to its historic houses, it would explain that it acquires, restores, and maintains the properties to prompt appreciation of history and to educate members of the public visiting the houses.

### (o) Part XVII, Information Regarding Transfers to and Transactions and Relationships with Noncharitable Exempt Organizations

This part was designed for Form 990, does not apply to many private foundations, and was added in 1988 in response to a congressional mandate that the IRS explore connections between charitable and noncharitable organizations. The IRS is searching for relationships that allow benefits, or the use of a foundation's assets, to flow from the foundation to a noncharitable exempt organization.

The questions in this part allow the IRS to scrutinize any asset sales or purchases, rental of facilities, loans, and the like to assure excessive or inadequate amounts are not paid by a foundation. These transactions are not necessarily prohibited, but could evidence a taxable expenditure[119] or a self-dealing transaction.[120] The foundation with such a transaction(s) has an extra burden to prove that the amounts paid are reasonable and serve its charitable purposes.

When these payments are made to an unaffiliated noncharitable organization at fair market value, the answer to question 1b can be *No*. All transactions with a related entity must be reported.

Question 1a asks whether cash or assets of the foundation or the noncharitable exempt organization have been transferred from one to the other without consideration or receipt of more than a nominal value. A contribution from a noncharitable entity to a foundation is such a transfer, but need not be reported. A *Yes* answer to question 1b may indicate that the foundation made a grant to a noncharitable organization. If so, the foundation must reveal the charitable purposes served by the transfer and report its expenditure responsibility exercised over the payment. The instructions are very specific and should be consulted if these transactions are to be reported. This part indicates yet another type of special records required to be kept by a foundation. To answer correctly, the foundation having the described relationship will want to establish subcodes or new departments in its chart of accounts to tabulate the answers.

---

119. *See* § 9.1.
120. *See* § 5.2.

Question 2 innocently asks the private foundation to list the names and nature of the relationships to any noncharitable exempt organizations. Two factors must be present to identify a related organization:

1. A historical and continuing relationship exists when two organizations participate in a joint effort to achieve a common purpose(s). This type of relationship is said to exist also if the foundation simply shares facilities, equipment, or paid staff.

2. Common control, whereby one or more of the officers, directors, or trustees (managers) of one organization are elected or appointed by those of the other. Similarly, control is found when 25 percent or more of the managers are interlocking.

## § 12.3  COMPLIANCE ISSUES

Between 1970 and 1999, Form 990-PF, including all attachments, was required to be made available for inspection at foundation offices, or the foundation could furnish a free copy to any person requesting inspection. A notice of availability was placed in a newspaper having general circulation in the county in which the foundation's principal office was located.

### (a)  Document Dissemination Rules

The public inspection requirements have been largely supplanted by mandatory document dissemination rules—rules that have been applicable to other tax-exempt organizations.[121]

These rules[122] require private foundations, including nonexempt charitable trusts and nonexempt private foundations, that file Form 990-PF, *Return of Private Foundation*, to have the returns available for anyone that asks to inspect them, free of charge. When one so requests, an "exact" copy of the forms must be provided for a "reasonable fee" (described later) plus actual postage costs. Alternatively, the forms can be made available electronically. The annual information return must be furnished for three years beginning on the actual date the returns are filed, whether on the normal deadline or on a delinquent date. The foundation's application for recognition of tax exemption must also be provided.[123] *Exact* means all schedules, attachments, and supporting

---

121. IRC § 6104(d).
122. Reg. § 301.6104(d)-1.
123. The process of seeking recognition of exemption is discussed in Chapter 2. This rule applies only after the IRS has made its final determination of the organization's exempt status. A pending application need not be furnished. If the organization no longer has a copy and its application was filed before July 15, 1987 (the initial effective date of the disclosure rules), it is relieved of responsibility of furnishing a copy of it.

documents, including any amendments, including the list of contributor names, addresses, and donation amounts and property type. (Public charities and other types of tax-exempt organizations are not required to disclose their donors' names.) Any correspondence to and from the IRS, including requests for additional information and an appeal for adverse determination in connection with the filing for determination of tax-exempt status, must also be provided. Forms 4720[124] and 990-T, Exempt Organization Business Income Tax Return,[125] must also be made available for public inspection. Note the requirement for public availability of Form 4720 is only provided in the regulation cited. The instructions to that form, IRS Life Cycle Diagrams, IRS Publication 4221, and the instructions to Form 990-PF make no mention of the requirement.

Form 990-PF has been available since 1969.[126] The returns are also available under Freedom of Information rules requiring copies to be provided by the IRS for a modest fee. The system is severely flawed, due partly to the weakness of retrieval systems for returns in various IRS service centers throughout the country and limited IRS staffing. A large number of requests for copies of the forms went unanswered. Congress first responded to pressure for public disclosure of the forms by public charities and other types of tax-exempt organizations by requiring that nonprofit organizations themselves make the returns available for inspection in their offices. Few nonprofit organizations, including foundations, have been confronted by persons availing themselves of the right to inspect Forms 990 since this privilege came into the tax law. Some expected this "evolution to soon lead to [a] markedly higher level of account-ability by charities and other nonprofits,"[127] which has certainly been the case.

**Public Communication Device.**   It is incumbent on private foundations filing Form 990-PF to present themselves effectively to the public. The suggestions for reporting and disclosure of compensation of officials (Part VIII), grant programs (Part XV), and direct charitable activities (Part IX) must particularly be carefully prepared with a view to public inspection.

**Prices and Timing.**   A reasonable fee of no more than the IRS's per-page copying charge[128]—currently $1.00 for the first and $0.15 for each subsequent page of the returns requested—plus the actual postage costs incurred by the foundation in mailing the copies, may be chargeable. When a foundation that requires advance payment receives a written request with no or insufficient payment, it must notify the person making the request within seven days from

---

124. Exhibit 12.6.
125. Exhibit 12.4.
126. *See* § 1.3.
127. Steuerle, "The Coming Revolution in the Nonprofit Sector," *Exempt Org. Tax Rev.* 313 (Sept. 1998).
128. Reg. § 601.702(f)(5)(iv)(B).

the receipt date of its prepayment policy and the amount due. Copies must be provided within 30 days from the date payment is received. Requests can be ignored if the fee is not paid within 30 days, or if the check received in payment does not clear on deposit. If the foundation does not require prepayment and the fee for copying and postage will exceed $20, the requester's consent to the charge will have to be obtained prior to sending the copies. Payment must be accepted in cash, money order, or by either check or credit card. Checks need not be accepted if payment is allowed by credit card. Foundations are required to respond to requests for information about fees that will be charged for copies, such as how many pages are contained in the application or the information returns.

For requests made *in person* at the foundation's principal, regional, or district offices, copies must be furnished during regular business hours on the same day unless the request is unreasonably burdensome. Examples of such a burden include a request received 10 minutes before the office closes, a volume of requests beyond the foundation's capability to respond, or the absence of responsible staff members who are working off-site or attending a conference. A request delayed by this type of situation must be fulfilled on the next business day or as soon as the condition ceases to exist, but no longer than five business days later. Copies requested *by mail* must be mailed within 30 days from receipt of the request that contains an address or fax number to which the copies are to be sent or 30 days from receipt of a required prepayment. A mailed request is considered to have been received seven days after the postmark or private delivery mark date. Requests delivered by electronic mail or facsimile are deemed received on the date of successful transmission.

Copies are considered to have been provided on the date of the postmark or private delivery mark date. Copies can be provided by electronic mail if the requestor consents; these copies are treated as provided on the date transmitted.

**Requests for Partial Copies.** A requester is able to ask for a complete or partial copy of the exemption application and return documents. The requester can specifically request a copy of particular parts or schedules included in the documents. For example, if the requester only wants a copy of Part V—the schedule reflecting compensation of officers and key employees—a copy of that particular part and its attachments, if any, must be provided.

**Processing Agent.** A foundation is able to hire a "local agent" to process requests made in person. This type of an agent must be located in reasonable proximity to the principal, district, or regional office of the foundation; the name, address, and phone number of the agent must be immediately given to requesters. Copies must be provided under the same rules outlined earlier regarding timing and pricing. Once the foundation transfers the request to the agent, it will not be required to respond further, though it will be responsible and can be penalized if the agent fails to follow the rules.

**Internet Posting.** Instead of furnishing copies, a foundation is able to make the returns widely available through electronic media. A foundation is able to satisfy its public inspection requirement either through its own website or through a database of other exempt organizations on another site. The site must contain instructions to enable the user to access, download, view, and print the posted documents in a format that exactly reproduces the image of the original documents filed with the IRS. No fee can be charged. The documents are considered *widely available* only if they are posted in an accessible format that allows any individual access to forms without special computer software or hardware (other than software that is readily available to members of the public without payment of any fee). The regulations acknowledge that the commonly used HTML format does not produce an exact image as does the PDF format. Foundations were allowed a one-year transition until June 8, 2000, to adopt a format that is fully compliant. Copies must be made available for inspection in the foundation's offices. Entities maintaining web pages for this purpose must have procedures for ensuring the reliability and accuracy of the documents posted on the page; take reasonable precautions to prevent alteration, destruction, or accidental loss of the documents; and correct any problems with the site.

**Local and Regional Offices.** If a foundation has more than one office, such regional or district offices must also satisfy the same requirements as the principal office, beginning 30 days after the returns are filed. An office is considered a regional or district office when it has paid employees working in the office for at least 120 hours per week, including full-time and part-time persons, without regard to the number of employees. A site that provides only exempt function services, such as day care or classes, and that has no administrative staff (other than managers of the site), is not an office at which inspection is required.

**No Office/Off-Site Inspections.** If a foundation has no permanent office or office hours, the returns must be made available at a reasonable location, at a reasonable time, and within two weeks of the receipt of a request for inspection. Instead of providing an off-site place for inspection, a foundation in this circumstance can send the requested copies for free to the requester, or if the requester consents in advance, charge the prescribed fee.

**Disclosures Required.** A copy of the entire Form 990-PF must be furnished upon request for either viewing or copying. The names and addresses of the foundation's contributors are subject to public inspection and cannot be omitted from the copy made available to the public as they can be for other types of tax-exempt organizations. Form 990-T filed by a foundation to report its unrelated business income[129] became subject to the disclosure requirements after August 17, 2006, and must be made available in a similar fashion.[130]

**Harassing Requests.**  If the foundation receives an excessive number of requests, it can apply to the IRS key district office to be excused from the disclosure requirements. As an example, the receipt of 200 requests following a national news report about the foundation is not considered harassment. Receipt of 100 requests from known supporters of another organization opposed to the policies and positions the organization advocates is considered disruptive to the organization's operations and thereby constitutes harassment. If more than two requests are received from the same person or address within 30 days, or if more than four requests are made within one year, the excessive requests can be ignored.

**Penalties.**  A $5,000 penalty is assessable against the person who is required to comply with these disclosure requirements and willfully refuses to furnish copies of the documents. The penalty applies with respect to each such return or application.

**Copies from the IRS.**  As in the past, the request to see a copy of a return can also be sent to the district director of the IRS in the area in which the foundation is located, or to the National Office of the IRS. Form 4506-A is used to request a copy of any return; the same photocopying fee described earlier will be imposed.[131]

## (b)  Where and When to File Form 990-PF

Effective January 1, 1997, all exempt organization returns, including Form 990-PF, are to be filed in the Ogden, Utah, Service Center. Before this centralization, notices regarding attachments or unanswered questions were common, even when the forms were prepared correctly. Improved handling has occurred as expertise has been developed by the section of this Service Center devoted especially to exempt organizations. When a foundation is unable to prepare the form in a timely fashion, an extension of time of up to six months can be requested. The extension does not apply to payment of the excise tax.

Form 990-PF must be filed on or before the fifteenth day of the fifth month following the end of the tax year. The due date cannot be on the weekend or federal holiday; instead the return will be due on the next business day. Form 8868 is an automatic three-month extension to file the return if it is filed by the

---

129. *See* Chapter 11.
130. IRC § 6104(d)(1)(A)(ii).
131. These regulations took effect March 13, 2000.

due date and includes any balance due. An additional three months may be requested on Form 8868 (page 2), but reasonable cause must be shown for the additional time requested.

The penalty for late filing is $20 for each day the failure continues ($100 for a large foundation with gross receipts in excess of $1 million for the tax year), unless the foundation can show the failure was due to reasonable causes. The maximum penalty for each return is $10,000 or 5 percent of the gross receipts of the foundation for the year. For a large foundation, the maximum is $50,000. In its instructions, the IRS cautions the preparer that penalties are imposed for failure to submit a complete and accurate return. The IRS thoughtfully reminds the organization that the reports are open to public inspection, and recommends that an effort be made to complete the report correctly.

Beginning in 2007 for tax year 2006 returns, private foundations and charitable trusts are required to file Form 990-PF electronically regardless of their asset size. The electronic filing requirements, however, only apply to entities that file at least 250 returns, including income tax, excise tax, employment tax, and information returns, during a calendar year. Thus, for example, if the foundation has 245 employees, it must file Form 990-PF electronically, because each Form W-2 and quarterly Form 941 is considered a separate return; thus, the organization files 250 returns (245 W-2s, four 941s, and one 990-PF).

## (c) First-Year Issues

When a new foundation's first tax year should begin is not stipulated in an IRS procedure or ruling. The IRS instructions to Form 990-PF direct all private foundations to file, including those whose applications for exemption are pending. The recognition of its tax-exempt status is granted retroactively to the date the foundation was effectively created as a legal entity so long as the foundation files Form 1023 within 27 months of the date of its creation. Therefore, the first tax year is normally treated as beginning on the date of creation. Often, however, the foundation has no assets until after it has received IRS approval for its tax exemption. In ruling on the consequence of foundation terminations,[132] the IRS said a foundation that gave away all of its assets, but did not terminate its existence, did not have to file until it received new assets. Additionally, the penalty for failure to file Form 990-PF is limited to a percentage of gross receipts, resulting in no penalty if there are no receipts.[133] Nevertheless, a new foundation with no assets may still choose to file. One advantage to filing a no activity return is to allow the foundation in the subsequent year when it becomes funded to qualify for the 1 percent tax rate.

---

132. *See* § 13.1.
133. IRC § 6652(c)(1)(A)(ii).

Form 4720 is due to be filed by the 15th day of the 5th month following the private foundation's year end and is filed separately from Form 990-PF. It is common that the mistake or violation is discovered after the filing deadline. Such a discovery necessitates the filing of a delinquent return for the year in which the violation occurred. A penalty for failure to file the return on time of 5 percent of the penalty tax shown due on the return is imposed for each month that the return is late, not exceeding 25 percent in the aggregate. An additional penalty for failure to pay the tax in a timely manner is also imposed. This penalty is equal to 5 percent of the tax on the return for each month that the payment is late, not exceeding 25 percent in the aggregate. Another issue when the problem is discovered after the filing of the return is whether an amended Form 990-PF should be filed to disclose the rule violation failure in Part VII-B in the year the failure occurred. The instructions to neither Form 990-PF nor Form 4720 provide for amendment of the originally filed return that omitted the disclosure, though some recommend such a correction to the prior return.

Certainly for the year in which the foundation has any assets, Form 990-PF should be filed. For purposes of making minimum distribution requirement calculations, the foundation's tax year begins on the day it is created rather than the day it first receives assets.[134] Both the average market valuation and payout percentage ratios are calibrated according to the number of days in the new or terminating foundation's year.

## (d) Reporting Violations and Other IRS Issues

A private foundation that violates one of the sanctions discussed in Chapters 5 through 9 is expected to disclose the mistake on Form 990-PF in Part VII-B. Additionally, Form 4720, illustrated in Exhbit 12.6, is filed separately to report the problem and calculate any penalties that are due. If the failure to follow the rules was due to reasonable causes and not willful disregard for the rules, the penalties, except those imposed for self-dealing, can be abated if the problem has been corrected. A request for abatement can be requested with Form 4720 with an explanation of the type illustrated in Exhibits 6.3 and 9.14 and 9.15. The particular rules for reporting the failure and methods for correcting the problem are unique to each violation.[135]

A private foundation may wish to change its fiscal year, its accounting method, its mission, its organizational documents, start a scholarship plan, or make other changes. Form 990-PF, in Part VII-A discussed above, asks whether any changes have occurred. The foundation may, or may not, need to, or want to, seek IRS approval for the changes. Simply submitting the information with Form 990-PF is permitted, but no response is received from the IRS when that

---

134. *See* § 6.2.
135. *See* §§ 6.6(c), 7.4, 8.4, 9.8.

choice is made.[136] Chapter 2 also discusses when an amended return should be filed and how to prepare for an IRS examination.

In a private ruling that reminds private foundations that they are potentially subject to most federal tax code provisions, the IRS approved the maintenance of a foundation's financial and grant-making records by electronic means.[137] The conclusion was based on rules applicable to all return filers. Any person (including exempt organizations for this purpose) required to file a return of information with respect to income must keep "such permanent books of account or records, including inventories, as are sufficient to establish the amount of gross income, deductions, credits, and other matters required to be shown by such person in any return of such tax or information."[138] "Machine-sensitive data media used for recording, consolidating, and summarizing accounting transactions and records with a taxpayer's automatic data processing system (ADP) are records" for this purpose.[139] All requirements that apply to hard copy books and records apply as well to machine-sensible books and records within an ADP system.[140] Audit trails that connect the electronic records to the tax returns should be established.[141] Hard copy records created or received in the course of business may be retained on microfiche or microfilm format or retained as machine-sensitive records.[142] The IRS, however, reserves the right to request hard copy printouts of electronic records in connection with an examination.

To promote efficiencies and streamline its operations, the foundation requesting the ruling plans to originate and maintain all books and records pertaining to operations electronically, including the tracking of investments, charitable activities, and all other matters. It will not retain printed copies of documents. The foundation proposes to conduct all charitable program activity by e-mail. Grantees will complete application forms online at the foundation's website. The application, including signatures of appropriate officials, will be returned by e-mail. All information used by the foundation to evaluate potential grantees, executed grant agreements, expenditure responsibility agreements, grant disbursement records, progress and final grantee reports, and any additional information gathered by the foundation in connection with each grant will be maintained electronically. Information received physically will be converted (scanned) into electronic form. The electronic grant files will contain a summary describing the terms of the grant; expected outcomes; milestones to those outcomes to be evaluated; the results of any financial, legal, or other due

---

136. *See* § 2.7 for discussion of the choices.
137. Priv. Ltr. Rul. 200324057.
138. Reg. § 1.6001-1(a).
139. Rev. Rul. 71-20, 1971-1 C.B. 392.
140. Rev. Proc. 98-25, 1998-1 C.B. 689.
141. *Id.* § 5.03.
142. Rev. Proc. 81-46, 1981-2 C.B. 621; Rev. Proc. 97-22, 1997-1 C.B. 652.

diligence; and any special conditions of the grant. All information required to be maintained in physical, hard copy books and records will be retained electronically. The ruling was based on the following stipulations:

- The foundation generates complete records of its charitable activities, including grants, loans, program-related investments, and other disbursements electronically, and retains these records in electronic form.

- The pre-grant inquiry, written agreements and follow-up reports, and return disclosures required for expenditure responsibility grants[143] are obtained and retained electronically.

- An electronic signature of a grantee's authorized official on an expenditure responsibility agreement will be considered binding.[144]

- The foundation retains the electronic records for a period sufficient to comply with federal tax law, including evidence of adherence to return disclosure rules, and make the records available to the service upon request.[145]

- The foundation retains the capability to conduct on-site investigations and reviews of the uses made of the funds granted.

- The foundation continues to file the annual return Form 990-PF in paper format until the IRS adopts electronic filing of the form.

## (e)  Employment Tax Considerations

When a private foundation compensates persons for services rendered to conduct the foundation programs, administration, and property management, compensation reporting issues must be considered. A private foundation is subject to the same rules that are applicable to public charities, other tax-exempt organizations, and for-profit taxpayers. The concepts defining taxable income[146] apply to determine when employee benefits are taxable, when a worker is treated as an independent contractor rather than an employee, and the amounts of tax, if any, that must be paid on behalf of or withheld from compensation payments. The IRS has very good publications and guidance on these matters that should be studied to determine a private foundation's tax compliance responsibilities.[147]

---

143. *See* § 9.6.
144. Pursuant to the Electronic Signatures in Global and National Commerce Act of 2000; *see* Exhibits 9.9 and 9.10 for examples of such agreements.
145. Reg. § 1.6001-1(e) provides "so long as the contents thereof may become materials in the administration of any internal revenue law."
146. IRC §§ 61-132.
147. *See Tax Planning and Compliance,* Chapter 25.

Special issues arise when a foundation participates in programs outside the United States. Tax withholding generally is not required on funds granted to a foreign organization or individuals for programs to be conducted outside of the United States[148] because they are gifts. The U.S. organization expects no services or goods to be provided in return so its payment is not compensatory.[149] However, a domestic foundation should consider the terms of the tax treaty between the United States and the countries into which the foundation is granting money. Certainly if workers are paid individually in foreign countries or foreign workers are hired to work in the United States, the rules of both countries must be respected. Addressing the concerns of U.S. foundations that bring foreign scholars to the United States, the IRS ruled no withholding was required in a situation where a portion of its funding would be spent by the foreign recipient to attend conferences and seminars in the United States.[150]

## (f) Reporting Requirements for Offshore Investments

An increasing number of foundations hold offshore investments in recent years. In diversifying their portfolios, tax-exempt organizations have been advised to purchase international securities, often through U.S.-based mutual funds.[151] In considering such investments, readers should study the checklists in Exhibits 8.1 and 11.3. The tax reporting for such domestic funds and outright purchase of marketable securities of an international company through a U.S. financial institution does not bring any unique reporting requirements. The dividends, interest, and resulting capital gains from such passive security investments are reported on Forms 990 or 990-PF and subject to the excise tax on investment income of a private foundation.[152]

Some of these passive investments are made in the form of so-called offshore hedge funds organized in either partnership or corporate form. Income of a hedge fund organized as a partnership is treated as being earned proportionately by and reportable by each partner, including those that are tax-exempt.[153]

The exempt investor receives and must report on Form 990 an allocated part of the dividends, interest, capital gains, and other income from derivatives, options, notional contracts, and the like. The partnership reports the income and must furnish the organization with a Form K-1 that contains details necessary for correct tax reporting. When an investment is made in corporate form, the issues discussed below influence the tax reporting. Additional tax reporting

---

148. There may be tax issues in foreign jurisdictions.
149. Rev. Rul. 2003-12, 2003-1 C.B. 283.
150. Priv. Ltr. Rul. 200529004.
151. *See* § 8.2 for discussion of prudent investor rules that recommend diversification of investment assets.
152. *See* § 12.2(b).
153. IRC § 702.

obligations can arise from hedge fund investments. Most costly is normal income tax that may be due on part or all of the fund income that is classified as unrelated business taxable income (UBTI). The taxable income usually results when the fund uses margin or other borrowed funds, called "acquisition indebtedness" to leverage the investments.[154] When UBTI is realized, the exempt must report it on Form 990-T and pay the normal income tax as if it were a nonexempt corporation or trust.[155] In order to offer protection to their investors, fund sponsors many times create a "blocker" structure to keep any taxable income from passing through the offshore hedge fund to the investor.

There are numerous variations on the theme of blocker structures, but the essence is that the investment activities potentially producing UBTI are held in a "blocker corporation." The corporate form serves to block any UBTI from flowing through to the exempt investor. Most of these corporate offshore hedge funds are controlled tax-wise by U.S. antideferral regimes for controlled foreign corporations (CFCs) and passive foreign investment companies (PFICs). Exempt organizations coming under CFC rules must report income currently even if the income is merely accumulated instead of being actually distributed. A CFC is a foreign corporation in which significant "U.S. shareholders" own more than 50 percent of the total combined voting power or value on any day during the corporation's tax year.[156] To be classified as a "U.S. shareholder," an organization must own at least 10 percent of the voting stock of the corporation. Of course, if the exempt organization has no UBTI from "debt financing" its stock purchase, these antideferral rules merely affect the timing of reporting dividend income subject only to the 1 or 2 percent excise tax.

The foreign corporation tax rules under which an offshore hedge fund is most likely to qualify, assuming it accepts U.S. investors, is the PFIC. Like the CFC rules, the PFIC tax laws were established as an antideferral regime—or at the least, a regime that would make income deferral an expensive proposition. A foreign corporation will be a PFIC if 75 percent or more of its gross income for the tax year consists of passive income, or 50 percent or more of the average fair market value of its assets consists of assets that produce, or are held for the production of, passive income.[157]

The general rule for a PFIC is that no taxes are due until there is an actual distribution of accumulated dividends or until the shareholder disposes of shares it owns. This allowable deferral of income is of little significance to exempts that have not "debt-financed" their purchase of PFIC stock, except to be concerned about proper reporting and timing of the dividend income subject to section 4940 excise taxes. If an organization does have debt-financed stock,

---

154. *See* § 11.4.
155. *See* Blazek, *IRS Form 990 Tax Preparation Guide for Nonprofits*.
156. IRC § 957(a).
157. IRC § 297(a).

deferring the UBTI produced comes at a high price. Whenever the deferred income is reported, all of the income is taxed as ordinary income even though some capital gains may have been included. In addition to the taxes due on the debt-financed income, an "interest penalty" must be paid.[158] To avoid the ordinary income classification for all income and to avoid the interest penalty, the organization may wish to make a qualified electing fund election. If this type of an election is made, the organization currently includes its pro rata share of the offshore hedge fund's ordinary and long-term gains in income for each tax year, and pays tax thereon even though such income and gains are not actually distributed.[159]

In addition to the complexities noted, there are other tax reporting forms to be filed in connection with foreign investments, particularly when the investment exceeds $100,000. If the investment entity is a foreign corporation, Form 926 and/or Form 5471 may be required. For PFIC corporate forms, Form 8621 may need to be filed. For a partnership investment entity, Form 8865 may be required. Prudent organizations will take the additional costs of meeting the filing requirements and enhanced auditing fees into account in evaluating the potential return on such foreign investment vehicles.

---

158. IRC § 1291(c)(3).

159. For a more detailed discussion of the QEF election and other tax aspects of foreign alternative investments, see Nelson, "The Tax Consequences of Passive Offshore Investments" 17 *Taxation of Exempts* 152 (Jan./Feb. 2006); Haag, "Hedge Fund Investments of Private Foundations and Educational Endowments," 50 *Exempt. Org. Tax Rev.* (No. 2) 261 (Nov. 2005).

**EXHIBIT 12.1**

Mock-Up of Form 990-PF, Return of Private Foundation (including cross-references to book chapters)

| Cross-Reference: Chapters and Form 990-PF | |
| --- | --- |
| Part I | Chapter 10 §§ 3–5 and Chapter 12 § 1(a)-(c) |
| Part II | Chapter 12 § 1(d) |
| Part III | Chapter 12 § 1(e) |
| Pat IV | Chapter 10 § 4 and Chapter 12 § 1(f) |
| Part V | Chapter 10 § 2 and Chapter 12 § 2(a) |
| Part VI | Chapter 10 § 1 and Chapter 12 § 2(b) |
| Part VII | Chapter 12 § 2(c)-(d) |
| Part VIII | Chapter 5 §§ 6–7 and Chapter 12 § 2(e) |
| Part IX | Chapters 6 § 5(b), 8 § 3, and 12 § 2(f)-(g) |
| Part X | Chapter 6 §§ 1–3 and Chapter 12 § 2(h) |
| Part XI | Chapter 6 § 4 and Chapter 12 § 2(i) |
| Part XII | Chapter 6 § 5 and Chapter 12 § 2(j) |
| Part XIII | Chapter 6 § 7 and Chapter 12 § 2(k) |
| Part XIV | Chapter 3 §1 and Chapter 12 § 2(i) |
| Part XV | Chapters 4 §§ 1–7, 6 § 5, 9 §§ 3–6, and 12 § 2(m) |
| Part XVI | Chapter 11 and Chapter 12 § 2(n) |
| Part XVII | Chapter 9 § (8) |

| Form **990-PF** | **Return of Private Foundation** | OMB No. 1545-0052 |
|---|---|---|
| | or Section 4947(a)(1) Trust Treated as Private Foundation | **20**13 |
| Department of the Treasury<br>Internal Revenue Service | ► Do not enter Social Security numbers on this form as it may be made public.<br>► Information about Form 990-PF and its separate instructions is at *www.irs.gov/form990pf*. | Open to Public Inspection |

For calendar year 2013 or tax year beginning _____, 2013, and ending _____, 20___

| Name of foundation | | A Employer identification number |
|---|---|---|
| Environmentalist Fund | | 77-7777777 |

| Number and street (or P.O. box number if mail is not delivered to street address) | Room/suite | B Telephone number (see instructions) |
|---|---|---|
| 1111 Any Street | | 444-444-4466 |

City or town, state or province, country, and ZIP or foreign postal code

Hometown, TX 77777-7777

**G** Check all that apply: ☐ Initial return ☐ Initial return of a former public charity
☐ Final return ☐ Amended return
☐ Address change ☐ Name change

**C** If exemption application is pending, check here ► ☐

**D** 1. Foreign organizations, check here . . . ► ☐
2. Foreign organizations meeting the 85% test, check here and attach computation . . ► ☐

**E** If private foundation status was terminated under section 507(b)(1)(A), check here . . . . ► ☐

**H** Check type of organization: ☑ Section 501(c)(3) exempt private foundation
☐ Section 4947(a)(1) nonexempt charitable trust ☐ Other taxable private foundation

**I** Fair market value of all assets at end of year *(from Part II, col. (c), line 16)* ► $ **22,474,800.**

**J** Accounting method: ☐ Cash ☑ Accrual
☐ Other (specify) _____
*(Part I, column (d) must be on cash basis.)*

**F** If the foundation is in a 60-month termination under section 507(b)(1)(B), check here . . ► ☐

**Part I** Analysis of Revenue and Expenses *(The total of amounts in columns (b), (c), and (d) may not necessarily equal the amounts in column (a) (see instructions).)*

| | | (a) Revenue and expenses per books | (b) Net investment income | (c) Adjusted net income | (d) Disbursements for charitable purposes (cash basis only) |
|---|---|---|---|---|---|
| 1 | Contributions, gifts, grants, etc., received (attach schedule) | 2,510,000. | | | |
| 2 | Check ► ☐ if the foundation is **not** required to attach Sch. B | | | | |
| 3 | Interest on savings and temporary cash investments | 10,000. | 12,000. | | |
| 4 | Dividends and interest from securities . . . . | 380,000. | 380,000. | | |
| 5a | Gross rents . . . . . . . . | 75,000. | 30,000. | | |
| b | Net rental income or (loss) _____ 14,800. | | | | |
| 6a | Net gain or (loss) from sale of assets not on line 10 | 399,000. | | | |
| b | Gross sales price for all assets on line 6a _____ | | | | |
| 7 | Capital gain net income (from Part IV, line 2) . . | | 980,000. | | |
| 8 | Net short-term capital gain . . . . . . | | | | |
| 9 | Income modifications . . . . . . . | | | | |
| 10a | Gross sales less returns and allowances _____ 2,500. | | | | |
| b | Less: Cost of goods sold . . . _____ 1,000. | | | | |
| c | Gross profit or (loss) (attach schedule) . . . . | 1,500. | | 1,500. | |
| 11 | Other income (attach schedule) . . . . . | 442,000. | 342,000. | 20,000. | |
| 12 | **Total.** Add lines 1 through 11 . . . . . | 3,817,500. | 1,744,000. | 21,500. | |
| 13 | Compensation of officers, directors, trustees, etc. | 92,000. | | | 97,000. |
| 14 | Other employee salaries and wages . . . . . | 240,000. | 10,000. | 1,000. | 241,800. |
| 15 | Pension plans, employee benefits . . . . | 28,000. | 2,500. | 400. | 33,200. |
| 16a | Legal fees (attach schedule) . . . . . | 20,000. | 4,000. | 3,000. | 15,000. |
| b | Accounting fees (attach schedule) . . . . | 20,000. | 2,000. | 500. | 17,000. |
| c | Other professional fees (attach schedule) . . . | 80,000. | 10,000. | | 72,000. |
| 17 | Interest . . . . . . . . . . | 24,000. | 7,200. | | 6,000. |
| 18 | Taxes (attach schedule) (see instructions) . . . . | 55,000. | 24,000. | | |
| 19 | Depreciation (attach schedule) and depletion . . | 35,200. | 28,080. | | |
| 20 | Occupancy . . . . . . . . . | 20,000. | | | 23,000. |
| 21 | Travel, conferences, and meetings . . . . | 40,000. | 4,000. | 1,000. | 36,000. |
| 22 | Printing and publications . . . . . . | 88,000. | 2,000. | | 90,000. |
| 23 | Other expenses (attach schedule) . . . . . | 97,400. | 11,200. | | 88,500. |
| 24 | **Total operating and administrative expenses.** Add lines 13 through 23 . . . . . . . | 839,600. | 104,980. | 5,900. | 719,500. |
| 25 | Contributions, gifts, grants paid . . . . . | 450,000. | | | 450,000. |
| 26 | **Total expenses and disbursements.** Add lines 24 and 25 | 1,289,600. | 104,980. | 5,900. | 1,169,500. |
| 27 | Subtract line 26 from line 12: | | | | |
| a | **Excess of revenue over expenses and disbursements** | 2,527,900. | | | |
| b | **Net investment income** (if negative, enter -0-) . | | 1,639,020. | | |
| c | **Adjusted net income** (if negative, enter -0-) . . | | | 15,600. | |

For Paperwork Reduction Act Notice, see instructions.      Cat. No. 11289X      Form **990-PF** (2013)

**EXHIBIT 12.1**

*(Continued)*

Form 990-PF (2013)
Page **2**

| Part II | Balance Sheets | Attached schedules and amounts in the description column should be for end-of-year amounts only. (See instructions.) | Beginning of year (a) Book Value | End of year (b) Book Value | End of year (c) Fair Market Value |
|---|---|---|---|---|---|
| | 1 | Cash—non-interest-bearing . . . . . . . . | | | |
| | 2 | Savings and temporary cash investments . . . . . . . | 250,000. | 451,600. | 451,600. |
| | 3 | Accounts receivable ▶ _ _ _ _ _ _ _ 12,000. | | | |
| | | Less: allowance for doubtful accounts ▶_ _ _ _ _ _ _ | 8,000. | 12,000. | 12,000. |
| | 4 | Pledges receivable ▶ _ _ _ _ _ _ _ _ | | | |
| | | Less: allowance for doubtful accounts ▶_ _ _ _ _ _ _ | | | |
| | 5 | Grants receivable . . . . . . . . . . . | | | |
| | 6 | Receivables due from officers, directors, trustees, and other disqualified persons (attach schedule) (see instructions) . . | | 4,000. | 4,000. |
| | 7 | Other notes and loans receivable (attach schedule) ▶ _ _ _ _ _ | | | |
| | | Less: allowance for doubtful accounts ▶ _ _ _ _ _ | | | |
| Assets | 8 | Inventories for sale or use . . . . . . . . | 1,500. | 2,000. | 3,000. |
| | 9 | Prepaid expenses and deferred charges . . . . . . | 4,500. | 9,200. | 9,200. |
| | 10a | Investments—U.S. and state government obligations (attach schedule) | | | |
| | b | Investments—corporate stock (attach schedule) . . . . | 18,300,000. | 19,195,000. | 19,195,000. |
| | c | Investments—corporate bonds (attach schedule) | | | |
| | 11 | Investments—land, buildings, and equipment: basis ▶ _ _ _ 1,000,000. | | | |
| | | Less: accumulated depreciation (attach schedule) ▶ _ _ _ 150,900. | 131,800. | 849,100. | 1,250,000. |
| | 12 | Investments—mortgage loans . . . . . . . . | | | |
| | 13 | Investments—other (attach schedule) . . . . . . . | 200,000. | 800,000. | 800,000. |
| | 14 | Land, buildings, and equipment: basis ▶ _ _ _ _ 250,000. | | | |
| | | Less: accumulated depreciation (attach schedule) ▶ _ _ _ 2,500. | | 247,500. | 250,000. |
| | 15 | Other assets (describe ▶ Statement 14 _ _ _ _ _ _ ) | | 500,000. | 500,000. |
| | 16 | Total assets (to be completed by all filers—see the instructions. Also, see page 1, item I) . . . . . . . | 18,895,800. | 22,070,400. | 22,474,800. |
| Liabilities | 17 | Accounts payable and accrued expenses . . . . . . | 100,000. | 50,000. | |
| | 18 | Grants payable . . . . . . . . . . . . | 200,000. | 100.000. | |
| | 19 | Deferred revenue . . . . . . . . . . . . | | | |
| | 20 | Loans from officers, directors, trustees, and other disqualified persons | | | |
| | 21 | Mortgages and other notes payable (attach schedule) . . . | | 590,000. | |
| | 22 | Other liabilities (describe ▶ Statement 16 _ _ _ _ ) | | 20,000. | |
| | 23 | Total liabilities (add lines 17 through 22) . . . . . . | 300,000. | 760,000. | |
| Net Assets or Fund Balances | | Foundations that follow SFAS 117, check here . . ▶ ☑ and complete lines 24 through 26 and lines 30 and 31. | | | |
| | 24 | Unrestricted . . . . . . . . . . . . . | 18,595,800. | 21,310,400. | |
| | 25 | Temporarily restricted . . . . . . . . . . | | | |
| | 26 | Permanently restricted . . . . . . . . . . | | | |
| | | Foundations that do not follow SFAS 117, check here ▶ ☐ and complete lines 27 through 31. | | | |
| | 27 | Capital stock, trust principal, or current funds . . . . . | | | |
| | 28 | Paid-in or capital surplus, or land, bldg., and equipment fund | | | |
| | 29 | Retained earnings, accumulated income, endowment, or other funds | | | |
| | 30 | Total net assets or fund balances (see instructions) . . . | 18,595,800. | 21,310,400. | |
| | 31 | Total liabilities and net assets/fund balances (see instructions) . . . . . . . . . . . . . . . | 18,895,800. | 22,070,400. | |

| Part III | Analysis of Changes in Net Assets or Fund Balances | | |
|---|---|---|---|
| 1 | Total net assets or fund balances at beginning of year—Part II, column (a), line 30 (must agree with end-of-year figure reported on prior year's return) . . . . . . . . . . . . . . . . . . . . | 1 | 18,595,800. |
| 2 | Enter amount from Part I, line 27a . . . . . . . . . . . . . . . . . . . . . . | 2 | 2,527,900. |
| 3 | Other increases not included in line 2 (itemize) ▶ See Statement 17 _ _ _ _ _ _ _ _ _ _ | 3 | 186,700. |
| 4 | Add lines 1, 2, and 3 . . . . . . . . . . . . . . . . . . . . . . . . | 4 | 21,310,400 |
| 5 | Decreases not included in line 2 (itemize) ▶ _ _ _ _ _ _ _ _ _ _ _ _ _ _ _ | 5 | |
| 6 | Total net assets or fund balances at end of year (line 4 minus line 5)—Part II, column (b), line 30 . . | 6 | 21,310,400. |

Form **990-PF** (2013)

EXHIBIT **12.1**

(*Continued*)

Form 990-PF (2013)                                                                                                         Page **3**

## Part IV — Capital Gains and Losses for Tax on Investment Income

| (a) List and describe the kind(s) of property sold (e.g., real estate, 2-story brick warehouse; or common stock, 200 shs. MLC Co.) | (b) How acquired P—Purchase D—Donation | (c) Date acquired (mo., day, yr.) | (d) Date sold (mo., day, yr.) |
|---|---|---|---|
| **1a**  Publicly-traded securities | D | Various | Various |
| **b** | | | |
| **c** | | | |
| **d** | | | |
| **e** | | | |

| (e) Gross sales price | (f) Depreciation allowed (or allowable) | (g) Cost or other basis plus expense of sale | (h) Gain or (loss) (e) plus (f) minus (g) |
|---|---|---|---|
| **a**  1,000,000. | | 20,000. | 980,000. |
| **b** | | | |
| **c** | | | |
| **d** | | | |
| **e** | | | |

Complete only for assets showing gain in column (h) and owned by the foundation on 12/31/69

| (i) F.M.V. as of 12/31/69 | (j) Adjusted basis as of 12/31/69 | (k) Excess of col. (i) over col. (j), if any | (l) Gains (Col. (h) gain minus col. (k), but not less than -0-) or Losses (from col. (h)) |
|---|---|---|---|
| **a** | | | 980,000. |
| **b** | | | |
| **c** | | | |
| **d** | | | |
| **e** | | | |

| | | | | |
|---|---|---|---|---|
| **2** | Capital gain net income or (net capital loss) { If gain, also enter in Part I, line 7 / If (loss), enter -0- in Part I, line 7 } | **2** | | 980,000. |
| **3** | Net short-term capital gain or (loss) as defined in sections 1222(5) and (6): If gain, also enter in Part I, line 8, column (c) (see instructions).  If (loss), enter -0- in Part I, line 8 . . . . . . . . . . . | **3** | | 0. |

## Part V — Qualification Under Section 4940(e) for Reduced Tax on Net Investment Income

(For optional use by domestic private foundations subject to the section 4940(a) tax on net investment income.)

If section 4940(d)(2) applies, leave this part blank.

Was the foundation liable for the section 4942 tax on the distributable amount of any year in the base period?          ☐ Yes ☑ No
If "Yes," the foundation does not qualify under section 4940(e). Do not complete this part.

**1**   Enter the appropriate amount in each column for each year; see the instructions before making any entries.

| (a) Base period years Calendar year (or tax year beginning in) | (b) Adjusted qualifying distributions | (c) Net value of noncharitable-use assets | (d) Distribution ratio (col. (b) divided by col. (c)) |
|---|---|---|---|
| 2012 | 1,900,000. | 22,500,000. | 0.084444 |
| 2011 | 1,500,000. | 22,000,000. | 0.068182 |
| 2010 | 2,000,000 | 21,000,000. | 0.095238 |
| 2009 | 1,400,000. | 25,000,000. | 0.056000 |
| 2008 | 1,000,000. | 20,000,000. | 0.050000 |

| | | | | |
|---|---|---|---|---|
| **2** | **Total** of line 1, column (d) . . . . . . . . . . . . . . . . . | **2** | | 0.353864 |
| **3** | Average distribution ratio for the 5-year base period—divide the total on line 2 by 5, or by the number of years the foundation has been in existence if less than 5 years  . . . . . . | **3** | | 0.070773 |
| **4** | Enter the net value of noncharitable-use assets for 2013 from Part X, line 5 . . . . . . | **4** | | 22,458,000. |
| **5** | Multiply line 4 by line 3  . . . . . . . . . . . . . . . . . | **5** | | 1,589,420. |
| **6** | Enter 1% of net investment income (1% of Part I, line 27b)  . . . . . . . . . . | **6** | | 16,390 |
| **7** | Add lines 5 and 6  . . . . . . . . . . . . . . . . . . . | **7** | | 1,605,810 |
| **8** | Enter qualifying distributions from Part XII, line 4 . . . . . . . . . . . . . . | **8** | | 1,919,500. |

If line 8 is equal to or greater than line 7, check the box in Part VI, line 1b, and complete that part using a 1% tax rate. See the Part VI instructions.

Form **990-PF** (2013)

## EXHIBIT 12.1

*(Continued)*

Form 990-PF (2013)                                                                                           Page **4**

## Part VI — Excise Tax Based on Investment Income (Section 4940(a), 4940(b), 4940(e), or 4948—see instructions)

| | | | |
|---|---|---|---|
| **1a** | Exempt operating foundations described in section 4940(d)(2), check here ▶ ☐ and enter "N/A" on line 1. Date of ruling or determination letter: _____ _____ _____ **(attach copy of letter if necessary—see instructions)** | | |
| **b** | Domestic foundations that meet the section 4940(e) requirements in Part V, check here ▶ ☑ and enter 1% of Part I, line 27b . . . . . . . . . . . . . . | **1** | 16,390. |
| **c** | All other domestic foundations enter 2% of line 27b. Exempt foreign organizations enter 4% of Part I, line 12, col. (b). | | |
| **2** | Tax under section 511 (domestic section 4947(a)(1) trusts and taxable foundations only. Others enter -0-) | **2** | 0. |
| **3** | Add lines 1 and 2 . . . . . . . . . . . . . . . . . . . . . . . . . | **3** | 16,390. |
| **4** | Subtitle A (income) tax (domestic section 4947(a)(1) trusts and taxable foundations only. Others enter -0-) | **4** | 0. |
| **5** | **Tax based on investment income.** Subtract line 4 from line 3. If zero or less, enter -0- . . . . | **5** | 16,390. |
| **6** | Credits/Payments: | | |
| **a** | 2013 estimated tax payments and 2012 overpayment credited to 2013    **6a**    16,790. | | |
| **b** | Exempt foreign organizations—tax withheld at source . . . . .    **6b** | | |
| **c** | Tax paid with application for extension of time to file (Form 8868) .    **6c** | | |
| **d** | Backup withholding erroneously withheld . . . . . . . . .    **6d**    250. | | |
| **7** | Total credits and payments. Add lines 6a through 6d . . . . . . . . . . | **7** | 17,040. |
| **8** | Enter any **penalty** for underpayment of estimated tax. Check here ☑ if Form 2220 is attached | **8** | |
| **9** | **Tax due.** If the total of lines 5 and 8 is more than line 7, enter **amount owed** . . . . . ▶ | **9** | 0. |
| **10** | **Overpayment.** If line 7 is more than the total of lines 5 and 8, enter the **amount overpaid** . . ▶ | **10** | 650. |
| **11** | Enter the amount of line 10 to be: **Credited to 2014 estimated tax** ▶   650.   **Refunded** ▶ | **11** | 0. |

## Part VII-A — Statements Regarding Activities

| | | | Yes | No |
|---|---|---|---|---|
| **1a** | During the tax year, did the foundation attempt to influence any national, state, or local legislation or did it participate or intervene in any political campaign? . . . . . . . . . . . . . . . . . | **1a** | | ✓ |
| **b** | Did it spend more than $100 during the year (either directly or indirectly) for political purposes (see Instructions for the definition)? . . . . . . . . . . . . . . . . . . . . . . | **1b** | | ✓ |
| | *If the answer is "Yes" to 1a or 1b, attach a detailed description of the activities and copies of any materials published or distributed by the foundation in connection with the activities.* | | | |
| **c** | Did the foundation file **Form 1120-POL** for this year? . . . . . . . . . . . . . . . | **1c** | | ✓ |
| **d** | Enter the amount (if any) of tax on political expenditures (section 4955) imposed during the year: **(1)** On the foundation. ▶ $ _____ **(2)** On foundation managers. ▶ $ _____ | | | |
| **e** | Enter the reimbursement (if any) paid by the foundation during the year for political expenditure tax imposed on foundation managers. ▶ $ _____ | | | |
| **2** | Has the foundation engaged in any activities that have not previously been reported to the IRS? . . . . *If "Yes," attach a detailed description of the activities.* | **2** | | ✓ |
| **3** | Has the foundation made any changes, not previously reported to the IRS, in its governing instrument, articles of incorporation, or bylaws, or other similar instruments? *If "Yes," attach a conformed copy of the changes* . . | **3** | | ✓ |
| **4a** | Did the foundation have unrelated business gross income of $1,000 or more during the year? . . . . . | **4a** | ✓ | |
| **b** | If "Yes," has it filed a tax return on **Form 990-T** for this year? . . . . . . . . . . . . | **4b** | ✓ | |
| **5** | Was there a liquidation, termination, dissolution, or substantial contraction during the year? . . . . . *If "Yes," attach the statement required by General Instruction T.* | **5** | | ✓ |
| **6** | Are the requirements of section 508(e) (relating to sections 4941 through 4945) satisfied either: ● By language in the governing instrument, or ● By state legislation that effectively amends the governing instrument so that no mandatory directions that conflict with the state law remain in the governing instrument? . . . . . . . . . . . . . | **6** | ✓ | |
| **7** | Did the foundation have at least $5,000 in assets at any time during the year? *If "Yes," complete Part II, col. (c), and Part XV* | **7** | ✓ | |
| **8a** | Enter the states to which the foundation reports or with which it is registered (see instructions) ▶ TX | | | |
| **b** | If the answer is "Yes" to line 7, has the foundation furnished a copy of Form 990-PF to the Attorney General (or designate) of each state as required by *General Instruction G? If "No," attach explanation* . . . . . | **8b** | ✓ | |
| **9** | Is the foundation claiming status as a private operating foundation within the meaning of section 4942(j)(3) or 4942(j)(5) for calendar year 2013 or the taxable year beginning in 2013 (see instructions for Part XIV)? *If "Yes," complete Part XIV* . . . . . . . . . . . . . . . . . . . . . . . . . . | **9** | | ✓ |
| **10** | Did any persons become substantial contributors during the tax year? *If "Yes," attach a schedule listing their names and addresses* . . . . . . . . . . . . . . . . . . . . . . . . . | **10** | | ✓ |

Form **990-PF** (2013)

**EXHIBIT 12.1**

*(Continued)*

| Form 990-PF (2013) | | | Page **5** |
|---|---|---|---|

**Part VII-A** Statements Regarding Activities *(continued)*

| | | | |
|---|---|---|---|
| 11 | At any time during the year, did the foundation, directly or indirectly, own a controlled entity within the meaning of section 512(b)(13)? If "Yes," attach schedule (see instructions) . . . . . . . . . . . | **11** | ✓ |
| 12 | Did the foundation make a distribution to a donor advised fund over which the foundation or a disqualified person had advisory privileges? If "Yes," attach statement (see instructions) . . . . . . . . . . . | **12** | ✓ |
| 13 | Did the foundation comply with the public inspection requirements for its annual returns and exemption application? | **13** | ✓ |

Website address ▶ www.environmentalistfund.org

14 The books are in care of ▶ Mary Goodbooks _____ Telephone no. ▶ ___ 444-444-4444 ___
Located at ▶ 1011 Main Street. Hometown, TX _____ ZIP+4 ▶ _77777-7777_

15 Section 4947(a)(1) nonexempt charitable trusts filing Form 990-PF in lieu of **Form 1041**—Check here. . . . . . . . ▶ ☐
and enter the amount of tax-exempt interest received or accrued during the year . . . . . ▶ | **15** | N/A

| | | | Yes | No |
|---|---|---|---|---|
| 16 | At any time during calendar year 2013, did the foundation have an interest in or a signature or other authority over a bank, securities, or other financial account in a foreign country?. . . . . . . . . . . . . **16** | | | ✓ |

See the instructions for exceptions and filing requirements for Form TD F 90-22.1. If "Yes," enter the name of the foreign country ▶

**Part VII-B** Statements Regarding Activities for Which Form 4720 May Be Required

File Form 4720 if any item is checked in the "Yes" column, unless an exception applies.

| | | | Yes | No |
|---|---|---|---|---|
| 1a | During the year did the foundation (either directly or indirectly): | | | |
| | **(1)** Engage in the sale or exchange, or leasing of property with a disqualified person? . . ☐ Yes ☑ No | | | |
| | **(2)** Borrow money from, lend money to, or otherwise extend credit to (or accept it from) a disqualified person? . . . . . . . . . . . . . . . ☑ Yes ☐ No | | | |
| | **(3)** Furnish goods, services, or facilities to (or accept them from) a disqualified person? . . ☐ Yes ☑ No | | | |
| | **(4)** Pay compensation to, or pay or reimburse the expenses of, a disqualified person? . . ☑ Yes ☐ No | | | |
| | **(5)** Transfer any income or assets to a disqualified person (or make any of either available for the benefit or use of a disqualified person)? . . . . . . . . . ☐ Yes ☑ No | | | |
| | **(6)** Agree to pay money or property to a government official? (**Exception.** Check "No" if the foundation agreed to make a grant to or to employ the official for a period after termination of government service, if terminating within 90 days.) . . . . . . ☐ Yes ☑ No | | | |
| b | If any answer is "Yes" to 1a(1)–(6), did **any** of the acts fail to qualify under the exceptions described in Regulations section 53.4941(d)-3 or in a current notice regarding disaster assistance (see instructions)? . . . . . . . | **1b** | ✓ | |
| | Organizations relying on a current notice regarding disaster assistance check here . . . . . . ▶☐ | | | |
| c | Did the foundation engage in a prior year in any of the acts described in 1a, other than excepted acts, that were not corrected before the first day of the tax year beginning in 2013? . . . . . . . . . | **1c** | | ✓ |
| 2 | Taxes on failure to distribute income (section 4942) (does not apply for years the foundation was a private operating foundation defined in section 4942(j)(3) or 4942(j)(5)): | | | |
| a | At the end of tax year 2013, did the foundation have any undistributed income (lines 6d and 6e, Part XIII) for tax year(s) beginning before 2013? . . . . . . . . . . . ☐ Yes ☑ No | | | |
| | If "Yes," list the years ▶ 20___ , 20___ , 20___ , 20___ | | | |
| b | Are there any years listed in 2a for which the foundation is **not** applying the provisions of section 4942(a)(2) (relating to incorrect valuation of assets) to the year's undistributed income? (If applying section 4942(a)(2) to **all** years listed, answer "No" and attach statement—see instructions.) . . . . . . . . | **2b** | | |
| c | If the provisions of section 4942(a)(2) are being applied to **any** of the years listed in 2a, list the years here. ▶ 20___ , 20___ , 20___ , 20___ | | | |
| 3a | Did the foundation hold more than a 2% direct or indirect interest in any business enterprise at any time during the year? . . . . . . . . . . . . . . . . . ☐ Yes ☑ No | | | |
| b | If "Yes," did it have excess business holdings in 2013 as a result of **(1)** any purchase by the foundation or disqualified persons after May 26, 1969; **(2)** the lapse of the 5-year period (or longer period approved by the Commissioner under section 4943(c)(7)) to dispose of holdings acquired by gift or bequest; or **(3)** the lapse of the 10-, 15-, or 20-year first phase holding period? *(Use Schedule C, Form 4720, to determine if the foundation had excess business holdings in 2013.)* . . . . . . . . . . . . . | **3b** | | |
| 4a | Did the foundation invest during the year any amount in a manner that would jeopardize its charitable purposes? | **4a** | | ✓ |
| b | Did the foundation make any investment in a prior year (but after December 31, 1969) that could jeopardize its charitable purpose that had not been removed from jeopardy before the first day of the tax year beginning in 2013? | **4b** | | ✓ |

Form **990-PF** (2013)

**EXHIBIT 12.1**

*(Continued)*

Form 990-PF (2013)                                                                                                    Page **6**

| **Part VII-B** | **Statements Regarding Activities for Which Form 4720 May Be Required** *(continued)* | | |
|---|---|---|---|

**5a** During the year did the foundation pay or incur any amount to:

   **(1)** Carry on propaganda, or otherwise attempt to influence legislation (section 4945(e))?   ☐ **Yes** ☑ **No**

   **(2)** Influence the outcome of any specific public election (see section 4955); or to carry on, directly or indirectly, any voter registration drive?   ☐ **Yes** ☑ **No**

   **(3)** Provide a grant to an individual for travel, study, or other similar purposes?   ☐ **Yes** ☑ **No**

   **(4)** Provide a grant to an organization other than a charitable, etc., organization described in section 509(a)(1), (2), or (3), or section 4940(d)(2)? (see instructions)   ☑ **Yes** ☐ **No**

   **(5)** Provide for any purpose other than religious, charitable, scientific, literary, or educational purposes, or for the prevention of cruelty to children or animals?   ☐ **Yes** ☑ **No**

 **b** If any answer is "Yes" to 5a(1)–(5), did **any** of the transactions fail to qualify under the exceptions described in Regulations section 53.4945 or in a current notice regarding disaster assistance (see instructions)?    **5b**   ✓

   Organizations relying on a current notice regarding disaster assistance check here    ► ☐

 **c** If the answer is "Yes" to question 5a(4), does the foundation claim exemption from the tax because it maintained expenditure responsibility for the grant?    ☑ **Yes** ☐ **No**

   *If "Yes," attach the statement required by Regulations section 53.4945–5(d).*     See attachment

**6a** Did the foundation, during the year, receive any funds, directly or indirectly, to pay premiums on a personal benefit contract?    ☐ **Yes** ☑ **No**

 **b** Did the foundation, during the year, pay premiums, directly or indirectly, on a personal benefit contract?    **6b**   ✓

   *If "Yes" to 6b, file Form 8870.*

**7a** At any time during the tax year, was the foundation a party to a prohibited tax shelter transaction?    ☐ **Yes** ☑ **No**

 **b** If "Yes," did the foundation receive any proceeds or have any net income attributable to the transaction?    **7b**

| **Part VIII** | **Information About Officers, Directors, Trustees, Foundation Managers, Highly Paid Employees, and Contractors** |
|---|---|

**1** List all officers, directors, trustees, foundation managers and their compensation (see instructions).

| (a) Name and address | (b) Title, and average hours per week devoted to position | (c) Compensation (If not paid, enter -0-) | (d) Contributions to employee benefit plans and deferred compensation | (e) Expense account, other allowances |
|---|---|---|---|---|
| Jane E. Environmentalist 1111 Any Street, Hometown, TX 77777-7777 | President 2.00 | 0. | 0. | 0. |
| John J. Environmentalist 1111 Any Street, Hometown, TX 77777-7777 | Vice President 2.00 | 0. | 0. | 0. |
| John J. Environmentalist, Jr. 1111 Any Street, Hometown, TX 77777-7777 | Sec/Treasurer 1.00 | 0. | 0. | 0. |
| Joanne Liberalminded 1111 Any Street, Hometown, TX 77777-7777 | Executive Director 40.00 | 80,000. | 12,000. | 0. |

**2** Compensation of five highest-paid employees (other than those included on line 1—see instructions). If none, enter "NONE."

| (a) Name and address of each employee paid more than $50,000 | (b) Title, and average hours per week devoted to position | (c) Compensation | (d) Contributions to employee benefit plans and deferred compensation | (e) Expense account, other allowances |
|---|---|---|---|---|
| None | | | | |
| | | | | |
| | | | | |
| | | | | |
| | | | | |

**Total** number of other employees paid over $50,000    ►    0.

Form **990-PF** (2013)

**EXHIBIT 12.1**

*(Continued)*

Form 990-PF (2013)                                                                                                Page **7**

**Part VIII** Information About Officers, Directors, Trustees, Foundation Managers, Highly Paid Employees, and Contractors *(continued)*

**3** Five highest-paid independent contractors for professional services (see instructions). If none, enter "NONE."

| (a) Name and address of each person paid more than $50,000 | (b) Type of service | (c) Compensation |
|---|---|---|
| None | | |
| | | |
| | | |
| | | |
| | | |
| | | |

**Total** number of others receiving over $50,000 for professional services . . . . . . . . . . . . . . ▶ |

**Part IX-A** **Summary of Direct Charitable Activities**

| List the foundation's four largest direct charitable activities during the tax year. Include relevant statistical information such as the number of organizations and other beneficiaries served, conferences convened, research papers produced, etc. | Expenses |
|---|---|
| **1** Collected and published statistics on water usage in state. Distributed publication to 52 municipalities, 250 school districts, and media within a 20-county area most affected by declining water table. Sponsored public meetings at which scientists performing study explained methodology and results. | 524,000. |
| **2** | |
| **3** | |
| **4** | |

**Part IX-B** **Summary of Program-Related Investments** (see instructions)

| Describe the two largest program-related investments made by the foundation during the tax year on lines 1 and 2. | Amount |
|---|---|
| **1** New Energy Solution - a start-up engineering firm inventing pollution measuring devices. | |
| | 500,000. |
| **2** | |
| All other program-related investments. See instructions. | |
| **3** | |
| **Total.** Add lines 1 through 3 . . . . . . . . . . . . . . . . . . . . . . . . . . . . . . ▶ | 500,000. |

Form **990-PF** (2013)

**EXHIBIT 12.1**

*(Continued)*

# § 12.3 COMPLIANCE ISSUES

**Part X** Minimum Investment Return (All domestic foundations must complete this part. Foreign foundations, see instructions.)

| | | | |
|---|---|---|---|
| 1 | Fair market value of assets not used (or held for use) directly in carrying out charitable, etc., purposes: | | |
| a | Average monthly fair market value of securities | 1a | 20,000,000. |
| b | Average of monthly cash balances | 1b | 1,000,000. |
| c | Fair market value of all other assets (see instructions) | 1c | 1,800,000. |
| d | **Total** (add lines 1a, b, and c) | 1d | 22,800,000. |
| e | Reduction claimed for blockage or other factors reported on lines 1a and 1c (attach detailed explanation) . . . . . . . . . . 1e | 0. | |
| 2 | Acquisition indebtedness applicable to line 1 assets | 2 | 0. |
| 3 | Subtract line 2 from line 1d | 3 | 22,800,000. |
| 4 | Cash deemed held for charitable activities. Enter 1 ½ % of line 3 (for greater amount, see instructions) | 4 | 342,000. |
| 5 | **Net value of noncharitable-use assets.** Subtract line 4 from line 3. Enter here and on Part V, line 4 | 5 | 22,458,000 |
| 6 | **Minimum investment return.** Enter 5% of line 5 | 6 | 1,122,900 |

**Part XI** Distributable Amount (see instructions) (Section 4942(j)(3) and (j)(5) private operating foundations and certain foreign organizations check here ► ☐ and do not complete this part.)

| | | | |
|---|---|---|---|
| 1 | Minimum investment return from Part X, line 6 | 1 | 1,122,900 |
| 2a | Tax on investment income for 2013 from Part VI, line 5 . . . 2a 16,390 | | |
| b | Income tax for 2013. (This does not include the tax from Part VI.) . . . 2b 21,261 | | |
| c | Add lines 2a and 2b | 2c | 37,651 |
| 3 | Distributable amount before adjustments. Subtract line 2c from line 1 | 3 | 1,085,249 |
| 4 | Recoveries of amounts treated as qualifying distributions | 4 | |
| 5 | Add lines 3 and 4 | 5 | 1,085,249 |
| 6 | Deduction from distributable amount (see instructions) | 6 | |
| 7 | **Distributable amount** as adjusted. Subtract line 6 from line 5. Enter here and on Part XIII, line 1 | 7 | 1,085,249 |

**Part XII** Qualifying Distributions (see instructions)

| | | | |
|---|---|---|---|
| 1 | Amounts paid (including administrative expenses) to accomplish charitable, etc., purposes: | | |
| a | Expenses, contributions, gifts, etc.—total from Part I, column (d), line 26 | 1a | 1,169,500. |
| b | Program-related investments—total from Part IX-B | 1b | 500,000. |
| 2 | Amounts paid to acquire assets used (or held for use) directly in carrying out charitable, etc., purposes | 2 | 250,000. |
| 3 | Amounts set aside for specific charitable projects that satisfy the: | | |
| a | Suitability test (prior IRS approval required) | 3a | |
| b | Cash distribution test (attach the required schedule) | 3b | |
| 4 | Qualifying distributions. Add lines 1a through 3b. Enter here and on Part V, line 8, and Part XIII, line 4 | 4 | 1,919,500. |
| 5 | Foundations that qualify under section 4940(e) for the reduced rate of tax on net investment income. Enter 1% of Part I, line 27b (see instructions) | 5 | 16,390 |
| 6 | **Adjusted qualifying distributions.** Subtract line 5 from line 4 | 6 | 1,903,110. |

**Note.** The amount on line 6 will be used in Part V, column (b), in subsequent years when calculating whether the foundation qualifies for the section 4940(e) reduction of tax in those years.

Form **990-PF** (2013)

**EXHIBIT 12.1**

*(Continued)*

Form 990-PF (2013)                                                                                          Page **9**

| **Part XIII** | **Undistributed Income** (see instructions) | **(a)** Corpus | **(b)** Years prior to 2012 | **(c)** 2012 | **(d)** 2013 |
|---|---|---|---|---|---|
| 1 | Distributable amount for 2013 from Part XI, line 7 . . . . . . . . . . . . . . | | | | 1,085,249 |
| 2 | Undistributed income, if any, as of the end of 2013: | | | | |
| a | Enter amount for 2012 only . . . . . . | | | 0. | |
| b | Total for prior years: 20___,20___,20___ | | 0. | | |
| 3 | Excess distributions carryover, if any, to 2013: | | | | |
| a | From 2008 . . . . . . | | | | |
| b | From 2009 . . . . . . | | | | |
| c | From 2010 . . . . . . | | | | |
| d | From 2011 . . . . . . | | | | |
| e | From 2012 . . . . . . 200,000. | | | | |
| f | **Total** of lines 3a through e . . . . . | 200,000. | | | |
| 4 | Qualifying distributions for 2013 from Part XII, line 4: ► $ 1,919,500. | | | | |
| a | Applied to 2012, but not more than line 2a . | | | 0. | |
| b | Applied to undistributed income of prior years (Election required—see instructions) . . . | | 0. | | |
| c | Treated as distributions out of corpus (Election required—see instructions) . . . . . | 0. | | | |
| d | Applied to 2013 distributable amount . . | | | | 1,085,249 |
| e | Remaining amount distributed out of corpus | 834,251. | | | |
| 5 | Excess distributions carryover applied to 2013 | 0. | | | 0. |
| | *(If an amount appears in column (d), the same amount must be shown in column (a).)* | | | | |
| 6 | **Enter the net total of each column as indicated below:** | | | | |
| a | Corpus. Add lines 3f, 4c, and 4e. Subtract line 5 | 1,034,251 | | | |
| b | Prior years' undistributed income. Subtract line 4b from line 2b . . . . . . . . | | 0. | | |
| c | Enter the amount of prior years' undistributed income for which a notice of deficiency has been issued, or on which the section 4942(a) tax has been previously assessed . . . . | | 0. | | |
| d | Subtract line 6c from line 6b. Taxable amount—see instructions . . . . . . | | 0. | | |
| e | Undistributed income for 2012. Subtract line 4a from line 2a. Taxable amount—see instructions . . . . . . . . . . . . | | | 0. | |
| f | Undistributed income for 2013. Subtract lines 4d and 5 from line 1. This amount must be distributed in 2014 . . . . . . . . . | | | | 0. |
| 7 | Amounts treated as distributions out of corpus to satisfy requirements imposed by section 170(b)(1)(F) or 4942(g)(3) (see instructions) . | 500,000. | | | |
| 8 | Excess distributions carryover from 2008 not applied on line 5 or line 7 (see instructions) . | 0. | | | |
| 9 | **Excess distributions carryover to 2014.** Subtract lines 7 and 8 from line 6a . . . | 534,251. | | | |
| 10 | Analysis of line 9: | | | | |
| a | Excess from 2009 . . . . . | | | | |
| b | Excess from 2010 . . . . . | | | | |
| c | Excess from 2011 . . . . . | | | | |
| d | Excess from 2012 . . . . . | | | | |
| e | Excess from 2013 . . . . . 534,251. | | | | |

Form **990-PF** (2013)

EXHIBIT **12.1**

(*Continued*)

Form 990-PF (2013)
Page **10**

**Part XIV** **Private Operating Foundations** (see instructions and Part VII-A, question 9)

N/A

**1a** If the foundation has received a ruling or determination letter that it is a private operating foundation, and the ruling is effective for 2013, enter the date of the ruling . . . . . . ▶

**b** Check box to indicate whether the foundation is a private operating foundation described in section ☐ 4942(j)(3) or ☐ 4942(j)(5)

| | Tax year | Prior 3 years | | | |
|---|---|---|---|---|---|
| | **(a)** 2013 | **(b)** 2012 | **(c)** 2011 | **(d)** 2010 | **(e)** Total |
| **2a** Enter the lesser of the adjusted net income from Part I or the minimum investment return from Part X for each year listed . . . . . . . | | | | | |
| **b** 85% of line 2a . . . . . . . | | | | | |
| **c** Qualifying distributions from Part XII, line 4 for each year listed . . . . | | | | | |
| **d** Amounts included in line 2c not used directly for active conduct of exempt activities . . | | | | | |
| **e** Qualifying distributions made directly for active conduct of exempt activities. Subtract line 2d from line 2c . . . | | | | | |
| **3** Complete 3a, b, or c for the alternative test relied upon: | | | | | |
| **a** "Assets" alternative test—enter: | | | | | |
| **(1)** Value of all assets . . . . . | | | | | |
| **(2)** Value of assets qualifying under section 4942(j)(3)(B)(i) . . . . | | | | | |
| **b** "Endowment" alternative test—enter ²⁄₃ of minimum investment return shown in Part X, line 6 for each year listed . . | | | | | |
| **c** "Support" alternative test—enter: | | | | | |
| **(1)** Total support other than gross investment income (interest, dividends, rents, payments on securities loans (section 512(a)(5), or royalties) . . . . | | | | | |
| **(2)** Support from general public and 5 or more exempt organizations as provided in section 4942(j)(3)(B)(iii) . . . . | | | | | |
| **(3)** Largest amount of support from an exempt organization . . . | | | | | |
| **(4)** Gross investment income . . . | | | | | |

**Part XV** **Supplementary Information (Complete this part only if the foundation had $5,000 or more in assets at any time during the year—see instructions.)**

**1** **Information Regarding Foundation Managers:**

**a** List any managers of the foundation who have contributed more than 2% of the total contributions received by the foundation before the close of any tax year (but only if they have contributed more than $5,000). (See section 507(d)(2).)

See Statement 18

**b** List any managers of the foundation who own 10% or more of the stock of a corporation (or an equally large portion of the ownership of a partnership or other entity) of which the foundation has a 10% or greater interest.

None

**2** **Information Regarding Contribution, Grant, Gift, Loan, Scholarship, etc., Programs:**

Check here ▶ ☐ if the foundation only makes contributions to preselected charitable organizations and does not accept unsolicited requests for funds. If the foundation makes gifts, grants, etc. (see instructions) to individuals or organizations under other conditions, complete items 2a, b, c, and d.

**a** The name, address, and telephone number or e-mail address of the person to whom applications should be addressed:

See Statement 19

**b** The form in which applications should be submitted and information and materials they should include:

See Statement for Line 2a

**c** Any submission deadlines:

See Statement for Line 2a

**d** Any restrictions or limitations on awards, such as by geographical areas, charitable fields, kinds of institutions, or other factors:

See Statement for Line 2a

Form **990-PF** (2013)

**EXHIBIT 12.1**

*(Continued)*

**Part XV** Supplementary Information (continued)

**3** Grants and Contributions Paid During the Year or Approved for Future Payment

| Recipient | If recipient is an individual, show any relationship to any foundation manager or substantial contributor | Foundation status of recipient | Purpose of grant or contribution | Amount |
|---|---|---|---|---|
| Name and address (home or business) | | | | |
| **a** *Paid during the year* | | | | |
| See Statement 20 | | | | |
| Total . . . . . . . . . . . . . . . . . . . . . . . . . . ► **3a** | | | | 450,000. |
| **b** *Approved for future payment*<br>HomeTown Campaign to Clean Up America<br>1111 Any Street<br>Hometown, TX 77777 | N/A | 509(a)(1) | General Support | 100,000. |
| Total . . . . . . . . . . . . . . . . . . . . . . . . . . ► **3b** | | | | 100,000. |

Form **990-PF** (2013)

EXHIBIT **12.1**

*(Continued)*

Form 990-PF (2013)                                                                                                      Page **12**

## Part XVI-A   Analysis of Income-Producing Activities

Enter gross amounts unless otherwise indicated.

| | Unrelated business income | | Excluded by section 512, 513, or 514 | | (e) Related or exempt function income (See instructions.) |
|---|---|---|---|---|---|
| | (a) Business code | (b) Amount | (c) Exclusion code | (d) Amount | |
| **1** Program service revenue: | | | | | |
| a _____ | | | | | |
| b _____ | | | | | |
| c _____ | | | | | |
| d _____ | | | | | |
| e _____ | | | | | |
| f _____ | | | | | |
| g Fees and contracts from government agencies | | | | | |
| **2** Membership dues and assessments  . . . . | | | | | |
| **3** Interest on savings and temporary cash investments | | | 14 | 10,000. | |
| **4** Dividends and interest from securities  . . . . | | | 14 | 380,000. | |
| **5** Net rental income or (loss) from real estate: | | | | | |
| a Debt-financed property  . . . . . . . . | 531120 | 8,880. | 16 | 5,920. | |
| b Not debt-financed property  . . . . . . | | | | | |
| **6** Net rental income or (loss) from personal property | | | | | |
| **7** Other investment income  . . . . . . . . | | | | | |
| **8** Gain or (loss) from sales of assets other than inventory | | | 18 | 399,000. | |
| **9** Net income or (loss) from special events  . . . | | | | | |
| **10** Gross profit or (loss) from sales of inventory  . . | | | | | 1,500. |
| **11** Other revenue: a Income from options | | | 19 | 2,000. | |
| b MNO Corp. (Sub. S distribution) | 531310 | 100,000. | | | |
| c Oil & Gas Royalties | | | 15 | 300,000. | |
| d Pass through K-1 Income | | | 14 | 20,000. | |
| e Program-related interest | | | | | 20,000. |
| **12** Subtotal. Add columns (b), (d), and (e)  . . . . | | 108,880. | | 1,116,920. | 21,500. |
| **13** Total. Add line 12, columns (b), (d), and (e)  . . . . . . . . . . . . . . . . . 13 | | | | | 1,247,300. |

(See worksheet in line 13 instructions to verify calculations.)

## Part XVI-B   Relationship of Activities to the Accomplishment of Exempt Purposes

| Line No. ▼ | Explain below how each activity for which income is reported in column (e) of Part XVI-A contributed importantly to the accomplishment of the foundation's exempt purposes (other than by providing funds for such purposes). (See instructions.) |
|---|---|
| 10 | Income from the sale of environmental educational brochures and publications. |
| 11e | Interest on program-related investment. See Part IX-B for a description. |
| | |

Form **990-PF** (2013)

**EXHIBIT 12.1**

*(Continued)*

# TAX COMPLIANCE AND ADMINISTRATIVE ISSUES

## Part XVII — Information Regarding Transfers To and Transactions and Relationships With Noncharitable Exempt Organizations

| | | Yes | No |
|---|---|---|---|
| 1 | Did the organization directly or indirectly engage in any of the following with any other organization described in section 501(c) of the Code (other than section 501(c)(3) organizations) or in section 527, relating to political organizations? | | |
| a | Transfers from the reporting foundation to a noncharitable exempt organization of: | | |
| | (1) Cash . . . . . . . . . . . . . . . . . . . . . . . . . . . . . .  **1a(1)** | | ✓ |
| | (2) Other assets . . . . . . . . . . . . . . . . . . . . . . . . .  **1a(2)** | | ✓ |
| b | Other transactions: | | |
| | (1) Sales of assets to a noncharitable exempt organization . . . . . . . . . . . .  **1b(1)** | | ✓ |
| | (2) Purchases of assets from a noncharitable exempt organization . . . . . . . . . . .  **1b(2)** | | ✓ |
| | (3) Rental of facilities, equipment, or other assets . . . . . . . . . . .  **1b(3)** | | ✓ |
| | (4) Reimbursement arrangements . . . . . . . . . . . . . . . . . .  **1b(4)** | | ✓ |
| | (5) Loans or loan guarantees . . . . . . . . . . . . . . . . . . . .  **1b(5)** | | ✓ |
| | (6) Performance of services or membership or fundraising solicitations . . . . . . . .  **1b(6)** | | ✓ |
| c | Sharing of facilities, equipment, mailing lists, other assets, or paid employees . . . . . . . . .  **1c** | | ✓ |
| d | If the answer to any of the above is "Yes," complete the following schedule. Column **(b)** should always show the fair market value of the goods, other assets, or services given by the reporting foundation. If the foundation received less than fair market value in any transaction or sharing arrangement, show in column **(d)** the value of the goods, other assets, or services received. | | |

| (a) Line no. | (b) Amount involved | (c) Name of noncharitable exempt organization | (d) Description of transfers, transactions, and sharing arrangements |
|---|---|---|---|
| N/A | | | |
| | | | |
| | | | |
| | | | |
| | | | |
| | | | |
| | | | |
| | | | |
| | | | |
| | | | |
| | | | |
| | | | |
| | | | |

**2a** Is the foundation directly or indirectly affiliated with, or related to, one or more tax-exempt organizations described in section 501(c) of the Code (other than section 501(c)(3)) or in section 527? . . . . . . . . ☐ Yes ☑ No

**b** If "Yes," complete the following schedule.

| (a) Name of organization | (b) Type of organization | (c) Description of relationship |
|---|---|---|
| N/A | | |
| | | |
| | | |
| | | |

**Sign Here**

Under penalties of perjury, I declare that I have examined this return, including accompanying schedules and statements, and to the best of my knowledge and belief, it is true, correct, and complete. Declaration of preparer (other than taxpayer) is based on all information of which preparer has any knowledge.

▶ _____ | _____ ▶ _____

Signature of officer or trustee | Date | Title

May the IRS discuss this return with the preparer shown below (see instructions)? ☑ Yes ☐ No

**Paid Preparer Use Only**

| Print/Type preparer's name | Preparer's signature | Date | Check ☑ if self-employed | PTIN |
|---|---|---|---|---|
| A Good Accountant | | | | P9999999 |

| Firm's name ▶ A Good Accountant | Firm's EIN ▶ 55-5555555 |
|---|---|
| Firm's address ▶ 444 Any Street, Hometown, TX 77777-7777 | Phone no. 444-555-6666 |

Form **990-PF** (2013)

**EXHIBIT 12.1**

*(Continued)*

| Schedule B<br>(Form 990, 990-EZ,<br>or 990-PF)<br>Department of the Treasury<br>Internal Revenue Service | **Schedule of Contributors**<br><br>▶ Attach to Form 990, Form 990-EZ, or Form 990-PF.<br>▶ Information about Schedule B (Form 990, 990-EZ, or 990-PF) and its instructions is at *www.irs.gov/form990*. | OMB No. 1545-0047<br><br>20**13** |
|---|---|---|

| Name of the organization | Employer identification number |
|---|---|
| Environmentalist Fund | 77-7777777 |

**Organization type** (check one):

Filers of:                     Section:

Form 990 or 990-EZ       ☐ 501(c)(    ) (enter number) organization

                                    ☐ 4947(a)(1) nonexempt charitable trust **not** treated as a private foundation

                                    ☐ 527 political organization

Form 990-PF                 ☑ 501(c)(3) exempt private foundation

                                    ☐ 4947(a)(1) nonexempt charitable trust treated as a private foundation

                                    ☐ 501(c)(3) taxable private foundation

---

Check if your organization is covered by the **General Rule** or a **Special Rule.**

**Note.** Only a section 501(c)(7), (8), or (10) organization can check boxes for both the General Rule and a Special Rule. See instructions.

**General Rule**

☑  For an organization filing Form 990, 990-EZ, or 990-PF that received, during the year, $5,000 or more (in money or property) from any one contributor. Complete Parts I and II.

**Special Rules**

☐  For a section 501(c)(3) organization filing Form 990 or 990-EZ that met the 33⅓ % support test of the regulations under sections 509(a)(1) and 170(b)(1)(A)(vi) and received from any one contributor, during the year, a contribution of the greater of **(1)** $5,000 or **(2)** 2% of the amount on (i) Form 990, Part VIII, line 1h, or (ii) Form 990-EZ, line 1. Complete Parts I and II.

☐  For a section 501(c)(7), (8), or (10) organization filing Form 990 or 990-EZ that received from any one contributor, during the year, total contributions of more than $1,000 for use *exclusively* for religious, charitable, scientific, literary, or educational purposes, or the prevention of cruelty to children or animals. Complete Parts I, II, and III.

☐  For a section 501(c)(7), (8), or (10) organization filing Form 990 or 990-EZ that received from any one contributor, during the year, contributions for use *exclusively* for religious, charitable, etc., purposes, but these contributions did not total to more than $1,000. If this box is checked, enter here the total contributions that were received during the year for an *exclusively* religious, charitable, etc., purpose. Do not complete any of the parts unless the **General Rule** applies to this organization because it received *nonexclusively* religious, charitable, etc., contributions of $5,000 or more during the year   .   .   .   .   .   .   .   .   .   .   .   .   .   .   .   .   .   .   .   .   ▶ $ _____

**Caution.** An organization that is not covered by the General Rule and/or the Special Rules does not file Schedule B (Form 990, 990-EZ, or 990-PF), but it **must** answer "No" on Part IV, line 2, of its Form 990; or check the box on line H of its Form 990-EZ or on its Form 990-PF, Part I, line 2, to certify that it does not meet the filing requirements of Schedule B (Form 990, 990-EZ, or 990-PF).

---

For Paperwork Reduction Act Notice, see the Instructions for Form 990, 990-EZ, or 990-PF.   Cat. No. 30613X   Schedule B (Form 990, 990-EZ, or 990-PF) (2013)

**EXHIBIT 12.1**

*(Continued)*

Page **2**

| Name of organization | Employer identification number |
|---|---|
| Environmentalist Fund | 77-7777777 |

**Part I**    Contributors (see instructions). Use duplicate copies of Part I if additional space is needed.

| (a) No. | (b) Name, address, and ZIP + 4 | (c) Total contributions | (d) Type of contribution |
|---|---|---|---|
| 1 | Jane & John Environmentalist<br><br>333 First Street<br><br>Hometown, TX 77777-0077 | $ 1,000,000. | Person ☐<br>Payroll ☐<br>Noncash ☑<br>(Complete Part II for noncash contributions.) |
| 2 | Big Foundation<br><br>123 Main Street<br><br>Big Town, TX 77711-0011 | $ 1,500,000. | Person ☑<br>Payroll ☐<br>Noncash ☐<br>(Complete Part II for noncash contributions.) |
| 3 | Big Company<br><br>555 Smith Street<br><br>Hometown, TX 77777-0177 | $ 10,000. | Person ☐<br>Payroll ☐<br>Noncash ☑<br>(Complete Part II for noncash contributions.) |
| | | $ | Person ☐<br>Payroll ☐<br>Noncash ☐<br>(Complete Part II for noncash contributions.) |
| | | $ | Person ☐<br>Payroll ☐<br>Noncash ☐<br>(Complete Part II for noncash contributions.) |
| | | $ | Person ☐<br>Payroll ☐<br>Noncash ☐<br>(Complete Part II for noncash contributions.) |

EXHIBIT **12.1**

*(Continued)*

Schedule B (Form 990, 990-EZ, or 990-PF) (2013)                                                                Page **3**

| Name of organization | Employer identification number |
|---|---|
| Environmentalist Fund | 77-7777777 |

**Part II** Noncash Property (see instructions). Use duplicate copies of Part II if additional space is needed.

| (a) No. from Part I | (b) Description of noncash property given | (c) FMV (or estimate) (see instructions) | (d) Date received |
|---|---|---|---|
| 1 | Gift of 10,000 shares of Clean Air Industries NYSE | $ 1,000,000. | 4/15/2013 |

| (a) No. from Part I | (b) Description of noncash property given | (c) FMV (or estimate) (see instructions) | (d) Date received |
|---|---|---|---|
| 3 | Used computers | $ 10,000. | 5/01/2013 |

| (a) No. from Part I | (b) Description of noncash property given | (c) FMV (or estimate) (see instructions) | (d) Date received |
|---|---|---|---|
| | | $ | |

| (a) No. from Part I | (b) Description of noncash property given | (c) FMV (or estimate) (see instructions) | (d) Date received |
|---|---|---|---|
| | | $ | |

| (a) No. from Part I | (b) Description of noncash property given | (c) FMV (or estimate) (see instructions) | (d) Date received |
|---|---|---|---|
| | | $ | |

| (a) No. from Part I | (b) Description of noncash property given | (c) FMV (or estimate) (see instructions) | (d) Date received |
|---|---|---|---|
| | | $ | |

Schedule B (Form 990, 990-EZ, or 990-PF) (2013)

**EXHIBIT 12.1**

*(Continued)*

# TAX COMPLIANCE AND ADMINISTRATIVE ISSUES

Schedule B (Form 990, 990-EZ, or 990-PF) (2013)        Page **4**

| Name of organization | Employer identification number |
|---|---|
| Environmentalist Fund | 77-7777777 |

**Part III**   *Exclusively* **religious, charitable, etc., individual contributions to section 501(c)(7), (8), or (10) organizations that total more than $1,000 for the year.** Complete columns **(a)** through **(e)** and the following line entry.
For organizations completing Part III, enter the total of *exclusively* religious, charitable, etc.,
contributions of **$1,000 or less** for the year. (Enter this information once. See instructions.) ▶   $ _____

Use duplicate copies of Part III if additional space is needed.

| (a) No. from Part I | (b) Purpose of gift | (c) Use of gift | (d) Description of how gift is held |
|---|---|---|---|
| -------- | | | |

**(e) Transfer of gift**

| Transferee's name, address, and ZIP + 4 | Relationship of transferor to transferee |
|---|---|
| | |

| (a) No. from Part I | (b) Purpose of gift | (c) Use of gift | (d) Description of how gift is held |
|---|---|---|---|
| -------- | | | |

**(e) Transfer of gift**

| Transferee's name, address, and ZIP + 4 | Relationship of transferor to transferee |
|---|---|
| | |

| (a) No. from Part I | (b) Purpose of gift | (c) Use of gift | (d) Description of how gift is held |
|---|---|---|---|
| -------- | | | |

**(e) Transfer of gift**

| Transferee's name, address, and ZIP + 4 | Relationship of transferor to transferee |
|---|---|
| | |

| (a) No. from Part I | (b) Purpose of gift | (c) Use of gift | (d) Description of how gift is held |
|---|---|---|---|
| -------- | | | |

**(e) Transfer of gift**

| Transferee's name, address, and ZIP + 4 | Relationship of transferor to transferee |
|---|---|
| | |

Schedule B (Form 990, 990-EZ, or 990-PF) (2013)

**EXHIBIT 12.1**

*(Continued)*

Form 990-PF

| Form **2220** | **Underpayment of Estimated Tax by Corporations** | OMB No. 1545-0142 |
|---|---|---|
| Department of the Treasury Internal Revenue Service | ►**Attach to the corporation's tax return.**<br>►**Information about Form 2220 and its separate instructions is at www.irs.gov/form2220.** | 2013 |

| Name | Employer identification number |
|---|---|
| Environmentalist Fund | 77-7777777 |

**Note:** *Generally, the corporation is not required to file Form 2220 (see Part II below for exceptions) because the IRS will figure any penalty owed and bill the corporation. However, the corporation may still use Form 2220 to figure the penalty. If so, enter the amount from page 2, line 38 on the estimated tax penalty line of the corporation's income tax return, but* **do not** *attach Form 2220.*

### Part I — Required Annual Payment

| | | | | |
|---|---|---|---|---|
| 1 | Total tax (see instructions) . . . . . . . . . . . . . . . . . . . . | | **1** | 16,390. |
| 2a | Personal holding company tax (Schedule PH (Form 1120), line 26) included on line 1 | **2a** | | |
| b | Look-back interest included on line 1 under section 460(b)(2) for completed long-term contracts or section 167(g) for depreciation under the income forecast method . . | **2b** | | |
| c | Credit for federal tax paid on fuels (see instructions) . . . . . . . . . | **2c** | | |
| d | **Total.** Add lines 2a through 2c . . . . . . . . . . . . . . . . . | | **2d** | |
| 3 | Subtract line 2d from line 1. If the result is less than $500, **do not** complete or file this form. The corporation does not owe the penalty . . . . . . . . . . . . . . . . . . . . . | | **3** | 16,390. |
| 4 | Enter the tax shown on the corporation's 2012 income tax return (see instructions). **Caution: If the tax is zero or the tax year was for less than 12 months, skip this line and enter the amount from line 3 on line 5** . . | | **4** | 13,325. |
| 5 | **Required annual payment.** Enter the **smaller** of line 3 or line 4. If the corporation is required to skip line 4, enter the amount from line 3 . . . . . . . . . . . . . . . . . . . . . . . | | **5** | 13,325. |

### Part II — Reasons for Filing

Check the boxes below that apply. If any boxes are checked, the corporation **must** file Form 2220 even if it does not owe a penalty (see instructions).

| | | |
|---|---|---|
| 6 | ☐ | The corporation is using the adjusted seasonal installment method. |
| 7 | ☐ | The corporation is using the annualized income installment method. |
| 8 | ☑ | The corporation is a "large corporation" figuring its first required installment based on the prior year's tax. |

### Part III — Figuring the Underpayment

| | | | (a) | (b) | (c) | (d) |
|---|---|---|---|---|---|---|
| 9 | **Installment due dates.** Enter in columns (a) through (d) the 15th day of the 4th (**Form 990-PF filers:** Use 5th month), 6th, 9th, and 12th months of the corporation's tax year . . . . . . . . . . | **9** | 5/15/2013 | 6/15/2013 | 9/15/2013 | 12/15/2013 |
| 10 | **Required installments.** If the box on line 6 and/or line 7 above is checked, enter the amounts from Schedule A, line 38. If the box on line 8 (but not 6 or 7) is checked, see instructions for the amounts to enter. If none of these boxes are checked, enter 25% of line 5 above in each column . . . . . | **10** | 3,331. | 4,864. | 4,098. | 4,098. |
| 11 | Estimated tax paid or credited for each period (see instructions). For column (a) only, enter the amount from line 11 on line 15 . . . . | **11** | 4,790. | 4,000. | 4,000. | 4,000. |
| | *Complete lines 12 through 18 of one column before going to the next column.* | | | | | |
| 12 | Enter amount, if any, from line 18 of the preceding column . . . . | **12** | | 1,459. | 595. | 497. |
| 13 | Add lines 11 and 12 . . . . . . . . . . . . . . . | **13** | | 5,459. | 4,595. | 4,497. |
| 14 | Add amounts on lines 16 and 17 of the preceding column . . . . . | **14** | | | | |
| 15 | Subtract line 14 from line 13. If zero or less, enter -0- . . . . . . | **15** | 4,790. | 5,459. | 4,595. | 4,497. |
| 16 | If the amount on line 15 is zero, subtract line 13 from line 14. Otherwise, enter -0- . . . . . . . . . . . . . . . . . | **16** | | 0. | 0. | |
| 17 | **Underpayment.** If line 15 is less than or equal to line 10, subtract line 15 from line 10. Then go to line 12 of the next column. Otherwise, go to line 18 . . . . . . . . . . . . . . . . . | **17** | | | | |
| 18 | **Overpayment.** If line 10 is less than line 15, subtract line 10 from line 15. Then go to line 12 of the next column . . . . . . . . | **18** | 1,459. | 595. | 497. | |

Go to Part IV on page 2 to figure the penalty. Do not go to Part IV if there are no entries on line 17—no penalty is owed.

For Paperwork Reduction Act Notice, see separate instructions.　　　　Cat. No. 11746L　　　　Form **2220** (2013)

EXHIBIT 12.1

(Continued)

Form 2220 (2013)  Environmentalist Fund                     77-7777777        Page **2**

## Part IV  Figuring the Penalty

| | | (a) | (b) | (c) | (d) |
|---|---|---|---|---|---|
| 19 | Enter the date of payment or the 15th day of the 3rd month after the close of the tax year, whichever is earlier (see instructions). *(Form 990-PF and Form 990-T filers:* Use 5th month instead of 3rd month.) . . . . . . . . . . . . . . . .  **19** | | | | |
| 20 | Number of days from due date of installment on line 9 to the date shown on line 19 . . . . . . . . . . . . . **20** | | | | |
| 21 | Number of days on line 20 after 4/15/2013 and before 7/1/2013  **21** | | | | |
| 22 | Underpayment on line 17 × $\frac{\text{Number of days on line 21}}{365}$ × 3%  **22** | $ | $ | $ | $ |
| 23 | Number of days on line 20 after 6/30/2013 and before 10/1/2013  **23** | | | | |
| 24 | Underpayment on line 17 × $\frac{\text{Number of days on line 23}}{365}$ × 3%  **24** | $ | $ | $ | $ |
| 25 | Number of days on line 20 after 9/30/2013 and before 1/1/2014  **25** | | | | |
| 26 | Underpayment on line 17 × $\frac{\text{Number of days on line 25}}{365}$ × 3%  **26** | $ | $ | $ | $ |
| 27 | Number of days on line 20 after 12/31/2013 and before 4/1/2014  **27** | | | | |
| 28 | Underpayment on line 17 × $\frac{\text{Number of days on line 27}}{365}$ × 3%  **28** | $ | $ | $ | $ |
| 29 | Number of days on line 20 after 3/31/2014 and before 7/1/2014  **29** | | | | |
| 30 | Underpayment on line 17 × $\frac{\text{Number of days on line 29}}{365}$ × *%  **30** | $ | $ | $ | $ |
| 31 | Number of days on line 20 after 6/30/2014 and before 10/1/2014  **31** | | | | |
| 32 | Underpayment on line 17 × $\frac{\text{Number of days on line 31}}{365}$ × *%  **32** | $ | $ | $ | $ |
| 33 | Number of days on line 20 after 9/30/2014 and before 1/1/2015  **33** | | | | |
| 34 | Underpayment on line 17 × $\frac{\text{Number of days on line 33}}{365}$ × *%  **34** | $ | $ | $ | $ |
| 35 | Number of days on line 20 after 12/31/2014 and before 2/16/2015  **35** | | | | |
| 36 | Underpayment on line 17 × $\frac{\text{Number of days on line 35}}{365}$ × *%  **36** | $ | $ | $ | $ |
| 37 | Add lines 22, 24, 26, 28, 30, 32, 34, and 36 . . . . . . . .  **37** | $ | $ | $ | $ |

| 38 | **Penalty.** Add columns (a) through (d) of line 37. Enter the total here and on Form 1120, line 33; or the comparable line for other income tax returns. . . . . . . . . . . . . . . . . . . . . . . . . . . . . . . **38** | $ | | | 0. |

*Use the penalty interest rate for each calendar quarter, which the IRS will determine during the first month in the preceding quarter. These rates are published quarterly in an IRS News Release and in a revenue ruling in the Internal Revenue Bulletin. To obtain this information on the Internet, access the IRS website at *www.irs.gov*. You can also call 1-800-829-4933 to get interest rate information.

Form **2220** (2013)

## Exhibit 12.1

*(Continued)*

**Statement 1**
**Form 990-PF, Part 1, Line 6a**
**Net Gain (Loss) from Noninventory Sales Per Books**
**Assets Not Included in Part IV**

| | | | |
|---|---|---|---|
| Description: | Donated Computers | | |
| Date Acquired: | 5/1/2013 | | |
| How Acquired: | Donated | | |
| Date Sold: | 7/15/2013 | | |
| To Whom Sold: | XYZ Corporation | | |
| Gross Sales Price: | $ 9,000 | | |
| Cost or Other Basis: | $ 10,000 | | |
| Basis Method: | FMV on date of gift | | |
| Depreciation: | 0 | | |
| | | Gain (Loss) | $ (1,000) |
| | | Total | $ (1,000) |

**Statement 2**
**Form 990-PF, Part 1, Line 10c**
**Gross Profit (Loss) From Sales of Inventory**

| Items Sold | | Amount |
|---|---|---|
| Educational brochures | | $ 2,500 |
| | | |
| Gross Sales | | $ 2,500 |
| Less Returns & Allowances | | 0 |
| Net Sales | | $ 2,500 |
| Less Cost of Goods Sold | | 1,000 |
| Gross Profit From Sales of Inventory | Total | $ 1,500 |

**Statement 3**
**Form 990-PF, Part I, Line 11**
**Other Income**

| | | |
|---|---|---|
| Income from options | | $ 2,000 |
| MNO Corp. (Sub. S distribution) | | 100,000 |
| Oil & Gas royalties | | 300,000 |
| Passthrough K-1 income | | 20,000 |
| Program related interest | | 20,000 |
| | Total | $ 442,000 |

EXHIBIT 12.1

(Continued)

**Statement 4**
**Form 990-PF, Part 1, Line 16a**
**Legal Fees**

|  | (a) Expenses Per Books | (b) Net Investment Income | (c) Adjusted Net Income | (d) Charitable Purposes |
|---|---|---|---|---|
| Contracts, loans, corporate matters | $ 20,000 | $ 4,000 | $ 3,000 | $ 15,000 |
| Total | $ 20,000 | $ 4,000 | $ 3,000 | $ 15,000 |

**Statement 5**
**Form 990-PF, Part 1 Line 16b**
**Accounting Fees**

|  | (a) Expenses Per Books | (b) Net Investment Income | (c) Adjusted Net Income | (d) Charitable Purposes |
|---|---|---|---|---|
| Tax Compliance / auditing | $ 20,000 | $ 2,000 | $ 500 | $ 17,000 |
| Total | $ 20,000 | $ 2,000 | $ 500 | $ 17,000 |

**Statement 6**
**Form 990-PF, Part 1 Line 16c**
**Other Professional Fees**

|  | (a) Expenses Per Books | (b) Net Investment Income | (c) Adjusted Net Income | (d) Charitable Purposes |
|---|---|---|---|---|
| Hydrology consultants | $ 70,000 |  |  | $ 72,000 |
| Investment managers | 10,000 | $ 10,000 |  |  |
| Total | $ 80,000 | $ 10,000 | $ - | $ 72,000 |

**Statement 7**
**Form 990-PF, Part 1 Line 18**
**Taxes**

|  | (a) Expenses Per Books | (b) Net Investment Income | (c) Adjusted Net Income | (d) Charitable Purposes |
|---|---|---|---|---|
| Ad valorem / production tax | $ 15,000 | $ 15,000 |  |  |
| Excise tax on investment income | 10,000 |  |  |  |
| Income tax 990-T | 9,000 |  |  |  |
| Property Tax | 21,000 | 9,000 |  |  |
| Total | $ 55,000 | $ 24,000 | $ - | $ - |

**EXHIBIT 12.1**

*(Continued)*

**Statement 8**
**Form 990-PF, Part I, Line 23**
**Other Expenses**

| | (a) Expenses Per Books | (b) Net Investment Income | (c) Adjusted Net Income | (d) Charitable Purposes |
|---|---|---|---|---|
| Insurance | $ 6,000 | $ 1,000 | | $ 7,000 |
| Memberships | 6,000 | | | 6,500 |
| Office Supplies and expenses | 20,000 | 2,000 | | 18,000 |
| Passthrough K-1 expenses | 3,400 | 3,400 | | |
| Rental Expenses | 12,000 | 4,800 | | |
| Research programs / fees | 40,000 | | | 45,000 |
| Website design / upkeep | 10,000 | | | 12,000 |
| Total | $ 97,400 | $ 11,200 | $ - | $ 88,500 |

**Statement 9**
**Form 990-PF, Part II, Line 6**
**Receivables Due from Officers, Directors, Trustees, and Key Employees**

| Receivables Reported Separately | | Book Value | Fair Market Value |
|---|---|---|---|
| Borrower's Name: | Jane E. Environmentalist | | |
| Borrower's Title: | President | | |
| Date of Note: | 11/1/2013 | | |
| Maturity Date: | 11/1/2013 | | |
| Repayment Terms: | Due immediately | | |
| Interest Rate: | 5.00% | | |
| Security Provided: | None | | |
| Purpose of Loan: | To pay legal bill | | |
| Consideration: | Cash | | |
| Balance Due: | | $ 4,000 | $ 4,000 |
| Legal bill of Jane E. Environmentalist was mistakenly paid by the foundation in 2013. In 2014, as soon as the error was discovered, Ms. Environmentalist Paid back the entire amount plus interest. | Total | $ 4,000 | $ 4,000 |

**EXHIBIT 12.1**

*(Continued)*

**Statement 10**
**Form 990-PF, Part II, Line 10b**
**Investments - Corporate Stocks**

| Corporate Stocks | Valuation Metod | Book Value | Fair Market Value |
|---|---|---|---|
| ABC Securities, 20,000 shs | Mkt Val | $ 725,000 | $ 725,000 |
| DEF Incorporated, 15,000 shs | Mkt Val | 145,000 | 145,000 |
| GHI Company, 5,000 shs | Mkt Val | 265,000 | 265,000 |
| JKL, Inc., 12,000 shs | Mkt Val | 570,000 | 570,000 |
| MNO Enterprises (Sub. S) | Mkt Val | 990,000 | 990,000 |
| Clean Air Industries, 160,000 shs | Mkt Val | 16,500,000 | 16,500,000 |
| Total | | $ 19,195,000 | $ 19,195,000 |

**Statement 11**
**Form 990-PF**
**Investments - Land, Buildings, and Equipment**

| Category | Basis | Accum. Deprec. | Book Value | Fair Market Value |
|---|---|---|---|---|
| Buildings | $ 600,000 | $ 7,700 | $ 592,300 | $ 300,000 |
| Land | 150,000 | | 150,000 | 450,000 |
| Mineral Interests | 250,000 | 143,200 | 106,800 | 500,000 |
| Total | $ 1,000,000 | $ 150,900 | $ 849,100 | $ 1,250,000 |

**Statement 12**
**Form 990-PF, Part II, Line 13**
**Investments - Other**

| Other Investments | Valuation Metod | Book Value | Fair Market Value |
|---|---|---|---|
| PQR Partnership | Mkt Val | $ 800,000 | $ 800,000 |
| Total | | $ 800,000 | $ 800,000 |

**Statement 13**
**Form 990-PF, Part II, Line 14**
**Land, Buildings and Equipment**

| Category | Basis | Accum. Deprec. | Book Value | Fair Market Value |
|---|---|---|---|---|
| Buildings | $ 200,000 | $ 2,500 | $ 197,500 | $ 100,000 |
| Land | 50,000 | | 50,000 | 150,000 |
| Total | $ 250,000 | $ 2,500 | $ 247,500 | $ 250,000 |

**EXHIBIT 12.1**

*(Continued)*

**Statement 14**
**Form 990-PF, Part II, Line 15**
**Other Assets**

|  | Book Value | Fair Market Value |
|---|---|---|
| Program-related loan - New Energy Solution | $ 500,000 | $ 500,000 |
| Total | $ 500,000 | $ 500,000 |

**Statement 15**
**Form 990-PF, Part II, Line 21**
**Mortgages and Other Notes Payable**

| Mortgages Payable | Balance Due |
|---|---|
| Bank of America | $ 590,000 |
| Total Mortgages Payable | $ 590,000 |

**Statement 16**
**Form 990-PF, Part II, Line 22**
**Other Liabilities**

| | |
|---|---|
| Open Options | $ 20,000 |
| Total | $ 20,000 |

**Statement 17**
**Form 990-PF, Part III, Line 3**
**Other Increases**

| | |
|---|---|
| Unrealized appreciation of investments | $ 186,700 |
| Total | $ 186,700 |

**Statement 18**
**Form 990-PF, Part XV, Line 1a**
**Foundation Managers - 2% or More Contributors**

Jane E. Environmentalist
John J. Environmentalist

**EXHIBIT 12.1**

*(Continued)*

**Statement 19**
**Form 990-PF, Part XV, Line 2a - d**
**Application Submission Information**

| | |
|---|---|
| Name of Grant Program: | Environmental Studies |
| Name: | Mary Goodbooks |
| Care Of: | Environmentalist Fund |
| Street Address: | 1011 Main Street |
| City, State, Zip Code: | Hometown, TX 77777-7777 |
| Telephone Number: | 444-444-4444 |
| Form and Content: | Description of programs with budgets (<6 pages); Form 990 and audit (if available) of most recent year and board list. |
| Submission Deadlines: | March 1st and September 1st |
| Restrictions on Awards: | The fund supports innovative programs to enhance protection of the environment. See www.environmentalistfund.org for more information. |

**Statement 20**
**Form 990-PF, Part XV, Line 3a**
**Recipients Paid During the Year**

| Name and Address | Donee Relationship | Foundation Status | Purpose of Grant | Amount |
|---|---|---|---|---|
| Hometown Cpgn to Clean Up America<br>1111 Any Street<br>Hometown, TX 77777 | N/A | 509(a)(1) | General Support | $ 200,000 |
| Natl Cpgn to Clean Up America<br>2525 Capital Street<br>Capital City, DC 01010 | N/A | 509(a)(1) | General Support | 50,000 |
| Smart Growth Institute<br>404 Fourth Street<br>Hometown, TX 77777 | N/A | 509(a)(2) | Research and dissemination of educational materials regarding livable communities. | 100,000 |
| Hometown Public Schools<br>303 Academic Row<br>Hometown, TX 77777 | N/A | 509(a)(1) | Develop teacher curriculum and support field trips focused on environmental issues. | 100,000 |
| Save the Bay Project<br>3 Shoreline Drive<br>Beachville, TX 77776 | N/A | 509(a)(3)<br>Type III | Educational materials and website. | 100,000 |

Adjustment for grant to Save the Bay Project not treated as a qualifying distribution.         (100,000)

Total    $    450,000

**EXHIBIT 12.1**

*(Continued)*

Attachment to Part VII-B, Question 5c

Expenditure Responsibility Statement for the year 2013
Pursuant to IRC Regulation §53.4945-5(d)(2), the ENVIRONMENTALIST FUND provides the following information:

(i) Grantee:       Save the Bay Project
                 3 Shoreline Drive
                 Beachville TX  77733

(ii) Amount of Grant:    December 28, 2013        $ 100,000

(iii) Purpose of grant: The Save the Bay Project (SBP) is a nonprofit corporation dedicated to saving marine life. SBP was created by Gulf Coast citizens unrelated to the fund's disqualified persons. This grant was for development of educational materials and creation of a web-site. SBP is classified as a 509(a)(3) Type III (non-functionally integrated) organization therefore, the fund is not claiming a qualifying distribution for this grant.

(iv) & (vi)Reports: The SBP is obligated to submit a full and complete report of its expenditures pursuant to the grant by October 1, 2014.

(v) Diversions: To the knowledge of the grantor, no funds have been diverted to any activity other than the activity for which the grant was originally made.

(vii) Verification: Reports not yet due.

**EXHIBIT 12.1**

*(Continued)*

| No. | Description | Date Acquired | Date Sold | Cost/ Basis | Bus. Pct. | Cur 179/ SDA | Prior 179/ SDA/ Depr. | Method | Life | Current Depr. |
|---|---|---|---|---|---|---|---|---|---|---|
| | **12/31/13** | | | | | | | | | |

**12/31/13**    **2013 Federal Book Summary Depreciation Schedule**    **Page 1**

Environmentalist Fund    77-7777777

| No. | Description | Date Acquired | Date Sold | Cost/ Basis | Bus. Pct. | Cur 179/ SDA | Prior 179/ SDA/ Depr. | Method | Life | Current Depr. |
|---|---|---|---|---|---|---|---|---|---|---|
| | Form 990/990-PF | | | | | | | | | |
| | **Buildings** | | | | | | | | | |
| 3 | Bldg - Investment portion | 7/01/13 | | 600,000 | | | | S/L | 39 | 7,700 |
| 4 | Bldg - Charitable portion | 7/01/13 | | 200,000 | | | | S/L | 39 | 2,500 |
| | Total Buildings | | | 800,000 | | 0 | 0 | | | 10,200 |
| | **Land** | | | | | | | | | |
| 1 | Land - Investment portion | 7/01/13 | | 150,000 | | | | | | 0 |
| 2 | Land - Charitable portion | 7/01/13 | | 50,000 | | | | | | 0 |
| | Total Land | | | 200,000 | | 0 | 0 | | | 0 |
| | **Miscellaneous** | | | | | | | | | |
| 5 | Mineral interests | 4/01/13 | | 250,000 | | | 118,200 | S/L | 10 | 25,000 |
| | Total Miscellaneous | | | 250,000 | | 0 | 118,200 | | | 25,000 |
| | Total Depreciation | | | 1,250,000 | | 0 | 118,200 | | | 35,200 |
| | Grand Total Depreciation | | | 1,250,000 | | 0 | 118,200 | | | 35,200 |

EXHIBIT 12.1

(*Continued*)

## Annual Tax Compliance Checklist for Private Foundation (PF)

PF's Name: _____    Prepared by: _____

Date: _____

### Federal Tax-exempt Status

Review Form 1023 and determination letter for exempt status and purposes originally represented to the IRS.                                                                                    _____

Was there any new programs or substantial change(s) in PF's exempt purpose(s)? [§18.3]     _____

    Review the minutes of director's meetings.

    Should change be reported on Form 990-PF?                                           _____

    Has there been a substantial contraction or termination?                          _____

Was there a change in the charter or bylaws to be attached?                                _____

Should PF consider conversion to a public charity? [§12.4]                                 _____

Could PF qualify as a Private Operating Foundation? [§15.5]                                _____

Ask for copies of any IRS notices and reports of IRS exam.                                 _____

    Review reports for corrections and other compliance issues raised.                 _____

### State and Local Taxes

Does PF properly claim sales tax exemption?                                                _____

Is PF's address and status with State office(s) current?                                  _____

Must the PF collect sales tax on goods or services sold?                                   _____

    If so, are timely returns filed? Is tax deposited on time?                         _____

Does the organization pay real or personal property tax?                                   _____

    Would use of property qualify it for exemption?                                    _____

    Has property classed as exempt-use been converted to investment-use property?      _____

Instruct PF to send copy of 990-PF to State Attorney General(s).                           _____

    Are there other state return filing requirements?                                  _____

### § 4941 Self-Dealing

Secure list of officers/directors, managers, significant staff.                            _____

Update disqualified persons ("DPs") and substantial contributor record [Ch.14].           _____

Did a sale, exchange, or other transaction involving property of any sort occur between the PF and its DPs? [§14.2]                                                                              _____

    Did the PF reimburse a DP for exempt function expenses? [§14.7]                     _____

    Was interest-free loan being repaid? [§14.3]                                       _____

    If the PF shares people or space, does PF have an Expenditure Documentation Policy? [Exhibit 14.2]                                                                          _____

## EXHIBIT 12.2

Annual Tax Compliance Checklist for Private Foundation (long version)

© 2013 Jody Blazek. Paragraph references to Blazek, *Tax Planning Compliance for Tax-Exempt Organizations*, 5th Edition, supplemented annually, John Willey & Sons.

**Annual Tax Compliance Checklist for Private Foundation (PF), page 2**

### § 4941 Self Dealing, Continued

Did a <$5,000 transaction occur during "normal course" of retail business? [§14.1(c)]  _____

Were benefit tickets accepted for PF grant? [§14.5(c)]  _____

Does the PF pay for DP's memberships or pledges? [§14.5(c)]  _____

Does the PF indirectly do business with a DP or his/her business? [§14.8]  _____

For property bequeathed to the PF, should distributions from estate be delayed until property sold or divided? [§14.9]  _____

### §4942 Mandatory Distribution Requirement

Review the following issues to determine if the PF has spent a sufficient amount on its charitable programs. Review calculation of minimum investment return: [§15.2]

    Are methods of valuation consistently applied?  _____

    Are non-readily marketable asset valuations updated at least annually?  _____

    Are exempt function assets excluded?  _____

    Is dual-use property reasonably allocated?  _____

    Can >1-1/2% cash reserves be justified?  _____

    Can a discount be applied to valuation of non-marketable assets?  _____

    Has real estate/mineral interest declined in value since last appraisal?  _____

Do all grants reported in Part XV count as qualifying distributions? [§15.4]  _____

    Any grants to organizations controlled by the PF?  _____

    Any redistributions to be offset against corpus?  _____

    Grant made to non-functionally integrated Type III SO?  _____

    Grant made to private foundation?  _____

Must portion of program expenses be reported in column (c) to offset revenues from exempt activities?_____

Is Part I, column (d) prepared on a cash basis? [§15.4]  _____

Should PF seek approval for Set-Aside of funds for program better accomplished over several years?  _____

Does Part XIII reflect satisfaction of the minimum distribution requirements? [§15.6]  _____

Determine if adjustments to "qualifying distributions" are needed for the following. [§15.3]

    Sale/disposition of exempt asset(s) previously classified as qualifying distribution?  _____

    Amounts not redistributed in a timely manner by another private foundation or controlled org?  _____

    Set-asides not used for the specified purpose?  _____

    Grant funds returned by grantee?  _____

If foundation is a private operating foundation, verify data to complete Part XIV [§15.5]:

    Amount spent for active conduct of programs  _____

    Value of assets devoted to active programs  _____

    Evaluate character of grants to other organizations to distinguish active program activity  _____

    Determine if individual grant program qualifies as an active exempt function activity  _____

Does POF describe active programs it conducts in Part IX?  _____

### EXHIBIT 12.2

*(Continued)*

© 2013 Jody Blazek. Paragraph references to Blazek, *Tax Planning Compliance for Tax-Exempt Organizations*, 5th Edition, supplemented annually, John Willey & Sons.

**Annual Tax Compliance Checklist for Private Foundation (PF), page 3**

### §4943 Excess Business Holdings

If the PF owns more than 2% of a corporation, partnership, or other business holding, ascertain whether disqualified persons' holdings must be aggregated. [§16.1]

Calculate permitted holdings to identify whether excess business holdings exist.

If the PF has permitted temporary excess business holdings acquired through gift or bequest, evaluate status of planning for timely disposition of excess?

### §4944 Jeopardizing Investments

Review PF's investment listing to evaluate presence of jeopardizing investments. [§16.2]

    Is the fair market value of assets less than cost basis?

    Does PF hold properties that produce no income?

If net capital loss reported, review past years of investment returns for trend indicating jeopardizing investments.

Does PF use outside alternative investment advisors?

Does PF have "alternative investments"?

    If so, complete Checklist for Alternative Investments. [Exhibit 19.11]

### §4945 Taxable Expenditures

Obtain a list of grants paid during year.

Determine if PF spent money for any of following: [Answers should be NO]

    Organizations listed as 509(a)(3) Type III - Other*

    Organizations classified as private foundations*

    Organizations classified as other than a permitted public charity*

    *unless Expenditure Responsibility exercised.

    Lobbying or a grant to finance lobbying [§17.1]

    Political campaign [§17.1]

    Unapproved individual grant for study, travel, or similar [§17.3]

    Support of noncharitable program [§17.7]

Are files (IRS approves electronic) maintained to evidence charitable nature of the PF's activities?

    (For example: files for grantees, programs, exhibitions, class schedules, articles published)

Do grant files contain a Grants Checklist [Exhibit 17.2] and Grant Transmittal Letter [Exhibits 17.3 and 17.4] for each grant paid?

Did the PF make an expenditure responsibility grant to another PF, Type III non-func.int. SO, or a non-(c)(3) entity? [§17.6] If so, were following prepared?

    Control Checklist of 7 Steps [Cklt. 17.5]

    Pre-grant inquiry [Checklist 17.6]

    Expenditure responsibility agreement [Cklt. 17.7 & 17.8]

    Report in Form 990-PF for current and prior year ER grants [Exhibit 17.9]

---

**EXHIBIT 12.2**

*(Continued)*

© 2013 Jody Blazek. Paragraph references to Blazek, *Tax Planning Compliance for Tax-Exempt Organizations*, 5th Edition, supplemented annually, John Willey & Sons.

**Annual Tax Compliance Checklist for Private Foundation (PF), page 4**

**§4945 Taxable Expenditures, Continued**

Is the list of grantees for Part XV designed to reflect the purpose of each grant and summarized to reflect the PF's mission? i.e., does this part paint a clear picture of type of programs the PF wants to support?_____

**Violations of §4941/4945 Sanctions**

Did a violation of §4941-4945 rules occur? _____

Verify correct answers given in Part VII-B. A "Yes" indicates Form 4720 may need to be filed. _____

Coordinate answer to Quest. 5(c) of Part VII-B with attachment of Expenditure Responsibility Report(s).\_\_\_\_\_

Should a Form 4720 be prepared? _____

    Has violation been corrected? [§§14.10,15.6,16.4,17.8] _____

    Can the penalty be abated for reasonable cause? _____

    Have practices to avoid such acts in the future been adopted? _____

**§4940 Investment Excise Tax**

Does the PF maintain records to support allocation to identify disbursements directly related to its investments, grant-making and program activity, and management and general expenses? See Exp.Alloc.Memo. [§13.3] _____

Are expense allocations consistent with prior years? _____

Is the tax basis of assets (donee's basis for gifts received) maintained separately from the book basis? [§13.2] _____

Consider distribution of substantially appreciated property (rather than cash) to grantees to reduce excise tax on capital gain from sale of the property. [§13.4] _____

Should PF plan timing of qualifying distributions to reduce its excise tax to 1%? [§13.4] _____

Does PF properly report all investment income? Most all types of income are now taxable, including gains from sale of exempt function property [§13.1] _____

Does PF have unrelated business income? [ Ch. 21] If so: _____

    Complete UBI checklist and prepare Form 990-T. _____

    Is the unrelated income excluded from Part I, column (b)? _____

Was excise tax paid in a timely fashion? [§13.6] _____

    Should Form 2220 be attached to Form 990-PF? _____

    Must large corporation method for estimating be used? _____

    Is tax properly paid electronically? _____

**Filing Requirements**

Has PF followed the public disclosure rules for its past three years of 990-PFs, 990-Ts and Form 1023? [§18.3(a)] _____

All PFs and PFs converting to public status must file 990-PF regardless of support, even if zero. [§12.4]\_\_\_\_\_

Was an extension(s) of time requested on Form 8868? _____

If the return is being filed late, has penalty abatement been requested? _____

If the PF wants to change its fiscal year, set up due date for automatic change for next year? [§18.3(b)]_____

**EXHIBIT 12.2**

---

*(Continued)*

© 2013 Jody Blazek. Paragraph references to Blazek, *Tax Planning Compliance for Tax-Exempt Organizations*, 5th Edition, supplemented annually, John Willey & Sons.

## § 12.3 COMPLIANCE ISSUES

**Annual Tax Compliance Checklist for Private Foundation (PF), page 5**

### Filing Requirements, Continued

Does the PF need to file Form 3115 to adopt change in tax accounting method? [§18.3(c)] _____

Does Part XVI-A, Analysis of Income Producing Activity, indicate PF has unrelated business income? _____
If so, has Form 990-T been filed? _____

Investigate application of exceptions and modifications that exclude or modify unrelated income from tax. [§21.9 & §21.10] _____

Does the EO make payments for personal services? If so, _____

Determine whether PF has a policy to distinguish between employees and independent contractors. [§24.1] _____

Does PF comply with Federal/state payroll withholding/reporting requirements (including ACA)? _____

Are payroll taxes deposited in a timely fashion? _____

Is withholding required for payments to foreign persons? _____

Are Forms 941, 5500, W-2, and other tax reports timely filed? _____

### Contributions Received

Has substantial contributor list been updated? [§12.1] _____

Has the PF received gifts of property (other than listed securities) for which Form 8283 is required? _____

Must sales of $5,000+ donated property made within three years from date of gift be reported on Form 8282? _____

Has PF furnished its funders §170 donation acknowledgments indicating no benefits provided? [§24.2] (Provision of benefits would indicate self-dealing.) _____

### EXHIBIT 12.2

---

*(Continued)*

© 2013 Jody Blazek. Paragraph references to Blazek, *Tax Planning Compliance for Tax-Exempt Organizations*, 5th Edition, supplemented annually, John Willey & Sons.

## Exhibit 12.3

---

Annual Tax Compliance Checklist for Private Foundation (short version)

PF's Name _____ Prepared by _____ with _____ Date _____

**If the answer to any of these questions is yes, complete long form checklist.**

### § 4941 Self-Dealing [Ch. 5]

Did PF have financial transactions with disqualified persons? _____

Did the PF reimburse exempt function expenses? _____

For property bequeathed to the PF, should distributions from _____
estate be delayed until property sold or divided?

### § 4942 Mandatory Distribution Requirement [Ch. 6]

Does Part XIII or XIV indicate PF failed to spend a sufficient amount on its _____
charitable programs?
There are returned grants to be added back. _____

### § 4943 Excess Business Holdings [Ch. 7]

Does PF own more than 2% of corporation, partnership, or other business? _____

### § 4944 Jeopardizing Investments [Ch. 8]

Does PF's investment list reflect significant declines in value? _____

### § 4945 Taxable Expenditures [Ch. 9]
Did the PF spend money on:

Organizations not listed as public charities in Pub 78 or classified as 509(a)(3) _____

Lobbying or a grant to finance lobbying _____

Political campaign _____

Unapproved individual grant _____

PF does not maintain grant files with Grants Checklist _____

### § 4940 Investment Excise Tax [Ch. 10]

Consider accuracy of expense allocations. _____

Is all revenue, other than exempt function, taxable? _____

Estimated tax payments not made in timely fashion. _____

Can PF time capital gains to reach the 1% tax rate? _____

### Other Tax Compliance Issues

PF failed to publicly disclose past three years of 990-PFs and Form 1023. _____

Part XVI-A indicates PF has unrelated business income. _____

PF makes payments for personal services. _____

PF failed to furnish its funders § 170 donation ltr indicating no benefits _____
provided? (Provision of benefits would indicate self-dealing.)
There are change(s) to report to IRS. _____

PF does not have local and state exemptions in place. _____

| Form **990-T** | **Exempt Organization Business Income Tax Return**<br>**(and proxy tax under section 6033(e))** | OMB No. 1545-0687 | |
|---|---|---|---|
| | For calendar year 2013 or other tax year beginning _____, 2013, and ending _____, 20 __ .<br>▶ See separate instructions. | **2013** | |
| Department of the Treasury<br>Internal Revenue Service | ▶ **Information about Form 990-T and its instructions is available at** *www.irs.gov/form990t.*<br>▶ **Do not enter SSN numbers on this form as it may be made public if your organization is a 501(c)(3).** | Open to Public Inspection for<br>501(c)(3) Organizations Only | |

| A ☐ Check box if<br>address changed | Name of organization ( ☐ Check box if name changed and see instructions.) | | **D** Employer identification number<br>(Employees' trust, see instructions.) |
|---|---|---|---|
| **B** Exempt under section<br>☑ 501( **c** )( **3** )<br>☐ 408(e)  ☐ 220(e)<br>☐ 408A  ☐ 530(a)<br>☐ 529(a) | Print<br>or<br>Type | **Environmentalist Fund** | 77-7777777 |
| | | Number, street, and room or suite no. If a P.O. box, see instructions.<br>**1111 Any Street** | **E** Unrelated business activity codes<br>(See instructions.) |
| | | City or town, state or province, country, and ZIP or foreign postal code<br>**Hometown, TX 77777-7777** | 900003 |
| **C** Book value of all assets<br>at end of year<br>**22,070,400** | **F** Group exemption number (See instructions.) ▶ | | |

**G** Check organization type ▶ ☑ 501(c) corporation  ☐ 501(c) trust  ☐ 401(a) trust  ☐ Other trust

**H** Describe the organization's primary unrelated business activity. ▶ **Sub-S Corporation Distribution**

**I** During the tax year, was the corporation a subsidiary in an affiliated group or a parent-subsidiary controlled group? . . ▶ ☐ Yes ☑ No
If "Yes," enter the name and identifying number of the parent corporation. ▶

**J** The books are in care of ▶ **Mary Goodbooks**     Telephone number ▶   **444-444-4444**

### Part I  Unrelated Trade or Business Income

| | | | (A) Income | (B) Expenses | (C) Net |
|---|---|---|---|---|---|
| **1a** | Gross receipts or sales | | | | |
| **b** | Less returns and allowances _____ **c** Balance ▶ | **1c** | | | |
| **2** | Cost of goods sold (Schedule A, line 7) . . . . . | **2** | | | |
| **3** | Gross profit. Subtract line 2 from line 1c . . . . . | **3** | | | |
| **4a** | Capital gain net income (attach Form 8949 and Schedule D) | **4a** | | | |
| **b** | Net gain (loss) (Form 4797, Part II, line 17) (attach Form 4797) | **4b** | | | |
| **c** | Capital loss deduction for trusts . . . . . . . | **4c** | | | |
| **5** | Income (loss) from partnerships and S corporations (attach statement)ST | **5** | 100,000 | | 100,000 |
| **6** | Rent income (Schedule C) . . . . . . . . . | **6** | | | |
| **7** | Unrelated debt-financed income (Schedule E) . . . . . | **7** | 45,000 | 36,120 | 8,880 |
| **8** | Interest, annuities, royalties, and rents from controlled organizations (Schedule F) | **8** | | | |
| **9** | Investment income of a section 501(c)(7), (9), or (17) organization (Schedule G) | **9** | | | |
| **10** | Exploited exempt activity income (Schedule I) . . . . . | **10** | | | |
| **11** | Advertising income (Schedule J) . . . . . . . | **11** | | | |
| **12** | Other income (See instructions; attach schedule.) . . . . | **12** | | | |
| **13** | **Total.** Combine lines 3 through 12 . . . . . . . . | **13** | 145,000 | 36,120 | 108,880 |

### Part II  Deductions Not Taken Elsewhere (See instructions for limitations on deductions.) (Except for contributions, deductions must be directly connected with the unrelated business income.)

| | | | | |
|---|---|---|---|---|
| **14** | Compensation of officers, directors, and trustees (Schedule K) . . . . . . . . | **14** | | |
| **15** | Salaries and wages . . . . . . . . . . . . . . . . . . . . . | **15** | | |
| **16** | Repairs and maintenance . . . . . . . . . . . . . . . . . . . | **16** | | |
| **17** | Bad debts . . . . . . . . . . . . . . . . . . . . . . . | **17** | | |
| **18** | Interest (attach schedule) . . . . . . . . . . . . . . . . . . | **18** | | |
| **19** | Taxes and licenses . . . . . . . . . . . . . . . . . . . . | **19** | | |
| **20** | Charitable contributions (See instructions for limitation rules.) . . . . . . . . . | **20** | 10,788 | |
| **21** | Depreciation (attach Form 4562) . . . . . . . **21** | 7,700 | | |
| **22** | Less depreciation claimed on Schedule A and elsewhere on return . . **22a** | 7,700 | **22b** | 0 |
| **23** | Depletion . . . . . . . . . . . . . . . . . . . . . . . | **23** | | |
| **24** | Contributions to deferred compensation plans . . . . . . . . . . . . | **24** | | |
| **25** | Employee benefit programs . . . . . . . . . . . . . . . . . . | **25** | | |
| **26** | Excess exempt expenses (Schedule I) . . . . . . . . . . . . . . . | **26** | | |
| **27** | Excess readership costs (Schedule J) . . . . . . . . . . . . . . . | **27** | | |
| **28** | Other deductions (attach schedule) . . . . . . . . . . . . . . . . | **28** | | |
| **29** | **Total deductions.** Add lines 14 through 28 . . . . . . . . . . . . . | **29** | 10,788 | |
| **30** | Unrelated business taxable income before net operating loss deduction. Subtract line 29 from line 13 | **30** | 98,092 | |
| **31** | Net operating loss deduction (limited to the amount on line 30) . . . . . . . . . | **31** | | |
| **32** | Unrelated business taxable income before specific deduction. Subtract line 31 from line 30 . . . | **32** | 98,092 | |
| **33** | Specific deduction (Generally $1,000, but see line 33 instructions for exceptions.) . . . . . | **33** | 1,000 | |
| **34** | **Unrelated business taxable income.** Subtract line 33 from line 32. If line 33 is greater than line 32, enter the smaller of zero or line 32 . . . . . . . . . . . . . . . . . . . . . . . . . | **34** | 97,092 | |

For Paperwork Reduction Act Notice, see instructions.     Cat. No. 11291J     Form **990-T** (2013)

**EXHIBIT 12.4**

Mock-up of Form 990-T, Exemption Organization Business Income Tax Return

Form 990-T (2013)  Environmentalist Fund                          77-7777777        Page **2**

### Part III  Tax Computation

**35** **Organizations Taxable as Corporations.** See instructions for tax computation. Controlled group members (sections 1561 and 1563) check here ▶ ☐ **See instructions** and:

**a** Enter your share of the $50,000, $25,000, and $9,925,000 taxable income brackets (in that order):
**(1)** $ _____  **(2)** $ _____  **(3)** $ _____

**b** Enter organization's share of: **(1)** Additional 5% tax (not more than $11,750)  $ _____
**(2)** Additional 3% tax (not more than $100,000)  . . . . . . . . .  $ _____

**c** Income tax on the amount on line 34 . . . . . . . . . . . . . . . ▶ | **35c** | 21,261

**36** **Trusts Taxable at Trust Rates.** See instructions for tax computation. Income tax on the amount on line 34 from: ☐ Tax rate schedule or ☐ Schedule D (Form 1041) . . . . . ▶ | **36** |

**37** **Proxy tax.** See instructions . . . . . . . . . . . . . . . . . . ▶ | **37** |

**38** Alternative minimum tax . . . . . . . . . . . . . . . . . . | **38** |

**39** **Total.** Add lines 37 and 38 to line 35c or 36, whichever applies . . . . . . . . . | **39** | 21,261

### Part IV  Tax and Payments

| | | | | |
|---|---|---|---|---|
| **40a** | Foreign tax credit (corporations attach Form 1118; trusts attach Form 1116) . | **40a** | | |
| **b** | Other credits (see instructions) . . . . . . . . . . . | **40b** | | |
| **c** | General business credit. Attach Form 3800 (see instructions) . . . | **40c** | | |
| **d** | Credit for prior year minimum tax (attach Form 8801 or 8827) . . . . | **40d** | | |
| **e** | **Total credits.** Add lines 40a through 40d . . . . . . . . . . | | **40e** | 0 |
| **41** | Subtract line 40e from line 39 . . . . . . . . . . . . . . | | **41** | 21,261 |
| **42** | Other taxes. Check if from: ☐ Form 4255 ☐ Form 8611 ☐ Form 8697 ☐ Form 8866 ☐ Other (attach schedule) . | | **42** | |
| **43** | **Total tax.** Add lines 41 and 42 . . . . . . . . . . . . . . | | **43** | 21,261 |
| **44a** | Payments: A 2012 overpayment credited to 2013 . . . . . . | **44a** | 4,050 | |
| **b** | 2013 estimated tax payments . . . . . . . . . . . | **44b** | | |
| **c** | Tax deposited with Form 8868 . . . . . . . . . . . | **44c** | | |
| **d** | Foreign organizations: Tax paid or withheld at source (see instructions) . | **44d** | | |
| **e** | Backup withholding (see instructions) . . . . . . . . . | **44e** | | |
| **f** | Credit for small employer health insurance premiums (Attach Form 8941) . | **44f** | | |
| **g** | Other credits and payments: ☐ Form 2439 ____ ☐ Form 4136 ____ ☐ Other ____ Total ▶ | **44g** | | |
| **45** | **Total payments.** Add lines 44a through 44g . . . . . . . . . . | | **45** | 4,050 |
| **46** | Estimated tax penalty (see instructions). Check if Form 2220 is attached . . . . . . . . ▶ ☑ | **46** | | |
| **47** | **Tax due.** If line 45 is less than the total of lines 43 and 46, enter amount owed . . . . ▶ | **47** | | 17,211 |
| **48** | **Overpayment.** If line 45 is larger than the total of lines 43 and 46, enter amount overpaid . . ▶ | **48** | | |
| **49** | Enter the amount of line 48 you want: Credited to 2014 estimated tax ▶ ____ Refunded ▶ | **49** | | |

### Part V  Statements Regarding Certain Activities and Other Information (see instructions)

| | | Yes | No |
|---|---|---|---|
| **1** | At any time during the 2013 calendar year, did the organization have an interest in or a signature or other authority over a financial account (bank, securities, or other) in a foreign country? If YES, the organization may have to file Form TD F 90-22.1, Report of Foreign Bank and Financial Accounts. If YES, enter the name of the foreign country here ▶ ---------- | | ✓ |
| **2** | During the tax year, did the organization receive a distribution from, or was it the grantor of, or transferor to, a foreign trust? . If YES, see instructions for other forms the organization may have to file. | | ✓ |
| **3** | Enter the amount of tax-exempt interest received or accrued during the tax year ▶ $ | | |

**Schedule A—Cost of Goods Sold.** Enter method of inventory valuation ▶

| | | | | | | | |
|---|---|---|---|---|---|---|---|
| **1** | Inventory at beginning of year | **1** | | **6** | Inventory at end of year . . . | **6** | |
| **2** | Purchases . . . . . . | **2** | | **7** | **Cost of goods sold.** Subtract line 6 from line 5. Enter here and in Part I, line 2 . . . . . . | **7** | |
| **3** | Cost of labor . . . . . . | **3** | | | | | |
| **4a** | Additional section 263A costs (attach schedule) . . . . | **4a** | | | | | |
| **b** | Other costs (attach schedule) | **4b** | | **8** | Do the rules of section 263A (with respect to property produced or acquired for resale) apply to the organization? . . . . . . . . . | Yes | No ✓ |
| **5** | **Total.** Add lines 1 through 4b | **5** | | | | | |

Under penalties of perjury, I declare that I have examined this return, including accompanying schedules and statements, and to the best of my knowledge and belief, it is true, correct, and complete. Declaration of preparer (other than taxpayer) is based on all information of which preparer has any knowledge.

**Sign Here** ▶ _____ Signature of officer ▶ _____ Date _____ Title

May the IRS discuss this return with the preparer shown below (see instructions)? ☑Yes ☐No

| **Paid Preparer Use Only** | Print/Type preparer's name | Preparer's signature | Date | Check ☑ if self-employed | PTIN P9999999 |
|---|---|---|---|---|---|
| | Firm's name ▶ **A Good Accountant** | | | Firm's EIN ▶ 55-5555555 | |
| | Firm's address ▶ **444 Any Street Hometown, TX 77777** | | | Phone no. 444-555-6666 | |

Form **990-T** (2013)

**EXHIBIT 12.4**

*(Continued)*

Form 990-T (2013)　　Environmentalist Fund　　　　　　　　　　　　　　　　　　77-7777777　　Page **3**

## Schedule C—Rent Income (From Real Property and Personal Property Leased With Real Property)
(see instructions)

**1.** Description of property

(1)

(2)

(3)

(4)

| **2.** Rent received or accrued | | **3(a)** Deductions directly connected with the income in columns 2(a) and 2(b) (attach schedule) |
|---|---|---|
| **(a)** From personal property (if the percentage of rent for personal property is more than 10% but not more than 50%) | **(b)** From real and personal property (if the percentage of rent for personal property exceeds 50% or if the rent is based on profit or income) | |
| (1) | | |
| (2) | | |
| (3) | | |
| (4) | | |
| Total | Total | |

**(c) Total income.** Add totals of columns 2(a) and 2(b). Enter here and on page 1, Part I, line 6, column (A)　　▶

**(b) Total deductions.** Enter here and on page 1, Part I, line 6, column (B) ▶

## Schedule E—Unrelated Debt-Financed Income (see instructions)

| **1.** Description of debt-financed property | **2.** Gross income from or allocable to debt-financed property | **3.** Deductions directly connected with or allocable to debt-financed property | |
|---|---|---|---|
| | | **(a)** Straight line depreciation (attach schedule) | **(b)** Other deductions (attach schedule)  See St 2 |
| (1) **Office Building** | 75,000 | 7,700 | 52,500 |
| (2) | | | |
| (3) | | | |
| (4) | | | |

| **4.** Amount of average acquisition debt on or allocable to debt-financed property (attach schedule) | **5.** Average adjusted basis of or allocable to debt-financed property (attach schedule) | **6.** Column 4 divided by column 5 | **7.** Gross income reportable (column 2 × column 6) | **8.** Allocable deductions (column 6 × total of columns 3(a) and 3(b)) |
|---|---|---|---|---|
| (1) 448,860 | 748,100 | 60.0000 % | 45,000 | 36,120 |
| (2) | | % | | |
| (3) | | % | | |
| (4) | | % | | |
| | | | Enter here and on page 1, Part I, line 7, column (A). | Enter here and on page 1, Part I, line 7, column (B). |
| Totals  .  .  .  .  .  .  .  .  .  .  .  .  .  .  .  .  .  .  ▶ | | | 45,000 | 36,120 |

Total dividends-received deductions included in column 8   .  .  .  .  .  .  .  .  .  .  .  .  .  .  ▶

## Schedule F—Interest, Annuities, Royalties, and Rents From Controlled Organizations (see instructions)

| | | Exempt Controlled Organizations | | | |
|---|---|---|---|---|---|
| **1.** Name of controlled organization | **2.** Employer identification number | **3.** Net unrelated income (loss) (see instructions) | **4.** Total of specified payments made | **5.** Part of column 4 that is included in the controlling organization's gross income | **6.** Deductions directly connected with income in column 5 |
| (1) | | | | | |
| (2) | | | | | |
| (3) | | | | | |
| (4) | | | | | |

Nonexempt Controlled Organizations

| **7.** Taxable Income | **8.** Net unrelated income (loss) (see instructions) | **9.** Total of specified payments made | **10.** Part of column 9 that is included in the controlling organization's gross income | **11.** Deductions directly connected with income in column 10 |
|---|---|---|---|---|
| (1) | | | | |
| (2) | | | | |
| (3) | | | | |
| (4) | | | | |
| | | | Add columns 5 and 10. Enter here and on page 1, Part I, line 8, column (A). | Add columns 6 and 11. Enter here and on page 1, Part I, line 8, column (B). |
| Totals  .  .  .  .  .  .  .  .  .  .  .  .  .  .  .  .  .  .  .  .  .  .  .  .  .  .  .  ▶ | | | | |

Form **990-T** (2013)

## EXHIBIT 12.4

### (Continued)

Form 990-T (2013)    Environmentalist Fund                                                77-7777777          Page **4**

## Schedule G—Investment Income of a Section 501(c)(7), (9), or (17) Organization (see instructions)

| **1.** Description of income | **2.** Amount of income | **3.** Deductions directly connected (attach schedule) | **4.** Set-asides (attach schedule) | **5.** Total deductions and set-asides (col. 3 plus col. 4) |
|---|---|---|---|---|
| (1) | | | | |
| (2) | | | | |
| (3) | | | | |
| (4) | | | | |
| **Totals** . . . . . . . . . ▶ | Enter here and on page 1, Part I, line 9, column (A). | | | Enter here and on page 1, Part I, line 9, column (B). |

## Schedule I—Exploited Exempt Activity Income, Other Than Advertising Income (see instructions)

| **1.** Description of exploited activity | **2.** Gross unrelated business income from trade or business | **3.** Expenses directly connected with production of unrelated business income | **4.** Net income (loss) from unrelated trade or business (column 2 minus column 3). If a gain, compute cols. 5 through 7. | **5.** Gross income from activity that is not unrelated business income | **6.** Expenses attributable to column 5 | **7.** Excess exempt expenses (column 6 minus column 5, but not more than column 4). |
|---|---|---|---|---|---|---|
| (1) | | | | | | |
| (2) | | | | | | |
| (3) | | | | | | |
| (4) | | | | | | |
| **Totals** . . . . . . . . . ▶ | Enter here and on page 1, Part I, line 10, col. (A). | Enter here and on page 1, Part I, line 10, col. (B). | | | | Enter here and on page 1, Part II, line 26. |

## Schedule J—Advertising Income (see instructions)

### Part I    Income From Periodicals Reported on a Consolidated Basis

| **1.** Name of periodical | **2.** Gross advertising income | **3.** Direct advertising costs | **4.** Advertising gain or (loss) (col. 2 minus col. 3). If a gain, compute cols. 5 through 7. | **5.** Circulation income | **6.** Readership costs | **7.** Excess readership costs (column 6 minus column 5, but not more than column 4). |
|---|---|---|---|---|---|---|
| (1) | | | | | | |
| (2) | | | | | | |
| (3) | | | | | | |
| (4) | | | | | | |
| **Totals** (carry to Part II, line (5)) . . ▶ | | | | | | |

### Part II    Income From Periodicals Reported on a Separate Basis (For each periodical listed in Part II, fill in columns 2 through 7 on a line-by-line basis.)

| **1.** Name of periodical | **2.** Gross advertising income | **3.** Direct advertising costs | **4.** Advertising gain or (loss) (col. 2 minus col. 3). If a gain, compute cols. 5 through 7. | **5.** Circulation income | **6.** Readership costs | **7.** Excess readership costs (column 6 minus column 5, but not more than column 4). |
|---|---|---|---|---|---|---|
| (1) | | | | | | |
| (2) | | | | | | |
| (3) | | | | | | |
| (4) | | | | | | |
| **Totals from Part I** | | | | | | |
| **Totals, Part II** (lines 1-5) . . . . ▶ | Enter here and on page 1, Part I, line 11, col. (A). | Enter here and on page 1, Part I, line 11, col. (B). | | | | Enter here and on page 1, Part II, line 27. |

## Schedule K—Compensation of Officers, Directors, and Trustees (see instructions)

| **1.** Name | **2.** Title | **3.** Percent of time devoted to business | **4.** Compensation attributable to unrelated business |
|---|---|---|---|
| (1) | | % | |
| (2) | | % | |
| (3) | | % | |
| (4) | | % | |
| **Total.** Enter here and on page 1, Part II, line 14 . . . . . . . . . . . . . . . . . . . . . . . ▶ | | | |

Form **990-T** (2013)

**EXHIBIT 12.4**

*(Continued)*

Form **2220**

Form 990-T

**Underpayment of Estimated Tax by Corporations**

Department of the Treasury
Internal Revenue Service

► Attach to the corporation's tax return.
► Information about Form 2220 and its separate instructions is at *www.irs.gov/form2220.*

OMB No. 1545-0142

**20**13

| Name | Employer identification number |
|------|-------------------------------|
| Environmentalist Fund | 77-7777777 |

**Note:** *Generally, the corporation is not required to file Form 2220 (see Part II below for exceptions) because the IRS will figure any penalty owed and bill the corporation. However, the corporation may still use Form 2220 to figure the penalty. If so, enter the amount from page 2, line 38 on the estimated tax penalty line of the corporation's income tax return, but* **do not** *attach Form 2220.*

**Part I    Required Annual Payment**

| | | | |
|---|---|---|---|
| 1 | Total tax (see instructions) . . . . . . . . . . . . . . . . . . . . . . | **1** | 21,261 |
| 2a | Personal holding company tax (Schedule PH (Form 1120), line 26) included on line 1 | **2a** | |
| b | Look-back interest included on line 1 under section 460(b)(2) for completed long-term contracts or section 167(g) for depreciation under the income forecast method . . | **2b** | |
| c | Credit for federal tax paid on fuels (see instructions) . . . . . . . . . . | **2c** | |
| d | **Total.** Add lines 2a through 2c . . . . . . . . . . . . . . . . . . | **2d** | 0 |
| 3 | Subtract line 2d from line 1. If the result is less than $500, **do not** complete or file this form. The corporation does not owe the penalty . . . . . . . . . . . . . . . . . . . . . | **3** | 21,261 |
| 4 | Enter the tax shown on the corporation's 2012 income tax return (see instructions). **Caution:** *If the tax is zero or the tax year was for less than 12 months, skip this line and enter the amount from line 3 on line 5* . . | **4** | 0 |
| 5 | **Required annual payment.** Enter the **smaller** of line 3 or line 4. If the corporation is required to skip line 4, enter the amount from line 3 . . . . . . . . . . . . . . . . . . . . . | **5** | 21,261 |

**Part II    Reasons for Filing—**Check the boxes below that apply. If any boxes are checked, the corporation **must** file Form 2220 even if it does not owe a penalty (see instructions).

| | |
|---|---|
| 6 | ☐ The corporation is using the adjusted seasonal installment method. |
| 7 | ☑ The corporation is using the annualized income installment method. |
| 8 | ☐ The corporation is a "large corporation" figuring its first required installment based on the prior year's tax. |

**Part III    Figuring the Underpayment**

| | | | (a) | (b) | (c) | (d) |
|---|---|---|---|---|---|---|
| 9 | **Installment due dates.** Enter in columns (a) through (d) the 15th day of the 4th (*Form 990-PF filers:* Use 5th month), 6th, 9th, and 12th months of the corporation's tax year . . . . . . . . . . . | **9** | 4/15/2013 | 6/15/2013 | 9/15/2013 | 12/15/2013 |
| 10 | **Required installments.** If the box on line 6 and/or line 7 above is checked, enter the amounts from Schedule A, line 38. If the box on line 8 (but not 6 or 7) is checked, see instructions for the amounts to enter. If none of these boxes are checked, enter 25% of line 5 above in each column . . . . . . . . . . . . . . . . . . | **10** | 0 | 0 | 0 | 0 |
| 11 | Estimated tax paid or credited for each period (see instructions). For column (a) only, enter the amount from line 11 on line 15 . . . . | **11** | 4,050 | | | |
| | ***Complete lines 12 through 18 of one column before going to the next column.*** | | | | | |
| 12 | Enter amount, if any, from line 18 of the preceding column . . . . | **12** | | 4,050 | 4,050 | 4,050 |
| 13 | Add lines 11 and 12 . . . . . . . . . . . . . | **13** | | 4,050 | 4,050 | 4,050 |
| 14 | Add amounts on lines 16 and 17 of the preceding column . . . . . | **14** | | | | |
| 15 | Subtract line 14 from line 13. If zero or less, enter -0- . . . . . | **15** | 4,050 | 4,050 | 4,050 | 4,050 |
| 16 | If the amount on line 15 is zero, subtract line 13 from line 14. Otherwise, enter -0- . . . . . . . . . . . . . . . . | **16** | | 0 | 0 | |
| 17 | **Underpayment.** If line 15 is less than or equal to line 10, subtract line 15 from line 10. Then go to line 12 of the next column. Otherwise, go to line 18 . . . . . . . . . . . . . . . . . | **17** | | | | |
| 18 | **Overpayment.** If line 10 is less than line 15, subtract line 10 from line 15. Then go to line 12 of the next column . . . . . . . . . | **18** | 4,050 | 4,050 | 4,050 | |

**Go to Part IV on page 2 to figure the penalty. Do not go to Part IV if there are no entries on line 17—no penalty is owed.**

For Paperwork Reduction Act Notice, see separate instructions.     Cat. No. 11746L     Form **2220** (2013)

**EXHIBIT 12.4**

*(Continued)*

Form 2220 (2013)   Environmentalist Fund                                    77-7777777          Page **2**

## Part IV  Figuring the Penalty

|  |  |  | (a) | (b) | (c) | (d) |
|---|---|---|---|---|---|---|
| 19 | Enter the date of payment or the 15th day of the 3rd month after the close of the tax year, whichever is earlier (see instructions). *(Form 990-PF and Form 990-T filers: Use 5th month instead of 3rd month.)* . . . . . . . . . . . . . . . | 19 | | | | |
| 20 | Number of days from due date of installment on line 9 to the date shown on line 19 . . . . . . . . . . . . . . | 20 | | | | |
| 21 | Number of days on line 20 after 4/15/2013 and before 7/1/2013 | 21 | | | | |
| 22 | Underpayment on line 17 × $\frac{\text{Number of days on line 21}}{365}$ × 3% | 22 | $ | $ | $ | $ |
| 23 | Number of days on line 20 after 6/30/2013 and before 10/1/2013 | 23 | | | | |
| 24 | Underpayment on line 17 × $\frac{\text{Number of days on line 23}}{365}$ × 3% | 24 | $ | $ | $ | $ |
| 25 | Number of days on line 20 after 9/30/2013 and before 1/1/2014 | 25 | | | | |
| 26 | Underpayment on line 17 × $\frac{\text{Number of days on line 25}}{365}$ × 3% | 26 | $ | $ | $ | $ |
| 27 | Number of days on line 20 after 12/31/2013 and before 4/1/2014 | 27 | | | | |
| 28 | Underpayment on line 17 × $\frac{\text{Number of days on line 27}}{365}$ × 3% | 28 | $ | $ | $ | $ |
| 29 | Number of days on line 20 after 3/31/2014 and before 7/1/2014 | 29 | | | | |
| 30 | Underpayment on line 17 × $\frac{\text{Number of days on line 29}}{365}$ × *% | 30 | $ | $ | $ | $ |
| 31 | Number of days on line 20 after 6/30/2014 and before 10/1/2014 | 31 | | | | |
| 32 | Underpayment on line 17 × $\frac{\text{Number of days on line 31}}{365}$ × *% | 32 | $ | $ | $ | $ |
| 33 | Number of days on line 20 after 9/30/2014 and before 1/1/2015 | 33 | | | | |
| 34 | Underpayment on line 17 × $\frac{\text{Number of days on line 33}}{365}$ × *% | 34 | $ | $ | $ | $ |
| 35 | Number of days on line 20 after 12/31/2014 and before 2/16/2015 | 35 | | | | |
| 36 | Underpayment on line 17 × $\frac{\text{Number of days on line 35}}{365}$ × *% | 36 | $ | $ | $ | $ |
| 37 | Add lines 22, 24, 26, 28, 30, 32, 34, and 36 . . . . . . . | 37 | $ | $ | $ | $ |
| 38 | **Penalty.** Add columns (a) through (d) of line 37. Enter the total here and on Form 1120, line 33; or the comparable line for other income tax returns . . . . . . . . . . . . . . . . . . . . . . . . . . | 38 | $ | | | 0 |

*Use the penalty interest rate for each calendar quarter, which the IRS will determine during the first month in the preceding quarter. These rates are published quarterly in an IRS News Release and in a revenue ruling in the Internal Revenue Bulletin. To obtain this information on the Internet, access the IRS website at *www.irs.gov*. You can also call 1-800-829-4933 to get interest rate information.

Form **2220** (2013)

## EXHIBIT 12.4

*(Continued)*

Form 2220 (2013)    Environmentalist Fund                                        77-7777777    Page 3

**Schedule A**    Adjusted Seasonal Installment Method and Annualized Income Installment Method
(see instructions)

**Form 1120S filers:** *For lines 1, 2, 3, and 21, below, "taxable income" refers to excess net passive income or the amount on which tax is imposed under section 1374(a), whichever applies.*

**Part I**    Adjusted Seasonal Installment Method (**Caution:** *Use this method only if the base period percentage for any 6 consecutive months is at least 70%. See instructions.*)

| | | | (a) First 3 months | (b) First 5 months | (c) First 8 months | (d) First 11 months |
|---|---|---|---|---|---|---|
| 1 | Enter taxable income for the following periods: | | | | | |
| a | Tax year beginning in 2010 | 1a | | | | |
| b | Tax year beginning in 2011 | 1b | | | | |
| c | Tax year beginning in 2012 | 1c | | | | |
| 2 | Enter taxable income for each period for the tax year beginning in 2013 (see instructions for the treatment of extraordinary items) . | 2 | | | | |
| 3 | Enter taxable income for the following periods: | | First 4 months | First 6 months | First 9 months | Entire year |
| a | Tax year beginning in 2010. | 3a | | | | |
| b | Tax year beginning in 2011 | 3b | | | | |
| c | Tax year beginning in 2012 | 3c | | | | |
| 4 | Divide the amount in each column on line 1a by the amount in column (d) on line 3a | 4 | | | | |
| 5 | Divide the amount in each column on line 1b by the amount in column (d) on line 3b | 5 | | | | |
| 6 | Divide the amount in each column on line 1c by the amount in column (d) on line 3c | 6 | | | | |
| 7 | Add lines 4 through 6 | 7 | | | | |
| 8 | Divide line 7 by 3.0 | 8 | | | | |
| 9a | Divide line 2 by line 8 | 9a | | | | |
| b | Extraordinary items (see instructions) | 9b | | | | |
| c | Add lines 9a and 9b . | 9c | | | | |
| 10 | Figure the tax on the amount on line 9c using the instructions for Form 1120, Schedule J, line 2 (or comparable line of corporation's return) | 10 | | | | |
| 11a | Divide the amount in columns (a) through (c) on line 3a by the amount in column (d) on line 3a | 11a | | | | |
| b | Divide the amount in columns (a) through (c) on line 3b by the amount in column (d) on line 3b | 11b | | | | |
| c | Divide the amount in columns (a) through (c) on line 3c by the amount in column (d) on line 3c | 11c | | | | |
| 12 | Add lines 11a through 11c . | 12 | | | | |
| 13 | Divide line 12 by 3.0 . | 13 | | | | |
| 14 | Multiply the amount in columns (a) through (c) of line 10 by columns (a) through (c) of line 13. In column (d), enter the amount from line 10, column (d) | 14 | | | | |
| 15 | Enter any alternative minimum tax for each payment period (see instructions) | 15 | | | | |
| 16 | Enter any other taxes for each payment period (see instructions) | 16 | | | | |
| 17 | Add lines 14 through 16 | 17 | | | | |
| 18 | For each period, enter the same type of credits as allowed on Form 2220, lines 1 and 2c (see instructions) | 18 | | | | |
| 19 | Total tax after credits. Subtract line 18 from line 17. If zero or less, enter -0- . | 19 | | | | |

Form **2220** (2013)

**EXHIBIT 12.4**

*(Continued)*

Form 2220 (2013)    Environmentalist Fund                                            77-7777777              Page **4**

**Part II    Annualized Income Installment Method**

| | | | (a) | (b) | (c) | (d) |
|---|---|---|---|---|---|---|
| | | | First **2** months | First **3** months | First **6** months | First **9** months |
| 20 | Annualization periods (see instructions) . . . . . . . . | 20 | | | | |
| 21 | Enter taxable income for each annualization period (see instructions for the treatment of extraordinary items) . . . | 21 | 0 | 0 | 0 | 0 |
| 22 | Annualization amounts (see instructions) . . . . . . . | 22 | 6 | 4 | 2 | 1.33333 |
| 23a | Annualized taxable income. Multiply line 21 by line 22 . . . | 23a | 0 | 0 | 0 | 0 |
| b | Extraordinary items (see instructions) . . . . . . . . | 23b | | | | |
| c | Add lines 23a and 23b . . . . . . . . . . . . . . | 23c | 0 | 0 | 0 | 0 |
| 24 | Figure the tax on the amount on line 23c using the instructions for Form 1120, Schedule J, line 2 (or comparable line of corporation's return) . . . . . . . . . . . . . | 24 | 0 | 0 | 0 | 0 |
| 25 | Enter any alternative minimum tax for each payment period (see instructions) . . . . . . . . . . . . . . . | 25 | | | | |
| 26 | Enter any other taxes for each payment period (see instructions) | 26 | | | | |
| 27 | Total tax. Add lines 24 through 26 . . . . . . . . . | 27 | 0 | 0 | 0 | 0 |
| 28 | For each period, enter the same type of credits as allowed on Form 2220, lines 1 and 2c (see instructions) . . . . . . | 28 | | | | |
| 29 | Total tax after credits. Subtract line 28 from line 27. If zero or less, enter -0- . . . . . . . . . . . . . . | 29 | | | | |
| 30 | Applicable percentage . . . . . . . . . . . . . . | 30 | 25% | 50% | 75% | 100% |
| 31 | Multiply line 29 by line 30 . . . . . . . . . . . . | 31 | 0 | 0 | 0 | 0 |

**Part III    Required Installments**

| | | | 1st installment | 2nd installment | 3rd installment | 4th installment |
|---|---|---|---|---|---|---|
| | **Note:** *Complete lines 32 through 38 of one column before completing the next column.* | | | | | |
| 32 | If only Part I or Part II is completed, enter the amount in each column from line 19 or line 31. If both parts are completed, enter the **smaller** of the amounts in each column from line 19 or line 31 . . | 32 | 0 | 0 | 0 | 0 |
| 33 | Add the amounts in all preceding columns of line 38 (see instructions) . . . . . . . . . . . . . . . . | 33 | | | | |
| 34 | **Adjusted seasonal or annualized income installments.** Subtract line 33 from line 32. If zero or less, enter -0- . . . | 34 | 0 | 0 | 0 | 0 |
| 35 | Enter 25% of line 5 on page 1 of Form 2220 in each column. **Note:** *"Large corporations," see the instructions for line 10 for the amounts to enter* . . . . . . . . . . . . . | 35 | 5,315 | 5,315 | 5,315 | 5,316 |
| 36 | Subtract line 38 of the preceding column from line 37 of the preceding column . . . . . . . . . . . . . | 36 | | 5,315 | 10,630 | 15,945 |
| 37 | Add lines 35 and 36 . . . . . . . . . . . . . | 37 | 5,315 | 10,630 | 15,945 | 21,261 |
| 38 | **Required installments.** Enter the **smaller** of line 34 or line 37 here and on page 1 of Form 2220, line 10 (see instructions) . | 38 | 0 | 0 | 0 | 0 |

Form **2220** (2013)

EXHIBIT **12.4**

*(Continued)*

**Form 4562**

Department of the Treasury
Internal Revenue Service  (99)

**Depreciation and Amortization**
**(Including Information on Listed Property)**
► See separate instructions.          ► Attach to your tax return.

OMB No. 1545-0172

**2013**

Attachment
Sequence No. **179**

| Name(s) shown on return | Business or activity to which this form relates | Identifying number |
|---|---|---|
| Environmentalist Fund | Office Building Rental | 77-7777777 |

**Part I**  Election To Expense Certain Property Under Section 179
**Note:** *If you have any listed property, complete Part V before you complete Part I.*

| | | | |
|---|---|---|---|
| 1 | Maximum amount (see instructions) . . . . . . . . . . . . . . . . | 1 | 125,000 |
| 2 | Total cost of section 179 property placed in service (see instructions) . . . . . . . | 2 | |
| 3 | Threshold cost of section 179 property before reduction in limitation (see instructions) . . . . . . | 3 | 500,000 |
| 4 | Reduction in limitation. Subtract line 3 from line 2. If zero or less, enter -0- . . . . . . . . | 4 | |
| 5 | Dollar limitation for tax year. Subtract line 4 from line 1. If zero or less, enter -0-. If married filing separately, see instructions . . . . . . . . . . . . . . . . . . . . . . | 5 | |

| 6 | (a) Description of property | (b) Cost (business use only) | (c) Elected cost | |
|---|---|---|---|---|
| | | | | |
| | | | | |

| | | | |
|---|---|---|---|
| 7 | Listed property. Enter the amount from line 29 . . . . . . . . . . **7** | | |
| 8 | Total elected cost of section 179 property. Add amounts in column (c), lines 6 and 7 . . . . | 8 | |
| 9 | Tentative deduction. Enter the **smaller** of line 5 or line 8 . . . . . . . . . . . | 9 | |
| 10 | Carryover of disallowed deduction from line 13 of your 2012 Form 4562 . . . . . . . . | 10 | |
| 11 | Business income limitation. Enter the smaller of business income (not less than zero) or line 5 (see instructions) | 11 | |
| 12 | Section 179 expense deduction. Add lines 9 and 10, but do not enter more than line 11 . . . . . | 12 | |
| 13 | Carryover of disallowed deduction to 2014. Add lines 9 and 10, less line 12 ► | **13** | |

**Note:** *Do not use Part II or Part III below for listed property. Instead, use Part V.*

**Part II**  Special Depreciation Allowance and Other Depreciation **(Do not** include listed property.) (See instructions.)

| | | | |
|---|---|---|---|
| 14 | Special depreciation allowance for qualified property (other than listed property) placed in service during the tax year (see instructions) . . . . . . . . . . . . . . . . . . . | 14 | |
| 15 | Property subject to section 168(f)(1) election . . . . . . . . . . . . . . . | 15 | |
| 16 | Other depreciation (including ACRS) . . . . . . . . . . . . . . . . . | 16 | |

**Part III**  MACRS Depreciation **(Do not** include listed property.) (See instructions.)

**Section A**

| | | | |
|---|---|---|---|
| 17 | MACRS deductions for assets placed in service in tax years beginning before 2013 . . . . . . | 17 | |
| 18 | If you are electing to group any assets placed in service during the tax year into one or more general asset accounts, check here . . . . . . . . . . . . . . . . . . . . . ► ☐ | | |

**Section B—Assets Placed in Service During 2013 Tax Year Using the General Depreciation System**

| (a) Classification of property | (b) Month and year placed in service | (c) Basis for depreciation (business/investment use only—see instructions) | (d) Recovery period | (e) Convention | (f) Method | (g) Depreciation deduction |
|---|---|---|---|---|---|---|
| 19a 3-year property | | | | | | |
| b 5-year property | | | | | | |
| c 7-year property | | | | | | |
| d 10-year property | | | | | | |
| e 15-year property | | | | | | |
| f 20-year property | | | | | | |
| g 25-year property | | | 25 yrs. | | S/L | |
| h Residential rental property | | | 27.5 yrs. | MM | S/L | |
| | | | 27.5 yrs. | MM | S/L | |
| i Nonresidential real property | 07/01/13 | 600,000 | 39 yrs. | MM | S/L | 7,700 |
| | | | | MM | S/L | |

**Section C—Assets Placed in Service During 2013 Tax Year Using the Alternative Depreciation System**

| | | | | | | |
|---|---|---|---|---|---|---|
| 20a Class life | | | | | S/L | |
| b 12-year | | | 12 yrs. | | S/L | |
| c 40-year | | | 40 yrs. | MM | S/L | |

**Part IV**  Summary  (See instructions.)

| | | | |
|---|---|---|---|
| 21 | Listed property. Enter amount from line 28 . . . . . . . . . . . . . . . . | 21 | |
| 22 | **Total.** Add amounts from line 12, lines 14 through 17, lines 19 and 20 in column (g), and line 21. Enter here and on the appropriate lines of your return. Partnerships and S corporations—see instructions . | 22 | 7,700 |
| 23 | For assets shown above and placed in service during the current year, enter the portion of the basis attributable to section 263A costs . . . . . . . . | 23 | |

For Paperwork Reduction Act Notice, see separate instructions.          Cat. No. 12906N          Form **4562** (2013)

**EXHIBIT 12.4**

*(Continued)*

Form 4562 (2013)                                                                                                                                                          Page **2**

**Part V** Listed Property (Include automobiles, certain other vehicles, certain computers, and property used for entertainment, recreation, or amusement.)

**Note:** For any vehicle for which you are using the standard mileage rate or deducting lease expense, complete **only** 24a, 24b, columns (a) through (c) of Section A, all of Section B, and Section C if applicable.

**Section A—Depreciation and Other Information (Caution:** See the instructions for limits for passenger automobiles.)

24a Do you have evidence to support the business/investment use claimed? ☐ Yes ☐ No | 24b If "Yes," is the evidence written? ☐ Yes ☐ No

| (a)<br>Type of property (list vehicles first) | (b)<br>Date placed in service | (c)<br>Business/investment use percentage | (d)<br>Cost or other basis | (e)<br>Basis for depreciation (business/investment use only) | (f)<br>Recovery period | (g)<br>Method/Convention | (h)<br>Depreciation deduction | (i)<br>Elected section 179 cost |
|---|---|---|---|---|---|---|---|---|
| **25** Special depreciation allowance for qualified listed property placed in service during the tax year and used more than 50% in a qualified business use (see instructions) . | | | | | **25** | | | |
| **26** Property used more than 50% in a qualified business use: | | | | | | | | |
| | | % | | | | | | |
| | | % | | | | | | |
| | | % | | | | | | |
| **27** Property used 50% or less in a qualified business use: | | | | | | | | |
| | | % | | | | S/L – | | |
| | | % | | | | S/L – | | |
| | | % | | | | S/L – | | |
| **28** Add amounts in column (h), lines 25 through 27. Enter here and on line 21, page 1 . | | | | | | **28** | | |
| **29** Add amounts in column (i), line 26. Enter here and on line 7, page 1 . . . . . . . . . . | | | | | | | **29** | |

**Section B—Information on Use of Vehicles**

Complete this section for vehicles used by a sole proprietor, partner, or other "more than 5% owner," or related person. If you provided vehicles to your employees, first answer the questions in Section C to see if you meet an exception to completing this section for those vehicles.

| | (a)<br>Vehicle 1 | | (b)<br>Vehicle 2 | | (c)<br>Vehicle 3 | | (d)<br>Vehicle 4 | | (e)<br>Vehicle 5 | | (f)<br>Vehicle 6 | |
|---|---|---|---|---|---|---|---|---|---|---|---|---|
| **30** Total business/investment miles driven during the year (**do not** include commuting miles) . | | | | | | | | | | | | |
| **31** Total commuting miles driven during the year | | | | | | | | | | | | |
| **32** Total other personal (noncommuting) miles driven . . . . . . . . | | | | | | | | | | | | |
| **33** Total miles driven during the year. Add lines 30 through 32 . . . . . . | | | | | | | | | | | | |
| **34** Was the vehicle available for personal use during off-duty hours? . . . . . | Yes | No | Yes | No | Yes | No | Yes | No | Yes | No | Yes | No |
| **35** Was the vehicle used primarily by a more than 5% owner or related person? . . | | | | | | | | | | | | |
| **36** Is another vehicle available for personal use? | | | | | | | | | | | | |

**Section C—Questions for Employers Who Provide Vehicles for Use by Their Employees**

Answer these questions to determine if you meet an exception to completing Section B for vehicles used by employees who **are not** more than 5% owners or related persons (see instructions).

| | | Yes | No |
|---|---|---|---|
| **37** | Do you maintain a written policy statement that prohibits all personal use of vehicles, including commuting, by your employees? . . . . . . . . . . . . . . . . . . . . . . . . | | |
| **38** | Do you maintain a written policy statement that prohibits personal use of vehicles, except commuting, by your employees? See the instructions for vehicles used by corporate officers, directors, or 1% or more owners . . | | |
| **39** | Do you treat all use of vehicles by employees as personal use? . . . . . . . . . . . . . | | |
| **40** | Do you provide more than five vehicles to your employees, obtain information from your employees about the use of the vehicles, and retain the information received? . . . . . . . . . . . . . . | | |
| **41** | Do you meet the requirements concerning qualified automobile demonstration use? (See instructions.) . . . | | |
| | **Note:** If your answer to 37, 38, 39, 40, or 41 is "Yes," do not complete Section B for the covered vehicles. | | |

**Part VI** Amortization

| (a)<br>Description of costs | (b)<br>Date amortization begins | (c)<br>Amortizable amount | (d)<br>Code section | (e)<br>Amortization period or percentage | (f)<br>Amortization for this year |
|---|---|---|---|---|---|
| **42** Amortization of costs that begins during your 2013 tax year (see instructions): | | | | | |
| | | | | | |
| | | | | | |
| **43** Amortization of costs that began before your 2013 tax year . . . . . . . . . . . . . | | | | **43** | |
| **44** **Total.** Add amounts in column (f). See the instructions for where to report . . . . . . . . . | | | | **44** | |

Form **4562** (2013)

**EXHIBIT 12.4**

(Continued)

| 2013 | Federal Statements | Page 1 |
|---|---|---|
| | Environmentalist Fund | 77-7777777 |

**Statement 1**
**Form 990-T, Part I, Line 5**
**Income (Loss) from Partnerships and S Corporations**

| Name | Gross Income | Deductions | Income (Loss) |
|---|---|---|---|
| Sub-S MNO corporation | $ 100,000. | $ 0. | $ 100,000. |
| | | Total | $ 100,000. |

**Statement 2**
**Form 990-T, Schedule E, Line 3b**
**Other Deductions Allocable to Debt-Financed Property**

Office Building
| | |
|---|---|
| Cleaning and Maintenance | $ 12,000. |
| Interest | 18,000. |
| Taxes | 22,500. |
| Total | $ 52,500. |

**EXHIBIT 12.4**

*(Continued)*

EXHIBIT 12.5

---

Description of Major Private Foundation Organizational Issues

---

**GRANTS PROGRAM**

*Define Mission*

Decide whether the foundation will make grants to other organizations or conduct self-initiated programs or both. Identify the foundation's charitable objectives by describing the types of concerns the foundation will support (religious study, ecumenical initiatives, animal protection, youth sports, women's issues, etc.). Consider producing a brochure or similar document or report describing the foundation's charitable purposes.

*Describe Eligibility*

Describe criteria for grant recipients (e.g., type of program, age of organization, budget size, or level of administrative costs). Decide what financial documentation will be required—financial statements issued by independent CPAs, Forms 990, budgets for future periods. Consider producing a standard application for grantees. Decide what follow-up reports, if any, will be required from grantees.

*Funding Profile*

Determine the types of grants the foundation will make. Will it fund capital improvements (bricks and mortar), special projects, operating budgets, scholarships, and so on? Should the foundation make challenge or matching grants? Will the foundation make multi-year commitments?

*Grants Budget*

Will the foundation target its annual giving to equal the 5 percent amount it is minimally required to pay out or some higher amount based on its current or future funding? Establish a grant decision-making system, including attention to setting annual deadline(s) for grant applications, designing matrix for evaluating requests for funding, scheduling site visits, and setting deadline(s) for funding decisions.

**DOCUMENTATION AND RECORD KEEPING**

*Financial Records*

Establish financial accounting and filing systems to track and capture the foundation's monetary transactions in a meaningful fashion. Study available software and optimally choose a program that contains an integrated general ledger and a grants management system. Design a chart of accounts with a view to ease of reporting on Form 990-PF. Evaluate usefulness and redesign, if necessary and possible, reports generated by investment managers to reflect monthly valuations of assets, year-end gain and loss schedules, and valuation reports.

*Grant Records*

Consider custom designing a computer database to monitor the foundation's grant awards, payments, achievements of grantees, and other information needed to evaluate success of

EXHIBIT **12.5**   (Continued)

grants program over the years. Establish a filing system for grant requests received, awarded, currently active, paid in the past, rejected, and so on. Tailor the Checklists in Chapter 9 to fit the foundation's situation regarding accumulating information about prospective grantees to avoid taxable expenditures. Evaluate follow-up information to require from grantees, such as newsletters, statistical evaluations, or annual reports. Establish timetable for grant pledge due dates and follow-up reports.

*Internal Controls*

Consult an accountant for assistance in adopting an internal control system designed to protect the foundation's assets. Issues to consider may include who signs checks, who approves disbursements, where stock certificates are stored, and who opens bank statements among other issues. Adopt a conflict of interest policy to protect against self-dealing violations.

## COMPLIANCE WITH PRIVATE FOUNDATION SANCTIONS

*Compliance Calendars*

Create system for monitoring compliance with overall and special private foundation rules, including the following:

- Calendar of filing deadlines for federal and state information, payroll, and other returns shown in Exhibit 12.7
- Deposit dates for excise tax
- Amounts required and deadlines for meeting minimum distribution requirements
- Follow-up status reports for expenditure responsibility grants
- Scholarship recipient report deadlines

*Board Responsibilities*

Plan meeting of board of trustees or directors at least annually, if not more often. Maintain minutes of meetings that reflect efforts to accomplish exempt purposes and satisfy fiduciary duties. Establish committees, if needed, to manage designated aspects of the foundation's operations: investments, grants, active projects, personnel, and so on.

*Conservation of Assets*

Develop an investment policy for safeguarding the foundation's assets. Decide whether an independent investment counselor should be engaged to manage properties. Appoint a committee of the board to regularly monitor investment results. Routinely evaluate investment managers to compare expected with actual returns on the money. Establish permanent filing system for equipment and other fixed assets to contain purchase vouchers, guarantees, insurance coverage, bids for acquisition, and other pertinent information concerning property the foundation owns.

*Local Authorities*

Determine if any tax on real and intangible personal property or income of the foundation is due and whether any other reports are due to the state or local government.

**Exhibit 12.5** (Continued)

*Other State Filings*

Most private foundations are exempted from state income and corporate taxes upon submission of determination of federal exemption and other evidence of charitable activities.

*Solicitation Registration*

Foundations that conduct fund-raising campaigns may have additional filing requirements.

Request for Abatement Under IRC Section 4962

| | | | |
|---|---|---|---|
| Form **4720** | **Return of Certain Excise Taxes Under Chapters 41 and 42 of the Internal Revenue Code** | | OMB No. 1545-0052 |
| Department of the Treasury Internal Revenue Service | (Sections 170(f)(10), 664(c)(2), 4911, 4912, 4941, 4942, 4943, 4944, 4945, 4955, 4958, 4959, 4965, 4966, and 4967) ▶ Information about Form 4720 and its separate instructions is at *www.irs.gov/form4720.* | | **2013** |

For calendar year 2013 or other tax year beginning _____ , 2013, and ending _____ , 20 ___

Name of organization or entity
**Environmentalist Fund**

Employer identification number
**77-7777777**

Number, street, and room or suite no. (or P.O. box if mail is not delivered to street address)
**1111 Any Street**

City or town, state or province, country, and ZIP or foreign postal code
**Hometown, TX 77777-7777**

Check box for type of annual return:
☐ Form 990   ☐ Form 990-EZ
☑ Form 990-PF
☐ Form 5227

|  | | Yes | No |
|---|---|---|---|
| A | Is the organization a foreign private foundation within the meaning of section 4948(b)? | | ✓ |
| B | Has corrective action been taken on any taxable event that resulted in Chapter 42 taxes being reported on this form? (Enter "N/A" if not applicable) | ✓ | |

If "Yes," attach a detailed description and documentation of the corrective action taken and, if applicable, enter the fair market value of any property recovered as a result of the correction ▶ $ __**80.**__ . If "No," (i.e., any uncorrected acts or transactions), attach an explanation (see instructions).   See Statement 1

**Part I   Taxes on Organization** (Sections 170(f)(10), 664(c)(2), 4911(a), 4912(a), 4942(a), 4943(a), 4944(a)(1), 4945(a)(1), 4955(a)(1), 4959, 4965(a)(1), and 4966(a)(1))

| | | | |
|---|---|---|---|
| 1 | Tax on undistributed income—Schedule B, line 4 | 1 | 0. |
| 2 | Tax on excess business holdings—Schedule C, line 7 | 2 | 0. |
| 3 | Tax on investments that jeopardize charitable purpose—Schedule D, Part I, column (e) | 3 | 0. |
| 4 | Tax on taxable expenditures—Schedule E, Part I, column (g) | 4 | 0. |
| 5 | Tax on political expenditures—Schedule F, Part I, column (e) | 5 | 0. |
| 6 | Tax on excess lobbying expenditures—Schedule G, line 4 | 6 | 0. |
| 7 | Tax on disqualifying lobbying expenditures—Schedule H, Part I, column (e) | 7 | 0. |
| 8 | Tax on premiums paid on personal benefit contracts | 8 | 0. |
| 9 | Tax on being a party to prohibited tax shelter transactions—Schedule J, Part I, column (h) | 9 | 0. |
| 10 | Tax on taxable distributions—Schedule K, Part I, column (f) | 10 | 0. |
| 11 | Tax on a charitable remainder trust's unrelated business taxable income. Attach statement | 11 | 0. |
| 12 | Tax on failure to meet the requirements of section 501(r)(3)-Schedule M, Part II, line 2 | 12 | 0. |
| 13 | **Total** (add lines 1–12) | 13 | 0. |

**Part II-A   Taxes on Managers, Self-Dealers, Disqualified Persons, Donors, Donor Advisors, and Related Persons** (Sections 4912(b), 4941(a), 4944(a)(2), 4945(a)(2), 4955(a)(2), 4958(a), 4965(a)(2), 4966(a)(2), and 4967(a))

| | (a) Name and address of person subject to tax. City or town, state or province, country, ZIP or foreign postal code | (b) Taxpayer identification number |
|---|---|---|
| a | Jane Environmentalist 1111 Any Street, Hometown, TX  77777-7777 | 444-44-4444 |
| b | | |
| c | | |

| | (c) Tax on self-dealing—Schedule A, Part II, col. (d), and Part III, col. (d) | (d) Tax on investments that jeopardize charitable purpose—Schedule D, Part II, col. (d) | (e) Tax on taxable expenditures—Schedule E, Part II, col. (d) | (f) Tax on political expenditures—Schedule F, Part II, col. (d) |
|---|---|---|---|---|
| a | 8. | | | |
| b | | | | |
| c | | | | |
| Total | 8. | 0. | 0. | 0. |

| | (g) Tax on disqualifying lobbying expenditures—Schedule H, Part II, col. (d) | (h) Tax on excess benefit transactions—Schedule I, Part II, col. (d), and Part III, col. (d) | (i) Tax on being a party to prohibited tax shelter transactions—Schedule J, Part II, col. (d) | (j) Tax on taxable distributions—Schedule K, Part II, col. (d) |
|---|---|---|---|---|
| a | | | | |
| b | | | | |
| c | | | | |
| Total | 0. | 0. | 0. | 0. |

| | (k) Tax on prohibited benefits—Sch L, Part II, col. (d), and Part III, col. (d) | (l) Total—Add cols. (c) through (k) |
|---|---|---|
| a | | 8. |
| b | | |
| c | | |
| Total | 0. | 8. |

For Privacy Act and Paperwork Reduction Act Notice, see the separate instructions.   Cat. No. 13021D   Form **4720** (2013)

**EXHIBIT 12.6**

Mock-up of Form 4720, Return of Certain Excise Taxes under Chapters 41 and 42 of the Internal Revenue Code

Form 4720 (2013)    Environmentalist Fund                                77-7777777        Page **2**

| Part II-B | **Summary of Taxes** (See **Tax Payments** in the instructions.) | | |
|---|---|---|---|
| 1 | Enter the taxes listed in Part II-A, column (I), that apply to managers, self-dealers, disqualified persons, donors, donor advisors, and related persons who sign this form. If all sign, enter the total amount from Part II-A, column (I) . . . . . . . . . . . . . . . . . . . | **1** | 8. |
| 2 | **Total tax.** Add Part I, line 13, and Part II-B, line 1 . . . . . . . . . . . . . | **2** | 8. |
| 3 | Total payments including amount paid with Form 8868 (see instructions) . . . . . . . | **3** | 0. |
| 4 | **Tax due.** If line 2 is larger than line 3, enter amount owed (see instructions) . . . . . ▶ | **4** | 8. |
| 5 | **Overpayment.** If line 2 is smaller than line 3, enter the difference. This is your refund . . ▶ | **5** | |

### SCHEDULE A—Initial Taxes on Self-Dealing (Section 4941)

| Part I | **Acts of Self-Dealing and Tax Computation** |
|---|---|

| (a) Act number | (b) Date of act | (c) Description of act |
|---|---|---|
| 1 | 11/01/2013 | Payment of the President's bill for legal services |
| 2 | | |
| 3 | | |
| 4 | | |
| 5 | | |

| (d) Question number from Form 990-PF, Part VII-B, or Form 5227, Part VI-B, applicable to the act | (e) Amount involved in act | (f) Initial tax on self-dealing (10% of col. (e)) | (g) Tax on foundation managers (if applicable) (lesser of $20,000 or 5% of col. (e)) |
|---|---|---|---|
| 1a(2) | 80. | 8. | |
| | | | |
| | | | |
| | | | |

| Part II | **Summary of Tax Liability of Self-Dealers and Proration of Payments** |
|---|---|

| (a) Names of self-dealers liable for tax | (b) Act no. from Part I, col. (a) | (c) Tax from Part I, col. (f), or prorated amount | (d) Self-dealer's total tax liability (add amounts in col. (c)) (see instructions) |
|---|---|---|---|
| Jane Environmentalist | 1 | 8. | 8. |
| | | | |
| | | | |
| | | | |

| Part III | **Summary of Tax Liability of Foundation Managers and Proration of Payments** |
|---|---|

| (a) Names of foundation managers liable for tax | (b) Act no. from Part I, col. (a) | (c) Tax from Part I, col. (g), or prorated amount | (d) Manager's total tax liability (add amounts in col. (c)) (see instructions) |
|---|---|---|---|
| | | | |
| | | | |
| | | | |

### SCHEDULE B—Initial Tax on Undistributed Income (Section 4942)

| | | | |
|---|---|---|---|
| 1 | Undistributed income for years before 2012 (from Form 990-PF for 2013, Part XIII, line 6d) . | **1** | |
| 2 | Undistributed income for 2012 (from Form 990-PF for 2013, Part XIII, line 6e) . . . . . | **2** | |
| 3 | Total undistributed income at end of current tax year beginning in 2013 and subject to tax under section 4942 (add lines 1 and 2) . . . . . . . . . . . . . . . . . . . | **3** | 0. |
| 4 | **Tax**—Enter 30% of line 3 here and on Part I, line 1 . . . . . . . . . . . . . . | **4** | 0. |

Form **4720** (2013)

## Exhibit 12.6

(*Continued*)

# § 12.3 COMPLIANCE ISSUES

## SCHEDULE C—Initial Tax on Excess Business Holdings (Section 4943)

**Business Holdings and Computation of Tax**

If you have taxable excess holdings in more than one business enterprise, attach a separate schedule for each enterprise. Refer to the instructions for each line item before making any entries.

Name and address of business enterprise

Employer identification number . . . . . . . . . . . . . . . . . . . ▶

Form of enterprise (corporation, partnership, trust, joint venture, sole proprietorship, etc.) . . ▶

|   |   |   | (a) Voting stock (profits interest or beneficial interest) | (b) Value | (c) Nonvoting stock (capital interest) |
|---|---|---|---|---|---|
| 1 | Foundation holdings in business enterprise . . | 1 | % | % | |
| 2 | Permitted holdings in business enterprise . . | 2 | % | % | |
| 3 | Value of excess holdings in business enterprise | 3 | | | |
| 4 | Value of excess holdings disposed of within 90 days; or, other value of excess holdings not subject to section 4943 tax (attach statement) | 4 | | | |
| 5 | Taxable excess holdings in business enterprise — line 3 minus line 4 . . . . . . . . . | 5 | | | |
| 6 | **Tax**—Enter 10% of line 5 . . . . . . . | 6 | | | |
| 7 | **Total tax**—Add amounts on line 6, columns (a), (b), and (c); enter total here and on Part I, line 2 | 7 | 0. | | |

## SCHEDULE D—Initial Taxes on Investments That Jeopardize Charitable Purpose (Section 4944)

**Part I    Investments and Tax Computation**

| (a) Investment number | (b) Date of investment | (c) Description of investment | (d) Amount of investment | (e) Initial tax on foundation (10% of col. (d)) | (f) Initial tax on foundation managers (if applicable)— (lesser of $10,000 or 10% of col. (d)) |
|---|---|---|---|---|---|
| 1 | | | | | |
| 2 | | | | | |
| 3 | | | | | |
| 4 | | | | | |
| 5 | | | | | |

**Total**—Column (e). Enter here and on Part I, line 3 . . . . . . . . . . . . . . .   0.

**Total**—Column (f). Enter total (or prorated amount) here and in Part II, column (c), below . . . . .   0.

**Part II    Summary of Tax Liability of Foundation Managers and Proration of Payments**

| (a) Names of foundation managers liable for tax | (b) Investment no. from Part I, col. (a) | (c) Tax from Part I, col. (f), or prorated amount | (d) Manager's total tax liability (add amounts in col. (c)) (see instructions) |
|---|---|---|---|
| | | | |
| | | | |
| | | | |
| | | | |

Form **4720** (2013)

**EXHIBIT 12.6**

*(Continued)*

# TAX COMPLIANCE AND ADMINISTRATIVE ISSUES

## SCHEDULE E—Initial Taxes on Taxable Expenditures (Section 4945)

**Part I**  Expenditures and Computation of Tax

| (a) Item number | (b) Amount | (c) Date paid or incurred | (d) Name and address of recipient | (e) Description of expenditure and purposes for which made |
|---|---|---|---|---|
| 1 | 100,000. | 12/28/2013 | Save the Bay Project | See Part XV for purpose |
| 2 | | | | |
| 3 | | | | |
| 4 | | | | |
| 5 | | | | |

| (f) Question number from Form 990-PF, Part VII-B, or Form 5227, Part VI-B, applicable to the expenditure | (g) Initial tax imposed on foundation (20% of col. (b)) | (h) Initial tax imposed on foundation managers (if applicable)—(lesser of $10,000 or 5% of col. (b)) |
|---|---|---|
| 5a(4) | | |
| | | |
| | | |
| | 0. | |

**Total**—Column (g). Enter here and on Part I, line 4 . . . . . . . . . .  0.

**Total**—Column (h). Enter total (or prorated amount) here and in Part II, column (c), below  .  .  .  .  .  .  .  .  .  .  .  .  0.

**Part II**  Summary of Tax Liability of Foundation Managers and Proration of Payments

| (a) Names of foundation managers liable for tax | (b) Item no. from Part I, col. (a) | (c) Tax from Part I, col. (h), or prorated amount | (d) Manager's total tax liability (add amounts in col. (c)) (see instructions) |
|---|---|---|---|
| | | | |
| | | | |
| | | | |
| | | | |

## SCHEDULE F—Initial Taxes on Political Expenditures (Section 4955)

**Part I**  Expenditures and Computation of Tax

| (a) Item number | (b) Amount | (c) Date paid or incurred | (d) Description of political expenditure | (e) Initial tax imposed on organization or foundation (10% of col. (b)) | (f) Initial tax imposed on managers (if applicable) (lesser of $5,000 or 2½% of col. (b)) |
|---|---|---|---|---|---|
| 1 | | | | | |
| 2 | | | | | |
| 3 | | | | | |
| 4 | | | | | |
| 5 | | | | | |

**Total**—Column (e). Enter here and on Part I, line 5 .  .  .  .  .  .  .  .  .  .  0.

**Total**—Column (f). Enter total (or prorated amount) here and in Part II, column (c), below  .  .  .  .  .  0.

**Part II**  Summary of Tax Liability of Organization Managers or Foundation Managers and Proration of Payments

| (a) Names of organization managers or foundation managers liable for tax | (b) Item no. from Part I, col. (a) | (c) Tax from Part I, col. (f), or prorated amount | (d) Manager's total tax liability (add amounts in col. (c)) (see instructions) |
|---|---|---|---|
| | | | |
| | | | |
| | | | |
| | | | |

Form **4720** (2013)

---

**EXHIBIT 12.6**

(*Continued*)

# § 12.3 COMPLIANCE ISSUES

## SCHEDULE G—Tax on Excess Lobbying Expenditures (Section 4911)

| | | |
|---|---|---|
| 1 | Excess of grassroots expenditures over grassroots nontaxable amount (from Schedule C (Form 990 or 990-EZ), Part II-A, column (b), line 1h). (See the instructions before making an entry.)  . . | **1** |
| 2 | Excess of lobbying expenditures over lobbying nontaxable amount (from Schedule C (Form 990 or 990-EZ), Part II-A, column (b), line 1i). (See the instructions before making an entry.)  . . . . . | **2** |
| 3 | Taxable lobbying expenditures—enter the larger of line 1 or line 2  . . . . . . . . . . . . | **3** |
| 4 | **Tax**—Enter 25% of line 3 here and on Part I, line 6  . . . . . . . . . . . . . . . . | **4** | 0. |

## SCHEDULE H—Taxes on Disqualifying Lobbying Expenditures (Section 4912)

**Part I**  **Expenditures and Computation of Tax**

| (a) Item number | (b) Amount | (c) Date paid or incurred | (d) Description of lobbying expenditures | (e) Tax imposed on organization (5% of col. (b)) | (f) Tax imposed on organization managers (if applicable)— (5% of col. (b)) |
|---|---|---|---|---|---|
| 1 | | | | | |
| 2 | | | | | |
| 3 | | | | | |
| 4 | | | | | |
| 5 | | | | | |

**Total**—Column (e). Enter here and on Part I, line 7 .  .  .  .  .  .  .  .  .  .          0.

**Total**—Column (f). Enter total (or prorated amount) here and in Part II, column (c), below  .  .  .  .  .  .          0.

**Part II**  **Summary of Tax Liability of Organization Managers and Proration of Payments**

| (a) Names of organization managers liable for tax | (b) Item no. from Part I, col. (a) | (c) Tax from Part I, col. (f), or prorated amount | (d) Manager's total tax liability (add amounts in col. (c)) (see instructions) |
|---|---|---|---|
| | | | |
| | | | |
| | | | |
| | | | |
| | | | |

## SCHEDULE I—Initial Taxes on Excess Benefit Transactions (Section 4958)

**Part I**  **Excess Benefit Transactions and Tax Computation**

| (a) Transaction number | (b) Date of transaction | (c) Description of transaction |
|---|---|---|
| 1 | | |
| 2 | | |
| 3 | | |
| 4 | | |
| 5 | | |

| (d) Amount of excess benefit | (e) Initial tax on disqualified persons (25% of col. (d)) | (f) Tax on organization managers (if applicable) (lesser of $20,000 or 10% of col. (d)) |
|---|---|---|
| | | |
| | | |
| | | |
| | | |
| | | |

Form **4720** (2013)

## Exhibit 12.6

(Continued)

Form 4720 (2013)   Environmentalist Fund                                                77-7777777        Page **6**

**SCHEDULE I—Initial Taxes on Excess Benefit Transactions** (Section 4958) *Continued*

**Part II**  Summary of Tax Liability of Disqualified Persons and Proration of Payments

| (a) Names of disqualified persons liable for tax | (b) Trans. no. from Part I, col. (a) | (c) Tax from Part I, col. (e), or prorated amount | (d) Disqualified person's total tax liability (add amounts in col. (c)) (see instructions) |
|---|---|---|---|
| | | | |
| | | | |
| | | | |
| | | | |
| | | | |
| | | | |

**Part III**  Summary of Tax Liability of 501(c)(3), (c)(4) & (c)(29) Organization Managers and Proration of Payments

| (a) Names of 501(c)(3), (c)(4) & (c)(29) organization managers liable for tax | (b) Trans. no. from Part I, col. (a) | (c) Tax from Part I, col. (f), or prorated amount | (d) Manager's total tax liability (add amounts in col. (c)) (see instructions) |
|---|---|---|---|
| | | | |
| | | | |
| | | | |
| | | | |
| | | | |
| | | | |

**SCHEDULE J—Taxes on Being a Party to Prohibited Tax Shelter Transactions** (Section 4965)

**Part I**  Prohibited Tax Shelter Transactions (PTST) and Tax Imposed on the Tax-Exempt Entity (see instructions)

| (a) Transaction number | (b) Transaction date | (c) Type of transaction 1 —Listed 2 —Subsequently listed 3 —Confidential 4 —Contractual protection | (d) Description of transaction |
|---|---|---|---|
| 1 | | | |
| 2 | | | |
| 3 | | | |
| 4 | | | |
| 5 | | | |

| (e) Did the tax-exempt entity know or have reason to know this transaction was a PTST when it became a party to the transaction? Answer **Yes** or **No** | (f) Net income attributable to the PTST | (g) 75% of proceeds attributable to the PTST | (h) Tax imposed on the tax-exempt entity (see instructions) |
|---|---|---|---|
| | | | |
| | | | |
| | | | |
| | | | |

**Total**—Column (h). Enter here and on Part I, line 9 . . . . . . . . . . . . . . . . . . . | 0.

Form **4720** (2013)

**EXHIBIT 12.6**

*(Continued)*

Form 4720 (2013)     Environmentalist Fund                                 77-7777777      Page **7**

**Part II**    **Tax Imposed on Entity Managers** (Section 4965) *Continued*

| (a) Name of entity manager | (b) Transaction number from Part I, col. (a) | (c) Tax—enter $20,000 for each transaction listed in col. (b) for each manager in col. (a) | (d) Manager's total tax liability (add amounts in col. (c)) |
|---|---|---|---|
|  |  |  |  |
|  |  |  |  |
|  |  |  |  |
|  |  |  |  |
|  |  |  |  |
|  |  |  |  |
|  |  |  |  |

**SCHEDULE K—Taxes on Taxable Distributions of Sponsoring Organizations Maintaining Donor Advised Funds** (Section 4966). See the instructions.

**Part I**    **Taxable Distributions and Tax Computation**

| (a) Item number | (b) Name of sponsoring organization and donor advised fund | (c) Description of distribution |
|---|---|---|
| 1 |  |  |
| 2 |  |  |
| 3 |  |  |
| 4 |  |  |

| (d) Date of distribution | (e) Amount of distribution | (f) Tax imposed on organization (20% of col. (e)) | (g) Tax on fund managers (lesser of 5% of col. (e) or $10,000) |
|---|---|---|---|
|  |  |  |  |
|  |  |  |  |
|  |  |  |  |

**Total**—Column (f). Enter here and on Part I, line 10  . . . . . .

**Total**—Column (g). Enter total (or prorated amount) here and in Part II, column (c), below  . .

**Part II**    **Summary of Tax Liability of Fund Managers and Proration of Payments**

| (a) Name of fund managers liable for tax | (b) Item no. from Part I, col. (a) | (c) Tax from Part I, col. (g) or prorated amount | (d) Manager's total tax liability (add amounts in col. (c)) (see instructions) |
|---|---|---|---|
|  |  |  |  |
|  |  |  |  |
|  |  |  |  |
|  |  |  |  |
|  |  |  |  |

Form **4720** (2013)

**EXHIBIT 12.6**

(*Continued*)

Form 4720 (2013)   Environmentalist Fund                                                            77-7777777          Page **8**

### SCHEDULE L—Taxes on Prohibited Benefits Distributed From Donor Advised Funds (Section 4967).
See the instructions.

**Part I    Prohibited Benefits and Tax Computation**

| (a) Item number | (b) Date of prohibited benefit | (c) Description of benefit |
|---|---|---|
| 1 | | |
| 2 | | |
| 3 | | |
| 4 | | |
| 5 | | |

| (d) Amount of prohibited benefit | (e) Tax on prohibited benefit (125% of col. (d)) (see instructions) | (f) Tax on fund managers (if applicable) (lesser of 10% of col. (d) or $10,000) (see instructions) |
|---|---|---|
| | | |
| | | |
| | | |
| | | |
| | | |

**Part II    Summary of Tax Liability of Donors, Donor Advisors, Related Persons and Proration of Payments**

| (a) Names of donors, donor advisor, or related persons liable for tax | (b) Item no. from Part I, col. (a) | (c) Tax from Part I, col. (e) or prorated amount | (d) Donor, donor advisor, or related persons total tax liability (add amounts in col. (c)) (see instructions) |
|---|---|---|---|
| | | | |
| | | | |
| | | | |
| | | | |

**Part III    Tax Liability of Fund Managers and Proration of Payments**

| (a) Names of fund managers liable for tax | (b) Item no. from Part I, col. (a) | (c) Tax from Part I, col. (f) or prorated amount | (d) Fund managers total tax liability (add amounts in col. (c)) (see instructions) |
|---|---|---|---|
| | | | |
| | | | |
| | | | |
| | | | |

Form **4720** (2013)

**EXHIBIT 12.6**

*(Continued)*

Form 4720 (2013)    Environmentalist Fund                                77-7777777        Page 9

## Schedule M—Tax on Failure to Meet the Community Health Needs Assessment Requirements (Sections 4959 and 501(r)(3)). (See instructions.)

**Part I**    Name of Hospital Facility and Summary of Failure to Meet Section 501(r)(3)

| (a) Item number | (b) Name of facility | (c) Description of the failure | (d) Tax year hospital facility last conducted a CHNA | (e) Tax year hospital facility last adopted an implementation strategy |
|---|---|---|---|---|
| 1 | | | | |
| 2 | | | | |
| 3 | | | | |
| 4 | | | | |
| 5 | | | | |

**Part II**    Computation of Tax

| | | | |
|---|---|---|---|
| 1 | Number of hospital facilities operated by the hospital organization that failed to meet the Community Health Needs Assessment requirements of section 501(r)(3) . . . . . . . . . . . . . . . . . | 1 | |
| 2 | **Tax**—Enter $50,000 multiplied by line 1 here and on Part I, line 12 . . . . . . . . . . . . | 2 | |

Form **4720** (2013)

## Exhibit 12.6

### (Continued)

Under penalties of perjury, I declare that I have examined this return, including accompanying schedules and statements, and to the best of my knowledge and belief it is true, correct, and complete. Declaration of preparer (other than taxpayer) is based on all information of which preparer has any knowledge.

**Sign Here**

▶ _____      _____      _____
Signature of officer or trustee                                                          Title                           Date

▶ _____      _____
Signature (and organization or entity name if applicable) of manager, self-dealer, disqualified person, donor, donor                Date
advisor, or related person

▶ _____      _____
Signature (and organization or entity name if applicable) of manager, self-dealer, disqualified person, donor, donor                Date
advisor, or related person

▶ _____      _____
Signature (and organization or entity name if applicable) of manager, self-dealer, disqualified person, donor, donor                Date
advisor, or related person

▶ _____      _____
Signature (and organization or entity name if applicable) of manager, self-dealer, disqualified person, donor, donor                Date
advisor, or related person

May the IRS discuss this return with the preparer shown below? (see instructions)  . . . . . . . . . . . .  ☑ Yes   ☐ No

**Paid Preparer Use Only**

| Print/Type preparer's name | Preparer's signature | Date | Check ☑ if self-employed | PTIN |
|---|---|---|---|---|
| A Good Accountant | | | | P9999999 |
| Firm's name   ▶  Smith & Jones LLP | | | Firm's EIN ▶ | 55-5555555 |
| Firm's address ▶   444 Any Street, Hometown, TX  77777 | | | Phone no. | 444-555-6666 |

Form **4720** (2013)

**EXHIBIT 12.6**

*(Continued)*

| 2013 | Federal Statements | Page 1 |
|---|---|---|
| | Environmentalist Fund | 77-7777777 |

**Statement 1**
**Form 4720, Line B**
**Description of Corrective Action Taken**

Correction of Self-Dealing:

As soon as the Fund realized it had paid an expense of the President, repayment of the expense was requested and received.

Correction of Taxable Expenditure:

Our foundation follows a system for identifying qualifying grantees that prior to December 28, 2013, provided we would obtain the following information from grantees:

• Grant request describing charitable nature of programs,
• IRS Determination Letter,
• Form 990 for most recent year, and
• Page from IRS EO Select Check on which grantee name appears as public charity.

As reflected on the attachment to Part XV, line 3, we made a grant to a §509(a)(3) organization that we determined was a Type III, non-functionally integrated, supporting organization. Thus the grant to Save the Bay Project did not constitute a qualifying distribution as we recognize on the return by not counting it as such (see Form 990-PF Statement 20). We had attended a seminar that talked about the new rules from the Pension Protection Act and understood we would not treat such grants as qualifying. We knew that our other grants and program expenditures would exceed the required amount. The problem, however, was that we did not understand that we were required to exercise expenditure responsibility (ER) in connection with the grant. It was only when, on January 10, 2014, we received a letter from our accountants outlining the new PPA rules that we discovered the need to follow expenditure responsibility steps. We took those steps as soon as possible. Our pre-grant inquiry had actually been performed ahead and the ER agreement was executed by January 20, 2014. With the report in this return, we are now current with the ER requirements. Our failure to perform ER was inadvertent and unintended. Pursuant to Internal Revenue Code §4962, we respectfully request that the first tier §4945 penalty for failure to report, or initial tax of $20,000, be abated because the failure was due to reasonable causes and without willful neglect. Therefore, we submit we are entitled to an abatement of the tax because it meets the requirements of §4962 and the instructions to Form 4720. I swear that this information is true and correct and that the foundation's failure to exercise expenditure responsibility was inadvertent and without intention or knowledge on my part or on the part of any of Environmental's other officers to violate the rules.

*Jane Environmentalist*

Jane E. Environmentalist, President

**Exhibit 12.6**

*(Continued)*

EXHIBIT 12.7

Annual Filing Requirements for a Private Foundation

---

## Annual Information Returns

| | |
|---|---|
| Form 990-PF | Filed by all private foundations annually by 15th day of 5th month following the end of the fiscal year. |
| Form 990-T Foreign Investments | Income tax return to report unrelated business income and calculate tax due annually. See Exhibit 8.1 (page 3) for filings for alternative investments. |
| State Reports | A copy of Form 990-PF is filed with each state in which the foundation is registered and possibly other states in which the foundation does business, including soliciting contributions, conducting programs, engaging employees, or maintaining financial accounts. |

## Employment Taxes

| | |
|---|---|
| Form 941 | Employment tax return reporting tax withheld and due, filed quarterly on April 30, July 31, October 31, and January 31. |
| Forms 5500 | PFs with employee benefit and pension plans must annually report their participant statistics and other details. |
| Depository Receipts | Federal, and some state, taxes are paid directly to a bank (with Form 8109), not mailed to the IRS when the tax liability exceeds $500. |
| Form W-2 | On calendar year basis, employees' total wages and taxes are reported to individual employees on this form by January 31. |
| Form W-4 | Completed (for PF's files) by each employee that evidences number of exemptions claimed for income tax withholding. |
| W-9 | Completed (for PF's files) by each independent contractor claiming the PF need not backup withhold tax from them. |
| Form 1099 | Non-employee fees, interest, rent, prizes, or other compensation paid to independent contractors is reported annually by January 31. If the PF does not have Form W-9 verifying the social security number, backup withholding of 20 percent of each payment is required. |
| Unemployment Tax | A private foundation is exempt from federal unemployment taxes but may be subject state taxes on workers. |

## Other State Taxes

| | |
|---|---|
| Sales Tax | Sales of goods and services may be subject to sales tax. State and local exemptions and reporting requirements vary. Exemption from paying sales tax on purchases of goods to conduct exempt programs may be exempt under state law. |

## Exhibit 12.7  (Continued)

| Local Property | Some states collect tax on real and intangible personal property. |
|---|---|
| Other State Filings: | Private foundations are exempted from state income and corporate franchise taxes upon submission of evidence of Federal exemption. |

## Exhibit 12.8

### Donor Acknowledgment

*For a private foundation contributor to be able to claim a charitable contribution deduction, the foundation must furnish a written receipt containing the information shown in this sample receipt.*

Written by SAMPLE FOUNDATION

To Private Foundation Contributor

Thank you for your donation of          DATE          AMOUNT

Cash          _____          _____

Other property:

_____          _____          _____

_____          _____          _____

Your gifts will be devoted to our exempt purposes, and Sample Foundation has not furnished any benefits or services required to be valued in consideration for this gift.

_____          _____

Date                              Responsible person

# CHAPTER THIRTEEN

# Termination of Foundation Status

Congress, in its deliberations that concluded with the Tax Reform Act of 1969, decided that private foundations should not be able to receive tax benefits in exchange for the promise of use of their assets for charitable purposes and, subsequently, avoid the carrying out of these responsibilities. The following is an explanation of the rationale underlying the termination requirements:

> Under prior law, an organization was exempt if it met the requirements of the code, whether or not it sought an "exemption certificate" from the Internal Revenue Service.
>
> If an organization did not continue to meet the requirements for exemption, if it committed certain specifically prohibited acts (sec. 503), or if it dealt in certain prohibited ways with its accumulated earnings (sec. 504), it lost its exempt status. This loss of exempt status might relate back to the time the organization first violated the code's requirements. However, if the violation occurred after the contributions had been made to the organization, no deductions were disallowed to such contributors. Also, the organization's income tax exemption was not disturbed for years before the organization's first violation.
>
> Congress was concerned that in many cases under prior law the loss of exempt status would impose only a light burden on many foundations. This was true in those circumstances, for example, where the foundation had already received sufficient charitable contributions to provide its endowment and where the

foundation could retain its exemption as to its current income by qualifying under an exemption category other than § 501(c)(3).[1]

The consequence was enactment of IRC § 507. This statutory provision imposes an onerous termination tax on any private foundation that has committed willful repeated acts or a single willful and flagrant act (or failure(s) to act) and permits the IRS to involuntarily require such a private foundation to terminate. This body of law provides the framework for a variety of mergers, consolidations, conversions, and other structural changes desirable for some private foundations. The statutory scheme distinguishes between two distinct types of terminations:

*Type 1.* This type of termination[2] renders the foundation subject to a termination tax[3] unless the IRS permits abatement. This section pertains to two different circumstances under which a private foundation might go out of existence as follows:

1.  An involuntary termination initiated by the IRS for reasons of repeated and flagrant violations of the private foundation sanctions.[4]

2.  A private foundation that has operated in accordance with the foundation rules can notify the IRS of its intention to terminate its existence and request abatement of the termination tax. A private foundation is not treated as having terminated for purposes of the termination tax rules unless it gives notification of its intent to do so.[5] As explained,[6] the successor foundation inherits all of the tax attributes and obligations of the foundation that is going out of existence so that technically such a foundation is not treated as having terminated.

*Type 2.* Under this type of termination,[7] a private foundation ceases to be classified as a private foundation under one of three different circumstances:

1.  A private foundation can transfer all of its assets to one or more organizations that qualify as public charities and go out of existence.[8]

2.  Based on its intention to reform its sources of support and/or the nature of its activities, a private foundation can qualify itself as a public charity.

1.  Joint Committee on Internal Revenue Taxation, *General Explanation of Tax Reform Act of 1969*, 91st Cong., 2d Sess. 54–55 (1970).
2.  IRC § 507(a).
3.  *See* § 13.5.
4.  Those described in §§ 15.3–15.5. *See* also § 13.2.
5.  Reg. § 1.507-1(b)(7).
6.  *See* § 13.7.
7.  IRC § 507(b).
8.  *See* § 13.3.

This type of a foundation notifies the IRS of its intention by seeking what is called a *60-month termination*.[9]

3.   A private foundation transfers all or part of its assets to one or more other private foundations that inherit all of its tax attributes and obligations so that it is not treated as having terminated.[10]

It has been held that the notice element in the termination requirements is reflective of Congress's intent in 1969 to provide the IRS and appropriate state officials with a means to gain more and ongoing information about the activities of private foundations.[11] A foundation must carefully follow the rules for ending its existence because missteps can be costly. The termination tax is equal to the lower of (1) aggregate tax benefits resulting from the tax-exempt status of the foundation or (2) the value of its net assets of the foundation.[12] To understand the reason the new guidance was possible, it is useful to focus on the words *except as provided in subsection (b)*. The termination tax is imposed only in the two enumerated circumstances listed above.

Inasmuch as split-interest trusts are, for various tax law purposes, treated as private foundations,[13] the IRS occasionally issues private letter rulings concerning application of the private foundation status termination rules to these trusts.[14]

## § 13.1   VOLUNTARY TERMINATION

A private foundation may wish to end its existence or change its classification as a private foundation for a number of reasons. Some foundations are created and have charter provisions that provide they exist for a limited number of years. Second-generation trustees may choose to divide up a private foundation's assets into several foundations so each can manage their own. A foundation's mission may be accomplished by spending its assets to buy a historic building and donating the site to a preservation society. In a rare circumstance, there could be some action[15] that would be impermissible if the organization remains a private foundation. These organizational changes are referred to as *voluntary terminations*.

---

9.   *See* § 13.4.

10.   *See* § 13.5.

11.   *Gladney v. Commissioner*, 745 F.2d 955 (5th Cir. 1984), *cert. den.*, 474 U.S. 923 (1985).

12.   IRC § 507(c).

13.   *See* § 3.7.

14.   E.g., Priv Ltr. Rul. 200208039.

15.   The self-dealing rules of IRC § 4941 prohibit, for example, the purchase or sale of an asset by a private foundation to its insiders and vice versa; *see* § 5.4.

The language of the statute[16] starts with the pronouncement that a private foundation can only terminate, which commonly means to cease to exist, if it gives advance notice to the IRS of its intention to do so and either pays back all the tax benefits it and its donors ever received or secures IRS abatement of such tax through a private ruling.[17] Although this requirement is lifted for many types of private foundation reformations, that possibility is buried deep in the long and complicated regulations. An advance ruling request as to this type of termination of private foundation status should be sought by means of filing an IRS form.[18] The regulations, however, provide that a transfer of all of the assets of a private foundation for charitable purposes does not result in its termination unless it elects to notify the IRS of its intention to do so.[19]

In an effort to discourage unnecessary ruling requests, the IRS in 2002 and early 2003 issued two revenue rulings on foundation transformations.[20] The first ruling pertains to the transfer of assets between commonly controlled private foundations.[21] Next the IRS addressed private foundations transferring assets to public charities.[22] The rulings, in essence, state that there is no need to notify the IRS prior to making transfers of this nature.

The basis of this conclusion is the regulation provision cited above that provides that a foundation does not terminate for these purposes unless it notifies the IRS of its intention to do so.

If a private foundation transfers all or part of its assets to one or more private foundations and one or more public or publicly supported charities, or to an organization operated for testing for public safety, pursuant to a liquidation, merger, redemption, recapitalization, or other adjustment, organization, or reorganization, the transferor private foundation will not have accomplished a voluntary termination.[23] Neither a transfer of all of the assets of a private foundation nor a significant disposition of assets[24] by it will result in a termination of the private foundation status of the transferor private foundation unless it elects to terminate under the voluntary termination provision or the involuntary termination rules apply.[25]

---

16. IRC § 507(b)(1)(B).
17. *See* § 13.2.
18. IRS Form 8940, Request for Miscellaneous Determination. A private foundation would submit information on this form to accomplish what the form identifies as type (h), Termination of private foundation status under IRC § 607(1)(B)—advance ruling request or (i), Termination of private foundation status under IRC § 507(b)(1)(B)—60-month period ended.
19. Reg. § 1.507-1(b)(7).
20. Rev. Ruls. 2002-28, 2002-1 C.B. 941, and 2003-13, 2003-1 C.B. 305.
21. *See* § 13.5.
22. *See* § 13.4.
23. Reg. § 1.507-1(b)(6); *see* §§ 13.4 and 13.5.
24. Reg. § 1.507-3(e)(2).
25. Reg. § 1.507-1(b)(7), (8).

Voluntary termination of private foundation status does not relieve a private foundation, or any disqualified person[26] with respect to the private foundation, of liability for any of the private foundation excise taxes with respect to acts or failures to act prior to termination or for any additional taxes imposed for failure to correct the acts or failures to act.[27] If any liability for a private foundation excise tax is incurred by a private foundation before or in connection with a transfer, transferee liability may be applied against the transferee organization for payment of the taxes.

## § 13.2 INVOLUNTARY TERMINATION

A private foundation's private foundation status may be involuntarily terminated if the IRS notifies the organization that because of willful, flagrant, or repeated acts or failures to act giving rise to one or more of the private foundation excise taxes, the organization is liable for the termination tax.

Under the involuntary termination rule, the phrase *willful repeated acts (or failures to act)* means at least two acts or failures to act that are voluntary, conscious, and intentional.[28] This type of an act (or failure to act) is one that is voluntarily, consciously, and knowingly committed in violation of any of the private foundation rules[29] and that appears to a reasonable person to be a gross violation of the rules.[30] An act or failure to act may result in termination of the private foundation's private foundation status, even though the tax is imposed on the foundation's managers rather than on the private foundation itself. A failure to timely correct the act or acts, or failures to act, that gave rise to liability for tax under any of the private foundation rules, may be a willful and flagrant act (or failure to act).[31]

No motive to avoid legal restrictions or the incurrence of tax is necessary to make an act or failure to act willful. A private foundation's act or failure to act is not willful, however, if the private foundation, or its manager if applicable, does not know that the act or failure to act is an act of self-dealing, a taxable expenditure, or other act or failure to act giving rise to liability for one or more of the private foundation taxes.

---

26. *See* Chapter 4.
27. Reg. § 1.507-1(b)(2).
28. IRC § 507(a)(2); Reg. § 1.507-1(c)(1). In addition to this form of termination, the IRS may attempt a jeopardy assessment under IRC § 6861, which in this context is likely, on challenge (IRC § 7429), to be abated by a court (e.g., *George F. Harding Museum v. United States*, 674 F. Supp. 1323 (N.D. Ill. 1987)).
29. Other than IRC §§ 4940 (Chapter 10) or 4948 (§ 3.8.)
30. Reg. § 1.507-1(c)(2).
31. Reg. § 1.507-1(c)(4).

## § 13.3 TRANSFER OF ASSETS TO A PUBLIC CHARITY

A private foundation, with respect to which there has not been any act or acts described in the involuntary termination rules, may voluntarily terminate its private foundation status by distributing all of its net assets to one or more public or publicly supported organizations and institutions,[32] each of which has been in existence and so described for a continuous period of at least 60 calendar months immediately preceding the distribution.[33] The statute is somewhat confusing because it only mentions "organizations described in section 170(b)(1)(A) (other than in clauses (vii) and (viii)"[34] and specifically excludes supporting organizations. The regulations expand qualifying public charity recipients to include those that are service provider publicly supported charities[35] and supporting organizations.[36] The IRS has verified the inclusion of all three types of public charities as eligible recipients of assets from a terminating foundation.[37]

The IRS ruled that, in measuring this 60-month period, the recipient organization may be an organization that has been in existence for less than 60 months where (1) it was formed as a result of a consolidation of two organizations, both of which would have qualified as eligible public or publicly supported entities and would have been in existence for the requisite 60 months had the consolidation not occurred, and (2) the successor organization was formed for the same purposes and carried on the same activities as the two consolidating organizations.[38]

A private foundation terminating in this manner is not required to notify the IRS and does not incur a termination tax, thereby obviating the necessity of any abatement.[39] An organization that terminates its private foundation status by transferring its assets to a qualified public or publicly supported charity remains subject to the private foundation rules until the required distribution of all of its net assets has been completed.[40] Likewise, an organization that remains in existence after terminating its private foundation status under these rules must file an application for recognition of exemption[41] (unless exempt from that requirement) if it wishes to be regarded as a charitable organization, since it is treated as a newly created organization.[42]

---

32. Reg. § 1.507-2(a)(2)(ii), (3). *See* Chapter 15.
33. IRC § 507(b)(1)(A).
34. *See* §§ 15.3, 15.4.
35. *See* § 15.5.
36. *See* § 15.6.
37. *See* § 13.3(b); Rev. Rul. 2003-13, 2003-1 C.B. 305.
38. Rev. Rul. 75-289, 1975-2 C.B. 215.
39. Reg. § 1.507-2(a)(1). In general, Blazek, "Assessing Options for Terminating Private Foundation Status," 12 *J. Tax Exempt Orgs.* 199 (Mar./Apr. 2001).
40. Reg. § 1.507-(a)(4).
41. *See* § 2.4.
42. Rev. Rul. 74-490, 1974-2 C.B. 171.

A private foundation meets the requirement that it "distribute all of its net assets" within the meaning of these rules only if it transfers all of its right, title, and interest in and to all of its net assets to one or more qualified public or publicly supported charities.[43]

## (a) Terms of Transfer

In order to effectuate this type of transfer, a transferor private foundation may not impose any material restrictions or conditions that prevent the transferee public charity from freely and effectively employing the transferred assets, or the income derived from the assets, in furtherance of its tax-exempt purposes. Whether or not a particular condition or restriction imposed on a transfer of assets is *material* must be determined from all of the facts and circumstances of the transfer.[44] Some of the more significant facts and circumstances to be considered in making this determination are whether the public or publicly supported charity is the owner in fee of the assets it receives from the private foundation, whether the assets are held and administered by the public charity in a manner consistent with one or more of its tax-exempt purposes, whether the governing body of the public charity has the ultimate authority and control over the assets, and the income derived from them, for its tax-exempt purposes, and whether, and to what extent, the governing body of the public charity is organized and operated so as to be independent from the transferor.[45]

**Acceptable Terms.** The presence of some or all of the following four factors is not considered to prevent the transferee from freely and effectively employing the transferred assets, or the income derived from them, in furtherance of its tax-exempt purposes:

1. The fund is given a name or other designation that is the same as or similar to that of the transferor private foundation or otherwise memorializes the creator of the private foundation or his or her family.

2. The income and assets of the fund are to be used for a designated purpose or for one or more particular organizations that are not private

---

43. Reg. § 1.507-2(a)(7).
44. Reg. § 1.507-2(a)(8)(i).
45. *Id.* Whether a governing body is "independent from the transferor" is to be determined from all of the facts and circumstances (Reg. § 1.507-(a)(8)(ii)). Some of the more significant facts and circumstances to be considered are (1) whether, and to what extent, members of the governing body are individuals selected by the transferor private foundation or its disqualified persons, or are themselves such disqualified persons; (2) whether, and to what extent, members of the governing body are selected by public officials acting in their capacities as such; and (3) how long a period of time each member of the governing body may serve (*id.*).

foundations, and the use is consistent with the charitable, educational, or other basis for the tax-exempt status of the public charity.

3.  The transferred assets are administered in an identifiable or separate fund, provided that the public charity is the legal and equitable owner of the fund and exercises ultimate and direct authority and control over the fund, as, for example, a fund to endow a chair at a university or a medical research fund at a hospital.

4.  The transferor private foundation transfers property the continued retention of which by the transferee is required by the transferor and is important to the achievement of charitable or other similar purposes in the community.[46]

**Unacceptable Terms.** The presence of any of the following seven factors is considered to prevent the transferee from freely and effectively employing the transferred assets, or the income derived from them, in furtherance of its tax-exempt purposes:

1.  The transferor private foundation, a disqualified person with respect to it, or any person or committee designated by, or pursuant to the terms of an agreement with, such a person (collectively, the "grantor"), reserves the right, directly or indirectly, to name the persons to which the transferee public charity must distribute, or to direct the timing of these distributions as, for example, by a power of appointment.

2.  The terms of the transfer agreement, or any express or implied understanding between the transferor and the transferee, require the public charity to take or withhold action with respect to the transferred assets that is not designed to further one or more of the tax-exempt purposes of the public charity, and the action or withholding of action would, if performed by the transferor private foundation with respect to the assets, have subjected the transferor to one or more of the private foundation excise taxes.[47]

3.  The public charity assumes leases, contractual obligations, or liabilities of the transferor private foundation, or takes the assets of the transferor private foundation subject to the liabilities (including obligations under commitments or pledges to grantees of the transferor private foundation), for purposes inconsistent with the purposes or best interests of the public charity.

---

46.  Reg. § 1.507-(a)(8)(iii).
47.  Other than with respect to the minimum investment return requirement of IRC § 4942(e). *See* Chapter 6.

4. The transferee public charity is required by any restriction or agreement (other than a restriction or agreement imposed or required by law or regulatory authority), express or implied, to retain, or not to dispose of, any securities or other investment assets transferred to it by the private foundation, either permanently or for an extended period of time.

5. An agreement is entered into between the transferor private foundation and the transferee public charity in connection with the transfer of securities or other property that grants to persons connected with the transferor private foundation a first right of refusal to purchase at fair market value the transferred securities or other property, when and if disposed of by the public charity, unless the securities or other property were purchased or otherwise received by the transferor private foundation subject to the right of first refusal prior to October 9, 1969.

6. An agreement is entered into between the transferor private foundation and the transferee public charity that establishes irrevocable relationships with respect to the maintenance or management of assets transferred to the public charity, such as continuing relationships with banks, brokerage firms, investment counselors, or other advisors with regard to the investments or other property transferred to the public charity.

7. Any other condition is imposed on action by the public charity that prevents it from exercising ultimate control over the assets received from the private foundation for purposes consistent with its tax-exempt purposes.[48]

With respect to the first of these seven factors, the IRS will examine carefully whether the seeking of advice by the transferee from, or the giving of advice by, any grantor after the assets have been transferred to the transferee constitutes an indirect reservation of a right to direct the distributions. In such a case, the reservation of this type of right will be considered to exist where the only criterion considered by the public charity in making a distribution of income or principal from a grantor's fund is advice offered by the grantor. Whether there is a reservation of this type of right is to be determined on the basis of all of the facts and circumstances.[49]

## (b) Reservation of Rights

As illustrated by the acceptable and unacceptable conditions outlined in the preceding lists, the transfer of private foundation assets must be complete. The recipient public charity must have absolute dominion and control over the use

---

48. Reg. § 1.507-2(a)(8)(iv).
49. Reg. § 1.507-2(a)(8)(iv)(A)(1).

of the assets it receives. Similar to terms allowed for donor-designated funds, however, the foundation officials can ask that they be allowed to advise, or make suggestions, about the use of its funds. The regulations outline the conditions under which a foundation may reserve such rights in regard to the transfer of its assets.

**Acceptable Rights.** The presence of some or all of the following five factors indicates that the reservation of this type of right does not exist:

1. There has been an independent investigation by the staff of the public charity, evaluating whether the grantor's advice is consistent with specific charitable needs most deserving of support by the recipient charity (as determined by it).

2. The public charity has promulgated guidelines enumerating specific charitable needs consistent with the charitable purposes of the public charity, and the grantor's advice is consistent with these guidelines.

3. The public charity has instituted an educational program publicizing these guidelines to donors and other persons.

4. The public charity distributes funds in excess of amounts distributed from the grantor's fund to the same or similar types of organizations or charitable needs as those recommended by the donor.

5. The solicitations for funds of the public charity specifically state that the public entity will not be bound by advice offered by the grantor.[50]

**Unacceptable Rights.** The presence of some or all of the following four factors indicate that the reservation of a right exists:

1. The solicitation of funds by the public charity states or implies, or a pattern of conduct on the part of that charity creates an expectation, that the grantor's advice will be followed.

2. The advice of the grantor (whether or not restricted to a distribution of income or principal from the grantor's trust or fund) is limited to distributions of amounts from the grantor's fund (and certain factors are not present).[51]

3. Only the advice of the grantor as to distributions of the grantor's fund is solicited by the public charity, and no procedure is provided for considering advice from persons other than the grantor with respect to the fund.

---

50. Reg. § 1.507-2(a)(8)(iv)(A)(2).
51. Namely, the first two of the factors in text accompanied by *supra* note 43.

4.  For the year involved and all prior years the public charity follows the advice of all grantors with respect to their funds substantially all of the time.[52]

The presence of any of the foregoing factors is, as noted, considered as preventing the transferee from "freely and effectively" utilizing the transferred assets or income from them in furtherance of exempt purposes. To have application of these rules be deemed something less than a full transfer for termination purposes, however, a restriction, right, or condition must also be material.[53]

## (c)  Eligible Public Charity Recipients

The statute describes the type of public charities to which a private foundation can transfer all of its assets to those qualified as institutions and certain public charities.[54] The list is expanded in private rulings to include service-providing public charities and supporting organizations.[55] A ruling was issued to clarify the eligibility of all public charities.[56] The ruling takes into account the basic fact situations in which this type of transfer may occur. The four situations discussed in this ruling are predicted on the following assumptions:

- The private foundation has not committed either willful repeated acts (or failures to act), or a willful and flagrant act (or failure to act), giving rise to tax liability under the private foundation rules.

- The foundation is not a private operating foundation.

- The transferee organization or organizations are not controlled, directly or indirectly, by the foundation or by one or more disqualified persons with respect to it.

- The foundation has not previously terminated (or had terminated) its private foundation status.

- The transferee organization(s) is a public charity (an entity described in IRC § 509(a)(1), (2), or (3)) that retains its public charity classification for at least three years following the date of the distribution.

---

52.  Reg. § 1.507-2(a)(8)(iv)(A)(3).
53.  *See* text accompanied by *supra* note 41.
54.  IRC § 507(b)(1)(A), i.e., churches, schools, hospitals and medical research organizations, university support organizations, governmental units, and donative public charities as described in §§ 15.3, 15.4.
55.  Listed in IRC § 170(b)(1)(a)(viii).
56.  Rev. Rul. 2003-13, 2003-1 C.B. 305.

- The foundation does not impose any material restrictions on the transferred assets.
- The foundation retains sufficient income or assets to pay any private foundation taxes, such as the tax on investment income for the portion of the tax year prior to the distribution, and pays these taxes when due.

**Situation 1.** A private foundation (PF) distributes, pursuant to a plan of dissolution, all of its net assets to a public charity (PC). PC is a public charity by reason of classification as an institution or a donative publicly supported charity.[57] PC has been in existence and a public charity for a continuous period of at least 60 calendar months immediately preceding the distribution. After PF completes the transfer, it files articles of dissolution with the appropriate state authority.

**Situation 2.** The facts are the same as in the first situation, except that PC has been in existence for fewer than 60 calendar months immediately preceding the distribution. Moreover, it was not formed as a result of a consolidation of other public charities of the same classification that would have been in existence for a continuous period of 60 calendar months prior to the distribution had they continued in existence.

**Situation 3.** The facts are the same as in the first situation, except that PC is a public charity by reason of classification as a service provider publicly supported charity.[58]

**Situation 4.** The facts are the same as in the first situation, except that PC is a public charity by reason of classification as a supporting organization.[59]

**IRS Conclusions.** In Situation 1, the distribution was made in accordance with the rules concerning favored terminations. This means that PF's status as a private foundation is terminated at the time of the distribution to PC. PF is not subject to the termination tax. PF is not required to give notice to the IRS to terminate its foundation status.

The distributions in Situations 2, 3, and 4 were not made in accordance with the favored termination rules. Thus, the status of PF as a private foundation is not terminated until it gives notice to the IRS. If PF does provide the notice (and thus terminates), it must ask for abatement of, or become subject to, the termination tax. If, however, PF does not have any net assets on the day it

---

57. Types of charities included are listed in *supra* note 54. Also, *see* §§ 15.3, 15.4.
58. *See* § 15.5.
59. *See* § 15.7.

provides the notice (such as because it gives the notice the day after it distributed all of its net assets), the tax is zero.

In all four situations, the distributions do not constitute an investment by PF for purposes of the investment income tax.[60] Therefore, the distributions do not give rise to net investment income. In these situations, the distributions are to tax-exempt charitable organizations, which are not disqualified persons. Thus, the self-dealing rules are not implicated.[61] In these instances, the payments are made in accomplishment of charitable purposes and are not to organizations controlled by PF. Thus, the transfers are qualifying distributions. These distributions do not cause PF to have excess business holdings, nor are they jeopardizing investments. Further, the distributions are to public charities and thus are not taxable expenditures, and, therefore, expenditure responsibility is not required.

A private foundation that terminates its private foundation status under these rules must inform the IRS on Form 990-PF of the details of the transactions.[62] A certified copy of the resolution or plan of liquidation or dissolution along with the names of recipient organizations and full description of the assets transferred must be attached. A private foundation seeking to terminate its private foundation status under these rules may rely on a ruling issued to a potential distributee that the distributee is a public or publicly supported charitable organization.

An advance ruling request as to this type of termination of private foundation status should be sought by means of filing an IRS form.[63]

The IRS occasionally issues rulings as to this type of termination of private foundation status.[64]

## § 13.4  OPERATION AS A PUBLIC CHARITY

A tax-exempt organization that has been classified as a public charity might become reclassified as a private foundation under a variety of circumstances. An organization might receive an unexpected level of support from a few major donors and less than expected support from modest donors that cause it to fail the test. A mature organization that has accumulated properties might begin to receive investment income that equals more than two-thirds of its total annual revenues and similarly cease to be publicly supported. In all of these cases, the formerly public charity becomes reclassified as a private foundation.

---

60. *See* § 13.5 discussion entitled "Section 4940."
61. *See* § 13.5 discussion entitled "Section 4941."
62. *See* Section T of IRS instructions to Form 990-PF.
63. IRS Form 8940.
64. E.g., Priv. Ltr. Rul. 200103079.

A private foundation, as to which there has not been any act or acts described in the involuntary termination rules, can voluntarily terminate its private foundation status if the organization:

- Meets the requirements of one or more of the sets of rules concerning organizations that are not private foundations for a continuous period of 60 calendar months,[65]

- Properly notifies the IRS before the commencement of the 60-month period that it is terminating its private foundation status, and

- Properly establishes immediately after the expiration of this period that it has complied with the requirements of the rules whereby an organization can qualify as not being a private foundation.[66]

The IRS is authorized to issue an advance ruling that an organization can be expected to satisfy the requirements of these rules during a 60-month termination period where that expectation is reasonable.[67] This type of a ruling was issued in the case of a private foundation that was operating as a supporting organization,[68] being supportive of another private foundation that was itself operating during a 60-month termination period as a publicly supported organization.[69] Once the supporting organization's termination period ends, it must establish to the satisfaction of the IRS that the supported organization was in fact a public or publicly supported charity during the supporting organization's termination period.[70]

A private foundation that terminates its private foundation status by commencing operation as a public charity does not incur a termination tax and, therefore, an abatement of the tax is not required.[71] The regulations state the information that must be contained in the requisite notification[72] but require only information "as is necessary" to cause this type of termination.[73] A Form 990-PF is filed by the converting private foundation for each year of the

---

65. Reg. § 1.507-2(d).
66. IRC § 507(b)(1)(B); Reg. § 1.507-2(b)(1).
67. Reg. § 1.507-2(e).
68. *See* § 15.7.
69. *See* §§ 15.2–15.4.
70. Rev. Rul. 78-386, 1978-2 C.B. 179. The IRS ruled that a private operating foundation (*see* § 3.1) could be expected to qualify as a publicly supported charity by reason of the facts-and-circumstances test (*see* § 15.4(c)) (Priv. Ltr. Rul. 200623068). In another instance, the IRS ruled that a private foundation can be converted to an operating educational organization (§ 15.3(b)) (Priv. Ltr. Rul. 200620036).
71. Reg. § 1.507-2(b)(2). The IRS ruled that an IRC § 4947(a)(2) trust (*see* § 3.6) must terminate its private foundation status pursuant to IRC § 507 before it can acquire public charity status under IRC § 509(a)(3) (Rev. Rul. 76-92, 1976-1 C.B. 160).
72. Reg. § 1.507-2(b)(3), (5).
73. Reg. § 1.507-2(b)(4), (5).

60-month or five-year period,[74] except for the last year. If the foundation will qualify as a public charity, it files a Form 990 for the final year of the termination period.[75]

In one instance, a private foundation filed the requisite notice with the IRS that it was terminating its private foundation status by operating as a public or publicly supported charity for a continuous 60-month period beginning with the first day of its next tax year. In conjunction with that notice, filed on February 1, the private foundation also gave notice that it was changing its annual accounting period from a calendar year to a fiscal year beginning April 1. The IRS ruled that the private foundation could begin the 60-month period required for termination of its private foundation status with its tax year beginning April 1, rather than postpone the commencement of that period to January 1.

## § 13.5 MERGERS, SPLIT-UPS, AND TRANSFERS BETWEEN FOUNDATIONS

When one private foundation "transfers its assets to another private foundation, pursuant to any liquidation, merger, redemption, recapitalization, or other adjustment, organization, or reorganization, the transferee (recipient) foundation shall not be treated as a newly created organization."[76] Furthermore, the transferor foundation will not have involuntarily terminated its private foundation status and need not notify the IRS in advance of its intentions.[77] A common use of this rule is to transfer assets of a private foundation to one or more other private foundations in division of assets because the trustees of the original foundation are not getting along; as the IRS discreetly stated the matter in one case, the "charitable interests" of the trustees of a foundation have "diverged," with the foundation thus finding it "difficult" to "develop a unified approach to grant making."[78] Another somewhat frequent use of this rule is in connection with mergers; in one instance, the IRS applied it in connection with a proposed merger of a private operating foundation and a private nonoperating foundation controlled by the same individuals, where the operating foundation will be the surviving entity.[79]

When 25 percent or more of a foundation's assets are transferred, called a "significant disposition of assets" to one or more other private foundations, the

---

74. *See* Chapter 12.
75. Internal Revenue Manual 7.26.7.5.6.3 (2).
76. IRC § 507(b)(2).
77. Rev. Rul. 2002-28, 2002-1 C.B. 942. *See* Priv. Ltr. Rul. 200421010 for an example of a subsequent look by the IRS at these issues.
78. Priv. Ltr. Rul. 201130006.
79. Priv. Ltr. Rul. 201321024.

recipient private foundation(s) "shall be treated as possessing those attributes and characteristics of the transferor."[80] As discussed in detail below, excess business holdings, cumulative contributions to define substantial contributors, and other tax attributes transfer proportionately along with the assets whether the transferor foundation is commonly controlled or not. When the recipient private foundation is not commonly controlled,[81] one attribute that does not transfer is the aggregate tax benefits in excess of the fair market value of assets transferred.

If a private foundation was organized as a corporation, has its corporate status administratively revoked, and cannot be reinstated as a corporation, its board of directors can create a successor transferee corporation. For federal tax purposes, the transferor foundation will remain in existence as a corporation, being deemed under the check-the-box regulations to be an association taxable as a corporation.[82] The foundation that lost its status as a corporation under state law can terminate its private foundation status pursuant to the federal tax law by utilizing the reorganization approach.[83]

## (a) IRS Road Map for Reforming a Foundation

The IRS in 2002 addressed three types of private foundation reorganizations involving commonly controlled private foundations.[84] The ruling described the filing obligations and excise tax issues that arise when a private foundation transfers assets to one or more other private foundation. The ruling is based on the following presumptions, the last of which limits the applicability of the ruling to commonly controlled foundations:

- All of the foundations involved are classified as tax-exempt organizations, are treated as private foundations, and are not private operating foundations.

- None of the foundations involved has committed willful and flagrant acts, or failures to act, giving rise to tax under Chapter 42 so as to be subject to the termination tax.

---

80. Reg. § 1.507- 3(a)(1).
81. Within the meaning of Reg. § 1.482-1(a)(3) according to Reg. § 1.507- 3(a)(2)(ii). The IRS chose not to give any further definition of these terms for this purpose. The instructions to Form 990 for purposes of reporting compensation paid by related organizations state that control exists where 50 percent or more of the officers, directors, and trustee directors of one organization are also officials of the second, or over 50 percent of the second are appointed by the first organization.
82. Reg. § 301.7701-2(b)(2), 3(c)(v).
83. Priv. Ltr. Rul. 200607027.
84. Rev. Rul. 2002-28, 2002-1 C.B. 941. Due to the complicated nature of the issues involved, the IRS limited this ruling to private foundation transformations. See § 13.3 for discussion of a subsequent ruling on transfers of foundation assets to public charities.

- The private foundations have not terminated under § 507(a)(2) or (b)(1).
- The transferor foundation has outstanding expenditure responsibility grants requiring future monitoring and reports.
- All of the foundations, both the transferor(s) and transferee(s), are effectively controlled, either directly or indirectly, by the same persons.

The ruling considers the reporting requirements and factors that carry over to the successor foundations in the following three situations:

*Situation 1:* PF P split into PFs X, Y, and Z.

*Situation 2:* PF T (a trust) transfers assets to PF W (nonprofit corporation).

*Situation 3:* PF J and PF K merge to create PF V.

---

**SITUATION 1**

A private foundation, due to the divergent interests of its current directors, distributes all of its remaining assets in equal shares to three other private foundations. Pursuant to the plan of dissolution, the foundation satisfies all of its outstanding liabilities, causes the recipient foundations to satisfy its expenditure responsibility reporting requirements, and, after all of its assets is transferred, files articles of dissolution with the appropriate state authority.

**SITUATION 2**

The trustees of a private foundation trust create a not-for-profit corporation to carry on the trust's charitable activities, which the trustees have determined can be more effectively accomplished by operating in corporate form. All of the trust's assets and liabilities are transferred to the new not-for-profit corporation.

**SITUATION 3**

Two private foundations that confine their grant-making activities to programs in the particular city in which they are located transfer all their assets and liabilities to a newly formed private foundation.

---

## (b) Questions Answered in Ruling

The IRS poses and answers the following four questions.

*Question 1.* If a private foundation transfers all of its assets to one or more private foundations, is the transferor foundation required to notify the IRS of its plans to terminate its private foundation status and pay the termination tax?

*Answer.* The IRS answer is *no* to both parts of the question. Advance IRS notification is not required when a private foundation voluntarily disposes of a significant portion of its assets to one or more private foundations.[85] A transfer of all of a private foundation's assets to one or more private foundations

---

85. Other than transfers for full and adequate consideration or distributions out of current income; IRC § 507(b)(2); Reg. § 1.507-3(c)(1).

constitutes a significant disposition.[86] In Situations 1, 2, and 3, described above, no termination has occurred.[87] Finally there is clarity that the termination tax language that prompted so many private letter ruling requests over the past decades does not always apply. It is now clear that the transfer of assets from one private foundation to another does not constitute a termination unless the private foundation voluntarily provides notice of its intent to terminate. According to the ruling, the fact that the foundation dissolves under state law has "no effect on whether it terminated its private foundation status for federal tax purposes." If the foundation chooses to provide notice, and thereafter voluntarily terminate, it is potentially subject to the termination tax, unless it requests and achieves abatements of the tax. If the foundation has no assets on the day it provides notice (e.g., it provides notice at least one day after it transfers all of its assets), the termination tax will be zero. The answer is true even if the ruling does not apply because the foundations involved are not commonly controlled.

*Question 2.* What are a private foundation's tax return filing obligations after it transfers all of its assets to one or more transferee private foundations and:

a. Its legal existence is dissolved, or

b. It continues to exist in a dormant condition?

*Answer.* A private foundation that has disposed of all its assets must file a Form 990-PF for the tax year of the disposition and comply with any expenditure responsibility reporting obligations on the return. Although the ruling does not mention it, any unfinished steps in the expenditure responsibility process, such as securing and reporting follow-up grantee reports, become the obligation of the transferee foundation(s). These filing requirements apply both for a private foundation that terminates by giving notice and one that does not terminate its private foundation status pursuant to the conclusion to question 1. The due date of the return is the fifteenth day of the fifth month following complete liquidation, dissolution, or termination.

The transferor foundation attaches a statement to its Form 990-PF for the year in which it has a liquidation, dissolution, termination, or substantial contraction.[88] A certified copy of the liquidation plan or resolutions (if any), schedule of the names and addresses of all recipients of assets, and an explanation of the nature and fair market value of the assets to each recipient is requested.[89] If the foundation has ceased to exist, the "Final" box on page 1 of the form is checked. If the entity remains in existence as a dormant shell without

---

86. Reg. § 1.507-3(c)(2).
87. Notice is not required; Regs. §§ 1.507-(b)(6), 1.507-3(d).
88. IRC § 6043.
89. By General Instruction T for Form 990-PF.

equitable title to any assets and without activity, it does not need to file returns in the following tax years.[90] If, in later years, it receives new assets or resumes activities, it must resume filing Form 990-PF. The ruling also says such a shell foundation should remain qualified as a tax-exempt organization eligible to receive charitable contributions.

*Question 3.* If a private foundation transfers all of its assets to one or more private foundations that are effectively controlled,[91] directly or indirectly, by the same person or persons who effectively control the transferor foundation, what are the implications under the private foundation rules?[92]

*Answer.* The IRS's answer to this question focuses on the fact that the successor foundation(s) inherit virtually all of the tax attributes of the transferor foundation. The recipient private foundation is not considered a newly created organization[93] whether it is commonly controlled or not. All tax obligations and attributes stemming from the listed code sections above, with one important exception noted below in answer to question 4, carryover to the successor foundations. If a private foundation incurs liability for one or more of the taxes imposed under chapter 42 (or any penalty resulting therefrom) prior to, or as a result of, making the asset transfer(s), in any case where transferee liability applies, each transferee foundation is treated as receiving the transferred assets subject to the liability to the extent that the transferor foundation does not satisfy the liability.[94] Further, a substantial contributor with respect to the transferor foundation is treated as a substantial contributor with respect to each recipient foundation receiving its assets, whether or not such person meets the $5,000, 2 percent test with respect to the transferee(s) at any time.[95] The consequences of the transfers and resulting carryovers are described below for each applicable code section.

*Section 4940.* The transfers do not give rise to net investment income and are not subject to the investment income tax. The basis for this answer is the fact that the transferred assets do not represent taxable income.[96] Private foundations each year pay an excise tax on net investment income at the rate of 1 or 2 percent. Only four specific types of income are subject to the tax: dividends, interest, rents, and royalties. From an accounting standpoint, the value of the net assets received by the transferee(s) would be reported as a donation if the recipient foundation is not commonly controlled. When the recipient foundation is

---

90. Reg. § 1.507-3(a)(10). Some question whether this no-filing rule could apply in other circumstances.
91. Within the meaning of Reg. § 1.507-3(a)(2) defined in § 1.507-3(a)(9), by reference to § 1.482-1(a)(3).
92. *See* Chapters 5–10 for additional discussion of these Code sections.
93. IRC § 507(b)(2).
94. Reg. § 1.507-3(a)(4).
95. Reg. § 1.507-3(a)(3).
96. *See* § 10.3.

controlled by one or more of the same persons that controlled the transferor, the value of the assets transferred is not reported as revenue, but instead would be reflected as an extraordinary increase in net assets.[97] The recipient foundations may use their proportionate share of any excess tax paid by the transferor to offset their own tax liability. This transfer could occur on the transferor's final return in the form of a special request that its tax credit be applied to its transferee(s). Since the IRS has acknowledged that the transferee is entitled to the funds, it might be preferable simply to request a refund. In the authors' experience, a transfer of tax deposits from one entity to another is sometimes a flawed process. When underpayment penalties will not result, it would be preferable to avoid this issue by causing the final return to reflect a tax liability rather than an overpayment of tax. Since an overpayment of tax is an asset, a foundation with such a receivable should specify in the transfer documents that it is donating the overpayment to the transferee. This step may protect it from an assertion that it has not transferred all of the assets. An unanswered question is the impact of the transfer on the estimated tax requirements for the transferee foundation(s). When the tax attributes carry over, theoretically it would be reasonable to allow the successor to base its safe estimate amount on the transferor's tax liability for the prior year. Absent guidance, the successor should follow the normal rules for newly created private foundations that require tax deposits based on its actual income received throughout the year using the annualization method provided in the instructions for Form 2220. Another investment income issue not mentioned in the ruling or the regulations is the calculation of depreciation or depletion on investment properties, such as rental buildings, mineral interests, and assets utilized to manage such properties. Again due to the carryover of tax attributes, the foundation receiving such assets would continue to follow the tax methodology and basis used by the transferor for those assets. Similarly, the basis of transferred assets for purposes of calculating taxable gain or loss for an investment property subject to the excise tax on investment income would be the same as the tax basis for the transferor.

*Section 4941.* The transfers do not constitute self-dealing.[98] The reason for this conclusion is the fact that the foundations involved in these transfers are tax-exempt charitable organizations. Self-dealing occurs only in transactions between a foundation and its disqualified persons. In planning for a transfer to another foundation, the possibility that relatives not currently treated as disqualified persons might become disqualified should be anticipated. Certain relatives, particularly aunts, uncles, nieces, and nephews, who are not treated as

---

97. The accounting presentation for such transactions involving nonprofit organizations are evolving but are governed generally by Statement of Financial Accounting Standard No. 136.
98. *See* Chapter 5.

disqualified persons in respect to the transferor could have some connection to relatives of board members or businesses owned by the transferee foundation. This caution is indicated when the transfers involve excess business holdings or partial interests in property that might need to be disposed of as a result of the transfers.[99]

*Section 4942.* The transfers do not constitute qualifying distributions for the transferor foundation because the foundations are commonly controlled. A transfer to an uncontrolled foundation does qualify, as discussed below. The transferee foundation assumes its proportionate share of the transferor foundation's undistributed income and reduces its distributable amount by its proportionate share of the transferors' excess qualifying distributions.[100] To understand this conclusion, one must start with the fact that the transferor foundation is required to meet its own distribution requirements for the year in which the transfer occurs.[101] Generally this payout amount is equal to 5 percent of the average value of the transferor's investment (referred to as nonexempt function) assets for the year preceding the transfer, called its "minimum investment return." Assume a foundation has $10 million of investment assets; the distributable amount equals $500,000 less its excise tax on investment income for the year, plus returned grants previously claimed as distributions. This "undistributed income," adjusted for over- or underdistributions from prior years, must be paid out before the end of the foundation's next succeeding year. The payout requirement is satisfied by payments of qualifying distributions: charitable grants, expenditures for its own charitable programs, and administrative expenses.

*Final-year issues.* The final year for the transferor foundation ends on the day it is dissolved. In many circumstances, the year will, therefore, be less than a full 12 months. A distributable amount is calculated for the transferor foundation as if it continued in existence. If the recipient foundation(s) is commonly controlled, the distributable amount must be paid out by the transferee(s). That amount equals 5 percent of the average value of its assets for the months of the year it is in existence. For a tax year of less than 12 months, the payout percentage is apportioned for the number of days it was in existence. Assume a calendar-year foundation distributes all of its assets to a successor foundation and dissolves its charter as a nonprofit corporation on June 30. The required payout percentage equals the number of days it was in existence, or 182 days, over 365 days times 5 percent, or 2.5 percent. If, for example, the average value of investment assets equals $10 million, a payout amount of $250,000, adjusted for over- or underdistributions, must be spent for charitable purposes by the transferee(s) foundation because it inherits all of the tax attributes of the transferor foundation.

---

99. The rules concerning co-owned property are discussed in § 5.4(e).
100. *See* § 6.6; in Rev. Rul. 78-387, 1978-2 C.B. 270, the IRS reached the same conclusion.
101. Reg. § 1.507-3(a)(5).

Multiple successor transferees, such as those in ruling Situation 1, become proportionately responsible to distribute or succeed to any excess distributions. In Situation 2, the newly created nonprofit corporation would be solely responsible for, or accede to, any under- or overdistributions from the charitable trust. Last, in Situation 3, the new private foundation would inherit the remaining distribution requirement or excess distribution carryover of both of its transferors.

It is important to note that the ruling stipulating the results in the above paragraph applies to foundations that are effectively controlled. The definition of *qualifying distributions* includes any amount paid to accomplish a charitable purpose, other than a contribution to a foundation controlled directly or indirectly by the foundation or one or more disqualified persons in respect to the foundation.[102] Therefore, the transfer of assets to an uncontrolled foundation offsets the distribution requirement in the final tax year if the foundation follows the redistribution requirements.[103]

The requirement that the transferee foundation(s) make qualifying distributions on behalf of the transferor necessitates good planning and attention to this detail and timing details. Normally newly created private foundations, such as the successors in Situations 2 and 3, have no distribution requirements in the first year. However, the next succeeding year of the transferor is the year the transferee receives its assets. Thus the remaining distributable amount must be paid out in that year.

Consider Situation 2 and assume charitable trust T transfers assets on November 1 and closes its 10-month tax year with a remaining distributable amount. Assume that recipient nonprofit corporation W is created on November 1 and adopts a calendar tax year so that it has a two-month tax year beginning on that date. W would be required before December 31 of the transfer year to complete the required distributions for Trust T. Similarly the newly created foundation V in Situation 3 would be required to satisfy the remaining payout requirements for foundations J and K before the end of their first tax year.[104] When the transferee foundation(s) has already been in existence (as may be the case in Situation 1), the transferor's remaining distributable amount would be payable in addition to any requirement it had from its own succeeding tax year. Conversely the transferor's excess distribution carryovers would be available to offset the transferee's distributable amount.[105] It is important to note that the above provisions do not apply when a foundation transfers its assets to a private foundation(s) that its disqualified persons do not effectively control. The transfer of assets to an uncontrolled foundation is considered to be a

---

102. *See* § 6.5(a).

103. IRC § 4942(g)(3).

104. The principal author of the ruling, Theodore R. Lieber, of the Exempt Organizations, Tax Exempt and Government Entities Division, said he had not anticipated the hardship this might create when the transfers occur late in the tax year.

105. A chart illustrating the application of carryovers can be found in § 6.4, Exhibit 6.2.

qualifying distribution and an expenditure responsibility report is due in its final return.[106]

*Section 4943.* Whether the transfer causes a transferee(s) foundation to have excess business holdings[107] depends on the facts and circumstances of the combined ownership after the transfer. When the foundations involved in the transfers are effectively controlled, the disqualified persons, including substantial contributors, of both the transferor and transferee foundations are treated as disqualified persons of the transferee in determining whether the transferee has excess business. In addition, the transferee's holding period includes both the time the transferred assets were held by the transferor(s) and by itself.

*Section 4944.* The transfers of assets do not constitute investments jeopardizing the transferor foundation's exempt purposes.[108] Whether or not an asset is a jeopardizing investment is determined at the time of its acquisition. The determination of jeopardy for an asset received by the transferee foundation would be based on the facts and circumstances existing when the transferor originally acquired it. If jeopardy is found to have existed, the transferee is responsible to remove the asset from jeopardy and pay the penalties due.

*Section 4945.* The transferor foundation is not required to exercise expenditure responsibility with respect to the transfers.[109] With respect to any outstanding grants it had previously made, the transferor foundation is required to exercise expenditure responsibility until the time it disposes of all of assets and make reports of such grants on its final Form 990-PF. Expenditure responsibility is an obligation that a private foundation incurs when it makes a grant to another private foundation, to a noncharitable tax-exempt organization, or to a nonexempt business for a charitable project or program-related investment.[110] The obligation to make a report and monitor expenditure responsibility with respect to outstanding grants transfers with the assets to transferee foundation(s). When multiple transferee foundations are involved, each is responsible to monitor and report on outstanding grants. That responsibility, however, can be shared, or assumed, by any one or more of the transferees in regard to particular grants. When assets are transferred by a private foundation to one or more other foundations that it does not control, the transfer requires an expenditure responsibility report in its final return. These transfers occur without consideration and can therefore be treated as qualifying distributions.[111] The uncontrolled transferee foundation, however, has no responsibility to exercise expenditure responsibility and report on outstanding grants of its transferor.

---

106. Reg. § 1.507-3(a)(7) provides that reporting is not required once the foundation has disposed of all of its assets.
107. *See* Chapter 7.
108. *See* Chapter 8.
109. Reg. § 1.507-3(a)(9)(iii), Example 2.
110. *See* § 9.6.
111. *See* text accompanied by *supra* note 99.

*Question 4.* If a private foundation transfers all of its assets to one or more private foundations that are effectively controlled, directly or indirectly, by the same person or persons who effectively control the transferor foundation, what are the implications for the transferor foundation's aggregate tax benefits?[112]

*Answer.* The transferor foundation's aggregate tax benefits are transferred to the transferee foundations in proportion to the assets received by each transferee. The *aggregate tax benefits*,[113] as the words imply, represent all of the tax savings realized to the foundation and its funders during the foundation's lifetime. When there is more than one transferee, the benefit is allocated to the successors by multiplying the amount by a fraction, the numerator of which is the fair market value of the assets, less encumbrances, transferred to such transferee and the denominator of which is the fair market value of the assets of the transferor, less encumbrances, immediately before the transfer.[114] The impact of this provision is to subject other assets and future enhancements in assets of a commonly controlled transferor to the termination tax for acts it might not have committed. Also, if it is ever determined that a transferee foundation committed willful violations of the private foundation sanctions itself, the termination tax could equal not only those benefits accrued since it received the transfer but also that of the transferor up to the value of all of its assets at the time of its termination. When the transferee foundation is not effectively controlled by the transferor foundation, the carryover is limited to the fair market value of assets received.

## (c) Unanswered Question

The 2002 and 2003 IRS rulings that provide guidance for private foundation transfers specifically state they pertain to the carryover of tax attributes to one or more other private foundations that are effectively controlled by the transferor(s). Thus for those transferee private foundations that are not controlled by the same person(s), some unanswered questions remain. The statute does not contain any mention of the controlled/uncontrolled distinction when it clearly states that the transferee shall not be treated as a newly created organization. The regulations repeat that characteristic and as a general rule provide that the successor organization inherits the tax attributes and characteristics of the transferor.[115] There are several matters, however, on which the regulations do make a distinction between a controlled and uncontrolled transferee private foundation:

- Carryover of aggregate tax benefits to an uncontrolled transferee private foundation is limited to the fair market value of the asset received.[116]

---

112. IRC § 507(d).
113. Defined in § 13.6.
114. Reg. § 1.507-3(a)(2).
115. IRC § 507(b)(2).
116. Reg. § 1.507-3(a)(2)(ii).

- Transfer of less than 100 percent can be treated as a qualifying distribution without regard to whether the transferee private foundation is controlled by the transferor private foundation.[117]

- Responsibility to continue to perform expenditure responsibility ceases when transferee private foundation is not controlled.[118] Controlled transferee private foundations, instead, must continue to monitor and report such grants made previously by the transferor. Responsibility is a shared obligation that may be allocated when there are several transferees.[119]

- Expenditure responsibility need not be exercised by the transferor following the year of a complete transfer of assets (to one or more controlled or uncontrolled private foundations) because no returns are filed once the private foundation has no assets.[120]

- Excess qualifying distributions carry over to a controlled transferee private foundation(s) when 100 percent of assets are transferred.[121]

Those matters on which the regulations provide for carryover of tax attributes without regard to the fact that transferee private foundation(s) is (are) controlled by persons in control of the transferor include:

- A substantial contributor as it regards the transferor private foundation becomes a substantial contributor of the one or more transferee private foundations.[122]

- The tax basis of the transferring private foundation's assets is retained.[123]

- Transferee private foundation(s) inherit(s) liability for any private foundation taxes incurred by the transferor.[124]

- Holding period for business holdings for purposes of measuring excessive amounts under IRC § 4943 includes the time assets were held by the transferor.[125]

The regulations provide methodology for allocating tax attributes in the ratio of assets transferred.[126] See Exhibit 13.1.

---

117. Reg. § 1.507-3(a)(5); IRC § 4942(g)(1)(A).
118. Reg. § 1.507-3(a)(7).
119. Reg. § 1.507-3(a)(9).
120. Reg. § 1.507-3(a)(7).
121. Reg. § 1.507-3(a)(9)(i).
122. Reg. § 1.507-3(a)(3).
123. Reg. § 1.507-3(a)(3).
124. Reg. § 1.507-3(a)(4).
125. Reg. § 1.507-3(a)(6).
126. Reg. § 1.507-3(a)(2), Examples 1–3; Reg. § 1.507-3(a)(9)(iii), Examples 2.

**Transfers between Private Foundations**

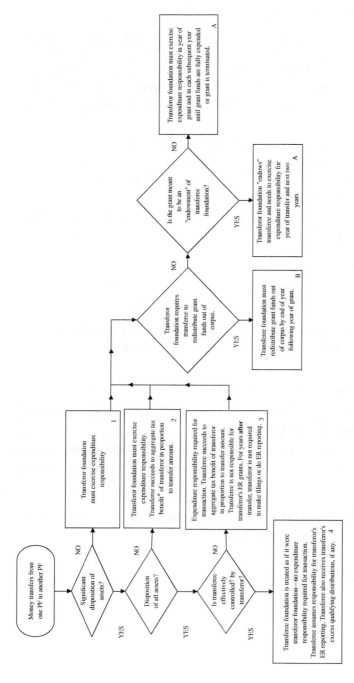

**Exhibit 13.1**

Transfers between Private Foundations

*Source:* Amanda Adams, Blazek & Vetterling Tax Manager, and Jeffrey Haskell, Senior Vice President, Legal Affairs, Foundation Source. Reprinted with permission.

The difficult, and still unanswered, questions involve a private foundation that remains in existence after it has transferred more than 25 percent, but less than 100 percent, of its assets. A partial liquidation or merger occurs when a private foundation disposes of more than 25 percent of its assets in one year or in a series of related transfers in what is called a "significant disposition." In this type of a case, a termination is deemed to occur that invokes the "not treated as a new entity" provisions of the termination rules.[127] Attributes and responsibilities are transferred whether or not the transferee private foundation(s) is controlled by the transferor private foundation following the rules. The regulations do not provide any additional guidance for these types of transfers. Presumably the tax attributes will follow the assets in proportion to the value of the assets transferred. Issues to consider in this regard follow.

- Does the specific tax basis follow the particular assets transferred? Yes.[128] A planning opportunity might exist here. Even though the tax rate is low, many foundation assets have unrealized appreciation that cause a 1 to 2 percent tax when they are sold. The 1 percent rate is not available in a new foundation's first tax year.

- How are accumulated excess qualifying distributions allocated when a series of transfers occurs over the year? Consider the situation in which the transferor has carryovers attributable to several years. Whether or not the transferee receives its proportionate share of each year or on some first in, first out (FIFO)–type method is not provided.

- Must the transferor private foundation exercise expenditure responsibility (ER) as it regards the transfer? The answer is *Yes*, if the transferor remains in existence.[129] Ongoing ER is not required for a complete transfer of assets for the practical reason that future tax returns are not required. Absent clean guidance and since ER is relatively easy to perform, a prudent private foundation will exercise ER. To avoid the possibility that ER will perpetually be required, the agreements should stipulate that the asset transfer create an endowment (requires no more than three years).[130]

- Must the transferee foundation make an "out-of-corpus" distribution for the transferor private foundation to treat the transfer as a qualifying distribution?[131] Before answering this question, it is important to note the transferring private foundation should inform the transferee of the

---

127.  Reg. § 1.507-3(c)(1).
128.  Reg. § 1.507-3(a)(8)(ii)(a).
129.  *See* the last sentence of Example (2) in Regs. § 1.507-3(a)(9)(iii), Reg. § 1.507-3(a)(7).
130.  *See* § 17.6(c).
131.  *See* § 15.4(b).

amount it is treating as a qualifying distribution. When the transferee private foundation is controlled by the transferor private foundation, and all assets are transferred, there is no grant, and therefore the transfer does not satisfy the distribution requirements of the transferor. When the transferee is not controlled, there can be a qualifying distribution reportable by the transferor. Correspondingly, the transferee must redistribute to the extent the transferring private foundation claims the transfers as qualifying distributions.

### (d)  Non-Control, Complete Assets Transfer

Subsequent to the foregoing, the IRS issued private letter rulings to two private foundations with identical exempt purposes, where, to realize administrative cost savings and eliminate duplication of efforts, one of the foundations (PF1) plans to transfer all of its assets to the other (PF2), then dissolve.[132] These private foundations are not controlled by the same persons. This transaction resulted in the following 20 rulings:

1.  This transfer of assets is a liquidation and merger.[133]

2.  Therefore, this asset transfer is not a "voluntary termination"[134] of PF1's status as a private foundation.

3.  Therefore, PF1 will not be subject to the termination tax.[135]

4.  Therefore, PF2 will not be treated as a "newly created organization" but will be regarded as possessing certain tax attributes and characteristics of PF1.[136]

5.  This asset transfer will not adversely affect the tax-exempt status[137] of PF1.

6.  This asset transfer will not adversely affect the exempt status of PF2.

7.  PF2 will succeed to the "aggregate tax benefit"[138] of PF1 but not in excess of the fair market value of the assets transferred.

8.  Inasmuch as the transferred assets will not constitute investment income, the receipt of these assets will not be investment income[139] to PF2.

---

132. Priv. Ltr. Ruls. 201013065, 201013066.
133. *See* text accompanied by *supra* note 76.
134. *See* § 13.1.
135. *See* § 13.6.
136. *See* text accompanied by *supra* note 76.
137. *See* § 2.5.
138. *See* text accompanied by *infra* note 152.
139. *See* text accompanied by *supra* note 96.

9.  If PF1 is liable for the investment income tax and this liability is not satisfied, PF2 will receive the transferred assets subject to this liability and will be required to satisfy it.

10. If PF1 is entitled to an investment income tax refund, the right to the refund will be included in the transferred assets, but PF2 may not use this right to receive the refund to offset its liability for the tax.

11. The assets transfer will not constitute an act of self-dealing because neither private foundation is a disqualified person with respect to the other.[140]

12. No part of the transfer of the assets will constitute a qualifying distribution for PF1, except to the extent that PF2 makes a timely redistribution of the funds that it treats as a distribution out of corpus.[141]

13. The assets transfer will not constitute a prohibited investment[142] by PF1.

14. The receipt of these assets by PF2 will not constitute a prohibited investment.

15. The assets transfer will not be a taxable expenditure[143] by PF1.

16. As to any obligation PF1 has to exercise expenditure responsibility[144] at the time of the transfer, PF2 will not be required to exercise expenditure responsibility.

17. PF1 will have to comply with certain information reporting requirements[145] for the tax year of the transfer.

18. PF1 is required to file an annual information return[146] for the tax year in which it transfers the assets to PF2.

19. If, after the assets transfer, PF1 does not have legal or equitable title in any assets and does not engage in any activity, it is not required to file an annual information return for any year following the year of the transfer.

20. PF1 will have to file certain information with the IRS with respect to the transaction (with the annual return referenced in number 18) because it will constitute the type of dissolution that triggers the requirement.[147]

The IRS issues private letter rulings concerning these types of adjustment, organization, or reorganization involving private foundations.[148]

---

140. *See* § 4.7.
141. *See* § 6.5.
142. *See* text accompanied by *supra* note 108.
143. *See* Chapter 9.
144. *See* § 9.6.
145. *See* § 9.6(h).
146. *See* Chapter 12.
147. *See* text accompanied by *supra* note 88.
148. E.g., Priv. Ltr. Rul. 8629062.

## § 13.6 TERMINATION TAX

There is imposed on each organization, the private foundation status of which is terminated, a tax equal to the lower of (1) the amount that the organization substantiates by adequate records or other corroborating evidence as the *aggregate tax benefit* resulting from the tax-exempt status of the organization as a charitable entity or (2) the value of the net assets of the organization.[149] The aggregate tax benefit resulting from the tax-exempt status of a private foundation is the sum of:

1. Aggregate increases in income, estate, and gift taxes that would have been imposed with respect to all substantial contributors[150] to the private foundation if deductions for all contributions made by the substantial contributors to the private foundation after February 28, 1913, had been disallowed.

2. Aggregate increases in income taxes that would have been imposed with respect to the income of the foundation for tax years beginning after December 31, 1912, if it had not been exempt from tax (or, if a trust, the amount by which its income taxes were reduced because it was permitted to deduct charitable contributions in excess of 20 percent of its taxable income).

3. Any amounts succeeded to from transferor private foundations.[151]

4. Interest on the foregoing increases in tax from the first date on which each increase would have been due and payable to the date on which the organization ceases to be a private foundation.[152]

In computing the amount of the aggregate increases in tax under item (1), all deductions attributable to a particular contribution for income, estate, or gift tax purposes must be included. Thus, the aggregate tax benefit in respect to a single contribution may exceed the fair market value of the property transferred.[153]

In respect to the amount of the tax benefit as stated in the second of these items in the case of a trust, one court found the provision "ambiguous."[154] Specifically, the applicable law[155] describes the tax benefit of a trust as including the aggregate increases in tax that would be imposed if "deductions under section 642(c) . . . had been limited to 20 percent of the taxable income of the

---

149. IRC § 507(c); Reg. § 1.507-4.
150. *See* § 4.1.
151. IRC § 507(b)(2).
152. IRC § 507(d); Reg. § 1.507-5(a).
153. Reg. § 1.507-5(b).
154. *Peters v. United States*, 80-2 U.S.T.C. ¶ 9510 (Ct. Cl. 1980).
155. IRC § 507(d)(1)(B)(ii).

trust (computed without the benefit of section 642(c) but with the benefit of section 170(b)(1)(A))." The court reached the conclusion that the provision requires a two-step calculation. The first step is to apply the pertinent charitable contribution deduction rule, which is the charitable deduction available to individuals for up to 50 percent of the donor's contribution base.[156] The second step is to apply a deduction of 20 percent of the trust's taxable income, rather than the full (100 percent) deduction normally allowed,[157] against the trust income remaining after the charitable deduction. This interpretation thus produces a 60 percent (50 percent plus 20 percent of 50 percent) deduction, which in turn produces the amount retained by the trust in calculating the tax benefit to be recaptured. Pursuant to this reading of the statute, this portion of the termination tax equals 40 percent of the value of the trust's deduction, namely, the 100 percent deduction taken by the trust minus the 60 percent deduction the trust can retain.

In computing the value of the net assets of a private foundation, the amount of the value is determined at whichever time the value is higher: the first day on which action is taken by the organization that culminates in its ceasing to be a private foundation (that is, the date the organization submitted notice it was terminating its private foundation status) or the date on which it ceases to be a private foundation (that is, the date a willful and flagrant act, failure to act, or a series of repeated acts or failures to act first occurred).[158] The term *net assets* means the gross assets of a private foundation reduced by all its liabilities, including appropriate estimated and contingent liabilities (such as any private foundation excise taxes or winding-up expenses).[159]

## § 13.7 ABATEMENT

The IRS has discretion to abate an unpaid portion of the assessment of a termination tax or any liability in respect to the tax, if a private foundation distributes all of its net assets to one or more eligible public or publicly supported organizations, each of which has been in existence and so described for a continuous period of at least 60 calendar months, or if the private foundation gives effective assurance to the IRS that its assets will be used for charitable purposes.[160]

Abatement of the unpaid portion of the assessment of a termination tax will occur only where the IRS determines that the requisite corrective action

---

156. IRC § 170(b)(1)(A). *See* § 14.1(b).
157. IRC § 642(c).
158. IRC § 507(e); Reg. § 1.507-7(a)–(c).
159. Reg. § 1.507-7(d).
160. IRC § 507(g); Reg. § 1.507-9(a).

has been taken.[161] The appropriate state officer has one year from the date of notification[162] that a notice of deficiency of termination tax has been issued to advise the IRS that corrective action has been initiated (by the state officer or a recipient public or publicly supported charity) pursuant to state law as may be ordered or approved by a court of competent jurisdiction.[163] On receipt of certification from the state officer that corrective action has been taken, the IRS may abate the termination tax assessment, unless the IRS determines that the action is not sufficiently corrective, in which case action on the assessment and collection of the tax may be suspended until corrective action[164] is obtained, or assessment and collection of the tax may be resumed.[165]

161. Reg. § 1.507-9(b)(1).
162. IRC § 6104(c).
163. Reg. § 1.507-9(b)(2).
164. Reg. § 1.507-9(c).
165. Reg. § 1.507-9(b)(3).

# CHAPTER FOURTEEN

# Charitable Giving Rules

## § 14.1  GENERAL RULES

Federal law provides an income tax charitable contribution deduction. Consequently, individuals who itemize deductions, as well as corporations, can deduct, subject to varying limitations, an amount equivalent to the value of a contribution made to a qualified charitable donee.[1] In general, a *contribution* is a payment where the donor does not expect anything of consequence in return for having made the gift.[2] A *charitable contribution* is a gift to or for the use of a qualified charitable entity, such as a private foundation.[3]

---

1. IRC § 170(a)(1). In general, *Charitable Giving*.
2. The U.S. Supreme Court observed that a "payment of money [or transfer of property] generally cannot constitute a charitable contribution if the contributor expects a substantial benefit in return" (*United States v. American Bar Endowment*, 477 U.S. 105, 116–117 (1986)). The income tax charitable deduction regulations and the business expense deduction regulations reflect this concept (Reg. §§ 1.170A-1(c)(5), 1.170A-1(h)(1), 1.162-15(b)).
3. IRC § 170(c). The IRS stated that a contribution to a single-member limited liability company, which is a disregarded entity for federal tax purposes, where the company is wholly owned and controlled by a U.S. charitable organization, is deductible, with the gift treated as being to a branch or a division of the charity (Notice 2012-52).

## (a) Deduction Variables

The extent of the income tax charitable deduction is dependent in part on whether the charitable donee is a public charity or a private foundation.[4] Another basic element in determining whether, or the extent to which, a contribution to charity is deductible is the nature of the property contributed: capital gain property or ordinary income property.[5] Other distinctions may be made between current giving or planned giving, between gifts of money and gifts of property, and between outright gifts, partial interest gifts, and gifts by means of a trust. The amount of a qualified charitable contribution of an item of property is normally based on its fair market value (with no tax imposed on the increase, if any, over what the donor paid for the property, or the capital gain).[6]

## (b) Percentage Limitations

The deductibility of charitable contributions for a tax year can be restricted by percentage limitations, which in the case of individuals are a function of the donor's *contribution base.* For nearly all individuals, the contribution base is the same as adjusted gross income.[7] These percentage limitations are:

- 50 percent of contribution base for gifts of money and ordinary income property to public charities and certain operating foundations.[8]

- 30 percent of contribution base for contributions of long-term capital gain property to public charities and certain foundations.[9]

- 30 percent of contribution base for contributions of cash and ordinary income property to private foundations and certain other recipients.[10]

- 50 percent of contribution base for contributions of capital gain property to public charities where the amount of the contribution is reduced by all of the unrealized appreciation in the value of the property.[11]

- 20 percent of contribution base for contributions of capital gain property to charitable organizations other than public charities and operating foundations, principally standard private foundations.[12]

---

4. *See* Chapter 15.
5. *See* § 14.2.
6. E.g., *Campbell v. Prothro*, 209 F.2d 331 (5th Cir. 1954).
7. IRC § 170(b)(1)(F).
8. This limitation is not stated as such in the federal statutory tax law but is embodied in an overall limitation on charitable gifts that can be deducted annually, in IRC § 170(b)(1)(A).
9. IRC § 170(b)(1)(C)(i).
10. IRC § 170(b)(1)(B)(i).
11. IRC § 170(b)(1)(C)(iii).
12. IRC § 170(b)(1)(D)(i).

When an individual makes charitable contributions that exceed the percentage limitations for the year, generally the excess may be carried forward and deducted in subsequent years, up to five.[13]

Deductible charitable contributions by corporations in a tax year may not exceed 10 percent of pretax net income.[14] A corporation using the accrual method of accounting can elect to treat a charitable contribution as having been paid in a tax year if it is actually paid during the first 2½ months of the following year.[15] Special rules apply as to the deductibility of corporate gifts of inventory,[16] of scientific property used for research,[17] and of computer equipment and technology for elementary or secondary school purposes.[18] There are carryover rules in this context.[19] The making of a charitable gift by a business corporation is not considered to be an act outside the entity's corporate powers as long as the general interests of the corporation and its shareholders are advanced.

For many years, the amount of itemized deductions that were otherwise claimable was reduced to the extent a taxpayer's adjusted gross income was above an amount—sometimes referred to as the *Pease limitation*. This reduction was phased out for 2006–2009, then repealed as of 2010. This repeal was extended through 2012. Legislation signed into law on January 2, 2013, extended repeal of the Pease limitation on adjusted gross income at or below $250,000 in the case of individuals, $275,000 in the case of heads of households, $300,000 in the case of married individuals filing jointly and surviving spouses, and $150,000 in the case of married individuals filing separately. After 2013, these amounts are adjusted for inflation. At income levels above these thresholds, the Pease limitation applies to reduce itemized deductions, including the income tax charitable deduction, by the lesser of 3 percent of the excess of adjusted gross income above the threshold amounts or 80 percent of the amount of itemized deductions that are otherwise allowable.[20]

## (c)  Estate and Gift Tax Deductions

There are charitable contribution deductions in the estate and gift context as well. A charitable estate tax deduction is allowed for the value of all transfers from a decedent's estate to or for the use of charitable organizations.[21] A charitable gift tax deduction is available for transfers by gift to or for the use

---

13. IRC § 170(d)(1), (b)(1)(C)(ii), (b)(1)(B), and (b)(1)(D)(ii).
14. IRC § 170(b)(2).
15. IRC § 170(a)(2).
16. IRC § 170(e)(3).
17. IRC § 170(e)(4).
18. IRC § 170(e)(6).
19. IRC § 170(d)(2).
20. IRC § 68.
21. IRC § 2055.

of charitable organizations.[22] The extent of these charitable deductions is not dependent on whether the charitable donee is a public charity or a private foundation; percentage limitations do not apply to these deductions.

## § 14.2 GIFTS OF APPRECIATED PROPERTY

A charitable gift of property to a private foundation or other charitable organization may involve an outright gift of the property or of a partial interest in the property. The property may be personal property or real property, tangible property or intangible property. The gift may be limited by one or more of the percentage rules or entail a reduction of the otherwise deductible amount.[23] The income tax rules, or the estate and gift tax rules, may be involved.

In the case of a charitable contribution of property, a critical determination in ascertaining the extent of the charitable deduction often is the fair market value of the property. As a general rule, the fair market value of an item of property is the price at which the property would change hands between a willing buyer and a willing seller, neither being under any compulsion to buy or sell and both having reasonable knowledge of relevant facts.[24] The IRS amplified this rule, holding that the "most probative evidence of fair market [value] is the price at which similar quantities of . . . [the property] are sold in arm's-length transactions."[25] The IRS also determined that the fair market value of gift property is determined by reference to the "most active and comparable marketplace at the time of the donor's contribution."[26] The fair value of property is frequently the subject of litigation.[27]

Inasmuch as the charitable deduction for a gift of property is often based on the fair market value of the property, a donor can be economically benefited where the property has increased in value since the date on which the donor acquired the property. Property in this condition has *appreciated* in value; it is known as *appreciated property.* Where certain requirements are satisfied, a donor is entitled to a charitable deduction based on the full fair market value of the property.[28]

This rule—allowance of the charitable deduction based on the full value of an item of property—is one of the rules in the tax law that is most beneficial to donors. This is particularly the case when it is considered that the donor in this circumstance is not usually required to recognize any gain on the transfer. The

---

22. IRC § 2522.
23. *See* § 14.4.
24. Reg. § 1.170A-1(c)(2).
25. Rev. Rul. 80-69, 1980-1 C.B. 55.
26. Rev. Rul. 80-233, 1980-2 C.B. 69.
27. E.g., *Hilborn v. Commissioner,* 85 T.C. 677 (1985); *Droz v. Commissioner,* 71 T.C.M. 2204 (1996).
28. IRC § 170(a); Reg. § 1.170A-(c)(1).

gain is the amount that would have been recognized had the donor sold the property; it is sometimes referred to as the *appreciation element*.

The ability of a donor to have a charitable deduction, for a contribution of property, based on the fair market value of the property is dependent on several factors. Chief among these are:

- The nature of the property contributed.
- The tax classification of the charitable donee.
- The use to which the charitable donee puts the property.

As to the first of these factors, the federal tax law categorizes items of property as follows:

- Long-term capital gain property.
- Short-term capital gain property.
- Ordinary income property.

An item of *long-term capital gain property* is a capital asset that has appreciated in value which, if sold, would result in long-term capital gain.[29] One feature of this type of property is that it must have been held by the owner for at least 12 months.[30] Property that is deductible on the basis of its fair market value is long-term capital gain property. Other property is *ordinary income property* or *short-term capital gain property*; this is property that, if sold, would give rise to ordinary income or short-term capital gain, respectively. For these purposes, ordinary income and short-term capital gain are regarded as the same.

*Automobiles, boats, and airplanes.* The deduction for a gift of a used automobile, boat, or airplane valued at more than $500 is limited to the actual proceeds of sale by the recipient charity, unless the charity retains the item for its exempt use or makes repairs.[31] The donor acknowledgment must reflect whether the car, boat, or plane was sold or retained and used by the charity and, unlike most donor receipts,[32] must be attached to the donor's income tax return. Only if the charity keeps the vehicle for use in its charitable programs, referred to as *significant intervening use*, or makes material improvements to the vehicle may the deduction be equal to the fair market value.[33] New Form 1098, *Contributions of Motor Vehicles, Boats, and Airplanes*, was issued for charities receiving such

---

29. IRC § 170(b)(1)(C)(iv).
30. IRC §§ 1(h) and 1223.
31. Effective January 1, 2005, American Jobs Creation Act of 2004 (P.L. 108-357), amending IRC § 170(f)(12).
32. *See Charitable Giving* § 24.2(b).
33. IRS Notice 2005-44.

donations. The form must be attached to the tax return of persons claiming a deduction for such a donation.

*Patents and other intellectual property.* The year-of-gift deduction for donations of patents, copyrights, and other intellectual property is limited to the lesser of the taxpayer's basis in the property or its fair market value.[34] To the extent the property produces income in future years, additional gifts may be deemed to occur. Once the donor informs it of such a gift, the recipient charity must file Form 8899 by January 31 each year following the gift to report any income it receives on the property.[35]

## § 14.3 DEDUCTIBILITY OF GIFTS TO FOUNDATIONS

As discussed,[36] one of the factors governing the deductibility of gifts is whether the charitable donee involved is a public charity or a private foundation. In part, this distinction is reflected in the percentage limitations, which are more restrictive with respect to gifts to private foundations than is the case with gifts to public charities. To recapitulate:

- A deductible contribution of money to a private foundation by an individual is limited in any one year to an amount equal to 30 percent of the donor's adjusted gross income.[37] (The percentage is 50 percent in the case of these gifts to public charities and private operating foundations.)

- A deductible contribution of appreciated property to a private foundation by an individual is limited in any one year to an amount equal to 20 percent of the donor's adjusted gross income.[38] (The percentage is 30 percent in the case of such gifts to public charities or private operating foundations.)

Aside from the percentage limitations, the ability in instances of gifts of property to base the charitable deduction on the full fair market value of the property turns on this public charity/private foundation dichotomy. As a general rule, the only time the deduction can be based on the property's full value and enable the donor to avoid recognition of the capital gain element is when the charitable donee is a public charity or private operating foundation. By contrast, where a contribution is made to a charitable organization that is not a public charitable organization, a deduction reduction rule usually applies.

---

34. IRC § 170(m).
35. Temp. Reg. § 1.6050L-2T.
36. *See* § 14.2.
37. IRC § 170(b)(1)(B)(i).
38. IRC § 170(b)(1)(D)(i).

# § 14.4 DEDUCTION REDUCTION RULES

In the federal income tax scheme relating to deductible charitable giving, there are three deduction reduction rules. One of them is unique to private foundations.

## (a) Capital Gain Property Deduction Rule

The deduction reduction rule that is unique to private foundations is this: When a charitable gift of capital gain property is made, the amount of the charitable deduction that would otherwise be determined must be reduced by the amount of gain that would have been long-term capital gain if the property contributed had been sold by the donor at its fair market value, determined at the time of the contribution.[39] This rule does not apply, however, with respect to a gift to a:

- Private operating foundation,
- Pass-through foundation, or
- Common fund foundation.[40]

Where this rule applies, the charitable deduction that would otherwise be determined must be reduced by the amount of the unrealized appreciation in value. The charitable deduction under these rules is confined to the basis in the property. This rule applies:

- Irrespective of whether the donor is an individual or a corporation,
- Irrespective of whether the charitable contribution is made to or for the use of a charitable organization, and
- To a gift of property prior to application of one or more of the appropriate percentage limitations.

## (b) Qualified Appreciated Stock Rule

A significant exception to the deduction reduction rule for private founda-tions[41] was added to the law in 1984 and set to expire with respect to contributions made after December 31, 1994.[42] Congress twice temporarily

---

39. IRC § 170(e)(1)(B)(ii); Reg. § 1.170A-4 (b)(2)(i).
40. IRC § 170(e)(1)(B)(ii), by cross-reference to the three types of private foundations referenced in IRC § 170(b)(1)(E).
41. This rule is the subject of § 14.4(a).
42. IRC § 170(e)(5)(D). A donor of qualified appreciated stock to a private foundation in 1994, who had a carryover of his or her charitable deduction by reason of the annual percentage limitation for that year (*see* text accompanied by *supra* note 12), was entitled to base the deduction in the subsequent year(s) on the full value of the stock (i.e., was entitled to IRC § 170(e)(5) treatment for the carryover amount) (e.g., Priv. Ltr. Rul. 9424040).

restored this authorization, making it available during the period July 1, 1996, through June 30, 1998.[43] These time constraints motivated those who wanted to form foundations and fund them with qualified appreciated stock to act within the deadlines.[44] In 1998, however, Congress extended this rule beginning July 1, 1998, and made it permanent.[45]

The exception to this deduction reduction rule is that it does not apply in the case of a contribution of *qualified appreciated stock*.[46] That is, where this exception is applicable, the charitable deduction for a contribution of stock to a private foundation is based on the fair market value of the stock at the time of the gift.

Basically, the term *qualified appreciated stock* means any stock:

- For which (as of the date of the contribution) market quotations are readily available on an established securities market.
- That is capital gain property.[47]

It is the view of the IRS that stock that cannot be sold or exchanged by reason of the securities law rules confining sales of control stock to small portions[48] cannot qualify as qualified appreciated stock.[49] Moreover, the IRS ruled that stock traded by means of the Over-the-Counter Bulletin Board Service is not qualified appreciated stock because market quotations are not readily available, in that they can be obtained only by consulting a broker, subscribing to a service, or obtaining a copy of the one newspaper that lists the stock.[50] By contrast, the IRS ruled that stock to be contributed to a private foundation was qualified appreciated stock, because the market quotations for the stock were readily available due to accessibility to the information on Internet sites.[51]

In the sole case on the point, a court held that stock contributed to a private foundation did not give rise to a charitable contribution deduction based on its fair market value, because the stock did not constitute qualified appreciated stock.[52] The stock involved was that of a bank holding company. The shares were not listed on the New York Stock Exchange, the American Stock Exchange, or any city or regional stock exchange, nor were the shares regularly traded in

---

43. IRC § 170(e)(5)(D), as revised by § 1206 of the Small Business Job Protection Act of 1996 and § 602 of the Taxpayer Relief Act of 1997.
44. E.g., as to the expiration date of May 31, 1997, Langley, "A Tax Break Prompts Millionaires' Mad Dash to Create Foundations," *Wall St. J.*, January 27, 1997, at 1.
45. IRC § 170(e)(5)(D), repealed by enactment of the Tax and Trade Relief Extension Act of 1998.
46. IRC § 170(e)(5)(A).
47. IRC § 170(e)(5)(B).
48. Securities and Exchange Commission Rule 144.
49. Priv. Ltr. Rul. 9247018, *aff'd*, Priv. Ltr. Rul. 9320016.
50. Priv. Ltr. Rul. 9504027.
51. Priv. Ltr. Rul. 200702031.
52. *Todd v. Commissioner*, 118 T.C. 334 (2002).

the national or any regional over-the-counter market for which published quotations are available. The shares were not those of a mutual fund. A brokerage firm occasionally provided a suggested share price based on the net asset value of the bank. The procedure for someone wishing to purchase or sell shares of the corporation was to contact an officer of the bank or a local stock brokerage firm specializing in the shares. An attempt would be made to match a potential seller with a potential buyer; the shares were not sold frequently. The court held that the stock could not constitute qualified appreciated stock because the market quotations requirement was not satisfied.

Further, qualified appreciated stock does not include any stock contributed to a private foundation to the extent that the amount of stock contributed (including prior gifts of stock by the donor) exceeds 10 percent (in value) of all of the outstanding stock of the corporation.[53] In making this calculation, an individual must take into account all contributions made by any member of his or her family.[54] The fact that a private foundation disposed of qualified appreciated stock is irrelevant in making this computation.[55]

In applying this limitation with respect to future contributions of qualified appreciated stock, the values of prior contributions of the same stock are based on the value of the stock at the time of the original contributions. That is, for this purpose, the prior contributions of stock are not revalued each time there is another contribution of the same stock.

From time to time, the IRS issues private letter rulings as to stock that constitutes qualified appreciated stock[56] and stock that does not so qualify.[57]

## (c) Other Deduction Reduction Rules

Two other deduction reduction rules may apply:

1. In the case of a contribution of ordinary income (inventory or certain depreciable property) property to a charity (public or private), the donor must reduce the deduction by the amount of any gain.[58]

---

53. IRC § 170(e)(5)(C)(i). This rule is applicable only in the case of a contribution to which IRC § 170(e)(1)(B)(ii) applies (*see supra* note 34) but for this rule. These rules are, of course, rules in the income tax charitable contribution context. Therefore, a stock contribution to a private foundation by an estate is not subject to the 10 percent limitation, because that gift would presumably give rise to an estate tax charitable deduction but not an income tax charitable deduction (Priv. Ltr. Rul. 200112022).
54. IRC § 170(e)(5)(C)(ii). The term *member of the family* means an individual's brothers and sisters (whether by whole or half blood), spouse, ancestors, and lineal descendants (IRC § 267(c)(4)).
55. Priv. Ltr. Rul. 200112022.
56. E.g., Priv. Ltr. Rul. 199925029.
57. E.g., Priv. Ltr. Rul. 199915053.
58. IRC § 170(e)(1)(A); Reg. § 1.170A-4(a)(1).

2. A donor who makes a gift of long-term capital gain tangible personal property (artwork, patent, and such) to a public charity must reduce the deduction by the amount of the gain that would have been recognized had the donor sold the property instead, where the use of the property by the charitable donee is not related to its tax-exempt purposes.[59]

## § 14.5 PLANNED GIVING REVISITED[60]

A charitable deduction for a contribution of less than the donor's entire interest in the property—a gift of a *partial interest*—including the right to use the property, generally is denied. There are exceptions for certain gifts of interests in trust, gifts of an outright remainder interest in a personal residence or farm, gifts of an undivided portion of one's entire interest in a property, gifts of easements with respect to real property granted in perpetuity to a public charity exclusively for contribution purposes, and a gift of a remainder interest in real property that is granted to a public charity exclusively for conservation purposes.

The general rule is that there is no charitable deduction for a contribution of a remainder interest in property unless it is in trust and the trust is a charitable remainder trust (annuity trust or unitrust) or pooled income fund. Defective charitable split-interest trusts may be re-formed to preserve the charitable deduction. Other charitable gifts of remainder interests may be made by means of the charitable gift annuity. Contributions of income interests in property may be made by means of charitable lead trusts.

## § 14.6 ADMINISTRATIVE CONSIDERATIONS

Federal tax law contains many requirements to which a private foundation (or any other charitable organization) must adhere in the administration of a charitable giving program. Chief among these rules are the mandates for gift record-keeping, substantiation, disclosure, appraisal, and reporting.

### (a) Record-Keeping Rules

As to any type of monetary gift, the donor must, as a condition of a charitable deduction, maintain a bank record or a written communication from the donee showing the name of the donee organization, the date of the contribution, and the amount of the contribution.[61] Some charitable organizations elect to provide this

---

59. IRC § 170(e)(1)(B)(i); Reg. § 1.170A-4(b)(2)(ii). The concept of *unrelated use* is discussed in Chapter 11.
60. A discussion of planned giving from the perspective of private foundations is the subject of § 2.4.
61. IRC § 170(f)(17).

information to their donors as a matter of donor relations. Likewise, some charities, in providing this information, include the information required pursuant to the substantiation rules in the same letter, irrespective of the amount of the contribution. These considerations, however, are of less concern to donee private foundations because the substantiation rules almost always apply.

### (b)  Substantiation Rules

A federal income tax charitable contribution deduction is not available in the case of any charitable contribution of $250 or more unless the donor has contemporaneous written substantiation from the donee charitable organization.[62] This written acknowledgment of the gift must (as illustrated in Exhibit 12.8) provide:

- The amount of any money contributed.
- A description of any property contributed.
- A statement as to whether the charitable donee provided any goods or services in consideration for the gift.[63]

In situations where the charity has provided goods or services to the donor in exchange for making the contribution, this contemporaneous written acknowledgment must include a good faith estimate of the value of the goods or services.[64] Unlike the fundraising practices engaged in by many public charities, however, a private foundation is unlikely to provide any goods or services to a donor in exchange for a gift, because this type of transaction may be self-dealing.[65]

Usually, a charitable donee provides the substantiation information to a donor by means of a letter. Courts are holding, however, that in the absence of a qualifying letter, the requisite substantiation information can be found in other documents pertaining to the gift, such as a gift agreement[66] or a deed.[67]

This rule is somewhat of an anomaly in the private foundation setting. It requires a written acknowledgment, often involving one individual. Suppose individual A establishes a private foundation as a trust, where A is the sole trustee. When A funds the foundation during his or her lifetime, A must make

---

62. IRC § 170(f)(8).
63. Reg. § 1.170A-3(f)(2)(i) and (ii). *See* § 16.2, note 9, for a discussion of this rule in the donor-advised fund context.
64. Reg. § 1.170A-3(f)(2)(iii).
65. Were that to occur, the transaction may well be an act of self-dealing, as discussed in § 5.8(e), assuming the donor is a disqualified person with respect to the foundation (*see* Chapter 4).
66. *RP Golf, LLC v. Commissioner* (2012).
67. *Simmons v. Commissioner* (2009), *aff'd*, D.C. Cir. (2011); *Averyt v. Commissioner* (2012).

the requisite substantiation on a timely basis to himself or herself (assuming, of course, that the gift is in excess of $250, which is almost certain to be the case).[68]

## (c)  Disclosure Rules

A charitable organization must provide a written disclosure statement to donors who make a *quid pro quo contribution* in excess of $75.[69] This disclosure must inform the donor that the amount of the contribution that is deductible for federal income tax purposes is limited to the excess of any money (and the value of any property other than money) the donor contributed over the value of goods or services provided by the charity. The disclosure must also provide the donor with a good faith estimate of the value of the goods or services the donor received. The charitable organization may use any reasonable methodology in making a good faith estimate, as long as it applies the methodology in good faith.[70] A penalty is imposed on charitable organizations that do not satisfy these disclosure requirements.[71] Again, a quid pro quo transaction is arguably prohibited self-dealing for a disqualified person.[72] Usually only a foundation conducting a public fund-raising campaign, a rare instance, would be subject to this rule.

## (d)  Appraisal Rules

There are requirements that apply to contributions of nearly all types of property where the value of the property is in excess of $5,000.[73] By virtue of a rule important to private foundations, however, these requirements do not apply to gifts of money and publicly traded securities.

In the case of real estate, artwork, interests in partnerships, and similar types of gifts to which these requirements apply, the donor must obtain a *qualified appraisal* and attach an *appraisal summary* to the return on which the deduction is claimed.[74] This qualified appraisal must be received by the donor before the due date (including extensions) of the return on which the deduction for the contributed property is claimed.[75] A *qualified appraisal* is an appraisal document that:

- Relates to an appraisal that is made not earlier than 60 days prior to the date of contribution of the appraised property.

---

68. The U.S. Tax Court held that the substantiation rules must be complied with where the donor and the principal representative of the done charity is the same individual (*Villareale v. Commissioner* (2013)).
69. IRC § 6115.
70. Reg. § 1.6115-(a)(1).
71. IRC § 6714.
72. See discussion of incidental and tenuous benefits in § 5.8(d).
73. Reg. § 1.170A-3(c)(1)(i).
74. Reg. § 1.170A-3(c)(2)(i)(A), (B).
75. Reg. § 1.170A-3(c)(3)(iv)(B).

- Is prepared, signed, and dated by a *qualified appraiser*.
- Contains the requisite information.
- Does not involve a prohibited type of appraisal fee.[76]

The information that must be in a qualified appraisal for the charitable deduction to be allowed[77] includes:

- A description of the property in sufficient detail.
- The date of contribution of the property.
- The terms of any agreement between the parties relating to any subsequent disposition of the property.
- The qualifications of the qualified appraiser.
- The appraised fair market value of the property on the contribution date.
- The method of valuation used to determine the value of the property.[78]

A qualified appraiser is an individual who meets all the following requirements.

- The individual either:
  - Has earned an appraisal designation from a recognized professional appraiser organization for demonstrated competency in valuing the type of property being appraised, or
  - Has met certain minimum education and experience requirements. For real property, the appraiser must be licensed or certified for the type of property being appraised in the state in which the property is located. For property other than real property, the appraiser must have successfully completed college or professional-level coursework relevant to the property being valued, must have at least two years of experience in the trade or business of buying, selling, or valuing the type of property being valued, and must fully describe in the appraisal his or her qualifying education and experience.
- The individual regularly prepares appraisals for which he or she is paid.
- The individual demonstrates verifiable education and experience in valuing the type of property being appraised. To do this, the appraiser can make a declaration in the appraisal that, because of his or her background, experience, education, and membership in professional associations, he or she is qualified to make appraisals of the type of property being valued.

---

76. Reg. § 1.170A-3(c)(3)(i).
77. Reg. § 1.170A-3(c)(2).
78. Reg. § 1.170A-3(c)(3)(ii).

- The individual has not been prohibited from practicing before the IRS under § 330(c) of title 31 of the United States Code at any time during the three-year period ending on the date of the appraisal.

- The individual is not the donor or donee of the property, or other type of excluded individual.[79]

In addition, the appraiser must complete Form 8283, Section B, Part III. More than one appraiser may appraise the property, provided that each complies with the requirements, including signing the qualified appraisal and Form 8283, Section B, Part III.

## (e) Reporting Requirements

A charitable donee that sells, exchanges, consumes, or otherwise disposes of gift property, having a value of $5,000 or more, within three years after the date of the contribution of the property must file an information return[80] with the IRS.[81] This information return must contain:

- The name, address, and taxpayer identification number of the donor and donee.

- A sufficient description of the property.

- The date of the contribution.

- The amount received on the disposition.

- The date of the disposition.

A copy of the information return must be provided to the donor and retained by the charitable organization.

## (f) State Fundraising Regulation

Nearly all of the states and some cities have a *charitable solicitation act.* This is a statute requiring a charitable organization soliciting contributions in the state to, in advance of the fundraising, register with the state. Thereafter, annual reports are required, and several other obligations may be imposed on the charity. These acts are rarely applicable to private foundations, however, which, by nature, infrequently solicit charitable gifts.[82]

---

79. This definition is contained in Reg. § 1.170A-13(c)(5) before revision for changes to IRC § 170(f)(11) by the Pension Protection Act. See IRS Publication 561, *Determining the Value of Donated Property.*
80. IRS Form 8282.
81. IRC § 6050L.
82. This body of law is detailed in *Fundraising*, Chapters 3–4.

# CHAPTER FIFTEEN

# Private Foundations and Public Charities

# § 15.1  DISTINCTIONS BETWEEN PUBLIC AND PRIVATE CHARITIES

The significance of public charity status for organizations that are tax-exempt charitable organizations[1] is multifaceted, and is of utmost importance to both private and public exempt organizations. Knowing the meaning of the four parts of a particular section of the Internal Revenue Code[2] is the key to understanding the concept of public charities. *All* charitable organizations, other than those included in the four subsections in the following list, are private foundations and are subject to the operational constraints imposed on private foundations.[3] The four categories of public charities are:

1.  § 501(a)(1)—Organizations engaging in inherently public activity and those supported by the public

2.  § 509(a)(2)—Organizations supported by fee-for-service revenue

3.  § 509(a)(3)—Supporting organizations

4.  § 509(a)(4)—Organizations that test for public safety

Private foundations must comply with a variety of special rules and sanctions; these constraints generally are not applicable to public charities. Therefore, it is useful, when possible, to obtain and maintain public charity status.[4] The important attributes of private foundations, as compared with the public charities (in parentheses) include (as illustrated in Exhibit 15.1):

- The charitable giving rules differ between public charities and private foundations.[5] The percentage limitation on deductions for charitable contributions by individuals to private foundations is 30 percent of adjusted gross income for gifts of money and 20 percent for gifts of appreciated property. (Up to 50 percent of an individual's income can be deducted for cash gifts to public charities and 30 percent for gifts of

---

1.  That is, organizations that are described in IRC § 501(c)(3) and tax-exempt by reason of IRC § 501(a).
2.  IRC § 509.
3.  *See* Chapters 5–9.
4.  Despite the fact that these rules have been in existence in excess of 40 years, there still is confusion surrounding them. This phenomenon was reflected in a decision by a federal court of appeals, which twice misstated the law as to private foundations and public charities, yet nonetheless managed to reach the correct conclusion (*Stanbury Law Firm, P.A. v. Internal Revenue Service*, 221 F.3d 1059 (8th Cir. 2000)).
5.  *See* Chapter 14.

**EXHIBIT 15.1**

Differences between Public and Private Charitable Organizations

| | Charitable Deduction | Excise Tax | Activities | Minimum Distribution Requirements | Annual Filings |
|---|---|---|---|---|---|
| Private Foundations (PFs) | • Limited to 30% of adjusted gross income for cash<br>• Other property limited to 20% and basis<br>• Limits on grants to other PFs<br>• Self-initiated projects | • 1–2% of investment income<br>• 10–30% of disqualified transactions | • Grants to other organizations<br>• No lobbying | • 5% of fair market value for investment assets | • All must file Form 990-PF |
| Private Operating Foundations (POFs) | • Limited to 30% for appreciated property, 50% for cash | • Same as for PFs<br>• No lobbying | • Carries out self-initiated projects | • 3⅓% fair market value investment assets | • Same as for private foundation |
| Public Charities | • Same as for POFs | • No tax on income (except UBI)<br>• Excise tax on excess lobbying activities | • Can lobby<br>• Grant-making or carry out own projects | • None<br>• No excess accumulation of surplus | • File if gross revenue over $25,000. Form 990 or 990-EZ, 990N, if < $25,000. |

■  **717**  ■

appreciated property.) To illustrate, assume that an individual with an income of $1 million wants to annually give $500,000 in cash for charitable pursuits. If it is given to a private foundation, $300,000 of the annual gift would be deductible for the year of the gift. The full $500,000 is deductible for the gift year if it is given to a public charity.

- Appreciated property generally is not fully deductible when given to a private foundation—only the basis of real estate, closely held company stock, or other types of property is deductible.[6] The fair market value of shares of qualified appreciated stock contributed to a private foundation may, however, be fully deductible.[7] A full deduction for the market value of the property is potentially available for a gift of this type of property to a public charity.

- An excise tax of 1 to 2 percent must be paid on a private foundation's investment income.[8] There is no tax on investment income for a public charity unless the unrelated business income tax applies.[9]

- A private foundation cannot buy or sell property, nor enter into most self-dealing transactions with its directors, officers, contributors, or their family members. Public charities can have business dealings with their insiders, within limits.[10]

- Annual information returns must be filed by private foundations regardless of revenue levels and value of assets. A return is not required for certain public organizations, and a short form is available for many others.[11]

- Private foundations cannot make grants to noncharitable organizations (albeit for charitable purposes) without compliance with expenditure responsibility rules, which require contracts and follow-up procedures.[12] No such policing of grant monies is required for public charities.

- Lobbying activity by private foundations is generally not permitted, while a limited amount of lobbying is allowed by public charities. Absolutely no political campaign activity is permissible for public or private charities.[13]

- A private foundation's annual spending for grants to other organizations and charitable projects must meet the minimum distribution requirements. A public charity rarely has any specific spending requirement.[14]

---

6. IRC § 170(e)(1)(B), (e)(5).
7. *See* § 14.4(b).
8. *See* Chapter 10.
9. *See* Chapter 11.
10. *See* Chapter 5 (concerning private inurement and self-dealing).
11. *See* Chapter 12.
12. *See* § 9.6.
13. *See* Chapter 9.
14. *See* Chapter 6.

- Holding more than 20 percent of a business enterprise, including shares owned by board members and contributors, is generally prohibited for private foundations,[15] as are jeopardizing investments.[16] Limits of this nature are not placed on most public charities.

## § 15.2 EVOLUTION OF LAW OF PRIVATE FOUNDATIONS

Essential to an understanding of the special federal tax rules applicable to private foundations is the tax law definition of the term *private foundation*. Prior to enactment of the Tax Reform Act of 1969, however, there was no statutory definition of that term. Up to that time, a private foundation generally was recognized as a charitable organization to which contributions could be made that were deductible in an amount up to 20 percent of an individual donor's adjusted gross income, in contrast to contributions to churches, schools, hospitals, and other public charities, which were deductible to the extent of 30 percent of the individual donor's adjusted gross income.[17]

This 30 percent/20 percent dichotomy was introduced in the federal tax law in 1954, when Congress acted in recognition of the fact that there are distinctive differences in the nature of charitable organizations. In that year, Congress permitted an extra 10 percent deduction (from 20 percent to 30 percent) for contributions to churches, educational institutions, and hospitals, and enacted other provisions in their favor. In 1964, the privileged class of 30 percent organizations was expanded to include other public and publicly supported organizations, and a five-year carryover of excess contributions was added for gifts to these organizations.

By the mid-1960s, the likelihood that alleged private foundation abuses would eventually result in statutory modifications was on the increase. A *Treasury Department Report on Private Foundations*, issued in 1965, emphasized the view that there was a need for more public involvement in the operation of philanthropic institutions that benefit from preferential treatment under the tax laws. Failing direct public involvement, the *Treasury Report* stated that there should be an assurance through other means (namely, governmental regulation) that funds set aside for appropriate charitable purposes will find their way promptly into the hands of those institutions where there is assurance of public control and operation.

Congress, having become convinced that there were problems concerning charitable organizations that needed remedy, believed that these problems were especially prevalent in the case of organizations in the 20 percent deduction category. On the other hand, it was also apparent that most organizations in the 30 percent deduction group were not involved in these problems. Consequently,

---

15. *See* Chapter 7.
16. *See* Chapter 8.
17. IRC § 170(b)(1) (pre–1969 Act).

in enacting a definition of the term *private foundation*, Congress conjured up a statute that provides that a private foundation is any domestic or foreign charitable organization,[18] other than four categories of organizations.[19] Indeed, the law presumes that every charitable organization is a private foundation and places the burden of demonstrating that it is not a private foundation on the charitable organization.[20] Organizations that are deemed not to be private foundations are *public charities*.

The organizations that comprise nearly all public charities[21] are those that either have broad public support or involvement or that actively function in a supporting relationship to public or publicly supported charities.[22] The fourth category of nonprivate foundation includes the organizations organized and operated exclusively for testing for public safety.[23] Contributions to public safety testing organizations are not deductible; according to the 1965 *Treasury Report*, these organizations are more analogous to business leagues, social welfare organizations, and similar tax-exempt groups than to private foundations.

Despite the technicalities of the term *private foundation* accorded to it by Congress, a private foundation essentially is a charitable organization that is funded from one source (usually one individual, family, or corporation). While private foundations may receive a consistent flow of ongoing donations, most do not. Most foundations receive a significant part, and in some cases all, of their funding from investment income earned on their endowments and other unrestricted fund balances. The typical private foundation makes grants for charitable purposes to other organizations rather than conduct its own programs. The *private* aspect of a private foundation, then, principally reflects the nature of its financial support as well as the nature of its governance.

There are, therefore, four general categories of charitable organizations that are *not* private foundations. These are the *public* institutions, the *publicly supported* charitable organizations, the *supporting* organizations, and organizations that test for public safety. An organization may not escape private foundation status by qualifying for tax exemption as a social welfare organization if it also meets the definition of a charitable organization.[24]

If an organization was a private foundation on October 9, 1969, or became a private foundation on a subsequent date, the organization must be treated as a private foundation for all periods after that date unless its private foundation

---

18. That is, an organization described in IRC § 501(c)(3) (and exempt from federal income taxation under IRC § 501(a) for that reason).
19. IRC § 509(a); Reg. §§ 1.509(d)-1, 1.509(e)-1.
20. IRC § 508(b).
21. That is, entities described in IRC § 509(a)(1), (2), or (3).
22. Reg. § 1.509(a)-1.
23. That is, entities described in IRC § 509(a)(4).
24. Gen. Couns. Mem. 37485.

status is terminated.[25] If an organization qualifies as a charitable entity and was a private foundation on October 9, 1969, it must be treated as a private foundation for all subsequent periods, even though it may also satisfy the requirements for another category of tax-exempt status.[26] Thus, for example, a charitable organization in existence on October 9, 1969, is treated as a private foundation (absent termination of status) even though it also qualified as an exempt social welfare organization.[27]

A charitable organization that cannot (or subsequently fails to) qualify as a public charity becomes, by operation of law, a private foundation, due to the statutory presumption to that effect.[28]

# § 15.3   ORGANIZATIONS WITH INHERENTLY PUBLIC ACTIVITY

Churches, schools, colleges, universities, hospitals, medical research organizations, and governmental units qualify as public charities by reason of the inherently exempt nature of their program activities. These include many of the *institutions* to be found in the charitable sector.[29]

Organizations in other categories of nonprivate foundation status may also have the attributes of institutions (such as museums and libraries), but they must qualify, if they can, under another category of public charity. The institutions that are public charities in this category are those that satisfy the requirements of at least one category of public institution. That is, these public institutions are not private foundations by reason of the nature of their programmatic activities (rather than by reason of how they are funded[30] or their relationship with one or more other tax-exempt organizations).[31]

## (a)   Churches and Similar Entities

A church or a convention or association of churches is a public charity.[32] The IRS formulated criteria that it uses to ascertain whether a religious organization constitutes a *church*. Originally these criteria, unveiled in 1977, were in a list of 14 elements, not all of which needed to be satisfied. These elements include a distinct legal existence, a recognized creed, an ecclesiastical government, a

---

25. IRC § 501(b). The termination rules are the subject of Chapter 13.
26. Reg. § 1.509(b)-1(a).
27. E.g., Priv. Ltr. Rul. 200846041. *See* § 1.4.
28. IRC § 508(b).
29. IRC § 509(a)(1). These institutions essentially are those in the former 30 percent deduction category (*see* § 15.2) (Reg. §§ 1.170A- 9(a)(3), 1.509(a)-2).
30. *See* §§ 15.4, 15.5.
31. *See* § 15.7.
32. IRC § 170(b)(1)(A)(i); Reg. § 1.170A-9(a). An example of a religious organization that failed to qualify as a church and constituted a private foundation appears in *First Church of In Theo v. Commissioner*, 56 T.C.M. 1045 (1989).

distinct religious history, a literature of its own, and schools for the religious instruction of youth and preparation of its ministers.

Over the ensuing years, however, the federal tax law in this context has radically changed. In part this is due to a shift in emphasis by the IRS, which has downgraded in importance some of the criteria in the 14-element list, concluding they are common to tax-exempt organizations in general.[33] It is currently the position of the agency that, to be a church, an organization must have a defined congregation of worshippers, an established place of worship, and regular worship services.[34] Coincidentally, a major court opinion held that, for a religious entity to qualify as a church, it must meet an *associated test*.[35] This test and the contemporary IRS ruling policy are much the same. Thus, today the IRS is issuing private letter rulings, finding that an organization is not a church, because it did not satisfy the IRS core criteria,[36] it failed the associational test,[37] or both.[38]

The IRS ruled that a tax-exempt organization, the membership of which is composed of churches of different denominations, qualifies as an association of churches.[39] Another type of religious public charity is the integrated auxiliary of a church; in one instance, however, the IRS revoked the exempt status of an ostensible auxiliary when the agency discovered that it was formed without the knowledge of the church.[40]

## (b) Educational Institutions

An "educational organization which normally maintains a regular faculty and curriculum and normally has a regularly enrolled body of pupils or students in attendance at the place where its educational activities are regularly carried on" is a public charity.[41] This type of institution is essentially a school; consequently it must have as its primary function the presentation of formal

---

33. E.g., Priv. Ltr. Rul. 200727021.
34. E.g., Tech. Adv. Mem. 200437040.
35. *Foundation of Human Understanding v. United States*, 2009-2 U.S.T.C. ¶ 50,519 (U.S. Ct. Fed. Cl. (2009), *aff'd*, 614 F.3d 1383 (Fed. Cir. 2010), *cert. den.*, 131 S. Ct. 1676 (2011)). Thereafter, the U.S. Tax Court found a religious organization to be a church, on the basis of the traditional IRS criteria and without reference to the *Foundation of Human Understanding* opinion (*Chambers v. Commissioner*, 101 T.C.M. 1550 (2011)).
36. E.g., Priv. Ltr. Rul. 201242014. Because of the place-of-worship requirement, the IRS has held that an entity conducting services by means of the Internet cannot qualify as a church (e.g., Priv. Ltr. Rul. 201232034), nor can an entity that conducts its services by tele-conference (e.g., Priv. Ltr. Rul. 200926049).
37. E.g., Priv. Ltr. Rul. 201232034.
38. E.g., Priv. Ltr. Rul. 201221022. In general, *Tax-Exempt Organizations*, § 10.3; *Tax Compliance*, § 3.2.
39. Rev. Rul. 74-224, 1974-1 C.B. 61.
40. Priv. Ltr. Rul. 201246037.
41. IRC § 170(b)(1)(A)(ii).

instruction.[42] Thus, a tax-exempt organization that has as its primary function the presentation of formal instruction, has courses that are interrelated and given in a regular and continuous manner (thereby constituting a regular curriculum), normally maintains a regular faculty, and has a regularly enrolled student body in attendance at the place where its educational activities are regularly carried on, qualifies as an educational institution that is a public charity.[43]

Educational institutions qualifying for public charity status include primary, secondary, preparatory, and high schools, and colleges and universities.[44] For purposes of the charitable contribution deduction and nonprivate foundation status, these organizations also encompass federal, state, and other public schools that otherwise qualify, although their tax exemption may be a function of their status as governmental units. An organization cannot achieve public charity status as an operating educational institution where it is engaged in educational and noneducational activities (e.g., a museum operating a school), unless the latter activities are merely incidental to the former.[45] Thus, the IRS denied public charity status to an organization the primary function of which was not the presentation of formal instruction but the operation of a museum.[46]

An organization may be regarded as presenting formal instruction even though it lacks a formal course program or formal classroom instruction. Thus, an organization that provided elementary education on a full-time basis to children at a facility maintained exclusively for that purpose, with a faculty and enrolled student body, was held to be a public charity despite the absence of a formal course program.[47] Similarly, an organization that conducted a survival course was granted public charity classification, even though its course periods were only 26 days and it used outdoor facilities more than classrooms, since it

---

42. Reg. § 1.170A-9(b). In one instance, an organization was held to not lose its IRC § 170(b)(1)(A)(ii) classification where it made a grant of over one-half of its annual income to another organization, because the grant did not affect its instructional activities and involved almost none of its employees' time and effort (Gen. Couns. Mem. 38437).

43. Rev. Rul. 78-309, 1978-2 C.R. 123.

44. Examination guidelines for colleges and universities generally defined a *university* as an institution of higher learning with teaching and research facilities, comprising an undergraduate school that awards bachelor's degrees and a graduate school and professional schools that award master's or doctor's degrees. A *college* is generally referred to as a school of higher learning that grants bachelor's degrees in liberal arts or sciences; the term is also frequently used to describe undergraduate divisions or schools of a university that offer courses and grant degrees in a particular field. The term *school* is defined as a division of a university offering courses of instruction in a particular profession. (Ann. 93-2, 1993-2 I.R.B. 39 § 342.1.) In general, the term *school* is also applicable to institutions of learning at the primary and secondary levels of education.

45. Reg. § 1.170A-9(b).

46. Rev. Rul. 76-167, 1976-1 C.B. 329.

47. Rev. Rul. 72-430, 1972-2 C.B. 105.

had a regular curriculum, faculty, and student body.[48] By contrast, a tax-exempt organization, the primary activity of which was providing specialized instruction by correspondence and a 5- to 10-day seminar program of personal instruction for students who completed the correspondence course, was ruled not to be an operating educational organization "since the organization's primary activity consist[ed] of providing instruction by correspondence."[49] In another instance, tutoring on a one-to-one basis in its students' homes was ruled insufficient to make a tutoring organization an operating educational entity.[50]

The fact that an otherwise qualifying organization offers a variety of lectures, workshops, and short courses concerning a general subject area, open to the general public and to its members, is not sufficient for it to acquire nonprivate foundation status as an educational institution.[51] This is because such an "optional, heterogeneous collection of courses is not formal instruction" and does not constitute a curriculum.[52] Where the attendees are members of the general public and can attend the functions on an optional basis, there is no "regularly enrolled body of pupils or students."[53] Further, where the functions are led by various invited authorities and personalities in the field, there is no "regular faculty."[54]

Even if an organization qualifies as a school or other type of "formal" educational institution, it will not be able to achieve tax-exempt status if it maintains racially discriminatory admissions policies[55] or if it benefits private interests to more than an insubstantial extent.[56] As an illustration of the latter point, an otherwise qualifying school, that trained individuals for careers as political campaign professionals, was denied exempt status because of the secondary benefit accruing to entities of a national political party and its candidates, since nearly all of the school's graduates become employed by or consultants to these entities or candidates.[57]

---

48. Rev. Rul. 73-434, 1973-2 C.B. 71. Also Rev. Rul. 79-130, 1979-1 C.B. 332; Rev. Rul. 73-543, 1973-2 C.B. 343, *clar. by* Ann. 74-115, 1974-52 I.R.B. 29; Rev. Rul. 75-215, 1975-1 C.B. 335; Rev. Rul. 72-101, 1972-1 C.B. 144; Rev. Rul. 69-492, 1969-2 C.B. 36; Rev. Rul. 68-175, 1968-1 C.B. 83.

49. Rev. Rul. 75-492, 1975-2 C.B. 80.

50. Rev. Rul. 76-384, 1976-2 C.B. 57. Also Rev. Rul. 76-417, 1976-2 C.B. 58.

51. Rev. Rul. 78-82, 1978-1 C.B. 70.

52. Rev. Rul. 62-23, 1962-1 C.B. 200.

53. Rev. Rul. 64-128, 1964-1 (Part I) C.B. 191.

54. Rev. Rul. 78-82, 1978-1 C.B. 70.

55. *Bob Jones University v. United States*, 461 U.S. 574 (1983).

56. Reg. § 1.501(c)(3)-1(c)(1).

57. *American Campaign Academy v. Commissioner*, 92 T.C. 1053 (1989). In general, Hopkins, Gross, and Schenkelberg, *Nonprofit Law for Colleges and Universities: Essential Questions and Answers for Officers, Directors, and Advisors* (Hoboken, NJ: John Wiley & Sons, 2011).

## (c)  Hospitals and Other Medical Organizations

An "organization the principal purpose or functions of which are the providing of medical or hospital care or medical education or medical research, if the organization is *a hospital*," is a public charity.[58]

For public charity classification purposes, the term *hospital* includes federal government hospitals, state, county, and municipal hospitals that are instrumentalities of governmental units, rehabilitation institutions, outpatient clinics, extended care facilities, or community mental health or drug treatment centers, and cooperative hospital service organizations,[59] if they otherwise qualify. The term does not include, however, convalescent homes, homes for children or the aged, or institutions the principal purpose or function of which is to train disabled individuals to pursue a vocation,[60] nor does it include free clinics for animals.[61] For these purposes, the term *medical care* includes the treatment of any physical or mental disability or condition, whether on an inpatient or outpatient basis, as long as the cost of the treatment is deductible[62] by the person treated.[63]

*Medical research organizations* directly engaged in the continuous active conduct of medical research in conjunction with a hospital can qualify as a public charity. The term *medical research* means the conduct of investigations, experiments, and studies to discover, develop, or verify knowledge relating to the causes, diagnosis, treatment, prevention, or control of physical or mental diseases and impairments of human beings. To qualify, an organization must have the appropriate equipment and professional personnel necessary to carry out its principal function.[64] Medical research encompasses the associated disciplines spanning the biological, social, and behavioral sciences.

An organization, to be a public charity under these rules, must have the conduct of medical research as its principal purpose or function[65] and be primarily engaged in the continuous active conduct of medical research in conjunction with a hospital, which itself is a public charity. The organization need not be formally affiliated with a hospital to be considered primarily engaged in the active conduct of medical research in conjunction with a hospital. There must, however, be a joint effort on the part of the research organization and the hospital pursuant to an understanding that the two organizations will maintain continuing close cooperation in the active conduct of medical

---

58.  IRC § 170(b)(1)(A)(iii).
59.  Cf. Rev. Rul. 76-452, 1976-2 C.B. 60.
60.  Reg. § 1.170A-9(c)(1).
61.  Rev. Rul. 74-572, 1974-2 C.B. 82.
62.  IRC § 213.
63.  Reg. § 1.170A-9(c)(1).
64.  Reg. § 1.170A-9(c)(2)(iii).
65.  Reg. § 1.170A-9(c)(2)(iv).

research.[66] An organization will not be considered to be "primarily engaged directly in the continuous active conduct of medical research" unless it, during the applicable computation period,[67] devotes more than one-half of its assets to the continuous active conduct of medical research or it expends funds equaling at least 3.5 percent of the fair market value of its endowment for the continuous active conduct of medical research.[68] If the organization's primary purpose is to disburse funds to other organizations for the conduct of research by them or to extend research grants or scholarships to others, it is not considered directly engaged in the active conduct of medical research.[69]

### (d) Public College Support Foundations

Public charity status is provided for certain organizations providing support for public colleges and universities.[70] These entities are useful in attracting private giving for these institutions, with the gifts usually not subject to the direction of the particular state legislature.

Specifically, the organization must normally receive a substantial part of its support (exclusive of income received in the exercise or performance of its tax-exempt activities) from the United States and/or direct or indirect contributions from the public. It must be organized and operated exclusively to receive, hold, invest, and administer property and to make expenditures to or for the benefit of a college or university (including a land grant college or university) that is a public charity and that is an agency or instrumentality of a state or political subdivision thereof, or that is owned or operated by a state or political subdivision thereof or by an agency or instrumentality of one or more states or political subdivisions.

These expenditures include those made for any one or more of the regular functions of colleges and universities, such as the acquisition and maintenance of real property comprising part of the campus area; the construction of college or university buildings; the acquisition and maintenance of equipment and furnishings used for, or in conjunction with, regular functions of colleges and universities; or expenditures for scholarships, libraries, and student loans.[71]

---

66. Reg. § 1.170A-9(c)(2)(vii).
67. Reg. § 1.170A-9(c)(2)(vi)(a).
68. Reg. § 1.170A-9(c)(2)(v)(b).
69. Reg. § 1.170A-9(c)(2)(v)(c). For purposes of the charitable contribution deduction, the organization must be committed, during the calendar year in which the contribution is made, to expend the contribution for medical research before January 1 of the fifth calendar year that begins after the date the contribution is made (Reg. § 1.170A- 9(c)(2)(ii), (viii)). In general, Hyatt and Hopkins, *The Law of Tax-Exempt Healthcare Organizations, Fourth Edition* (Hoboken, NJ: John Wiley & Sons, 2013).
70. IRC § 170(b)(1)(A)(iv).
71. Reg. § 1.170A-9(b)(2).

Another frequently important feature of the state college- or university-related foundation is its ability to borrow money for or on behalf of the supported institution, with the indebtedness bearing tax-excludible interest.[72]

### (e)   Governmental Units

The United States, District of Columbia, states, possessions of the United States, and their political subdivisions are classified as governmental units.[73] An important point is that this type of a unit qualifies as a public charity without regard to its sources of support, partly because, by its nature, it is responsive to all citizens.[74] The regulations do not contain an additional definition or explanation of the meaning of the term. A *governmental unit* presumably encompasses not only political subdivisions of states and the like, but also government instrumentalities, agencies, and entities referenced by similar terms. The distinction between a *political subdivision* and an *instrumentality* was made by the IRS in 1975, when it observed that a county is a political subdivision of a state and that an association of counties is a wholly owned instrumentality of the counties,[75] on the basis of criteria promulgated in 1957.[76]

An unincorporated intergovernmental cooperative organization established by an act of a state legislature on behalf of a consortium of 11 of the state's public school districts was found to be a private foundation, not a governmental unit, for two reasons:[77]

1.   Its source of support was a private foundation that granted the money to undertake the curriculum research and development.

2.   Although the cooperative arguably was an instrumentality of the state, it had no sovereign powers, such as the right of eminent domain, the power to assess and collect taxes, or police powers. The fact that it was an integral part of a group of governmental units—the public schools by which it was established—did not make it a governmental unit.

## § 15.4   PUBLICLY SUPPORTED ORGANIZATIONS— DONATIVE ENTITIES

One way for a charitable organization to avoid private foundation status is to receive its financial support from a suitable number of sources. A publicly supported charity is the antithesis of a private foundation, in that

---

72.   IRC § 103.
73.   IRC § 170(c)(1).
74.   IRC § 170(b)(1)(A)(v); Reg. § 1.170A-9(d).
75.   Rev. Rul. 75-359, 1975-2 C.B. 79.
76.   Rev. Rul. 57-128, 1957-1 C.B. 311.
77.   *Texas Learning Technology Group v. Commissioner*, 958 F.2d 122 (5th Cir. 1992).

the latter customarily derives its financial support from one source, while a publicly supported organization is primarily supported by the public. The law in this area principally concerns the process for determining *public* support.

There are essentially two ways by which a charitable organization can be supported for federal tax law purposes. One is to be an organization whose revenues come from a range of gifts and grants—a *donative* charitable entity.[78] The other is to be an organization that is primarily supported by an appropriate combination of fee-for-service (exempt function) revenue, gifts, and grants—a *service provider* charitable entity.[79] The rules concerning the donative type of organization were enacted in 1954; the rules concerning the service provider type of organization were introduced in 1969. Thus, Congress has provided two definitions of the same type of organization (in a generic sense); although there are substantive differences between the two sets of rules, many charitable organizations are able to satisfy the requirements of both.[80]

## (a)  General Rules

An organization is a publicly supported organization, as a donative charitable organization, if it is a charitable entity that "normally receives a substantial part of its support" (other than income from the performance of an exempt function) from a governmental unit[81] or from direct or indirect contributions from the public.[82]

Organizations that qualify as donative publicly supported entities generally are entities such as museums of history, art, or science; libraries; community centers to promote the arts; organizations providing facilities for the support of an opera, symphony orchestra, ballet, or repertory drama group; organizations providing some other direct service to the general public; and organizations such as the American Red Cross or the United Givers Fund.[83]

The principal way for an organization to be a publicly supported organization under these rules is for it to normally derive at least one-third of its

---

78.  IRC §§ 170(b)(1)(A)(vi), 509(a)(1).

79.  IRC § 509(a)(2). *See* § 15.5.

80.  The donative type of publicly supported organization is generally perceived as the preferred category of the two. For example, only a charitable organization that satisfies the requirements of the donative organization rules (or the rules pertaining to public institutions (*see* § 15.3)) is able to maintain a pooled income fund (IRC § 642(c)(5)(A)).

81.  IRC § 170(c)(1).

82.  IRC § 170(b)(1)(A)(vi). The U.S. Tax Court, faced with interpreting the regulations accompanying IRC § 170(b)(1)(A)(vi), found them "almost frighteningly complex and technical" (*Friends of the Society of Servants of God v. Commissioner*, 75 T.C. 209, 213 (1980)).

83.  Reg. § 1.170(A)-9(e)(1)(ii). An organization otherwise qualifying as a public institution (*see* § 15.3) may nonetheless qualify under IRC § 170(b)(1)(A)(vi) (Rev. Rul. 76-416, 1976-2 C.B. 57).

support from qualifying contributions and grants.[84] Thus, an organization classified as a publicly supported entity under these rules must maintain a support fraction, the denominator of which is total eligible support received during the computation period and the numerator of which is the amount of support from eligible public and/or governmental sources for the period. An organization's support is determined under the method of accounting on the basis of which the organization regularly computes its income in keeping its books.

**Two Percent Gifts.**  A 2 percent ceiling is generally imposed on contributions and grants in calculating public support. Only this threshold amount of a particular gift or grant is counted as public support, whether that contributor or grantor is an individual, corporation, trust, private foundation, or other type of entity (taking into account amounts given by related parties).

Consider, for example, an organization receiving total support of $1 million during the measuring period. In such a case, all contributions and grants up to $20,000 are counted as public support. If one person gave a total of $80,000, or $20,000 each year, only $20,000 is counted. The $1 million organization must receive at least $333,334 in public contributions or grants of $20,000 or less each. It could receive $666,666 from one source and $10,000 from 33 sources, or $20,000 from 17 sources, for example.

> A public gift or grant = Up to and no more than 2% of total support
> $20,000 = 2% of $1 million

Therefore, the total amount of support by a donor or grantor is included in full in the denominator of the support fraction, and the amount determined by application of the 2 percent limitation is included in the numerator of the support fraction. The latter amount is the amount of support in the form of direct contributions and/or grants from the public. Donors or grantors who stand in a defined relationship to one another (such as spouses) must be considered as one source for purposes of computing the 2 percent limitation amount. Support received from governmental units and/or other donative publicly supported organizations is considered to be a form of indirect contributions from the public (in that these grantors are considered conduits of direct public support).[85]

For these purposes, the legal nature of the donors or grantors is not relevant. That is, in addition to individuals, public support can be derived from for-profit entities (including corporations and partnerships) and nonprofit entities (including various forms of tax-exempt organizations). For example, the IRS ruled that contributions made by a business league to a charitable organization seeking designation as a donative publicly supported entity are subject to this

---

84. Reg. § 1.170A-9(e)(2).
85. *Id.*

2 percent limitation.[86] (It frequently happens, therefore, that private founda-tions are sources of public support, albeit subject to the 2 percent inclusion limit.) The fact that contributions are restricted or earmarked does not detract from their qualification as public support.[87]

The 2 percent limitation does not generally apply to support received from other donative publicly supported organizations nor to support from governmen-tal units[88]—that is, this type of support is, in its entirety, public support.[89] Organizations classified as other than private foundations because of their inher-ently public activities also meet the requirements of a donative publicly supported organization.[90] The 2 percent limitation, therefore, does not apply with respect to contributions from these organizations. For example, the limitation does not apply to support from a church, since "in general, churches derive substantial amounts of their support from the general public" and, therefore, contributions from a church are considered indirect public support.[91] Likewise, financial support of a charitable organization from a governmental unit was ruled to not be subject to the limitation because the funds were considered grants for the benefit of the public, rather than gross receipts for specific services.[92] Assistance from a foreign government may be considered allowable support in determining an organization's qualifications as a donative publicly supported entity.[93] By contrast, the 2 percent limitation is applicable to amounts received from a supporting organization.[94]

Nonetheless, the 2 percent limitation applies with respect to support received from a donative publicly supported charitable organization or gov-ernmental unit if the support represents an amount that was expressly or impliedly earmarked by a donor or grantor to the publicly supported organi-zation or unit of government as being for or for the benefit of the organization asserting status as a publicly supported charitable organization.[95] Earmarked contributions constitute support of the intermediary organization under these rules to the extent that they are treated as contributions to the organization under the law concerning the charitable deduction, except where the intermediary

---

86. Rev. Rul. 77-255, 1977-2 C.B. 74.
87. Priv. Ltr. Rul. 8822096.
88. IRC § 170(c)(1).
89. Reg. § 1.170A-9(e)(6)(i).
90. Rev. Rul. 76-416, 1976-2 C.B. 57.
91. Rev. Rul. 78-95, 1978-1 C.B. 71.
92. Priv. Ltr. Rul. 200515021.
93. Rev. Rul. 75-435, 1975-2 C.B. 215.
94. Priv. Ltr. Rul. 9203040, where the IRS also ruled that contributions to the supporting organization are not forms of support to the affiliated supported organization at the time they are made to the supporting organization. The supporting organization requirements are the subject of § 15.7. This private letter ruling also stated that the special rule by which supporting organization grants to service provider publicly supported charities retain their character as investment income (see § 15.5(a), text accompanied by notes 165–168) does not apply to these grants made to donative publicly supported charitable organizations.
95. Reg. §§ 1.170A-9(e)(6)(v), 1.509(a)-3(j)(3).

organization receives the contributions as the agent for the donor for delivery to the ultimate recipient.[96]

All contributions made by a donor and any person or persons standing in a relationship to the donor that is described in the disqualified persons rules[97] must be combined and treated as if made by a single person.[98] These rules stipulate a combination of "a corporation of which persons described in subparagraph (A), (B), (C), or (D) own more than 35 percent of the total combined voting power."[99] An unanswered question in this regard is whether a grant from a private foundation must be combined with donations of that foundation's disqualified persons for this purpose. The regulations do not follow the same alpha labels but indicate that "for purposes of subparagraph (1)(iii)(a) and (v) of this paragraph, the term 'combined voting power' includes voting power represented by holdings of voting stock, actual or constructive (under section 4946(a)(3)), but does not include voting rights held only as a director or trustee."[100]

The Internal Revenue Code provides that *only* for purposes of calculating excess business holdings, a private foundation (i) that is effectively controlled directly or indirectly by the same person or persons, or (ii) to which substantially all of the contributions were made by the same person or persons, or members of their families, is a disqualified person.[101] However, such a direction regarding the combination of private foundation and its disqualified persons is not contained in the public support test regulations. For purposes of the service provider rules,[102] there is no 2 percent test; instead, support from a substantial contributor is excluded entirely, but there is no requirement that all disqualified persons be combined. The provisions of the tax regulations[103] also have no discussion of the 2 percent limitation. Nor do the instructions for Form 990, Schedule A, on which the support ratios are reported and calculated, address the issue.[104]

---

96. Gen. Couns. Mem. 39748. This conclusion is based on the fact that the extent of deductibility of gifts to private foundations is not dependent on any earmarking (e.g., IRC § 170(b)(1)(E)(ii)) and, thus, that gifts to nonprivate foundations should not be treated any differently. In 1992, the IRS, in Gen. Couns. Mem. 39875, withdrew Gen. Couns. Mem. 39748. This occurred because the IRS is rethinking its position concerning *donor-directed funds* and believes that the conclusion reached in the now-withdrawn general counsel memorandum was being applied in circumstances beyond those contemplated. The IRS ruled, however, that contributions to a donative publicly supported organization will constitute *support* under these rules, even though some of the contributors may designate their gifts for one of two specific projects, as long as all of the contributions are expended for the organization's exempt purposes (Priv. Ltr. Rul. 9203040).

97. IRC § 4946(a)(1)(C) through (a)(1)(G).

98. Reg. § 1.170A-9(a)(6).

99. IRC § 4946(a)(1)(E).

100. Reg. § 53.4946-1(a)(5).

101. IRC § 4946(a)(1)(H).

102. IRC § 509(a)(2).

103. Reg. § 1.509(a)-3

104. The authors expect a gift by the donor and his or her private foundation could reasonably be combined for the IRC § 509(a)(1) 2 percent limitation purposes, but cannot prove it.

## (b)  Support Test

A matter that can be of considerable significance in enabling a charitable organization to qualify as a donative publicly supported organization is the meaning of the term *support*. For this purpose, *support* means amounts received as gifts, grants, contributions, net income from unrelated business activities, gross investment income,[105] tax revenues levied for the benefit of the organization and either paid to or expended on behalf of the organization, and the value of services or facilities (exclusive of services or facilities generally furnished to the public without charge) furnished by a governmental unit to the organization without charge.[106] All of these items are amounts that, if received by the organization, comprise the denominator of the support fraction, as shown in Exhibits 15.2–15.4. *Support* does not include any gain from the disposition of property that would be considered as gain from the sale or exchange of a capital asset, or the value of exemption from any federal, state, or local tax or any similar benefit.[107] Also, funding in the form of a loan does not constitute support.[108]

Sponsorship payments that are acknowledged by the tax-exempt organization without quantitative and qualitative information so as to avoid classification as advertising revenue[109] can be treated as contributions for public support purposes.[110]

In constructing the support fraction, an organization must exclude from both the numerator and the denominator amounts received from the exercise or performance of its exempt purpose or function and contributions of services for which a deduction is not allowable.[111] An organization will not be treated as meeting the support test, however, if it receives *almost all* of its support from gross receipts from related activities and an insignificant amount of its support from governmental units and the public.[112] Moreover, the organization may exclude from both the numerator and the denominator of the support fraction an amount equal to one or more qualifying unusual grants.[113]

In computing the support fraction, the organization's support that is *normally* received must be determined. This is reference to support received over a five-year period, consisting of its current tax year (the test year) plus the four tax years immediately preceding the current tax year.[114] If the requisite support is received over this period, the organization is considered to have met

---

105.  IRC § 509(e).
106.  IRC § 509(d); Reg. § 1.170A-9(e)(7)(i).
107.  IRC § 509(d).
108.  E.g., Priv. Ltr. Rul. 9608039.
109.  Reg. § 513-4(c)(2)(iv).
110.  Reg. § 1.170A-9(e)(6).
111.  Reg. § 1.170A-9(e)(7)(i).
112.  Reg. § 1.170A-9(e)(7)(ii).
113.  Reg. § 1.170A-9(e)(6)(ii), (iii). E.g., Rev. Rul. 76-440, 1976-2 C.B. 58. *See* § 15.5(c).
114.  Reg. § 1.170A-9(e)(4)(i).

| SCHEDULE A (Form 990 or 990-EZ) | **Public Charity Status and Public Support** | OMB No. 1545-0047 |
|---|---|---|
| | Complete if the organization is a section 501(c)(3) organization or a section 4947(a)(1) nonexempt charitable trust. | 2013 |
| Department of the Treasury Internal Revenue Service | ► Attach to Form 990 or Form 990-EZ. ► Information about Schedule A (Form 990 or 990-EZ) and its instructions is at *www.irs.gov/form990*. | Open to Public Inspection |
| Name of the organization | | Employer identification number |

**Part I**  Reason for Public Charity Status (All organizations must complete this part.) See instructions.

The organization is not a private foundation because it is: (For lines 1 through 11, check only one box.)

1 ☐ A church, convention of churches, or association of churches described in **section 170(b)(1)(A)(i).**

2 ☐ A school described in **section 170(b)(1)(A)(ii).** (Attach Schedule E.)

3 ☐ A hospital or a cooperative hospital service organization described in **section 170(b)(1)(A)(iii).**

4 ☐ A medical research organization operated in conjunction with a hospital described in **section 170(b)(1)(A)(iii).** Enter the hospital's name, city, and state:
-------------------------------------------------------------------

5 ☐ An organization operated for the benefit of a college or university owned or operated by a governmental unit described in **section 170(b)(1)(A)(iv).** (Complete Part II.)

6 ☐ A federal, state, or local government or governmental unit described in **section 170(b)(1)(A)(v).**

7 ☐ An organization that normally receives a substantial part of its support from a governmental unit or from the general public described in **section 170(b)(1)(A)(vi).** (Complete Part II.)

8 ☐ A community trust described in **section 170(b)(1)(A)(vi).** (Complete Part II.)

9 ☐ An organization that normally receives: (1) more than 33⅓% of its support from contributions, membership fees, and gross receipts from activities related to its exempt functions—subject to certain exceptions, and (2) no more than 33⅓% of its support from gross investment income and unrelated business taxable income (less section 511 tax) from businesses acquired by the organization after June 30, 1975. See **section 509(a)(2).** (Complete Part III.)

10 ☐ An organization organized and operated exclusively to test for public safety. See **section 509(a)(4).**

11 ☐ An organization organized and operated exclusively for the benefit of, to perform the functions of, or to carry out the purposes of one or more publicly supported organizations described in section 509(a)(1) or section 509(a)(2). See **section 509(a)(3).** Check the box that describes the type of supporting organization and complete lines 11e through 11h.

    **a** ☐ Type I    **b** ☐ Type II    **c** ☐ Type III–Functionally integrated    **d** ☐ Type III–Non-functionally integrated

  **e** ☐ By checking this box, I certify that the organization is not controlled directly or indirectly by one or more disqualified persons other than foundation managers and other than one or more publicly supported organizations described in section 509(a)(1) or section 509(a)(2).

  **f** If the organization received a written determination from the IRS that it is a Type I, Type II, or Type III supporting organization, check this box . . . . . . . . . . . . . . . . . . . . . . . . ☐

  **g** Since August 17, 2006, has the organization accepted any gift or contribution from any of the following persons?

| | | Yes | No |
|---|---|---|---|
| (i) A person who directly or indirectly controls, either alone or together with persons described in (ii) and (iii) below, the governing body of the supported organization? . . . . . . . . . . . . . . | 11g(i) | | |
| (ii) A family member of a person described in (i) above? . . . . . . . . . . . . . | 11g(ii) | | |
| (iii) A 35% controlled entity of a person described in (i) or (ii) above? . . . . . . . . . . | 11g(iii) | | |

  **h** Provide the following information about the supported organization(s).

| (i) Name of supported organization | (ii) EIN | (iii) Type of organization (described on lines 1–9 above or IRC section (see instructions)) | (iv) Is the organization in col. (i) listed in your governing document? | | (v) Did you notify the organization in col. (i) of your support? | | (vi) Is the organization in col. (i) organized in the U.S.? | | (vii) Amount of monetary support |
|---|---|---|---|---|---|---|---|---|---|
| | | | Yes | No | Yes | No | Yes | No | |
| (A) | | | | | | | | | |
| (B) | | | | | | | | | |
| (C) | | | | | | | | | |
| (D) | | | | | | | | | |
| (E) | | | | | | | | | |
| Total | | | | | | | | | |

For Paperwork Reduction Act Notice, see the Instructions for Form 990 or 990-EZ.    Cat. No. 11285F    Schedule A (Form 990 or 990-EZ) 2013

**EXHIBIT 15.2**

2013 Form 990, Schedule A, Part I

# PRIVATE FOUNDATIONS AND PUBLIC CHARITIES

**Part II**    **Support Schedule for Organizations Described in Sections 170(b)(1)(A)(iv) and 170(b)(1)(A)(vi)**
(Complete only if you checked the box on line 5, 7, or 8 of Part I or if the organization failed to qualify under Part III. If the organization fails to qualify under the tests listed below, please complete Part III.)

## Section A. Public Support

| Calendar year (or fiscal year beginning in) ▶ | (a) 2009 | (b) 2010 | (c) 2011 | (d) 2012 | (e) 2013 | (f) Total |
|---|---|---|---|---|---|---|
| **1** Gifts, grants, contributions, and membership fees received. (Do not include any "unusual grants.") . . . | | | | | | |
| **2** Tax revenues levied for the organization's benefit and either paid to or expended on its behalf . . . | | | | | | |
| **3** The value of services or facilities furnished by a governmental unit to the organization without charge . . . . | | | | | | |
| **4** **Total.** Add lines 1 through 3 . . . . | | | | | | |
| **5** The portion of total contributions by each person (other than a governmental unit or publicly supported organization) included on line 1 that exceeds 2% of the amount shown on line 11, column (f) . . . . | | | | | | |
| **6** **Public support.** Subtract line 5 from line 4. | | | | | | |

## Section B. Total Support

| Calendar year (or fiscal year beginning in) ▶ | (a) 2009 | (b) 2010 | (c) 2011 | (d) 2012 | (e) 2013 | (f) Total |
|---|---|---|---|---|---|---|
| **7** Amounts from line 4 . . . . . . | | | | | | |
| **8** Gross income from interest, dividends, payments received on securities loans, rents, royalties and income from similar sources . . . . . . . . . | | | | | | |
| **9** Net income from unrelated business activities, whether or not the business is regularly carried on . . . . | | | | | | |
| **10** Other income. Do not include gain or loss from the sale of capital assets (Explain in Part IV.) . . . . . . | | | | | | |
| **11** **Total support.** Add lines 7 through 10 | | | | | | |

**12** Gross receipts from related activities, etc. (see instructions) . . . . . . . . . . . . **12** ▢

**13** **First five years.** If the Form 990 is for the organization's first, second, third, fourth, or fifth tax year as a section 501(c)(3) organization, check this box and **stop here** . . . . . . . . . . . . . . . . . . . . . . . . . . ▶ ▢

## Section C. Computation of Public Support Percentage

**14** Public support percentage for 2013 (line 6, column (f) divided by line 11, column (f)) . . . .    **14**    %

**15** Public support percentage from 2012 Schedule A, Part II, line 14 . . . . . . . . . .    **15**    %

**16a** **33¹⁄₃% support test—2013.** If the organization did not check the box on line 13, and line 14 is 33¹⁄₃% or more, check this box and **stop here.** The organization qualifies as a publicly supported organization . . . . . . . . . . . . ▶ ▢

   **b** **33¹⁄₃% support test—2012.** If the organization did not check a box on line 13 or 16a, and line 15 is 33¹⁄₃% or more, check this box and **stop here.** The organization qualifies as a publicly supported organization . . . . . . . ▶ ▢

**17a** **10%-facts-and-circumstances test—2013.** If the organization did not check a box on line 13, 16a, or 16b, and line 14 is 10% or more, and if the organization meets the "facts-and-circumstances" test, check this box and **stop here.** Explain in Part IV how the organization meets the "facts-and-circumstances" test. The organization qualifies as a publicly supported organization . . . . . . . . . . . . . . . . . . . . . . . . . . . . . ▶ ▢

   **b** **10%-facts-and-circumstances test—2012.** If the organization did not check a box on line 13, 16a, 16b, or 17a, and line 15 is 10% or more, and if the organization meets the "facts-and-circumstances" test, check this box and **stop here.** Explain in Part IV how the organization meets the "facts-and-circumstances" test. The organization qualifies as a publicly supported organization . . . . . . . . . . . . . . . . . . . . . . . . ▶ ▢

**18** **Private foundation.** If the organization did not check a box on line 13, 16a, 16b, 17a, or 17b, check this box and see instructions . . . . . . . . . . . . . . . . . . . . . . . . . . . . . . . . ▶ ▢

**EXHIBIT 15.3**

2013 Form 990, Schedule A, Part II

# § 15.4 PUBLICLY SUPPORTED ORGANIZATIONS—DONATIVE ENTITIES

**Part III**   **Support Schedule for Organizations Described in Section 509(a)(2)**
(Complete only if you checked the box on line 9 of Part I or if the organization failed to qualify under Part II. If the organization fails to qualify under the tests listed below, please complete Part II.)

## Section A. Public Support

| Calendar year (or fiscal year beginning in) ▶ | (a) 2009 | (b) 2010 | (c) 2011 | (d) 2012 | (e) 2013 | (f) Total |
|---|---|---|---|---|---|---|
| **1** Gifts, grants, contributions, and membership fees received. (Do not include any "unusual grants.") | | | | | | |
| **2** Gross receipts from admissions, merchandise sold or services performed, or facilities furnished in any activity that is related to the organization's tax-exempt purpose . . . | | | | | | |
| **3** Gross receipts from activities that are not an unrelated trade or business under section 513 | | | | | | |
| **4** Tax revenues levied for the organization's benefit and either paid to or expended on its behalf . . . | | | | | | |
| **5** The value of services or facilities furnished by a governmental unit to the organization without charge . . . . | | | | | | |
| **6** **Total.** Add lines 1 through 5 . . . . | | | | | | |
| **7a** Amounts included on lines 1, 2, and 3 received from disqualified persons . | | | | | | |
| **b** Amounts included on lines 2 and 3 received from other than disqualified persons that exceed the greater of $5,000 or 1% of the amount on line 13 for the year | | | | | | |
| **c** Add lines 7a and 7b . . . . . . | | | | | | |
| **8** **Public support** (Subtract line 7c from line 6.) . . . . . . . . | | | | | | |

## Section B. Total Support

| Calendar year (or fiscal year beginning in) ▶ | (a) 2009 | (b) 2010 | (c) 2011 | (d) 2012 | (e) 2013 | (f) Total |
|---|---|---|---|---|---|---|
| **9** Amounts from line 6 . . . . . . | | | | | | |
| **10a** Gross income from interest, dividends, payments received on securities loans, rents, royalties and income from similar sources . | | | | | | |
| **b** Unrelated business taxable income (less section 511 taxes) from businesses acquired after June 30, 1975 . . . . . | | | | | | |
| **c** Add lines 10a and 10b . . . . . | | | | | | |
| **11** Net income from unrelated business activities not included in line 10b, whether or not the business is regularly carried on | | | | | | |
| **12** Other income. Do not include gain or loss from the sale of capital assets (Explain in Part IV.) . . . . . . . | | | | | | |
| **13** **Total support.** (Add lines 9, 10c, 11, and 12.) . . . . . . . . . | | | | | | |

**14** **First five years.** If the Form 990 is for the organization's first, second, third, fourth, or fifth tax year as a section 501(c)(3) organization, check this box and **stop here** . . . . . . . . . . . . . . . . . . . . . . . . . . . . . . . ▶ ☐

## Section C. Computation of Public Support Percentage

| | | |
|---|---|---|
| **15** Public support percentage for 2013 (line 8, column (f) divided by line 13, column (f)) . . . . . | **15** | % |
| **16** Public support percentage from 2012 Schedule A, Part III, line 15 . . . . . . . . . . . | **16** | % |

## Section D. Computation of Investment Income Percentage

| | | |
|---|---|---|
| **17** Investment income percentage for **2013** (line 10c, column (f) divided by line 13, column (f)) . . . | **17** | % |
| **18** Investment income percentage from **2012** Schedule A, Part III, line 17 . . . . . . . . . . | **18** | % |

**19a** **33$\frac{1}{3}$% support tests—2013.** If the organization did not check the box on line 14, and line 15 is more than 33$\frac{1}{3}$%, and line 17 is not more than 33$\frac{1}{3}$%, check this box and **stop here.** The organization qualifies as a publicly supported organization . ▶ ☐

**b** **33$\frac{1}{3}$% support tests—2012.** If the organization did not check a box on line 14 or line 19a, and line 16 is more than 33$\frac{1}{3}$%, and line 18 is not more than 33$\frac{1}{3}$%, check this box and **stop here.** The organization qualifies as a publicly supported organization ▶ ☐

**20** **Private foundation.** If the organization did not check a box on line 14, 19a, or 19b, check this box and see instructions ▶ ☐

Schedule A (Form 990 or 990-EZ) 2013

## EXHIBIT 15.4

2013 Form 990, Schedule A, Part III

the one-third public support test for its current tax year and the immediately succeeding tax year. For example, if an organization's current tax year is calendar year 2014, the computation period for measuring public support pursuant to these rules is calendar years 2010 through 2014. If the support fraction requirement is satisfied on the basis of the support received over this five-year period, the organization satisfies this support test for 2014 and 2015.

There are several issues that can arise in computing the public support component (the numerator) of the support fraction for donative publicly supported organizations, including:

- Whether or not a contribution or grant is from a qualifying publicly supported charity.[115]

- Whether or not a contribution or grant from a qualifying publicly supported charity or governmental unit is a pass-through transfer from another donor or grantor.[116]

- Whether or not a "membership fee" constitutes a contribution rather than a payment for services.[117]

- Whether or not a payment pursuant to a government contract is support from a governmental unit (a grant) rather than revenue from a related activity (exempt function revenue).[118]

---

115. IRC § 170(b)(1)(A)(vi) (donative organization).

116. *See* § 3.2.

117. Reg. § 1.170A-9(e)(7)(iii). E.g., *The Home for Aged Men v. United States*, 80-2 U.S.T.C. ¶ 9711 (N.D. W.Va. 1980), *aff'd unrep. dec.* (4th Cir. 1981), where the court found that funds provided to a home for the aged by new admittees are not membership fees but are items constituting exempt function income, with the result that the organization was determined to be a private foundation. Also *Williams Home, Inc. v. United States*, 540 F. Supp. 310 (W.D. Va. 1982), where funds conveyed to a home for aged women as a condition of admission were held to not be contributions; *see* § 15.6(c).

118. Reg. § 1.170A-9(e)(8). An amount paid by a governmental unit to an organization is not regarded as received from the exercise or performance of its tax-exempt functions (and thus can qualify as eligible support) if the purpose of the payment is primarily to enable the organization to provide a service to the direct benefit of the public, rather than to serve the direct and immediate needs of the payor (Reg. § 1.170A-9(e)(8)(ii)). In application of this rule, the IRS determined that payments by the U.S. Department of Health and Human Services to a professional standards review organization are not excludible gross receipts but are includible support, because the payments compensate the professional standards review organization for a function that promotes the health of the beneficiaries of governmental health-care programs in the areas in which the organization operates, thus enabling the organization to be classified as an entity described in IRC § 170(b)(1)(A)(vi) (Rev. Rul. 81-276, 1981-2 C.B. 128). By contrast, Medicare and Medicaid payments to tax-exempt health-care organizations constitute gross receipts derived from the performance of exempt functions, and thus are not includible support, because the patients control the ultimate recipients of the payments by their choice of a health-care provider, so that they, not the governmental units, are the payors (Rev. Rul. 83-153, 1983-2 C.B. 48).

- Whether or not an organization is primarily dependent on gross receipts from related activities.[119]

Government support for an organization that produces a television program aired on government and local access channels; that conducts forums for educating citizens and communities on issues of local interest; that produces and coordinates a training program for city officials and local government employees, businessmen, and interested citizens; that promotes city government month; and that encourages local governments to develop new ways to improve services and operations was found to be a contribution.[120] The language used in the ruling expands the regulation description of the condition under which a government grant is treated as a donation as follows:

> A grant is normally made to encourage the grantee organization to carry on certain programs or activities in furtherance of its exempt purposes. It may contain certain terms and conditions imposed by the grantor to insure the grantee's programs or activities are conducted in a manner compatible with the grantor's own programs and policies and beneficial to the public. The grantee may also perform a service or produce a work product which incidentally benefits the grantor, because of the imposition of terms and conditions, the frequent similarities of public purposes of grantor and grantee, and the possibility of benefit resulting to the grantor, amounts received as grants for the carrying on of exempt activities are sometimes difficult to distinguish from amounts received as gross receipts from the carrying on of exempt activities. The fact that the agreement, pursuant to which payment is made, is designated a contract or a grant is not controlling.

A court held that investment income generated by an endowment fund cannot be regarded as public support, notwithstanding the fact that the endowment principal originated with public contributions.[121] This correct decision may be contrasted with one where a court failed to distinguish between investment income as public support—which it is not—and grants from trusts

---

119. Reg. § 1.170A-9(e)(7)(ii). One of the similarities between a donative publicly supported organization and a state-university related foundation (*see* § 15.3(d)) is that both must normally receive a substantial part of their support from governmental sources and/or contributions from the public. There is a difference, however, in respect to the measurement of allowable governmental support. For purposes of publicly supported organizations (IRC § 170(b)(1)(A)(vi)), governmental sources are a state, a U.S. possession, a political subdivision of the foregoing, or the United States or the District of Columbia (IRC § 170(c)(1)), while for purposes of the state university related "foundation" (IRC § 170(b)(1)(A)(iv)), governmental sources are the United States or a state, or any political subdivision thereof. Thus, the sources of qualifying government support for an IRC § 170(b)(1)(a)(vi) entity are broader than those for an IRC § 170(b)(1)(A)(iv) organization (Rev. Rul. 82-132, 1982-2 C.B. 107).

120. Priv. Ltr. Rul. 200515021.

121. *Trustees for the Home for Aged Women v. United States*, 86-1 U.S.T.C. ¶ 9290 (D. Mass. 1986).

that are funded with investment income—which clearly constitute public support, limited perhaps by the 2 percent limitation.[122]

In making these computations, care must be taken in a situation where the organization being evaluated under these rules previously had to make changes in its operations to qualify as a charitable entity. The position of the IRS is that the rules that require, as discussed, a determination of the extent of broad public financial support in prior years "presuppose" that the organization was organized and operated exclusively for charitable purposes and otherwise qualified as a charitable entity during those years. Consequently, support received by an organization in these circumstances in one or more years in which it failed to meet the requirements for a charitable entity cannot be considered in ascertaining its status as a publicly supported charitable organization.[123]

## (c) Facts and Circumstances Test

One of the defects of the donative organization support rules is that organizations that are not private foundations in a generic sense, because they have many of the attributes of a public organization, may be classified as private foundations because they cannot meet the precise mechanical one-third test. Organizations in this position include museums and libraries that principally rely on their endowments for financial support and thus have little or no need for contributions and grants. Although the statutory law is silent on the point, the tax regulations offer some relief in this regard, by means of the *facts and circumstances test.*

The history of the organization's fundraising efforts and other factors can be considered as an alternative method to the strict mathematical formula for qualifying for public support under the general donative charitable entity rules. This test is not available in connection with the service provider entity rules. These factors must be present for this test to be met:[124]

- Public support must be at least 10 percent of the total support; the higher the better.

---

122. *St. John's Orphanage, Inc. v. United States*, 89-1 U.S.T.C. ¶ 9176 (Ct. Cl. 1989).
123. Rev. Rul. 77-116, 1977-1 C.B. 155. The IRS likewise asserted that support received by an organization prior to the date of the filing of its application for recognition of tax exemption, where the application was filed after the 15-month period (*see* § 2.5), cannot be used in ascertaining public charity status (Rev. Rul. 77-469, 1977-2 C.B. 196; Rev. Rul. 77-208, 1977-1 C.B. 153). A charitable organization filed an annual information return (*see* Chapter 12) showing a public support ratio, by reason of IRC § 170(b)(1)(A)(vi), of 99 percent, even though virtually all of its income was derived from a trust; the IRS concluded that an incomplete return was filed for purposes of imposition of penalties (IRC §§ 6501(c)(3), 6652(c)(1)) (Tech. Adv. Mem. 200047048).
124. Reg. § 1.170A-9(e)(3). An illustration of an organization that failed both the general rules and the facts and circumstances test appears in *Collins v. Commissioner*, 61 T.C. 593 (1974).

- The organization must have an active "continuous and bona fide" fundraising program designed to attract new and additional public and governmental support. Consideration will be given to the fact that, in its early years of existence, the charitable organization may limit the scope of its solicitations to those persons deemed most likely to provide seed money in an amount sufficient to enable it to commence its charitable activities and to expand its solicitation program.

- Other favorable factors must be present, such as:
  - The composition of the board is representative of broad public interests.
  - Support comes from governmental and other sources representative of the general public.
  - Facilities and programs are made available to the general public, such as those of a museum or symphony society.
  - Programs appeal to a broad-based public.[125]

The higher the percentage of support from public or governmental sources, the less is the burden of establishing the publicly supported nature of the organization through the other factors—and the converse is also true.

Concerning the governing board factor, the organization's nonprivate foundation status will be enhanced where it has a governing body that represents the interests of the public, rather than the personal or private interests of a limited number of donors. This can be accomplished by the election of board members by a broad-based membership or by having the board composed of public officials, persons having particular expertise in the field or discipline involved, community leaders, and the like.

As noted, one of the important elements of the facts and circumstances test is the availability of public facilities or services. Examples of entities meeting this requirement are a museum that holds its building open to the public, a symphony orchestra that gives public performances, a conservation organization that provides educational services to the public through the distribution of educational materials, and an old age home that provides domiciliary or nursing services for members of the general public.[126]

---

125. Reg. § 1.170A-9(e)(3). In a case concerning the public charity status of a home for the elderly, a court held that the practice of the home to encourage lawyers to mention to their clients the possibility of bequests to the home was inadequate compliance with the requirement of an ongoing development program (*The Home for the Aged Men v. United States*, 80-2 U.S.T.C. ¶ 9711 (N.D. W. Va. 1980), *aff'd unrep. Dec.* (4th Cir. 1981)).

126. The *reliance* rules (*see* § 15.11) for donative publicly supported organizations are in Reg. §§ 1.170A-9(e)(4)(v), 1.170A-9(e)(6)(iv).

## (d) Community Foundations

A community trust (or community foundation) may qualify as a donative publicly supported charity if it attracts, receives, and depends on financial support from members of the general public on a regular, recurring basis. Community foundations are designed primarily to attract large contributions of a capital or endowment nature from a small number of donors, with the gifts often received and maintained in the form of separate trusts or funds. They are generally identified with a particular community or area and are controlled by a representative group of persons from that community or area. Individual donors relinquish control over the investment and distribution of their contributions and the income generated from them, although donors may designate the purposes for which the assets are to be used, subject to change by the governing body of the community trust.[127]

A community foundation, to qualify as a publicly supported organization, must meet the support requirements for a donative publicly supported charity[128] or meet the facts and circumstances test for donative charities.[129] As to the latter, the requirement of attraction of public support will generally be satisfied if a community foundation seeks gifts and bequests from a wide range of potential donors in the community or area served, through banks or trust companies, through lawyers or other professional individuals, or in other appropriate ways that call attention to the community foundation as a potential recipient of gifts and bequests made for the benefit of the community or area served. A community foundation is not required to engage in periodic, community-wide fundraising campaigns directed toward attracting a large number of small contributions in a manner similar to campaigns conducted by a community chest or united fund.[130]

A community foundation wants to be treated as a single entity, rather than as an aggregation of funds. To be regarded as a component part of a community foundation, a trust or fund must be created by gift or like transfer to a community foundation that is treated as a separate entity and may not be subjected by the transferor to any material restriction[131] with respect to the transferred assets.[132] To be treated as a separate entity, a community foundation must be appropriately named, be so structured as to subject its funds to a common governing instrument, have a common governing body, and prepare periodic financial reports that treat all funds held by the community foundation as its funds.[133] The governing body of a community foundation must have the

---

127. Reg. § 1.170A-9(e)(10).
128. *See* § 15.4(b).
129. *See* § 15.4(c).
130. Reg. § 170A-9(e)(10).
131. *See* § 13.3(a).
132. Reg. § 1.170A-9(e)(11)(ii). E.g., Priv. Ltr. Rul. 200204040.
133. Reg. § 1.170A-9(e)(11)(iii)–(vi). E.g., Priv. Ltr. Rul. 201307008, superseded by Priv. Ltr. Rul. 201322046, superseded by Priv. Ltr. Rul. 201403016.

power to modify any restriction on the distribution of funds where it is inconsistent with the charitable needs of the community, must commit itself to the exercise of its powers in the best interests of the community foundation, and must commit itself to seeing that the funds are invested pursuant to accepted standards of fiduciary conduct.[134]

Grantors, contributors, and distributors to community trusts may rely on the publicly supported charity status of these trusts under circumstances that are the same as those applicable to reliance in the case of other categories of public charities[135] or of private operating foundations.[136]

A private foundation can make a grant to a designated fund within a community foundation or other charitable entity that maintains a donor-advised fund program.[137] A foundation can receive a payout credit for the grant,[138] even though it acquires the ability to make recommendations as to distributions to other charitable organizations from the fund. This assumes, of course, that all of the appropriate requirements are satisfied, particularly the absence of prohibited material restrictions.[139] Grants of this nature are regarded as made to the charitable organization to maintain the program and not to a discrete fund (which would likely be a private foundation).[140]

There is nothing in the law that expressly requires a community foundation to serve only a *community*. Indeed, some community foundations operate programs nationwide. Nonetheless, the concept of community foundation (and even the term) would seem to lead to the conclusion that the grant-making activities and other programs of a community foundation should be confined to the foundation's community.

### (e) Community Foundation Compliance Check Project

The IRS, in mid-2007, commenced a compliance check project in connection with the operations of community foundations. This compliance check project was launched with the IRS mailing Community Foundations Questionnaires to 3,700 organizations.

**Demographics.** An organization receiving one of these questionnaires is provided the opportunity to convince the IRS that it is not a community foundation, by identifying itself as a private foundation or a form of public

---

134. Reg. § 1.170A-9(e)(11)(v). Reg. § 1.170A-9(e)(14) provides rules for trusts or funds that cannot qualify as component parts of a community foundation.

135. *See* § 15.11.

136. *See* § 15.1. The reliance rule for community trusts appears at Reg. § 1.508-1(b)(4)(i). Also Rev. Proc. 77-20, 1977-1 C.B. 585.

137. Donor-advised funds are the subject of Chapter 16.

138. *See* Chapter 6.

139. *See* § 16.5.

140. E.g., Priv. Ltr. Rul. 9807030.

charity other than a community foundation. Some of the recipients of the questionnaire are not community foundations.

If the entity is a community foundation, it is requested to identify its legal form, such as a corporation or trust. If the latter, a question asks if the trust is aggregated into a single entity.[141] A community foundation is asked if its "area of service" is defined by geography. If the answer is *Yes*, the community foundation is to identify the geographic area it serves. If the answer is *No*, the community foundation is asked for its definition of the community it serves.

**Revenue and Assets.**  A community foundation is requested to identify its annual support in the form of percentages of contributions and grants, membership fees, investment income, exempt function revenue (such as income from sale of merchandise or performance of services), net income from unrelated business, tax revenues levied for its benefit, the value of services or facilities furnished to the foundation by a governmental unit without charge, and other income.

A community foundation is asked to report the fair market value of its assets at the end of the year. These entities are also asked to provide the amount of assets and the number of accounts in unrestricted funds, designated funds, donor-advised funds, and other funds. The organization is asked if it has "component parts"; if it does, it is asked to report the percentage of the total value of its fund that are component parts.

**Investments.**  Community foundations are asked to list their investments by type and the amounts invested within each type. If investment advice is received from outside firms, the name and address of the firm or firms is to be provided. If donors are able to recommend that their account assets be invested in a particular investment firm or in a particular asset, the community foundation is requested to describe its policy in this regard.

**Grant-Making.**  Community foundations are requested to report the number of grants, and the total value of grants, made during the year. If the organization permits donors to recommend or offer advice as to charitable grant recipients or projects, it is requested to describe its "process and policy for soliciting, reviewing, and accepting or rejecting advice." The community foundation is asked to report the number and value of grants made during the year that were based on donor advice. It is also requested to identify the percentage and total value of annual grants made to charities that serve communities outside the community or geographic area the foundation serves.

**Relationships.**  The community foundation is asked if any member of its governing body or any of its officers has a business or family relationship with

141. *See* § 15.4(d), text accompanied by notes 131–133.

an individual, business, or organization that the foundation is "involved with" or with which it does business. If the answer to this question is *Yes*, the foundation is to identify the trustee, director, and/or officer; the entity with which the relationship exists; and the nature of the relationship.

The community foundation is also asked if any of its board members or officers is related (by family or business ties) to one another. If so, the individual's name and title is to be reported, and the nature of the family or business relationship identified.

**Fees.** The community foundation is asked to report whether its trustees or fund managers are paid and, if so, the total amounts paid. If a state or local law governs fees imposed on its fund accounts, the foundation is asked to report the type and amount of fees allowed by law. If there is no such law, the organization is asked whether it has an established fee schedule for fees paid by a fund and, if it does, to provide a copy of the schedule.

The community foundation is also asked whether a fund pays fees apart from fees paid to trustees or fund managers. If it does, it is to report the amount paid during the year by amount and fee type, including custodial fees, investment advisor fees, distribution fees, up-front brokerage (or financial management) fees, and trailing fees for sales.

The community foundation is further asked whether a fund pays fees for investment advisory services to an entity that is independent of the financial institutions providing trust or custodial services. If the answer to the question is *Yes*, the foundation is to identify the entity and the amount of fees paid to it during the year.

**Staff.** The community foundation is asked to report the total amount paid to its staff. The number of staff in the categories of administration, finance, grant-making, fundraising, and other is also to be reported. If one person performs "multiple tasks," the tasks performed are to be explained. The foundation is asked for the number of staff that reviews donor advice for grants and for an explanation of the background and qualifications of staff members who work with donors on "advice and review of grant recommendations."

## § 15.5 SERVICE PROVIDER ORGANIZATIONS

A charitable organization can be a publicly supported organization as a *service provider* entity. Qualification for the service provider category of public charities is measured by sources of revenue, but there are significant differences in relation to the donative entity rules.[142] Public support for this purpose includes *exempt function income*, as shown in Exhibit 15.4, and thus this category

---

142. The Supreme Court referred to organizations of this nature as "nonprofit service provider[s]" (*Camps Newfound/Owatonna, Inc. v. Town of Harrison, Maine*, 520 U.S. 564, 572 (1997)).

usually includes organizations receiving a major portion of their support from fees and charges for activity participation, such as day care centers, animal shelters, theaters, and educational publishers.

A two-part support test must be met to qualify under this category:

1. Investment income cannot exceed one-third of the total support. (Total support basically means the organization's gross revenue except for capital gains or the value of exemptions from local, state, or federal taxes.)

2. More than one-third of the total support must be received from of a combination of:

   ○ Gifts, grants, contributions, and membership dues received from nondisqualified persons.

   ○ Admissions to exempt function facilities or performances, such as theater or ballet performance tickets, museum or historical site admission fees, movie or video tickets, seminar or lecture fees, and athletic event charges.

   ○ Fees for performance of services, such as school tuition, day care fees, hospital room and laboratory charges, psychiatric counseling fees, testing fees, scientific laboratory fees, library fines, animal neutering charges, and athletic facility fees.

   ○ Sales of merchandise related to the organization's activities, including books and educational literature, pharmaceuticals and medical devices, handicrafts, reproductions and copies of original works of art, by-products of a blood bank, and goods produced by disabled workers.[143]

Exempt function revenues received from one source are not counted if they exceed $5,000 or 1 percent of the support of the organization, whichever is higher.

Subject to certain limitations,[144] the support must come from *permitted sources*. Thus, an organization seeking to qualify under this one-third support test must construct a *support fraction*, with the amount of support received from permitted sources constituting the numerator of the fraction and the total amount of support received being the denominator.[145]

---

143. An organization claimed that the sale of pickle cards (a type of gambling) was revenue constituting a form of public support; the IRS not only disagreed but also found, as did a court, that the revenue was unrelated business income (*Education Athletic Association, Inc. v. Commissioner*, 77 T.C.M. 1525 (1999)).

144. *See* text accompanying *infra* notes 193–199.

145. IRC § 509(a)(2)(A); Reg. § 1.509(a)–3(a)(2).

*Permitted sources* are governmental units,[146] certain public and publicly supported organizations,[147] and persons other than disqualified persons[148] with respect to the organization. Thus, with one exception,[149] support (other than from disqualified persons) from another service provider publicly supported entity, a supporting organization,[150] any other tax-exempt organizations (other than governmental units, public institutions, and donative publicly supported organizations), a for-profit organization, or an individual constitutes public support for the service provider publicly supported organization, albeit confined by these limitations. For these purposes, an organization's support is determined under the method of accounting on the basis of which the organization regularly computes its income in keeping its books.[151]

The term *support*[152] means (in addition to the categories of public support referenced above) (1) net income from unrelated business activities,[153] (2) gross investment income,[154] (3) tax revenues levied for the benefit of the organization and either paid to or expended on behalf of the organization, and (4) the value of services or facilities (exclusive of services or facilities generally furnished to the public without charge) furnished by a governmental unit to the organization without charge. The term does not include any gain from the disposition of property that would be considered as gain from the sale or exchange of a capital asset, or the value of exemption from any federal, state, or local tax or any similar benefit.[155] Also, funding in the form of a loan does not constitute support.[156] These items of support are combined to constitute the denominator of the *support fraction.*

Sponsorship payments that are acknowledged by the tax-exempt organization without quantitative and qualitative information so as to avoid classification as advertising revenue[157] can be treated as contributions for public support purposes.[158] This parallels rules applicable in the donative publicly supported charity context.[159]

---

146. IRC § 170(c)(1).
147. These are the organizations described in IRC § 509(a)(1) (*public* and *donative*) entities described in §§ 15.3 and 15.4.
148. *See* Chapter 4.
149. *See* § 15.5(d).
150. *See* § 15.7.
151. Reg. § 1.509(a)-3(k). *See* Exhibit 15.4.
152. IRC § 509(d).
153. *See* Chapter 11.
154. IRC § 509(e).
155. IRC § 509(d).
156. E.g., Priv. Ltr. Rul. 9608039.
157. Reg. § 513-4(c)(2)(iv).
158. Reg. § 1.509(a)-3(f)(1).
159. *See* § 15.4(b).

## (a)  Investment Income Test

An organization, to avoid private foundation classification, by being a *service provider* publicly supported entity, also must normally receive not more than one-third of its support from the sum of (1) gross investment income,[160] including interest, dividends, payments with respect to securities loans, rents, and royalties, and (2) any excess of the amount of unrelated business taxable income over the amount of the tax on that income.[161] To qualify under this test, an organization must construct a *gross investment income fraction*, with the amount of gross investment income and any unrelated income (less the tax paid on it) received constituting the numerator of the fraction and the total amount of support received being the denominator.[162] In certain instances it may be necessary to distinguish between *gross receipts* and *gross investment income*.[163] For example, interest income earned on a portfolio of microloans that pay dividend and interest income is gross receipts from exempt function activity, not investment income for this purpose.[164]

For these purposes, amounts received by a putative service provider publicly supported organization from (1) an organization seeking classification as a supporting organization[165] by reason of its support of the would-be publicly supported organization or from (2) a charitable trust, corporation, fund, or association or a split-interest trust,[166] which is required by its governing instrument or otherwise to distribute, or which normally does distribute at least 25 percent of its adjusted net income to the putative publicly supported organization, and where the distribution normally comprises at least 5 percent of the would-be publicly supported organization's adjusted net income, retain their character as gross investment income (i.e., are not treated as gifts or contributions) to the extent that the amounts are characterized as gross investment income in the possession of the distributing organization. Where an organization, as described here, makes distributions to more than one putative service provider publicly supported organization, the amount of gross investment income deemed distributed is prorated among the distributees.[167] Further, where this type of an organization expends funds to provide goods, services, or facilities for the direct benefit of a putative service provider publicly supported organization, the amounts are treated as gross investment income to the beneficiary organization to the

---

160.  IRC § 509(e).
161.  IRC § 509(a)(2)(B).
162.  Reg. § 1.509(a)-3(a)(3).
163.  Reg. § 1.509(a)-3(m).
164.  Priv. Ltr. Rul. 200508018.
165.  *See* § 15.7.
166.  IRC § 4947(a)(2); *see* Chapter 3.
167.  Reg. § 1.509(a)-5(a)(1).

extent that the amounts are so characterized in the possession of the organization distributing the funds.[168]

As noted, these rules provide that an organization having or seeking nonprivate foundation status as a service provider publicly supported entity may not normally receive more than one-third of its support each tax year from a combination of gross investment income and any excess of unrelated business taxable income over the tax on that income.[169] This provision arose in 1975[170] because the Senate adopted amendments to postpone depreciation recapture where a controlled subsidiary operating an unrelated trade or business is liquidated into a parent tax-exempt corporation.[171] The Senate acted in this regard for the benefit of the Colonial Williamsburg Foundation, which liquidated a wholly owned subsidiary in 1970 so as to qualify as a publicly supported charity under these rules. The House of Representatives responded with another amendment,[172] however, to treat income from an unrelated trade or business acquired by an organization after June 30, 1975, the same as investment income for these purposes.[173] The House amendment was designed to prevent a change of form, as to the operation of an unrelated business to enable a charitable organization to convert from a private foundation to a publicly supported charity—albeit grandfathering in prior transactions such as the Colonial Williamsburg liquidation.

## (b)  Concept of *Normally*

These support and investment income tests are computed on the basis of the nature of an organization's *normal* sources of support. An organization is considered as *normally* receiving one-third of its support from permitted sources and not more than one-third of its support from gross investment income for its current tax year and immediately succeeding tax year if, for the measuring period, the aggregate amount of support received over the period from permitted sources is more than one-third of its total support and the aggregate amount of support over the period from gross investment income is not more than one-third of its total support.[174]

In computing the support fraction, the organization's support that is *normally* received must be determined. This is reference to support received over a five-year period, consisting of its current tax year (the test year) plus the

---

168.  Reg. § 1.509(a)-5(a)(2).
169.  IRC § 509(a)(2)(B)(ii).
170.  P.L. 94-81, 94th Cong., 1st Sess. (1975).
171.  IRC §§ 1245(b)(7), 1250(d)(9). *See* 121 Cong. Rec. 22264 (1975).
172.  IRC § 509(a)(2)(B)(ii).
173.  *See* 121 Cong. Rec. 24812 (1975). Also Reg. § 1.509(a)-3(a)(3).
174.  Reg. § 1.509(a)-3(c)(1)(i).

four tax years immediately preceding the current tax year.[175] If the requisite support is received over this period, the organization is considered to have met the one-third public support test for its current tax year and the immediately succeeding tax year. For example, if an organization's current tax year is calendar year 2014, the computation period for measuring public support pursuant to these rules is calendar years 2010 through 2014.[176] If the support fraction requirement is satisfied on the basis of the support received over this five-year period, the organization satisfies this support test for 2014 and 2015.

If, in an organization's current tax year, there are substantial and material changes in its sources of support (e.g., an unusually large contribution or bequest), other than changes arising from unusual grants, the computation period becomes the tax year of the substantial and material changes and the four immediately preceding tax years.[177]

A *substantial and material change* in an organization's support may cause it to no longer meet either the public support test or the investment income test of these rules and thus no longer qualify as a service provider publicly supported charity. Nonetheless, its status as a publicly supported charity under these rules, with respect to a grantor or contributor, will not be affected until notice of a change of status is communicated to the public. If the grantor or contributor was either aware of or responsible for the substantial and material change, or acquired knowledge that the IRS had given notice to the organization that it had lost its designation as a service provider publicly supported charitable organization, however, then the status would be affected.[178] But the foregoing rule does not apply if, under appropriate circumstances, the grantor or contributor acted in reliance on a written statement by the grantee organization that the grant or contribution would not cause the organization to lose its nonprivate foundation classification.[179] This statement must be signed by a responsible officer of the organization and must set forth sufficient information to assure a reasonably prudent person that the grant or contribution would not cause loss of the organization's classification as a publicly supported entity.

## (c) Unusual Grants

Under the *unusual grant* rule, a contribution may be excluded from the numerator of the one-third support fraction and from the denominator of both the one-third support and one-third gross investment income fractions. When inclusion of this type of a gift would cause loss of public charity status, the exception is very important. A grant is unusual if it is an unexpected and

---

175. Reg. § 1.509(a)-3(c)(1)(i).
176. *See* Exhibit 15.4.
177. Reg. § 1.509(a)-3(c)(1)(ii).
178. Reg. § 1.509(a)-3(c)(1)(iii)(a); *see* § 15.10.
179. Reg. § 1.509(a)-3(c)(1)(iii)(b).

substantial gift attracted by the public nature of the organization *and* received from a disinterested party.[180] A number of factors are taken into account, and no single factor is determinative. The positive factors are shown in the following list, along with their opposites, or negative factors, in parentheses.[181]

1. The contribution is received from a party with no connection to the organization. (The gift is received from a person who created the organization, is a substantial contributor, a board member, a manager, or related to such a person.)[182]

2. The gift is in the form of cash, marketable securities, or property that furthers the organization's exempt purposes. (The property is illiquid, difficult to dispose of, and not pertinent to the organization's activities.) A gift of a painting to a museum, or a gift of wetlands to a nature preservation society would be useful and appropriate property.

3. No material restrictions or conditions are placed on the transfer.

4. The organization attracts a significant amount of support to pay its operating expenses on a regular basis, and the gift adds to an endowment or pays for capital items. (The gift pays for operating expenses for several years and is not added to an endowment.)

5. The gift is a bequest. (The gift is an inter vivos transfer.)

6. An active fundraising program exists and attracts significant public support. (Fund solicitation programs are limited or unsuccessful.)

7. A representative and broad-based governing body controls the organization. (Related parties control the organization.)

8. Prior to the receipt of the unusual grant, the organization qualified as a publicly supported entity. (The unusual grant exclusion was relied on in the past to satisfy the test.)

The IRS provided an illustration of the unusual grant rule in the case of an organization that received a large inter vivos gift of undeveloped land from a disinterested party, with the condition that the land be used in perpetuity to further its tax-exempt purpose of preserving the natural resources of a particular town. The IRS ruled that the gift constituted an unusual grant and, thus, that the organization's nonprivate foundation status was not adversely affected, even though all of the aforementioned factors were not satisfied and the

---

180. Thus, the term *unusual grant* is somewhat of a misnomer; a better term would have been *unexpected grant*, and the term should also reflect the fact that it also applies with respect to contributions.

181. Reg. § 1.509(a)-3(c)(3). Similar rules for IRC § 170(b)(1)(A)(vi) organizations ("donative"— *see* § 15.4) are stated in Reg. § 1.170A-9(e)(6)(ii), (iii).

182. *See* Chapter 4.

organization had previously received an unusual grant ruling. The IRS cited the following facts as being of "particular importance": The donor was a disinterested party, the organization's operating expenses were paid for primarily through public support, the gift of the land furthered the tax-exempt purpose of the organization, and the contribution was in the nature of new endowment funds because the organization was relatively new.[183]

As an illustration of a proposed contribution that was not sufficiently unusual, an individual agreed to fund the construction of a new facility of a charity if the gift was classified as an unusual grant. The prospective donor had provided a majority of this entity's funding since its inception. The chair and president of the charity is the donor's spouse. The executive director of the charity is the donor's daughter. The IRS concluded that the proposed gift had not been attracted by reason of the charity's publicly supported nature but rather by the charity's historic relationship with the donor. The agency concluded that the proposed gift was "not unusual or unexpected" and that the donor "has shown a history of providing support [to this charity], in significant amounts, to the point where the proposed [gift] of the given amount is not unusual."[184]

The IRS surprisingly ruled, in a situation involving the reorganization of a service provider organization resulting in a second service provider organization and a supporting organization with respect to them, that payments from the original service provider organization to the new one would qualify as unusual grants.[185] This ruling seems inconsistent with the rules that the grant not be derived from a person that created the organization and that, otherwise, disinterested parties be involved.

A potential grantee organization may request a ruling from the IRS as to whether an unusually large grant may be excluded under this exception.[186] The IRS has promulgated "safe haven" criteria that, if satisfied, automatically cause a contribution or grant to be considered *unusual*, if the gift or grant, by reason of its size, would otherwise adversely affect the organization's public status. If the first four factors in the preceding list are present, unusual grant status can automatically be claimed and relied on. As to item 4, the terms of the grant cannot provide for more than one year's operating expense.[187] If the grant is payable over a period of years, it can be excluded each year,[188] but any income earned on the sums would be included.[189]

---

183. Rev. Rul. 76-440, 1976-2 C.B. 621.
184. Priv. Ltr. Rul. 201239011.
185. Priv. Ltr. Rul. 200437036.
186. Reg. § 1.509(a)-3(c)(5)(ii). Advance approval from the IRS that a potential grant or contribution constitutes an unusual grant should be sought by means of filing Form 8940.
187. Rev. Proc. 81-7, 1981-1 C.B. 621.
188. Reg. § 1.170A- 9(e)(6)(ii)(c).
189. These rules do not preclude a potential donee or grantee organization from requesting a ruling from the IRS as to whether a proposed gift or grant, with or without the characteristics, will constitute an unusual gift or grant.

The form requires information submitted on Form 990, Schedule A, to evidence the organization's qualification to exclude the grant. As a practical matter, this guideline relieves the organization of the need to seek IRS approval for the exclusion. Though not required, the organization might choose, in Schedule A, Part IV, to describe its responses to the eight previously mentioned factors in order to provide evidence of its eligibility to exclude the grant as unusual.

These rules may be illustrated as follows:

> During the years 2010 to 2014, A, a publicly supported organization,[190] received total support of $350,000. Of this amount, $105,000 was received from grants, contributions, and receipts from admissions that constituted qualifying public support.[191] Of this amount, $150,000 was received in the form of grants and contributions from persons who were disqualified persons because they were substantial contributors.[192] The remaining $95,000 was gross investment income.[193] Among the contributions was a gift of $50,000 from X, who was not a substantial contributor to A prior to the making of this gift. All of the other requirements of the guidelines were met with respect to X's contribution. If X's contribution is excluded from A's support as an unusual grant, A will have received, for the years 2010 to 2014, $105,000 from public sources, $100,000 in grants and contributions from disqualified persons, and $95,000 in gross investment income. Therefore, if X's contribution is excluded from A's support, A meets the requirements for being a service provider publicly supported organization for the year 2010, because more than one-third of its support is from "public" sources and no more than one-third of its support is gross investment income. Thus, X's contribution would adversely affect the publicly supported status of A, and, since the guidelines are met, the contribution is excludible as an unusual grant. X will not be considered responsible for a "substantial and material" change in A's support.

> The computations to show the effect of excluding X's contribution from A's support are as follows:

| | | |
|---|---|---|
| Total support for A during 2010–2014 | $350,000 | |
| Less: Contribution from X | 50,000 | |
| Total support of A less X's contribution | $300,000 | |
| Gross investment income received by A as a percentage of A's total support (less X's contribution) | $95,000/$300,000 = 31.67% | |
| Public support received by A as a percentage of A's total support (less X's contribution) | $105,000 | = 35% |

> Under the same facts, except that for the years 2009 to 2013 A received $100,000 in grants and contributions from disqualified persons, the result would be different.

---

190. In this example, the organization is a service provider public charity.
191. IRC § 509(a)(2)(A)(i), (ii).
192. *See* § 4.1.
193. IRC § 509(e).

In this case, if X's contribution is excluded as an unusual grant, A will have received $105,000 from public sources, $50,000 in grants and contributions from disqualified persons, and $95,000 in gross investment income. If X's contribution is excluded from A's support, A will have received more than one-third of its support from gross investment income and thus not meet all of the requirements of the support test for 2014. Consequently, even though the guidelines are satisfied, X's contribution is not excludible as an unusual grant because it would not adversely affect the status of A as a publicly supported organization.

The computations to show the effect of excluding X's contribution from A's support are as follows:

| | |
|---|---|
| Total support for A during 2010–2014 | $300,000 |
| Less: Contribution from X | 50,000 |
| Total support of A (less X's contribution) | $250,000 |
| Gross investment income received by A as a percentage of A's total support (less X's contribution) | $95,000/$250,000 = 38% |

As part of the reorganizations of charitable entities,[194] it is common for one charitable entity to transfer assets to a new parent or new subsidiary. Because the transfer is part of the reorganization and where the amount is unusual, the IRS will allow the transferee to disregard the amount transferred in determining its status as a publicly supported entity.[195]

## (d)  Limitations on Support

The support taken into account in determining the numerator of the support fraction under these rules concerning gifts, grants, contributions, and membership fees must come from permitted sources. Thus, transfers from disqualified persons cannot qualify as public support under the service provider organization's rules. In computing the amount of support received from gross receipts that is allowable toward the one-third support requirement, however, gross receipts from related activities (other than from membership fees) received from any person or from any bureau or similar agency of a governmental unit are includible in any tax year to the extent that these receipts do not exceed the greater of $5,000 or 1 percent of the organization's support for the year.[196] Thus, it is frequently significant to determine precisely the persons who are the actual payors (rather than a single entity/payor). The fact that contributions are restricted or earmarked does not detract from their qualification as public support.[197]

---

194. *See infra* notes 317, 318.

195. E.g., Priv. Ltr. Rul. 8510068.

196. Reg. § 1.509(a)-3(b)(1). The term *person*, as used in IRC § 509(a)(2)(A)(ii), includes IRC § 509(a)(1) organizations, so that, for example, rent paid to a tax-exempt medical center by related hospitals constitutes support subject to the $5,000/1 percent limitation (Gen. Couns. Mem. 39104).

197. Priv. Ltr. Rul. 8822096.

In one instance, a nonprofit blood bank entered into agreements with hospitals it supplied with blood, by which the hospitals were responsible for collecting charges from the patients and reimbursing the blood bank. Because of the existence of an agency relationship, the amounts paid to the hospitals were treated as though paid directly by the patients to the blood bank. Thus, each patient was considered a separate payor for purposes of the $5,000 or 1 percent support test.[198] Similarly, because Medicare and Medicaid patients control the recipients of the payments by their choice of a health-care provider, each patient (rather than a governmental unit) is a payor for purposes of this support test.[199]

The phrase government *bureau or similar agency*[200] means a specialized operating (rather than policy-making or administrative) unit of the executive, judicial, or legislative branch of government, usually a subdivision of a department of government. Therefore, an organization receiving gross receipts from both a policy-making or administrative unit (e.g., the Agency for International Development, AID) and an operational unit of a department (e.g., the Bureau for Latin America, an operating unit within AID) is treated as receiving gross receipts from two agencies, with the amount from each separately subject to the $5,000 or 1 percent limitation.

A somewhat comparable *permitted sources* limitation excludes support from a disqualified person, including a *substantial contributor*.[201] A *substantial contributor* is a person who contributes or bequeaths an aggregate amount of more than $5,000 to a charitable organization, where that amount is more than 2 percent of the total contributions and bequests received by the organization before the close of its tax year in which the contribution or bequest from the person is received.[202] Thus, transfers from a substantial contributor (or any other type of disqualified person) cannot qualify as public support under the service provider organizations rules.[203] As discussed, however, grants from governmental units and certain public and publicly supported organizations[204] are not subject to this limitation.[205]

The income tax regulations define the various forms of support referenced in the service provider organization rules: *gift*, *contribution*, or *gross receipts*;[206]

---

198. Rev. Rul. 75-387, 1975-2 C.B. 216.
199. Rev. Rul. 83-153, 1983-2 C.B. 48.
200. Reg. § 1.509(a)-3(i).
201. *See* § 4.1.
202. IRC § 507(d)(2)(A).
203. Since the concept of *disqualified person* is inapplicable in the context of the donative publicly supported charity (*see* § 15.2), however, a contribution from a person who would be a disqualified person under the service provider organization rules may be, in whole or in part, public support under the donative organization rules.
204. *See* §§ 15.3, 15.4.
205. *See* text accompanied by *supra* notes 136, 137.
206. Reg. § 1.509(a)-3(f).

*grant* or *gross receipts;*[207] *membership fees;*[208] *gross receipts* or *gross investment income;*[209] and *grant* or *indirect contribution.*[210] For example, the term *gross receipts* means amounts received from a related activity where a specific service, facility, or product is provided to serve the direct and immediate needs of the payor, while a *grant* is an amount paid to confer a direct benefit on the general public.[211] Any payment of money or transfer of property without adequate consideration is generally considered a gift or contribution. The furnishing of facilities for a rental fee or the making of loans as part of an exempt purpose will likely give rise to gross receipts rather than gross investment income. The fact that a membership organization provides services, facilities, and the like to its members as part of its overall activities will not result in the fees received from members being treated as gross receipts rather than membership fees.

## § 15.6 COMPARATIVE ANALYSIS OF THE TWO CATEGORIES OF PUBLICLY SUPPORTED CHARITIES

The principle underlying the two discrete categories of publicly supported organizations—the donative and the service provider organizations—is much the same, in that both types of entities generally must, to qualify, receive at least one-third of their support from public sources. The principal difference is the definition of public support. Conceptually, the donative organization is one that is principally funded with contributions and grants, while the service provider organization is one that is principally funded with exempt function revenue (such as revenue generated from the sale of publications, admission to programs, and student tuition).

### (a) Definition of *Support*

The items of gross income included in the requisite *support* are different for each category and do not equal total revenue in an accounting sense under either class. *Support* forms the basis of public status for both categories, and the calculations are made on a four-year moving average basis using the cash method of accounting.[212] For purposes of the donative publicly supported

---

207. Reg. § 1.509(a)-3(g).
208. Reg. § 1.509(a)-3(h).
209. Reg. § 1.509(a)-3(m).
210. Reg. § 1.509(a)-3(j).
211. E.g., the IRS ruled that Medicare and Medicaid payments made to health-care organizations constitute gross receipts from the conduct of a related activity rather than grants (Rev. Rul. 83-153, 1983-2 C.B. 48).
212. Reg. § 1.509(a)-3(k).

organizations rules, certain revenues are not counted as support and are not included in the numerator or the denominator:[213]

- Exempt function revenue, or that amount earned through charges for the exercise or performance of exempt activities, such as admission tickets and patient fees.
- Capital gains or losses.
- Unusual grants.

For purposes of the service provider publicly supported organizations rules, total revenue less capital gains or losses and unusual grants equals total support.

## (b)  Major Gifts and Grants

Contributions and grants received are counted as public support differently for each category. For planning purposes, these rules are extremely important to consider. Under the donative publicly supported organizations category, a particular giver's donations or grantor's grants are counted only up to an amount equal to 2 percent of the total support for the four-year period. Gifts and grants from other public charities and governmental entities are not subject to this 2 percent floor.[214]

For purposes of the service provider publicly supported organizations rules, all gifts, grants, and contributions are counted as public support, except those received from disqualified persons.[215] Such a person may be a substantial contributor, or one who gives over $5,000 if such amount is more than 2 percent of the organization's aggregate contributions for its life, or a relative of such a person. For purposes of the service provider publicly supported organizations rules, gifts from these insiders are not counted in the numerator at all. Subject to the 2 percent ceiling, their gifts are counted for purposes of donative publicly supported organizations. Significantly, only donative publicly supported organizations can qualify under the *facts and circumstances test*, meaning the amount of public support can be as low as 10 percent. *Unusual grants* are excluded from gross revenue in calculating total support for both types.[216]

## (c)  Types of Support

Not all revenue is counted as support. The basic definition of *support* excludes capital gains from the sale or exchange of capital assets. Some types of gross revenue are counted differently under differing circumstances.

---

213. Reg. § 1.170A-9(e)(7).
214. *See* § 15.4(a).
215. Disqualified persons are the subject of Chapter 4.
216. *See* § 15.5(c).

*Membership fees* for both classes may represent donations or charges for services rendered. In some cases a combined gift and payment for services may be present, and the facts in each circumstance must be examined to properly classify the revenue. A membership fee is a donation if it is paid by members to support the goals and interests they have in common with the organization, rather than to purchase admission, merchandise, services, or the use of facilities. The regulations say that when services are provided to members as a part of overall activity, the payment may still be classified as member dues (donations).[217] If instead the organization solicits membership fees as a means to sell goods and services to the general public, the so-called membership fees are treated as gross receipts. Particularly for purposes of the donative publicly supported organizations rules, this distinction is very important, because exempt function fees are not included in the public support calculation.

*Grants for services* to be rendered for the granting organization, such as a state government's funding for home health care, are treated under both categories as exempt function income, not donations or grants.[218] A grant is normally made to encourage the grantee organization to carry on certain programs or activities in furtherance of its own exempt purposes; no economic or physical benefit accrues to the grant-maker.[219] *Gross receipts*, however, result whenever the recipient organization performs a service or provides a facility or product to serve the needs of the grantor.

Under both categories, this distinction is important to determine amounts qualifying as contributions. For status as a service provider publicly supported organization, the distinction has yet another dimension. Only the first $5,000 of fees for these services received from a particular person or organization is includible in public support.[220] Monies received from a third-party payor, such as Medicare or Medicaid patient receipts,[221] or blood bank charges collected by a hospital as agent for a blood bank,[222] are attributed to gross receipts from the individual patients.

As noted throughout, Congress continually examines the business, and ostensibly commercial and competitive, activities of most categories of tax-exempt organizations; the service provider entities may receive more scrutiny in this regard than the donative entities, since the nature of their revenues has the

---

217. Reg. § 509(a)-3(h).
218. Rev. Rul. 83-153, 1983-2 C.B. 48, provided similar treatment for state agency payments to a youth care facility.
219. Reg. § 1.509(a)-3(g).
220. IRC § 509(a)(2)(A)(ii).
221. Rev. Rul. 83-153, 1983-2 C.B. 48, stated that these payments are gross receipts from an exempt function, not a government grant, because individuals choose their own health-care providers.
222. Rev. Rul. 75-387, 1975-2 C.B. 216.

potential of appearing competitive with for-profit organizations, particularly in instances of sales of products or the provision of services.

For purposes of annual reporting, unrelated business, limits on deductions for donors, and most other tax purposes, the two categories are virtually the same, with one important exception: To receive a terminating distribution from a private foundation upon its dissolution, the charity must be a donative publicly supported charitable organization.[223]

*Investment income* is subject to a specific no-more-than-one-third test under the service provider publicly supported organizations rules, while donative publicly supported organizations can receive up to two-thirds of their total support from investment income.

Another distinction between these two types of organizations is that supporting organization payments to a service provider publicly supported organization retain their character as investment income (where applicable),[224] while the same payments to a donative publicly supported organization can be considered as grants[225] (although likely subject to the 2 percent limitation).[226]

As discussed earlier in connection with the rules pertaining to the donative publicly supported charitable organization,[227] care must be taken in making these computations in relation to an organization that failed to qualify as a charitable entity during one or more years, since the IRS asserts that support received by an organization during the period of its disqualification cannot be taken into account in determining its foundation/public charity status.[228]

## § 15.7 SUPPORTING ORGANIZATIONS

Another category of charitable organization that is deemed to not be a private foundation is the *supporting organization.*[229]

Charitable supporting organizations usually are those entities that are not themselves publicly supported nor qualified public institutions, but are instead sufficiently related to one or more organizations that are publicly supported or are otherwise public entities so that the requisite degree of public control and involvement is considered present. Thus, the supported or benefited

---

223. IRC § 507(b)(1)(A). Also *see* § 13.3.
224. *See* text accompanied by *supra* notes 150–161.
225. Reg. § 1.509(a)-3(j).
226. Gen. Couns. Mem. 39748 was issued in 1988 to clarify this subject and was later withdrawn by Gen. Couns. Mem. 39875.
227. IRC § 170(b)(1)(A)(vi) (*see* § 15.4).
228. Rev. Rul. 77-116, 1977-1 C.B. 155.
229. IRC § 509(a)(3). The U.S. Tax Court concluded that an organization claiming to be a supporting organization (with that status ignored by the court), that passively rented commercial real estate and distributed its net revenue to a public charity, was instead a (nonexempt) feeder organization (IRC § 502; *see Tax-Exempt Organizations*, § 27.13) (*CRSO v. Commissioner*, 128 T.C. 153 (2007)).

organization is usually a public charity,[230] while the organization that is not a private foundation by virtue of these rules is characterized as a supporting organization. Certain types of noncharitable tax-exempt organizations may be supported organizations.[231] The supported organization generally may be a foreign organization as long as it otherwise qualifies as an eligible entity.[232]

A supporting organization must be organized, and at all times thereafter operated, exclusively for the benefit of, to perform the functions of, or to carry out the purposes of one or more eligible supported organizations.[233] Thus, if the IRS discovers that a supported organization is not a qualified one, it will revoke the organization's supporting organization status.[234]

A supporting organization also must be operated, supervised, or controlled by one or more qualified supported organizations,[235] supervised or controlled in connection with one or more such organizations, or operated in connection with one or more such organizations.[236] These organizations are sometimes referred to as Type I, II, or III organizations, respectively.[237] However, inasmuch as Type III supporting organizations are classified as either functionally integrated Type III supporting organizations or other Type III supporting organizations,[238] there are four types of supporting organizations.[239]

A supporting organization must not be controlled directly or indirectly by one or more disqualified persons (other than foundation managers or eligible public charitable organizations).[240]

A supporting organization may evolve out of a public or publicly supported charity.[241] To qualify as a supporting organization, a charitable organization must meet both an organizational test and an operational test.[242]

### (a) Organizational Test

A supporting organization must be organized exclusively to support or benefit one or more specified public institutions, publicly supported charitable

---

230. *See* §§ 15.3–15.5, 15.8.

231. *See* § 15.8.

232. Rev. Rul. 74-229, 1974-1 C.B. 142. *See*, however, § 15.7(g), text accompanied by *infra* note 326.

233. IRC § 509(a)(3)(A), Reg. § 1.509(a)-4(a)(2).

234. The authors expect a gift by the donor and his or her private foundation could reasonably be combined for the IRC § 509(a)(1) 2 percent limitation purposes, but cannot prove it.

235. The term *supported organization* is defined in IRC § 509(f)(3).

236. IRC § 509(a)(3)(B). Also Reg. §§ 1.509(a)-4(a)(3), 4(f)(2).

237. The *Type III supporting organization* is defined in IRC § 4943(f)(5)(A).

238. See text accompanied by *infra* note 304.

239. In general, Reg. §§ 1.509(a)-4(f)(4), (g)(1)(i). Also, *supra* note 237.

240. IRC § 509(a)(3)(C); Reg. § 1.509(a)-(a)(4). *See* § 15.7(i).

241. E.g., Priv. Ltr. Rul. 8825116.

242. Reg. § 1.509(a)-4(b).

organizations, or certain noncharitable exempt organizations.[243] Its articles of organization[244] must limit its purposes to one or more of the purposes that are permissible for a supporting organization,[245] may not expressly empower the organization to engage in activities that are not in furtherance of these purposes, must state the specified public institution or publicly supported organization (or institutions and/or organizations) on behalf of which it is to be operated, and may not expressly empower the organization to operate to support or benefit any other organizations.[246]

To qualify as a supporting organization, an organization's stated purposes may be as broad as, or more specific than, the purposes that are permissible for a supporting organization. Thus, an organization formed "for the benefit of" one or more public institutions and/or publicly supported organizations will meet this organizational test, assuming the other requirements are satisfied. An organization that is "operated, supervised, or controlled by" or "supervised or controlled in connection with" one or more public institutions and/or publicly supported organizations to carry out their purposes will satisfy these requirements if the purposes as stated in its articles of organization are similar to, but no broader than, the purposes stated in the articles of the supported public organization or organizations.[247]

An organization will not meet this organizational test if its articles of organization expressly permit it to operate to support or benefit any organization other than its specified supported organization or organizations. The fact that the actual operations of the organization have been exclusively for the benefit of one or more specified public institutions or publicly supported organizations is not sufficient to permit it to satisfy this organizational test.[248]

## (b) Operational Test

A supporting organization must be operated exclusively to support or benefit one or more specified qualified supported organizations.[249] Unlike the definition of the term *exclusively*, as applied in the context of charitable

---

243. IRC § 509(a)(3)(A).
244. Reg. § 1.501(c)(3)-1(b)(2).
245. IRC § 509(a)(3)(A).
246. Reg. § 1.509(a)-4(c)(1). The U.S. Tax Court applied these regulations in concluding that an organization was not a supporting organization because the organizational documents of the entity expressly empowered it to benefit organizations other than specified publicly supported organizations (*Trust Under the Will of Bella Mabury v. Commissioner*, 80 T.C. 718 (1983)).
247. Reg. § 1.509(a)-4(c)(2).
248. Reg. § 1.509(a)-4(c)(3).
249. IRC § 509(a)(3)(A).

organizations generally, which means *primarily*,[250] the term *exclusively* in this context means *solely*.[251]

The supporting organization must engage solely in activities that support or benefit one or more eligible supported organizations.[252] These activities may include making payments to or for the use of, or providing services or facilities for, individual members of the charitable class benefited by the specified public or publicly supported organization.[253] A supporting organization may make a payment indirectly through another unrelated organization to a member of a charitable class benefited by a specified public or publicly supported organization, but only where the payment constitutes a grant to an individual rather than a grant to an organization.[254] The IRS ruled that a supporting organization operating for the benefit of a community college may make grants to a capital fund for advancement of a business incubator program, because the resulting educational opportunities are expected to contribute importantly to the college's teaching program.[255]

An organization is regarded as operated exclusively to support or benefit one or more specified public or publicly supported organizations even if it supports or benefits a charitable organization, other than a private foundation, that is operated, supervised, or controlled directly by or in connection with the public or publicly supported organizations.[256] Consequently, it is possible for a supporting organization to ultimately support or benefit a public institution or publicly supported organization by supporting or benefiting another supporting organization, although it is the view of the IRS Chief Counsel that this possibility was not intended and that perhaps the regulations should be revised to preclude that possibility.[257] An organization will not be regarded as operated exclusively, however, if any part of its activities is in furtherance of a purpose other than supporting or benefiting one or more specified eligible supported organizations.[258]

---

250. *See* § 1.6.

251. Reg. § 1.509(a)-4(e)(1).

252. Reg. § 1.509(a)-4(e)(1), (2).

253. Nonetheless, Congress mandated the promulgation of new regulations (*see* Reg. § 1.509(a)-4(i)(3)(iii)) requiring Type III supporting organizations that are not functionally integrated Type III supporting organizations to make distributions of a percentage of either income or assets to supported organizations (Pension Protection Act of 2006, Pub. L. No. 109-280 § 1241(d)). *See* text accompanied by *infra* notes 312–319.

254. The criteria used to distinguish grants to individuals from grants to organizations are the same as those used in the private foundation taxable expenditures context (Reg. § 53.4945-4(a)(4); *see* Chapter 9).

255. Priv. Ltr. Rul. 200614030. The IRS also ruled that any benefit to the companies that receive investment capital from the fund would be incidental (*see* § 5.2).

256. Reg. § 1.509(a)-4(e)(1).

257. Gen. Couns. Mem. 39508.

258. Reg. § 1.509(a)-4(e)(1).

The concept of the supporting organization includes, but is not confined to, one that pays more than a suitable amount of its income to one or more eligible supported organizations. A supporting organization may carry on a discrete program or activity that supports or benefits one or more supported organizations. For example, a supporting organization, supportive of the academic endeavors of the medical school at a university, was used to operate a faculty practice plan in furtherance of the teaching, research, and service programs of the school.[259] As another illustration, a supporting organization to an entity that provided residential placement for mentally and physically disabled adults had as its supportive programs the construction and operation of a facility to provide employment suitable to disabled persons and to establish an information center about the conditions of disabled individuals.[260] A supporting organization may also engage in fundraising activities, such as solicitations of contributions and grants, special events, and unrelated trade or business activities, to raise funds for one or more supported organizations or for other permissible beneficiaries.[261]

A supporting organization has many characteristics of a private foundation, such as, as noted, the absence of any requirement to be publicly supported.[262] Thus, like a private foundation, a supporting organization can be funded entirely by investment income; it can satisfy the operational test by engaging in investment activities (assuming charitable ends are being served).[263]

This being the state of the law on the supporting organization operational test, it was surprising to learn that the IRS retroactively revoked[264] the tax-exempt and public charity status of a supporting organization inasmuch as the organization never made any grants to its supported organization, stating that this failure to fund was a violation of the operational test applicable to charitable organizations[265] as a condition of exemption.[266] The dual status was lost because, as the ruling stated the matter, the organization "failed to contribute any contributions to the intended supported organization." The IRS thus confused the general operational test, used for purposes of qualification for exemption, and the supporting organization rules. From an exemption and supporting organization status standpoint, this organization did not violate any

---

259. Priv. Ltr. Rul. 9434041, superseded by Priv. Ltr. Rul. 9442025.
260. Priv. Ltr. Rul. 9438013.
261. Reg. § 1.509(a)-4(e)(2).
262. *See* text accompanied by *supra* note 209.
263. This point is illustrated by the case styled *Henry E. & Nancy Horton Bartels Trust for the Benefit of the University of New Haven v. United States*, 209 F.3d 147 (2d Cir. 2000). This aspect of the law does not, however, cause the investment activity to be an exempt function to the extent that the unrelated debt-financed income rules (*see* § 11.4) become inapplicable.
264. *See Tax-Exempt Organizations*, § 26.3.
265. *See* § 1.6.
266. Priv. Ltr. Rul. 200903081.

rule. As noted, it can be a charitable purpose for an organization to hold property, including investment property, for another charitable organization; it is common, for example, for a supporting organization to hold an endowment fund. There is no general payout requirement for supporting organizations.

## (c) Specified Public Charities

As noted, a supporting organization must be organized and operated to support or benefit one or more *specified* supported organizations.[267] This specification must be in the supporting organization's articles of organization, although the manner of the specification depends on which of the types of relationships with one or more eligible supported organizations is involved.[268]

Generally it is expected that the articles of organization of the supporting organization will designate (i.e., *specify*) each of the specified supported organizations by name.[269] If the relationship is one of *operated, supervised, or controlled by* or *supervised or controlled in connection with*, however, designation by name is not required as long as the articles of organization of the supporting organization require that it be operated to support or benefit one or more beneficiary organizations that are designated by class or purpose and that include one or more supported organizations, as to which there is one of the foregoing two relationships (without designating the organizations by name), or public institutions or publicly supported charities that are closely related in purpose or function to supported organizations, as to which there is one of the two relationships (again, without designating the organizations by name).[270] Therefore, if the relationship is one of *operated in connection with*, generally the supporting organization must designate the specified supported organizations by name.[271]

Where the relationship is other than *operated in connection with*, the articles of organization of a supporting organization may permit the substitution of one eligible organization within a designated class for another eligible organization either in the same or a different class designated in the articles of organization, permit the supporting organization to operate for the benefit of new or additional eligible organizations of the same or a different class designated

---

267. IRC § 509(a)(3)(A).
268. Reg. § 1.509(a)-4(c)(1).
269. Reg. § 1.509(a)-4(d)(2)(i).
270. Reg. § 1.509(a)-4(d)(2)(i)(b). The IRS denied an organization supporting organization/public charity classification where, after payment of a certain amount to qualified supported organizations, the supporting requirements would not be met (Rev. Rul. 79-197, 1979-2 C.B. 204).
271. Reg. § 1.509(a)-4(d)(4). In one case, the U.S. Tax Court generally ignored these regulations and found compliance with the specificity requirement of IRC § 509(a)(3)(A) merely by reading the statutory provision in light of the facts of the case (*Warren M. Goodspeed Scholarship Fund v. Commissioner*, 70 T.C. 515 (1978)).

in the articles of organization, or permit the supporting organization to vary the amount of its support among different eligible supported organizations within the class or classes of organizations designated by the articles of organization.[272]

These rules were illustrated in the reasoning followed by the IRS in according supporting organization classification to a tax-exempt community trust.[273] The community trust was created by a publicly supported community chest to hold endowment funds and to distribute the income from the endowment to support public or publicly supported charities in a particular geographic area. A majority of the trustees of the community trust were appointed by the governing body of the community chest. The trust was required by the terms of its governing instrument to distribute its income to public or publicly supported charities in a particular area, so that, the IRS held, even though the public or publicly supported charities were not specified by name, the trust qualified as a supporting organization because the community chest was specified by the requisite class or purpose, in that the trust was organized and operated exclusively for the benefit of this class of organizations. Inasmuch as the community chest appointed a majority of the trust's trustees, the trust was ruled to be *operated, supervised, or controlled by* the community chest, so that the *specification* requirement was met.[274]

In another case, an organization, attempting to qualify pursuant to the "supervised or controlled in connection with" category of supporting organization, was unable to satisfy the "class or purpose" test. This organization, according to its articles of incorporation, exists to conduct and support activities "for the benefit of, to perform the functions of, and/or to carry out the purposes of" other organizations "which support, promote and/or perform public health and/or Christian objectives, including but not limited to Christian evangelism, edification, and stewardship." A court of appeals agreed with the IRS and took the position that the "class or purpose" exception applies only where the class of beneficiaries is "readily identifiable." [275] The appellate court noted that, in this charitable organization's articles of incorporation, there is no "geographic limit" and no "limit by type" of supported organization.[276] The court agreed with the government that "it would be difficult, if not impossible, to determine whether the [f]oundation will receive oversight from a readily identifiable class of publicly supported organizations." [277] The organization retained its tax-exempt status but as a private foundation.

An organization that is *operated in connection with* one or more eligible supported organizations can satisfy the specification requirement even if its

---

272. Reg. § 1.509(a)-4(d)(3).
273. Reg. § 1.170A-9(e)(11).
274. Rev. Rul. 81-43, 1981-1 C.B. 350.
275. *Polm Family Foundation v. United States*, 644 F.3d 406 (D.C. Cir. 2011).
276. *Id.*
277. *Id.*

articles of organization permit an eligible supported organization that is designated by class or purpose to be substituted for the supported organizations designated by name in its articles, but "only if such substitution is conditioned upon the occurrence of an event which is beyond the control of the supporting organization."[278] This type of event is stated as being one such as loss of tax exemption, substantial failure or abandonment of operations, or dissolution of the eligible supported organization or organization designated in the articles of organization.[279] In one case, the trustee of a charitable entity had the authority to substitute other charitable beneficiaries for those named in its articles whenever, in the trustee's judgment, the charitable uses had become "unnecessary, undesirable, impracticable, impossible, or no longer adapted to the needs of the public." A court held that the organization failed the organizational test, and thus was a private foundation, because the events that could trigger the substitution of beneficiaries were "within the trustee's control for all practical purposes" since the standard "require[d] the trustee to make a judgment as to what is desirable and what are the needs of the public."[280] The court stated that the organizational test is essential to qualification of organizations as supporting entities because the "public scrutiny [necessary to obviate the need for governmental regulation as a private foundation] derives from the publicly supported beneficiaries, which, in turn, oversee the activities of the supporting organization" and "this oversight function is substantially weakened if the trustee has broad authority to substitute beneficiaries and, thus, it is essential that such authority be strictly limited."[281]

A supporting organization that has one or more public institutions and/or publicly supported charities designated by name in its articles of organization may have in the articles a provision that permits it to operate for the benefit of a beneficiary organization that is not a public or publicly supported charity, but only if the supporting organization is currently operating for the benefit of a public or publicly supported charity and the possibility of its operating for the benefit of an organization other than a public or publicly supported charity is a "remote contingency."[282] Should that contingency occur, however, the supporting organization would then fail to meet this operational test.[283] Moreover, under these circumstances, the articles of organization of a supporting organization can permit it to vary the amount of its support between different designated organizations as long as it meets the requirements with respect to at least one beneficiary organization.[284]

---

278. Reg. § 1.509(a)-4(d)(4)(i)(a).
279. *Id.*
280. *William F., Mable E., and Margaret K. Quarrie Charitable Fund v. Commissioner*, 70 T.C. 182, 187 (1978), *aff'd*, 603 F.2d 1274 (7th Cir. 1979).
281. *Id.*, 70 T.C. at 190.
282. Reg. § 1.509(a)-4(d)(4)(i)(b).
283. Reg. § 1.509(a)-4(d)(4)(ii).
284. Reg. § 1.509(a)-4(d)(4)(i)(c).

A grandfather provision in the federal tax regulations states that a supporting organization will be deemed to meet the specification requirement even though its articles of organization do not designate each supported organization by name—despite the nature of the relationship—if there has been a historical and continuing relationship between the supporting organization and the supported organizations and, by reason of the relationship, there has developed a substantial identity of interests between the organizations.[285]

In general, the federal tax law is vague as to how a supported organization with respect to a supporting organization can be changed, without loss of the supporting organization's public charity status. In a rare private letter ruling on the subject, the IRS ruled that a tax-exempt organization could retain its status as a supporting organization, notwithstanding a transaction in which a supported organization was substituted.[286] An exempt university caused a related support organization to become affiliated with another entity that also functions to support and benefit the university. This ruling is of limited utility in planning a supporting organization substitution, however, because, under the facts of the ruling, the functions of the supporting organization remained essentially the same and it will continue to indirectly support the university.

### (d)  Required Relationships

As noted, to meet these requirements, an organization must be operated, supervised, or controlled by or in connection with one or more eligible supported organizations. Thus, if an organization does not stand in at least one of the required relationships to one or more eligible supported organizations, it cannot qualify as a supporting organization.[287] Regardless of the applicable relationship, it must be ensured that the supporting organization will be *responsive* to the needs or demands of one or more eligible supported organizations and that the supporting organization will constitute an *integral part* of or maintain a *significant involvement* in the operations of one or more qualified supported organizations.[288]

### (e)  Operated, Supervised, or Controlled by (Type I)

The distinguishing feature of the relationship between a supporting organization and one or more eligible supported organizations encompassed by the phrase *operated, supervised, or controlled by* is the presence of a substantial degree of direction by one or more supported organizations in regard to the policies, programs, and activities of the supporting organization—a relationship

---

285.  Reg. § 1.509(a)-4(d)(2)(iv). E.g., *Cockerline Memorial Fund v. Commissioner*, 86 T.C. 53 (1986).
286.  Priv. Ltr. Rul. 200731034.
287.  Reg. § 1.509(a)-4(f)(1).
288.  Reg. § 1.509(a)-4(f)(3).

comparable to that of a subsidiary and a parent.[289] This is, as noted, also referred to as a Type I supporting organization.

This relationship is established by the fact that a majority of the officers, directors, or trustees of the supporting organization are either composed of representatives of the supported organizations or at least appointed or elected by the governing body, officers acting in their official capacity, or the membership of the supported organizations.[290] This relationship will be considered to exist with respect to one or more supported organizations and the supporting organization considered to operate *for the benefit of* one or more different supported organizations only where it can be demonstrated that the purposes of the former organizations are carried out by benefiting the latter organizations.[291]

## (f)  Supervised or Controlled in Connection with (Type II)

The distinguishing feature of the relationship between a supporting organization and one or more eligible supported organizations encompassed by the phrase *supervised or controlled in connection with* is the presence of common supervision or control by the persons supervising or controlling both the supporting organization and the supported organizations to ensure that the supporting organization will be responsive to the needs and requirements of the supported organizations.[292] This is, as noted, also referred to as a Type II supporting organization. Therefore, in order to meet this requirement, the control or management of the supporting organization must be vested in the same individuals who control or manage the supported organizations.[293]

A supporting organization will not be considered to be in this relationship with one or more eligible supported organizations if it merely makes payments (mandatory or discretionary) to one or more named supported organizations, regardless of whether the obligation to make payments to the named beneficiaries is enforceable under state law and the supporting organization's governing instrument contains the private foundation rules provisions.[294] According to the regulations, this arrangement does not provide a sufficient connection between the payor organization and the needs and requirements of the supported organizations to constitute supervision or control in connection with these organizations.[295]

---

289. Reg. § 1.509(a)-4(f)(4), (g)(1)(i).
290. Reg. § 1.509(a)-4(g)(1)(i).
291. Reg. § 1.509(a)-4(g)(1)(ii).
292. Reg. §§ 1.509(a)-4(f)(4), 1.509(a)-4(h)(1).
293. Reg. § 1.509(a)-4(h)(1).
294. IRC § 508(e)(1)(A), (B).
295. Reg. § 1.509(a)-4(h)(2).

## (g) Operated in Connection with (Type III)

Qualification as a supporting organization by reason of the *operated in connection with* relationship entails the loosest of relationships between a supporting organization and one or more supported organizations; this relationship usually is more of a programmatic one than a governance one. This is, as noted, also referred to as a Type III supporting organization. A court nicely observed that this category of supporting organization involves the "least intimate" of the three types of relationships.[296] The IRS believes that most of the abuses concerning supporting organizations reside within this relationship and thus generally disfavors it. Often the IRS views this relationship as the most tenuous one; the agency refers to these entities as "razor edge" organizations.[297]

**Overview.** An organization is a Type III supporting organization only if it meets five tests: (1) it is not disqualified by reason of the rules concerning acceptance of contributions from controlling donors,[298] (2) it does not support any foreign supported organizations,[299] (3) it satisfies a notification requirement,[300] (4) it meets a responsiveness test,[301] and (5) it meets one of two integral part tests.[302]

**Notification Requirement.** For each of its tax years, a Type III supporting organization must provide the following documents to each of its supported organizations: (1) a written notice, addressed to the principal officer of the supported organization, describing the type and amount of all of the support the supporting organization provided to the supported organization during the supporting organization's tax year immediately preceding the tax year in which the notice is provided; (2) a copy of the supporting organization's annual information return that was most recently filed as of the date the notification is provided; and (3) a copy of the supporting organization's governing documents as in effect on the date the notification is provided (unless previously provided and not amended).[303]

---

296. *Lapham Foundation, Inc. v. Commissioner*, 84 T.C.M. 586, 593 (2003), *aff'd*, 389 F.3d 606 (6th Cir. 2004).

297. *IRS Exempt Organizations Continuing Professional Education Program* textbook for fiscal year 2001, at 110.

298. *See* text accompanied by *infra* notes 324–325.

299. *See* text accompanied by *infra* note 326.

300. *See* text accompanied by *infra* note 304.

301. *See* text accompanied by *infra* notes 305–308.

302. *See* text accompanied by *infra* notes 303–322. In general, Reg. § 1.509(a)-4(i)(1).

303. Reg. § 1.509(a)-4(i)(2).

**Responsiveness Test.** A supporting organization meets the responsiveness test if it is responsive to the needs or demands of a supported organization.[304] Generally,[305] to meet this test, a supporting organization must satisfy two sets of requirements.

First, (1) one or more trustees, directors, or officers of the supporting organization must be elected or appointed by the trustees, directors, officers, or membership of the supported organization; (2) one or more members of the governing body of the supported organization must also be trustees, directors, or officers of, or hold other important offices in, the supporting organization; or (3) the trustees, directors, or officers of the supporting organization must maintain a close and continuous working relationship with the trustees, directors, or officers of the supported organization.[306]

Second, the trustees, directors, or officers of the supported organization must, by reason of one of the foregoing three types of relationships, have a significant voice in the investment policies of the supporting organization, the timing of grants, the manner of making grants, and the selection of grant recipients by the supporting organization, and in otherwise directing the use of the income and assets of the supporting organization.[307]

**Integral Part Test—Functionally Integrated Organizations.** A supporting organization meets an integral part test and thus is considered functionally integrated with a supported organization if it (1) engages in activities substantially all of which directly further the exempt purposes of one or more supported organizations, (2) is the parent of each of its supported organizations, or (3) supports a governmental supported organization.

A supporting organization meets the first of these requirements if it engages in activities substantially all of which directly further the exempt purposes of one or more supported organizations to which the supporting organization is responsive by performing the functions of, or carrying out the purposes of, the supported organization(s), and but for the involvement of the supporting organization would normally be engaged in by the supported organization(s).

Activities *directly further* the exempt purposes of one or more supported organizations only if they are conducted by the supporting organization. Holding title to and managing exempt-use assets[308] are activities that directly further the exempt purposes of a supported organization. By contrast, generally fundraising, making grants (whether to a supported organization or third parties), and investing and managing nonexempt-use

---

304. Reg. § 1.509(a)-4(i)(3)(i).
305. There is an exception for pre–November 20, 1970, organizations (Reg. § 1.509(a)-4(i)(3)(v)).
306. Reg. § 1.509(a)-4(i)(3)(ii).
307. Reg. § 1.509(a)-4(i)(3)(iii).
308. *See* text accompanied by *infra* note 316.

assets are not activities that directly further the exempt purposes of a supported organization.

The making or awarding of grants, scholarships, or other payments to individual beneficiaries who are members of the charitable class benefited by a supported organization is an activity directly furthering the exempt purposes of the supported organization if (1) the beneficiaries are selected on an objective and nondiscriminatory basis; (2) the trustees, directors, and officers of the supported organization have a significant voice in the timing of the payments, the manner of making them, and the selection of recipients; and (3) the making or awarding of the payments is part of an active program of the supporting organization that directly furthers the exempt purposes of the supported organization and in which the supporting organization maintains significant involvement.

For purposes of the second of these requirements, a supporting organization is the parent of a supported organization if the supporting organization exercises a substantial degree of direction over the policies, programs, and activities of the supported organization and a majority of the trustees, directors, and officers of the supported organization is appointed or elected, directly or indirectly, by the governing body, members of the governing body, or officers of the supporting organization.[309]

**Integral Part Test—Non–Functionally Integrated Organizations.** In general, a supporting organization meets an integral part test and is considered non–functionally integrated where it satisfies a distribution requirement and an attentiveness requirement.[310]

With respect to each tax year, a supporting organization must, to be in compliance with these rules, distribute to or for the use of one or more supported organizations an amount equaling or exceeding the supporting organization's distributable amount for the year, on or before the last day of the year.[311]

The *distributable amount* for a tax year is an amount equal to the greater of 85 percent of the supporting organization's adjusted net income. This is determined by applying the principles of the adjusted net income rules[312] for the tax year immediately preceding the tax year of the required distribution or the minimum asset amount for the immediately preceding tax year, reduced by the amount of any income taxes imposed on the supporting organization during the immediately preceding tax year. A supporting organization's *minimum asset amount* for its immediately preceding tax year is 3.5 percent of the

---

309. Reg. § 1.509(a)-4(i)(4).
310. Reg. § 1.509(a)-4(i)(5)(i)(A). There is an exception for pre–November 20, 1970, trusts (Reg. § 1.509(a)-4(i)(5)(i)(B)).
311. Reg. § 1.509(a)-4(i)(5)(ii)(A).
312. IRC § 4942(f); Reg. § 53.4942(a)-2(d). *See* § 6.8, text accompanied by note 290.

aggregate fair market value of all of the organization's non-exempt-use assets in the year, with certain adjustments and certain added amounts.[313]

For purposes of determining its distributable amount for a tax year, a supporting organization determines its minimum asset amount by determining the aggregate fair market value of all of its non-exempt-use assets in the immediately preceding tax year. This determination is made using the preexisting valuation methods.[314] The aggregate fair market value of the assets may not be reduced by any amount that is set aside. The non-exempt-use assets of a supporting organization are all of its assets other than (1) certain future interests in the income or corpus of any real or personal property, (2) assets of an estate before their distribution, (3) present interests in certain trusts, (4) any pledge of money or property, and (5) assets that are used (or held for use) to carry out the exempt purposes of the supporting organization's supported organization(s) (known as *exempt-use assets*) by either the supporting organization or one or more supported organizations but only if the supporting organization makes the asset available to the supported organization(s) at no cost (or nominal rent) to the supported organization(s).[315]

The amount of a distribution made to a supported organization is the amount of cash distributed or the fair market value of the property distributed as of the date the distribution is made. The amount of a distribution is determined on the cash receipts and disbursements method of accounting. Distributions by a supporting organization that count toward the distribution requirement include (1) any amount paid to a supported organization to accomplish the supported organization's exempt purposes, (2) any amount paid by the supporting organization to perform an activity that directly furthers the exempt purposes of the supported organization but only to the extent the amount exceeds any income derived by the supporting organization from the activity, (3) any reasonable and necessary administrative expenses paid to accomplish the exempt purposes of the supported organization (other than expenses incurred in the production of investment income), (4) any amount paid to acquire an exempt-use asset, and (5) any amount set aside for a specific project that accomplishes the exempt purposes of a supported organization as long as certain criteria are satisfied.[316]

If with respect to a tax year, an excess amount is created, the amount may be used to reduce the distributable amount in any of the five tax years immediately following the tax year in which the excess amount is created. An *excess amount* is created for a year if the total distributions made in that year that count toward

---

313. Reg. § 1.509(a)-4T(i)(5)(ii)(B). This payout requirement is currently the subject of proposed and temporary regulations because the originally proposed regulations utilized a different distribution regime (akin to the general mandatory payout rule (*see* Chapter 6)).
314. *See* § 6.3.
315. Reg. § 1.509(a)-4T(i)(5)(ii)(8).
316. Reg. § 1.509(a)-4(i)(6).

the distribution requirement exceed the supporting organization's distributable amount for the year.[317]

A non–functionally integrated Type III supporting organization that fails to meet this distribution requirement will not be classified as a private foundation for the year in which it fails to meet the requirement if the organization establishes to the satisfaction of the IRS that the (1) failure was due solely to unforeseen events or circumstances that are beyond the organization's control, a clerical error, or an incorrect valuation of assets; (2) failure was due to reasonable cause and not to willful neglect; and (3) distribution requirement is met within 180 days after the organization is first able to distribute its distributable amount notwithstanding the unforeseen events or circumstances, or 180 days after the date the incorrect valuation or clerical error was or should have been discovered.[318]

Regarding the attentiveness requirement, with respect to each tax year, a non–functionally integrated Type III supporting organization must distribute at least one third of its distributable amount to one or more supported organizations that are attentive to the operations of the supporting organization and to which the supporting organization is responsive.[319]

A supported organization is *attentive* to the operations of a supporting organization during a year if, in the year, at least one of the following requirements is satisfied:

1.  The supporting organization distributes to the supported organization amounts equaling or exceeding 10 percent of the supported organization's total financial support (or perhaps the support of a division of the organization) received during the supported organization's last tax year ending before the beginning of the supporting organization's tax year.

2.  The amount of support received from the supporting organization is necessary to avoid interruption of the conduct of a particular function or activity of the supported organization. The support is necessary if the supporting organization or the supported organization earmarks the support for a particular program or activity of the supported organization, even if the program or activity is not the supported organization's primary program or activity as long as the program or activity is a substantial one.

3.  Based on the consideration of all pertinent factors, including the number of supported organizations, the length and nature of the relationship between the supported organization and supporting organization, and the purpose to which the funds are put, the amount of support received

---

317.  Reg. § 1.509(a)-4(i)(7).
318.  Reg. § 1.509(a)-4(i)(5)(ii)(F).
319.  Reg. § 1.509(a)-4(i)(5)(iii)(A).

from the supporting organization is a sufficient part of a supported organization's total support (or perhaps that of a division) to ensure attentiveness. Normally, the attentiveness of a supported organization is influenced by the amounts received from the supporting organization. Thus, the more substantial the amount involved in terms of a percentage of the supported organization's total support, the greater the likelihood that the required degree of attentiveness will be present. However, in determining whether the amount received from a supporting organization is sufficient to ensure the attentiveness of the supported organization to the operations of the supporting organization, evidence of actual attentiveness by the supported organization is of almost equal importance. A supported organization is not considered to be attentive solely because it has enforceable rights against the supporting organization under state law.[320]

In determining whether a supported organization is attentive to the operations of a supporting organization, any amount received from the supporting organization that is held by the supported organization in a donor-advised fund[321] is disregarded.[322]

**Contributions from Controlling Donors.** For any tax year, a supporting organization is not a Type I or Type III entity if it accepts a contribution from a person (other than another category of public charity)[323] who directly or indirectly controls, alone or together with family members or certain controlled entities, the governing body of a specified publicly supported organization supported by the supporting organization.[324]

**Foreign Supported Organizations.** A supporting organization is not a Type III entity if its supports any supported organization organized outside of the United States.[325]

**Pending Regulation Projects.** Seven regulation projects are embedded in the preamble to these final regulations or in the final regulations themselves:

1. Proposed regulations are to be issued that amend the responsiveness test[326] by clarifying that Type III supporting organizations must be responsive to all of their supported organizations.

---

320. Reg. § 1.509(a)-4(i)(5)(iii)(B).
321. *See* Chapter 16.
322. Reg. § 1.509(a)-4(i)(5)(iii)(C).
323. That is, an organization described in IRC § 509(a)(1), (2), or (4). *See* §§ 15.3–15.5, 15.13.
324. IRC § 509(f)(2); Reg. § 1.509(a)-4(f)(5).
325. Reg. § 1.509(a)-4(i)(10).
326. *See* text accompanied by *supra* notes 305–308.

2. Proposed regulations are to be issued that provide clarification, in connection with supporting organizations that are charitable trusts and satisfaction of the significant voice test, where the trust instrument specifies the recipients, timing, manner, and amount of grants.[327]

3. Proposed regulations are to be issued that will provide a new definition of the term *parent*, in the context of the integral part test for functionally integrated Type III supporting organizations,[328] which addresses the power to remove and replace trustees, directors, and officers of the supporting organization.

4. Proposed regulations are to be issued that will provide guidance on how supporting organizations can qualify as functionally integrated entities by supporting a governmental entity.[329]

5. Proposed regulations are to be issued that will more fully describe the expenditures (including expenditures for administrative and additional charitable activities) that do and do not count toward the distribution requirement.

6. Proposed regulations are to be issued as to whether program-related investments may count toward the distribution requirement for non–functionally integrated Type III supporting organizations.

7. A regulation has been reserved to address the definition of the term *control* in the rules concerning the relationship test for Types I or III supporting organizations in the context of contributions from controlling donors.[330]

## (h) Application of Excess Benefit Transactions Rules

An excise tax is imposed on disqualified persons if they engage in one or more excess benefit transactions with public charities and social welfare organizations.[331] A grant, loan, compensation, or other similar payment (e.g., an expense reimbursement)[332] by any type of supporting organization to a substantial contributor or a person related to a substantial contributor, as well as a loan provided by a supporting organization to certain disqualified

---

327. *See* text accompanied by *supra* note 308.
328. *See* text accompanied by *supra* note 310.
329. Reg. § 1.509(a)-4(i)(4)(iv).
330. Reg. § 1.509(a)-4(f)(5)(ii).
331. IRC § 4958. *See Tax-Exempt Organizations*, Chapter 21.
332. A *similar payment* does not include, for example, a payment made pursuant to a bona fide sale or lease of property with a substantial contributor (Joint Committee Explanation at 358).

persons with respect to the supporting organization, is an automatic excess benefit transaction.[333] Thus, the entire amount paid to the substantial contributor, disqualified persons, and related parties is an excess benefit.[334] The legislation enacting this law provides that these rules apply to transactions occurring after July 25, 2006.[335]

Nonetheless, the IRS does not consider a payment made pursuant to a written contract that was binding on August 17, 2006 (the date the legislation was signed into law), to be an excess benefit transaction if (1) the contract was binding at all times after August 17, 2006, and before payment is made, (2) the contract is not modified during that period, and (3) the payment pursuant to the contract is made on or before August 17, 2007.[336]

Similarly, as to arrangements that are not governed by a binding written contract described above, involving an employment relationship in existence, or other legal obligation in effect, as of August 17, 2006, the IRS will not consider a payment pursuant to such an arrangement to be an excess benefit transaction under this law, provided that (1) the terms of the arrangement are not modified after August 17, 2006, (2) any services are performed and any goods were delivered as required by the arrangement no later than December 31, 2006, and (3) the payment is made no later than August 17, 2007.

### (i) Limitation on Control

A supporting organization may not be controlled directly or indirectly by one or more disqualified persons, other than foundation managers and one or more supported organizations.[337] An individual who is a disqualified person with respect to a supporting organization (e.g., a substantial contributor) does not lose that status because a beneficiary public or publicly supported charity appoints or designates him or her to be a foundation manager of the supporting organization to serve as the representative of the public or publicly supported charity.[338]

---

333. IRC § 4958(c)(3). For purposes of the *similar payment* rule, the term *substantial contributor* does not include an eligible supported organization (other than a supporting organization) (IRC § 4958(c)(3)(C)(ii)). Likewise, for purposes of the loan rule, the term *disqualified person* does not include an eligible supported organization (other than a supporting organization) (IRC § 4958(c)(3)(A)(i)(II)). There was an anomaly here, in that, when these rules were originally written, these exclusions failed to include the types of noncharitable organizations that qualify as supported organizations (*see* § 15.8) (Pension Protection Act of 2006, Pub. L. No. 109-280, 109th Cong., 2nd Sess. (2006) § 1242). This matter was remedied by subsequent legislation (Tax Technical Corrections Act of 2007, Pub. L. No. 110-172, 110th Cong., 1st Sess. (2007) § 3(i)).
334. Cf. § 16.9, text accompanied by notes 105–106.
335. Pension Protection Act of 2006, § 1242(c)(2).
336. Notice 2006-109, 2006-51 I.R.B. 1121, § 4.
337. IRC § 509(a)(3)(C).
338. Reg. § 1.509(a)-4(j)(1).

A supporting organization is considered *controlled* if the disqualified persons, by aggregating their votes or positions of authority, may require the organization to perform any act that significantly affects its operations or may prevent the supporting organization from performing such an act. Generally, control exists if the voting power of these persons is 50 percent or more of the total voting power of the organization's governing body, or if one or more disqualified persons have the right to exercise veto power over the actions of the organization. All pertinent facts and circumstances, including the nature, diversity, and income yield of an organization's holdings, the length of time particular securities or other assets are retained, and its manner of exercising its voting rights with respect to securities in which members of its governing body also have some interest, will be taken into consideration in determining whether a disqualified person does in fact indirectly control an organization. Supporting organizations are permitted to establish, to the satisfaction of the IRS, that disqualified persons do not directly or indirectly control them.[339]

For example, this control element may be the difference between the qualification of an organization as a supporting organization and its qualification as a common fund private foundation. This is because the right of the donors to designate the recipients of the organization's gifts can constitute control of the organization by disqualified persons, namely, substantial contributors.[340]

In one instance, the IRS found indirect control of a supporting organization by, in effect, legislating an expanded definition of the term *disqualified person.* The matter involved a charitable organization that made distributions to a university. The organization's board of directors was composed of a substantial contributor to the organization, two employees of a business corporation of which more than 35 percent of the voting power was owned by the substantial contributors, and one individual selected by the university. None of the directors had veto power over the organization's actions. Conceding that the organization was not directly controlled by disqualified persons, the IRS said that "one circumstance to be considered is whether a disqualified person is in a position to influence the decisions of members of the organization's governing body who are not themselves disqualified persons." Thus, the IRS decided that the two directors who were employees of the disqualified person corporation should be considered disqualified persons for purposes of applying the 50 percent control rule. This position in turn led to the conclusion that the organization was indirectly controlled by disqualified persons and, therefore, could not be a nonprivate foundation by virtue of being a qualifying supporting organization.[341]

---

339. Reg. § 1.509(a)-4(j)(2).
340. Rev. Rul. 80-305, 1980-2 C.B. 71. For a discussion of common fund foundations, *see* § 3.3, and of *substantial contributors, see* § 4.1.
341. Rev. Rul. 80-207, 1980-2 C.B. 193.

The operation of these rules is further illustrated by two IRS rulings. One instance concerned a charitable trust formed to grant scholarships to students graduating from a particular public high school. The sole trustee of the trust was the council of the city in which the school was located, and its funds were managed by the city's treasurer. The school system was an integral part of the city's government. One of the purposes of the city, as outlined in its charter, was to provide for the education of its citizens. The IRS granted the trust classification as a supporting organization (and thereby determined it was not a private foundation),[342] using the following rationale:

- The city, being a governmental unit,[343] was a qualified supported entity.[344]

- Because of the involvement of the city council and treasurer, the trust satisfied the requirements of the "operated, supervised, or controlled by" relationship.

- The organizational test was met because of the similarity of educational purpose between the trust and the city.

- The "exclusive" operation requirement was deemed met because the trust benefited individual members of the charitable class aided by the city through its school system.

- The trust was not controlled by a disqualified person (other than a public or publicly supported charity).

By contrast, the IRS considered the public or publicly supported charity status of a charitable trust formed to grant scholarships to students graduating from high schools in a particular county. The scholarship recipients were selected by a committee composed of officials and representatives of the county.

The trustee of the trust was a bank. The IRS denied the trust classification as a supporting organization (and thereby determined that it was a private foundation),[345] using the following rationale:

- The high schools were qualified supported organizations.[346]

- Since the trustee was independent of the county, neither the *operated, supervised, or controlled by* nor the *supervised or controlled in connection with* relationship was present.

342. Rev. Rul. 75-436, 1975-2 C.B. 217.
343. IRC §§ 170(c)(1), 170(b)(1)(A)(v).
344. IRC § 509(a)(1).
345. Rev. Rul. 75-437, 1975-2 C.B. 218.
346. IRC §§ 170(b)(1)(A)(ii) or (v); 509(a)(1).

- The integral part test of the *operated in connection with* relationship was not met because of the independence of the trustee, the county's lack of voice in the trust's investment and grant-making policies, and the absence of the necessary elements of significant involvement, dependence on support, and sufficient attentiveness.

- The responsiveness test of the same relationship was not met because the beneficiary organizations were not named and lacked the power to enforce the trust and compel an accounting.

- The trust failed the organization test because its instrument lacked the requisite statement of purpose and did not *specify* the publicly supported organizations.

The U.S. Tax Court demonstrated a disposition to avoid this type of stringent reading of these requirements. In finding a scholarship-granting charitable trust to be a public charity pursuant to the *operated in connection with* requirements, the court ruled that it satisfied the responsiveness and integral part tests even though the school was not a named beneficiary of the trust and the funds were paid directly to the graduates rather than to the school or a school system.[347] This, a prior, and a subsequent tax court holding[348] indicate that the courts will not be giving these exceedingly complex and intricate regulations an overly technical interpretation, but will apply them in a commonsense manner to effectuate the intent of Congress.

A supporting organization must annually demonstrate that it is not controlled, directly or indirectly, by one or more disqualified persons (other than its managers and supported organization(s)); this is done by means of a certification on its annual information return.[349]

## (j)  Hospital and Other Reorganizations

A contemporary application of the supporting organization rules may be seen in hospital reorganizations. These are occurring for a variety of reasons, including facilitation of compliance with governmental reporting requirements, separation of assets to limit liability, enhancement of the ability to expand facilities, and development of a more flexible framework within which to

---

347. *Nellie Callahan Scholarship Fund v. Commissioner*, 73 T.C. 626 (1980).

348. *Warren M. Goodspeed Scholarship Fund v. Commissioner*, 70 T.C. 515 (1978); *Cockerline Memorial Fund v. Commissioner*, 86 T.C. 53 (1986).

349. IRC § 6033(l)(3). It is intended that supporting organizations be able to certify that the majority of the organization's governing body is comprised of individuals who were selected on the basis of their special knowledge or expertise in the particular field or discipline in which the supporting organization is operating or because they represent the particular community that is served by the supported public charity(ies) (Joint Committee Explanation at 359).

conduct and expand management functions. Thus, many institutions perceived as hospitals today are really an aggregation of organizations, including one or more entities that are actually qualified as hospitals,[350] one or more other types of charitable entities (including, perhaps, a related foundation used for development purposes), and one or more for-profit entities (housing assets and functions, such as a parking garage, and billing, collection, and land management). Under emerging concepts, control is being shifted away from a true hospital organization and all of these entities are instead coordinated by a multientity health-care system, which itself is a charitable entity, and are managed by a parent organization that also is a charitable entity. The hospital entity (or entities) remains in being, but with its oversight functions transferred to the parent and the services it performs for other organizations in the system transferred to an organization that provides centralized management and other support services for the system. The management entity, controlled by the parent, provides a variety of services, such as investment management, fundraising, shared service arrangements, and the provision of data processing services. The management entity of a hospital system (or similar collection of institutions) can qualify as a supporting organization, with the nexus to the other organizations in the system based on any of the three relationships available to supporting organizations.[351] Other reorganizations of hospitals and similar entities are occurring without the use of a supporting organization.[352]

Following a study of the federal tax implications of the structure of systems of health-care organizations, prompted by the many ruling requests concerning hospital reorganizations, the Chief Counsel's office of the IRS prepared a summary of its view of the law regarding the applicability of the supporting organization concept in this context. The conclusion of the study was that a parent management organization of a system of hospitals and related health-care entities can qualify as a supporting organization only (assuming that only the relationship embraced by the phrase *supervised or controlled in connection with* applies) where the parent and each of the qualified supported organizations have management or control vested in the same persons.[353] That is, according to this view, it is not sufficient that management or control be vested in representatives or appointees of the supported organizations.

This study reflects the general concern at the IRS with the concept of a parent entity being a supporting organization for a subordinate organization. That is, the IRS generally believes that a supporting organization should be subordinate to, rather than the parent of, the supported organization or organizations.

---

350. IRC § 170(b)(1)(A)(iii).
351. E.g., Priv. Ltr. Rul. 8210120.
352. E.g., Priv. Ltr. Rul. 8226127.
353. Gen. Couns. Mem. 39508.

Nonetheless, hospital reorganizations have evolved to the point that, as a practical matter, the IRS cannot preclude an entity from achieving supporting organization classification simply because of its status as a parent organization.

It has become common for this type of reorganization to be approved by the IRS, but on the condition that the federal anti-kickback restrictions in connection with the referral of Medicare or Medicaid patients[354] are not being violated.[355]

Other types of tax-exempt organizations engage in comparable reorganizations, using a supporting organization.[356]

Sometimes these reorganizations generate issues as to the ongoing tax-exempt status of one or more organizations, including supporting organizations. If the functions of an entity are not inherently exempt, the organization may nonetheless be able to successfully gain or retain exemption on the basis of operation as an *integral part* of one or more parent organizations; under this approach, the functions do not have to be inherently exempt.[357] The IRS issues rulings, applying the integral part doctrine in this manner, from time to time.[358]

Recent years have witnessed a spate of conversions of tax-exempt hospitals to for-profit entities. These transactions take many forms, one of which is sale of the hospital assets, with the selling entity remaining as a charitable organization, albeit engaged in other programs (such as community education or a variety of social services). Issues can arise when the selling entity has one or more supporting organizations. When the selling entity becomes a private foundation,[359] the supporting organization will lose its public charity status, unless it becomes a supporting organization for one or more other qualified organizations. Otherwise, if the charitable entity that once was a hospital can continue to be a public charity on another basis (other than as a supporting organization), the entity that was a supporting organization with respect to the hospital can continue to be a supporting organization with respect to the public charity.[360]

## (k)  Use of For-Profit Subsidiaries

For a time, there was an issue as to whether a supporting organization can have a for-profit subsidiary. The difficulty was this: The law requires that a supporting organization be organized and operated *exclusively* for the benefit or

---

354. 42 U.S.C. § 1320a-7(b)(1), (2).

355. E.g., Priv. Ltr. Rul. 9426040.

356. E.g., Priv. Ltr. Rul. 8719038.

357. E.g., Rev. Rul. 78-41, 1978-1 C.B. 148 (a fund created by a tax-exempt hospital to satisfy its malpractice claims was held to be an IRC § 501(c)(3) entity); Rev. Rul. 75-282, 1975-2 C.B. 201(an organization formed by a tax-exempt conference of churches to make mortgage loans to affiliated churches was held to qualify under IRC § 501(c)(3)).

358. E.g., Priv. Ltr. Rul. 200038049.

359. E.g., Priv. Ltr. Rul. 9715031.

360. E.g., Priv. Ltr. Rul. 9643039.

other support of one or more public charities.[361] This is a literal use of the word *exclusively*: Congress meant *exclusively*, rather than merely *primarily*. The question then was whether the very use of a for-profit subsidiary would violate the *exclusively* standard and thus cause the supporting organization to lose its public charity status on that basis.

The mystery intensified when, in 1993, the IRS ruled that a charitable organization that is a supporting organization can establish and operate a wholly owned for-profit subsidiary without jeopardizing its tax-exempt status.[362] This ruling was silent, however, on the impact of the use of the subsidiary on the organization's supporting organization status. Nonetheless, three years later, the IRS ruled that a supporting organization can, without jeopardizing its public charity status, utilize a for-profit subsidiary.[363] Later in 1996, the IRS ruled as to the tax consequences of liquidation of a for-profit subsidiary into a supporting organization.[364]

Thus, unless the IRS or a court alters this policy position, it seems clear that a supporting organization can, without endangering its tax classifications, hold and otherwise utilize a for-profit subsidiary.[365]

## (I)  Department of Treasury Study

The Department of the Treasury was directed by Congress to undertake a study on the organization and operation of supporting organizations, to consider whether (1) the deductions allowed for income, estate, or gift taxes for charitable contributions to supporting organizations are appropriate in consideration of the use of contributed assets or the use of the assets of such organizations for the benefit of the person making the charitable contribution, and (2) these issues are also issues with respect to other forms of charitable organizations or charitable contributions.[366]

The Treasury Department issued this report in early December 2011. The report focuses on both supporting organizations and donor-advised funds.[367] This report summarizes these two bodies of law, including the rules enacted in 2006; provides a statistical analysis of supporting organizations and donor-advised funds; and answers questions posed by Congress. Overall, this report

---

361. *See* text accompanied by *supra* note 224.
362. Priv. Ltr. Rul. 9305026.
363. Priv. Ltr. Rul. 9637051.
364. Priv. Ltr. Rul. 9645017.
365. Because a supporting organization is a public charity and not a private foundation, the excess business holdings rules (*see* Chapter 7) do not apply.
366. Pension Protection Act of 2006, Pub. L. No. 109-280, 109th Cong., 2nd Sess. (2006) § 1226.
367. *See* § 16.9, text accompanied by note 120. Because the analysis of the two topics is integrated in the report, the elements of it pertaining to donor-advised funds are included in this summary.

concludes that supporting organizations and donor-advised funds "play an important role in the charitable sector."

**Statistics.**   The  statistics utilized by the Treasury Department are for 2006, the first year for which complete data were available for use in time for this report. Supporting organizations received $94.1 billion, had outlays of $72.5 billion, including $11.5 billion in grants, $4 billion in payments to affiliates, and $46.9 billion in program expenditures. As of the close of that year, supporting organizations had a net worth of $226.7 billion.

The report observes that supporting organizations that "support organizations that provide medical and dental care for low-income households, work with hospital patients and employees, and conduct health research had the largest [amount of] revenue, expenses, and net worth."

Organizations sponsoring donor-advised funds received $59.5 billion, including $9 billion in contributions to the funds. These sponsoring organizations had total expenses of $37.7 billion, including $5.7 billion in grants paid from donor-advised fund assets, $6.8 billion in other grants made, and $20.7 billion in program expenses. These organizations had a net worth of $211.3 billion at the end of the year. The 2,398 organizations sponsoring donor-advised funds had 160,000 of them, entailing assets valued at $31.1 billion as of the end of the year.

The report notes that, beginning with 2006, the annual information return (Form 990) was redesigned, requiring sponsoring organizations to report the aggregate value of assets held in, the aggregate contributions to, and the grants from their donor-advised funds. This data, the report adds, will make it possible to calculate aggregate payout rates at the sponsoring organization level and compare the payout rates of these aggregate donor-advised funds with those of private foundations.

The report references sponsoring organizations that have a "national reach" and have as their primary role services as "intermediaries between donors and a broad range of charities providing direct charitable services by sponsoring and maintaining donor-advised funds and other similar charitable funds." These are referred to as *national donor-advised funds*. A subset of national donor-advised funds is those that are sponsored by charitable affiliates of financial institutions—accorded the (unfortunate) name of *commercial national donor-advised funds.*

Aggregate donor-advised funds that are commercial national donor-advised funds had an average of $424.5 million in total assets and median assets of $58.9 million. The average payout rate across all aggregate donor-advised funds in 2006 was 9.3 percent. Among the commercial national donor-advised funds, the average payout rate was 14.2 percent. This led the report to conclude that it would be "premature to recommend a distribution requirement for [donor-advised funds] at this point."

**Overall Conclusions.** The report states that the Pension Protection Act "appears to have provided a legal structure to address abusive practices and accommodate innovations in the sector without creating undue additional burden or new opportunities for abuse."

As for public comments received by Treasury, the report observes that respondents "generally praised the relative benefits of [supporting organizations] to the supported organizations compared to the benefits that charities derive from [donor-advised funds] and private foundations." Also, "[t]here is a consensus among the respondents that [donor-advised funds] have been a helpful development for donors in the charitable sector."

The final component of this report is a collection of answers to questions posed by Congress. As to the workability of the charitable contribution deduction in these contexts, the report concludes that the charitable deduction rules "for gifts to [donor-advised funds] and [supporting organizations], which are the same as the rules for gifts to other public charities, appear to be appropriate." Concerning distribution requirements, the report states, as noted, that "it would be premature to make a recommendation regarding distribution requirements for [donor-advised funds] on the basis of this first year of reported data." The report is of the view that "it is consistent to treat donations to [donor-advised funds] and [supporting organizations] that comply with existing legal requirements as completed gifts even if the donor retains non-binding advisory rights."

The report concludes with this: "The [Pension Protection Act] enacted provisions designed to mitigate undue donor influence on [supporting organizations] and [donor-advised fund] sponsoring organizations and to increase the required transparency of these organizations. New reporting requirements will make more data available to federal and state regulators, as well as to researchers, the press, and the general public. As the effects of the [Pension Protection Act] and new regulations become clearer over time, Treasury looks forward to working with Congress to determine whether additional legislation or reporting is necessary."

## (m)  IRS Ruling Policy

As IRS rulings are indicating, the law in place prior to enactment of the additional supporting organization rules in 2006[368] was amply adequate to resolve misuse of these entities. In one instance, two donors established a supporting organization; the organization made interest-only, noncollateralized loans to them (some within days of the ostensible gift) and was lax in enforcing the terms of the notes, such as the repayment requirement. Monies granted to public charities by the organization were used to pay tuition for the

---

368.  Pension Protection Act of 2006 (Pub. L. No. 109-280, 109th Cong., 2nd Sess. (2006)).

benefit of the donors' children and to pay a portion of their tithing obligations. The IRS concluded that the supporting organization was formed for these individuals' "personal benefit" and that it was used for "tax-avoidance" purposes; it revoked the organization's tax exemption retroactively to the date of its inception on the grounds of private inurement, prohibited transactions, and misstatement of a material fact on its application for recognition of exemption.[369]

A similar retroactive revocation of exemption occurred earlier, with the individuals who formed the supporting organization agreeing with the IRS that the arrangement constituted an "abusive trust" and a "sham."[370]

An individual, having acquired valuable stock options and facing serious tax troubles, contacted a promoter in response to an advertisement. The promoter devised a "comprehensive master financial plan" consisting of a loss-of-income insurance program, an equity management mortgage, various estate planning techniques, and a supporting organization. The entity, ostensibly a supporting organization, loaned the funds to this individual and his or her spouse, comprising this mortgage. The IRS revoked the tax-exempt status of the supporting organization on the grounds of private inurement, use of the entity for tax-avoidance purposes, and advancement of the financial interests of the promoter and others. The IRS also concluded that the organization did not qualify as any type of supporting organization[371] and was controlled by disqualified persons with respect to it.[372] The revocation was made retroactive to the date of formation of the organization, inasmuch as the application for recognition of exemption failed to mention this tax shelter scheme.[373]

IRS efforts in this context continue. In one instance, the tax-exempt status of a supporting organization was retroactively revoked because its primary activity was the making of loans to disqualified persons.[374] This occurred in another case, where the supporting organization was created as part of a "structure of multiple entities designed to shift income and reduce or eliminate taxes" used to "facilitate a circular tax avoidance scheme."[375] In still another instance, retroactive revocation occurred where the entity's dissolution clause allowed distributions to organizations other than the specified supported organizations, its trustee was empowered to change the primary supported organization at will, and the trustee (the only individual controlling the organization) was a disqualified person with respect to the entity.[376]

---

369. Priv. Ltr. Rul. 200844022.
370. Priv. Ltr. Rul. 200810025.
371. *See* §§ 15.7(e)–15.7(g).
372. *See* § 15.7(i).
373. Priv. Ltr. Rul. 201004046.
374. Priv. Ltr. Rul. 201007076.
375. Priv. Ltr. Rul. 201052022.
376. Priv. Ltr. Rul. 201115030.

## § 15.8  CHANGE OF PUBLIC CHARITY CATEGORY

### (a)  From § 509(a)(1) to § 509(a)(2) or Vice Versa

Sometimes the sources of a public charity's support change, causing it to fail to qualify under one category or another. When the change indicated is reclassification from (a)(1) to (a)(2) or vice versa, the organization must decide whether to submit the correct information in the current Form 990 filed in Ogden, Utah, or to the Cincinnati, Ohio, office. Currently the determination letter is only updated in Cincinnati. Sometimes it is a matter of the organization's officials being tolerant of uncertainty. The factors to consider in making the choice include the following:

- The IRS does not issue amended or new determination letters or update its Business Master File simply on the basis of a change reported on Form 990, Schedule A.

- Private foundations need not exercise expenditure responsibility in making a grant to either category, so a new determination letter is not critical.

- IRS Publication 78 makes no distinction in its labeling of public charities, so the public charity/private foundation category is not entered into that IRS record (as of June 3, 2008).

- The Ohio Key District Office does not charge a user fee for submission of the information.

### (b)  From § 509(a)(3) to § 509(a)(1) or § 509(a)(2)

Many charities classified as § 509(a)(3) supporting organizations actually receive revenues that also qualify them as a § 509(a)(1) or (2) public charity. Faced with the punitive restraints placed on supporting organizations discussed previously, the IRS fortunately designed a process to facilitate receipt of new public charity classification for those that can qualify.[377] A request for reclassification, which must be submitted in accordance with the rules for seeking rulings and the like,[378] must include a prominent notice as to the reclassification being sought (for example, in capital letters) and either (1) a copy of the organization's annual information return (including Schedule A) for the year immediately preceding the year in which the request is made, or (2) the organization's support information for its most recent five years. Response time for these requests has been only a few weeks or days in some cases with a new

---

377. This procedure, originally the subject of Ann. 2006-93, 2006-48 I.R.B. 1017, was revised, updated, and published as Ann. 2009-62, 2009-33 I.R.B. 247
378. Rev. Proc. 2014-4, 2014-1 I.R.B. 125.

determination provided. It has taken more than a month for the change to enter the IRS Business Master File and Publication 78.

### (c)   From a § 509(a)(3) Type III to a § 509(a)(3) Type I or II

The above-mentioned announcement was unfortunately limited in its scope. A Type III supporting organization that changes its organizational structure and seeks reclassification as a Type I or II supporting organization, in the authors' experience, is asked to submit information comparable to that submitted on Schedule D of Form 1023, which is normally filed when the organization seeks initial qualification as a supporting organization. The requested information and time for the IRS to review it means this type of change can be complex and time consuming.

### (d)   IRS Recognition of Change in Status

The IRS issued procedures with respect to the issuance of determination letters and rulings as to public charity (private foundation status, operating foundation status,[379] and exempt operating foundation status).[380]

This guidance addresses the matter of change in public charity status. The rule states that an organization is not required to obtain another determination letter to *qualify* for its new public charity status, but "in order for IRS records to *recognize* any change in public charity status, an organization must obtain a new determination of foundation [i.e., public charity] status" (emphasis added). The IRS has issued Form 8940 to allow a public charity to seek reclassification of foundation status, including a voluntary request from a public charity for private foundation status.

A private foundation may qualify as an operating foundation without an IRS determination letter, but the IRS will not "recognize such status in IRS records" without a new letter. An organization claiming to be an exempt operating foundation must obtain a determination letter recognizing that status (so as to be exempt from the foundation tax on net investment income).

The IRS also issues determination letters as to the type of supporting organization, whether a Type III supporting organization is functionally integrated with one or more supported organizations,[381] and whether a nonexempt charitable trust[382] (an IRC § 4947(a)(1) entity) can constitute a supporting organization.[383]

---

379.  *See* § 3.1.
380.  Rev. Proc. 2014-10, 2014-2 I.R.B. 293. Exempt operating foundations are the subject of § 3.1(i).
381.  *See* § 15.7(e)–(h).
382.  *See* § 3.6.
383.  These determination letters are requested by following the general procedures for seeking determination letters in the TE/GE context (currently Rev. Proc. 2014-4, 2014-1 I.R.B. 125).

## § 15.9 NONCHARITABLE SUPPORTED ORGANIZATIONS

Certain tax-exempt organizations that are not charitable entities qualify as supported organizations; this means that the charitable organization that is supportive of one or more of these noncharitable entities is able to avoid classification as a private foundation on the ground that it is a supporting organization.

This point of law is contained in a rather cryptic passage in the Internal Revenue Code, which states that, for purposes of the supporting organization rules, "an organization described in paragraph (2) [§ 509(a)(2)] shall be deemed to include an organization described in section 501(c)(4) [social welfare organization], (5) [agricultural, horticultural, or labor organization], or (6) [trade, business, and professional association and other forms of business leagues] which would be described in paragraph (2) if it were an organization described in section 501(c)(3)."[384]

This provision means that a tax-exempt charitable entity may be operated in conjunction with a social welfare, agricultural, horticultural, or labor organization, or a business league, and thus qualify as a supporting organization if the supported organization meets the one-third support test of the rules concerning the service provider organization.[385] These organizations frequently meet this support requirement simply because they have a membership that pays dues. This rule is principally designed to preserve nonprivate foundation status for related "foundations" and other funds (e.g., scholarship and research funds) operated by the specified noncharitable organizations. This type of supporting organization is often in an awkward position: It must be charitable in function to be tax-exempt yet be supportive of a noncharitable entity to avoid being considered a private foundation.

## § 15.10 RELATIONSHIPS CREATED FOR AVOIDANCE PURPOSES

The income tax regulations contain rules to ensure that the requirements concerning service provider publicly supported organizations and supporting organizations are not manipulated to avoid private foundation status for charitable organizations. Thus, if a relationship between a would-be service provider publicly supported organization and a putative supporting organization is established or availed, and one of the purposes of the relationship is to avoid classification as a private foundation with respect to either organization, the character and amount of support received by the ostensible supporting organization will be attributed to the would-be service provider publicly supported organization for purposes of determining whether the

---

384. IRC § 509(a), last sentence.
385. Reg § 1.509(a)-4(k). Also Rev. Rul. 76-401, 1976-2 C.B. 175.

latter meets the one-third support test and the one-third gross investment income test.[386]

If an organization seeking qualification as a service provider publicly supported organization fails to meet either the one-third support test or the one-third gross investment income test by reason of the application of the foregoing rules or the rules with respect to retained character of gross investment income, and the organization is one of the specified organizations[387] for whose support or benefit an organization seeking the qualification is operated, the would-be supporting organization will not be considered to be operated exclusively to support or benefit one or more eligible public or publicly supported organizations.[388]

For purposes of determining whether an organization meets the gross investment income test in the rules concerning the service provider publicly supported organization,[389] amounts received by the organization from an organization seeking categorization as a supporting organization, by reason of its support of the would-be publicly supported organization, retain their character as gross investment income (rather than gifts or contributions) to the extent that the amounts are characterized as gross investment income in the possession of the distributing organization. The rule is also applicable with respect to support of a would-be publicly supported organization from a charitable trust, corporation, fund, association, or similar organization that is required by its governing instrument or otherwise to distribute, or that normally does distribute, at least 25 percent of its adjusted net income to the organization and the distribution normally comprises at least 5 percent of the distributee organization's adjusted net income. (There is no similar rule in connection with the donative publicly supported organizations.)

## § 15.11   RELIANCE BY GRANTORS AND CONTRIBUTORS

### (a)   Verifying an Organization's Public Charity Status

After passage of the Pension Protection Act in August 2006, grantors and, in particular, private foundations and donor-advised funds faced the need to determine whether supporting organizations are Type I, II, or III entities.[390] Most IRS determination letters and IRS databases did not reflect that information. In December 2006, the IRS issued guidance in the form of a notice stating:[391]

---

386.  Reg. § 1.509(a)-5(b).
387.  IRC § 509(a)(3)(A).
388.  Reg. § 1.509(a)-5(c).
389.  IRC § 509(a)(2)(B).
390.  *See* § 6.6.
391.  Notice 2006-109, 2006-51 I.R.B. 1121.

> Until further guidance is issued, for purposes of §§ 4942, 4945, and 4966 (as applicable) a grantor, acting in good faith, may rely on information from the IRS Business Master File ("BMF") or the grantee's current IRS letter recognizing the grantee as exempt from federal income tax and indicating the grantee's public charity classification in determining whether the grantee is a public charity under §§ 509(a)(1), (2), or (3). In addition, a grantor, acting in good faith, may rely on a written representation from a grantee and specified documents as described in A and B[392] below in determining whether the grantee is a Type I, Type II, or functionally integrated Type III supporting organization. The good faith requirement is not satisfied if the collected specified documents are inconsistent with the written representation. In each case, the grantor must verify that the grantee is listed in Publication 78, *Cumulative List of Organizations Described in Section 170(c) of the Internal Revenue Code of 1986,* or obtain a copy of the current IRS letter recognizing the grantee as exempt from federal income tax.

Although the above notice contained helpful information, a couple of significant problems remained for many grantors.[393] Some IRS determination letters do not include the public charity designation under § 509. If the determination letter is silent, the only permitted way to determine § 509 status is by consulting the Business Master File. Many private foundations and donor-advised funds have difficulty in making use of the IRS Business Master File, particularly in attempting to download it and integrate it into existing grant-making software.

In March 2007, the IRS, in an exempt organization update, announced that a grantor could rely on certain qualified third parties, such as GuideStar, to obtain IRS Business Master File information.[394] The IRS also confirmed that, alternatively, a grantor could rely on the grantee's current IRS letter, provided that the letter indicated the grantee's public charity status under § 509.

A private foundation can rely on the public charity classification of a grantee organization that files Form 8734 within 90 days of the end of its advance ruling period, until the IRS has made a final determination.[395] Previously, one could call the IRS Determinations Group in Cincinnati to inquire whether a Form 8734 had been filed and what its status was. This policy changed in the fall of 2004: until a determination has been made, customer service personnel will provide no information, because the IRS now considers the information confidential. In such a case, a prudent private foundation may choose not to rely on the grantee's evidence that the filing was made within 90 days and is still pending, even if it remains listed in Publication 78. A literal reading of the regulation cited in Rev. Proc. 89–23 validates this position. The regulation actually uses the word

---

392. *See* Exhibit 9.3 for an example of certification.
393. These problems were noted in a letter from the Council on Foundations to the IRS dated February 1, 2007.
394. IRS EO Update 2007-8, March 27, 2007.
395. Reg. § 1.170A-9(e)(5)(iii)(b).

*final* to refer to the type of IRS ruling or determination letter that a PF can rely on to evidence public status.[396] Some argue that public status can be relied on until such time as the IRS publishes notification of revocation in the Internal Revenue Bulletin and/or changes the classification in Publication 78. Foundation Source Senior Vice-President Jeffrey D. Haskell disagrees and laments this conclusion that reliance does not mature until a final determination is published. He refers to the 90-day period after the end of the advance ruling as an awkward "twilight" period.[397]

## (b)  Reliance on Current Determination Letter

Once an organization has received a determination from the IRS classifying it as a publicly supported organization, the treatment of grants and contributions and the status of grantors and contributors to it generally are not affected by reason of a subsequent revocation of the determination by the IRS until notice of the revocation is communicated to the general public. This is not the case, however, where the grantor or contributor had knowledge of the revocation or was in part responsible for or was aware of the act, the failure to act, or the substantial and material change on the part of the organization that gave rise to the revocation of status.[398]

The IRS, in 1989, issued guidelines in this regard.[399] Under these guidelines, a private foundation's grant will not cause the foundation to be considered to be responsible for, or aware of, a substantial and material change in the recipient organization's sources of support that results in the loss of the recipient's status as a publicly supported organization, if three conditions are met at the time of the making of the grant. These conditions are (1) the recipient organization has received a ruling or determination letter, or an advance ruling or determination letter, that it is a publicly supported organization; (2) notice of a change in the recipient's status as a publicly supported organization has not been made to the public (such as by publication in the Internal Revenue Bulletin), and the private foundation has not acquired knowledge that the IRS has given notice to the recipient that it will lose that status; and (3) the recipient is not controlled directly or indirectly by the private foundation.

A principal and fundamental difficulty with the reliance rules prior to this time is that a grantor or contributor would not in fact be able to rely on the ruling that the grantee or donee was a publicly supported charity (or private operating foundation). The grantor or donor was expected to obtain a written statement

---

396. Reg. § 1.509(a)-7(a); Rev. Proc. 89-23, 1989-1 C.B. 844.

397. "Is It Really a Public Charity?" 143 *Trusts & Estates 51* (2004).

398. Reg. § 1.509(a)-7. As discussed throughout, the reliance rules are essentially the same regarding IRC §§ 170(b)(1)(A)(vi) and 509(a)(2) organizations and private operating foundations.

399. Rev. Proc. 89-23, 1989-1 C.B. 844.

and pertinent financial data from the grantee or donee, review the information under the constraints of a reasonably prudent person test, and make an independent determination of the effect of the gift or grant on the grantee's or donee's nonfoundation status. The concern was that the gift or grant would constitute a substantial and material change in the support of the recipient entity, thereby causing loss of its publicly supported charity or private operating foundation status, with the attendant adverse consequences to the grantor or donor.[400] For a contributor, the loss would likely mean that the contributor's deduction is confined by the 20 percent limitation rather than the 50 percent or 30 percent limitation.[401] For a private foundation, the change in the grantee's classification may cause the grant to be a taxable expenditure.[402]

These requirements, by imposing the need for an extensive investigation and analysis, frequently eliminated any authentic *reliance* opportunity for grantors and contributors. A private foundation may lack the resources to conduct the necessary investigations and consequently confine its grants to institutions that are clearly public or publicly supported charities, so as to avoid the expenditure responsibility requirements.[403] The only alternatives, before the IRS provided some relief in this regard in 1981 and 1989, were for the grantor or donor to seek an unusual grant ruling or to voluntarily undertake to assume expenditure responsibility.

The IRS, in 1981, promulgated guidelines, which still apply when a private foundation makes a grant to a controlled recipient, for determining when a contributor or grantor will not be considered responsible for *substantial and material* changes in the sources of financial support for an organization that, as the result of the transfer, loses its classification as a publicly supported organization. (In the parlance of the law, such a shift from categorization as a publicly supported charity to a private foundation is known as *tipping*.) The essence of these guidelines, which are designed to provide a "safe haven" rule, is this: A grantor or donor will not be considered to be responsible for a substantial and material change in a recipient's support if the total of the grants or gifts from a grantor or donor for a tax year is no more than 25 percent of the total support received by the recipient organization—other than the grant or gift from the grantor or donor, a foundation manager, or related parties—during the immediately preceding four tax years. In the case of an organization in existence for less than five tax years, the number of years of its existence immediately preceding the tax year at issue is substituted for the four-year period, as long as the organization has been in existence at least one tax year consisting of at least eight months.[404]

---

400. Reg. § 1.509(a)-3(c)(1)(iii). Also Reg. § 1.170A-9(e)(4)(v); Rev. Proc. 89-23, 1989-1 C.B. 844 § 3.01.
401. *See* § 14.3.
402. *See* § 9.4.
403. *Id*. The 2008 Form 990 extended the four-year test to five years, as discussed in § 15.4.
404. Rev. Proc. 81-6, 1981-1 C.B. 620. Also Rev. Proc. 89-23, 1989-1 C.B. 844 § 3.02.

The following example illustrates the application of this rule:

A was determined by the IRS to be a publicly supported charity and received total support of $340,000 in 2009–2013. X, a private foundation, granted A $30,000 in 2014. X had contributed $40,000 of A's total support during 2009–2013. Even if A is later determined to be a private foundation for 2014, X will not be considered to be responsible for a substantial and material change in A's sources of support, resulting in the loss of A's public charity status. The grant in 2014 was only 10 percent of A's total support during 2009–2013, less the grants from X during that period ($300,000).

The computations are as follows:

| | |
|---|---|
| Total support received by A during 2009–2013 | $340,000 |
| Less: Total support provided by X during 2009–2013 | −40,000 |
| Total support, for purposes of guidelines, received by A during 2009–2013 | $300,000 |
| Total support provided by X as a percentage of A's total support, for purposes of guidelines, during 2009–2013 | = 10% |

To an extent, contributors may rely on the listing of an organization in the publication by the IRS of its cumulative list of charitable organizations.[405] As a general rule, a contribution by a donor who is unaware of the recipient organization's loss of charitable status will give rise to a charitable deduction where made on or before the date of a public announcement (such as by publication in the Internal Revenue Bulletin) stating that the contributions are no longer deductible. The same is true with respect to the recipient organization's public charity status. As noted previously, however, the IRS reserves the authority to disallow the charitable deduction where the donor (1) had knowledge of the revocation of status, (2) was aware that the revocation was imminent, or (3) was in part responsible for or was aware of the activities or deficiencies on the part of the organization that gave rise to the loss of qualification.[406]

In the process of finalizing the Tax Reform Act of 1984, the House-Senate conferees directed the Department of the Treasury to amend the tax regulations to permit greater reliance by private foundations on IRS classifications concerning new organizations during the first five years of their existence and in any other circumstances in which the Treasury Department concludes that greater reliance is appropriate.[407] Regulations to this end have not been promulgated.

---

405. Publication No. 78, *Cumulative List of Organizations Described in Section 170(c) of the Internal Revenue Code*; available on the Internet at www.irs.ustreas.gov.
406. Rev. Proc. 82-39, 1982-2 C.B. 759.
407. H. Rep. No. 98-861, 98th Cong., 2d Sess. 1090 (1984).

## § 15.12   OTHER RULES

If a charitable organization was a private foundation on October 9, 1969, it will be treated as a private foundation for all periods thereafter (or until terminated)[408] even though it may also qualify as some other type of tax-exempt organization.[409] In other words, an organization cannot hope to avoid private foundation status by claiming it also qualifies as, for example, a social welfare organization.[410]

If an organization was a private foundation on October 9, 1969, and it is subsequently determined that it no longer qualifies as a charitable entity, it will continue to be treated as a private foundation (until terminated).[411] In other words, an organization cannot avoid private foundation status by converting to a taxable entity.

## § 15.13   PUBLIC SAFETY ORGANIZATIONS

Another category of organization that is deemed to not be a private foundation is an organization that is organized and operated exclusively for testing for public safety.[412] These entities are described in the analysis of charitable organizations, but they are not eligible to receive deductible charitable contributions.

## § 15.14   TERMINATION OF PUBLIC CHARITY STATUS

On occasion, a charitable organization will be required to be a private foundation, having once qualified as a public charity. This usually happens when an organization ceases to constitute a publicly supported charity, with no likelihood of meeting a public support test[413] or otherwise remaining a public charity. When the basis for being a public charity ceases to exist, the presumption that the organization is a private foundation[414] is activated, and the entity becomes a private foundation. The revised Form 990 Schedule A prompts such an organization to file Form 990-PF, rather than 990, when the new five-year tests reflect lack of requisite public support for the prior and current year.[415]

The process of transformation from public charity status to private foundation status is informal. The IRS should be notified of the change in status by

---

408. *See* Chapter 13.
409. Reg. § 1.509(b)-1(a).
410. IRC § 501(c)(4).
411. Reg. § 1.509(b)-1(b).
412. IRC § 509(a)(4).
413. *See* §§ 15.4, 15.5.
414. IRC § 508(b).
415. *See* Exhibits 15.2–15.4 and discussion in § 15.4.

letter, and, beginning with the appropriate tax year involved, the organization should cease filing the annual information return expected of tax-exempt organizations in general (Form 990) and commence filing the annual return required of private foundations (Form 990-PF).[416] At that point, of course, the organization becomes subject to the entire panoply of private foundation rules, including payment of the tax on investment income.[417]

Oddly, while it is easy—as a matter of law (because of the presumption)—for an organization to shed public charity status and become a private foundation, it is often difficult for the IRS to cope with the request and recognize the change. It is, admittedly, uncommon for a charity to come forward and ask the agency to change it from a public charity to a private foundation;[418] the IRS is used to the reverse.[419] All too often, the IRS will not know how to process the submission. It is obviously favorable, however, from the government's standpoint, to have a charitable organization become a private foundation—if only because it starts paying taxes.

Once the letter requesting the change in status is submitted to the IRS, the agency may not accept on its face the organization's statement that it no longer meets a public support test. Instead, the IRS may be expected to request that the organization submit the requisite financial information (usually on Form 8734) so that it can make an independent review of the data. The IRS will compare this information to that filed in prior years, and perhaps send a letter requesting additional information. This, in turn, is certain to be followed by a lengthy letter from the IRS explaining why the organization does not qualify as a public charity. (The charitable organization, of course, already possesses this information, which is why the submission was made in the first instance.) Thereafter, the IRS will request that the organization execute, in duplicate, a form that is normally utilized following an adverse (from the organization's viewpoint) audit (Form 6018, titled *Consent to Proposed Adverse Action*). This form will assign an effective date for the conversion.

---

416. *See* Chapter 12.
417. *See* Chapter 10.
418. On one occasion, an IRS representative, having received this type of a request, sent a memorandum to legal counsel for the organization in response, saying that he had a "senior agent" and his manager review the submission, and reporting that they "said it was a unique situation in that most organizations do not notify the Service when they may be considered a private foundation."
419. *See* Chapter 13.

# CHAPTER SIXTEEN

# Donor-Advised Funds

One of the most controversial entities in the realm of charitable organizations is the *donor-advised fund*. These funds are created and maintained within public charities,[1] such as community foundations, colleges and universities, churches, and charitable gift funds. Indeed, these funds were initiated by community foundations, which have existed since the early 1900s. Today, there are about 400 community foundations and a growing number of charitable gift funds, accounting for billions of dollars in assets and income.

Thus, while this giving vehicle has been part of the federal tax law of charity for nearly a century, only recently has it become the subject of considerable scrutiny and criticism. Indeed, several federal tax issues are involved, all resting on the fundamental fact that the donor-advised fund can be an alternative to a private foundation. Some choose to state the matter somewhat differently, regarding donor-advised funds as a means of sidestepping or avoiding the private foundation rules. A statutory definition of donor-advised funds and two

---

1. It is incontrovertible that use of a donor-advised fund amounts to avoidance of the private foundation rules. Indeed, it can be said that every public charity is a mechanism for sidestepping these rules. The point is that this is an avoidance of a set of rules in a lawful manner. The U.S. Supreme Court long ago observed: "The legal right of a taxpayer to decrease the amount of what otherwise would be his taxes, or altogether to avoid them, by means which the law permits, cannot be doubted" (*Gregory v. Helvering*, 293 U.S. 465, 469 (1935)). More recently, an appellate court wrote that "[w]e recognize that it is axiomatic that taxpayers lawfully may arrange their affairs to keep taxes as low as possible" (*Neonatology Associates P.A. v. Commissioner*, 2002-2 U.S.T.C. ¶ 50,550 (3rd Cir. 2002)).

private foundation-like prohibitions were effective for tax years beginning after August 17, 2006.[2]

## § 16.1   BASIC DEFINITIONS

A donor-advised fund is not a separate legal entity. Rather, as noted, it is a fund within an organization that is a public charity. This type of fund is often referred to as an *account* or sometimes as a *subaccount* of the host organization.

These accounts can be in the name of an individual, family, corporation, private foundation, or cause; they can be used to facilitate anonymous gifts. They often bear the name of the contributor or the contributor's family or business. Because of its name, a donor-advised fund can appear to be a separate legal entity—seemingly a charitable organization with many of the attributes of a private foundation.

The donor-advised fund is to be contrasted with the *donor-directed fund*. In the case of a donor-directed fund, the donor or a designee of the donor retains the right to direct the investment of the fund's assets and/or to direct grants from the fund for charitable purposes. By contrast, with the donor-advised fund, the donor has the ability (but not a legal right) to make recommendations (proffer advice) as to investment policy and/or the making of grants.

The donor-advised fund has, as noted, long been a staple of community foundations.[3] In recent years, other types of charitable organizations and commercial investment companies have created donor-advised funds, recognized as public charities by the IRS. As long as the use of these funds was confined to community foundations, there was no controversy; the attention accorded these funds, including criticism, started when their use was extended to other public charities.

These funds can, as noted, be viable alternatives to the formation of private foundations. The individual or individuals involved may wish to avoid the responsibilities imposed by law (including annual reporting to the IRS and other foundation regulatory requirements) of operating a private foundation. With a donor-advised fund, as opposed to a private foundation, there is no need for a board of trustees (with the concomitant requirements of board meetings, maintenance of meeting minutes, election and supervision of officers and employees, and the like). Contributions to these funds are deductible pursuant to the rules concerning public charities, not private foundations. Another factor may be that the amount of money or property involved is too small to warrant the establishment of a private foundation.

---

2. *See* § 16.9.
3. *See* § 15.4(d). In general, Hoyt, *Legal Compendium for Community Foundations* (Washington, DC: Council on Foundations, 1996).

## § 16.2  GENERAL CONCEPT OF A GIFT

One of the legal issues raised by donor-advised funds is whether the transfer to the fund constitutes a gift. That is, the question arises as to whether the transfer to the fund is incomplete, in that the donor, by reserving an ability to advise, has retained some form of "right" that precludes the transfer from being a completed gift.

There must be a gift before there can be a charitable gift. Integral to the concept of the charitable contribution deduction is the fundamental requirement that the payment of money or property to a charitable organization be transferred pursuant to a transaction that constitutes a gift. Although the Internal Revenue Code does not define the word *gift*, the federal income tax regulations contain this definition: A *contribution* is a "voluntary transfer of money or property that is made with no expectation of procuring financial benefit commensurate with the amount of the transfer."[4] This definition reflects the observation of the United States Supreme Court, years ago, that a *gift* is a transfer motivated by "detached or disinterested generosity."[5] Any condition (see below) by which the donor retains complete dominion and control over the transferred property makes the gift incomplete.[6] An incomplete gift cannot give rise to a deductible contribution.

The Supreme Court also ruled, in the context of determining the concept of a *charitable gift*, that a "payment of money [or a transfer of property] generally cannot constitute a charitable contribution if the contributor expects a substantial benefit in return."[7] Subsequently, the Supreme Court wrote that an exchange having an "inherently reciprocal nature" is not a gift and thus cannot be a charitable gift when the recipient is a charity.[8] At the same time, when a benefit to a donor arising out of a transfer to a charitable organization is *incidental*, the benefit will not defeat the charitable deduction.[9]

Thus, a *charitable gift* can be defined as a voluntary transfer of money or property to a charitable organization without actual or anticipated receipt by the donor of more than incidental economic considerations or benefits in return. The value inherent in any economic consideration or benefit received in return, other than an incidental one, must be subtracted from the value of

---

4. Reg. § 1.170A-1(c)(5).
5. *Commissioner v. Duberstein*, 363 U.S. 278, 285 (1960), quoting from *Commissioner v. LoBue*, 351 U.S. 243, 246 (1956).
6. Reg. § 25.2511-2(b).
7. *United States v. American Bar Endowment*, 477 U.S. 105, 116–117 (1986). *See* Chapter 14, note 2.
8. *Hernandez v. Commissioner*, 490 U.S. 680, 692 (1989).
9. E.g., Rev. Rul. 81-307, 1981-2 C.B. 78.

the total gift to determine the value (if any) of the actual gift (the deductible portion).[10]

In most situations, once a donor has made a gift to a charity, the gift becomes the property of the charitable organization, and the donor retains none or perhaps a little authority over the use (including investment) or expenditure of the funds. The issue in this context is the extent of any donor control that may arise when a gift is made to a donor-advised fund, that is, when a transfer is made but the donor or a designee retains the ability to make recommendations as to subsequent transfers of the fund's income.

At this time, this issue is receiving scrutiny by Congress, the Department of the Treasury, and the IRS. The principal reason for this development is the *charitable gift funds* established by commercial investment management firms.[11]

The traditional type of donor-advised funds is that which, as noted, is a component entity of a community foundation. A monumental rivalry for millions of dollars in charitable gifts is under way between community foundations and charitable gift funds, and this activity is helping to stimulate and maintain the government's interest in this area. This focus has brought intense scrutiny of donor-advised funds.

This use of charitable gift funds involves the law concerning conditional gifts. A *conditional gift* is one that is made subject to the occurrence of an event, either before (*condition precedent*) or after (*condition subsequent*). This matter concerns conditions subsequent, namely, gifts made to a charitable organization containing binding covenants on the charitable donee.

---

10. *See* § 14.6(b). This concept is also reflected in the charitable gift substantiation rules, which require a good faith estimate of any goods or services provided to a donor in consideration of the contribution (*see* § 14.6(a)). The U.S. Tax Court held that contributions to a charitable organization were not deductible because the substantiation requirements were not met (*Addis v. Commissioner*, 118 T.C. 528 (2002), *aff'd*, 374 F.3d 881 (9th Cir. 2004), *cert. den.*, 543 U.S. 1151 (2005)). The court concluded that certain "expectations" of the donors amounted to a "service," so that the expectations had to be valued and reflected in the substantiation document for the contributions to be deductible. This is a troublesome decision in the donor-advised fund setting, inasmuch as donors to these funds clearly have an expectation that the charitable donee will give attention to and usually follow their recommendations. If this decision is correct, charitable organizations must now be ever so cautious in preparing the substantiation documents, in that they must not only value what they *provided* in exchange for the gift, they must also peer into the misty reaches of donor motivation and intent to discern what donors *expect to be provided* (and value that). Query then: Does the expectation a donor has when making a gift designated for a donor-advised fund, as to forthcoming recommendations (advice), have to be reflected in the substantiation document?

11. E.g., Langley, "You Don't Have to Be a Rockefeller to Set Up Your Own Foundation," *Wall St. J.*, February 12, 1998, at 1. The IRS announced, in its Implementing Guidelines for the government's fiscal year 2002, that it is viewing the tax-exempt organizations sector as a cluster of *market segments*, to be analyzed by rounds of statistical studies; among the first six of these segments to be reviewed is community foundations (read: donor-advised funds).

Usually, with respect to the tax consequences of conditional gifts, the only party that may be subject to any risk is the donor who is taking a full charitable deduction yet may not lawfully be allowed to do so. The tax-exempt status of the charitable donee may, however, be implicated.[12]

Conditions subsequent that are not negligible can defeat the income tax charitable deduction. In one case, donors gifted real property to a charitable trust but retained control over its future occupancy and sale; the entire federal income tax charitable contribution deduction was disallowed because of these retained rights (although they were incapable of valuation).[13] The charitable deduction for a gift of a rare book collection to a charity was disallowed because the donor retained an unlimited right of access to the collection and the right to deny access to it to others.[14] An illustration of a negligible or incidental condition subsequent was a gift of theatrical materials to a public library, where the materials could not be copied or removed from the library without the donor's permission.[15]

## § 16.3 TYPES OF DONOR FUNDS

Until the enactment of legislation in 2006, the Internal Revenue Code and the income tax regulations offered only two significant methods for donors to charitable organizations to exercise any posttransfer control or direction over the use of money or property irrevocably transferred to charity for which the donor is entitled to a charitable deduction in the year of the transfer. One method is the use of a special type of private foundation that is, in essence, a donor-directed fund.[16] This entity is referred to as the common fund foundation.[17] The other method is utilization of the community foundation or community trust.[18] The community foundation regulations and another regulation[19] only allow donor designation at the time of the gift and donor advice (not donor direction) after the date of the gift. The 2006 legislation introduced a third approach in this context, introducing statutory law concerning donor-advised funds.[20]

Relevant to the concept of a charitable gift and the matter of reciprocal benefits to donors is the fact that the federal law, as noted, distinguishes

---

12. E.g., *Fund for Anonymous Gifts v. Internal Revenue Service*, 97-2 U.S.T.C. ¶ 50,710 (D.D.C. 1997), *on appeal, suspended* (D.C. Cir. Mar. 16, 1998). *See*, however, text accompanied by *infra* note 39.
13. *Darling v. Commissioner*, 43 T.C. 520 (1965).
14. Rev. Rul. 77-225, 1977-2 C.B. 73.
15. *Lawrence v. United States*, 75-1 U.S.T.C. ¶ 9165 (C.D. Cal. 1974).
16. See text accompanied by *infra* notes 20–21.
17. *See* § 3.3.
18. Reg. § 1.170A-9(e)(10).
19. *See* text accompanied by *infra* note 22.
20. *See* § 16.9.

between donor-advised funds and donor-directed funds. To reiterate, the latter type of fund involves an arrangement between a charitable organization and a donor whereby the donor retains one or more rights as to the subsequent investment and/or disposition of the subject of the gift. By contrast, a donor-advised fund does not have the feature of donor direction, but allows the donor to tender advice as to subsequent investment and/or disposition of the subject of the gift.

Until 2006, there was little specific law on donor-advised funds and donor-directed funds, however. The closest reference in the Internal Revenue Code to the concept was the provision authorizing the common fund foundation; deductible charitable contributions are allowed in these circumstances.[21] This is the case even though the donor and his or her spouse can annually designate public charities to which the foundation must grant the income and principal of the original contribution. Thus, the common fund foundation is a type of private foundation closely comparable to a donor-directed fund.

In the case of community foundations, which hold themselves out as a bundle of donor-advised funds, a donor at the time of the gift (i.e., at the time of creation of the component fund) is permitted to designate the charitable purpose of the gift or the specific charity that will receive the income or principal, consistent with the community foundation's exempt purposes.[22] These regulations do not permit the donor to direct, aside from the original designation, which charity may receive distributions or the timing of the distributions to the charitable recipient.[23] The donor may also offer nonbinding advice to the community fund manager regarding payouts from the component fund. (When a donor offers advice of this nature, the IRS is likely to carefully examine the facts involved to determine whether the giving of the "advice" by the donor is in actuality an indirect reservation of a right to direct the distributions.)

There is, nonetheless, a determination from the IRS that is somewhat pertinent to this analysis.[24] This private letter ruling involved a private foundation, the trustees of which determined to transfer all of its assets to a community foundation, which in turn would place the assets in a donor-advised fund. (The private letter ruling does not define this term.) The private foundation would remain in existence for the sole purpose of advising the community foundation on the use of the fund for charitable purposes. The IRS ruled that retention of this ability to make this type of recommendation would not constitute a prohibited material restriction as that term is used for purposes of the private foundation termination provisions.[25]

---

21. IRC § 170(b)(1)(A)(vii).
22. Reg. §§ 1.170A-9(e)(11)(B), 1.507-2(a)(8)(iii)(B).
23. Cf. Reg. § 1.507-2(a)(8)(iv)(A)(1).
24. Tech. Adv. Mem. 8836033.
25. *See* Chapter 13.

A private foundation can make a grant (qualifying distribution) to a donor-advised fund in satisfaction of the foundation's mandatory payout require-ments.[26] These distribution requirements can be satisfied even though the private foundation's governing board retains the ability to make recommenda-tions as to the subsequent granting of the money.[27]

The law concerning *prohibited material restrictions*[28] is similar to the concepts distinguishing donor-directed funds and donor-advised funds. This body of law is in the federal income tax regulations.[29] The test under these restrictions is whether the transferee of assets is prevented from freely and effectively employ-ing the transferred assets or the income from them for charitable purposes. For example, if the transferor reserved the right to direct one or more public charities to which the transferee must distribute the transferred assets and/or income, that would constitute a prohibited material restriction. The same is true with respect to restrictions on the ability of the transferee to maintain or manage the assets and with respect to any other condition imposed on the transferee that prevents it from exercising ultimate control over the assets received by the transferor.

The previously referenced IRS determination[30] holds that the ability to make the recommendation expressed by the trustees of the private foundation does not constitute a prohibited material restriction.[31]

The IRS ruled that a donor is entitled to a charitable contribution deduction for a gift of money or other property where the donor, or the donor's investment manager, retains the power, under certain conditions, to manage the gift property in a designated account.[32]

A significant (albeit unfortunate) court opinion concerning donor-advised funds concluded that an organization that operated such a fund could not be tax-exempt as a charitable entity, although the case was more about tax fraud and private benefit.[33] Because of the fund's promotional materials, which emphasized donor self-interest rather than charitable intent, the court observed that the organization "served significant non-exempt purposes that focused primarily on providing personal, rather than public, benefits." It wrote that the organization's operations were "characterized at the least by willful neglect, and, more than likely, an active willingness to participate in a scheme designed to produce impermissible tax benefits." These materials and operations sug-gested, the court wrote, that the "donors in question did not truly relinquish

---

26. *See* Chapter 6.
27. E.g., Priv. Ltr. Rul. 9807030.
28. *See* § 16.5.
29. Reg. § 1.507-2(a)(8)(iii).
30. *Supra* note 22.
31. The identical conclusion was subsequently reached in Priv. Ltr. Rul. 9807030.
32. Priv. Ltr. Rul. 200445023.
33. *New Dynamics Foundation v. United States*, 2006-1 U.S.T.C. ¶ 50,286 (U.S. Ct. Fed. Cl. 2006).

ownership and control over the donated funds and property" but rather treated the organization as a "conduit for accomplishing the twin tax avoidance goals of building up their assets tax-free and then siphoning off the accumulated wealth to pay for personal expenditures." This case was an aberration, certainly not in the donor-advised or donor-directed mainstream; it is essentially a private benefit doctrine case with unusually ugly facts.

## § 16.4   IRS CHALLENGES TO DONOR FUNDS

The IRS challenged the donor-advised fund/donor-directed fund technique in court; the government lost the case for reasons articulated in an opinion issued in 1987.[34] The IRS attempted to deny tax-exempt status to a public charity maintaining donor-advised funds, contending that the entity was merely an association of donors for which commercial services were being performed for fees, and that the entity was violating the prohibitions on private inurement and private benefit.[35] The IRS asserted that the organization's "activities are all originated, funded, and controlled by small related groups, by single individuals, or by families" and that "these individual donors retain full control of the funds."[36]

The court, however, found that donors to the organization "relinquish all ownership and custody of the donated funds or property" and that the organization is "free to accept or reject any suggestion or request made by a donor."[37] Indeed, the court enthused that the "goal" of the organization "is to create an effective national network to respond to many worthy charitable needs at the local level which in many cases might go unmet" and that its activities "promote public policy and represent the very essence of charitable benevolence as envisioned by Congress in enacting" tax-exempt status for charitable organizations.[38]

Ten years later, the IRS prevailed on the point.[39] The entity involved was structured much the same as the collective of donor-advised funds in the previous case. The trustee of the fund was bound by the donor's enforceable conditions as to disposition of its funds to ultimate charities. Nonetheless, the fund was ruled to not be tax-exempt as a charitable organization. The court wrote: "The manner in which the fund's investment activity would be conducted makes clear that one of the purposes of the fund is to allow persons to take a charitable deduction for a donation to the fund while retaining

---

34. *National Foundation, Inc. v. United States*, 87-2 U.S.T.C. ¶ 9602 (Cl. Ct. 1987).
35. *See* § 5.1.
36. *National Foundation, Inc. v. United States*, 87-2, U.S.T.C. ¶ 9602 (Ct. Cl. 1987), at 89,830.
37. *Id.* at 89,831.
38. *Id.* at 89,832.
39. *Fund for Anonymous Gifts v. Internal Revenue Service*, 97-2 U.S.T.C. ¶ 50,710 (D.D.C. 1997), *on appeal, suspended* (D.C. Cir. Mar. 16, 1998).

investment control over the donation."[40] This opinion did not differentiate between material and other restrictions.

The IRS's victory was short-lived, however. This decision was appealed, which led to settlement negotiations.[41] The trustee of the fund agreed, as requested by the IRS, to eliminate the language in the fund's document that gave donors the control that was found by the lower court to be unwarranted private benefit. Nonetheless, for more than one year, the IRS refused to grant the fund recognition of tax-exempt status, eventually causing the court of appeals, in frustration, to vacate the district court's decision and to direct that court to issue an order that the fund is an exempt charitable entity.[42]

The government was of the view that this amendment did not "sufficiently address the inadequacies" of the fund's operations. It contended that the administrative record showed that the fund would not "take complete control over the contributions." Rather, the government was of the view that the fund would "adhere to the directions of its donors regarding the investment and the ultimate distribution of the contributed funds." This amendment did not, the government asserted, prevent the fund from "providing investment services and acting as an administrative conduit for its donors' funds."[43]

In the IRS's first private letter ruling on the point, the agency held that the establishment by a charitable organization of a donor-advised gift fund program did not jeopardize the organization's exempt status.[44]

## § 16.5 PROHIBITED MATERIAL RESTRICTIONS

One of the reasons for focus on these types of donor funds is the need for a judgment as to whether a transaction, which is otherwise a charitable gift,[45] is not, in law, a completed gift at all because the donor retains too much control over the subsequent use and disposition of the gift money or property. At least in the context of donor-advised gift funds (and thus presumably in most other donor fund contexts, including donor-directed funds), the IRS uses the criteria provided in the private foundation termination rules to determine whether a completed gift has been made.

A charitable organization can terminate its private foundation status by transferring all of its income and assets to one or more public charities.[46] An

---

40. *National Foundation, Inc. v. United States*, 87-2 U.S.T.C. ¶ 9602 (Ct. Cl. 1987), at 89,854.
41. *See* § 16.6.
42. *Fund for Anonymous Gifts v. United States*, 99-1 U.S.T.C. ¶ 50,440 (D.C. Cir. 1999). The Fund for Anonymous Gifts eventually became reorganized as a tax-exempt, public charity, by ruling dated February 27, 2003, as the result of mediation with the IRS.
43. *IRS Exempt Organizations Continuing Professional Education Text for Fiscal Year 2000*, Technical Topic P 2 B (2).
44. Priv. Ltr. Rul. 200149045.
45. *See* § 16.2.
46. *See* § 13.3.

issue that can arise is whether the transfer is in fact a completed one. The income tax regulations provide criteria for making this determination.

The regulations concerning termination of private foundation status focus on whether a grantor private foundation has transferred "all of its right, title, and interest in and to" the funds (including any property) transferred.[47] To effectuate such a transfer, a grantor private foundation "may not impose any material restriction or condition" that prevents the grantee from "freely and effectively employing the transferred assets, or the income derived therefrom, in furtherance of its exempt purposes."[48] Whether a particular condition or restriction imposed on a transfer of assets is *material* must be determined from all of the facts and circumstances of the transfer.[49]

The presence of some or all of the following nonadverse factors (or positive characteristics) is not considered as preventing the grantee from "freely and effectively employing the transferred assets, or the income derived therefrom, in furtherance of its exempt purposes":

*Name.* The transfer is to a fund that is given a name or other designation that is the same as or similar to that of the grantor private foundation or otherwise memorializes the creator of the foundation or his or her family.

*Purpose.* The income and assets of the fund are to be used for a designated purpose or for one or more particular public charities, and that use is consistent with the public charity's charitable purpose.

*Administration.* The transferred money or property is administered in an identifiable or separate fund, some or all of the principal of which is not to be distributed for a specified period, if the grantee public charity is the legal and equitable owner of the fund and the governing body of the public charity exercises ultimate and direct authority and control over the fund.[50]

*Retention requirement.* The grantor private foundation transfers property the continued retention of which by the grantee is required by the transferor if the retention is important to the achievement of charitable purposes (the *nonadverse factors*).[51]

The presence of any of seven factors is considered as preventing the grantee from "freely and effectively employing the transferred assets, or the income derived therefrom, in furtherance of its exempt purposes" (the *adverse factors*).[52]

---

47. IRC § 507(b)(1)(A).
48. Reg. § 1.507-2(a)(8)(i).
49. *Id.*
50. A donor-advised fund established within a community trust must be administered in or as a component part of the trust (Reg. § 1.170A-9(e)(1)). *See* § 13.5(d).
51. Reg. § 1.507-2(a)(8)(iii).
52. Reg. § 1.507-2(a)(8)(iv).

The first of these factors concerns control over distributions. The issue is whether the transferor private foundation, a disqualified person with respect to it (such as a board member, officer, or substantial contributor), or any person or committee designated by, or pursuant to the terms of an agreement with, such a person (collectively, the *grantor*) reserved the right, directly or indirectly, to name the persons to which the transferee public charity must distribute, or to direct the timing of such distributions.[53]

With respect to this factor, the IRS will carefully examine whether the seeking of advice by the transferee from, or the giving of advice by, any grantor after the assets have been transferred to the transferee constitutes an indirect reservation of a right to direct the distributions.[54] In such a case, the reservation of this type of a right will be considered to exist when the only criterion considered by the public charity in making a distribution of income or principal from a grantor's fund is advice offered by the grantor.[55] Whether there is a reservation of this type of right is to be determined on the basis of all of the facts and circumstances.[56] In making this determination, the elements contained in the six factors, in addition to the five factors (both of which are discussed next), are to be taken into consideration.[57]

The presence of some or all of the following six factors indicates that the reservation of this type of right does not exist:

1. There has been an independent investigation by the staff of the public charity evaluating whether the grantor's advice is consistent with specific charitable needs most deserving of support by the recipient charity (as determined by it).

2. The public charity has promulgated guidelines enumerating specific charitable needs consistent with the charitable purposes of the public charity.

3. The grantor's advice is consistent with these guidelines.

4. The public charity has instituted an educational program publicizing these guidelines to donors and other persons.

5. The public charity distributes funds in excess of amounts distributed from the grantor's fund to the same or similar types of organizations or charitable needs as those recommended by the grantor.

---

53. Reg. § 1.507-2(a)(8)(iv)(A)(1).
54. *Id.*
55. *Id.*
56. *Id.*
57. *Id.*

6. The solicitations for funds of the public charity specifically state that the public entity will not be bound by advice offered by the grantor (the *six factors*).[58]

The presence of some or all of the following five factors indicates that the reservation of a right exists:

1. The solicitation of funds by the public charity states or implies that the grantor's advice will be followed.

2. A pattern of conduct on the part of that charity creates an expectation that the grantor's advice will be followed.

3. The advice of a grantor (whether or not restricted to a distribution of income or principal from the grantor's trust or fund) is limited to distributions of amounts from the grantor's fund (and certain factors are not present (namely, the first two of the six factors).

4. Only the advice of the grantor as to distributions from the grantor's fund is solicited by the public charity, and no procedure is provided for considering advice from persons other than the grantor with respect to the fund.

5. For the year involved and all prior years, the public charity follows the advice of all grantors with respect to their funds substantially all of the time (the *five factors*).[59]

The other factor of the seven factors that may be relevant pertains to any agreement entered into between the transferor private foundation and the transferee public charity "which establishes irrevocable relationships with respect to the maintenance or management of assets transferred to the public charity."[60] This factor is additionally described by a reference to relationships "such as continuing relationships with banks, brokerage firms, investment counselors, or other advisors with regard to the investments or other property transferred to the public charity."[61]

Of the seven factors, the remaining five are irrelevant to this matter. They pertain to certain mandatory actions or withholding of actions, assumptions of leases, retentions of investment assets, rights of first refusal, and any other condition that prevents the transferee public charity "from exercising ultimate control over the assets received from the transferor private foundation for purposes consistent with its exempt purposes."[62]

---

58. Reg. § 1.507-2(a)(8)(iv)(A)(2).
59. Reg. § 1.507-2(a)(8)(iv)(A)(3).
60. Reg. § 1.507-2(a)(8)(iv)(F).
61. *Id.*
62. Reg. § 1.507-2(a)(8)(iv)(B)–(E), (G).

The presence of any of the seven factors is, as noted, considered as preventing the transferee from "freely and effectively" utilizing the transferred assets or income from them in furtherance of charitable purposes. To have application of these rules be deemed to cause something less than a full transfer, for purposes of termination of private foundation status and thus for purposes of determining whether a transfer is a qualifying distribution,[63] however, a restriction, right, or condition must also be material.[64]

Whether a particular condition or restriction imposed on a transfer of assets is *material* must be determined from all of the facts and circumstances of the transfer.[65] The tax regulations state that some of the "more significant" facts and circumstances to be considered in making this determination are whether:

1. The public charity is the owner in fee of the assets it received from the private foundation.

2. The assets are to be held and administered by the public charity in a manner consistent with one or more of its exempt purposes.

3. The governing body of the public charity has the ultimate authority and control over the assets and the income derived from them.

4. The extent to which the governing body of the public charity is organized and operated so as to be independent from the transferor (the *materiality factors*).[66]

As to the fourth of these factors, it also must be determined from all of the facts and circumstances.[67] Some of the "more significant" of these facts and circumstances to be considered are:

- Whether, and to what extent, members of the governing body are individuals selected by the transferor private foundation or its disqualified persons, or are themselves disqualified persons with respect to the foundation.

- Whether, and to what extent, members of the governing body are selected by public officials acting in their capacities as such.

- How long a period of time each member of the governing body may serve in that capacity (the independence factors).[68]

---

63. *See* § 6.5.
64. Reg. § 1.507-2(a)(8)(i).
65. *Id.*
66. *Id.*
67. Reg. § 1.507-2(a)(8)(ii).
68. *Id.*

In one instance, a private foundation proposed to provide an endowment to fund the operating expenses of a public charity, including those for construction of a facility. The funds were to be paid to an escrow agent, who would hold the funds until certain conditions were satisfied. The purpose for establishment of the endowment, before construction took place, was to assure bond holders and contributors that funds would be available to support the entity. In finding the restrictions not to be "material," the IRS observed that the private foundation had given up any right to control use of the funds in the grantee's possession, other than through the restrictions set forth in the escrow agreement; the private foundation retained no right of reversion or other interest in the transferred assets; ultimate distribution of the funds would occur within a reasonable period of time; and the ultimate grantee was a public charity.[69]

## § 16.6 DEPARTMENT OF JUSTICE POSITION

A case in this area was appealed.[70] Following the organization's loss in the lower court and during the appellate process, settlement negotiations ensued. In a letter to the fund involved, dated June 4, 1998, the Tax Division of the Department of Justice (Tax Division) proposed that the fund's trust agreement be amended to state that the "Trustee shall only accept gifts that are free of any 'material restrictions or conditions' within the meaning of Section 1.507–2(a)(8) of the Income Tax Regulations."

The Tax Division also wanted this language: "The Trustee shall establish procedures that insure complete and independent control and discretion over the Fund's assets. The Trustee agrees that it is not obligated to use or contribute [grant] donated funds in the manner requested by the donor of the funds." This settlement proposal was rejected by the fund.

By letter dated October 16, 1998, the Tax Division proposed the following language: "The Trustee may not receive any contribution, donation, gift, bequest or devise that is not a transfer of all the donor's right, title, and interest or is subject to a restriction or condition that prevents the Trustee from freely and effectively employing the transferred assets, or income therefrom, in furtherance of the Fund's exempt purposes. The Trustee may not receive any contribution, donation, gift, bequest or devise that is subject to any condition or term that prevents the Trustee from obtaining the ultimate authority and control over the assets, and the income derived from them, at the time of the transfer."

---

69. Priv. Ltr. Rul. 9014004.
70. *See supra* note 42.

As discussed earlier,[71] the trustee of the fund agreed to a provision of this nature; nonetheless, the continuing inability of the parties to resolve the issue led to a court order as to tax exemption for the fund.

## § 16.7 PUBLIC CHARITY STATUS OF FUNDS

Another issue being raised by the functions of charitable organizations that maintain donor-advised funds—particularly those that maintain these funds as their sole function, such as charitable gift funds and *national foundations*[72]—is whether these entities qualify as publicly supported charities.

Community foundations, charitable gift funds, and other entities maintaining donor-advised funds to a significant extent are classified as donative-type publicly supported charities.[73] This is because the contributions to these organizations, albeit earmarked for donor-advised funds, are treated, in whole or in part, as public support for the charity. The IRS, however, has been fretting over the propriety of treating donor-advised funds as publicly supported charities, on the theory that these charities may not be *supported* in a technical, legal sense.

When a grant is made from a donor-advised fund to a charity—which may be termed the *ultimate beneficiary*—the grant amount can be regarded (in whole or in part) as public support for the ultimate beneficiary. For some time, it was the view of the IRS that these gifts to charities maintaining donor-advised funds amounted to public support for both the "intermediate" and "ultimate" beneficiary charities.[74] As the controversy widened, however, the IRS withdrew its views on the subject.[75]

The IRS is not troubled by the concept that "earmarked" gifts are forms of public support for the "ultimate" charitable recipient. It is the treatment of these gifts as public support for the "intermediate" entity—the collective of donor-advised funds—that the IRS has said is giving it pause.[76]

The IRS's publication[77] feigns objectivity in places, then loses even that in others. Thus, it was written: "There is no authority in the regulations or elsewhere that the earmarked funds are treated as support for the intermediary organizations as well as the ultimate recipient." It is true that the law is silent on the point, but that does not necessarily mean that this dual characterization of

---

71. *See* § 16.4.
72. A term of disparagement once promoted by certain members of congressional staff to describe these entities is *accommodation charities*.
73. *See* § 15.4.
74. Gen. Couns. Mem. 39748.
75. Gen. Couns. Mem. 39875.
76. *1995 Exempt Organizations Continuing Professional Education Technical Instruction Program Textbook*, which contains an essay on donor-advised and donor-directed funds.
77. IRS CPE text FY 2000, *supra* note 39.

the funds for tax purposes is inappropriate. This is particularly the case with donor-advised funds, where the gifts are not earmarked as a matter of law.[78]

This analysis posited a second approach, in that it applied the distinction between contributions to a charitable organization and those *for the use of* a charitable organization.[79] The idea is that only contributions to a charitable organization can be treated as public support, as the charity is free to use the gifts in its charitable program. The IRS essay asserts that an earmarked gift and a gift "for the use of" a charity are similar in that "both have qualities of property held in trust." That is, this view asserts that the intermediary entity is the functional equivalent of a trustee for the ultimate charity, so that these earmarked contributions ought not to be regarded as public support for the intermediate entity (the organization housing charitable gift funds).

There are fundamental problems with this approach. This analysis often fails to differentiate between donor-advised funds and donor-directed funds. Given the limited recommendatory authority associated with the former, it is not credible to assert that the arrangement involves a trust relationship. Also, it is common for donors to make restricted gifts, where the restriction is a programmatic one (such as for research or scholarships); there is no authority for a proposition that these restrictions give rise to a trust. Moreover, the statutory definition of *support*[80] does not embody this dubious dichotomy in this context between gifts to and for the use of charity.

## § 16.8 INTERRELATIONSHIP OF PRIVATE FOUNDATION RULES

Of great concern to the IRS in approving tax exemption for donor-advised funds, particularly those created by for-profit financial institutions, is the potential for avoidance of the minimum distribution requirements.[81] This is one of the reasons the IRS regards certain donor-advised funds as "aggressive tax avoidance schemes."[82] Because they qualify as public charities, charitable

---

78. Nonetheless, in one set of circumstances, the IRS ruled that contributions to a donor-advised fund may be treated as support from the general public (in this instance, under IRC § 170(b)(1)(A)(vi)) to the charity that maintains the fund (Priv. Ltr. Rul. 200037053). In a second determination, the IRS reached a like conclusion (Priv. Ltr. Rul. 200150039). In *The Fund for Anonymous Gifts v. Commissioner*, on remand from a decision that the fund qualifies as a charitable organization (*supra* note 42), the lower court ruled, in September 2001, that the administrative record does not support a "reasonable expectation" that the fund will qualify as a publicly supported charity, due in part to a "lack of any plan to solicit the general public for support." The matter was settled, however, with the IRS recognizing the fund as a tax-exempt public supported charity.
79. *See Charitable Giving*, § 10.2.
80. IRC § 509(d).
81. *See* Chapter 6.
82. IRS CPE Text FY 2000, Technical Topic P, 1.

organizations administering donor-advised funds are not subject to the mandatory payout rules.

Nonetheless, the IRS expects donor-advised funds to adhere to certain of the private foundation rules, if tax exemption is to be recognized. The following expected representations are being required, at least in certain circumstances:[83]

The organization expects that its grants for the year will equal or exceed 5 percent of its average net assets on a fiscal-year rolling basis. (This is adherence to the private foundation payout requirements.[84]) If this level of grant activity is not attained, the organization will identify the named accounts (donor-advised funds) from which grants over the same period totaled less than 5 percent of each account's average assets. The organization will contact the donor-advisors of these accounts to request that they recommend grants of at least this amount. If a donor-advisor does not provide the qualified grant recommendations, the organization is authorized to transfer an amount up to 5 percent of assets from the donor-advisor's named account to the charity or charities selected by the organization.

The organization will add language to its promotional materials stating that the organization will investigate allegations of improper use of grant funds for the private benefit of donor-advisors.

The organization will add language to its grantee letters to the effect that grants are to be used by grantees exclusively in furtherance of charitable purposes and cannot be used for the private benefit of donor-advisors. (This is intended to parallel the prohibitions on private foundations as to the making of taxable expenditures.)[85]

Making a charitable gift to create a donor-advised fund is relatively easy compared to the establishment of a new private foundation. No new trust or nonprofit corporation comes into existence, and IRS recognition of tax-exempt status of the fund is not necessary. Often community foundations and commercial gift funds have preprinted master documents designed to meet the standards regarding donor advice. Many of these organizations provide guidelines that stipulate the parameters within which grant recommendations will be acted on. Forms for creating designated accounts for some funds are available on the Internet for immediate completion if one so desires. Administration of a donor-advised fund is normally also far less of a burden than managing an independent private foundation. Annual information returns are not necessary for these accounts because they are not separate entities. Though an annual administrative fee is customarily charged for each designated account, the annual cost of accounting for the investments and grants, and preparing annual IRS and state reports for the typical private foundation, can be far more costly.

---

83. These are referenced in IRS CPE Text FY 2000, Technical Topic P, 2C.
84. *See* Chapter 6.
85. *See* Chapter 9.

To further compare to the establishment of an independent private foundation, donor-advised funds are free of some constraints that make a private foundation unacceptable. The excise tax on investment income[86] is not imposed on the assets held in donor-advised accounts. Of particular concern for the type of assets limited in their deductibility to the donor's basis, such as land or tangible personal property, the income tax deductibility limits are more favorable.[87] The self-dealing rules do not apply to prohibit transactions between the donor and the fund,[88] although as a practical matter many organizations managing donor-advised funds do not accept the type of assets that might present this issue. The excess business holdings rules[89] are imposed on donor-advised funds; the jeopardizing investment rules[90] that place specific limitations on the type of assets a private foundation may hold are not so imposed. Last, and sometimes most important, the taxable expenditure rules do not apply to require special steps to be taken before the fund can make grants for individual scholarships and fellowships, or donations to foreign organizations and projects.

In contrast, the most significant disadvantage of a donor-advised fund in comparison to a private foundation is the donor's lack of control. Donors are prohibited from placing material restrictions on the funds.[91] Grant recipients may be recommended, but not required. Geographic location may be limited to the area in which the community foundation is established, whereas a private foundation has no such restrictions absent enhanced record-keeping requirements for certain foreign and individual grants. For donors that desire privacy, the different disclosure rules for public charities may be desirable. Private foundations have to include a listing of their contributors in their annual information returns that will have to be provided to anyone who asks.[92] Public charities may exclude a listing of their donors. Although being subject to the ultimate control of an independent board may be undesirable while the donor(s) is living, the fund's existence within an established, presumably everlasting, charitable organization may be advantageous when succession is uncertain. Most funds allow the appointment of substitute or successor advisors.

## § 16.9 STATUTORY CRITERIA

Legislation that generally took effect for tax years beginning after August 17, 2006, brought a statutory definition of the term *donor-advised fund*. Essentially, it is a fund or account that is (1) separately identified by reference to contributions

---

86. *See* Chapter 10.
87. *See* § 14.4.
88. *See* Chapter 5.
89. *See* Chapter 7, § 16.9.
90. *See* Chapter 8.
91. *See* § 16.5.
92. *See* § 12.3.

of one or more donors, (2) that is owned and controlled by a sponsoring organization, and (3) as to which a donor or a donor advisor[93] has, or reasonably expects to have, advisory privileges with respect to the distribution or investment of amounts held in the fund or account by reason of the donor's status as a donor.[94] A *sponsoring organization* is a public charity that maintains one or more donor-advised funds.[95] A donor-advised fund does not include funds that make distributions only to a single identified organization or governmental entity, or certain funds where a donor or donor advisor provides advice as to which individuals receive grants for travel, study, or other similar purposes.[96]

A distribution from a donor-advised fund is taxable if it is to (1) a natural person or (2) any other person for a noncharitable purpose unless expenditure responsibility is exercised with respect to the distribution.[97] A tax, of 20 percent of the amount involved, is imposed on the sponsoring organization.[98] Another tax, of 5 percent, is imposed on the agreement of a fund manager[99] to the making of a taxable distribution, where the manager knew that the distribution was a taxable one.[100] The tax on fund management is subject to a joint and several liability requirement.[101] This tax does not apply to a distribution from a donor-advised fund to most public charities,[102] the fund's sponsoring organization, or another donor-advised fund.[103]

If a donor, donor advisor, or a person related to a donor or donor advisor with respect to a donor-advised fund provides advice as to a distribution that results in any of those persons receiving, directly or indirectly, a benefit that is more than incidental, an excise tax equal to 125 percent of the amount of the benefit is imposed on the person who advised as to the distribution and on the

---

93. That is, a person appointed or designated by a donor.
94. IRC § 4966(d)(2)(A).
95. IRC § 4966(d)(1).
96. IRC § 4966(d)(2)(B). The IRS has the authority to exempt a fund or account from treatment as a donor-advised fund under certain circumstances (IRC § 4966(d)(2)(C)). Exercising this authority, the IRS announced that certain employer-sponsored disaster relief assistance funds do not constitute donor-advised funds (Notice 2006-109, 2006-51 I.R.B. 1121 § 5.01).
97. IRC § 4966(c)(1). This is termed a *taxable distribution*. The expenditure responsibility rules are the subject of § 9.6.
98. IRC § 4966(a)(1).
99. This term embraces trustees, directors, officers, and executive employees of a sponsoring organization (IRC § 4966(d)(3)).
100. IRC § 4966(a)(2). This tax is confined to $10,000 per transaction (IRC § 4966(b)(2)).
101. IRC § 4966(b)(1).
102. That is, organizations described in IRC § 170(b)(1)(A), other than a *disqualified supporting organization*, which is a Type III supporting organization (other than a functionally integrated one) and certain Type I and II supporting organizations (IRC § 4966(d)(4)). *See* § 15.7(e)–(g).
103. IRC § 4966(c)(2).

recipient of the benefit.[104] Also, if a manager of the sponsoring organization agreed to the making of the distribution, knowing that the distribution would confer more than an incidental benefit on a donor, donor advisor, or related person, the manager is subject to an excise tax equal to 10 percent of the amount of the benefit.[105] These taxes are subject to a joint and several liability requirement.[106]

A grant, loan, compensation, or other similar payment (e.g., reimbursement of expenses) from a donor-advised fund to a person that, with respect to the fund, is a donor, donor advisor, or a person related to a donor or donor advisor automatically is treated as an excess benefit transaction for intermediate sanctions law purposes.[107] This means that the entire amount paid to any of these persons is an excess benefit.[108] Donors and donor advisors with respect to a donor-advised fund (and related persons) are disqualified persons for intermediate sanctions law purposes with respect to transactions with the donor-advised fund (although not necessarily with respect to transactions with the sponsoring organization).[109]

The private foundation excess business holdings rules[110] apply to donor-advised funds.[111] For this purpose, the term *disqualified person* means, with respect to a donor-advised fund, a donor, donor advisor, member of the family of either, or a 35 percent controlled entity of any such person.[112]

In the facts of the first IRS private letter ruling applying this law, a charitable organization maintaining donor-advised funds was the recipient of gifts of a corporation's nonvoting stock from two brothers, founders of the corporation; the gifts were placed in donor-advised funds. The brothers were disqualified persons. After these gifts and after transfer of all of the voting stock of the

---

104. IRC § 4967(a)(1). The term *incidental* is not defined in this context. A summary of this legislation, however, states that "there is a more than incidental benefit if, as a result of a distribution from a donor-advised fund, a donor, donor advisor, or related person with respect to such fund receives a benefit that would have reduced (or eliminated) a charitable contribution deduction if the benefit was received as part of the contribution to the sponsoring organization" (Joint Committee Explanation at 350). This suggests that at least one way to define the term *incidental* is to use the definition of the term in the charitable giving context where a charitable deduction is not otherwise reduced by reason of an inconsequential benefit. Definitions of tenuous and incidental benefits applicable to private foundations can be found in § 5.8(d) (also *see Charitable Giving*, § 3.1(c)).

105. IRC § 4967(a)(2). The maximum amount of this tax per distribution is $10,000 (IRC § 4967 (c)(2)). This tax and the tax referenced in *supra* note 96 may not be imposed if a tax with respect to the distribution has been imposed pursuant to the intermediate sanctions rules (IRC § 4967(b)); *see Tax-Exempt Organizations*, Chapter 21.

106. IRC § 4967(c)(1).

107. IRC § 4958(c)(2).

108. Cf. § 15.7(h), text accompanied by notes 332–335.

109. IRC § 4958(f)(7).

110. *See* Chapter 7.

111. IRC § 4943(e)(1).

112. IRC § 4943(e)(2).

corporation to another public charity, however, the disqualified persons owned less than 20 percent of the voting stock, causing the nonvoting stock to be permitted holdings. The second public charity was not a disqualified person with respect to the charitable donee. Thus, the sponsoring organization, and of course its funds, was ruled to not have any excess business holdings.[113]

Contributions to a sponsoring organization for maintenance in a donor-advised fund are not eligible for a charitable deduction for federal income tax purposes if the sponsoring organization is a fraternal society, a cemetery company, or a veterans' organization.[114] Contributions to a sponsoring organization for such maintenance are not eligible for a charitable deduction for federal estate or gift tax purposes if the sponsoring organization is a fraternal society or a veterans' organization.[115] Contributions to a sponsoring organization for such maintenance are not eligible for a charitable deduction for income, estate, or gift tax purposes if the sponsoring organization is a Type III supporting organization (other than a functionally integrated Type III supporting organization).[116] A donor must obtain, with respect to each charitable contribution to a sponsoring organization to be maintained in a donor-advised fund, a contemporaneous written acknowledgment from the sponsoring organization that the organization has exclusive legal control over the funds or assets contributed.[117]

A sponsoring organization is required to disclose on its annual information return the number of donor-advised funds it owns, the aggregate value of assets held in the funds at the end of the organization's tax year, and the aggregate contributions to and grants made from these funds during the year.[118] When seeking recognition of tax-exempt status, a sponsoring organization must disclose whether it intends to maintain donor-advised funds.[119] As to this latter rule, the organization must provide information regarding its planned operation of these funds, including a description of procedures it intends to use to (1) communicate to donors and donor advisors that assets held in the funds are the property of the sponsoring organization and (2) ensure that distributions from donor-advised funds do not result in more than incidental benefit to any person.[120]

---

113. Priv. Ltr. Rul. 201311035.

114. IRC § 170(f)(18)(A)(i). *See Tax-Exempt Organizations*, §§ 19.4, 19.6, 19.11, respectively.

115. IRC §§ 2055(e)(5)(A)(i), 2522(c)(5)(A)(i).

116. IRC §§ 170(f)(18)(A)(ii), 2055(e)(5)(A)(ii), 2522(c)(5)(A)(ii).

117. IRC §§ 170(f)(18)(B), 2055(e)(5)(B), 2522(c)(5)(B). This requirement is in addition to other charitable giving substantiation requirements (*see Charitable Giving*, § 21.1).

118. IRC § 6033(k).

119. IRC § 508(f).

120. Joint Committee Explanation at 350.

## § 16.10 DEPARTMENT OF TREASURY STUDY

The Department of the Treasury was directed by the Congress to undertake a study on the organization and operation of donor-advised funds, to consider whether (1) the deductions allowed for income, estate, or gift taxes for charitable contributions to sponsoring organizations of donor-advised funds are appropriate in consideration of the use of contributed assets or the use of the assets of such organizations for the benefit of the person making the charitable contribution, (2) donor-advised funds should be required to distribute for charitable purposes a specified amount in order to ensure that the sponsoring organization with respect to the donor-advised fund is operating in a manner consistent with its tax exemption or public charity status, (3) the retention by donors to donor-advised funds of "rights or privileges" with respect to amounts transferred to such organizations (including advisory rights or privileges with respect to the making of grants or the investment of assets) is consistent with the treatment of these transfers as completed gifts, and (4) these issues are also issues with respect to other forms of charitable organizations or charitable contributions.[121]

## § 16.11 CONGRESSIONAL RESEARCH SERVICE STUDY

The Congressional Research Service (CRS) issued a report, dated July 11, 2012, that includes statistics on donor-advised funds, using data derived from Forms 990 for 2008.

### (a) Statistics

In 2008, more than 181,000 individual donor-advised fund accounts were maintained. In that year, there were about 1,818 organizations maintaining at least one donor-advised fund account. Approximately one-third of organizations claiming to have donor-advised funds reported that only one fund was maintained. About one-half of all sponsoring organizations reported that five or fewer funds were held.

Thus, according to this report, a small percentage of sponsoring organizations held a large number of donor-advised fund accounts. Fifty-one organizations (about 3 percent of all sponsoring organizations) reported having 500 or more individual donor-advised funds. More than 121,000 of all fund accounts (or two-thirds of them) are maintained by organizations that have at least 500 individual accounts. The report observes that the fact that a large proportion of individual donor-advised fund accounts are maintained by a small number of sponsoring organizations explains why the number of donor-advised funds per

---

121. Pension Protection Act of 2006, Pub. L. No. 109-280 § 1226. This report was issued in December 2011. *See* § 15.7(l).

organization (100) is "highly skewed." Also: "Since most [donor-advised fund] accounts are held by organizations maintaining multiple [fund] accounts, little is known about the characteristics of the majority of individual [fund] accounts."

For the year, sponsoring organizations reported $29.5 billion in donor-advised fund assets. On average, assets per donor-advised funds had a value of about $162,000. Nearly all donor-advised fund assets (87 percent) are held by sponsoring organizations that maintain 100 or more individual fund accounts.

Total contributions to donor-advised funds were reported to be $7.1 billion. These contributions represented approximately 3.3 percent of total individual giving. On average, sponsoring organizations received $3.9 million in contributions. The average contribution per fund account was $39,103.

Sponsoring organizations reported paying out $7 billion in grants. On average, $38,641 in grants were paid per donor-advised funds. Out of the 1,828 sponsoring organizations included in the sample, an estimated 453 did not pay out any grants. The organizations that sponsored donor-advised funds but did not pay grants held $280.4 million in assets in 2008.

The average payout rate across sponsoring organizations was 13.1 percent. The median payout rate was 6.1 percent; this average was said to be "skewed" by the payout rates of organizations with "unusually large payouts." Forty-three percent of sponsoring organizations had an average payout of less than 5 percent. Twenty-six percent did not report a payout.

This study included a review of 21 "commercial" organizations maintaining donor-advised funds. In 2008, 46.7 percent of individual fund accounts were maintained by these organizations. For the year, 34.3 percent of donor-advised fund assets, 39.2 percent of fund contributions, and 39.7 percent of fund grants involved "commercial" sponsoring organizations.

The average payout rate for commercial donor-advised funds was 26.5 percent. The report observed that, since commercial sponsoring organizations "tend to sponsor a large number of individual accounts (2,720 on average), it is possible that there is substantial variation in payout rates across individual accounts that is masked by the aggregate nature of available payout data."

## (b)  Policy Considerations

This report extensively addressed the matter of a minimum distribution requirement for donor-advised funds. It noted that the Treasury's position on a minimum payout for donor-advised funds was that it is premature to consider it based on one year of data. Yet, both the 2006 and 2008 data indicate a payout ratio in the aggregate that was higher than that of private foundations (but considerable variability in these ratios across sponsoring organizations).

The Treasury report stated that the payout rates for donor-advised funds in the aggregate in 2006 "appear to be high for most categories of [fund] sponsoring organizations." This statement, said the CRS, "seems to imply that observing an overall payout rate higher than that for foundations is a rationale for not imposing a minimum payout requirement" in the donor-advised fund context. The CRS, however, wrote that "there is ample reason to reject the notion that an aggregate payout ratio higher than that of private foundations provides a good rationale for not imposing such requirements on a per [fund] account basis." Yet, the CRS noted, although for sponsoring organizations maintaining a single fund account the average payout rate was 10.6 percent, over one-half of these organizations did not make any distribution and over 70 percent made a distribution of less than 5 percent. The CRS concluded that "there is likely to be substantial variation in payout rates at the individual account level across all sponsoring organizations."

The CRS report, not so subtly advocating consideration of a minimum payout rate for individual donor-advised funds, stated that a minimum rate imposed on sponsoring organizations would be "relatively meaningless," given the data. This approach, the CRS report stated, "would also create an incentive for donors who wished to accumulate funds and maintain endowments while paying little or nothing in grants to move to the larger [fund] sponsors, including commercial [donor-advised funds]."

This report also recalled that the Treasury report rejected application of private foundation rules to donor-advised funds on the ground that, as a matter of law, control of the fund is in the sponsoring organization (a public charity). The CRS report rejected this, writing that "donors appear to have actual control of grant-making because sponsoring organizations typically follow their advice." The report states that, "[i]n considering this issue, one question is whether the restricted legal rights of the donor or actual practice should determine the appropriate treatment."

The report raised the issue as to whether commercial donor-advised funds and national ones lacked a charitable purpose. It noted that some have suggested "tighter regulations and greater restrictions" for these sponsors. Also referenced was, in the case of commercial donor-advised funds, a "tension" between the "needs of charitable organizations . . . and the incentive to maintain large investment accounts."

Another proposal discussed in the CRS report is the one to restrict the duration of donor-advised funds. This could be done by limiting the life of these accounts or by limiting the period of years that advisory rights would be effective. The report states that this approach "would be an alternative or perhaps addition to a payout requirement to insure that the amounts in [fund] accounts are used for charitable purposes in some reasonable time period."

The CRS report bemoaned the fact that "all reporting is done at the aggregate [donor-advised fund] sponsor level, which means there is information only by inference concerning the shares of accounts that have low or no payout ratios." It stated: "Requiring reporting on individual [fund] accounts is an option that could improve understanding of how [donor-advised funds] operate and provide better oversight."

The report stated: "Useful information that could be provided by [donor-advised fund] sponsors could include the share of their [fund] accounts that made no distributions, the share that made distributions of less than 5 [percent], or a general distribution of accounts across different payout intervals." Also: "Information on investment fees and administrative costs of managing the [donor-advised funds], separated from other costs, could also be useful." Further: "Additional information could help policy makers evaluate whether giving through [donor-advised funds] is achieving charitable giving policy goals."

The CRS report concluded with this: "In some ways, the fundamental policy issue about how freely to allow donors to make contributions that are not immediately used for charitable purposes is whether such arrangements increase charitable giving per dollar of cost or decrease it. Allowing for contributions to accumulate and earn a tax-free return increases the benefit to the donor and thus may increase contributions to funds or foundations, albeit at an additional cost. Such arrangements can also reduce current charitable giving by encouraging fund accumulation, a concern that presumably motivated the minimum distribution rules for private foundations. [Donor-advised funds] differ from foundations in some ways, including the legal technicalities, but in practice, are very similar. One concern that remains for both foundations and [donor-advised funds] is how soon donations are put to charitable use."

# CHAPTER SEVENTEEN

# Corporate Foundations[1]

Tax-exempt charitable organizations that are affiliated with for-profit corporations, and usually controlled by them, are almost always private foundations (generically, corporate foundations). This private foundation status arises, in large part, because the related for-profit corporation typically is the sole funder of the corporate foundation.

## § 17.1 CORPORATE FOUNDATION OVERVIEW

Among the four features of a conventional private foundation is the characteristic that it is funded from one source.[2] Because the typical foundation related to a for-profit business is financially supported only by that business entity, the corporate foundation usually is a private foundation. It is possible for a charitable organization that is controlled by a for-profit entity to be a public charity—most likely, a donative-type publicly supported organization[3]—but these types of affiliated charities are rare.

---

1. Virginia C. Gross, Polsinelli PC, provided invaluable assistance in the preparation of this chapter.
2. *See* § 1.2.
3. *See* § 15.4. For example, the affiliated charitable organization could be principally funded by the employees of the related for-profit business (perhaps because of an employer matching-gift program) or perhaps by a suitable number of members of the public.

The corporate foundation is a separate legal entity[4] and must be operated primarily for charitable purposes.[5] Most frequently, the corporate foundation is a corporation.[6] The governing board of a corporate foundation is subject to the same requirements as to duties and responsibilities that are applicable to charitable organizations generally.[7] As noted, the corporate foundation is usually controlled by a for-profit business; this control element is almost always manifested by ex officio positions[8] and/or the ability of the related business entity to appoint (and remove) at least a majority of the trustees or directors of the foundation.[9]

Thus, in several ways, a corporate foundation is the alter ego of the for-profit business related to it. The two organizations usually have similar names (such as the XYZ Corporation and the XYZ Foundation), and the foundation's governing board is likely to be populated with present and former executives (indeed, as noted, probably at least a majority) of the related company. The name of the for-profit company usually brings recognition to the name of the corporate foundation; more substantially, the charitable works of the corporate foundation bring positive public recognition to the for-profit company and serve as evidence of the company's commitment to advancement of charitable causes.

The corporate foundation (assuming it is a private foundation) is subject to all of the requirements of law imposed on private foundations. There are, however, unique aspects of private foundation law as they relate to corporate foundations. These aspects arise because the related for-profit business almost always is an insider for private inurement doctrine purposes[10] and a disqualified person for private foundation law purposes.[11] As to the private foundation rules, the body of law that is most likely to be applicable is that pertaining to self-dealing.[12]

## § 17.2  REASONS FOR ESTABLISHMENT OF A CORPORATE FOUNDATION

A corporate foundation is a legitimate recipient of the related for-profit business's contributions, which presumably are, in whole or in part, deductible

---

4.  *See* § 1.7.
5.  *See* § 1.6.
6.  *See Nonprofit Governance* § 1.1(a).
7.  *See id.* §§ 1.4, 1.5.
8.  For example, the chief executive officer of the related business corporation is automatically the president of the corporate foundation and/or the treasurer of the business corporation is also the foundation's treasurer. Another model has the executive committee of the for-profit corporation serving as the full board of the foundation.
9.  *See Nonprofit Governance* §§ 1.3(c), (d).
10.  *See* § 17.3.
11.  *See* § 17.4.
12.  *See* § 17.5.

by the donor.[13] The investment income generated by the company's gifts (money or other property) is not subject to income tax[14] and provides a source of additional funding of the corporate foundation's grants. In most instances, a corporate foundation serves as a vehicle for a more focused and stable charitable grant-making program than the for-profit company could achieve within itself. Additionally, a corporate foundation may engage in program activities that the for-profit company itself cannot conduct using deductible charitable gifts; thus, a corporate foundation enables the related company to use its tax-deductible contributions to engage in charitable activities such as grants to individuals[15] and foreign charities.[16]

A separate corporate foundation allows for increased awareness and branding of the charitable objectives of the for-profit corporation. Foundations of this type facilitate the creation and maintenance of an increased charitable asset base by means of solicitation and receipt of contributions from employees of the related for-profit business and perhaps contributions and grants from others. Overall, these foundations provide for a more "tax-efficient manner" of conducting a charitable grant-making program, in relation to what the related for-profit company could do on its own.

## § 17.3 PRIVATE INUREMENT DOCTRINE

Private foundations are subject to the doctrine of private inurement.[17] The various forms of private inurement are transactions or other arrangements with persons who are insiders with respect to the foundation. An insider is a person who has a unique relationship with a charitable organization, by which that person can cause application of the organization's funds or assets for the private purpose of the person by reason of the person's exercise of control or influence over, or being in a position to exercise that control or influence over, the organization. The for-profit business that is operated in tandem with the corporate foundation is almost certainly an insider with respect to the foundation.[18]

The federal tax law does not prohibit transactions between charitable organizations and their insiders; they are, however, subject to the requirement that the terms and conditions of the transaction (or other arrangement) be reasonable. Thus, any transaction between a corporate foundation and its insiders must be tested against the standard of reasonableness. (Positive public

---

13. IRC § 170(a)(1). *See* Chapter 14; *Charitable Giving*, § 6.13.
14. It is, however, subject to an excise tax. *See* Chapter 10.
15. *See* § 9.3.
16. *See* § 9.5.
17. *See* § 5.1.
18. In the unlikely event that the private inurement doctrine is inapplicable in this context, the private benefit doctrine would probably apply (*see* § 5.2).

recognition accorded a for-profit company due to the charitable activities of its corporate foundation is not the type of private benefit that is a transgression of the doctrine of private inurement.[19]) The sanction for violation of the private inurement doctrine is revocation (or denial) of the charitable organization's tax-exempt status.

## § 17.4 DISQUALIFIED PERSONS RULES

As noted, the for-profit business that is associated with a corporate foundation is highly likely to be a disqualified person, probably as a substantial contributor.[20] Corporations, partnerships, and/or trusts, as to which the for-profit entity has more than a 35 percent interest, are also disqualified persons with respect to a corporate foundation.[21] Generally, a for-profit organization affiliated with a corporate foundation cannot be a foundation manager with respect to the foundation, even if the for-profit entity controls the foundation, because foundation managers usually are individuals.[22]

The directors and officers of a for-profit organization that controls a corporate foundation are not, by statute, disqualified persons (for that reason) with respect to the foundation. If, however, the for-profit organization is significantly involved in the management of a related corporate foundation (an inadvisable practice),[23] the IRS might assert (the agency has yet to do so) that officers and/or employees of the company are foundation managers with respect to the foundation.[24] In one instance, the IRS determined that employees of a bank that was the trustee of a private foundation were foundation managers, because "they [were] free, on a day-to-day basis, to administer the trust and distribute the funds according to their best judgment."[25] Also, in a determination concerning paid admissions to fundraising functions, the IRS found self-dealing in connection with a transaction involving a company's executive, not because the executive was a disqualified person but because the executive was functioning as an agent of the related company.[26]

---

19. *See*, e.g., *Charitable Giving*, § 3.1(c).
20. *See* § 4.1.
21. *See* §§ 4.5, 4.6.
22. *See* § 4.2. A for-profit corporation that is a director or the trustee of a private foundation, however, is a disqualified person.
23. *See Tax-Exempt Organizations*, § 29.2.
24. The IRS, in a misapplication of the law, found that the activities of a wholly owned for-profit subsidiary were attributable to a tax-exempt parent entity (causing retroactive revocation of exemption) (Priv. Ltr. Rul. 200842050). This type of attribution of activities is to be made where the parent is involved in the management of the subsidiary on a day-to-day basis; it is not to be made merely on the basis of the existence of control (unavoidable where the subsidiary is wholly owned).
25. Rev. Rul. 74-287, 1974-1 C.B. 327.
26. *See* § 17.5(c), text accompanied by *infra* note 40.

# § 17.5   SELF-DEALING RULES

In general, self-dealing between a private foundation and a disqualified person with respect to it is essentially forbidden.[27] This prohibition thus obviously extends to transactions or other arrangements between a corporate foundation and the for-profit business that is related to it. (As is the case with the private inurement doctrine,[28] positive public recognition accorded a for-profit company due to the charitable activities of its corporate foundation is not the type of private benefit that is a transgression of the self-dealing rules.[29])

## (a)   Payment of Compensation and Reimbursements

The payment of compensation by a private foundation to a disqualified person generally constitutes an act of self-dealing.[30] An important exception to this general rule allows payment of compensation by a private foundation to a disqualified person where the compensation is for personal services, reasonable, and necessary for advancement of the foundation's exempt purposes. It is the view of the IRS that a private foundation may, without engaging in an act of self-dealing, share the services of employees of the disqualified person, with the foundation reimbursing the disqualified person for its allocable share of the cost of the services, where the services are reasonable, necessary, and not excessive.[31] It is essential, however, for the availability of this exception, that the services be personal services, which means that the services must be professional and managerial, not merely operational, in nature.[32]

The foregoing rules also apply in connection with the payment to or reimbursement of the expenses of a disqualified person.[33]

## (b)   Sharing of Facilities

It is common for a corporate foundation to share offices and the like (such as equipment and supplies) with its related for-profit company. Yet, the general rule is that self-dealing includes the "furnishing of goods, services, or facilities" between (to or from) a private foundation and a disqualified person.[34] Nonetheless, the IRS has been rather generous in permitting shared office space and facilities.[35] Still, as a general principle, it is preferable for a corporate foundation

---

27. *See* § 5.3.
28. *See* §§ 5.1, 17.3.
29. This is a type of incidental and tenuous benefit (*see* § 17.5(e)).
30. *See* § 5.6.
31. Priv. Ltr. Rul. 7952117.
32. *See* § 5.6(a).
33. *See* § 5.6(f).
34. *See* § 5.9(a).
35. *See* § 5.9(b).

(and private foundations generally) to procure goods, services, equipment, and the like from sources other than the related company (or other disqualified persons).

The furnishing of goods, services, or facilities by a disqualified person to a private foundation is not self-dealing when done without charge and where the goods, services, or facilities that are furnished are used exclusively for charitable purposes. This includes rental arrangements.[36] Thus, the for-profit business can, without causing self-dealing, allow its corporate foundation to use its office space and equipment without charge. By contrast, a payment of rent by the corporate foundation to the related for-profit company would be an act of self-dealing.

If a corporate foundation and a related for-profit company are to have adjoining rented office space, each entity should enter into separate lease agreements with the property owner (assuming that person is not a disqualified person with respect to the foundation). Any remodeling costs should be borne by the entity receiving the benefit of the remodeling. The cost of any remodeling benefiting both parties should be allocated equally between the two organizations or borne solely by the for-profit company. The for-profit company may allow the foundation to utilize certain of its areas, such as a lobby/reception area, library, conference rooms, kitchen, mailroom, and/or restrooms, without charge.

A corporate foundation and a related for-profit company may share certain office equipment owned by the company. The foundation may use this equipment without charge. Detailed records of this use could be maintained, however, to enable the company, should it choose to do so, to allocate to the foundation its share of maintenance costs for the equipment. The foundation should pay its allocable share of these costs, if any, directly to the third-party service provider (assuming it is not a disqualified person with respect to the foundation). If leased equipment is shared, the foundation and company should enter into separate leases with the lessor (assuming it is not a disqualified person with respect to the foundation); the rental amounts should be based on actual use as established by detailed records. The foundation and company may jointly purchase a common telephone system; the two entities should have separate outside telephone lines and individual telephone instruments, and be billed separately by the telephone company.

A corporate foundation and its related for-profit company may share office and certain other supplies, such as refreshments and postage. Detailed records should be maintained by the foundation with respect to such a supplies-sharing arrangement to ensure that it does not pay more than its share of the costs. The foundation should pay its share of these costs directly to the third-party vendors (assuming none of them is a disqualified person with respect to the foundation).

---

36. *See* § 5.3(b).

A corporate foundation and its related for-profit company may share the cost of a receptionist. This individual should be an employee of both organizations and be entitled to each entity's benefits. Each organization should enter into a contract with this individual, with compensation based on a determination of the reasonable value of the employee's services to the organization. Sharing of other employees, if any, should be in accordance with similar arrangements, unless one or more employees are paid solely by the for-profit company.

The situation may arise where, due to sick leave, vacations, and the like, support staff from one entity would render services to the other on a temporary basis. If an employee of the for-profit company provided services to the corporate foundation under these circumstances, the foundation should pay the employee directly for the services (unless they are provided to the foundation at no charge). Likewise, if one of the foundation's employees provided services to the company under these circumstances, the employee should be directly compensated by the company.

In one instance, a corporate foundation and its related for-profit company proposed to open a bank account for the purpose of making payments of premiums on group insurance policies or other similar benefits covering the employees of both entities. The two organizations would each deposit into this account its share of the premium payments; a single check would be drawn against the account each month for the total premium payment for each policy or other benefit. Both organizations represented to the IRS that this type of arrangement would prevent administrative difficulties that could arise on the part of the third-party provider (which was not a disqualified person with respect to the foundation) if separate checks were issued by the company and the foundation each month for each policy or other benefit. The IRS ruled that the establishment and use of this account would not constitute one or more acts of self-dealing.[37]

## (c)  Provision of Tangible Benefits

The provision of a tangible economic benefit to a related for-profit business by a corporate foundation generally constitutes an act of self-dealing. The principal exception is the incidental and tenuous benefit,[38] which in this context means an intangible, indirect promotion benefit accruing to the company as an unavoidable consequence of conduct of the foundation's charitable activities.

For example, self-dealing would arise if a for-profit company advertised that it was sponsoring a community event, where the cost of the sponsorship was borne by the corporate foundation. Likewise, a corporate foundation that

---

37. Priv. Ltr. Rul. 9312022, which also pertains to the five paragraphs preceding this one.
38. *See* § 17.5(e).

works to promote the arts would engage in self-dealing if it paid for a work of art to be placed on or near a building owned by the related for-profit company, where the artwork improved the look of the building and/or its surroundings, and thus enhanced public perception of the company and its business.

One of the rare instances of any law on this point pertains to the pesky matter of purchase of tickets to fundraising events.[39] In one instance (reflective of a common practice), a corporate foundation purchased tickets to fundraising activities sponsored by various charitable organizations. The foundation provided an individual, who was the chair of the board and chief executive officer of the related company, and his guests, with paid admission to several of the fundraising functions. This individual was not a director, officer, or employee of the foundation. He attended the events; the directors and officers of the foundation used the remaining admissions. The IRS ruled that the furnishing of the admissions to the foundation's managers was not self-dealing because their attendance at the functions was reasonable and necessary to the performance of their evaluation and oversight tasks for the foundation.[40] By contrast, the use of the tickets by the company executive was found to be self-dealing inasmuch as the executive was attending the charitable functions as an agent of the company and not as a representative of the foundation.

Corporate foundations cannot avoid self-dealing by paying only the charitable portion of the cost of a ticket to a fundraising event and having the related for-profit corporation pay the costs allocable to the noncharitable portion. The IRS ruled that this bifurcation approach results in self-dealing inasmuch as the event can be attended only by paying both portions of the ticket price. A corporate foundation's payment of the charitable portion, the IRS reasoned, relieved the for-profit business's obligation to pay that element of the payment, which resulted in an economic benefit to the for-profit company and thus self-dealing.[41]

### (d)  Grant-Making

Corporate foundations need to be cautious in their grant-making policies and practices, being concerned about grants that benefit, or may benefit, or may be perceived as benefiting the related for-profit company. Again, any grant from a corporate foundation confers a private benefit on the related company; yet this alone is insufficient to constitute self-dealing (or private inurement).[42] The related company will thus benefit, directly or indirectly, incidentally or otherwise, from each related corporate foundation grant. The objective obviously

---

39.  *See* § 5.8(f).
40.  Tech. Adv. Mem. 8449008.
41.  E.g., Priv. Ltr. Rul. 9021066.
42.  *See* § 17.5(e).

should be to avoid conferring an unwarranted benefit on the related company as the consequence of a corporate foundation grant; this is often a question of judgment. There is little law to guide a corporate foundation in this regard.

Corporate foundation programs that are among the most problematic in this regard are the making of scholarship grants to employees of the related for-profit company and disaster relief grants to this category of employees. The federal tax law in these contexts has developed largely in connection with the taxable expenditures rules.[43]

One way to cause self-dealing is by transfer of a private foundation's income or assets to a grantee under circumstances where the item is considered transferred for the benefit of a disqualified person.[44] Under this body of law, the grantee can be a qualified charity and the purpose of the grant can be furtherance of charitable purposes, yet it is still self-dealing because an inappropriate benefit was provided to a disqualified person. This is an area of considerable traps, if only because many think of self-dealing transactions as transactions directly with disqualified persons.

The IRS ruled that a grant-making program was conducted by a charitable organization in a way so as to create substantial benefits for a business interest. Grants were made to writers who produced manuscripts that a for-profit company published; substantial royalties were paid to the parties. Finding that the grants were, in substance, compensation for the writers' services, the IRS concluded that private inurement had occurred and revoked the organization's tax-exempt status.[45]

## (e)  Incidental and Tenuous Benefits

As reflected throughout, the self-dealing rules include an exception for incidental and tenuous benefits provided to disqualified persons.[46] This exception is critical to the functioning of corporate foundations; the mere existence of these entities necessarily and unavoidably confers a benefit on the related company.

One example of this type of incidental benefit is the commonality of names of the two entities. As an illustration, a disqualified person with respect to a private foundation contributed real estate to the foundation for the purpose of building a neighborhood recreation center in an underprivileged area. As a condition of this contribution, the foundation agreed to use the disqualified person's name as part of the name of the center. Inasmuch as this benefit to the disqualified person was merely incidental, the naming of the center in this

---

43.  *See* § 17.5(d).
44.  *See* § 5.8(c).
45.  Rev. Rul. 66-104, 1966-1 C.B. 135. This was not a self-dealing case.
46.  *See* § 5.8(d).

manner does not constitute self-dealing. This point carries over into the corporate foundation context.

As another illustration, a private foundation and a public charity entered into an agreement pursuant to which the foundation agreed to make a sizeable grant to the charity if the charity changed its name to include that of a substantial contributor to the foundation and agreed to refrain from thereafter changing its name for 100 years. The IRS ruled that the public recognition this disqualified person received from this name change was an incidental and tenuous benefit, so that the making of this grant would not be self-dealing.[47]

Public recognition is another element usually protected by this exception. Thus, for example, a corporate foundation proposed to make a grant to a public charity in support of an annual educational competition organized by the charity. Participants in the competition were ninth-to-twelfth-grade students. The competition culminated in a banquet at which awards were presented to the winners. The foundation agreed to be the primary sponsor of this competition for five years; the charity agreed to rename the competition and banquet, using the name of the for-profit company that was the sole funder of the foundation. The IRS concluded that the public recognition this company was to receive as a consequence of the foundation's grant was an incidental and tenuous benefit.[48]

Additionally, the IRS considered a grant by a corporate foundation to a public broadcasting company for the purpose of underwriting a program, which featured credits at the beginning and close of the weekly telecast. These credits included the showing of the foundation's logo, which was identical to the related company's logo, and messages generally favorable to the company and its product line. The station published messages about the company, along with other corporate underwriters, in its viewers' guide. The IRS ruled that the television and viewing guide credits were merely an "inconsequential amount of commercial benefit."[49]

Other forms of private benefit may be shielded by this exception. Two classic IRS rulings illustrate the basic concept. In one, a for-profit corporation contributed parklands and money to a charitable organization, retaining the right to use as a brand symbol a scenic view located in the park. The IRS ruled that the tax-exempt status of the charitable organization was not jeopardized by this arrangement, in that the beneficial use of the park, subsidized by the donor, flowed principally to the public and that any identification of the donor's

---

47. Rev. Rul. 73-407, 1973-2 C.B. 383.
48. Priv. Ltr. Rul. 7817081.
49. Priv. Ltr. Rul. 8644003. Federal law requires these noncommercial stations to identify (albeit in a nonpromotional manner) the sponsors of broadcast segments, thus restricting the import of this ruling, which is somewhat inconsistent with the IRS's posture on other occasions where the provision of goodwill was found to be self-dealing (see § 5.8(c)).

business interest by visitors to the park was incidental to this primary public benefit.[50] In the other ruling, a for-profit corporation provided a substantial portion of the support of a charitable organization operating a replica of a nineteenth-century village. Although the corporation benefited by having the village named after it, by having its name associated with the village in conjunction with its advertising program, and by having its name mentioned in each publication of the charitable organization, the IRS ruled that these benefits are "merely incidental to the benefits flowing to the general public," so that the exempt status of the charitable organization operating the village was not jeopardized.[51]

The incidental and tenuous benefits exception thus applies in connection with benefits received by businesses related to corporate foundations for grants made in the community in which the foundation and the related for-profit entity reside. For example, a grant by a private foundation to the governing body of a city for the purpose of alleviating slum conditions of one of the city's neighborhoods is not an act of self-dealing merely because a related for-profit business is located in the same geographic area where the grant will be applied.[52] In addition, a for-profit corporation that was a substantial contributor to a private foundation was found to benefit only in an incidental manner from a grant by the private foundation to a local university to establish an educational department in manufacturing engineering. While the for-profit business would encourage its employees to enroll in the program and would recruit graduates from the program, it would not receive any preferential treatment regarding these activities, and its employees would compete for admission to the program on an equal basis with the public. Thus, this grant was ruled by the IRS not to constitute an act of self-dealing.[53]

Matching gift and similar programs can be shielded from self-dealing penalties by this exception. In one instance, a corporate foundation proposed to match, within certain limits, contributions to educational institutions made by full-time employees, who have completed a minimum of one year of service, of the related for-profit company. This foundation also proposed to provide financial assistance to any publicly supported charity on whose behalf any full-time employee of the company, with at least one year of service, has been serving as a volunteer for at least one year. Further, this foundation gives particular attention to grant applications from public charities that have been endorsed by local charities, the formation of which was encouraged by the company, that function in each community in which the company maintains a plant or office. The IRS ruled that, as to each of these programs, the financial

---

50. Rev. Rul. 66-358, 1666-2 C.B. 218.
51. Rev. Rul. 77-367, 1977-2 C.B. 193.
52. Reg. § 53.4941(d)-2(f)(9), Example 1.
53. Rev. Rul. 80-310, 1980-2 C.B. 319.

benefit of the foundation's grants accrues directly and entirely to the qualified public charities, and that the public recognition and goodwill enjoyed by the company as a result of the programs constitutes an incidental or tenuous benefit.[54]

### (f)  Corporate Reorganizations and Stock Transfers

Under certain circumstances, a transaction between a private foundation and a corporation that is a disqualified person with respect to the foundation is not considered self-dealing if the transaction takes place pursuant to a liquidation, merger, redemption, recapitalization, or other corporate adjustment, organization, or reorganization.[55] This exception to the self-dealing rules can be important for company foundations holding one or more forms of securities issued by the related for-profit company.

This exception is available where all securities of the same class as that held are subject to the same terms and those terms provide for receipt by the foundation of no less than fair market value. The issuer corporation must make a bona fide offer on a uniform basis to the foundation and to all other persons who hold the securities. Compensating the company foundation with property, such as debentures, for its stock while the other holders of identical stock received cash would not be a transaction that comports with the uniform-basis rule.[56]

In one instance, a private foundation organized as a trust owned approximately 9 percent of the preferred stock of a corporation, which was a disqualified person with respect to the trust. Under the corporation's articles of incorporation, the corporation was annually required to invite tenders, from all of the holders of preferred stock, to be made by a certain date. The maximum price at which the stock could be offered was $104 per share, plus any accumulated or unpaid dividends. The corporation was required to accept the tender of not more than 2,400 shares starting with tenders having the lowest prices. If more than 2,400 shares were tendered in any year, the shares to be purchased of tenders made at the same price had to be selected by lot or in another manner as the directors selected. The trustees of the trust sought to tender the trust's shares for $104 per share each year, provided that the fair market value per share equaled or was less than $104, until all of the shares held by the trust had been redeemed. The IRS held that any redemptions by the corporation of the preferred stock tendered by the trust would not constitute

---

54.  Priv. Ltr. Rul. 8004086. The IRS added that any "secondary intangible benefit" derived by this company in the form of "increased morale and satisfaction" is likewise an incidental or tenuous benefit.

55.  *See* § 5.8(a).

56.  Reg. § 53.4941(d)-3(d).

self-dealing, with the agency basing its holding on the fact that all of the corporation's preferred stock had to be tendered in accordance with the same terms and conditions.[57] Thus, this exception from the self-dealing rules for certain securities redemptions was satisfied.

## § 17.6 OTHER PRIVATE FOUNDATIONS RULES

The relationship between a company foundation and the related for-profit company can implicate federal tax private foundations rules other than those concerning self-dealing.

### (a) Mandatory Payout Rules

In connection with the mandatory payout rules,[58] the value of any stock owned by a company foundation that was issued by the related for-profit company will be included in the foundation's asset base for purposes of calculating the required amount of qualifying distributions.[59] The foundation could satisfy some or all of its payout obligation for one or more years by distributing some or all of this stock to one or more qualifying distributees.[60]

### (b) Excess Business Holdings Rules

In connection with the excess business holdings rules,[61] any stock owned by a company foundation that was issued by the related for-profit company will be taken into account in determining whether the foundation has permitted or excess business holdings.[62]

### (c) Jeopardizing Investments Rules

In connection with the jeopardizing investments rules,[63] it is highly unlikely that stock owned by a company foundation that was issued by the related for-profit company will be considered a jeopardizing investment.[64] This is the case if only because of the exception from these rules for property that is contributed to a private foundation.[65]

---

57. Priv. Ltr. Rul. 8425080.
58. *See* Chapter 6.
59. *See* § 6.2(a).
60. *See* § 6.5(a).
61. *See* Chapter 7.
62. *See* §§ 7.1, 7.2.
63. *See* Chapter 8.
64. *See* § 8.1(a).
65. *See* § 8.1(b).

## (d)  Taxable Expenditures Rules

In connection with the taxable expenditures rules,[66] a grant by a company foundation that provides an unwarranted benefit to the related for-profit company may be considered a distribution for noncharitable purposes.[67] Company foundation programs that are among the most problematic in this regard include the making of scholarship grants to employees of the related for-profit company. The IRS developed guidelines for use by these foundations in determining whether grants of this nature are forms of qualifying distributions[68] and thus are not taxable expenditures.[69]

Another law area involving company foundations that raises taxable expenditures issues is the matter of disaster relief programs involving employees of the related for-profit company. The IRS has vacillated on this topic, first approving these programs, then disapproving them, and more recently edging toward approval of many of them.[70] The legitimate concern of the IRS is whether a charitable class is being served,[71] whether there is private inurement or unwarranted private benefit,[72] and otherwise whether the program is designed to provide a type of welfare benefit to the employees.

The most recent pronouncement by the IRS on the subject of this type of disaster assistance program came in the form of a series of private letter rulings made public in late 2008.[73] This emergency assistance program was maintained by a system of health-care institutions to provide grants and/or loans to current and former employees of the system and/or their families and those of system affiliates. Beneficiaries of the program were confined to individuals who are needy and suffered economic hardship due to accident, loss, or disaster; the pool of eligible grantees numbered approximately 5,000 individuals. A committee administered the program, which entailed an emergency assistance fund; there was a formal application process, objective criteria, committee review procedure, limits on allowable assistance, and elaborate record-keeping practices. The IRS ruled that operation of this fund would not adversely affect the tax-exempt status of the institutions in the system, holding that the class of eligible beneficiaries was "sufficiently large and open-ended to constitute a charitable class," observing that support for the fund would be derived only from employee contributions and gifts from the public (that is, none of the entities in the system will provide any financial support for the program).

---

66. *See* Chapter 9.
67. *See* § 9.8.
68. *See* Chapter 6.
69. *See* § 9.3(e).
70. *See* § 9.3(b).
71. *See Tax-Exempt Organizations*, § 6.3(a).
72. *See* §§ 5.1, 5.2.
73. E.g., Priv. Ltr. Rul. 200839034.

## (e) Economic Returns

In connection with the excise tax on investment income,[74] securities issued by the related for-profit company may be held by a company foundation; any resulting dividend and/or interest income is subject to taxation.[75] Likewise, any capital gain incurred because of a sale or other disposition of this type of stock will be subject to this tax.[76]

---

74. *See* Chapter 10. In general, Shevlin, "A Legal Guide to Corporate Philanthropy," 55 *Exempt Org. Tax Rev.* (no. 3), 281 (Mar. 2007); Nooney and Mehlman, "The Corporate Foundation: Five Traps for the Unwary," 28 *Exempt Org. Tax Rev.* (no. 1), 41 (April 2000).
75. *See* § 10.3(c), (d).
76. *See* § 10.3(b).

# About the Authors

**BRUCE R. HOPKINS** is a senior partner in the law firm of Polsinelli PC, practicing in the firm's Kansas City, Missouri office. He specializes in the representation of private foundations and other tax-exempt organizations. His practice ranges over the entirety of law matters involving exempt organizations, with emphasis on the formation of nonprofit organizations, acquisition of recognition of tax-exempt status for them, the private inurement and private benefit doctrines, the intermediate sanctions rules, legislative and political campaign activities issues, public charity and private foundation rules, unrelated business planning, use of exempt and for-profit subsidiaries, joint venture planning, tax shelter involvement, review of annual information returns, Internet communications developments, the law of charitable giving (including planned giving), and fundraising law issues.

Mr. Hopkins served as Chair of the Committee on Exempt Organizations, Tax Section, American Bar Association; Chair, Section of Taxation, National Association of College and University Attorneys; and President, Planned Giving Study Group of Greater Washington, D.C.

Mr. Hopkins is the series editor of Wiley's Nonprofit Law, Finance, and Management Series. In addition to being co-author of *Private Foundations: Tax Law and Compliance, Fourth Edition*, he is the author of *The Law of Tax-Exempt Organizations, Tenth Edition*; *The Planning Guide for the Law of Tax-Exempt Organizations: Strategies and Commentaries*; *Bruce R. Hopkins Nonprofit Law Library* (e-book); *Tax-Exempt Organizations and Constitutional Law: Nonprofit Law as Shaped by the U.S. Supreme Court*; *IRS Audits of Tax-Exempt Organizations: Policies, Practices, and Procedures*; *The Tax Law of Charitable Giving, Fifth Edition*; *The Law of Fundraising, Fifth Edition*; *The Tax Law of Associations*; *The Tax Law of Unrelated Business for Nonprofit Organizations*; *The Nonprofits' Guide to Internet Communications Law*; *The Law of Intermediate Sanctions: A Guide for Nonprofits*; *Starting and Managing a Nonprofit Organization: A Legal Guide, Sixth Edition*; *Nonprofit Law Made Easy*; *Charitable Giving Law Made Easy*; *Private Foundation Law Made Easy*; *650 Essential Nonprofit Law Questions Answered*; *The First Legal Answer Book for Fund-Raisers*; *The Second Legal Answer Book for Fund-Raisers*; *The Legal Answer Book for Nonprofit Organizations*; *The Second Legal Answer Book for Nonprofit Organizations*; and *The Nonprofit Law Dictionary*. He is the co-author, with Thomas K. Hyatt, of *The Law of Tax-Exempt Healthcare Organizations, Fourth Edition*; with Alicia M. Kirkpatrick, of *The Law of Fundraising, Fifth Edition*; with David O. Middlebrook, of *Nonprofit Law for Religious Organizations: Essential Questions & Answers*; with Douglas K. Anning, Virginia C. Gross, and Thomas J.

Schenkelberg, of *The New Form 990: Law, Policy and Preparation*; also with Ms. Gross, of *Nonprofit Governance: Law, Practices & Trends*; and with Ms. Gross and Mr. Schenkelberg, of *Nonprofit Law for Colleges and Universities: Essential Questions and Answers for Officers, Directors, and Advisors*. He also writes *Bruce R. Hopkins' Nonprofit Counsel*, a monthly newsletter, published by John Wiley & Sons.

Mr. Hopkins maintains a website providing information about the law of tax-exempt organizations, at www.nonprofitlawcenter.com. Material posted on this site includes current developments outlines concerning this aspect of the law, summaries of court opinions, discussions of his books, various indexes for his newsletter, and a "What's New" listing of recent developments in exempt organizations law.

Mr. Hopkins received the 2007 Outstanding Nonprofit Lawyer Award (Vanguard Lifetime Achievement Award) from the American Bar Association, Section of Business Law, Committee on Nonprofit Corporations. He is listed in *The Best Lawyers in America*, Nonprofit Organizations/Charities Law, 2007–2014.

Mr. Hopkins earned his JD and LLM degrees at the George Washington University National Law Center and his BA at the University of Michigan. He is a member of the bars of the District of Columbia and the state of Missouri. He is on the adjunct faculty of the University of Kansas School of Law.

**JODY BLAZEK** is a partner in Blazek & Vetterling LLP, a Houston CPA firm focusing on tax and financial planning for exempt organizations and the individuals who create, fund, and work with them. BV serves over 400 nonprofit organizations providing financial reports and tax compliance and planning services.

Ms. Blazek's accounting career has concentrated on nonprofit organizations for over 38 years. This focus began with KPMG (then Peat Marwick) when she studied and interpreted the Tax Reform Act of 1969 as it related to charitable organizations and the creation of private foundations. From 1972 to 1981 she gained nonprofit management experience as treasurer of the Menil Interests, where she worked with John and Dominique de Menil to plan the Menil Collection, The Rothko Chapel, and other projects of the Menil Foundation. She reentered public practice in 1981 to found the firm she now serves.

She is the author of six books in the Wiley Nonprofit Series: *Nonprofit Financial Planning Made Easy* (2008); *IRS Form 1023 Preparation Guide* (2005); *IRS Form 990 Tax Preparation Guide for Nonprofits* (2004); *Tax Planning and Compliance for Tax-Exempt Organizations, Fourth Edition* (2004); *and Private Foundations: Tax Law and Compliance, Third Edition* (2008); and *The Legal Answer Book for Private Foundations* (2002), the latter two volumes co-authored with Bruce R. Hopkins.

Ms. Blazek serves on the Panel of the Nonprofit Sector, Transparency and Financial Accountability Work Group.

Ms. Blazek is past Chair of the Tax-Exempt Organizations Resource Panel and a member of Form 1023 and 999 Revision Task Forces for the American Institute of Certified Public Accountants; she serves on the national editorial board of Tax Analysts' *The Exempt Organization Tax Review* and the AICPA's *The Tax Advisor*; and is an advisor to the Volunteer Service Committee of the Houston Chapter of Certified Public Accountants. She is a founding director of Texas Accountants and Lawyers for the Arts and a member of the board of the Anchorage Foundations, Houston Artists Fund, and the River Pierce Foundation. Ms. Blazek is a frequent speaker at nonprofit symposia, including AICPA Not-for-Profit Industry Conference; University of Texas Law School Nonprofit Organizations Institute; Texas, New York, Arizona, and Washington State CPA Societies' Nonprofit Conferences; conference of Southwest Foundations and Association of Small Foundations; and Nonprofit Resource Center's Nonprofit Legal and Accounting Institute, among others.

Jody Blazek received her BBA from University of Texas at Austin in 1964 and took selected taxation courses at South Texas School of Law. She and her husband, David Crossley, nurture two sons, Austin and Jay Blazek Crossley.

# About the Online Resources

*Private Foundations: Tax Law and Compliance, Fourth Edition* is complemented by a number of online resources.

For a list of all Wiley books by Bruce R. Hopkins, please visit www.wiley.com/go/hopkins. Wiley books by Jody Blazek include *Tax Planning and Compliance for Tax-Exempt Organizations, Fifth Edition; Revised Form 990; Form 1023 Preparation Guide; Nonprofit Financial Planning Made Easy;* and *The Private Foundation Legal Answer Book,* co-authored with Bruce Hopkins.

Also, please visit www.wiley.com/go/privatefoundations and enter the password *funding123* to download various tables in PDF format and other documents to use alongside this fourth edition. These include the following:

- Appendix A—Sources of Law
- Appendix B—Internal Revenue Code Sections
- Table of Cases
- Table of IRS Revenue Rulings and Revenue Procedures
- Table of IRS Determinations Cited in Text
- Table of IRS Private Determinations Discussed in *Bruce R. Hopkins' Nonprofit Counsel*
- Table of IRS Private Letter Rulings, Technical Advice Memoranda, and General Counsel Memoranda

# Index

Leases and rental arrangements
(*Continued*)
private inurement, § 5.1
rental income, §§ 10.3(e), 11.2,
11.2(b)
sale, exchange, or leasing of
property, §§ 5.3(a), 5.4, 5.4(c)
Legislative activities
grants to charities that lobby,
§ 9.1(c)
monitoring grant requirements,
§ 9.6(d)
nonpartisan analysis, study, or
research, § 9.1(d)
private foundation restrictions,
§§ 9.1, 9.1(a), 9.1(b), 15.1
proposal, § 10.7
public charities, § 15.1
self-defense exception, § 9.1(e)
Legislative history, §§ 1.1, 1.10
excess business holding rules,
§ 7.1(c)
mandatory distribution
requirement, § 6.8
private foundation tax law, § 15.2
Life insurance, gifts of, § 2.4(c)
Limited liability companies (LLCs),
§§ 3.1(a), 5.4(e), 6.5(a), 6.5(b)
Liquidation, §§ 1.9, 13.5, 13.5(c)
Loans and extensions of credit
interest-free loans, § 5.5(b)
loan guarantee for benefit of
disqualified person, § 5.8(g)
to make expenditures for tax-
exempt purpose, § 6.5(a)
private inurement, § 5.1
program-related investments,
§ 8.3
as self-dealing, §§ 5.3(a), 5.5, 5.5(a),
5.5(b)
undoing loan to correct self-
dealing, § 5.15(a)(iii)

unrelated business income tax
exceptions, § 11.2
Lobbying activities, § 9.1. *See also*
Legislative activities
Lobbying Disclosure Act of 1995,
§ 9.1(a)
Long-term capital gain property, gifts
of, §§ 14.1(b), 14.2, 14.4(a), 14.4(c)
Look-through rule, § 9.4(d)
Low-profit limited liability
companies, § 8.3

## M
Managers
Form 990-PF, Part VIII, information
about, § 12.2(e)
jeopardizing investments, excise
taxes for, §§ 8.4, 8.4(a)
taxable expenditures, liability for
excise taxes, §§ 9.10(a), 9.10(c)
termination tax and involuntary
termination of foundation,
§ 13.2
Medical research organizations,
§ 15.3, 15.3(c)
Membership dues or fees, §§ 5.8(e),
15.6(c)
Merchandise, sale of, § 11.1(b),
11.2(d), 11.4(b), Ex. 11.2
Mergers, §§ 13.5, 13.5(a)–(d)
Mexico, § 9.5
Mineral interests, §§ 6.3(b), 6.3(f),
10.3(f), 11.2(a)
Minimum distribution requirement,
§§ 1.4(e), 15.1, 16.8
Minimum investment return (MIR),
§§ 3.1(d), 6.1, 6.2
acquisition indebtedness, § 6.2(f)
assets held for future charitable use,
§ 6.2(e)
dual-use property, §§ 6.2(a), 6.2(d)

individual grant programs,
§ 3.1(c)
overview, § 3.1
qualifying distributions, § 3.1(d)
significant involvement, § 3.1(c)
support test, §§ 3.1(d), 3.1(e), 3.1(f)
types of, § 3.1
Professional advisors, reliance on
advice of, §§ 1.10, 5.15(e), 5.16,
8.4(b)
Professional fees, §§ 10.4(a), 12.1(b)
Profits interest of partner, § 4.3
Program-related investments, §§ 8.1,
8.3, 9.6(c), 11.3(b), 12.2(g)
Prohibited transactions, foreign
private foundations, § 3.8
Property tax exemptions, § 2.5(g)
Proprietorships, excess business
holding rules, § 7.2(b)
Prudent investor, § 1.1
Prudent investor rule, §§ 8.1(a), 8.2
Prudent man rule, § 8.2. *See also*
Prudent investor rule
Prudent trustee, § 8.2
Public charities, §§ 1.1, 1.2
categories of, §§ 15.1, 15.2,
15.8(a)–(c)
charitable contribution deductions,
§§ 14.1(a), 14.2, 14.3
conversion to supporting
organization, § 13.4
donative entities, §§ 15.4,
15.4(a)–(e)
eligible recipients of assets of
private foundation, § 13.3(c)
grants to, §§ 1.6, 9.4, 9.4(a)–(c)
private charities compared, § 15.1,
Ex. 15.1
private foundation operating as,
§ 13.4
private foundation presumption,
§§ 1.1, 2.6, 15.14

reclassification, §§ 13.4, 15.8(a)–(c)
specified public charities, §§ 15.7(a),
15.7(b), 15.7(c), 15.7(g)
and supporting organizations,
§ 15.7. *See also* Supporting
organizations
termination of status as, § 15.14
transfer of assets to and voluntary
termination of private
foundation, §§ 13.1, 13.3,
13.3(a)–(c), 16.5
verifying status as, §§ 9.4(c),
15.11(a), 15.11(b)
Public institutions, §§ 15.2, 15.3,
15.3(a)–(e)
Public officials, § 4.8
Public safety organizations, §§ 15.2,
15.13
Publicly supported charitable
organizations, §§ 15.2, 15.4,
15.4(a)–(e), 15.5, 15.5(a)–(d),
15.6

## Q

Qualified appreciated stock rule,
§§ 14.4(b), 15.1
Qualified organization contract
research, § 3.4
Qualifying distributions, § 1.4(e)
and Charitable Giving Act of 2003,
§ 6.5(c)
direct charitable expenditures,
§ 6.5(b)
direct grants, § 6.5(a)
to foreign recipients, § 6.5(e)
Form 990-PF, Part XII, § 12.2(j)
overview, § 6.5
private operating foundations,
§ 3.1(d)
set-asides, §§ 6.5, 6.5(d)
test, § 3.1(h)